Women

A Feminist Perspective

Fifth Edition

Edited by

Jo Freeman

Mayfield Publishing Company

Mountain View, California
London • Toronto

Library of Congress Cataloging-in-Publication Data

Women : a feminist perspective / edited by Jo Freeman.—5th ed.
     p.   cm.
  Includes bibliographical references and index.
  ISBN 1-55934-111-4
  1. Women—United States—Social conditions.   2. Feminism—United
States.   I. Freeman, Jo.
HQ1426.W62   1994
305.42'0973—dc20   94–16032
                                                                         CIP

Manufactured in the United States of America
10   9   8   7   6   5

Mayfield Publishing Company
1280 Villa Street
Mountain View, California 94041

Sponsoring editor, Franklin C. Graham; production editors, Carol Zafiropoulos and Sharon Montooth; manuscript editor, Beverly Zegarski; text and cover designer, Claire Seng-Niemoeller; cover photography, James Bryant/Visicom Design Group. The text was set in 11.5/12 Perpetua by ExecuStaff and printed on 50# Text White Opaque by Maple Vail Book Manufacturers.

Text Credits

Contents

Part Four
Words and Images

Part Five
Institutions of Social Control

Part Six
Feminism in Perspective

Part Seven
Feminism and Diversity

Preface

THE FIRST EDITION OF this book was put together as a labor of love and published primarily as an act of faith. It had its genesis in 1968, at the first national conference of what was to become the younger branch of the women's liberation movement. Many of us at that conference had just begun reading everything we could find on women, and in that traditional era we were appalled at the scarcity of perceptive writings and only occasionally delighted by a gem that sparkled with new ideas. There were no books or anthologies presenting a feminist perspective on women's status, and those books about women that were not written from a wholly traditional view generally discounted feminism as outmoded, extreme, or both.

Ironically for a group that has since produced so much writing, most of us then felt unable to express our rising consciousness in words. Why not, we thought, do the next best thing? Why not bring together those few existing pieces that were worthwhile and save other women the task of seeking them out? That was a job I took on. Unfortunately, at the same time, I started working for my Ph.D. in political science. It took two years longer to publish the anthology than it did to get the degree.

During the years I worked on the book it grew and changed with the movement. Of the earliest selections, only two made it to the first edition. The rest represented the new research of that time, the new thinking, and the new interpretations of old research inspired by the women's liberation movement.

The first-edition articles came from a variety of sources. I placed ads in most of the burgeoning feminist media, and some organizations, notably the Women's History Research Library of Berkeley and KNOW of Pittsburgh, included special notices with their regular mailings. The response was overwhelming. Hundreds of articles and proposals poured in, and well over a year was spent reading and editing them.

From the beginning the standards were high. This book was to contain pieces that were comprehensive, lucidly written, and well grounded in scholarly research. Needless to say, the submissions I received in response to ads were not uniform in style and approach; nor did they cover all the topics needed. Hence I also collected movement pamphlets and other publications on women, attended feminist meetings, and audited panel discussions on women at professional meetings to find potential authors.

During this period both scholarly and popular writing on women was increasing exponentially, with feminist insights sparking analysis of the contradictions in women's lives in every conceivable sphere. Simultaneously, it was becoming harder and harder to interest a publisher in the book. Some who had expressed tentative interest when I first began sending out the prospectus decided as the book took shape that "this women's thing" was a fad and what market there was, was already glutted. Then one of my authors discussed the book with the traveling editor of a small house on the West Coast. That editor was Alden Paine. He wrote to me; I sent the manuscript; and after I agreed to decrease its length by one-third, National Press Books (soon to become Mayfield Publishing Company) sent me a contract.

As the book went to press, almost everything about it (except the quality of the articles) was an unknown. Owing to its size and recent name change, the publisher was unknown. I was an unknown. All but a few of the authors were unknowns. The potential readership was unknown. All publishing involves some risk, but this was extraordinary. Within two years we knew that love and faith had carried the day. Women's studies courses grew and spread, and both teachers and students found the volume an appropriate introductory text. The reason the courses spread, even in an atmosphere of skepticism and a period of declining college enrollments, is that feminism is not a fad, but a national consciousness that is fundamentally changing the fabric of all our lives.

The first edition of this book took seven years to complete. The second, third, and fourth editions took only about two and a half years each. The fifth took three and a half years. The authors of this edition had an extraordinary number of problems that delayed delivery of their chapters. Several had illnesses or accidents; two lost the sight of one eye (fortunately, only temporarily); one lost her house (and research) in the Oakland fire; many had reached the age where they had to take time out for aging parents; and I spent five months running for the New York State Assembly. Afterward, I had extra time on my hands, so I was able to do some of the work for many of them. But while I could update the statistics, clarify the citations, reorganize their research, and improve their language, only the authors could finalize their manuscripts. The uncertainty of when, or if, a chapter would arrive (and some never did) added to the usual hard decisions about what to delete and what to add. In one case I went through four authors for a particular topic before I got a usable manuscript; in many others the promised piece simply never arrived or was inadequate.

The evolution of this book illustrates the growth and development of feminist scholarship. Papers submitted for the first edition tended to be light on data and heavy on expression of personal feelings. Most authors tried to say a little bit about everything because women were so conscious of the interconnections between the various facets of their existence. Articles for the second edition were well substantiated but still dealt with broad themes, and thus it was the easiest edition to do. Papers sent in for consideration for the third edition sometimes drowned in data and were too narrow for this particular book. "Bring back the rhetoric," my readers complained. Many of the fourth edition submissions were less interested in analyzing institutions and presenting basic facts than they were in exploring the usefulness of different theoretical frameworks. The issues and approaches those writers wished to pursue were more appropriate for advanced courses than an introductory one. The nemesis of the fifth edition was literature reviews. After twenty-five years of feminist scholarship, the field has matured to the point that many of today's young scholars are spending their time critiquing what those that went before them have said rather than the subjects that they wrote about. Although this book certainly relies on the extensive literature for facts and ideas, it doesn't publish literature reviews. Trying to persuade newly minted scholars that they should think for themselves and not just report what others have thought was my hardest (and least successful) editorial task. Sometimes I just had to find a new author.

Through all these changes I have tried to maintain the standards set in the first edition of providing solid, accurate, and up-to-date information along with a critical analysis that interpreted the facts from a feminist perspective. As in previous editions, I encouraged authors to use the most recent data and to double-check for accuracy. More often I checked, and revised, them myself. During the editing of the second edition, I had an office in the Department of Labor in Washington, D.C., and I learned how to locate and use the tons of statistics the government produces each year. Before editing the third edition, I went to law school. Consequently, the statistics and legal citations in this edition have all been carefully scrutinized and often revised. For this edition I spent many days in the documents department of Brooklyn College Library, whose cooperative staff were extremely resourceful in locating obscure government publications.

As in the previous three editions, Howard Hayghe of the Bureau of Labor Statistics was a gold mine of information; he never failed to come through with a necessary number or an explanation of why there wasn't one. All references to "unpublished data from the Bureau of Labor Statistics" in the different chapters are a tribute to his contribution. In addition, I phoned many different subunits in the Bureau of the Census, the Bureau of Justice Statistics, the Department of Education, and the Department of Health and Human Services to find the best sources. As I had learned in previous years, there is often a lot of valuable information around that isn't in university libraries or isn't catalogued in a way that makes it accessible. Networking through the telephone is often the only way to find such information. We hoped to have 1990 Census data for the fifth edition, but the compilation and publication of that data are taking longer than in the past due to staff and budget cuts. As it is, a lot of detailed data are still not available. Unlike the Bureau of Labor Statistics, the Census Bureau refuses to release unpublished data—even those that will be published before the actual publication date of this book.

We also made use of the latest new tool for researchers—the Internet—and through it, access to electronic databases and to other scholars through mailing lists. When I wanted to know if any states had added equal rights amendments to their constitutions since I last counted many years ago, I put a query on the "net." Stephanie Ann Webster, a law student at the University of Virginia, answered and told me she had researched that very question thoroughly a couple years ago, and unfortunately the answer was no. Some had tried; none had succeeded. When I was reading page proofs for my chapter on women and the law, the Supreme Court announced its decision on the use of sex in peremptory challenges of jurors. In the old days, I would not have been able to get a copy of the decision fast enough to add it to my chapter (maybe a cite to its existence, but not a discussion or a quote). A legal list I subscribe to "owned" by Cornell University School of Law "mailed" a synopsis the next day; when I couldn't find a copy of the entire decision at Cornell's "gopher server," Peter Martin, a professor at Cornell Law School, e-mailed it to me in pieces. Thanks to both of these helpful people and the Internet this book is a little bit more current than it would have been.

As with every edition, this book contains not only an enormous amount of painstaking research and original thinking but some information that cannot easily be found anywhere else. The reader will find this a useful reference book as well as a general text. What can't be found in the articles can probably be found in sources cited in the footnotes. But while accuracy, thoroughness, and the use of the most recent data are stressed throughout, the true strength of the book rests not in its facts but in its ideas, and in the comprehensive orientation provided by a feminist perspective.

Introduction

WHEN THE FIRST edition of this book was conceived and compiled twenty-five years ago, there was a fairly uniform feminist perspective. There were, to be sure, fights among feminists (especially academics), but the fundamental viewpoint that was emerging was a shared one. This was true for only a few years. Since then feminist ideas, like the movement itself, have flowed in every direction, entering cracks and crevices not even imagined at that time. New ideas have flowered that are so different from the original ones that the title of this book, *A Feminist Perspective*, seems more appropriate than ever. As I review the Introductions to previous editions, they seem almost archaic.

Since this is an introductory text on women, not on the women's movement, there has been no attempt to reflect the many analyses and conflicts over issues that have developed in the last fifteen years. Instead, the book still tries to present basic data and a feminist analysis about which there is still some agreement. However, the newest issues, the ones that cause so much heat at feminist conferences, are often ones on which there is no feminist consensus. Thus, insofar as these new issues are touched on by the authors, they are each from that author's feminist perspective. This book still has a point of view, but it is found less consistently than in previous editions.

The book has also been revised and somewhat reorganized to reflect what our surveys tell us is reader demand. And, as in the past, some standard pieces were lost because the authors were not available. The organization of the book still allows readers to begin by looking at their own lives, then moves out in widening circles to bring in the social and historical context of women's present-day status. This edition, however, concludes with *two* sections on feminism. One is historical, and the other better reflects the diversity of present-day feminist views from the perspective of authors who do not share the dominant white, middle-class, heterosexual culture.

In Part I, Carole J. Sheffield provides an overview of the different ways in which a woman's body is controlled and, through it, women as a group. Beginning with Lucy Stone's admonition that a woman's right to herself is the most fundamental one of all, Sheffield argues that such practices as rape, wife assault, the sexual abuse of children, and sexual harassment form a system of *sexual terrorism* "by which males frighten, and by frightening, control and dominate females." Susan Ehrlich Martin explores one form of abuse, sexual harassment, in depth, showing how reluctantly our society has come to recognize that what men view as merely a sport is in fact a crime against women and a form of illegal sex discrimination. Nancy Russo and Jody Horn ask what are a woman's options to an unwanted pregnancy, particularly looking at abortion and the consequences to women if that were no longer one of our choices. Barbara Katz Rothman and Mary Beth Caschetta point out how both reproductive and mothering functions have been co-opted by the medical establishment. Nancy Henley and Jo Freeman look at how women must restrict their body language in order to avoid being misinterpreted.

Women's relationships throughout the life cycle are explored in Part II. The family has been the primary social institution to structure women's lives, and the patriarchal family has been perhaps the single most pervasive and effective means of confining and controlling women's activities. Naomi Gerstel and Harriet Engel Gross put the family in a historical context, showing how different family forms and different systems of production have interacted with patriarchal norms about women's place. Hilary M. Lips shows how women learn their place through lessons in femininity. Janet M. Steil explains why inequality in marital relationships still persists despite an acceptance of egalitarian rhetoric. Michele Hoffnung explores the contradictions of the motherhood mystique and the conflict it creates with other important aspects of women's lives. Laurie Russell Hatch analyzes the situation of older women—whether or not they buy into the myth that marriage is their most important product, they are still left with less in the end.

Women's work and the occupations in which they most frequently find themselves are examined in Part III. Nancy Thornborrow and Marianne Sheldon provide an overview of women's economic situation, with particular attention to why women's wages are so low. Mary Frank Fox focuses on higher education for women—an institution that effectively decides many women's future. Brigid O'Farrell looks at women in blue-collar occupations, comparing those that are traditional women's jobs with women's attempts to break into "nontraditional" ones that pay much higher wages. Evelyn Nakano Glenn and Roslyn L. Feldberg show how the channeling of women into clerical work has led to decreased benefits. Debra Kaufman profiles some of the professions and how they are structured around the typical male life-style. What comes through loud and clear is that income is more directly related to the sex of the typical employee than to the requirements of the job; that is, "men's" jobs pay more than "women's" jobs regardless of the skill or education required.

Part IV reintroduces a section on Words and Images that was in the first edition of this book but was dropped from intervening ones. In it, Joan C. Chrisler and Elayne A. Saltzberg look at how society's standards of beauty shift, but always in such a way as to make women feel inadequate. Gloria Steinem shows how advertisers of beauty products use women's magazines to control these standards and increase profits through her history of *Ms.* magazine's efforts to survive without complying with advertisers' demands. Karen L. Adams and Norma C. Ware show how everyday conversation reinforces prescribed sex role behaviors in our society. Gloria Cowan examines the conflict among feminists over pornography and whether or not its images structure male behavior toward women.

Overt Institutions of Social Control are analyzed in Part V. Jo Freeman looks at the history of women's constitutional rights and public policy on women, which were significantly changed by the new feminist movement. Ruth Mandel surveys women's efforts to obtain power in traditional political institutions and the consequences for women of that effort. Martha J. Reineke analyzes how myths, rituals, and symbols are used to socialize and control women. Rose Weitz calculates the price of independence by looking at the fate of women who would live without men: spinsters, widows, nuns, and particularly lesbians. Alice Abel Kemp examines poverty: why women are poor and why welfare doesn't help very much. Stephanie Golden shows how traditional attitudes toward women contribute to their homelessness.

Part VI puts feminism in historical perspective. Marlene LeGates looks at women's protests before there was a feminist ideology to justify them as well as the intellectual history behind the growth of that ideology. Jo Freeman takes up the story with Suffrage, illuminating the continuity of feminist activity as well as the emergence of a new movement in the mid 1960s that led to a great leap forward. Carol White argues that African-American women have their own history of feminist activity, reflecting the particular conditions of their racial community. Susan E. Marshall looks at the rhetoric of the antifeminist back-lash to both the Suffrage and the women's liberation movements, and Michael S. Kimmel looks at the ways in which men have responded to feminism.

Diversity has become a talisman of our time, and this book reflects that in Part VII. As more and more women from different ethnic and minority groups have paid attention to feminism, they have redefined and reinterpreted it to fit their needs. Elizabeth Almquist surveys a variety of minority groups to add to our knowledge of how experiencing different situations in our society create different concerns. Pauline Terrelonge advocates the relevance of femi-nism to black women and identifies barriers to its active acceptance. *Black* was the accepted term when she first wrote her piece for the second edition, so we've retained it. Denise Segura and Beatriz M. Pesquera define and describe several Chicana feminisms. Ilsa M. Glazer examines how feminism has affected the Jewish community and how Jewish women have affected feminism. Lisa Ransdell looks at lesbian feminism and the important role of lesbians in the feminist movement.

The articles in this book are not merely a critique of society; implicitly, they take to task the scholarly disciplines whose research and concepts they draw upon. These disciplines, like the institutions and agencies of society at large, are dominated by those on the inside. They still reflect, to a great degree, the traditionalist point of view and with it a desire to explain, justify, and maintain the status quo of human and institutional relationships. The result is too often a consistency of approach that is almost stifling. It may be politically convenient to view the world through the most comfortable lenses, but the resulting distortion is scientifically unacceptable. Only when one changes position, views the world from another stance, and relaxes one's claim to a monopoly on truth can new knowledge be gained. These chapters show how feminist thought contributes to this process by providing alternative perspectives from which to reexamine basic concepts in many spheres of learning. They not only point out the sexist prejudices of old research but also show how new human opportunities can be created by changing outworn institutions and values. A feminist perspective is practical as well as theoretical; it illuminates possibilities for the future as well as criticizes the limitations of the present. It is the readers of this book, each new generation, who must learn from them and put them into practice.

The Contributors

Jo Freeman is the author of *The Politics of Women's Liberation* (winner of a 1975 American Political Science Association prize as the Best Scholarly Work on Women and Politics) and the editor of *Social Movements of the Sixties and Seventies* (1983). She has a Ph.D. in Political Science from the University of Chicago (1973) and a J.D. from New York University School of Law (1982). Her articles on feminism, social movements, law, public policy, sex-role socialization, organizational theory, education, federal election law, and party politics have been published in *The Nation, Ms., Valparaiso Law Review, Transaction, School Review, Liberal Education, American Journal of Sociology, Intellect, Political Science Quarterly, Acta Sociologica, Prospects, Signs, Pace Law Review,* and numerous anthologies.

Karen L. Adams is an associate professor in the English department of Arizona State University and is currently the director of the Linguistics/TESL programs. She is also affiliated faculty in the Women's Study Program. She has a Ph.D. in linguistics from the University of Michigan. Her research and teaching interests deal with the relationship between language and society. She has recently given courses and organized conferences on the relationship of language to power. Her recent publications and research are concerned with the structure of political debates and style differences between male and female candidates from different regions of the United States.

Elizabeth M. Almquist is regents professor of sociology at the University of North Texas, where her research centers on inequalities of gender, race, and social class. Her articles on women, work, and politics have appeared in *Gender and Society, Signs: Journal of Women in Culture and Society, Sex Roles, Journal of Marriage and the Family, Merrill Palmer Quarterly,* and *Social Science Quarterly*. She is beginning a historical study of women in a ranch community in Wyoming. She is a past president of the Southwestern Sociological Association (1986), is currently (1993–94) chair of the Section on Sex and Gender of the American Sociological Association, and will be president of the Southwestern Social Science Association in 1995.

Mary Beth Caschetta is a treatment advocate for low-income HIV-positive women in New York City. A medical sociologist and lesbian feminist, she has been published concerning women's health in the *Journal of the American Medical Women's Association,* the *Sex Information and Education Council of the U.S. Report,* the *New England Journal of Medicine,* and the *Encyclopedia of Childbirth.*

Joan C. Chrisler is associate professor of psychology at Connecticut College. She has published extensively on the psychology of women and women's health and is particularly known for her work on weight and eating behavior and on psychosocial aspects of the menstrual cycle. She has coedited three books: *New Directions in Feminist Psychology* with Doris Howard (Springer, 1992), *Variations on a Theme: Diversity and the Psychology of Women* with Alyce Huston Hemstreet (SUNY Press, forthcoming), and *Lectures on the Psychology of Women* with Carla Golden and Patricia Rozee (McGraw-Hill, forthcoming).

Gloria Cowan is a professor of psychology at California State University, San Bernardino. She is on the coordinating committee of the Women's Studies Program and director of the MA in General-Experimental Psychology. Her current research concerns pornography, gender and power strategies, and women's hostility toward other women. She is currently working on two projects on pornography. One project relates high school students' beliefs about the causes of rape to their exposure to pornography, and the other concerns defining "degrading/dehumanizing" pornography. She was selected as outstanding professor at California State University, San Bernardino, in 1991–92.

Roslyn L. Feldberg is a sociologist who studies women's employment and works in coalitions to promote pay equity and policies that make it easier to encompass the work-family connection for the varying configurations of contemporary families. Her recent publications include *Hidden Aspects of Women's Work* (coedited by Chris Bose and Natalie Sokoloff) and articles on comparable worth. As associate director of labor relations at the Massachusetts Nurses Association, Dr. Feldberg is beginning a study of the origins and meanings of part-time work among nurses.

Mary Frank Fox is associate professor of sociology, School of History, Technology, and Society, Georgia Tech. Her work focuses upon women and men in occupations and organizations, especially scientific and academic ones. Her current research, supported by the National Science Foundation, is a study with H. Etzkowitz of women in doctoral education in scientific and engineering fields. Her work has been published in over twenty different scholarly journals and collections. She is associate editor of the journal, *Sex Roles*; member of editorial boards of *Work and Occupations* and *The American Sociologist*; and past associate editor of *Gender & Society*. She is a member of the Council of the Sex and Gender Section of the American Sociological Association.

Naomi Gerstel is a professor of sociology at the University of Massachusetts, Amherst, where she teaches courses on gender, the family, and family and work. Her current research, funded by the National Science Foundation and The Russell Sage Foundation, is on the impact of state policy on the strategies for survival developed by the homeless. With Harriet Gross, she coauthored *Commuter Marriage* and coedited *Work and Family*. Her articles on caregiving as well as on divorce appeared in journals such as *Gender & Society, Journal of Marriage and the Family, Social Problems, The Gerontologist,* and *Social Forces.*

Ilsa M. Glazer, an anthropologist, is assistant professor in the Department of Behavioral Sciences at Kingsborough Community College of the City University of New York. The present article is based on three years of field-work among New York Jewish women. She has written extensively on Zambian women in development: as Ilsa Schuster, she published *The New Women of Lusaka* (Mayfield) and many articles on Zambian women's occupational groups, politics, family life, and social life. She has also written numerous articles on interfemale aggression cross culturally, on Israeli kibbutz women, and on the human rights of Palestinian women. Her writing is based on fourteen years of residence in Zambia and Israel. Her doctorate is from the University of Sussex, England. Her current research is on black-Jewish relations in New York City.

Evelyn Nakano Glenn teaches at the University of California, Berkeley, where she is professor of ethnic studies and women's studies. Her research focuses on women's work, with particular emphasis on race and gender hierarchies and the impact of technology. In addition to coauthoring many articles on clerical work, she has written extensively on the work and family lives of racial ethnic women. She is the author of *Issei, Nisei Warbride: Three Generations of Japanese American Women in Domestic Service,* and co-editor of *Mothering: Ideology, Experience and Agency.* She is currently writing a book on the race and gender construction of women's work, based on a comparative historical study of African-American, Latina, and Asian American women's labor.

Stephanie Golden is a freelance journalist and medical writer whose involvement with homelessness goes back to the late 1970s, when she began trying to understand "shopping bag ladies." For four years she was a volunteer at a private shelter for homeless women in Manhattan. This experience formed the core of her book *The Women Outside: Myths and Meanings of Homelessness* (University of California Press, 1992), which was a finalist for the Robert F. Kennedy Book Award. She has also written for the *San Francisco Chronicle, New York Newsday, City Limits,* and *New Directions for Women.* The essay appearing here was first published in *Frontiers: A Journal of Women Studies* 11 (2,3): 1–7, 1990.

Harriet Engel Gross, professor of sociology at Governors State University, long interested in family analysis, is currently researching the history of adoption and its implications for open adoption. She is involved in a long term study of open adoption families and is particularly interested in these as new family forms.

Laurie Russell Hatch is associate professor of sociology at the University of Kentucky, where she teaches courses on gender, inequality, aging, and contemporary social theory. She is a member of Sociologists for Women in Society and has served on the Women's Studies Advisory Board and various women's studies committees at the University of Kentucky. Her research on gender and aging has been published in *Gender and Society, Journal of Marriage and the Family,* and *Research on Aging.* She is currently working on a book entitled *Gender and Aging in Perspective: A Life-Course Approach.*

Nancy Henley is professor of psychology at the University of California at Los Angeles. Her research in recent years has focused on gender and communication and on attitudes toward women. Dr. Henley's published works include *Body Politics: Power, Sex and Nonverbal Communication* (1977), *Language and Sex: Difference and Dominance* (coedited with Barrie Thorne, 1975), *Gender and Nonverbal Behavior* (coedited with Clara Mayo, 1981), and *Language, Gender and Society* (coedited with Barrie Thorne and Cheris Kramarae, 1983), as well as numerous articles and book chapters.

Michele Hoffnung is professor of psychology and director of women's studies at Quinnipiac College in Hamden, Connecticut. She is the editor of *Roles Women Play: Readings Toward Women's Liberation* (1971) and the author of *What's a Mother to Do: Conversations on Work and Family* (1992), as well as articles about childbirth, child care, motherhood, and feminist teaching and curriculum change. She is currently working on a longitudinal study of college women's expectations for, and experiences with, balancing employment and family roles, and writing a lifespan development psychology textbook.

Jody D. Horn is research analyst for Starr Litigation Services, Inc., where she conducts studies of jury decision making. She is also a doctoral candidate in the School of Justice Studies at Arizona State University. Her dissertation is on the rhetoric of rights for U.S. women, involving a sociolegal rights analysis of the *U.N. Convention on the Elimination of All Forms of Discrimination Against Women.*

Debra Renee Kaufman is professor of sociology and the coordinator of the women's studies program at Northeastern University in Boston, Massachusetts. Her book length scholarly works include: *Achievement and Women: Challenging the Assumptions* (1982, coauthored with B. Richardson and nominated for the C. Wright Mills Award for notable contributions to sociological thought); *Public/Private Spheres: Women Past and Present* (edited volume, Northeastern University Customs Textbooks, Spring 1989); *Rachel's Daughters: Newly Orthodox Jewish Women,* which explores the relationship between fundamentalist religious right women and feminism during the final decades of this century (nominated for three awards). She is the author of numerous articles and chapters on women, work, the family, and feminist methodology and theory. She is currently working on identity politics and concepts of the other as she analyzes the data she collected during her semester stay as a visiting scholar at Brigham Young University where she interviewed both Mormon and Jewish feminists. She was the twenty-third annual Robert D. Klein lecturer at Northeastern University in recognition of her outstanding scholarly achievement, professional contribution, and creative classroom activity.

Alice Abel Kemp is an associate professor of sociology at the University of New Orleans and director of the women's studies program. She is the author of a sociology/Women's Studies textbook, *Women's Work: Degraded and Devalued,* published in 1994 by Prentice Hall and is currently working on a feminist family text with two colleagues. Her research and publications center on women's labor force participation, occupational sex segregation, race and gender inequality, and poverty. She is also a seminar leader for Landmark Education Corporation.

Michael S. Kimmel is a sociologist at the State University of New York at Stony Brook where he teaches courses on gender, social theory, and human sexuality. His books include *Against the Tide: Pro-Feminist Men in the United States,* a documentary history (Beacon, 1992), *Men Confront Pornography* (Crown, 1990), *Men's Lives* (2nd edition, Macmillan, 1992), *Changing Men* (Sage, 1987), and the forthcoming *Manhood: The American Quest* (HarperCollins, 1995). He is the editor of *masculinities,* a scholarly journal on gender issues, the book series on Men and Masculinity at University of California Press, and he edits a research series on Men and Masculinities at Sage Publications. He is the spokesperson for the National Organization for Men Against Sexism.

Marlene LeGates teaches history and women's studies at Capilano College, North Vancouver, British Columbia, and at the University of British Columbia, Vancouver. She has a Ph.D. in history from Yale University, has served as coordinator of the Women's Studies Program, coordinator of International Women's Day activities, and chair of the Status of Women Committee of the College-Institute Educators' Association. Having lectured and written on topics within the history of feminism, she is presently finishing a book tentatively titled *Making Waves: A History of Feminism in Europe and North America,* which will be published in January 1996.

Hilary M. Lips is a professor of psychology and director of the Center for Gender Studies at Radford University in Virginia, where she teaches courses in social psychology, the psychology of women, and the psychology of sex and gender. Her books include *Sex and Gender: An Introduction* and *Women, Men, and Power,* for which she received the Distinguished Publication Award from the Association for Women in Psychology. Her current research focuses on gender and self-concept as factors in mathematics and science achievement and on reactions to powerful women.

Ruth B. Mandel is professor at the Eagleton Institute of Politics at Rutgers University and director of Eagleton's Center for the American Woman and Politics (CAWP). She writes and speaks widely about women and leadership, with particular emphasis on women as political candidates, women in office, women's political networks, and the "gender gap." Her book, *In the Running: The New Woman Candidate* (Beacon Press, 1983), describes women's experiences campaigning for political office. In 1984, she was executive producer of *Not One of the Boys,* a sixty-minute film created by CAWP to document the progress women are making and the obstacles they encounter as they enter political life.

Mandel oversees the center's work with women public officials, has co-directed a national research program to study the impact of women in public office, and is developing summer institutes and other educational programs to interest young women in political leadership. A member of the Faculty of Arts and Sciences at Rutgers, Mandel currently teaches graduate and undergraduate courses on women and American politics and women and political leadership.

Susan E. Marshall is associate professor of sociology and former director of the Women's Studies Program at the University of Texas at Austin. She is the author of numerous articles on U.S. antifeminist movements, women's right-wing political organizations, the politics of the Equal Rights Amendment, and gender and race differences in political attitudes. She is currently completing a social history of the American antisuffrage movement.

Susan Ehrlich Martin is a health scientist administrator in the Prevention Research Branch at the National Institute of Alcohol Abuse and Alcoholism of NIH. She is currently directing the programs on alcohol and interpersonal violence, drunk driving, and alcohol in the worksite. She is author of *Breaking and Entering: Policewomen on Patrol* (1980) and *On the Move: The Status of Women in Policing* (1990) and editor of *Alcohol and Interpersonal Violence: Fostering Multidisciplinary Perspectives* (1993) and articles on law, criminal justice, and alcohol policy that have appeared in *Criminology, Justice Quarterly,* and *Accident Analysis and Prevention.* She is currently working on a book on women as criminal justice professionals.

Brigid O'Farrell is a senior associate at the Center for Women Policy Studies in Washington, D.C. Her research focus is organizational change, which includes issues of equal employment policy, unions, child care, and work/family. Recent publications include "Unions, Hard Hats, and Women Workers," with Suzanne Moore (in *Women and Unions: Forging a Partnership,* 1993), *Work and Family: Policies for a Changing Work Force* coedited with Marianne Ferber and LaRue Allen (1991), and *Pay Equity: Empirical Inquires* coedited with Robert Michael and Heidi Hartmann (1989). She is currently working on a volume of oral histories by women in the labor movement. She has an Ed.M. in social policy from Harvard University.

Beatriz M. Pesquera is associate professor and director of the Chicana/Chicano Studies Program at the University of California, Davis. She has published articles on Chicanas' employment and familial experiences and on Chicana feminism. She is co-editor (with Adela de la Torre) of *Building with Our Hands: New Directions in Chicana Studies.* She is currently completing a book on the intersection of employment and family among Chicana workers, and with Denise Segura, is preparing a manuscript on Chicana feminism. During 1990–91, she was a Rockefeller Humanist-in-Residence at the Southwest Institute for Research on Women at the University of Arizona, Tucson.

Lisa Ransdell received her Ph.D. in sociology from The Ohio State University in 1990. She is director of Women's Programs and adjunct assistant professor of sociology/anthropology and women's studies at Denison University in Granville, Ohio. Her research and teaching interests center on women's health issues, the U.S. feminist movement, and the social construction of sexual identities. She also speaks and consults on sexual harassment and workplace diversity.

Martha J. Reineke received her Ph.D. from Vanderbilt University in 1983. She is associate professor of religion and director of the graduate program in women's studies at the University of Northern Iowa where she teaches courses in Women's Studies, religion and society, and world religions. Her published works include articles in *Philosophy and Theology, Feminist Ethnics,* and *Soundings.* She is currently working on a book, influenced by Julia Kristeva and René Girard, in which she will probe the coincidence of violence and the sacred in the history of Western culture from a feminist perspective.

Barbara Katz Rothman is professor of sociology at Baruch College and the Graduate Center of the City University of New York. She is the author of *In Labor: Women and Power in the Birthplace,* a comparison of the medical and midwifery models of childbirth; and of *The Tentative Pregnancy: Prenatal Diagnosis and the Future of Motherhood,* a study of women's experiences with amniocentesis and selective abortion; and most recently, *Recreating Motherhood: Ideology and Technology in a Patriarchal Society,* a feminist analysis of changing ideas about motherhood in America; and *Centuries of Solace,* with Wendy Simonds.

Nancy Felipe Russo is professor of psychology and women's studies at Arizona State University, where her research focuses on women's health (physical and mental) and achievement issues. Currently, she is exploring the intersection of childbearing, violence, and health issues for women of varying ethnicity. A former president of the Division of the Psychology of Women of the American Psychological Association (APA), she serves as editor of the *Psychology of Women Quarterly* and was a member of APA's task force on Male Violence Against Women. The report of that Task Force, *No Safe Haven: Violence Against Women at Home, at Work and in the Community* (Washington, D.C.: APA), is the most recent of her more than 140 publications related to women's issues.

Elayne A. Saltzberg is a doctoral candidate in clinical psychology at the University of Rhode Island, where she is currently writing her dissertation on the impact of breast cancer surgery on women's body image and sexual functioning. She earned her masters degree in psychology at Connecticut College where she conducted research on gender and exercise participation. She has published several articles on body image issues, and she is presently examining the impact of the pursuit of beauty on women's health.

Denise A. Segura is associate professor of sociology at the University of California, Santa Barbara, where she also serves as the associate director of the Center for Chicano Studies Research and participates on the Advisory Board of the Women's Studies Program. She has received numerous awards, most recently a 1993–94 U.C. Management Fellowship and a 1991–92 Ford Foundation Postdoctoral Fellowship. She teaches courses on women and work, racial ethnic families, and Chicana studies. Her research focuses on the complex interplay of class, race-ethnicity, and gender in women's lives with emphasis on Chicana/Mexicana women. Her articles have appeared in *Signs: Journal of Women in Culture and Society, Gender and Society, Aztlán, A Journal of Chicano Studies, Sociological Perspectives,* and numerous anthologies in sociology and women's studies. At present, she is writing a coauthored book (with Beatriz M. Pesquera) on the contemporary and historical dimensions of Chicana feminism. She is a single parent of three children who support her academic endeavors lovingly.

Carole J. Sheffield is a professor of political science and women's studies at The William Paterson College of New Jersey. She was a founding member of the college's Women's Studies Program and has served as its director. She teaches in both the Women's Studies and the Race and Gender Programs. She has recently completed an in-house study of campus violence and also published a study on women's experiences of obscene phone calls. Sheffield lectures widely and continues to publish on issues of feminism and sexual violence. Her current interest is on sexual terrorism in the popular culture.

Marianne B. Sheldon received her Ph.D. in history from the University of Michigan. She is currently a professor of history at Mills College in Oakland, California. She teaches courses on the history of women, children, and the family including an undergraduate interdisciplinary seminar on women and work in America with Dr. Nancy M. Thornborrow. Her current research focuses on the development of group medical practice in the United States.

Janice M. Steil received her Ph.D. from Columbia University in 1979, after which she joined the faculty of the Derner Institute of Advanced Psychological Studies at Adelphi University. She is a social psychologist with interests in the psychology of justice, psychology and gender, and power. For the last ten years, she has been studying these issues in the context of dual-career marriages.

Dr. Steil has published reports of her work in varied psychological and feminist journals including *The Journal of Social and Personal Relations, The Journal of Experimental Social Psychology, Psychology of Women Quarterly,* and *Sex Roles.* She has given invited talks at conferences and universities in Europe and Asia as well as the United States, has contributed chapters to both undergraduate and graduate texts, and is currently working on a book for Sage Press entitled *Marital Equality: Benefits and Barriers.*

In addition to her teaching, research, and writing, Dr. Steil has done a number of invited book reviews, served on the program committee of the Eastern Psychological Association, and is currently serving as an associate editor for *Psychology of Women Quarterly,* the journal of Division 35 of the American Psychological Association, which focuses on psychology and women.

Gloria Steinem is one of the country's most widely read and critically acclaimed writers and editors. She travels as a lecturer and feminist organizer and appears frequently on television and radio as an interviewer and spokeswoman on issues of equality. She is currently an editorial consultant and writer for *Ms.* magazine, the international feminist bimonthly that she co-founded in 1972. *Moving Beyond Words,* a collection of essays, will be published by Simon & Schuster in the spring of 1994. Her best-seller, *Revolution from Within: A Book of Self-Esteem,* was published in 1992 by Little, Brown & Co. Gloria Steinem helped to found, and continues to serve as board member or advisor, for the

Ms. Foundation for Women, the National Women's Political Caucus, the Women's Action Alliance, and the Coalition of Labor Union Women. She is president of Voters for Choice, a nonpartisan political action committee that supports pro-choice candidates.

In 1984, **Pauline Terrelonge** was an assistant professor of political science and Afro-American and African studies at the University of Michigan at Ann Arbor. She holds advanced degrees in law and political science. She has taught courses on women in political theory, black women in America, and legal policy. She is the author of articles in a number of scholarly journals on the subject of black politicians in American society and has done research on women in the Caribbean. Her current work is on United States immigration policy. She has been practicing law in San Francisco for the past ten years.

Nancy M. Thornborrow received her Ph.D. in economics from the University of California, San Diego. She is currently a professor of economics at Mills College in Oakland, California. Her research and teaching interests lie in the fields of labor and macroeconomics. With Dr. Marianne Sheldon, she teaches an undergraduate interdisciplinary seminar entitled "Women at Work in America." She is currently investigating female labor supply issues in the health care field.

Norma C. Ware is a research fellow in the program in medical anthropology at Harvard Medical School. She received her Ph.D. in anthropology and linguistics from the University of Michigan. She has done research on factors predicting the choice of a scientific major for college men and women, on the prevalence and correlates of bulimia in college women, and on the present life patterns of men and women who graduated from college in the mid 1970s. Her present research interests center on the relationship between culture and mental health.

Rose Weitz is a full professor in the Sociology Department at Arizona State University. She received her Ph.D. in 1978 from Yale University, specializing in the sociology of gender and the sociology of health and illness. She is the author of *Life with AIDS* (Rutgers University Press, 1991) and is co-author of *Labor Pains: Modern Midwives and Home Birth* (Yale University Press, 1988). Currently, she is writing a textbook on the sociology of health and illness for Wadsworth Publishing.

Carol Wayne White is an assistant professor in the Religion Department of Bucknell University, where she teaches courses in philosophy of religion, feminist theology, and contemporary religious thought. She has a Ph.D. in philosophy of religion and theological studies from the Iliff School of Theology and University of Denver (1993). Her recent publications and research are concerned with the intersection between French poststructuralism, feminism, and philosophical theology.

Sexual Terrorism

Carole J. Sheffield

> No two of us think alike about it, and yet it is clear to me, that question underlies the whole movement, and our little skirmishing for better laws, and the right to vote, will yet be swallowed up in the real question, viz: Has a woman a right to herself? It is very little to me to have the right to vote, to own property, etc., if I may not keep my body, and its uses, in my absolute right. Not one wife in a thousand can do that now.
> —Lucy Stone, in a letter to Antoinette Brown, July 11, 1855

THE RIGHT OF MEN TO control the female body is a cornerstone of patriarchy. It is expressed by their efforts to control pregnancy and childbirth and to define female health care in general. Male opposition to abortion is rooted in opposition to female autonomy. Violence and the threat of violence against females represent the need of patriarchy to deny that a woman's body is her own property and that no one should have access to it without her consent. Violence and its corollary, fear, serve to terrorize females and to maintain the patriarchal definition of woman's place.

The word *terrorism* invokes images of furtive organizations of the far right or left, whose members blow up buildings and cars, hijack airplanes, and murder innocent people in some country other than ours. But there is a different kind of terrorism, one that so pervades our culture that we have learned to live with it as though it were the natural order of things. Its target is females—of all ages, races, and classes. It is the common characteristic of rape, wife battery, incest, pornography, harassment, and all forms of sexual violence. I call it *sexual terrorism* because it is a system by which males frighten and, by frightening, control and dominate females.

The concept of terrorism captured my attention in an "ordinary" event. One afternoon I collected my laundry and went to a nearby laundromat. The place is located in a small shopping center on a very busy highway. After I had loaded and started the machines, I became acutely aware of my environment. It was just after 6:00 P.M. and dark, the other stores were closed, the laundromat was brightly lit, and my car was the only one in the lot. Anyone passing by could readily see that I was alone and isolated. Knowing that rape is often a crime of opportunity, I became terrified. I wanted to leave and find a laundromat that was busier, but my clothes were well into the wash cycle, and, besides, I felt I was being "silly," "paranoid." The feeling of terror persisted, so I sat in my car, windows up and doors locked. When the wash was completed, I dashed in, threw the clothes into the dryer, and ran back out to my car. When the clothes were dry, I tossed them recklessly into the basket and hurriedly drove away to fold them in the security of my home.

1

Although I was not victimized in a direct, physical way or by objective or measurable standards, I felt victimized. It was, for me, a terrifying experience. I felt controlled by an invisible force. I was angry that something as commonplace as doing laundry after a day's work jeopardized my well-being. Mostly I was angry at being unfree: a hostage of a culture that, for the most part, encourages violence against females, instructs men in the methodology of sexual violence, and provides them with ready justification for their violence. I was angry that I could be victimized by being "in the wrong place at the wrong time." The essence of terrorism is that one never knows when is the wrong time and where is the wrong place.

Following my experience at the laundromat, I talked with my students about terrorization. Women students began to open up and reveal terrors that they had kept secret because of embarrassment: fears of jogging alone, shopping alone, going to the movies alone. One woman recalled feelings of terror in her adolescence when she did child care for extra money. Nothing had ever happened, and she had not been afraid of anyone in particular, but she had felt a vague terror when being driven home late at night by the man of the house.

The male students listened incredulously and then demanded equal time. The harder they tried, the more they realized how very different—qualitatively, quantitatively, and contextually—their fears were. All agreed that, while they experienced fear in a violent society, they did not experience terror, nor did they experience fear of rape or sexual mutilation. They felt more in control, either from a psychophysical sense of security that they could defend themselves or from a confidence in being able to determine wrong places and times. All the women admitted feeling fear and anxiety when walking to their cars on the campus, especially after an evening class or activity. None of the men experienced fear on campus at any time. The men could be rather specific in describing where they were afraid: in Harlem, for example, or in certain parts of downtown Newark, New Jersey—places that have a reputation for violence. But either they could avoid these places or they felt capable of self-protective action. Above all, male students said that they *never* feared being attacked simply because they were male. They *never* feared going to a movie or to a mall alone. Their daily activities were not characterized by a concern for their physical integrity.

The differences between men's and women's experiences of fear underscore the meaning of sexual terrorism: that women's lives are bounded by both the reality of pervasive sexual danger and the fear that reality engenders. In her study of rape, Susan Brownmiller argues that rape is "nothing more or less than a conscious process of intimidation by which all men keep all women in a state of fear."[1] In their study *The Female Fear,* Margaret T. Gordon and Stephanie Riger found that one-third of women said they worry at least once a month about being raped. Many said they worry daily about the possibility of being raped. When they think about rape, they feel terrified and somewhat paralyzed. A third of women indicated that the fear of rape is "part of the background" of their lives and "one of those things that's always there." Another third claimed they never worried about rape but reported taking precautions, "sometimes elaborate ones," to try to avoid being raped.[2]

Indeed, women's attempts to avoid sexual intrusion take many forms. To varying degrees, women change and restrict their behavior, life-styles, and physical appearances. They will pay higher costs for housing and transportation and even make educational and career choices to attempt to minimize sexual victimization.

Sexual terrorism includes nonviolent sexual intimidation and the threat of violence as well as overt sexual violence. For example, although an act of rape, an unnecessary hysterectomy, and the publishing of *Playboy* magazine appear to be quite different, they are in fact more similar than dissimilar. Each is based on fear, hostility, and a need to dominate women. Rape is an act of aggression and possession. Unnecessary hysterectomies are extraordinary abuses of power rooted in men's concept of women as primarily reproductive beings and in their need to assert power over that reproduction. *Playboy,* like all forms of pornography, attempts to control women through the power of definition. Male pornographers define women's sexuality for their male customers. The basis of pornography is men's fantasies about women's sexuality.

Components of Sexual Terrorism

The literature on terrorism does not provide a precise definition.[3] Mine is taken from Hacker, who says that "terrorism aims to frighten, and by frightening, to dominate and control."[4] Writers agree more readily on the characteristics and functions of terrorism than on a definition. This analysis will focus on five components to illuminate the similarities and distinctions between sexual terrorism and political terrorism. The five components are ideology, propaganda, indiscriminate and amoral violence, voluntary compliance, and society's perception of the terrorist and the terrorized.

An *ideology* is an integrated set of beliefs about the world that explains the way things are and provides a vision of how they ought to be. Patriarchy, meaning the "rule of the fathers," is the ideological foundation of sexism in our society. It asserts the superiority of males and the inferiority of females. It also provides the rationale for sexual terrorism. The taproot of patriarchy is the masculine/warrior ideal. Masculinity must include not only a proclivity for violence but also all those characteristics claimed by warriors: aggression, control, emotional reserve, rationality, sexual potency, etc. Marc Feigen Fasteau, in *The Male Machine,* argues that "men are brought up with the idea that there ought to be some part of them, under control until released by necessity, that thrives on violence. This capacity, even affinity, for violence, lurking beneath the surface of every real man, is supposed to represent the primal untamed base of masculinity."[5]

Propaganda is the methodical dissemination of information for the purpose of promoting a particular ideology. Propaganda, by definition, is biased or even false information. Its purpose is to present one point of view on a subject and to discredit opposing points of view. Propaganda is essential to the conduct of terrorism. According to Francis Watson, in *Political Terrorism: The Threat and the Response,* "Terrorism must not be defined only in terms of violence, but also in terms of propaganda. The two are in operation together. Violence of terrorism is a coercive means for attempting to influence the thinking and actions of people. Propaganda is a persuasive means for doing the same thing."[6] The propaganda of sexual terrorism is found in all expressions of the popular culture: films, television, music, literature, advertising, pornography. The propaganda of sexual terrorism is also found in the ideas of patriarchy expressed in science, medicine, and psychology.

The third component, which is common to all forms of political terrorism, consists of "indiscriminateness, unpredictability, arbitrariness, ruthless destructiveness and amorality."[7] Indiscriminate violence and amorality are also at the heart of sexual terrorism. Every female is a potential target of violence—at any age, at any time, in any place. Further, as we shall see, amorality pervades sexual violence. Child molesters, incestuous fathers, wife beaters, and rapists often do not understand that they have done anything wrong. Their views are routinely shared by police officers, lawyers, and judges, and crimes of sexual violence are rarely punished in American society.

The fourth component of the theory of terrorism is voluntary compliance. The institutionalization of a system of terror requires the development of mechanisms other than sustained violence to achieve its goals. Violence must be employed to maintain terrorism, but sustained violence can be costly and debilitating. Therefore, strategies for ensuring a significant degree of voluntary compliance must be developed. Sexual terrorism is maintained to a great extent by an elaborate system of sex-role socialization that in effect instructs men to be terrorists in the name of masculinity and women to be victims in the name of femininity.

Sexual and political terrorism differ in the final component, perceptions of the terrorist and the victim. In political terrorism we know who is the terrorist and who is the victim. We may condemn or condone the terrorist, depending on our political views, but we sympathize with the victim. In sexual terrorism, however, we blame the victim and excuse the offender. We believe that the offender either is "sick" and therefore in need of our compassion or is acting out normal male impulses.

Types of Sexual Terrorism

While the discussion that follows focuses on four types of sexual terrorism—rape, wife abuse, sexual abuse of children, and sexual harassment—recent feminist research has documented other forms of sexual terrorism, including threats of violence, flashing, street hassling, obscene phone calls, stalking, coercive sex, pornography, prostitution, sexual slavery, and femicide. What women experience as sexually intrusive and violent is not necessarily reflected in our legal codes, and those acts that are recognized as criminal are often not understood specifically as crimes against women—as acts of sexual violence.

Acts of sexual terrorism include many forms of intrusion that society accepts as common and are therefore trivialized. For example, a recent study of women's experiences of obscene phone calls found that women respondents overwhelmingly found these calls to be a form of sexual intimidation and harassment.[8] While obscene phone calls are illegal, only in rare cases do women report them and the police take them seriously. In contrast, some forms of sexual terrorism are so extraordinary that they are regarded not only as aberrant but also as incomprehensible. The execution of fourteen women students at the University of Montreal on December 6, 1989, is one example of this. Separating the men from the women in a classroom and shouting, "You're all fucking feminists," twenty-five-year-old Marc Lepine systematically murdered fourteen women. In his suicide letter, claiming that "the feminists have always enraged me," Lepine recognized his crime as a political act.[9] For many women, this one act of sexual terrorism galvanized attention to the phenomenon of the murder of women because they are women. "Femicide," according to Jane Caputi and Diane E. H. Russell, describes "the murders of women by men motivated by hatred, contempt, pleasure, or a sense of ownership of women."[10] Most femicide, unlike the Montreal massacre, is committed by a male acquaintance, friend, or relative. In *Surviving Sexual Violence,* Liz Kelly argues that sexual violence must be understood as a continuum—that is, "a continuous series of events that pass into one another" united by a "basic common character."[11] Viewing sexual violence in this way furthers an understanding of both the "ordinary" and "extraordinary" forms of sexual terrorism and the range of abuse that women experience in their lifetimes.

Many types of sexual terrorism are crimes, yet when we look at the history of these acts, we see that they came to be considered criminal not so much to protect women as to adjust power relationships among men. Rape was originally a violation of a father's or husband's property rights; consequently, a husband by definition could not rape his wife. Wife beating was condoned by the law and still is condemned in name only. Although proscriptions against incest exist, society assumes a more serious posture toward men who sexually abuse other men's daughters. Sexual harassment is not a crime, and only recently has it been declared an actionable civil offense. Crimes of sexual violence are characterized by ambiguity and diversity in definition and interpretation. Because each state and territory has a separate system of law in addition to the federal system, crimes and punishments are assessed differently throughout the country.

RAPE

Rape statutes have been reformed in the past decade, largely to remove the exemption for wife rape and to use gender-neutral language. The essence of the definition of rape, however, remains the same: sexual penetration (typically defined as penile-vaginal, but may include oral and anal sodomy or penetration by fingers or other objects) of a female by force or threat of force, against her will and without her consent.[12]

Traditional views of rape are shaped by male views of sexuality and by men's fear of being unjustly accused. Deborah Rhode argues, in *Justice and Gender,* that this reflects a "sexual schizophrenia." That is, forced sexual intercourse by a stranger against a chaste woman is unquestionably regarded as a heinous crime, whereas coercive sex that does not fit this model is largely denied.[13] Since most women are raped by men they know, this construction excludes many forms of rape.

Because rape is considered a sexual act, evidence of force and resistance is often necessary to establish the nonconsent needed to convict rapists. Such proof is not demanded of a victim of any other crime. If females do not resist rape as much as possible, "consent" is assumed.

By 1990, forty-two states had adopted laws criminalizing rape in marriage: sixteen states recognize that wife rape is a crime and provide no exemptions; twenty-six states penalize wife rape but allow for some exemptions under which husbands cannot be prosecuted for raping their wives. Eight states do not recognize wife rape as a crime.[14] In spite of statutory reform, wife rape remains a greatly misunderstood phenomenon, and the magnitude of sexual abuse by husbands is not known. In Diana E. H. Russell's pioneering study on rape in marriage, 14 percent of the female respondents reported having been raped by their husbands.[15] The prevalence of wife rape, however, is believed to be much higher; approximately 40 percent of women in battered women's shelters also report having been raped by their husbands.[16] Victims of wife rape, according to one study, are at a greater risk of being murdered by their husbands, or of murdering them, than women who are physically but not sexually assaulted.[17]

WIFE ABUSE

For centuries it has been assumed that a husband had the right to punish or discipline his wife with physical force. The popular expression "rule of thumb" originated from English common law, which allowed a husband to beat his wife with a whip or stick no bigger in diameter than his thumb. The husband's prerogative was incorporated into American law. Several states once had statutes that essentially allowed a man to beat his wife without interference from the courts.[18]

In 1871, in the landmark case of *Fulgham v. State,* an Alabama court ruled that "the privilege, ancient though it be, to beat her with a stick, to pull her hair, choke her, spit in her face or kick her about the floor or to inflict upon her other like indignities, is not now acknowledged by our law."[19] The law, however, has been ambiguous and often contradictory on the issue of wife abuse. While the courts established that a man had no right to beat his wife, it also held that a woman could not press charges against her abusive husband. In 1910, the U.S. Supreme Court ruled that a wife could not charge her husband with assault and battery because it "would open the doors of the court to accusations of all sorts of one spouse against the other and bring into public notice complaints for assaults, slander and libel."[20] The courts virtually condoned violence for the purpose of maintaining peace.

Laws and public attitudes about the illegality of wife abuse and the rights of the victim have been slowly evolving. During the 1980s, there was a proliferation of new laws designed to address the needs of victims of domestic violence and to reform police and judicial responses to wife abuse. These measures include temporary or permanent protection orders, state-funded or state-assisted shelters, state-mandated data collection, and proarrest or mandatory arrest policies.[21] Most states, however, continue to define domestic violence as a misdemeanor crime, carrying jail sentences of less than one year. Felony crimes are punishable by more than one year in jail, and police officers tend to arrest more often for felony offenses. The distinction between misdemeanor and felony crimes is also based on the use of weapons and the infliction of serious injuries.[22] While wife abuse is still considered a misdemeanor crime, a National Crime Survey revealed that at least 50 percent of the domestic "simple assaults" involved bodily injury as serious as or more serious than 90 percent of all rapes, robberies, and aggravated assaults.[23]

SEXUAL ABUSE OF CHILDREN

Defining sexual abuse of children is very difficult. The laws are complex and often contradictory. Generally, sexual abuse of children includes statutory rape, molestation, carnal knowledge, indecent liberties, impairing the morals of a minor, child abuse, child neglect, and incest. Each of these is defined, interpreted, and punished differently in each state.

The philosophy underlying statutory-rape laws is that a child below a certain age—arbitrarily fixed by law—is not able to give meaningful consent. Therefore, sexual intercourse with a female below a certain age, even with consent, is rape. Punishment for statutory rape, although rarely imposed, can be as high as life imprisonment. Coexistent with laws on statutory rape are laws on criminal incest. Incest is generally interpreted as sexual activity, most often intercourse, with a blood relative. The difference, then, between statutory rape and incest is the relation of the offender to the child. Statutory rape is committed by someone outside the family; incest, by a member of the family. The penalty for incest, also rarely imposed, is usually no more than ten years in prison. This contrast suggests that sexual abuse of children is tolerated when it occurs within the family and that unqualified protection of children from sexual assault is not the intent of the law.

SEXUAL HARASSMENT

Sexual harassment is a new term for an old phenomenon. The research on sexual harassment, as well as the legal interpretation, centers on acts of sexual coercion or intimidation on the job and at school. Lin Farley, in *Sexual Shakedown: The Sexual Harassment of Women on the Job,* describes sexual harassment as "unsolicited nonreciprocal male behavior that asserts a woman's sex role over her function as a worker. It can be any or all of the following: staring at, commenting upon, or touching a woman's body; requests for acquiescence in sexual behavior; repeated nonreciprocated propositions for dates; demands for sexual intercourse; and rape."[24]

In 1980 the Equal Employment Opportunity Commission issued federal guidelines that defined sexual harassment as any behavior that "has the purpose or effect of unreasonably interfering with an individual's work performance or creating an intimidating or hostile or offensive environment." Such behavior can include "unwelcome sexual advances, requests for sexual favors, and other verbal or physical conduct of a sexual nature."[25] It was not until six years later, however, that the Supreme Court, in *Meritor Savings Bank FSB v. Vinson,* ruled that sexual harassment was a form of sex discrimination under Title VII of the Civil Rights Act of 1964.[26]

In October 1991 national attention was focused on the issue of sexual harassment as a result of allegations made against Supreme Court Justice nominee Clarence Thomas by Professor Anita Hill. (Thomas was subsequently confirmed as a Supreme Court justice by a vote of fifty-two to forty-eight.) While there was a blizzard of media attention about sexual harassment, what emerged most clearly from the confirmation hearings was that the chasm between women's experiences of sexual harassment and an understanding of the phenomenon by society in general had not been bridged. Perhaps most misunderstood was the fact that Professor Hill's experience and her reaction to it were typical of sexually harassed women.[27]

Characteristics of Sexual Terrorism

Those forms of sexual terrorism that are crimes share several common characteristics. Each will be addressed separately, but in the real world these characteristics are linked together and form a vicious circle, which functions to mask the reality of sexual terrorism and thus to perpetuate the system of oppression of females. Crimes of violence against females (1) cut across socioeconomic lines; (2) are the crimes least likely to be reported; (3) when reported, are the crimes least likely to be brought to trial or to result in conviction; (4) are often blamed on the victim; (5) are generally not taken seriously; and (6) fuse dominance and sexuality.

VIOLENCE AGAINST FEMALES CUTS ACROSS SOCIOECONOMIC LINES

The question "Who is the typical rapist, wife beater, incest offender, etc.?" is raised constantly. The answer is simple: men. Female sexual offenders are exceedingly rare. The men who commit acts of sexual terrorism are of all ages, races, and religions; they come from all communities, income levels, and educational levels; they are married, single, separated, and divorced. The "typical" sexually abusive male does not exist.

One of the most common assumptions about sexual violence is that it occurs primarily among the poor, uneducated, and predominantly non-white populations. Actually, violence committed by the poor and nonwhite is simply more visible because of their lack of resources to secure the privacy that the middle and upper classes can purchase. Most rapes, indeed, most incidents of sexual assault, are not reported, and therefore the picture drawn from police records must be viewed as very sketchy.

The data on sexual harassment in work situations indicates that it occurs among all job categories and pay ranges. Sexual harassment is committed by academic men, who are among the most highly educated members of society. In a 1991 *New York Times* poll, five out of ten men said they had said or done something that "could have been construed by a female colleague as harassment."[28]

All the studies on wife abuse testify to the fact that wife beating crosses socioeconomic lines. Wife beaters include high government officials, members of the armed forces, businessmen, policemen, physicians, lawyers, clergy, blue-collar workers, and the unemployed.[29] According to Maria Roy, founder and director of New York's Abused Women's Aid in Crisis, "We see abuse of women on all levels of income, age, occupation, and social standing. I've had four women come in recently whose husbands are Ph.D.s—two of them professors at top universities. Another abused woman is married to a very prominent attorney. We counseled battered wives whose husbands are doctors, psychiatrists, even clergymen."[30]

Similarly, in Vincent De Francis's classic study of 250 cases of sexual crimes committed against children, a major finding was that incidents of sexual assault against children cut across class lines.[31] Since sexual violence is not "nice," we prefer to believe that nice men do not commit these acts and that nice girls and women are not victims. Our refusal to accept the fact that violence against females is widespread throughout society strongly inhibits our ability to develop meaningful strategies to eliminate it. Moreover, because of underreporting, it is difficult to ascertain exactly how widespread it is.

CRIMES OF SEXUAL VIOLENCE ARE THE LEAST LIKELY TO BE REPORTED

Underreporting is common for all crimes against females. There are two national sources for data on crime in the United States: the annual Uniform Crime Reports (UCR) of the Federal Bureau of Investigation, which collects information from police departments, and the National Crime Survey (NCS), conducted by the U.S. Department of Justice, which collects data on personal and household criminal victimizations from a nationally representative sample of households.

The FBI recognizes that rape is seriously underreported by as much as 80 to 90 percent. According to FBI data for 1990, 102,555 rapes were reported.[32] The FBI Uniform Crime Report for 1990 estimates that a forcible rape occurs every five minutes.[33] This estimate is based on reported rapes; accounting for the high rate of underreporting, the FBI estimates that a rape occurs every two minutes. The number of forcible rapes reported to the police has been increasing every year. Since 1986, the rape rate has risen 10 percent.[34]

The National Crime Survey (renamed in 1991 as the National Crime Victimization Survey) data for 1990 reports 130,260 rapes.[35] This data is only slightly higher than FBI data; researchers argue that NCS data has serious drawbacks as well.[36] Just as victims are reluctant to report a rape to the police, many are also reluctant to reveal their victimization to an NCS interviewer. In fact, the NCS does not ask directly about rape (although it will in the future). A respondent may volunteer the information when asked questions about bodily harm. The NCS also excludes children under twelve, thus providing no data on childhood sexual assault.

In April 1992 the National Victim Center and the Crime Victims Research and Treatment Center released a report entitled "Rape in America," which summarized two nationwide studies: the National Women's Study, a three-year longitudinal survey of a national probability sample of 4,008 adult women, and the State of Services for Victims of Rape, which surveyed 370 agencies that provide rape crisis assistance.[37] The National Women's Study sought information about the incidence of rape and information about a number of health issues related to rape, including depression, posttraumatic stress disorder, suicide attempts, and alcohol- and drug-related problems.

The results of the National Women's Study confirm a belief held by many experts that the UCR and NCS data seriously underrepresents the occurrence of rape. According to the National Women's Study, 683,000 adult women were raped during a twelve-month period from the fall of 1989 to the fall of 1990.[38] This data is significantly higher than UCR and NCS data for approximately the same period. Moreover, since rapes of female children and adolescents under the age of eighteen and rapes of boys or men were not included in the study, the 683,000 rapes of adult women do not reflect an accurate picture of all rapes that occurred during that period. The data in this study also confirms the claim that acquaintance rape is far more pervasive than stranger rape. While 22 percent of victims were raped by someone unknown to them, 36 percent were raped by family members: 9 percent by husbands or ex-husbands, 11 percent by fathers or stepfathers, 16 percent by other relatives. Ten percent were raped by a boyfriend or ex-boyfriend and 29 percent by nonrelatives such as friends or neighbors (3 percent were not sure or refused to answer).[39]

Perhaps the most significant finding of the National Women's Study is that rape in the United States is "a tragedy of youth."[40] The study found that 29 percent of rapes occurred to female victims under the age of eleven, 32 percent occurred to females between the ages of eleven and seventeen, and 22 percent occurred to females between the ages of eighteen and twenty-four.[41] Other research suggests that one in four women will be the victim of rape or an attempted rape by the time they are in their midtwenties, and at least three-quarters of those assaults will be committed by men known to the victims.[42] Lifetime probability for rape victimization is as high as 50 percent; that is, one out of two women will be sexually assaulted at least once in her lifetime.[43]

The FBI's Uniform Crime Report indexes 10 million reported crimes a year but does not collect statistics on wife abuse. Since statutes in most states do not identify wife beating as a distinct crime, incidents of wife abuse are usually classified under "assault and battery" and "disputes." Estimates that 50 percent of American wives are battered every year are not uncommon in the literature.[44] Recent evidence shows that violence against wives becomes greatest at and after separation.[45] Divorced and separated women account for 75 percent of all battered women and report being battered fourteen times as often as women still living with their partners.[46] These women are also at the highest risk of being murdered by their former husbands. Thirty-three percent of all women murdered in the United States between 1976 and 1987 were murdered by their husbands.[47]

"The problem of sexual abuse of children is of unknown national dimensions," according to Vincent De Francis, "but findings strongly point to the probability of an enormous national incidence many times larger than the reported incidence of the physical abuse of children."[48] He discussed the existence of a wide gap between the reported incidence and the actual occurrence of sexual assaults against children and suggested that "the reported incidence represents the top edge of the moon as it rises over the mountain."[49] Research definitions as to what constitutes sexual abuse and research methodologies vary widely, resulting in reported rates ranging from 6 percent to 62 percent for female children and 3 percent to 31 percent for male children.[50] David Finkelhor suggests that the lowest figures support the claim that child sexual abuse is far from a rare occurrence and that the higher reported rates suggest a "problem of epidemic proportions."[51]

In a study of 126 African-American women and 122 white women in Los Angeles County, 62 percent reported at least one experience of sexual abuse before the age of eighteen.[52] The same men who beat their wives often abuse their children. Researchers have found that "the worse the wife-beating, the worse the child abuse."[53] It is estimated that fathers may sexually abuse children in 25 percent to 33 percent of all domestic abuse cases. There is also a strong correlation between child abuse and the frequency of marital rape, particularly where weapons are involved.[54]

Incest, according to author and researcher Florence Rush, is the *Best Kept Secret*.[55] The estimates, however speculative, are frightening. In a representative sample of 930 women in San Francisco, Diana E. H. Russell found that 16 percent of the women had been sexually abused by a relative before the age of eighteen and 4.5 percent had been sexually abused by their fathers (also before the age of eighteen).[56] Extrapolating to the general population, this research suggests that 160,000 women per million may have been sexually abused before the age of eighteen, and 45,000 women per million may have been sexually abused by their fathers.[57]

Accurate data on the incidence of sexual harassment is impossible to obtain. Women have traditionally accepted sexual innuendo as a fact of life and only recently have begun to report and analyze the dimensions of sexual coercion in the workplace. Research indicates that sexual harassment is pervasive. In 1978 Lin Farley found that accounts of sexual harassment within the federal government, the country's largest single employer, were extensive.[58] In 1988 the U.S. Merit Systems Protection Board released an updated study that showed that 85 percent of working women experience harassing behavior at some point in their lives.[59]

In 1976 over nine thousand women responded to a survey on sexual harassment conducted by *Redbook* magazine. More than 92 percent reported sexual harassment as a problem, a majority of the respondents described it as serious, and nine out of ten reported that they had personally experienced one or more forms of unwanted sexual attentions on the job.[60] The Ad Hoc Group on Equal Rights for Women attempted to gather data on sexual harassment at the United Nations. Their questionnaire was confiscated by UN officials, but 875 staff members had already responded; 73 percent were women, and more than half of them said that they had personally experienced or were aware of incidents of sexual harassment at the UN.[61] In May 1975, the Women's Section of the Human Affairs Program at Cornell University in Ithaca, New York, distributed the first questionnaire on sexual harassment. Of the 155 respondents, 92 percent identified sexual harassment as a serious problem, 70 percent had personally experienced some form of sexual harassment, and 56 percent reported incidents of physical harassment.[62] A 1991 *New York Times*/CBS poll found that four out of ten women experienced sexual harassment at work, yet only 4 percent reported it.[63]

In *The Lecherous Professor,* Billie Wright Dziech and Linda Weiner note that the low reportage of sexual harassment in higher education is due to the victims' deliberate avoidance of institutional processes and remedies.[64] A pilot study conducted by the National Advisory Council on Women's Educational Programs on Sexual Harassment in Academia concluded:

> The sexual harassment of postsecondary students is an increasingly visible problem of great, but as yet unascertained, dimensions. Once regarded as an isolated, purely personal problem, it has gained civil rights credibility as its scale and consequences have become known, and is correctly viewed as a form of illegal sex-based discrimination.[65]

CRIMES OF VIOLENCE AGAINST FEMALES HAVE THE LOWEST CONVICTION RATES

The common denominator in the underreporting of all sexual assaults is fear. Females have been well trained in silence and passivity. Early and sustained sex-role socialization teaches that women are responsible for the sexual behavior of men and that women cannot be trusted. These beliefs operate together. They function to keep women silent about their victimization and to keep other people from believing women when they do come forward. The victim's fear that she will not be believed and, as a consequence, that the offender will not be punished is not unrealistic. Sex offenders are rarely punished in our society.

Rape has the lowest conviction rate of all violent crimes. The likelihood of a rape complaint ending in conviction is 2 to 5 percent.[66] While the intent of rape reform legislation was to shift the emphasis from the victim's experiences to the perpetrator's acts,[67] prosecutions are less likely to be pursued if the victim and perpetrator are acquainted, and juries are less likely to return a conviction in cases where the victim's behavior or *alleged behavior* (emphasis mine) departed from traditional sex-role expectations.[68]

Data on prosecution and conviction of wife beaters is practically nonexistent. This is despite the fact that battery is, according to the U.S. Surgeon General, the "single largest cause of injury to women in the U.S." and accounts for one-fifth of all emergency room visits by women.[69] Police departments have generally tried to conciliate rather than arrest. Guided by the "stitch rule," arrests were made only when the victim's injuries required stitches. Police routinely instructed the parties to "break it up" or "talk it out" or asked the abuser to "take a walk and cool off." Male police officers, often identifying with the male abuser, routinely failed to advise women of their rights to file a complaint.[70]

As a result of sustained political activism on behalf of abused women, many states have revised their police training and have instituted pro- or even mandatory arrest policies. In 1984 the Attorney General's Task Force on Family Violence argued that the legal response to such violence be predicated on the abusive act and not on the relationship between the victim and the abuser.[71] A key issue, however, is the implementation of such reform. The record shows that the criminal justice system has responded inconsistently.[72]

Studies in the late 1970s and 1980s showed that batterers receive minimal fines and suspended sentences. In one study of 350 abused wives, none of the husbands served time in jail.[73] And while the result of pro- and

mandatory arrest policies is a larger number of domestic violence cases entering the judicial system,[74] "there is considerable evidence that judges have yet
to abandon the historical view of wife abuse."[75] In 1981 a Kansas judge suspended the fine of a convicted assailant on the condition that he buy his wife
a box of candy.[76] In 1984 a Colorado judge sentenced a man to two years on
work release for fatally shooting his wife five times in the face. Although the
sentence was less than the minimum required by law, the judge found that
the wife had "provoked" her husband by leaving him.[77] Recent task force
reports on gender bias in the courts reveal a pattern of nonenforcement of
protective orders, trivialization of complaints, and disbelief of females when
there is no visible evidence of severe injuries.[78] In 1987 a Massachusetts trial
judge scolded a battered women for wasting his time with her request for a
protective order. If she and her husband wanted to "gnaw" on each other, "fine,"
but they "shouldn't do it at taxpayers' expense." The husband later killed his
wife, and taxpayers paid for a murder trial.[79]

The lack of support and protection from the criminal justice system
intensifies the double bind of battered women. Leaving the batterer significantly
increases the risk of serious injury or death, while staying significantly increases
the psychological terrorism and frequency of abuse. According to former
Detroit Police Commander James Bannon, "You can readily understand why
the women ultimately take the law into their own hands or despair of finding
relief at all. *Or why the male feels protected by the system in his use of violence*"
(emphasis mine).[80]

In his study of child sexual abuse, Vincent De Francis found that plea
bargaining and dismissal of cases were the norm. The study sample consisted
of 173 cases brought to prosecution. Of these, 44 percent (seventy-six cases)
were dismissed, 22 percent (thirty-eight cases) voluntarily accepted a lesser
plea, 11 percent (six cases) were found guilty of a lesser charge, and 2 percent (four cases) were found guilty as charged. Of the remaining thirty-five
cases, either they were pending (fifteen) or terminated because the offender
was committed to a mental institution (five) or because the offender absconded
(seven), or no information was available (eight). Of the fifty-three offenders
who were convicted or pleaded guilty, thirty offenders escaped a jail sentence.
Twenty-one received suspended sentences and were placed on probation,
seven received suspended sentences without probation, and two were fined a
sum of money. The other 45 percent (twenty-three offenders) received prison
terms from under six months to three years; five were given indeterminate
sentences—that is, a minimum term of one year and a maximum term subject to the discretion of the state board of parole.[81]

In Diana E. H. Russell's study of 930 women, 648 cases of child sexual
abuse were disclosed. Thirty cases—5 percent—were reported to the police;
four were cases of incestuous abuse, and twenty-six were extrafamilial child
sexual abuse. Only seven cases resulted in conviction.[82]

Most of the victims of sexual harassment in the Cornell University study
were unwilling to use available procedures, such as grievances, to remedy their
complaints, because they believed that nothing would be done. Their perception is based on reality; of the 12 percent who did complain, over half found
that nothing was done in their cases.[83] The low adjudication and punishment

rates of sexual-harassment cases are particularly revealing in light of the fact that the offender is known and identifiable and that there is no fear of "mistaken identity," as there is in rape cases. While offenders accused of familial violence—incest and wife abuse—are also known, concern with keeping the family intact affects prosecution rates.

BLAMING THE VICTIM OF SEXUAL VIOLENCE IS PERVASIVE

The data on conviction rates of men who have committed acts of violence against females must be understood in the context of attitudes about women. Our male-dominated society evokes powerful myths to justify male violence against females and to ensure that these acts will rarely be punished. Victims of sexual violence are almost always suspect. We have developed an intricate network of beliefs and attitudes that perpetuate the idea that "victims of sex crimes have a hidden psychological need to be victimized."[84] We tend to believe either that the female willingly participated in her victimization or that she outright lied about it. Either way, we blame the victim and excuse or condone the offender.

Consider, for example, the operative myths about rape, wife battery, incest, and sexual harassment.

RAPE

All women want to be raped.
No woman can be raped if she doesn't want it (you-can't-thread-a-moving-needle argument).
She asked for it.
She changed her mind afterward.
When she says no, she means yes.
If you are going to be raped, you might as well relax and enjoy it.

WIFE ABUSE

Some women need to be beaten.
A good kick in the ass will straighten her out.
She needs a punch in the mouth every so often to keep her in line.
She must have done something to provoke him.

INCEST

The child was the seducer.
The child imagined it.

SEXUAL HARASSMENT

She was seductive.
She misunderstood. I was just being friendly.

Underlying all the myths about victims of sexual violence is the belief that the victim causes and is responsible for her own victimization. In the National

Women's Study, 69 percent of the rape victims were afraid that they would be blamed for their rape, 71 percent did not want their family to know they had been sexually abused, and 68 percent did not want people outside of their family knowing of their victimization.[85] Diana Scully studied convicted rapists and found that these men both believed in the rape myths and used them to justify their own behavior.[86] Underlying the attitudes about the male offender is the belief that he could not help himself: that is, he was ruled by his biology and/or he was seduced. The victim becomes the offender, and the offender becomes the victim. These two processes, blaming the victim and absolving the offender, protect the patriarchal view of the world by rationalizing sexual violence. Sexual violence by a normal male against an innocent female is unthinkable; therefore, she must have done something wrong or it would not have happened. This view was expressed by a Wisconsin judge who sentenced a twenty-four-year-old man to ninety days' work release for sexually assaulting a five-year-old girl. The judge, claiming that the child was an "unusually promiscuous young lady," stated that "no way do I believe that [the defendant] initiated sexual contact."[87] Making a victim believe she is at fault erases not only the individual offender's culpability but also the responsibility of the society as a whole. Sexual violence remains an individual problem, not a sociopolitical one.

One need only read the testimony of victims of sexual violence to see the powerful effects of blaming the victim. From the National Advisory Council on Women's Educational Programs Report on Sexual Harassment of Students:

I was ashamed, thought it was my fault, and was worried that the school would take action against me (for "unearned" grades) if they found out about it.

This happened seventeen years ago, and you are the first person I've been able to discuss it with in all that time. He's still at _____, and probably still doing it.

I'm afraid to tell anyone here about it, and I'm just hoping to get through the year so I can leave.[88]

From *Wife-Beating: The Silent Crisis,* Judge Stewart Oneglia comments,

Many women find it shameful to admit they don't have a good marriage. The battered wife wraps her bloody head in a towel, goes to the hospital, and explains to the doctor she fell down the stairs. After a few years of the husband telling her he beats her because she is ugly, stupid, or incompetent, she is so psychologically destroyed that she believes it.

A battered woman from Boston relates,

I actually thought if I only learned to cook better or keep a cleaner house, everything would be okay. I put up with the beatings for five years before I got desperate enough to get help.[89]

Another battered woman said,

When I came to, I wanted to die, the guilt and depression were so bad. Your whole sense of worth is tied up with being a successful wife and having

a happy marriage. If your husband beats you, then your marriage is a failure, and you're a failure. It's so horribly the opposite of how it is supposed
to be.[90]

Katherine Brady shared her experience as an incest survivor in *Father's
Days: A True Story of Incest*. She concluded her story with the following:

> I've learned a great deal by telling my story. I hope other incest victims may
> experience a similar journey of discovery by reading it. If nothing else, I
> would wish them to hear in this tale the two things I needed most, but had
> to wait years to hear: "You are not alone and you are not to blame."[91]

SEXUAL VIOLENCE IS NOT TAKEN SERIOUSLY

Another characteristic of sexual violence is that these crimes are not taken
seriously. Society manifests this attitude by simply denying the existence of
sexual violence, denying the gravity of these acts, joking about them, and
attempting to legitimate them.

Many offenders echo the societal norm by expressing genuine surprise
when they are confronted by authorities. This seems to be particularly true
in cases of sexual abuse of children, wife beating, and sexual harassment. In
her study of incest, Florence Rush found that child molesters very often do
not understand that they have done anything wrong. Many men still believe
that they have an inalienable right to rule "their women." Batterers, for
example, often cite their right to discipline their wives; incestuous fathers cite
their right to instruct their daughters in sexuality. These men are acting on
the belief that women are the property of men.

The concept of females as the property of men extends beyond the family unit, as the evidence on sexual harassment indicates. "Are you telling me
that this kind of horsing around may constitute an actionable offense?" que-
ried a character on a television special on sexual harassment.[92] This represents
the typical response of a man accused of sexual harassment. Men have been
taught that they are the hunters, and women—all women—are fair game.
The mythology about the workaday world abounds with sexual innuendo. Concepts of "sleazy" (i.e., sexually accessible) nurses and dumb, big-breasted, blond
secretaries are standard fare for comedy routines. When the existence of sexual
violence can no longer be denied, a common response is to joke about it
in order to belittle it. "If you are going to be raped, you might as well enjoy
it" clearly belittles the violence of rape. The public still laughs when Ralph
threatens Alice with "One of these days, POW—right in the kisser." Recently,
a television talk-show host remarked that "incest is a game the whole family
can play." The audience laughed uproariously.

SEXUAL VIOLENCE IS ABOUT VIOLENCE, POWER, AND SEX

The final characteristic common to all forms of violence against females is
perhaps the most difficult to comprehend. During the past decade, many
researchers argued (as I did in earlier versions of this article) that sexual

violence is not about sex but about violence. I now believe, however, that the "either-or" dichotomy—either sexual violence is about sex or it's about violence—is false and misleading. Male supremacy identifies females as having a basic "flaw"—a trait that distinguishes males and females and legitimates women's inferior status. This "flaw" is female sexuality: it is tempting and seductive and therefore disruptive, capable of reproducing life itself and therefore powerful.[93] Through sexual terrorism men seek to bring this force under control. The site of the struggle is the female body and female sexuality.

Timothy Beneke, in *Men on Rape,* argues that "not every man is a rapist but every man who grows up in America and learns American English learns all too much to think like a rapist" and that "for a man, rape has plenty to do with sex."[94] Twenty years of research and activism have documented that women largely experience rape, battery, incest, and sexual harassment as violence. That women and men often have vastly different experiences is not surprising. Under patriarchy men are entitled to sex; it is a primary vehicle by which they establish and signal their masculinity. From the male perspective, female sexuality is a commodity, something they must take, dominate, or own. Our popular culture routinely celebrates this particular notion of masculinity. Women are permitted to have sex, but only in marriage (the patriarchal ideal), or at least in love relationships. Women earn their femininity by managing their sexuality and keeping it in trust for a potential husband. The double standard of sexuality leads inevitably to coercion and sexual violence.

Many believe that re-visioning rape as violence not only accurately reflects many women's experiences but also is a more productive strategy for reforming legislation and transforming public attitudes. While arguing that "theoretically and strategically" the "rape as violence" position is the better one, attorney and author Susan Estrich points out that such an approach obscures the reality that the majority of rapes are coerced or forced but unaccompanied by conventional violence.[95] In fact, one consequence of this approach is that it precludes protest from women who experience sexual intrusions in ways not typically seen as violent.

It is argued that in sexual harassment the motive is power, not sex. There is a wide consensus that sexual harassment is intended to "keep women in their place." Yet, the means by which this is attempted or accomplished are sexual: rude comments about sex or about a woman's body, pornographic gestures or posters, demands for sexual favors, rape, etc. Clearly, to the harassers, a woman's place is a largely sexual one; her very presence in the workplace sexualizes it. In the accounts of women's experiences with sexual harassment in *Sexual Harassment: Women Speak Out,*[96] themes of sexual power and sexual humiliation resonate in each essay.

In wife battery the acts of violence are intended to inflict harm on the woman and ultimately to control her, but the message of the violence is explicitly sexual. For example, the most common parts of a woman's body attacked during battering are her face and her breasts—both symbols of her sexuality and her attractiveness to men. During pregnancy, the focus of the attack often shifts to the abdomen—a symbol of her reproductive power. In addressing the "either-or" debate in the sexual abuse of children, David

Finkelhor points out "sex is always in the service of other needs. Just because it is infused with nonsexual motives does not make child sexual abuse different from other kinds of behavior that we readily call 'sexual'."[97]

Conclusion

The dynamic that underscores all manifestations of sexual terrorism is misogyny—the hatred of women. Violence against women is power expressed sexually. It is violence eroticized. Diana E. H. Russell argues that "we are socialized to sexualize power, intimacy, and affection, and sometimes hatred and contempt as well."[98] For women in the United States, sexual violence and its threat are central issues in their daily lives. Both violence and fear are functional. Without the power to intimidate and punish women sexually, the domination of women in all spheres of society—political, social, and economic—could not exist.

RESOURCES

Attorney General's Task Force on Family Violence, Final Report. Washington, DC, 1984.

Lee H. Bowker, Michelle Arbitell, and J. Richard McFerron. "On the Relationship Between Wife Beating and Child Abuse," in Kersti Yllo and Michele Bograd (eds.), *Feminist Perspectives on Wife Abuse.* Newbury Park, CA: Sage Publications, Inc., 1988.

Jacquelyn C. Campbell. "Women's Responses to Sexual Abuse in Intimate Relationships." *Health Care for Women International* 8 (1989).

Jane Caputi and Diana E. H. Russell. "Femicide: Speaking the Unspeakable," in "Everyday Violence Against Women, Special Report." *Ms.* 1, no. 2 (1990).

Crime in the United States: Uniform Crime Reports, 1990. Washington, DC: U.S. Department of Justice, 1991.

Criminal Victimization in the United States, 1990. Washington, DC: U.S. Department of Justice, 1992.

Laura L. Crites. "Wife Abuse: The Judicial Record," in Laura L. Crites and Winifred L. Hepperle, *Women, the Courts and Equality.* Beverly Hills, CA: Sage Publications, Inc., 1987.

Billie Wright Dziech and Linda Weiner. *The Lecherous Professor: Sexual Harassment on Campus* (2nd ed.). Chicago: University of Illinois Press, 1990.

Susan Estrich. *Real Rape.* Cambridge, MA: Harvard University Press, 1987.

David Finkelhor. *A Sourcebook on Child Sexual Abuse.* Beverly Hills, CA: Sage Publications, Inc., 1986.

David Finkelhor (ed.). *Child Sexual Abuse: New Theory and Research.* New York: The Free Press, 1984.

David Finkelhor and Kersti Yllo. *License to Rape: Sexual Abuse of Wives.* New York: The Free Press, 1985.

Ellen Goodman. "My Equal Rights Winners." *Boston Globe,* Aug. 25, 1987, p. 13.

Gail A. Goolkasian. "Confronting Domestic Violence: The Role of the Criminal Court Judges." Washington, DC: U.S. Department of Justice, National Institute of Justice, 1986.

Margaret T. Gordon and Stephanie Riger. *The Female Fear.* New York: The Free Press; 1989.

Caroline Wolf Harlow. "Female Victims of Violent Crime." Washington, DC: U.S. Department of Justice, 1991.

Liz Kelly. *Surviving Sexual Violence.* Minneapolis: University of Minnesota Press, 1988.

Elizabeth Kolbert. "Sexual Harassment at Work Is Pervasive, Survey Suggests." *New York Times,* Oct. 11, 1991, pp. 1, A17.

Mary P. Koss and Mary R. Harvey. *The Rape Victim: Clinical and Community Interventions* (2nd ed.). Newbury Park, CA: Sage Publications, Inc., 1991.

Gary D. LaFree. *Rape and Criminal Justice: The Social Construction of Sexual Assault.* Belmont, CA: Wadsworth Publishing Co., 1989.

Patrick A. Langan and Christopher Innes. "Preventing Domestic Violence Against Women." Washington, DC: U.S. Department of Justice, Bureau of Justice Statistics, 1986.

Tamar Lewin. "Law on Sex Harassment Is Recent and Evolving." *New York Times,* Oct. 8, 1991, p. A22.

Louise Malette and Marie Chalouh. *The Montreal Massacre.* Translated by Marlene Wildeman. Charlottetown, Prince Edward Island: Gynergy Books, 1991.

Andrea Parrot and Laurie Bechofer. *Acquaintance Rape: The Hidden Crime.* New York: John Wiley and Sons, Inc., 1991.

Rape in America: A Report to the Nation. Prepared by the National Victim Center and the Crime Victims Research and Treatment Center, New York, Apr. 23, 1992.

Deborah L. Rhode. *Justice and Gender: Sex Discrimination and the Law.* Cambridge, MA: Harvard University Press, 1989.

Diana E. H. Russell. *Rape in Marriage* (2nd ed.). Indianapolis: Indiana University Press, 1990.

Diana E. H. Russell. *The Secret Trauma: Incest in the Lives of Girls and Women.* New York: Basic Books, Inc., 1986.

Lynn Hecht Schafran. "Documenting Gender Bias in the Courts: The Task Force Approach." *Judicature* 70 (1987): 280, 283–84.

Claudine SchWeber and Clarice Feinman, eds. *Criminal Justice Politics and Women: The Aftermath of Legally Mandated Change.* New York: The Haworth Press, 1985.

Diana Scully. *Understanding Sexual Violence: A Study of Convicted Rapists.* Boston: Unwin Hyman, Inc., 1990.

Carole Sheffield. "The Invisible Intruder: Women's Experiences of Obscene Phone Calls." *Gender and Society* 3, no. 4 (1989): 483–88.

Carole Sheffield. "Sexual Terrorism: The Social Control of Women," in Beth B. Hess and Myra Marx Feree (eds.), *Analyzing Gender: A Handbook of Social Science Research.* Beverly Hills, CA: Sage Publications, Inc., 1987.

Elizabeth A. Stanko. *Intimate Intrusions: Women's Experiences of Male Violence.* London: Routledge and Kegan Paul, 1985.

Amber Coverdale Sumrall and Dena Taylor, *Sexual Harassment: Women Speak Out.* Freedom, CA: The Crossing Press, 1992.

U.S. House of Representatives. Hearings on Sexual Harassment in the Federal Government, Committee on the Post Office and Civil Service, Subcommittee on Investigations. Washington, DC: U.S. Government Printing Office, 1980.

Joan Zorza. "Woman Battering: A Major Cause of Homelessness." *Clearinghouse Review* (Special Issue) 24, no. 4 (1991): 421–29.

NOTES

1. Susan Brownmiller, *Against Our Will: Men, Women and Rape* (New York: Simon and Schuster, 1975), 5.

2. Gordon and Riger, 22.

3. Yonah Alexander, "Terrorism and the Mass Media: Some Considerations," in Yonah Alexander, David Carlton, and Paul Wilkinson (eds.), *Terrorism: Theory and Practice* (Boulder, CO: Westview Press, 1979), 159; Ernest Evans, *Calling a Truce to Terrorism: The American Response to International Terrorism* (Westport, CT: Greenwood Press, 1979), 3; Charmers Johnson, "Perspectives on Terrorism," in Walter Laquer (ed.), *The Terrorism Reader* (Philadelphia: Temple University Press, 1978), 273; Thomas P. Thornton, "Terror as a Weapon of Political Agitation," in Harry Eckstein (ed.), *The Internal War* (New York: Free Press, 1964), 73; Eugene Walter, *Terror and Resistance* (New York: Oxford University Press, 1969), 6; Francis M. Watson, *Political Terrorism: The Threat and the Response* (Washington, DC: R. B. Luce Co., 1976), 15; Paul Wilkinson, *Political Terrorism* (New York: John Wiley and Sons, 1974), 11.

4. Frederick F. Hacker, *Crusaders, Criminals and Crazies: Terrorism in Our Time* (New York: W. W. Norton and Co., 1976), xi.

5. Marc Feigen Fasteau, *The Male Machine* (New York: McGraw-Hill Book Co., 1974), 144.

6. Watson, 15.

7. Wilkinson, 17.

8. Sheffield, "Obscene Phone Calls," 487.

9. Malette and Chalouh, 100.

10. Caputi and Russell, 34.

11. Kelly, 76.

12. Estrich, 8; UCR, 43; Koss and Harvey, 4.

13. Rhode, 245.

14. Russell, *Rape in Marriage,* 21–22.

15. Ibid., xxii.

16. Ibid., xxvi.

17. Campbell, 340.

18. *Bradley v. State. I Miss.* (7 Walker) 150 (1824); *State v. Black,* 60 N.C. (Win.) 266 (1864).

19. *Fulgham v. State,* 46 Ala. 143 (1871).

20. *Thompson v. Thompson,* 218 U.S. 611 (1910).

21. SchWeber and Feinman, 30.

22. *Arrest in Domestic Violence Cases: A State by State Summary* (New York: National Center on Women and Family Law, Inc., 1987), 1.

23. Langan and Innes, 1.

24. Lin Farley, *Sexual Shakedown: The Sexual Harassment of Women on the Job* (New York: McGraw-Hill Book Co., 1978), 14–15.

25. U.S. House of Representatives, 1980: 8.

26. *Meritor Savings Bank FSB v. Vinson,* 477 U.S. 57 (1986).

27. Lewin, A22; *Sexual Harassment: Research and Resources. A Report in Progress* (New York: The National Council for Research on Women, 1991), 10–13.

28. Kolbert, 1.

29. Roger Langley and Richard C. Levy, *Wife-Beating: The Silent Crisis* (New York: E. P. Dutton, 1977), 43.

30. Ibid., 44.

31. Vincent De Francis, *Protecting the Child Victim of Sex Crimes Committed by Adults* (Denver: American Humane Society, 1969), vii.

32. UCR, 1991, 16.

33. Ibid., 7.

34. Ibid., 16.

35. *Criminal Victimization in the United States,* 1990, 5.

36. Koss and Harvey, 11–17.

37. *Rape in America,* 1.

38. Ibid., 2.

39. Ibid., 4.

40. Ibid., 3.

41. Ibid.

42. Parrot and Bechofer, ix.

43. Crites, 36.

44. Langley and Levy, 3.

45. Zorza, 423.

46. Harlow, 5.

47. Caputi and Russell, 35.

48. De Francis, vii.

49. Ibid.

50. Finkelhor, *Sourcebook,* 19.

51. Ibid.

52. Russell, *Secret Trauma,* 69.

53. Bowker et al., 164.

54. Ibid.

55. Florence Rush, *The Best Kept Secret* (Englewood Cliffs, NJ: Prentice-Hall, 1980), 5.

56. Russell, *Secret Trauma,* 10.

57. Ibid.

58. Farley, 31.

59. Rhode, 232.

60. Ibid., 20.

61. Ibid., 21.

62. Ibid., 20.

63. Kolbert, A17.

64. Dziech and Weiner, xxi.

65. Frank J. Till, *Sexual Harassment: A Report on the Sexual Harassment of Students* (Washington, DC: National Advisory Council on Women's Educational Programs, 1980), 3.

66. Rhode, 246.

67. Koss and Harvey, 5.

68. LaFree, 240.

69. Zorza, 243.

70. Rhode, 239.

71. *Attorney General's Task Force,* 4.

72. Ibid.

73. Rhode, 241.

74. Goolkasian, 3.

75. Crites, 41.

76. Ibid., 45.

77. Ibid.

78. Schafran, 280, 283–84.

79. Goodman, 13.

80. James Bannon, as quoted in Del Martin, *Battered Wives* (New York: Pocket Books, 1977), 115.

81. De Francis, 190–91.

82. Russell, *Secret Trauma,* 85.

83. Farley, 22.

84. Georgia Dullea, "Child Prostitution: Causes Are Sought" (*New York Times,* Sept. 4, 1979), p. C11.

85. *Rape in America,* 4.

86. Scully, 58.

87. Stanko, 95.

88. Till, 28.

89. Ibid., 115.

90. Ibid., 116.

91. Katherine Brady, *Father's Days: A True Story of Incest* (New York: Dell Publishing Co., 1981), 253.

92. Till, 4.

93. Sheffield, "Social Control," 172.

94. Timothy Beneke, *Men on Rape: What They Have to Say About Sexual Violence* (New York: St. Martin's Press, 1982), 16.

95. Estrich, 83.

96. Sumrall and Taylor.

97. Finkelhor, *New Theory,* 34.

98. Russell, *Secret Trauma,* 393.

Sexual Harassment: The Link Joining Gender Stratification, Sexuality, and Women's Economic Status

Susan Ehrlich Martin

JOKES ABOUT THE secretary taking dictation on the boss's lap have long been part of workplace lore, but there was little public recognition of sexual harassment as a feminist issue until October 1991. At that time the testimony of Law Professor Anita Hill before the Senate Judiciary Committee on national television during the confirmation hearings of Clarence Thomas transformed the scope and nature of sexual harassment into a public issue. It could no longer be dismissed as an individual problem often brought on by women whose demeanor or attire "asked for it" or a complaint initiated by a woman as an illegitimate way to get ahead on the job. As described in *Capitol Games: Clarence Thomas, Anita Hill, and the Story of a Supreme Court Nomination* by Timothy Phelps and Helen Winternitz, the hearings showed that sexual harassment includes a far wider scope of behaviors than previously recognized, that it is an illegal but widespread fact of life for millions of American women in the paid labor force, that women are increasingly vocal about their perceptions of what is unacceptable behavior, and that in growing numbers they are willing to assert rights that did not even exist fifteen years ago. The hearings also showed that there still is ample disagreement over how to define such instances and how to deal with them.

"Sexual harassment has a long past but a short history" (Fitzgerald 1990:41). Until 1976, when the term *sexual harassment* apparently first came into use, the phenomenon was literally unspeakable (MacKinnon 1979). Since that time, sexual harassment has come to be recognized as a pervasive and harmful social problem and as a form of behavior prohibited by the Supreme Court as sex discrimination under Title VII of the Civil Rights Act of 1964.

Understanding sexual harassment requires recognizing that it is central to maintaining women's subordinate social, economic, and sexual statuses and thus is closely related to other feminist issues. Along with rape, wife beating, prostitution, and pornography, it is one of the ways in which male control of women's sexuality shapes women's experience.

This article reviews recent studies of the nature and extent of sexual harassment, analyzes the meaning of harassment from a feminist perspective, and examines the responses of individuals to the harassment experience. It also examines the government's responses to the issue through the development of case law and public policy.

Definitions of Sexual Harassment

Various definitions of sexual harassment have been proposed. For example, MacKinnon (1979:1) termed it "the unwanted imposition of sexual requirements in the context of a relationship of unequal power"; Farley (1978:14–15) called it "unsolicited, nonreciprocal male behavior that asserts a woman's sex role over her functioning as a worker"; and Yale University defined it as "an attempt to coerce an unwilling person into a sexual relationship, to subject a person to unwanted attention or to punish a refusal to comply" (cited by Crocker, 1983:698). The definition of sexual harassment applicable throughout the federal civil service is "deliberate or repeated unsolicited verbal comments, gestures, or physical contact of a sexual nature which are unwelcome" (U.S. House of Representatives 1980:8). What is common to these definitions is that sexual harassment (1) is physical or verbal behavior that is sexual in nature (i.e., it makes the victim's sex salient over her occupational or other statuses); (2) is unwanted; and (3) implicitly or explicitly is experienced as a threat to the woman's job or ability to perform her work or educational activities.[1]

Problems arise in defining and identifying incidents of sexual harassment because harassing behavior is not always clearly different from other acts.[2] The same action, such as a man's putting an arm around a woman's shoulder, may be regarded by its recipient either as intentionally offensive or as a friendly gesture, and may be welcome or repugnant depending on the woman's interpretation of the man's intentions, her view of him, and the situation.[3]

Both the Senate hearings and several studies (Konrad and Gutek 1986; Rubin and Borgers 1990; Fitzgerald and Ormerod 1991) indicate that there is strong agreement that requests for sex that are linked to threats of retaliation for noncompliance and sexual coercion constitute sexual harassment. There continues to be confusion, however, surrounding behaviors that are more subtle, less serious, and more widespread. Women are more likely than men to view such actions as harassment.

Two primary types of sexual harassment have been identified by MacKinnon (1979) and subsequently by the courts: *quid pro quo harassment* and *harassment as a continuing condition of work*. Quid pro quo harassment involves a more or less explicit exchange: A woman must comply sexually or forfeit an employment or educational benefit. In such instances, the harasser tends to be an employer, supervisor, or teacher because his power to punish or reward rests on his occupational status. Male coworkers, classmates, and clients, however, may use informal authority in the work or academic setting or the power to give or withhold business or sales in order to harass. Quid pro quo harassment situations involve three elements: an advance, a response, and a consequence. Four different outcomes are possible: (1) an employer or instructor makes an advance, the woman declines it, and she is punished; (2) the employer or instructor makes an advance, the woman complies, but she does not receive the promised benefit; (3) the employer or instructor makes an advance, the woman complies, and she gains the benefit; (4) the employer or instructor makes an advance, the woman declines, and she receives no subsequent harassment or reprisal. Although each situation involves harassment, all successful legal cases against quid pro quo harassment have dealt with the first type, whereas courts have identified the second type as an additional illegal "condition of work."

Sexual harassment may also occur as a condition of work. Such harassment generally does not involve outright sexual demands (but see discussion of *Meritor v.Vinson* 477 US 57 [1986] on pages 37–40), but does include a variety of behaviors, such as touching, teasing, and making comments about a woman's appearance or sexuality; these require no response but make the woman's work environment unpleasant. Often such harassing behavior is less blatant or threatening than quid pro quo harassment, is condoned by management, and is regarded as "normal" male behavior or as an extension of the male prerogative of initiation in male–female interaction. For these reasons, women often do not define such behavior as sexual harassment and, when they do, they tend to be more reluctant to make formal complaints about it than about quid pro quo harassment.

Survey Findings Regarding Sexual Harassment

Knowledge is still limited about the frequency of various types of sexual harassment, the characteristics of victims and harassers, the conditions under which it occurs, its psychological and physical effects on the victims, and their responses to it. Most of the early studies involved nonrandom surveys with self-selected respondents, lacked a standard definition of sexual harassment, failed to specify the time period within which the respondent was to answer, and provided evidence that was stark but impressionistic rather than scientific (Safran 1976; Carey 1977; Kelber 1977; Silverman 1976–77). Several more recent studies have used random samples that permit more conclusive statistical analyses of the distribution of harassing behavior (Loy and Stewart 1984; Gutek et al. 1980; Gutek 1981; MSPB 1981; Benson and Thomson 1982; McCormack 1985; MSPB 1988). Loy and Stewart surveyed a random probability sample of 304 female and 203 male adult residents of Connecticut. Gutek et al., in 1980, pilot-tested interviews with 399 men and women, and subsequently (1981), Gutek interviewed 405 men and 827 women in the Los Angeles area using a random-digit-dialing selection procedure. Benson and Thomson sent questionnaires to a random sample of 400 female students in their senior year at the University of California at Berkeley and got 269 responses. McCormack (1985) conducted a survey of 1,178 randomly selected male and female students majoring in physics, chemistry, economics, and sociology at sixteen northeastern universities. The first study by the U.S. Merit Systems Protection Board (MSPB 1981) involved a stratified random sample of more than 23,000 civilian employees of the executive branch of the federal government and thus provides the fullest and most reliable picture of sexual harassment to date.[4]

EXTENT OF SEXUAL HARASSMENT

In the early studies estimates of the proportion of women experiencing sexual harassment on the job were so high that *Redbook* observed: "The problem is not epidemic; it is pandemic—an everyday, everywhere occurrence" (Safran 1976:217). Recent studies support this conclusion. Both the first and follow-up MSPB studies found that 42 percent of the female federal employees had experienced some form of sexual harassment in the workplace during the previous two years. The most severe type of harassment, actual or attempted rape or sexual assault, decreased from 1 percent to 1980 to .8 percent in 1987, and unwanted pressure for dates also fell (from 26 to 15 percent). The rate of all other types of harassment remained the same (9 percent faced pressure for sexual favors and 28 percent received suggestive looks or gestures in both years of the survey) or increased (the proportion of women that received unwanted letters, telephone calls, or materials of a sexual nature grew from 9 to 12 percent; deliberate touching, leaning over, cornering, or pinching increased from 15 to 26 percent; and the proportion experiencing sexual remarks, teasing, jokes, or questions grew from 33 to 35 percent) (MSPB 1988:16–17).

Loy and Stewart (1984:Table 3) found that almost half (49.8 percent) of the women surveyed had experienced at least one type of sexual harassment, with 37 percent reporting commentary harassment, 26 percent manhandling, 7 percent negotiation harassment and 2 percent assault. Reports of the frequency of sexual harassment in university settings vary depending on the definition and the population surveyed (females only or both sexes; undergraduates, graduates, faculty). For example, Metha and Nigg (1983) found that 13 percent of the female and 5 percent of the male students, faculty, and staff at Arizona State University experienced some form of harassment.

Benson and Thomson (1982:241) found that about 30 percent of the Berkeley seniors who responded had personally experienced at least one incident of sexual harassment during their college careers, although a larger proportion knew of incidents involving someone else and agreed that such occurrences were not rare. These incidents tended to take the form of gradual inducements not overtly linked to grades or to immediate sexual obligations. Instead, instructors displayed friendliness and offered extra help and flexible deadlines, which laid the groundwork for subsequent overtures. McCormack (1985) found only 2 percent of the male and 17 percent of the female students reported sexual harassment by a college instructor. Fitzgerald et al. (1988) found that more than 31 percent of the female students at two unidentified universities had experienced some form of sexual harassment, including 15 percent who had experienced seductive sexual approaches from their professors.

Based on their review of the findings from twenty-one studies of sexual harassment conducted mostly during the 1980s on a variety of campuses, Rubin and Borgers (1990:405) suggest that the incidence rate of 30 percent of the female students "may be a reliable estimate."

VICTIM CHARACTERISTICS

Women of all backgrounds and in all positions have been victims of harassment, although a woman's age, marital status, and education affect the likelihood of harassment. The first MSPB study found that the rate of harassment was directly proportional to the youth of the victim. Twice as many women between sixteen and nineteen years of age (67 percent) reported being harassed as did women between forty-five and fifty-four (33 percent) (MSPB 1981:43). More single (53 percent) and divorced (49 percent) women reported harassment than married (37 percent) and widowed women

(31 percent). Surprisingly, both MSPB studies found that harassment increased with the woman's education. The higher victimization rate of the more educated female employees appears to be related both to the difference in their attitudes (i.e., they defined more behaviors as harassment) and to their presence in nontraditional jobs (MSPB 1981:44; MSPB 1988:20). The race and ethnic background of the victim, however, made virtually no difference (MSPB 1981:44–45).

ORGANIZATIONAL CHARACTERISTICS

A number of organizational characteristics were also found by the MSPB studies to be related to sexual harassment, including agency, job classification, traditionalism of the job, gender of the victim's supervisor, and gender composition of the victim's work group. Incidents of harassment in the 1987 study varied from 29 to 52 percent of the respondents among federal agencies (MSPB 1988:18); the job classification of the victim showed only a modest relationship to victimization. The earlier study found that harassment occurred most frequently among trainees (51 percent); the proportions of women in professional and technical, clerical, and blue-collar positions that reported victimization were 41, 40, and 38 percent respectively (MSPB 1981:50). The differences between the trainees and other employees may reflect the younger age and greater powerlessness of the former. It is noteworthy that 53 percent of the women in nontraditional jobs but only 41 percent in traditional jobs reported unwanted sexual attention on the job (MSPB 1981:51). Women with a male supervisor were somewhat more likely to be sexually harassed (45 percent) than were those with a female supervisor (38 percent). In addition, the male–female ratio of the work group was strongly related to harassment. The greater the proportion of men in the work group, the more likely the women were to be harassed: 55 percent of those who worked in virtually all-male groups and 49 percent of those in predominantly male groups were subjected to harassment; 37 percent in predominantly female and only 22 percent in all-female work groups were victims of harassment (MSPB 1981:52). This difference may be related both to the statistically greater number of men in jobs that are nontraditional for women and to deliberate harassment by men as an expression of resentment of the presence of women in these jobs. Differences among salaries and grade levels and by region were minor, as were several other organizational characteristics, including privacy on the job, length of federal service, work schedule, typical working hours, and the size of the immediate work group (MSPB 1981:52–54).

THE HARASSERS

The typical harasser of female federal employees was a male coworker who was married, older than the victim, of the same race or ethnic background, and likely to have harassed others at work, according to descriptions of the victims (MSPB 1981:59–60). In the 1987 study, in 29 percent of the cases, women reported harassment by an immediate or higher-level supervisor (down from the 37 percent who reported victimization by supervisors in the 1980 study); 69 percent were bothered by a coworker or other federal employee with no supervisory authority over the victim (an increase from the 65 percent figure reported in 1980); and only 2 percent were bothered by a subordinate (a decrease from the 4 percent reported in 1980) (MSPB 1988:20). The 1980 study found that for the victim of rape or sexual assault, however, the supervisor was the perpetrator in 51 percent of the cases (MSPB 1981:60).

Loy and Stewart report somewhat different proportions of harassment by coworkers and supervisors. They found that 48 percent of the women reporting harassment had been victimized by an immediate or higher-level supervisor, and 50 percent reported harassment by a coworker (Loy and Stewart 1984: Table 8).

Fitzgerald et al. (1988) conducted a mail survey of 235 male faculty members employed at a prestigious university regarding social and sexual interactions with students, including gender harassment, seductive behavior, sexual bribery, sexual coercion, and sexual assault. More than a quarter of the sample stated that they had dated students, 26 percent had a sexual encounter or relationship with a student, but only one reported he believed he had sexually harassed a student, while 6 percent asserted they believed they had been sexually harassed by their women students. There were few differences among the men with respect to age, academic rank, or scholarly discipline. Written explanations by the men regarding their behavior indicate that they view their sexual relationships as ethically acceptable on the basis of mutual consent, the status and age of the student, the outcome of the relationship (i.e., marriage), and whether or not the student initiated the relationship.

To measure sexual harassment proclivities of men, Pryor (1987) asked male undergraduates at a large university to indicate on a five-point scale the likelihood they would sexually exploit a woman if they could be assured of not being caught and punished. This explored their willingness to use the social power inherent in a role or situation to elicit sex from another person through threat of punishment or promise of reward. He found that the likely harassers tend to view sex as a struggle between men and women, find it difficult to assume another's perspective, have higher rape proclivities, are high in authoritarianism, and tend to describe themselves in masculine terms that strongly differentiate them from stereotypical femininity. They also have a tendency to behave in sexually exploitive ways when their motives can be disguised by situational excuses.

EFFECTS OF SEXUAL HARASSMENT ON VICTIMS

Sexual harassment has psychological, social, and physical effects on its victims that in some cases "change lives" (Koss 1990). Like victims of rape and incest, sexually harassed women feel humiliated, ashamed, angry, and betrayed. Like the victims of sexual assault who report their cases, sexual harassment victims may experience a second injury when confronted by the institutional reaction to their claims. In one survey in which women could report multiple reactions, 78 percent reported feeling angry, 48 percent feeling upset, and 23 percent feeling frightened; an additional 27 percent mentioned feeling alienated, isolated, helpless, guilty, or another negative emotion (Silverman 1976–77). Many of the harassed victims feel the incident was their fault and that they were individually responsible as well as demeaned (Dziech and Weiner 1984;

Koss 1990; Rabinowitz 1990). Even victims who avoid self-blame recognize that others would judge them harshly if the situation became known (Jensen and Gutek 1982; Rabinowitz 1990). Others report physical symptoms, attitude changes including loss of ambition and self-confidence, a negative view of their work, and strained relations with men (Safran 1976; Silverman 1976–77; Lindsey 1977; New Responses, Inc. 1979; Schneider 1991). One-third of the victims—and 82 percent of the victims of sexual assault—reported suffering emotional and physical consequences (MSPB 1981:81). These symptoms led Tong (1984) to identify a "sexual harassment syndrome." In a study focused on victims of rape and attempted sexual assault on the job, Schneider (1991) found that 40 percent of these victims reported loss of interest in their jobs, an equal proportion believed they were taken less seriously as workers, and 20 percent believed they lost some career opportunity such as an expected pay increase or promotion.

Sexual harassment has harmful effects on college students as well. In addition to the psychological effects on the student's self-confidence, harassment may force a student to forfeit work, research, educational comfort, or a career as professors withhold legitimate opportunities from those who resist, or students withdraw rather than comply (Dziech and Weiner 1984). For example, a study conducted at Harvard in 1983 (cited in Fitzgerald and Schullman 1987) found that 15 percent of the graduate and 12 percent of the undergraduate students who experienced sexual harassment changed academic majors or educational programs as a result. Another study (Reilly et al. 1986) found that 30 percent of the student victims of sexual harassment reported a deterioration in their emotional condition, and 75 percent asserted that the quality of their schoolwork suffered. Benson and Thomson (1982:246–47) found that student victims reported disrupted intellectual development, confusion, self-doubt, distrust of male faculty in general, as well as feelings of helplessness—that nothing was likely to be done about a complaint. Women perceived that a victim was not likely to be believed when a tenured professor denied a complaint and that she would be labeled a "troublemaker" or suffer reprisals in the form of lowered grades and poor recommendations.

Although there is no way to estimate costs to individual victims, the MSPB estimated that the sexual harassment of women cost the federal government $267 million between May 1985 and May 1987. This figure encompasses the costs of job turnover, including the costs of offering a job to, doing background checks on, and training new employees; dollar losses due to emotional and physical stress, measured in terms of increased use of governmental health-benefit plans; and dollar losses due to absenteeism and lost individual and work-group productivity over a two-year period (MSPB 1988:39).

Analysis of Sexual Harassment

Sexual harassment is traditionally explained as either biologically based, "natural" behavior or as the idiosyncratic personal proclivity of a minority of men. One variation of this traditional perspective assumes that the human sex drive is stronger in men, leading them to act in sexually aggressive ways toward women. Another variation maintains that men and women are naturally attracted to each other and therefore inevitably engage in sexually oriented behavior in the workplace. A third variation suggests that sexually harassing behavior stems from the personal peculiarities of isolated, highly sexed individuals. What these variations have in common is their denial that sexual harassment at work has the intent or effect of discriminating against women or that it reduces women's chances to achieve social equality.

This traditional approach has several notable shortcomings. Most important is the failure to recognize that men and women are members of gender groups that have been socialized into learned gender scripts and work behaviors. Gender refers to patterned, socially-produced distinctions between females and males. It is not something inherent in people, but for the individual and the social group, it is "a daily accomplishment" (West and Zimmerman 1987) achieved through interactions that occur during participation in work organizations as well as in many other locations and relations (Acker 1992).

In rejecting a biologically deterministic approach, initially feminists focused on "sex roles" and observed that sexual behavior, like other kinds of social behavior, is learned, shaped by social rules and norms. Individuals can and do control impulses and conform with existing social rules. They noted that the traditional view trivializes sexual harassment by asserting that such behavior is "normal" or that it is futile to attempt to change human nature.

The "sex roles" or gender role approach regards gender as a category, social role, or identity of the individual. Recently, a "gendered organization" approach has expanded understanding of how gender differentiation and women's disadvantage are a pervasive feature of social and organizational life. Rather than treating gender as a fixed characteristic possessed by the individual or an addition to otherwise "gender neutral" social processes,

> advantage and disadvantage, exploitation and control, action and emotion, meaning and identity are patterned through and in terms of a distinction between male and female, masculine and feminine. Gender is . . . an integral part of those processes (Acker 1990:146).

These feminist approaches assert that sexual harassment involves use of power derived from the economic or occupational sphere to gain benefits, impose punishment, and assert dominance in the sexual sphere. Thus, economic inequality (i.e., employers' control over workers) and gender inequality (i.e., men's dominance over and control of women) reinforce each other, undercutting women's potential for social equality. Women's confinement to dead-end, low-paying, gender-stereotyped jobs and their subordination to male supervisors, employers, and instructors make them systematically vulnerable to sexual coercion; gendered workplace expectations are used to coerce women economically.

Because men dominate both the occupational sphere and the system of gender stratification that accords men higher status and authority over women, the power derived from one sphere supports that drawn from the other. Male superiors are unlikely to be sexually harassed by subordinates. But what occurs when there is status incongruity, such as when a woman supervises male subordinates? "Contrapower harassment" (Benson 1984) refers to sexual harassment that occurs when the victim has formal occupational power over the abuser. The MSPB data (1981:60) indicate that 4 percent of the female victims were harassed by a subordinate. Similarly, Benson (1984) provided anecdotal evidence to suggest that women instructors sometimes are sexually harassed by students.

A survey of 208 female instructors employed at a major university found that women professors experience a variety of unwanted behaviors, mostly from male students, which range from sexist comments to sexual assaults (Grauerholz 1989). Nearly half (47 percent) claimed to have experienced at least one of the following behaviors: sexist comments, undue attention, verbal sexual comments, written sexual comments, body language, physical advances, explicit sexual propositions, sexual bribery, sexual assault, or obscene phone calls. Not all these experiences were considered sexual harassment, although 44 percent of the respondents agreed that sexist comments constitute sexual harassment when directed at a professor from a student, and the majority agreed that all other behaviors described are sexual harassment.

Women's experience of contrapower harassment, usually in the form of sexist and verbal sexual comments,

> highlights the importance of gender in defining a woman's vulnerability to sexual harassment . . . and reflects women's experience in a culture in which coercive sexuality is widespread (Grauerholz 1989:798).

Thus both gender and occupational status define an individual's vulnerability to sexual harassment. Even in situations where a woman has clearly defined authority, gender continues to be one of the most salient and powerful variables governing work relations.

Regardless of a woman's status, she is vulnerable to men's definitions of the situation in gendered terms through interactions in which they assert gender dominance.

WOMEN IN THE OCCUPATIONAL SYSTEM

Organizational processes create gender distinctions, structure interaction in terms of gender, and influence the gender identity of workers (Acker 1990). Work organizations also create gendered job tasks and duties that press workers to construct and display gender as an integral part of their work. Occupations themselves are gender typed as the gender of job incumbents becomes associated with their primary tasks and jobs. These, then, acquire a gender character "which rubs off on the people who do them" (Cockburn 1988:169).

As a result of these processes, women workers (1) get lower pay than men on the average and lower pay for doing the same job; (2) are subordinated to male supervisors and depend on their goodwill and approval for getting, keeping, and advancing on the job; and (3) are concentrated in gender-stereotyped occupations and jobs. "Women's work" involves serving and nurturing men and caring for others. Opportunities for mobility up career ladders are limited; those that are open confer supervisory authority only over women and children. Occupational segregation contributes to the sexual harassment of women employed in both traditionally "women's jobs" and "men's work." The gendered structure of work opportunities and subordination to male supervisors across workplaces make it difficult and costly for female workers to reject the sexual advances of men in positions of authority.

Gendered images and expectations of women as wives, mothers, and sex objects, once labeled "sex-role spillovers" (Gutek and Morash 1982), in fact are extensions of women's domestic and reproductive roles into the workplace. Thus gendered meanings and relationships are embedded in the definition of the work roles themselves. Besides offering low pay, little prestige, and routine tasks, "women's jobs" are defined as those that involve service, emotional support, and being sexually attractive to men. Part of doing secretarial work is making coffee, running personal errands for the boss, and bolstering his sense of masculinity through flattery and deference (Kanter 1977). The definition of "waitressing" includes smiling, deferring, and exhibiting sexuality as part of the job (Hall 1993). While we now speak of "flight attendants" whose primary job is passenger safety (and many of whom are men), less than two decades ago the requirement that the "airlines stewardess" be unmarried and under thirty years of age indicates how integral sexuality was (and continues to be) to the definition of that job. Indeed,

> the very qualities which men find sexually attractive in the women they harass are the real qualifications for the jobs for which they hire them. It is this good-girl sexiness . . . that qualifies a woman for her job that leaves her open to sexual harassment at any time and to the accusation that she invites it (MacKinnon 1979:23).

"Token" women in male-dominated occupations also frequently suffer from sexual harassment. Those occupations require displays of masculine behavior as an integral part of the meaning of the work role; women's integration challenges the gender meanings connected to the work performance. Women's successful fulfillment of the occupational tasks highlights the incongruity between the worker's gender and the gendered work role, prompting a reinterpretation of the gender meanings embedded in the work role. For women, the apparent contradiction between the work tasks and gender scripts may lead to splitting the work role into two gendered forms in which women choose to emphasize their gender identity, enacting the role "like a woman," or emphasize their occupational identity and behaving "like a man." Each performance may involve interactions in which women are cast into and perform familiar gender stereotypes (e.g., "the mother," "the seductress," and "the bitch" [Kanter 1977:234–35]). Each also may lead to sexual harassment; the "seductress" is harassed because she "asks for it" by acting "sexy"; the "bitch" is punished for failing to do so.

The challenge to gender meanings also heightens men's resistance to such reinterpretation. One form of resistance is sexual harassment, particularly as a condition of work. Women's presence is regarded as an invasion of male economic turf (i.e., a challenge to men's better pay and supervisory authority), as an invasion of their social turf (e.g., army barracks, boardrooms, and police stations), and as a threat to their work and selves as "masculine." Men's harassment keeps women from working effectively, thereby "proving" women's unfitness for a "man's job" and, in some instances, driving out the female "invaders." In addition, male supervisors have ample opportunity for quid pro quo sexual harassment, since they are often in a position to "protect" the isolated woman or to give assignments that are more difficult and dangerous than those given to men for women who will not "cooperate."

A recent study reanalyzed the MSPB data to test the contributions of three hypothesized factors—power differentials, gender ratios in the workplace, and the effect of diffuse master status characteristics including gender, race, ethnicity—on the occurrence of seven types of unwanted behavior. These behaviors include actual or attempted sexual assaults; pressure for sexual favors; deliberate touching, leaning over, cornering, or pinching; sexually suggestive looks or gestures; letters, phone calls, or materials of a sexual nature; pressure for dates; and sexual teasing, jokes, remarks, or questions (Fain and Anderton 1987). The researchers found support for all three factors when they examined the proportion of female victims who reported each of the types of behavior by organizational, power, and other status characteristics. First, all seven types of sexual harassment were significantly less likely if the individual was a supervisor, supporting the argument that power inequalities affect workplace behavior. In addition, lower-status service workers were more likely to be harassed than higher-status professionals.

Each of the four status characteristics that reflect power relationships in society—education, ethnic group, marital status, and age—was significantly related to the likelihood of harassment. Women with high school education or less and those who were not currently married were more likely to have experienced all types of harassment; nonwhites were significantly more likely than whites to experience pressure for sexual favors, sexual gestures, and pressure for dates. The likelihood of harassment decreased with age.

Gender ratios also affected the likelihood of experiencing harassing behaviors, but in more complex ways. Women working in male-dominant groups generally were less likely to report being sexually harassed than women in female-dominated jobs, probably because they come to perceive men's behavior as "normal." Two groups of women in male-dominated workplaces, however, reported higher rates of harassment. These were women who identified the men's behaviors as sexual harassment (not as "normal") and women who were not married (and experienced higher rates of the potentially objectionable behavior). Thus while organizational factors are important, theories of gender-related behavior in the workplace must also examine and control for the larger context of social sexual relations.

SOCIALIZATION, CULTURAL NORMS, AND "DOING GENDER"

Sexual harassment, as well as the position of women in the occupational world, rests on the social arrangements between the sexes and their perpetuation through socialization to the cultural norms, expectations, and behaviors of persons. When a person is born, they are placed on a sex category, that is, labeled "male" or "female." Interactions with others throughout their lives then are based on "doing gender" or "managing situated conduct in light of normative conceptions of attitudes and activities appropriate for one's sex category" (West and Zimmerman 1989:127). In other words, they learn how to think and act as boys or girls, men or women in a variety of situations and interactions. Women are not born weak, passive, dependent, and receptive to male initiation. They are socially conditioned to develop these qualities, which are reinforced when they enact them, and expected to account for failures to live up to them. Similarly, men learn to act strong, dominant, independent, and aggressive and to initiate sexual interaction. Both men and women are continuously evaluated in terms of normative conceptions of appropriate attitudes and activities for their sex category. These permit men as a group to dominate women as a group through the privilege of initiating—and thereby controlling—intimate relationships. The social and sexual power that gender scripts, images, and norms give men over women is carried into the workplace and reinforced through male control of women's livelihood.

ACQUIESCENCE TO SEXUAL HARASSMENT

Despite folklore about "women who sleep their way to the top," there is little evidence that women advance on the job by using their sexuality to gain employment benefits. On the contrary, there is strong indication that acquiescence to sexual harassment has harmful effects on women's efforts to gain social and economic equality. Allegations of women's sexual complicity to gain employment benefits trivializes the magnitude of the problem of sexual harassment and obscures the nature of the situation faced by most women by putting it in false moral terms. For example, Phyllis Schlafly asserted that "sexual harassment on the job is not a problem for the virtuous woman except in the rarest of cases" (Rich 1981:A2). Such a statement implies that sexual harassment is the woman's fault. Rather than perceiving the woman as a victim of unwanted attention from someone with power over her livelihood, Schlafly blames the woman who "allows" herself to be harassed—or worse, elicits the harassment—because she is of dubious virtue. However, sexual harassment is not a question of "virtue"; it is a question of power. Women who acquiesce often are not in a position to refuse; their surrender is the price of survival. And while some women may gain benefits by providing "sexual favors," statistics on women's employment clearly indicate that these must be few in number, since as a group women fail to attain jobs for which they are qualified, much less to obtain undeserved advancement.

Both women and men feel injured by the benefits given to acquiescent women. But they direct their anger at the victims rather than looking at the system that permits the victimization. The acquiescence of a few women divides women as a group, thereby diminishing their ability to unite in fighting economic and sexual discrimination. Compliant women become the scapegoats for women's anger, which should properly focus on the men who offer economic rewards at a price, the work organization that permits harassment (often informally regarding it as a perquisite of male employees), or the sexual-stratification system that gives men power over women's livelihood and sexuality and perpetuates women's subordination and dependence.

Women's acquiescence to sexual harassment also reinforces the hostility of men to female coworkers. Many men who tolerate or accept a variety of other forms of favoritism in the distribution of job-related rewards, including relationships cultivated on the ball field, in the locker room, or at all-male clubs, are infuriated by the thought that women have and use "advantages" men do not have, making them feel "disadvantaged as a class" (Martin 1980). Men's anger at this form of injustice, however, is directed at both the compliant women and all women on the job, rather than at their male bosses (since it would be dangerous to express such jealousy and anger) or at the system that evades the merit principles it espouses. Such anger also serves as a convenient ego-protecting device, particularly for men of average competence. Stories or rumors about compliant women protect such men's sense of masculinity, which is threatened by the possibility that female coworkers are being advanced ahead of them because the women are more competent. By implying that the only way a woman can succeed is by using her sexuality rather than by performing better than male colleagues, the men can rationalize their failures, redirect their anger at a less threatening target, and thereby re-assert their superiority as males.

Individual Responses to Sexual Harassment: Strategies and Outcomes

During the Thomas confirmation hearings, the credibility of Anita Hill was questioned on the grounds that she had failed to speak out when she was harassed and instead continued to work for Thomas. Her behavior, however, was typical of sexual harassment victims. They have limited options for dealing with unwanted sexual attention, and each possible response poses costs and risks. They can adopt informal approaches, which include ignoring the harassment and asking the harasser to stop. They can quit the job or seek a transfer; students can change majors or courses. They can use formal grievance and complaint procedures or take legal action. Or they can acquiesce. What are the problems with each of these responses? Informal approaches may be ineffectual and may trigger escalation of the situation or retaliation. Escapist approaches can have substantial economic consequences: the loss of seniority, accumulated job knowledge, personal work-based ties, and income during the transition; the possibility of finding a new job only at a lower salary; and the acquisition of a reputation as an unstable worker. Formal complaints risk reprisals (including failure to be promoted, reduction in duties, dismissal, or, for students, lowered grades and poor recommendations); acquisition of a reputation for being a "troublemaker" among coworkers, who often "blame the victim"; and considerable expense if legal action is taken.

Given these options, most women workers seek to handle the situation informally—by either ignoring the behavior, avoiding the harasser, or asking him to stop. In the first MSPB study (1981:67), 61 percent of the victims reported ignoring the harassment and 48 percent asking the harasser to stop. Loy and Stewart (1984) found 32 percent ignoring the harasser and 39 percent asking him to stop. Respondents in both studies indicated that ignoring the harassment failed to end it and often made it worse. Asking the harasser to stop was effective for 54 percent of the women (MSPB 1981:67)—but ineffective in almost half the cases.

Findings from several studies suggest that the high turnover and absentee-ism rates for female workers are related to sexual harassment. In the initial MSPB study, 6 percent of all sexually harassed women (but 14 percent of the rape victims and 10 percent of the severely harassed women) reported sub-sequently quitting or transferring from their jobs (MSPB 1981:80). Loy and Stewart (1984: Table 4) found that 17 percent of victims reported quitting or transferring. Only a small proportion of victimized women sought a formal remedy by complaining through official channels (3 percent according to MSPB [1981:70] and 12.5 percent according to Loy and Stewart [1984:Table 4]). Schneider (1991) found that 19 percent of women victims of work-related attempted and actual sexual assault quit, while 67 percent of those women who remained in their jobs maintained a formal working relationship with their assailant. Further analyses revealed that being raped and harassment by a boss were not significant predictors of quitting. However, blatant economic coercion was. In this study, 21 percent of the victims filed a complaint. Their action was not related to the major characteristics of the assault encounter; but such a complaint occurred mostly when the assailant was an outsider. The vast majority of female victims did not complain through official channels due to ignorance of available remedies, the belief that formal action is less effective than informal treatment, and fear of making the situation worse. Fear of reprisals and negative outcomes appears to be well founded. Among MSPB respondents who had taken formal action, 41 percent found that their actions had no effect or made things worse (MSPB 1981:88–92).

Acquiescence is also an option. In the case of the less severely harassed women, this generally means tolerating suggestive looks, jokes, teasing, or pressure to go on dates. According to the MSPB study, 18 percent of the less severely harassed, 3 percent of the severely harassed, and 14 percent of the rape/assault victims reported that they "went along with the behavior," but only 8 percent of these women found that things had improved as a result (MSPB 1981:67).

Female students manage unwanted sexual attention in ways similar to those adopted by working women. Some, fearful of making a direct complaint, try to ignore the harassing behavior or use indirect strategies for stopping it. These strategies include directing discussion with the instructor back to the academic issue, bringing a friend to the instructor's office to avoid being alone with the instructor, and talking about a husband or boyfriend to indicate sexual unavailability. About 30 percent of the student victims did not directly communicate their displeasure to the harassing instructor; for almost all these women (thirteen out of fifteen), his unwanted behavior continued (Benson and Thomson 1982:244). The 70 percent who directly communicated their displeasure were more successful in stopping the harassment, although the professor's power tended to affect this outcome. Power was measured by three factors: whether the professor had tenure, whether he was in the student's chosen major field, and whether the student aspired to attend graduate school. The sexual harassment stopped in twenty-one of the twenty-four cases in which one or two of the three conditions were present. However, the harass-ment stopped in only five of the eleven instances in which all three were present (Benson and Thomson 1982:244). Even when the harassment stopped,

however, students who did not reciprocate sexual attention were often punished by the instructor's withdrawal of intellectual support and encouragement,
by his making critical comments about work that formerly had been praised,
and by his giving lower grades.

One option that is increasingly available to students as a growing number
of universities have policies and procedures for dealing with sexual harassment
is to make a formal complaint (Robertson et al. 1988). Nevertheless, only
about 5 percent of the undergraduate victims of sexual harassment report it
or file a grievance (Rabinowitz 1990). Their caution appears well justified.
When complaints were brought, informal methods were usually used to deal
with them; official investigations and the imposition of sanctions (usually only
a verbal warning) were rare.

In sum, findings from studies of women's responses suggest that ignoring
sexual harassment is not likely to end it, but that both informal confrontation
and formal complaints have risks and only modest success rates. Although there
is no single "right way" to deal with harassment, and although victims must
tailor their reaction to their individual situation, two strategies appear to be
advisable across the board. Students and workers should (1) learn about their
organization's formal grievance procedures and know who is responsible for
handling complaints and (2) discuss incidents they regard as potentially harassing with a trusted confidant to avoid self-blame and to gain support both in
dealing with feelings and in examining response options.

Organizational Responses to Sexual Harassment

Since the late 1970s, the federal government's response to pressure to prohibit
sexual harassment in the workplace has been the relatively swift establishment
of formal policy. Sexual harassment has been defined as an illegal form of sex
discrimination by the Equal Employment Opportunity Commission (EEOC)
and by the federal courts. Universities, often following the lead of major
higher-education professional organizations, have adopted policy guidelines and
grievance mechanisms for dealing with sexual harassment. Despite this clear
policy mandate, however, enforcement of the law remains weak. Punishment
of harassers is rare, and victims continue to suffer the triple burden of harassment, hostility and suspicion of coworkers, and reprisals by supervisors.
Furthermore, the structural context of inequality in the workplace and power
differentials in the university remain barely changed (Schneider 1985).

THE FEDERAL GOVERNMENT AND SEXUAL HARASSMENT

Before 1979, no federal agency had a policy prohibiting sexual harassment.
In 1979, apparently in response to adverse publicity regarding one government
agency (Ripskis 1979) and to pressure from organizations representing working
women, the House Committee on the Post Office and Civil Service held
hearings on sexual harassment in the federal government and called on the
U.S. Merit Systems Protection Board (MSPB) to conduct a study of sexual
harassment in the federal workplace. In addition, the Office of Personnel

Management issued a policy statement applicable throughout the federal government that defined sexual harassment, unequivocally declared that such harassment is unacceptable conduct in the workplace, and directed each federal agency to establish policies to reduce sexual harassment and grievance mechanisms to handle complaints (U.S. House of Representatives 1980:7–8).

In September 1980, the Equal Employment Opportunity Commission (EEOC) issued guidelines applicable to both federal and private employers that prohibit sexual harassment as a form of discrimination under Title VII of the Civil Rights Act of 1964. The guidelines declare that the degree of injury sufficient to support a finding of sexual harassment may occur under three sets of circumstances: (1) where the sexual conduct is made an explicit term or condition of an individual's employment (employment condition); (2) where submission to or rejection of the condition is used as a basis for employment decisions (employment consequence); and (3) where the condition creates an offensive, hostile, or intimidating work environment or interferes with job performance (offensive job interference) (Equal Employment Opportunity Commission 1980). The guidelines also make an employer liable for non-supervisory employees if it "knows or should have known" of the harassing behavior, and liable for supervisory employees "regardless of whether the employer knew" of the offense.[5]

Most universities receive federal funding and, therefore, must follow guidelines prohibiting discrimination on the basis of sex established by the Office of Civil Rights (OCR) of the U.S. Department of Education. Although the OCR did not promulgate guidelines regarding sexual harassment, it has maintained that sexual harassment is prohibited by Title IX of the Educational Amendments Act of 1972. In response, a number of colleges and universities have adopted explicit statements defining and condemning sexual harassment and have established grievance procedures to process sex-discrimination complaints, including those regarding sexual harassment.[6] Some, including Harvard and the University of California system, have issued "amorous relationship" statements that define sexual relationships or sex between teachers and students directly under their supervision as unprofessional conduct, even if the act is initiated by a student (Hoffman 1986:111). Although such statements are important and shift the burden of responsibility, how they are interpreted and applied will determine whether they signal a return to paternalistic rules or a way to empower women (Hoffman 1986).

DEVELOPMENT OF CASE LAW CONCERNING SEXUAL HARASSMENT

Although women who experience sexual harassment recognize that it was done to them *as* women, acceptance of the argument that it is sex discrimination prohibited by law took time. Ten years passed between the enactment of the Civil Rights Act of 1964 prohibiting employment discrimination on the basis of sex and an action before a federal court based primarily on sexual harassment. It was not until 1986 that the U.S. Supreme Court finally ruled on a sexual-harassment case. In *Meritor Savings Bank FSB v. Vinson* (477 US 57 [1986]), the Supreme Court clearly ruled that sexual harassment in employee relations is sex discrimination prohibited by Title VII, but left unresolved the specific issues of employer liability and standards of consent as well as the basic questions how gender, sexuality, and power are related.

In the early cases, the plaintiffs argued unsuccessfully that sexual harassment is an illegal form of sex discrimination (see *Corne v. Bausch and Lomb, Inc.,* 390 F. Supp. 161 [D.C. Ariz. 1975]; *Miller v. Bank of America,* 418 F. Supp. 233 [N.D. Calif. 1976] *reversed,* 600 F. 2d 211 [1979]; *Barnes v. Train,* Civ. No. 1828-73 [D.C.C. Aug. 9, 1974]; and *Tomkins v. Public Service Electric and Gas Co.* 422 F. Supp. 553 [D.J.J. 1976]). In *Corne,* for example, Jane Corne and Geneva DeVane alleged that the repeated verbal and physical sexual advances of their male supervisor made their jobs intolerable and forced them to choose between "putting up with being manhandled or being out of work" (Brief of Appellants at 17). They argued that their employer, Bausch and Lomb, Inc., was responsible because it had allowed them to be supervised by a man who sexually harassed them. The judge, however, dismissed the claim that the advances constituted sexual discrimination, stating that the supervisor's conduct was simply "a personal proclivity, peculiarity, or mannerism" (390 F. Supp. at 163) for which the employer could not be held liable. The court also found that the supervisor's behavior was not "based on sex" because the harassment might have been directed at male as well as at female employees. In addition, the judge expressed concern that granting relief in this case might lead to "a potential federal lawsuit every time an employee made an amorous or sexually-oriented advance toward another" (390 F. Supp. at 163–64). Similarly, in *Tomkins,* in denying that sexual harassment is either sex-based discrimination or employment related, the court stated:

> In this case the supervisor was male and the employee was female. But no immutable principle of psychology compels this alignment of parties. . . . While sexual desire animated the parties, or at least one of them, the gender of each is incidental to the claim of abuse. (422 F. Supp. at 556.)

A different conclusion, reached in *Williams v. Saxbe* (431 F. Supp. 654 [D.D.C. 1976] *reversed on other grounds sub. nom. Williams v. Bell,* 587 F.2d 1240 [D.C. Cir. 1978]), marked the turning of the tide. The court ruled that a male supervisor's retaliatory action against a female employee who refused his sexual advances constituted treatment "based on sex" within the meaning of Title VII of the Civil Rights Act of 1964, but whether an incident was employment related was left to be determined as a fact at trial.

The *Williams* result was followed by reversals on appeal in *Barnes* and *Tomkins* and similar rulings in several other cases (*Barnes v. Costle,* 561 F.2d 982 [D.C. Cir. 1977]; *Tomkins v. Public Service Electric and Gas Co.,* 568 F.2d 1044 [3d Cir. 1977]). In reversing *Barnes,* the Court of Appeals for the District of Columbia ruled that making sexual compliance a "job retention condition" imposed an employment requirement on a woman that would not be imposed on a man and for which the employer was held accountable. The court affirmed that, for discrimination in employment to be found, "it is enough that gender is a factor contributing to the discrimination in a substantial way" (561 F.2d at 990). In reversing *Tompkins,* the Court of Appeals for the Third Circuit affirmed that an unresponsive employer to whom a victim had complained was legally liable for the actions of its agent or supervisor. Other appellate courts, however, while agreeing that harassment involving injury to a plaintiff in the form of a tangible loss of job benefits (i.e., quid pro quo harassment) violated Title VII, differed with respect to the extent of employer liability.

In 1981, the Circuit Court of Appeals for the District of Columbia in *Bundy v. Jackson* (641 F.2d 934 [D.C. Cir. 1981]) expanded coverage in sex-discrimination cases to sexual harassment as a condition of work. It extended the phrases "terms, conditions, and privileges of employment" to cover nontangible injury to the victim, thus making sexual harassment in and of itself a violation of the law. The court found conditions of employment to include the psychological and emotional work environment and reasoned that unless employers are prohibited from maintaining a "discriminatory environment," they could sexually harass a female employee with impunity by carefully stopping short of firing her or taking other action against her when she resisted.

In the *Meritor* case, Plaintiff Michelle Vinson was hired by Sidney Taylor, a vice president and branch manager of Meritor Savings Bank, in 1974. After she became a teller, Taylor invited her to dinner and suggested they have sexual relations. At first, she refused Taylor's advances but, at his insistence and out of fear of losing her job, she acquiesced. Thereafter Vinson estimated she had intercourse with Taylor forty to fifty times between 1975 and 1977. She claimed that she did not report the problem to any of Taylor's superiors or use the bank's complaint procedure out of fear of Taylor. Taylor and the bank denied all allegations of sexual misbehavior on his part. The bank also claimed that because it did not know of the situation, it could not be held responsible (477 US at 61).

The District Court (23 Fair Empl. Prac. Cas. [BNA] 37 [D.D.C. 1980]) found that if there was a sexual relationship, it was voluntary, and thus denied Vinson's claim of sex discrimination. The Court of Appeals for the District of Columbia Circuit reversed and remanded (753 F.2d 141 *reh'g denied,* 760 F.2d 1330 [D.C. Cir. 1985]), finding that Vinson was a victim not of quid pro quo sexual harassment but of harassment of the type emanating from a hostile working environment. It held that the voluntariness of the sexual relationship was immaterial and that the employer was strictly liable for the sexual harassment of an employee by her or his supervisor or agent even if he did not have the authority to hire, fire, or promote, since the mere appearance of influence over job decisions gives him opportunity to impose on employees.

The Supreme Court unanimously affirmed that both types of sexual harassment identified in the EEOC guidelines are prohibited by Title VII and that in hostile-environment cases the victim does not necessarily have to demonstrate economic harm (*Meritor Savings Bank FSB v. Vinson* 477 US at 64). For sexual harassment to be actionable, the Court ruled "it must be sufficiently severe or pervasive to alter the conditions of [the victim's] employment and create an abusive work environment" (*id.* at 67 quoting *Henson v. Dundee,* 682 F.2d 897, 904 [11th Cir. 1982]). In addressing the issue of employer liability, however, the Supreme Court refused to rule definitively on liability for hostile-environment–type discrimination. Rejecting the standard recommended in the EEOC guidelines, a slim majority of the Court held that the Court of Appeals erred when it held employers automatically liable for sexual harassment by supervisors (*id.* at 72).

While the *Meritor* decision recognized hostile-work–environment claims, the language of the decision resulted in a higher threshold for finding an environment to be hostile than the standards set by the EEOC (Pollock 1990). For example, in determining whether the defendant's conduct was offensive, many cases decided by lower courts immediately following *Meritor* demanded such strict proof that the behavior was "unwelcome" that they denied women's experience (Pollock 1990).

Several recent decisions, however, promise recognition that a female victim will have a different perspective than a typical man. First, in a landmark decision (*Ellison v. Brady,* 924 F.2d 872 [9th Cir. 1991]), the Ninth U.S. Circuit ruled that the law covers any remark or behavior that a "reasonable woman" would find to be a problem. It acknowledged that a woman's perception might differ from that of a man, thus permitting a gender-conscious examination of sexual harassment. It overturned a lower court decision involving a woman who had been receiving love letters from another employee, which the lower court had ruled did not qualify as harassment. The appellate court remanded the case to the lower court for retrial using the perspective of "a reasonable woman." This represents a major legal shift, since the prevailing "reasonable person" standard, while appearing to be sex neutral, has tended to be interpreted from the male point of view.

Adopting this "reasonable woman" standard, a federal District Court in Jacksonville, Florida, agreed with complaints from a female welder that the "boys' club atmosphere" of the Jacksonville Shipyards, including a display of nude pinups, was offensive to women and, therefore, constituted illegal harassment (*Robinson v. Jacksonville Shipyards,* 760 F. Supp. 1486 [M.D. Fla. 1991]).

In a third case (*Jenson v. Eveleth Taconite Co.,* 824 S. Supp. 847 [D. Minn. 1993]), three women were permitted by a federal court to file the first class action sexual harassment lawsuit seeking relief on behalf of all female employees of their company (*Jenson v. Eveleth Taconite Co.,* 139 FRD 657 [D. Minn. 1991]). They claimed that their work environment was filled with sexually graphic materials, sexual insults, and unwanted touching by male colleagues and supervisors. In an interim ruling the judge rejected the company's claim that reactions to potentially offensive material are individual ones, and certified the class action, stating that the issue is "whether a reasonable woman would find the work environment hostile" (*Washington Post,* Dec. 18, 1991, p. D1). In 1993 the plaintiffs prevailed in their class-based claim of a hostile environment and were granted an injunction that required positive remedial steps by the company.

Further class action sexual harassment suits are likely to increase because the Civil Rights Act of 1991 permits victims of sex discrimination, including sexual harassment, to sue for monetary damages. Previously, a victim's only legal remedy had been an award of back pay if she was fired or demoted, which generally did not apply in hostile-environment cases. Now victims may get compensatory damages for nonfinancial losses such as emotional pain, suffering, inconvenience, and mental anguish up to $300,000.

In late 1993, the Supreme Court addressed the issue of what constitutes a harassing environment in *Harris v. Forklift Systems, Inc.* [Slip Opinion No.

92-1168]. In a unanimous decision reached in record time, the Court ruled that for a work environment to be sufficiently abusive under the law, the harassing conduct does not have to "seriously affect [an employee's] psychological well being" or lead her to "suffer injury." Instead, the Court adopted what it termed "a middle path between making actionable any conduct that is merely offensive and requiring the conduct to cause a psychological injury" (at 4) in determining what is sufficiently severe and pervasive to be actionable, based on the totality of the circumstances. Whether behavior rises to the level of an abusive environment depends on such factors as its frequency and severity and whether it physically threatens or humiliates the victim (rather than being "a mere offensive utterance") and/or unreasonably interferes with an employee's work performance.

Case law prohibiting sexual harassment as sex-based discrimination against students under Title IX of the Education Amendments Act is not well established, although most of the arguments are now similar to those already established under Title VII. In a lawsuit brought against Yale University (*Alexander v. Yale University*, 459 F. Supp. 1 [D. Conn. 1977] *reversed on other grounds*, 631 F.2d 178 [2d Cir. 1980]), a student alleged that her grade was adversely affected by her refusal to submit to her professor's sexual demands. Using reasoning developed in the context of employment discrimination cases, the court held that the student had stated a cause of action under Title IX, but dismissed the suit because the complainant had failed to prove that an improper advance had been made or that the student had been adversely affected. It also dismissed the claims of coplaintiffs alleging harm resulting from "contamination" of the educational environment. The Second Circuit Court of Appeals affirmed this reasoning, thereby establishing quid pro quo harassment as illegal but leaving open the issue of environmental harm. In *Moire v. Temple University School of Medicine* (613 F. Supp. 1360 [E.D. Pa. 1985] *affirmed* 800 F.2d 1136 [3d Cir. 1986]), the district court allowed a claim for sexual harassment based solely on environmental harm, although it found no merit in the particular allegation that because of her sex the complainant had been subjected to a harassing or abusive environment. The *Moire* court's explicit recognition that the EEOC guidelines are equally applicable to Title IX suggests that the courts will continue to decide claims of sexual harassment brought by students under Title IX using reasoning similar to that established under Title VII cases.[7]

The turnabout of the courts has been dramatic. Although the early cases involved blatant abuses of power by supervisors, the judges treated these abuses as matters of "natural" attraction or of the personal peculiarity of the supervisors unrelated to job conditions. As legal analyses clarified the relationship between sexual harassment and sex discrimination, as research supported the claims that sexual harassment is widespread and socially patterned, as the EEOC added its authority in support of the plaintiffs in a number of cases, and as the media called public attention to the issue, the courts could no longer sustain the traditional "personal proclivity" approach. They shifted to the view that sexual harassment is an illegal, socially imposed wrong—sex discrimination—not only when the victim faces tangible economic losses, but also when the harassment is made a condition of work. Thus, the law now acknowledges the socially defined character of sexual harassment by recognizing that the unwanted sexual advances are "based on sex" and that women are sexually harassed because they are women.

Despite this apparent progress, clear prohibition of sexual harassment is only the first step toward addressing the problems that sexual harassment poses for women. While the law provides victims with legal support, enforcement is weak, litigation is expensive, and women remain reluctant to invoke it. Grievance procedures rely principally on informal mediation; if a problem cannot be resolved informally, the mechanisms for redress break down, since few employers have policies for using sanctions and the government has no mechanisms to monitor policy statements or grievance procedures (Livingston 1982; Schneider 1985).

Women often fail to define certain offensive behaviors as sexual harassment, blame other women or themselves rather than the harasser for the experience (Jensen and Gutek 1982), and, when they do label the unwanted behavior as sexual harassment, tend to treat it as an individual matter to be handled informally. Their reluctance to take more formal action for fear of making things worse, particularly at a time of economic insecurity and reduced civil-rights law enforcement, appears to be well founded.

Even more frequent complaints and fuller enforcement through formal channels, however, only provide redress on a case-by-case basis without addressing the underlying structural causes of sexual harassment—the conditions of social and economic inequality. Thus, the elimination of sexual harassment in the workplace and educational setting may not bring fundamental change unless the root of the problem—the nature and structure of the environment in which women and men work and learn—is altered.

Conclusion

Sexual harassment in the university and the workplace must be recognized and treated as an oppressive form of sex discrimination that undercuts women's potential for independence and equality. It disrupts women's drive for autonomy outside of the home and family by sexualizing women's work role and by making sexuality a condition of economic survival. Women as a group suffer from two inequalities: gender inequality based on socially defined patterns of sexual initiative and acquiescence and economic inequality maintained by women's separate and subordinate place at work. Sexual harassment links these inequalities by expressing the unequal social power of women, sexualizing their subordination, and deepening their powerlessness as women.

NOTES

1. Although men have been victims of sexual harassment as well as women, the vast difference between the sexes in victimization rates and the meaning attached to sexual initiatives make sexual harassment primarily a problem of women. Only research findings on the sexual harassment of women are presented here, and the analysis of harassment is from the perspective of female victims.

2. Increasingly, studies have sought to classify the frequency and nature of various types of behavior that people regard as unwanted or offensive and those respondents' willingness to label

each as "sexual harassment." For example, Fitzgerald and Ormerod (1991) distinguished five types of harassment: gender harassment (i.e., verbal behavior such as jokes and innuendos that are aimed at women as women but may not be intended to elicit cooperation), seductive behavior (i.e., inappropriate and offensive but essentially sanction-free sexual advances), sexual bribery (i.e., solicitation of sexual activity by promise of reward), sexual coercion (coercion of sexual activity by threat of punishment), and sexual imposition (including attempts to touch or grab) or sexual assault.

3. One study found that more than 70 percent of the women surveyed would not call a behavior sexual harassment if the person doing it did not mean to be offensive (U.S. Merit Systems Protection Board [MSPB] 1981:29). Much of the recent psychological research on sexual harassment focuses on the cognitive processes involved in interpreting a behavior as harassing. Studies have found that (1) men tend to rate hypothetical scenarios (Gutek et al. 1983) and specific social-sexual behaviors (Gutek et al., 1980) as less harassing than do women and (2) lesbian women workers are more likely than are heterosexual ones to label a variety of specific social sexual behaviors directed at them as sexual harassment (Schneider 1982). Other studies have found that when behaviors are inconsistent with ordinary expectations of the actor's social role and thus appear to be inappropriate (e.g., enacted by a professor rather than by a fellow student), they are more likely to be viewed as incidents of sexual harassment (Pryor 1985). In interpreting ambiguous incidents, students put more weight on personal and interpersonal aspects of a relationship between the persons involved than the actual behavior, suggesting that people tend to emphasize the positive aspects of a relationship and to deny that sexual harassment exists (Cohen and Gutek 1985).

In a study of the effect of the account offered by the perpetrator for his behavior on the perceived seriousness of incidents, Hunter and McClelland (1991) compared excuses (where the actor rejects personal responsibility), justifications, and apologies. They found that the man's verbal explanation for his behavior influenced the perceived seriousness of the behavior almost as much as the offensive behavior itself. Apologies and those excuses that focus attention on one's temporary failure to follow culturally appropriate norms reduce the perceived seriousness of these sexual misbehaviors. Justifications and excuses that blame others for one's failure to act appropriately (e.g., "the guys dared me to do it") increase the perceived seriousness of the incident.

In an effort to explain individual perception of sexual harassment, Konrad and Gutek (1986) tested three theories related to perceptions of sexual harassment. They postulated that differences between men and women in the perception of sexual harassment were related to (1) differences in personal orientation to sexual harassment and to the definition of it, (2) differences in sexual experiences at work, and (3) differences due to gender-role spillover. They found support for all three explanations and concluded that women label more behaviors as sexual harassment than do men because of differences in both attitudes and experiences.

4. In 1978, the Civil Service Reform Act reorganized the Civil Service Commission by dividing it into two agencies: MSPB and the Office of Personnel Management. The MSPB hears and adjudicates appeals by federal employees complaining of adverse personnel actions, resolves cases charging prohibited personnel practices, and conducts special studies on the civil service and other executive branch merit systems. The Office of Personnel Management administers a merit system for federal employees, which includes recruitment, examination, training, and promotion on the basis of people's knowledge and skill.

5. Ironically, one employer—the Congress of the United States—was exempt from the guidelines. It was only in the month following the Thomas hearings, with the passage of the Civil Rights Act of 1991, that employees on Capitol Hill were extended the same right to a harassment-free workplace as all other government employees.

6. Robertson et al.'s (1988) survey of 311 institutions of higher learning regarding their policies and procedures related to sexual harassment found that 66 percent of all respondents had written policies and 46 percent had grievance procedures specifically designed to deal with sexual harassment complaints. Eighty percent of the public institutions, which are required by law to have such policies, have them, and 54 percent also have grievance procedures. In contrast, only 52 percent of the private schools have sexual harassment policies, and 38 percent have procedures for addressing complaints. Within the private school category, only 43 percent of the religiously affiliated schools but 74 percent of the nonaffiliated schools had such policies.

7. There is little doubt that an educational institution would be held liable for quid pro quo harassment under the *Meritor* decision. Title IX, however, is not currently a useful mechanism to

provide relief to most victims of sexual harassment in an educational institution since the only remedy it specifies is withdrawal of federal funding from the institution. It provides no monetary remedy for mental suffering and emotional distress caused by the harassment situation.

REFERENCES

Joan Acker. "Hierarchies, Jobs and Bodies: A Theory of Gendered Organizations." *Gender and Society* 4 (1990), 139–58.

Joan Acker. "Gendering Organizational Theory. Pp. 248–60 in Albert J. Mills and Peta Tancred, eds., *Gendering Organizational Analysis.* Newbury Park: Sage, 1992.

Donna J. Benson and Gregory E. Thomson. "Sexual Harassment on a University Campus: The Confluence of Authority Relations, Sexual Interest and Gender Stratification." *Social Problems* 29 (1982), 236–51.

Karen Benson. "Comment on Crocker's "An Analysis of University Definitions of Sexual Harassment.'" *Signs* 9 (1984), 516–19.

Sandra H. Carey. "Sexual Politics in Business" (unpublished paper, University of Texas, San Antonio, 1977).

Cynthia Cockburn. *In the Way of Women: Men's Resistance to Sex Equality in Organizations* (Ithaca, NY: ILR Press, 1991).

Aaron G. Cohen and Barbara A. Gutek. "Dimensions of Perceptions of Social-Sexual Behavior in a Work Setting." *Sex Roles* 13 (1985), 317–27.

Phyllis Crocker. "An Analysis of University Definitions of Sexual Harassment." *Signs* 8 (1983), 696–707.

Billie W. Dziech and Linda Weiner. *The Lecherous Professor: Sexual Harassment on Campus* (2nd ed.) (Urbana and Chicago: University of Illinois Press, 1990).

Equal Employment Opportunity Commission. "Discrimination Because of Sex Under Title VII of the Civil Rights Act of 1964, as Amended: Adoption of Interim Interpretive Guidelines." *Federal Register* 29 (1980), 1604 (Washington, D.C.: U.S. Government Printing Office).

Terri C. Fain and Douglas L. Anderton. "Sexual Harassment: Organizational Context and Diffuse Status." *Sex Roles* 17 (1987), 291–311.

Lin Farley. *Sexual Shakedown: The Sexual Harassment of Women on the Job* (New York: McGraw-Hill, 1978).

Louise F. Fitzgerald. "Sexual Harassment: The Definition and Measurement of a Construct." Pp. 21–44 in Michele A. Paludi, ed., *Ivory Power: Sexual Harassment on Campus* (Albany: SUNY Press, 1990).

Louise F. Fitzgerald and Mimi Ormerod. "Perceptions of Sexual Harassment: The Influence of Gender and Academic Context." *Psychology of Women Quarterly* 15 (1991), 281–94.

Louise F. Fitzgerald and S. L. Schullman. "The Development and Validation of an Objectively Scored Measure of Sexual Harassment in Higher Education: Some Extensions and Applications to Theory." Paper presented to the convention of the Association for Women in Psychology, Denver, Colo.

Louise F. Fitzgerald, Lauren Weitzman, Yael Gold, and Mimi Ormerod. "Academic Harassment: Sex and Denial in Scholarly Garb." *Psychology of Women Quarterly* 12 (1988), 329–40.

Elizabeth Grauerholz. "Sexual Harassment of Women Professors by Students: Power, Authority and Gender in a University Setting." *Sex Roles* 21 (1988), 78–99.

Barbara A. Gutek. "The Experience of Sexual Harassment: Results from a Representative Survey" Paper presented at the American Psychological Association annual meeting, Los Angeles, August 29, 1981.

Barbara A. Gutek and Bruce Morash. "Sex Ratios, Sex Role Spillover, and Sexual Harassment of Women at Work." *Journal of Social Issues* 38 (1982), 55–74.

Barbara A. Gutek, Charles Y. Nakamura, M. Gahart, I. Handschumacher, and Diane Russell. "Sexuality in the Workplace." *Basic and Applied Social Psychology* 1 (1980), 255–65.

Elaine J. Hall. "Smiling, Deferring and Flirting: Doing Gender by Giving 'Good Service.'" *Work and Occupations* 20 (1993), 452–71.

Frances L. Hoffman. "Sexual Harassment in Academia: Feminist Theory and Institutional Practice." *Harvard Educational Review* 56 (1986), 105–20.

Christopher Hunter and Kent McClelland. "Honoring Accounts for Sexual Harassment: A Factorial Survey Analysis." *Sex Roles* 24 (1991), 725–51.

Inger W. Jensen and Barbara A. Gutek. "Attributions and Assignments of Responsibility in Sexual Harassment." *Journal of Social Issues* 38 (1982), 121–36.

Rosabeth M. Kanter. *Men and Women of the Corporation* (New York: Basic Books, 1977).

Mim Kelber. "Sexual Harassment . . . the UN's Dirty Little Secret." *Ms.,* Nov. 1977, 51, 79.

Alison M. Konrad and Barbara A. Gutek. "Impact of Work Experiences on Attitudes Toward Sexual Harassment." *Administrative Science Quarterly* 31 (1986), 422–38.

Mary Koss. "Changed Lives: The Psychological Impact of Sexual Harassment." Pp. 73–92 in Michele A. Paludi, ed., *Ivory Power: Sexual Harassment on Campus* (Albany: SUNY Press, 1990).

Karen Lindsey. "Sexual Harassment on the Job." *Ms.,* Nov. 1977, 47–51, 74–78.

Jay Livingston. "Responses to Sexual Harassment on the Job: Legal, Organizational, and Individual Actions." *Journal of Social Issues* 38 (1982), 5–22.

Pamela Loy and Lee Stewart. "The Extent and Effects of the Sexual Harassment of Working Women." *Sociological Focus* 17 (1984), 31–43.

Catherine A. MacKinnon. *Sexual Harassment of Working Women: A Case of Sex Discrimination* (New Haven, Conn.: Yale University Press, 1979).

Catherine A. MacKinnon. "Feminism, Marxism, Method and the State: An Agenda for Action." *Signs* 7 (1982), 515–44.

Susan E. Martin. *"Breaking and Entering": Policewomen on Patrol* (Berkeley: University of California Press, 1980).

Arlene McCormack. "The Sexual Harassment of Students by Teachers: The Case of Students in Science," *Sex Roles* 13 (1985), 21–32.

A. Metha and J. Nigg. "Sexual Harassment on Campus: An Institutional Response." *Journal of the National Association of Women Deans and Counselors* 46 (1983), 9–15.

MSPB. See U.S. Merit Systems Protection Board.

Adrienne Munich. "Seduction in Academe." *Psychology Today,* Feb. 1978, 82–108.

Timothy M. Phelps and Helen Winternitz. *Capitol Games: Clarence Thomas, Anita Hill, and the Story of a Supreme Court Nomination.* New York: Hyperion, 1992.

Letty C. Pogrebin. "Sexual Harassment: The Working Woman." *Ladies Home Journal,* June 1977, 47.

Wendy Pollock. "Sexual Harassment: Women's Experience vs. Legal Definitions." *Harvard Women's Law Journal* 13 (1990), 35–85.

Project on the Status of Women in Education. *Sexual Harassment: A Hidden Issue* (Washington, D.C.: American Association of Colleges, 1978).

John B. Pryor. "The Lay Person's Understanding of Sexual Harassment." *Sex Roles* 5/6 (1985), 273–86.

John B. Pryor. "Sexual Harassment Proclivities in Men." *Sex Roles* 17 (1987), 269–90.

Vita C. Rabinowitz. "Coping with Sexual Harassment." Pp. 103–18 in Michele A. Paludi, ed., *Ivory Power: Sexual Harassment on Campus* (Albany: SUNY Press, 1990).

Mary Ellen Reilly, Bernice Lott, and Sheila M. Gallogly. "Sexual Harassment of University Students." *Sex Roles* 15 (1986), 333–58.

Spencer Rich. "Schlafly: Sexual Harassment on Job No Problem for Virtuous Woman." *Washington Post,* Apr. 22, 1981, A2.

Al Ripskis. "Sexual Harassment Rampant at HUD." *Impact* 7 (July/Aug. 1979), 1, 5, 7.

Claire Robertson, Constance E. Dyer, and D'Ann Campbell. "Campus Harassment: Sexual Harassment Policies and Procedures at Institutions of Higher Learning." *Signs* 13 (1988), 792–812.

Linda J. Rubin and Sherry B. Borgers. "Sexual Harassment in Universities During the 1980s." *Sex Roles* 23 (1990), 397–411.

Claire Safran. "What Men Do to Women on the Job: A Shocking Look at Sexual Harassment." *Redbook,* Nov. 1976, 149, 217–23.

Beth E. Schneider. "Consciousness About Sexual Harassment Among Heterosexual and Lesbian Women Workers." *Journal of Social Issues* 38 (1982), 75–97.

Beth E. Schneider. "Approaches, Assaults, Attractions, Affairs: Policy Implications of the Sexualization of the Workplace." *Population Research and Policy Review* 4 (1985), 93–113.

Beth Schneider. "Put up and Shut up: Workplace Sexual Assaults." *Gender and Society* 5 (1991), 533–48.

William C. Seymour. "Sexual Harassment: Finding a Cause of Action Under Title VII." *Labor Law Journal* 30 (Mar. 1979), 170–210.

Body Politics | Dierdre Silverman. "Sexual Harassment: Working Women's Dilemma." *Quest: A Feminist Quarterly* 3 (Winter 1976–77), 15–24.

Rosemarie Tong. *Women, Sex and the Law* (Totowa, N.J.: Rowman and Allanheld, 1984).

U.S. House of Representatives. *Hearings on Sexual Harassment in the Federal Government* (Committee on the Post Office and Civil Service, Subcommittee on Investigations, Washington, D.C.: U.S. Government Printing Office, 1980).

U.S. Merit Systems Protection Board. *Sexual Harassment in the Federal Workplace: Is It a Problem?* (Washington, D.C.: U.S. Government Printing Office, 1981).

U.S. Merit Systems Protection Board. *Sexual Harassment in the Federal Government: An Update* (Washington, D.C.: U.S. Government Printing Office, 1988).

Candace West and Don H. Zimmerman. "Doing Gender." *Gender and Society* 1 (1989), 125–51.

Unwanted Pregnancy and Its Resolution: Options, Implications

Nancy Felipe Russo and Jody D. Horn

EVERY YEAR, MORE THAN 6 million women in the United States between the ages of fifteen and forty-four become pregnant.[1] Despite the availability of contraception, more than half of those pregnancies are unintended; among teenagers, four out of five pregnancies are unintended.[2] An unintended pregnancy confronts a woman with a serious decision: to bear and keep the child, to bear it but give it up for adoption, or to have an abortion.[3] She does not make this decision in isolation. Personal and family resources, social pressures, legal constraints, and the availability of real options all affect what she decides to do.

Of the more than 3.4 million unintended pregnancies in 1987, 40 percent ended in childbirth, while 47 percent were terminated by induced abortion; 13 percent miscarried.[4] Age and marital status were related to the likelihood that a woman resolved an unintended pregnancy through abortion. Fifty-three percent of unintended pregnancies among women under age twenty-five (college age and younger) were aborted, compared with 35 percent among women twenty-five years and older. Unmarried women aborted 63 percent of their unintended pregnancies, compared with 21 percent of married women.[5]

Prior to 1967, abortion was not a legal option for most women in the United States. Estimates of the number of (predominantly illegal) abortions before that time range from a low of 200,000 to a high of 1.2 million per year.[6] Between 1967 and 1973 some states liberalized their abortion laws, so that a woman's ability to obtain an abortion depended largely on where she lived and how much money she could raise.[7]

In 1973 the U.S. Supreme Court ruled in *Roe v. Wade* that the constitutional "right of privacy . . . founded in the Fourteenth Amendment . . . is broad enough to encompass a woman's decision whether or not to terminate her pregnancy."[8] This ruling did not mean abortion became available "on demand." The Court ruled that a woman's right to an abortion may be counterbalanced by the state's interest in protecting maternal health and potential human life, interests that increase throughout the pregnancy. In the first trimester (i.e., under thirteen weeks of pregnancy), when abortion is clearly safer than childbirth, the decision to have an abortion rests solely with the woman and her physician. After the first trimester, the state "may regulate the abortion procedure to the extent that the regulation reasonably relates to the preservation and protection of maternal health."[9] At some point between twenty-four and twenty-eight weeks after conception, the fetus reaches a point of *viability;* that is, its brain and respiratory system have matured enough to enable it to survive outside the uterus (the exact point varies depending on access to high-tech medical care). The viability of the fetus permits the state to exercise its interest in protecting potential life. Regulation and prohibition of abortion are per-mitted except when they would endanger the life or health of the woman.

Legal abortion is not equally available to all women as a choice when faced with an unwanted pregnancy. Since *Roe,* the Supreme Court has permitted the states to impose ever greater regulations on when, where, and how abortions can be performed, particularly after the first trimester. Regulations vary by state and include denial of public funds for abortion, waiting periods, informed consent provisions, and parental notification requirements for minors. In addition, antiabortion groups have used harassment to stop the provision of legal abortion services, including picketing outside clinics, tracing patients' identities and invading their privacy, vandalizing and destroying facilities, and harassing the families of doctors at home or at their children's schools (see Table 1). In 1988, 49 percent of all nonhospital facilities and 85 percent of those doing more than 400 abortions per year experienced harass-ment by antiabortion groups; over a third experienced vandalism, bomb threats, or demonstrations resulting in arrests. The larger the facility, the more likely it was to be harassed.[10] In 1993, a physician at an abortion clinic was shot in the back and killed by an antiabortion protestor.[11]

One consequence of this harassment has been a shift in the availability of abortions from hospital settings to clinics and doctors' offices. In 1973, hospitals performed slightly more than half of all abortions. This number declined steadily to 7 percent by 1992. The number of hospitals doing abortions went from 1,468 in 1974 to 855 in 1992—one in six general hospitals—while the number of clinics increased from 536 to 889.[12] Hospital facilities are not necessary for an ordinary abortion; it can be done as an outpatient procedure. However, the clinics are concentrated in metropolitan areas, so the withdrawal of hospitals meant that by 1992 more than 90 percent of all abortion providers were located in or near cities. Rural women often must travel long hours, even days, to obtain an abortion. Waiting periods and requirements that necessitate return trips to the provider before an abortion may occur increase costs and create barriers that can become insurmountable for some women, particularly if they are young or poor. These barriers mean that the pregnant women who are least able to marshal resources, cope with stress, and care for themselves and their families are the women most likely to be denied the option of abortion.[13]

Option 1: Continuing the Pregnancy and Keeping the Child

During the two decades before *Roe,* an estimated 20 percent of the births to ever-married women were unwanted.[14] Although the proportion of unwanted births in 1978–1982 to ever-married women aged fifteen through forty-four dropped to 7.7 percent, by 1988 the figure had increased to 10.3 percent.[15] Increases were greatest for poor women and women with less than a high school education, particularly if they were African-American. Among women with less than a high school education in 1988, 44.5 percent of births to black women and 15.5 percent of births to white women were unwanted.[16]

Table . Incidents of Violence and Disruption Against Abortion Providers, 1993[1]

	1977–1983	1984	1985	1986	1987	1988	1989	1990	1991[2]	1992	1993	Total
Violence (number incidents)												
Murder	0	0	0	0	0	0	0	0	0	0	1	1
Bombing	8	18	4	2	0	0	2	0	1	1	1	37
Arson	13	6	8	7	4	4	6	4	10	16	9	87
Attempted bomb/arson	5	6	10	5	8	3	2	4	1	13	7	64
Invasion	68	34	47	53	14	6	25	19	29	26	24	345
Vandalism	35	35	49	43	29	29	24	26	44	116	113	543
Assault and battery	11	7	7	11	5	5	12	6	6	9	9	88
Death threats	4	23	22	7	5	4	5	7	3	8	78	166
Kidnapping	2	0	0	0	0	0	0	0	0	0	0	2
Burglary	3	2	2	5	7	1	0	2	1	5	3	31
Stalking[3]	–	–	–	–	–	–	–	–	–	–	188	188
Total	149	131	149	133	72	52	76	68	95	194	433	1,552
Disruption												
Hate mail and harassing calls	9	17	32	53	32	19	30	21	142	469	628	1,452
Bomb threats	9	32	75	51	28	21	21	11	15	12	22	297
Picketing	107	160	139	141	77	151	72	45	292	2,898	2,279	6,361
Total	125	209	246	245	137	191	123	77	449	3,379	2,929	8,110
Clinic blockades:												
Number incidents	0	0	0	0	2	182	201	34	41	83	66	609
Number arrests[4]	0	0	0	0	290	11,732	12,358	1,363	3,885	2,580	1,236	33,444

1. As of Monday, March 14, 1994. Numbers represent incidents reported to NAF (National Abortion Federation); actual numbers may be higher.
2. The sharp increase in numbers of incidents for 1991 may be partially attributable to the computerization of NAF's tracking and recording system in mid-1991.
3. Stalking is defined as the persistent following, threatening, and harassing of an abortion provider, staff member, or patient *away from* the clinic. Especially severe stalking incidents will be noted on NAF's Incidents of Extreme Violence fact sheet. Tabulation of stalking incidents began in 1993.
4. The "number of arrests" represents the total number of arrests, not the total number of *persons* arrested. Many blockaders are arrested multiple times.

Women of every income and educational level experience unwanted pregnancy. However, women who have lower self-esteem, lower income, and fewer years of education are at greatest risk for *repeated* unwanted pregnancy. This is true no matter how such pregnancies are resolved—indeed, women who have unwanted births also have a greater number of abortions than other women.[17] The women who have more than one abortion are often the same women who bear unwanted children.

Unwanted births do not necessarily translate into unwanted children. People change their minds—sometimes an unwanted birth results in a wanted child, and vice versa. Definitions of unwantedness, when applied to pregnancy and childbearing, are extremely complex. However, having a child who is *unwanted during pregnancy* does predict a higher risk of psychological and social disadvantage for the mother and resulting child.[18]

The negative physical, psychological, and social risks of unwanted childbearing vary with timing, spacing, and number of children, among other factors. Health problems include increased risk for illness and death for both mother and child. Psychological problems can be profound and long lasting. In one study, one out of three women still actively resented the baby at a one-year follow-up.[19] In another study of ninety-five women, a similar proportion had not adjusted to their children at a two-year follow-up (6 percent of the women had even attempted suicide).[20] A longer-term study found that 27 percent of 249 women denied a request for abortion had problems in adjusting to their children *seven years* after birth. Unmarried mothers were at particularly high risk for problems; over one-half of this group reported not adjusting to the child after seven years.[21]

Problems associated with unwanted childbearing are shaped by the fact that women who are already experiencing a variety of social and economic disadvantages are overrepresented among women who have unintended pregnancies and unwanted births.[22] Such disadvantages include poverty, lower level of education, forced marriage, teenage childbearing, single parenthood, larger family sizes, short childbirth intervals, and marital conflict and disruption.[23] Unwanted children are more likely to have chaotic and insecure family lives, perform more poorly in school, exhibit delinquent behavior, and require treatment for symptoms of psychological distress and psychopathology. As adults, unwanted children have been found to be more likely to engage in criminal behavior, receive welfare, and use psychiatric services.[24]

There is a strong link between child maltreatment, including child abuse and neglect, and unplanned and unwanted childbearing.[25] Mothers of abused and neglected children are more likely than other women to (1) have unplanned pregnancies, (2) have first births at a younger age, (3) have more births, (4) space their first two children more closely, and (5) have more children by different fathers.[26] Two of the strongest predictors of future child abuse are having two or more children under age five and less than a twelve-month spacing between the first two births.

Even in intact families with good economic circumstances, unwanted children are at higher risk for psychological and social problems. A study in Czechoslovakia[27] has documented differences between 220 unwanted children born in 1961 to 1963 and a matched control group. These children, who were defined as unwanted because they were born to women who were twice denied a request to abort them, were interviewed at ages nine, fourteen to fifteen, and twenty-one to twenty-three. The unwanted children were more likely to have poorer grades in school, be less liked by other children, and be regarded by teachers and parents as more anger-prone and irritable. They were also more likely to be involved with drugs and alcohol, engage in criminal behavior, have earlier initial sexual experiences, express lower job satisfaction, and, if married, have marital problems. During the 1990s, researchers began to study the children of these unwanted children and found negative second-generation effects. Given that one in five children born to married women in the United States during the 1950s and 1960s was unwanted,[28] these findings have disturbing implications.

Option 2: Abortion

About 1.5 million abortions, roughly 24 percent of all pregnancies, are performed each year in the United States (see Figure 1).[29] Based on 1987 figures, the majority of abortion patients are white (65 percent), under age twenty-five (59 percent), and unmarried (82 percent; 63 percent are never married). They have had no previous abortions (57 percent) and no previous live births (53 percent).[30]

WHO HAS ABORTIONS?

Women of color and poor women are overrepresented among abortion patients. Nonwhite women are 17 percent of the population of women of reproductive age[31] and 31 percent of abortion patients. Hispanic women (who may be of any race) are 8 percent of this population and 13 percent of abortion patients. More than one in three abortion patients were poor (with family incomes under $11,000 per year). After controlling for age, the abortion rate for poor women was more than three times that of women with higher family incomes (over $25,000 per year).

About 42 percent of abortion patients are Protestant; 32 percent are Catholic, and 1.4 percent Jewish. Sixteen percent describe themselves as Evangelical or "born-again" Christians. Although only about 3 percent of abortion patients say they have no preferred religion, such women have higher abortion rates than women in general. Using the abortion rate for all women as the comparison, Catholics have about the same rate as the national average; Protestants have a lower rate, followed by Jews, and then Evangelical Christians.[32]

Minors (patients under eighteen years of age) had nearly 12 percent of all abortions.[33] More than 98 percent of minors seeking abortion were unmarried; most were also nonmothers, white, and enrolled in school. Unfortunately, this global portrait masks substantial variation in the role obligations and life circumstances of these unmarried minors. Nearly 9 percent of unmarried minors were already mothers; nearly 16 percent of these mothers already had two children, and one in twenty-five was separated or divorced. These mothers, who were disproportionately women of color, were also more likely to be poor, drop out of school, and have no job. Table 2

Figure 1. Number of Legal Abortions, Abortion Rate per 1,000 Women Aged 15–44, and Percentage of Pregnancies Terminated by Abortion, by Race, 1973–1988

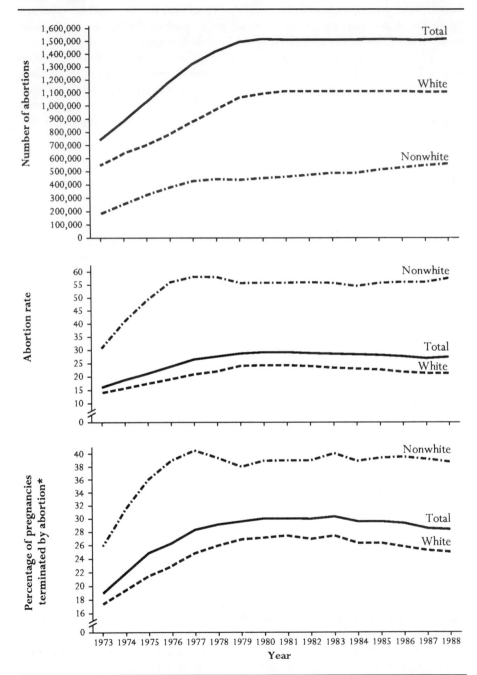

*Denominator is live births six months later (to match time of conception with abortions) and abortions. Pregnancies exclude miscarriages and stillbirths. Births and abortions are adjusted to age of woman at time of conception.

Source: Alan Guttamucher Institute, *Abortion Factbook 1992*. Data from the 1992 survey was published too late to be included in this figure.

Table 2. Percentage Characteristics of U.S. Abortion Patients: Unmarried Minors and Adults, by Motherhood

Characteristic	Unmarried minors			Unmarried adults			Married adults		
	Total (1,111)	Mothers (97)	Nonmothers (1,014)	Total (6,636)	Mothers (2,941)	Nonmothers (3,692)	Total (1,719)	Mothers (1,423)	Nonmothers (296)
Want no more children	10.0	28.2	7.8	27.7	47.6	11.9	56.3	63.2	23.0
Number of prior births									
0	91.3	0	100	55.6	0	100	17.2	0	100
1	7.4	84.5	0	23.2	52.4	0	26.8	32.4	0
2–3	1.4	15.5	0	18.1	40.8	0	47.8	57.9	0
4 or more				3.0	6.8	0	9.7	8.0	0
Number of prior abortions									
0	86.6	70.1	88.2	54.4	40.8	65.2	49.9	48.7	55.4
1	11.9	23.7	10.7	28.4	33.4	24.1	31.6	31.9	30.4
2	1.4	5.2	1.0	11.5	16.4	7.6	12.6	12.9	11.5
3 or more	0.2	1.0	0.1	5.7	9.0	3.2	5.8	6.5	2.6
Race/ethnicity									
Black	28.4	61.9	25.1	27.5	40.0	17.6	18.3	20.1	9.8
White	63.7	26.8	67.3	65.2	51.9	75.8	67.5	66.1	74.3
Hispanic[a]	8.9	16.5	8.2	11.4	13.9	9.4	18.5	19.8	12.2
Enrolled in school	86.2	61.9	88.6	27.3	15.5	36.7	11.0	8.4	23.3
Employed outside the home	39.2	33.0	39.8	74.1	64.6	81.7	65.6	63.2	76.7
Family income									
<$11,000	32.2	52.5	30.2	36.6	46.0	29.0	19.5	20.1	16.9
$11,000–$24,999	27.3	26.8	27.2	34.4	36.0	33.3	35.4	36.1	32.1
≥$25,000	40.6	20.6	42.5	28.9	18.0	37.7	45.0	43.7	51.1

Note: Analysis based on data set reported in Henshaw and Silverman (1988). Numbers may not total 100 percent due to rounding. Married minors (1.2 percent) were omitted because there were too few for meaningful comparisons.
a. Hispanics may be of any race.

contains a summary of the characteristics of unmarried minors and adult women (eighteen years of age and older) seeking abortion in 1987 based on AGI survey data.[34]

Nearly one out of two (48 percent) abortion patients are mothers. This figure includes 83 percent of married adults and 44 percent of unmarried adults. The family responsibilities of these mothers are considerable. Nearly two-thirds of married mothers and half of unmarried mothers who get abortions already have two or more children. A substantial proportion are caring for a child in diapers. In 1987, 12 percent of mothers seeking an abortion had a youngest child less than one year old; 25 percent had a youngest child less than two years of age.[35]

Mothers who obtain abortions—married or unmarried—are more likely to be women of color (black and Hispanic) than nonmothers who obtain abortions. Further, abortion patients who have at least one child under two years of age are more likely to be African-American and to be poor than are abortion patients with older children.[36] Unmarried African-American mothers in particular have substantial family obligations and scarce resources. In 1987, almost half of these women had two or more children and lived below the poverty line. Without the option of abortion, the childbearing burdens of these unmarried mothers would have been even greater; nearly two out of three already had had at least one abortion.[37]

WHEN AND HOW ARE ABORTIONS PERFORMED?

In 1987, more than nine out of ten abortions were performed at less than thirteen weeks after the onset of the woman's last menstrual period (LMP)[38]—when the fetus is less than two inches long and weighs less than one-half ounce. Over half (51 percent) of abortions were performed at eight weeks or less, before a fetus was even formed. More than 99 percent of abortions were performed before twenty-one weeks, less than one percent (.6 percent) at twenty-two weeks or later. Such late abortions typically occur *only when a defect in the fetus is discovered or the life of the mother is in danger if the pregnancy continues.*[39]

The low proportion of abortions performed after twenty weeks since a woman's last menstrual period (.6 percent) is significant, because it is not until between twenty-one and twenty-three weeks after LMP that rudimentary connections between the higher centers of the developing fetal brain (i.e., those located in the neocortex) and the rest of the fetal body begin to emerge. The neocortex is the most recently evolved part of the brain. It contains human consciousness, thinking, problem solving, and language—the brain functions that make humans unique as a species. Before the neocortex develops and is connected with the rest of the developing fetal body, the idea that a fetus can "think" or "feel pain" has no basis in biological fact. Further, it is not until about thirty-two weeks after the women's last menstrual period—and after the point of viability with high-tech medical care—that the neocortex begins to look and function like that of a newborn, with continuous electrical activity (brain waves) and periodic fluctuations suggestive of the normal sleep-wake cycle. At this point the major difference between a fetus and a newborn becomes size.[40]

The procedure employed to perform an abortion is largely a function of length of gestation. During the first trimester, vacuum aspiration is typically used to empty the contents of the uterus (normally a five-minute procedure requiring only local anesthesia). In the second trimester, dilation and evacuation (D&E) is typically used. Dilation of the cervix can take several hours (even overnight), but once dilation is complete, the procedure takes ten minutes or less. Approximately 3 percent of abortions involve induction of labor to expel the fetus. These contractions are painful and may last several hours. Less than .1 percent of abortions involve uterine surgery, hysterotomy, and hysterectomy.[41]

WHY DO WOMEN HAVE ABORTIONS?

In a 1987 study,[42] Aida Torres and Jacqueline Forrest asked a nationwide sample of 1,900 abortion patients to describe their reasons for abortion and identify the ones most important to them. Table 3 presents their answers.

Most women had several reasons for seeking an abortion—only 7 percent of women cited just one factor, and there were no strong patterns among the reasons. Reasons associated with developmental level/life stage clearly played a critical role in the abortion decision—11 percent of the women indicated their major reason for abortion was that they were "not mature enough" or were "too young" to have a child, 8 percent said they had all the children they wanted or had adult children, and another 21 percent gave "unready for the responsibility" as the most important reason. Interpersonal relationships and socioeconomic circumstances related to the woman's ability to care for current or future children were also significant; 23 percent mentioned that a husband or partner wanted the abortion; 68 percent said they couldn't afford a baby.

A substantial number of women's reasons for abortion reflect responsibilities to others or outside circumstances; these aspects of women's realities are sometimes lost in abortion policy debates. To examine these different types of reasons more closely, we regrouped and reanalyzed the data for unmarried minors, unmarried adults, and married adults.[43] Table 4 provides the reorganized categories for the three subgroups of particular interest.[44]

Inspection of Table 4 reveals that women's reasons for abortion vary with circumstances. For example, minors sought abortions largely because they believed they were too young or immature to raise a child. Among adults, mothers (married and unmarried) were more likely to say that their childbearing was completed, other children needed them, and they had current responsibilities for others as reasons for abortion. More than one out of three adult abortion patients, regardless of group, indicated that they could not afford to have a baby now. The reasonableness of these women's assessment of their ability to afford to have a child is supported by the finding that one-third of them live in families with total incomes of less than $11,000 a year.

In summary, women's motivations for abortion reflect a wide range of developmental levels, health conditions, competing role obligations, access to coping resources, and exposure to stressful life events such as marital conflict. The abortion decisions of these women reflect a desire to reduce the risk of physical, psychological, social, and economic disadvantages for themselves and

Table 3. Percentage of Abortion Patients Reporting That a Specific Reason Contributed to Their Decision to Have an Abortion

Reason	% mentioning reason (N=1,900)	% identifying reason as most important (N=1,773)
Woman is concerned about how having a baby could change her life	76	16
Woman can't afford baby now	68	21
Woman has problems with relationship or wants to avoid single parenthood	51	12
Woman is unready for responsibility	31	21
Woman doesn't want others to know she has had sex or is pregnant	31	1
Woman is not mature enough or is too young to have a child	30	11
Woman has all the children she wanted or has all grown-up children	26	8
Husband or partner wants woman to have an abortion	23	1
Fetus has possible health problem	13	3
Woman has health problem	7	3
Woman's parents want her to have abortion	7	0
Woman was victim of rape or incest	1	1
Other	6	3

Note: Adapted from Torres and Forrest (1988, p. 170).

their existing and future children. In doing so, they help to alleviate a host of social and economic problems that are undermining the functioning of the larger society.

OUTCOMES OF ABORTION

Abortion, like any other health or family decision, has both positive and negative outcomes. How serious the negative outcomes are varies enormously with the surrounding circumstances. In the United States, legal abortion is safer than either pregnancy or childbirth. About one out of 200,000 U.S. abortion patients dies (about half the risk of a penicillin shot). Risks of complications increase with duration of the pregnancy. From 1981 to 1985, the death rate per 100,000 legal abortions ranged from 0.2 (for women eight or fewer weeks since LMP) to 0.6 (nine to ten weeks LMP), 3.7 (sixteen to

Table 4. Percentages of Five Groups of Abortion Patients Giving Various Internal and External Reasons for Abortion: Unmarried Minors and Adult Women by Marital and Parental Status

Reasons	Unmarried minors	Unmarried adults		Married adults	
	Nonmothers (261)	Mothers (480)	Nonmothers (852)	Mothers (204)	Nonmothers (46)
I. Internal reasons	77.8	51.5	60.7	55.9	34.8
A. Not ready for childrearing	75.9	23.8	48.5	21.1	34.8
1. Too young/not mature enough to raise a(nother) child	61.3	—	16.1	—	—
2. Can't take the responsibility	33.3	22.3	35.8	18.6	34.8
B. Childbearing completed	—	17.9	—	39.7	—
C. Desire to avoid single parenthood	5.0	18.1	21.4	—	—
D. Health	—	—	—	10.8	6.5
1. Physical problems	—	—	—	7.8	6.5
II. External reasons	70.0	71.3	77.2	66.7	89.1
A. General situational factors	38.3	14.8	33.6	10.3	21.7
1. Education related	36.8	5.2	22.7	—	13.0
2. Job related/would interfere with job/career	8.8	7.1	15.0	6.9	13.0
B. Fetus related	6.5	8.1	11.2	11.8	23.9
1. Prescription medication	—	—	—	5.4	15.2
2. Diagnosed fetal defect	—	—	—	—	6.5
C. Partner related	11.9	24.0	19.0	17.2	28.3
1. Partner not ready/wants abortion	5.0	—	—	—	15.2
2. Relationship may break up/has broken up	—	7.7	—	5.9	10.9
D. Social disapproval of others	13.8	—	9.3	—	—
1. Doesn't want others to know pregnant	10.7	—	8.5	—	—
E. Other responsibilities/other children need me	—	18.5	—	17.2	—
F. Cannot afford to have a baby	28.4	40.0	44.2	34.3	41.3

Note: Analysis based on data set reported in Torres and Forrest (1988). Dashes indicate that subcategory had responses of less than 5%. Married minors (0.7%) and minors who were mothers (3.6%) were not included because there were too few for meaningful comparisons.

twenty weeks LMP), and 12.7 per 100,000 (twenty-one or more weeks LMP). The risk of dying from childbirth was greater than that of dying from an abortion at all but the last stage of pregnancy: 6.6 deaths per 100,000 live births.[45] Among women who have abortions in the first trimester, 97 percent have *no* complications or postabortion complaints; less than .5 percent require an additional surgical procedure and/or hospitalization.

The mental health risks of abortion, particularly of legal abortion conducted in the first trimester of pregnancy, are minimal compared to those from bearing an unwanted child. This does not mean that women who have abortions never have any psychological problems. Some do, just as some women have psychological problems associated with wanted and unwanted childbearing and adoption. A history of psychiatric disorder, lack of access to psychological, social, and economic resources, low expectations for coping, the meaningfulness of the pregnancy to the woman, level of stress from other life events, and powerlessness and feelings of coercion all appear linked to postpregnancy psychopathology in women, *whatever the outcome of the pregnancy.*

Women typically have both positive and negative emotions about their abortion experience. Positive emotions (relief and happiness) are more often and more strongly experienced than negative emotions (shame, guilt, regret, anxiety, and depression), both immediately after the abortion as well as in the months following. Thus, women can simultaneously feel a little guilty and *very* relieved and happy after having an abortion.[46]

In general, women's anxiety and depression levels are highest *before* their abortion. Immediately after the abortion they drop and continue dropping for several weeks later, until they are lower than they were *before* the abortion.[47] One of the largest studies[48] examined the well-being of 773 women who had one or more abortions in a national sample of 5,295 women followed over eight years. The most important factor in predicting a woman's postabortion well-being was her level of well-being *before* her first abortion. In addition, education and income were positively associated with enhanced well-being; larger family size was associated with decreased well-being. Once these factors were controlled, there was no relationship between having an abortion and level of well-being. Abortion's positive relationship to well-being thus appears to be through the important role that abortion plays in enabling women to time, space, and limit childbearing, acquire more education, and obtain better-paying jobs.

Option 3: Adoption

National data on adoption is scarce. Precisely how many children are placed for adoption, how many are adopted, and how many people want to adopt are not known.[49] Every year, there are about 50,000 unrelated adoptions (i.e., adoptions where parents are not related to the child) in the United States, but only about half of these involve infants.[50] Based on sample data, it is estimated that about 1 percent of women who are mothers (including all marital statuses) have given one or more children up for adoption.[51] About 2 percent of children born to never-married women are placed for adoption. There are marked ethnic and cultural differences in the use of adoption as an alternative to keeping the child or having an abortion. Never-married white women are more likely to place their children for adoption than are comparable black women (3.2 percent compared to 1.1 percent).[52] It has been suggested that black women are less likely to relinquish their children because adoption is viewed as a violation of black family norms, which emphasize keeping the child within the extended family unit.[53]

Rates of adoption are similar for both whites and blacks, but white women are more likely to adopt an *unrelated* child. In 1988, 1.4 percent of white women between the ages of twenty and fifty-four had adopted an unrelated child, compared to .8 percent of black women and .4 percent of Hispanic women.[54] Thus, although black children are less likely to be placed for adoption, they are also less likely to be adopted, and a review of waiting lists for adoption suggests that black children are overrepresented among children waiting for adoption.[55] A perception that one's child may not be readily adopted can affect the adoption decision. As one African-American woman described her visit to an adoption agency before choosing abortion:

> Next option was to visit an adoption facility. . . . I had volunteered in one when I was younger and I wanted to see if the conditions had changed much since then. Unfortunately, they hadn't, minority children sadly waiting for someone to adopt them. I realized that it was not an option for me and my minority child.[56]

WHY DO WOMEN CHOOSE ADOPTION?

There is no national study that systematically answers this question and compares reasons for adoption to those given for abortion or keeping the child. A retrospective study that asked thirty-eight women why they chose adoption found that the reasons given included providing a baby with a family (68 percent), being unprepared for parenthood (26 percent), wanting to finish school (26 percent), not being ready emotionally (21 percent), and lacking financial resources (18 percent).[57]

Another study focused on why adolescent mothers did *not* choose adoption over keeping their children. One half reported they were not emotionally prepared to place their child for adoption, and one-third said they couldn't relinquish a child after carrying it for nine months. In contrast, three-fourths who placed their child for adoption said they were unable to provide the kind of home environment needed for the child.[58]

OUTCOME OF ADOPTION

There is little scientific research on the psychological and social consequences of the adoption decision, and what there is generally ignores preexisting psychological conditions and other circumstances surrounding adoption that may contribute to postadoption psychological distress. There are studies that suggest that placing a child for adoption may pose some psychological risks for some women.[59] For example, one study of approximately eighty birth mothers found that 60 percent experienced emotional problems after relinquishing their child. In addition, 66 percent reported gynecological problems, and 60 percent reported other medical concerns.[60]

Other studies have reported that the psychological distress of relinquishing a child for adoption may last for long periods of time and affect the interpersonal relationships of the birth parents.[61] Unfortunately, this research is based on samples of people who are self-selected because of problems with adoption. For example, a study of 334 adults belonging to a national organization that began as an initial support group for people dealing with postadoption emotional responses found such individuals to perceive adoption as having a long-lasting negative impact in the areas of marriage, childbearing, and parenting. Such perceptions included marital conflict that emerges as a result of search activity (particularly if the mate is not the parent of the child) and overindulging and overprotecting other children in the family.[62] These individuals, who had relinquished their children when closed adoption records were the standard practice, had not adjusted to their decision and continued to express unresolved conflict over their past loss. They reported that their decision-making process was characterized by family opposition to their adoption decision, pressure by physicians or social workers to choose adoption, and a lack of financial resources. Sixty-five percent of this sample had initiated a search for the relinquished child.

In the words of a woman seventeen years after giving up her child for adoption:

> I don't think there is a woman alive who has been through this, as I have, who doesn't wonder what happened to her child. It doesn't make any difference how many other children you have, they never take the place of that one you "put out" for adoption. I would like to know if my first boy is happy and healthy, and if he forgives me. . . . I don't even know if he is alive or dead.[63]

The type of adoption procedure used may affect the level of postadoption psychological adjustment. Recent research suggests that adolescents who relinquish their children in an open adoption process in which they meet and approve of the adopting parents are generally satisfied with their decision. As adoption procedures change and open adoption becomes more widespread, more people may become comfortable with this option. If coercion is used to promote adoption as an alternative to abortion, however, the risk for psychological distress after adoption may also increase.

Several methodologically rigorous studies have identified adoptees as at higher risk for psychological and academic problems, particularly during elementary and high school years.[64] One study found that at five years of age, adopted children were rated by researchers (but not parents) as less confident, more fearful, and less task motivated than nonadopted children.[65] Adopted children have also been found to be more likely to be viewed by teachers, but not by parents, as having more personality problems, conduct disorders, and delinquency than nonadopted children.[66] A national health survey found that adopted children were more likely to have higher scores on a behavior problem index and more likely to have been treated by a psychologist or psychiatrist than nonadopted children.[67]

Brodzinsky has provided an eloquent summary of the findings in the scientific adoption literature:

> As a substitute form of child care for children whose parents cannot or will not provide for them, the practice of adoption has proved to be [a]...success. Children placed in adoptive homes...fare much better than children who live with birthparents who are ambivalent about raising them....Still...it would be inappropriate and unjustified to disregard what is becoming increasingly clear to adoption caseworkers, mental health professionals, and researchers alike: namely, that certain genetic and prenatal vulnerabilities...as well as intrapersonal, familial, and socio-cultural stresses associated with adoption render adoptees more vulner-able to a host of emotional and school-related problems than their nonadopted counterparts. To ignore or distort this situation...is to look at adoption through rose-colored glasses.[68]

The feasibility of adoption as an alternative to abortion clearly needs more thoughtful discussion. In addition to ethnic and cultural differences in attitudes toward adoption and preferences for adopting children of one's own race, there is a resistance to adopting children in poor health or who have birth defects. The fact that babies born to unmarried women are more likely to have low birth weight and other health problems has significant implications for adoption programs, as do the increasing rates of drug and alcohol abuse and AIDS among pregnant women. Although adoption—if chosen freely, without coercion—may indeed be a good alternative for some women, like all women's reproductive choices, it is an option with pros and cons, benefits and risks.

Implications of Restricting Women's Choice

The decision to bear and raise a child—or to avoid doing so through abortion or adoption—is complex and personal. In thinking about the state's interest in the outcome of a woman's pregnancy, it is instructive to consider how the United States might be different if women who sought abortions over the last decade had not been able to attain them.[69]

Given that the characteristics of abortion patients have not changed substantially over the past ten years, they can be used to roughly project the impact of denying abortion on various groups in society at high risk for many of the psychological and social problems linked to unwanted childbearing. In this alternative future, if abortion had been denied over the past ten years, the additional children born would include an estimated

- 15 million who were unwanted at some time during pregnancy
- 5 million born below the poverty line
- 12.2 million born to single-parent families
- 4.8 million born to women who were unemployed
- 1.7 million born to minors
- 4 million born into families who already had two or more children
- 3.8 million born to women whose youngest child was less than two years of age
- 2.25 million born to women abused during pregnancy

Although these estimates are rough, the size of the numbers leaves a large margin for error. However, they underscore the profound and far-reaching societal consequences of interfering with a woman's personal reproductive choices and suggest that society's best interests lie in leaving abortion decisions in the hands of individual women, without hurdles or restrictions.

NOTES

1. Koop, C. Everett (1987). The Surgeon General's report: The public health effects of abortion. In J. Douglas Butler & David F. Walbert (Eds.) (1990). *Abortion, medicine, and the law* (pp. 731–44). New York: Facts on File.

2. Forrest, Jacqueline (1987). Unintended pregnancy among American women. *Family Planning Perspectives, 19*(?), 76–77.

3. Actually, a large but unknown number of women bear but neither raise nor relinquish their children; the children end up in foster care when the women cannot care for them. In 1985, about 276,000 children were in foster care (sadly, only 66 percent of these children were actually able to be placed in foster family homes). Data on the number of years they have been in foster care,

how many of these children are legally relinquished and waiting to be placed for adoption, and how many are in foster care but not relinquished is not available (General Accounting Office [1989]. *Foster parents: Recruiting and preservice training practices need evaluation.* [GAO/HRD-89-86]. Washington, DC: USGAO).

4. Gold, Rachel B. (1990). *Abortion and women's health: A turning point for America?* New York: The Alan Guttmacher Institute.

5. Westoff, Charles W. (1988).

6. Tietze, Christopher, & Henshaw, Stanley K. (1986). *Induced abortion: A world review: 1986.* (6th ed.). New York: Alan Guttmacher Institute.

7. In the 1960s, thirteen states liberalized their abortion laws. By 1970, Alaska, Hawaii, New York, and Washington in effect had abortion on request (Tietze & Henshaw, 1986).

8. *Roe v. Wade,* 410 U.S. 113, 153 (1973).

9. *Id.* at 162.

10. Henshaw, Stanley K. (1991). The accessibility of abortion services in the United States. *Family Planning Perspectives, 23*(6), 250, Table 4 at 251. 1985 data is in Jacqueline D. Forrest & Stanley K. Henshaw (1987), The harassment of U.S. abortion providers. *Family Planning Perspectives, 19*(1), 9–13.

11. Abortion doctor shot dead at clinic protest. *Arizona Republic,* March 11, 1993, p. 1.

12. These numbers are not exact because not all facilities responded to the AGI surveys.

13. Henshaw, Stanley K., & Van Vort, Jennifer (1994). Abortion services in the United States, 1991 and 1992. *Family Planning Perspectives, 26*(3), 100–106.

14. Births are defined as unwanted in these studies if the woman says that she had not wanted to have a child (or another child) at the time of conception or at any point of time in the future. Unwanted births are distinguished from mistimed births, which are wanted at a future time but occur sooner than the woman prefers.

15. Data on unwanted conceptions and births comes from a series of national fertility surveys that began in 1955. The 1955 survey was based on currently married white women aged eighteen to thirty-nine, i.e., women at least risk for unwanted pregnancy. By 1973, researchers had realized that other women had babies, too; formerly married women, single mothers, and black women were included in the sample. However it was not until 1982 that the sample covered all women of childbearing age (ages fifteen to forty-four) in the United States. Thus, the pre-*Roe* studies underestimate the number of unwanted conceptions, and comparisons before 1982 are limited to ever-married women.

16. Williams, Linda B. (1991). Determinants of unintended childbearing among ever-married women in the United States: 1973–1988. *Family Planning Perspectives, 23*(5), 212–21.

17. Russo, Nancy Felipe, & Zierk, Kristin L. (1992). Abortion, childbearing, and women's well-being. *Professional Psychology, 23,* 269–80.

18. David, Henry P., Dytrych, Zdenek, Matejcek, Zdenek, & Schuller, Vratislav. (1988). *Born unwanted: Developmental effects of denied abortion.* New York: Springer.

19. Pare, C. M. B., & Raven, Hermione. (1970). Follow-up of patients referred for termination. *The Lancet, i,* 653–58.

20. Visram, S. (1971). A follow-up study of 95 women who were refused abortions on psychiatric grounds. In Norman Morris (Ed.), *Proceedings of the Third International Congress of Psychosomatic Medicine in Obstetrics and Gynaecology,* London, England.

21. Study described in David et al. (1988), pp. 47–48.

22. Westoff, Charles F. (1988). Contraceptive paths toward the reduction of unintended pregnancy and abortion. *Family Planning Perspectives, 20*(1), 4–13.

23. Russo, Nancy Felipe. (1992). Psychological aspects of unwanted pregnancy and its resolution. In J. Douglas Butler & David E. Walbert (Eds.), *Abortion, medicine, and the law* (4th ed.) (pp. 592–636). New York: Facts on File.

24. David et al. (1988); Forssman, Hans, & Thuwe, Inga (1966). One hundred and twenty children born after application for therapeutic abortion refused. *Acta Psychiatrica Scandinavia, 64,* 142–46; Blomberg, Stig (1980). Influence of maternal distress during pregnancy on postnatal development. *Acta Psychiatrica Scandinavia, 62,* 405–17; Terhune, Kenneth W. (1975). A review of the actual and expected consequences of family size. Calspan report no. DP-5333-G-1, USGPO.

25. Altemeier, William A., O'Connor, Susan, Vietze, Peter M., Sandler, Howard M., & Sherrod, Kathryn B. (1982). Antecedents of child abuse. *Behavioral Pediatrics, 100,* 823–29; Egeland, Byron, & Brunquell, Don (1979). An at-risk approach to the study of child abuse. *Journal of the*

American Academy of Child Psychiatry, 18, 219–35; Hunter, Rosemary S., Klistrom, Nancy, Kraybill, Ernest N., & Loda, Frank (1978). Antecedents of child abuse and neglect in premature infants: A prospective study in a newborn intensive care unit. *Pediatrics, 61,* 629–35; Murphy, Solbritt, Orkow, Bonnie, & Nicola, Ray M. (1985). Prediction of child abuse and neglect: A prospective study. *Child Abuse and Neglect, 9,* 225–35.

26. For a summary of these studies, see Zuravin, Susan (1987). Unplanned pregnancies, family planning programs, and child maltreatment. *Family Relations,* 135–39; Zuravin, Susan (1988). Fertility patterns: Their relationship to child physical abuse and child neglect. *Journal of Marriage and the Family, 50,* 983–93.

27. David et al. (1988).

28. Albeit by a different definition of unwanted than the Czech study.

29. The Alan Guttmacher Institute (AGI), which surveys abortion providers every two or three years, is the most reliable collector of statistics for legal abortions and is the source primarily relied on here. Their surveys represent at least 94 percent of all abortions. AGI has published data from eleven surveys of abortion providers between 1973 and 1992 in its journal *Family Planning Perspectives* (*FPP*). Some recent articles and some previously unpublished data can be found in *Abortion Factbook: 1992 Edition,* edited by Stanley K. Henshaw and Jennifer Van Vort (New York: AGI, 1992). Data from more recent surveys will be published in future issues of *FPP.* The results of the AGI surveys are summarized by the U.S. Department of Commerce in the *Statistical Abstract of the United States.*

30. Henshaw, Koonin, & Smith (1991).

31. Women aged fifteen through forty-four are considered the population of reproductive age.

32. Henshaw, Stanley K., & Silverman, Jane. (1988). The characteristics and prior contraceptive use of U.S. abortion patients. *Family Planning Perspectives, 20,* 158–68.

33. Henshaw & Silverman (1988). The highest abortion is for women aged eighteen and nineteen.

34. This data is based on a 1987 AGI survey of 9,480 women obtaining abortions at 103 clinics, hospitals, and doctors' offices—a nationally representative sample of abortion providers.

35. Russo, Nancy Felipe, Horn, Jody D., & Schwartz, Robert. (1992). U.S. abortion in context: Selected characteristics and motivations of women seeking abortions. *Journal of Social Issues, 48,* 183–202.

36. Regrettably, detailed information on other groups of women of color who are mothers with young children is not available.

37. Russo, Nancy Felipe, Horn, Jody D., & Tromp, Shannon. (1993). Childspacing intervals and abortion among blacks and whites: A brief report. *Women & Health, 20*(3), 43–52.

38. Henshaw, Stanley. (1990). Induced abortion: A world review, 1990. *Family Planning Perspectives, 22*(2), 76–89. Gestation is counted in different ways. A picture of an "eight-week fetus" looks very different depending if the starting point is the woman's last menstrual period (LMP), from conception or from implantation. Even these are arbitrary. There is no "moment" of conception. It takes about twenty-four hours for each set of twenty-three chromosomes contributed by the man and the woman to be organized into a new set of twenty-three *pairs* of chromosomes. Implantation refers to when the zygote burrows into the uterine wall and the woman actually becomes pregnant— an event that occurs several days after fertilization. Flowers, Michael J. (1992). Coming into being: The prenatal development of humans. In J. Douglas Butler & David E. Walbert (Eds.), *Abortion, medicine, and the law* (4th ed.). New York: Facts on File, 437–52.

39. Henshaw, Koonin, & Smith (1991).

40. Flowers (1992).

41. Henshaw, Stanley (1990).

42. These findings were based on responses of abortion patients to a self-administered questionnaire distributed to patients in a sample of thirty U.S. abortion facilities over a five-month period beginning in November 1987. Details of the sampling method and procedure are available in Torres, Aida, & Forrest, Jacqueline (1988). Why do women have abortions? *Family Planning Perspectives, 20,* 169–76.

43. Russo, Horn, & Schwartz (1992).

44. We do not report these reasons separately for African-Americans or Hispanic Americans because ethnicity plays little part in reasons for abortion when age, marital status, employment status, student status, and parental status are controlled.

45. Henshaw, Stanley (1990).

46. Adler, Nancy E. (1975). Emotional responses of women following therapeutic abortion. *American Journal of Orthopsychiatry, 45,* 446–54.

47. See Adler, Nancy E., David, Henry P., Major, Brenda N., Roth, Susan H., Russo, Nancy Felipe, & Wyatt, Gail E. (1992). Psychological factors in abortion: A review. *American Psychologist, 47,* 1194–1204, and Russo (1992) for reviews of this literature.

48. Russo & Zierk (1992).

49. Mosher, William. (1988). Fertility and family planning in the United States: Insights from the National Survey of Family Growth. *Family Planning Perspectives, 20*(5), 207–17.

50. Sobol, Michael P., & Daly, Kerry J. (1992). The adoption alternative for pregnant adolescents: Decision making, consequences, and policy implications. *Journal of Social Issues, 48,* 143–62.

51. Russo & Zierk (1992).

52. Bachrach, Christine A., Stolley, Kathy S., & London, Kathryn A. (1992). Relinquishment of premarital births: Evidence from national survey data. *Family Planning Perspectives, 24*(1), 27–32, 48.

53. Sobol & Daly (1992).

54. Bachrach, Christine A., Adams, Patricia F., Sambrano, Soledad, & London, Kathryn A. (1990). *Adoption in the 1980s: Advance data from vital and health statistics (No. 181).* Hyattsville, MD: National Center for Health Statistics, U.S. Public Health Service.

55. Munns, Joyce M., & Copenhaver, J. A. (1989). *The state of adoption in America.* Washington, DC: Child Welfare League.

56. Anonymous. (n.d.). *The voices of women. Abortion: In their own words.* Washington, DC: NARAL, 14.

57. Pannor, Reuben, Baran, Annette, & Sorosky, Arthur D. (1978). Birth parents who relinquished babies for adoption revisited. *Family Process, 17,* 329–37.

58. Resnick, Michael. (1987). *Adoption and parenting decision making among adolescent females.* Final report to the Office of Adolescent Pregnancy Prevention, U.S. Department of Health and Human Services.

59. Sorosky, Arthur, Baran, Annette, & Pannor, Reuben (1978). *The adoption triangle: The effects of the sealed record on adoptees, birth parents, and adoptive parents.* New York: Anchor Press.

60. Burnell, George M., & Norfleet, Mary Ann. (1979). Women who place their infant for adoption: A pilot study. *Patient Counseling and Health Education, 16,* 169–76.

61. Sorosky, Baran, & Pannor (1978).

62. Deykin, Eva, Campbell, Lee, & Patti, Patricia (1984). The postadoption experience of surrendering parents. *American Journal of Orthopsychiatry, 54,* 271–80.

63. Baran, Annette, Pannor, Reuben, & Sorosky, Arthur. (1977). The lingering pain of surrendering a child. *Psychology Today,* 58–88.

64. A more detailed discussion of this literature can be found in Brodzinsky, David. (1987). Looking at adoption through rose-colored glasses: A critique of Marquis and Detweiler's "Does Adoption Mean Different: An Attributional Analysis." *Journal of Personality and Social Psychology, 52,* 394–98.

65. Hoopes, Janet L. (1982). *Prediction in child development: A longitudinal study of adoptive and nonadoptive families.* New York: Child Welfare League of America.

66. Lindholm, Bryon W., & Touliatos, John (1980). Psychological adjustment of adopted and nonadopted children. *Psychological Reports, 46,* 307–10. See, e.g., Bohman, Michael. (1970). *Adopted children and their families: A follow-up study of adopted children, their background environment, and adjustment.* Stockholm, Sweden: Proprius; Seglow, Jean, Pringle, Mia Kellmer, & Wedge, Peter. (1972). *Growing up adopted.* Windsor, England: National Foundation for Educational Research in England and Wales.

67. Zill, Nicholas. (1985). *Behavior and learning problems among adopted children: Findings from a U.S. national survey of child health.* Paper presented at the meeting of the Society for Research in Child Development, Toronto, Canada (Apr. 1985).

68. Brodzinsky (1987).

69. This discussion is adapted from Russo, Horn, & Schwartz (1992).

Treating Health: Women and Medicine

Barbara Katz Rothman and Mary Beth Caschetta

WOMEN ARE NOT ONLY people: *Woman* is a subject one can specialize in within medicine. However, except for sex organs and reproduction, women have not been studied or treated adequately by the medical establishment. At the moment, when a woman enters the health delivery system, her body is essentially divided among specialists. Obstetricians and gynecologists, for example, are medicine's, and perhaps society's, generally recognized "experts" on the subject of women, though technically they provide care for only reproduction and the functioning of sex organs.[1] *Obstetrics* is the branch of medicine limited to the care of women during pregnancy, labor, and the time surrounding childbirth,[2] a practice that tried to supplant midwifery. Gynecology is the "science of the diseases of women, especially those affecting the sex organs."[3] Diseases that frequently affect women and do not involve the sex organs, such as thyroid disease, rheumatoid arthritis, adult-type diabetes, osteoporosis, and depression, have not been studied in women.[4] Conditions occurring more frequently in women of color, for example, hypertension, alcoholism, and cardiovascular diseases, have, until very recently, received no attention at all.

At its simplest, a medical specialty can be seen as arising out of preexisting needs. People have heart attacks: The medical specialty of cardiology develops. Or the amount of knowledge generated in a field grows so enormously that no one person can hope to master it all. Physicians then "carve out" their own areas of specialization. Increasing knowledge about cancer thus led to the specialty of, and the subspecialties within, oncology. By looking at the history of emerging specialties, their successes and failures, we can tell a lot about medical needs and knowledge. For instance, an attempt by urologists in 1891 to develop an "andrology" specialty for men came to nothing.[5] Technically, there is no "science" of the study of men, comparable to the specialties devoted to women and their reproductive functions. This may be because most of generalized medicine is already geared toward men and the male body, and women are treated as special cases in that they are different from men.

But the development of a medical specialty is not necessarily the creation of a key for an already existing lock. Medical needs do not necessarily predate the specialty, even though the specialty is presumably organized to meet those needs. This has been made quite clear in the work of Thomas Szasz on the expansion of medicine into such "social problem" areas as alcoholism, gambling, and suicide.[6] Medicine does not have "cures" for these problems, but by defining them in medical terms, as a sickness, the physician gains political control over the societal response: Punishment becomes "treatment," desired or not, successful or not. Similarly, medicine can be viewed as a tool in the political control over women's sexuality, childbirth, lactation, menopause, and general health and well-being. Such medical control has rarely been based on superior ability to deal with these concerns.

Exclusion of Women from Research

In 1985, the United States Public Health Service reported a general lack of research data on women and a limited understanding of women's general health needs.[7] Because menstrual cycles are said to constitute a separate variable affecting test results,[8] researchers have used menses as an excuse to exclude women from research. A woman's period "muddies" the research data, so to speak. Additionally, medical experts have been, and continue to be, reluctant to perform studies on women of childbearing age, because experimental treatments or procedures may affect their reproductive capabilities and/or a potential fetus.[9]

The exclusion of females from medical research is so institutionalized that even female rats are commonly excluded from early basic research, on which most medical decisions rest. The result of female exclusion from human research is that most medical recommendations made to the general population are extrapolated from the Caucasian male body.[10] Therefore, the original research on the ability of aspirin to prevent coronary artery disease was done exclusively on men,[11] although it had been known for some time that heart disease is a leading killer of women. The original testing of antidepressant drugs on men[12] did not anticipate the fact that the constant doses appropriate for men may in women sometimes be too high or too low, due to the natural hormonal changes during the menstrual cycle.[13]

As expected, this astounding lack of research concerning women's biology has enormous impact on the individual experiences of women seeking care and results in inadequate health care. For instance, more women than men die from heart disease each year, yet women with heart trouble are less likely to receive treatment, even when symptoms clearly indicate severe heart trouble exists.[14] And while lung cancer is the number-one cancer killer of women, they are twice as likely as men *not* to be tested for lung cancer.[15] Additionally, while AIDS is a leading killer of women in many urban areas, the official definition of AIDS—which is actually a series of infections and cancers that occur when the immune system is weakened by the human immunodeficiency virus (HIV)—did not originally include many of the HIV-related conditions in women because what is known about HIV disease is derived principally from research on men.[16] Therefore, significant numbers of women who die of HIV-related complications do so without an actual diagnosis of AIDS.[17]

The medical specialists clash over women and AIDS: Infectious disease experts claim not to know about the gynecological infections and cancers of HIV, and gynecologists claim not to understand the general manifestations of HIV. Internists generally do not look for HIV infection in women. Therefore undercounting of women in the epidemic is enormous: Women are denied disability entitlements to which they are entitled; their illness goes misdiagnosed and untreated; and research efforts are skewed, distorting general knowledge of the scope of the AIDS epidemic.

Problems with "Women" as a Medical Category

It is important to understand that the medical term *women* almost always assumes white, middle-class females. The significance of this short-sighted view of a diverse population is wide-reaching. For instance, biological racial differences and socioeconomic impacts on illness are only now coming to light, although they have long been suspected. Studies show that compared to whites, Asians may achieve significantly higher blood serum levels when given certain drugs; osteoporosis is more prevalent in white women; and black women have a significantly higher rate of low birth weights, a fact often blamed on inner-city socioeconomic status, yet Latina women in similar inner-city situations birth far fewer low-weight babies.[18] Nonetheless, until recently, medicine has ignored differences among real people, including gender and race.

Doctors, Midwives, and Other Struggles for Power

Jacoba Felice de Almania was a woman tried for the illegal practice of medicine in 1322. In her defense Almania had witnesses who testified that she never charged unless she cured and that her cures were successful where other, "legal" (male) practitioners had failed. However, since she had not attended a medical school (medical schools being closed to women), she was not licensed to practice medicine. That she saw women who did not want to go to a male practitioner and that she was successful did not matter. "Efficacy of treatment was not the criterion for determining who was or was not a legitimate medical practitioner, but the educational requirements and membership in the faculty of an organized group were the most important factors."[19] In essence, the statement behind professional control over medicine is: "We may not be able to help you, but we are the only ones qualified to try."

Vern Bullough, in his analysis of the development of medicine as a profession, writes about the situation during the Middle Ages: "One obvious group outside of the control of the university physician was the midwife, but during the period under study the university physician generally ignored this whole *area of medicine*. Midwives might or might not be qualified, but this *was not a matter of public concern*"[20] (emphasis added). More accurately, one might state not that physicians ignored this "area of medicine" but that midwifery and its concerns were outside the area of medicine, just as other matters that were undoubtedly of concern to women existed outside of the "public" concern. Until pregnancy and childbirth were defined as medical events, midwifery was in no sense a branch, area, or interest of medicine as a profession.

Medical expansion into the area of childbirth began before the development of asepsis, surgical techniques, or anesthesia—all of which are now considered the contributions of obstetrics. And yet, even without the technology, medicine had begun to redefine childbirth by the beginning of the nineteenth century. Childbirth came to be seen not as a family or religious event, but as a medical one, needing medical presence for its safe conduct.[21]

Midwives treated childbirth in the larger context of women's lives. Midwives did not and do not "deliver" babies. They teach women how to give birth. Brack has called the role of the midwife "total"—she helped both as teacher and as role model in the socialization of the mother to her new status. "The midwife's relation to the woman was both diffuse and affective, while the physician role demanded specificity and affective neutrality."[22] Midwives taught how to birth babies, how to nurse them, how to care for them and for the mother's own body. Physicians deliver babies and move on. The physician "isolated the laboring woman and her delivery of the infant from the rest of the childbearing experience, and defined it as a medical and surgical event which required specialized knowledge."[23] As one modern nurse-midwife has said of obstetrics residents: "They want us to stay with the woman in labor and just call them when she's ready to deliver. To them, that's the whole thing."

At the time that physicians were taking over control of childbirth, it is virtually unarguable that the noninterventionist, supportive techniques of the midwives were safer for both the birthing woman and her baby. The physicians' approaches included bleeding to "syncope" (until the woman fainted), tobacco infusion enemas, frequent nonsterile examinations, and other surgical and chemical interventions.[24] In the 1910s and 1920s, as American physicians successfully ousted midwives, the midwives' safety records remained better than the physicians'. In Newark from 1914 to 1916, a midwifery program achieved a maternal mortality rate as low as 1.7 per thousand, while in Boston, where midwives were banned, the rate was 6.5 per thousand. Similarly, the infant mortality rate in Newark was 8.5 per thousand, contrasted with 37.4 in Boston.[25] In Washington, as the percentage of births reported by midwives shrank from 50 percent in 1903 to 15 percent in 1912, infant mortality in the first day, first week, and first month of life all increased. New York's dwindling corps of midwives did significantly better than did New York doctors in preventing both stillbirths and postpartum infection.[26]

The physician's separation of the delivery of the baby from its larger socio-emotional context has its roots as far back as René Descartes's concept of mind–body dualism. To Descartes, the body was a machine whose structure and operation fall within the province of human knowledge, as distinguished from the mind, which God alone could know. Although even the Hippocratic principles state that the mind and body should be considered together, "most physicians, . . . irrespective of their professional activities and philosophical views on the nature of the mind, behave in practice as if they were still Cartesian dualists. Their conservative attitudes are largely a matter of practical convenience."[27]

The medical models used for convenience are that diseases are the bad guys that the good-guy medications can cure; that the body breaks down and needs repair; that the body can be repaired in the hospital like a car in the shop; and that once "fixed" the person can be returned to the community. The earliest models were largely mechanical; later models worked more with chemistry; and newer, more sophisticated medical writing describes computer-like programming. But the basic points remain the same. These models were useful when dealing with the problems facing medicine at the turn of the century: primarily bacterial and viral disease-causing agents and simple accidents and trauma. They have never worked well for understanding the problems that women face in dealing with doctors, including those encountered during the experience of childbirth. While midwives learned by apprenticeship, doctors were instructed in the use of forceps, as well as in the techniques of normal delivery, by "book learning," by discussion, by the use of wooden models, and infrequently by watching another doctor at work. Dorothy Wertz, in her study of the development of obstetrics, has pointed out that "by regarding the female body as a machine, European doctors found that they could measure the birth canal and predict whether or not the child could pass through."[28] Stories of women giving birth while their doctors scrub for a cesarean section are part of the lore of midwifery. Among the stories midwives tell one another are tales of women who were told that they could never deliver vaginally and then went on to have normal births of oversized babies.

In the nineteenth and early twentieth centuries midwives and physicians were in direct competition for patients, and not only for their fees. Newer, more clinically oriented medical training demanded "teaching material," so that even immigrant and poor women were desired as patients.[29] The displacement of the midwife by the male obstetrician can be better understood in terms of this competition than as an ideological struggle or as "scientific advancement." Physicians, unlike the unorganized, disenfranchised midwives, had access to the power of the state through their professional associations. They were thus able to control licensing legislation, restricting the midwife's sphere of activity and imposing legal sanctions against her in state after state.[30]

The legislative changes were backed up by the medical establishment's attempt to win public disapproval for midwifery and support for obstetrics. Physicians accused midwives of ignorance and incompetence and attacked midwifery practices as "meddlesome." Rather than upgrading the practice of midwifery by teaching the skills physicians thought necessary, the profession of medicine refused to train women either as midwives or as physicians.[31] Physicians argued repeatedly that medicine was the appropriate profession to handle birth because "normal pregnancy and parturition are exceptions and to consider them to be normal physiologic conditions was a fallacy."[32] Childbirth was redefined as a medical rather than a social event, and the roles and care surrounding it were reorganized to suit medical needs.[33]

Once professional dominance was established in the area of childbirth, obstetrics rapidly expanded into the relatively more sophisticated area of gynecology. The great obstetricians of the nineteenth century were invariably gynecologists (and of course were all men).[34] Among other effects, this linking of obstetrics and gynecology further reinforced the obstetrical orientation toward pathology.

Medical Control and Women

One of the earliest uses of the developing field of gynecology was the overt social control of women through surgical removal of various sexual organs. Surgical removal of the clitoris (clitoridectomy) or, less dramatically, its foreskin (circumcision) and removal of the ovaries (oopherectomy or castration) were used to check women's "mental disorders." The first gynecologist to do a clitoridectomy was an Englishman, in 1858.[35] In England, the procedure was harshly criticized and was not repeated by others after the death of the originator in 1860. In America, however, clitoridectomies were done regularly from the late 1860s until at least 1904,[36] and then sporadically until as recently as the late 1940s.[37] The procedure was used to terminate sexual desire or sexual behavior, something deemed pathological in women. Circumcisions were done on women of all ages to stop masturbation up until at least 1937.[38]

More widespread than clitoridectomies or circumcisions were oophe-rectomies for psychological "disorders." Interestingly, the female gonads were removed not when women were "too female"—i.e., too passive or dependent—but when women were too masculine—assertive, aggressive, "unruly." Oopherectomies for "psychiatric" reasons were done in America between 1872 and 1946.[39] (By the 1940s, prefrontal lobotomies were gaining acceptance as psychosurgery.)

The developing medical control of women was not limited to extreme cures for psychiatric problems. The physical health and stability of even the most socially acceptable women were questioned. Simply by virtue of gender, women were (and are) subject to *illness labeling.*

One explanation for women's vulnerability to illness labeling lies in the functionalist approach to the sociology of health. Talcott Parsons has pointed out that it is a functional requirement of any social system that there be a basic level of health of its members.[40] Any definition of illness that is too lenient would disqualify too many people from fulfilling their functions and would impose severe strains on the social system. System changes, such as war, can make changes in standards of health and illness generally set for members. This works on an individual level as well, standards of health and illness being related to social demands: A mild headache will excuse a student from attending class but not from taking final exams. A logical extension of this is that the less valued a person's or group's contribution to society, the more easily are such people labeled ill.

Women are not always seen as functional members of society, as people doing important things. This has historically and cross-culturally been especially true of the women of the upper classes in patriarchal societies, where it is a mark of status for a man to be able to afford to keep a wife who is not performing any useful function. A clear, if horrifying, example of this is the traditional Chinese practice of foot-binding. By crippling girls, men were able to show that they could afford to have wives and daughters who did nothing. It is a particularly disturbing example of conspicuous consumption. In their historical analysis of the woman patient, *Complaints and Disorders,* Barbara Ehrenreich and Deirdre English speak of the European-American "lady of leisure" of the late nineteenth and early twentieth centuries. "She was the social ornament that proved a man's success; her idleness, her delicacy, her child-like ignorance of 'reality' gave a man the 'class' that money alone could not provide."[41]

Menstruation and the Body as Machine

The practice of creating physical deformity in women can be seen in our history as well. A woman researcher who studied menstrual problems among college women between 1890 and 1920 found that women in the earlier period probably were somewhat incapacitated by menstruation, just as the gynecologists of the day were claiming. However, the researcher did not attribute the menstrual problems to women's "inherent disabilities" or "overgrowth of the intellect" as did the male physicians; she related it to dress styles. Women in the 1890s carried some fifteen pounds of skirts and petticoats, hanging from a tightly corseted waist. As skirts got lighter and waists were allowed to be larger, menstruation ceased to be the problem it had been.[42] In the interest of science, women might try the experiment of buckling themselves into a painfully small belt and hanging a fifteen-pound weight from it. One might expect weakness, fatigue, shortness of breath, even fainting, all the physical symptoms of women's "inherent" disability. And consider further the effects of bleeding as a treatment for the problem.

It follows from Parsons's analysis that, in addition to suffering by created physical disabilities (the bound feet of the Chinese, the deforming corsetry of our own history), women were more easily *defined* as sick when they were not seen as functional social members. At the same time in our history that the upper-class women were "delicate," "sickly," and "frail," the working-class women were well enough to perform the physical labor of housework, both their own and that of the upper classes, as well as to work in the factories and fields. "However sick or tired working class women might have been, they certainly did not have the time or money to support a cult of invalidism. Employers gave no time off for pregnancy or recovery from childbirth, much less for menstrual periods, though the wives of these same employers often retired to bed on all these occasions."[43] The working-class women were seen as strong and healthy; for them, pregnancy, menstruation, and menopause were not allowed to be incapacitating.

These two factors—the treatment of the body as a machine and the lesser functional importance assigned to women—still account for much of the medical treatment of women. Contemporary physicians do not usually speak of the normal female reproductive functions as diseases. The exception, to be discussed below, is menopause. The other specifically female reproductive functions—menstruation, pregnancy, childbirth, and lactation—are regularly asserted in medical texts to be normal and healthy phenomena. However, these statements are made within the context of teaching the medical "management," "care," "supervision," and "treatment" of each of these "conditions."

Understood in limited mechanical terms, each of these normal female conditions or happenings is a complication or stress on an otherwise normal system. Medicine has fared no better than has any other discipline in developing a working model of women that does not take men as the comparative norm. For example, while menstruation is no longer viewed as a disease, it is seen as a complication in the female system, contrasted to the reputed biological stability of the supposedly noncycling male.[44] As recently as 1961, the *American Journal of Obstetrics and Gynecology* was still referring to women's "inherent disabilities" in explanations of menstruation:

> Women are known to suffer at least some inconvenience during certain phases of the reproductive cycle, and often with considerable mental and physical distress. Woman's awareness of her inherent disabilities is thought to create added mental and in turn physical changes in the total body response, and there result problems that concern the physician who must deal with them.[45]

Premenstrual syndrome (PMS) is probably the most recent and most stunning example of the construction of women's normal functions as disease. According to the medical model, PMS manifests as emotional, physical, and behavioral conditions, characterized by more than 150 "symptoms," any number of which a woman might "suffer" during a specific phase of her menstrual cycle. Symptoms are always negative and include the following, to name a few: tension, irritability, forgetfulness, depression, mood swings, anger, muscle pains, cramps, craving for sweets or alcohol, headaches, crying jags, panic attacks, suicidal depressions, and bouts of violent or abusive behavior.[46]

The cause of PMS is thought to be a physiologic abnormality or an abnormal response to normal hormonal changes during the seventh to tenth day before the menstrual period starts. However, the most current research shows that no such abnormalities could be consistently identified and linked to women who are diagnosed as having PMS.[47] Nonetheless, an abundance of hypotheses link PMS to medical causes. For instance, the syndrome has been attributed to an overproduction of estrogen, under- and overproduction of progesterone, a disturbance in the estrogen/progesterone balance, water retention, salt retention, an insulin imbalance, a liver malfunction, stress, and inadequate nutrition.[48] To accommodate "treatment" for the new medical condition, PMS clinics have sprung up across the United Sates, offering "diagnoses" of the syndrome by pelvic exam and blood tests that cost anywhere from $200 to $500.[49]

There is much debate about whether PMS is a true medical entity or a social phenomenon that medicalizes the menstrual cycle in order to enforce social control over women. Emily Martin explores current conceptions of women's role in society and women's bodies by examining accounts of the language used to describe PMS and its foremost "symptom," anger.[50] Martin writes:

> The problems of men in these accounts are caused by outside circumstances and other people (women). The problems of women are caused by their own internal failure, seen as a biological malfunction. What is missing is any consideration of why, in Western societies, women might feel extreme rage at a time when their usual emotional controls are reduced.[51]

Pregnancy and the Mother-Host

Research on contraception displays mechanistic biases. The claim has been made that contraceptive research has concentrated on the female rather than the male because of the sheer number of potentially vulnerable links in the female chain of reproductive events.[52] Reproduction is clearly a more complicated process for the female than the male. While we might claim that it is safer to interfere in a simpler process, medicine has tended to view the number of points in the female reproductive process as distinct entities. Reproduction is dealt with not as a complicated organic process but as a series of discrete points, like stations on an assembly line, with more for female than for male.

The alternative to taking the female system as a complication of the "basic" or "simpler" male system is of course to take female as the working norm. In this approach, a pregnant woman is compared only to pregnant women, a lactating breast compared only to other lactating breasts. Pregnancy and lactation are accepted not only as nominally healthy variations but as truly normal states. To take the example of pregnancy, women *are* pregnant; pregnancy is not something they "have" or "catch" or even "contain." It involves physical changes; these are not, as medical texts frequently call them, "symptoms" of pregnancy. Pregnancy is not a disease, and its changes are no more symptoms than the growth spurt and development of pubic hair are symptomatic of puberty. There may be diseases or complications of pregnancy, but the pregnancy itself is neither disease nor complication.

In contrast, medicine's working model of pregnancy is a woman with an insulated parasitic capsule growing inside. The pregnancy, while physically located within the woman, is still seen as external to her, not a part of her. The capsule within has been seen as virtually omniscient and omnipotent, reaching out and taking what it needs from the mother-host, at her expense if necessary, while protected from all that is bad or harmful.

The pregnancy, in this medical model, is almost entirely a mechanical event in the mother. She differs from the nonpregnant woman only in the presence of this thing growing inside her. Differences other than the mechanical are accordingly seen as symptoms to be treated, so that the woman can be kept as "normal" as possible through the "stress" of the pregnancy. Pregnancy in this model is not seen necessarily as inherently unhealthy, but it is frequently associated with changes other than the growth of the uterus and its contents, and these changes are seen as unhealthy. For example, hemoglobin (iron) is lower in pregnant women than nonpregnant, making pregnant women appear (by nonpregnant standards) anemic. They are then treated for this anemia with iron supplements. Water retention, or edema, is greater in pregnant women than nonpregnant ones, so pregnant women are treated with limits placed on their salt intake and with diuretics. Pregnant women tend to gain weight over that accounted for by the fetus, placenta, and amniotic fluid. They are treated for this weight gain with strict diets, sometimes even with "diet pills." And knowing that these changes are likely to occur in pregnant women, American doctors generally have tried to treat all pregnant women with iron supplements, with limits on salt and calorie intake, and sometimes with diuretics. This attempt to cure the symptoms has brought up not only strict diets to prevent normal weight gain and diuretics to prevent normal fluid retention but also the dangerous drugs, from thalidomide to Bendectin, to prevent nausea. Each of these "cures" has had devastating effects: fetal malformation, maternal and fetal illness, even death.

What is particularly important to note is that these "treatments" of entirely normal phenomena are frequently not perceived by the medical profession as interventions or disruptions. Rather, the physician sees himself as assisting nature, restoring the woman to normality. Janet Bogdan, in her study of the development of obstetrics, reports that in the 1800s, a noninterventionist physician, as opposed to a "regular" physician, would give a laboring woman some castor oil or milk of magnesia, catheterize her, bleed her a pint or so, administer ergot, and use poultices to blister her. "Any of these therapies would be administered in the interests of setting the parturient up for an easier, less painful labor and delivery, while still holding to the belief that the physician was letting nature take its course."[53] Dorothy Wertz says that medicine currently has redefined "natural childbirth," in response to consumer demand for it, to include any of the following techniques: spinal or epidural anesthesia, inhalation anesthesia in the second stage of labor, forceps, episiotomy, induced labor.[54] Each of these techniques increases the risks of childbirth for mothers and babies.[55] Under the title "Normal Delivery," an obstetric teaching film shows "the use of various drugs and procedures used to facilitate normal delivery." Another "Normal Delivery" film is "a demonstration of a normal, spontaneous delivery, including a paracervical block, episiotomy."

As the technologies of both "curing" and "diagnosis" grow more powerful, the danger increases. The extraordinary rise in cesarean sections starting in the 1970s in the United States provides a striking example of this. Refinements in anesthesiology, and to a lesser extent in surgery itself, have made the cesarean section a much safer procedure in recent years. While it is not, and cannot be, as safe as an unmedicated vaginal birth—a section is major abdominal surgery, and all anesthesia entails risk—it is unquestionably safer today than it was twenty or forty years ago. Thus, the "cure" is more readily used. But what is the disease? The disease is labor, of course. While medicine now claims that pregnancy and labor are not diseases per se, they are always considered in terms of "riskiness": labor is at best "low risk" and is increasingly often defined as "high risk." At first only labors defined as high risk, but now even low-risk labors, are routinely being monitored electronically. The electronic fetal monitor has a belt that wraps around the pregnant belly, thus preventing normal walking and movement, and an electrode that goes into the vagina and literally screws into the top of the baby's head. Contractions, fetal heartbeat, and fetal scalp blood are all continuously monitored. With all of this diagnostic sophistication, "fetal distress" can be detected—and presumably cured, by cesarean section. The National Center for Health Services Research announced as far back as 1978 that electronic fetal monitoring may do more harm than good, citing among other things the dangers of the rapidly increasing cesarean section rate, but monitoring is still receiving widespread medical acceptance.[56]

Menopause and the End of the Femininity Index

The use of estrogens provides an even better example of how medicine views the body as a machine that can be "run" or managed without being changed. Estrogens are female hormones; in medicine they are seen as femininity in a jar. In the widely selling *Feminine Forever,* Dr. Robert A. Wilson, pushing "estrogen-replacement therapy" for all menopausal women, calls estrogen levels, as detected by examination of cells from the vagina, a woman's "femininity index."[57] As estrogen levels naturally drop off after menopause a woman, according to Wilson, is losing her femininity. Interestingly, estrogen levels are also quite low while a woman is breastfeeding, something not usually socially linked to a "loss of femininity."

Menopause remains the one normal female process that is still overtly referred to as a disease in the medical literature. To some physicians, menopause is a "deficiency disease," and the use of estrogens is restoring the woman to her "normal" condition. Here we must reconsider the question of women's functional importance in the social system. Middle-aged housewives have been called the last of the "ladies of leisure," having outlived their social usefulness as wife-mothers and having been allowed no alternatives. While oopherectomies and clitoridectomies are no longer being done on upper-class women as they were a hundred years ago, to cure all kinds of dubious ills, older women are having hysterectomies (surgical removal of the uterus) at alarming rates.[58] Much more typical of modern medicine, however, is the use of chemical rather than surgical "therapy." Because the social changes and demands for readjustment of middle age roughly coincide with the time of menopause, menopause becomes the "illness" for which women can be treated.

Estrogens have been used in virtually every stage of the female reproductive cycle, usually with the argument that they return the woman to normal or are a "natural" treatment. Estrogens are used to keep adolescent girls from getting "unnaturally" tall; to treat painful menstruation; as contraception, supposedly mimicking pregnancy; as a chemical abortion in the "morning after" pill; to replace supposedly missing hormones and thus to prevent miscarriages; to dry up milk and return women to the "normal" nonlactating state; and to return menopausal women to the "normal" cycling state. For all the claims of normality and natural treatment, at this writing approximately half of these uses of estrogens have been shown to cause cancer. The use of estrogens in pregnancy was the first to be proved carcinogenic: Daughters of women who had taken estrogens (notably DES, a synthetic estrogen) are at risk for the development of a rare cancer of the vagina.[59] The sequential birth-control pill was taken off the market as the danger of endometrial cancer (cancer of the lining of the uterus) became known,[60] and, similarly, estrogens taken in menopause have been shown to increase the risk of endometrial cancer by as much as fourteen times after seven years of use.[61]

The model of the body as a machine that can be regulated, controlled, and managed by medical treatments is not working. "Femininity" or physical "femaleness" is not something that comes in a jar and can be manipulated. Nor are women accepting the relegation to secondary functional importance, as wives and mothers of men. In rejecting the viewpoint that women bear men's children for them, women are reclaiming their bodies. When pregnancy is seen not as the presence of a (man's) fetus in a woman but as a condition of the woman herself, attitudes toward contraception, infertility, abortion, and childbirth all change. When pregnancy is perceived as a condition of the woman, then abortion, for example, is primarily a response to that condition.

Changing Feminist Perspectives

In the 1970s, the reemergence of the feminist movement brought about a new focus on women and health that called attention to medicine's treatment of female patients. Women's health advocates rejected not only the "specialty treatment" offered women by the medical establishment but in fact the whole medical system. These women opted for methods of care outside of the system altogether and urged the mobilization of self-help groups, self-examinations, and women's clinics. Self-help and lay midwifery groups have worked, and continue to work, outside of the medical system, redefining women's health. They taught, and continue to teach, women how to examine their own bodies, not in the never-ending search for pathology in which physicians are trained, but to learn more about health.

Contemporary women's health advocates also reject the specialty care approach, but do so by emphasizing women's inclusion into the system. These new feminists, operating at a time separated from their foremothers by a decade of conservative politics and an ailing, underfunded health care system, demand access to primary medical attention for women of all classes, colors, and cultures. Additionally, they emphasize a need for women's general health care that is based on a sound scientific understanding of female biology. These health advocates are geared toward consumerism within medicine, seeking better medical care and access for a wider range of services and a more inclusive population of women. Better trained, more knowledgeable, and more humane health care workers are a high priority, as is care that is based on the realities of women's lives.

Demanding better access, however, may not address the problem that medical care in the United States consists of an overmedicalization of the female body, a primary treatment focus on women's reproduction, and a general lack of information about female biology. And do we want physicians to be "treating" our health? Do we agree with what physicians consider to be illness in women? Do we want to urge comprehensive care that overmedicalizes the female body? It is entirely possible for a woman to fit herself for a diaphragm, do a pap smear and a beast examination (all with help and instruction if she needs it), and never adopt the patient role. It is also possible for a woman to go through a pregnancy and birth her baby with good, knowledgeable, caring help without becoming a patient under the supervision of a physician.

Women have been imbued with the medical model of women's bodies and health. And it is essential, whether working within or outside of the system, to redefine women in women's terms and to redefine physical normality within the context of the female body. This is not a problem unique to health. It is an essential feminist issue.

NOTES

1. Diana Scully and Pauling Bart, "A Funny Thing Happened on the Way to the Orifice: Women and Gynecology Textbooks," *American Journal of Sociology* 78 (1971), 1045–50.

2. *Gould Medical Dictionary,* 3rd ed. (New York: McGraw-Hill, 1972), 1056.

3. *Gould Medical Dictionary,* 658.

4. Karen Johnson and Charlea Massion, "Why a Women's Medical Specialty?" *Ms.* 11:3 (1991), 68–69.

5. G. J. Barker-Benfield, *The Horrors of the Half-Known Life* (New York: Harper and Row, 1976).

6. Thomas Szasz, *The Theology of Medicine* (New York: Harper Colophon, 1977).

7. U.S. Public Health Service, "Women's Health: Report of the Public Health Service Task Force on Women's Health Issues," Washington, D.C.: U.S. Department of Health and Human Services, 1985.

8. A. Hamilton and C. Perry, "Sex Related Differences in Clinical Drug Response: Implications for Women's Health," *Medical Women's Association* 38 (1983), 126–37.

9. Council on Ethical and Judicial Affairs of the American Medical Association, "Gender Disparities in Clinical Decision Making," *Journal of the American Medical Association* 266 (1991), 559–62.

10. Paul Cotton, "Is There Still Too Much Extrapolation from Data on Middle-Aged White Men?" *Journal of the American Medical Association* 263 (1990), 1049–50.

11. Joann E. Manson et al., "A Prospective Study of Aspirin Use and Primary Prevention of Cardiovascular Disease in Women," *Journal of the American Medical Association* 266 (1991), 521–27.

12. A. Raskin, "Age-Sex Differences in Response to Antidepressant Drugs," *Journal of Nervous Mental Disease* 159 (1974), 120–30.

13. Paul Cotton, "Examples Abound of Gaps in Medical Knowledge Because of Groups Excluded from Scientific Study," *Journal of the American Medical Association* 263 (1990), 1051–52.

14. N. K. Wenger, "Gender, Coronary Artery Disease, and Coronary Bypass Surgery," *Annals of Internal Medicine* 112 (1985), 557–58.

15. Council on Ethical and Judicial Affairs of the American Medical Association, "Gender Disparities in Clinical Decision Making," *Journal of the American Medical Association* 266 (1991), 559–62.

16. Howard Minkoff and Jack DeHovitz, "Care of Women Infected with the Human Immuno-deficiency Virus," *Journal of the American Medical Association* 266 (1991), 2253–58.

17. Susan Chu et al., "Impact of the Human Immunodeficiency Virus Epidemic on Mortality in Women of Reproductive Age, United States," *Journal of the American Medical Association* 264 (1990), 225–29.

18. Cotton, "Examples Abound," 1051–52.

19. Vern Bullough, *The Development of Medicine as a Profession* (New York and Switzerland: Karger, 1966), 101.

20. Bullough, *Development of Medicine,* 102.

21. Janet Carlisle Bogdan, "Nineteenth Century Childbirth: Its Context and Meaning" (paper presented at the third Berkshire Conference on the History of Women, June 9–11, 1976), 2.

22. Datha Clapper Brack, "The Displacement of the Midwife: Male Domination in a Formerly Female Occupation" (unpublished, 1976), 4.

23. Brack, "Displacement of the Midwife," 5.

24. Bogdan, "Nineteenth Century Childbirth."

25. Frances E. Kobrin, "The American Midwife Controversy: A Crisis in Professionalization," *Bulletin of the History of Medicine* (1966), 355.

26. Ibid.

27. René Dubos, *Man, Medicine and Environment* (New York: New American Library, 1968), 79.

28. Dorothy C. Wertz, "Childbirth as a Controlled Workspace: From Midwifery to Obstetrics" (paper presented at the 71st annual meeting of the American Sociological Association, 1976), 5.

29. Barbara Ehrenreich and Deirdre English, *Witches, Midwives and Nurses* (Old Westbury, N.Y.: Feminist Press, 1973), 33.

30. Brack, "Displacement of the Midwife."

31. Bogdan, "Nineteenth Century Childbirth," 8.

32. Kobrin, "American Midwife Controversy," 353.

33. Brack, "Displacement of the Midwife," 1.

34. G. J. Barker-Benfield, *The Horrors of the Half-Known Life* (New York: Harper and Row, 1976), 83.

35. Ibid., 120.

36. Ibid., 120.

37. Barbara Ehrenreich and Deirdre English, *Complaints and Disorders* (Old Westbury, N.Y.: Feminist Press, 1973).

38. Barker-Benfield, *Horrors of the Half-Known Life,* 120.

39. Ibid., 121.

40. Talcott Parsons, "Definitions of Health and Illness in Light of American Value Systems," in E. Gartly Jaco, ed., *Patients, Physicians and Illnesses* (New York: Free Press, 1958).

41. Ehrenreich and English, *Complaints and Disorders,* 16.

42. Vern Bullough and Martha Voght, "Women, Menstruation and Nineteenth-Century Medi-cine" (paper presented at the 45th annual meeting of the American Association for the History of Medicine, 1972).

43. Ehrenreich and English, *Complaints and Disorders,* 47.

44. Estelle Ramey, "Men's Cycles (They Have Them Too, You Know)," *Ms.* (1972), 8–14.

45. Milton Abramson and John R. Torghele, *American Journal of Obstetrics and Gynecology* (1961), 223.

46. Lynda Madaras and Jane Paterson, M.D., *Womancare: A Gynecological Guide to Your Body* (New York: Avon Books, 1984), 601.

47. Peter J. Schmidt, M.D., Lynnette K. Nieman, et al., "Lack of Effect of Induced Menses on Symptoms in Women with Premenstrual Syndrome," *The Journal of the American Medical Association* 324:17 (1991), 1174–79.

48. Madaras, 604.

49. Ellen Switzer, "PMS, the Return of Raging Hormones," *Working Woman,* Oct. 1983, 123–27.

50. Emily Martin, "Premenstrual Syndrome: Discipline, Work, Anger in Late Industrial Societies," in Thomas Buckley and Alma Gottlieb, ed., *Blood Magic: The Anthology of Menstruation* (Berkeley: University of California Press, 1988), 161–81.

51. Ibid., 174.

52. Sheldon Segal, "Contraceptive Research: A Male Chauvinist Plot?" *Family Planning Perspectives* (July 1972), 21–25.

53. Janet Carlisle Bogdan, "Nineteenth Century Childbirth: The Politics of Reality" (paper presented at the 71st annual meeting of the American Sociological Association, 1976), 11.

54. Wertz, "Childbirth as a Controlled Workspace," 15.

55. Doris Haire, *The Cultural Warping of Childbirth* (Hillside, N.J.: International Childbirth Education Association, 1972).

56. See Barbara Katz Rothman, *In Labor: Women and Power in the Birthplace* (New York: Norton, 1982), for a fuller discussion of the medicalization of the maternity cycle and developing alternatives.

57. Robert A. Wilson, *Feminine Forever* (New York: Pocket Books, 1968).

58. John Bunker, "Surgical Manpower," *New England Journal of Medicine* 282 (1970), 135–44.

59. Arthur Herbst, J. Ulfelder, and D. C. Poskanzer, "Adenocarcinoma of the Vagina," *New England Journal of Medicine* 284 (1971), 871–81.

60. Barbara Seaman and Gideon Seaman, *Women and the Crisis in Sex Hormones* (New York: Rawson Associates, 1977), 78.

61. Harry Ziel and William Finkle, "Estrogen Replacement Therapy," *New England Journal of Medicine* 293 (1975), 1167–70.

The Sexual Politics of Interpersonal Behavior

Nancy Henley and Jo Freeman

SOCIAL INTERACTION IS the battlefield on which the daily war between the sexes is fought. It is here that women are constantly reminded what their "place" is and here that they are put back in their place should they venture out. Thus, social interaction serves as the locus of the most common means of social control employed against women. By being continually reminded of their inferior status in their interactions with others and continually compelled to acknowledge that status in their own patterns of behavior, women may internalize society's definition of them as inferior so thoroughly that they are often unaware of what their status is. Inferiority becomes habitual, and the inferior place assumes the familiarity—and even desirability—of home.

Different sorts of cues in social interaction aid this enforcement of one's social definition, particularly the verbal message, the nonverbal message transmitted within a social relationship, and the nonverbal message transmitted by the environment. Our educational system emphasizes the verbal message but teaches us next to nothing about how we interpret and react to the nonverbal one. Just how important nonverbal messages are, however, is shown by the finding of Argyle et al.[1] that nonverbal cues have over four times the impact of verbal ones when verbal and nonverbal cues are used together. Even more important for women, Argyle found that female subjects were more responsive to nonverbal cues (compared with verbal ones) than male subjects. This finding has been confirmed in the extensive research of Rosenthal, Hall, and their colleagues.[2] In studies of subjects of all ages and from a variety of occupations and cultures, they found a small but consistent sex difference in sensitivity to nonverbal communication, females being better at decoding than males. If women are to understand how the subtle forces of social control work in their lives, they must learn as much as possible about how nonverbal cues affect people and particularly how they perpetuate the power and superior status enjoyed by men.

The World of Everyday Experience

Even if a woman encounters no one else directly in her day, visual status reminders permeate her environment. As she moves through the day, she absorbs many variations of the same status theme, whether or not she is aware of it. Male bosses dictate while female secretaries bend over their steno pads.

Male doctors operate while female nurses assist. At lunchtime, restaurants are populated with female table servers who wait on men. Magazine and billboard ads remind the woman that home maintenance and child care are her foremost responsibilities and that being a sex object for male voyeurs is her greatest asset. If she is married, her mail reminds her that she is a mere "Mrs." appended to her husband's name. When she is introduced to others or fills out a written form, the first thing she must do is divulge her marital status, acknowledging the social rule that the most important information anyone can know about her is her legal relationship to a man. Her spatial subordination is shown in ways parallel to that of other animal and human subordinates: Women's "territory" (office space at work, individual rooms, or space at home) tends to be less extensive and less desirable (e.g., not having office windows) than is men's. Women are not as free to move in others' territory or "open" territory (e.g., city streets) as are men.

Advertisements form a large part of our visual world, and the messages of advertisements are subtle but compelling in suggesting that the way the sexes are shown in them is the usual and appropriate arrangement. Sociologist Erving Goffman[3] describes six themes involving gender distinctions in advertising pictures: *relative size,* especially height, used to symbolize the greater importance of men than of women; *feminine touch* that is delicate, not truly grasping; *function ranking,* in which males direct and guide action while females are directed or watch; *the family,* in which fathers are linked with boys (and are distant) and mothers are linked with girls and girlhood; the *ritualization of subordination,* in which women, by lower spatial position, canting postures of the head and body, smiles, and clowning, display subordinate status to men; and *licensed withdrawal,* in which women are shown as relatively less oriented to the situation (often flooded with emotion or distracted by trivia) and are dependent on men. Goffman draws a parallel between the ritual of our everyday interaction and the hyperritualization of advertising: Our "natural expressions" are commercials too, performed to sell a view of the world and of female–male (as well as other) relationships.

Asymmetry in Social Interaction

Environmental cues set the stage on which the power relationships of the sexes are acted out and the assigned status of each sex is reinforced.[4] Earlier studies of the means by which power and status inequalities are communicated in interpersonal behavior, while generally not addressing inequality between the sexes, laid the foundation for its examination. For example, Goffman in 1956 illuminated many characteristics associated with status:

> Between status equals we may expect to find interaction guided by symmetrical familiarity. Between superordinate and subordinate we may expect to find asymmetrical relations, the superordinate having the right to exercise certain familiarities which the subordinate is not allowed to reciprocate. Thus, in the research hospital, doctors tended to call nurses by their first names, while nurses responded with "polite" or "formal" address. Similarly, in American business organizations the boss may thoughtfully ask the elevator man how his children are, but this entrance into another's life may be blocked to the elevator man, who can appreciate the concern but not return it. Perhaps the

clearest form of this is found in the psychiatrist–patient relation, where the psychiatrist has a right to touch on aspects of the patient's life that the patient might not even allow himself to touch upon, while of course this privilege is not reciprocated.

Rules of demeanor, like rules of deference, can be symmetrical or asymmetrical. Between social equals, symmetrical rules of demeanor seem often to be prescribed. Between unequals many variations can be found. For example, at staff meetings on the psychiatric units of the hospital, medical doctors had the privilege of swearing, changing the topic of conversation, and sitting in undignified positions; attendants, on the other hand, had the right to attend staff meetings and to ask questions during them . . . but were implicitly expected to conduct themselves with greater circumspection than was required of doctors. . . . Similarly, doctors had the right to saunter into the nurses' station, lounge on the station's dispensing counter, and engage in joking with the nurses; other ranks participated in this informal interaction with doctors, but only after doctors had initiated it.[5]

A status variable that illustrates rules of symmetry and asymmetry is the use of terms of address, widely studied by Brown and others.[6] In languages that have both familiar and polite forms of the second person singular ("you"), asymmetrical use of the two forms invariably indicates a status difference, and it always follows the same pattern. The person using the familiar form is always the superior to the person using the polite form. In English, the only major European language not to have dual forms of address, status differences are similarly indicated by the right of first-naming (addressing a person by his or her given name rather than surname): The status superior can first-name the inferior in situations in which the inferior must use the superior's title and last name. An inferior who breaks this rule by inappropriately using a superior's first name is considered insolent.[7]

According to Brown, the pattern evident in the use of forms of address applies to a very wide range of interpersonal behavior and invariably has two other components: (1) whatever form is used by a superior in situations of status inequality can be used reciprocally by intimates, and whatever form is used by an inferior is the socially prescribed usage for nonintimates; (2) initiation or increase of intimacy is the right of the superior. To use the example of naming again to illustrate the first component, friends use first names with each other, whereas strangers use titles and last names (although "instant" intimacy is considered proper in some cultures, such as our own, among status equals in informal settings). As an example of the second component, status superiors, such as professors, specifically tell status inferiors, such as students, when they may use the first name, and often rebuff the inferiors if they assume such a right without invitation.

The relevance of these patterns to status differences between the sexes is readily seen. The social rules say that all moves to greater intimacy are a male prerogative: It is boys who are supposed to call girls for dates, men who are supposed to propose marriage to women, and males who are supposed to initiate sexual activity with females. Females who make "advances" are considered improper, forward, aggressive, brassy, or otherwise "unladylike." By initiating intimacy, they have stepped out of their place and usurped a status prerogative. The value of such a prerogative is that it is a form of power. In interactions between the sexes, as in other human interactions, the one who has the right to initiate greater intimacy has more control over the relationship. Superior status brings with it not only greater prestige and greater privilege but also greater power.

Demeanor, Posture, and Dress

The advantages of superior status are exemplified in many of the means of communicating status. Like the doctors in Goffman's research hospital, men are allowed such privileges as swearing and sitting in undignified positions, but women are denied them. Although the male privilege of swearing is curtailed in mixed company, the body movement permitted to women may be circumscribed even in all-female groups. It is considered "unladylike" for a woman to use her body too forcefully, to sprawl, to stand with her legs widely spread, to sit with her feet up, or to cross the ankle of one leg over the knee of the other. Many of these positions are ones of strength or dominance.

Henley[8] reviewed the research evidence for sex differences in nonverbal behavior, linking it with evidence for differences due to power, status, or dominance. She concluded that the symbols and gestures used by males tend to be those of power and dominance, while the gestures of females tend to be those of subordination and submission. Wex[9] reached similar conclusions through her examination of the public postures of women and men photographed in Germany.[10] The more "feminine" a woman's clothes, the more circumscribed the use of her body. Depending on her clothes, she may be expected to sit with her knees together, not to sit cross-legged, or not even to bend over. Although these taboos seem to have lessened in recent years, how much so is unknown, and there are recurring social pressures for a "return to femininity," while etiquette arbiters assert that women must retain feminine posture no matter what their clothing.

Prior to the 1920s, women's clothes were designed to be confining and cumbersome. The dress-reform movement, which disposed of corsets and long skirts, was considered by many to have more significance for female emancipation than woman suffrage.[11] Today women's clothes are often designed to be revealing of their bodies, but women are expected to restrict their body movements to avoid revealing too much. Furthermore, because women's clothes are contrived to cling and reveal women's physical features, rather than to be loose as men's are, women must resort to purses instead of pockets to carry their belongings. These "conveniences" (purses) have become one of the surest signs of sex and thus have developed the character of a stigma, a sign of women's shame—for example, when they are used by comics to ridicule both women and transvestites.

Access to a Person's Self and Body

Women in our society are expected to reveal not only more of their bodies than men but also more of their minds and souls. Whereas men are expected to be stolid and impassive and not to disclose their feelings beyond certain limits, women are expected to express their feelings fully. Indeed, research evidence indicates that both sexes do act out these stereotypes: Hall's review of thirty-eight studies of females and males as nonverbal communicators showed females to be more expressive than males in almost two-thirds of the studies surveyed.[12] Does this mean that women are more emotional than men? Differences in emotional expression do not necessarily mean that the actual emotions are felt differently. Just as different cultures operate under different norms for the appropriateness of emotional display, so do women and men have different "display rules." For example, a study attempting to separate felt emotion from display rules found no sex differences in *emotional state* experienced by subjects in response to emotional stimuli, but did find women to show more *facial activity* than men.[13] Female socialization encourages generally greater expression of emotion than does male socialization (although expression of anger is more sanctioned for men than for women).

Both socialization and expectations of others (social norms) are probably implicated in the frequent research finding that females are more self-disclosing to others than males are.[14] Self-disclosure involves both expression of emotion and revelation of other personal and intimate information. Not only do we expect women to be more self-disclosing than men, but we see negative implications when women are not self-disclosing or when men are: A psychological study found that men who were very self-disclosing and women who were *not* very self-disclosing were considered by others to be more psychologically maladjusted than were nondisclosing men and disclosing women.[15] Such self-disclosure gives away knowledge about oneself, putting women at an immediate disadvantage relative to men: Knowledge, as is often noted, is power.

The inverse relationship between disclosure and power has been reported in Goffman's earlier cited observations in a research hospital and in other studies.[16] Self-disclosure is a means of enhancing another's power. When one person has greater access to information about another person, he or she has a resource the other person does not have. Thus, not only does power give status, but also status gives power. And those possessing neither must contribute to the power and status of others.

Another factor adding to women's vulnerability is that they are socialized to *care* more than men—especially about personal relationships. This puts them at a disadvantage, as Ross articulated in what he called the Law of Personal Exploitation: "In any sentimental relation the one who cares less can exploit the one who cares more." The same idea was stated more broadly by Waller and Hill as the Principle of Least Interest: "That person is able to dictate the conditions of association whose interest in the continuation of the affair is least."[17] In other words, women's caring, like their openness, gives them less power in a relationship.

One way to indicate acceptance of one's place and deference to those of superior status is to follow the rules of "personal space." Sommer has observed that dominant animals and human beings have a larger envelope of inviolability surrounding them—i.e., they are approached less closely—than those of lower status.[18] Various authors have subsequently shown that this rule applies between men and women, with women both having smaller personal space than men and tending to yield space to men when the two sexes come into proximity.[19] And women's time, like their space, can be invaded readily.[20]

Touching

Touching is one of the closer invasions of one's personal space, and in our low-contact culture it implies privileged access to another person. People who accidentally touch other people generally take great pains to apologize; people forced into close proximity, for example, in a crowded elevator, often go to extreme lengths to avoid touching. Even the figurative meanings of the word convey a notion of access to privileged areas—e.g., to one's emotions (one is touched by a sad story) or one's purse (one is touched for ten dollars). In addition, the act of touching can be a subtle physical threat.

Remembering the patterns that Brown found in terms of address, it is enlightening to consider the interactions between pairs of persons of different status and to picture who would be more likely to touch the other (put an arm around the shoulder or a hand on the back, tap the chest, hold the arm, or the like): teacher and student, master and servant, police officer and accused, doctor and patient, minister and parishioner, adviser and advisee, supervisor and worker, business executive and secretary. Again, we see that the form used by the status superior—touching—is the form used between intimates of equal status. It is considered presumptuous for a person of low status to initiate touch, like first-naming, with a person of higher status.

Some earlier observational and self-report studies indicated that females were touched more than males were, both as children (from six months on) and as adults. But we need more evidence than this to conclude that touching is associated with status; do other members of high-status groups touch members of low-status groups more than the reverse? In observations of incidents of touch in public urban places, higher-status persons did touch lower-status persons significantly more. In particular, men touched women more, even when all other variables were held constant.[21] Not only behaviors, but also social interpretations of behavior associate power/dominance with touch; as Hall notes, "People's beliefs, anecdote, self-report, [and] observational studies of socioeconomic status and age, and one true experiment favor either the power-privilege idea or the idea that relative dominance increases as a consequence of touch initiation."[22]

Some studies have attempted to determine whether the effect of touch on perceptions of dominance is to increase the perceived dominance of the toucher, decrease the perceived dominance of the person touched, or both.[23] Although the findings have been mixed, the preponderance of evidence seems to indicate that touching affects the perceived dominance of both the toucher and touched. In an observational study in public places, researchers found that when mixed-sex couples walked together in public, the female was most often on the side of the male's dominant hand; that is, she was on his right if he was right-handed and on his left if he was left-handed. These researchers speculated that such "strong-arming" reflected male dominance and would allow more convenient male touching of the female.[24]

This touching asymmetry becomes most ambiguous and problematic in heterosexual situations when females may protest males' touch as presumptuous only to be told they are too "uptight." Female office, restaurant, and factory workers and students are quite used to being touched by their male superordinates, but they are expected not to "misinterpret" such gestures as sexual advances. However, women who touch men may be interpreted as conveying sexual intent, as they have often found out when their intentions were quite otherwise. Such different interpretations are consistent with the status patterns found earlier. If touching indicates either power or intimacy, and women are deemed by men to be status inferiors, touching by women will be perceived as a gesture of intimacy, since power is not an acceptable interpretation.[25]

Gaze and Dominance

The most studied nonverbal communication among humans is probably eye contact, and here too we observe a sex difference. Researchers have found repeatedly that women look more at another person in a dyad than men do.[26] Exline, Gray, and Schuette suggest that "willingness to engage in mutual visual interaction is more characteristic of those who are oriented towards inclusive and affectionate interpersonal relations,"[27] but Rubin concludes that while "gazing may serve as a vehicle of emotional expression for women, [it] in addition may allow women to obtain cues from their male partners concerning the appropriateness of their behavior."[28] This interpretation is supported by the data of Efran and Broughton, which shows that male subjects too "maintain more eye contact with individuals toward whom they have developed higher expectancies for social approval."[29]

Looking, then, may be indicative of some dependency and subordination. However, looking can also be an aggressive and dominant gesture, when it becomes a stare. Dovidio and Ellyson write, "In humans as in other primates, the stare widely conveys messages of interpersonal dominance and control. Research conducted over the past 60 years suggests that, in general, staring at another person is a dominance gesture while breaking eye contact or not looking is a sign of submission."[30] How can the same gesture—looking at another—indicate both dominance and deference? Henley suggests that women may watch men when they are not being looked at, but lower or avert their gaze when a man looks at them, as submissive animals do when a dominant animal looks their way.[31]

Also, as Dovidio and Ellyson point out, the meaning of gaze depends on the context, and on the patterning of looking with other behaviors, most notably with speaking. A series of experiments by Ellyson, Dovidio, and their colleagues has developed a measure of "visual dominance": the ratio of [looking at another while speaking] to [looking at another while listening]. In peer interaction, we tend to look while listening more than we look while speaking; however, visually dominant people, both men and women, have a greater proportion of look/speak to look/listen than do nondominant people. People with higher status, expert power, or an orientation to interpersonal control all showed higher visual dominance ratios than did people without those characteristics. Gender also affects visual dominance behavior: In an experiment with mixed-sex pairs, both female and male experts showed greater visual dominance in interaction with nonexperts; when there was no differential expertise, men still showed greater visual dominance than did women.[32]

Like other tiny habits of which we are scarcely aware, women's "modest" eye lowering can signal submission or subordinate position even when that message is not intended.

Verbal Cues to Dominance

Gestures of dominance and submission can be verbal as well as nonverbal. Subtle verbal cues—especially paralinguistic features, such as emphasis, inflection, pitch, and noncontent sounds—are often classified with nonverbal ones in the study of interpersonal interaction, because they have similar regulating functions aside from the traditional verbal content. Other features of verbal interaction, such as frequency and length of utterance, turn-taking patterns, interrupting, and allowing interruption, also help to regulate inter-action and to establish dominance.

Sheer verbalization itself can be a form of dominance, rendering someone quite literally speechless by preventing that person from "getting a word in edgewise." Contrary to popular myth, men talk more than women, in both single-sex and mixed-sex groups. Within a group, a major means of asserting dominance is to interrupt. Those who want to dominate others interrupt more; those speaking will not permit themselves to be interrupted by their inferiors, but they will give way to those they consider their superiors.[33] It is not surprising, therefore, that Zimmerman and West found, in a sample of eleven natural conversations between women and men, that forty-six of the forty-eight interruptions were by males; other research on interruption con-sistently finds men interrupting more than women.[34]

In verbal communication, we find a pattern of differences between the sexes similar to that seen in nonverbal communication. It was observed earlier in this article that men have the privilege of swearing and hence have access to a vocabulary not customarily available to women. On the surface, this seems to be an innocuous limitation, but it is significant because of the psychological function of swearing: Swearing is one of the most harmless and effective ways of expressing anger. The common alternatives are to express one's feelings with physical violence or to suppress them and by so doing turn the anger in on oneself. The former is prohibited to both sexes (to different degrees), but the latter is decidedly encouraged in women.

Swearing is perhaps the most obvious sex difference in language usage. Of course, sex differences are to be found in phonological, semantic, and grammatical aspects of language as well as in word use.[35] Austin, for example, has commented that "in our culture little boys tend to be nasal . . . and little girls, oral," but that in the "final stages" of courtship the voices of both men and women are low and nasal.[36] The pattern cited by Brown,[37] in which the form appropriately used by status superiors is used between status equals in intimate situations, is again visible: In the intimate situation, the female adopts the vocal style of the male.

In situations in which intimacy is not a possible interpretation, it is not power but abnormality that is the usual interpretation. Female voices are expected to be soft and quiet—even when men are using loud voices. Women who do not fit this stereotype are often called *loud*—a word commonly applied derogatorily to other minority groups or out-groups.[38] One of the most popular derogatory terms for women is *shrill,* which, after all, simply means loud (applied to an out-group) and high-pitched (female).

Gestures of Submission

Henley and LaFrance suggest that the nonverbal asymmetry of male and female is paralleled by the asymmetry of racial/ethnic/cultural dominance.[39] In any situation in which one group is seen as inferior to another, they predict, that group will be more *submissive,* more *readable* (nonverbally expressive), more *sensitive* (accurate in decoding another's nonverbal expressions), and more *accommodating* (adapting to another's nonverbal behaviors). How true this is for racially and ethnically oppressed groups remains to be shown; in this review, however, we have seen that these characteristics are among the non-verbal behaviors of females. Recent research by Snodgrass supports the contention that decoding sensitivity is associated with dominance and authority rather than with gender per se.[40]

Other verbal characteristics of persons in inferior status positions are the tendencies to hesitate and apologize, often offered as submissive gestures in the face of threats or potential threats. If staring directly, pointing, and touching can be subtle nonverbal threats, the corresponding gestures of submission seem to be lowering the eyes from another's gaze, falling silent (or not beginning to speak at all) when interrupted or pointed at, and cuddling to the touch. Many of these nonverbal gestures of submission are very familiar. They are the traits our society assigns as desirable characteristics of females. Girls who have properly learned to be "feminine" have learned to lower their eyes, to remain silent, to back down, and to cuddle at the appropriate times. There is even a word for this syndrome that is applied only to females: *coy.*

Sexual Interaction

Sexual interaction is expressed through nonverbal communication: the caress, the gaze, coming close to each other, the warm smile, smelling the other, provocative postures and inviting gestures; much sexual contact, unlike other forms of human interaction, is *purely* nonverbal. Sexual interaction, like all interaction, is conditioned by the social context in which it takes place. One particularly compelling aspect of that social context is that males have more power, prestige, and status than do females, a fact that cannot but affect heterosexual interaction. If even casual relationships between females and males are caught up in the social system in which males wield power over females, how much more does this power system affect the sexual relationship, which we consider the ultimate intimacy? In addition, in both heterosexual and homosexual interactions, relationships are affected by other power and status dimensions, such as work status, wealth, race, age, and interpersonal dominance. This power too is often expressed nonverbally.

Unfortunately, little has been written on nonverbal behavior, power, and sexuality examined simultaneously. However, the research and ideas presented earlier in this article may be applied to the sexual sphere. First, much can be said about a sexual relationship after observing the mutuality or nonmutuality of various gestures. For example, we may already believe that the person who is more dominant in the relationship is the one who takes a superior position in intercourse, the one around whose pleasure sexual activity is structured, and the one upon whose climax it is terminated. Beyond that, when gestures are not mutual (or not balanced over time), one person may dominate by initiating touching, hand-holding, and kissing; maintaining gaze; putting an arm around the other's back when sitting; initiating moves to greater intimacy in the course of a relationship or a single encounter; exerting more influence over the couple's spacing, postures, and walking pace; getting to hold hands with the preferred or dominant hand; having the hand in front when walking holding hands; and terminating as well as initiating hand-holding and kissing. Subordination may be expressed by the person who shows more emotional expressivity, shows more facial and kinesic activity, is more self-disclosing, accommodates timing and action to the other, and exhibits the reciprocal behaviors of those described as dominant.

These questions of who touches, who initiates, and who terminates apply, of course, to both heterosexual and homosexual relationships. However, in the heterosexual relationship, we often have a good idea of what the answers will be; in fact, heterosexual custom has prescribed male leadership and dominance. But these are changing times, and many think that few aspects of our society are changing faster than are sexual relationships and female–male interactions. Many people today do not wish to have unequal sexual relationships or to express sexual inequality unconsciously. However, since we generally take body language for granted and do not attend to it much, it may be hard to change: Nonverbal expressions may lag behind changes in attitudes, values, and ideas. Slowness in changing this communication may keep us trapped in old modes of expression and old modes of relationship. No matter how egalitarian we may believe our relationships or sexual interactions to be, they will have an edge of inequality and imbalance until we bring our nonverbal expressions into line with our verbal ones.

Di*V*ering Interpretations of the Same Behavior

Status differences between the sexes mean that many of the same traits and actions are interpreted differently when displayed by each sex. A man's behavior toward a woman might be interpreted as an expression of either power or intimacy, depending on the situation. When the same behavior is engaged in by a woman and directed toward a man, it is more likely to be interpreted as a gesture of intimacy—and intimacy between the sexes is typically seen as sexual in nature. Recent research confirms that, when women display dominance gestures to men, they are rated higher on sexuality and lower in dominance than men are rated when making the same gestures to women.[41] Because our society's values say that women should not have power over men, women's nonverbal communication is rarely interpreted as an expression of power. If the situation precludes a sexual interpretation, women's assumption of the male prerogative may be dismissed as deviant (castrating, domineering, unfeminine, or the like). Women in supervisory positions thus often have a difficult time asserting their power nonverbally—gestures that are socially recognized as expressions of power when used by male supervisors may be denied or misinterpreted when used by women.

Change

Knowledge of the significance of nonverbal communication can help us to understand not only others' gestures but also our own, giving us a basis for social and personal change. However, just because certain gestures associated with males are responded to as powerful, women need not automatically adopt them. Rather than accepting "masculine" values without question, individual women will want to consider what they wish to express and how, and they will determine whether to adopt particular gestures or to insist that their own be responded to appropriately. There has been growing pressure on women to alter their verbal and nonverbal behavior[42] to the words and movements of "power"—i.e., to those associated with men—often with little thought of the implications. It would be mistaken to assume that such gestures are automatically better and that it is only women who should change. Revealing emotions rather than remaining wooden-faced and unexpressive, for example, may be seen as weak when only one person in an interaction is doing it; but, in the long run, openness and expressivity—by all people—may be better for the individual, the interpersonal relationship, and the society. Women who wish to change their nonverbal behavior can monitor it in various situations to determine when it contradicts their intention or is otherwise a disservice and only then change. They will wish to keep those behaviors that give them strength, whether those behaviors are traditionally associated with women or with men.

NOTES

1. Michael Argyle, Veronica Salter, Hilary Nicholson, Marylin Williams, and Philip Burgess, "The Communication of Inferior and Superior Attitudes by Verbal and Non-Verbal Signals," *British Journal of Social and Clinical Psychology*, 9 (1970), 222–31.

2. Robert Rosenthal, Judith A. Hall, M. Robin DiMatteo, Peter L. Rogers, and Dane Archer, *Sensitivity to Nonverbal Communication: The PONS Test* (Baltimore: Johns Hopkins University Press, 1979); Judith Hall, *Nonverbal Sex Differences: Communication Accuracy and Expressive Style* (Baltimore: Johns Hopkins University Press, 1984).

3. Erving Goffman, *Gender Advertisements* (New York: Harper and Row, 1979).

4. The term *power* is used here to mean social power, the ability to influence the behavior of others based on access to and control of resources; *status* refers to acknowledged prestige rankings within the social group; *dominance* is used to refer to a psychological tendency (desire to dominate) and immediate pairwise influence (rather than general social value or influence).

5. Erving Goffman, "The Nature of Deference and Demeanor," *American Anthropologist*, 58 (1956), 473–502; reprinted in Erving Goffman, *Interaction Ritual* (Garden City, N.Y.: Anchor, 1967).

6. Several studies are described in Roger Brown, *Social Psychology* (Glencoe, Ill.: Free Press, 1965), 51–100.

7. For discussion of these rules vis-à-vis women and men, see Sally McConnell-Ginet, "Address Forms in Sexual Politics," in Douglas Butturff and Edmund L. Epstein (eds.), *Women's Language and Style* (Akron, Ohio: University of Akron Press, 1978), 23–35.

8. Nancy M. Henley, *Body Politics: Power, Sex, and Nonverbal Communication* (Englewood Cliffs, N.J.: Prentice-Hall, 1977).

9. Marianne Wex, *Let's Take Back Our Space: "Female" and "Male" Body Language as a Result of Patriarchal Structures* (Hamburg: Frauenliteraturverlag Hermine Fees, 1979).

10. See also Susan J. Frances, "Sex Differences in Nonverbal Behavior," *Sex Roles,* 5 (1979), 519–35; Irene H. Frieze and Sheila J. Ramsey, "Nonverbal Maintenance of Traditional Sex Roles," *Journal of Social Issues,* 32, no. 3 (1976), 133–41; Marianne Lafrance and Clara Mayo, "A Review of Nonverbal Behaviors of Women and Men," *Western Journal of Speech Communication,* 43 (1979), 96–107; Clara Mayo and Nancy M. Henley (eds.), *Gender and Nonverbal Behavior* (New York: Springer-Verlag, 1981); Shirley Weitz, "Sex Differences in Nonverbal Communication," *Sex Roles,* 2 (1976), 175–84.

11. William L. O'Neill, *Everyone Was Brave: The Rise and Fall of Feminism* (Chicago: Quadrangle, 1969), 270.

12. Judith A. Hall, *Nonverbal Sex Differences* (Baltimore: Johns Hopkins University Press, 1984), 53.

13. Paul D. Cherulnik, "Sex Differences in the Expression of Emotion in a Structured Social Encounter," *Sex Roles,* 5 (1979), 413–24.

14. Eugenia P. Gerdes, John D. Gehling, and Jeffrey N. Rapp, "The Effects of Sex and Sex-Role Concept on Self-Disclosure," *Sex Roles,* 7 (1981), 989–98.

15. Valerian J. Derlega, Bonnie Durham, Barbara Gockel, and David Sholis, "Sex Differences in Self-Disclosure: Effects of Topic Content, Friendship, and Partner's Sex," *Sex Roles,* 7 (1981), 433–47.

16. For example, see Dan I. Slobin, Stephen H. Miller, and Lyman W. Porter, "Forms of Address and Social Relations in a Business Organization," *Journal of Personality and Social Psychology,* 8 (1968), 289–93.

17. Edward Alsworth Ross, *Principles of Sociology* (New York: Century, 1921), 136; Willard W. Waller and Reuben Hill, *The Family: A Dynamic Interpretation* (New York: Dryden, 1951), 191.

18. Robert Sommer, *Personal Space* (Englewood Cliffs, N.J.: Prentice-Hall, 1969), Chapter 2.

19. For example, see Frieze and Ramsey, "Nonverbal Maintenance of Traditional Sex Roles"; Henley, *Body Politics,* Chapter 2; Nancy M. Henley and Marianne LaFrance, "Gender as Culture: Difference and Dominance in Nonverbal Behavior," in Aaron Wolfgang (ed.), *Nonverbal Behavior: Perspectives, Applications, Intercultural Insights* (Lewiston, N.Y.: C. J. Hogrefe, 1984), 351–71.

20. Henley, *Body Politics,* Chapter 3.

21. Henley, *Body Politics,* Chapter 7; See also Brenda Major, Anne Marie Schmidlin, and Lynne Williams, "Gender Patterns in Social Touch: The Impact of Setting and Age," *Journal of Personality and Social Psychology,* 58 (1990), 634–43.

22. Hall, *Nonverbal Sex Differences,* 117.

23. Diana L. Summerhayes and Robert W. Suchner, "Power Implications of Touch in Male–Female Relationships," *Sex Roles,* 4 (1978), 103–10. Brenda Major and Richard Heslin, "Perceptions of Cross-Sex and Same-Sex Nonreciprocal Touch: It is Better to Give than to Receive," *Journal of Nonverbal Behavior,* 6 (1982), 148–62. Nancy M. Henley and Sean Harmon, "The Nonverbal Semantics of Power and Gender," in Steve L. Ellyson and John F. Dovidio (eds.), *Power, Dominance, and Nonverbal Behavior* (New York: Springer-Verlag, 1985), 151–64. Michael A. Goldberg and Barry Katz, "The Effect of Nonreciprocated and Reciprocated Touch on Power/Dominance Perception," *Journal of Social Behavior and Personality,* 5 (1990), 379–86.

24. Richard J. Borden and Gordon M. Homleid, "Handedness and Lateral Positioning in Heterosexual Couples; Are Men Still Strongarming Women?" *Sex Roles,* 4 (1978), 67–73.

25. See Henley, *Body Politics,* Chapter 11.

26. Both Henley, *Body Politics,* Chapter 9, and Judith A. Hall and Amy G. Halberstadt, "Smiling and Gazing," in Janet S. Hyde and Mark C. Linn (eds.), *The Psychology of Gender: Advances Through Meta-Analysis* (Baltimore: Johns Hopkins University Press, 1986), have reviewed this research, though they arrive at different conclusions. See also John F. Dovidio and Steve L. Ellyson, "Patterns of Visual Dominance Behavior in Humans," in Steve L. Ellyson and John F. Dovidio (eds.), *Power, Dominance, and Nonverbal Behavior* (New York: Springer-Verlag, 1985), 129–49.

27. Ralph Exline, David Gray, and Dorothy Schuette, "Visual Behavior in a Dyad as Affected by Interview Control and Sex of Respondent," *Journal of Personality and Social Psychology,* 1 (1965), 201–9; quotation, 207.

28. Zick Rubin, "Measurement of Romantic Love," *Journal of Personality and Social Psychology,* 16 (1970), 265–73; quotation, 272.

29. Jay S. Efran and Andrew Broughton, "Effect of Expectancies for Social Approval on Visual Behavior," *Journal of Personality and Social Psychology,* 4 (1966), 103–7; quotation, 103.

30. Dovidio and Ellyson, "Patterns of Visual Dominance Behavior," 129.

31. Henley, *Body Politics,* Chapter 9.

32. Dovidio and Ellyson, "Patterns of Visual Dominance Behavior"; see also John F. Dovidio, Clifford E. Brown, Karen Heltman, Steve L. Ellyson, and Caroline F. Keating, "Power Displays Between Women and Men in Discussion of Gender-Linked Tasks: A Multichannel Study," *Journal of Personality and Social Psychology,* 55 (1988), 580–87; John F. Dovidio, Steve L. Ellyson, Caroline F. Keating, Karen Heltman, and Clifford E. Brown, "The Relationship of Social Power to Visual Displays of Dominance Between Men and Women," *Journal of Personality and Social Psychology,* 54 (1988), 233–42.

33. Barbara Eakins and Gene Eakins, "Verbal Turn-Taking and Exchanges in Faculty Dialogue," in Betty Lou Dubois and Isabel Crouch (eds.), *Papers in Southwest English IV: Proceedings of the Conference on the Sociology of the Languages of American Women* (San Antonio, Tex.: Trinity University Press, 1976), 53–62.

34. Don Zimerman and Candace West, "Sex Roles, Interruptions and Silences in Conversation," in Barrie Thorne and Nancy Henley (eds.), *Language and Sex: Difference and Dominance* (Rowley, Mass.: Newbury House, 1975), 105–29. See also Candace West and Don Zimmerman, "Small Insults: A Study of Interruptions in Cross-Sex Conversations Between Unacquainted Persons," in Barrie Thorne, Cheris Kramarae, and Nancy Henley (eds.), *Language, Gender and Society* (Rowley, Mass.: Newbury House, 1983), 102–17.

35. See, for example, M. R. Key, *Male/Female Language* (Metuchen, N.J.: Scarecrow, 1975); Cheris Kramarae, *Women and Men Speaking* (Rowley, Mass.: Newbury House, 1981); Thorne, Kramarae, and Henley (eds.), *Language, Gender and Society;* Robin Lakoff, *Language and Woman's Place* (New York: Harper and Row, 1975); Sally McConnell-Ginet, Ruth Borker, and Nelly Furman (eds.), *Women and Language in Literature and Society* (New York: Praeger, 1980).

36. William M. Austin, "Some Social Aspects of Paralanguage," *Canadian Journal of Linguistics,* 11 (1965), 31–39; quotations, 34, 37.

37. Brown, *Social Psychology.*

38. Austin, "Some Social Aspects of Paralanguage," 38.

39. Henley and LaFrance, "Gender as Culture."

40. Sara E. Snodgrass, "Women's Intuition: The Effect of Subordinate Role upon Interpersonal Sensitivity," *Journal of Personality and Social Psychology,* 49 (1985), 146–55; Sara E. Snodgrass, "Further Effects of Role versus Gender on Interpersonal Sensitivity," *Journal of Personality and Social Psychology,* 62 (1992), 154–158.

41. Nancy M. Henley and Sean Harmon, "The Nonverbal Semantics of Power and Gender: A Perceptual Study," in Steve L. Ellyson and John F. Dovidio (eds.), *Power, Dominance, and Nonverbal Behavior* (New York: Springer-Verlag, 1985), 151–64.

42. E.g., Lakoff, *Language and Woman's Place;* Lynn Z. Bloom, Karen Coburn, and Joan Pearlman, *The New Assertive Woman* (New York: Dell, 1976).

Gender and Families in the United States: The Reality of Economic Dependence

Naomi Gerstel and Harriet Engel Gross

THE FAMILY, WE LIKE TO think, is, or at least should be, about love. Whatever we like to think, however, the realities of family life suggest otherwise. For women, men, and children alike, the family is, and long has been, an institution based on economic dependence. Despite women's unprecedented entry into the labor force, most women depend financially on husbands. Despite men's apparent financial independence, most depend on wives not only for "invisible" and unpaid household work but also for the income provided by their wives' paychecks. Despite children's growing assertions of independence, most offspring still depend on their parents for current and future class positions. Yet, although a division of labor links husband with wife and children with parents, ideologies transmute and mystify the economic significance of these exchanges, casting them in terms of love and companionship.

This chapter examines the economic bonds of family life and the ideologies that have grown up around them. First, we trace the historical origins and transformations of economic interdependence in colonial and industrial America. Next, we show how the historical legacy of nineteenth-century families, in both ideology and practice, continues to shape contemporary families. Finally, we discuss both how the growing participation of women in the labor force and current trends in the structure of families have altered, but not eliminated, the economic dependencies of men, and women, and children.

The Family as an Economic Unit: A Historical Perspective

COLONIAL FAMILIES

In colonial America, economic and family life were merged. The majority of husbands, wives, and children lived on farms or in artisan households. The colonial family was not self-sufficient, especially in New England: Colonial farmers engaged in a constant exchange of domestic goods and work with their neighbors and kin. Yet, in broad comparison to contemporary families, the colonial family depended primarily on goods it produced for itself and by itself.[1] A self-governing entity—or, more accurately, an entity governed by a patriarchal father—it formed a little "commonwealth."[2]

Copyright © 1995 by Naomi Gerstel and Harriet Engel Gross.

In ideology, if not always in practice, the colonial family was multi-generational. To be sure, extended kin did not typically share a household throughout the life course: Few people lived long enough to reside in a three-generation household, and inheritance practices forced children who did not inherit the family farm to leave when they married. Thus, at any one time in colonial America, most households were nuclear families.[3] Yet, ties between the generations were strong and important: The long-term security of family members and the continuity of family lineage took precedence over individual advancement.[4]

Despite the fact that most households were nuclear, a significant propor-tion of elderly parents lived with their children. One study found that although only 9 percent of households contained grandparents, 80 percent of persons over sixty-five who had living children resided with those children. A high adult-mortality rate, rather than a distaste for multigenerational households, explains the predominance of nuclear households.[5]

The authority of parents—vested mainly in fathers—typically overrode individual rights or claims to independence. In the North, male parents normally retained legal control of much of the family estate until death in order to ensure their material well-being in old age.[6] That control ensured the long-term obedience of children, which, in turn, shaped patterns of marriage. Sons had to wait for grants of land from their fathers before they could marry, whereas fathers delayed turning over that land as a way to determine when, and perhaps whom, their sons would marry.[7] So, too, fathers preferred daughters to marry in the order of their birth (otherwise, a prospec-tive suitor might well think something was wrong with an unmarried older daughter); and, indeed, New England older daughters typically married before their younger sisters.[8] However, even though the prescriptive literature of the day, written in scriptures and repeated in sermons of early New England, expressed the widespread injunction to "honor old age," such honor often was limited to those elderly parents who commanded economic resources. Only those with both productive land and economically dependent family members actually commanded much respect. For other elderly—often women—old age brought poverty and dishonor.[9]

Neither the nuclear family nor even extended kin defined the boundaries of colonial families. Servants who lived and worked in a household, whether or not they were related by blood, were viewed and treated often as family members by those with whom they shared a home. They provided labor, and in return they were taught productive skills, religious doctrine, and moral values. They were family members *because* they shared and worked in a household and were subject to the authority of its head, not because they were treated with nurturance, affection, or love. In fact, in colonial New England towns, the term *love* was reserved for the ideal relationship with persons outside the family.[10]

Most important, the nuclear family was a unit of production. Unlike the contemporary family, which purchases many of the goods and services it consumes, the colonial family shared in the production of most (although not all) of what it consumed. On farms in the North and South, colonial wives usually took care of the garden, animals, and house. They worked throughout the day and evening, managing the vegetable garden, gathering eggs, feeding chickens or milking cows, processing and preparing food, building and coaxing fires, or making clothes and quilts, often while they were pregnant or nursing.[11] Husbands plowed, planted, and harvested the fields. Yet husbands sometimes helped with the making of cloth, as wives sometimes helped with the hoeing.[12]

Just as colonial husbands and wives shared in production for household use, so, too, they shared in childrearing. Both fathers and mothers were deeply involved in caring for children, who were welcomed for their labor and for the security they promised in their parents' old age. Children did not simply "help"; they were an essential source of labor. These children rather quickly became "little adults": If not bound out as servants, daughters learned from and worked side by side with their mothers; sons, with their fathers.[13]

Living and working together, husbands and wives, parents and children, may well have developed strong feelings for one another. Yet, to imagine that such feelings were the primary bonds of colonial family life would be to distort these people's experience. Productive ties—among spouses and their children, extended kin, and even boarding servants—were explicitly the ties that bound colonial American families. This agrarian society was a "family economy," or a "family system of production."[14]

THE RISE OF INDUSTRIAL CAPITALISM AND THE BIRTH OF NEW FAMILY AND GENDER IDEOLOGIES

The late eighteenth and early nineteenth centuries were pivotal periods in the transformation of the family. From the "family economy" characterizing colonial America, industrial capitalism gradually fractured job site and household into separate spheres. A growing commercialization of agriculture, an increasing number of itinerant traders, and improvements in transportation made possible links to expanding national markets. At first, however, most families still lived in rural areas and still produced primarily for family consumption or local exchange. Fathers and their mature sons still farmed crops and raised livestock for the use of their own families. Mothers and daughters prepared the family's food and turned their talents and energies to the home production of textiles, which they made into clothes for household use. Only when there was a surplus were crops, livestock, and textiles put up for sale in the expanding market.[15]

Gradually, at different rates in different locales, land became more difficult to acquire, at least for those unwilling to migrate west. With the rise of factories, stores, and centralized workshops "manned" by a newly land-poor labor force, production slowly moved out of the home. No longer making all of their own clothes, often not growing much of their own food, families came to depend on cheap ready-made goods available for purchase. Without sufficient land to provide support or work for an entire family, and newly dependent on cash-producing pursuits, families had little choice but to send their children (in particular their young, single daughters, who, unlike sons, neither inherited land nor migrated west) to work in the new industrial and commercial enterprises owned and run by a growing entrepreneurial elite.[16]

As the century progressed, a number of forces in both the working and middle class converged to produce new images of family and gender relations common to both classes. The young "native" women factory operatives were gradually pushed out by employers who speeded up production and hired cheaper immigrant labor, by working-class men who fought for a male family wage, and by elite reformers who began to elaborate an ideology of a privatized "affectionate family" with clearly differentiated gender roles. These developments slowly became the basis for a new vision of the family, one not only spatially and temporally but also normatively distinct from work. This vision included new prescriptions for the roles of husbands, wives, and children. Although to some extent these roles were rooted in the pre-industrial past, they were also a forced adaptation to the emerging realities of industrial capitalism.

At the same time, at least among the growing urban elite, a new ideology for married women began to take hold. The Victorian "domestic code" or "cult of true womanhood," outlined in the prescriptive literature of the nineteenth century, cast women as moral guardians—pious, nurturant, and naturally domestic.[17] Wives' "proper place" became the home; their proper duties, "housework" and mothering.

Over the course of that century, "manliness became equated with success in the economic competition; indeed man's position in the household came to be described as bread*winner*."[18] Popular literature by midcentury created a mythology of the "self-made man": He no longer followed in his father's footsteps, but worked in jobs requiring "manly independence" and "individual exertions."[19] Simultaneously, because these urban men ventured daily into competitive and tension-filled jobs away from home, they and their wives increasingly believed home-based wives were essential to supply husbands with emotional support and children with care and guidance.

Changing views of husbands and wives operated in concert with changing images of parents and children. Over the course of the nineteenth century, urban middle-class children became "economically worthless"[20] as they, like their mothers, were thought best removed from paid employment. Not incidentally, during the same period, fertility was cut in half: In 1800, women gave birth to an average of 8.0 children; by 1900, that average had dropped to 3.7.[21] These declining birth rates, in concert with declining infant-mortality rates and changing cultural conditions, increased the emotional (as contrasted to economic) value of each child.

Children's work in the home, like their play, became increasingly construed as acts of character development, anticipating future—rather than embodying current—productive activity. So, too, girls' and boys' games became clearly differentiated. Whereas competitive play was promoted for little boys, the nineteenth century saw the creation of "playing house" as the preferred pastime of little girls.[22] Here, children were taught at an early age that women's family work was really play.

Having become "emotionally priceless," these middle-class children, boys and girls alike, were increasingly presented in the growing literature of child-rearing advice as needing their mother's homebound influence in order to maintain their innocence while developing a conscience or a sense of *self*-control.[23] At the same time, fathers' presumed and actual preoccupation with an increasingly separate occupational sphere conspired to reduce their prescribed contribution to the daily care of children.[24] Children's new innocence, their delicately balanced self-control, their differentiated gender "natures," and their fathers' absence required that mothers should focus all the more on the home. Middle-class women's domestication and purification, then, went hand in hand with a new "sentimentalization" of childhood.

With changes in its members' roles, the nineteenth-century family and home were increasingly heralded as secluded and subdued, cut off from the "public" world. Middle-class wives' residence in and guardianship of the home were proclaimed necessary to preserve the family as a private haven and, as important, to civilize the increasingly distant, harsh, and competitive world of commerce and politics. Not only the middle-class woman, but also the middle-class man, "was being enticed into the same darkened corner of history. The popular literature of the 1850's courted men away from their male associations—from taverns, political clubs, lodges--into the feminine world of the home."[25] To be sure, the husband was not expected to contribute to the care of house or children. But his nightly presence as companion to his wife and children in the newly private home was touted as essential to that home's emotional mission.

The conjugal unit gradually became, at least in the prescriptive literature of the day, a privatized emotional unit that produced an "affectionate family." In contrast to the colonial American family, which was defined in terms of productive contribution, nineteenth-century spouses were expected to unite on the basis of love, sexual attraction, and affection; husbands and wives were to become one another's primary companions, complementing one another with their special personalities as well as skills; and parents (especially mothers) were to become nurturant and self-sacrificing for their innocent children.[26]

IDEOLOGY VERSUS PRACTICE IN THE MIDDLE CLASS

The development in the nineteenth century of an ideology of the family as a private emotional unit, and the concomitant sentimentalization of its members' ties, masked the actual relations among those members. The obscured reality was that marriages were still based on economic exchange.

A telling indicator that women were oriented to marriage as an economic resource can be found in the records of those relatively few women who became financially independent. A study of over 100 spinsters from the northeastern United States found that these women self-consciously chose "single blessedness" if they could afford to do so.[27] Based on a survey of single women's reasons for their spinsterhood, a nineteenth-century reporter summarized her findings in the following way:

> I have a good job;
> I earn a good living;
> I am contented and happy;
> Why be encumbered?[28]

In addition, those well-educated women who eventually wed increasingly chose to marry late and to postpone childbearing.[29] Finally, nineteenth-century widows whose husbands left them a substantial inheritance were much less likely to remarry than were those left without means.[30] In practice, then, women seemed to marry for material consideration as much as, if not more than, for respect and emotional concern.

In fact, whatever they married for, the distinctly separate spheres of women and men led more to their emotional segregation than to their union. Women's common domestic location engendered sisterhood.[31] Because they inhabited the same worlds, women empathized with one another. Close relationships flourished outside the home: Middle-class women formed intense loyalties and deeply loving and dependent ties with women friends and kin. These often competed with conjugal ties for women's affection.[32] Although dependent on their husbands for economic support, many women did not, or could not, turn to those husbands for empathy or emotional care. Although middle-class men increasingly returned to the home as a nightly haven, working-class men spent their evenings in saloons, lodges, and clubs where male camaraderie prevailed.[33] As historian Stephanie Coontz observes, "By giving women sole responsibility for cleanliness, godliness, culture and manners, the domestic architects had constructed people that manly men could hardly bear to be around."[34] Ironically, for most women and some men, the separation of spheres impeded the very emotional ties that the ideology of marriage promised.

So, too, the ideology of marriage suggested that couples were bound by sexual attraction and physical love. Using diaries and a nineteenth-century survey on sexuality, recent research shows that Victorian women, at least in the middle class, viewed sexual intercourse as a normal part of married life and were orgasmic.[35] But most of these same women believed procreation, not pleasure, was the purpose of marital intercourse.[36] Women achieved freedom and autonomy—from the pain of childbearing, burden of childrearing, and unsatisfactory sex lives—by denying these sexual desires.[37] Thus, the ideal of companionate marriage, with its promise of emotional and sexual pleasure, was undermined by the actual conditions of adult lives.

Just as was true in their parents' generation, the family remained an important economic resource for middle-class children, albeit in an altered way. Although the inheritance of land was no longer an essential prerequisite for independence, their fathers' income provided these nineteenth-century children (especially sons) with the formal schooling and time necessary for preparation for high-status jobs.[38] So, too, parents, especially mothers, continued to provide the cultural background and training in conduct and language, as well as in physical appearance, that prepared their children to assume the family's class position.[39]

The family, broadly defined, remained an economic unit in still another sense. Like their colonial counterparts, elderly widows often moved in with their adult children and helped with domestic chores. If they could afford to, elderly parents remained an important source of financial assistance for their offspring.[40] Thus, extended kin were themselves central to the material well-being of the married pair.[41]

In sum, then, the ties binding nineteenth-century bourgeois families remained, at least in large part, material rather than emotional. The creation of separate spheres had transformed the character of, but had hardly sundered, their economic bonds.

VARIATIONS BY CLASS, ETHNICITY, REGION, AND RACE

Just as the ideology of the "affectionate family" masked material dependence in the nineteenth-century middle class, a family ideology with similar consequences took root in other social classes. No less than in the middle class, the ideology masked as it transformed family members' economic dependence.

In the urban working class, the reorganization of the family took place around the idea of the male earner's entitlement to a "family wage." Beginning in the 1830s, demands for a male "family wage" first served the working-class struggle to obtain for itself a decent standard of living. Yet, in the end, working men joined their industrial bosses to make the "family wage" an affirmation of men's market, and of women's and children's nonmarket, roles.[42] Although men no longer contributed to the household as a productive unit, their paychecks were essential to a family increasingly viewed as a unit of consumption, whose buying power was determined by the husband's income.

At the same time, the economic well-being of the family continued to depend on the unpaid work of wives at home. Hidden in the home, women's unpaid domestic efforts were rarely recognized as "real" work, but instead came to be viewed as pure and simple acts of love. Yet wives and mothers not only produced many services on which husbands depended (from cooking their meals to cleaning their homes and mending their clothes), but also reproduced—both literally and metaphorically—the very labor force on which industry depended. Receipt of the domestic services of wives helped to make it possible for husbands, working- and middle-class alike, to work outside the home; at the same time, the wives' provision of such services made it more difficult for the wives to do so.[43] The ideology that exalted and sentimentalized wives' domestic roles condemned those women forced to do wage work. It allowed and supported the establishment of low wage rates for women: "Working" women, in this conception, were only waiting for marriage and were working for "pin money."[44] Thus, both wives and husbands came to rely on each other for gender-based material support, even as the material basis of this mutuality was mystified.

Yet, the romantic veneer overlaying practical realities and material dependence was even thinner for those who were not privileged members of the urban bourgeoisie. As Stansell writes of nineteenth-century New York: "Like other family relationships, the marriages of laboring men and women harbored little explicit, articulated tenderness. Courting was a time for private strolls and seductions, but its end was a practical household arrangement based on reciprocal obligations."[45] This description characterizes most marriages and families outside of the privileged class.

Foreign Immigrants to the northeast.   Most foreign immigrants—albeit with differences by regions from which they came—practiced some aspects of the family- and gender-role patterns found in the middle class even as they diverged from others. Although their domestic work was often more strenuous and demanding than it was among their middle-class counterparts, immigrant women—whether Irish, German, Italian, or Polish—assumed primary responsibility for the care of their homes and children.[46] So, too, these women relied on the incomes, typically greater than their own, of fathers and husbands. The all-too-frequent loss of a man's economic support—whether through death or through desertion—often left them in devastating poverty.[47]

However, given hard times, low wages, and the instability of employment, an immigrant husband's income was rarely enough to support an entire family. Immigrant wives, like their single and widowed counterparts, were often forced to earn a wage in order to help support their families.[48] First- and second-generation immigrant women were nearly twice as likely to work for a wage as were women born to "native" parents.[49] The paid work they performed was shaped both by their gender and by their particular ethnic group. Thus, Polish wives often took in paying boarders for whom they cooked and cleaned. Italian wives took sewing into their homes. Irish wives, at least compared to other white ethnic groups, were particularly likely to work for pay outside of the home: Many of them took jobs working as domestics in the homes of white "natives."[50] Thus, it was the very presence of a large reservoir of such poor women who sewed, washed, cleaned, cooked, and served that made possible the Victorian "true womanhood" of the privileged class.

Neither were nineteenth-century children of the immigrant poor "sentimentalized." Children, as soon as they were old enough, left school and began working, turning over their wages to their families.[51] As Early found of the children of French Canadians newly immigrated to nineteenth-century Massachusetts: "Family survival was—literally—in their [the children's] hands."[52] In the big cities of the northeast, immigrant children helped their mothers with domestic work by not only sewing and cleaning but also toting water and scavenging for fuel.[53] These children also endured great misery as they worked in the mines, factories, and streets for low wages that they contributed to their families. Like their preindustrial counterparts, poor immigrant parents thought of childhood not as a separate stage of life, but rather as a time to begin to shoulder the burdens of labor. They struggled against elite reformers who believed the development of children's morality depended on the mothers' protection of children within the home.[54]

These immigrant families often relied quite heavily on the material contributions of kin and neighbor. Nineteenth-century relatives were a vital resource for one another. In a system of chain migration, kin often moved close to and helped one another find and keep jobs. Employers used these kin ties for industrial recruitment and training. In a "family economy," kin pooled resources and helped one another with housing as they borrowed and loaned household goods.[55] Immigrants engaged in a constant exchange with relatives and neighbors that was often crucial for survival. Thus, these immigrant families typically lived a dense communal existence in which all, regardless of age and gender, who could contribute materially were called upon to do so.

Southern White Rural Families. Nineteenth-century southern rural white families—especially those not members of the planter elite—established a "family economy" resembling in many ways that of their preindustrial counterparts. Although husbands and fathers were patriarchs and household heads, all family members were deeply involved in producing primarily for household use. Men were largely responsible for field work, and women were responsible for tending gardens, dairying, cooking, and producing cloth. Yet women often helped men, and men often helped women, with their respective labors. Economically valuable children were incorporated into the family's effort at survival, and vital exchange relationships were formed with kin. Here, the explicit link among family members was economic rather than emotional.[56]

In contrast, southern elite planters were "strongly influenced by the sentimentalization of family life and children that swept like a tidal wave over the wealthy...during the eighteenth and nineteenth centuries."[57] But only when white farmers owned a number of slaves did white women become fragile, sentimentalized "ladies of leisure." Just as Victorian womanhood in the North depended on the labor of poor immigrants, the leisured lady of the South depended on the labor of slaves. Yet even this lady of leisure worked to nurture her children and manage the domestic routines of slaves as her planter husband managed the routines of fieldwork.[58]

Black Families: Slave and Free. Among nineteenth-century black slaves, everyone—woman, man, boy, girl—who could work was put to work. Insofar as it did not interfere with black women's capacity to bear a future work force, slave owners—who upheld the ideology of virtue, innocence, and delicacy for their white wives and children—downplayed gender and age differences in the work assignments meted out to slaves.[59]

Owners sometimes presented (and perhaps viewed) themselves as authoritarian fathers; their plantations, as big families.[60] Yet most owners acted to encourage stable family life among slaves only insofar as it increased fertility, producing children who could be put to work or sold, or insofar as family ties provided labor incentive for adult slaves (who, when living with family, were less likely to run away and often worked harder to protect or hide the feebleness of kin).[61] But even this attenuated commitment to the slaves' family life broke down in many stages of the plantation owners' lifespan. When a young planter got married and was setting up a work force for a newly established plantation, many slave families were broken up when their members were proffered as wedding gifts. So, too, when an owner died, his slaves were often dispersed by sale or inheritance. Only in the middle phase of the plantation cycle would many slave owners encourage stability of slave families for both economic and moral reasons, finding these families to be a source of fertility and an incentive conducive to labor discipline.[62]

In contrast, among slaves themselves, the family became a basis for "resistance to dehumanization": They used it to create an organization of work and relationships different from that imposed by slave masters.[63] Often, slaves managed to keep up extensive kin networks and remained committed to marriage.[64] The strength of slaves' attachment to families was amply shown in their anguish when families were sold apart. Ironically, it was among blacks—denied economic resources—that family attachment may have attained the fullest expression of pure sentiment.

Yet, as part of this resistance, slaves, men as well as women, upheld a gender-based division of labor in their own quarters: Wives and daughters cooked and sewed while husbands and sons fished and hunted for prey.[65] Whether from their own cultural heritage or because of the conditions of their lives as slaves (in which owners encouraged the authority of males and handed out resources through them), slaves came to value husbands and fathers as heads of their households.[66] Overall, then, there were clear indications of the tenacity of the black family, with a commitment to gender-differentiated roles, despite the great adversity of slavery.

When freed, large numbers of blacks obtained marriage licenses to gain official recognition that they were legally wed even though doing so used up most of the few resources they had.[67] With the support of the church and legal system, freed blacks who remained in the South reestablished the authority of black men over black women and removed black women from field work and the whites' "big house" whenever they had the opportunity to do so. Yet black wives—typically responsible for their own family's housework—often joined their husbands in the fields, especially during planting and harvest time.[68] So, too, older black children in the South took care of younger siblings or worked in the fields.[69]

Those blacks who migrated to northern and southern cities faced problems in finding employment that also shaped their family lives. Concentrated in the lowest paying and most difficult jobs and excluded from union membership, black men—unlike their white immigrant counterparts—were typically unable to assist their relatives in finding work.[70] Black women also could only find jobs in circumscribed labor markets: In 1890, 90 percent of all black women who worked for pay were employed in just two sectors, personal service and agriculture;[71] between 1870 and 1910, close to 80 percent of nonfarm black women were employed in domestic service.[72] Though poorly paid and working under arduous conditions, black women—precisely because their jobs were highly segregated—were able to assist near and distant kin in locating and changing jobs. Employment often spread by word of mouth: Employers passed on the names of friends who were looking for household help; domestics assisted their daughters and other female kin in filling those jobs.[73] Moreover, freed black women's employment affected their probability of marriage: the smaller the wage difference between women and men, the less likely black women were to marry (or remarry).[74] The extended family became an important source of assistance: Grandmothers looked after grandchildren while their mothers worked; new arrivals boarded with kin, who helped them find jobs.[75] Many black women and their children, then, survived on the edges of poverty, dependent on the assistance of kin just as most white married women were dependent on the incomes of husbands.

Nineteenth-century industrial capitalism, then, wrought massive changes in the ideology and practices of American families as it fractured job site and household into separate spheres and provided a new basis for the segregation of women and men. The implementation of these changes varied by class, ethnicity, region, and race. Yet, overall, although the economic bonds of family members were transformed, among no group were they eliminated entirely.

Contemporary Families: Continuity and Commonality

Nineteenth-century developments set in place the basic scaffolding undergirding twentieth-century families. As the following sections will show, gender-linked material dependencies remain very much alive. Women retain their primary responsibility for care of home and children, and most remain economically dependent on husbands (or on husbands' counterparts in subsidies upheld or generated by the state). However, the majority of wives and mothers—across race and class—have added paid employment outside the home to their work inside it. This twentieth-century addition, and its ideological repercussions, has again transformed but not eliminated the economic dependencies of women and men.

GETTING MARRIED

The most fundamental continuity between the nineteenth century and the present is that marriage remains a near universal experience for American women. Just as 95 percent of women married in 1800,[76] 95 percent of both black and white women born before the end of World War II married. Although demographers now predict that a somewhat smaller proportion of women born recently will marry, they nonetheless expect that about 90 percent of young white and 80 percent of young black women are likely to do so.[77] To be sure, women now delay marriage.[78] And certainly, given these delays in concert with increased rates of divorce,[79] women of all races spend less time in first marriages than they did previously.[80] Yet, reduced mortality and high rates of remarriage (at least among whites) mean women spend more time in marriage than they did in the nineteenth century: In 1800, women spent about twenty-seven years in marriage; now, after a peak of forty-two years during the baby boom, they are married for an average total of thirty-five years.[81]

The slight decline in the rate of marriage has been accompanied by a steady rise in the rate of cohabitation. The number of unmarried cohabiting couples has gone from less than one-half million in 1960 to five times that many by 1990;[82] close to 40 percent of these couples have children present.[83] A number of factors, including increased sexual freedom and growing tolerance of singlehood, encourage cohabitation. Cohabitation, however, is not so much an alternative to marriage as a stage on the way to marriage: a majority (over 80 percent) of cohabitors expect to marry,[84] and "cohabitation seems to be most common among those who use or intend to use it as a stepping stone to marriage."[85]

Contemporary women's decision to marry, like that of their historical predecessors, is very much affected by economic considerations. Women with more financial resources, whether personal income or educational credentials likely to command future income, are less likely to get married than are other women, whereas the rate of marriage increases among men with greater financial resources.[86] Thus, as Goldscheider and Waite recently found, women use resources, whether from their own employment or from their parents, to "buy out of marriage."[87] Most, however, do not have the resources to "buy out."

When they choose a spouse, young women today are aware of their likely financial dependence. Examining the characteristics individuals hope to find in a potential spouse, a recent national survey found that men place more value than women on physical attractiveness, while women emphasize a potential mate's employment stability and earnings.[88] Similarly, another study found that young women do more "feeling work" on love, as they seek to redirect it in "realistic" or "practical" directions. Hochschild explains these differences by suggesting: "Young men hold hegemony over the courtship process while at the same time women, *for economic reasons,* need marriage more."[89]

BEING MARRIED: HOUSEWORK

Although women look to marriage for financial support more than men do, wives nonetheless continue to make important contributions to the economic well-being of families through their labors in the home. After getting married, contemporary wives—like their nineteenth-century counterparts—cook, clean, shop, and manage domestic routines. As much quantitative research has shown, domestic work, across race and class,[90] remains women's work. Husbands "help." But they do far less than their wives.[91] Women do from 70 to 80 percent of the total housework hours and most of the repetitive chores.[92] Although employed wives devote fewer hours to domestic labor than do housewives, they—no less than farm women—labor from dawn to dusk.[93]

Although its nature is obscured by popular and legal ideas, housework consists of economically valuable services. An increasing number of household tasks have their analogue in the marketplace. Prepared food is for sale in restaurants; transportation is available from buses and taxis; cleaning and child care are available from paid housekeepers and baby-sitters. Researchers who calculate the dollar value of housework, pricing it at its equivalent market price, estimate that such compensation would increase the family's income by as much as 60 percent.[94] In reality, then, husbands continue to rely on wives' family work just as wives rely on husbands' greater income.[95]

To be sure, the character of women's domestic work has changed over the course of the twentieth century. Women put less time into laundry and cooking but more into marketing. Much domestic labor has become "consumption work" that pulls women outside the home into shopping malls, supermarkets, and bank lines.[96] As Ruth Schwartz Cowan writes: "The automobile brought with it the woman driver and the suburbs. The peddler disappeared and so did the milkman, replaced by the supermarket—and the woman who drove to the shop."[97] And since the early part of the century, the reorganization of stores has intensified the efforts of shoppers. For example, in grocery stores, a known customer aided by helpful clerks who gave advice, knew products, and packed and delivered them has gradually been replaced by an unknown consumer who now "memorizes the location of goods, makes selections without consulting a clerk, loads the cart and pushes it to the checkout stand [where she] loads the goods onto the counter, placing purchases in bags and portering them home."[98] Such "self-service shopping" may not reduce costs, but it does intensify women's unpaid efforts outside the home.[99] Thus, the family's ability to function as the unit of consumption increasingly depends on the labors of wives.

Women themselves experience contradictory impulses with regard to their continued responsibility for housework. On the one hand, many women often resent the time-consuming, isolating, boring, and repetitive chores that much housework involves.[100] When they can find and afford it, many take advantage of alternatives available in the market by "subcontracting"[101] out part of the housework to poorer, often immigrant or black, women or to the growing number of firms that employ such women.[102] So, too, newly created food services—from the caterers serving the elite to the fast-food restaurants serving the many—now provide a good number of the meals once cooked at home. And, notably, women seem to be lowering their standards for house-work; one telling indicator is that in the last few years, the sale of paper plates has increased markedly while the sale of floor waxes has declined.[103]

On the other hand, some women find satisfaction in some of the work they do for their families; it is still both constituted and experienced as a "labor of love." Given the availability of commercial services and products, at least part of what was once compulsory is now voluntary: sewing, cooking, and gardening are sometimes freely chosen by women, who find such work enjoyable to themselves as well as useful to their husbands and children. Many believe that purchased services are not always equivalent to homemade ones; they lack the personal touch. Wives and mothers also gain a sense of control by managing a home and the routines of its members. Moreover, doing housework validates womanhood: Adult women create and experience their gender identity in the very process of doing domestic chores.[104] And women experience doing housework, especially making meals, as part of the important project of constructing a "family" out of a household; making meals gives the family a common social life while preserving the individuality of family members and affirming the woman's gendered self.[105] Finally, they know it will create conflict—and possibly more work for themselves—if they ask their husbands to take a greater share. Thus, recent studies show, often to the surprise of the researchers, that although there has been an increase in the proportion of women desiring greater help from their husbands, many women themselves do not want to give up, or fully to share, housework.[106] To understand all of women's family work simply as "oppressed labor" or to view women who choose to do housework as victims of false consciousness is to miss the point: Some housework produces a sense of achievement and harmony, just as women's control over their families' well-being affirms their gender identity.[107]

Women, then, resent their work in the home *and* resist forfeiting it. Yet, however they feel about housework, such work constrains women's ability to achieve financial independence. The more housework they do, the lower their wages;[108] the greater the household demands, the lower their labor-force participation.[109] Moreover, as economist Barbara Bergmann notes: "If she stops doing the housework, the marriage will probably end. So there is in reality

an exchange of the wife's housework for the husband's continuance in
the marriage, and for his continuing to supply her with room, board and
other benefits."[110]

PARENTING

Just as wives continue to do most of the housework, they also continue to
do most of the parenting. Here, too, husbands "help." Even women employed
full-time in demanding careers spend far more time with their children than
do their husbands. When fathers do spend time with children, their primary
activity is playing. Mothers are much more likely to engage in "custodial
activities" such as diapering, bathing, and feeding.[111]

Although women today have fewer children and have them later than they
did in the past,[112] childrearing remains a central activity in their lives. It is
often a primary arena in which wives exercise power, express creativity, as
well as work out unconscious desires rooted in their own experience as
children being mothered.[113] Whether for reasons conscious or unconscious,
parenting is a source of satisfaction that many women do not want to give
up. Fewer than 10 percent of young women become adults with no expectation
of having or desire for children.[114] Even career women, who often plan to
give birth at a time that will not interfere with their careers, find that it is
their jobs, rather than their children, they see as the interference.[115] Children,
then, continue to be seen as "emotionally priceless."

Yet the very parenting women cherish imposes constraints on other areas
of life—on marriage, leisure, and employment—which these women also
value. Both black and white wives with children, especially those with young
children, are less satisfied with their marriages and friends than are those
without children.[116] More important, even when they have similar education
and work experience, women who give birth to children while still in their
early twenties have lower wages than do those who delay childbirth.[117] Although parenting may be seen as standing outside a system of economic
exchange, mothering nonetheless reinforces wives' economic dependence on
their husbands. At the same time, husbands are able to maintain full involvement in their jobs or careers because their wives assume primary responsibility
for child care.

EMOTION WORK

Although women continue to perform much labor in the home, many think
that what distinguishes the modern family (with its roots a century old) and
what now binds family members is the provision of emotional support. Thus,
we say marriage and the family have become newly "companionate." Yet, in
fact, if the modern family provides emotional support, it does so primarily
for husbands and children. To be sure, many married women—especially in
the middle class—turn to their husbands and children for emotional support
and security. But they are much more likely to give than to receive.

Husbands turn to their wives as their only confidant—the person to whom
they disclose their personal feelings and concerns. In contrast, like their

nineteenth-century counterparts, wives typically have more than one confidant: they have close women friends and kin to whom they turn for emotional support.[118] At the same time, wives sustain marital conversations: They do more listening, more questioning, and less interrupting than do their husbands.[119] Perhaps for these reasons, husbands are more likely than are wives to say that their spouse is appreciative and affectionate and that their spouse understands them well.[120] So, too, women more often respond to their children's emotional demands, and thereby shield their husbands from those demands. Both by shielding and by comforting her husband, a wife makes an economic contribution in that "the emotional gratification provided by her enables the husband to devote himself more effectively to his role as the family breadwinner."[121]

KIN WORK

In addition to the "second shift"[122] of housework, parenting, and emotion work, women do a "third shift" of caring for those outside their households.[123] In particular, the work of "kinkeeping" depends on the efforts and resources of wives far more than husbands. Both husbands and wives, as well as siblings, believe that it is women as wives and adult daughters who should keep in touch with and care for kin.[124] Many studies suggest that they do: Women call, write, visit, and invite both their own and their husband's kin far more often than do men.[125] Although women's kinkeeping requires a great deal of physical and emotional labor, it is often taken for granted, invisible not only to policy makers and social analysts but sometimes dismissed or disparaged by providers themselves.[126] Because women think they should care for kin, but feel ambivalence and strain when doing so, they often feel guilty, stifling complaints about their own arduous labor.[127]

But there is variation among women, both by race and employment. Blacks, especially women but also men, spend far more time helping relatives than do whites.[128] Caregiving, for women and blacks, may originate in (and constitute an adaptation to) the experience of an uncertain or subordinate social location: It is both altruistic and self-interested, a demanding labor of love as well as a survival strategy.[129] So, too, kin work is affected by women's employment. Some studies suggest that because women do so much caregiving, their own employment suffers. Thus, women postpone entry into the labor force, limit their hours of work, take time off, and even quit jobs entirely in order to provide care for their aged kin.[130] Other research suggests that employment somewhat reduces the time daughters spend providing care, although that reduction appears to be offset by the employed daughter's substitution of financial for direct personal help.[131] When employed wives spend less time providing such care, their husbands do not substitute for their labor. In fact, husbands of employed women actually give less care than husbands of housewives.[132] Moreover, because wives (employed or not) do such work, husbands can invest themselves in their job.

In sum, like their nineteenth-century counterparts, wives make the "home a haven" by doing not only most of the housework and parenting but also emotion work and kinkeeping. An ideology still attaches to this work, turning it into pure and simple acts of love. Yet, such work contributes much to both the husband's economic success and the wife's economic dependence.

RETIREMENT AND WIDOWHOOD

The effects of this lifelong economic dependence in marriage follow women into retirement and widowhood. To some extent being married protects both men and women from being poor. While just 6 percent of married older women are poor, almost four times as many older widowed (20 percent) and divorced (24 percent) women are among the impoverished.[133] However, married women among the elderly face the risk of impoverishment should their husbands die, divorce, or enter a nursing home. For example, wives whose spouses require institutionalization are more likely than husbands to become impoverished before their institutionalized partners are covered by Medicaid. This is because the method for calculating eligibility for Medicaid does not take into account the fact that women live longer and are more likely to marry men older than themselves. Consequently, it is women who are more likely to face the problem of paying for the care of an institutionalized spouse.[134]

This same lack of recognition of distinctions between men's and women's longevity and likelihood of living in widowhood also characterizes the gender-neutral criteria that determine retirement and pension benefits. Gender-neutral criteria have the effect of disadvantaging women because their employment constraints (e.g., taking lower-paying, benefit-poor jobs to accommodate family responsibilities) and more frequent interruptions of jobs to care for their families limit the earnings on which retirement and pension eligibility are based.[135] Thus, despite dramatic gains in the economic status of the elderly since the early seventies,[136] the relatively low economic status of elderly widows remains a major policy concern in the United States.[137] Moreover, evidence indicates that the concentration of poverty among elderly women living alone will worsen as we move into the next century.[138] As with divorce, then so with widowhood; when women's marital status changes, the "mutual economic compact" that marriage entails is undermined and women's economic standing deteriorates overnight.[139]

Contemporary Families: Discontinuity and Diversity

The patterns that contemporary families share with their historical counterparts are matched by an equally important difference. While husbands and fathers continue to take little part in "women's sphere," wives and mothers are increasingly entering men's. We might expect these changes to make women economically independent of husbands. As we shall see, only a minority are. At the same time, these changes might make men—at least to some extent—dependent on the incomes of their wives. As we shall see, a majority are. If nineteenth-century marriage was based on the exchange of husbands' income for wives' domestic service, twentieth-century marriage is increasingly becoming one in which the economic bond of husband and wife is extended to the pooling of incomes.

Two oft-cited and connected demographic trends are particularly important for understanding this transformation. First, except for a brief period after World War II, the proportion of women in the labor force has increased steadily during the twentieth century. Before World War II, women in the labor force were primarily single. After that, although the unmarried were still more likely to be employed, the number and proportion of married women in the labor force increased steadily. Whereas only one-fifth of married women were in the labor force in 1950 (when they made up only 24 percent of employed women), by 1991 their participation was close to 60 percent (making up about half of all employed women). Among married women, the most rapid increase took place among mothers of preschool children: In 1950, only about 11 percent of these women were in the labor force, but since then the proportion has increased steadily, reaching 60 percent by 1991.[140]

Second, as we have seen, the early stages of industrial capitalism developed with—perhaps even depended on—married women's labor, paid and unpaid labor in and outside of the home. But, the logic of capitalism is to extend markets into previously excluded areas. Women's exit from the home both provides a new source of cheap labor and generates demands for the products of new industries. As employed wives necessarily do less household labor than do unemployed ones, their families must either do without the products of such labor or purchase them. Thus, the labor force expands as two-earner families provide a new market for prepared food, child care, and cleaning services. Indeed, since World War II, the fastest-growing sector of the economy has consisted not of products but of services—including, for example, retail trade, personal and business services, and food and health industries. Between 1970 and 1980, the service sector grew by close to 14 million jobs—a 31 percent growth in this sector's share of the labor market.[141] Of note, women assumed 75 percent of these new jobs.[142] This sector's growth, then, relied on a relatively large number of low-paid women workers, many of whom (especially when compared to their male counterparts in manufacturing) needed or were willing to work intermittently or part-time, with limited fringe benefits and chances for advancement.[143]

These two demographic trends are linked not only to one another but also to the family. The nineteenth-century construction of the husband as the family's breadwinner has set the stage in the twentieth century for the inferior position of women in the labor force. As Joan Smith writes: "The nature of jobs offered them in the growing service sector is shaped by the presumption that women still have access to sufficient support beyond their own earnings and are at best only partially committed to wage labor."[144] Thus, the growth of a service-dominated economy—based on the inclusion of women—depended on those very features of family life created by the exclusion of married women from employment in the industrializing economy of the nineteenth century.

In this sense, the twentieth century's economy inherited and made use of the nineteenth century's expectations for women's and men's family life. Yet, although these presumptions are made use of, the very conditions on which they were based have been transformed by women's labor force participation. This transformation takes different forms at different levels of the class structure and in different types of families.

DUAL-EARNER FAMILIES

Today, two or more jobs are typically required to meet a family's financial needs and, in the modal family, both husband and wife are employed. Approximately two-thirds of all married couples have more than one earner today, compared to less than one-half in 1960. The rate is slightly higher for blacks and slightly lower for Spanish-origin populations, but the trend to multiple earners is substantial for married-couple families in all groups.[145] A family's financial status is closely linked to wives, whose earnings contribute on average 31 percent of family income.[146] White married couples, for instance, had a median income in 1990 of $30,781 when the wife was a full-time homemaker, compared to $47,247 when she was employed. For blacks, the median income was $20,333 when the wife was a full-time homemaker, compared with $40,038 when she was in the labor force.[147]

Thus, while they have contributed little additional work at home, most husbands have become dependent on the earnings of their wives. At the same time, completely dependent wives now constitute a minority of all wives.[148] Yet, women's lower average earnings mean that wives still rely more than husbands do on their spouses for financial support and that unmarried mothers often face poverty.

Because wives in dual-earner families work for pay at the same time as they parent, keep house, and keep kin, many feel the strain of "juggling" these different tasks. Yet some researchers suggest that the sources of strain stem not so much from conflict among these tasks as from inadequacies within each of them.[149] Because women's wages are less than men's, because women's efforts at home so eclipse their husbands', because social supports for employed parents are so inadequate—employed wives feel the burdens of these tasks far more than do husbands. So too, as working wives continue to devote more than an extra month a year to housework, parenting, and kin work, their relative disadvantage both at home and in the marketplace is reinforced.[150] By contributing more to such family work requirements than her husband, the typical wife not only provides the "backstage support" for his relative economic success but also undermines her ability to pursue economic advantage. This in turn contributes to the wage gap between women and men that "keeps the cycle spinning."[151]

Moreover, given the wide cultural acceptance of husbands' lesser obligation for family care, an "economy of gratitude" develops whereby wives whose husbands "help" feel grateful but also guilty. At the same time and for the same reasons, husbands feel "put upon" by comparison with their male counterparts who do not "help."[152] This asymmetry in work effort and gratitude propels gender strategies wherein husbands resist efforts to get them to pull their own weight at home while wives either deny the imbalance, live with the stress this imbalance entails, or leave their marriages.

DIVORCE AND FEMALE-HEADED FAMILIES

While the labor force participation of women expanded, the two-parent family declined. By 1991, over half (61 percent) of all black families and one-fifth of white families with children under eighteen years old were headed solely by women.[153]

The increase in female-headed families is due in part to the increase in the divorce rate. In 1973, for the first time, the number of marriages ending in divorce exceeded the number ending in widowhood.[154] The incidence of divorce in the United States more than quadrupled between 1960 and 1990, to more than 1 million divorces annually.[155] Although the divorce rate declined slightly in the late 1980s, about half of the marriages of persons now in their thirties are likely to end in divorce.[156] What has not changed much is the placement of children: In 1990, 86 percent of children in single-parent families lived with their mothers; in the last few decades, there has been very little change in the proportion of children living with their fathers.[157]

The economic dependence of wives and mothers, particularly whites, on marriage becomes especially clear when marriages dissolve.[158] Growing divorce rates, accompanied by negligible alimony and unreliable child-support payments, have led an increasing number of women to rely on their own, typically low, earnings.[159] Whereas both marriage and divorce have relatively little effect on the economic status of black and white men, divorce is a key event accounting for a decline in the economic status, often even impoverishment, of white women. Although divorce is also associated with a drop in the economic status of black women, it is less important in accounting for these women's poverty. Recent national evidence suggests that white, but not black, men also suffer a drop in their family income in the first year following a divorce. However, the decline at this point for white men is much smaller than that for white or black women. Moreover, by the third year after divorce, men's family income, white as well as black, has increased, while the family income of still-divorced white and black women remains much lower than it was when they were married.[160]

The primary way poor white women, especially if they head households, can improve their economic situation is through remarriage.[161] Most divorced women—especially those who are uneducated, young, poor, and white—remarry if they have the opportunity to do so. And the most needy divorced women tend to remarry as quickly as they can, while those in more favorable economic conditions tend to be more deliberate about whether or when to remarry.[162] On remarriage, these women regain a standard of living almost equal to that of divorced men or women who stayed married.[163] The situation is quite different for black women.

VARIANTS ON A THEME: THE BLACK FAMILY AND POVERTY

Given the greater likelihood of poverty among black men, marriage does not serve as the economic safeguard for black women in the way it can for white women. The differences between white and black families are tied to both the poorer labor market prospects of black women and the decreasing labor-market status of black men.[164] Since 1960, the number of black men out of the labor force—because they are unemployed, are discouraged workers, are in correctional facilities, or are unaccounted for—has more than tripled. Thirty percent of working-aged black men are unemployed, discouraged workers, or unaccounted for, compared to only 11 percent in these categories for working aged white men.[165] Analysts of black family life suggest this worsening economic position of black males has been a major, if not the single, factor contributing to an increase in black female-headed households. Developing an "index of marriageable males" (which includes not only labor-force participation but also mortality and incarceration rates), Wilson and Neckerman reveal a long-term decline in the proportion of black men who are in a position to support a family. Their work, and the analyses of others, suggest that the economic position of black males, in concert with discriminatory political and cultural forces, forces many black women to leave or forego marriage.[166]

As a result, black women have higher divorce rates than do white women.[167] However, an even more striking feature—and the factor most different from those for whites—is the increase over the last two decades in the proportion of never-married black mothers.[168] The increase in the rate of never-married mothers is not a result of increasing rates of adolescent pregnancy. In fact, the rate of teenage pregnancy and child birth has declined sharply since the late 1950s. Rather, what has happened, particularly among black women, is a separation of childbearing from marriage. Although many of these women will eventually marry, childbearing often comes several years before marriage.[169]

Although both divorce and out-of-wedlock birth are *associated* with high rates of poverty,[170] recent research makes clear these are not the *cause* of poverty for blacks. As Mary Jo Bane found, three-quarters of whites who were poor in the first year after forming a female-headed or single-person household became poor simultaneously with that transition. In contrast, of the blacks who were poor after the transition, about two-thirds had also been poor before.[171] As Bane concludes: "Although there has indeed been a dramatic and shocking increase in female-headed households among blacks and an equally dramatic feminization of black poverty, one cannot conclude that much of the poverty could have been avoided had families stayed together."[172] Whereas for white women divorce is both cause and consequence of poverty, for black women poverty is a cause of divorce.

The primary way poor white women can improve their economic situation is through remarriage; among poor blacks, the situation is very different. Because of the lower earnings of black men, poor black women can expect fewer economic gains from remarriage than can white women. And, in fact, black women remarry far less often than do white women.[173]

In the absence of an economically viable marital bond, poor black women, like the nineteenth-century poor more generally, regularly turn to friends, neighbors, and extended kin for economic support. Since relations with friends and extended kin compose dense networks of exchange, these relationships are more stable than is marriage. Moreover, poor black women turn friends into "fictive kin," which means that these friends can be counted on to exchange money, goods, and services—not simply love. In the face of failure of the conjugal ties, blacks, then, adapt the language of kinship to the friends and neighbors on whom they rely.[174]

Overall, then, the economic bonds of black families—at least among the poor—differ from those of white families. Disadvantaged black men are, for whatever reasons, unable to provide women with economic security. Yet, this is not to say that economic ties among black families disappear altogether. Rather, they are reconstituted along different lines, emphasizing extended and fictive kin ties rather than conjugal ties.

PROFESSIONAL WOMEN AND DUAL-CAREER FAMILIES

As the high unemployment rate among black men has loosened the economic ties binding black families, so too has the growing (although still small) number of women who have well-paying careers loosened the economic ties binding affluent families. For these women, new career options provide alternatives to a forced marital dependency. Compared to those with fewer resources, better-educated and better-paid women are less likely to marry, or to have children if they do. They are also more likely to divorce and are less likely to remarry.[175] Ironically, then, although for very different reasons, the nineteenth-century bargain that marriage promised is collapsing for these professional women just as it is for poor black women.

But the parallels between these groups should not overshadow important differences. While poor black women reconstitute family as an economic unit around kin, professional wives may reconstitute marriage as a productive unit, albeit in a sense quite different from that of their historical counterparts. Thus, as recent research indicates, dual-career husbands and wives often bring their work home to get help from, and to give help to, a knowledgeable spouse.[176] In doing so, they may increase their own productivity. Not only are married men more productive in their professions than are their single counterparts, but also at least some married women professionals—including academics, research scientists, and lawyers—are more productive than are unmarried ones.[177] Thus, in relying on their mates, these dual-career spouses fortify an economic as well as emotional bond between each other. However, because of their ability to earn a good income, it is for such well-paid women that marriage and family can most readily be "freely chosen," based on and sustained by emotional dependence. They can be tied by emotional attachment precisely because they are least economically driven.

Yet we cannot be too sanguine about the combination of career and family for these women. Along with career gains, these married professional women often experience the anxiety that accompanies high expectations and token status. Typically, these women feel desperately pressed for time, giving up their own leisure and sleep to meet demands of both employment and family. Unlike men, these women discover that their job and family constantly intrude on each other.[178] Notwithstanding the media's celebrated creation, the "super-woman" who does it "all" is as unrealistic and pernicious an image as is her predecessor, the "supermom."[179]

LESBIAN AND GAY FAMILIES

A telling reflection of the ongoing importance of the economic underpinnings of marriage is the growing movement to legalize relationships of those who cohabit, whether heterosexual, lesbian, or gay. Among lesbians and gay men, this movement has taken two forms—attempts to legally marry and attempts to legitimate same-sex relationships via "domestic partnerships." The first—attempts to marry—has met with little success. In the 1970s, three cases concerning same-sex marriage were brought to the courts (*Baker v. Nelson* [1971], *Jones v. Hallahan* [1973], and *Singer v. Hara* [1974]); in all three cases, the courts denied the couples marriage licenses on the grounds that they could not reproduce.[180] Since the 1970s, no additional cases of same-sex couples seeking marriage have appeared in the U.S. courts. Nonetheless, a number of lesbian and gay couples have sought to "analogize a committed lesbian or gay relationship to a marriage" for a number of purposes. Many of these reasons are economic, including "renewing a lease held in the name of a deceased lover or asserting property rights in a former lover's assets."[181]

The second form many gays and lesbians have advanced is "domestic partnership"—generally defined as "a household partnership . . . used as a criterion for granting [those] benefits" accorded to married heterosexuals.[182] A few employers[183] have offered domestic partnership benefits, a number of cities[184] have enacted domestic partnership ordinances, and a few states are currently considering them. To make claims to domestic partnership benefits, couples often must show that their relationships closely approximate heterosexual marriage. That is, they must document that they are older than eighteen years of age, have been together for a certain period of time, are not married to anyone else, and form a single economic unit (in particular, they must show they share the common necessities of life and assume responsibility for each other's welfare). The material and economic outcomes of such partnerships are clear. Although domestic partnership ordinances provide different benefits in different locales, the benefits often sought and proffered include joint property and life insurance, sick and bereavement leave, health insurance, and annuity and pension rights.[185] So, too, the Lambda Defense League (an organization that has engaged in legal advocacy for and dissemination of information on lesbian and gay rights since 1973) recently issued a project publication "discussing issues of pivotal importance to gay and lesbian families." That publication emphasizes the considerable economic savings for those who successfully claim to be "family," including savings at the federal level entailed in spousal retirement plans, social security rights, housing eligibility, and inheritance benefits as well as "family" discounts to users of public accommodations (like frequent flyer plans and travel packages).[186]

While the large majority of Americans still oppose same-sex marriage,[187] a growing majority of Americans support these couples' claims to the economic benefits associated with marriage. For example, a 1989 Time/CNN poll found that over half of the respondents believed that lesbian and gay couples should enjoy the rights of inheritance equivalent to those of married couples and receive medical and life insurance benefits from a partner's policy.[188]

To be sure, there is debate within the lesbian and gay community as to whether they should seek the label and rights of marriage. Interestingly, it is a recognition of the potential of marriage to subordinate the interests of one partner to the interests of the other that lies behind some activists' reluctance to support efforts to legalize same-sex relationships.[189] Though the focus here is on escaping the restrictions of marriage, the logic of both positions rests on acknowledgment that marriage in our society does shape the material interests of those who enter it.

Conclusion

We have shown how the nineteenth-century construction of different spheres for men and women, and its attendant romanticization of family ties, accounts for both changing and enduring features of contemporary families. Our analysis of the relationship between that heritage and the realities of women's and men's lives over the course of this century highlights the fact that ideology never exerts its influence in a social vacuum. Instead, people's everyday experiences in given historical circumstances reverberate on ideology, revealing the interplay between them. But even more, we have seen how ideology and practice mutually constitute and reconstitute each other over time, so transformations in both develop out of the realities created by each.

Day-to-day realities in the "new" families of the nineties—female-headed, dual-earner, dual-career, and same-sex—derive from the legacy of the nineteenth-century relegation of woman to the home and the ideological celebration of her presence there. Trivialization of the considerable remaining work women do for their families—a residue of the devaluation that this work underwent over the course of the last century—hides that work's economic value and even conceals that it is work. Most family responsibilities, in turn, whether willingly pursued or begrudgingly resented, vitiate women's continued attachment to jobs or, at the very least, keep employed wives and mothers perpetually exhausted.

Moreover, woman's relative economic disadvantage on the job—also a throwback to nineteenth-century definitions of the worth of her labor both at home and in the market—ensures that women are likely to be poor if they head their own household, and that they probably will be obliged to subordinate job demands to family if they marry. In such ways have ideologies set in place and nourished the reality of gender inequality in the twentieth century.

At the same time, however, the new realities of women's lives in the twentieth century—their increasing labor-force participation, higher educational achievements, and growing necessity to manage a family alone—have in turn challenged prevailing ideologies and transformed the basis of women's personal identities, as well as the social landscape available to them. Now that women are no longer confined to the family, women's experiences in families, and in social life more generally, are changing beliefs and practices both in the home and away from it. In such ways have demographic and economic developments in this century produced new realities that constrain old ideologies and at least offer the promise of mitigating gender inequality.

An important conclusion results from this analysis. Some people argue that recent changes—from the decrease of single-earner families and the rising employment of women to the declining fertility and increasing divorce rates—are evidence for the imminent demise of the family. Many more believe that while families of the past were linked by strong economic bonds, the ties that bind contemporary families are made of a weak emotional twine. In contrast, we have argued that far from having lost its economic significance, the family is still the predominant economic lifeline for most women. Unfortunately, however, the premium put on the modern family's emotional life has eclipsed the family's remaining economic significance.

In fact, the family remains economically significant for all its members. Although it is true that men's economic fortunes do not plummet, as women's do, on divorce, married men and their children are increasingly relying both on their wives' unpaid domestic services and on their wives' wages to maintain their family's economic status. And even (perhaps especially) among those women spurning marriage—black impoverished and white affluent women—it is underlying economic exigencies that explain, as they constrain, such options. A common productive effort no longer constitutes family ties, but a common economic fate is still very much a family affair—even if this common fate, based as it is on exchange, is an unequal exchange. Whether affluent or poor, white or black, husbands, wives, and children are still economically intertwined—for better or worse—even as that union is mystified by notions of romantic and maternal love. These mystifications must be made visible if they are to be resisted effectively.

Moreover, the increasing requirement that there be two earners to ensure a family's economic solvency suggests that economic ties among family members will continue to shape emotional ones, just as the reverse will remain true. Thus, spouses and parents in dual-career marriages who put in long hours required by their jobs may find it harder and harder to fulfill the emotional goals they set for their families.[190]

Thus, we see a dialectic, as well, in the relative economic versus emotional tilt assigned to the family. While we have come to emphasize the family's emotional significance, we may have changed the conditions that could sustain such an emphasis. As others have suggested, the fifties may have been the last decade in which women's behavior and social norms coincided.[191] If this is so, we must come to terms with the new realities inhering in the fact that women need jobs and that our society needs their labor, just as that labor necessarily changes families. We can no longer afford to sustain an ideological eclipse of such economic realities if for no other reason than that such views so influence the state policies we get and ask for.

NOTES

1. James A. Henretta, "Families and Farms: Mentality in Pre-Industrial America." *William and Mary Quarterly* 35 (Jan. 1978), 15–17; Laurel T. Ulrich, *Good Wives, Image and Reality in the Lives of Women in Northern New England, 1650–1750* (New York: Oxford University Press, 1980), 51–68.

2. For use of the concept "little commonwealth" to describe the colonial family, see John Demos, *A Little Commonwealth: Family Life in Plymouth Colony* (New York: Oxford University Press, 1970). Although most people agree the colonial family was a "little commonwealth," historians have

disagreed about the relative power of men and women in colonial America. In the 1970s, some feminist historians (including Mary Ryan and Joan Wilson) argued that because women made essential contributions to household production, they wielded considerable power. In the 1980s, others (including Nancy Folbre and Mary Beth Norton) argued that such contributions did not ensure that women exercised family authority or control over economic resources. In a recent and insightful review of the data and argument, Toby Lee Ditz suggests that while colonial women may have had considerable influence and respect, these are not equivalent to power: "Control over resources is the crux of the matter. There was nothing in the wife's role as producer per se to dilute the husband's position as the ultimate arbiter of household business" (p. 128). See Mary Ryan, *Womanhood in America: From Colonial Times to the Present* (New York: Franklin Watts–New Viewpoints, 1979), 3–40; Joan Hoff Wilson, "The Illusion of Change: Women and the American Revolution," in Alfred Young, ed. (Dekalb, Ill.: Northern Illinois University Press, 1976), 383–445; Nancy Folbre, "Patriarchy in Colonial New England," *Review of Radical Political Economics* 12 (1980), 4–13; Mary Beth Norton, "The Evolution of White Women's Experience in Early America," *American Historical Review* 89 (June 1984), 593–619; Toby L. Ditz, *Property and Kinship* (Princeton, N.J.: Princeton University Press, 1986), 118–27.

3. Andrew Cherlin, "Changing Family and Household: Contemporary Lessons from Historical Research," in Ralph Turner and James Short, eds., *Annual Review of Sociology,* vol. 9 (Palo Alto, Calif.: Annual Reviews Inc., 1983), 52–54.

4. Michael Merrill, "Cash Is Good Enough to Eat: Self-Sufficiency and Exchange in the Rural Economies of the United States," *Radical History Review* 4 (Winter 1977), 42–71; Henretta, "Families and Farms," 3–32.

5. Tamara K. Haraven, "American Families in Transition: Historical Perspectives on Change," in Arlene S. Skolnick and Jerome H. Skolnick, eds., *Family in Transition,* 5th ed. (Boston: Little Brown and Co., 1986), 75.

6. Philip J. Greven, "Family Structure in Seventeenth-Century Andover, Massachusetts," in Michael Gordon, ed., *The American Family in Social Historical Perspective* (New York: St. Martin's Press, 1983), 136–54; Robert A. Gross, *The Minute Men and Their World* (New York: Basic Books, 1976), 210–13.

7. Greven, "Family Structure in Seventeenth-Century Andover, Massachusetts," 154–68.

8. Daniel S. Smith, "Parental Power and Marriage Patterns: An Analysis of Historical Trends in Hingham, Massachusetts," *Journal of Marriage and the Family* 35 (Aug. 1973), 219–28.

9. John Demos, "Old Age in Early New England," in Michael Gordon, ed., *The American Family in Social Historical Perspective* (New York: St Martin's, 1983), 269–305; Maris Vinovskis, "Aged Servants of the Lord: Changes in the Status and Treatment of the Elderly in Colonial America," in Matilda W. Riley, Ronald P. Abelews, Martin S. Teitelbaum, eds., *Aging from Birth to Death: Sociotemporal Perspectives* (Boulder, Colo.: Westview, 1982), 105–38.

10. Mary Ryan, "The Explosion of Family History," *Reviews in American History* 19 (Dec. 1982), 180–95.

11. Sara Evans, *Born for Liberty* (New York: Free Press, 1989), 28. As Evans points out, the character of colonial women's and men's labor depended on the region in which they lived. For example, while northern women made candles and cloth, few southern frontier women did so because such items were more readily available except when the tobacco economy experienced a recession (p. 29).

12. Alice Kessler-Harris, *Out to Work* (New York: Oxford University Press, 1982), Chapter 1.

13. Recent research has suggested that some of the characteristics associated with "the little adult" child were exaggerated in earlier research. Although children were certainly important for production, parents were not (as some had proposed) formal, distant, or particularly punitive toward their children, but instead were affectionate and kind. Although parents sometimes resorted to physical punishment and even to serious abuse, such offending adults were severely punished. See Linda Pollock, *Forgotten Children: Parent–Child Relations from 1500–1800* (New York: Cambridge University Press, 1983).

14. Although economy and family were merged throughout the colonies, the circumstances of these families varied considerably by geographic region. For example, the Chesapeake colonists of Maryland and Virginia experienced high mortality at a relatively young age (due to epidemics of typhoid and dysentery, and later malaria), a severely imbalanced sex ratio (with men far outnumbering women), and an immigrant-dominated population consisting of single, often indentured,

servants. These demographic facts had profound consequences for family life. Because the people immigrated as singles rather than in family groups, and because they died so young, kin networks remained small and underdeveloped compared to their northern counterparts. In the absence of older generations to control them, sons and daughters obtained relatively early autonomy in marriage decisions. Because parents, especially fathers, died young, many children were orphaned, and unstable family units were often held together by impoverished widows. Because there were so many available single men, after the death of a husband these widows remarried quickly and reinstated the same division of labor found in the North to ensure the economic survival of themselves and their progeny. Overall, although surviving family members worked together to provide for their needs, these southern colonists had far less developed family systems and controls. For a discussion of these southern colonists, see Lois Green Carr and Lorena S. Walsh, "The Planter's Wife: The Experience of White Women in Seventeenth Century Maryland," in Michael Gordon, ed., *The American Family in Social Historical Perspective* (New York: St. Martin's Press, 1983), 321–39; Daniel Blake Smith, "Mortality and Family in the Colonial Chesapeake," *Journal of American History* 8 (1978), 403–27; Daniel Blake Smith, "The Study of Family in Early America: Trends, Problems and Prospects," *William and Mary Quarterly* 39 (Jan. 1982), 3–28; Norton, "The Evolution of White Women's Experience in Early America," 597–601.

15. To be sure, these forces—the commercialization of agriculture, the growth of external markets, and the availability of transportation—varied in their force even within the northeast. Some communities were primarily subsistence-plus—they did not rely heavily on production for nonlocal markets—whereas others became highly commercialized. And, of course, these different rates of development were highly consequential for the development of family life. For a good discussion of such differences in the northern countryside, see Ditz, *Property and Kinship,* 3–14, 61–102, 157–73.

16. For good overviews of this transition, see Christopher Clark, "Household Economy, Market Exchange, and the Rise of Capitalism," *Journal of Social History* 13 (Winter 1979), 1800–1860; Kessler-Harris, *Out to Work,* 20–45.

17. A rich body of works documents the rise of this cult of domesticity or true womanhood. See, for example, Barbara Welter, "Cult of True Womanhood: 1820–1860," in Gordon, ed., *The American Family in Social Historical Perspective,* 372–92; Nancy Cott, *The Bonds of True Womanhood* (New Haven, Conn.: Yale University Press, 1977); Kathryn Kish Sklar, *Catherine Beecher: A Study in American Domesticity* (New Haven, Conn.: Yale University Press, 1973).

18. Julie Matthaei, *An Economic History of Women in America* (New York: Schocken Books, 1982), 105.

19. Mary Ryan, *Cradle of the Middle Class: The Family in Oneida County, New York, 1790–1865* (New York: Cambridge University Press, 1981), 146–47.

20. Viviana A. Zelizer, *Pricing the Priceless Child: The Changing Social Value of Children* (New York: Basic Books, 1985).

21. Susan C. Watkins, Jane A. Menken, and John Bongaarts, "Demographic Foundations of Family Change," *American Sociological Review* 52 (June 1987), 346–58.

22. Ryan, *Womanhood in America,* 134.

23. Ryan, *Cradle of the Middle Class,* 155–78.

24. Pleck and Rothman note that nineteenth-century middle-class fathers were still expected to take responsibility for the inculcation of practical skills, especially among their sons; but, when compared with colonial fathers, they were expected to be "far less involved" with their children. Elizabeth Pleck and Ellen Rothman, *The Legacies Book* (New York: Corporation for Public Broadcasting Project, 1987), 195. See also Ryan, *Cradle of the Middle Class,* 156–58.

25. Ryan, *Cradle of the Middle Class,* 147.

26. Carl Degler, *At Odds* (New York: Oxford University Press, 1980), 8–86; Ryan, *Womanhood in America,* 134–59. For an overview of the "affectionate family," see Pleck and Rothman, *The Legacy Book,* 180–95.

27. Lee V. Chambers-Schiller, *Liberty, A Better Husband: Single Women in America: The Generations of 1780–1840* (New Haven, Conn.: Yale University Press, 1984).

28. Cited in Ruth Freeman and Patricia Klaus, "Blessed or Not? The New Spinster in England and the United States in the Late Nineteenth and Early Twentieth Century," *Journal of Family History* 9 (Winter 1984), 404.

29. Gerda Lerner, "Single Women in Nineteenth Century Society: Pioneers or Deviants?" *Reviews in American History* 15 (Mar. 1987), 94–100.

30. Suzanne Lebsock, *The Free Women of Petersburg* (New York: W. W. Norton, 1984), 26–27.

31. Cott, *The Bonds of Womanhood,* 160–96.

32. Caroll Smith-Rosenberg, "The Female World of Love and Ritual: Relations Between Women in Nineteenth Century America," in Gordon, ed., *The American Family in Social Historical Perspective,* 411–35.

33. Herbert Gutman, "Work Culture and Society in Industrializing America: 1815–1919," *American Historical Review* 78 (1973), 531–88; Kathy Peiss, *Cheap Amusements* (Philadelphia: Temple University Press, 1986), 11–34; Ryan, *Cradle of the Middle Class,* 145–79.

34. Stephanie Coontz, *The Social Origins of Private Life: A History of American Families 1600–1900* (London: Verso, 1988), 222.

35. Carl N. Degler, "What Ought to Be and What Was: Women's Sexuality in the Nineteenth Century," *American Historical Review* 79 (1975), 1468–91; Carol Z. Stearns and Peter N. Stearns, "Victorian Sexuality: Can Historians Do It Better?" *Journal of Social History* 18 (Summer 1985), 625–34.

36. Estelle B. Freedman, "Sexuality in Nineteenth Century America: Behavior, Ideology and Politics," *Reviews in American History* 10 (Dec. 1982), 196–215.

37. Linda Gordon, *Women's Bodies, Women's Rights: A Social History of Birth Control in America* (New York: Grossman, 1976), 104–15.

38. Ryan, *Cradle of the Middle Class,* 155–79.

39. For an interesting analysis of this work, see Dorothy Smith, "Women's Inequality and the Family," in Naomi Gerstel and Harriet Gross, eds., *Families and Work* (Philadelphia: Temple University Press, 1987), 35–37.

40. Susan M. Juster and Maris A. Vinovskis, "Changing Perspectives on the American Family in the Past," in W. Richard Scott and James F. Short, eds., *Annual Review of Sociology,* vol. 13 (Palo Alto, Calif.: Annual Reviews, Inc., 1987), 210.

41. A substantial minority of Americans did share a home with nonkin, whether they were servants, apprentices, employees, boarders, or friends. Some scholars even suggest that if we compare the early twentieth century to any earlier period, the changing composition of households can more properly be described as the increasing exclusion of nonkin rather than kin. See, for example, Barbara Laslett, "Production, Reproduction, and Social Change: The Family in Historical Perspective," in James Short, ed., *The State of Sociology* (Beverly Hills, Calif.: Sage Publications, 1981), 167.

42. Martha May, "The Historical Problem of the Family Wage: The Ford Motor Company and the Five Dollar Day," in Gerstel and Gross, eds., *Families and Work,* 111–13.

43. Smith, "Women's Inequality and the Family," 23–54.

44. Kessler-Harris, *Out to Work,* 53.

45. Christine Stansell, *City of Women, Sex and Class in New York, 1789–1860* (Urbana and Chicago: University of Illinois, 1987), 77.

46. Matthaei, *An Economic History of Women in America,* 120–41.

47. For a discussion of the high rates of poverty among unmarried immigrant women in New York, see Stansell, *City of Women, Sex and Class in New York, 1789–1860,* especially 11–18, 43–52, 106–20.

48. Kessler-Harris, *Out to Work,* 45–73.

49. Suzanne W. Model, "Work and Family: Blacks and Immigrants from South and East Europe," in Virginia Yans McLaughlin, ed., *Immigration Reconsidered* (New York: Oxford University Press, 1990), 136.

50. Degler, *At Odds,* 132–43.

51. Christine Bose, "Household Resources and U.S. Women's Work: Factors Affecting Gainful Employment at the Turn of the Century," *American Sociological Review* 49 (Aug. 1984), 486; Elizabeth Ewen, *Immigrant Women in the Land of Dollars* (New York: Monthly Review Press), 104–6.

52. Francis H. Early, "The French-Canadian Economy and the Standard of Living in Lowell, Massachusetts, 1870," in M. Gordon, ed., *The American Family in Social Historical Perspective* (New York: St. Martin's Press, 1983), 491.

53. Stansell, *City of Women,* 50–52.

54. Christine Stansell, "Women, Children and the Uses of the Street: Class and Gender Conflict in New York City: 1850–1860," *Feminist Studies* 8 (Summer 1982), 309–36.

55. Tamara Hareven, "The Dynamics of Kin in an Industrial Community," in Gerstel and Gross, eds., *Families and Work,* 55–83; Virginia Yans-McLaughlin, *Family and Community: Italian Immigrants in*

Buffalo, 1880–1893 (Ithaca, N.Y.: Cornell University Press, 1977), 262–63; Suzanne W. Model, "Work and Family: Blacks and Immigrants from South and East Europe," in Virginia Yans-McLaughlin, ed., *Immigration Reconsidered* (New York: Oxford University Press, 1990), 132–36; Stansell, *City of Women*, 41–62.

56. Jean E. Friedman, *The Enclosed Garden: Women and Community in the Evangelical South, 1830–1900* (Chapel Hill, N.C.: University of North Carolina Press, 1985), 21–38. While we have focused here on the rural South, western migrants also recreated the preindustrial division of labor characteristic of colonial America and of the nineteenth-century south. The "affectionate family" with its cult of domesticity collapsed with migrations to the west. Men had more power (indeed, men typically decided when a family would move west, often against the protestations of their wives). Yet both husbands and wives contributed to what became once again a family explicitly united by the productive labors of its members. On reaching their destinations, these western wives cared for the home, dairy, hen house, and garden and spun the clothes their families wore, while husbands cleared and plowed the fields, cared for the tools, and hauled wood. However, this was a diminished family, whether compared to its colonial predecessor, southern rural families, or the eastern industrializing families that these women and men abandoned. In the west, the family had become a relatively isolated unit, with few external supports for its primary mission of economic survival. John Mack Farragher, *Women and Men on the Overland Trail* (New Haven, Conn.: Yale University Press, 1979), especially Chapters 3, 4, 5, and 7.

57. Jane Turner Censer, *North Carolina Planters and Their Children: 1800–1860* (Baton Rouge, La.: Louisiana State University Press, 1984), xiv.

58. For a discussion of work roles of planters' wives, see Anne Firor Scott, *The Southern Lady* (Chicago: University of Chicago Press, 1970), 28–33; Catherine Clinton, *The Plantation Mistress* (New York: Pantheon Books, 1984), 30–35. There is some disagreement about the relationship of these elite southern women to their children. Some, such as Phillip Greven, argue that the presence of slave nursemaids promoted and allowed distant, formal relationships between white parents and children. However, Jean Censer in her study of North Carolina planter families found affectionate relationships between parents and children, as she found mothers who focused on their offspring. See Phillip Greven, *The Protestant Temperament: Patterns of Child Rearing, Religious Experience and Self* (New York: Basic Books, 1977), 274–76; Censer, *North Carolina Planters*, 20–41.

59. Jacqueline Jones, *Labor of Sorrow, Labor of Love: Black Women, Work, and Family from Slavery to Present* (New York: Basic Books, 1986), 11–43.

60. Eugene D. Genovese, *Roll, Jordan, Roll—The World Slaves Made* (New York: Vintage Books, 1974), 70–75.

61. For the argument that slave-family ties produced incentives for labor, see Genovese, *Roll, Jordan, Roll*, 477–81; Degler, *At Odds*, 112–13.

62. Herbert G. Gutman, *The Black Family in Slavery and Freedom: 1750–1925* (New York: Pantheon, 1976), 129–37, 284–91, 310–17. In one study, only 13.6 percent of recently freed ex-slave couples said they had lived together without some disruption. And one-third of these disruptions were caused by sales. See John W. Blassingame, *The Slave Community* (New York: Oxford University Press, 1972), 90–92.

63. Genovese, *Roll, Jordan, Roll*, 319.

64. Gutman, *The Black Family in Slavery and Freedom*, 129–37, 284–91, 310–17.

65. Jacqueline Jones, "My Mother Was Much of a Woman: Black Women, Work and the Family Under Slavery," in Gerstel and Gross, eds., *Families and Work*, 95–96.

66. John E. Goldthorpe, *Family Life in Western Societies* (New York: Cambridge University Press, 1987), 191–92.

67. Gutman, *The Black Family in Slavery and Freedom*, 455–56.

68. Susan Mann, "Slavery, Sharecropping and Sexual Inequality," *Signs* 14 (Summer 1989), 783–84.

69. Jones, *Labor of Love, Labor of Sorrow*, 336–37.

70. John Bodnar, Michael Weber, and Roger Simon, "Migration, Kinship and Urban Adjustment," *Journal of American History* 66 (Jan. 1979), 554–57.

71. Claudia Goldin, *Understanding the Gender Gap* (New York: Oxford University Press, 1990), 75.

72. Suzanne W. Model, "Work and Family: Blacks and Immigrants from South and East Europe," in Virginia Yans McLaughlin, ed., *Immigration Reconsidered* (New York: Oxford University Press, 1990), 141.

73. Claudia Goldin, "Family Strategies and the Family Economy in the Late Nineteenth Century," in Theodore Hershberg, ed., *Philadelphia: Work, Space, Family, and Group Experience in the 19th Century* (New York: Oxford University Press, 1980), 305.

74. Lebsock, *Free Women of Petersburg,* 90; Suzanne W. Model, "Work and Family: Blacks and Immigrants from South and East Europe," 138.

75. Suzanne W. Model, "Work and Family: Blacks and Immigrants from South and East Europe," 138.

76. Susan Watkins, Jane A. Menken, and John Bongaarts, "Demographic Foundations of Family Change," *American Sociological Review* 52 (June 1987), 348.

77. Arthur J. Norton and Jean E. Moorman, "Current Trends in Marriage and Divorce Among American Women," *Journal of Marriage and the Family* 49 (Feb. 1987), 3–14.

78. In 1800, the median age at first marriage for females was twenty, but it had risen to twenty-two by 1890, when the first reliable census data became available. For the next fifty years it remained stable, with half of all eligible women marrying before the end of their twenty-first year. During the "baby-boom" years after World War II, the median age dropped steadily until it bottomed out at 20.1 in 1956. Thereafter women married at a later and later age; the median age peaked in 1990 at 23.9. The figure for 1800 comes from Susan Watkins, Jane A. Menken, and John Bongaarts, "Demographic Foundations of Family Change," *American Sociological Review* 52 (June 1987), 346–58. The other figures can be found in U.S. Bureau of Labor Statistics, "Marital Status and Living Arrangements: March 1990," *Current Population Reports,* Series P-20, no. 450, Table A-1, 67. "Median Age at First Marriage" is also graphed on p. 2. Other sources indicate that blacks used to marry earlier than did whites. Andrew J. Cherlin, *Marriage, Divorce, Remarriage* (Cambridge, Mass.: Harvard University Press, 1981), 94. Black women now delay marriage—although not motherhood, a point we return to—even longer than do whites. Suzanne M. Bianchi and Daphne Spain, *American Women in Transition* (New York: Russell Sage, 1986), 15.

79. For data on increases in divorce and declines in remarriage, see section "Divorce and Female-Headed Households."

80. The average time spent in first marriages has declined by ten or eleven years over the last three decades. Suzanne M. Bianchi and Daphne Spain, *American Women in Transition* (New York: Russell Sage, 1986), 85.

81. Watkins, Menken, Bongaarts, "Demographic Foundations of Family Change," 351.

82. U.S. Bureau of the Census, "Marital Status and Living Arrangements, March, 1990." *Current Population Reports,* Series P-20, no. 445 (Washington, D.C.: U.S. Government Printing Office, March 1990), Table 8, 65; Paul C. Glick, "American Families: As They Are and Were," in Arlene S. Skolnick and Jerome Skolnick, eds., *Family in Transition* (New York: HarperCollins Publisher, 1992), 94.

83. Larry Bumpass, James Sweet, and Andrew Cherlin, "The Role of Cohabitation in Declining Rates of Marriage," *Journal of Marriage and the Family* 53 (Nov. 1991), 919.

84. Bumpass, Sweet, and Cherlin, "The Role of Cohabitation," 922.

85. Koray Tanfer, "Patterns of Premarital Cohabitation Among Never-Married Women in the United States," *Journal of Marriage and the Family* 49 (Aug. 1987), 483–97 (quote on 493).

86. Hugh Carter and Paul C. Glick, *Marriage and Divorce: A Social and Economic Study,* 2d ed. (Cambridge, Mass.: Harvard University Press, 1976); Sharon K. Houseknecht, Suzanne Vaughan, and Anne Statham, "The Impact of Singlehood on the Career Patterns of Professional Women," *Journal of Marriage and the Family* 49 (May 1987), 353–66.

87. Francis K. Goldscheider and Linda J. Waite, "Sex Differences in the Entry into Marriage," *American Journal of Sociology* 92 (July 1986), 91–109.

88. Scott J. South, "Sociodemographic Differentials in Mate Selection Preferences," *Journal of Marriage and the Family* 53 (Nov. 1991), 937.

89. Arlie R. Hochschild, "Attending to, Codifying and Managing Feelings: Sex Differences in Love," in Laurel Richardson and Verta Taylor, eds., *Feminist Frontiers* (Reading, Mass.: Addison-Wesley, 1983), 250–62.

90. Most studies of housework do not specify class and race differences. However, of the studies that examine racial differences, two report that black husbands do more housework than do white husbands, and two studies show the opposite. The same inconsistency characterizes studies of class differences: High-income husbands do the least housework in one sample and the most in another. Overall, studies show that husbands, across class and race, do far less housework than their wives do. Peter Stein, "Men in Families," in Beth Hess and Marvin Sussman, eds., *Women and the Family, Two Decades of Change* (New York: Haworth Press, 1984), 151–52.

91. Estimates suggest that men spend only from 15 to 50 percent as much time doing domestic work as women do. For a review, see Shelley Coverman and J. Shelley, "Changes in Men's Housework and Child Care Time," *Journal of Marriage and the Family* 48 (May 1986), 413–22.

92. Myra Marx Ferree, "Beyond Separate Spheres: Feminism and Family Research," *Journal of Marriage and the Family* 52 (Nov. 1990), 875.

93. See Myra Marx Ferree's review essay: "Housework: Rethinking the Costs and Benefits," in Irene Diamond, ed., *Families, Politics and Public Policy: A Feminist Dialogue on Women and the State* (New York: Longman, 1983), 148–69; Sara F. Berk, *The Gender Factory: The Apportionment of Work in American Households* (New York: Plenum Press, 1985); Dana Hiller and W. W. Philliber, "The Division of Labor in Contemporary Marriage: Expectations, Perceptions, and Performance," *Social Problems* 33 (Feb. 1986), 191–201; Donna Hodgkins Berardo, Constance L. Shehan, and Gerald R. Leslie, "A Residue of Tradition: Jobs, Careers, and Spouses' Time in Housework," *Journal of Marriage and the Family* 49 (May 1987), 381–90.

94. Researchers have used a number of different techniques for assessing the dollar value of housework. Few suggest that the salary of a paid housecleaner is equivalent to the value of homemakers' labor. Some economists do suggest the use of a "shadow wage" (in which the value of housework is the wage the homemaker herself could earn on a full-time job). Others use the occupational-components approach, in which the hours a housewife puts into particular jobs (e.g., her work as a nurse, chauffeur, dietitian, housecleaner, etc.) are multiplied by the wages for those particular jobs. However, each of these techniques has its own flaws (e.g., the shadow-wage method pays highly educated women more than less-educated women for the same job of housework; the occupational components method gives all women the same wage for similar tasks, although skill levels vary enormously). For a discussion of these different methods, see Bergmann, *The Economic Emergence of Women* (New York: Basic Books, 1986), 206–9.

95. See Naomi Gerstel, Catherine Riessman, and Sarah Rosenfield, "Explaining the Symptomatology of Separated and Divorced Women and Men," *Social Forces* 64 (Sept. 1985), 84–101.

96. Batya Weinbaum and Amy Bridges, "The Other Side of the Paycheck: Monopoly Capital and the Structure of Consumption," *Monthly Review* 28 (July–Aug. 1976), 88–103.

97. Ruth Schwartz Cowan, "Women's Work, Housework and History: The Historical Roots of Inequality in Work-Force Participation," in Gerstel and Gross, eds., *Families and Work,* 171.

98. Nona Y. Glazer, "Servants to Capital: Unpaid Domestic Labor and Paid Work," in Gerstel and Gross, eds., *Families and Work,* 241.

99. Ibid., 246–48.

100. Catherine White Berheide, "Women's Work in the Home: Seems Like Old Times," in Beth Hess and Marvin Sussman, eds., *Women and the Family: Two Decades of Change* (New York: Haworth Press, 1984), 38–55.

101. Rosanna Hertz uses the term *subcontracting* and discusses hired help in *Dual-Career Couples in the Corporate World* (Berkeley: University of California Press, 1986), 160–84.

102. Because so much of domestic work is not reported, reliable figures on it are difficult to obtain. However, census reports provide some data that are useful, at least for comparative purposes. In 1987, the census showed that 16,000 men and 284,000 women were employed as full-time "private-household" service workers (U.S. Department of Labor, "Weekly Earnings of Wage and Salary Workers," *News Release* #87-165 [1987], Table 3). However, as other occupations have become available to women, the proportion of women doing domestic work—either full- or part-time— has declined steadily; at the turn of the century, in 1900, 29 percent of women in the labor force were domestics; before World War II, in 1940, the proportion had declined to 18 percent; by 1950, it was again cut in half to 9 percent; by 1970, the proportion had declined to 4 percent; and by 1985, it was down to 1.2 percent. (Figure for 1987 from *Employment and Earnings* [Jan. 1988], 159, 179. Remaining data from U.S. Bureau of the Census, *Historical Statistics of the United States from the Colonial Times to the Present,* Series D [1976], 140, 182–232.) As Judith Rollins (*Between Women: Domestics and Their Employers* [Philadelphia: Temple University Press, 1985], 56–59) points out, the representation of immigrants in domestic service is increasing as that of blacks is declining: she claims that 38 percent of all domestic workers were black in 1970, only 32 percent were in 1979, and 22.6 percent were in 1987. *Employment and Earnings* (Jan. 1988), 187. Figures on commercial cleaning services are not available, but as Rollins writes: "It may be assumed that if the number of women doing domestic work continues to decrease, such companies will proliferate" (p. 58).

103. These figures are from SAMI Burke, Inc., a New York marketing research company, cited in "Housekeeping Today: Just a Lick and a Promise," *New York Times,* Aug. 20, 1987, C6.

104. Berk, *The Gender Factory,* 201.

105. Marjorie L. DeVault, *Feeding the Family* (Chicago: University of Chicago Press, 1991), 95–121.

106. Both Arlene Skolnick (in *Embattled Paradise* [New York: Basic Books, 1991], 193) and Joseph H. Pleck (in *Working Wives/Working Husbands* [Beverly Hills, Calif.: Sage, 1985], 82–90) report a small increase in the proportion of women who now desire greater "help" with housework from their husbands. Moreover, although polls show that most women do not want more "help" in housework, increasing numbers of highly educated, younger women are more likely to want such help. See Joseph Pleck, "The Work-Family Role System," in Rachel Kahn-Hut, Arlene Kaplan Daniels, and R. Colvard, eds., *Women and Work: Problems and Perspectives* (New York: Oxford University Press, 1982), 105. See also Ferree's specification of the circumstances under which women feel justified in asking their husbands to help with housework. Myra Marx Ferree, "The Struggles of Super-woman," in Christine Bose, Roslyn Feldberg, and Natalie Sokoloff, eds., *Hidden Aspects of Women's Work* (New York: Praeger, 1987), 161–80. For other discussions of women's resistance to asking husbands for more help, see Joanne Vanek, "Household Work, Wage Work, and Sexual Equality," in A. S. Skolnick and J. Skolnick, eds., *Families in Transition* (Boston: Little Brown and Co., 1983), 176–89; Sara Yogev, "Do Professional Women Have More Egalitarian Marital Relationships?" *Journal of Marriage and the Family* 43 (Nov. 1981), 865–71.

107. See the concluding chapter in Berk's *The Gender Factory* for an insightful analysis of the ways women manufacture gender identity by doing housework.

108. As Shelley Coverman has shown, the number of hours men or women spend in housework is negatively associated with wages from jobs. "Gender, Domestic Labor, and Wage Inequality," *American Sociological Review* 48 (1983), 623–36.

109. Berk, *The Gender Factory,* 199–211.

110. Bergmann, *The Economic Emergence of Women,* 210.

111. William Marsiglio, "Paternal Engagement Activities with Minor Children," *Journal of Marriage and the Family* 53 (Nov. 1991), 979; Ralph LaRossa, *Becoming a Parent* (Beverly Hills, Calif.: Sage, 1986), 106–14; Cynthia Darling-Fisher and Linda Beth Tiedje, "The Impact of Maternal Employment Characteristics on Fathers' Participation in Child Care," *Family Relations* 39 (Nov. 1990), 21.

112. In 1900, wives had an average of 3.7 children. By the 1940s, the rate had fallen to fewer than 3 births. In the "baby-boom" years that followed the war, the number went back up to 3.6. By 1990, the fertility rate had fallen to 1.9. (1900 data from Watkins, Menken, and Bongaarts, "Demographic Foundations of Family Change," 346; 1990 data from A. Skolnick, *Intimate Environment* [New York: HarperCollins Publisher, 1992], 339.) In 1989, one-third of all births were to women in their thirties, up from 19 percent in 1976. U.S. Bureau of the Census, "Fertility of American Women: June, 1989," *Current Population Reports,* Series P-20, no. 436 (Washington D.C.: U.S. Government Printing Office, 1989), 12.

113. Nancy Chodorow, *The Reproduction of Mothering* (Berkeley: University of California Press, 1978), 77–92; Judith Gardner, "Self Psychology as Feminist Theory," *Signs* 12 (Summer 1987), 768–71.

114. Judith Blake, "Is Zero Preferred? American Attitudes Toward Childlessness in the 1970's," *Journal of Marriage and the Family* 41 (Aug. 1979), 245–57. Although only 10 percent of women expect to remain childless, demographers predict that a far higher proportion will end their reproductive years without giving birth. See Digest, "Fertility Rate Edges Up, but Record Proportions of Women Are Expected to Remain Childless," *Family Planning Perspectives* 18 (July–Aug. 1986), 178.

115. Pamela Daniels and Kathy Weingarten, *Sooner or Later: The Timing of Parenthood in Adult Lives* (New York: W. W. Norton, 1982), 128–29.

116. Sara McLanahan and Julia Adams, "Parenthood and Psychological Well-Being," in W. Richard Scott and James Richard Short, eds., *Annual Review of Sociology* 13 (1987), 237–57.

117. Digest, "Labor Market Rewards: Women Who Postpone Families till Later Ages," *Family Planning Perspectives* 18 (Nov.–Dec. 1986), 271–72.

118. Wenda Dickens and Daniel Perlman, "Friendship over the Life-Cycle," in Steve Duck and Robin Gilmour, eds., *Personal Relationships,* vol. 2. (New York: Academic Press, 1981), 91–121.

119. Pamela Fishman, "Interaction: The Work Women Do," *Social Problems* 25 (1978), 397–406.

120. Beth Vanfossen, "Sex Differences in the Mental Health Effects of Spouse Support and Equity," *Journal of Health and Social Behavior* 22 (1981), 130–43; A Campbell, Phillip Converse,

and W. Rodgers, *The Quality of American Life: Perceptions, Evaluations and Satisfactions* (New York: Russell Sage Foundation, 1976).

121. Janet Finch, *Married to the Job, Wives' Incorporation in Men's Work* (London: George Allen and Unwin, 1983), 84.

122. Arlene Hochschild, *The Second Shift* (New York: Avon, 1989).

123. Naomi Gerstel and Sally Gallagher, "Caring for Kith and Kin: Gender, Employment, and the Privatization of Care," *Social Problems*, forthcoming (1994).

124. See Marjorie Cantor, "Strain Among Caregivers: A Study of Experience in the United States," *Gerontologist* 23 (Dec. 1983), 597–604.

125. Micaeli Di Leonardo, "The Female World of Cards and Holidays: Women, Families, and the Work of Kinship," *Signs* 12 (Spring 1987), 440–53; Carolyn J. Rosenthal, "Kinkeeping in the Family Division of Labor," *Journal of Marriage and the Family* (May 1985), 965–74; Naomi Gerstel, "Divorce and Kinkeeping: The Importance of Gender," *Journal of Marriage and the Family* 50 (Feb. 1988), 209–21; Naomi Gerstel and Sally Gallagher, "A Redistribution of Caregiving: The Effects of Women's Employment on the Caregiving of Women and Men" (paper presented at the Eastern Sociological Society Meeting, Boston, Mass., Apr. 1991); Emily K. Abel, "Family Care of the Frail Elderly," in Emily K. Abel and Margaret K. Nelson, eds., *Circles of Care: Work and Identity in Women's Lives* (New York: State University of New York Press, 1990), 71–73; Jane Aronson, "Women's Sense of Responsibility for the Care of Old People: 'But Who Else Is Going to Do It?' " *Gender and Society* 6 (Mar. 1992), 16–20.

126. Aronson, "Women's Sense of Responsibility," 16–20; Naomi Gerstel, "The Third Shift: Gender, Difference, and Women's Caregiving" (paper presented at Talks on Gender and Meaning, Smith College, Northampton, Mass., Oct. 1992), 16–19; Naomi Gerstel and Sally Gallagher, "Kinkeeping and Distress: Gender, Recipients of Care, and Work-Family Conflict," *Journal of Marriage and the Family* 55 (Aug. 1993), 598–607.

127. Aronson, "Women's Sense of Responsibility," 21–24.

128. Charles Mindel, Charles H., Roosevelt Wright, and Richard Starrett, "Informal and Formal Health and Social Support Systems of Black and White Elderly: A Comparative Cost Approach," *The Gerontologist* 26 (Jan. 1986), 282–84; Gerstel, "The Third Shift," 17–21.

129. Gerstel, "The Third Shift," 17–21.

130. Elaine Brody, M. Kleban, P. Johnsen, C. Hoffman, and Carma Schoonover, "Work Status and Parent Care: A Comparison of Four Groups of Women," *The Gerontologist* 17 (1987), 201–8.

131. Alice Rossi and Pete Rossi, *Of Human Bonding* (New York: Aldine de Gruyer, 1990); Gerstel and Gallagher, "Caring for Kith and Kin."

132. Gerstel and Gallagher, "A Redistribution of Caregiving."

133. Madonna Harrington Meyer, "Family Status and Poverty Among Older Women: The Gendered Distribution of Retirement Income in the United States," *Social Problems* 37 (Nov. 1990), 551–63.

134. Robyn I. Stone, "The Feminization of Poverty Among the Elderly," in Margaret L. Andersen and Patricia H. Collins, eds., *Race, Class, and Gender: An Anthology* (Belmont, Calif.: Wadsworth, 1992), 209.

135. Meyer, "Family Status and Poverty Among Older Women." Even as late as 1989 (that is, after twenty years of women's relatively high labor force participation), only 36 percent of women but 42 percent of men have pension coverage. U.S. Bureau of the Census, "Pension Plan Coverage of Workers by Selected Characteristics: 1989," no. 595, *Statistical Abstracts of the United States: 1991.*

136. In the 1970s changes in income transfer policies targeted at older widows did attempt to increase their share of the couple's income after their husbands' deaths. In 1972 there was an increase of social security survivor benefits from 82.5 percent of the deceased spouse's benefit to 100 percent along with an increase on the limit placed on the maximum reduction in widows' benefits due to early receipt. In 1974, a change in pension laws increased the percentage of husbands who chose pensions that continued to pay benefits to their widows. See Karen C. Holden, "Women's Economic Status in Old Age and Widowhood," in Martha N. Ozawa, ed., *Women's Life Cycle and Economic Insecurity* (New York: Greenwood, 1989), 163.

137. Karen C. Holden, "Women's Economic Status in Old Age and Widowhood," 145. Not surprisingly, given the difference in their financial well-being, elderly men are more satisfied with their financial situation than elderly women. Neal Krause, "Stressful Events and Life Satisfaction Among Elderly Men and Women," *Journal of Gerontology* 46 (Mar. 1991), S84–S92.

138. Davis and her colleagues conclude, "While most of the older population will fare well economically over the next 30 years, the proportion of women with incomes below 150% of poverty

will remain high: 45 percent in 1987 and 45 percent in 2020. . . . Among widows the situation is slightly worse, with the proportion who are poor or near-poor rising until the turn of the century. . . . By 2020 poverty among the elderly will be almost exclusively a problem of elderly women." K. Davis, P. Grant, and D. Rowland, "Alone and Poor: The Plight of Elderly Women," *Generations* 14 (Summer 1990), 43–45.

139. Martha N. Ozawa, "Conclusions: Women and Society," in Ozawa, *Women's Life Cycle and Economic Insecurity,* 194.

140. 1950 data from Arland Thornton and Deborah Freedman, "The Changing American Family," *Population Bulletin* 38 (Oct. 1983), 24; 1991 data from U.S. Department of Labor, Bureau of Labor Statistics, March 1991 (unpublished data).

141. Of course, in addition to the growth that replaced women's previously directed family work, expansion of business and industry services has also been a part of the growth of this sector.

142. Joan Smith, "The Paradox of Women's Poverty: Wage Earning Women and Economic Transformation," *Signs* 10 (Winter 1984), 302.

143. Ibid., 291–310. For a discussion of factors affecting women's employment since World War II, see Bergmann, *The Economic Emergence of Women;* and Natalie J. Sokoloff, "What's Happening to Women's Employment: Issues for Women's Labor Struggles in 1980–1990," in Christine Bose, Roslyn Feldberg, and Natalie Sokoloff, eds., *Hidden Aspects of Women's Work* (New York: Praeger, 1987), 14–45.

144. Smith, "The Paradox of Women's Poverty," 308.

145. Jane Riblett Wilkie, "The Decline in Men's Labor Force Participation and Income and the Changing Structure of Family Economic Support," *Journal of Marriage and the Family* 53 (Feb. 1991), 112.

146. Wives who worked full-time, year round (53 percent) contributed 40 percent to family income. U.S. Bureau of Labor Statistics, *Current Population Survey,* Table 24, Mar. 1991, unpublished data.

147. U.S. Bureau of the Census, *Current Population Reports,* Series P-60, no. 174, "Money Income of Households, Families and Person in the United States: 1991."

148. For a discussion of wives' declining dependence on husbands' income, see Annemette Sorensen and Sara McLanahan, "Married Women's Economic Dependency: 1940–1980," *American Sociological Review* 93 (Nov. 1987), 659–87.

149. Faye Crosby, *Juggling: The Unexpected Advantage of Balancing Career and Home for Women and Their Families* (New York: Free Press, 1991). Crosby argues that combining these roles often brings advantages, not only for wives but for husbands and children as well.

150. Arlene Hochschild, *The Second Shift* (New York: Avon, 1990).

151. Hochschild, *The Second Shift,* 254.

152. Hochschild, *The Second Shift;* Dana Vanoy-Hiller and William Philliber, *Equal Partners: Successful Women in Marriage* (Newbury Park, Calif.: Sage, 1989).

153. U.S. Department of Labor, Bureau of Labor Statistics, Mar. 1991 (unpublished data).

154. Paul Glick and Sung-Ling Lin, "Recent Changes in Divorce and Remarriage," *Journal of Marriage and the Family* 48 (Nov. 1986), 737–47.

155. Ibid., Table 3.

156. Paul C. Glick, "American Families: As They Are and Were," 96.

157. U.S. Bureau of the Census, *Current Population Reports,* Series P-20, no. 450, "Marital Status and Living Arrangements, March, 1990" (Washington, D.C.: U.S. Government Printing Office, 1990).

158. Millman argues that there is a deep symbolic relationship between love and money in our culture, often not acknowledged until marriages and families break up. "The perspective of marriage changes with divorce: going into marriage people think of the union primarily in terms of love. Going out, they see it in terms of money." Marcia Millman, *Warm Hearts and Cold Cash: The Intimate Dynamics of Families and Money* (New York: Free Press, 1991), 135.

159. Using a national survey, Duncan and Hoffman found the majority of both black (83 percent) and white (57 percent) women received no alimony or child support in the first year after marital dissolution, and that both the incidence and amount of such transfers declined as time passed. Greg J. Duncan and Saul D. Hoffman, "A Reconsideration of the Economic Consequences of Marital Dissolution," *Demography* 22 (Nov. 1985), 490. Moreover, as Weitzman found in her California study, only 15 percent of divorced women are awarded any alimony at all. The median child-support

payment ordered by the courts covers less than half of the actual cost of raising children. Furthermore, in 53 percent of the cases, women did not receive the court ordered payments. Leonore
Weitzman, *The Divorce Revolution* (New York: Basic Books, 1985), 167–74, 270–72, 283–84. Finally,
using national data, Rogers found that far fewer black (29 percent) than white (79 percent) women
were awarded support. Harrell R. Rodgers, *Poor Women, Poor Families* (Armonk, N.Y.: M. E. Sharpe,
1986), 51–53; and Seltzer found that among those who do make at least one child-support payment,
the mean monthly contribution was less than $200. Judith Seltzer, "Relationships Between Fathers
and Children Who Live Apart: The Father's Role After Separation," *Journal of Marriage and the Family*
53 (Feb. 1991), 87.

160. Duncan and Hoffman, "A Reconsideration of the Economic Consequences of Marital
Dissolution," 488–90.

161. Duncan, *Years of Poverty, Years of Plenty*. To be sure, there was a sharp decline in remarriage
in the 1970s, but the rate rebounded in the 1980s.

162. Paul Glick and Sung-Ling Lin, "Remarriage After Divorce: Recent Changes and Demographic Variations," *Sociological Perspectives* 30 (Mar. 1987), 67.

163. Cherlin, "Women and the Family," 92.

164. For example, see William Julius Wilson and Kathryn Neckerman, "Poverty and Family
Structure," in Sheldon H. Danziger and Daniel Weinberg, eds., *Fighting Poverty: What Works and What
Doesn't* (Cambridge, Mass.: Cambridge University Press, 1986), 242–46, 253–59; Rose M. Brewer,
"Black Women in Poverty: Some Comments on Female-Headed Households," *Signs* 13 (Winter
1988), 331–39.

165. Center for the Study of Social Policy, "The 'Flip Side' of Black Families Headed by
Women: The Economic Status of Black Men," in Robert Staples, ed., *The Black Family: Essays and
Studies* (Belmont, Calif.: Wadsworth, 1986), 232–38. For a lucid summary of the factors producing
the worsening economic position of black men, see Maxine Bacca Zinn, *Minority Families in Crisis:
The Public Discussion* (Memphis, Tenn.: Center for Research on Women, 1987), 15–23.

166. Wilson and Neckerman, 253; Brewer, 333–39; Rodgers, 51–53; Tom Joe, "The Other
Side of Black Female-Headed Families: The Status of Black Men," *Family Planning Perspectives* 19
(Mar.–Apr. 1987), 77–76; Maxine Bacca Zinn and D. Stanley Eitzen, *Diversity in American Families*
(New York: Harper and Row, 1987), 237; Robert Staples, "Changes in Black Family Structure: The
Conflict Between Family Ideology and Structural Conditions," in Staples, 25. Affirming the continuing
significance of African-American men's economic marginality, Lichter and his colleagues show that
the influence of differential marriage markets is only a partial factor contributing to continued racial
differences. Daniel T. Lichter, Felicia B. Le Clere, and Dianna K. McLaughlin, "Local Marriage
Markets and the Marital Behavior of Black and White Women," *American Journal of Sociology* 96
(Jan. 1991), 843–67.

167. In 1986, the proportion of divorced women among black women was more than twice
that among white women (323 versus 145 per 1,000 married women). U.S. Bureau of the Census,
"Marital Status and Living Arrangements," *Current Population Reports* P-20, no. 418 (Washington, D.C.:
U.S. Government Printing Office, March 1986), Table D, 7. For comparisons of black and white
women's marital status from 1947 to 1980, see William Julius Wilson and Kathryn M. Neckerman,
"Poverty and Family Structure," in Danziger and Weinberg, eds., *Fighting Poverty: What Works and What
Doesn't*, 238.

168. Analyzing data from 1950 to 1980 on increases in female-headed households, Garfinkel
and McLanahan show that among whites, the increase in mother-only families during each decade
was due primarily to the growing prevalence of formerly married mothers. (Among whites, this
accounted for about 45 percent of the growth in the 1950s and 1960s, and about 57 percent in
the 1970s.) In contrast, among blacks, although during the 1950s about half of the increase in
families headed by women was due to increases in formerly married mothers, they accounted for
less than 30 percent of the increase during the 1960s and less than 3 percent in the 1970s. The
decline in the relative importance of formerly married mothers was replaced by an increase in never-
married mothers. Among blacks, never-married mothers accounted for about 9 percent of the
growth in the 1950s, 20 percent in the 1960s, and 23 percent in the 1970s. Irwin Garfinkel and
Sara S. McLanahan, *Single Mothers and Their Children* (Washington, D.C.: The Urban Institute Press,
1986), 53.

169. The rate of total teenage childbearing increased sharply after World War II, reached a
peak in 1957, then declined in the 1980s. However, the birth rate for unmarried teenage women

rose almost uninterruptedly from the 1940s to late 1980, due to the rise of teenage sexual activity and the lowered inclination for and postponement of marriage. Black women have had much higher rates of out-of-wedlock childbearing than have white women since at least 1940. In 1988, the birth rate for unmarried black teenagers remained much higher than that of whites—about four times the rate—but the white teen rate increased much faster. Andrew Cherlin, *Marriage, Divorce, Remarriage* (Cambridge, Mass.: Harvard University Press, 1981), 95–97; Andrew Cherlin, "Women and the Family," in Sara E. Rix, ed., *The American Woman, 1987–1988* (New York: W. W. Norton, 1987), 77–78; Maris A. Vinovskis, *An Epidemic of Adolescent Pregnancy? Some Historical and Policy Considerations* (New York: Oxford University Press, 1988), 25–30; Arland Thornton, "The Changing American Family," *Population Bulletin* 38 (Oct. 1983), 20; Kristin Luker, "Dubious Conceptions: The Controversy over Teen Pregnancy," in Arlene Skolnick and Jerome Skolnick, eds., *Family in Transition* (New York: HarperCollins Publisher, 1992), 162.

170. Although most researchers suggest that poverty is a major factor causing out-of-wedlock births, there is still considerable debate about the relative impact of economic disadvantage versus other cultural and social factors. As Kenneth Clark argued about blacks in the mid-sixties: "In the ghetto, the meaning of the illegitimate child is not ultimate disgrace. . . . On the contrary, a child is a symbol of the fact that she [the mother] is a woman and she may gain from having something of her own" (Kenneth Clark, *Dark Ghetto* [New York: Harper and Row, 1965], 72). For recent quantitative evidence that differences in attitudes or norms may be important in the explanation of high rates of black adolescent intercourse and childbearing, see Frank F. Furstenberg, S. Philip Morgan, Kristin Moore, and James L. Peterson, "Race Differences in the Timing of Adolescent Intercourse," *American Sociological Review* 52 (Aug. 1987), 511–18. However, as Carol Stack's ethnographic research has shown, favorable attitudes toward out-of-wedlock births in the black ghetto may well be tied to the economic value of children in such communities: Black children are not only symbols of their mothers' adulthood but also involve the mothers in—indeed, provide access to—dense networks whose members exchange resources and information. Thus, the normative system itself may well be tied to economic disadvantage (Carol Stack, *All Our Kin, Strategies for Survival in a Black Community* [New York: Harper and Row, 1974]). Surveys show that only a small minority of black or white teenagers today actually expect and want to become parents before marriage (William J. Wilson, *The Truly Disadvantaged* [Chicago: University of Chicago Press, 1986], 74). Other recent survey research shows that black teenagers' high level of out-of-wedlock birth is associated with a number of social conditions, including being a member of a lower social class as well as residing in an innercity ghetto neighborhood, growing up in single-parent families (rather than two-parent or two-generation ones), having a large number of siblings, and experiencing loose parental control of dating. (See Larry Bumpass and Sara McLanahan, "Unmarried Motherhood: A Note on Recent Trends, Composition, and Black–White Differences" [paper presented at the Annual Meeting of the Population Association of America, Chicago, April 29–May 2, 1987], cited and discussed in Digest, *Family Planning Perspectives* 19 [Sept.–Oct. 1987], 220; Dennis P. Hogan and Evelyn M. Kitagawa, "The Impact of Social Status, Family Structure and Neighborhood on the Fertility of Black Adolescents," *American Journal of Sociology* 90 [Jan. 1985], 825–55.) Overall, then, although norms and economic status may be inextricably intertwined, no available evidence would lead us to dismiss economic disadvantage as a major factor explaining out-of-wedlock pregnancy and birth.

171. Bane, "Household Composition and Poverty," 227.

172. Ibid., 231.

173. Duncan and Hoffman, "A Reconsideration of the Economic Consequences of Marital Dissolution," 493–95.

174. Carol Stack, *All Our Kin, Strategies for Survival in a Black Community*.

175. Cherlin, "Women and the Family."

176. Hertz, *More Equal than Others*.

177. Although we are suggesting that some of this increased productivity may come from the reconstitution of the dual-career family, Epstein explains this seeming anomaly by suggesting: "While we might expect the obligations of marriage and family to hold women back . . . married women are simply considered more normal than single adults. They pose fewer problems to co-workers and clients. . . . Most professional men . . . are more comfortable with women colleagues who carry the protective status of being married . . . and married women make contacts through their husbands." Epstein, *Women in Law,* 342. For additional data and a discussion of greater productivity of married professional women compared to their single counterparts, see Jonathan Cole, *Fair Science: Women in the Scientific Community* (New York: Free Press, 1979), 65–66, 252; Helen S. Astin and

Diane E. Davis, "Research Productivity Across the Life and Career Cycles: Facilitators and Barriers for Women," in Mary Frank Fox, ed., *Scholarly Writing and Publishing* (Boulder, Colo., and London: Westview Press, 1985), 148, 153–55.

178. Rosabeth Moss Kanter, *Men and Women of the Corporation* (New York: Basic Books, 1977); Robert Rapoport and Rhona Rapoport, *Dual-Career Families Re-Examined* (New York: Harper Colophon, 1976); Colleen L. Johnson and Frank A. Johnson, "Role Strain in High-Commitment Career Women," *Journal of American Academy of Psychoanalysts* 4 (1976), 13–36.

179. Ferree, "The Struggles of Superwoman," 161–80.

180. Alissa Friedman, "The Necessity for State Recognition of Same-Sex Marriage: Constitutional Requirements and Evolving Notions of Family," *Berkeley Women's Law Journal* (1987–88), 134–70; Gretchen Stiers, "Transforming Family: Meanings, Practices and Laws Concerning Same-Sex Marriages," unpublished dissertation proposal, University of Massachusetts, Amherst, 1992.

181. Friedman, "The Necessity for State Recognition of Same-Sex Marriage," 141.

182. Lambda Legal Defense and Education Fund, *Domestic Partnership: Issues and Legislation* (New York: Sept. 1990).

183. Ben and Jerry Ice Cream, the *Village Voice,* the National Organization for Women, and Lotus.

184. Some of the cities that have enacted domestic partnership legislation or registration or executive orders include West Hollywood, Berkeley, Santa Cruz, Ithaca, Seattle, Laguna Beach, Los Angeles, Tacoma Park, Madison, and Washington, D.C.

185. Jean Seligman, "Variations on a Theme," in Arlene Skolnick and Jerome Skolnick, eds., *Family in Transition* (New York: HarperCollins Publisher, 1992), 162. Lambda Legal Defense and Education Fund, *Domestic Partnership: Issues and Legislation.*

186. Lambda Legal Defense and Education Fund, *Domestic Partnership: Issues and Legislation,* 4–6.

187. A 1988 General Social Survey, using a national sample of U.S. residents, found that only a total of 9 percent of the respondents either "strongly agreed" or "agreed" that "homosexual couples should have the right to marry" (General Social Survey, National Opinion Research Center, University of Chicago, Chicago, Illinois, 1988), Question 526J, 578.

188. Stiers, "Transforming Family," 14.

189. Friedman, "The Necessity for State Recognition of Same-Sex Marriage," 142; Paula Ettlebrick, "Since When Is Marriage a Path to Liberation?" *Outlook* 2 (Fall 1989), 14.

190. William Kingston and Steven L. Nock, "Time Together Among Dual-Earner Couples," *American Sociological Review* 52 (June 1987), 391–400; Bradley K. Googins, *Work Family Conflicts: Private Lives, Public Responses* (New York: Auburn House, 1991).

191. Suzanne M. Bianchi and Daphne Spain, *American Women in Transition* (New York: Russell Sage Foundation, 1986).

Gender-Role Socialization: Lessons in Femininity

Hilary M. Lips

WHEN TWO RESEARCHERS examined the creative writing of elementary-school children attending a "young authors conference" in Michigan, their findings with respect to gender roles were striking: Male characters outnumbered female ones in stories written by both girls and boys, and male characters were credited with more attributes—both positive ones, such as courageous and determined, and negative ones, such as mean and nasty—than were female characters (Trepanier & Romatowski, 1985). Most striking of all was the difference in the occupational roles assigned to female and male characters: Of 127 occupations assigned by the young authors to their protagonists, 111 (87 percent) were assigned to males and only 16 (13 percent) to females. The occupational assignments clearly reflected the assumption that females' capabilities limited them to gender-stereotypic jobs: The few roles allotted to female characters included those of princess, cook, hula dancer, teacher, babysitter, nurse, and housekeeper.

It is early indeed that children show an awareness of the message that males are active while females watch from the sidelines, and that females are generally less interesting and less important than males are and have narrower horizons and less impact on the world than males do. The (often inadvertent) bearers of this message include parents, peers, and teachers, with reinforcement from a variety of media sources and cultural institutions.

Childhood Socialization

PARENTS

Perhaps because it is one of the earliest distinguishing pieces of information available about a child, gender appears to be an important dimension of socialization for parents in virtually every cultural, ethnic, and class group. Among white, middle-class North American parents, female infants are viewed, as early as twenty-four hours after birth, as softer and more delicate than are their male counterparts (Rubin, Provenzano, & Luria, 1974). Mothers playing with another woman's six-month-old infant have been found to offer gender-stereotypic toys and to smile at and hold the baby more closely when told it is a girl than when told it is a boy (Will, Self, & Datan, 1976). Furthermore, parents provide their daughters and sons with different kinds of toys, games, and environmental surroundings (Bradbard, 1985; Lytton & Romney, 1991; Miller, 1987; Peretti & Sydney, 1985; Rheingold & Cook, 1975).

Though parents do not treat their young daughters and sons as differently as gender norms might suggest (Lytton & Romney, 1991), some apparently "minor" differences in childhood can lay the groundwork for larger differences later on. In this sense, parental gender-role socialization has a more global impact than merely the communication of a particular set of "gender-appropriate" behaviors. Girls and boys are taught by their parents to take different approaches to problem solving, to challenge, and to life in general. Specifically, parents are more likely to encourage dependency in daughters than in sons (Lytton & Romney, 1991). Noting the research showing that parents give male infants more stimulation and varied responses than they give to females, give more contingent responses to boys than to girls, and allow boys more freedom to explore than they do girls, Jeanne Block (1984) argued that boys are socialized to "develop a premise system that presumes or anticipates mastery, efficacy, and instrumental competence" (p. 131). The socialization practices directed at girls tend toward "fostering proximity, discouraging independent problem solving by premature or excessive intervention, restricting exploration, and discouraging active play" (p. 111). Speaking in even stronger terms, Block suggested that the end result of the differing patterns of socialization for females and males is that boys develop " 'wings'—which permit leaving the nest, exploring far reaches, and flying alone" (p. 137), while girls develop " 'roots'- —roots that anchor, stabilize and support growth" (p. 138), but allow fewer chances to master the environment.

Block's conclusions are supported by a wealth of research besides her own. For example, one study showed that parents used different strategies when working on jigsaw-puzzle and memory tasks with their six-year-old sons and daughters. They were more likely to try to teach general problem-solving strategies to their sons and to make specific solution suggestions to their daughters. With a daughter, parents were more likely to work with the child cooperatively and to provide her with information about whether her performance was correct. With a son, parents were more likely to be physically uninvolved in the task but to direct and order the child's activities and to give him praise (such as "You did well") or negative reactions (such as "Stop acting silly") (Frankel & Rollins, 1983). What these parents seemed to be communicating to their children is that it is more important for the sons than for the daughters that they not only solve this problem, but also learn how to solve others like it—and that they do it, as far as possible, on their own.

Other research also shows that parental behavior toward children may lay the groundwork for gender differences in patterns of thinking and problem solving. North American mothers' speech to their female and male toddlers differs significantly on dimensions thought to stimulate cognitive development. In one study, mothers used more questions, more numbers, more verbal teaching, and more action verbs when talking to their sons than they did when talking to their daughters (Weitzman, Birns, & Friend, 1985). Moreover, parents tend to expect more of their children in gender-stereotypic areas of performance and to communicate these differential expectations to children at a young age. For example, after tracking 1,100 children semester by semester over the first three grades of school, one research team found that boys developed higher expectations for their performance in mathematics than girls did, despite the fact that arithmetic marks and general aptitude were similar for girls and boys in the first grade. Boys' higher expectations for their own performance seemed to be related not to past performance or to teachers' evaluations but rather to mothers' expectations for their children's performance (Baker & Entwisle, 1987; Entwisle & Baker, 1983).

Even the different toys and play activities parents encourage for girls and boys influence not only children's conceptions of what activities are appropriate for females and males but also what thinking, problem-solving, and social skills these children develop. For example, when mechanical toys such as models and tools are defined as "boys' toys" and are not given to girls, the outcome is a chance for boys to develop both their spatial ability and the attitude that this ability is a peculiarly masculine one. A study by Cynthia Miller (1987) used adults' ratings to classify children's toys on twelve functional dimensions, illustrating that the toys selected as appropriate for boys and girls do differ in the kinds of skills they promote. Toys rated as "boys' toys" were also rated as high in the promotion of symbolic or fantasy play, competition, constructiveness (adding pieces or combining with another toy to create something new), handling, sociability, and aggressiveness; "girls' toys" were rated higher on manipulability (ease of removing and replacing parts), creativity, nurturance, and attractiveness.

Although parents in various cultural groups differ in the rules they attach to gender, it is not unusual to find that parents (particularly fathers, according to some research) pay more attention to boys than to girls, emphasize cooperation and nurturance more for girls and achievement and autonomy more for boys. For example, a study of Mexican families by Phyllis Bronstein (1984) showed that, when interacting with their school-aged children, fathers but not mothers listened more to boys than to girls and were more likely to show boys than to show girls how to do things. In contrast, they treated girls especially gently, but with a lack of full attention and a readiness to impose opinions on them. Overall, these fathers were communicating to their children that what boys have to say is more important than what girls have to say and that boys are more capable than girls are of learning new skills.

Within North American society, there are variations among groups in gender-role socialization. A number of studies have shown that gender stereotyping tends to be stronger and restrictions on girls greater in working-class than in middle-class families (McBroom, 1981; Rubin, 1976). Perhaps as a result, middle-class children's ideas about gender roles reflect more sharing of characteristics between the sexes than do those of working-class children (Romer & Cherry, 1980). Ethnicity is also linked to variations in parental gender-role socialization. Romer and Cherry (1980) found that black children viewed men and women as being equally emotionally expressive, whereas children from Jewish and Italian families thought it more characteristic of women than of men. Studies of both Mexican-American and Puerto Rican families indicate greater emphasis on feminine subservence and the wife-mother role for women than in non-Hispanic families (Garcia, 1991; Mirande, 1977; Fitzpatrick, 1971). The opposite is true of black families. While black parents are more concerned than white parents that girls be feminine and boys masculine (Dugger, 1991; Price-Bonham & Skeen, 1983), research suggests that they are less likely than are white families to polarize *behavioral* expectations. The female role in particular differs from that of white middle-class Americans. In black families female strength, independence, and resourcefulness are admired; weakness is not.

PEERS

As soon as they are old enough to have peers outside the home, children begin to rely heavily on these peers as a source on information and approval about social behavior. Peer interactions promote gender-role socialization first of all by a tendency to segregate the sexes. School-aged children tend to play in same-sex groups (Katz & Boswell, 1984; Maccoby, 1990), thus minimizing contact between girls and boys and promoting an "us–them" rhetoric that contributes to the exaggeration of female–male differences, self-serving gender prejudice on the part of both groups, and a tendency to react negatively to children who "break the rules" by behaving in non–gender-stereotypic ways. There is some evidence that peers even help to shape girls' and boys' different orientations toward mastery and power.

Researchers have found consistently that children evaluate their own gender group more positively than they do the other (Etaugh, Levine, & Mennella, 1984; Olsen & Willemsen, 1978). There is also strong evidence that preschoolers, kindergartners, and elementary-school children are active and effective at maintaining gender-stereotypic behavior in their peers. Very young children make harsh judgments about and punish other children, especially boys, who violate gender stereotypes (Fagot, 1977, 1984, 1985; Langlois & Downs, 1980). The girl who tries to join a boys' game is likely to be told "You can't play--you're a girl"; the boy who picks up a girls' toy is likely to be taunted "now you're a girl." Young children are also active in reinforcing peers who engage in gender-appropriate behavior, and the peers do adjust their behavior to conform to the gender roles thus enforced (Lamb, Easterbrooks, & Holden, 1980; Lamb & Roopnarine, 1979). When researchers interviewed children in kindergarten and in the second, fourth, and sixth grades about their attitudes toward hypothetical peers who violated gender-role norms, the vast majority of the children, while indicating that cross-gender behavior was not wrong, said that they would prefer not to associate with children who violated these norms (Carter & McCloskey, 1983/84). Reactions to cross-gender behavior were more negative among older than among younger children, suggesting that children become more sure of their gender stereotypes as they progress through elementary school. These children also reported that they would react more negatively toward males than toward females who exhibited cross-gender behavior. The negative reactions listed by children in the interviews indicate just how strong the gender stereotypes can be at a young age: "I would push him and call him a weirdo"; "I'd probably hit him and take away the doll"; "I'd call him a sissy and make fun of him"; "I wouldn't go anywhere near him." Other research indicates that same-sex peers are the most effective socializers: Girls respond more to the pressures of female peers, boys to those of male peers (Fagot, 1985). It is not clear whether children are aware of their power to keep their peers "in line" with gender-role expectations or even exactly what motivates them to exert these pressures. It is evident, however, that peers do act as strict enforcers of gender-role norms in the areas of activities, toy preference, friendship choices, and traits.

Not only do peers enforce gender roles in specific content areas, but they also play an important part in the creation and maintenance of gender-differentiated approaches to power, mastery, and influence. Among toddlers, the beginnings of gender differences in power and effectiveness can be noted in the finding that girls paired with male playmates behave more passively than do girls paired with other girls or than boys paired with either girls or boys, and that vocal prohibitions (such as "Stop! Don't do that!") are most likely to be ignored when addressed to a boy by a girl (Jacklin & Maccoby, 1978). Power is still problematic for females, even in elementary school. A study of first- and second-graders in same-sex groups showed that, although both the female and male groups were structured by power hierarchies that were maintained in essentially similar ways, reactions to power holders differed in female and male groups. Boys who held top positions in the hierarchy were liked and accepted by their peers; powerful girls, in contrast, were rejected (Jones, 1983).

Among preschoolers, boys make a greater number of influence attempts on their male and female peers than girls do—a difference that is almost entirely due to boys' greater use of "direct" requests and that becomes more pronounced with age (Serbin, Sprafkin, Elman, & Doyle, 1982). Between the ages of three and five years, boys become more likely to use influence attempts, such as ordering a peer to "give me the truck," announcing "you have to give me the truck," or specifying roles, as in "pretend you're the doctor." Across the same ages, girls become more likely to use "indirect" requests, in which either the request is implied rather than clearly spelled out (e.g., "I need the truck"), or it is bracketed in polite phrases (e.g., "May I please have the truck?"). Furthermore, boys become less and less responsive with age, from three to five, to peer influence attempts, particularly indirect requests, whereas the responsiveness of girls to influence attempts seems to be relatively stable across the same ages. Another interesting finding is that girls in this age range are more effective in their direct requests of other girls than in those of boys. The researchers suggest that the social effectiveness that girls experience with other girls, relative to boys, helps to perpetuate the high levels of same-sex play found in preschool classrooms, and that this sex segregation, in turn, fosters the development of increasingly differentiated verbal social influence styles and perhaps differences in cognitive and social problem-solving skills.

Even the way that children talk to one another underlines and reinforces differences in gender roles with respect to power. Research by Austin, Salehi, and Leffler (1987), who studied the discourse of samples of mainly white children from working- and middle-class homes, uncovered gender differences in the degree to which children "took charge" of conversations as opposed to simply facilitating continuing interaction. Boys of all ages studied (preschool, third, and sixth grades) were more likely than were girls to initiate conversations and to use verbal (e.g., "Hey, look at me") and nonverbal (e.g., tapping another child on the arm) attention-getting devices. Girls were more likely than were boys to say things that facilitated an ongoing conversational theme and to use reinforcers, especially positive ones, that acknowledged their partner's speech or behavior. These gender differences are similar to those that have been found for adults and suggest that peers play a role in the early development of patterns of conversational dominance by males. There may also be long-term consequences of these different interaction styles. Girls become accustomed through childhood patterns of female–female interaction to a cooperative style of communication that encourages listening and turn-taking in speaking. As young women, they may later feel uncomfortable and ineffective when they are working or socializing with males who take a more competitive approach to social interaction, in which speakers restrict one another's access to the conversation (Maccoby, 1990).

Peers may play a more important role in socialization for some groups than for others. For example, Ladner (1971), studying girls in a lower-class black American inner-city community, noted that the peer group had a broader function for these children than for their middle-class counterparts. The girls tended to have a lot of unsupervised contact with peers and began at an early age to rely heavily on them for company, emotional support, advice, comfort, and other intangible resources that might, in other groups, be expected to come from parents. Thus, according to Ladner, in poor inner-city communities, peers are an extremely important force in shaping black American girls' images of womanhood.

TEACHERS

Teachers' behavior adds to gender-role–socialization pressure as soon as children enter the educational system. Part of teacher influence occurs through the teachers' choice of textbooks and other curriculum materials that depict gender in traditional ways and present females as invisible or incompetent (e.g., Hahn & Blankenship, 1983; Marten & Matlin, 1976; Pursell & Stewart, 1990; United States Commission on Civil Rights, 1980; Weitzman & Rizzo, 1974). Moreover, teachers reinforce sex-differentiated activity patterns by introducing toys and play activities in gender-stereotypic ways (Serbin, Connor, & Citron, 1981; Serbin, Connor, & Iler, 1979). In one study, researchers asked teachers of preschoolers to introduce one of three toys to their classes each day: a magnetic fishing set, a set of sewing cards, and a number puzzle. To introduce the toy, they were to show it to the class and then call on four to six children to assist in demonstrating the toy and to try it out. When the toy in question was a fishing set (a stereotypically masculine toy), these teachers were far more likely to call on boys than on girls to demonstrate it, thus effectively restricting the play experience of the girls. For the other two toys, rated by observers as feminine and neutral respectively, the teachers showed no overall preference for either girls or boys as demonstrators (Serbin, Connor, & Iler, 1979). In a second study, the same researchers showed that gender-stereotyped introductions of toys to preschoolers lead the children to make gender-stereotypic toy choices. For example, when a teacher introduced a set of trucks and cars by saying "Daddies can go to work and drive a trailer truck" and then called on only boys to demonstrate the trucks, girls were much less likely to play with the trucks than they were when the teacher introduced the toys by saying "We can pretend to be policemen and policewomen driving the police car" and called on children of both sexes to demonstrate.

Perhaps the most important influence of teachers on the development of gender roles, however, is that teachers respond differently to girls and boys. Even in preschool, teachers, apparently unaware of the differential treatment they are handing out, pay more attention to boys and respond more to boys who act aggressive and to girls who act dependent (Serbin & O'Leary, 1975). Moreover, these researchers found that teachers actually teach boys more than they teach girls, with boys twice as likely as girls to receive individual instruction in how to do things. For example, in one classroom where the children were making paper baskets, it was necessary to staple the paper handles onto each basket. The teacher circulated through the room, helping each child individually to do this task. With boys, she held the handle in place and allowed the child to staple it; for girls, unless the child spontaneously stapled the handle herself, the teacher simply took the basket and stapled it for her rather than showing her how to do it.

Even teachers' evaluations of the intellectual competence of children is biased by gender-role considerations. For example, a preschool child's compliance to teachers does not significantly predict teachers' evaluations of that child's competence, providing the child is a boy. However, for girls, compliance to teachers is a significant factor in teacher evaluation of intellectual competence, with the less compliant girls being viewed as less competent (Gold, Crombie, & Noble, 1987). Even gender stereotypes with respect to physical appearance affect teachers' reactions to their young students. For example, the stereotype that females should be dainty and petite disadvantages girls who do not fit this mold. In one study, teachers of children in kindergarten through fourth grade rated each child's academic, athletic, and social skills. Girls who were larger and heavier than their peers were rated by teachers as lower in all three areas of skill. Moreover, teachers gave lower grades to these large girls. The same pattern was not found for teachers' ratings of boys (Villimez, Eisenberg, & Carroll, 1986).

In elementary-school classrooms, girls and boys are treated in ways that tend to produce relatively more feelings of control among boys and relatively more feelings of helplessness among girls. From preschool onward, teachers focus more on boys, spend more time interacting with boys than with girls, allow boys to talk and to interrupt them more in class, and even have more out-of-class conversations with boys (e.g., BenTsvi-Mayer, Hertz-Lazarowitz, & Safir, 1989; Brophy, 1985; Ebbeck, 1984). In addition, teachers punish girls and boys for different kinds of behaviors: girls for academic mistakes and boys for being disruptive. In contrast, when teachers praise students, they are more likely to be responding to good appearance or conduct for girls and good academic performance for boys (Dweck, 1975; Dweck, Goetz, & Strauss, 1980; Dweck & Leggett, 1988; Elliott & Dweck, 1988). Teachers also encourage girls and boys to react differently to the children's own mistakes. Boys are given more precise feedback and are encouraged to keep trying until they get the right answer; girls are more often told not to worry about a mistake, and teachers spend less time with them suggesting new approaches and encouraging them to keep trying. In fact, girls are often simply left in the dark about whether their answers are right or wrong (Sadker & Sadker, 1985).

Studies of teacher–student interactions that have included race as a variable suggest strongly that the classroom is a place where white middle-class conceptions of gender roles are enforced. Among elementary-school students, Irvine (1985) found that white females received significantly less total communication from teachers than did white males or black females or males. Moreover, when teacher–student interactions are examined across grade levels, it becomes clear that black females are being socialized by teachers to join their white sisters in invisibility. In early elementary school (grades K through 2), black girls do not receive less teacher feedback than do their male counterparts; by later grades (3 through 5), however, they fit the pattern of inconspicuousness and low salience to the teacher that holds for white girls from the beginning (Irvine, 1986). Irvine suggests that it is because black girls are not socialized to the passive and submissive behaviors encouraged in white girls that they receive more teacher attention than do white girls in the early grades. As noted by Lightfoot (1976), black female students in the classroom may be more likely to be seen as "assertive and bossy" than as fitting the white-female-student image of "submissive and cuddly" (p. 259). However, as found by Irvine (1986), as black girls move from lower to upper elementary-school grades, there is a significant decline in the total amount of teacher feedback they receive, in the amount of positive teacher feedback they receive, and in the number of opportunities to respond in class they are given. As Irvine notes, "Black female students present an active, interacting and initiating profile in the early grades but join their white female counterparts in the later grades in what appears to be traditional female sex role behaviors" (p. 20). The teachers in Irvine's study were predominantly white and female; this research leaves unanswered questions as to the importance of teacher race and sex, and of the race and gender composition of the classroom, in producing the patterns Irvine found.

Other research supports the notion that children's approach to school achievement is influenced by gender-role socialization and that these gender roles vary among ethnic groups. Studies of white middle-class children show that, as early as the third grade, boys begin to predict more successful performance for themselves than do females (Erkut, 1983; Vollmer, 1984). However, when samples include a high proportion of black and low-socioeconomic-status children, gender differences in expectations for success on specific tasks are not found (Fulkerson, Furr, & Brown, 1983). One reason for this may be that teachers tend to hold lower academic expectations for black males than for black females (Ross & Jackson, 1991). Even when it comes to actual achievement, the mediation of gender roles by cultural and ethnic factors is evident. In mathematics achievement, where studies of white middle-class children have generally shown an advantage for boys, some studies of black American children show no gender differences (Fulkerson, Furr, & Brown, 1983), and research on children of a number of different racial backgrounds in Hawaii shows a consistent advantage for females (Brandon, Newton, & Hammond, 1987).

SPECIFIC CONSEQUENCES OF CHILDHOOD SOCIALIZATION

Aggression.   Researchers generally agree that boys are more likely than are girls to behave in aggressive ways. The difference was noted by Maccoby and Jacklin (1974), after an extensive review of the literature, as one of the few female–male behavioral differences that is found consistently. Since then, the greater tendency of male than of female children toward such physical aggression as hitting and pushing has been demonstrated repeatedly in free-play situations (e.g., Archer & Westeman, 1981; Di Pietro, 1981), and boys have also been found to surpass girls in the use of verbal aggression such as insults (Barrett, 1979). Although well established, however, gender differences in aggression are neither large nor completely consistent. They are largest in situations in which expectations for female and male behavior differ most strongly (Eagly & Steffen, 1986). Janet Hyde's (1984) analysis of 143 studies indicated that the amount of variation in the aggressive behavior measured in these studies that can be attributed to gender is about 5 percent. Some researchers have noted that the apparent overall gender difference can sometimes be traced to extremely aggressive behavior by a few boys (Archer & Westeman, 1981).

It is clear that socialization plays an important part in the formation of whatever gender differences in aggression exist. For example, while cross-cultural research shows that, within any given society, boys tend to be at least slightly more aggressive than girls, the variation *among* societies in children's aggressive behavior is far more dramatic than is the gender difference. In some societies, children of both sexes have violent temper tantrums and learn to scream insults as soon as they learn to speak; in others, children tend not to quarrel at all. In fact, in any particular society, the level of aggression displayed by children of one sex is strongly and positively related to the level of aggression displayed by the other (Rohner, 1976, pp. 61–62). Clearly, social reactions to and tolerance of aggression affect the likelihood that children of either sex will engage in it.

Researchers have shown that, when girls and boys are similarly rewarded for aggressive behaviors, girls are as aggressive as boys (Bandura, 1973). It has been established, however, that boys are more rewarded by their peers than females are for aggressive behavior and that aggression in females meets with disapproval, even among children. One study showed that aggression by girls in the classroom was far more likely to be ignored, by both peers and teachers, than was aggression by boys. For the girls in this study, more than 50 percent of their aggressive actions received no response whatsoever (Fagot & Hagan, 1985). Since any response, either positive or negative, is better than none at all for maintaining a behavior, it is easy to see the large part that the social environment plays in making boys more aggressive than girls.

Performance on cognitive tests: language and mathematics.   For years, it was consistently reported in the psychological literature that females outperformed males on verbal tasks, while males outperformed females on quantitative and spatial tasks (Anastasi, 1937/1958; Hyde, 1981; Maccoby & Jacklin, 1974; Tyler, 1947/1965). Research comparing test performances of samples of children between 1947 and 1983 shows that gender differences in verbal performance, as well as in other cognitive skill areas, have declined drastically over the years (Feingold, 1988). A recent review of 165 studies found no gender differences in verbal performance, either across all types of verbal tests or within such specific tests as vocabulary, reading comprehension, and essay writing (Hyde & Linn, 1988). However, some researchers continue to report gender differences in verbal performance. For instance, a study of high school students in Japan and the United States indicated that in both countries girls averaged significantly higher scores than boys on a word fluency test (Mann, Sasanuma, Sakuma, & Masaki, 1990).

The gender gap in mathematics performance is also decreasing (Friedman, 1989; Hyde, Fennema, & Lamon, 1990) and is often negligible. The latter review showed that gender differences in mathematics performance were greater for white Americans than for black, Hispanic, or Asian Americans or for Canadian or Australian samples. A similar pattern of larger gender differences in samples of white American students than in studies based on minority samples is reported by Friedman (1989).

Until early adolescence, most studies show no gender differences in performance on general mathematics achievement tests—a finding that holds across a variety of cultures (Lummis & Stevenson, 1990). Girls show a slight advantage in computation in elementary and middle school. Some studies find that boys do better than girls on one type of quantitative performance, mathematical problem solving, as early as the first grade (Lummis & Stevenson, 1990). However, gender differences favoring males in mathematical problem solving appear most reliably in high school and are maintained or increased in college. About 43 percent of high school females and 57 percent of high school males would score above the average score for the whole high school sample (Hyde et al., 1990).

On the whole, gender differences seem to be smallest, and may favor females, when the samples studied are from the general population. The differences are larger with more selective samples and appear largest for samples of highly precocious persons (Hyde et al., 1990). There are some indications that gender and social class interact with respect to mathematics achievement test results. Smaller gender differences in performance are found in samples from lower than from higher socioeconomic groups (Fischbein, 1990).

Despite the finding that by high school males tend to outperform females on standardized tests of mathematical problem solving, girls often obtain higher grades in mathematics than boys do (Kimball, 1989). This fact, along with the wide individual variation within each gender group, is frequently ignored when people use cognitive gender differences as a basis for arguing that girls and boys are naturally suited for different kinds of tasks and should prepare for different kinds of work.

Because the differences are so small, they cannot explain the large differences in occupation. For example, Hyde (1981), making the initial assumption that a person would have to be in the top 5 percent of the range of spatial abilities to be qualified for a profession such as engineering, calculated that, if spatial ability were the only determining factor, the ratio of males to females in such professions would be 2 to 1. Since the ratio of men to women in engineering is currently 25 to 1, gender differences in spatial ability could conceivably explain only a small part of the male dominance of the engineering professions.

The gender difference in mathematics achievement is linked more strongly to gender-role socialization than to ability differences. Parents and teachers have differing expectations for girls and boys, and these expectations are communicated early. One study of the parents of mathematically gifted children in the Johns Hopkins Talent Search found that the boys' parents were considerably more likely than were the girls' parents even to be aware that their child was mathematically talented (Tobias, 1982), and parents of boys were more likely than were parents of girls to have given their children science-related gifts, such as science kits, telescopes, and microscopes (Astin, 1974). Parents tend to credit their sons' success in mathematics more to talent and their daughters' success more to effort (Yee & Eccles, 1988). Furthermore, even within the same class, girls and boys tend not to get the same education. When one team of researchers observed thirty-three second-grade teachers in the classroom, they found that these teachers spent more time teaching reading than mathematics to individual girls and more time teaching mathematics than reading to individual boys (Leinhardt, Seewald, & Engel, 1979).

A large-scale study of Baltimore first-graders indicates that, even as children enter school, girls and boys have already begun to learn that different things are important (Entwisle, Alexander, Pallas, & Cardigan, 1987). At this stage, academic competence and the student role formed a more important and distinct aspect of self-concept for boys than for girls. Boys were more concerned with learning quickly; girls were more concerned with obeying rules and being honest. Being able to do arithmetic was an important aspect of the academic self-concept for boys; for girls, it was irrelevant. The girls did not view their ability in mathematics as relevant to their academic self-image, even though they did as well in mathematics as the boys did and were exposed to the same mathematics instruction classes as the boys. Where do these differences come from? The study suggests that, for girls at least, they originate partly in parental expectations—and parental expectations of girls focus strongly on "being good" rather than on academic achievement. However, when data for black children and white children in this study are examined separately, it appears that black parents give a less gender-stereotypic message about mathematics to their daughters than white parents do. For black girls, but not for white girls, parents' mathematics-achievement expectations were significant predictors of their daughters' academic self-image.

Socialization in Adolescence

By adolescence, the impact of gender-role socialization centers on two major issues: vocational decisions and sexuality. For girls much more than for boys, these two issues are linked, since the girls have observed by this time that adult women make a lot more compromises between work and family relationships than men do. As girls struggle with decisions in these areas, parental, peer, and teacher socialization influences continue to be important. A theme from childhood that continues to be present is that girls are frequently given the message that they have little control over their lives.

For girls, physical maturation—such as the development of breasts and a more sexually mature appearance—is associated with early pressures in the direction of the traditional female role. Parents, worried about pregnancy, often place new restrictions on girls at this stage, so that growing up is associated with a feeling of loss of freedom rather than with one of expanding horizons (Golub, 1983; Katz, 1986). Under such conditions, early marriage, or even pregnancy, is sometimes idealized by the young girl as an escape from parental pressures and a chance to take control of her life and to prove that she is grown up and responsible. This kind of situation can tip the balance of the career versus family conflict in the direction of family at such an early age that the girl does little exploration of occupation-related possibilities. A girl who is physically well developed at an early age faces especially strong pressure to emphasize relationships at the expense of achievement. She receives reinforcement earlier than do her peers for following a traditional feminine "script," reducing the likelihood that she will explore less traditional alternatives, such as a career (Katz, 1986). Also, to the extent that males keep the role of initiator in the heterosexual dating arena, a girl often finds herself in a situation where she is passively waiting to be "asked out" rather than feeling that she has active control over her relationships or her leisure time. In the realm of sexuality also, girls have traditionally been taught that whatever control they have is of a reactive (and negative) nature—the power to say no (or, in special circumstances, yes), but not that to initiate sexual interactions. Thus, even if a girl has survived childhood with her sense of control and effectiveness intact, the interpersonal issues she encounters in adolescence are likely to shake her feelings of efficacy.

A common gender stereotype is that women are less motivated than are men by a need for achievement, but research has not supported this notion. What the research does suggest is that women, from adolescence onward, are faced with pressures to balance their achievement needs against their desire for relationships, and for marriage and family. For female adolescents planning their future, the potential conflict between work and family life can be intense. Young women are more likely than are young men to expect to have to be flexible in their work roles in order to have a family life (Herzog & Bachman, 1982). Thus, even a young woman with high occupational aspirations and commitment has probably learned to consider her future parental and spouse-support roles as more important than, or even incompatible with, her future work role. Such considerations are frequently encouraged by parents and teachers, and they may snowball as female adolescents watch their peers and siblings begin to marry. A girl is led to feel at this stage that she cannot, or should not, assert the independent control of her life that choosing a demanding occupational path entails. She is encouraged to prepare for a variety of options and to remain flexible, rather than to become committed to a particular personal goal (Angrist, 1969). The message received by adolescent girls is often that they will have to adapt their career goals to the needs of a future spouse and family. Moreover, the pressure to make marriage and family a primary concern increases as these young women approach the end of their schooling or when they become involved seriously with a particular boyfriend (Weitzman, 1984).

Children list parents as one of the primary sources of information about education and occupations (Farmer, 1985; Kidd, 1984). Furthermore, parental encouragement and expectations, and the values parents place on achievement and on the homemaker role for women, are influential for educational and occupational plans. It has long been acknowledged, for example, that parental encouragement to attend college is linked to high occupational aspirations among teenage girls (Picou & Curry, 1973). In a rare longitudinal study that followed adolescents and their parents from seventh to twelfth grades, Perrone (1973) showed that changes in the behavior parents valued in their daughters seemed to precede changes in the daughters' occupational values. When the daughters reached early high school, many parents began to value their development of homemaking skills and domestic orientation. The communi-cation of these values may have been important in the development of new occupational values among the daughters, for by late high school these girls' most frequently voiced occupational values had changed from self-fulfillment to working with people and helping others. At this stage, for the first time in this study, their occupational aspirations were lower than were those of their male counterparts.

By the end of high school, many girls have finally accepted the message that having a marriage, home, and family will conflict with occupational goals—and they reduce their occupational goals accordingly. In fact, gender-role socialization apparently leads women to lower their vocational goals even before they begin the process of choosing a specific occupation. According to a model proposed by Corder and Stephan (1984), young women plan their future in two stages: First they decide how they will combine family and work roles, then they decide on an occupation. In the first stage, because they perceive that men dislike career-oriented women and because they have been taught to value marriage and family more than a career, most adolescent women rule out occupations that are high in prestige or in required commit-ment. Then, in the second stage, the choice of a specific occupation is made from a range that has been drastically limited by decisions made in the first stage. Corder and Stephan's research supports not only their notion of a two-stage process in adolescent women's vocational decisions but also the validity of the young women's perceptions of men's preferences. The adolescent men in their sample showed a definite lack of enthusiasm for future marriage to career-oriented women.

Young women's sensitivity to men's preferences may be a factor in these women's avoidance of mathematical and technical fields. Male high school and college students believe more strongly than their female peers do that women are not suited to mathematics and science (Temple & Lips, 1989) and that women will have difficulty combining family responsibilities with demanding scientific careers (Lips, 1992). Concomitantly, among both black and white college women, aspiring to careers in male-dominated occupations is asso-ciated with less traditional attitudes toward gender roles (Murrell, Frieze, & Frost, 1991).

Research indicates that young women are continuing to base their occupational choices on gender-stereotyped perceptions of family roles (Leslie, 1986). Such choices, rather than reflecting a lack of awareness of the options available to women, may, as Jane Gaskell (1985) argues, indicate their realistic assessment of the situation. In her study of high-school girls from working-class families, Gaskell (1981) found that many of them were choosing business courses and planning for clerical jobs, even though they readily admitted that they found the courses boring. They persisted in this choice, however, because they knew it would lead to employment, and finding a job after graduation was crucial. Moreover, these young women were reluctant to plan for demanding occupations, since their own family experiences led them to believe that, if they married, they would have the primary responsibility for domestic work and that their paid work outside the home would have to take second priority. Thus, a young woman's realistic assessment of a gender-unequal labor market and family support system may lead her to make traditional choices when planning her future work. They employment situation may be assessed somewhat differently by girls from upper middle-class families, who do have more options for continuing their education. Among these young women, there has been an increase in the percentage who aspire to high-status, nontraditional occupations (Geller, 1984; Institute for Women's Policy Research, 1991).

An important factor in socialization for achievement is the presence of models. Where girls are provided with achieving female models, their attitudes toward success and career attainment seem to be favorably affected. The literature on maternal employment indicates that, in middle-class families, daughters of employed mothers have higher educational and occupational aspirations than do daughters of women who are full-time homemakers (Etaugh, 1974; Hoffman, 1984; Stein & Bailey, 1973). Daughters of employed women also regard the professional competence of women more highly than do daughters of women who are full-time homemakers (Baruch, 1972), and there is a correspondence between mothers' and daughters' career interests and aspirations (Zuckerman, 1981). Among black female university students, those pursuing nontraditional careers were more likely than were their more traditional counterparts to have mothers who were well educated and were working in nontraditional fields themselves (Burlew, 1982).

Parental socialization of daughters for work is an area in which race and class differences in the conception of gender roles are substantial. For example, most researchers agree that in white working-class families, the pressures on daughters to conform to the traditional female role are greater than those that exist in white middle-class families (McBroom, 1981). However, in black working-class families, the notion of what is "traditional" for women is quite different from the notion of the full-time homemaker role idealized by working-class whites. For black women, it is, in fact, "traditional" to participate in the labor force, and some researchers have argued that black women's long-term experience in the work force has profoundly influenced these black women's ideology of gender (Gump, 1980; Malson, 1983). For example, in a heterogeneous sample of urban black women interviewed by Malson (1983), 95 percent had mothers who had been employed, usually full-time, when they were children. As Malson quotes one of these women, "I'd never known a woman who stayed home with children . . . I did not know any housewives. That form of life was kind of alien. I did not even know that was possible. When I found out that people actually only stayed home and did nothing but raise children and clean house, I thought it was fascinating. . . I always assumed I'd work and have children" (p. 107).

Research suggests that black females are socialized to assume that they must take some economic responsibility for family support (Peters & de Ford, 1978; Smith, 1982). It is sometimes assumed that this means that these women place less value on family roles than on work roles, but this assumption is not supported by evidence. Young black women have been found to be equally predisposed toward work and homemaking–childrearing (Engram, 1980; Gump, 1975). In fact, a recent study of gender-role attitudes among southern college students revealed that blacks were more likely than were whites to believe that a woman's real fulfillment in life comes from motherhood, *and* that blacks were more likely than whites to believe that it was appropriate for a mother with school-aged children to work outside the home (Lyson, 1986). It is clear that the black students had not been socialized as strongly as had the white students to see motherhood and employment as mutually exclusive.

Black women are not the only group for whom cultural traditions and some isolation from mainstream middle-class socialization pressures have resulted in less gender-stereotyped perceptions of work. One team of researchers studying the attitudes of seventh-grade Navajo children in reservation schools found them to have less gender-stereotyped perceptions of occupations than had any other group studied (Beyard-Tyler & Haring, 1984). The researchers attribute the lack of sterotyping to lack of information about the dominant culture; however, an additional factor is probably the longstanding tradition of flexibility in male–female work roles among the Navajo (Griffin, 1984).

In school settings, the role of teachers and counselors in guiding women toward particular occupational choices can be crucial. Unfortunately, the evidence indicates that such resource persons are generally not very good at providing students with information about options that are gender-nontraditional (Eccles & Hoffman, 1984). For young minority women, this problem is compounded by the dual effects of racism and sexism. Studies have found that black female students tend to be steered toward low-level, blue-collar jobs, while their white counterparts are oriented toward white-collar occupations (Baker & Levenson, 1975) and that counselors discourage minority women from going to college or channel them into traditional nonscientific majors (Alexander, 1979). This problem has been noted as an especially strong reason for Native American women's clustering in low-paid occupations (Metoyer, 1979; Abella, 1984). In fact, the low occupational status of both Native American women (Abella, 1984) and Hispanic-American women (Ortiz & Cooney, 1984) has been linked to low levels of education—a factor that may well reflect teacher and counselor influence.

Most of the literature on women's socialization in adolescence is characterized by a concern with the tension implicit in the role demands placed on women. According to tradition, women are supposed to be preparing to be wives and mothers, yet increasingly they are also expected to be preparing for a lifetime of employment. Much of this preparation takes place in the context of expectations that, in most marriages, when work and family demands conflict, the woman will have to make more compromises than the man will and the woman will be saddled with more than half of the domestic responsibilities. If, as they contemplate this prospect, young women feel ambivalent about the wholehearted pursuit of achievement goals, as studies show they do (Weitzman, 1984), it is hardly surprising. It seems a reasonable prediction that, even if socialization pressures on girls increasingly stress achievement, girls' realistic appraisal of the difficulties of combining family and job demands in a culture that still refuses to consider women's occupational lives as comparable in importance to men's occupational lives will contribute to reluctance to pursue demanding careers. By the time young women reach the end of adolescence, they have accumulated years of experience of being less influential than males—of receiving less attention, getting less feedback, being taken less seriously. It would be surprising indeed if most of these young women, finding themselves at the point in their lives where the pressures to find a marriage partner and start a family are strongest, were to resist social expectations and to refuse to marry unless they had an agreement with their partner of complete equality or to decide not to marry or have children at all.

Finally, there is no reason to assume that the family goals that young women have been taught to value are any less important than the achievement goals so often stressed for young men (Eccles, 1987). If members of either gender group choose at times to compromise work success in favor of family obligations, there is perhaps more cause for celebration than alarm—except that in our present society the economic costs of such choices are substantial, and they fall disproportionately on women. As young women face choices about work and family, there is much in their socialization that has prepared them for the necessary compromises and less that has prepared them for the necessary firmness in pursuit of their own goals. The challenge for them, and for society as a whole, is to find an appropriate balance.

REFERENCES

Abella, Judge Rosalie S. (1984). *Equality in employment: A royal commission report.* Ottawa: Canadian Government Publishing Centre.

Alexander, Vicki (1979). The nature of professional training for minority women: An overview. In Lucy Ann Geiselman (Ed.), *The minority woman in America: Professionalism at what cost?* (pp. 15–25). San Francisco: University of California.

Anastasi, Anne (1937/1958). *Differential psychology: Individual and group differences in behavior.* New York: Macmillan.

Angrist, Shirley S. (1969). The study of sex roles. *Journal of Social Issues, 25,* 215–32.

Archer, John, & Westeman, Karin (1981). Sex differences in the aggressive behaviour of school-children. *British Journal of Social Psychology, 20,* 31–36.

Astin, Helen (1974). Sex differences in mathematical and scientific precocity. In Julian C. Stanley, D. P. Keating, & Lynn Fox (Eds.), *Mathematical talent: Discovery, description and development.* Baltimore: Johns Hopkins University Press.

Austin, Ann M. B. A., Salehi, Mahshid, & Leffler, Ann (1987). Gender and developmental differences in children's conversations. *Sex Roles, 16* (9/10), 497–510.

Baker, David P., & Entwisle, Doris R. (1987). The influence of mothers on the academic expectations of young children: A longitudinal study of how gender differences arise. *Social Forces, 65* (3), 670–94.

Baker, Sally Hillsman, & Levensen, Bernard (1975). Job opportunities of black and white working-class women. *Social Problems, 2,* 510–33.

Bandura, Albert (1973). *Aggression: A social learning analysis.* Englewood Cliffs, NJ: Prentice-Hall.

Barrett, David E. (1979). A naturalistic study of sex differences in children's aggression. *Merrill Palmer Quarterly, 25* (3), 193–203.

Baruch, Grace K. (1972). Maternal influence upon college women's attitudes toward women and work. *Developmental Psychology, 6,* 32–37.

BenTsvi-Mayer, S., Hertz-Lazarowitz, R., & Safir, M. P. (1989). Teachers' selections of boys and girls as prominent pupils. *Sex Roles, 21,* 231–45.

Beyard-Tyler, Karen, & Haring, Marilyn J. (1984). Navajo students respond to nontraditional occupations: Less information, less bias? *Journal of Counseling Psychology, 31* (2), 270–73.

Block, Jeanne H. (1984). Psychological development of female children and adolescents. In Jeanne H. Block, *Sex role identity and ego development* (pp. 126–42). San Francisco: Jossey-Bass.

Block, Jeanne H., Block, Jack, & Morrison, A. (1981). Parental agreement-disagreement on child-rearing orientations and gender-related personality correlates in children. *Child Development, 52,* 965–74.

Bradbard, Marilyn R. (1985). Sex differences in adults' gifts and children's toy requests at Christmas. *Psychological Reports, 56,* 969–70.

Brandon, Paul R., Newton, Barbara J., & Hammond, Ormond W. (1987). Children's mathematics achievement in Hawaii: Sex differences favoring girls. *American Educational Research Journal, 24* (3), 437–61.

Bronstein, Phyllis (1984). Differences in mothers' and fathers' behavior toward children: A cross-cultural comparison. *Developmental Psychology, 20* (6), 995–1003.

Brophy, J. (1985). Interactions of male and female students with male and female teachers. In L. C. Wilkinson & C. B. Marrett (Eds.), *Gender influences in classroom interaction* (pp. 115–42). Orlando, FL: Academic Press.

Burlew, Ann Kathleen (1982). The experiences of black females in traditional and nontraditional professions. *Psychology of Women Quarterly, 6* (3), 312–26.

Carter, D. Bruce, & McCloskey, Laura A. (1983/84). Peers and the maintenance of sex-typed behavior: The development of children's conceptions of cross-gender behavior in their peers. *Social Cognition, 2* (4), 294–314.

Corder, Judy, & Stephan, Cookie White (1984). Females' combinations of work and family roles: Adolescents' aspirations. *Journal of Marriage and the Family, 46,* 391–402.

Di Pietro, Janet A. (1981). Rough and tumble play: A function of gender. *Developmental Psychology, 17* (1), 50–58.

Dugger, K. (1991). Social location and gender-role attitudes: A comparison of black and white women. In J. Lorber & S. A. Farrell (Eds.), *The social construction of gender* (pp. 38–59). Newbury Park, CA: Sage.

Dweck, Carol S. (1975). The role of expectations and attributions in the alleviation of learned helplessness. *Journal of Personality and Social Psychology, 31,* 674–85.

Dweck, Carol S., Goetz, Therese E., & Strauss, Nan L. (1980). Sex differences in learned helplessness: IV: An experimental and naturalistic study of failure generalization and its mediators. *Journal of Personality and Social Psychology, 38,* 441–52.

Dweck, Carol S., & Leggett, Ellen L. (1988). A social-cognitive approach to motivation and personality. *Psychological Review, 95,* 256–73.

Eagly, Alice H., & Steffen, Valerie J. (1986). Gender and aggressive behavior: A meta-analytic review of the social psychological literature. *Psychological Bulletin, 100,* 309–30.

Ebbeck, M. (1984). Equity issues for boys and girls: Some important issues. *Early Child Development and Care, 18* (1/2), 119–31.

Eccles, Jacquelynne S. (1987). Gender roles and women's achievement-related decisions. *Psychology of Women Quarterly, 11* (2), 135–72.

Eccles, Jacquelynne S., & Hoffman, Lois W. (1984). Sex roles, socialization, and occupational behavior. In H. W. Stevenson & A. E. Siegel (Eds.), *Research in child development and social policy: Volume 1* (pp. 367–420). Chicago: University of Chicago Press.

Elliott, E. S., & Dweck, Carol S. (1988). Goals: An approach to motivation and achievement. *Journal of Personality and Social Psychology, 54,* 5–12.

Engram, E. (1980). Role transition in early adulthood: Orientations of young black women. In La Frances Rodgers-Rose (Ed.), *The black woman.* Beverly Hills, CA: Sage Publications.

Entwisle, Doris R., Alexander, Karl L., Pallas, Aaron M., & Cardigan, Doris (1987). The emergent academic self-image of first graders: Its response to social structure. *Child Development, 58* 1190–1206.

Entwisle, Doris R., & Baker, D. P. (1983). Gender and young children's expectations for performance in arithmetic. *Developmental Psychology, 19* (2), 200–209.

Erkut, Sumru (1983). Exploring sex differences in expectancy, attribution, and academic achievement. *Sex Roles, 9,* 217–31.

Etaugh, Claire (1974). Effects of maternal employment on children: A review of recent research. *Merrill Palmer Quarterly, 20,* 71–98.

Etaugh, Claire, Levine, Diane, & Mennella, Angela (1984). Development of sex biases in children: 40 years later. *Sex Roles, 10,* 911–22.

Fagot, Beverly I. (1977). Consequences of moderate cross-gender behavior in preschool children. *Child Development, 48,* 902–7.

Fagot, Beverly I. (1984). Teacher and peer reactions to boys' and girls' play styles. *Sex Roles, 11,* 691–702.

Fagot, Beverly I. (1985). Beyond the reinforcement principle: Another step toward understanding sex role development. *Developmental Psychology, 21* (6), 1097–1104.

Fagot, Beverly I., & Hagan, Richard (1985). Aggression in toddlers: Responses to the assertive acts of boys and girls. *Sex Roles, 12* (3/4), 341–51.

Farmer, Helen S. (1985). Model of career and achievement motivation for women and men. *Journal of Counseling Psychology, 32,* 363–90.

Feingold, A. (1988). Cognitive gender differences are disappearing. *American Psychologist, 43* (2), 95–103.

Fischbein, S. (1990). Biosocial influences on sex differences for ability and achievement test results as well as marks at school. *Intelligence, 14* (1), 127–39.

Fitzpatrick, J. (1971). *Puerto Rican Americans: The meaning of migration.* Englewood Cliffs, NJ: Prentice-Hall.

Frankel, Marc T., & Rollins, Howard A., Jr. (1983). Does mother know best? Mothers and fathers interacting with preschool sons and daughters. *Developmental Psychology, 19* (5), 694–702.

Friedman, L. (1989). Mathematics and the gender gap: A meta-analysis of recent studies on sex differences in mathematical tasks. *Review of Educational Research, 59* (2), 185–213.

Fulkerson, Katherine Fee, Furr, Susan, & Brown, Duane (1983). Expectations and achievement among third-, sixth-, and ninth-grade black and white males and females. *Developmental Psychology, 19* (2), 231–36.

Garcia, A. M. (1991). The development of Chicana feminist discourse. In J. Lorber & S. A. Farrell (Eds.), *The social construction of gender* (pp. 269–87). Newbury Park, CA: Sage.

Gaskell, Jane (1981). Sex inequalities in education for work: The case of business education. *Canadian Journal of Education, 6* (2), 54–72.

Gaskell, Jane (1985). Course enrollment in the high school: The perspective of working-class girls. *Sociology of Education, 58,* 48–59.

Geller, Gloria (1984). Aspirations of female high school students. *Resources for Feminist Research, 13* (1), 17–19.

Gold, Dolores, Crombie, Gail, & Noble, Sally (1987). Relations between teachers' judgments of girls' and boys' compliance and intellectual competence. *Sex Roles, 16* (7/8), 351–58.

Golub, Sharon (1983). Menarche: The beginning of menstrual life. *Women & Health, 8* (2/3), 17–36.

Griffin, J. (1984). Culture contact, women and work: The Navajo example. *Social Science Journal, 21* (4), 29–39.

Gump, Janice (1975). A comparative analysis of black and white women's sex-role attitudes. *Journal of Consulting and Clinical Psychology, 43,* 858–63.

Gump, Janice (1980). Reality and myth: Employment and sex role ideology in black women. In F. Denmark & J. Sherman (Eds.), *The psychology of women.* New York: Psychological Dimensions.

Hahn, C., & Blankenship, G. (1983). Women and economics textbooks. *Theory and Research in Social Education, 11* (3), 67–75.

Herzog, A. R., & Bachman, J. G. (1982). *Sex-role attitudes among high school seniors.* Ann Arbor, MI: Institute for Social Research, University of Michigan.

Hoffman, Lois W. (1984). Maternal employment and the young child. In M. Perlmutter (Ed.), *Mother/child interaction and parent/child relations in child development* (pp. 101–28). Hillsdale, NJ: Lawrence Erlbaum Associates.

Hyde, Janet S. (1981). How large are cognitive gender differences? A meta-analysis using ω and δ. *American Psychologist, 36,* 892–901.

Hyde, Janet S. (1984). How large are gender differences in aggression? A developmental meta-analysis. *Developmental Psychology, 20* (4), 722–36.

Hyde, Janet S., Fennema, Elizabeth, & Lamon, S. J. (1990). Gender differences in mathematics performance: A meta-analysis. *Psychological Bulletin, 107* (2), 139–55.

Hyde, Janet S., & Linn, Marcia C. (1988). Gender differences in verbal ability: A meta-analysis. *Psychological Bulletin, 104* (1), 53–69.

Institute for Women's Policy Research (1991). *The thirty-five million: The status of young women* (research-in-brief). Washington, DC: Author.

Irvine, Jacqueline Jordan (1985). Teacher communication patterns as related to the race and sex of the student. *Journal of Educational Research, 78* (6), 338–45.

Irvine, Jacqueline Jordan (1986). Teacher–student interactions: Effects of student race, sex, and grade level. *Journal of Educational Psychology, 78* (1), 14–21.

Jacklin, Carol Nagy, & Maccoby, Eleanor Emmons (1978). Social behavior at thirty-three months in same-sex and mixed-sex dyads. *Child Development, 49,* 557–69.

Jones, Diane C. (1983). Power structures and perceptions of power holders in same-sex groups of young children. *Women and Politics, 3,* 147–64.

Katz, Phyllis A. (1986). Gender identity: Development and consequences. In R. D. Ashmore & F. K. Del Boca (Eds.), *The social psychology of female–male relations* (pp. 21–67). Orlando, FL: Academic Press.

Katz, Phyllis A., & Boswell, S. L. (1984). Sex-role development and the one-child family. In T. Falbo (Ed.), *The single-child family.* New York: Guilford Press.

Kidd, J. M. (1984). Young people's perceptions of their occupational decision-making. *British Journal of Guidance and Counseling, 12,* 15–38.

Kimball, Meredith (1989). A new perspective on women's math achievement. *Psychological Bulletin, 105,* 198–214.

Ladner, Joyce A. (1971). *Tomorrow's tomorrow: The black woman.* Garden City, NY: Doubleday.

Lamb, Michael E., Easterbrooks, M. Ann, & Holden, George W. (1980). Reinforcement and punishment among preschoolers: Characteristics, effects, and correlates. *Child Development, 51,* 1230–36.

Lamb, Michael E., & Roopnarine, Jaipaul L. (1979). Peer influences on sex-role development in preschoolers. *Child Development, 50,* 1219–22.

Langlois, Judith H., & Downs, A. Chris (1980). Mothers, fathers, and peers as socialization agents of sex-typed play behaviors in young children. *Child Development, 51,* 1237–47.

Leinhardt, G., Seewald, A. M., & Engel, M. (1979). Learning what's taught: Sex differences in instruction. *Journal of Educational Psychology, 71,* 432–39.

Leslie, Leigh A. (1986). The impact of adolescent females' assessments of parenthood and employment on plans for the future. *Journal of Youth and Adolescence, 15,* 29–50.

Lewis, Diane K. (1975). The black family: Socialization and sex roles. *Phylon, 36* (3), 221–37.

Lightfoot, S. L. (1976). Socialization and education of young black girls in school. *Teachers College Record, 78,* 239–62.

Lips, Hilary M. (1992). Gender- and science-related attitudes as predictors of college students' academic choices. *Journal of Vocational Behavior, 40,* 62–81.

Lummis, M., & Stevenson, H. W. (1990). Gender differences in beliefs and achievement: A cross-cultural study. *Developmental Psychology, 26* (2), 254–63.

Lyson, Thomas A. (1986). Race and sex differences in sex role attitudes of southern college students. *Psychology of Women Quarterly, 10* (4), 421–28.

Lytton, H., & Romney, D. M. (1991). Parents' differential socialization of boys and girls: A meta-analysis. *Psychological Bulletin, 109* (2), 267–96.

Maccoby, Eleanor E. (1990). Gender and relationships: A developmental account. *American Psychologist, 45* (4), 513–20.

Maccoby, Eleanor E., & Jacklin, Carol N. (1974). *The psychology of sex differences.* Stanford, CA: Stanford University Press.

Malson, Michelene Ridley (1983). Black women's sex roles: The social context for a new ideology. *Journal of Social Issues, 39* (3), 101–14.

Mann, V. A., Sasanuma, S., Sakuma, N., & Masaki, S. (1989). Sex differences in cognitive abilities: A cross-cultural perspective. *Neuropsychologia, 28* (10), 1063–77.

Marten, Laurel A., & Matlin, Margaret W. (1976). Does sexism in elementary school readers still exist? *The Reading Teacher, 29,* 767–76.

McBroom, William H. (1981). Parental relationships, socioeconomic status, and sex role expectations. *Sex Roles, 7,* 1027–33.

Metoyer, Cheryl A. (1979). The Native American woman. In Eloise C. Snyder (Ed.), *The study of women: Enlarging perspectives of social reality* (pp. 329–35). New York: Harper & Row.

Miller, Cynthia L. (1987). Qualitative differences among gender-stereotyped toys: Implications for cognitive and social development in girls and boys. *Sex Roles, 16* (9/10), 473–87.

Mirande, Alfredo (1977). The Chicano family: A reanalysis of conflicting views. *Journal of Marriage and the Family, 39,* 747–56.

Murell, Audrey J., Frieze, Irene Hanson, & Frost, Jacquelyn L. (1991). Aspiring to careers in male- and female-dominated professions: A study of black and white college women. *Psychology of Women Quarterly, 15* (1), 103–26.

Olsen, Nancy J., & Willemsen, Eleanor W. (1978). Studying sex prejudice in children. *The Journal of Genetic Psychology, 133,* 203–16.

Ortiz, Vilma, & Cooney, Rosemary Santana (1984). Sex-role attitudes and labor force participation among young Hispanic females and non-Hispanic white females. *Social Science Quarterly, 65* (2), 392–400.

Peretti, Peter O., & Sydney, Tiffany M. (1984). Parental toy choice stereotyping and its effect on child toy preference and sex-role typing. *Social Behavior and Personality, 12* (2), 213–16.

Perrone, Philip A. (1973). A longitudinal study of occupational values in adolescents. *Vocational Guidance Quarterly, 22,* 116–23.

Peters, M., & de Ford, C. (1978). The solo mother. In R. Stables (Ed.), *The black family: Essays and studies.* Belmont, CA: Wadsworth.

Picou, J. Steven, & Curry, Evans W. (1973). Structural, interpersonal and behavioral correlates of female adolescents' occupational choices. *Adolescence, 8,* 421–32.

Pollard, D. S. (1982, November). Perspectives of black parents regarding the socialization of their children. Paper presented at the Seventh Conference on Empirical Research in Black Psychology, Hampton, Virginia.

Price-Bonham, Sharon, & Skeen, Patsy (1982). Black and white fathers' attitudes toward children's sex roles. *Psychological Reports, 50,* 1187–90.

Pursell, P., & Stewart, L. (1990). Dick and Jane in 1989. *Sex Roles, 22* (3/4), 177–85.

Reid, Pamela Trotman (1985). Sex-role socialization of black children: A review of theory, family, and media influence. *Academic Psychology Bulletin, 7,* 201–12.

Rheingold, Harriet L., & Cook, Kaye V. (1975). The contents of boys' and girls' rooms as an index of parents' behaviors. *Child Development, 46,* 459–63.

Rohner, Ronald P. (1976). Sex differences in aggression: Phylogenetic and enculturation perspectives. *Ethos, 4* (1), 57–72.

Romer, Nancy, & Cherry, Debra (1980). Ethnic and social class differences in children's sex-role concepts. *Sex Roles, 6,* 245–63.

Ross, Sandra I., & Jackson, Jeffrey M. (1991). Teachers' expectations for black males' and black females' academic achievement. *Personality and Social Psychology Bulletin, 17* (1), 78–82.

Rubin, Jeffrey Z., Provenzano, Frank J., & Luria, Zella (1974). The eye of the beholder: Parents' views on sex of newborns. *American Journal of Orthopsychiatry, 44,* 512–19.

Rubin, Lillian (1976). *Worlds of pain: Life in the working class family.* New York: Basic Books.

Sadker, Myra, & Sadker, David (1985, March). Sexism in the schoolroom of the '80s. *Psychology Today, 19,* 54–57.

Serbin, Lisa A., Connor, Jane M., & Citron, Cheryl C. (1981). Sex-differentiated free play behavior: Effects of teacher modeling, location and gender. *Developmental Psychology, 17,* 640–46.

Serbin, Lisa A., Connor, Jane M., & Iler, Iris (1979). Sex-stereotyped and non-stereotyped introductions of new toys in the preschool classroom: An observational study of teacher behavior and its effects. *Psychology of Women Quarterly, 4,* 261–65.

Serbin, Lisa A., & O'Leary, K. Daniel (1975, December). How nursery schools teach girls to shut up. *Psychology Today, 9* (7), 56–58, 102–3.

Serbin, Lisa A., Sprafkin, Carol, Elman, Meryl, & Doyle, Anna-Beth (1982). The early development of sex-differentiated patterns of social influence. *Canadian Journal of Behavioural Science, 14* (4), 350–63.

Smith, Elsie J. (1982). The black female adolescent: A review of the educational, career, and psychological literature. *Psychology of Women Quarterly, 6* (3), 261–88.

Stein, Aletha H., & Bailey, Margaret M. (1973). The socialization of achievement orientation in females. *Psychological Bulletin, 80* (5), 345–66.

Temple, Linda, & Lips, Hilary M. (1989). Gender differences and similarities in attitudes toward computers. *Computers in Human Behavior, 5,* 215–26.

Tobias, Sheila (1982, January). Sexist equations. *Psychology Today,* 14–17.

Trepanier, Mary L., & Romatowski, Jane A. (1985). Attributes and roles assigned to characters in children's writing: Sex differences and sex-role perceptions. *Sex Roles, 13* (5/6), 263–72.

Tyler, Leona (1947/1965). *The psychology of human differences.* New York: Appleton-Century-Crofts.

U.S. Commission on Civil Rights (1980). *Characters in textbooks.* Washington, D.C.: U.S. Government Printing Office.

Vaughn, Brian E., Block, Jeanne H., & Block, Jack (1988). Parental agreement on child rearing during early childhood and the psychological characteristics of adolescents. *Child Development, 59,* 1020–33.

Villimez, Carolyn, Eisenberg, Nancy, & Carroll, James L. (1986). Sex differences in the relation of children's height and weight to academic performance and to others' attributions of competence. *Sex Roles, 15* (11/12), 667–81.

Vollmer, Fred (1984). Sex differences in personality and expectancy. *Sex Roles, 11,* 1121–39.

Weitzman, Lenore J. (1984). Sex-role socialization: A focus on women. In Jo Freeman (Ed.), *Women: A Feminist Perspective,* third edition (pp. 157–237). Palo Alto, CA: Mayfield.

Weitzman, Lenore J., & Rizzo, Diane (1974). *Images of males and females in elementary school textbooks.* New York: National Organization for Women's Legal Defense and Education Fund.

Weitzman, Nancy, Birns, Beverly, & Friend, Ronald (1985). Traditional and nontraditional mothers' communication with their daughters and sons. *Child Development, 56,* 894–98.

Will, Jerrie, Self, Patricia, & Datan, Nancy (1976). Maternal behavior and perceived sex of infant. *American Journal of Orthopsychiatry, 46,* 135–39.

Yee, Doris K., & Eccles, Jacquelynne S. (1988). Parent perceptions and attributions for children's math achievement. *Sex Roles, 19,* 317–33.

Zuckerman, Diana M. (1981). Family background, sex-role attitudes, and life goals of technical college and university students. *Sex Roles, 7,* 1109–26.

Supermoms and Second Shifts: Marital Inequality in the 1990s

Janice M. Steil

I. A Historical Context

The status of married women has been described as extending along a continuum from wife as property to wife as equal partner, with wife as complement and wife as junior partner as intermediary steps (Scanzoni, 1972). Prior to the Civil War married women had many duties but few rights. They were not permitted to control their property, even when it was theirs by inheritance. A husband had the right to his wife's wages, to decide on the education and religion of their children, and to punish his wife if she displeased him. The wife's property status was based on the English common law, which declared that

> the legal existence of the wife is merged in that of the husband so that, in law, the husband and wife are one person. . . . The husband's dominion over the person and property of the wife is fully recognized. She is utterly incompetent to contract in her own name. He is entitled to her society and her service; to her obedience and her property. . . . In consideration of his married rights the husband is bound to furnish the wife a home and suitable support (*Phillips v. Graves*, 1870).

II. The Persistence of Inequality

Over the last two decades there has been increased interest in the other end of the spectrum, wife as equal partner. A 1989 Gallup poll of 1,234 randomly selected adults from across the country found that a majority (57 percent) now believe that the ideal marriage is one in which both the husband and the wife have jobs and share in the responsibilities of childrearing and caring for the home (DeStefano & Colasanto, 1990). This marks an increase of 9 percent over a twelve-year period. A significant minority (37 percent), however, maintained that the traditional roles of man as provider and woman as homemaker are best. But what do these findings really mean? Is an endorsement of wives "having jobs" an endorsement of wives having jobs of equally high status and pay with an equal responsibility to provide for their families financially? Is an endorsement of "sharing" in childrearing and caring for the

I wish to thank Shielagh Shusta, Karen Bruchhauser, and Susan Rosenbluth, students at the Derner Institutute who helped in the preparation of this chapter. I also thank Faye Crosby, Francine Deutsch, and Judy Worell for their many perceptive comments on an earlier version.

149

home an endorsement of husbands' having equal responsibility or spending equal time in either realm?

In the same Gallup poll in which 57 percent of respondents endorsed sharing, over 70 percent reported that women did all or most of the laundry, meal preparation, gift buying, childcare, shopping, dish washing, and bill paying. Husbands reportedly did more than wives on three tasks: minor home repairs, yard work, and car maintenance. Looking at this issue from the other direction, the percentage of husbands in dual-earner families who shared the work of the home equally has been shown to range from a low of 2 percent to a high of 20 percent (Ferree, 1991; Hochschild, 1989; Nyquist, Slivken, Spence, & Helmreich, 1985).

And what about women's jobs? A look at employment statistics shows that women continue to be employed in numbers and hours and for earnings well below those of men (Bureau of Labor Statistics, 1990; Taueber, 1991). Indeed, even when dual-earner wives achieve high-status positions, their careers are likely to be considered secondary. Both men and women generally report that a husband's job is more important than his wife's. As a result, employed wives are more likely than their husbands to take time off if children are sick or problems with childcare arise. Eighty-nine percent of the Gallup poll respondents said that the wife rearranged her schedule when a child became ill (DeStefano & Colasanto, 1990). Are husbands, then, still entitled to their wives' "society and service"? Are wives still entitled to "suitable support"? Or have behavioral changes failed to keep pace with attitudinal shifts?

THE ALLOCATION OF DOMESTIC WORK

According to some estimates, employed wives in the 1980s did 60 to 64 percent of the total housework, compared to the 67 to 70 percent of all household labor they did in the 1970s (Berk, 1985; Ferree, 1991). Others, using aggregate time measures, suggest that husbands now typically do about 20 percent of the household work, compared to the approximately 15 percent that they did earlier. As with the Gallup poll respondents, *what* husbands and wives do continues to be divided along gender lines. Further, the tasks that wives do are more likely to be those that are done on a daily basis, while those that husbands do are intermittent and discretionary. This results in a significant difference in the number of hours husbands and wives spend in household work.

Berk (1985) found that wives averaged approximately eight and one-half hours per day on household work, compared to husbands' three and one-quarter hours per day, or thirty-five hours more per week. Huber and Spitze (1983) found that full-time housewives spent fifty-two hours per week, employed wives twenty-six hours per week, and husbands about eleven hours per week. Hochschild (1989) labeled women's extra hours of work at home the "second shift." According to Hochschild, woman's second shift is equal to an extra month of twenty-four-hour days every year.

Overall, research studies have found the following:

1. Over the last two decades all women have reduced their time in housework. Employed wives have reduced their time in household work more

than unemployed wives, but neither group has reduced it by much (Berk, 1985; Coverman & Sheley, 1986; Ferree, 1991).

2. Husbands have not picked up the slack, and husbands of both employed and unemployed women do considerably less housework than their wives (Pleck, 1985; Huber & Spitze, 1983).

3. Employed women more often purchase household services than rely on additional assistance from family members. Yet, only between 14 and 20 percent of wives obtained paid housekeeping help on a regular basis (typically one day a week). Employed women are no more likely than nonemployed women to have cleaning help. It is a matter of who can afford it (Berheide, 1984; DeStefano & Colasanto, 1990).

4. Husbands of employed wives have increased the social time they spend with their children, especially when they are of preschool age, but not time spent in physical care (Pleck, 1985; Thompson & Walker, 1989). Both parents do almost equal amounts of educating and socializing of children, but wives do much more of the day-to-day physical care (Hochschild, 1989).

DECISION MAKING

Some studies have assessed the relative equality of relationships by asking partners how decision making is shared. A review of decision-making studies conducted in the 1960s and 1970s showed that women who worked outside the home had more influence in decision making than women who were housewives. Overall, however, there was little evidence that egalitarian decision making was the norm (Steil, 1983). A study of over 7,000 married men and women published the same year as the review of earlier studies showed some change. Approximately 60 percent of respondents reported relatively equal influence in decision making. The more a woman earned, the greater her influence (Blumstein & Schwartz, 1983).

RELATIONSHIP MAINTENANCE

Other studies have asked respondents what was important to them in a relationship. Of 144 elements, men and women rated being committed to the relationship, being sociable and pleasant to be with, leading an interesting and varied life, taking care of the children, and being attentive as the most important. Both men and women reported that women contributed far more in each of these areas than their partners (VanYperen & Buunk, 1990).

Kidder, Fagan, and Cohn (1981) asked men and women what they each contributed to their relationship. Men reported that they contributed more than women in three areas: finances, intelligence, and physical attractiveness. Women reported that they contributed more in six areas: (1) liking the other person and showing it, (2) committing oneself to the other person and the future of the relationship, (3) remembering special occasions, (4) being thoughtful about sentimental things, (5) showing affection, and (6) contributing time and effort to household responsibilities.

EQUALITY VERSUS INEQUALITY

Steil and Whitcomb (1992) asked dual-career husbands and wives how they conceptualized marital equality. Respondents were asked if they knew any couples who had a relationship they considered equal. They were then asked to identify what it was about that couple's relationship that led them to characterize it as equal. They were also asked if they knew of a couple whose relationship they would characterize as unequal and what it was that made them think of it that way.

The most frequent response to both questions was "task sharing." This was true despite the fact that the majority of respondents in this sample employed outside help with housework and all had help with childcare. One male respondent described a couple whose marriage he considered equal as follows: "They both have important, demanding jobs, and they share pretty much equally in the at-home and childcare duties." A female respondent described a couple whose "marriage is unequal because the wife has much more responsibility for the child and the home and doesn't think that it's appropriate to challenge it. She's a career woman and just assumes those responsibilities. She's content with what I think of as real inequality." For this sample, then, the distribution of responsibility at home and at work was the most salient indicator of the relative equality or inequality of the relationships.

Relationship characteristics was the second most frequent response. This category included items such as the ability to communicate, equal commitment, a sense of reciprocity, and mutual respect. Equal voice in decision making was mentioned with moderate frequency, but it was mentioned more in its absence as an indicator of unequal relationships than it was in its presence, as an indicator of equality. Resources, in terms of earning equal pay or having similar jobs, was mentioned somewhat infrequently and cited primarily as a characteristic of equal relationships.

The respondents in this study judged relationships as equal using the same standards as the social scientists. Across all criteria, studies show little evidence that equality is the norm. Husbands continue to bear a disproportionate responsibility for the financial support of the family. Women's careers are still considered secondary, and wives still bear the disproportionate responsibility for the home, children, and relationship maintenance.

III. The Benefits of Equality

A number of sociological and psychological investigators have assessed the relationship between the relative equality of a marriage and the partners' satisfaction with their relationships and psychological well-being.

DECISION MAKING AND SATISFACTION

Gray-Little and Burks (1983) reviewed twelve studies assessing the relationship between equality, measured as influence in decision making, and marital satisfaction. The highest levels of marital satisfaction were linked to perceptions of equal influence in eight of the twelve studies and to husband-dominant decision making in two. Wife dominance was reported least often and was associated with the lowest satisfaction levels. Syncratic decision making, in which most decisions were made jointly, was associated with greater satisfaction than autonomic decision making, in which equal numbers of separate decisions were made by each partner.

Lange and Worell (1990) looked at personal power using an adapted measure of decision-making say. They found that husbands were more satisfied with their relationships when say in decision making was equal or when they had more voice than their wives. Husbands were least satisfied with their relationships when their wives had more influence in decision making than husbands did. Women were more satisfied with relationships when voice in decision making was equal than when there was an imbalance in either direction. Furthermore, individuals who reported an equal balance of power gave and received higher levels of communal nurturance (i.e., positive regard, empathy, affirmation, and acceptance) than those in relationships of unequal power balance, regardless of which partner was more dominant.

Two other studies looked at influence in decision making but focused on the effects on the dominant partner when the relative say was unequal. These studies found that respondents who perceived themselves as controlling decision making rated themselves more favorably than their partners; expressed less affection for their partners; were less attracted to their partners, less satisfied and less happy with the relationship; and had lower levels of sexual satisfaction (Kipnis, Castell, Gergen, & Mausch, 1976; Kipnis, Cohn, & Catalno, 1979).

RESPONSIBILITY SHARING AND DYSPHORIA

Other studies have examined the relationship between equality and spouses' psychological well-being, specifically depressive or dysphoric symptomatology (e.g., feeling blue, feeling worthless, tiring easily, or losing interest in sex). Each study used different measures, and none of the studies actually selected their samples on the basis of whether or not the marriage was equal or unequal. Indeed, most relationships were unequal. Some assessed the extent to which husbands "help," which is very different from husbands' and wives' having equal responsibility. Yet, even with these caveats, the studies suggest that more equal relationships are psychologically beneficial, especially for women.

VanFossen (1981) found that employed wives who described their relationships as "reciprocal" were less likely to be depressed than those whose relationships were perceived as unreciprocal. As well, all wives, whether or not they were employed, were less depressed when they perceived their husbands as willingly "helpful," as compared to when they did not. Ross, Mirowsky, and Huber (1983) found that the more a husband helped, the less depression his wife reported, and this was true for all wives, whether or not they worked outside the home. Both of these studies used large national samples. A study examining the relationship between equality and well-being among Hispanic women found the same results. The more their husbands helped at home, the less mental distress Hispanic wives reported (Kranau, Greer, & Valencia-Weber, 1982).

Steil and Turetsky (1987) assessed equality in terms of responsibility across three areas: decision making, childcare, and a number of traditionally male and female domestic tasks. The sample consisted of 815 dual-earner couples.

Employed mothers reported less equality in their relationships than husbands or employed wives without children. Responsibility for childcare was reported as unequal by husbands and wives alike, but the more responsibility a husband assumed, the fewer dysphoric symptoms his wife experienced. Employed mothers who had equal responsibility for decision making reported fewer symptoms than mothers who had either more or less responsibility than their partners. Finally, increased household responsibility was associated with fewer dysphoric symptoms for childless husbands but, contrary to prediction, with increased symptomatology for mothers. A number of studies have found that the more hours of household work men do, the more couples fight about housework (Berk, 1985; Blumstein & Schwartz, 1983). Thus, a possible explanation for the mothers' increased symptomatology is that the stress of the arguments undermined the benefits of the help.

These studies assessed relationship equality in a number of different ways. Yet, across these diverse measures the general pattern of findings seems to support equality as a desirable basis for marriage. More equal relationships were characterized by more communal nurturance, more mutually supportive communication, less manipulative forms of influence, and greater sexual and marital satisfaction. Greater equality was also consistently associated with less dysphoric symptomatology for wives, who were usually the underbenefited partner when relationships were unequal.

IV. Explaining Inequality

TIME AVAILABILITY

If equality is indeed beneficial, why does inequality persist? One explanation focuses on the issue of time availability. Because husbands spend more time in outside employment, they simply do not have the same amount of time as their wives do to spend on household labor. This explanation is essentially unsupported by the empirical evidence. While there is some evidence that husbands may decrease their household labor when their work demands increase (Biernat & Wortman, 1991), there is little evidence of the reverse. Husbands do not increase their participation in household labor in any significant way when work demands lessen.

The reverse is true for women. According to Pleck (1985), wives appear to reduce their family time relatively little when employed, and wives who are employed the same number of hours as their husbands nonetheless perform much more family work. Even if a husband is unemployed, he does much less housework than a wife who puts in a forty-hour week. According to Blumstein and Schwartz (1983), this is the case even among couples who profess egalitarian ideals, including equal sharing of the work that has to be done in the house.

RESOURCE DIFFERENCES

A second explanation posits that wives have less influence and do more work at home because they provide fewer outside resources to the family (Blood & Wolfe, 1960; Scanzoni, 1972). Husbands' jobs provide more money and status than wives', and these are exchanged for greater authority and less work at home (Scanzoni, 1972). Indeed, the more successful a husband is, the less power his wife is likely to have (see Steil, 1983, for a review). Further, the higher a husband's income, the more likely his wife is to endorse the legitimacy of his power (Scanzoni, 1972). For husbands, then, access to resources *is* exchanged for greater power at home.

But does access to resources reap the same rewards for women? The most stringent test of resource theory to date showed that women whose salaries and job prestige exceeded their husbands' still didn't achieve equality. Women who earned one-third more than their spouses had more say in decision making and did less childcare and housework than women who earned a third less than their husbands. Yet, in neither case was the sharing equal. Women retained greater responsibility for household tasks and childcare, while their husbands maintained a greater say in financial matters (Steil & Weltman, 1991). Access to resources, then, is not associated with identical outcomes for husbands and wives. It does not make work allocations gender-free, and resources alone do not equalize the burden for men and women of integrating the responsibilities of work and family life. While access to material resources may be a prerequisite to change, it is not by itself sufficient to achieve such change.

THE CULTURAL CONTEXT: THE PROVIDER ROLE

The resource position is unable to fully explain the gender gap in household labor and child care because it fails to consider the social context in which negotiations over equal sharing take place. Our society continues to endorse separate gender roles, and these give different meaning to the waged work of husbands and wives (Thompson & Walker, 1989).

Sixty percent of wives with children under the age of six are now employed. Twenty-seven percent of wives now have higher earnings than their husbands (Bureau of Labor Statistics, 1991), yet wives' earnings are still considered secondary because, culturally, their husbands retain the role of primary provider. Thompson and Walker (1989) assert that in working-class families, husbands of women with full-time, unionized jobs see their wives' paid work as making an essential contribution to the whole family because it provides almost half (45 percent) of the family income, yet these wives are still seen as secondary wage earners rather than as coproviders. In white middle-class families, a wife may be seen as working out of choice rather than necessity. As a result, her employment is viewed not from the perspective of family provision but as an opportunity for self-development that conflicts with her primary role of nurturer.

In 1983, Blumstein and Schwartz, studying a national sample of adults, found that less than one-quarter of all wives felt that it was not important for their husbands to furnish them with financial security. Other studies have found that between 52 and 54 percent of wives, and 68 percent of husbands, in dual-earner couples believed that earning income is *solely* the husband's responsibility (Haas, 1986; Vannoy-Hiller & Philliber, 1989). Even though the women in these studies were employed, the majority said that earning income was their husband's responsibility, and 68 percent of their husbands agreed.

The higher a man's income relative to his wife's, the better he feels about himself as a parent and as a spouse (Biernat & Wortman, 1991). The higher a woman's income relative to her husband's, the worse she feels about herself as a spouse. Women still expect to be supported by their husbands, and husbands' identity and self-esteem are still largely derived from success in the provider role. While there is some variability—black couples have the most experience with sharing family income provision, and white middle- and upper-class couples have the least—endorsement of the husband's provider role seems to pervade both racial and class differences.

When a wife earns more than her husband, it creates tensions that partners address in a number of ways. Hochschild (1989) has shown that couples will go to great lengths to conceal a high-earning wife's income. Biernat and Wortman (1991) found that when academic women earned more than their partners, their husbands did less childcare. After eliminating a number of possible explanations, they concluded that these high-earning wives "absolved" their husbands from childcare responsibilities in order to compensate for the negative feelings evoked by their high salaries. Other studies have shown that women in nontraditional managerial and professional positions are more likely to become divorced, leave the labor force, or move to a lower-status position than women in traditional jobs. This pattern is more salient when the wife's position is similar in status to her husband's than when her position is of lower status (Philliber & Hiller, 1983).

COSTS OF SUPPORTING AND VIOLATING THE MALE PROVIDER ROLE

Most women in heterosexual relationships seem to believe that husbands can and should earn more than their wives (Haas, 1986). They are apprehensive of the potential costs to themselves, their partners, and the relationship when this norm is violated. Yet endorsing the male provider role entails its own costs. In couples where either spouse endorses the provider role, the husband is more powerful, regardless of his partner's income (Blumstein & Schwartz, 1983). When a husband earns more than his wife, he says that his career is more important than hers and she agrees. When a wife earns more than her husband, neither husbands nor wives say that the wife's career is more important (Steil & Weltman, 1991). Yet, in at least three studies of dual-career couples, the best predictor of the relative equality of the relationship was how important a wife said her career was relative to her spouse's career (Biernat & Wortman, 1991; Steil & Turetsky, 1987; Steil & Weltman, 1991). Endorsement of the male provider role leads women to view their husbands' job as primary and to minimize the importance of their own work. Yet the less important they say their own job is relative to their husbands', the less likely they are to achieve equal sharing at home.

THE PROVIDER ROLE: LESBIAN RELATIONSHIPS

Lesbian relationships offer a marked contrast to the gender-role–based relationships of heterosexual marriages. Women in lesbian relationships generally forego any expectation of economic security provided by marriage and accept a lifelong responsibility to support themselves (Eldridge & Gilbert, 1990). As a result, two-paycheck families are far more common among lesbian than heterosexual couples. Lange and Worell (1990), in a study that compared 100 women in heterosexual and lesbian relationships, found that women in lesbian relationships were more likely to be employed, were more likely to be employed full-time, and, on average, earned higher salaries than their heterosexual counterparts.

Others have found that lesbian, as compared to heterosexual, relationships are more likely to resemble friendships with the added component of romantic and erotic attraction (Peplau, 1981). Instead of treating one another as "husband" and "wife," homosexual partners have been found to treat one another as best friends and to develop patterns of interaction based on the unique individual characteristics of each partner (Harry & DeVall, 1978). There has been little empirical support for the stereotype of one partner assuming a traditionally masculine role while the other assumes a traditionally feminine role (Bell & Weinberg, 1978; Blumstein & Schwartz, 1983; Lynch & Reilly, 1985/86; Peplau, Cochran, Rook, & Padesky, 1978).

Peplau and her colleagues found that 97 percent of a sample of lesbian women said that partners should have exactly equal say in relationships (Peplau, Cochran, Rook, & Padesky, 1978). Kurdek and Schmitt (1986) found that lesbian partners had higher shared decision-making scores than either male gay, heterosexual married, or heterosexual cohabiting couples. Lange and Worell (1990), using a multi-item measure of perceived personal and partner power, found that 63 percent of the heterosexual sample and 84 percent of the lesbian sample were in relationships characterized by a balance of power between partners. Furthermore, equal power was consistently associated with greater relationship satisfaction (Eldridge & Gilbert, 1990; Lange & Worell, 1990) and liking for each other (Caldwell & Peplau, 1984).

Does access to resources work the same way in lesbian relationships? The evidence is mixed. Caldwell and Peplau (1984) found that women with lower income tended to have less power. Blumstein and Schwartz (1983), in a study of over 6,000 couples, found that for partners in male gay, heterosexual married, and heterosexual cohabiting couples, the amount of money earned affected relative power in the relationship. Lesbian relationships were the only ones in which power balance was not determined by either partner's income. The authors concluded that men, who have learned in the workplace that money equals power, have imposed this same equation at home. All lesbian relationships are not equal. However, women in relationships with other women may be more likely to have a partner who shares that ideal, and they may be less likely to adopt traditional gender roles that impede the achievement of equality.

V. Gender Differences in Entitlement

Inequality persists due to the acceptance of separate gender roles more than any other factor. For a man, the provider role carries the obligation to earn and provide for his family. This entitles him to put his career above his wife's, frees him from a number of responsibilities at home, and entitles him to greater influence. For a woman, the provider role is not socially approved. It is incongruent with her gender role and assumed to interfere with her role as nurturer. Thus, even when she earns more than her husband, she is not entitled to view her career as primary or to significantly decrease her house-hold work. Unlike her husband, it would not be acceptable for her to claim that her waged work kept her from her children (Thompson & Walker, 1989). Thus, women more than men continue to adapt their work schedules around their children. Husbands, employers, and women themselves continue to view childcare as the woman's rather than the family's responsibility, just as provid-ing is viewed as the man's responsibility. This allows husbands to put their waged work ahead of other family responsibilities. It also allows employers to continue to define equality at work as equality with men under conditions established for men without home responsibility (Cook, 1992).

THE ROLE OF SOCIAL COMPARISONS

Separate gender roles create fundamental differences in men's and women's sense of responsibilities and entitlements. These are internalized in the socialization process (see Steil, in press, for a more complete discussion of gender differences in entitlement) and maintained through a process of social comparison that relies on comparisons to similar, usually same-sex, others: I am entitled to what others like me are entitled to.

Hochschild (1989, p. 49) relates the story of Nancy, an avowed egalitarian: "In the past, Nancy had compared her responsibilities at home, her identity, her life to Evan's (her husband)." Yet, as time went on, Nancy changed her comparison:

> Now, to avoid resentment, she seemed to compare herself more to other working mothers. By this standard she was doing great. Nancy also compared herself to single women who had moved further ahead in their careers, but they fit into another mental category. . . . A single woman could move ahead in her career, but a married woman has to do a wife's work and mother's work as well. She did not make this distinction for men.

When Nancy compared her responsibilities at home, her identity, and her life to Evan's, she found herself dissatisfied with her life. So she switched her comparison to other working mothers and improved her self-evaluation.

Studies show that Nancy is not unique. Like Nancy, most women compare themselves to other women rather than to their husbands (Hay & Steil, 1992). And, as for Nancy, this serves to reduce their dissatisfaction with their re-lationships. VanYperen and Buunk (1991) found that women who compared themselves to other women were more satisfied with their marriages and their lives than women who compared their lives to those of their partners. They also compared for different reasons. Women who compare to other women are more likely to say they do so for reasons of similarity. As one woman said, "Women think along the same lines about relationships. Our needs as females are different from those of men." Women who compare themselves to their spouses are more likely to say they do so for reasons of fairness. A woman who compared herself to her husband said, "[I'd compare to] my partner definitely, because as partners, we are equal and should be putting in and getting out the same things in the relationship" (Hay & Steil, 1992).

Hochschild concluded that only 18 percent of the wives in her study were married to men who shared the "second shift." Yet, most of the other wives were not trying to change the division of labor. They were either "super-moming, cutting back their hours at work, or cutting back at home. They complained, they joked, they sighed fatalistically, they collected a certain moral credit for doing so much" (Hochschild, 1989, p. 259). They accepted the burdens of the "second shift" as "their" problem. They lacked a sense of entitlement to equal sharing and consequently lacked the moral outrage necessary to sustain the press for change in the face of their husbands' resistance.

The literature shows that women in unequal relationships pay significant costs in terms of career achievement, loss of leisure, and impaired well-being. They experience increased fatigue and dysphoria as well as lowered self-esteem. Men also pay a cost in being part of a less-satisfying relationship and in the loss of close relationships with their children. Yet, when women and men were asked who benefits most from an equal relationship, the most frequent response (56 percent) by men and women alike was "both." The second most frequent response as to who benefits most was "women" (29 percent). Not a single man or woman said that husbands would be the primary beneficiaries of equal relationships (Steil & Whitcomb, 1992). Thus, while men have much to gain, they are also perceived as having much to lose (Crosby, 1991). As a result, husbands are unlikely to provide the impetus for change. Indeed, they will resist it. Furthermore, due to the confidential and privatized nature of relationships, it is unlikely that the major impetus for change will come from without. This means the burden is on women to renegotiate traditional gender roles. On some level, women already know the costs of inequality. They are delaying marriage and childbearing. They also fear the possibility of divorce. Yet, as women disproportionately bear the costs of relationships that are unequal, so they must disproportionately assume the burden of initiating and enforcing change.

Seven years ago, after reviewing the literature on inequality in intimate relationships, I concluded that women, if they are to achieve equality, must perceive it as their entitlement (Steil, 1984). The first step may require a change in women's object of comparison: we are entitled not to what others like us (other tired, employed mothers) are entitled to, but to the same responsibilities and entitlements as our partners. Only then can women achieve equality.

REFERENCES

Bell, Alan, & Weinberg, Martin (1978). *Homosexualities: A study of diversity among men and women.* New York: Simon and Schuster.

Berheide, Catherine W. (1984). Women's work in the home: Seems like old times. *Marriage and Family Review,* 7(3–4), 37–55.

Berk, Sarah F. (1985). *The gender factory: The apportionment of work in American households.* New York: Plenum.

Biernat, Monica, & Wortman, Camille B. (1991). Sharing of home responsibilities between professionally employed women and their husbands. *Journal of Personality and Social Psychology,* 60, 844–60.

Blood, Robert O., & Wolfe, Donald M. (1960). *Husbands and wives.* New York: Free Press.

Blumstein, Philip, & Schwartz, Pepper (1983). *American couples.* New York: William Morrow.

Bureau of Labor Statistics (1990). *Employment and earnings,* vol. 37.

Bureau of Labor Statistics (1991). *Employment and earnings,* vol. 38.

Caldwell, Mayta, & Peplau, Letitia Anne (1984). The balance of power in lesbian relationships. *Sex Roles, 10,* 587–99.

Cook, Alice (1992). Can work requirements accommodate to the needs of dual-earner families? In Suzan Lewis, Dafna Izraeli, & Helen Hootsmans (Eds.), *Dual-earner families.* London: Sage.

Coverman, Shelley, & Sheley, Joseph (1986). Change in men's housework and child-care time. *Journal of Marriage and the Family, 48*(2), 413–22.

Crosby, Faye (1991). *Juggling.* New York: Free Press.

DeStefano, Linda, & Colasanto, Diane (1990). The gender gap in America: Unlike 1975, today most Americans think men have it better. *Gallup Poll News Service, 54*(37), 1–7.

Eldridge, Natalie S., & Gilbert, Lucia A. (1990). Correlates of relationship satisfaction in lesbian couples. *Psychology of Women Quarterly, 14,* 43–62.

Ferree, Myra Marx (1991). The gender division of labor in two-earner marriages. *Journal of Family Issues, 12*(2), 158–80.

Gray-Little, Bernadette, & Burks, Nancy (1983). Power and satisfaction in marriage: A review and critique. *Psychological Bulletin, 93*(3), 513–38.

Haas, Linda (1986). Wives' orientation toward breadwinning: Sweden and the United States. *Journal of Family Issues, 7*(4), 358 -81.

Harry, Joseph (1983). Gay male and lesbian relationships. In E. Macklin & R. Rubin (Eds.), *Contemporary families and alternative lifestyles* (pp. 216–33). Newbury Park, CA: Sage.

Harry, Joseph, & DeVall, William (1978). *The social organization of gay males.* New York: Praeger.

Hay, Jennifer, & Steil, Janice (1993). *Social comparison choices and entitlement in intimate relationships.* Paper presented at the meeting of the Eastern Psychological Association, Washington, DC.

Hochschild, Arlie (1989). *The second shift.* New York: Viking.

Huber, Joan, & Spitze, Glenna (1983). *Sex stratification, children, housework, and jobs.* New York: Academic Press.

Kidder, Louise, Fagan, Michelle, & Cohn, Ellen (1981). Giving and receiving: Social justice in close relationships. In Melvin Lerner & Sally Lerner (Eds.), *The justice motive in social behavior* (pp. 235–59). New York: Plenum Press.

Kipnis, David, Castell, Patricia J., Gergen, Mary, & Mausch, Donna (1976). Metamorphic effects of power. *Journal of Applied Psychology, 61,* 127–35.

Kipnis, David, Cohn, Ellen S., & Catalno, Ralph (1979). *Power and affection.* Paper presented at the meeting of the Eastern Psychological Association.

Kranau, Edgar J., Greer, Vicki, & Valencia-Weber, Gloria (1982). Acculturation and the Hispanic woman: Attitudes toward women, sex role attribution, sex role behavior, and demographics. *Hispanic Journal of Behavioral Sciences, 4*(1), 21–40.

Kurdek, Lawrence A., & Schmitt, J. Patrick (1986). Relationship quality of partners in heterosexual married, heterosexual cohabiting, and gay and lesbian relationships. *Journal of Personality and Social Psychology, 51,* 711–20.

Lange, Shirley, & Worell, Judith (1990). *Satisfaction and commitment in lesbian and heterosexual relationships.* Paper presented at the meeting of the American Psychological Association, Boston, Massachusetts.

Lynch, Jean M., & Reilly, Mary E. (1985/86). Role relationships: Lesbian perspectives. *Journal of Homosexuality, 12*(2), 53–69.

Nyquist, Linda, Slivken, Karla, Spence, Janet, & Helmreich, Robert L. (1985). Household responsibilities in middle-class couples: The contribution of demographic and personality variables. *Sex Roles, 12*(1/2), 15–34.

Peplau, Letitia Anne (1981). What homosexuals want. *Psychology Today,* Mar. 1981, 28–38.

Peplau, Letitia Anne, Cochran, Susan, Rook, Karen, & Padesky, Christine (1978). Loving women: Attachment and autonomy in lesbian relationships. *Journal of Social Issues, 34,* 7–27.

Philliber, William W., & Hiller, Dana V. (1983). Relative occupational attainments of spouses and later changes in marriage and wife's work experience. *Journal of Marriage and the Family, 45,* 161–70.

Phillips v. Graves (1870), quoted in J. M. Krauskopf, Partnership marriage: Legal reforms needed, in J. Chapman and M. Gates (Eds.), *Women into wives: The legal and economic impact of marriage.* Beverly Hills, CA: Sage, 1977.

Pleck, Joseph H. (1985). *Working wives, working husbands.* Beverly Hills, CA: Sage.

Ross, Catherine, Mirowsky, John, & Huber, Joan (1983). Dividing work, sharing work, and in-between: Marriage patterns and depression. *American Sociological Review, 48,* 809–23.

Scanzoni, John (1972). *Sexual bargaining: Power politics in the American marriage.* Englewood Cliffs, NJ: Prentice-Hall.

Steil, Janice M. (1983). Marriage: An unequal partnership. In B. Wolman and G. Stricker (Eds.), *Handbook of marriage and the family* (pp. 49–59). New York: Plenum.

Steil, Janice M. (1984). Marital relationships and mental health: The psychic costs of inequality. In J. Freeman (Ed.), *Women: A feminist perspective* (3rd ed.). Mountain View, CA: Mayfield.

Steil, Janice M. (in press). Equality and entitlement in marriage. In Melvin Lerner & Gerald Mikula (Eds.), *Justice in Close Relationships: Entitlement and the affectional bond.* New York: Plenum.

Steil, Janice M., & Turetsky, Beth (1987). Is equal better? The relationship between marital equality and psychological symptomatology. In S. Oskamp (Ed.), *Applied social psychology annual* (pp. 73–95). Beverly Hills, CA: Sage.

Steil, Janice M., & Weltman, Karen (1991). Marital inequality: The importance of resources, personal attributes, and social norms on career valuing and the allocation of domestic responsibilities. *Sex Roles, 24*(3/4), 161–79.

Steil, Janice M., & Whitcomb, Juliet (1992). *Conceptualizing equality.* Paper presented at the Sixth International Conference on Close Relationships, Orono, Maine.

Taueber, Cynthia Murray (1991). *Statistical handbook on women in America,* Chart B1-20, p. 85. Phoenix, AZ: Oryx Press.

Thompson, Linda, & Walker, Alexis J. (1989). Gender in families: Women and men in marriage, work and parenthood. *Journal of Marriage and the Family, 51,* 845–71.

VanFossen, Beth E. (1981). Sex differences in the mental health effects of spouse support and equity. *Journal of Health and Social Behavior, 22*(June), 130–43.

Vannoy-Hiller, Dana, & Philliber, William W. (1989). *Equal partners: Successful women in marriage.* Newbury Park, CA: Sage.

VanYperen Nico, & Buunk, Bram (1990). A longitudinal study of equity and satisfaction in intimate relationships. *European Journal of Social Psychology, 20,* 287–309.

VanYperen Nico, & Buunk, Bram (1991). Sex-role attitudes, social comparison, and satisfaction with relationships. *Social Psychology Quarterly, 54*(2), 169–80.

Motherhood: Contemporary Conflict for Women

Michele Hoffnung

THE POWER OF ideology is demonstrated forcefully in the contemporary concept of motherhood. We all know about motherhood, or at least we think we know. We hold a set of assumptions and beliefs founded on the premise that the mother-child unit is basic, universal, and psychologically most suited for both the healthy development of the child and the fulfillment of the mother. "The experts have no doubts: they are unanimous in their statement that only the mother, and no one else, should take care of her child. No other question is answered so definitely and plainly. The mother is the person to look after her child."[1] Since raising children is useful work, necessary for the continuation of society, satisfying to human generative impulses, and highly valued in the lives of women who mother, it is easy for us to believe these "experts" and accept the motherhood mystique.

Yet mothering within this narrow definition conflicts with other important aspects of women's lives—productive work, companionate marriage, economic independence. Mothering is done at home, outside the world of achievement, power, and money. It consequently pulls women who mother away from the public world back into the private world for at least part of their adult lives.

It is this aspect of motherhood, its limiting effect on women's public participation at a time when women have won access to the public world, that must inform the next stages of feminist activity for social change. It is not enough for women to be able to do men's work as well as women's; it is necessary to reconsider the value of mothering and to reorder public priorities so that caring for children counts in and adds to the lives of women and men. Until children are valued members of society and child care is considered work important enough to be done by both men and women, the special burdens and benefits of motherhood will keep women in second place.

Historical Perspective

Mothering has not always been the same. Recent work by social historians indicates that our modern notion of motherhood has its roots in the nineteenth century.

> The most important function of the morally superior nineteenth-century women was bearing and raising children. In the Victorian period motherhood came to have the emotional and semisacred connotations that tempt one to write it with a capital "M." The mother's task was to care for her children

physically, preserve their moral innocence, protect them from evil influences, and inspire them to pursue the highest spiritual values. If woman failed in this duty, she jeopardized the whole progress of civilization, an awesome responsibility indeed. . . . This glorification of motherhood and exaggeration of its responsibilities was as new an element in Anglo-American culture as the opinion that females were particularly virtuous. Indeed, the two ideas evolved together and reinforced one another in eighteenth and nineteenth century thought.[2]

Prior to this glorification of motherhood by the nineteenth-century middle class, the bearing and rearing of children were integrated into the other work women did and were not women's most important work. In a subsistence farm economy, survival required women as well as men to place productive work before reproductive concerns. Women and men worked side by side, in and around the home. Women were responsible for food and clothing production for the family, which involved many complicated skills, as well as cooking, laundering, cleaning, and child care.[3] Infants were tended when possible and were sometimes played with, but were never the center of their mothers' attention. Their care was largely the task of older siblings. Those children who survived infancy quickly took their places in the social and economic life of the family.[4]

Industrialization simultaneously disrupted the unity of home and workshop, decreased patriarchal power, and devalued women's work within the family. Life in industrial society is characterized by distinct separations: work from play, production from reproduction, adulthood from childhood. Adults work; children play. Work takes place in the office or factory, relaxation in the home. Activities done outside the home are reimbursed with money; inside the home activities are done for love. Within this new set of values, which emerged during the nineteenth century, women were assigned to the home as non-producing homemakers. In this context, mother-work became the focus of their attention. As work was transformed into wage labor in factory or office, the family took on new meaning. It became a refuge, the place to which Dad and kids would come to recover from the pressure and pain of alienated work and school.[5] The burden of providing the comforts of home was assigned to women.

The combination of homemaking and child care was a full-time job, but it carried none of the economic benefits that employment outside the home provided. Although reproductive tasks were more physically demanding in days gone by, they were not severed from the productive work of the family or imbued with heavy psychological significance. In contrast to the economic value of women's work in the past, today a woman's devotion to "women's work" makes her dependent on the people she tends. It results in an economic dependence on her husband—a man chosen for love—and a psychological dependence on her children as products of her mothering.

Other historic changes have also made more choices possible for women. Prior to the nineteenth century, abstinence was the only effective method of controlling fertility.[6] Technological improvements and political struggles have made contraception relatively safe, effective, and available in the twentieth century. With the repeal of restrictive birth control legislation in the 1960s, heterosexual intimacy became no longer inseparable from maternity. Although most babies worldwide are still unplanned,[7] in our country the birthrate has been decreasing steadily since the nineteenth century;[8] in the last three decades alone, the fertility rate of American women has fallen nearly 50 percent.[9] Many women have made a dramatic choice to have fewer children, to end their childbearing earlier, or to start their families later.

This steady decrease in the number of births per woman reflects more than the availability of contraception. It also reflects a perception on the part of more women that life has exciting and rewarding experiences to offer in addition to childbearing and that these are within their reach. "Decreased fertility rates are a consequence of increased educational and occupational aspirations and pressures by women. To regulate her reproductive life a woman must also come to believe that it is morally right to control her own body and she must acquire knowledge regarding how best and most safely to do so."[10]

These increased educational and occupational opportunities are also consequences of economic and political changes. Although gender differences persist in education,[11] today girls, like boys, are educated to compete to get ahead, to believe in and strive for individual success—first in school and then in a competitive labor market—and to value persistent independence. Coeducation, contraception, and the need for wage laborers have promoted the integration of women into the economic system; feminism has promoted the integration of women into the political system.

At the same time, women are still trained to be the foundation of the family as wives and mothers. Their early socialization encourages a connected sense of self, a sense of interdependence in relation to others that makes the activity of caring for others' needs vital to their own well-being. Women feel connected to their children and to other family members as well; typically they do not envision their own development separate from that relational context.[12] As a result, the nineteenth-century notion that "women's place is in the home" lingers on as "women's *essential* place is in the home."

Psychological Conflict and Material Cost

There are two sets of expectations for women. There are those made possible by industrialization—individuality, successful accomplishment, equality; and there are those born of the patriarchal tradition—the public domain belongs to men, wives and their services belong to their husbands, and family life is the responsibility of women. Although these expectations conflict, the conflict is not always acute. Most girls learn to compartmentalize, to keep separate the feelings associated with achievement from those associated with femininity, and to handle the two as mutually exclusive.[13] Separation is one strategy for coping with essentially contradictory expectations.[14] Indeed, the very structure of modern life makes this distinction appear "natural." Girls succeed in school; then, at home, as daughters and sisters, they assist in feminine pursuits.

Daughters are encouraged to prepare for work, but they are also expected to become mothers later. Through school, during the early years on a job, or in a childless marriage, middle-class women may notice contradictions, feel anger about sex discrimination at work or about unequal responsibility for housework at home, or feel guilt about their shortcomings; but to a large extent they can manage to fulfill both sets of expectations.

The selection of a career, however, expresses clearly the consequences of this contradiction. Almost all college women expect to work at some time in their lives, almost all desire marriage and children, and almost all stress the centrality of family life to their future plans. The way they accomplish this goal is by remaining flexible in their career choices. For men, career is the central choice; by contrast, Shirley Angrist and Elizabeth Almquist, in a study of college women, found that

> choices are not so concrete, not so specific, and far from wide-ranging. The extreme changeability of occupational choices, the lack of decisiveness in their plans, the resort to a short list of predominately "women's" fields, the tendency to postpone a definite choice and to vacillate—all these tell us that while [women] students perceive pressure to make decisions about their post-college lives, the particular occupation chosen is only one and perhaps not even the central component of their thinking about the future.[15]

In a study of Barnard College undergraduates, Mirra Komarovsky found that occupation was an important part of these young women's self-image; the students were highly motivated to find high-status and high-paying occupations. Almost all wanted motherhood as well; 85 percent said they wished in fifteen years to be married career women with children. In spite of the increased importance of career, however, these women students exhibited indecision and dramatic shifts in occupational decision making similar to that found by Angrist and Almquist.[16]

In a study of women students at a public university, Kristine Baber and Patricia Monaghan found that all intended to have careers, and almost all expected to be mothers of two or more children as well. While their career choices were for the most part nontraditional, their plans for motherhood included delayed childbearing, extended maternity leaves, and part-time work. These strategies for combining work and motherhood are likely to leave some of them without jobs (since employers need not wait out six- or twelve-month leaves) and many of them behind their male colleagues who maintain full-time status.[17]

In interviews with middle-class suburban women who had at least one preschool child, I found that those who were employed were those who remembered having career aspirations as children.[18] Their particular fields of employment, however, were not necessarily related to their early aspirations or to their academic training. Most of them wanted to work, but, for most, family responsibilities came first, so work had been adjusted. Some had enjoyed working, had stopped to raise their children, and were considering career changes when they returned to the ranks of the employed. Others had given up careers such as teaching for jobs such as waitressing while their children were young. Still others had continued their careers while tending their children with the help of their husbands, paid mother substitutes, or day-care centers. All these employed mothers, however, had achieved some form of job flexibility. They had rearranged hours, changed jobs, or changed pace to encompass the demands of children as well as work. Faced with two sets of expectations at the same time, they had readjusted work.

Both work and family require emotional investment, time, and energy; there are many external and internal pressures that push women to devote their major energies to the family. As a result, women often shy away from commitment to high-powered careers. As mothers, they often are employed outside their homes, but they select jobs based on the scheduling needs of their families rather than the needs of their own career development.

The conflict between individual achievement and feminine responsibility, therefore, is not just internal. It places constraints on women's commitment to employment. It pushes women to limit the careers they consider possible to less lucrative female occupations, to give up what they have accomplished for mother-work, or to spread themselves very thin. The resulting part-time or intermittent employment patterns contribute to the large wage differential between women and men.[19] Motherhood as we know it has substantial material costs for women.

Infant care is a twenty-four-hour-a-day job. Although no particular part of it is especially difficult, child-centered care is constantly demanding. The feeding, bathing, and laundry routine involves a lot of physical labor. Beyond the child's infancy or with additional children, the job becomes much more difficult. For women who have been working, as is true for most women before their first child is born,[20] the changes from having a work schedule to being in demand constantly, from having adult to infant company, from feeling competent to feeling like a novice require a great deal of adjustment. Although many mothers try, few accomplish this transition without suffering tension, depression, or emotional trauma. Postpartum depression is one of the first signs of difficulty. The excitement and rewards of the new mothering role partially offset the disruption. Motherhood, a very special aspect of being a woman, opens up the joy of intimate contact with a growing, developing infant, the sense of importance that nurturing holds for most women, and the personal growth that comes from facing and mastering a new developmental stage. Modern mothering ideals, however, require selflessness from women who have been socialized by their experiences at school and at work to be selves. This conflict of values is why the early mothering years are characterized by pain and conflict.

The difficulties are heightened by the fact that, while many lofty phrases are penned in tribute to mother-work, that work is accorded very low prestige. Our society values money, power, and achievement, none of which are associated with child care. Women who are used to achieving in their own right and earning their own paychecks become defined as someone's wife and someone's mother. They also become financially dependent on the income of their husbands. Later, when the children leave home, there are new costs. Mothers still have half or more of their lives ahead of them, but their "priority" role, raising the children, is over.[21] Their years of full-time work in the home leave them unprepared for life after active mothering; their work skills are rusty, their training is dated, and they are unsure of themselves. Alternatively, mothers who choose to continue their employment face the difficulties peculiar to this option: double demands, two jobs at once, and guilt.

Mother-work, therefore, extracts a great cost from women. Although it carries heavy responsibility, it brings none of the material rewards of employment. It is demeaned and trivialized in the mass media, which use it to sell a multitude of housekeeping products. It is not integrated with productive work; rather, it conflicts with work or career, thereby limiting a woman's independence, achievement, earnings, and status.[22]

The Motherhood Mystique

Motherhood, as we know it, is only one possible childrearing arrangement. It has the aura, however, of being "natural" and unchanging. Because of this aura, our contemporary definition has been referred to as the *motherhood mystique*.[23] It has four aspects: (1) ultimate fulfillment *as a woman* is achieved by becoming a mother; (2) the body of work assigned to mothers—caring for child, home, and husband—fits together in a noncontradictory manner; (3) to be a good mother, a woman must like being a mother and all the work that goes with it; (4) a woman's intense, exclusive devotion to mothering is good for her children.

Becoming a mother introduces a woman into a new league, the league of "real" women. Once a pregnancy begins to show, women who may never have spoken to the expectant mother before become friendly and offer helpful advice. Giving birth proves womanhood, as combat proves manhood. Successful combat, however, requires physical training and intellectual rigor; successful birth requires only conception and the unfolding of the physiological processes. Endeavors that a woman has been devoted to for years tend to be overlooked in the general excitement created by pregnancy and birth. Hospitals and families act as though all else the woman has done or been is now unimportant; being a mother will absorb her, interest her, and define her.[24] This is very different from the view of fathers, who are expected to be interested in and delighted by their children but whose other interests and employment are expected to continue. This aspect of the motherhood mystique is a denial of a woman as a multifaceted person.

In spite of strong social approval for childbearing, women find that giving birth does not provide ultimate fulfillment. Fulfillment comes not from the experience of a biological event but rather from development of and dedication to values, interests, and competencies over time. Nor does giving birth ensure a perfect relationship with a new and perfect being. Relationships are never perfect and always require time and energy. The gap between many a new mother's expectations of fulfillment and the reality of exhaustion and distraction is often shocking.[25] Whereas almost everybody gets excited about pregnancy and birth, no one gets excited about colicky babies and dirty diapers. After being the center of attention during labor and delivery, a new mother soon finds herself very much alone at home. The birth of a first child is, therefore, "an event causing the greatest discontinuity of personality in American middle-class women," especially if the birth is not followed by full-time involvement outside the home.[26]

The second aspect of the motherhood mystique is the assumption that care of the child, home, and husband consists of complementary roles. For middle-class women this is not true; conflict exists among the roles of mother, homemaker, and wife. Although couples usually expect the birth of their baby to enhance their relationship, in fact the first baby's birth has been shown to cut conversation time between parents almost in half and to shift the topics of conversation from the parents' relationship, their inner feelings, or sex to the child. The two become parents first and marriage partners second.[27] The child becomes the focus of the wife's attention, often causing the husband to resent being ousted from first place in her consideration. There is conflict between the needs and demands of children for attention, their noise, and their activity and a husband's need for order, peace, and food at the end of a workday. In addition, the modern companionate marriage assumes a strong common bond between husband and wife in the preparental stage. The traditional wife-mother-homemaker and husband-father-breadwinner division of labor that often follows the birth of the first child dramatically changes the former quasi egalitarian relationship between the parents. With the child come new problems, worries, and inner conflicts, and, because their roles are now so different, the husband and wife are often pulled apart. Some of the role changes bring tension. The wife may envy the husband's freedom. The husband may feel additional financial pressure and envy his wife's self-regulated schedule.

In a study of infant care in which more than seven hundred mothers of infants were interviewed, John and Elizabeth Newson found significant dissatisfaction with the mother role among middle-class women in Nottingham, England.[28] These women expected to be social assets to their husbands. Babies and young children, however, interfered with this goal by disturbing the cleanliness of their homes, their intellectual pursuits, and their previously well-ordered lives. Mary Boulton also found differences between white middle-class and working-class English families in their expectations of the conjugal relationships. Middle-class mothers expected companionate marriages and less sex-typed division of labor and were less happy with the marital changes that children brought. In both groups, however, the husbands' degree of help and understanding had a strong positive influence on the women's experience of motherhood.[29]

Motherhood, therefore, is a complicated set of roles that results in ambivalent feelings on the part of women. There are the love, intimacy, and caring that make it personal, intense, and special, but there are also the very real changes in women's bodies, free time, work, and marriage relationships. These lead to conflicting feelings in most mothers: feelings of intense need and suffocation, of sublime selflessness and supreme selfishness.[30]

Since the third aspect of the motherhood mystique is that, to be a good mother, a woman must like being a mother, ambivalent feelings lead to guilt and worry about mothering adequacy. Angela McBride writes of "the anger-depression-guilt-go-round" that is a "normal-crazy" part of the motherhood experience.[31] As people women have different personalities, talents, and temperaments, but as mothers they are expected to be continually patient, even-tempered, and consistent. When they fail to meet these impossible expectations, they fear that they are bad mothers, that they are failing their children. In the past, when child care was not expected to be the focus of a mother's life, there were less self-consciousness and guilt associated with the role. Now women turn to experts—pediatricians, psychologists, social workers—to tell them what to do and try to measure their behavior in terms of the pundits' advice.[32] The whole experience becomes more tormented and less satisfying; it loses the spontaneity and genuine warmth of unmediated intimate relations.

This self-conscious, guilt-ridden striving might be justified if the fourth aspect of the mystique—that exclusive, full-time mothering is best for child development—were true, but that is not at all clear. Having one person on twenty-four-hour duty is not optimal for meeting the developmental needs of a child. The most even-tempered mother will at times be tired, self-absorbed, occupied with other things, or under the weather. The child is then subject to adult anger, annoyance, or inattention when she or he may have real needs. In contrast, when Mom feels good, she may shower attention on the child at a time when the child needs most to be left alone. Assigning child care to a single adult leaves both the adult and the child subject to the needs, feelings, and demands of the other without relief. Children are consequently overmothered and undermothered by turns. When mothers feel guilty or worried, they pour attention on their children; when they feel angry or preoccupied, there is no one else to whom the child can turn. In each situation, the children are bound into the personality dynamics of the mothers. "The result of the exclusiveness of the mother-child relationship is that no one can prevent this relationship from becoming too narrow. It makes personality absorption practically unavoidable."[33]

This is the aspect of the mother-child relationship that has led to the concept of "momism." *Momism* has become a catchword for blaming a mother for living out her needs through her children, for being overbearing and overabsorbing.[34] Blaming Mom, however, is blaming the victim. Because a mother gives up so much to be a mother, because she is educated and achievement oriented, because there is so little family or community support for the contemporary mother, the child has come to mean too much to her. The child cannot grow freely but must succeed for the mother to show that she has done a good job and that her sacrifices have been worth it. Since a woman often puts aside any personal ambition for motherhood, the child may be expected to succeed in her stead, to act out her ambitions for her. Or the child may become a substitute for the mother's ambitions, a product she can be proud of as well as a child. The workplace values of achievement and success are extended to the kin relationship.

Women sacrifice to do what is "best" for their children, but it simply is not best.

> The way we institutionalize motherhood in our society—assigning sole responsibility for child care to the mother, cutting her off from the easy help of others in an isolated household, requiring round-the-clock tender, loving care, and making such care her exclusive activity—is not only unique, but not even a good way for either women or—if we accept as criterion the amount of maternal warmth shown—for children. It may, in fact, be the worst. It is as though we had selected the worst features of all the ways motherhood is structured around the world and combined them to produce our current design.[35]

A longitudinal study of New York City and suburban families with mothers at home and fathers at work clearly demonstrates this point. Sylvia Brody and Sidney Axelrod found that very few women "mothered adequately." Adequate mothering required mothers who were emotionally stable *and* educated *and* not distressed by their economic conditions *and* who had satisfactory marriages. As we know, most mothers do not have all these advantages. The majority of the mothers Brody and Axelrod studied did not, and these mothers almost had "to ignore signs of distress in the child, to make too hasty judgments of the child's behavior, or to rationalize that it is the child's unalterable nature to act as he does."[36]

The Contemporary Problem

In spite of the contradictions, most women want to be mothers, and most mothers want at least two children.[37] The contemporary problem is how to fit motherhood into their lives without relinquishing their other activities or narrowing their ambitions. Women have many reasons for wanting children—liking for children, desiring to experience pregnancy and childbirth, demonstrating being an adult, establishing a family like their family of origin, resolving an uncertain identity, conforming to social expectations. Some of these have to do with pronatalist social pressure—pressure from family, church, and media that pushes women to have children.[38] Liberation for women means freedom from the single, socially assigned role of mother, freedom to choose whether to be mothers. But self-fulfillment for most contemporary women includes a sexual relationship and motherhood as well as ego-creative work that expresses individuality.[39] Motherhood is a very limited choice, if a woman must accept the entire motherhood mystique, which denies the importance of nonmaternal pursuits. The contemporary question is: How can motherhood be organized so that it will be better for both women and children than is currently the case?

There is a related problem for men. In this world of largely contractual work relationships, the responsibility for nurturing one's offspring—some of the time—has its special rewards. Being in intimate physical and emotional contact with a child develops a father's loving and caring feelings, establishes a closeness between himself and his child, and keeps him in tune with the experiences of his child's mother. The way contemporary fatherhood is conducted denies men these rewards. Although many people think that fathers today are more involved with their children than fathers past, contemporary evidence indicates that women still carry more than 90 percent of the responsibility for the children.[40] This lack of paternal involvement puts traditional demands on mothers and leads to marital conflict, while increasing fathers' involvement relieves some of the pressure on a couple to switch from shared roles before the birth of a child to the sex-stereotyped roles (discussed earlier) when the first child is born.

Given the biological demands of pregnancy and lactation, however, as well as the historical connection between mothers and children, it would be a mistake to take the focus off mothers while examining the problems of childrearing. How can a mother fit childrearing into her life? A good place to begin the examination is with the last generation of mothers. Pauline Bart, in a pioneering study of depression in middle-aged women, found that it was "women who play the traditional feminine role—who are housewives, are not aggressive, are centered on their children, who in short, have 'bought' the cultural proscriptions—who are most prone to depression when their children leave."[41] Utilizing anthropological and epidemiological data as well as interviews with twenty hospitalized middle-aged women, she found that overinvolved and overprotective relationships with their children could be pathological for mothers in middle age.

"Today's midlife women had lived by the old rules —rules that promised [a woman] kudos, congratulations, and fulfillment of self for giving up her own life to meet her responsibilities to others."[42] Lillian Rubin conducted a series of interviews with normal middle-aged women who had devoted themselves to the responsibilities of childrearing and now were in the post-parental stage of their lives. Rubin found that the women were unprepared for life after children; neither they nor their husbands had looked ahead. The problems of these midlife women suggest a way of considering the issue of motherhood for young women. Active mothering is a stage in life, not an ultimate fulfillment or a lifelong job. Women's life expectancies are long, family size is typically small, and children grow up and move away. Young women must prepare for satisfying employment and must not consider childrearing their life work. As one of Rubin's interviewees said, "Motherhood self-destructs in twenty years."[43]

Louise Kapp Howe has identified three major employment patterns that women follow after leaving school. The first is to work for a few years and then to give up employment and become a homemaker. This pattern used to be the dominant one. The second is to follow the same pattern as men, to begin work after leaving school and to continue working until retirement. This pattern is most frequent among women who have no children, black women, and women in professional and managerial careers. The third pattern is to work until having children, take time off to raise them, and then return or try to return to work. The time off for full-time mothering used to be five to ten years, but the interval has been getting shorter. The prevalence of this pattern has grown the fastest during this century.[44]

Kathleen Gerson argues, however, that a growing percentage of young women (those born after 1944) are joining the work force with a commitment that resembles that of male workers—namely, "steady, long-term, full-time workplace attachment." The career woman, whether she combines motherhood and employment or forgoes motherhood, is no longer unusual.[45] Based on conversations with my college students and teenaged children and their friends, contemporary young women do expect to have careers.

Clearly, several life plans are possible. Each has its attendant problems; only choosing to be childless avoids this conflict.

The women Lillian Rubin spoke with who had devoted themselves to full-time mothering had many fears and doubts to overcome in going to work. They also had to deal with resistance on the part of their husbands and the lack of interesting, challenging, decently paying jobs for inexperienced middle-aged women.[46] Women may reduce these problems somewhat by planning to work in the future, but staying home full-time for twenty or so years to tend to the needs of others is not good preparation for successful accomplishment in much of the public world.[47] It tracks women into service jobs, extensions of mothering, when they are ready for employment. This path of "family first, then career" has been a difficult one for women to follow, in part because these women have not planned ahead. I suspect it will become even more difficult to follow when women do plan ahead, because it will push them to get childbearing out of the way early, and that decision has been shown to have particularly limiting effects on women's educational and occupational achievement.[48] In practice, first births are rarely planned; I found that when they were planned it was usually in conjunction with an active career, never with a future one.[49]

Establishing a career and then taking time out works well for some women. It is this option that attracts many women to teaching or nursing, because these careers offer some flexibility for fitting in families. For many women, however, it is frustrating and boring to be home once they have established a career, and many careers (particularly those that are less traditionally "female") do not allow for a time-off period long enough to raise a child or two to school age. This pattern of career choice results in severe limitation of the areas of women's public participation to a few sex-stereotyped jobs.

Many contemporary mothers are living out the "both" option; they cannot or do not choose to stay home with their young children. Since World War II, there has been a dramatic shift in the patterns of employment for married women in the United States. Before 1940, if a woman worked, she did so prior to marriage. After 1940, married women in their late thirties started to return to work.[50] In recent years, this trend for married women to be in the labor force has expanded to include women with children, even women with preschool children. In 1988, 53 percent of mothers with children under the age of three were in the labor force, and 51 percent of mothers with infants under the age of one were in the labor force. Of the mothers of preschoolers who were not employed, 25 percent said they would choose to work if safe and affordable child care were available.[51] For a variety of reasons, more than half the mothers with preschoolers are now employed.

When midlife comes and children go, women who have jobs or careers are better prepared for the postparental stage of life. But, during the years when a woman simultaneously works and cares for a young family, her life is physically demanding and involves constant compromise. Mothers who work full-time report more conflicts with work, family, achievement, and individual concerns than do other mothers, although the reported intensity of their conflicts is no greater.[52] In the past, the extended family—primarily grandmothers and aunts—shared child care, providing variety for children and relief, as well as sociability, for mothers, but today many families are geographically isolated from relatives. When female relatives are nearby, women often have their help, but they then have less help from their husbands.[53]

The most pressing problem for working mothers is lack of time—there are more tasks to be done than there are hours in the day. Working mothers have less leisure time than do other adults, full-time mothers, fathers, or nonparents. What they long for is some time for themselves.[54] They have child-care help during their working hours, but they continue to do housework—research indicates that they have no more paid household help than do full-time mothers. The amount of paid household help a family has appears to depend on the husband's income, not on the wife's employment status. In other words, when the husband's salary is high, the couple is more likely to hire help than when it is low, regardless of whether the wife has a job or is a full-time homemaker.[55]

Families in which fathers are present have the option of sharing respon-sibilities between husband and wife. There is considerable evidence that, when the wife is employed, the husband does more house and child care than when the wife is home, although he does not share the burden equally. Kathryn Walker found that husbands of working wives assisted one to three hours per day, whereas the wives spent four to eight hours on housework.[56] I found that husbands of working mothers took more responsibility for child care than did those of nonemployed mothers; most helped, and a few shared the respon-sibility. None of the husbands of nonemployed mothers shared responsibility, and some did not help either.[57] Joseph Pleck found that the full-time employed wife's share of the domestic tasks was three times as great as that of her full-time employed husband.[58] Nonetheless, husbands of employed wives do a higher percentage of the couples' total family work than do husbands of homemakers. Dual-earner husbands do 30 to 35 percent; sole-earner husbands 20 percent.[59] Even when the father helps, the working mother is typically the one responsible for making the arrangements and assigning the tasks. She usually has the "executive decision-making responsibilities over child and family matters."[60] And, of course, many working mothers have no husbands.

Although many fathers help, child care and housework are done for the most part by women, mothers, or mother substitutes. Women choosing or being forced by circumstances both to work outside the home and do child care and housework are faced with serious constraints. A few have the option of hiring a full-time housekeeper-mother substitute to keep household and child well tended while they vigorously pursue their careers. This is the female equivalent to having a wife.[61] Many others give their careers less than they would if they did not have a family to care for as well.[62] Lydia O'Donnell has distinguished between "labor-force attachment" and "labor-force involvement." She found that the seventy-four mothers in her study limited their employment so that they could continue to spend time with their children. They saw paid work as playing a limited role in their lives. They were "involved" but not "attached."[63] In an earlier study, Margaret Poloma interviewed fifty-two married women doctors, lawyers, and professors and found that they rejected the view of themselves as "career" women. They experienced very little strain between their professional and family roles because they routinely resolved any role conflicts in favor of home.[64] In these studies, we see employed women whose commitment is first and foremost to family.

Nonetheless, many mothers do work, and many are committed to careers. For women who are in professional and managerial jobs, the time pressures are even more intense. These careers are structured for the lives that men lead; they assume that one is not hampered by home and child-care responsibilities. They require enormous time and energy as well as the flexibility to leave work late or to come in early. Such demands conflict with the needs of a family. Professional and managerial women report major concern over conflicts between their careers and children. Their concerns include fatigue, emotional depletion, and, in many cases, guilt.

Not all career commitments are consistent with active mothering or fathering. An active parent must be willing to give up some of the other pursuits that engage adults, at least for a while. This continues to be a major barrier to women's achievement. There is no reason, however, why only mothers should be active parents.

A Question of Values

The role of mother brings with it benefits as well as limitations. Children affect parents in ways that lead to personal growth, enable reworking of childhood conflicts, build flexibility and empathy, and provide intimate, loving human connections. "Little People are more curious than cautious"; they expand their caretakers' worlds by their activity levels, their imaginations, and their inherently appealing natures.[65] Although motherhood is not enough to fill an entire life, for most mothers it is one of the most meaningful experiences in their lives.

The option that most reduces the costs for young women who want to be mothers is to prepare to combine work and family. Accepting the continuing importance of employment in their lifetimes enables women to take their career choices and training seriously, to select mates who are more inclined to share the responsibility of family care, and to resist the pressures of the motherhood mystique. This option provides the most opportunity for women, men, and children. It is also the option most associated with better health for women. Women with several key roles, such as employment, marriage, and parenthood, are more likely to be healthy than are women with few roles. Multiple roles provide more privileges, more resources, and more avenues for self-esteem and social involvement. Women without multiple key roles are more subject to boredom, social isolation, and stress. Employment is the single most important factor. Employed women have the best health; full-time homemakers have the worst health.[66]

For women, relinquishing sole responsibility for childrearing and family care is necessary if they are to become equal participants in the productive activities of the public world. By defining ultimate fulfillment for women through maternity, the motherhood mystique limits all women, not just mothers, to secondary status outside the home; maternal responsibilities, or potential ones, are always expected to come first. When mothers reject the mystique and take their productive lives as seriously as they do their family responsibilities, they help to create a different view of women.

In my research with preschool mothers, the quality that related most positively to adjustment and satisfaction was "strategic planning" or the extent of control a woman exerted over her life. Strategic planning implies perceiving options and making choices rather than simply drifting into stereotypical roles. Strategic planning was a quality that showed up again and again in the lives of the career women I spoke with, so often that it appeared to represent nothing less than an approach to life. While women without careers sometimes planned systematically, those with careers characteristically did. Career women also held a different set of assumptions about the division of labor with their spouses. They were unlikely to assume that family responsibilities were solely their own and likely to establish shared, rather than traditional, conjugal roles.[67]

Employed mothers who choose to work, and choose their work, are happier than those who are forced to work at jobs that are demanding but give them little control. Women who become full-time homemakers because the job fits their skills and desires are happier and healthier than women who become full-time homemakers out of a sense of feminine duty.[68] Women do best when they consider the role of full-time homemaker as they would consider any job rather than assume it is their fate. This means weighing the alternatives. It also means discussing the terms of homemaking with their mates rather than taking on all associated tasks singlehandedly.

For women to give up full responsibility for child and family care, however, men must change as well. Fathers must be more active as caretaking parents. Sharing responsibility for both family life and financial support enables men to be closer to their children, less at the mercy of their employers, and better friends with their wives. In fact, many critics of the masculine sex-role stereotype consider that "being with children and joining in the immediacy of their emotional life may be a route toward reclaiming the spontaneous emotional awareness that . . . masculine training drove into hiding so long ago."[69]

Children, perhaps, will gain the most if they are released from their intense one-to-one relationships with their mothers. Having two, or more, involved caretakers broadens a child's experience and makes him or her less dependent on a single personality.[70] Nurture by men, as well as by women, can alter the formation of sex-typed personality structures in young children that have been associated with exclusively women-nurtured girls and boys.[71] Two caretaking parents provides children with more accessible fathers and a more balanced view of their mothers.

Many individual women and couples have forged ahead and have created their own alternatives. They split shifts, or job share, or find good day care, or form cooperatives with other couples like themselves.[72] For the most part, however, women have been trapped. They have borne the burden of rearing their children, because as individuals they lacked the insight or resources to alter the traditional arrangement.

More support services for parents are needed. Nonprofit neighborhood and work-based child-care centers, flex-time work schedules, and reliable after-school programs are a few solutions that have been implemented in some places. But there is no way to accomplish these changes on a large scale without an accompanying change in social values.[73] Our society does not value children. Children are viewed as enjoyable objects, necessary to complete a family, but not as valuable or inspiring members of society. There is little recognition on the part of adult society that children contribute something special to the family, the neighborhood, and the community. Children traditionally were valuable as additional productive members of the family; now they are costly. Women traditionally had few options outside of marriage and motherhood, but they were important economic contributors to the family. Now women have more options. More young women are learning to value the place of work in their lives. More young men are seeking wives who have professions. But the problems for women combining career and family have not been solved. There is no place for kids in the lives of two independent spouses—unless they share responsibilities or hire a nanny. That situation requires a change in social values.

In *Juggling,* an important new book about combining work and motherhood, Faye J. Crosby argues that placing blame for the strain women experience when they work outside the home in addition to mothering is a form of blaming the victim. While many women's lives are indeed strained, much of the strain comes from the stresses within the individual roles that have been assigned to women rather than the combination of work and family roles. The nature of the jobs women have and/or the structure of their family roles cause conflict, not their combination. Crosby amply documents that women benefit from juggling career and family, just like men do. Women suffer more than men, however, because of the sexist gender imbalances at home and at work. Men do not do their share of family work; women earn less money and have less authority at the office.[74] Again, this requires a change in social values.

What Is to Be Done

Changing social values is necessary, but it hardly serves as an answer to women who are now facing or contemplating motherhood. While there is accumulating evidence that employed mothers feel better about themselves, report more satisfaction with their lives, and have higher self-esteem than do their non-employed counterparts, it is helpful to consider what factors contribute to the satisfactory combination of work and family roles.[75]

A woman's attitude toward her work is perhaps most important. Women who are more deeply committed to the work force seem to be more satisfied with their jobs. They also have high self-esteem and attach importance to intrinsic aspects of their work, viewing it as a source of enrichment.[76] They consider their employment a legitimate priority.

Family support is another important factor. Women with families supportive of their employment report greater job satisfaction, whereas women who perceive their husbands to be unfavorable toward their working report less job satisfaction, as do those whose children are unfavorable. Husbands' and children's attitudes, not surprisingly, are correlated.[77] Unfavorable family attitudes result in more conflict between home and work responsibilities.

Child care is the most important support service employed mothers require. Mothers with high-quality, reliable child care are content; those without it are subject to anxiety and guilt.[78] Whether the child care is provided in the form of a baby-sitter, a neighbor's home, a licensed home, or a day-care center, when the mother is comfortable with the style of care, she has little guilt or regret.

Women who are career oriented do not necessarily fit the stereotype of absent, uninvolved mothers, nor are they generally less family oriented than are their homebound counterparts. In a comparative study of working and nonworking mothers of infants, both groups saw the mother role as important. They differed in the predictable directions, however, in how important they considered the homemaker role and the work role. They also differed in their perceptions of their children's needs. Career-oriented working mothers were less anxious than were home mothers about separation from their infants, were only moderately apprehensive about alternate care, and were unlikely to believe that infant distress at separation was due to their absence.[79]

In my study of preschool mothers, the career-oriented women were no less family oriented than the full-time homemakers. They valued other commitments, particularly their work, but they valued their families and family life no less as a result. All maintained a commitment to being good mothers, though they differed in some of their ideas about what good mothering entailed. For some it meant being full-time caretaker of the children; for others it included good alternate care. All the mothers, in fact, used alternate care for their children some of the time, but employed career women used it more regularly and, perhaps because of that, were often more careful about its selection.[80]

Career-oriented women consider their need to work as legitimate, which places the needs of their families in a somewhat different light. This, with support from their families, enables them to reduce the amount of conflicting responsibilities at home and at work and consequently to increase their life satisfaction.

In an effort to understand how women cope effectively in the "male" professions, Janet Gray distributed questionnaires to 232 married women doctors, lawyers, and professors. She found that these women took their careers very seriously. They worked hard to avoid limiting their professional involvement. Five of the coping strategies that they reported using were positively related to satisfaction with their lives. First was having family members share household tasks. Second was reducing standards within certain roles, such as standards of household cleanliness. Third was careful scheduling and organizing of activities. Fourth was having family members help to resolve conflicts. Fifth was considering personal interests important. Strategies that were negatively related to satisfaction were eliminating roles, keeping roles totally separate, attempting to meet fully all expectations, overlapping roles, and having no conscious strategy for dealing with role conflicts. Almost all the women studied felt that the rewards of combining career and family were well worth the associated strain.[81]

Social values have to change if motherhood is to be a less conflictual part of women's lives, as do the values of individual women and men. Rejecting stereotypical roles and relationships and putting careers and family—as well as husband and wife—on more equal footing can make the both option more successful. These changes can reduce, although they cannot eliminate, the costs of motherhood for contemporary women.

NOTES

1. Jan Hendrick van den Berg, *Dubious Maternal Affection* (Pittsburgh, Pa.: Duquesne University Press, 1972), 9–10.

2. Barbara Harris, "Careers, Conflict, and Children: The Legacy of the Cult of Domesticity," in Alan Roland and Barbara Harris, eds., *Career and Motherhood: Struggles for a New Identity* (New York: Human Sciences Press, 1979), 71.

3. See John Mack Faragher, *Women and Men on the Overland Trail* (New Haven, Conn.: Yale University Press, 1979), chapter 2, for a detailed description of the division of labor between the sexes in subsistence farm families of the Midwest.

4. Phillipe Aries, in *Centuries of Childhood* (New York: Knopf, 1962), has pointed out that childhood itself is a relatively recent invention.

5. Eli Zaretsky, *Capitalism, the Family, and Personal Life* (New York: Harper Colophon, 1976).

6. Bernice Lott, *Becoming a Woman* (Springfield, Ill.: Charles C. Thomas, 1981), 206. James Mohr, in *Abortion in America* (New York: Oxford, 1978), chapter 4, points out that from 1840 to 1880 abortion was widely used by native-born women to limit family size.

7. Linda Gordon, *Women's Body: Women's Right* (New York: Grossman Publishers, 1976), 403.

8. Robert Wells, "Women's Lives Transformed: Demographic and Family Patterns in America, 1600–1970," in Carol Ruth Berkin and Mary Beth Norton, eds., *Women of America: A History* (Boston: Houghton Mifflin, 1979), 18.

9. In 1960 the fertility rate per one thousand women ages fourteen to forty-four was 118.0 children; in 1970, it was 87.9; in 1980, it was 68.4; in 1988, it was 67.2. See National Center for Health Statistics, *Vital Statistics of the United States, 1988,* vol. 1, Natality. DHHS pub. no. (PHS) 89-1100, Public Health Service (Washington, D.C.: U.S. Government Printing Office, 1990), 1.

10. Lott, *Becoming a Woman,* 213.

11. Susan Chira, "Bias Against Girls Is Found Rife in Schools with Lasting Damage," *New York Times,* 12 Feb. 1992, pp. A1, 27.

12. While young boys too develop this ethic of care, they are more likely to learn to give it up in their quest for a masculine identity that stresses autonomy in relation to others. See Jean Baker Miller, *Toward a New Psychology of Women* (Boston: Beacon Press, 1986), and Carol Gilligan, Janie Victoria Ward, and Jill McLean Taylor, eds., *Mapping the Moral Domain* (Cambridge, Mass.: Harvard University Press, 1988).

13. Matina Horner, "Femininity and Successful Achievement: A Basic Inconsistency," in Michele Hoffnung Garskof, ed., *Roles Women Play* (Monterey, Calif.: Brooks/Cole, 1971), 98. Although Horner's empirical work has not been successfully replicated, her descriptions of the problems for women are still apt.

14. Janet Dreyfus Gray, in "The Married Professional Woman: An Examination of Her Role Conflicts and Coping Strategies," *Psychology of Women Quarterly,* 1983, 7(3), 235–43, points out that this is a less effective coping strategy among married professional women.

15. Shirley S. Angrist and Elizabeth M. Almquist, *Careers and Contingencies* (New York: Dunellen, 1975), 67.

16. Mirra Komarovsky, *Women in College: Shaping New Feminine Identities* (New York: Basic Books, 1985), part II.

17. Kristine M. Baber and Patricia Monaghan, "College Women's Career and Motherhood Expectations: New Options, Old Dilemmas," *Sex Roles,* 1988, 3/4, 189–203.

18. Michele Hoffnung, "Working Mothers: Alternatives to Stereotyped Mothering" (paper presented to the National Conference on Feminist Psychology, Dallas, Mar. 1979).

19. Jacquelynne S. Eccles, "Gender Roles and Women's Achievement-Related Decisions," *Psychology of Women Quarterly,* 1987, 11, 135–72.

20. Michele Hoffnung, *What's a Mother to Do? Conversations on Work and Family* (Pasadena, Calif.: Trilogy Books, 1992), found that twenty out of thirty mothers had worked at least one year before having a child; fifteen of these twenty had worked more than one year.

21. These women are in their forties and fifties. In earlier times, active mothering would span forty years rather than the current twenty, and the average woman's life was shorter. See Mary P. Ryan, *Womanhood in America: From Colonial Times to the Present,* 2d ed. (New York: New Viewpoints, 1979), 26.

22. Katherine Gieve, ed., *Balancing Acts: On Being a Mother* (London: Virago Press, 1988), presents thirteen personal descriptions of the contradictions between motherhood and maintaining a place in the outside world by women with a variety of backgrounds and circumstances.

23. Angela Baron McBride, *The Growth and Development of Mothers* (New York: Harper and Row, 1973), chapter 1.

24. Michele Hoffnung Garskof, "The Psychology of the Maternity Ward: A Study in Dehumanization," in *Proceedings of the First International Childbirth Conference* (Stamford, Conn.: New Moon Publications, 1973).

25. See Louis Genevie and Eva Margolis, *The Motherhood Report* (New York: Macmillan, 1987), for a report on a survey of 870 mothers that richly illuminates the gap between women's expectations and experiences of motherhood.

26. Helena Znaniecki Lopata, *Occupation Housewife* (New York: Oxford University Press, 1971), 200. Lopata's extensive interviews with women in the Chicago area led her to the conclusion that only full-time involvement outside the home reduced this discontinuity, since it prevented the abrupt and complete change in life activity that usually accompanies the birth of the first child.

27. Unpublished data by Feldman (1962) as reported in Edward Pohlman, *Psychology of Birth Planning* (Cambridge, Mass.: Schenkman, 1969), chapter 6.

28. John Newson and Elizabeth Newson, *Infant Care in an Urban Community* (London: George Allen and Unwin, 1963).

29. Mary Georgina Boulton, *On Being a Mother* (London: Tavistock Publications, 1983).

30. Jane Lazarre, in *The Mother Knot* (New York: McGraw-Hill, 1976), gives an excellent personal account of these ambivalent feelings.

31. McBride, *The Growth and Development of Mothers,* chapter 3.

32. Norman K. Denzin, *Children and Their Caretakers* (New Brunswick, N.J.: Transaction Books, 1973). See also Elaine Heffner, *Mothering* (New York: Anchor, 1980), which stresses the need to trust oneself as a mother.

33. Van den Berg, *Dubious Maternal Affection,* 74.

34. Philip Wylie, *Generation of Vipers* (New York: Farrar, 1942); Hans Sebald, *Momism: The Silent Disease of America* (Chicago: Nelson Hall, 1976).

35. Jessie Bernard, *The Future of Motherhood* (New York: Penguin, 1974), 9.

36. Sylvia Brody and Sidney Axelrod, *Mothers, Fathers, and Children* (New York: International Universities Press, 1978), 238–39.

37. Judith Guss Teicholz, in "Psychological Correlates of Voluntary Childlessness in Married Women" (paper presented to the Eastern Psychological Association, Washington, D.C., Mar. 1978), reports that, although fertility rates have decreased, statistics do not indicate an increase in the number of married couples who have chosen to remain childless. Throughout the twentieth century, a constant 5 percent of the married population has chosen childlessness. In 1988 5.4 percent of wives expected to have no children. U.S. Bureau of the Census, *Statistical Abstract of the United States: 1990,* 110th ed. (Washington, D.C., 1990), 70. Surveys of women students in my classes over the years consistently indicate that about 80 percent want to have two children. In 1988 the average number of children expected by currently married women was 2.2. National Center for Health Statistics, *Health, United States, 1989* (Hyattsville, Md.: Public Health Services, 1990), 95.

38. Pohlman, in *Psychology of Birth Planning,* chapter 4, presents a detailed discussion of reasons. See Ellen Peck and Judith Lenderowitz, *Pronatalism* (New York: Crowell, 1974), for a full discussion of pronatalism.

39. Esther Menaker, "Some Inner Conflicts of Women in a Changing Society," in Roland and Harris, *Career and Motherhood,* 90.

40. Ralph LaRossa, "Fatherhood and Social Change," in Michael S. Kimmel and Michael A. Messner, eds., *Men's Lives,* 2d ed. (New York: Macmillan, 1992), 521–35.

41. Pauline Bart, "The Loneliness of the Long-Distance Mother," in Jo Freeman, ed., *Women: A Feminist Perspective,* 2d ed. (Palo Alto, Calif.: Mayfield Publishing Co., 1979), 257.

42. Lillian B. Rubin, *Women of a Certain Age: The Midlife Search for Self* (New York: Harper and Row, 1979), 6.

43. Ibid., 120.

44. Louise Kapp Howe, "The World of Women's Work," in Jeffrey P. Rosenfeld, ed., *Relationships: The Marriage and Family Reader* (Glenview, Ill.: Scott, Foresman and Co., 1982), 216–17.

45. Kathleen Gerson, *Hard Choices: How Women Decide About Work, Career, and Motherhood* (Berkeley: University of California Press, 1985), 7.

46. Rubin, *Women of a Certain Age,* chapters 7 and 8. Gail Sheehy, in *Passages: Predictable Crises of Adult Life* (New York: Dutton, 1976), also discusses these problems.

47. Tillie Olson's "Tell Me a Riddle," in Tillie Olson, *Tell Me a Riddle* (New York: Dell Laurel Edition, 1976), 72–125, is a wonderful story about how the assignment of full-time home and child care changes the character of a woman.

48. Harriet B. Presser, "Social Factors Affecting the Timing of the First Child," in Warren B. Miller and Lucille F. Newman, eds., *The First Child and Family Formation* (Chapel Hill: University of North Carolina, Carolina Population Center, 1978), 159. See also Pamela Daniels and Kathy Weingarten, *Sooner or Later: The Timing of Parenthood in Adult Lives* (New York: Norton, 1982).

49. Hoffnung, *What's a Mother to Do?* chapter 10.

50. Valerie Kincade Oppenheimer, *The Female Labor Force in the United States: Demographic and Economic Factors Governing Its Growth and Changing Composition* (Westport, Conn.: Greenwood Press, 1970), chapter 1.

51. Jennifer Watson, *Women, Work and the Future: Workforce 2000* (Washington, D.C.: National Commission on Working Women for Wider Opportunities for Women, Jan. 1989).

52. Dona Alpert and Amy Culbertson, "Daily Hassles and Coping Strategies of Dual-Earner and Nondual-Earner Women," *Psychology of Women Quarterly,* 1987, 11, 359–66.

53. Michele Hoffnung, "Teaching About Motherhood: Close Kin and the Transition to Motherhood," *Women's Studies Quarterly,* 1988, 16, 3 and 4, 48–57.

54. Faye J. Crosby, *Juggling: The Unexpected Advantages of Balancing Career and Home for Women and Their Families* (New York: The Free Press, 1991), chapter 1.

55. Myra H. Strober, "Market Work, Housework and Child Care: Buying Archaic Tenets, Building New Arrangements," in Phyllis W. Berman and Estelle R. Ramey, eds., *Women: A Developmental Perspective* (Bethesda, Md.: U.S. Department of Health and Human Services, 1982), 210–14.

56. As reported in Alice H. Cook, *The Working Mother* (Ithaca, N.Y.: Cornell University Press, 1978), 29.

57. Hoffnung, *What's a Mother to Do?* 183–84.

58. Joseph Pleck, "The Work-Family Role System," in R. Kahn-Hut, A. Daniels, and R. Colvard, eds., *Women and Work* (New York: Oxford University Press, 1982), 101–10.

59. Joseph H. Pleck, *Working Wives, Working Husbands* (Beverly Hills, Calif.: Sage Publications, 1985), chapter 7.

60. S. Shirley Feldman and Sharon C. Nash, "The Effects of Family Formation on Sex-Stereotypic Behavior: A Study of Responsiveness to Babies," in Miller and Newman, eds., *The First Child and Family Formation,* 159.

61. Gail Sheehy, in *Pathfinders* (New York: Morrow, 1981), describes this as her personal solution.

62. Barbara Harris, in "Two Lives, One 24-Hour Day," in Roland and Harris, eds., *Careers and Motherhood,* presents a personal and intelligent discussion of these problems.

63. Lydia N. O'Donnell, *Unheralded Majority: Contemporary Women as Mothers* (Lexington, Mass.: Lexington Books, 1985), 58–60.

64. Cited in Gray, "The Married Professional Woman," 236.

65. Richard Q. Bell and Lawrence V. Harper, *Child Effects on Adults* (Hillsdale, N.J.: Lawrence Erlbaum Associates, 1977), 214, 65.

66. Lois M. Verbrugge, "Role Responsibilities, Role Burdens, and Physical Health," in Faye J. Crosby, ed., *Spouse, Parent, Worker. On Gender and Multiple Roles* (New Haven, Conn.: Yale University Press, 1987), 154–66; Paula R. Pietromonaco, Jean Manis, and Katherine Frohardt-Lane, "Psychological Consequences of Multiple Social Roles," *Psychology of Women Quarterly,* 1986, 10, 373–82.

67. Hoffnung, *What's a Mother to Do?* chapter 10.

68. Grace Baruch, Rosalind Barnett, and Carol Rivers, *Lifeprints: New Patterns of Love and Work for Today's Women* (New York: McGraw Hill, 1983), in a survey of three hundred women, found that control over her work, whether it was paid work or homemaking, was key to a woman's sense of well-being.

69. Joseph H. Pleck and Jack Sawyer, *Men and Masculinity* (Englewood Cliffs, N.J.: Prentice-Hall, 1974), 53. See also Marc Feigin Fasteau, *The Male Machine* (New York: McGraw-Hill, 1974); Deborah S. David and Robert Brannon, eds., *The Forty-Nine Percent Majority* (Reading, Mass.:

Addison-Wesley, 1976); Joe L. Dubbert, *A Man's Man* (New York: Random House, 1974); Barbara Katz-Rothman, "Fathering as a Relationship," in Michael S. Kimmel and Michael A. Messner, eds., *Men's Lives,* 2d ed. (New York: Macmillan, 1992), 535–38, for discussions of weaknesses in the male role definition and the positive value of child care in men's lives.

70. Bruno Bettelheim, *The Children of the Dream* (London: Macmillan, 1969), 305–6.

71. See Dorothy Dinnerstein, *The Mermaid and the Minotaur: Sexual Arrangements and Human Malaise* (New York: Harper and Row, 1976); and Nancy Chodorow, *The Reproduction of Mothering: Psychoanalysis and the Sociology of Gender* (Berkeley: University of California Press, 1978).

72. Robert Rapoport and Rhonda Rapoport, *Working Couples* (New York: Harper Colophon, 1979); and Karen Wolk Feinstein, ed., *Working Women and Families* (Beverly Hills, Calif.: Sage, 1979).

73. See Alan Pifer, "Women Working: Toward a New Society," in Feinstein, ed., *Working Women and Families,* 13–34, for fuller discussion of this issue.

74. Crosby, *Juggling,* chapters 3 and 7.

75. Eccles, "Gender Roles," 135–72.

76. Paul J. Andrisani, "Job Satisfaction Among Working Women," *Signs: Journal of Women in Culture and Society,* 1978, 3, 588–607.

77. Nancy M. Rudd and Patrick C. McKenry, "Family Influences on the Job Satisfaction of Employed Mothers," *Psychology of Women Quarterly,* 1986, 10, 363–72.

78. Hoffnung, *What's a Mother to Do?*

79. Ellen Hock, Karen Christman Morgan, and Michael D. Hock, "Employment Decisions Made by Mothers of Infants," *Psychology of Women Quarterly,* 1985, 9, 383–402.

80. Hoffnung, *What's a Mother to Do?*

81. Gray, "The Married Professional Woman," 235–43.

Gray Clouds and Silver Linings: Women's Resources in Later Life

Laurie Russell Hatch

A HUNDRED YEARS AGO few people lived long enough to become old. Only 4 percent of the U.S. population was sixty-five years of age or older in 1900. By 1990, the proportion of Americans this age had grown to 12.5 percent. It is expected to rise to 13 percent by the year 2000 and to 22 percent by the year 2030 (U.S. Dept. of Health and Human Services, 1992, p. 19). As the older population has grown in the United States, it has become heavily female. Life expectancies for both women and men have increased over the century, but gains have been greater for women (Nathanson, 1990). As of 1990, there were 149 women for every 100 men in the sixty-five-and-older group, and 259 women for every 100 men in the eighty-five-and-older group (U.S. Bureau of the Census, 1992, pp. 23–178, Table 2-2).

Although women make up 59 percent of Americans sixty-five and older and 72 percent of those eighty-five and older, old-age economic and health programs are oriented more toward men's needs and life-course experiences than they are to women's. Old-age benefit programs are based on men's work histories and job characteristics. Women are penalized economically for the unpaid family labor they have performed throughout their lives. Older women are more likely than men to suffer from long-term, chronic health problems, but the central focus of the compensation programs of the U.S. health care system is on short-term acute illnesses (Hess, 1985).

Health and economic limitations are serious problems, clouding the horizon for many women as they grow older. At the same time, women experience many strengths and joys in later life, particularly such "silver linings" as nurturing friendships. Most older women evaluate their lives positively.

This chapter examines resources that support and enhance women's well-being in later life, as well as resource limitations that challenge and detract from older women's quality of life. The role of old-age programs, including Social Security and Medicare, is of particular concern. A central assumption underlying this examination is that although old age presents special challenges to women, it is not an isolated stage of life. In large part, the resources available to older women derive from the opportunities and constraints they have experienced over a lifetime.

Economic Resources

Economic resources illustrate well such life-course effects. Gender differences in work history, occupation, and industrial placement are important factors in explaining women's inferior economic status and greater risks for poverty at all ages (Bielby and Baron, 1986; England, 1982; England, Farkas,

Kilbourne, and Dou, 1988; Hodson and England, 1986).[1] Women's lifetime work in the labor force and in unpaid family roles determines the sources as well as the amount of their income in old age.

WOMEN'S PAID WORK AND OLD-AGE INCOME

Social Security and private pension programs are the two major sources of income in old age (Holden, 1989). For both of these sources, greater benefits are provided by lengthy and continuous labor force histories and occupations with higher pay. These features are associated more closely with non-Latino white men's employment experiences than with those of women (or racial-ethnic men).[2]

Social Security benefits are calculated by averaging workers' lifetime earnings (Meyer, 1990).[3] In addition to women's lower average earnings, many women have had periods of zero earnings during child-rearing years. Thus, benefits tend to be considerably lower for women than for men. Women's Social Security benefits, whether spousal or earned, average just 70 percent those of men. At the same time, women are more likely to rely on Social Security as their principal—or only—source of income. One-third of older unmarried women who receive Social Security benefits rely on this source for over 90 percent of their income (Arendell and Estes, 1991).

Like Social Security, private pensions provide greater benefits to those with higher earnings and longer, more continuous labor force histories. Among women and men who receive income from a private pension, women's average benefits are one-half those of men. However, women are also less likely to receive *any* income from a private pension source. Only 10 percent of older women receive any private pension income, compared to 27 percent of older men (Meyer, 1990).[4] Many of today's older women do not meet eligibility criteria for private pensions because of their delayed and interrupted paid work careers. Pension eligibility or vesting is determined by the number of continuous years of employment. The specific number of years required varies across different occupations and industries (Holden,1989). In addition, the jobs women hold tend to be clustered in the retail trade and service sectors, which are less likely than other industries to offer any pension plan at all (Holden, 1989; O'Rand and Henretta, 1982). Thus, women are less likely to receive pension income than men even when they have participated continuously in the labor force.

WOMEN'S UNPAID WORK

Neither public nor private benefit programs recognize unpaid work performed within the home, though society in general and capitalism in particular benefit from such labor (Cowan, 1987; DeVault, 1987; Glazer, 1987). The family labor that is performed primarily by women would be costly if it were purchased in the marketplace (Vanek, 1984), but it is not defined as "work"—by society at large, or even by women themselves (Daniels, 1987). As such, domestic labor—women's labor—is invisible. Financial resources over the life course are foregone, including incomes that could have been earned in the work force, as well as Social Security credits and private pension benefits that would otherwise have been accumulated.

It is well known that women perform the bulk of housework and child care (Hiller and Philliber, 1986; Bielby and Bielby, 1988) and that women often interrupt or delay their paid work careers to bear and rear children (Treiman, 1985). Women are also the primary care providers for elderly who need some help to perform activities of daily life and remain living in their homes (as opposed to institutional residence, such as in a nursing home). National data reveal that 29 percent of these home care providers are daughters, 23 percent are wives, and 20 percent are other female relatives and nonrelatives. Husbands represent 13 percent of home caregivers to the elderly. Only 9 percent are sons, most of whom lack female siblings who might otherwise provide parent care. Other male relatives and nonrelatives make up the remaining 7 percent of community care providers (Stone, Cafferata, and Sangl, 1987).[5,6]

In addition to gender differences in the likelihood of taking on a caregiving role, women and men differ in the types and amount of unpaid care they provide. Women typically give greater amounts of care and for longer periods of time (Horowitz, 1985; Stoller, 1983; Young and Kahana, 1989). Female caregivers are also more likely to provide direct, hands-on types of assistance, especially personal care tasks such as dressing and feeding (Dwyer and Coward, 1991; Finley, 1989; Horowitz, 1985). These gender differences are less pronounced among spouses than other types of caregivers. In general, husbands and wives provide more hours and a broader range of care than other types of caregivers. However, married women are more likely to be institutionalized than married men, indicating that husbands withdraw from the caregiving role sooner than wives (Stoller, 1992; Stone, Cafferata, and Sangl, 1987).[7] Wives, daughters, and other female caregivers are also less likely than male caregivers to have supplementary assistance from other family members (Stoller and Cutler, 1992; Stone, Cafferata, and Sangl, 1987).

Unpaid and unrecognized[8] as "workers," women's caregiving efforts can jeopardize their economic well-being. Women are more likely than men to reduce their hours of employment to care for a family member (White-Means and Thornton, 1990). Among older persons, women are more likely than men to retire early when an ill or disabled family member requires care (Szinovacz, 1989). Not surprisingly, women's current income is diminished when they curtail their hours of work or leave the labor force (Stoller, 1992). Less obvious is the fact that women's future economic well-being also is affected. Private pension benefits may be diminished or nullified with early labor force withdrawal. This is especially a problem for women whose paid work careers were interrupted in earlier years. These women will have greater difficulties meeting pension eligibility criteria. In addition, Social Security benefits are reduced when workers retire early. Although women can expect to live an additional two decades or more following early retirement, their Social Security benefits will remain at the reduced level (Arendell and Estes, 1991; Stoller, 1992).[9]

Other economic costs of caregiving are more direct. Caregiving assistance often includes financial assistance to older family members in need.[10] Sons are more apt to provide economic aid to an older parent than they are to perform more personal types of caregiving assistance. However, daughters are as likely as sons to give economic aid to elderly parents, and they are far more likely to provide personal care as well (Horowitz, 1985; Stoller, 1983). Gender differences in economic (and other) costs[11] of caregiving can also be inferred by the fact that daughters are three times more likely than sons to share their households with an ill or disabled elderly parent (Brody and Schoonover, 1986).

MARITAL STATUS AND SPOUSAL BENEFITS

At all stages of the life course, married women and men are better off economically than their unmarried counterparts (Keith, 1986). Though both spouses are at greater risk for economic difficulties upon widowhood, divorce, or separation, women are more likely to experience substantial declines in income when marriage ends and thus have a greater risk of falling into poverty (Holden, Burkhauser, and Myers, 1986; Keith, 1986, 1988). Older women are also far more likely to be single than older men. In 1990, among those age sixty-five and older, 60 percent of women but only 25 percent of men were unmarried. Among those eighty-five and older, 90 percent of women were unmarried compared to half of all men (computed from U.S. Bureau of the Census, 1992, Table 6-2). Women's greater likelihood of being single is due to their greater longevity, their tendency to marry men several years older than themselves, and their lower rates of remarriage (Sweet and Bumpass, 1987, pp. 41, 194; Grambs, 1989, p. 132).

The economic protection marriage provides to older women is shown clearly by the poverty rates for women in different marital groups. In 1987 only 6 percent of married women age sixty-five and over were poor, whereas over one-fifth of widowed and divorced women in this age group fell into the poverty category (U.S. Bureau of the Census, 1989, Table 8). Unmarried racial-ethnic women are especially likely to be poor. Among unmarried African-American women, for example, almost half of those sixty-five and older have below-poverty incomes (U.S. Bureau of the Census, 1989, Table 8).

Risks for poverty also are great for displaced homemakers (Arendell and Estes, 1991; Grambs, 1989, p. 167). These are women who become divorced or widowed after spending their adult lives providing care and household services to their families. Estimated at almost 11.5 million women in total, over 8 million displaced homemakers are fifty-five years of age or older. Suddenly faced with the need to support themselves financially, these women have little chance of finding adequate employment. Their job prospects have deteriorated even further in recent years due to cuts in federal employment and training programs. Displaced homemakers are not eligible for unemployment benefits or for Social Security credits (Arendell and Estes, 1991).

In theory, spousal benefits from private pensions and Social Security are available to provide economic resources for older displaced homemakers. In reality, spousal benefits are typically low, and in the case of private pension benefits, often nonexistent (Arendell and Estes, 1991; Meyer, 1990). Many private pension programs do not contain provisions for spousal benefits. Those that do have spousal provisions usually pay no more than a half-benefit when the wage-earning spouse dies. For couples who divorce, the allocation of private pension benefits depends upon the state in which they live. In most states, private pensions are considered the sole property of the wage earner.

In California and other states with community property laws, private pension benefits are more likely to be considered marital property and divided between the spouses (Meyer, 1990).

Social Security has a dual-eligibility structure. Those who are currently or previously married can derive benefits either from their own work force participation or from the earnings record of their spouse. Virtually all men receive Social Security benefits based on their own earnings record, but a whopping 99 percent of those receiving spousal benefits are women (Meyer, 1990). Spousal benefits are paid out at the rate of one-half the earner's (i.e., husband's) benefits. However, many women who are eligible for Social Security payments from their own labor force histories receive the spousal benefit because their own earnings-related benefits are even lower. Karen Holden (1982) found that spousal benefits were higher than earner benefits for 84 percent of women who were eligible for either type of benefits but who had one or more earning periods with zero earnings. Thus, most married women who are employed will never realize the Social Security contributions they made. The benefits these women receive are the same as if they had never been employed.

Even spousal benefits are not provided when marriages last less than ten years. For those who are no longer married, the relative amount of spousal benefit depends upon how the marriage was terminated: widowed women receive a larger benefit than divorced women. With widowhood, spousal benefits are calculated at two-thirds the couple's total Social Security benefit, whereas divorced partners split the total benefit based on their own relative portions. Divorced husbands generally receive two-thirds of the couple's benefit and divorced wives one-third (Meyer, 1990). Further, although the average age of women's widowhood in the United States is fifty-five, Social Security spousal benefits do not become available until the age of sixty. This "widow's gap" creates a period of great economic insecurity for many women (Kinderknecht, 1989).

Thus, not only do women's family and paid work experiences put them at an economic disadvantage in old age; women are also penalized by the ways in which old-age benefit programs are structured. Social Security as well as private pension programs continue to reflect traditional assumptions about gender roles within the family, including the meaning of "productive" versus "unproductive" (i.e., paid versus unpaid) labor.

Health Resources

A precious resource at any age, good health is less likely to be taken for granted among the elderly. Old age should not be equated with poor health (Stahl and Feller, 1990), but it is true that *physical* health problems and disabilities are more common in later life (Verbrugge, 1989). Contrary to popular belief, *mental* distress does not increase with age. Psychological disorders are found more frequently among younger than older age groups (Feinson, 1990).

There are important differences in the physical and mental health of older women and men. Government programs to help meet some of the health care needs of the elderly (Ferraro and Wan, 1990) are oriented more toward men's needs than toward women's (Hess, 1985), even though women constitute a larger proportion of the older population.

PHYSICAL HEALTH AND LONGEVITY

Probably the most striking gender-linked health difference is that women live longer, a phenomenon observed in all developed countries. In the United States, gender differences in life expectancy have increased over the course of the twentieth century but seem to have stabilized in recent years (Nathanson, 1990). At birth, American women can expect to live seventy-eight years, or seven years longer than men.[12] For those who reach age sixty-five, women can expect to live an additional nineteen years—four years more than men of the same age (U.S. Department of Health and Human Services, 1991, p. 11). We do not yet have a clear understanding of why women live longer than men. Potentially important factors identified to date include genetic and hormonal influences and the greater tendency among men to engage in risky behaviors such as smoking, drinking, driving, and violence (Nathanson, 1990).

Women's longevity is a mixed blessing. In addition to the fact that many women live out their later years in dire economic circumstances, older women are more likely than men to suffer from debilitating chronic illnesses (Verbrugge, 1985, 1989) including arthritis, high blood pressure, diabetes, allergies, anemia, migraine, sciatica (a painful condition affecting the hip or its nerves), most orthopedic problems, and most digestive and urinary problems (except hernias and ulcers). Due in large part to the types and severity of illnesses they are prone to develop, older women typically have greater mobility limitations than older men and greater difficulties performing various personal care activities such as bathing (Verbrugge, 1985).

In contrast, the list of chronic illnesses older men are more likely to suffer from is shorter—heart disease, respiratory diseases, arteriosclerosis, pneumonia, and emphysema/asthma—but they are at greater risk for life-threatening health problems. Men are more likely than women to die from diseases of the heart, malignant neoplasms (cancer), and injuries, which represent three of the four leading causes of death among older persons (Herzog, 1989; Verbrugge, 1989).[13] Thus, while many women's later years are characterized by painful and limiting yet nonfatal health conditions, men typically die sooner, having experienced fewer or briefer periods of chronic illness and disability (Verbrugge, 1989).

Older women are more likely than older men to spend some portion of their lives in a nursing home (46 percent compared to 28 percent) and to spend a significant amount of time there prior to death (Kemper and Murtaugh, 1991). Women's greater risk for institutional residence is due to a combination of factors including their higher disability levels, greater longevity, and higher rates of living alone (Kemper and Murtaugh, 1991; Steinbach, 1992; Verbrugge, 1989). Those who live alone generally receive less health care assistance from family and friends in the community and thus are more likely to enter a nursing home when they require long-term care (Chappell, 1991; Steinbach, 1992; Wolinsky, Callahan, Fitzgerald, and Johnson,

1992). As Lois Verbrugge (1989, p. 64) has noted with respect to nursing home admissions, "There is more to becoming a resident there than just health status."

Although nearly half of all women age sixty-five and older live in a nursing home at some point during their lives, the major U.S. health care program for the elderly (Medicare) is intended primarily to meet acute-care needs. Medicare covers 44 percent of the health costs of older married couples and even less (33 percent) of the health costs of older single women. These differences are due to the fact that Medicare does not cover the long-term care that is needed by many older women and thus pays a lower proportion of women's health costs than those of men. Given that older women are more likely to be poor than older men and less likely to have private health coverage, they are harder pressed to cover out-of-pocket health care costs (Arendell and Estes, 1991).

The program that does cover long-term institutional care, Medicaid, is available only when individuals have exhausted most of their economic resources. Medicaid is a program intended for the poor of all ages rather than specifically for the elderly (U.S. Senate, Special Committee on Aging, 1991). However, due to increasingly restricted eligibility requirements, only 40 percent of poor elderly were eligible for this program as of 1987 (Arendell and Estes, 1991). Clearly, women's greater needs for long-term institutional care are far from being met by Medicaid. Further, Medicaid reinforces gender disparities in economic resources by making benefits contingent on poverty status.

Not only nursing home residents but their community-dwelling spouses as well are required to "spend down" to meet Medicaid eligibility requirements. Because elderly men are likely to be married and cared for by their spouse until institutional care becomes necessary, spousal impoverishment is a greater problem for women (England, Keigher, Miller, and Linsk, 1991). In 1988 Medicaid requirements were revised to reduce impoverishment among community spouses. The new provisions allow community spouses a monthly income equal to 122 percent of the poverty level and allowances for shelter costs (if housing exceeds 30 percent of the allowed monthly income). Spouses of institutionalized elderly also are now able to retain either $12,000 or one-half of the couple's combined assets (whichever is greater), to a maximum of $60,000. These new maximum provisions may still not prevent serious financial hardships for many spouses (Meyer and Quadagno, 1990). Those who had a modest amount of assets as a couple must live out the remainder of their lives with only half of that sum.

With few exceptions, elderly of both genders prefer to live in the community rather than in an institution (Béland, 1987). Some community-based services for long-term care are available through Medicaid, but they are quite limited in scope. In addition, confusing Medicaid regulations hinder the ability of eligible (i.e., poor) elderly to make use of the services that are available (U.S. Senate, Special Committee on Aging, 1991). The result is that families— and more accurately, *women*—are the major caregivers to disabled elderly residing in the community, providing 75 to 80 percent of all community-based elder care (Coward, 1987; Stone, Cafferata, and Sangl, 1987; Ward, Sherman, and LaGory, 1984).

MENTAL HEALTH

Considering their greater risks for economic hardships, widowhood, and chronic illnesses, it is not surprising that depression is greater among older women than older men (Herzog, 1989). Depression is assessed by standardized tests such as the DSM-III and by clinicians' assessments (Feinson, 1987). Gender differences in depression are not confined to the elderly, but are observed among younger age groups as well (Herzog, 1989). In contrast, men are more likely to be diagnosed with antisocial personality disorders, including drug and alcohol abuse (Lennon, 1987). Consideration of all types of psychological disorders reveals similar levels of psychological impairment among older women and men (Feinson, 1987).

When older persons are asked to evaluate their own mental health, both women and men report generally high levels of happiness and satisfaction with their lives (Baur and Okun, 1983). In Lucille Bearon's (1989) recent study of older women, most said that their lives could not be better. It is possible that older women scale down their expectations because they perceive few opportunities for change. At the same time, the positive views many older women express about their lives should not be discounted. Most of the women in Bearon's study emphasized positive elements in their lives over the negative ones, counting "their blessings, not their problems" (p. 778).

Social Resources

Along with health and economic resources, social resources are important determinants of life quality for women and men of all ages (Ishii-Kuntz, 1990). Social resources can buffer stressful life experiences by helping individuals to clarify their situations, develop strategies and plans for action, and reinforce their self-identities (Krause, 1986). Because the elderly are more likely to experience role losses due to retirement and widowhood, social resources have been considered especially important for their well-being (Adams, 1987; Morgan, 1984).[14]

INTERACTION WITH FAMILY AND FRIENDS

Women and men tend to differ in their social relationships at younger as well as older ages. These differences include quantitative as well as qualitative dimensions. Men typically have larger social networks, while women have richer, more intimate relationships with friends and family (Connidis and Davies, 1992; Depner and Ingersoll-Dayton, 1988; Wright, 1989). Women are also more likely than men to report continuity in their relationships over the life course, remaining emotionally close to friends made at younger ages (Roberto and Kimboko, 1989).

Women attach particular importance to the role of confiding in their friendships (Wright, 1989). They are likely to confide in other women—their mothers, sisters, and friends—and to have more than one confidant. This is true for unmarried women as well as those who are married. In contrast, men of all ages are more likely to rely on women for emotional intimacy.

Unmarried men usually name a woman as confidant (but this pattern may be more characteristic of heterosexual men than it is of unpartnered gay men).[15] Married men almost always name their spouse as confidant (Depner and Ingersoll, 1982; Wright, 1989). When marriage ends, most men but few women are deprived of their primary or sole confidant.

In addition, women seem better able than men to develop and maintain other types of social relationships when they become divorced or widowed (Kohen, 1983; Keith, 1986; Morgan, 1984). Leslie Morgan's longitudinal study (which followed the same individuals over time) found that women interacted with fewer family members after they were widowed, but their remaining family contacts increased in intensity. Intensity of contacts for male widowers remained stable or declined over time. Overall, although women are at greater risk for widowhood than men, most older women are not at risk for loneliness and social isolation (Babchuck and Anderson, 1989; Essex and Nam, 1987; Kohen, 1983).

ORGANIZATIONAL PARTICIPATION

Like younger persons, elderly belong to a wide variety of organizations—community, political, professional, and religious groups, to name a few broad categories (Grambs, 1989, pp. 98–103). Organizational membership and participation can provide valued resources to older persons. For example, church groups often provide financial, emotional, and health care support to older members in need (Hatch, 1991; Taylor and Chatters, 1986). Participation in organizations also can promote the self-esteem and life satisfaction of the elderly as well as provide them with opportunities for social activities and interaction (Daley, Applewhite, and Jorquez, 1989; Walls and Zarit, 1990).

Older women are more likely than older men to have mobility limitations that restrict their ability to leave their homes (Verbrugge, 1989). However, age-related declines in women's organizational involvement are smaller than the declines observed among men. This gender difference is linked to the different types of organizations to which men and women tend to belong. Men are more likely to belong to professional or national service associations. Typically geared toward their occupations or other economically oriented connections, men's organizational participation often declines greatly when they retire. Women are more likely to belong to neighborhood, community, and religious organizations. Their participation is little affected by retirement (deVaus and McAllister, 1987; McPherson and Smith-Lovin, 1982).

Involvement in religious organizations is important for many women. Women of all ages attend religious services and activities more frequently than men, and they express greater religious commitment (deVaus and McAllister, 1987; Taylor, 1986). Older women, in particular, often are perceived as the mainstay of their religions (Grambs, 1989, p. 102). A study by Jane Peterson (1990) documents the active, valued roles of older African-American women in their churches. These "wise women" provide continuity in knowledge and tradition to younger generations. In turn, the women derive status and respect from their contributions.

Conclusions

The economic, health, and social resources of older women differ in important ways from those of older men. Overall, older women have fewer economic resources and poorer physical health than older men. At the same time, most older women express satisfaction with their lives and are no more likely than older men to be diagnosed with a psychological impairment. With respect to social resources, women seem to be clearly advantaged. In particular, same-sex friendships among older women afford nurturance and self-expression as well as companionship. Involvement in organizations, including religious groups, is also an invaluable social resource for many older women.

Older women also differ in important ways from one another. Race, ethnicity, and social class are critical determinants of resources across the life course. It is important to recognize that these dimensions, as well as gender and age, are linked together inextricably, shaping individuals' experiences, opportunities, and identities throughout their lives. Marital status and sexual orientation also have profound effects on individuals' lives, but very little is known about the latter with respect to older women's resources.[16]

Changes in social policies and programs can and should be made. However, the economic disadvantages and health care problems of older women—both as givers as well as receivers of care—reflect deep-seated structural inequalities in society that social policy reforms alone cannot eliminate (Arendell and Estes, 1991). Large-scale changes in societal institutions, including the economy and the family, must also take place to address the structural sources of gender-based inequalities that are present at all ages and that culminate in later life.

NOTES

1. As discussed in the chapter by Alice Abel Kemp in this volume, adult women have greater risks for poverty than men at all ages. It is important to note that the proportion of elderly poor would be higher if poverty were defined the same way for persons over sixty-five as it is for those under sixty-five. Under the dubious assumption that elderly people require less money for food than younger people, the federal government uses two different poverty lines (Margolis, 1990, pp. 11–13). Thus, an unmarried sixty-four-year-old with an annual income of $6,930 would be designated as poor in 1991, while a sixty-five-year-old with an identical income would not.

2. This chapter uses the term *racial-ethnic* to designate members of historically disadvantaged racial and ethnic groups.

3. Specifically, Social Security benefits are calculated by averaging workers' earnings over thirty-five years, or by averaging income earned between the ages of twenty-one and sixty-two, excluding the five lowest-earning years (Meyer, 1990).

4. Racial-ethnic men also are significantly less likely to receive private pension income (Dressel, 1991).

5. Caregiver categories add to 101 percent due to rounding. These figures are for persons designated as the primary caregiver to community-dwelling elderly.

6. The gendered pattern of caregiving is even stronger among Latin Americans, whose ranked hierarchy of caregivers has been reported as (1) wife, (2) sister or other adult female blood relative, (3) female in-laws, (4) male blood relatives including spouses, and (5) male in-laws (Henderson, 1990).

7. This finding has been interpreted as evidence that husbands have less tolerance than wives for the demands of caregiving. Other researchers have concluded more simply that husbands are not quite as dependable as wives in providing long-term care (see Stoller, 1992).

8. The taken-for-granted nature of women's unpaid work is underlined by the finding that husbands are often praised for their caregiving efforts, while wives' efforts are unremarked (Stoller, 1992). In a similar vein, married sons usually expect and receive support from their wives in providing care to the son's parents, while married daughters express appreciation when their husbands do not object to the time and effort the daughters expend in caring for their own parents (Horowitz, 1985).

9. This is pertinent to women who rely on Social Security benefits derived from their own earnings records. However, women who depend on spousal benefits from Social Security will receive reduced benefits for the duration of their lifetime when their husbands retire early due to illness or for other reasons (Kinderknecht, 1989).

10. Dependency is not inevitable in old age. Contingent upon their health and economic status, some individuals require assistance at earlier ages, while others remain independent throughout their lives (Spitze and Logan, 1992; Stahl and Feller, 1990).

11. Many caregivers derive feelings of satisfaction from their efforts (Abel, 1989, 1990). However, in addition to economic burdens arising from caregiving, emotional and physical costs have been documented. Research indicates that these caregiving burdens are disproportionately experienced by women (Barusch and Spaid, 1989; George and Gwyther, 1986; Moen, Dempster-McClain, and Williams, 1992; Stoller and Pugliesi, 1989; Young and Kahana, 1989).

12. Life expectancies are lower for racial-ethnic group members than for non-Latino whites, within gender groups. At birth, African-American women have a life expectancy of seventy-three years, compared to seventy-nine years for white women. The figures for African-American men and white men are sixty-five and seventy-two years, respectively. All figures are for persons born in 1988 (U.S. Department of Health and Human Services, 1991, p. 11).

13. Diabetes, the fourth leading cause of death among the elderly, does not show a gender-linked pattern of mortality (Verbrugge, 1989).

14. This does not mean that greater amounts of social interaction invariably produce greater well-being. Interaction can have negligible or even harmful effects, depending upon the type and source of support (Bankoff, 1983; Morgan, 1989). However, researchers agree that friendships promote elders' well-being (Lee and Ihinger-Tallman, 1980; Lee and Ishii-Kuntz, 1987), probably because friendships are volitional and can be terminated when they are no longer rewarding (Lee and Shehan, 1989).

15. Emotional intimacy between partners is an important element of enduring gay relationships (Lee, 1990).

16. Gerontological studies seldom provide information on respondents' sexual orientations. Most researchers (as well as policymakers) implicitly assume that elders are heterosexual (Cruikshank, 1990; Quam and Whitford, 1992), and those who do study homosexuality among the aged have difficulties obtaining representative samples; older lesbians and gay men are especially wary of disclosing their sexual identities (Adelman, 1990). Nevertheless, an intriguing argument made by some gerontologists is that lesbians and gay men may adapt better to aging because they are not restricted by traditional gender roles and thus have greater flexibility in responding to life changes (Quam and Whitford, 1992).

BIBLIOGRAPHY

Abel, Emily K. 1989. Family care of the frail elderly: Framing an agenda for change. *Women's Studies Quarterly* 17 (1/2):75–85.

Adams, Rebecca G. 1987. Patterns of network change: A longitudinal study of friendships of elderly women. *The Gerontologist* 27(2):222–27.

Adelman, Marcy. 1990. Stigma, gay lifestyles, and adjustment to aging: A study of later-life gay men and lesbians. *Journal of Homosexuality* 20(3/4):7–32.

Arendell, Terry, and Carroll L. Estes. 1991. Older women in the post-Reagan era. In *Critical perspectives on aging: Toward a political and moral economy of aging,* ed. Meredith Minkler and Carroll L. Estes, 209–26. Amityville, NY: Baywood.

Babchuck, Nicholas, and Trudy B. Anderson. 1989. Older widows and married women: Their intimates and confidants. *International Journal of Aging and Human Development* 28(1):21–35.

Bankoff, Elizabeth A. 1983. Social support and adaptation to widowhood. *Journal of Marriage and the Family* 45(4):827–39.

Barusch, Amanda S., and Wanda M. Spaid. 1989. Gender differences in caregiving: Why do wives report greater burden? *The Gerontologist* 29(5).667–76.

Baur, Patricia A., and Morris A. Okun. 1983. Stability of life satisfaction in late life. *The Gerontologist* 23(3):261–65.

Bearon, Lucille B. 1989. No great expectations: The underpinnings of life satisfaction for older women. *The Gerontologist* 29(6):772–78.

Béland, Francois. 1987. Living arrangement preferences among elderly people. *The Gerontologist* 27(6):797–803.

Bielby, Denise D., and William T. Bielby. 1988. She works hard for the money: Household responsibilities and the allocation of work effort. *American Journal of Sociology* 93(5):1031–59.

Bielby, William T., and James N. Baron. 1986. Men and women at work: Sex segregation and statistical discrimination. *American Journal of Sociology* 91(4):759–99.

Brody, Elaine M., and Claire B. Schoonover. 1986. Patterns of parent-care when adult daughters work and when they do not. *The Gerontologist* 26(4):372–81.

Chappell, Neena L. 1991. Living arrangements and sources of caregiving. *Journal of Gerontology* 46(1):S1–8.

Connidis, Ingrid Arnet, and Lorraine Davies. 1992. Confidants and companions: Choices in later life. *Journal of Gerontology* 47(3):S115–22.

Cowan, Ruth Schwartz. 1987. Women's work, housework, and history: The historical roots of inequality in work-force participation. In *Families and work,* ed. Naomi Gerstel and Harriet Engel Gross, 164–77. Philadelphia, PA: Temple University.

Coward, Raymond T. 1987. Factors associated with the configuration of the helping networks of noninstitutionalized elders. *Journal of Gerontological Social Work* 10(1/2):113–32.

Cruikshank, Margaret. 1990. Lavender and gray: A brief survey of lesbian and gay aging studies. *Journal of Homosexuality* 20(3/4):77–87.

Daley, John Michael, Steven R. Applewhite, and James Jorquez. 1989. Community participation of the elderly Chicano: A model. *International Journal of Aging and Human Development* 29(2):135–50.

Daniels, Arlene Kaplan. 1987. Invisible work. *Social Problems* 34:403–15.

Depner, Charlene, and Berit Ingersoll. 1982. Employment status and social support: The experience of the mature woman. In *Women's retirement: Policy implications for recent research,* ed. Maximiliene Szinovacz, 61–76. Beverly Hills, CA: Sage.

Depner, Charlene, and Berit Ingersoll-Dayton. 1988. Supportive relationships in later life. *Psychology and Aging* 3:348–57.

DeVault, Marjorie L. 1987. Doing housework: Feeding and family life. In *Families and work,* ed. Naomi Gerstel and Harriet Engel Gross, 178–91. Philadelphia, PA: Temple University.

deVaus, David, and Ian McAllister. 1987. Gender differences in religion: A test of the structural location theory. *American Sociological Review* 52:472–81.

Dressel, Paula L. 1991. Gender, race, and class: Beyond the feminization of poverty in later life. In *Critical perspectives on aging: The political and moral economy of growing old,* ed. Meredith Minkler and Carroll L. Estes, 245–52. Amityville, NY: Baywood.

Dwyer, Jeffrey W., and Raymond T. Coward. 1991. Gender, family, and long-term care of the elderly. In *Gender, families, and elder care,* ed. Jeffrey W. Dwyer and Raymond T. Coward, 3–17. Newbury Park, CA: Sage.

England, Paula. 1982. The failure of human capital theory to explain sex segregation. *The Journal of Human Resources* 17(3):358–70.

England, Paula, George Farkas, Barbara Stanek Kilbourne, and Thomas Dou. 1988. Explaining sex segregation and wages: Findings from a model with fixed effects. *American Sociological Review* 53(Aug.):544–58.

England, Suzanne E., Sharon M. Keigher, Baila Miller, and Nathan L. Linsk. 1991. Community care policies and gender justice. In *Critical perspectives on aging: The political and moral economy of growing old,* ed. Meredith Minkler and Carroll L. Estes, 227–44. Amityville, NY: Baywood.

Essex, Marilyn J., and Sunghee Nam. 1987. Marital status and loneliness among older women: The differential importance of close family and friends. *Journal of Marriage and the Family* 49(1):93–106.

Feinson, Marjorie Chary. 1987. Mental health and aging: Are there gender differences? *The Gerontologist* 27(6):703–11.

Feinson, Marjorie Chary. 1990. The distribution of distress by age and gender: Examining data from community surveys. In *The legacy of longevity: Health and health care in later life,* ed. Sidney M. Stahl, 115–39. Newbury Park, CA: Sage.

Ferraro, Kenneth F., and Thomas T. H. Wan. 1990. Health needs and services for older adults: Evaluating policies for an aging society. In *The legacy of longevity: Health and health care in later life,* ed. Sidney M. Stahl, 235–54. Newbury Park, CA: Sage.

Finley, Nancy J. 1989. Theories of family labor as applied to gender differences in caregiving for elderly parents. *Journal of Marriage and the Family* 51(Feb.):79–86.

Glazer, Nona Y. 1987. Servants to capital: Unpaid domestic labor and paid work. In *Families and work,* ed. Naomi Gerstel and Harriet Engel Gross, 236–55. Philadelphia, PA: Temple University.

Grambs, Jean D. 1989. *Women over forty: Visions and realities.* New York: Springer.

Hatch, Laurie Russell. 1991. Informal support networks of older African-American and white women: Examining effects of family, paid work, and religious participation. *Research on Aging* 13(2):144–70.

Henderson, J. Neil. 1990. Alzheimer's disease in cultural context. In *The cultural context of aging: Worldwide perspectives,* ed. Jay Sokolovsky, 315–30. New York: Bergin & Garvey.

Herzog, A. Regula. 1989. Methodological issues in research on older women. In *Health and economic status of older women,* ed. A. Regula Herzog, Karen C. Holden, and Mildred M. Seltzer, 133–48. New York: Baywood.

Hess, Beth B. 1985. Aging policies and old women: The hidden agenda. In *Gender and the life course,* ed. Alice S. Rossi, 319–31. New York: Aldine.

Hiller, Dana V., and William W. Philliber. 1986. The division of labor in contemporary marriage: Expectations, perceptions, and performance. *Social Problems* 33(3):191–201.

Hodson, Randy, and Paula England. 1986. Industrial structure and sex differences in earnings. *Industrial Relations* 25(1):16–32.

Holden, Karen C. 1982. Supplemental OASI benefit to homemakers through current spouse benefits, a homemaker's credit and child-care drop-out years. In *A challenge to Social Security: The changing roles of women and men in American society,* ed. Richard V. Burkhauser and Karen C. Holden, 41–72. New York: Academic Press.

Holden, Karen C. 1989. Economic status of older women: A summary of selected research issues. In *Health and economic status of older women,* ed. A Regula Herzog, Karen C. Holden, and Mildred M. Seltzer, 24–32. Amityville, NY: Baywood.

Holden, Karen C., Richard V. Burkhauser, and Daniel A. Myers. 1986. Income transitions at older stages of life: The dynamics of poverty. *The Gerontologist* 26(3):292–97.

Hooyman, Nancy R. 1992. Social policy and gender inequities in caregiving. In *Gender, families, and elder care,* ed. Jeffrey W. Dwyer and Raymond T. Coward, 181–201. Newbury Park, CA: Sage.

Horowitz, Amy. 1985. Sons and daughters as caregivers to older parents: Differences in role performance and consequences. *The Gerontologist* 25(6):612–17.

Ishii-Kuntz, Masako. 1990. Social interaction and psychological well-being: Comparison across stages of adulthood. *International Journal of Aging and Human Development* 30(1):15–36.

Keith, Pat M. 1986. The social context and resources of the unmarried in old age. *International Journal of Aging and Human Development* 23(2):81–96.

Keith, Pat M. 1988. Finances of unmarried elderly people over time. *International Journal of Aging and Human Development* 26(3):211–23.

Kemper, Peter, and Christopher M. Murtaugh. 1991. Lifetime use of nursing home care. *The New England Journal of Medicine* 324(9):595–600.

Kinderknecht, Cheryl H. 1989. What's out there and how to get it: A practical resource guide for the helpers of older women. In *Women as they age: Challenge, opportunity, and triumph,* ed. J. Dianne Garner and Susan O. Mercer. New York: The Haworth Press.

Kohen, Janet A. 1983. Old but not alone: Informal social supports among the elderly by marital status and sex. *The Gerontologist* 23(1):57–63.

Krause, Neal. 1986. Social support, stress, and well-being among older adults. *Journal of Gerontology* 41(4):512–19.

Lee, Gary R., and Marilyn Ihinger-Tallman. 1980. Sibling interaction and morale: The effects of family relations on older people. *Research on Aging* 2(3):367–91.

Lee, Gary R., and Masako Ishii-Kuntz. 1987. Social interaction, loneliness, and emotional well-being among the elderly. *Research on Aging* 9(4):459–82.

Lee, Gary R., and Constance L. Shehan. 1989. Retirement and marital satisfaction. *Journal of Gerontology* 44(6):S226–30.

Lee, John Alan. 1990. Can we talk? Can we *really* talk? Communication as a key factor in the maturing homosexual couple. *Journal of Homosexuality* 20(3/4):143–68.

Lennon, Mary Clare. 1987. Sex differences in distress: The impact of gender and work roles. *Journal of Health and Social Behavior* 28(Sept.):290–305.

Margolis, Richard J. 1990. *Risking old age in America.* Boulder, CO: Westview.

McPherson, J. Miller, and Lynn Smith-Lovin. 1982. Women and weak ties: Differences by sex in the size of voluntary organizations. *American Journal of Sociology* 87(4):883–904.

Meyer, Madonna Harrington. 1990. Family status and poverty among older women. The gendered distribution of retirement income in the United States. *Social Problems* 37(4):551–63.

Meyer, Madonna Harrington, and Jill Quadagno. 1990. The dilemma of poverty-based long-term care. In *The legacy of longevity: Health and health care in later life,* ed. Sidney M. Stahl, 255–69. Newbury Park, CA: Sage.

Moen, Phyllis, Donna Dempster-McClain, and Robin M. Williams, Jr. 1992. Successful aging: A life-course perspective on women's multiple roles and health. *American Journal of Sociology* 97(6):1612–38.

Morgan, David L. 1989. Adjusting to widowhood: Do social networks really make it easier? *The Gerontologist* 29(1):101–7.

Morgan, Leslie A. 1984. Changes in family interaction following widowhood. *Journal of Marriage and the Family* 46(May):323–31.

Nathanson, Constance A. 1990. The gender-mortality differential in developed countries: Demographic and sociocultural dimensions. In *Gender, health and longevity: Multidisciplinary perspectives,* ed. Marcia G. Ory and Huber R. Warner, 3–23. New York: Springer.

O'Rand, Angela M., and John C. Henretta. 1982. Delayed career entry, industrial pension structure, and early retirement in a cohort of unmarried women. *American Sociological Review* 47(June):365–73.

Peterson, Jane W. 1990. Age of wisdom: Elderly black women in family and church. In *The cultural context of aging: Worldwide perspectives,* ed. Jay Sokolovsky, 213–27. New York: Bergin & Garvey.

Quam, Jean K., and Gary S. Whitford. 1992. Adaptation and age-related expectations of older gay and lesbian adults. *The Gerontologist* 32(3):367–74.

Roberto, Karen A., and Priscilla J. Kimboko. 1989. Friendships in later life: Definitions and maintenance patterns. *International Journal of Aging and Human Development* 23(1):9–19.

Spitze, Glenna, and John R. Logan. 1992. Helping as a component of parent-adult child relations. *Research on Aging* 14(3):291–312.

Stahl, Sidney M., and Jacquelyn Rupp Feller. 1990. Old equals sick: An ontogenetic fallacy. In *The legacy of longevity: Health and health care in later life,* ed. Sidney M. Stahl, 21–34. Newbury Park, CA: Sage.

Steinbach, Ulrike. 1992. Social networks, institutionalization, and mortality among elderly people in the United States. *Journal of Gerontology* 47(4):S183–90.

Stoller, Eleanor P. 1983. Parental caregiving by adult children. *Journal of Marriage and the Family* 45(Nov.):851–58.

Stoller, Eleanor P. 1992. Gender differences in the experiences of caregiving spouses. In *Gender, families, and elder care,* ed. Jeffrey W. Dwyer and Raymond T. Coward, 46–64. Newbury Park, CA: Sage.

Stoller, Eleanor P., and Stephen J. Cutler. 1992. The impact of gender on configurations of care among married elderly couples. *Research on Aging* 14(3):313–30.

Stoller, Eleanor P., and Karen L. Pugliesi. 1989. Other roles of caregivers: Competing responsibilities or supportive resources. *Journal of Gerontology* 44(6):S231–38.

Stone, Robyn I., Gail Lee Cafferata, and Judith Sangl. 1987. Caregivers of the frail elderly: A national profile. *The Gerontologist* 27(5):616–26.

Sweet, James A., and Larry L. Bumpass. 1987. *American families and households.* New York: Russell Sage.

Szinovacz, Maximiliane. 1989. Decision-making on retirement timing. In *Dyadic decision making,* ed. David Brinberg and James Jaccard, 286–310. New York: Springer.

Taylor, Robert J. 1986. Religious participation among elderly blacks. *The Gerontologist* 26(6):630–36.

Taylor, Robert J., and Linda M. Chatters. 1986. Church-based informal support among elderly blacks. *The Gerontologist* 26(6):637–42.

196

Relationships, Family, and the Life Cycle

Treiman, Donald J. 1985. The work histories of women and men: What we know and what we need to find out. In *Gender and the life course,* ed. Alice S. Rossi, 213–31. New York: Aldine.

U.S. Bureau of the Census. Poverty in the United States, 1987. *Current Population Reports,* P-60, no. 163. Washington, DC: GPO.

U.S. Bureau of the Census. 1992. Sixty-five plus in America. *Current Population Reports,* P-23, no. 178. Washington, DC: GPO.

U.S. Department of Commerce. 1992. *1990 Census of Population and Housing.* Summary Tape File 1C. Washington, DC: Data User Service Division.

U.S. Department of Health and Human Services. 1991. *Vital Statistics of the United States, 1988,* vol. 2, sec. 6. DHHS pub. no. (PHS) 91-1104. Washington, DC: GPO.

U.S. Department of Health and Human Services. 1992. *Health United States 1991 and Prevention Profile.* DHHS pub. no. (PHS) 92-1232. Washington, DC: GPO.

U.S. Senate, Special Committee on Aging. 1991. *Developments in Aging, 1990: Volume 1.* Washington, DC: GPO.

Vanek, Joann. 1984. Housewives as workers. In *Work and family: Changing roles of men and women,* ed. Patricia Voydanoff, 89–110. Palo Alto, CA: Mayfield.

Verbrugge, Lois M. 1985. An epidemiological profile of older women. In *The physical and mental health of aged women,* ed. Marie R. Haug, Amasa B. Ford, and Marian Shea, 41–64. New York: Springer.

Verbrugge, Lois M. 1989. Gender, aging, and health. In *Aging and health: Perspectives on gender, race, ethnicity, and class,* ed. Kyriakos S. Markides, 23–78. Newbury Park, CA: Sage.

Walls, Carla Tooles, and Steven H. Zarit. 1990. Informal support from black churches and the well-being of elderly blacks. *The Gerontologist* 31(4):490–95.

Ward, Russell A., Susan R. Sherman, and Mark LaGory. 1984. Subjective network assessments and subjective well-being. *Journal of Gerontology* 39(1):93–101.

White-Means, Shelley I., and Michael C. Thornton. 1990. Labor market choices and home health care provision among employed ethnic caregivers. *The Gerontologist* 30(6):769–75.

Wolinsky, Fredric D., Christopher M. Callahan, John F. Fitzerald, and Robert J. Johnson. 1992. The risk of nursing home placement and subsequent death among older adults. *Journal of Gerontology* 47(4):S173–82.

Wright, Paul H. 1989. Gender differences in adults' same- and cross-gender friendships. In *Older adult friendship: Structure and process,* ed. Rebecca G. Adams and Rosemary Blieszner, 197–221. Newbury Park, CA: Sage.

Young, Rosalie, and Eva Kahana. 1989. Specifying caregiver outcomes: Gender and relationship aspects of caregiver strain. *The Gerontologist* 29(5):660–66.

Women in the Labor Force

Nancy M. Thornborrow and Marianne B. Sheldon

Introduction

Women have always worked. Throughout the twentieth century women's work has increasingly meant participation in the paid labor force in addition to household production. By the year 2005, women are projected to be 47.4 percent of that paid labor force.[1] Yet, as recently as 1991, women working full-time had median annual earnings equal to only 69 percent of men's, and women with college degrees had annual median earnings only $1,436 higher than those of men with high school degrees.[2] This chapter examines the differences in women's work experiences by looking at the evolution of women's work, at the occupational and earnings patterns of contemporary women, and at what opportunities the labor force is likely to hold for women in the coming decades. Significant changes are projected in female participation rates by race and ethnicity, which, along with changes in the demographic composition of the population, will alter the labor force in the twenty-first century.

Historical Background

Preindustrial America was an underdeveloped, labor-scarce society in which all persons, male and female, young and old, married and unmarried, were required to work for survival. In the agrarian household economy of the seventeenth and eighteenth centuries, women's labor was essential to the survival of the family, the primary economic unit of production. The division of labor was generally along sex lines, with women processing and preparing for consumption the commodities produced by men in the fields. Nevertheless, the economic contributions of men and women converged in the basically self-sufficient agrarian household, in which the woman's position was sometimes described as that of "helpmeet."

Women's household tasks varied somewhat depending upon the family's wealth, race, size, and location, but in general they were physically demanding and time consuming. Women were responsible for the preparation of food, clothing, and certain other household products such as soap and candles as well as for the care of children and the household. Other common tasks included tending vegetable gardens and dairies and raising chickens. Only women in families with numerous servants were able to reduce this burden, but even then, because they were responsible for the supervision of servants, they needed extensive knowledge of these tasks. The skill and strength needed for these household activities were valued in this culture. Indeed, Protestant religious doctrine as well as the imperative for labor meant that work was viewed as a religious and civic duty of all citizens.[3]

The economic activities of some women extended beyond their homes. Those women able to produce a surplus of some commodity for sale or barter became involved in the monetary and legal activities of the larger economy. In addition, the frontier character of early American society contributed to a situation in which sex roles were less strictly defined than in English society at this time or American society in later eras. At least some women worked at tasks generally considered men's work or ran their own businesses, frequently when there were no men present to perform such tasks. Women were expected to help their husbands in their trades and, under some circumstances, to continue them as widows. Single women and widows were expected to support themselves.[4] Accordingly, English common law, which merged the legal identity of a married woman with that of her husband, was modified to fit the conditions of this labor-scarce, wilderness, agrarian economy. For example, as "feme sole traders" a small number of women acquired the right to enter into contracts, buy and sell property, sue, and have power of attorney in the absence of their husbands.[5]

Finally, the family also served as a school for young persons and a welfare institution for persons unable to care for themselves. Women as members of families were thus integrally linked to the larger communities in which they lived. Nevertheless, law, religion, and tradition all operated to establish a hierarchical, patriarchal order. All members of the household owed obedience to its male head, and it was he who formally spoke for all of them. The earnings of married women, their property, and even their clothing belonged to their husbands.[6]

For African-American women, the majority of whom were slaves in early America, life was very different. They worked alongside male slaves in the fields and households of their white masters and were also responsible for domestic chores in their own homes. Thus, while a strict sexual division of labor prevailed in the slave quarters, the division of labor performed for the master was less clearly based upon gender considerations:

> The dual status of a bondswoman—a slave and a female—afforded her master a certain degree of flexibility in formulating her work assignments. When he needed a field hand, her status as an able-bodied slave took precedence over gender considerations, and she was forced to toil alongside her menfolk. At the same time, the master's belief that most forms of domestic service required the attentions of a female reinforced the traditional role of woman as household worker.[7]

Industrialization marks an important watershed in the history of women's work both within the household and outside of it. The production of goods in the preindustrial era had been geared to a subsistence economy, but the market revolution of the late eighteenth century increasingly brought all economic activities into the market system, thereby promoting economic specialization and the consequent removal of production from the household. The emergence of a factory system in the late eighteenth and early nineteenth centuries had dramatic consequences for women's productive role. Although the transformation was slow and gradual, products once produced by women for household consumption increasingly came to be available at shops or from peddlers. The eclipse of the preindustrial household economy resulted in an increased separation of the spheres of home and work as well as a widening gap between the work activities of men and women. More and more, the nature of women's participation in the economy was transformed from that of producer to that of consumer. At the same time, as the scope of women's domestic obligations narrowed and the level of skill needed to run a household declined, the esteem once accorded women's domestic realm gradually began to diminish.[8]

While industrialization thus altered women's work lives within their homes, it also opened up to certain women new opportunities and occupations. The need of factories for workers in an economy characterized by a shortage of labor encouraged would-be manufacturers to employ women and children. For young, unmarried women, work in the mills was their first major opportunity to earn wages outside of the household. However, by the mid-nineteenth century, the growth of immigration created for industrialists a cheaper alternative to the employment of the daughters of Yankee farmers.[9]

The gradual disappearance of the preindustrial family economy was accompanied by the tremendous influx of men and women into the manufacturing and service work force, but not into the same jobs. Generally, throughout the nineteenth century and into the twentieth century, women worked in jobs with other women rather than with men. In addition, most of these jobs were created by industrialization rather than being ones from which men were displaced. Nevertheless, in 1900 the largest single employment category for women remained domestic service, which employed about 28.7 percent[10] of the female work force. This category was, however, in a permanent decline; more women were working in the sewing trades, textile manufacturing, laundry work, and retail sales. The increasing access of women to secondary and higher education facilitated their entry into teaching, nursing, and clerical work. The expansion of industrial capitalism was thus characterized by the sex-typing of jobs. Distinctions by marital status, race, ethnicity, and class were also important. The highest status female jobs (clerical work, retail sales, teaching) usually went to native-born, white women. Immigrant women were more likely to find employment in the expanding factory sector. Until World War I most African-American women were excluded from factory work and were able to find employment only as domestic servants, laundry workers, and agricultural workers.[11]

Until about 1890, with the exception of African-American women,[12] only unmarried women worked for wages. After that, factors such as the decline in the birthrate and the growth of labor-saving household technology along with the expansion of job opportunities created circumstances that gradually encouraged increasing numbers of married women to enter the paid labor force. In addition, many other married women contributed to the family income by taking work into their homes.

> In the end, crowding and competition exacerbated the problems women faced as workers. They sacrificed higher wages for the relative satisfactions of working with compatriots or of doing respected work. Sexual divisions in the job market tended to restrict vocational ambition, bunched together

women of like ethnic and racial groups, and limited some jobs to women of particular racial and ethnic backgrounds. Even an expanding pool of jobs could not prevent the resulting cycle of deteriorating work conditions, low wages, and squalid home lives. The result was to raise again the issue of whether home and work roles could ever be compatible, and to destroy, at least temporarily, any possibility that the two could sustain each other.[13]

Women's Employment Today

Even in the last decade of the twentieth century the work experiences of men and women continue to be very different. Furthermore, women are not a homogeneous group in the work force. They remain separated by dimensions of race, class, ethnicity, age, marital status, education, and culture. These variables along with institutional forces continue to shape women's labor force experiences.

LABOR FORCE STATISTICS

The data necessary to examine changes and trends in women's labor force participation are collected by the Census Bureau and analyzed by the Bureau of Labor Statistics (BLS). The census is only conducted every ten years. Since the 1930s, data for the intervening years are estimated by sampling the population monthly and compiling the results into the Current Population Survey (CPS), commonly referred to as the household survey. It is from this source that labor force statistics such as the monthly unemployment rate are calculated. Estimates based on sample data will differ from census figures because of inherent errors associated with using a subset of the population to generalize about the population itself. As a result, the census and household survey data are not interchangeable.

The labor force is composed of two groups of people: the employed and the unemployed. The BLS has very strict definitions of these two categories. Persons sixteen years of age and older who worked for at least one hour per week for pay or are employed for fifteen hours or more a week without pay in a family enterprise (including farming) or are not at work at their regular jobs because of illness, bad weather, a strike, or for personal reasons are considered employed. Those actively seeking work, on temporary layoff who expect to be recalled to their jobs, or scheduled to begin a job within thirty days are considered unemployed. The unemployment rate is the percentage of the labor force categorized as unemployed, not simply people without jobs. The total labor force includes not only the civilian employed and unemployed, but also resident members of the armed forces. The labor force participation rate measures the percentage of the population in the total labor force. A separate participation rate is calculated for the civilian population. In addition, participation rates by age, sex, race, and ethnicity can be calculated. So, for example, the labor force participation rate for married women is the number of married women, both employed and unemployed, divided by the total number of married women in the population.

Changes in the composition of the labor force can occur as a result of changes in the composition of the population or changes in the participation rates of various groups within the population. Throughout the twentieth century women increased their share of the labor force as a result of increasing rates of participation. As seen in Table 1, over this same period the participation rates of men were declining. By 1990 women comprised 44.9 percent of the labor force, and 57.5 percent of all women were labor force participants; in contrast, men were 55.1 percent of the labor force, and 76.5 percent of all men were labor force participants. White women in the first few decades of the twentieth century had low though steadily increasing rates of participation. African-American women have historically had higher rates of labor force participation than white women; their 1890 rates were not achieved by white women until 1960.[14] However, by 1990 the participation rates of both groups had nearly equalized; by the year 2005, participation rates for white women are predicted to surpass those of African-American women.[15]

Table 1.   Labor Force Participation Rates, Selected Years, 1890–1992 (Total Labor Force)

Year[a,b]	Males	Females	Females as a percentage of the labor force
1890	84.3	18.2	17.0
1900	85.7	20.0	18.1
1920	84.6	22.7	20.4
1930	82.1	23.6	21.9
1940	82.5	27.9	25.2
1945	87.6	35.8	29.2
1947	86.8	31.8	27.4
1950	86.7	33.9	29.0
1955	85.9	35.7	30.7
1960	83.9	37.8	32.5
1965	81.3	39.3	34.3
1970	80.3	43.4	37.2
1975	78.4	46.4	39.3
1980	77.8	51.6	42.0
1985	76.7	54.5	43.7
1990	76.5	57.5	44.9
1992	75.9	57.8	45.1

a. Figures for 1947 and after include persons sixteen years old and over; for the years prior to 1947, those fourteen years old and over are included.
b. Figures for 1950 and subsequent years include employed and unemployed civilians plus members of the armed forces stationed within the United States *only*.
Sources: U.S. Department of Commerce, Bureau of the Census, *Historical Statistics of the United States, Colonial Times to 1970,* Bicentennial Edition, Part I (1975), pp. 131–32; U.S. Department of Labor, Bureau of Labor Statistics, *Handbook of Labor Statistics* (1985), pp. 6–7; U.S. Department of Labor, Bureau of Labor Statistics, *Employment and Earnings* (January 1993), p. 14.

Women's labor force participation rate varies throughout the life cycle but now resembles the male pattern of highest participation in the middle years. As can be seen in Figure 1, this has not always been true. Prior to the 1940s most women worked before marriage and then withdrew; those with consistent work histories were predominantly single. After World War II married women began to reenter the work force when their children were older; today most women stay in the labor force continuously. Table 2 shows rates of participation by age, race, and ethnicity for women since 1975. The pattern differs between white and African-American women, with white women having highest rates of participation at earlier ages (twenty to twenty-four) in 1975, 1980, and 1985, and African-American women experiencing their maximum participation rates at ages twenty-five through thirty-four in 1975 and 1980. However, in 1990 the peak participation for both groups occurred at ages thirty-five through forty-four.

One of the most significant phenomena of the latter half of the twentieth century has been the increased participation of married women in the paid labor force. In 1940 married women were 30 percent of the female labor force, by 1960 they had grown to 55.5 percent; this percentage has remained relatively constant over the last thirty years. Prior to World War II, family responsibilities, social prejudice, and government policy discouraged married women from working. As early as the 1820s and 1830s, trade unions supported

Figure 1. Women's Labor Force Participation Rates, 1940–1990.

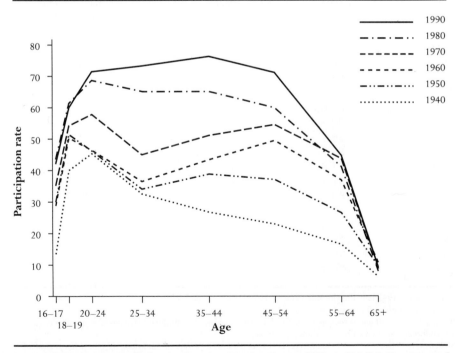

Sources: U.S. Department of Labor, *Employment and Earnings* (January 1991), p. 164; U.S. Department of Labor, *Handbook of Labor Statistics* (1985), pp. 26–27; and U.S. Department of Commerce, *Statistical Abstract of the United States 1942,* p. 57.

Table 2. Female Labor Force Participation Rates by Race, Hispanic Origin*, and Age

	16–17	18–19	20–24	25–34	35–44	45–54	55–64	65+
1975								
White	42.7	60.4	65.5	53.8	54.9	54.3	40.6	8.0
Black	25.0	43.8	55.9	62.8	62.0	56.6	43.1	10.7
Hispanic	NA	NA	NA	NA	NA	NA	NA	NA
1980								
White	47.2	65.1	70.6	64.8	65.0	59.6	40.9	7.9
Black	24.6	45.0	60.2	70.5	68.1	61.4	44.8	10.2
Hispanic	29.9	50.4	57.0	54.0	55.3	54.5	34.7	5.7
1985								
White	45.2	64.8	73.8	70.9	71.4	64.2	41.5	7.0
Black	27.6	47.9	62.5	72.4	74.8	65.7	45.3	9.4
Hispanic	26.5	49.2	57.7	57.1	59.1	55.1	36.4	5.9
1990								
White	45.8	63.9	73.7	74.2	76.7	71.4	45.6	8.5
Black	26.5	46.2	62.3	72.3	77.6	70.5	43.2	9.9
Hispanic	28.3	48.0	59.2	61.4	66.0	58.8	39.6	7.3

* Hispanics may be of any race.
Sources: *Handbook of Labor Statistics* (August 1989), Table 5, pp. 25–30 (1975–88 data); *Employment and Earnings* (January 1991), Table 3, pp. 164–66 (1990 black and white data); U.S. Department of Labor, Bureau of Labor Statistics, unpublished data, Current Population Survey.

the idea of paying men an amount sufficient to care for a wife and dependent children, i.e., a "family wage." By the 1920s the family wage had become the standard.[16] During World War II women were needed to work in factories and offices. However, when the war ended they were encouraged to return to their homes and family responsibilities, and many did. In spite of strong prejudice and discriminatory laws that existed until the mid 1960s, married women continued to enter the labor force; by 1992 their participation rate was 59.4 percent.[17] Even today tax laws, originally designed for families with dependent wives, discourage married women's participation.[18]

Table 3 shows female labor force participation by race and marital status. The Bureau of Labor Statistics, using data from the Current Population Survey, has compiled estimates going back to 1954 of labor force participation by race, sex, and marital status. Recent work by Claudia Goldin[19] using census data produced the estimates in Table 3. The data show significant differences between white and nonwhite women for both single and married women, though the patterns are quite different. In 1890, single white women had rates 20 percentage points lower than nonwhite women, but by 1930 that gap had nearly closed, and since that time white single women have experienced higher rates of participation. Conversely, married nonwhite women have always participated in the labor force at higher rates than have white married women. Among nonwhite women, one reason for African-American wives' greater rates of participation is to enhance low family incomes.[20] Some historians have

Table 3.   Female Labor Force Participation by Marital Status and Race

	Single			Married		
	Total	White	Nonwhite	Total	White	Nonwhite
1890	40.5	38.4	59.5	4.6	2.5	22.5
1900	43.5	41.5	60.5	5.6	3.2	26.0
1920	46.4	45.0	58.8	9.0	6.5	32.5
1930	50.5	48.7	52.1	11.7	9.8	33.2
1940	45.5	45.9	41.9	13.8	12.5	27.3
1950	50.6	51.8	40.0	21.6	20.7	31.8
1960	47.5	48.5	39.7	30.6	29.8	40.5
1970	51.0	52.1	43.6	39.5	38.5	50.0
1980	61.5	64.2	49.4	50.1	49.3	59.0
1988		68.6	56.4		55.8	64.4

Single includes unknown marital status for 1890, 1900, and 1920.
For various years, the data assume that all fourteen- and fifteen-year-olds are unmarried.
From 1940–1988 data are for married women with a spouse present.
From 1890–1960 data include those fifteen years of age and older; from 1970–1980 data include those sixteen years of age and older.
Source: Claudia Goldin, *Understanding the Gender Gap* (New York: Oxford University Press, 1990), Table 2.1, p. 17.

suggested that cultural differences made the responses of African-American married women to economic hardship different from those of poor white immigrant families. Instead of allowing children to drop out of school and work to help support the family, as was the case in many immigrant families, African-American wives assumed a larger part of the burden of supporting the family themselves.[21]

Until recently, participation rates for men by race have not shown the large differences that have existed for women. Beginning in 1954 the male rate was 85.4 percent for whites and 85 percent for nonwhites; however, by 1975 the rate for African-American males had dropped to 70.9 percent, while the rate for white males was 78.9 percent. If the dimension of marital status is added for males, single white and nonwhite participation rates were similar in 1960 (55.6 percent for whites and 55 percent for nonwhites) and increased to 73.6 percent for whites and 63.9 percent for nonwhites by 1987. For married men with spouses present, the rates for whites and nonwhites were nearly the same (89 percent and 87.9 percent) in 1960 but declined over the next three decades to 78.8 percent and 77.2 percent, respectively, in 1987.[22] So, while single men and women of all races increased their labor force participation, it was married men of all races whose participation dropped during the last half of the twentieth century.

In 1960 the participation rates for women with children under six were quite different for married women than for widowed, divorced, and separated women: 18.6 percent versus 40.5 percent.[23] By 1991 the rates for the two groups had virtually equalized, with married women working at the rate of 59.9 percent and widowed, divorced, and separated women at 59.8 percent.[24] Between 1975 and 1991 the participation rate for white married women with children under six rose from 34.7 percent to 59 percent; for African-American women it rose from 54.9 percent to 73.4 percent. Also, between 1975 and 1991, for white wives with children one year or less the rate rose from 29.2 percent to 54.9 percent; for African-Americans from 50 percent to 66.9 percent.[25]

Several factors contributed to women's joining and staying in the labor force.[26] For white married women who could rely on financial support from their husbands, the decision to work outside the home was considered a choice; for single and nonwhite women the decision to work may have been one more of necessity. The increase in real hourly wages throughout the first seven decades of the twentieth century[27] gave all women an incentive to work for pay and made staying at home cost more because of earnings foregone. However, for married women the increase in their husbands' real wages decreased their need to work outside their homes. Empirical evidence shows that this ambiguous wage effect, in fact, resulted in increased participation by married women. However, since 1973 a halt in real wage growth, in combination with three recessions, has caused real family incomes to stagnate.[28] Many women have joined the labor force in an attempt to maintain or improve their families' standard of living.[29] In 1990, 57.4 percent of white, 65.8 percent of African-American, and 50.6 percent of Hispanic married couples had wives in the labor force.[30]

An important additional factor in encouraging females' participation has been their increasing level of educational attainment.[31] Between 1940 and 1991 the percentage of white women completing four or more years of high school rose from 28.1 percent to 79.9 percent; those completing four or more years of college increased from 4.0 percent to 19.3 percent.[32] The percentage of African-American women completing four or more years of high school rose from 8.4 percent to 66.7 percent; the percentage completing four or more years of college increased from 1.2 percent to 11.6 percent between 1940 and 1991.[33] Because women were investing more time and money in acquiring human capital in the form of education and training, a decision to remain out of the paid labor force became an even more costly one. By refusing to participate, they would not only fail to recoup their educational investment but would also forego the higher earnings associated with higher levels of education. Of all women over age twenty-five in 1992, 74 percent of those with a college degree were in the labor force, compared to 65.4 percent of those with a high school diploma. Those without a diploma had participation rates of only 29.4 percent.[34]

Other possible factors contributing to women's increased participation are changes in family size and structure;[35] changes in occupational distribution as the economy moved from heavy manufacturing to service sector employment, thereby expanding opportunities for female employment; the contemporary women's movement; increased opportunities for women generated by equal opportunity laws over the last thirty years; and changes in social attitudes toward married women's working[36] making the decision to work an easier one.

WAGE DIFFERENTIALS

There are two main sources for income and earnings data: (1) the Current Population Survey, described earlier, and (2) establishment data, which are payroll reports from employers. The CPS surveys the earnings of wage and salary workers in all occupations and industries in both the private and public sectors by population characteristics. Each year the Department of Commerce uses this monthly survey data from sixty thousand households to compile its annual report on the money income of households, families, and persons in the United States. The establishment survey gathers industry information on nonfarm average hourly earnings, employment, hours of work, and productivity by detailed industry. The data are collected by the Bureau of Labor Statistics (BLS) from monthly questionnaires mailed to a sample of over 350,000 establishments employing over forty-one million workers, full or part time, who receive pay during the payroll period. The data from both surveys are published monthly in a BLS publication, *Employment and Earnings.* Because the data come from two different sources, they are complementary though not interchangeable.

Wages differ by occupation, industry, and location. The wage rate itself is the price of labor per hour of work and ideally would include all forms of labor compensation. Unfortunately, data on fringe benefits is often unavailable, so a substitute measure, average hourly earnings, is used as a proxy for the wage rate. Average hourly earnings are calculated by dividing weekly earnings by weekly hours of work. The establishment survey reports average earnings data; the household survey reports median earnings data. The Department of Commerce reports both average and median earnings based on the household survey data. In making comparisons, year-round (fifty or more weeks per year), full-time (thirty-five or more hours per week) median earnings are used.[37] Many women work part-time, and inclusion of their lower earnings would make the female earnings as a percent of male earnings even smaller.

The annual full-time, year-round median female earnings as a percentage of male full-time, year-round median earnings showed a remarkable consistency between 1955 and 1980, hovering around the 60 percent mark.[38] However, throughout the 1980s the percentage began to increase, and by 1991 the ratio of female to male annual full-time median earnings rose to 68.9 percent.[39] There are, therefore, two phenomena that need to be explained: (1) what accounts for the slight narrowing of the wage gap,[40] and (2) why does the gap persist?

Some of this improvement represents real increases in incomes for women; however, some reflects the fact that men's real incomes were actually lower in 1991 than twenty years previously.[41] Particularly hard hit were less-educated men, whose real wages have been dropping since 1969, while wages for less-educated women remained relatively constant.[42] Women are making improvements in average hourly earnings and average weekly earnings; however, because they tend to work fewer hours, their annual wages continue to lag behind men's by more than the hourly differential.[43] The 1991 ratio of female to male full-time median weekly earnings for persons age twenty-five and older shows a larger improvement for women; the ratio is 73.8 percent.[44]

Table 4 shows median full-time, year-round earnings for 1990 by sex, race, Hispanic origin, and educational attainment. Human capital theory argues that those persons who invest in skills and training in the form of higher education will be more productive and, therefore, will receive higher compensation in terms of wages in the labor market.[45] The data in Table 4 show that women,

Table 4. Median Year-Round Full-Time Earnings for Persons Aged Twenty-Five and Over by Sex, Race, Hispanic Origin, and Years of School Completed, 1990

	All races	*White*	*Black*	*Hispanic*
Females				
All	20,556	20,759	18,838	16,480
1–3 years high school	13,858	14,010	13,643	12,586
4 years high school	17,412	17,552	16,531	16,298
1–3 years college	21,324	21,547	19,922	20,881
4 years college	26,828	26,822	26,881	22,555
5+ years college	31,969	31,991	31,119	30,133
Males				
All	29,987	30,598	22,176	20,556
1–3 years high school	20,452	21,048	16,778	17,868
4 years high school	25,872	26,526	20,271	20,932
1–3 years college	30,865	31,336	25,863	26,380
4 years college	37,283	38,263	30,532	33,074
5+ years college	47,131	47,787	36,851	42,315

Data are for those working fifty or more weeks per year, thirty-five or more hours per week.
Data are for highest grade of schooling attended, whether or not the grade was completed.
Persons of Hispanic origin may be of any race.
Source: U.S. Dept. of Commerce, *Money Income of Households, Families and Persons in U.S.: 1990*, Series P-60, no. 174, Table 29, pp. 129–55.

regardless of race or ethnicity, have lower median earnings than men with the same education. In fact, the median earnings for full-time, year-round employed women with four years of college in 1990 was only 37.7 percent more than the median earnings of men with only four years of high school. However, while large discrepancies exist among men and between men and women of the same educational attainment, among women these differences are much smaller. African-American women with four years of college had slightly higher median earnings than white women of the same educational level in 1990; Hispanic and African-American women with four years of high school had similar earnings, but Hispanic women with four years of college earned less than either African-American or white women. The improvement in women's educational attainment has been a factor in reducing the female/male wage gap.

Table 5 shows median full-time earnings by educational attainment, sex, race, Hispanic origin, and age for 1990. White female earnings peak for all educational attainment levels between ages thirty-five and forty-four, while for white males the peak is much higher and occurs later. The earnings profile for white women is rather flat, with at most a $4,000 difference over the life cycle. For men the profiles are steeper, and differences over the life cycle are greater. For African-American and Hispanic workers the data is incomplete, but the male profiles are steeper and higher than the female profiles. Among women the profiles are very similar, with whites only slightly higher than African-Americans. White and African-American women aged twenty-five

Table 5. Median Year-Round, Full-Time Earnings by Years of Schooling
Completed, Sex, Race, Hispanic Origin, and Age, 1990

Female	*25–34*	*35–44*	*45–54*	*55–64*	*65+*
White					
All	19,947	21,833	21,113	19,358	18,675
4 years high school	16,481	18,733	18,460	17,373	18,089
4 years college	25,733	29,650	26,684	25,765	(B)
Black					
All	17,121	20,875	19,699	15,648	(B)
4 years high school	14,132	18,033	18,954	15,174	(B)
4 years college	25,019	28,683	(B)	(B)	(B)
Hispanic					
All	15,538	17,829	17,742	14,027	(B)
4 years high school	14,632	17,150	18,357	(B)	(B)
4 years college	22,881	(B)	(B)	(B)	(B)
Male	*25–34*	*35–44*	*45–54*	*55–64*	*65+*
White					
All	25,767	32,750	35,364	31,655	27,469
4 years high school	22,985	27,472	31,255	29,211	24,733
4 years college	31,320	41,227	46,051	49,482	41,889
Black					
All	19,200	26,023	25,965	22,868	(B)
4 years high school	17,197	21,778	26,426	22,192	(B)
4 years college	27,626	33,673	36,405	(B)	(B)
Hispanic					
All	18,180	22,291	22,247	23,285	(B)
4 years high school	18,721	22,864	24,754	(B)	(B)
4 years college	30,800	35,736	(B)	(B)	(B)

Data are for those working fifty or more weeks per year, thirty-five or more hours per week.
Data are for highest grade of schooling attended, whether or not the grade was completed.
Persons of Hispanic origin may be of any race.
(B) base for derived figures is less than 75,000.
Source: U.S. Dept. of Commerce, *Money Income of Households, Families and Persons in the U.S.: 1990*, Series P-60, no. 174, Table 29, pp. 128–55.

through thirty-four with four years of college earned roughly 80 percent of their white male counterparts' wage. The higher earnings of younger women have helped to narrow the female/male wage gap. If these differentials can be maintained or improved over the life cycle, then a further narrowing of the gap will occur. In fact, white, young (age twenty-five through forty-four), and well-educated women made significant gains in the labor force relative to their male counterparts throughout the decade of the 1980s. So, while in 1990 the wage differential between African-American and white women narrowed for those with similar educational backgrounds, the differential between men and women remained large.[46]

Human capital theory predicts that wages will be a function of factors other than education. Perhaps the wage differentials observed are a result of differences in levels of experience between males and females. A glance back at Figure 1 shows that certainly in the past women exhibited discontinuous or intermittent work patterns, but the women of 1990 demonstrate both high and continuous levels of participation to age fifty-five. These more continuous levels of participation provide a partial explanation for some of the reduction in the female/male earnings gap.

OCCUPATION

While occupation can be analyzed on the basis of numerous characteristics such as status and prestige, this chapter examines occupation as a key determinant of wages. Today those with higher levels of education are able to enter professional and managerial fields that pay higher salaries. If women do not prepare for the higher paying fields, or if they choose lower paying occupations, then these factors might be an explanation of the wage gap. Table 6 shows both the percentage of each broad occupational category that is female and the occupational distribution of the labor force by sex and race for 1990. The percentage of women in every occupational category, with the exception of service occupations, increased between 1972 and 1990.[47] The largest gains

Table 6. Occupational Distribution of the Labor Force by Sex and Race, 1990

| | Percentage of employed labor force | | | | | | | |
| | Males | | | Females | | | | |
Occupational category	Total	White	Black	Total	White	Black	% Female	Median earnings* (F/M)
Executive, administrative, and managerial	13.8	14.6	6.8	11.1	11.6	7.5	40.0	65.4
Professional specialty	12.0	12.3	6.5	15.1	15.6	11.2	51.2	74.2
Technicians and related support	3.0	3.1	2.2	3.5	3.5	3.6	64.7	66.9
Sales occupations	11.2	11.8	5.8	13.1	13.6	9.4	49.2	57.8
Administrative support, including clerical	5.9	5.5	9.1	27.8	28.2	26.1	79.8	75.5
Service occupations	9.8	8.7	18.2	17.7	16.4	27.3	60.1	71.9
Precision production, craft, and repair	19.4	20.0	15.6	2.2	2.1	2.3	8.5	64.8
Operators, fabricators, and laborers	20.6	19.4	32.7	8.5	7.8	12.2	25.5	69.3
Farming, forestry, and fishing	4.9	4.6	3.2	1.0	1.1	0.3	16.0	82.1
Total	100.0	100.0	100.0	100.0	100.0	100.0		

* Full-time, year-round median earnings.
Source: U.S. Department of Labor, *Employment and Earnings* (January 1991), p. 184. Note: Figures may not add to totals because of rounding.

were in the executive, administrative, and managerial category, which went from 20 percent to 40 percent female,[48] and the technicians and related support category, which went from 38 percent to 64.7 percent female. The distribution appears to be shifting from jobs requiring less education and training to those requiring more, which also command higher wages. This occupational movement explains some of the narrowing of the wage gap.

Table 6 shows the occupational distribution among women by race. In 1990 white women continued to have a higher representation in executive, administrative, managerial, and professional specialties; however, African-American women made significant increases between 1970 and 1990 in the percentage of women in those categories.[49]

Table 6 also displays the ratio of female to male wages by major occupational categories. In 1990 women's wages varied between 57.8 percent and 82.1 percent of men's wages. However, within any one category there are many levels of jobs, and women are likely to be at the lower end. Some argue that wage differentials are a result of women's lower levels of experience and will gradually close; others see them as evidence of a "glass ceiling" for female workers.

Many do not accept women's occupational choice as an explanation of wage differentials.[50] They see women's occupational choices as restricted by societal pressure, the sex-typing of occupations, women's maternal responsibilities, and discrimination. Women's wages, they argue, reflect the fact that women are concentrated in a few occupational categories whose economic contribution has been monetarily devalued. This hypothesis is known as occupational crowding or occupational segregation.[51] What evidence exists for this hypothesis? In 1990 24 percent of women were employed in six of over five hundred narrowly defined occupational categories: secretary, bookkeeper, registered nurse, cashier, elementary teacher, waitress/waiter.[52] Each of these occupations was more than 80 percent female in 1990.[53] Even in these narrowly defined categories, men had higher wages.[54] If we expand these categories slightly, in 1990 70.6 percent of all women were employed in the following six areas: nurses and health technicians, elementary and secondary school teachers, sales clerks in retail trade, clerical workers, apparel and textile workers, and service workers (including waitresses, dental assistants, and cleaning persons).[55] In 1990 28 percent of all women worked in clerical and administrative support.[56]

Changes in the occupational picture by sex are revealed in Table 7 by the percentage of the labor force that was female in 1960, 1970, 1980, and 1990 in ten traditionally male and nine traditionally female occupations. The table shows that while women are still a minority in all the male occupations, they are in fact entering them; however, there is no similar movement of men into female occupations.

Studies of occupational segregation often use a Duncan index[57] to calculate the percentage of workers who would have to change from female occupations to male occupations in order to eliminate occupational segregation.[58] In 1960 approximately 62 percent of women would have had to move to male occupations in order to eliminate gender-based occupational segregation; by 1980 the percentage had only improved by 5 percentage points to 57 percent.[59] The same study, in comparing occupational segregation by race rather than by

Table 7. Percentage of Female Workers in Traditionally Male and Female Occupations in 1960, 1970, 1980, and 1990

Traditionally male occupations

		Percent female		
Occupation	*1960*	*1970*	*1980*	*1990*
Engineers	0.8	1.6	4.6	9.1
Lawyers and judges	3.5	4.8	13.8	24.4
Physicians	6.9	9.2	13.3	20.7
Economists	14.5	11.2	29.3	43.9
Clergy	2.3	2.9	5.8	10.4
Insurance sales	9.7	12.4	25.2	35.3
Managers and administrators	14.4	16.6	27.7	38.1
Carpenters	0.3	1.3	1.6	1.7
Bus drivers	10.1	30.0	45.8	48.1
Police and detectives	2.7	3.5	7.8	14.6

Traditionally female occupations

		Percent female		
Occupation	*1960*	*1970*	*1980*	*1990*
Registered nurses	97.5	97.3	95.9	94.3
Librarians	85.6	81.9	82.6	81.3
Teachers, except postsecondary	71.6	70.2	70.7	74.6
Bank tellers	69.3	86.2	91.2	89.8
Secretaries	97.2	97.6	98.8	98.7
Typists	95.1	94.2	96.9	94.4
Dress makers	96.7	95.1	93.5	93.4
Dental assistants	—	97.9	98.0	97.1
Child care workers	—	93.0	93.4	95.6

Sources: Bureau of the Census, *Census of the Population* (Washington, D.C.: G.P.O., 1960, 1970, 1980); and Bureau of the Census, *1990 Census of Population, Supplemental Report of Detailed Occupations and Other Characteristics from the EEO File for the U.S.* (October 1992).

gender, calculated a Duncan index of 28 percent for white women versus African-American women in 1980 and an index of 33 percent for white men versus African-American men in 1980. These numbers represent significant improvements over the measures in 1960, when the index for women was 56 percent and the one for men was 50 percent.[60] Reductions in gender segregation in the workplace appear more difficult to achieve than reductions in segregation by race.

DISCRIMINATION

Economists define discrimination as the valuation in the labor market of personal characteristics of a worker that are not related to productivity. Such a definition determines discrimination by looking at market outcomes in terms of wages, occupational attainment, or levels of employment. Certainly the data examined thus far imply significant differences between women and men with respect to these broad measures. Discrimination that is observed in the labor market can be a result of a variety of premarket conditions: some easily measured like differences in educational background, health, and marital status and some very difficult to measure like differences in socialization for work or motivation. Discrimination that happens in the labor market itself can be a result of prejudice on the part of employers, fellow employees, or customers;[61] market power exercised by either employers[62] or labor unions; or statistical discrimination in which an employer evaluates potential employees on the basis of observable characteristics, e.g., race or sex, which may not be correlated with productivity.

Numerous empirical studies have been conducted in an effort to account for the wage differences between women and men. Analyses using the human capital variables, e.g., education, occupation, experience, along with a list of other personal characteristics indicating labor force attachment, have attempted to explain the wage gap. Estimates implied that as much as 55 percent[63] of the wage gap remained unexplained when men and women of identical characteristics were compared; some have interpreted this to be a measure of the percentage of the wage gap due to discrimination.[64]

The results of this type of analysis are hotly debated. The empirical question that needs to be answered is whether the differences observed between women's and men's wages are the result of pre–labor market discrimination, labor market discrimination, or some combination of factors created by cultural attitudes toward women and by the dual roles of homemaker and labor force participant that many women assume. These factors create a causality problem in attempting to quantify discrimination: women seeing restricted opportunities in the labor market due to discrimination may be influenced in their decisions about market work. The human capital analysis described above fails to quantify such a phenomenon. While there seems to be universal agreement that women are subject to discrimination, the extent due to labor market forces as opposed to other forces, many of a very circular and subtle nature, is more difficult to establish. However, determining the source of discrimination is essential in suggesting solutions.

SUGGESTIONS TO CLOSE THE PAY GAP

The above analysis suggests that some of the pay differential between women and men will disappear as women acquire more skills and training, enter higher paying male-dominated occupational categories, and continue working over the life cycle. Others have suggested that women need to organize themselves to challenge the status quo.[65] While union membership has declined from its peak of 33 percent of nonagricultural employment in 1953 to only 16 percent in 1990,[66] unions are still effective in elevating the earnings of their members.[67] In 1990 21.4 percent of male and 14.9 percent of female full-time workers were represented by unions.[68] Among white women, 14 percent of the full-time employed were represented by unions; their median earnings were 36 percent higher than those of white female nonunion workers and were 91.8 percent of median total white male earnings.[69] Among African-American full-time female workers, 21.2 percent were represented by unions; their median earnings were 40.9 percent higher than those of African-American women not represented by unions and were 81.1 percent of median total white male earnings.[70] For full-time employed Hispanic women, 14.2 percent were represented by unions; they made 38 percent higher median earnings than those not represented by unions and made 73.8 percent of median total white male earnings in 1990.[71]

While the earnings gains for women as a result of union membership are significant, the percentage of women whose wages are set by unions has declined 3.1 percentage points since 1983; the decline for men over the same period was 6.3 percentage points.[72] However, the sector suffering the smallest decline was the government sector, which employs many women.[73] Because unions are required to bargain for their members without regard to race, gender, or ethnicity, they must make nondiscriminatory wages their goal. In those fields where wages are depressed due to occupational crowding, unions may be effective in bargaining with management for higher compensation. Perhaps as a way to encourage organization among women, unions have also come out in favor of pay equity schemes.

PAY EQUITY

Economic theory argues that wage differentials exist in response to market conditions. High wages are the result of strong demand for the product or service a person's labor produces in combination with a small supply of individuals capable of providing that labor. Those who press for pay equity do so on the grounds that occupational crowding has resulted in low wages in traditionally female occupations.

What is a pay equity scheme?[74] The idea of pay equity is to set wages based on job characteristics such as knowledge, skill, effort, responsibility, and working conditions and their worth within the firm rather than based on the market's demand for the specific job. Many schemes to evaluate jobs already exist and are used in both the private and public sectors. The simplest and most usual type of evaluation survey assigns points to job characteristics based on standard personnel practices. These points are weighted by the importance assigned each factor by the firm, and a score is assigned to each job that reflects the value of that job to the employer. Wages are then assigned relative to the scores. This essentially allows for two very different jobs to be compared and equal wage rates assigned to persons whose jobs were scored the same.

Figure 2 shows the results of a 1974 pay equity study done for the state of Washington. Each point represents a job category placed by its monthly salary and evaluation points. Jobs dominated by at least two-thirds of one sex are designated by different symbols. The line passing through the figure predicts "average" or expected salaries based on evaluation points. At each evaluation level, virtually all of the female-dominated jobs pay amounts below the predicted monthly salary, whereas nearly all of the male-dominated jobs pay amounts above the predicted monthly salary. The ratio of female to male

Figure 2. Scatter Diagram of 1974 Study of Washington State Government Job Classes by Monthly Salary and Evaluation Points.

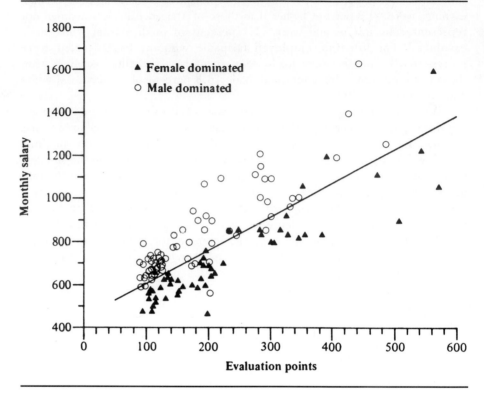

Source: Helen Remick, "Major Issues in a Priori Applications," in Helen Remick, ed., *Comparable Worth and Wage Discrimination* (Philadelphia: Temple University Press, 1984), p. 103.

compensation for jobs of equal value, i.e., that were scored the same, was about 80 percent.[75]

Proponents of pay equity believe that giving equal pay for jobs of equal value is essential to overcome the low wages caused by institutional factors and occupational crowding[76] so unambiguously displayed in Figure 2. They feel that job evaluation procedures could be effectively used in the public sector and in the private sector on a firm-by-firm basis. In fact, they argue that higher wages in traditional female jobs would help to eliminate discrimination by attracting more men to those fields. Opponents of comparable worth believe that it would be expensive and arbitrary and would cause unemployment and dislocation in the labor market.[77] They argue that if wages are to provide economic signals for resource allocation, wage setting will disrupt that process and distort the labor supply. And, critics continue, biases of the evaluators and sex bias in existing market wages would undoubtedly affect the scores of jobs in the rating system.

Finally, if women are to close the pay gap with men, recognition of their dual roles as mothers and labor force participants in the form of child care policies will be required. In 1990 Congress provided major support for child care.[78] And in February 1993, Congress passed the family leave bill, guaranteeing workers up to twelve weeks of unpaid leave for medical emergencies.[79] Without adequate family and child-centered public policies, women, particularly those with young children, will be unable to gain the training and experience necessary to participate fully in the paid labor force.

Female Labor in the Twenty-First Century

Demographers expect a significant change in the racial and ethnic composition of the labor force in the first part of the twenty-first century.[80] Over the period 1990–2005, the number of men in the labor force is projected to increase by only 16 percent. This projection reflects a continued decline in the white male participation rate, with rates for African-American, Hispanic, and Asian males increasing slightly.[81] Women, in contrast, will increase their labor force numbers by 26 percent during the same years.[82] White women, who contributed nearly half the additions to the labor force between 1975 and 1990, are projected to have a declining share of the labor force in the year 2005. This decline will not be as a result of declining rates of participation but rather as a result of the decline in the growth rate of the white female population. In addition, white women, whose labor force participation rates increased steadily throughout the twentieth century, began to slow their rates of increase in 1985. This trend is expected to continue, with women aged twenty through twenty-four projected to have the smallest increases in participation rates; women in the fifty-five to sixty-four age bracket are projected to have higher rates of labor force participation, reflecting a continuation of work patterns already established. In the year 2005 white women's share of the labor force will drop from 35.4 percent in 1990 to 34.8 percent.[83] At the same time African-American, Hispanic, and Asian women will see their shares of the labor force grow. African-American women are projected to increase their share from 5.4 percent to 5.9 percent; Hispanic women will expand from 3.1 percent to 4.6 percent; and Asian women will move from 1.4 percent to 2.1 percent of the labor force in the year 2005.[84]

What will this change in the racial and ethnic composition of the female labor force mean for occupational distribution and female/male wage differentials? The occupational picture for women is a mixed one.[85] Women are well represented in some of the occupational categories that are expected to enjoy the largest rates of growth in the first decade of the twenty-first century: health care workers and personal services. They are underrepresented in another set of fast-growing jobs: math and computer science, lawyers and judges, and protective services. Even more importantly, they are over-represented in all of the slowest growing or declining occupations: private household and clerical workers. African-American and Hispanic women are the most over-represented in all the occupational categories that are the slowest growing. The areas that are the fastest growing are those requiring higher levels of educational achievement.[86] Closing the female/male pay gap will require women in the labor force to have higher educational levels. Otherwise, they will not be able to move into the higher paying, faster growing sectors of the economy, and the female/male wage differential will not improve.

Certainly women have made significant gains into the paid labor force in the twentieth century. Women's ability to retain and improve on their past success will depend on many factors detailed in this chapter as well as the general condition of the economy.

NOTES

1. Howard N. Fullerton, "Labor Force Projections: The Baby Boom Moves On," *Monthly Labor Review* (November 1991), Table 5, p. 41.

2. U.S. Bureau of the Census, *Money Income of Households, Families and Persons in U.S.: 1991,* Series P-60, no. 180 (Washington, D.C.: U.S. G.P.O.), Table 29, pp. 116 and 130. Numbers are for persons age twenty-five and over.

3. Mary Beth Norton, *Liberty's Daughters: The Revolutionary Experience of American Women, 1750–1800* (Boston: Little, Brown and Co., 1980), chap. 1., and Alice Kessler-Harris, *Out to Work: A History of Wage-Earning Women in the United States* (New York: Oxford University Press, 1982), chap. 1.

4. See Laurel Thatcher Ulrich, *Good Wives: Image and Reality in the Lives of Women in Northern New England, 1650–1750* (New York: Alfred A. Knopf, 1987), chaps. 1 and 2, and Kessler-Harris, *Out to Work: A History of Wage-Earning Women in the United States,* chap. 1.

5. Marylynn Salmon, *Women and the Law of Property in Early America* (Chapel Hill: University of North Carolina Press, 1986).

6. Mary P. Ryan, *Womanhood in America: From Colonial Times to the Present,* 2nd ed. (New York: New Viewpoints, 1979), pp. 3–18, and John Demos, *A Little Commonwealth: Family Life in Plymouth Colony* (New York: Oxford University Press, 1970), pp. 80–81, 144, and 182–88.

7. Jacqueline Jones, *Labor of Love, Labor of Sorrow: Black Women, Work, and the Family from Slavery to the Present* (New York: Basic Books, 1985), p. 28.

8. Suzanne Lebsock, *The Free Women of Petersburg: Status and Culture in a Southern Town, 1784–1860* (New York: W. W. Norton & Co., 1984), pp. 48–50, and chap. 6, and Nancy F. Cott, *The Bonds of Womanhood: "Woman's Sphere" in New England, 1780–1835* (New Haven, Conn.: Yale University Press, 1977), chap. 1.

9. Kessler-Harris, *Out to Work: A History of Wage-Earning Women in the United States,* chaps. 2 and 3.

10. U.S. Department of Commerce, Bureau of the Census, *Historical Statistics of the United States, Colonial Times to 1970,* Bicentennial Edition, Part I (1975), p. 140.

11. Kessler-Harris, *Out to Work: A History of Wage-Earning Women in the United States,* chap. 5.

12. Although immediately after the Civil War, married African-American women appeared interested in devoting themselves to caring for their homes and families, by the 1870s their labor force participation rate began to rise. See Jones, *Labor of Love, Labor of Sorrow: Black Women, Work, and the Family from Slavery to the Present,* chaps 2, 3, and 4.

13. Kessler-Harris, *Out to Work: A History of Wage-Earning Women in the United States,* p. 141.

14. Nancy Woloch, *Women and the American Experience* (New York: Alfred A. Knopf, 1984), p. 544, and U.S. Department of Labor, *Handbook of Labor Statistics* (August 1989), Table 5, pp. 25–30.

15. Fullerton, "Labor Force Projections: The Baby Boom Moves On," Table 2, p. 34.

16. See Martha May, "The Historical Problem of the Family Wage: The Ford Motor Company and the Five Dollar Day," in *Families and Work* (Philadelphia: Temple University Press, 1987), pp. 111–31.

17. *Employment and Earnings* (January 1993), p. 182.

18. Current laws essentially provide a bonus to a married couple with a nonemployed wife and penalties for a married two-earner couple or a single-parent wage earner. See Barbara Bergmann, *The Economic Emergence of Women* (New York: Basic Books, Inc., 1986), pp. 218–25.

19. Claudia Goldin, *Understanding the Gender Gap* (New York: Oxford University Press, 1990).

20. For a summary of studies comparing African-American and white female labor force participation, see Claudia Goldin, "Female Labor Force Participation: The Origin of Black and White Differences, 1870 to 1880," *Journal of Economic History 37* (March 1977), pp. 87–108.

21. See Elizabeth H. Pleck, "A Mother's Wages: Income Earning Among Married Italian and Black Women 1896–1911," in Michael Gordon, ed., *The American Family in Social Historical Perspective,* 2nd ed. (New York: St. Martin's Press, 1978), pp. 367–92.

22. Cynthia Taeber, ed., *Statistical Handbook on Women in America* (Phoenix, Ariz.: The Oryx Press, 1991), Table B3-4, p. 105.

23. U.S. Department of Commerce, *Statistical Abstract of the United States 1992,* Table 620, p. 388.

24. Ibid.

25. Ibid., Table 621, p. 388.

26. For a review of causes of increasing female participation, see James P. Smith and Michael P. Ward, "Time-Series Growth in the Female Labor Force," *Journal of Labor Economics* 3, pt. 2 (January 1985), pp. 559–90.

27. Clarence D. Long, "The Illusion of Wage Rigidity: Long and Short Cycles in Wages and Labor," *Review of Economics and Statistics* (May 1960); Albert Rees, *New Measures of Wage Earner Compensation in Manufacturing, 1914–57,* occasional paper 75 (New York: National Bureau of Economic Research, 1960); and Standard Bureau of Labor Statistics series, as published in *Economic Indicators and Economic Report of the President, 1990.*

28. Families are groups of two or more persons (one of whom is the householder) related by birth, marriage, or adoption and residing together. Median family income, expressed in 1990 dollars, for white families was lower in 1990 than in 1973 ($37,076 in 1973 compared with $36,915 in 1990). For African-American families the numbers were $21,398 in 1973 and $21,423 in 1990; for Hispanic families the numbers were $25,654 in 1973 and $23,431 in 1990. Source: U.S. Department of Commerce, *Money Income of Households, Families and Persons in U.S.: 1990,* Table B-4, p. 201.

29. In 1990 white married-couple families with wives not in the labor force had median incomes of $30,781, compared with $47,247 for white married-couple families with wife labor participants. The comparable numbers for African-American married-couple families are $20,333 and $40,038; for Hispanic married-couple families the numbers are $21,168 and $34,778. Source: U.S. Department of Commerce, *Money Income of Households, Families and Persons in U.S.: 1990,* Table 13, pp. 53–55.

30. Ibid.

31. See Ralph E. Smith, "The Movement of Women into the Labor Force," in Ralph E. Smith, ed., *The Subtle Revolution* (Washington, D.C.: The Urban Institute, 1979), 1–29.

32. Taeuber, ed., *Statistical Handbook on Women in America,* Table D4-10, p. 308; and *Statistical Abstract of the United States 1992,* Table 220, p. 144.

33. Ibid.

34. Bureau of Labor Statistics, unpublished data.

35. See, for example, David Shapiro and Lois B. Shaw, "Growth in the Labor Force Attachment of Married Women: Accounting for Changes in the 1970s," *Southern Economic Journal* 50, no. 2 (October 1983), pp. 461–73.

36. A. Cherlin and P. B. Walters, "Trends in United States Men's and Women's Sex-Role Attitudes: 1972 to 1978," *American Sociological Review* (August 1981), pp. 453–60.

37. Because the distribution of earnings is positively skewed, arithmetic mean or "average" earnings will always be higher than the median or middle earnings. Large individual earnings figures pull the mean in their direction. In making comparisons over time or between groups, using the median or middle value conveys the best measure of typical earnings.

38. U.S. Bureau of Labor Statistics, *U.S. Working Women: A Databook 1955–1975,* Bulletin 1977; U.S. Bureau of the Census, *Money Income of Households, Families and Persons in the United States,* Current Population Reports Series P-60, various issues.

39. Numbers for persons twenty-five years and older, working fifty weeks or more, thirty-five or more hours per week. Source: U.S. Bureau of the Census, *Money Income of Households, Families and Persons in the United States 1991,* Current Population Report Series P-60, no. 180, Table 29, pp. 116 and 130.

40. See Elaine Sorensen, *Exploring the Reasons Behind the Narrowing of the Gender Gap in Earnings* (Washington, D.C.: Urban Institute Press, 1991).

41. Ibid., Table B-14, Appendix B, p. 25.

42. Rebecca M. Blank, as reported in the *New York Times,* July 26, 1992, p. 18. See also U.S. Bureau of the Census, *Money Income of Households, Families and Persons in the United States,* Current Population Report Series P-60, various issues.

43. Michael W. Horrigan and James P. Markey, "Recent Gains in Women's Earnings: Better Pay or Longer Hours?" *Monthly Labor Review* (July 1990), pp. 11–17.

44. U.S. Bureau of Labor Statistics, *Employment and Earnings* (January 1992, Table 54), p. 221.

45. It is notable that in the nineteenth century as access to education improved, women still had difficulty in finding ways to utilize that education in jobs.

46. See Myra Strober, "The MBA: Same Passport to Success for Women and Men?" in *Women in the Workplace,* ed. Phyllis A. Wallace (Boston, Mass.: Auburn House Publishing Co., 1982), pp. 25–44, and Robin L. Bartlett and Timothy I. Miller, "Executive Earnings by Gender: A Case Study," *Social Science Quarterly,* vol. 69, no. 4 (December 1988), pp. 892–909.

47. U.S. Bureau of Labor Statistics, *Employment and Earnings* (January 1984 and 1991).

48. This large change was partially because the major category "managers" was redefined to include support professions that are heavily female.

49. See Amott and Matthaei, *Race, Gender, and Work,* Table 6-1, p. 158; and Daniel O. Price, *Changing Characteristic of the Negro Population* (Washington, D.C.: U.S. Department of the Census, 1969).

50. See for example, Barbara Bergmann, *The Economic Emergence of Women* (New York: Basic Books, Inc., 1986), pp. 87–145.

51. See Barbara Reskin and Heide Hartmann, eds., *Women's Work, Men's Work: Sex Segregation on the Job* (Washington, D.C.: National Academy Press, 1986).

52. *Employment and Earnings* (January 1991, Table 22), pp. 186–90.

53. Ibid.

54. *Employment and Earnings* (January 1991, Table 56), pp. 223–27.

55. *Employment and Earnings* (January 1991, Table 22).

56. Ibid.

57. The index is calculated by summing the absolute differences between the percent of men and women employed in different occupations and dividing by 2. The index can range between zero, implying the male/female occupational distributions are identical, to 100, implying that there is complete occupational segregation by sex.

58. Suzanne Bianchi and Nancy Rytina, "Decline in Occupational Sex Segregation During the 1970s: Census and CPS Comparisons," *Demography* 23 (February 1986), p. 81.

59. Victor Fuchs, "Women's Quest for Economic Equality," *Journal of Economic Perspectives* 3, no. 1 (Winter 1989), pp. 26–29.

60. Ibid.

61. Gary Becker, *The Economics of Discrimination,* 2nd ed. (Chicago: University of Chicago Press, 1971).

62. For discussion of monopsonistic discrimination see Joan Robinson, *Economics of Imperfect Competition* (London: Macmillan, 1933).

63. See for example, Mary Corcoran and Greg J. Duncan, "Work History, Labor Force Attachment, and Earnings Differences Between the Sexes," *Journal of Human Resources* 14, no. 1 (Winter 1979), pp. 3–20.

64. For this approach, see Ronald Oaxaca, "Male-Female Wage Differentials in Urban Labor Markets," *International Economic Review* 14 (October 1973), pp. 693–709.

65. For a discussion of women and unions, see Richard B. Freeman and Jonathan S. Leonard, "Union Maids: Unions and the Female Labor Force," in C. Brown and J. Pechman, eds., *Gender in the Workplace* (Washington, D.C.: Brookings Institution, 1987), pp. 189–212.

66. *Employment and Earnings,* Table 59 (January 1991), p. 230.

67. There are various problems associated with using nonunion/union earnings ratios as a measure of union wage influence: union status of workers is correlated with other factors that affect wage rates, union and nonunion wage rates are interdependent, and union members take a larger percentage of their total compensation in the form of fringe benefits than do nonunion workers. See Bruce E. Kaufman, *The Economics of Labor Markets,* 3rd ed. (Chicago: The Dryden Press, 1991), pp. 583–617.

68. *Employment and Earnings,* Table 57 (January 1991), p. 228.

69. Ibid., Tables 57 and 59, pp. 228 and 230.

70. Ibid.

71. Ibid.

72. U.S. Department of Commerce, *Statistical Abstract of the United States 1991*, Table 697, p. 425.

73. Ibid.

74. For a comprehensive overview of comparable worth, see Paula England, *Comparable Worth Theories and Evidence* (New York: Aldine De Gruyter, 1992).

75. Helen Remick, "Major Issues in a Priori Applications," in Helen Remick, ed., *Comparable Worth and Wage Discrimination* (Philadelphia: Temple University Press, 1984), pp. 102–3.

76. See Barbara Bergmann, "The Economic Case for Comparable Worth," in Heidi Hartmann, ed., *Comparable Worth: New Directions for Research* (Washington, D.C.: National Academy Press, 1985), pp. 75–85; and Barbara Bergmann, "Does the Market for Women's Labor Need Fixing?" *Journal of Economic Perspectives* 3, no. 1 (Winter 1989), pp. 43–60.

77. See Mark Killingsworth, *The Economics of Comparable Worth* (Kalamazoo, Mich.: W. E. Upjohn Institute, 1990); and Mark Aldrich and Robert Buchele, *The Economics of Comparable Worth* (Cambridge, Mass.: Ballinger, 1986).

78. *The New York Times,* "U.S. Plan on Child Care Is Reported to Be Stalled," January 27, 1991.

79. Ibid., February 5, 1993.

80. See Ronald Kutscher, "New BLS Projections: Findings and Implications," *Monthly Labor Review* (November 1991), pp. 3–12; and Fullerton, "Labor Force Projections: The Baby Boom Moves On," pp. 31–44.

81. Fullerton, "Labor Force Projections: The Baby Boom Moves On," pp. 31 and 36.

82. Ibid., p. 31.

83. Kutscher, "New BLS Projections: Findings and Implications," p. 6.

84. Ibid.

85. Ibid., p. 9.

86. Ibid., pp. 10–12.

Women and Higher Education: Gender Differences in the Status of Students and Scholars

Mary Frank Fox

IN THE NINETEENTH-century movement for women's rights, feminists thought that higher education would lead not only to equal suffrage but also to widespread political, legal, and economic reforms of benefit to women (Antler, 1982:15). It is unclear whether gains in education lead or follow women's progress in other areas, and increased levels of education have not resulted "as a matter of course" in political or social gains for women (Schwager, 1987:335). However, women's educational attainment is related to their participation and role in the economy. To begin with, the more education a woman has, the more likely she is to be employed. Of all women twenty-five years of age or over who had not graduated from high school, less than one in three (29 percent) were in the labor force in 1992. With higher levels of education, rates of labor force participation rose sharply, so that among women who had completed high school, well over half (57 percent) were in the labor force; among those with some college, two thirds (66 percent) were employed, and among those with a bachelor's degree or higher, the proportion employed was 75 percent (U.S. Department of Education, NCES, 1993:Table 366).

Men use their educational credentials for initial entry to jobs and then rely on job-related "experience" for advancement (Featherman, 1980). For women, however, formal credentials remain critical throughout their working lives (Featherman, 1980). In other words, the direct effect of education on occupational status is stronger for women (Sewell, Hauser, and Wolf, 1980). Although women cannot expect to gain the same returns (salary, occupational rank, advancement) on their education as men do (Featherman and Hauser, 1976:481, U.S. Department of Education, NCES, 1993:Table 369), if women's credentials are "less than the best," women can suffer even greater inequality (see, for example, Fox, 1981:81).

Finally, because higher education influences the next generation and reflects social trends in American society, the standing of women as faculty indicates the position and plight of women in the professions and sets an example to students of the status of women in society.

Women as Students in Higher Education: Historical Background

In America's colonial era, educational opportunities were almost nonexistent
for women. The town schools of New England generally excluded girls or
admitted them for just a few hours per day at inconvenient times when boys
were not in attendance (Woody, 1966:177). The few colleges of this era were
given over to the training of ministers; since women were barred from the
ministry, they were excluded from these schools. Only in the wealthiest
families, where a system of tutorial education prevailed, did girls sometimes
get instruction in arts, letters, and literature. For the vast majority of women,
education was simply an apprenticeship in the home, where they learned
domestic arts and skills.

At the beginning of the eighteenth century, however, the seminary or
academy schools began to open, and these schools became the prevailing form
of education available to women. The seminary or academy schools frequently
emphasized "flashy accomplishments of little substantial value" (Woody,
1966:399) and have been sorely criticized for their cursory and superficial curriculum. Still, along with courses of music, dancing, and fancy
needlework, these schools provided rudimentary training in grammar, composition, rhetoric, geography, and arithmetic. Further, the seminary schools
nurtured women's aspirations. The experience of taking classes, competing,
and winning prizes gave these young students a taste for a new role—beyond
that of merely being a daughter (or wife) (Gordon, 1979). Most important,
the seminary and academy schools, which flourished throughout New England,
the mid-Atlantic, and the deep South, secured public recognition of and
support for female education (Woody, 1966). From the seminary schools,
higher education for women got its start.

The seminary schools of the postrevolutionary, American Federal era
flourished in an ideology—called Republican Motherhood—unknown in
Europe at the time. That ideology assigned to women a political role as educators of the next generation of sons, and thus as educators for the independence of the nation (Kerber, 1976, 1980). This put some premium on
rationality and literacy for women—within the confines of women's domestic responsibilities.

During the nineteenth century, women's education also advanced with the
growth of normal schools established to train teachers for the growing system
of public education. The expansion in public education during this period raised
great concern about the costs it incurred. Because female teachers earned
about one-quarter to one-third of the salaries of male teachers, they provided
a cost-saving solution (see Woody, 1966:492–93). Thus, women were in demand for the public schools and for the institutes in which teachers trained.
In consequence—and as an indicator —during the antebellum years, one out
of five white women (and one out of four native-born white women) taught
sometime during their lives (Bernard and Vinovskis, 1977).

These teaching institutes had several notable effects. First, they provided
solid and useful preparation in principles of education and practices of teaching.
Second, the development of teaching as an occupation for women marked a
new phase in the life cycle of nineteenth-century women: it added three or

more years of education and, critically, made women's life cycle more complex by providing an option of remaining single (Allmendinger, 1979; Schwager, 1987). Finally, the normal schools gave an impetus to women's education throughout the nineteenth century. But the pace of progress was halting.

Before the Civil War, only three private colleges (Oberlin, Hillsdale, and Antioch) and two public colleges (Utah and Iowa) admitted women. This coeducational experiment was not one of parallel education for women and men, however; rather, it was one of women's conventional value for men on campus. The history of Oberlin College is a striking example.

Founded as a self-subsidizing school with a farm attached to it, Oberlin College enrolled men students who produced crops to help pay for their education. It became apparent, however, that a domestic labor force was necessary to clean, cook, launder, and mend clothes—and women students fit the bill. Once admitted, women students attended no classes on Mondays when they did laundry, and each day they cooked, waited on tables, and served meals. They were also regarded as a "balance" to men's mental and emotional development, altogether duplicating the conventional role of women in the family (Conway, 1974:6). Throughout the debate on the Oberlin experiment, not one serious discussion occurred on what coeducation might do for women—except to prepare them for marriage. As Conway (1974) points out, this argument of coeducation's benefit for men has a contemporary ring to it found in the rationale for admitting women to elite men's colleges during the 1970s.

Not until the later part of that century did advanced education on a par with that of men become available to women. Again, "demand" factors were important. The shortage of male students and dwindling enrollments during the Civil War encouraged administrators to open their doors to female students (Graham, 1978). First-rate women's colleges also opened—starting with Vassar College in 1865, followed by Smith and Wellesley in 1875, Bryn Mawr in 1885, and Mt. Holyoke in 1888. Modeled on a classical and literary curriculum, these women's colleges provided an education for women that was not merely "compensatory" to or for that of male students (Conway, 1974:8). Spurred on by the women's rights movement, enrollment in these women's colleges increased by 348 percent between 1890 and 1910. And at coeducational colleges, the number of women students grew by even more—438 percent—during that same period (Antler, 1982:18).

At the end of the nineteenth century, higher education for women emphasized the development of character, the pursuit of culture, and the ideals of liberal arts—especially at women's colleges (Antler, 1982). All of this was consistent with prevailing notions of femininity and traditional values of womanhood and thus justified "the experiment in female education" (Antler, 1982:20). After the turn of the century, however, the goals of women's education took other directions—focusing first on service and utility to society and community and later on vocational and life preparation (Antler, 1982). During the early 1920s, especially, college curricula for women began to incorporate career preparation. This shift toward career was most apparent at the women's colleges, since state schools had always emphasized vocational training as part of their mandate to the public.

Yet the focus on career preparation faltered severely in the next decades. Between the 1930s and 1960s, college women married earlier, bore more children, and turned their attention to homemaking in greater proportions than did the graduates of the early 1920s (Antler, 1982:29; Perun and Giele, 1982). Studies indicate that during this period—and especially during the 1950s—few college women had clear vocational goals, and most attended for the general education, prestige, and social life. Thus, college had come to occupy an interlude between high school and marriage (and motherhood) for young women (Antler, 1982; Chafe, 1972; Graham, 1978:770–71).

In the late 1960s and early 1970s, however, a resurgence in the women's movement, a decline in fertility, and a dramatic increase in female labor force participation ushered in an era of changes in women's role in work, society, and education. Nonetheless, as we shall see, certain patterns—especially the sex segregation of educational fields and the male dominance of educational institutions—continue to restrict women's prospects in higher education.

Women as Students: Recent Data and Trends

Until recently, men were more likely to attend college than were women. Parents were more apt to encourage and finance the education of sons, and admissions standards favored males (see Frazier and Sadker, 1973:146–47). In the past two decades, however, the proportion of women going on to college has been growing, while the proportion of men has remained stable. Women now receive over half of all bachelor's and master's degrees and almost two-fifths of all doctoral and first professional degrees (Figure 1).

However, women's proportion of bachelor's degrees has not increased in a simple linear fashion over the century (see Figure 1). Before World War II, women's proportion of bachelor's degrees was higher than in the early postwar years. Their proportion of bachelor's degrees dipped particularly in 1949–50. During these postwar years, the G.I. Bill dramatically changed women's role in higher education. Passed by a Congress nervous about the unemployment of returning veterans, the G.I. Bill democratized higher education for men while taking no particular notice of women. In 1946–47, when veterans first arrived in the classrooms, prewar enrollment rates of colleges doubled overnight (Hornig, 1984:33). Eventually, one-third of America's returning veterans enrolled in college, and only 3 percent of all veterans were women (Clifford, 1983:8).

Beyond overall proportions of women attaining degrees, gender patterns in higher education also vary with racial and ethnic status. In 1990, the proportion of degrees awarded to women compared to men was lowest among Asians (except women's proportion for professional degrees, which was lowest among Hispanics) and highest among blacks at all degree levels (Table 1).

In assessing women's status in higher education, we must look beyond degrees to fields of study. Although fields of study are not as segregated as they were formerly, men and women continue to concentrate in different areas. At the bachelor's level, men are at least twice as likely as are women to concentrate in computer and physical sciences and are seven times more likely

Figure 1. Percentage of Degrees Earned by Women, 1919–20 to 1985–1990.

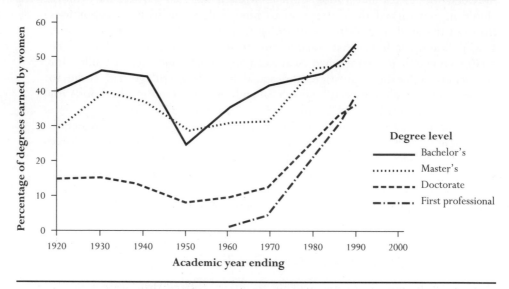

Sources: 1919–20 to 1949–50 data from Douglas Adkins, *The Great American Degree Machine* (Berkeley, Calif.: Carnegie Commission on Higher Education, 1975), Table A-2, and from National Center for Education Statistics, *Digest of Education Statistics, 1981* (Washington, D.C.: U.S. Government Printing Office, 1981), Table 95. 1960–61 to 1975–76 data from Mary Lou Randour, Georgia Strasburg, and Jean Lipman-Blumen, "Women and Higher Education: Trends in Enrollment and Degrees Earned," *Harvard Educational Review* 52 (May 1982): Table 4. 1979–80 data from National Center for Education Statistics, *Degrees Awarded to Women: 1979 Update* (Washington, D.C.: U.S. Department of Education), Tables 1, 3, 5, 7. 1985–86 data from Center for Education Statistics, *Bachelor's and Higher Degrees Conferred in 1985–86* (Washington, D.C.: U.S. Department of Education), Table 1. 1990 data from U.S. Department of Education, National Center for Education Statistics, *National Higher Education Statistics* (Fall 1990).

Table 1. Percent of Degrees Awarded to Women by Institutions of Higher Education, by Racial/Ethnic Group, 1989–1990

| | Degree | | | |
Racial/ethnic group	BA	MA	PhD	First professional
White non-Hispanic	53.2	55.2	41.6	37.2
Black non-Hispanic	61.9	64.1	53.7	51.0
Hispanic	54.5	54.9	46.3	40.3
Asian or Pacific Islander	49.8	43.3	29.5	41.6
American Indian/Alaskan native	57.6	58.1	50.5	47.5

Source: U.S. Department of Education, National Center for Education Statistics. *Digest of Education Statistics.* Washington, D.C.: U.S. Government Printing Office, 1993: Tables 255, 258, 261, 264.

to specialize in engineering. Women, in contrast, are more than three times more likely than are men to major in education and five times more likely to concentrate in health fields (nursing, health services, and health technologies) (see Table 2). Over the past fifteen years, the big change has been in the proportion of women taking undergraduate business degrees. In 1989,[1] business

Table 2. Distribution of Bachelor's Degrees, by Gender and Discipline
Division, 1971 and 1989

| | Percentage of degrees awarded | | | |
| | Women | | Men | |
Discipline division	1971	1989	1971	1989
Agriculture and natural resources	.1	.8	2.5	1.9
Architecture and environmental design	.2	.7	1.0	1.2
Area studies	.4	.4	.2	.3
Biological sciences	2.9	3.4	5.3	3.7
Business and management	2.9	21.6	22.1	27.3
Communications	1.0	5.5	1.5	4.0
Computer and information science	.1	1.8	.4	4.4
Education	26.0	14.1	9.5	4.5
Engineering	.1	2.2	10.4	15.3
Fine and applied arts	4.9	4.4	2.6	3.0
Foreign languages	4.2	1.5	1.1	.6
Health professions	5.4	9.4	1.2	1.9
Home economics	3.0	2.5	.1	.3
Law	(*)	.2	.1	.2
Letters	12.2	5.9	6.0	3.8
Library science	.3	(*)	(*)	(*)
Mathematics	2.6	1.3	3.2	1.7
Military science	(*)	(*)	.1	(*)
Physical sciences	.8	1.0	3.9	2.5
Psychology	4.6	6.4	4.4	2.9
Public affairs and services	1.2	3.4	1.0	3.3
Social sciences	15.8	9.0	20.6	12.4
Theology	.3	.2	.6	.9
Interdisciplinary studies	1.1	4.3	2.1	3.8

(*) less than .05 percent.
Note: Total may not add to 100.0 percent because of rounding.
Sources: For 1971: U.S. Department of Education. *Degrees Awarded to Women.* Washington, D.C.: U.S. Government Printing Office, 1981: Table 2. For 1989: U.S. Department of Education, National Center for Education Statistics. "Racial/Ethnic Trends in Degrees Conferred by Institutions of Higher Education, 1978–79 Through 1988–89," E.D. TABS, Table 3, January 1991.

was the single most popular undergraduate degree for both women and men. The consequence in jobs and managerial opportunities remains to be seen.

Finally, it is important to look to the trends in professional and graduate education—since this education is a prelude to and prerequisite for employment in higher-ranking positions in professions, business, and government. Although women have made some striking gains in graduate and professional education, gender differences still prevail, especially in fields of concentration.

Twenty-five years ago, women earned only about 3 percent of all professional (e.g., medical, dental, law, veterinary) degrees awarded; throughout the 1960s and early 1970s, that proportion grew very slowly. But in the mid-1970s, women began making strides in professional education; between 1970 and 1975, the proportion of professional degrees awarded to women grew from 7 to 16 percent, and by 1979 women were earning 24 percent of all professional degrees. In 1990, women's proportion of professional degrees increased to 39 percent (see Figure 1). However, men continue to predominate in the most powerful and prestigious areas in professional education.

Women's proportion of medical degrees increased from 8 percent in 1970 to 34 percent in 1990 (Table 3). Yet among physicians, the highly remunerative, surgical areas are overwhelmingly male domains. Across surgical specialties (excluding obstetrics/gynecology), 95 percent of the physicians are men. Even among physicians under age thirty-five—the most recently trained—89 percent of those in surgical areas are men (American Medical Association, 1990: calculated from Tables B-2 and B-4). Overall, the specialties with the highest proportions of women are those in the lower-status and less remunerative areas—pediatrics, child psychiatry, physical medicine and rehabilitation, public health, and psychiatry. Among physicians under thirty-five, pediatrics and child psychiatry are still the specialties with the highest proportion of female practitioners, followed by dermatology, obstetrics/gynecology, and psychiatry (American Medical Association, 1990:calculated from Tables B-2 and B-3).

Women's proportion of law degrees rose from 5 percent in 1970 to 29 percent in 1980; in 1990, women earned 42 percent of all law degrees (Table 3). However, in the practice of law, women are concentrated in trust, estate, tax, and family specialties (Epstein, 1983).

As with professional education, women have made gains in attainment of doctoral degrees. However, the trend is one of variable rather than steady improvement. Between the two world wars—in 1920, 1930, 1940—women received between 13 percent and 15 percent of all doctorates. That proportion dropped to 10 percent in 1950 and did not begin to rise until about 1970. In 1970, women earned 14 percent of all doctorates, and the proportion rose

Table 3. Percent of First Professional Degrees Earned by Women in Dentistry, Medicine, and Law, 1956 to 1990

	Professional degree		
Academic year ending	Dentistry	Medicine	Law
1956	1.1	5.1	3.5
1960	.8	5.5	2.5
1966	1.0	6.6	3.5
1970	.9	8.4	5.4
1975	3.1	13.1	15.1
1980	13.3	23.4	30.2
1985	20.7	30.4	38.5
1990	30.9	34.2	42.2

Sources: For 1956–1985: U.S. Department of Education. *Digest of Education Statistics, 1990.* Washington, D.C.: U.S. Government Printing Office, 1991: Table 231. For 1990: U.S. Department of Education, National Center for Education Statistics. *Digest of Education Statistics.* Washington, D.C.: U.S. Government Printing Office, 1993: Table 250.

to 23 percent in 1975. By 1980, women accounted for 28 percent of the doctoral degrees awarded; in 1990, they earned 36 percent (see Figure 1).

These gains notwithstanding, gender differences among doctorates prevail. In 1989, nearly half of women's doctorates were in education or psychology, which accounted for 30 and 14 percent, respectively, of the doctorates received by women. Women doctorates also clustered in biological sciences, social sciences, health professions, and literature (letters) (see Table 4). Thus, women are being awarded doctorates largely in traditionally female areas, which are relatively "glutted" with people holding doctoral degrees (Ekstrom, 1979:1). Men, in contrast, are distributed in a larger number of fields and are more likely than are women to be awarded degrees in computer science,

Table 4. Distribution of Doctoral Degrees, by Gender and Discipline Division, 1971 and 1989

| | Percentage of degrees awarded | | | |
| | Women | | Men | |
Discipline division	1971	1989	1971	1989
Agriculture and natural resources	(*)	1.8	3.8	4.2
Architecture and environmental design	(*)	.2	(*)	.3
Area studies	(*)	.4	(*)	.3
Biological sciences	13.0	9.9	11.1	9.9
Business and management	(*)	2.3	(*)	3.7
Communications	(*)	.9	(*)	.6
Computer and information science	(*)	.6	(*)	2.0
Education	29.6	29.8	18.3	12.8
Engineering	(*)	3.1	13.1	18.2
Fine and applied arts	3.0	2.4	1.7	2.0
Foreign languages	6.4	1.9	1.7	.7
Health professions	1.7	6.3	1.4	2.7
Home economics	1.6	1.6	(*)	.3
Law	0	.2	(*)	.2
Letters	12.4	6.1	6.7	4.0
Library science	(*)	.3	(*)	.1
Mathematics	2.0	1.3	4.0	3.1
Physical sciences	5.3	5.8	15.0	13.7
Psychology	9.3	14.1	4.9	6.3
Public affairs and services	(*)	1.7	(*)	1.1
Social sciences	11.0	7.2	11.4	8.6
Theology	(*)	1.1	1.0	4.5
Interdisciplinary studies	(*)	.9	(*)	.8

(*) less than .05 percent.
Note: Total may not add to 100.0 percent because of rounding.
Sources: For 1971: U.S. Department of Education. *Degrees Awarded to Women.* Washington, D.C.: U.S. Government Printing Office, 1981: Table 6. For 1989: U.S. Department of Education, National Center for Education Statistics. "Racial/Ethnic Trends in Degrees Conferred by Institutions of Higher Education, 1978–79 Through 1988–89," E.D. TABS, Table 5, January 1991.

engineering, mathematics, physical science, and other technical fields (see Table 4)—more lucrative employment areas.

Among minority women, the clustering of doctorates in female-typed fields is even more marked. Minority women are concentrated specifically in the field of education. In 1991, nearly half (48 percent) of the doctorates awarded to black women and almost one-third (29 percent) of those awarded to Hispanic women were in education (U.S. Department of Education, NCES, 1993:calculated from Table 262).

BEYOND ENROLLMENT: GENDER-BIASED PROCESSES IN HIGHER EDUCATION

To fully understand the disparate status of the women and men in American colleges and universities, we must look beyond simple enrollment data and trends to the socialization and experiences of students.

Even when men and women attend the same institution, occupy the same classroom, and share the same teachers, their educational experiences differ (Association of American Colleges, 1982). In faculty interaction with students, a "subtle and silent language" prevails. Studies indicate that, in their interaction with students, faculty encourage male as compared to female students by making more eye contact with men, nodding and gesturing in response to men's questions, assuming a position of attentiveness when men speak, and taking a location near men (see Association of American Colleges, 1982:7; Thorne, 1979).

Observers frequently note that even the brightest and most talented female students tend to remain silent in the classroom, while their male counterparts dominate the discussion (Sterglanz and Lyberger-Ficek, 1977; Speizer, 1982). Faculty promote and reinforce the invisibility of women students by subtle practices such as calling directly on men but not on women, addressing men by name more often than they do women, giving men more time to answer a question before going on to another student, interrupting women more frequently or allowing them to be interrupted, and crediting the contributions of men but not those of women (Association of American Colleges, 1982). These practices convey messages about women's value and status in the classroom and signal their exclusion as significant members of the college community. This, in turn, depresses women's intellectual development, undermines their confidence, and dampens their aspirations both in and out of school.

Such patterns are especially consequential for the undergraduates—since, at this level, education is largely a formal classroom process. Graduate education, in contrast, is an informal process of interaction, socialization, and alliance. Yet here again men's and women's experiences are very different. In their doctoral training, men and women are about equally likely to receive a research or teaching assistantship sometime during graduate school (National Research Council, 1983). But women see faculty and research advisors much less frequently than do men (Holmstrom and Holmstrom, 1974; Kjerulff and Blood, 1973), and their interaction and communication with faculty are less relaxed and egalitarian (Kjerulff and Blood, 1973). Further, women tend to regard themselves as students rather than as colleagues of faculty and report that they are taken less seriously than are male graduate students (Berg and Ferber, 1983; Holmstrom and Holmstrom, 1974; see also Freeman, 1979). In short, in graduate and professional education, women report that they are more marginal—especially outside of formal classroom proceedings. As one woman at Berkeley put it:

> Have I been overtly discriminated against? Probably no. Have I been encouraged, congratulated, received recognition, gotten a friendly hello, a solicitous "can I help you out?" The answer is no. Being a woman here just makes you tougher, work harder, and hope that if you get a 4.0 GPA, someone will say "You're good." (Quoted in Association of American Colleges, 1982·1.)

To understand the implications of this pattern, one must appreciate the consequences of faculty alliance in graduate education. For their favored students, faculty provide the research training and experience necessary for professional and intellectual development. They nominate preferred students for fellowships and awards and take a stand for them in the perennial disputes surrounding qualifying examinations and degree requirements. They provide professional visibility by introducing their protégés at meetings and conferences and by coauthoring papers and articles with them. Faculty selectively provide students the opportunity to pose important questions, to solve problems, and to set professional goals. Ultimately, the faculty help their favored students to locate good jobs and thus place them on the road of career mobility.

Women's limited interaction with faculty lessens their opportunities for advancement. This exclusion is not a simple function of overt discrimination. Rather, it is linked more subtly to the character of dominance and control within higher education. Like other organizations and institutions in our society, academia is largely a "male milieu." The men have grown up together, have played, learned, and competed together. They share certain language, traditions, and understandings—in and out of the work setting (see Epstein, 1970:167–76; Epstein, 1974). When these professionals choose protégés or apprentices, they look to fledglings in whom they can see a reflection of themselves. In such a system of mentor/protégé relations, women are more likely to be "outsiders" and, as such, are infrequently identified as successors of the men in control. Thus, in an organization that operates by way of sponsorship and support, the women students are more likely to be left to struggle along on their own.

Of course, the presence of women faculty and mentors can change the balance of interaction and support. One study reports a strong positive correlation between the proportion of female faculty and the number of women students who are subsequently cited for achievement (Tidball, 1973). And women holding doctoral degrees who had female dissertation advisors are reported to publish significantly more than do women who had male advisors (Goldstein, 1979). Moreover, since both men's and women's aspiration levels are a function of their real and perceived opportunities (Kanter, 1977), the presence and availability of female mentors can broaden women's sense of possibilities.

During the last twenty years, women's studies programs have been one expression of the feminist movement on campuses.[2] In their course offerings and research on women, women's studies have helped to correct scholarship's longstanding oversight of (or bias in) the study of women. Focusing upon women's problems, activities, and contributions, women's studies scholarship has regarded women as a primary subject of study and gender as a fundamental factor in the creation and development of knowledge and society. Treating women as writers and historical figures and examining their roles in law, the economy, politics, arts, and popular culture, women's studies have critiqued "publicly acceptable prejudice against women" (Tobias, 1978:82). In this way, women's studies have proceeded on a principle that changing what and how women are (or are not) studied may affect the way in which women live (Boxer, 1988:73). Thus, unlike other areas of study, women's studies join theory and practice, academics and activism—although the extent of this unity varies considerably among women's studies programs.

One organizational controversy remains unresolved: should women's studies scholarship and courses be taught in separate academic programs or be integrated throughout the academy? Separation can engender a ghettoization of feminist scholarship and perhaps a false illusion of academic influence. However, autonomy comes with separation. The development of critical scholarship, of challenges to established modes of thought, and of constructions of women as the subject of study may flourish better under independent organizational conditions. Further, introducing women's studies scholarship throughout the curriculum may fall within the rubric of integration, but the question remains as to whether the faculty at large (compared to a women's studies faculty in particular) can be charged with this task. One resolution is to clearly site the development of women's studies scholarship within women's studies programs, but to provide means for the integration of that knowledge throughout departments.[3]

Women as Faculty in Higher Education

As faculty, women are segregated in the tasks they perform, the places they teach, the fields they occupy, and the ranks they hold. Across each dimension (task, place, position), women receive lower rewards (Fox, 1985).

Female academics are underrepresented in research universities and located disproportionately in two-year colleges—where teaching loads are heavy and service demands are high (see Table 5). In fact, among full-time teaching faculty, almost 30 percent of the women teach thirteen or more hours a week, whereas only 15 percent of the men teach this much (Ekstrom, 1979:2). Women are concentrated disproportionately in state colleges and satellite campuses rather than in the doctoral-granting universities that have resources for the research and publication on which academic eminence and recognition are based. At the top of the academic hierarchy, in the prestigious and powerful places that set the pace and dominate the standards of scholarly work, even fewer women are present (see Graham, 1978:768).

Women are located not only in less prestigious places, but also in the less powerful fields and disciplines within academia. Academic men are

Table 5. Women as a Percentage of Total Full-Time Instructional Faculty, by
Institutional Type and by Rank: 1987, 1991

Institutional type, 1987	Percent women
Public research	21
Private research	19
Public doctoral	24
Private doctoral	27
Public comprehensive	29
Private comprehensive	28
Liberal arts	29
Public 2-year	38
All institutions	27

Across institutions, by rank, 1991

Rank	Percent women
Professor	15
Associate professor	28
Assistant professor	40
Instructor	47
Lecturer	52

Sources: For institutional type: U.S. Department of Education, National Center for Education Statistics.
NSOPP-88 Faculty Summary. For rank: U.S. Department of Education, National Center for Educa-
tion Statistics. *Digest of Educational Statistics.* Washington, D.C.: U.S. Government Printing Office, 1993:
Table 219.

concentrated in the sciences, social sciences, and professional schools. Women,
in contrast, are clustered in the arts, humanities, and services associated with
more marginal areas of education, public health, and welfare (Bognanno, 1987;
Fox, 1981).

Moreover, the higher the rank, the fewer the women. Among all full-time
instructional faculty, 49 percent of the women compared to 70 percent of the
men are tenured (U.S. Department of Education, NCES, 1993:Table 231).
Across fields and institutions, 40 percent of the assistant professors are women,
but only 28 percent of the associate professors and 15 percent of the full
professors are women (Table 5). It is, instead, in the subprofessorial ranks
where we find highly disproportionate concentrations of women. At the
instructor and lecturer levels, women account for about one-half of the faculty
(Table 5).

These subprofessorial appointments are often marginal positions that
fluctuate with enrollments, unexpected leaves of absence, and other departmental exigencies (see Hornig, 1979; Van Arsdale, 1978). Many of these
appointments are part-time or part-year positions. For university administrators, appointing faculty to adjunct or temporary appointments provides a
big benefit: it keeps salary levels down, avoids long-term commitments, and
relieves "regular" faculty of tedious undergraduate courses. But for those who
hold these posi-tions, the costs are high: part-time and adjunct appointments

rarely carry fringe benefits, they never provide leaves or sabbaticals, and they offer no security or chance for tenure. Further, because these faculty are rarely represented by unions or professional associations, they are exempt from formal grievance procedures (Tuckman et al., 1978). Perhaps most important, part-time, adjunct, and subprofessorial appointees are ineligible for outside research funding—thus reducing their chance to establish an independent scholarly record and obtain better prospects for themselves (Hornig, 1979).

As university resources have dwindled and budgets have decreased, the number of full-time faculty has declined dramatically. Between 1970–71 and 1982–83, the ratio of full-time to part-time faculty decreased from 3.5:1 to 2.1:1—a remarkable dive in a single decade (Bowen and Schuster, 1985:5). By 1990, the ratio had decreased further to 1.75:1 (U.S. Department of Education, NCES, 1992:calculated from Table 209). Across institutional types, women hold a disproportionate number of the part-time appointments: 45 percent of the female and 31 percent of the male faculty in higher education had such an appointment in 1989 (U.S. Department of Education, NCES, 1992:calcu-lated from Table 209).

The growth in part-time, temporary, and subprofessorial appointments creates a permanent, marginally employed faculty who exist on the fringes of academic life (see Wilke, 1979). These faculty suffer from a humiliating absence of status and from indignities, which range from denial of clerical help, to exclusion from departmental meetings and isolation from contact with "regular faculty" (see Van Arsdale, 1978). That this class of faculty is disproportionately female is an indication of, and blight on, the status of women in higher education.

Women's depressed status as faculty members is tied partially to the socialization processes and to the restrictive political and economic structures that produce gender inequalities throughout the labor force. But beyond these factors, women in higher education are disadvantaged by particular features of the academic organization itself.

First, women faculty, like women graduate students, are constrained by the male culture of academia. In this milieu, men share traditions, styles, and understandings about rules of competing, bartering, and succeeding. They accept one another, they support one another, and they promote one another. Because women are more likely to be outsiders to this male milieu, and its informal network of information and resources, they are disadvantaged in job prospects, research information, and professional opportunities and services. As one woman in science put it:

> Sooner or later I and those around me knew I was not one of the boys. Professional identification in the absence of colleague identification gets you only so far. When somewhere along the line the boys start boosting their buddies in a kind of "quid pro quo" competition, you realize you've had it. You don't have the "quo" for the "quid." You don't have any coattails, and everyone knows it. The shift may be subtle or it may come as a jolt, but it *does* come. In school, the boys took you more or less seriously because you got the highest grades in courses and helped them study for exams. But now that everyone has degree in hand, they don't need you anymore (Tidball, 1974:56–57).

Since the academic culture is not only male but also white, these problems are compounded for nonwhite women.

In addition, the normative standards of academic work create a bias in evaluation. In scholarly and scientific work, standards are both "absolute" and "subjective." Work is measured against a standard of absolute excellence, and this, in turn, is a subjective assessment. Thus, in academia, the evaluative criteria are vague, the process of appraisal is highly inferential, and the decisions for reward are judgmental.

In such a context, stereotyped and sex-biased reactions abound. Studies indicate that the more loosely defined and subjective the criteria, the more likely white males are perceived to be and evaluated as the superior candidates, and the more likely gender bias is to operate (see Deux and Emswiller, 1974; Nieva and Gutek, 1980; Pheterson et al., 1971; Rosen and Jerdee, 1974). In academia, conditions are then prime for bias in recruitment, hiring, and promotion, and women are among the casualties of the system.

Although this bias is a violation of federal law, seeking legal redress is a costly process (see Theodore, 1986). Further, an irony of academic life is that scholars and scientists have counted since childhood on their individual achievement and performance to win them recognition and reward. And, as a group, they regard the rules of their work—the standards, the evaluation, and the rewards—as legitimate. Consequently, academics tend to attribute their failure to individual performance rather than to institutional structure (Cole and Cole, 1973:254–59; Fox, 1981:82). In this way, the norms of science and scholarship—with their emphasis on individual attainment and meritocratic reward—help to dampen collective alienation and response in academia.

Finally, women's disadvantaged status in academia is perpetuated by the very sex segregation that is an index of their subordination. Inequality in the status of the sexes is more tenable when it is less evident, and the segregation of men and women in different units, departments, and institutions makes their discrepant ranks and rewards less apparent and visible. This reduces potential strain and, in doing so, helps to perpetuate the discrepant status of the men and women without threatening academia's ideology of universalism and objectivity (Fox, 1985).

Title IX and Prospects for Women in Higher Education

In 1972, Congress prohibited sex discrimination in higher education by adding Title IX to the Education Amendments Act. Its key stipulation states:

> No person in the United States, shall, on the basis of sex, be excluded from participation in, be denied the benefits of, or be subjected to discrimination under any education program or activity receiving Federal financial assistance [20 U.S.C. §1681].

Because colleges and universities receive federal assistance in grants, contracts, loan programs, and student aid, the act applies to higher-education institutions along with elementary and secondary schools. Title IX covers employment in education as well as almost every aspect of student life. Thus, the act prohibits sex discrimination in admissions to educational institutions (except admissions to private and single-sex institutions); curricular and extracurricular programs; student services and benefits such as counseling, health care, and financial aid; and hiring and promotion within educational agencies and institutions.

With this mandate, Title IX has altered the most obvious and blatant discriminatory practices in higher education, especially in admissions. As late as the early 1970s, women were subject to inequitable quota and admissions standards in colleges and universities. At Cornell University's College of Agriculture, for example, women were admitted to the program only if they had SAT scores thirty to forty points higher than those of the entering males; at Pennsylvania State University, a male applicant was five times more likely to be accepted than a female; and at the University of North Carolina, admission of female students was restricted by policies that required women to live in dormitories, of which there were only a few, whereas men could live off-campus (National Advisory Council on Women's Educational Programs, 1981:25). Title IX has eliminated the most flagrant of these practices—at least as they operate on the formal level.

Yet the area in which Title IX has been most acutely seen and felt is in athletics. Before Title IX, female athletes were a rarity on our college campuses. Men dominated the playing fields, courts, and pools; they got the athletic scholarships and awards; and they obtained public attention and acclaim for athletic accomplishment. The few female athletes, in contrast, struggled along without facilities, funding, or rewards. With Title IX, however, women's participation in college athletics greatly expanded (National Advisory Council on Women's Educational Programs, 1981).

Beyond athletics and formal discrimination in admissions, however, Title IX has had limited impact. It has not reduced informal sources of bias in higher education—the classroom procedures, interaction processes, and systems of faculty support discussed earlier. To correct these disparities, one step would be an increase in female faculty, especially in the higher ranks. The presence and availability of female faculty would serve to broaden women's aspirations, to increase their opportunities for interaction with faculty, and most important, to reduce the male dominance of educational practices and processes.

Yet, with the stagnation of affirmative-action programs in the university and with a low public demand for redress of sex discrimination, women have not increased their proportions as faculty—particularly tenured faculty—in higher education. Between 1976 and 1991, the proportion of women among all full professors increased from 10 percent to just 15 percent (U.S. Department of Education, 1987b:Appendix Table A; and Table 5 of this chapter). Instead, women academics remain limited in number and are clustered in the lower ranks, where they have little visibility and influence. Although Title IX covers employment as well as student life, the act has had little influence on the proportions of female faculty.

Finally, while Title IX may be one factor in the increased female enrollments in higher education, it has had limited effect on the segregation of male and female students into different areas of study. Women continue to be restricted, especially in their technical and scientific training, which has profound consequences for their occupational options. Because they have been diverted from high-school mathematics courses, in particular, many women lack the critical "filter" subject necessary for education in 75 percent of all college and university majors, including the business, medicine, science, engineering, and architecture programs (Sell, 1974), which lead to higher-paying jobs. To correct these patterns, schools must make clear to students the lifetime consequences of both technical and nontechnical preparation and must remove the barriers that surround numbers, logic, and problem solving as male domains.

As an act for gender equity in education, Title IX has provided a broad mandate. But legislation lives and dies by its enforcement, not by its mandate (Scott, 1974:402). To achieve gender equity in education, we must confront the practices that track men and women into different curricular areas and activities and that socialize them for different occupational outcomes. Such action requires effective monitoring, strong enforcement, and firm sanctions for noncompliance with policies of equity. These, in turn, demand the awareness, support, and effort of political institutions. Institutional action can help to break the patterns and processes that restrict women's options and constrain their possibilities throughout work and society.

NOTES

1. For some data, the most recent time point available is 1989 (rather than 1990). This is because (1) certain government data for 1990 are preliminary (unverified), or (2) categories for 1990 are different than those for the earlier time point (1971) in tables, and thus do not allow appropriate comparisons between times.

2. The 1990 edition of the National Women's Studies Association Directory lists 142 institutions that offer undergraduate majors in women's studies.

3. I thank Donna Hughes for her perspective on this.

REFERENCES

Allmendinger, David. "Mount Holyoke Students Encounter the Need for Life Planning, 1837–1850." *History of Education Quarterly* 19(Spring 1979):27–46.

American Medical Association (AMA). Department of Physician Data Services. *Physician Characteristics and Distribution in the U.S.* Chicago, Ill.: AMA, 1990.

Antler, Joyce. "Culture, Service, and Work: Changing Ideals of Higher Education for Women." In *The Undergraduate Woman,* pp. 15–41. Edited by P. Perun. Lexington, Mass.: Lexington Books, 1982.

Association of American Colleges. "The Classroom Climate: A Chilly One for Women?" Washington, D.C.: Association of American Colleges, Project on the Status and Education of Women, 1982.

Berg, H. M. and Ferber, Marianne. "Women and Men Graduate Students: Who Succeeds and Why." In *Journal of Higher Education* 54(Nov/Dec 1983):629–48.

Bernard, Richard and Vinovskis, Maris. "The Female School Teacher in Ante-Bellum Massachusetts." *Journal of Social History* 10(Spring 1977):332–45.

Bognanno, Mario. "Women in Professions: Academic Women." In *Working Women: Past, Present, Future,* pp. 245–64. Edited by K. Koziara, M. Moskow, and L. Tanner. Washington, D.C.: The Bureau of National Affairs, 1987.

Bowen, Howard and Schuster, Jack. *American Professors.* New York: Oxford University Press, 1986.

Boxer, Marilyn. "For and About Women: The Theory and Practice of Women's Studies in the United States." In *Reconstructing the Academy,* pp. 69–103. Edited by E. Minnich, J. O'Barr, and R. Rosenfeld. Chicago: University of Chicago Press, 1988.

Chafe, William. *The American Woman: Her Changing Social, Economic, and Political Roles, 1920–1970.* New York: Oxford University Press, 1972.

Clifford, Jeraldine Joncich. "Shaking Dangerous Questions from the Crease: Gender and American Higher Education." *Feminist Studies* 3(Fall 1983):3–62.

Cole, Jonathan R. and Cole, Stephen. *Social Stratification in Science.* Chicago: University of Chicago Press, 1973.

Conway, Jill. "Perspectives on the History of Women's Education in the United States." *History of Education Quarterly* 14(Spring 1974):1–12.

Deux, K. and Emswiller, T. "Explanations of Successful Performance in Sex-Linked Tasks." *Journal of Personality and Social Psychology* 22(1974):80–85.

Ekstrom, Ruth S. "Women Faculty: Development, Promotion, Pay." *Findings: Educational Testing Service* 5(1979):1–5.

Epstein, Cynthia Fuchs. *Woman's Place: Options and Limits in Professional Careers.* Berkeley, Calif.: University of California Press, 1970.

Epstein, Cynthia Fuchs. "Bringing Women In: Rewards, Punishments, and the Structure of Achievement." In *Women and Success: The Anatomy of Achievement,* pp. 13–21. Edited by R. Kundsin. New York: William Morrow and Co., 1974.

Epstein, Cynthia Fuchs. *Women in Law.* Garden City, N.Y.: Anchor Books, 1983.

Featherman, David. "School and Occupational Careers: Constancy and Change in Worldly Success." In *Constancy and Change in Human Development,* pp. 675–738. Edited by O. G. Brimm and J. Kagan. Cambridge, Mass.: Harvard University Press, 1980.

Featherman, David and Hauser, Robert. "Sexual Inequalities and Socioeconomic Achievement in the U.S." *American Sociological Review* 41(June 1976):462–83.

Fox, Mary Frank. "Sex, Salary, and Achievement: Reward-Dualism in Academia." *Sociology of Education* 54(April 1981):71–84.

Fox, Mary Frank. "Location, Sex-Typing, and Salary Among Academics." *Work and Occupations* 12(May 1985):186–205.

Frazier, Nancy and Sadker, Myra. *Sexism in School and Society.* New York: Harper and Row, 1973.

Freeman, Jo. "How to Discriminate Against Women Without Really Trying." In *Women: A Feminist Perspective,* 2nd edition, pp. 217–32. Edited by J. Freeman. Palo Alto, Calif.: Mayfield Publishing, 1979.

Goldstein, Elysee. "Effect of Same-Sex and Cross-Sex Role Models on the Subsequent Academic Productivity of Scholars." *American Psychologist* 34(May 1979):407.

Gordon, Ann. "The Young Ladies Academy of Philadelphia." In *Women of America: A History,* pp. 68–91. Edited by C. Berkin and M. B. Norton. Boston: Houghton Mifflin Co., 1979.

Graham, Patricia A. "Expansion and Exclusion: A History of Women in American Higher Education." *Signs* 3(Summer 1978):759–73.

Holmstrom, Engininel and Holmstrom, Robert. "The Plight of the Woman Doctoral Student." *American Educational Research Journal* 11(Winter 1974):1–17.

Hornig, Lilli S. *Climbing the Academic Ladder: Doctoral Women Scientists in Academe.* Washington, D.C.: National Academy of Sciences, 1979.

Hornig, Lilli S. "Women in Science and Engineering: Why So Few." *Technology Review* 87(Nov/Dec 1984):31–47.

Kanter, Rosabeth Moss. *Men and Women of the Corporation.* New York: Basic Books, 1977.

Kerber, Linda. "The Republican Mother: Women and the Enlightenment—An American Perspective." *American Quarterly* 28(Summer 1976):187–205.

Kerber, Linda. *Women of the Republic: Intellect and Ideology in Revolutionary America.* Chapel Hill: University of North Carolina Press, 1980.

Kjerulff, Kristen H. and Blood, Milton R. "A Comparison of Communication Patterns in Male and Female Graduate Students." *Journal of Higher Education* 44(Nov 1973):623–32.

National Advisory Council on Women's Educational Programs. *Title IX: The Half Full, Half Empty Glass.* Washington, D.C.: U.S. Government Printing Office, 1981.

National Research Council. Committee on the Education and Employment of Women in Science and Engineering. *Climbing the Ladder: An Update on the Status of Doctoral Women Scientists and Engineers.* Washington, D.C.: National Academy Press, 1983.

National Research Council. *Summary Report 1986: Doctorate Recipients from United States Universities.* Washington, D.C.: National Academy Press, 1987.

Nieva, Veronica and Gutek, Barbara A. "Sex Effects on Evaluation." *Academy of Management Review* 5(1980):267–76.

Perun, Pamela and Giele, Janet. "Life After College: Historical Links Between Women's Work and Women's Education." In *The Undergraduate Woman*, pp. 375–98. Edited by P. Perun. Lexington, Mass.: Lexington Books, 1982.

Pheterson, G. T., S. B. Kiesler, and P. A. Goldberg. "Evaluation of the Performance of Women as a Function of Their Sex, Achievement, and Personal History." *Journal of Personality and Social Psychology* 19(1971):110–14.

Rosen, B. and Jerdee, T. H. "Influence of Sex-Role Stereotypes on Personnel Decisions." *Journal of Applied Psychology* 59(1974):9–14.

Schwager, Sally. "Educating Women in America." *Signs* 12(1987):333–72.

Scott, Ann. "It's Time for Equal Education." In *And Jill Came Tumbling After*, pp. 399–409. Edited by J. Stacey, S. Bereaud, and J. Daniels. New York: Dell Publishing, 1974.

Sell, Lucy. "High School Math as a Vocational Filter for Women and Minorities." Berkeley: University of California at Berkeley, 1974.

Sewell, William, Robert Hauser, and Wendy Wolf. "Sex, Schooling, and Occupational Status." *American Journal of Sociology* 86(1980):551–83.

Speizer, Jeanne. "Students Should Be Seen *and* Heard." In *The Undergraduate Woman*, pp. 401–4. Edited by P. Perun. Lexington, Mass.: Lexington Books, 1982.

Sterglanz, Sarah Hall and Lyberger-Ficek, Shirley. "Sex Differences in Student–Teacher Interactions in the College Classroom." *Sex Roles* 3(1977):345–52.

Theodore, Athena. *The Campus Troublemakers: Academic Women in Protest*. Houston: Cap and Gown Press, 1986.

Thorne, Barrie. "Claiming Verbal Space: Women's Speech and Language in the College Classroom." Paper presented at the Research Conference on Educational Environments and the Undergraduate Woman. Wellesley, Mass.: Wellesley College, September 1979.

Tidball, M. Elizabeth. "Perspective on Academic Women and Affirmative Action." *Educational Record* 54(Spring 1973):130–35.

Tidball, M. Elizabeth. "Women Role Models in Higher Education." In *Graduate and Professional Education of Women*, pp. 56–59. Proceedings of the Conference of the AAUW. Washington, D.C.: American Association of University Women, 1974.

Tobias, Sheila. "Women's Studies: Its Origin, Organization, and Prospects." In *The Higher Education of Women*, pp. 80–94. Edited by H. Astin. New York: Holt, Rinehart, and Winston, 1978.

Tuckman, Howard P., Jaime Caldwell, and William Volger. "Part-Timers and the Academic Labor Market of the Eighties." *American Sociologist* 13(Nov 1978):184–95.

U.S. Department of Education, National Center for Education Statistics. *Degrees Awarded to Women: 1979 Update*. Washington, D.C.: U.S. Department of Education, 1981a.

U.S. Department of Education, National Center for Education Statistics. *Faculty, Salary, Tenure, Benefits, 1980–81*. Washington, D.C.: U.S. Government Printing Office, 1981b.

U.S. Department of Education, National Center for Education Statistics. HEGIS Survey XX. "Salaries, Tenure, and Fringe Benefits for Full Time Instructional Faculty." Washington, D.C.: U.S. Government Printing Office, 1986.

U.S. Department of Education, National Center for Education Statistics. *Digest of Education Statistics, 1992*. Washington, D.C.: U.S. Government Printing Office, 1991, 1992, and 1993.

U.S. Department of Education, National Center for Education Statistics. "Racial/Ethnic Trends in Degrees Conferred by Institutions of Higher Education, 1978–79 Through 1988–89." E.D. TABS. January 1991.

Van Arsdale, George. "De-Professionalizing a Part-Time Teaching Faculty." *American Sociologist* 13(Nov 1978):195–201.

Wilke, Arthur. *The Hidden Professoriate: Credentialism, Professionalism, and the Tenure Crisis*. Westport, Conn.: Greenwood Press, 1979.

Woody, Thomas. *A History of Women's Education in the United States*, vol. 1. New York: Octagon Books, 1966.

Women in Blue-Collar Occupations: Traditional and Nontraditional

Brigid O'Farrell

BLUE COLLARS AND hard hats symbolize workers who do manual labor: skilled craft workers, semiskilled operatives, and unskilled laborers. Carpenters on construction sites, motor inspectors in steel mills, and sewing machine operators in garment factories are all blue-collar workers involved in the production process, making and repairing goods and equipment. In the United States, there are over thirty million blue-collar workers. Women have always been part of this work force, which includes slightly over five million women, representing 17 percent of all blue-collar workers.

Women and men in blue-collar work face many similar rewards and problems on the job. They work because of economic necessity, as well as for a sense of challenge, accomplishment, and companionship, needs most fully met in skilled trade occupations such as electrician, carpenter, and plumber. But even skilled, well-paying construction work has been characterized as physically hard and dangerous, with little security or respect. As a group, blue-collar workers are less well paid than managerial, technical, and professional workers. New technology and a more competitive world economy have led to decreasing skill levels and increasing unemployment for women and men.

Clear differences also exist between women and men in blue-collar jobs. Women have been excluded from the skilled crafts and unskilled labor jobs. They have been limited to a relatively small number of low-wage, semiskilled operative jobs in the textile, apparel, and electronics industries. During the past two decades some change has occurred, however, and the work experiences of these women now fall into two distinct categories: nontraditional and traditional.[1]

In nontraditional or male-dominated jobs, women are a considerably smaller proportion of the occupation (less than 20 percent) than their share of the total employed population, which in 1993 was 46 percent (Rytina and Bianchi, 1984; U.S. Department of Labor, 1994). Under equal employment opportunity (EEO) legislation passed in the 1960s, a small number of women have gained access to nontraditional work as plumbers, machinists, auto workers, and laborers. A few jobs, such as typesetter and compositor in the printing industry, have changed from predominantly men to predominantly women. The majority of women, however, continue to work in operative jobs traditionally held by women. In 1993, 39 percent of all operatives and 86 percent of sewing machine operators were women (U.S. Department of Labor, 1994).

The distinction between traditional and nontraditional work provides the organizational framework for this chapter. The first section describes the women who do traditional blue-collar work in terms of their economic and family status, education, race, and ethnicity. Four factors are then outlined that distinguish female-dominated jobs from other blue- and white-collar jobs: skill level, working conditions, unemployment, and unionization. The second section analyzes the progress and problems in integrating women into nontraditional craft, operative, and laborer jobs. Characteristics of the women in these jobs and the barriers they must overcome are discussed. The final section summarizes four themes that suggest that the employment of women in traditional jobs, the slow progress in integrating women into nontraditional jobs, and the development of new female-dominated jobs have more to do with organizational constraints and government policies than with the preferences of individual women. The implications for women are assessed in the context of the broader changes occurring in blue-collar work.

Traditional Occupations: Machine Operators

The first industrial factory workers were women operatives in the New England textile mills in the 1800s. By 1830, thirty-nine thousand of the fifty-five thousand mill workers were young farm women. Textile owners used newspapers and company recruiters to find women for the lowest-paying, least-skilled jobs. Hiring women freed men for agricultural work, western expansion, and new skilled factory work (Wertheimer, 1984).

As the industrial revolution progressed, it further contributed to the segregation of paid work by sex and to the practice of paying women less than a living wage. In industries that continued to depend more heavily on workers than on machines, such as textiles and electronics, hiring women became a business necessity. Plants were located where there were large populations of potential women workers. Employers assumed that women would remain economically dependent on their fathers or husbands and therefore did not need a living wage. Rather than liberating women, paid work in factories reinforced women's economic dependence and traditional roles as wives and mothers (Tentler, 1979; Kessler-Harris, 1982).

Milkman (1983) offers a striking comparison between the electronics and auto industries at the turn of the century. In the electrical products industry, women were actively recruited because the industry remained labor intensive and women could be hired for less money than men to do the least skilled jobs. Women rapidly became 30 percent of the work force. In the auto industry, by contrast, technology and the moving assembly line became the major expense. Since the industry was not labor intensive, Henry Ford could pay higher wages to men and act on his stated preference of not hiring women and children. Thus, women were excluded from some of the highest paying industrial jobs at that time, and the auto industry work force remains less than 10 percent women.

Today, within the skilled occupational category of precision production, craft, and repair there are a small number of women in female-dominated trades. In 1993, for example, 91,000 dressmakers (94 percent) and 212,000 electrical and electronic equipment assemblers (67 percent) were women. Over 4.1 million women, however, work in the semiskilled and unskilled category of operators, fabricators, and laborers. Most operate winding, twisting, separating, filling, painting, slicing, and sewing machines. This section describes the background women bring to these jobs, the characteristics of the jobs themselves, and efforts to improve the wages and working conditions through both informal actions on the job and more formally through labor unions.

WHO ARE THE WOMEN OPERATIVES?

Like the vast majority of employed women and men, women operatives work because they and their families need the money. Eighty-one percent of these women work full-time, but their median annual earnings (Table 1) were only $14,976 in 1993, barely above the federal poverty level of $13,924 for a family of four (U.S. Bureau of the Census, 1993). When part-time workers are included, the median earnings for women machine operators is only $10,845.

In 1987, among married couples, two-thirds of the women in the operator, fabricator, and laborer category were married to men in blue-collar jobs with combined earnings of approximately $30,000. Blue-collar wives now contribute about 45 percent of family income (Rosen, 1987; U.S. Bureau of the Census, 1991). Among two-parent families with children in this income

Table 1. Median Earnings for Women and Men in Full-Time Blue-Collar Occupations, 1993

Occupation (full-time, year-round)	Men		Women	
	Weekly	Annual[a]	Weekly	Annual
Precision production, craft, and repair	$511	$26,572	$344	$17,888
Mechanics and repairers	$503	$26,156	$526	$27,352[b]
Construction trades	$495	$25,740	—	—[c]
Precision production	$531	$27,612	$319	$16,588
Operators, fabricators, and laborers	$399	$20,748	$288	$14,976
Machine operators, assemblers, inspectors	$407	$21,164	$284	$14,768
Transportation and material moving	$456	$23,712	$358	$18,616
Handlers, equipment cleaners, helpers, and laborers	$319	$16,588	$286	$14,872
Total work force	$514	$26,728	$395	$20,540

a. Annual estimates are based on median weekly earnings multiplied by fifty-two weeks.
b. Between 1983 and 1993 men's wages steadily increased. Because the sample for women was small (less than one hundred), women's wages fluctuated. In six years they were higher than men's. In five years they were lower.
c. Data not shown where base is less than fifty thousand and the sample is very small.
Source: U.S. Department of Labor, *Employment and Earnings*, Table 56 (January 1994).

range, the standard of living remained stagnant during the last ten years. One study, analyzing the Current Population Survey of sixty thousand households in March of 1980 and 1990, found that increases in wives' hours of work were offset by a decline in men's real hourly wages (Joint Economic Committee, 1992). Even though the wages are low, money is a primary reason for blue-collar women to enter the labor force and a major source of job satisfaction (Walshok, 1981; O'Farrell and Harlan, 1982; Rosen, 1987).

Most operative jobs require no formal background or training and can be learned in a matter of days or weeks. Thus, these jobs represent relatively good opportunities for women with little education, training, experience, and/or limited use of English. For example, 36 percent of women aged twenty-five or older in operative jobs have received less than a high school education, compared to 6 percent of women in white-collar jobs (U.S. Bureau of the Census, 1991). Young women who have received little or no job training in high school may see these jobs as temporary opportunities before they go back to school or enter training programs (Green, 1983). They continue to offer opportunities to immigrant women who speak little English, from Portuguese women in the garment and electronics factories of New England (Rosen, 1987) to Chicana women in the canneries of northern California (Zavella, 1987).

Historically, operative jobs have been held by white women, often from first- and second-generation immigrant families. Increasingly, however, these jobs are being held by women of color (Table 2). Amott and Mathaei (1991) conclude that the increase in women of color in manufacturing, which includes most of the craft, operative, and laborer occupations, reflects a decline in the quality of jobs and subsequent movement of white women into higher paying or higher status clerical and professional work. Within operative work, Rosen (1987), in her study of over four hundred women factory workers in New England, found that the best wages in unionized jobs were held by younger American-born women rather than the Portuguese immigrants or older

Table 2. Percent of Working Women Employed in Manufacturing by Racial-Ethnic Group, 1900–1980

	1900	*1930*	*1960*	*1980*
African-American	2.6	8.4	15.5	18.4
European American	32.6	21.2	18.5	12.6
American Indian	24.9	37.6	18.1	17.0
Chinese American	41.1	20.8	24.0	20.8
Japanese American	7.7	12.2	19.0	12.5
Filipina American	n.a.	15.3	17.4	13.8
Chicana	n.a.	24.7	29.1	26.0
U.S. Puerto Rican	n.a.	n.a.	69.3	29.1
Island Puerto Rican	14.6	52.4	31.3	22.0

Notes. Use Amott and Mathaei (1991) for a listing of occupations and a discussion of comparability issues across censuses years, Asian American data only for Hawaii for all years, 1980 data for American Indians include Eskimo and Aleut peoples, for 1900–1960, African American and European American include Latinas.
Source: Amott and Mathaei (1991), Table 10-8, p. 331

women. In a study of vocational high school students in New York City, Baker and Levenson (1975) found that the tracking of black and Hispanic women into the least skilled and lowest paying operative jobs begins in high school.

The majority of women operatives, regardless of racial or ethnic background, see few alternatives to their work and find ways to adjust to semi-skilled, high-pressure jobs that have poor working conditions and the constant threat of unemployment. At the same time, these women take pride in doing their jobs well, earning money, and contributing to their families' well-being and their own sense of self-esteem. Like men in less skilled, low-opportunity jobs, association with coworkers provides an alternative but not the only source of job satisfaction (see, for example, Green, 1983; Sacks and Remy, 1984; Rosen, 1987; Bookman and Morgen, 1988). Ferree (1985) suggests that balancing factory work (as well as other types of traditional female employment) with family responsibilities is personally important and rewarding to working-class women, fulfilling both psychological and economic needs. Full-time housework may be undesirable as well as economically infeasible.

JOB SKILLS AND PRESSURES

Dexterity, patience, and speed are the primary requirements of operative jobs. There is little autonomy, responsibility, challenge, or opportunity in most of these jobs. Machine operator jobs continue to reflect the early principles of scientific management established by Frederick Taylor in the early 1900s. Tasks are broken down into the smallest possible specialties and coordinated according to detailed rules; workers are closely monitored for performance and productivity. A punch press operator in a large firm manufacturing sophisticated industrial machines explains her job this way:

> The set up man has the machine all ready. It is a bench press. Not very big . . . you can fit it right on the table. I sit and I take these little tweezers, I have two kinds of tweezers, and I take these little pieces [disc about the size of a dime] and put them on the press . . . and there are two round tools that you put on, I hit two buttons on either side, which is an excellent safety device, and the die comes down and punches it . . . see that little notch, the die cut that. You just sit there and sit there and sit there and punch and punch . . . I did 3,200 last night. (O'Farrell, unpublished)

Punching thirty-two hundred pieces in a shift was not considered very good (less than five hundred pieces an hour). This woman got less money in her paycheck than coworkers who punched six hundred pieces an hour because they are paid on a piecework basis. These jobs are dominated by piecework payment systems originally introduced with scientific management as a way to reduce costs by controlling production in labor-intensive jobs (Milkman, 1983). Lamphere (1984) describes the system in a garment factory:

> Piece rates were based on the decimal system, so that they were easy to computerize. But they were also calculated to baffle the workers, since garments were batched in dozens and most sewers kept their eyes on a clock that ticks away in sixty-minute hours. In the official system, the hour is

divided into 100 parts, so that 10 minutes is really .167 of an hour. Thus, a piece rate of .073 meant that an operation had to be performed on a dozen garments in 4.38 minutes if the sewer was to earn . . . base rates on which the piece rates were figured. (Lamphere, 1984:250)

Lamphere figured that to earn the minimum wage by working all day on the same t-shirts with a rate of .073 she would have to sew a dozen garments, setting two sleeves each, every 6.3 minutes, completing seventy-six dozen garments in a day.

Despite technological advances in machines and production processes, many operative jobs remain labor intensive, and piecework payment continues to be a primary method of production control. For example, Fox (1991:37) describes work done primarily by Hispanic, Native American, Asian, and black women in an electronics plant in New Mexico as "winding, stacking, potting, snagging, clamping, waxing, or winding daisies." Yet he found that because of the rapid changes in designs as products were modified and refined, management favored manual over automated construction because people can be retrained more quickly and cheaply than automatic assembly machines can be redesigned and rebuilt.

While some women find doing piecework a challenge, many find it a source of stress and pressure even though it offers more money and they have some control. According to the women Rosen (1987:58) interviewed, trying to work fast enough and at the same time complete the work with care is very trying and very difficult: "Working fast earns you 'good money,' but at the same time, whether you're making pajamas or auto parts, it's hard work and you have to work like a demon." Another woman described her job as tedious, nerve-racking, and painstaking.

Both women and men do operative work, but men's wages are higher than women's (see Table 1). In part this is because men are in different industries and do different jobs. For example, machine operators in metal and plastics are only 16 percent women, while those in textile and apparel are 74 percent women. Within the printing operative category, however, printing press operators are only 16 percent women, while typesetters and compositors are 66 percent women. There are several competing theories to explain wage differences between women and men (see, for example, Blau and Ferber, 1986; Michael, et al., 1989). For operative jobs, however, there is evidence that lower wages for women are the result of discriminatory corporate policies. War Labor Board hearings in the 1940s documented cases where, based on elaborate job studies, men and women were doing work requiring similar levels of skill and responsibility, yet the women were deliberately paid less (Chafe, 1972). More recently, Hams (1984) has described how her union fought and won a comparable pay lawsuit to upgrade the pay of operative jobs done by women and based on wage differences established in the 1940s.

Some variation also exists in skill level among operative jobs and in how different women perceive them. Depending on the machines involved, the work being done, and the alternatives available, some jobs can offer challenge and satisfaction, often in comparison to other jobs the women have held, including housework. Regardless of the real or perceived skill involved or the pressure or challenge of piecework systems, the conditions under which these women work are considered poor. We turn to three major areas of concern: lack of time, physical difficulty, and health and safety hazards.

WORKING CONDITIONS

Operative jobs are not nine-to-five jobs. Like other blue-collar workers, the majority of operatives work shifts: the day shift from 7:00 A.M. to 3:00 P.M., the second shift from 3:00 P.M. to 11:00 P.M., or the graveyard shift from 11:00 P.M. to 7:00 A.M. They punch a time clock, have two fifteen-minute breaks, and get twenty to thirty minutes for lunch. One of the major complaints women workers express is lack of time, especially for themselves, both on and off the job. The women describe themselves as tired whether or not they are satisfied with their jobs, and especially if they are active in a union. As Cathy Creer, who works the second shift in an electronics factory in the Northeast, said, "I'm home by 12:10 A.M. By the time I shower, have a bite to eat, maybe read the *Town Crier* or whatever, it's 1:00 A.M. And you get those nights when you are overtired and you can't get to sleep. When the kids are in school, I'll be up at 6:30. From 1:30 to 6:30—so I average five hours a night. But you get used to it" (Rosen, 1981:9).

Like other blue-collar workers, women operatives prefer jobs that do not involve heavy lifting and are relatively clean. While women's factory work has often been distinguished from men's by being designated as light and clean, in fact it is often dirty and heavy. In a study of Wisconsin apprentices, for example, Briggs (1979) found women doing dirty, heavy work in over half of the seventy-eight plants studied.

Finally, health and safety problems have become an increasingly important concern for blue-collar workers. In 1991 twenty-five workers, mostly black women, were killed by a fire in a chicken processing plant in North Carolina when the exits were locked. This incident was reminiscent of the Triangle Shirtwaist Company fire of 1911, in which 146 women were killed because "factory doors were locked each working day to keep the women in" (Wertheimer, 1977:310). Women risk getting brown lung disease in cotton mills, and textile and apparel workers are exposed to high noise levels, excessive heat, humidity, poor lighting, toxic chemicals, and dust.

The electrical products industry, whose work force is 30 percent women, ranks third among those industries most likely to expose workers to carcinogens (National Commission on Working Women, 1984). According to Fox:

> The "clean industry" may not have smoke stacks or visible piles of scrap, but it is an industry based on chemicals with lethal effects. . . . Scores of the chemicals used in electronics are known to cause, when inhaled or absorbed to excess, drunkenness, nerve damage, hormonal disruption, heart rhythm problems, kidney, lung, or thyroid damage, cancers, mental dysfunction, and emotional disturbance. (Fox, 1991:310)

On-the-job pressures and poor working conditions are important concerns for women operatives, but they are often overshadowed by the threat of having no job at all. While high rates of unemployment have recently come to public attention as a concern for blue-collar men, they have long been a concern for women operatives.

UNEMPLOYMENT

Blue-collar unemployment and the decline of the U.S. industrial base became the focus of public attention during the 1980–82 recession, when steel workers as well as textile workers began losing their jobs. Production workers in manufacturing declined from over fourteen million in 1980 to slightly more than twelve million in 1992. The apparel industry went from over one million to 852,000 during that period. None of the women's operative jobs are found in the Department of Labor's job growth projections, but they account for three of the thirteen fastest declining jobs (U.S. Department of Labor, 1991a).

Temporary layoff and permanent job loss are two forms of unemployment that are common concerns for women in operative jobs. Women in Rosen's (1987) sample experienced an average of between three and four layoffs during the previous ten years, some temporary, but just as often "for good." Seasonal layoffs may leave workers without employment for a few weeks or a few months. Some women like to use this time to catch up on housework and be with their children, provided the women get some form of unemployment compensation and are not the sole support of their families. For women who are supporting families, however, even a temporary layoff can be devastating (Schlozman, 1975; Rosen, 1987).

Permanent job loss occurs through plant closings, regional shifts in production work, and the transfer of production jobs to Third World countries. For example, many jobs have shifted from north and east to south and west, causing regional unemployment, particularly in industries such as textiles and electronics that traditionally employ women. The majority of unemployed factory women find other operative jobs, although almost always at lower wages, with reduced health and pension benefits and loss of seniority, which makes them even more vulnerable to layoffs in the future. This is as true for garment workers in New England as for cannery workers in California (Rosen, 1987; Zavella, 1987).

UNIONIZATION

Despite high levels of unemployment, women operatives have not passively accepted their employment situation. They have actively fought to improve their wages and working conditions, with some limited success. Informally, they have developed resistance strategies on the shop floor, such as the pacing of work to regulate output exemplified by Rhode Island jewelry workers (Shapiro-Perl, 1984). In California's Silicon Valley, home work is developing as an alternative to the factory setting, in part because women may have more control over their work (Katz and Kemnitzer, 1984). Home work, however, is more likely to benefit professional men and women. Home-based operatives continue a long tradition of immigrant women with few skills, low wages, no benefits, and little control over their work (Boris and Daniels, 1989; Ferber and O'Farrell, 1989).

More than other groups of working women, operatives have also fought to change their employment situation through labor unions and the collective bargaining process. Women operatives have played an active role in union history (Kessler-Harris, 1982; Wertheimer, 1984; Baron, 1991). By 1840, they had organized a major association of mill workers in Massachusetts to protest wage cuts, work speedup, and long hours. At the turn of the century, two unions, the International Ladies' Garment Workers Union (ILGWU) and the Amalgamated Clothing Workers Union (now ACTWU), emerged, primarily representing women. Women factory workers were active participants, although not always successful, in the organizing efforts of the industrial unions beginning in the 1930s.

Today, only 12 percent of workers in the private sector belong to a labor union, and most growth has occurred in the public sector, where, for example, 37 percent of government workers are union members. Blue-collar workers, however, are still more likely to belong to a labor union (e.g., 25 percent of craft workers and 26 percent of operatives) than technical workers (10 percent) or service workers (14 percent). Women now account for over a third of all union members. Union women earn more than nonunion women across all occupations (U.S. Department of Labor, 1993a; Spalter-Roth, Hartmann, and Collins, 1994) and are more likely to have benefits such as pension plans and health care, as well as formal procedures for upgrade, layoff, and grievances. They have lower wages and benefits than union men, however, although some unions have fought through grievances, collective bargaining, and the courts to upgrade the operative jobs (Hams, 1984; Freeman and Leonard, 1987).

Despite differences within unions, it is clear that union membership is what makes many operative jobs better than alternative clerical and sales jobs (Rosen, 1987). Contrary to popular beliefs, studies show no differences between men and women in their willingness to join unions, but there is increasing recognition that gender, race, and ethnicity may play an important role when organizing women factory workers (Bookman, 1988; Zavella, 1988; Lamphere and Grenier, 1988).

In general, however, union membership reflects the occupational segregation of the workplace; most women are concentrated in a few unions, and those unions are predominantly female. The ILGWU, for example, is 90 percent women. However, women are not well represented in the leadership positions of their unions. This is slowly beginning to change with the efforts of organizations like the Coalition of Labor Union Women and the increasing activism of women's committees, conferences, and labor education programs at both the national and local levels (Wertheimer, 1984; Milkman, 1985; Roby, 1987; Needleman and Tanner, 1987; Cobble, 1993).

The vast majority of women in traditional operative jobs, however, remain unorganized. In fact, union membership is declining for all blue-collar workers. The decline in part reflects the general economic shift from a manufacturing to a service economy and the dramatic cutbacks beginning with the 1980–82 recession in industries like auto and steel, which have been union strongholds.

At the same time, employers have become increasingly aggressive, sophisticated, and sometimes illegal in their antiunion activities (Freeman and Medoff, 1984; Herrera and Marklin, 1994). Lamphere and Grenier (1988) document the effectiveness of these techniques, as well as the new participative management procedures, to defeat a union drive at a new plant in the Southwest, where Hispanic women were involved in making surgical sutures. Solving these problems requires changes in the current labor laws, established in the 1930s and 1940s, including improved enforcement of laws (U.S. Department of Labor, 1993b; Cobble, 1994; Needleman, 1994).

Despite current difficulties, unions continue to offer an opportunity for women to improve wages and working conditions, especially at a time when government regulation is being reduced. New union initiatives to organize and represent women workers and the increasingly active leadership of women within unions should be of particular benefit to women operatives in the future.

Nontraditional Occupations: Carpenters, Machinists, and Laborers

During World War II, women in unprecedented numbers entered skilled blue-collar jobs traditionally held by men. The government actively recruited women and pressured resistant employers to hire them, although there was considerable segregation of women within their new occupations and industries (Milkman, 1987). The number of women building ships, for example, went from thirty-six in 1940 to 160,000 in 1942. Similar efforts were then made to return women to traditional jobs and to their homes after the war (Chafe, 1972). During the 1970s, women again began to enter nontraditional jobs, but at a much slower pace, under equal employment legislation.

The small successes achieved in the 1970s, however, came to a virtual halt in the 1980s. Progress for women is slowest in the blue-collar skilled jobs. As shown in Table 3, women continue to hold only 1.9 percent of construction trade jobs, and they are only 4 percent of welders and 4 percent of machinists. Men of color have had somewhat more success; in the construction trades 7 percent of those employed are black, and 10 percent are of Hispanic origin. In 1990, according to the Bureau of Apprenticeship (U.S. Department of Labor, 1992), people of color, pre-dominantly men, were 22.5 percent of registered apprentices, compared to 7.1 percent female.

Until recently, many employers and scholars have attributed this slow progress to the lack of available, qualified, interested women and the hostility women face from male coworkers. Research, however, also points to the resistance of employers to hiring women and the persistence of organizational barriers, both in schools and in the job market, as important factors restricting job integration for women in blue-collar jobs. Employers acknowledge that even limited progress would not have occurred without the threat of costly lawsuits and the use of controversial measures such as goals and timetables under the equal employment opportunity laws (Reskin, 1984; Reskin and Hartmann, 1986). Economic and technological change also play a critical role.

This section describes the women who are now in nontraditional jobs, their relationships with male coworkers, the organizational barriers and corporate constraints that continue to limit their interest and opportunities, and the unions that represent them. The research reported here provides a sound basis for challenging theories and policies that fault only the qualifications and initiative of individual women for the slow progress toward

Table 3. Women in Selected Nontraditional Occupations (Numbers in Thousands)

Occupation	1983		1993	
	Total employed	Percent women	Total employed	Percent women
Precision production, craft, and repair	*12,328*	*8.1*	*13,326*	*8.6*
Mechanics and repairers	3,906	2.8	4,416	3.5
Auto mechanics	800	0.5	854	0.6
Telephone installers	247	9.9	188	12.5
Construction trades	3,784	1.9	5,004	1.9
Carpenters	1,160	1.4	914	2.1
Painters	473	4.9	548	5.2
Precision production	3,685	21.5	3,758	23.6
Machinists	471	4.1	441	4.0
Sheetmetal workers	127	4.5	106	7.1
Operators, fabricators, and laborers	*16,091*	*26.6*	*17,038*	*24.5*
Machine operators, assemblers, inspectors	7,744	42.1	7,415	38.7
Lathe and turning mach.	78	9.2	57*	8.5*
Welders and cutters	692	5.3	539	3.5
Transportation and material moving	4,201	7.8	5,004	9.3
Truck drivers	1,771	2.1	2,786	4.5
Industrial truck and tractor operators	369	5.6	432	7.3
Handlers, cleaners, helpers, laborers	4,147	16.8	4,619	18.3
Construction laborer	595	2.1	658	3.5
Laborers, except construction	1,024	19.4	1,127	17.0

* 1990 data; 1993 not available.
Source: U.S. Department of Labor, *Employment and Earnings,* Table 2 (January 1984), Table 22 (January 1994).

integration. Job integration for women is a complex process in which the interests and qualifications of individual women interact with important organizational factors.

WHO ARE THE WOMEN IN NONTRADITIONAL JOBS?

Another woman said she had worked in factories, driven school buses, and found part-time work in stores, unable all along to support herself and her four children. . . . To that woman and others who followed, being allowed to shovel in a coal mine was a victory. (The President's Commission on Coal, 1980)

There is growing evidence that significant numbers of women are interested and respond positively when nontraditional jobs are made available. Women have both fought for and responded to opportunities at construction sites and in coal mines, steel mills, manufacturing plants, and apprenticeship programs, to name a few. Their stories of challenges and setbacks, work and families, are told in their own words in Schroedel (1985) and Martin (1988) as well as in *Tradeswomen,* a quarterly magazine published in San Francisco for women in blue-collar work.

High schools, vocational schools, and federal job-training programs, however, continue to track women into traditional jobs, and young women continue to view work as a temporary phenomenon (Reskin and Hartmann, 1986; Harlan and Steinberg, 1989; Wolfe, 1991). Berryman and Waite (1987), for example, in their analysis of the National Longitudinal Survey of Youth Labor Market Behavior, found that high school girls planning to allocate more time to homemaking than to the labor force were less likely to choose nontraditional occupations. Consequently, women seeking nontraditional jobs are often in their late twenties or their thirties with experience trying to support themselves and their families in traditional female jobs.

Many of these women have had some exposure to nontraditional jobs in the past, often through family members who worked in the trade or industry. They are more likely to be white, high school graduates, and single heads of families than are women in traditional jobs. Few women of color have entered nontraditional jobs, and those who have report some negative experiences. In one study, minority women stated that they believed they were more likely than white women to be kept in the lowest level and least desirable nontraditional jobs (Harlan and O'Farrell, 1982). Deaux and Ullman (1983) found minority women concentrated in the job of janitor in the steel mills they studied.

Women who stay in nontraditional jobs report that they are satisfied with their work, and they are more satisfied with the pay and work content than women in traditional jobs, white- or blue-collar (see, for example, Walshok, 1981; O'Farrell and Harlan, 1982; Schroedel, 1985; Martin, 1988). Money is the primary reason given for working in these jobs. Anna Brinkley, an electrician, explains:

> The bottom line was the dollar. I mean, it was the money. Money meant independence, being able to support my family without having a man around, if I couldn't find a decent man to relate to the family. In other words, a trade meant not being financially dependent on a man. (Schroedel, 1985:191)

But women also value the jobs because they are more challenging and interesting and provide more opportunity than their previous traditional jobs. These findings have been confirmed in studies of women coal miners (Hammond and Mahoney, 1983), women truckers (Lembright and Riemer, 1982), and women rapid transit workers (Swerdlow, 1989). Fran Krauss, an iron worker who did office work for seven years before becoming an apprentice, describes her work:

> The trade is broken down into several areas: rebar, structural work, rigging, bridgework, and miscellaneous. . . . Part of the job involves going out on

girders carrying pieces of iron called stairway supports. . . . Another important part of the trade is rigging and crane work. It's a part of the trade that I really love. . . . Just recently I got to do a rigging job that was really fast-paced and I had to look at prints, know what iron had to go up, lay it out and put it on the crane. Everyone else was ready to drag up (quit), but I loved it. (Martin, 1988:105–6)

Some evidence also exists that after women are in these jobs for a year or two, aspects unique to nontraditional work, such as having to learn new skills or working with male coworkers, become less important, and women's attitudes and concerns about wages and working conditions are similar to those of men on the jobs (McIlwee, 1982).

Unfortunately, very little information is available about the women who leave nontraditional jobs. It is difficult to find the women and collect longitudinal data, particularly when companies fear more discrimination lawsuits. Limited data in the steel industry (Deaux and Ullman, 1983) found no difference in turnover rates for women and men, and Glover (1989) reports that in recent data from New York State women were more likely to complete apprenticeship programs than men. Waite and Berryman (1985) found that being in a nontraditional job did not affect turnover for women in the military or civilian sectors. They conclude that policies that begin to equalize work conditions for women and men also begin to equalize their aggregate quit rates.

Some evidence does exist, however, that turnover may be higher for the pioneers, the very first women to try nontraditional jobs (Meyer and Lee, 1978). Pioneers, first defined by Walshok (1981) in a study of women in thirty-one different nontraditional jobs, are a special group of women. They have reached their jobs through personal initiative, often filing union grievances and going to state and federal agencies with charges of sex discrimination to open up these jobs. They describe themselves and are described by others as fighters—brave, rugged, tough, aggressive, confident, and willing to take a chance. They face more difficulties, particularly harassment, than those women who follow them (Harlan and O'Farrell, 1982; O'Farrell and Harlan, 1982; Schroedel, 1985).

HARASSMENT ON THE JOB

Harassment of women in nontraditional blue-collar jobs continues to be a well-documented and often-cited problem limiting women's interest and tenure in nontraditional work. The harassment takes many forms of both mental and physical abuse and comes from supervisors as well as coworkers (Reskin and Padavic, 1988; Martin, 1988; Swerdlow, 1989; Padavic and Reskin, 1990; Moccio, 1991). Studies have consistently found that about 20 to 30 percent of the women interviewed report harassment (e.g., Meyer and Lee, 1978; O'Farrell and Harlan, 1982; Gruber and Bjorn, 1982; Deaux and Ullman, 1983; Padavic and Reskin, 1990).

Such harassment is most severe for the first women, but appears to lessen over time, be directed to a few women, and come from relatively few men. In a study of women in an auto plant, for example, Gruber and Bjorn (1982) found that sexual harassment on nontraditional jobs was most severe for women who were either unmarried, young, black, or in lower status jobs. These findings are based on studies of industrial work sites rather than construction sites, however, where even less progress has been made (Moccio, 1991; Le Breton and Loevy, 1992).

It is important to more fully understand men's reactions to women in these jobs because they directly affect women's abilities to learn jobs through procedures such as on-the-job training, as well as the general quality of work life on a day-to-day basis. Three groups of men have been identified: a small group of very hostile men; a small group of actively supportive men; and the majority, who are ambivalent and can be swayed one way or the other. These groups are found in studies of police work (Martin, 1980, 1990), production plants (Gray, 1984; O'Farrell and Moore, 1993), and transit work (Swerdlow, 1989).

For the relatively small proportion of hostile men, hostility toward women seems firmly rooted in sexist beliefs about women and their proper role, attitudes that are unlikely to change. These men may see their jobs degraded and their masculinity threatened (Martin, 1980; Williams, 1989; O'Farrell and Moore, 1993), but they can be prohibited from acting on these feelings by clear policies that prohibit aggressive acts against women. At the same time women can actively work with the small groups of supportive men to bring about change in both people and policies (Gray, 1984; O'Farrell and Moore, 1993; Colatosti and Karg, 1992; O'Farrell, 1993).

The majority of men, however, appear to be more neutral, and their attitudes and behaviors subject to change. When men are hostile it is, in part, rooted in a fear of job loss and a concern for fairness. For example, Swerdlow (1989) found less hostility from men when jobs were not threatened by layoff, as suggested by Harlan and O'Farrell (1982). In addition, once men see that women are qualified and can actually do the work involved, they are more positive about working with women. Conversely, having unqualified women on the job has a very negative impact on men's attitudes and reactions. Therefore, hostility can be somewhat reduced, for example, by training programs that adequately prepare women with the necessary technical skills (Meyer and Lee, 1978; Kane and Miller, 1981; Deaux and Ullman, 1983; Gray, 1984; Glover, 1989; Johnson, 1991).

While male hostility is clearly a severe problem for many women, and one prohibited by law, it is a barrier that has less effect on women's entry and retention in nontraditional jobs than originally thought. Waite and Berryman (1985) found that coworker responses were not critical predictors of women's retention in craft jobs, and Padavic and Reskin (1990), in their study of over two hundred women in a utility company, found that harassment and hostility reduced women's liking for their nontraditional jobs but caused no appreciable impact on their interest in the work. Despite her share of harassment, Fran Krauss concludes:

> Those of us already in the trades see ourselves as a wedge in the door; we've got to hold the door open so that more women can come in behind us. I hope more women get into ironwork. It's so beautiful up there early in the morning when the sun comes up. The air is nice and clean and you never feel boxed in. It's like being on a mountain without having to go to the mountains. (Martin, 1988:108)

We turn now to the organizational barriers that constrain women's mobility and affect men's attitudes as well.

ORGANIZATIONAL CONSTRAINTS

The pace of integration in male-dominated blue-collar jobs is affected by organizational barriers in the areas of recruitment, training, and promotion as well as by the overall economic climate in specific industries and the degree of technological change. Efforts to overcome these constraints are also influenced by the enforcement of equal employment opportunity laws, most recently the Civil Rights Act of 1991. Recent research documents examples of organizational and economic constraints and procedures to overcome such barriers (see reviews by O'Farrell and Harlan, 1984; Roos and Reskin, 1984; Reskin and Hartmann, 1986; Glover, 1989; Johnson, 1991).

Traditional recruiting sources and the lack of vocational training, especially in shop and math, are important barriers to women in both construction and industrial craft jobs. Traditional recruiting sources for young men, such as high school shop classes, trade schools, and the military service, involve few women. Consequently, women may not hear about jobs and are unfamiliar with the skills involved. Women already employed in traditional female jobs, particularly operative factory jobs, may also be discouraged from bidding for entry-level nontraditional jobs because plant seniority systems and related wage scales could result in a short-term loss of pay, benefits, and seniority, while requiring additional job training. Such training may be available only in off-the-job hours, making it difficult for women with family responsibilities, and informal training may not be forthcoming from male coworkers or supervisors, especially for the pioneer women (Kelley, 1982; Harlan and O'Farrell, 1982; O'Farrell and Harlan, 1984; Strauss, 1992).

Corporations, unions, and government agencies have developed outreach and training programs to overcome these barriers. Such programs include active community recruitment, careful screening, and classes in basic tools and language. Tours of the workplace, hands-on experience, and using women already in nontraditional jobs as recruiters have all been somewhat effective. Federally funded recruitment and training programs targeted for low-income women have also successfully prepared women and minorities to enter apprenticeships.

A major problem is that such programs are not always offered without strong government pressure. Corporate managers themselves report that little change would occur without the threat of government lawsuits or the cancelation of lucrative government contracts (O'Farrell and Harlan, 1984). Under the Reagan and Bush administrations, however, EEO enforcement agencies have been openly opposed to affirmative action programs. Wider Opportunities for Women reported that in 1978 there were over 150 programs generally able to recruit and train more women applicants for apprenticeships than they could place. By 1982, fewer than fifty outreach and training programs remained, and one building contractor concluded: "There's no way we're going to comply with [affirmative action] regulations; we know they're going to be weakened or eliminated" ("Women Hard Hats," 1982).

For women in entry-level nontraditional jobs, there is the question of whether they will move to the most skilled jobs. The largest increase in the number of women in nontraditional jobs has been in the entry-level laborer and operative categories. In a coal mine, for example, this means work shoveling coal onto conveyor belts in tunnels that may be no more than three feet high, laying tracks, dragging heavy power cables, and spraying walls with limestone. But many of these jobs are dead ends with little opportunity for advancement for women or men.

Once hired, mobility within a company to the highest paying skilled jobs is often determined by rules governing job ladders, promotion systems, wage scales, training programs, and seniority systems. Research in large industrial factories and utility companies suggests that women and minorities are placed on job ladders with the least opportunity for moving to the most skilled jobs (Harlan and O'Farrell, 1982; Strauss, 1992). Patterns of segregation may then be reinforced, limiting women's mobility by seniority systems that have generally been upheld by the courts (Kelley, 1982; O'Farrell and Harlan, 1984; Strauss, 1992). In a study of over seven thousand factory workers, Harlan and O'Farrell (1982) found newly hired women concentrated in job categories with the lowest wages and least opportunities for advancement.

Recruitment, hiring, and mobility problems are compounded by the effects of the economy on real opportunities to move into the most skilled jobs. In declining industries, newly recruited women with little seniority are the first laid off. In mining and manufacturing, industrial retrenchment has taken a clear toll on job integration. Between 1980 and 1992, production workers in the mining industry declined from 762,000 to 450,000. Durable goods, e.g., steel and industrial equipment, declined from almost 8.5 million to 7.0 million workers (U.S. Bureau of the Census, 1993). The number of workers employed by the steel industry, for example, which had made some progress in hiring and training women under a 1974 affirmative action agreement with the federal government, declined from 726,000 workers in the late 1970s to 390,000 in 1982 (U.S. Department of Labor, 1984). Consequently, there were fewer women in the steel industry in 1980 than before the agreement was signed (Deaux and Ullman, 1983). By 1992, the number of production workers in blast furnaces and basic steel products was down to 191,000.

In a large plant mass-producing aircraft engines, marine turbines, gears, and power generators, the layoff of about three thousand workers between 1986 and 1989 eliminated many of the gains women had made under a government affirmative action program begun in 1978 (Strauss, 1992). This was the result of layoffs coupled with an affirmative action program that did not enable women with seniority to move into skilled jobs and did not provide adequate training or placement for newly hired women. Swerdlow (1989) found less hostility from men when jobs were not threatened, as suggested by Harlan and O'Farrell (1982).

Skilled blue-collar jobs are also vulnerable to technological change, deskilling, and displacement. In the telephone company, for example, one entry-level craft job predominantly held by men became 30 percent female under an affirmative action agreement, but that job was slated for complete automation and was no longer a step in the progression to skilled work

(Hacker, 1979). By 1990, the number of telephone installers nationwide had declined from 247,000 to 193,000, while the percentage but not the number of women had increased (see Table 3). In the meat packing industry, a combination of retrenchment and technological change had a discriminatory effect on women and blacks just as equal employment laws opened up opportunities (Remy and Sawyers, 1984).

The combined effect of organizational barriers, reduced government enforcement of EEO laws, and the general decline in blue-collar jobs due to economic and technological factors has contributed to the slow progress of job integration and may, in fact, be contributing to the development of new sex segregation of jobs. In a study of women's inroads into male occupations, Reskin and Roos (1990) found three male blue-collar jobs that had a disproportionate increase in the number of women—bakers, typesetters, and bus drivers (see Table 4). Among bakers the actual number of workers declined. While the number of women bakers increased substantially, they were in the less skilled, lower paying jobs in the grocery store bakeries and school cafeterias. Among printers, once the quintessential craft workers, typesetters and compositors changed from being almost all men to two-thirds women. Employers replaced the noisy, dirty, hot metal composing room with a clean, well-lit, air-conditioned office, while paying women less for the new type of work. Among bus drivers, now 52 percent female, women are concentrated in the part-time school bus driver category. These changes are attributed to men abandoning deteriorating jobs to women or not being interested in the newly developing, lower paying, part-time jobs.

Despite these problems, women will continue to seek nontraditional blue-collar jobs. Growth is projected in the construction, transportation, and electronic equipment industries. Between 1988 and 2000, under moderate projections, the number of truck drivers is expected to grow by 15 percent, and carpenters and automotive mechanics by 16 percent (U.S. Bureau of the Census, 1991). Shortages in newly developing skilled jobs are anticipated as well.

There is also renewed interest in integrating these jobs on the part of the government. In 1990, the secretary of labor announced a multidepartmental

Table 4.   Occupations with Disproportionate Increase of Women, 1970–1990

	Percent female		
Occupation	*1970*	*1980*	*1990*
Precision production, craft, and repair			
Baker	25.4	40.7	44.3
Machine operators, assemblers, inspectors			
Typesetters and compositors	16.8	55.7	68.0
Transportation and material moving			
Bus drivers	28.3	45.8	51.6

Sources: 1970, 1980 data adapted from Reskin and Roos (1990); 1990 data from U.S. Department of Labor, *Employment and Earnings,* Table 22 (1991a).

initiative to help women gain access to the skilled trades that focuses on increased recruitment and training but also recognizes the need to enforce the laws (U.S. Department of Labor, 1991b). In 1991, the president signed into law the Nontraditional Employment for Women Act to encourage the training, placement, and retention of low-income women in jobs traditionally held by men. The Women's Bureau is funding several demonstration programs. In 1992, a second act, the Women in Apprenticeship Occupations and Nontraditional Occupations Act, provided $750,000 for technical assistance to employers and unions to assist them in successfully integrating women in apprenticeship and nontraditional jobs such as carpenter, painter, or welder. The effectiveness of these efforts remains to be seen, but coupled with a gradually improving economy, they provide a basis for some optimism. An alternative source of pressure for continued change is the labor movement, using collective bargaining, grievance procedures, and legal actions.

THE ROLE OF LABOR UNIONS

Until recently, workers in blue-collar jobs predominantly held by men were the most highly organized in the country. In 1980, for example, 49 percent of construction craft workers (except carpenters), 55 percent of machinists, 61 percent of metal craft workers, and 85 percent of automobile workers and equipment operatives were organized (U.S. Department of Labor, 1981). The EEO laws assumed that unions were part of the problem for women workers. Craft unions excluded women from membership, and industrial unions accepted the assignment of men and women to different jobs with different wages and seniority systems (Milkman, 1987; Wertheimer, 1984).

Federal laws hold unions along with employers responsible for discriminatory practices. For example, unions have been charged with implementing discriminatory hiring and placement procedures in the building trades and negotiating discriminatory seniority systems in industrial factories (Wallace and Driscoll, 1981; Kelley, 1982). However, unions have supported equal opportunity legislation and have been able to use the laws to gain benefits for their members that could not be negotiated exclusively through collective bargaining. The most notable examples are pregnancy disability, equal pay for equal work, and equal pay for comparable worth (Newman and Wilson, 1981; Milkman, 1985, 1987; Freeman and Leonard, 1987; Needleman and Tanner, 1987).

Today, union leaders and members continue to be a problem for some women and a source of support for others. Membership is declining, however, in the skilled unions, adding to resistance and decreasing effectiveness. Between 1979 and 1991 the carpenters union lost 132,000 members, while the steelworkers lost over 500,000 (U.S. Bureau of the Census, 1993). At the same time, women are increasingly learning to work with unions to integrate jobs through grievance procedures, women's committees, running for office, and using the courts (Freeman and Leonard, 1987; Strauss, 1992; O'Farrell and Moore, 1993; O'Farrell, 1993; Colatosti and Karg, 1992).

Unions must be held accountable for any policies or procedures that are discriminatory. On a day-to-day basis, unions can and should play a much more active role for women in nontraditional jobs by negotiating nondiscriminatory wages and working conditions, identifying discriminatory practices, informing workers about their rights, providing financial and legal assistance, helping to reduce coworker hostility, monitoring affirmative action agreements, and representing women with grievances. Women in turn offer a source of new members and new leadership. While job integration strategies can be divisive, they can also provide opportunities for new alliances among women and men.

Conclusions

Blue-collar occupations for men and women are changing in response to new technologies and a more competitive world economy. Declining productivity and rising unemployment in industrial manufacturing and the general trend away from manufacturing and toward a service economy are altering both the size and the shape of blue-collar work. This work, however, will remain an important part of the American economy for the foreseeable future.

The majority of women blue-collar workers continue to be employed in low-skill, low-paying operative jobs with poor working conditions and high unemployment. These traditional jobs, increasingly held by minority women, are the most vulnerable to technological displacement and national and international relocation. Some women have moved to more skilled nontraditional jobs, particularly entry-level jobs, but progress has been slow, and there is evidence that new patterns of female predominance may be developing. Some nontraditional jobs are also being deskilled or eliminated through new technology and plant closings.

Four themes emerge from our review of women's experiences in both traditional and nontraditional blue-collar jobs to help explain women's continued segregation in low-status jobs. The first theme is the responsiveness of women to real opportunities. When jobs have been available, women have taken them. At the turn of the century, women took newly created jobs in textile and electronics firms. During World War II and more recently under the equal employment laws, they have moved into skilled blue-collar jobs despite individual and organizational barriers. The second theme is the willingness of companies to hire women despite cultural norms to the contrary if doing so meets business needs. This was forcefully demonstrated in the electronics industry, which became 30 percent female in the early 1900s, and more recently in the printing industry.

The third theme is the importance of government policy to force employers to hire women and improve wages and working conditions when the employers are not motivated by their own economic concerns. Both during World War II and under the more recent equal employment laws, resistant employers have hired women in nontraditional jobs and increased wages in traditional jobs as a result of strong government intervention, sometimes with union support. Employers themselves have sometimes reported that changes would not have been made without government pressure.

The fourth theme is the need to actively recruit women and remove organizational barriers when changes in established employment policies are first made. Simply saying that jobs are available for women is not sufficient to overcome previous restrictions. Textile factory owners actively recruited women in the 1800s, as did electronics firms in the early 1900s. The government established child care centers and undertook a massive advertising campaign to recruit women during World War II. Outreach and recruitment as well as changes in some basic organizational structures such as job bidding systems were necessary to attract substantial numbers of women beyond the pioneers into nontraditional jobs in the 1970s.

These themes suggest that the slow pace of integration has at least as much to do with a lack of opportunities, employer resistance, organizational barriers, and government policies as with the choices of individual women. Nontraditional jobs can be integrated by women, and wages and working conditions in traditional jobs can be improved. Labor law reform will help by making union membership more available to women. In the long term, however, job integration and job improvement call for a continued federal presence to enforce existing employment legislation combined with a healthy, growing economy. Industrial policy related to the new global economy and international division of labor needs to look seriously at the effects on women. Including women in retraining for new semiskilled and skilled jobs is critical. Women and men in blue-collar jobs, however, must work together to overcome problems of foreign competition, technological change, health and safety problems, and employer resistance both to unions and affirmative action.

NOTES

1. *Traditional* and *nontraditional* are standard terms used to describe jobs usually performed by workers of one sex and considered atypical for workers of the other sex. They are not based on workers' abilities to do different jobs, and, as we discuss in this chapter, jobs have changed from one category to the other over time.

2. In 1983, the Census Bureau and the Department of Labor eliminated the terms *blue-collar* and *white-collar* from their occupational classification systems and made extensive changes in the reporting categories, making comparisons between 1970 and 1990 difficult. For example, the category "blue-collar craft and kindred" became "precision, production, craft, and repair." "Dressmaker" was moved from the operative to the skilled category, thus upgrading the occupation but distorting the increase in the number of women in the total traditionally male skilled jobs. Using a special recoded sample, however, Rytina and Bianchi compared 1970 and 1980 census data and found almost no change in occupational segregation for women in blue-collar jobs, similar to the findings of Beller and Han (1984).

REFERENCES

Amott, Teresa L. and Julie A. Mathaei. 1991. *Race, Gender, and Work.* Boston: South End Press.

Baker, Sally H. and Bernard Levenson. 1975. "Job Opportunities of Black and White Working-Class Women." *Social Problems* 2:510–33.

Baron, Ava (Ed.). 1991. *Work Engendered: Toward a New History of American Labor.* Ithaca, NY: Cornell University Press.

Beller, Andrea H. and Kee-ok Kim Han. 1984. "Occupational Segregation: Prospects for the 1980s." In *Sex Segregation in the Workplace: Trends, Explanations, Remedies,* ed. B. F. Reskin. Washington, DC: National Academy Press.

Berryman, Sue E. and Linda J. Waite. 1987. "Young Women's Choice of Nontraditional Occupations." In *Ingredients for Women's Employment Policy,* ed. C. Bose and G. Spitze. Albany: State University of New York Press.

Blau, Francine D. and Marianne A. Ferber. 1986. *The Economics of Women, Men, and Work.* Englewood Cliffs, NJ: Prentice-Hall.

Bookman, Ann. 1988. "Unionization in an Electronics Factory: The Interplay of Gender, Ethnicity, and Class." In *Women and the Politics of Empowerment,* ed. A. Bookman and S. Morgen. Philadelphia: Temple University Press.

Bookman, Ann and Sandra Morgen. 1988. *Women and the Politics of Empowerment.* Philadelphia: Temple University Press.

Boris, Eileen and Cynthia R. Daniels (Eds.). 1989. *Homework: Historical and Contemporary Perspectives on Paid Labor at Home.* Urbana: University of Illinois Press.

Briggs, Norma. 1979. "Apprenticeship." In *Women in the U.S. Labor Force,* ed. A. F. Cahn. New York: Praeger.

Chafe, William H. 1972. *The American Woman: Her Changing Social, Economic, and Political Roles, 1920–1970.* London: Oxford University Press.

Cobble, Sue (Ed.). 1993. *Women and the Labor Movement: Forging a Partnership.* Ithaca, NY: Industrial and Labor Relations Press.

Cobble, Dorothy Sue. 1994. "Making Postindustrial Unionism Possible." Research report prepared for the Women's Bureau. Washington, DC: U.S. Department of Labor.

Colatosti, Camille and Elissa Karg. 1992. *Stopping Sexual Harassment: A Handbook for Union and Workplace Activists.* Detroit, MI: Labor Notes.

Deaux, Kay K. and Joseph C. Ullman. 1983. *Women of Steel: Female Blue-Collar Workers in the Basic Steel Industry.* New York: Praeger.

Ferber, Marianne and Brigid O'Farrell with La Rue Allen (Ed.). 1991. *Work and Family: Policies for a Changing Workforce.* Washington, DC: National Academy Press.

Ferree, Myra Marx. 1985. "Between Two Worlds: German Feminist Approaches to Working-Class Women and Work." *Signs* 10:517–36.

Fox, Steve. 1991. *Toxic Work.* Philadelphia: Temple University Press.

Freeman, Richard B. and Jonathan S. Leonard. 1987. "Union Maids: Unions and the Female Work Force." In *Gender in the Workplace,* ed. C. Brown and J. A. Pechman. Washington, DC: The Brookings Institution.

Freeman, Richard B. and James L. Medoff. 1984. *What Do Unions Do?* New York: Basic Books.

Glover, Robert W. 1989. "Apprenticeship: A Route to the High-Paying Skilled Trades for Women?" In *Job Training for Women: The Promise and Limits of Public Policies,* ed. S. L. Harlan and R. J. Steinberg. Philadelphia: Temple University Press.

Gray, Stan. 1984. "Sharing the Shop Floor: Women and Men on the Assembly Line." *Radical America* 18:69–88.

Green, Susan S. 1983. "Silicon Valley's Women Workers: A Theoretical Analysis of Sex Segregation in the Electronics Industry Labor Market." In *Women and Men and the International Division of Labor,* ed. J. Nash and M. P. Fernandez-Kelly. Albany: State University of New York Press.

Gruber, James E. and Lars Bjorn. 1982. "Blue-Collar Blues: The Sexual Harassment of Women Autoworkers." *Work and Occupations* 9:271–97.

Hacker, Sally L. 1979. "Sex Stratification, Technological and Organizational Change: A Longitudinal Case Study of AT&T." *Social Problems* 26:539–57.

Hammond, Judith A. and Constance W. Mahoney. 1983. "Reward-Cost Balancing Among Women Coal Miners." *Sex Roles* 9:17–29.

Hams, Marcia. 1984. "Women Taking Leadership in Male-Dominated Locals." *Women's Rights Law Reporter* 8:71–82.

Harlan, Sharon L. and Brigid O'Farrell. 1982. "After the Pioneers: Prospects for Women in Nontraditional Blue-Collar Jobs." *Work and Occupations* 9:363–86.

Harlan, Sharon L. and Ronnie J. Steinberg (Eds.). 1989. *Job Training for Women: The Promise and Limits of Public Policies.* Philadelphia: Temple University Press.

Herrera, Yvette and Anne Marie Marklin. 1994. "Heroines and Hurdles: A Look at Women's Struggle for a Voice in the Workplace Through Unionization." Research report prepared for the Women's Bureau. Washington, DC: U.S. Department of Labor.

Johnson, Wendy. 1991. "Model Programs Prepare Women for Skilled Trades." In *Women, Work, and School,* ed. L. Wolfe. Boulder, CO: Westview Press.

Joint Economic Committee. 1992. "Families on a Treadmill: Work and Income in the 1980s." Staff Study, U.S. Congress.

Kane, Roslyn D. and Jill Miller. 1981. "Women and Apprenticeship: A Study of Programs Designed to Facilitate Women's Participation in the Skilled Trades." In *Apprenticeship Research: Emerging Findings and Future Trends,* ed. V. B. Briggs and F. F. Foltman. Ithaca, NY: ILR Publications Division, Cornell University.

Katz, Naomi and David S. Kemnitzer. 1984. "Women and Work in Silicon Valley: Options and Futures." In *My Troubles Are Going to Have Trouble with Me,* ed. K. B. Sacks and D. Remy. New Brunswick, NJ: Rutgers University Press.

Kelley, Mary Ellen. 1982. "Discrimination in Seniority Systems: A Case Study." *Industrial and Labor Relations Review* 36, no. 1 (Oct.):40–55.

Kessler-Harris, Alice. 1982. *Out to Work: A History of Wage-Earning Women in the United States.* New York: Oxford University Press.

Lamphere, Louise. 1984. "On the Shop Floor: Multi-Ethnic Unity Against the Conglomerate." In *My Troubles Are Going to Have Trouble with Me,* ed. K. B. Sacks and D. Remy. New Brunswick, NJ: Rutgers University Press.

Lamphere, Louise and Guillermo J. Grenier. 1988. "Participative Management: Organizing in the Sunbelt." In *Women and the Politics of Empowerment,* ed. A. Bookman and S. Morgen. Philadelphia: Temple University Press.

Le Breton, Lauric Wasserman and Sara Segal Loevy. 1992. *Breaking New Ground: Worksite 2000.* Chicago: Chicago Women in Trades.

Lembright, Muriel F. and Jeffrey W. Riemer. 1982. "Women Truckers' Problems and the Impact of Sponsorship." *Work and Occupations* 9:457–74.

Martin, Molly. 1988. *Hard-Hatted Women: Stories of Struggle and Success in the Trades.* Seattle: Seal Press.

Martin, Susan E. 1980. *Breaking and Entering: Policewomen on Patrol.* Ewing, NJ: University of California Press.

Martin, Susan E. 1990. *On the Move: The Status of Women in Policing.* Washington, DC: The Police Foundation.

McIlwee, Judith. 1982. "Work Satisfaction Among Women in Nontraditional Occupations." *Work and Occupations* 9:299–366.

Meyer, Herbert and Mary D. Lee. 1978. *Women in Traditionally Male Jobs: The Experiences of Ten Public Utility Companies* (R&D Monograph no. 65). Washington, DC: Employment and Training Administration, U.S. Department of Labor.

Michael, Robert T., Heidi Hartmann, and Brigid O'Farrell (Eds.). 1989. *Pay Equity: Empirical Inquiries.* Washington, DC: National Academy Press.

Milkman, Ruth. 1983. "Female Factory Labor and Industrial Structure: Control and Conflict over 'Woman's Place' in Auto and Electrical Manufacturing." *Politics and Society* 12:159–203.

Milkman, Ruth (Ed.). 1985. *Women, Work, and Protest: A Century of U.S. Women's Labor History.* Boston: Routledge & Kegan Paul.

Milkman, Ruth. 1987. *Gender at Work: The Dynamics of Job Segregation by Sex During World War II.* Urbana: University of Illinois Press.

Moccio, Francine. 1991. "Contradicting the 'Common Sense' of Gender Identity: Women as Construction Workers." Institute for Women and Work, Cornell University, unpublished.

National Commission on Working Women. 1984. "Caution, Your Work May Be Hazardous to Your Health." *Women at Work* (Summer):3–4.

Needleman, Ruth. 1994. "Raising Visibility, Reducing Marginality: A Labor Law Reform Agenda for Working Women of Color." Research report prepared for the Women's Bureau. Washington, DC: U.S. Department of Labor.

Needleman, Ruth and Lucretia Dewey Tanner. 1987. "Women in Unions: Current Issues." In *Working Women: Past, Present, Future,* ed. K. S. Koziara, M. H. Moskow, and L. D. Tanner. Washington, DC: The Bureau of National Affairs, Inc.

Newman, Winn and Carole W. Wilson. 1981. "The Union Role in Affirmative Action." *Labor Law Journal* (June):323–42.

O'Farrell, Brigid. 1987. "Women in Blue-Collar Occupations: Traditional and Nontraditional." In *Women Working: Theories and Facts in Perspective,* ed. A. H. Stromberg and S. Harkess. Mountain View, CA: Mayfield Publishing Company.

O'Farrell, Brigid. 1993. *Nontraditional Employment Training (NET) Project Technical Assistance Package for Working with Unions.* Washington, DC: Wider Opportunities for Women.

O'Farrell, Brigid. *We Pay Union Dues: Women, Unions, and Nontraditional Blue-Collar Jobs.* Unpublished.

O'Farrell, Brigid and Sharon L. Harlan. 1982. "Craftworkers and Clerks: The Effect of Male Coworkers' Hostility on Women's Satisfaction with Nontraditional Jobs." *Social Problems* 29:252–65.

O'Farrell, Brigid and Sharon L. Harlan. 1984. "Job Integration Strategies: Today's Programs and Tomorrow's Needs." In *Sex Segregation in the Workplace: Trends, Explanations, Remedies,* ed. B. F. Reskin. Washington, DC: National Academy Press.

O'Farrell, Brigid and J. Suzanne Moore. 1993. "Unions, Hard Hats, and Women Workers." In *Women and the Labor Movement: Forging a Partnership,* ed. Sue Cobble. Ithaca, NY: Industrial and Labor Relations Press.

Padavic, Irene and Barbara F. Reskin. 1990. "Men's Behavior and Women's Interest in Blue-Collar Jobs." *Social Problems* 37:613–28.

The President's Commission on Coal. 1980. *The American Coal Miner: A Report on Community and Living Conditions in the Coalfields.* Washington, DC: U.S. Government Printing Office.

Remy, Dorothy and Larry Sawyers. 1984. "Economic Stagnation and Discrimination." In *My Troubles Are Going to Have Trouble with Me,* ed. K. B. Sacks and D. Remy. New Brunswick, NJ: Rutgers University Press.

Reskin, Barbara F. (Ed.). 1984. *Sex Segregation in the Workplace: Trends, Explanations, Remedies.* Washington, DC: National Academy Press.

Reskin, Barbara F. and Heidi I. Hartmann (Eds.). 1986. *Women's Work, Men's Work: Sex Segregation on the Job.* Washington, DC: National Academy Press.

Reskin, Barbara F. and Irene Padavic. 1988. "Supervisors as Gatekeepers: Male Supervisors' Response to Women's Integration in Plant Jobs." *Social Problems* 35, 536–50.

Reskin, Barbara F. and Patricia A. Roos. 1990. *Job Queues, Gender Queues: Explaining Women's Inroads into Male Occupations.* Philadelphia: Temple University Press.

Roby, Pamela. 1987. "Union Stewards and Women's Employment Conditions." In *Ingredients for Women's Employment Policy,* ed. C. Bose and G. Spitze. Albany: State University of New York Press.

Roos, Patricia A. and Barbara F. Reskin. 1984. "Institutional Factors Contributing to Sex Segregation in the Workplace." In *Sex Segregation in the Workplace: Trends, Explanations, Remedies,* ed. B. F. Reskin. Washington, DC: National Academy Press.

Rosen, Ellen I. 1981. *Between the Rock and the Hard Place: Employment and Unemployment Among Blue-Collar Women.* Newton, MA: Social Welfare Research Institute, Boston College.

Rosen, Ellen Israel. 1987. *Bitter Choices: Blue-Collar Women In and Out of Work.* Chicago: University of Chicago Press.

Rytina, Nancy F. and Suzanne M. Bianchi. 1984, March. "Occupational Reclassification and Changes in Distribution by Gender." *Monthly Labor Review* 107:11–17.

Sacks, Karen B. and Dorothy Remy (Eds.). 1984. *My Troubles Are Going to Have Trouble with Me: Everyday Trials and Triumphs of Women Workers.* New Brunswick, NJ: Rutgers University Press.

Schlozman, Kay L. 1975. "Women and Unemployment: Assessing the Biggest Myths." In *Women: A Feminist Perspective* (1st ed.), ed. J. Freeman. Palo Alto, CA: Mayfield.

Schroedel, Jean R. 1985. *Alone in a Crowd: Women in the Trades Tell Their Stories.* Philadelphia, PA: Temple University Press.

Shapiro-Perl, Nina. 1984. "Resistance Strategies: The Routine Struggle for Bread and Roses." In *My Troubles Are Going to Have Trouble with Me,* ed. K. B. Sacks and D. Remy. New Brunswick, NJ: Rutgers University Press.

Spalter-Roth, Roberta, Heidi Hartmann and Nancy Collins. 1994. "What Do Unions Do for Women?" Research report prepared for the Women's Bureau. Washington, DC: U.S. Department of Labor.

Strauss, Susan. 1992. "Strategy for Failure: Affirmative Action in a Mass Production Context." In *Union Voices: Labor's Responses to Crisis,* ed. G. Adler and D. Suarez. Albany: State University of New York Press.

Swerdlow, Marian. 1989. "Men's Accommodations to Women Entering a Nontraditional Occupation: A Case of Rapid Transit Operatives." *Gender and Society* 3:373–87.

Tentler, Leslie W. 1979. *Wage-Earning Women: Industrial Work and Family Life in the United States, 1900–1930.* Oxford: Oxford University Press.

U.S. Bureau of the Census. 1991. *Statistical Abstract of the United States:* (111th ed.). Washington, DC: U.S. Government Printing Office.

U.S. Bureau of the Census. 1993. *Statistical Abstract of the United States:* (113th ed.). Washington, DC: U.S. Government Printing Office.

U.S. Department of Labor. Bureau of Apprenticeship and Training. 1992. Personal communication.

U.S. Department of Labor. Bureau of Labor Statistics. 1981. *Earnings and Other Characteristics of Organized Workers: May 1980* (Bulletin 2105). Washington, DC: U.S. Government Printing Office.

U.S. Department of Labor. 1984, Jan. *Employment and Earnings.*

U.S. Department of Labor. 1991a, Nov. *Monthly Labor Review.*

U.S. Department of Labor. Women's Bureau. 1991b. *Directory of Nontraditional Training and Employment Programs Serving Women.* Washington, DC: U.S. Government Printing Office.

U.S. Department of Labor. 1993a, Jan. *Employment and Earnings.*

U.S. Department of Labor. Women's Bureau. 1993b, Dec. 15. "Statement of Karen Nussbaum Before the Commission on the Future of Worker/Management Relations." Washington, DC: U.S. Department of Labor.

U.S. Department of Labor. 1994, Jan. *Employment and Earnings.*

Waite, Linda J. and Sue E. Berryman. 1985. "Women in Nontraditional Occupations, Choice and Turnover." Santa Monica, CA: The Rand Corporation.

Wallace, Phyllis A. and James W. Driscoll. 1981. "Social Issues in Collective Bargaining." In *U.S. Industrial Relations, 1950–1980: A Critical Assessment,* ed. J. Stieber et al. Madison, WI: Industrial Relations Research Association.

Walshok, Mary Lindenstein. 1981. *Blue Collar Women: Pioneers on the Male Frontier.* Garden City, NY: Anchor.

Wertheimer, Barbara. 1977. *We Were There: The Story of Working Women in America.* New York: Pantheon Books.

Wertheimer, Barbara. 1984. "The United States of America." In *Women and Trade Unions in Eleven Industrialized Countries,* ed. A. H. Cook, V. R. Lorwin, and A. K. Daniels. Philadelphia: Temple University Press.

Williams, Christine. 1989. *Gender Differences at Work: Women and Men in Nontraditional Occupations.* Berkeley: University of California Press.

Wolfe, Leslie R. (Ed.). 1991. *Women, Work, and School: Occupational Segregation and the Role of Education.* Boulder, CO: Westview Press.

"Women Hard Hats Losing Ground as Slump, Budget Cuts Take Toll." 1982, April. *Wall Street Journal.*

Zavella, Patricia. 1987. *Women's Work and Chicano Families: Cannery Workers of the Santa Clara Valley.* Ithaca, NY: Cornell University Press.

Zavella, Patricia. 1988. "The Politics of Race and Gender: Organizing Chicana Cannery Workers in Northern California." In *Women and the Politics of Empowerment,* ed. A. Bookman and S. Morgen. Philadelphia: Temple University Press.

Clerical Work: The Female Occupation

Evelyn Nakano Glenn and Roslyn L. Feldberg

EVERY WEEKDAY, FROM nine in the morning until five in the evening, in offices all over the country, accounts are checked, correspondence typed, inventories tallied, bills prepared, appointments booked, records filed, and documents reproduced. This "paperwork" is carried out in small offices of one or two persons and in corporate headquarters with hundreds of workers, in private industry and in public agencies. Some of the people are all-around workers, carrying out myriad different activities each day; others are single-function clerks, repeating the same small task over and over. Some work with paper, pencil, and perhaps a typewriter; others work with electronic equipment linking them to a computer system that automatically handles many complex clerical operations.

The five most frequently found titles among the 18.64 million people engaged in clerical activities are secretary, bookkeeper, computer operator, general office clerk, and receptionist. These five categories account for nearly half of all clerical workers, but there are numerous other titles classified as "administrative support including clerical," including bank teller, data-entry keyer, stock clerk, reservation agent, counter clerk, keypuncher, telephone operator, and file clerk.

All of these people are engaged in what is called *white-collar* work (to contrast it with blue-collar manual labor). Features that have traditionally characterized clerical occupations include the following: the work is "clean"— it takes place indoors in relatively safe, clean, and comfortable surroundings and involves no great physical exertion; it is "mental"; it relies to some extent on a worker's judgment and requires a literate work force that is able to read, write, and manipulate symbols; and it lacks a distinctive product—its outcome is not a concrete commodity but rather a flow of documents and communication. In addition, the clerical worker has traditionally enjoyed certain advantages in work life over the factory employee: a fixed weekly salary rather than hourly wages, more regular hours, greater job security, smaller fluctuations in salary during hard times, and greater opportunities for advancement.[1] These supposed advantages have conferred on clerical work a status above blue-collar, sales, and service occupations. At the same time, those in the other white-collar occupations—managers and professionals—have looked down on clerical work as more routine, offering less scope for independent decisions. In addition, the workers' hours, movements, and work patterns are subject to closer controls. Although there have been many changes (which will be described later), these features are still prominent in popular conceptions of clerical work.

Clerical Work as a Female Occupation

Aside from the work itself, the most distinctive feature of clerical work is the gender of the people who do it: they are overwhelmingly female. In the United States in 1990 four out of five clerical workers (80.0 percent) were women. In two of the largest categories, secretaries and receptionists, the proportions rose to 99.0 and 97.0 percent. Overall, 14.9 million women were engaged in clerical work in 1990. Over one-quarter (27.7 percent) of all employed women were in this category.[2] Clerical work is therefore, absolutely and proportionally, the largest single occupation for women. The degree to which clerical work is common to women was confirmed by a personal experience. Recently in an all-female discussion section of a sex-roles course, the instructors asked how many students had ever done office work. Out of twenty-five women present, twenty-three raised their hands, including the two instructors.

Considering these numbers and percentages, it can be argued that clerical work represents the prototypical female employment experience. We shall explore this tie between women and clerical work by examining a set of interrelated questions: How did clerical work become a large and predominantly female occupation? How has the concentration of women in this occupation affected wages, status, and working conditions? What has been the impact of economic and organizational changes on the role and function of clerical work? What effects have these factors had on the quality of work life for this group of women workers? What is the outlook for, and what are the possible outcomes of, organizing clerical workers? What form might a largely woman-based organizing movement take?

In addressing these questions, the following line of argument will be developed. There have been two seemingly contradictory trends in clerical work. The increased size and complexity of organizations mean that internal control, coordination, and communications become increasingly critical for organizational survival. Since these activities rely largely on clerical labor, clerical work takes on a more central role in the economy. But, while clerical work has become more important, organizations have pushed toward streamlining and mechanizing the work to increase efficiency in and control over the work process. This has degraded the work, lowered the status of clerical workers, and further restricted opportunities for advancement. Thus, clerical workers as a group have become a large and important part of the economy, while their jobs and status have become less desirable. The combination of these two trends can be expected to strengthen the impetus for workers to organize--to use the untapped power of clerical workers as leverage to improve their wages and conditions relative to other groups.

The Feminization of Clerical Work

The office setup of a typical large organization is structured in the following way. At the top, occupying the highest positions, are the officers and top managers, all men. Each has at least one private secretary and/or administrative assistant. Below them are other managers, mostly men, graded into many levels. Several of them may share the services of a single secretary or call on a pool of typists and/or clerks. Below them are several specialized sections, divided according to function—for example, accounting, billing, and inventory control. Each section has many women clerks engaged in the routine tasks of record-keeping, coding and processing information, and communication. The supervisor of each section is frequently a woman promoted from the ranks. In addition, there may be a photocopy or reproduction unit made up of a mixed group of young men and women and a data-processing unit where women operators enter information into the computer system via electronic terminals. An office manager, usually a man, may be responsible for overall office administration. Most large organizations also have a separate computer department, consisting of computer operators, programmers, and systems analysts who oversee the operations of the centralized data system.

In short, there are three separate groups of office jobs differing in gender composition. One group, the clerical, is clearly female (secretaries, typists, data-entry operators); the second, the managerial, is clearly male (vice-president, product manager, sales manager); the third, the technical, is mixed sex (computer operators, programmers, and systems analysts). Furthermore, each group of jobs is organized into a hierarchy that is also sex-typed.[3] Management is a male hierarchy, although it frequently includes female supervisors at the lowest levels. The clerical staff is largely a female hierarchy. The technical category is also gender-stratified, with the lower-ranked jobs filled by both men and women, while the higher-ranked jobs—upper-level programmers and systems analysts—are held almost exclusively by men. Occasionally one hears of a clerk who trains to be a systems analyst or a secretary who rises to become an officer in the company. This kind of story generates excitement precisely because it is a freak occurrence.

. The segregation of jobs by sex is so universal that the office structure is frequently viewed as a "natural" situation. Does not having men in authority and women in subordinate positions reflect their places in society as a whole? Moreover, do not the requirements for clerical and managerial jobs fit the stereotypes for feminine and masculine traits? Women are said to make good clerks because they are conscientious about details, have nimble hands for operating office machines, and are sufficiently submissive to take orders well. In contrast, managerial traits—rationality, decisiveness, objectivity, and assertiveness—are seen as exclusively masculine qualities.

The appearance of naturalness is shattered by a historical survey, which reveals that the sex composition of jobs shifts over time. Jobs that were once predominantly male sometimes come to be occupied primarily by females, and vice versa. When the work force of an occupation changes from largely male or mixed sex to predominantly female, the process is called *feminization*. Accompanying the shift in sex may be a change in the actual activities of the job or in the traits that are seen as necessary for the job.

Changes in both sex composition and job activities have taken place in the office. The present division of labor in the large office is a fairly recent phenomenon. Until 1910, office work was done almost exclusively by men. Clerks were few in number, constituting only 2.6 percent of the labor force in 1900.[4] Until the last years of the nineteenth century, most businesses were small, local, family-owned enterprises.[5] The offices were made up of a handful of clerks, at most. The head clerk had extensive responsibilities, many of which would be labeled managerial today.[6] His advice might be sought by his employer, because of his familiarity with the details of the business. He might be expected to carry on the business when the owner was absent or away. Braverman notes:

> This picture of the clerk as assistant manager, retainer, confidant, management trainee, and prospective son-in-law can of course be overdrawn. There were clerks—hard-driven copyists in law offices, for example—whose condition and prospects in life were little better than those of dock workers. But by and large, in terms of function, authority, pay, tenure of employment (a clerical position was usually a lifetime post), prospects, not to mention status and even dress, the clerks stood much closer to the employer than to factory labor.[7]

The ground for women's entrance into the offices was prepared during the Civil War, when women were hired to work in the government because of the shortage of male labor. The "experiment" was successful, for the women proved to be good workers and economical, working for only one-half to two-thirds the wages paid to men.[8]

The large-scale entry of women into offices, however, did not begin until the end of the nineteenth century. This period was one of rapid growth and consolidation of corporations.[9] The economy came to be dominated by enterprises with national markets and substantial financing by banks. The size of organizations mushroomed and with it the volume of communication, record-keeping, and related activities. Hence there was a burgeoning demand for clerical labor, met by an influx of workers into the field. As shown in Table 1, the clerical work force grew from an estimated 91,000 in 1870 to more than 770,000 by 1900, doubling in the next ten-year period to 1,885,000. Except for 1929–35, during the Depression, the clerical work force has grown substantially every decade. As impressive as the overall growth was, the most striking trend was the increasing proportion of women. While the size of the occupation increased by a factor of eight between 1870 and 1900, the proportion of women increased by a factor of 340. The number of women entering clerical work then began to exceed the number of men, so that by the late 1920s a tipping point had been reached, at which over half of all the clerical workers were women.

Women, far from being seen as naturally suited to office work, were at first considered an oddity. An 1875 engraving depicts the ludicrousness of women in offices by showing them crocheting, dressing each other's hair, reading *Harper's Bazaar,* and spilling ink; a man, presumably the owner, has just walked in and is dumbstruck. A lively debate was carried on in the pages of popular and business magazines from the 1890s through the 1920s by attackers and defenders of women in offices.[10] During the 1920s and 1930s, many popular novels and short stories depicted the lives and loves of the "office girl," in which the principal conflict was romance and marriage versus career and spinsterhood.[11]

Table 1. Growth of the Clerical Force, 1870–1987[a]

	1870	1880	1890	1900	1910	1920	1930	1940	1950	1960	1970	1980	1990
Total clerical workers (in thousands)	91	186	490	770	1,885	3,311	4,274	4,847	7,635	9,783	13,714	18,105	18,641
as percentage of employed persons	.7%	1.1%	2.1%	2.6%	5.1%	8.0%	9.0%	9.1%	12.8%	14.7%	17.4%	18.6%	15.8%
Female clerical workers (in thousands)	2	8	83	204	677	1,601	2,223	2,549	4,597	6,629	10,233	14,502	14,875
as percentage of all clerical workers	2.4%	4.3%	16.9%	26.5%	35.9%	48.4%	52.0%	52.6%	60.2%	67.8%	74.6%	80.1%	79.8%

a. Figures are not strictly comparable due to reclassifications of occupational categories. For example, after 1980, the category "clerical and kindred" was relabeled "administrative support, including clerical" and "cashiers"—the second largest occupation classified as clerical prior to 1980—was transferred to "sales occupations." If cashiers were still included in 1990, the total "clerical" would be 21,133,000, or 17.9 percent of all employed persons.

Sources: For total clerical workers and female clerical workers, 1870 to 1940: compiled from Janet M. Hooks, *Women's Occupations Through Seven Decades*, U.S. Department of Labor, Women's Bureau, Bulletin no. 218 (Washington, D.C.: U.S. Government Printing Office, 1947), Tables 11A, 11B. For employed persons, 1870 to 1940: U.S. Bureau of the Census, *Historical Statistics: Abstracts of the United States*, Series D57-71. For 1950 to 1970: U.S. Bureau of the Census, *Statistical Abstract of the United States* (Washington, D.C.: U.S. Government Printing Office, 1972), Table 366. For 1980: *Employment and Earnings* 28 (Jan. 1981), U.S. Bureau of Labor Statistics, Table 23. For 1990: *Employment and Earnings* 38 (Jan. 1991), U.S. Bureau of Labor Statistics, Table 22.

Faced with this skepticism about their desirability, why did increasing numbers of women go into clerical work rather than other occupations? Clearly, the large number of jobs created by changes in corporate structure provided one necessary condition. Another important factor, according to some writers, was the impact of the typewriter, which was invented in 1873.[12] The Remington Company trained women to demonstrate the new machines, so that from the beginning the machines were operated by women. Typing in offices became identified as a feminine specialty.

Although this may have facilitated women's entry into the field, it would not have made a difference if there were not a large supply of available women to do the work.[13] Women constituted an untapped reservoir of educated and cheap labor. Women in that era were more likely to have finished high school (a requisite) than men.[14] And those men who had the requisite education could find better opportunities elsewhere. In contrast, women with high school education had few options that were more attractive. Factory and sales jobs were lower in status and in pay.[15] There is also scattered evidence that clerical workers received higher wages, particularly in the early period, than did teachers.[16]

Part of the reason men had better opportunities was that, while clerks were growing more numerous, another category was also increasing in size. Managers were needed to help coordinate the diverse activities and departments of the new organizations. A new stratum of hired managers, replacing the old-style owner-manager, was inserted between the top officers and the clerks. Henceforth, this new stratum became the dominant group in the office, taking over the planning and decision making, leading one observer to call this the era of the "managerial revolution."[17]

The rise of managers and the feminization of clerical work fundamentally altered the meaning and status of clerical work. Increasingly, it meant that the carrying out of routine tasks was planned, set up, and supervised by others. A clerical job came to be viewed less and less as a stepping-stone to business success. A survey conducted in the late 1920s showed that 88 percent of the office managers "felt they needed 'clerks who are satisfied to remain clerks.' "[18] Thus, women entered the work force in occupations that no longer offered the traditional advantages of white-collar jobs: they found themselves in dead-end occupations that were declining in status, and, to make matters worse, wages did not rise as expected.

In fact, most writers argue that the wages of clerical workers actually declined in relation to manual labor, both in the early period and in the years following World War II.[19] Evidence on this point is scattered. Although available data indicate a fall in average office wages compared to average factory wages over the last ninety years, the degree and timing of the fall are difficult to pin down. Data from different historical periods are not comparable because the definitions of office work sometimes differ, and men's and women's wages are not reported separately.

Prior to 1920, we find no systematic evidence of decline. National wage data for the years 1890 to 1926 (shown in Table 2) indicate marked fluctuations in the relative wage advantage of clerical workers in manufacturing and steam railways over other wage earners in those industries. Overall, however, the

Table 2. Average Yearly Wages for Clerical and Wage Workers in Manufacturing and Steam Railways, 1890–1926

Workers	1890	1900	1910	1920	1926
Clerical, in manufacturing and steam railways	$848	$1,011	$1,156	$2,160	$2,310
Wage, in manufacturing	439	435	558	1,358	1,309
Wage, in steam railways	560	548	677	1,817	1,613
Clerical wages as proportion of other manufacturing wages	193.2%	232.4%	207.2%	159.0%	176.5%

Source: U.S. Bureau of the Census, *Historical Statistics of the United States: Colonial Times to 1970*, bicentennial ed., Part 2, Series D (Washington, D.C.: U.S. Government Printing Office, 1975), 779–93.

clerical workers earned substantially more than other wage earners during the entire thirty-six-year period.[20] Data on postal employees and government employees (not shown in the table) indirectly confirm the relatively higher clerical salaries during this period.

It is only after 1920 that systematic data separate men's and women's wages. For the period from 1920 through World War II, the most systematic data were collected by New York State, which surveyed office workers employed in factories as well as all workers employed by these establishments. Table 3 presents information for five representative years. Note that clerical women during the entire period earned much less than clerical men (usually 50 to 60 percent) and somewhat less than factory men. The only group over which they have an advantage is factory women, and this declines over time.

In the post–World War II era, there is much clearer evidence of an overall decline (not due to a greater proportion of low-wage women). As Table 4 shows, clerical women's wages declined markedly in relation to men's blue-collar wages between 1939 and 1960. The advantage that clerical women enjoyed over blue-collar women also shrank. Since 1960, women clerical wages have stabilized at 70 to 72 percent of men operative wages and have fluctuated

Table 3. Average Weekly Wages for Office Workers and All Workers[a] in New York Manufacturing Industries, 1914–1947

Workers	1914	1924	1934	1944[b]	1947
Office	$19.18	$33.58	$32.45	$42.99	$47.74
Women office	c	21.29	21.15	34.60	40.76
All factory	11.82[d]	26.22	21.97	47.71	53.96
All women factory	c	16.65	14.90	38.46	39.62

a. Including office workers.
b. Wages for years after 1939 are not comparable with earlier years because of some changes in classification.
c. Breakdown by sex not available.
d. Average for last seven months of the year.
Source: New York State Department of Labor, *Handbook of New York Labor Statistics, 1948,* Special Bulletin no. 226 (1949), Tables D4 and D12.

Table 4. Median Yearly Wage or Salary Income for Year-Round, Full-Time Clerical Workers and Operatives by Sex, 1939–1990

Workers/Operatives	1939	1949	1960	1970	1980	1990
Clerical workers, women	$1,072	$2,235	$3,586	$5,539	$10,997	$18,475
Clerical workers, men	1,564	3,136	5,247	8,652	18,247	26,192
Operatives, women	742	1,920	2,970	4,465	9,440	14,606
Operatives, men	1,268	2,924	4,977	7,644	15,702	21,988
Women clerical workers Wages as percentage of men operatives' wages	84%	76%	72%	72%	70%	84%
Women clerical workers Wages as percentage of women operatives' wage	144%	116%	121%	124%	116%	126%

Sources: For 1949: U.S. Bureau of the Census, *1950 Census of the Population of the United States: Special Reports, Vol. 4*, P-E no. 1B, Table 20. For all other years: U.S. Bureau of the Census, *Current Population Reports*, Series P-60, no. 69, Table A-10 (for 1939 and 1960), no. 80, Table 55 (for 1970), no. 132, Table 55 (for 1980), and no. 174, Table 32 (for 1990). The figures given for all years except 1949 are for year-round full-time workers. Those for 1949 are for all year-round workers.

between 116 and 123 percent of women operative wages. Because men predominate in the operatives category, and women in the clerical category, the average combined male–female clerical earnings were lower than the average combined male–female blue-collar earnings.

Racial Stratification

One feature of clerical work that did not change with feminization was the overwhelmingly white racial character. Clerical work remained a white-dominated preserve through the 1950s. Historically, color bars kept blacks, Hispanics, and Asian Americans out of offices, forcing them to concentrate in low-status blue-collar jobs, especially in service—as private household workers, cleaners, food-service workers, and the like. As recently as 1950, for example, only one in twenty black women in the labor force was employed in a clerical position, making up a little over 1 percent of the total (Table 5). It was not until the 1960s, with the civil rights movement and the implementation of equal opportunity legislation, that minorities were able to enter white-collar work in any significant numbers. With the barriers down, minority women poured into clerical work in the 1960s and 1970s; thus, by 1980, one out of every four black women workers was employed in a clerical position. As white women moved out of their extreme concentration in clerical work in the late 1980s, the gap between the percent of black women workers employed in clerical positions and the proportion of white women so employed declined to 2 percentage points in 1990. However, if we examine where black women are located, we see that, although they are now included in the clerical ranks, they remain segregated within particular specialties and sectors. Black women are concentrated in public-sector employment (government) and are found disproportionately in lower level, "back-room," mass-production jobs

Table 5. Number and Percentage of Black Women Workers Employed in Clerical Occupations

	1950	*1960*	*1970*	*1980*	*1990*
Number	100,868	181,678	634,208	1,200,516	1,579,311
As percent of black women workers	5.3%	7.4%	19.2%	25.8%	26.1%
As percent of all clerical workers	1.3%	1.8%	4.6%	6.6%	8.5%

Sources: For 1950, U.S. Bureau of the Census, *U.S. Census of Population: 1950. Vol. IV, Special Reports,* Part 3, Chapter B, *Nonwhite Population by Race* (Washington, D.C.: U.S. Government Printing Office, 1953), Table 9; for 1960, U.S. Bureau of the Census, *U.S. Census of Population: 1960. Subject Reports, Nonwhite Population by Race,* Final Report PC(2)1C (Washington, D.C.: U.S. Government Printing Office, 1963), Table 37; for 1970, U.S. Bureau of the Census, *Census of Population: 1970, Subject Reports, Negro Population,* Final Report PC(2)1B (Washington, D.C.: U.S. Government Printing Office, 1973), Table 7; for 1980, U.S. Bureau of the Census, *1980 Census of Population, Vol. 1, Characteristics of the Population,* Chapter C, *General Social and Economic Characteristics,* Part 1, *United States Summary* PC801C1 (Washington, D.C.: U.S. Government Printing Office, 1983), Table 89; for 1990, *Employment and Earnings,* 38, January 1991, Table 21. Last line of table computed from these sources and from Table 1, this chapter.

as file clerks, data-entry keyers, and messengers. They are underrepresented in private industry and in higher level jobs, especially in the more visible positions requiring contact with managers and clients—for example, bookkeepers, secretaries, and payroll clerks.[21]

The Functions of Clerical Work

The role of clerical work in organizations and in the economy has been altered as well as increased over time. In the early stages of industrialization, the accounting, record-keeping, and other office operations were incidental to the main productive activities of a company. The amount of clerical labor expended for a given unit of goods produced was relatively small. In more advanced stages of capitalism, however, the accounting and record-keeping functions became much more complex. The number of intermediate stages between production and consumption—wholesaling, transportation, advertising, marketing—increased, and at each stage clerical operations need to be performed. Finally,

> just as in some industries the labor expended upon marketing begins to approach the amount expended upon the production of the commodities being sold, so in some industries the labor expended upon the mere transformation of the form of value (from the commodity form into the form of money or credit)—including the policing, the cashiers and collection work, the record-keeping, the accounting, etc.—begins to approach or surpass the labor used in producing the underlying commodity or service.[22]

In short, in large-scale modern organizations, clerical operations are no longer incidental functions but important processes in their own right.

An equally important trend in the past quarter-century has been a shift of economic growth from manufacturing to the service and financial sectors. These sectors rely on clerical labor in the same way that manufacturing industries rely on blue-collar labor—for the production of the main goods for exchange. The so-called office industries (principally banking, insurance, and finance) deal almost solely with the accounting and transfer of values. To a lesser but still considerable extent, service industries and public agencies — such as educational institutions and auto registration bureaus— rely heavily on office functions to do their work. Thus, they become "semiclerical" industries. The office and semiclerical industries together now employ a larger and larger share of the work force.

The sheer numbers of workers employed in clerical work have made it important to the economy. But the services that the office and semiclerical industries provide to other sectors of the economy have made these industries vital even for basic production activity. The net result is that clerical work is increasingly central to the operation of the economy as a whole.

These developments constitute what has been called a paperwork revolution. The incredible growth of these clerical occupations in turn has significance for issues of gender equality. Women have traditionally been seen as an auxiliary work force, a secondary group of workers who carry out the least essential activities, while men carry out the central ones. The paperwork revolution changes that pattern. Functions previously seen as auxiliary are now central to the running of industrial organizations, and it is women who are carrying out these functions. For the first time since the early 1800s, women predominate in a job category that is central to the industrial economy. They can no longer be viewed simply as auxiliary workers. As a collectivity, therefore, women clerical workers have a great deal of potential power, perhaps equal to that of male production workers—but as yet unrealized.

The Changing Conditions in the Office

The realization of this potential power is made problematic, however, by a second and related trend. The very size and centrality of clerical operations has made managers eager to bring office work under closer managerial control.[23] As a result of their efforts to do so, the features that once distinguished clerical work are being eroded, and the line between it and manual work is becoming blurred.[24]

Most people are aware of the principle of subdivision as it applies to the organization of blue-collar production. Tasks are broken down into small segments so that each worker does one part of the overall work. An unskilled worker can be trained quickly to carry out these narrow tasks, and should the worker leave, she or he can be easily replaced by another unskilled worker. Mechanization speeds up the work by substituting machine power for human energy. The pace of the machine controls the pace of the work. With more sophisticated machinery, many operations can be carried out automatically.

These principles of subdivision and mechanization can also be applied to paperwork—and have been since the rise of the large office. The initial thrust for reorganization of clerical work occurred in the office industries. Operations such as handling correspondence were studied and then standardized. Where possible, the operation was divided into subtasks assigned to different pools of workers. By the second decade of the century scientific management had been introduced into office routines.[25] Extensive time-and-motion studies were conducted on the minutest details—opening file drawers, taking off a paper clip, and so forth. Office machines, both simple and complex, were also introduced, but more slowly. Extensive mechanization and automation occurred after World War II.[26]

These changes in the office have been uneven. There are numerous small offices today that scarcely differ from their nineteenth-century counterparts. Even in large corporations, pockets of the "preindustrial office" have survived. Private secretaries have been largely exempt from the rationalizing trend, and they usually perform a variety of tasks from composing letters and answering the telephone to running personal errands. They have frequent personal contact with their superiors. Since the secretary's whole position is defined by her attachment to a particular person, some observers have labeled her the "office wife."[27] This personal tie to her boss effectively screens her from organizational scrutiny of her activities. Until recently, corporations were willing to tolerate this situation, even encouraging it for the sake of managerial morale. Having a secretary to carry out time-consuming routine chores was a perquisite of executive status.

In recent years, the drive for managerial control over employees' time and output has taken on added momentum. The first step in control is to gather the scattered secretaries and place them in a pool where they can be centrally supervised. Private secretaries are increasingly reserved for the highest ranks of managers. Lesser lights must make do with the shared services of pools.

Pools of typists and clerks have existed for some time, but now their use is more extensive and they are more highly organized. We observed an example of the new pooling system in a branch office of a firm we will call Public Utility. The office was reorganized when an IBM word-processing system was installed, and it is now typical of clerical industries in the way routine correspondence is handled.

Middle-level managers (called *clients* in this system) share the services of two major pools of clerks. The word-processing unit, made up of ten to twelve women, does all typing. Clients submit material to be typed on dial dictation equipment; the word-processing clerks transcribe the material into typed form, using semiautomatic machines. The work flow is continuous, unvaried, and fast. The administrative-service center performs all nontyping services, such as answering telephones and scheduling appointments. Instructions for carrying out tasks are written in manuals. For example, precise instructions are given for routing telephone calls and delivering the mail. A third group does all copying and reproduction work.

These new pooling arrangements have been facilitated by technological advancements. For example, output machines with memory capacity can type more than a hundred "personal" letters per hour. Canned paragraphs, stored in the memory, are melded with names, addresses, and "personal greetings" from a computer list as the letter is typed on the printer. The typist types only the names, addresses, and greetings. The impetus to subdivide the work process can best be understood, however, not as a response to technological advances but as part of a drive to attain control over the cost of clerical services and to assure reliability and standardization in the work process. Since the automated systems require workers to use standard forms, they also make it easier for management to trace errors and to assess each worker's productivity, whether it be number of lines typed or the number of telephone calls answered.[28]

Pooling breaks down personal ties and makes secretaries interchangeable. A secretary noted about the administrative-service center at her company: "Each secretary has a backup. . . . She cannot leave her workstation to go to the bathroom, get a drink, go to lunch, or whatever unless the other secretary is there. . . . Each secretary has a job description. If [a secretary] is on vacation or out ill, her backup will handle both jobs."

Even the savings made possible by having fewer secretaries servicing more managers are not enough for some companies. To further cut costs, employers are reducing the number of permanent employees by subcontracting clerical functions to outside agents. Secretaries at one company do very little typing. Smaller typing jobs are assigned to an in-house word-processing center using typists employed by a subcontractor, while large jobs are sent to an off-site subcontractor who picks up jobs to be done and drops off finished work twice each day. Some corporations are experimenting with "vendorizing" their administrative-service centers. The centers are contracted to outside vendors who hire, train, and pay the secretaries. Although these vendor-on-premise (VDP) secretaries work alongside regular employees, they are not technically employees of the corporation, which therefore has no legal liability for them. The corporation does not assume any of the long-term costs of permanent employees, such as medical and pension benefits. A regular employee described the case of a VDP secretary who wanted to work at a high-technology firm so much that she found out who got the contract and applied to the vendor for a job. However, she was soon disillusioned, discovering she was not entitled to the same kind of training that corporation employees received. The regular employee described her friend's experience:

> I guess the transition period, the way they [the vendor] handled it, was just totally unreal. They [the secretaries] were given a job description: "Here this is your job, this is what you will do; this is your equipment, learn it." She didn't know the people; she didn't know where they were located. She went home . . . so torn because of the lack of training . . . and the noncaring attitude.[29]

The Experiences of Clerical Workers

What impact do conditions have on the workers themselves? How do the women feel about their jobs? For the past nineteen years, we have been studying clerical work. In 1975 and 1976, we conducted in-depth interviews with thirty female clerical workers in a variety of jobs in many different organizations. Their responses were as varied as their own situations. Additional interviews, conducted in a large insurance and utility company between 1978 and 1980 as part of a larger study, revealed similar patterns of responses. We have continued to track trends in the 1980s, particularly changes growing out of office automation.

PAY

Women clerical workers are not poorly paid in comparison to other women workers, but their wages reflect the disadvantaged position of women in relation to men. In 1990, the median yearly earnings of women clerical workers employed full-time year-round was $18,475. This figure was only 84 percent of the median earnings of male operatives, whose jobs require less education and training; and it was only 70.5 percent of earnings of male clerical workers.[30]

Another important yardstick is the standard of living made possible by earnings. According to a 1985 U.S. Department of Labor Consumer Survey, a single person living independently spent an average of $13,353 for all living expenses and purchases of goods and services, exclusive of income taxes. If taxes are added in, we see that the median clerical salary was sufficient to maintain an "average" standard of living for a single individual. It was clearly inadequate for a woman head of household with dependents. For example, the average expenditure for two-person households was $22,056, and that for three-person households was $26,781.[31] Thus, most clerical women with families are dependent on another person's income to maintain a moderate standard of living.

The salaries among the women we interviewed in Boston were typical in that they averaged slightly above what the Labor Department estimated to be a budget for an "intermediate" standard of living for a single person in the Boston area, but well below what was needed for an intermediate standard for a woman head of household with two dependents.[32] Also striking was the wide range of salaries, with women doing similar work being paid very different amounts. Five of the thirty women (16.7 percent) earned *below* the intermediate standard for even a single individual. Half of the thirty women thought their wages should be higher, primarily because they believed that their work was worth more. The responses of the other half, who judged their salaries appropriate, were interesting. Nine said that the work they did or their own qualifications were not worth more, and five said that other women doing comparable work received similar wages. Perhaps these workers had internalized the low value accorded their work by society and the company, accepted other women's low wages as the appropriate comparison, or realized they had little hope of earning more. Whatever the reason, their acceptance dissipated the feeling that they deserved a living wage.

In the 1980s, wages of women clerical workers rose more rapidly than did those of male clerical workers and female blue-collar workers. However, not all workers benefited from the gains. While employers offer higher wages to attract new workers, they do not adjust the wages of long-term employees to reflect these people's contributions and experience. Thus, older employees suffer from "salary compression." During a recent union meeting, a secretary with seventeen years' service complained, "The longer you work at Harvard, the lower your pay."

DESKILLED JOBS

Clerical jobs have been deskilled in two ways. First, the *variety* of skills required in all-around jobs is not needed in the growing number of limited-function jobs. An administrative-services clerk, who had formerly worked in smaller offices, complained that she was unable to keep up her typing skills. All typing was done in the word-processing unit. She did not want to type full-time, so she did not get to type at all. Second, the *level* of skills required has been degraded. Complete accuracy is not essential in typing because the new equipment corrects errors semiautomatically. Even literacy, long a hallmark of clerical occupations, is being programmed out of some traditional specialties. The file clerk in automated systems does not need to know the sequence of the alphabet or numbers. She simply places the documents to be filed on the plate of the machine as quickly as possible.

OVERQUALIFIED WORKERS

A related outcome is that many women feel that their abilities and skills go unused. Many women are simply *overeducated.* Our sample of thirty women included sixteen with at least some college education. This proportion was much higher than in the general clerical population; figures for 1976 show that 28.4 percent of all clerical workers had at least some college, and 6.7 percent had four or more years. By 1987, 40 percent of clerical workers had some college, and 12.6 percent had four or more years[33] (see Table 6). One of the college-educated women in our sample noted: "The things on the job description any sixth grader could do."

College-educated women are not alone in feeling that their jobs are too limited. Many of the noncollege women are *overskilled.* They have received training in stenography or other specialties in high school or in vocational

Table 6. Educational Attainment of Clerical Workers Aged Twenty-Five to Sixty-Four,[a] March 1987

	Total employed (thousands)	*Years of school completed*			
		Fewer than 12 years	*12 years*	*1–3 years of college*	*4 or more years of college*
Number	14,076[b]	744	7,638	3,917	1,778
Percentage	100%	5.3%	54.3%	27.8%	12.6%

a. Includes men.
b. Numbers do not add exactly to total because they were calculated from percentages.
Source: U.S. Department of Labor, Bureau of Labor Statistics, "Labor Market Success Continues to Be Linked to Education," *News,* Sept. 28, 1987.

institutions. These skills are either obsolete or in limited demand because of the new systems. The women expressed their convictions of being underused by such statements as "I could do more," "I can handle more responsibility," "There's no way I would not welcome more challenging work," or "I feel misplaced."

CAREER LADDERS

Because of the sex-segregated office hierarchies described earlier, clerical jobs do not link up to professional or managerial ladders. Many workers find themselves at the tops of their ladders in a few years, with nowhere to go. Although there are few advantages to staying in the job, there are also few benefits from changing. The worker typically finds she can move only horizontally or downward. One woman expressed frustration that she was at a dead end in her current job, then concluded: "It took me ten years of seniority to get a month's vacation. If I left and went to another job, I don't know how long it would take."

JOB SECURITY

Just as a blue-collar assembly-line worker can be easily replaced, the clerical worker in a highly rationalized clerical job finds she has a precarious hold on her position. Caplow points out the basic similarities of semiskilled factory work and clerical jobs in large offices in this regard:

> The modern technics [*sic*] of job classification and personnel selection, developed in connection with large-scale production, are designed above all to facilitate the interchangeability of personnel. One method of ensuring interchangeability is to reduce each complex operation to a series of simple operations which require no extraordinary ability. . . . At the same time, the formal qualifications required for employment are standardized by the educational process, so that there are comparatively few differences that matter between one worker and another.[34]

Many clerical workers are acutely aware that they are expendable. A worker notes: "We laugh around here and say, 'Clericals? They're the throw-aways.' I feel like clerical workers are like machines. When the machines break down, you just replace them." An insurance company clerk says, "I'm a number. That's all anybody is at *X*. If you die, they replace you the next day. You can always be replaced." A clerk in administrative services describes the manuals the clerks are required to write, listing their duties and specifying exactly how each of their clients likes to have his mail delivered. She says, "If I'm out, my fill-in should be able to do what I do . . . It's like writing yourself out of a job."

CONTROL OVER THE WORKER

The private secretary and the limited-function clerk provide illustrations of the two main forms of control over the office worker. The secretary experiences personal control by her immediate boss. By definition, she is doing a good job if he is pleased by her performance. By the same token, the boss screens the secretary from direct company control. Several secretaries mentioned that their bosses safeguarded their time or protected them from unpleasant company assignments. The basis of control, therefore, is highly personal, with all of the problems of arbitrariness that this entails.

In contrast, clerks in pooled arrangements are subject primarily to impersonal controls; that is, formal rules are applied (e.g., clocking in) and external checks of performance are built into the work routine. The supervisor makes no special effort to keep track of workers' performance—the worker is, for example, simply visible at her designated post. A supervisor at a large insurance company claims she can tell at a glance whether one of her charges is doing her assigned task. The total output of a clerk is automatically counted by her machine.

This automatic counting represents the latest form of impersonal control, electronic monitor. Workers have always been subject to constant surveillance by superiors, but they could contrive to look busy without actually doing assigned tasks. With electronic monitor, it is harder to avoid scrutiny; the very equipment that the worker uses is her inspector. Automated equipment can monitor work in a variety of ways. The terminals on which data-entry clerks work keep track of the number of key strokes and documents completed. Automatic call distributors used in the telephone work of reservations clerks and customer-service representatives give each call to the first unengaged line and keep track of how long each call takes and the amount of time a line is "down." In addition to providing an electronic record of the worker's day, the equipment allows supervisors to "listen in" on calls at any time. Thus, not only the quantity, but also the quality, of the clerk's activity is open to inspection.

STRESS

Whereas a secretary can get angry at her boss for exercising control, a word-processing clerk cannot easily target her resentment. She may be angry at her supervisor while realizing that the supervisor has no real power, or she may feel generally angry at "them" (the anonymous big bosses). Frequently, she experiences the anger as a pervasive sense of tension or a feeling of being in a fishbowl. The combination of close monitoring and pressure for productivity thus creates anxiety and stress. Workers in production units complain about the constant pace and the lack of slack periods or frequent-enough breaks. Responding to a checklist of health problems, women most often mentioned suffering from frequent insomnia and headaches. These responses parallel the findings of a survey conducted by the National Association of Working Women, 9 to 5, which reported that, although managerial women were more likely to describe their jobs as very stressful, lower level workers, including clerical workers, were more likely to report symptoms of stress and stress-related illnesses.[35]

THE MEANING OF WORK

The many negative job conditions do not mean women find no meaning or satisfaction in their jobs. We found that, on the whole, the women were committed to working, if not to their specific jobs. In addition to the income, which they clearly saw as most important, the women found meaning in three areas. First, work provided opportunities to form and maintain social connections. Second, it gave direction and purpose to their lives by structuring their time and getting them involved in "useful" activity. Third, for some women, particularly married women with children, it provided an identity separate from their family roles.[36]

COPING AND RESISTANCE

Since the women sought meaning in their work, and their particular jobs sometimes frustrated this desire, they responded in a number of ways. A few, whose jobs allowed the latitude, informally expanded their jobs, gradually taking over new responsibilities (but they were not given titles or salaries commensurate with their actual activities). Some, particularly the college graduates, intended to leave the clerical field altogether. The majority, however, felt they had limited options and tried to find what satisfactions they could on the job—by being particularly "nice" to one another, by viewing the materials they typed as critical to the company, or by simply doing their often limited jobs well. At the same time, they protected themselves from attempts to exploit their eagerness to do something meaningful. They shrugged off compliments and rejected ploys designed to get them to do extra work. They also found creative ways to evade or resist control by electronic monitor. Some data-entry keyers said they pressed certain keys, such as the space bar, repeatedly to raise their key-stroke count. Telephone clerks arranged to call people back with additional information to increase their call count and to give themselves extra time to complete work.

Organizing

None of the women in our original study spontaneously suggested organizing or unionization as a possible strategy for dealing with her problems. Yet in the later study, when asked about the idea of an organization for clerical workers, over 50 percent of the women working in a nonunion company said it was a good idea. The main reason given was that a union would back them up in case of a dispute with management and would thus prevent individual workers from having to fight alone. Interestingly, higher pay was not the most frequently mentioned reason, even though it is the most easily documented benefit of unionization—in 1990, clerical workers represented by unions earned 34 percent more than did nonrepresented workers.[37] Despite clerical workers' own sentiments and the evident advantages of unionization, these workers remain the largest category of unorganized wage workers.

Experienced labor organizers generally consider clerical workers the most difficult segment of labor to organize, and they have made relatively little effort to unionize it. A variety of arguments have been put forward to explain the difficulties of organizing clerical personnel. Most explanations focus on two characteristics: their gender and their lack of worker consciousness.

One line of argument is that women see themselves as secondary workers. Their primary commitment is to their present or future family roles. Therefore, their wages and working conditions are not of sufficient importance to motivate them to join unions. A second line of argument focuses on women's socialization. Women are trained to take a subordinate position to men. Their situation in the office does not strike them as unfair; thus they are unlikely to organize in opposition to authority.[38] A related argument is that, also as a result of socialization, women accept exploitation because they have been trained to think it unladylike to fight back. According to one writer:

> A great majority of office workers are female and have been socialized into anti-militant values, militancy having been equated by their parents with unfeminine attitudes. Furthermore, the single office girl might prefer the prestige of a white collar job to the demotion in status involved in joining a union and thereby becoming less attractive (perhaps even declasse) to the young executive she had her eye on.[39]

This quote also illustrates another common view: that clerks fail to identify as workers because they identify with management. In the case of men, it is because they aspire to managerial positions.[40] In the case of women, it is because they hope to marry into management.[41] Lockwood cites a union official who says the personal relations between managers and clerical workers make it unlikely that the latter will unite to oppose management.[42] In addition, common dress, common working conditions, and overlapping job activities encourage clerks to see themselves as part of management.

Another belief illustrated by the above quote and elaborated by Lockwood is that clerical workers are particularly status-conscious.[43] Their marginal social positions make them snobbish and anxious about their status. To protect themselves, they set up artificial barriers between themselves and the working class.

More and more women see themselves as serious long-term workers. Out of the thirty women we interviewed, twenty-seven planned to be working five years in the future, some outside the field of clerical work, but most within it. This is a realistic expectation, given the emerging pattern for women of more continuous participation in the labor force. Seven out of ten women between the ages of eighteen and fifty-four are employed.[44] Several trends indicate that women are likely to spend more years in the labor force. First, single women have traditionally high rates of employment, and more young women are remaining single today. Second, labor force participation among married women with children has increased phenomenally over the past twenty years. Third, women are having fewer children, which means that they will be taking fewer years out for childbearing and child rearing.[45] In fact, a study of work-life expectancies indicated that the work life of women born in the 1960s can be expected to average nearly 30 years.[46] Certainly the women we interviewed took their earning power seriously. Being able to make a living—being economically independent—was an important source of pride and self-esteem.

Whether women consider union activity "unfeminine" is harder to determine directly. What is clear is that about half of the women we interviewed, when asked directly, supported the idea of a union. Those who opposed the idea expressed concern that unions represented another outside force, another "they," which would impose conditions the women might not want. Such an expression can hardly be taken to mean that women accept subordination easily. Moreover, we note that nationally 59 percent of clerical workers in 1988 were married.[47] It is unlikely that they reject union activity for the sake of snaring a manager into marriage.

We found little evidence that clerks identify with management in opposition to their own self-interest. To be sure, private secretaries took personal pride in their bosses' successes. However, clerks in other categories were keenly aware of the dichotomy between boss and worker. Many of them resented what they perceived as attempts by management to manipulate them through false compliments. Others complained about having no say over where they worked or what they did. They could be transferred from one section to another or have their jobs changed arbitrarily. Powerlessness of the individual worker was one of the main reasons given for supporting a union. As one worker said, "If we had unions, we could stick together and help each other instead of one person defending herself." Another woman displayed a wily cynicism about managerial pronouncements. She said that when the company instituted pools, workers were told that the new systems would be more democratic. She shrewdly pointed out that pool clerks were paid 20 percent less than secretaries.

We would argue, therefore, that female character and lack of worker consciousness are not impenetrable barriers to organizing. The fact remains that clerical workers have not been organized. Why? An important part of the answer is that not much effort has been put into organizing them. Many are employed in sectors of the economy that are newer and not unionized—for example, service industries.[48] Unions have generally concentrated on improving wages and benefits and increasing membership in industries in which they are already established, rather than organizing new industries.

Another part of the answer lies in the nature of the labor market in which women work. Most explanations of the absence of unions overlook this factor. Women confront a sex-segregated labor market. They are crowded into a few sex-typed occupations. The occupations dominated by women are those in which it is difficult to control entry (i.e., monopolize jobs) and in which there is a surplus of qualified workers who are not in the labor force at a given time.[49] Any worker can be easily replaced from this available labor pool. Under these conditions, it is difficult for women to develop collective strength.

Still another part of the answer lies in the composition of the clerical work force. Clerical workers are extremely diverse; they come from widely varied educational and social backgrounds. Our own sample of thirty women reflects the range: the occupations of their fathers covered the thirteen major groupings used by the U.S. Census. Their own educations varied from less than high school to postgraduate college degrees. Because of the limited job options open to women, due to sex-typing of jobs, women with diverse qualifications end up in a common occupation. The current situations of these women were equally varied. Among the married women, some were married to professionals, others to semiskilled or unskilled workers. This fits the national picture. Of all married female clerical workers with employed husbands in 1988, 51 percent had white-collar husbands and 49 percent blue-collar husbands.[50] Since these women lack a shared class situation, it should not be surprising that they lack a sense of common identity.

Despite the barriers to organizing, there has been a great increase in organizing activity among women clerical workers. Ironically, the very changes in technology and organization that managers are introducing into offices may help to create conditions that encourage organization among workers. As common disadvantages become more widespread, they may overshadow the absence of common class background. Some evidence suggests that employed women come to judge their social class from their own occupations rather than from those of their husbands or their fathers.[51]

In addition, there has been a general trend toward unionization among white-collar workers, and growing efforts have been made to organize clerical workers. Organized labor has stepped up its campaign to organize state and municipal employees and has also begun making inroads in the private sector. Grassroots groups have sprung up among women office and service workers in the larger cities. Ten of these groups are now affiliated in a national organization known as 9 to 5 (previously called Working Women), which has twenty-five chapters throughout the United States and an "action alert network" of active members in one hundred cities. Several other groups—Women Organized for Employment, in San Francisco; Women Employed, in Chicago; and Women Office Workers, in New York—remain independent but have reciprocal information exchanges with 9 to 5. Using political and educational strategies, these groups work to empower women office workers so they can improve their situation in the office. For example, 9 to 5 installed a toll-free "hot line on job problems" (1-800-522-0925) staffed by two full-time counselors. In 1991, over seventy thousand calls were made to that number. The most commonly reported problems were sexual harassment and difficulties around pregnancy disability/maternity leave. Nine to 5 responded with a new publication, *The 9 to 5 Guide to Combating Sexual Harassment,* in June 1992.[52] These organizations also work for changes in employer policies (such as job posting), for workplace improvements (such as back-pay settlements and training programs), to inform the public about the conditions office workers face, and to build organizations for office workers.

A second level of organization has developed in the form of new unions, separate locals of established unions, or separate unions affiliated with internationals. Boston's Local 925 of the Service Employees International Union (SEIU) began as a spinoff of the Boston chapter of 9 to 5. While the Boston 9 to 5 group continues its educational and politicizing activities, Local 925 evolved into District 925 (SEIU), an organization with a national jurisdiction and the rights of a local. Other partnerships link District 65 (Distributive Workers of America) with the United Automobile Workers and the Harvard Union of Clerical and Technical Workers with the American Federation of State, County and Municipal Employees, while other unions—including the Office and Professional Employees International Union, the Hotel Employees and Restaurant Employees International Union, and the Teamsters—organize particular areas of the clerical work force.

There are two possible—and not mutually exclusive—outcomes of clerical organizing. One is that clerical workers will receive increased material benefits in the form of higher wages, shorter hours, better medical insurance, and other traditional union goals. Another is that the quality of work life will be improved through changes in the organization of work activities.

The history of organized labor indicates that the first set of goals is likely to be achieved, but the second is not. However, the degree to which issues of quality of work life are addressed will depend partly on which forms of organizing predominate and what kinds of unions are formed. At one time, it seemed that the women's movement would provide a model for a different kind of organizing among clerical workers. Although the uncertain future of the women's movement makes that prospect seem less likely, the grassroots organizing of what might be called the preunion groups continues to borrow heavily from the techniques of the women's movement. These include the use of group support to help women identify common problems, consciousness-raising activities (such as public speakouts), and interpersonal strategies for changing worker–boss relationships. The shift toward forming unions necessarily involves other methods of organizing, yet it may not signal the end of a unique kind of organizing among clerical workers.

The successful effort by Local 34 of the Hotel Employees and Restaurant Employees International Union (HERE) to organize clerical and technical workers at Yale in 1983–84 is a model of grassroots organizing centered on women workers' concerns. The first eighteen months were devoted to building rank-and-file support through home visits and lunch meetings. A four-hundred-member organizing committee was in place before the union even distributed membership cards. During the contract negotiations Local 34 rejected narrowing their tactics to simply withholding labor. While they had a brief strike to buttress their demands, they simultaneously worked to rally broad-based support from faculty and students and other employees within the university as well as from outside religious and political organizations and the black community in New Haven. The union's goals were linked to larger issues of achieving economic justice for women and minorities, recognizing the value of women's work, and encouraging Yale to be a responsible citizen in the community.[53] Similarly, in May 1988, the Harvard Union of Clerical and Technical Workers won an election, the culmination of ten years of organizing efforts. Here too, much of the organizing was done in small groups, and issues of economic justice, child care for workers' children, and the university's responsibility to the community were addressed.

The Yale drive, the Harvard drive, and other recent organizing drives in large and small workplaces testify to clerical workers' growing self-confidence, militance, and commitment to democratic principles.[54] These organizing drives also testify to the growing recognition among male unionists that women clerical workers are serious workers who will strengthen the union movement. In the Yale drive, members of Local 35 (HERE), the largely male blue-collar union at Yale, raised their dues to contribute to the organizing efforts of clerical and technical workers: the parent union HERE supplied considerable financial support and experienced organizers while respecting local autonomy.[55] At Harvard, despite a split between the local organizing committee and its original supporting union, the union movement remained committed to the drive; another major union, the American Federation of State, County and Municipal Employees, stepped in with substantial financial and technical support without interfering with local grassroots control.[56]

Employers obviously take clerical organizing seriously. Both Yale and Harvard delayed the union efforts at their respective schools through challenges to the National Labor Relations Board. When these challenges failed, both waged sophisticated and expensive antiunion campaigns. Only after losing its appeal to the NLRB to overturn the election did Harvard concede the results and recognize the union in November 1988.

The late 1980s proved to be a difficult time for unions. Many were losing members and had little success in organizing. But organizing among clerical workers is continuing. SEIU 925 has had at least two or three organizing victories in small offices in each of the past two years, as well as a major victory at the University of Cincinnati in 1989. A campaign at Kent State University is currently under way. Likewise, the union that grew out of the Harvard Union of Clerical and Technical Workers continues to organize. It won major campaigns at the University of Minnesota and the University of Illinois in 1991 and was engaged in three other university campaigns under way at this moment.[57]

Clerical workers are beginning to gain recognition as workers in the popular culture too, as in the film and television show *Nine to Five*. Moreover, they are including in their organizing issues that directly challenge sexist practices and identify unique aspects of women's work experience—such as pay equity (comparable worth) and protection against sexual harassment. Such organizing seems to proceed from a vision of active, autonomous locals and a full voice for workers. If the organizing succeeds on these grounds, it is more likely to lead to demands for fundamental changes in the workplace than if more traditional approaches are used.

It is an exciting future to contemplate. When clerical women organize widely, they will become one of the largest groups within the union movement. They may well alter the issues and concerns addressed by organized labor.

NOTES

1. U.S. Bureau of Labor Statistics, *Trends of Earnings Among White Collar Workers During the War*, Bulletin no. 783 (Washington, D.C.: U.S. Government Printing Office, 1944). Also Grace Coyle, "Women in the Clerical Occupations," *Annals of the American Academy of Political and Social Sciences* 143 (1929), 180–87.

2. U.S. Bureau of Labor Statistics, *Employment and Earnings* 38 (Jan. 1991), Table 22, 21.

3. See Rosabeth Kanter, "Women and the Structure of Organizations," in Marcia Millman and Rosabeth Kanter, eds., *Another Voice* (New York: Anchor, 1975). Also Rosabeth Kanter, *Men and Women of the Corporation* (New York: Basic, 1977).

4. The best descriptions of the historical changes in office work are Margery Davies, "Women's Place Is at the Typewriter: The Feminization of the Clerical Labor Force," *Radical America* 8 (1974), 1–28; Harry Braverman, *Labor and Monopoly Capital* (New York: Monthly Review Press, 1974), Chapter 15; C. Wright Mills, *White Collar* (New York: Oxford University Press, 1956).

5. Daniel Bell, "The Breakup of Family Capitalism," in Bell, *The End of Ideology*, rev. ed. (New York: Collier, 1961.

6. Mary Kathleen Benet, *The Secretarial Ghetto* (New York: McGraw-Hill, 1972).

7. Braverman, *Labor and Monopoly Capital*, 294.

8. Davies, "Women's Place Is at the Typewriter."

9. Bell, "The Breakup of Family Capitalism."

10. Davies, "Women's Place Is at the Typewriter."

11. Judith Smith, "The New Woman Knows How to Type: Some Connections Between Sexual Ideology and Clerical Work, 1900–1930" (paper presented at the Berkshire Conference on the History of Women, Radcliffe College, Cambridge, Mass., 1974).

12. Writers who have made this point include Coyle, "Women in the Clerical Occupations"; Davies, "Women's Place Is at the Typewriter"; Janet Hooks, *Women's Occupations Through Seven Decades,* Women's Bureau Bulletin, no. 218 (Washington, D.C.: U.S. Government Printing Office, 1944); Bruce Bliven, Jr., *The Wonderful Writing Machine* (New York: Random House, 1954); and Elizabeth F. Baker, *Technology and Woman's Work* (New York: Columbia University Press, 1964).

13. The introduction of new technologies is often related to changes in the sex composition of an occupation. Jo Freeman (personal communication) points out that sometimes a new labor force is introduced because the older group of workers will not or cannot use the new technology. We would argue against strictly technological determination, however. The replacement of frame-spinning machinery with mule-spinning machinery in the 1840s coincided with a changeover from a predominantly female to a predominantly male labor force in textiles. Mule-spinning equipment was considered unsuitable for women, partly because it was awkward to use with long skirts. Mule spinning had been widely used for many years in England prior to its use in the United States. Due to the shortage of male labor, its introduction into American factories was delayed for many years. Thus, we would argue that a changeover in labor force accompanying technological change occurs only when there is an available alternate labor pool. See Edith Abbott, *Women in Industry* (New York: Appleton, 1910), especially 91–92.

14. Valerie K. Oppenheimer, *The Female Labor Force in the United States: Demographic and Economic Factors Governing Its Growth and Changing Composition,* Population Monograph Series, no. 5 (Berkeley: University of California, 1970).

15. Robert Smuts, *Women and Work in America,* rev. ed. (New York: Schocken, 1971).

16. U.S. Bureau of the Census, *Historical Statistics of the United States: Colonial Times to 1970,* bicentennial ed., part 2 (Washington, D.C.: U.S. Government Printing Office, 1975), 168. Also Elyce Rotella, "Occupational Segregation and the Supply of Women to the American Clerical Labor Force, 1870–1930" (paper presented at the Berkshire Conference on the History of Women, Radcliffe College, Cambridge, Mass., 1974).

17. James Burnham, *The Managerial Revolution* (New York: John Day, 1941).

18. Coyle, "Women in the Clerical Occupations."

19. For example, Braverman, *Labor and Monopoly Capital;* Mills, *White Collar;* and Coyle, "Women in the Clerical Occupations."

20. Braverman (*Labor and Monopoly Capital*) uses the 1900 data on manufacturing and steam railway workers and contrasts them with 1971 data on clerical and manual wages to illustrate the erosion of clerical wages. The contrast implies a dramatic decline over the seventy years. As Table 2 shows, the 1900 figures are the point of maximum difference, 56 percent greater than 1890, thus accentuating the apparent decline of clerical wages.

21. *Employment and Earnings* 38 (Jan. 1991), U.S. Department of Labor, Table 22.

22. Braverman, *Labor and Monopoly Capital,* 302.

23. Alfred Vogel, "Your Clerical Workers Are Ripe for Unionism," *Harvard Business Review* 49 (1971), 48–54.

24. Evelyn N. Glenn and Roslyn L. Feldberg, "Degraded and Deskilled: The Proletarianization of Clerical Work," *Social Problems* 25 (1977), 52–64.

25. Influential proponents of scientific management in offices were William Henry Leffingwell, *Scientific Office Management* (Chicago: Shaw, 1917), and Lee Galloway, *Office Management: Its Principles and Practices* (New York: Ronald Press, 1918).

26. Jon M. Shepard, *Automation and Alienation: A Study of Office and Factory Workers* (Cambridge, Mass.: M.I.T. Press, 1972).

27. Benet, *The Secretarial Ghetto;* and Kanter, *Men and Women of the Corporation.*

28. For further discussions of technology and changing conditions in the office, see U.S. Department of Labor, Women's Bureau Bulletin, no. 218, *Women and Office Automation: Issues for the Decade Ahead* (Washington, D.C.: U.S. Government Printing Office, 1985); National Research Council, *Computer Chips and Paper Clips* (Washington, D.C.: National Academy Press, 1987); and Daniel Marschall and Judith Gregory, eds., *Office Automation, Jekyll or Hyde?* (Cleveland, Ohio: Working Women's Education Fund, 1983).

29. Interview conducted by Sue Funari, 1987.

30. U.S. Bureau of the Census, "Money Income of Households, Families and Persons in the United States: 1990," *Current Population Reports,* Series P-60, no. 174 (Washington, D.C.: U.S. Government Printing Office, 1991), Table 32.

31. U.S. Department of Labor, Bureau of Labor Statistics, "Consumer Expenditure Survey Results from 1985," *News,* USDL no. 87-399, September 24, 1987.

32. See U.S. Bureau of Labor Statistics, *Autumn 1981 Urban Family Budgets and Comparative Indexes for Selected Urban Areas* (Boston) (Washington, D.C.: U.S. Government Printing Office, April 1981). Budget figures are presented for lower, intermediate, and higher budgets for families of four. Figures for single individuals and single heads of families are computed from these basic figures using equivalence scales from Table A-1, "Revised Scale of Equivalent Income for Urban Families of Different Size, Age, and Composition," which is available from regional Bureau of Labor Statistics offices.

33. U.S. Bureau of Labor Statistics, "Labor Market Success Continues to Be Linked to Education," *News* USDL no. 87-415 (Washington, D.C.: U.S. Government Printing Office, Jan. 21, 1987).

34. Theodore Caplow, *The Sociology of Work* (New York: McGraw-Hill, 1954), 85.

35. National Association of Working Women, 9 to 5, *National Survey on Women and Stress* (Cleveland, Ohio: 1984). See also Suzanne Haynes and M. Feinlab, "Women, Work and Coronary Heart Disease," *American Journal of Public Health* (1980).

36. Roslyn L. Feldberg and Evelyn N. Glenn, "Category or Collectivity: The Consciousness of Clerical Workers" (paper presented at the meeting of the Society for the Study of Social Problems, Chicago, 1977).

37. *Employment and Earnings* (January 1991), Table 60.

38. Albert Blum, *Management and the White Collar Union* (New York: American Management Association, 1964).

39. Elliot Krause, *The Sociology of Occupations* (Boston: Little, Brown, 1971), 86.

40. Mills, *White Collar.*

41. Krause, *The Sociology of Occupations.*

42. David Lockwood, *The Black-Coated Worker* (London: Unwin University Books, Allen & Unwin, 1958).

43. Ibid.

44. Susan E. Shank, "Women and the Labor Market: The Link Grows Stronger," *Monthly Labor Review* (March 1988), 3–8; *Employment and Earnings* (January 1991), Table 3.

45. Ibid.; see also Allyson Sherman Grossman, "Women in the Labor Force: The Early Years," *Monthly Labor Review* 98 (1975), 3–9.

46. U.S. Bureau of Labor Statistics, *Worklife Estimates: Effects of Race and Education,* Bulletin no. 2254 (Washington, D.C.: U.S. Government Printing Office, 1986), Table A-4.

47. U.S. Bureau of Labor Statistics, unpublished data from March 1988 Current Population Survey. We thank Mary Sullivan of the Boston Regional Office of the BLS for tracking down these data.

48. Martin Oppenheimer, "Women Office Workers: Petty Bourgeoisie or New Proletarians?" *Social Scientist,* Monthly Journal of the Indian School of Social Sciences, Trivandrum, Kerala, nos. 40–41. For statistics on rates of union representation by industry, see U.S. Department of Labor, Bureau of Labor Statistics, Bulletin no. 2105, *Earnings and Other Characteristics of Organized Labor, May 1980* (Washington, D.C.: U.S. Government Printing Office, 1981); and *Employment and Earnings,* January 1988, Table 60.

49. See Caplow, *The Sociology of Work,* Chapter 10, for a discussion of these and related points. An economist, Mary Stevenson, in "Wage Differences Between Men and Women: Economic Theories," in Ann H. Stromberg and Shirley Harkess, eds., *Women Working* (Palo Alto, Calif.: Mayfield, 1978), 89–107, analyzes the impacts of occupational segregation and consequent crowding of women's occupations on women's wages.

50. U.S. Bureau of the Census, "Household and Family Characteristics, March 1988," *Current Population Reports,* Series P-20, no. 437 (Washington, D.C.: U.S. Government Printing Office, 1988), calculated from Table 6.

51. Kathleen Ritter and Lowell Hargens, "Occupational Positions and Class Identifications of Married Women: A Test of the Asymmetry Hypothesis," *American Journal of Sociology* 80 (Jan. 1975), 934–48.

52. Karen Nussbaum, president, SEIU District 925, telephone interview, 1992.

53. Molly Ladd Taylor, "Women Workers and the Yale Strike," *Feminist Studies* 11 (1985), 463–65.

54. See Cynthia B. Costello, "On the Front: Class, Gender and Conflict in the Insurance Workplace," Ph.D. dissertation, Department of Sociology (Madison: University of Wisconsin, 1984).

55. Taylor, "Women Workers and the Yale Strike," 466.

56. Kristine Rondeau, President, Harvard Union of Clerical and Technical Workers, personal communication, 1988.

57. Karen Nussbaum, telephone interview, 1992; Kristine Rondeau, telephone interview, 1992.

Professional Women: How Real Are the Recent Gains?

Debra Renee Kaufman

TODAY THERE ARE JUST under fifty million women in the civilian labor force. Nearly ten million women, or one out of every five of those employed, hold professional or managerial positions. In law, medicine, postsecondary education, and business, the number of women has increased significantly during the last ten years. But the gains that women have made in the professions have been hard won and may well prove even harder to maintain. As Epstein warned in 1970, "No matter what sphere of work women are hired for or select, like sediment in a wine bottle they seem to settle to the bottom" (1970b, p. 2). What women are allowed to do remains limited, and barriers still restrict their mobility in the professional world. In professions that are as male-dominated today as they were a decade ago, women are still likely to be overrepresented in low-paid and low-prestige subspecialties. However, when men enter female-dominated professions, they usually rise to the top.

Society has various expectations of and beliefs about its professionals. It assumes that they will abide by a code of ethics in dealing with their colleagues and clients and that they will belong to a professional association entrusted with enforcing this code. Since professionals are considered best qualified to judge each other's work, they are expected to submit to the judgment of their colleagues. Professionals are expected to make decisions without pressure from clients, the public, or an employing agency. It is believed that professional work benefits the public.

In many respects, professionals represent the elite cadre of society's work force. Since professions carry a high degree of honor and status in our society, their members can expect greater rewards for their services. Professional prestige is partly attributable to the fact that professionals are highly educated. Their specialized training allows them to draw on a body of knowledge unavailable to lay people. The exclusivity of the professions is also a result of their legal right to exercise a virtual monopoly over the delivery of their

The author would like to acknowledge the help of the Center for Labor Market Studies, Northeastern University, Boston, Massachusetts, for their assistance with the census data. She would also like to thank Jyoti Puri for her persistence and patience in locating pertinent data from the American Medical Association, American Bar Association, Bureau of Labor Statistics, Center for Educational Statistics, and Department of Labor. Shirley Selhub was helpful in collecting data about women and management, and the U.S. Women's Bureau was particularly helpful in forwarding the most recent releases on the glass ceiling initiative. This chapter is rewritten in memory of Pat Golden, who worked diligently to ensure that women and minorities were well represented in the professions at Northeastern University.

287

service. Professionals are thought to derive a great deal of fulfillment from their work and to enjoy a high degree of autonomy. It is not clear, however, that professional women enjoy these advantages to the same extent as do their male colleagues. Even when women are willing and able to make the commitment to a professional career, most find themselves located in subsidiary positions within prestige professions or in positions that do not accord them the autonomy, prestige, or pay customarily associated with the professional image (see Table 1).

Table 1 shows that, from the beginning of this century to the present, the professions have been clearly sex-segregated. In the 1990s the prestige professions

Table 1.   Percent Female in Eight Selected Professions, 1900–1980

Profession	1990	1980	1970	1960	1950	1940	1930	1920	1910	1900
Physicians[a]	21.0	13.4	9.3	6.8	6.5	4.7	4.4	5.0	6.0	5.6
Lawyers and judges	24.4	12.8	4.9	3.5	3.5	2.5	2.1	1.4	0.5	.8
Clergy	10.4	5.8	2.9	2.3	4.1	2.7	2.2	1.4	0.5	3.1
Professors[b]	40.5	36.6	28.6	21.9	23.3	26.5	32.5	30.2	18.9	6.3
Social workers[c]	69.0	64.9	62.8	62.7	69.1	64.3	78.7			
Nurses[d]	94.3	95.9	96.1	97.5	97.6	97.8	98.1	96.3	92.9	93.6
Librarians[e]	81.3	82.5	82.0	85.5	88.5	89.5	91.3	88.2	78.5	74.7
Teachers[f]	74.7	70.8	69.5	72.5	78.8	75.3	81.8	84.5	80.1	74.5
Managers[g]	42.2	30.5	18.5							

a. Osteopaths were included with physicians in 1910, 1970, and 1980.

b. For "professors" we have used the category "teachers, college and university" in the 1970 and 1980 censuses. "College presidents, professors, and instructors" was used for the others.

c. From 1930 to 1960, the decennial reports use the category "social and welfare workers," but the 1930 count is not comparable to those that came afterward. Prior to 1920, social and welfare workers were included in the group "religious, charity, and welfare workers."

d. The category used for 1970 and 1980 is "registered nurses"; that for 1950 and 1960 is "nurses, professional"; that for 1940 is "nurses and student nurses." Before 1930, the category is "trained nurses."

e. In 1910, "librarians" includes librarian assistants.

f. "Teachers" is a composite figure for elementary- and secondary-school teachers from 1960 to 1980. The 1940 and 1950 reports use "teachers (not elsewhere classified)," and those for 1910 to 1930 use "teachers (school)" as the category. Prior to 1910, "teachers" included all teachers of every kind.

g. Managers is from "executive, administrative and managerial occupations," which is a broad category, unlike the professional specialty occupations in this table. In 1980 several management-related occupations were relocated into this category. These were heavily female, which partially accounts for the large increase in percent of female "managers" from 1970.

Sources: For 1990: *Supplementary Report Series, Detailed Occupation and Other Characteristics from the EEO File for the U.S.,* Table 1. For 1980: 1980 Census of Population, Vol. 1, *Characteristics of the Population,* Chapter D, Detailed Population Characteristics, Part 1, United States Summary, Section A, Table 276, "Detailed Occupations of the Experienced Civilian Labor Force and Employed Persons by Sex, 1980 and 1970." *Supplementary Report from the 1980 Census of Population,* Table 1, "Detailed Occupations and Years of School Completed, by Age for Civilian Labor Force, by Sex, Race, and Spanish Origin: 1980," PC80-51-8. For 1970: *Nineteenth Decennial Census of the United States,* Vol. 1, *Characteristics of the Population,* Part 1, Section 2, Table 221, "Detailed Occupations of Experienced Civilian Labor Force and Employed Persons by Sex, 1970 and 1960," p. I-1718. For 1960 and 1950: *Eighteenth Decennial Census of the United States,* Vol. 1, *Characteristics of the Population,* Part 1, Table 201, "Detailed Occupations of Experienced Labor Force, by Sex, for the United States, 1960 and 1950," p. I-522. For 1940: *Sixteenth Decennial Census of the United States: Population: Comparative Occupation Statistics for the United States, 1870 to 1940,* Table 2, "Persons 14 Years Old and over in the Labor Force (Except New Workers), 1940," p. 49. For 1930, 1920, and 1910: *Fifteenth Decennial Census: Population: General Report on Occupations,* Table 1, "Gainful Workers 10 Years Old and over, by Occupation and Sex, with the Occupations Arranged According to the Classification of 1930, for the United States, 1930, 1920, and 1910," Vol. 5, p. 20. For 1900: *Twelfth Decennial Census: Population: Part 2,* Table 91, "Total Persons 10 Years of Age and over in the United States Engaged in Each Specified Occupation (in Detail), Classified by Sex, 1900," p. 505.

remain male-dominated: only 8.4 percent of the clergy, 21.4 percent of lawyers and judges, 20.4 percent of physicians, and 40.9 percent of college and university teachers were women. Conversely, the percentages of women who are social workers (68.9 percent), teachers except college and university (74.8 percent), registered nurses (94.3 percent), and librarians (87.6 percent) indicate that those professions remain female-dominated (*Employment and Earnings,* Jan. 1992, Table 22). The male-dominated professions are overwhelmingly white. In the female professions, African-American women are approaching parity with their proportion of the population. This is not true of Hispanic women (*Employment and Earnings,* Jan. 1993, Table 22). Perhaps even more revealing about women's status in the professions is that the female-dominated occupations, although classified by the Bureau of the Census as professions, are often referred to in the sociological literature as the "semi-professions" (Etzioni, 1969; Ritzer, 1972; England, 1992).

We see that this distinction is more than academic when we realize that the term *profession* seems to be reserved for only those careers structured for the lives that men lead. Such careers are predicated on the notion that the professional is relatively free from child-care and home responsibilities. This permits great investments of time, energy, devotion, and "overtime" work, which are not possible for someone whose primary obligation is to a family. Extensive, difficult, and often expensive schooling is also required for the pursuit of such careers. "Continuity is usually essential," writes Oppenheimer, "and the freedom to move or to stay put, depending on the exigencies of the career, may be an important factor in whether or not success is achieved" (1970, p. 115).

The Female-Dominated Professions

While the female-dominated occupations, like other professions, require advanced education and specific credentials, they often lack the authority, autonomy, and monopoly over a knowledge base that characterize the prestige and male-dominated professions. Oppenheimer suggests that the major female-dominated professions stand in direct contrast to the male-dominated ones:

> All of [the female-dominated professions] depend on skilled but cheap labor in fairly large quantities . . . most of the training for them is acquired *before* employment, and career continuity is not essential. They exist all over the country, and hence mobility—or the lack of it—is not usually a serious handicap. Diligence and a certain devotion to the job are required, but long-range commitments and extensive sacrifices of time and energy are not necessary. Employment in most of these occupations relatively infrequently puts the female worker in a supervisory position over male employees, though she may be in a position of relative power over those outside the organization. Nurses, for example, may initiate action for patients, but their authority to do so is derived from the attending physician; furthermore, the authority and the task have a distinctly feminine flavor—that of the nurturing female. Social workers are often in power positions vis-à-vis clients, but these clients are

not in the work organization and are in a notoriously poor position to effect changes anyway. (Oppenheimer, 1970, p. 114)

While all women are affected by this pattern, black professional women are especially vulnerable. They are heavily concentrated in the lower-paying specialties in the female-dominated professions, serving black clients and generally poor and working-class people in the public sector (Sokoloff, 1986, pp. 24–25).

Men assume the more respected positions of authority and power in female-dominated professions, positions quite consonant with societal views about men's "natural" roles. Male nurses, for instance, tend to be promoted to administrative jobs more frequently than are female nurses (Butter et al., 1987, p. 134). Among teachers, women are more likely to teach at less prestigious levels of education than are men. In 1992, 98.6 percent of prekindergarten and kindergarten and 85.4 percent of elementary-school teachers were women, compared to 55.5 percent of secondary-school teachers (*Employment and Earnings,* Jan. 1993, Table 22).

The Prestige Professions

Despite the increasing number of women earning doctorates, completing professional degrees, and entering the professions, the prestige professions and the prestige specialties within them still remain male-dominated. Medicine, law, academia, science, and management have a similar gender hierarchy.

MEDICINE

Throughout the first seventy years of this century, the proportion of women among active American physicians remained essentially unchanged, at around 7 percent. Many factors have contributed to this low percentage—from early gender-role socialization to discrimination in admission practices and policies of medical schools. However, in the last two decades, changes in federal law and in custom have helped women more than quadruple their enrollment in medical schools. In 1964–65, 7.7 percent of the first-year medical students in America were women (Association of American Medical Colleges, 1982); in 1991–92 women were 39.9 percent (Association of American Medical Colleges, 1992, Table I). In 1976–77 (Vetter and Babco, 1987, Table 3-2, p. 72), women accounted for 19.2 percent of all those who obtained medical degrees in America; by 1990–91 they were 35.9 percent (Association of American Medical Colleges, 1992). As of 1992, women constituted 20.4 percent of all practicing physicians (*Employment and Earnings,* Jan. 1993, Table 72), and 29.5 percent of all medical residents in America (Association of American Medical Colleges, 1992, Table 4).

However, it is after medical school that the recent gains women have made come into question. Female physicians, for instance, tend to concentrate in such specialties as pediatrics, psychiatry, public health, physical medicine (rehabilitation), and preventive medicine, while men concentrate in high-status and high-pay surgical specialties (Lorber, 1984; Butter et al., 1987; Vetter and Babco, 1987; Hodson and Sullivan, 1990). Despite steady increases, women are primarily located in the less prestigious areas of the medical profession and consequently earn less in each specialty (Bowman and Gross, 1986; Butter et al., 1987; Association of American Medical Colleges, 1992). In part, this may be because men are more likely to practice in independent or group practices and women are more likely to be found in salaried positions (Bowman and Gross, 1986).

LAW

Women have made great strides in the legal profession, increasing from 5.3 percent of those receiving law degrees in 1969–70 (NCES, 1992, Table 244) to 42.6 percent in 1991–92 (American Bar Association, 1992). In 1992, 21.4 percent of all lawyers were women (*Employment and Earnings,* Jan. 1993, Table 22). However, as with medicine, the gains women have made are tempered by the different career patterns women lawyers face compared to those of their male colleagues. While women have been able to enter areas formerly denied to them—such as small private companies, large corporate firms, law school faculties, and the judiciary (Hodson and Sullivan, 1990)—they are still heavily clustered in the less prestigious areas of family law, trusts and estates, and tax. Even their Wall Street advances from associates to partners must be interpreted with caution (Epstein, 1980, 1988). Although more women are making gains in the profession, such advancements may have a different meaning now than they would have had earlier.

> For women and minority associates, there is a greater chance of becoming partner, but that position may be a junior partnership bringing a proportionately smaller share of profits at the end of the year. It may also have less power and influence attached to it. There is some suspicion on the part of the older women attorneys that this is the kind of partnership young women are likely to get as the firms are feeling pressed to promote their women associates. Although this is definitely a step upward compared to the past, it does not mean that women have "made it" in relation to men who are rising in the hierarchy. (Epstein 1980, p. 308)

ACADEME

Just over 40 percent of university and college teachers in 1992 were women (*Employment and Earnings,* Jan. 1993, Table 22). Nonetheless, as in other male-dominated professions, many disparities exist between male and female professors. Academic women are concentrated in lower-ranked and nontenured positions; they work mainly in less prestigious institutions and fields; they are often segregated in areas with predominantly female student bodies; and, even within the same academic rank or category of institutional affiliation, they do not earn as much as men do (National Center for Education Statistics, 1992, Tables 212–16, 218–19, 224). Even in traditional women's fields, men are more likely to be at the highest levels of the professions. Men direct the libraries, schools of social work, and teacher-training institutions for elementary and secondary education (Theodore, 1986, p. xix). Outside of education depart-ments, employment of minority women is virtually nonexistent in all types of schools.

Women faculty in the professional schools fare particularly poorly compared to men. In 1991–92, women were only 26.2 percent of full-time and 24.3 percent of part-time faculty in law degree–granting programs but were 42.6 percent of the student body (American Bar Association, 1992, p. 66). Women were 28.5 percent of full-time medical school faculty that year, while composing nearly 40 percent of the student body (Association of American Medical Colleges, 1992, Figure 1). Irrespective of the professional school and the timing of their first appointment, women are located at the bottom of the academic hierarchy. If women are disproportionately on nontenure track appointments, and if such appointments are in the lower ranks, as the data suggest, it is not certain that women, over time, will achieve either professional security or equality in ranks with men.

SCIENCE AND ENGINEERING

In 1992, women accounted for 17.5 percent of the science and engineering work force, up from 9 percent in 1976 (*Employment and Earnings,* Jan. 1993, Table 22). Women account for a larger share of employment in science than they do in engineering. Again, as with the other male-dominated professions, women are not randomly distributed in science or engineering. Almost half of all women scientists and engineers are concentrated in psychology or in the life and biological sciences (National Science Foundation, 1990, p. 4). Women represent less than 10 percent of all engineers. Among engineers, only 6.9 percent of aerospace, 6.3 percent of chemical, and 7.9 percent of civil engineers were women (*Employment and Earnings,* Jan. 1993, Table 22).

Sokoloff (1986) suggests that a split is developing in the organization of the professions. Two sets of jobs seem to be emerging: those with high prestige, good pay, autonomy, and opportunity for growth, and those that are more routinized, poorly paid, and less autonomous. She also notes that shifts in sex segregation have been often followed by declines in earnings or career possibilities (1986, p. 34). Therefore, numerical growth may not offset segregation patterns within the professions. This has led some authors to conclude that desegregation in the male-dominated professions has not substantially changed the sex-segregation patterns within those professions (see also England, 1992).

MANAGEMENT

Over the past decade many scholars have argued that managerial careers have become professional careers (Kanter, 1977; Kaufman and Fetters, 1980, 1983). Like the professions, managerial careers often require licensing and professional schooling. In 1992, women in the United States represented 41.5 percent of all persons employed in managerial, executive, and administrative occupations, indicating an increase from 26.5 percent in 1978 (*Employment and Earnings,*

Jan. 1993, Table 22). These gains are also reflected in the dramatic increase in the number of women receiving their bachelor's and master's degrees in business management over the last two decades. In 1970–71, women earned 9.1 percent of the bachelor's and 3.9 percent of the master's degrees awarded. By 1989–90 they earned 46.7 percent of the bachelor's degrees and 34 percent of the master's degrees (NCES, 1992, Table 263). Much of this significant gain can be attributed to the women's movement, affirmative action, and the passage in 1972 of Title IX of the Education Amendments, which prohibited sex discrimination in institutions of higher education and thus opened business schools to women who had been excluded or dissuaded from enrolling in them before that time.

However, despite these real gains, closer inspection of women's distribution within this occupational category clearly reflects the same pattern as that in the other prestigious, high-paying, and male-dominated professions: Women are more likely to be managers in areas where the pay and prestige are less and where there are already more women employees at lower levels. Women (and minorities) are more often found in staff (e.g., personnel and labor relations) than in line (marketing and sales) positions. This distinction is important since line positions are considered to be important entry points to upper-management jobs (Levine, 1991, p. 4).

Although more women hold management positions than at any other time, few have made the breakthrough to top-level executive positions. Findings from a 1991 study done by the Feminist Majority Foundation indicate that of the 6,502 jobs at the vice-presidential level and higher within the nation's largest corporations, only 175, or 2.6 percent, were held by women (reported in the *New York Times,* September 11, 1991, p. B11). According to a survey of seven hundred companies by Korn Ferry, a leading executive recruiting firm, women and minorities were virtually the same percentage of officials with ranks of vice-president or higher as they were a decade ago (Department of Labor Library Information Brief No. 1, May 1991, p. 3).

In conclusion, there are fewer women in the prestige professions than there are men, female professionals generally still occupy the least prestigious specialties within those professions, and females earn less for comparable work. These facts suggest that women still face stern barriers to their entry into and advance through the professional ranks.

Sex-Typing and the Professions

Not only have the professions been segregated by sex, but also they have been greatly affected by the even more invidious process of sex-typing. When a majority of those in a profession are of one sex, the "normative expectation" develops that this is how it *should* be (Epstein, 1970b). The model of the practitioner then takes on the personality and behavioral characteristics associated with that sex. For instance, in our study of accountants, the quality most frequently cited for success and mobility by both young and old, male and female respondents was "executive presence" (Kaufman and Fetters, 1983). This term almost perfectly matches what is called in the sociological literature the *male managerial behavioral model*—characterized by aggressiveness, decisiveness, competitiveness, and risk taking. In fact, so identified is *male* with *manager* that one writer has stated: "The good manager is aggressive, authoritative, firm and just. He is not feminine" (McGregor, 1967, p. 23). The high-status professions and the prestige specialties in our society are identified with the instrumental, rigorous, "hard-nosed" qualities identified as masculine, not with the "softer," more expressive, nurturing modes of behavior identified as feminine. Since the characteristics associated with the most valued professions are also those associated with men, women fail to meet one of the most important professional criteria: they are not men.

Research on the subject has clearly shown that traits customarily associated with femininity, and consequently with women, are not as highly valued in our society as are traits stereotypically associated with men. The belief in strong gender differences persists, although leading scholars clearly state that the overlap between the sexes on most personality and behavioral measures is extensive. Jacklin and Maccoby, for instance, in a thorough review of the subject, argue that gender differences in fear, timidity, anxiety, competitiveness, and dependence among young children remain open to debate because of insufficient or ambiguous evidence (1975). They also assert that there is little scientific support for gender differences in such areas as achievement motivation, risk taking, task persistence, or other related skills. Yet these traits are typically associated with men in our society and with the pursuit of a successful professional career (Kaufman & Richardson, 1982).

Other studies (Rosenkrantz et al., 1968; Broverman et al., 1970, 1972) have revealed a deep conviction in our society that men and women manifest different characteristics, as well as showing that there is a more positive evaluation of those characteristics ascribed to men. Perhaps their most surprising finding was that even mental-health clinicians ascribed specific traits to each sex and agreed that a normal, healthy adult more closely reflects those traits ascribed to a healthy male that it does those ascribed to a healthy female (Broverman et al., 1970). The clinicians portrayed healthy female adults as more submissive, less independent, less adventurous, less objective, more easily influenced, less aggressive, less competitive, more excitable in minor crises, more emotional generally, more conceited about their appearance, and more apt to have their feelings hurt. This childlike portrait led the authors to remark that "this constellation seems a most unusual way of describing *any* mature healthy individual" (p. 5, emphasis mine).

Such stereotypes follow women into the workplace. Even when women do the same work as men, they are not perceived as being as competent as men, and their work is not perceived to be as prestigious (England, 1992). In a fine and thorough review of the social-psychological literature on sex-related stereotypes, O'Leary (1977) notes that Feldman-Summers and Kiesler (1974) were unable to find a single occupation in which women were expected to outperform males, even in elementary-school teaching and nursing. Touhey (1974a) emphasizes that anticipating greater participation by women in high-status professions has resulted in a decline in the way both males and females perceive the prestige of those occupations. However, the converse was found when men entered female-dominated professions (Touhey, 1974b). In a study by Bass, Krussell, and Alexander (1971), 174 male managers and staff personnel perceived women as unable to supervise men and as less dependable than men. In another study of managers' perceptions of sex differences, particularly perceptions relevant to the promotion of women, Rosen and Jerdee (1978) found that male managers and administrators held uniformly more negative perceptions of women compared to men on each of four scales: aptitudes, knowledge, and skills; interest and motivation; temperament; and work habits and attitudes. Generally, women were perceived as having aptitudes, knowledge skills, and interests and motivations compatible with routine clerical roles and not managerial roles (p. 841). In this study, virtually every perceived difference between male and female employees was unfavorable to women aspiring to higher-level occupations (p. 843). In contrast, Reskin and Hartmann cite other studies that suggest that negative correlations about women supervisors are weaker among women, well-educated males, and workers with female bosses (1986).

In their study, Rosen and Jerdee (1973) found that males and females often were treated differently in their managerial roles. In a simulated situation, "supervisor" subjects promoted men more often, gave men more career development opportunities, trusted men more in handling personnel problems, and granted men leaves of absence for child-care duties less often than they did with hypothetical female counterparts. However, we need not rely on hypothetical supervisors to know that gender biases exist. Women earn less than men do in almost every occupation and within almost all specialties (*Employment and Earnings,* Jan. 1993, Table 56; England, 1992). Perhaps the best indicator that women are less valued in our society simply because they are female comes from a number of studies documenting that women possessing the *identical* qualifications and skills as men fare more poorly in obtaining professional-type jobs (Dipboye, Fromkin, and Wibac, 1975; Fidell, 1970; Shaw, 1972; Zikmund, Hitt, and Pickens, 1978; Firth, 1982).

The Fidell study (1970) was particularly eye opening for people just entering graduate school and planning for an academic career. Fidell sent one of two forms to all colleges and universities that were offering graduate degrees in psychology in 1970. Each form contained ten paragraphs describing professional characteristics of ten hypothetical psychologists. The person most closely associated with departmental hiring was asked to participate in the study by judging the "candidates" and their chances of obtaining full-time positions. Form A used masculine first names; form B, feminine first names. Except for the names and pronouns, the wording on both forms was identical. Fidell found that men received higher levels of appointments; the positions were more likely to be on tenure track; and only men were offered full professorships (pp. 1096–97).

Since the prestige professions are sex-typed, the expectations for men and women differ from the moment people make a decision to train for a career. As graduate students, women are not expected to be as dedicated, ambitious, or serious about their studies as men are. It is assumed that marriage and child rearing will eventually interrupt their studies and certainly their careers. The data suggest that such interruptions are indeed more disruptive for women than they are for men. In a reanalysis of a nationwide sample of graduate students, Feldman (1975) found that divorced men were unhappier with the graduate-student role than were single or married men, whereas divorced women among all graduate students were the happiest. He concluded that "apparently divorced men are burdened with greater responsibilities than their single or married counterparts, while divorced women have reduced their responsibilities and are thus freer to pursue the student role" (p. 227).

One fact reported in all studies on the division of labor at home among two-earner families is that employed married women spend far more time on housework than employed husbands. Pleck (1985, 1989) implies that except for the "fun" parts of child care, there has not been a major shift in the division of labor between men and women.

Indeed, professional women, like other working women, see the private sphere as still primarily a woman's responsibility. Cultural norms that reinforce the links between women, personal life, domesticity, and child rearing are deeply entrenched. One study of upper middle-class professionals found that women rated themselves lower on their performance as wives and mothers than men rated themselves as husbands and fathers. One possibility for women's lower ratings is that these professionally employed women used unemployed wives and mothers as the point of comparison for their own behavior. Interestingly, the higher the incomes of successful academic women in this study, the more work they did around the house. However, the more money their husbands made, the more frequently these women absolved their husbands from domestic responsibilities. Businesswomen in this study reported that they were happiest when their husbands' careers took precedence over their own (reported in *Boston Globe Sunday Magazine,* October 27, 1991, p. 37).

The full-time employed wife–mother bears the largest burden for managing the home and children. Her share of domestic activities is three times as great as that of her full-time employed husband (Pleck, 1982). These findings may not simply reflect a generation lag: in Komarovsky's study of Columbia University male students, even the "liberated" males in her sample expressed concern about the combination of motherhood and career for their future wives (1976). The majority of the men believed that home and child-care responsibilities were still primarily the concern of the wife–mother (p. 33). Professional careers are designed not for women with families, but rather for men who are free of family obligations. For the professional man, frequent absences from home, tardiness for dinner, and "overtime" work are not only expected but also accepted as evidence that he is a good provider and therefore a good parent and spouse. Such is not the case for the professional woman. (For an excellent discussion of some of these points, see Coser and Rokoff, 1971.)

Multiple-role conflict is but one area in which differences exist between men and women who pursue professional careers. Another difference has to do with the timing of that endeavor. Hochschild argues that age is measured against one's achievements. Getting there first is an important element of success. "If jobs are scarce and promising reputations important, who wants a 50 year old mother-of-three with a dissertation almost completed?" (1975, p. 61). Referring specifically to the academic arena, Hochschild states that "time is objectified in the academic vita which grows longer with each article and book, and not with each vegetable garden, camping trip, political meeting or child" (p. 62). A successful professional career requires early achievement and uninterrupted competition for continued success—timing based on a male pattern.

In almost every particular, professional life is oriented more toward males than toward females. Because women are expected to behave in a generally "softer" way than are men, they may be perceived as unsuited for the combative style expected from many professionals. Even smiling might be bad for women's business careers because it is interpreted by male coworkers as a sign of submission (Varro, 1982). This is substantiated by studies suggesting that the way women talk, gesture, smile, touch, sit, walk, and use space communicates their dependent and inferior status in our society. (For a comprehensive review see Frieze et al., 1978, especially Chapter 16; and Thorne et al., 1983.) Some feminists have openly challenged the "success ethic" and the values of the professional life, arguing for a more humane (if not feminine) style in the workplace. However, such changes demand a total restructuring of the attitudes and behavior now common in the professions and a redefining and revaluing of what is feminine. The incentives for such change are few, particularly in a tight economy, and, as the following section shows, change generally comes quite slowly.

Historical Review

The discouraging picture painted in the preceding discussion still represents an improvement over the past. The professions at the top of the American occupational hierarchy—medicine, law, and higher education—began as medieval guilds from which women were virtually excluded. In the thirteenth century, European medicine became firmly established as a secular science, and physicians were trained in the universities. Since females were excluded from the universities, they were denied the key resource to become professionals. However, there was little that we would recognize as science in the late medieval training. Physicians rarely saw any patients, and no experimentation of any kind was taught. Medicine was sharply differentiated from surgery; the dissection of bodies was considered sacrilegious. In contrast, women healers of the same time, who were often labeled witches, had an experimental and empirical base to their healing. "It was witches who developed an extensive understanding of bones, muscles, herbs, and drugs, while physicians were still deriving their prognoses from astrology"; in fact, "Paracelsus, considered the 'father of modern medicine', burned his text on pharmaceuticals, confessing that he had learned from the Sorceress all he knew" (Ehrenreich and English, 1973, p. 17).

The key point is that neither knowledge, techniques, nor results defined the professional. What defined the professional was access to the universities. Society barred women from practicing medicine as professionals by denying them access to university training. By the fourteenth century, the church had explicitly legitimized the professionalism of male practitioners by denouncing healing without university training as heresy. Medieval writings on the subject asserted that "if a woman dare to cure without having studied, she is a witch and must die" (Ehrenreich and English, 1973, p. 19).

The development of the American medical profession was quite different, but the results were the same—women were effectively barred from the profession. By the early nineteenth century, there were many formally trained doctors—"regular" doctors, as they called themselves. At the same time, the popular health movement and numerous other groups with new medical philosophies were establishing their own schools open to women and to blacks. Frightened by these new movements, the "regulars" established the American Medical Association in 1847, thereby asserting themselves as the only legitimate spokespersons for the medical profession. Noting that by definition a profession has authority to select its own members and to regulate their practice, Ehrenreich and English (1973) emphasize that the "regular" doctors were a formidable obstacle to women. The rare woman who did make it into a "regular" medical school faced a series of "sexist hurdles" that only the most motivated women could manage:

> First there was the continuous harassment—often lewd—by the male students. There were professors who wouldn't discuss anatomy with a lady present. There were textbooks like a well-known 1848 obstetrical text which states, "She (Woman) has a head almost too small for intellect but just big enough for love." There were respectable gynecological theories of the injurious effects of intellectual activity on the female reproductive organs. . . . Having completed her academic work, the would-be woman doctor usually found the next steps blocked. Hospitals were usually closed to women doctors, and even if they weren't, the internships were not open to women. If she did finally make it into practice, she found her brother "regulars" unwilling to refer patients to her and absolutely opposed to her membership in their medical societies. (Ehrenreich and English, 1973, p. 29)

By the early twentieth century, "irregular" schools and their students were routinely closed out of the medical profession. Tough licensing laws, requiring extended college and clinical training, sealed the doctors' monopoly on medical practice (Ehrenreich and English, 1973, p. 33).

Law, like medicine, began as a medieval guild and has been, until very recently, a male bastion. Women in law, until the last decade, have been "sex segregated in an occupational hierarchy: the lawyers and judges are almost invariably men, while the clerks, paralegal workers and secretaries who work for them are usually women" (Patterson and Engleberg, 1978, p. 277).

It was even more difficult for women to enter the legal profession than it was for them to become doctors. The first woman to be admitted to the practice of law in the United States was Belle Mansfield in 1869. Less than one year later, Myra Bradwell was refused admission to the bar in Illinois solely on the basis of her sex. In the nineteenth century, the legal profession was more highly organized and protected by government than was medicine (Brownlee and Brownlee, 1976, p. 264). Law schools did not admit women until the 1890s, and then did so only reluctantly. And after completing their studies, "even if women did achieve professional acceptance, they usually supported themselves through salaried positions, generally with insurance companies or government agencies, rather than through independent practice" (p. 289). Patterson and Engleberg note that even now women lawyers are still more likely than are men to turn to government positions. But what is more important, the authors find that when a man enters a government position, he uses it as a stepping-stone into private practice, whereas a woman tends to stay put, making it a career (p. 282).

Prior to 1920, women's admission to law schools was not critical because preparation to practice law could be done by apprenticeships. In 1920, the American Bar Association officially endorsed law school as the desired preparation for the practice of the profession. But it was not until 1972 that women were finally admitted to *all* law schools (Fossum, 1980).

The recruitment of women into the now female-dominated professions has had a different historical pattern. Shortages of cheap skilled labor—particularly during wars, recessions, and depressions--have accounted for a good deal of the recruitment of women into teaching and nursing. There were several advantages to using females as teachers. Women were available in great numbers, and they were willing to work for low wages. Moreover, this profession did not challenge the cultural ideal of women's "natural" place. Who could be more "naturally" equipped to teach children than women?

Nursing, too, began as an occupation dominated by men. But, when the Civil War created a shortage of male nurses, women entered the field in significant numbers (Brownlee and Brownlee, 1976, p. 264). The Brownlees contend that the transformation of nursing into a woman's profession did not occur until there was a "sustained entry of educated women who reduced wages below what productivity justified" (p. 264). These were, for the most part, educated women who had been closed out of the prestige professions. Ehrenreich and English, for instance, note that Dorothea Dix and Florence Nightingale did not "begin to carve out their reform careers until they were in their thirties and faced with the prospect of a long useless spinsterhood" (1973, p. 38).

In nursing, female attributes seemed more important than competence or skill; good nurses were essentially ones who looked good and possessed "character." Ehrenreich and English suggest that the "ideal lady" of the nineteenth century was simply transplanted from home to hospital.

> To the doctor, she brought the wifely virtue of absolute obedience. To the patient, she brought the selfless devotion of a mother. To the lower level hospital employee she brought the firm but kindly discipline of a household manager accustomed to dealing with servants. (Ehrenreich and English, 1973, pp. 36–37)

Nursing itself was hard labor; therefore, while the educators remained upper class, the practitioners were mostly working-class and middle-class women. When a group of English nurses proposed that nursing model itself after the medical profession, with examinations and licensing, Nightingale claimed that "nurses cannot be examined any more than mothers" (cited in Ehrenreich and English, 1973, p. 37). The occupations of nursing and teaching were extensions of women's "natural" domestic roles.

Keeping Women Down: The Subtle Art of Practicing the Professions

How can we explain women's continuing secondary status within the professions? As we have seen, the prestige professions are defined primarily in terms of men and the lives they lead. The processes that maintain this male model are usually well beyond a woman's control, however committed or dedicated she may be. No matter what her personal characteristics, a woman is often assigned the stereotypical characteristics of her sex, and despite her efforts to transcend these stereotypes, certain structural features of the professions work against her upward mobility.

The invisible barriers found in many professional organizations that appear to block the advancement opportunities of minorities and women in the public and private sectors of the economy are referred to as the "glass ceiling." The glass ceiling is often the result of a failure of professional business organizations to adhere to affirmative action programs, to monitor programs specifically established to promote women and minorities, and/or a failure to make clear the standards of performance and the resources necessary for advancement often obtained through informal mentoring.

In 1989, the Office of Federal Contract Compliance Programs of the Department of Labor interviewed nine Fortune 500 establishments as a pilot study of the glass ceiling phenomenon. Although the researchers had initially intended to study the highest levels of management within those companies, they had to shift their focus downward when they found that there were no minorities or women at the very top levels. The glass ceiling not only existed but also was lower than expected. The study cited the lack of informal mentoring as one of the single most important factors in keeping women in the lowest managerial positions. Other attitudinal and organizational practices that worked against women and minorities included the use of executive search firms that were not aware of affirmative action obligations, the failure to assign minorities and women to career-enhancing assignments, and the lack of a formal system to monitor how personnel were given consideration for develop-ment opportunities and for financial compensation by senior-level executives and corporate decision makers (Dept. of Labor, 1991, p. 5). These processes are similar to the mechanisms that operate to keep women out of the top positions in law, medicine, science, and academia.

"Interaction in professions, especially in their top echelons," Epstein points out, "is characterized by a high degree of informality, much of it within an exclusive, club-like context" (1970a, p. 968). Hughes notes that the "very word 'profession' implies a certain social and moral solidarity, a strong dependence of one colleague upon the opinions and judgments of others" (1962, p. 125). Those who bear certain characteristics (black, Jewish, female, etc.) are at an immediate disadvantage in such a collegial context. As Hughes (1945) suggested years ago, such statuses condition what is considered an "appropriate" set of characteristics for acceptance by one's peers as a professional; he describes these as "auxiliary characteristics." Such auxiliary characteristics as race, religion, ethnicity, and sex are "the bases of the colleague group's definition of its common interests, of its informal code, and of selection of those who become the inner fraternity" (p. 355). Hughes's fraternal imagery is apt; like fraternal societies, the collegial group depends on "common background, continual association and affinity of interest" (Epstein, 1970a, p. 972). Almost by definition, women and other low-status groups are exclud-ed from such brotherly associations.

Professional "standards of excellence" allegedly establish the criteria for recruitment and advancement in one's field. Excellence, however, like any other social reality, is not universally manifest, but must be defined and interpreted. As Epstein (1970a) notes, fine distinctions between good and superior performances require subtle judgments, and such judgments are rendered by one's peers. In many ways, one's acceptance into and success within the professions are contingent on one's acceptance into the informal circles.

> The professions depend on intense socialization of their members, much of it by immersion in the norms of professional culture even before entry; and later by the professionals' sensitivity to his peers. . . . Not only do contacts with professional colleagues act as a control system, they also provide the wherewithal by which the professional may become equipped to meet the highest standards of professional behavior. (Epstein, 1970a, p. 972)

Those who do not conform because they lack important "auxiliary characteristics" create dilemmas for themselves and for others. For example, the protégé system is one of the mechanisms whereby one's name and work become known in the upper echelons of one's profession. According to Epstein (1970a, 1970b) and White (1970), the men who dominate the top echelons of most professions may be reluctant to adopt female protégés. White claims that "a man . . . may believe that she is less likely to be a good gamble, a risk for him to exert himself for, or that she is financially less dependent upon a job" (p. 414). The man may also fear others' suspicion of a sexual liaison as a byproduct of such close and intense work. Although it is not unusual for a senior executive to be a mentor to a rising male star, this acceptable practice immediately becomes suspect if a young female receives it. A lack of sponsorship means a woman is more likely to be excluded from those crucial arenas where professional identity and recognition are established.

Collegial contacts are important for more than one's professional identity and acceptance into the profession. Social psychologist White (1970) interviewed women scholars at the Radcliffe Institute who had been awarded fellowships to continue their professional interests on a part-time basis while raising their families. The women thought that access to stimulating colleagues was as important as was the opportunity to be intellectually engaged in a project. White concluded that "appraisals of their work by others, coupled with acceptance and recognition by people whose professional opinions were relevant and appropriate, made a significant difference in determining whether a woman felt like a professional, and whether she in turn had a strong sense of commitment to future work" (p. 413). Furthermore, she suggests that "challenging interaction with other professionals is frequently as necessary to creative work as is the opportunity for solitude and thought" (p. 414).

Collegial contacts are also crucial for survival.

> There are elaborate social systems in all parts of academic and business life, and purely technical training is rarely enough. The aspiring young scientist must be knowledgeable about many aspects of institutions, journals, professional meetings, methods of obtaining source materials, and funding grant applications. Knowing how to command these technical and institutional facilities requires numerous skills, many unanticipated by the young student. . . . This is the kind of learning we speak of as "caught," and not taught, and it is a valued by-product of acceptance and challenging association with other professionals. (White, 1970, p. 414)

If women are excluded from male networks, they remain not only marginal but also invisible when such important professional decisions as selection for promotion, tenure, research grants, coeditorships, summer teaching, and departmental privileges are under consideration (Hughes, 1973). My research (Kaufman, 1978) suggests that women academicians are less likely than are men to include people of higher rank in their collegial networks and are more likely to claim their colleague-friends as professionally unimportant to their careers.

It is within the collegial arena that judgments are made and standards are set. It is within the collegial arena that the ongoing dynamics of professional life are carried out. If women are denied access to this arena (even if they have formed their own networks), they are left out of the power centers of their professions. Moreover, their exclusion from male networks prevents the breakdown of myths about professional women. If women and men operate in different networks, gender-role stereotypes remain unchallenged (Kaufman and Richardson, 1982).

Conclusion

How real are women's most recent gains in the professions? Despite their increasing numbers in male-dominated professions, women still constitute a disproportionately small percentage of those practicing the professions. Moreover, even in female-dominated professions, women are second to men in that their positions tend to carry less prestige.

Perhaps the most difficult task in assessing women's gains is measuring the "cost" of success. Even when women have been able to achieve high-pay, high-prestige positions within the professions, the costs for such success have been high. Many have had to give up or delay marriage, family, and significant relationships. Those who have not given up family have had to add to their demanding career commitments the major responsibilities of managing home and child-care tasks. In our society, both families and professional careers are "greedy" institutions. Until changes occur, women who want both can expect to face conflicting and overwhelming demands. Moreover, until we change the normative expectations about a woman's place both within the professions and within the home, so that both demands and rewards are equal to those of men, we must continue to question the gains women have made.

REFERENCES

American Bar Association. Fall 1992. *A Review of Legal Education in U.S.* American Bar Association, Section of Legal Education, Indianapolis, Indiana.
Association of American Medical Colleges. 1982. *Women in Medicine Statistics.* Washington, D.C.: Association of American Medical Colleges.
Association of American Medical Colleges. 1988. *Women in Medicine Statistics.* Washington, D.C.: Association of American Medical Colleges.
Association of American Medical Colleges. June 1992. *Women in Medicine Statistics.* Washington, D.C.
Bass, B. M., Krussell, J., and Alexander, R. A. 1971. "Male Managers' Attitudes Toward Working Women." *American Behavioral Scientist* 15:77–83.

Bowman, M., and Gross, M. 1986. "Overview of Research on Women in Medicine—Issues for Public Policymakers." *Public Health Reports* 101 (September–October):513–21.

Broverman, I. K., Broverman, D. M., Clarkson, F. E., Rosenkrantz, P. S., and Vogel, S. R. 1970. "Sex Role Stereotypes and Clinical Judgments of Mental Health." *Journal of Consulting and Clinical Psychology* 34:1–7.

Broverman, I. K., Vogel, S. R., Broverman, D. M., Clarkson, F. E., and Rosenkrantz, P. S. 1972 "Sex Role Stereotypes: A Current Appraisal." *Journal of Social Issues* 28(3):59–78.

Brownlee, W. E., and Brownlee, M. 1976. *Women in the American Economy: A Documentary History 1675–1929.* New Haven, Conn.: Yale University Press.

Bulletin. August 1987. Office of Education Research and Improvement. U.S. Department of Education. Center for Education Statistics.

Butter, I., Carpenter, E., Kay, B., and Simmons, R. 1987. "Gender Hierarchies in the Health Labor Force." *International Journal of Health Services* 17(I):133–49.

Coser, R., and Rokoff, G. 1971. "Women in the Occupational World: Social Disruption and Conflict." *Social Problems* 18(4):535–52.

Department of Labor Library Information Brief No. 1. May 1991. *From the Glass Slipper to the Glass Ceiling: Women's Emergence in the Marketplace.* Department of Labor Library, Washington, D.C.

Dipboye, R. L., Fromkin, H. L., and Wibac, K. 1975. "Relative Importance of Applicant's Sex, Attractiveness, and Scholastic Standing in Evaluation of Job Applicant Resumes." *Journal of Applied Psychology* 60(February):39–43.

Ehrenreich, Barbara, and English, Dierdre. 1973. *Witches, Midwives, and Nurses: A History of Women Healers.* Old Westbury, N.Y.: Feminist Press.

Employment and Earnings. January 1993. Annual 1992 Averages, Household Data, Table 22, "Employed Civilians by Detailed Occupation, Sex, Race and Hispanic Origin." Washington, D.C.: U.S. Bureau of Labor Statistics.

England, Paula. 1992. *Comparable Worth.* New York: Aldine De Gruyter.

Epstein, Cynthia. 1970a. "Encountering the Male Establishment: Sex-Status Limits on Women's Careers in the Professions." *American Journal of Sociology* 75(6):965–82.

Epstein, C. 1970b. *Woman's Place: Options and Limits in Professional Careers.* Berkeley: University of California Press.

Epstein, C. 1980. "The New Women and the Old Establishment." *Sociology of Work and Occupations* 7(3):291–316.

Epstein, C. 1981. *Women in Law.* New York: Basic Books.

Epstein, Cynthia Fuchs. 1988. *Deceptive Distinctions.* New Haven, Conn.: Yale University Press and Russell Sage Foundation.

Etzioni, A., ed. 1969. *The Semi-Professions and Their Organizations.* New York: Free Press.

Feldman, S. 1975. "Impediment or Stimulant? Marital Status and Graduate Education." In *Changing Women in a Changing Society,* ed. Joan Huber. Chicago: University of Chicago Press.

Feldman-Summers, S., and Kiesler, S. B. 1974. "Those Who Are Number Two Try Harder: The Effects of Sex on Attributions of Causality." *Journal of Personality and Social Psychology* 30(6):846–55.

Fidell, Linda. 1970. "Empirical Verification of Sex Discrimination in Hiring Practices in Psychology." *American Psychologist* 25(12):1094–98.

Firth, M. 1982. "Sex Discrimination in Job Opportunities for Women." *Sex Roles* 8(8):891–901.

Fossum, Donna. 1980. "Women Law Professors." *American Bar Foundation Research Journal* 4(Fall):906–14.

Frieze, I. H., Parsons, J., Johnson, P., Ruble, D., and Zellman, G. 1978. *Women and Sex Roles.* New York: W. W. Norton and Co.

Hochschild, A. R. 1975. "Inside the Clockwork of Male Careers." In *Women and the Power to Change,* ed. F. Howe. New York: McGraw-Hill Book Co.

Hodson, Randy, and Teresa Sullivan. 1990. *The Social Organization of Work.* Belmont, Calif.: Wadsworth Publishing Co.

Hughes, E. 1945. "Dilemmas and Contradiction of Status." *American Journal of Sociology* 50:353–59.

Hughes, E. 1962. "What Other?" In *Behavior and Social Processes,* ed. A. Rose, 23–28. Boston: Houghton Mifflin Co.

Hughes, Helen. 1973. *The Status of Women in Sociology, 1968–72.* Washington, D.C.: American Sociological Association.

Jacklin, C., and Maccoby, E. 1975. "Sex Differences and Their Implications for Management." In *Bringing Women into Management,* ed. F. Gordon and M. Strober. New York: McGraw-Hill Book Co.

Kanter, Rosabeth. 1977. *Men and Women of the Corporation.* New York: Basic.

Kaufman, D. 1978. "Associational Ties in Academe: Some Male and Female Differences." *Sex Roles* 4(1):9–21.

Kaufman, Debra, and Michael Fetters. 1980. "Work Motivation and Job Values Among Professional Men and Women: A New Accounting." *Journal of Vocational Behavior* 17:251–62.

Kaufman, D., and Fetters, M. 1983. "The Executive Suite: Are Women Perceived as Ready for the Managerial Climb?" *Journal of Business Ethics* 2:203–12.

Kaufman, D., and Richardson, B. 1982. *Achievement and Women: Challenging the Assumptions.* New York: Free Press.

Komarovsky, M. 1976. *Dilemmas of Masculinity.* New York: W. W. Norton and Co.

Levine, Linda. 1991. "The 'Glass Ceiling': Access of Women and Minorities to Management Positions." Congressional Research Service, number 91-623E. Library of Congress (August 19).

Lorber, J. 1984. *Women Physicians: Careers, Status and Power.* New York: Tavistock.

McGregor, D. 1967. *The Professional Manager.* New York: McGraw-Hill Book Co.

Mincer, J., and Polachek, S. 1974. "Family Investments in Human Capital: Earnings of Women." *Journal of Political Economy* 82(2, part II):S76–108.

National Center for Educational Statistics. 1992. *Digest of Education Statistics.* U.S. Department of Education, Office of Educational Research and Improvement. Washington, D.C.: U.S. Government Printing Office.

National Science Foundation. 1990. *Women and Minorities in Science and Engineering.* Washington, D.C.: Division of Science Resources Studies, Surveys and Analysis Section.

O'Leary, Virginia. 1977. *Toward an Understanding of Women.* Monterey, Calif.: Brooks/Cole Publishing Co.

Oppenheimer, V. K. 1970. *The Female Labor Force in the U.S.: Demographic and Economic Factors Governing Its Growth and Changing Composition.* University of California at Berkeley Population Monographs, no. 5. Berkeley: University of California.

Patterson, M., and Engleberg, L. 1978. "Women in Male-Dominated Professions." In *Women Working,* ed. A. Stromberg and S. Harkess, 201–25. Palo Alto, Calif.: Mayfield Publishing Co.

Pleck, J. 1982. "The Work-Family Role System." In *Women and Work,* ed. R. Kahn-Hut, A. Daniels, and R. Colvard, 101–10. New York: Oxford University Press.

Pleck, Joseph. 1985. *Working Wives/Working Husbands.* Beverly Hills, Calif.: Sage.

Pleck, Joseph. 1989. *Family Supportive Employer Policies and Men's Participation.* Washington, D.C.: U.S. Government Printing Office, U.S. Department of Labor, Women's Bureau.

Professional Women and Minorities: A Manpower Data Resource Service. 9th ed. March 1991. Washington, D.C.: Commission on Professionals in Science and Technology.

Reskin, B., and Hartmann, H. (eds.). 1986. *Women's Work, Men's Work.* Washington, D.C.: National Academy of Science.

Ritzer, G. 1972. *Man and His Work, Conflict and Change.* New York: Appleton-Century-Crofts.

Rosen, B., and Jerdee, T. 1973. "The Influence of Sex-Role Stereotypes on Evaluations of Male and Female Supervisory Behavior." *Journal of Applied Psychology* 57(1):185–218.

Rosen, B., and Jerdee, T. 1978. "Perceived Sex Differences in Managerially Relevant Characteristics." *Sex Roles* 4(6):837–43.

Rosenkrantz, P. S., Vogel, S. R., Bee, H., Broverman, I. K., and Broverman, D. M. 1968. "Sex-Role Stereotypes and Self-Concepts in College Students." *Journal of Consulting and Clinical Psychology* 32(3):287–95.

Shaw, E. A. 1972. "Differential Impact of Negative Stereotyping in Employee Selection." *Personnel Psychology* 25(2):333–38.

Sokoloff, N. 1986. "A Profile of the General Labor Force and the Professions: A Review of the Aggregate Gender and Race Segregation Literature." Paper presented at the American Sociological Association, New York, August 1986.

Theodore, A. 1986. *The Campus Troublemakers: Academic Women in Protest.* Houston, Tex.: Cap and Gown Press.

Thorne, Barrie, Kramarae, Cheris, and Henley, Nancy (eds.). 1983. *Language, Gender and Society.* Rowley, Mass.: Newbury House.

Touhey, J. C. 1974a. "Effects of Additional Men on Prestige and Desirability of Occupations Typically Performed by Women." *Journal of Applied Social Psychology* 4(4):330–35.

Touhey, J. C. 1974b. "Effects of Additional Women Professionals on Ratings of Occupational Prestige and Desirability." *Journal of Personality and Social Psychology* 29(1):86–89.

U.S. Bureau of Labor Statistics. 1980. *Perspectives on Working Women: A Databook.* Bulletin 2080, table 11, p. 10. Washington, D.C.: U.S. Government Printing Office.

U.S. Department of Labor. *A Report on the Glass Ceiling Initiative.* Washington, D.C.: U.S. Government Printing Office.

Varro, B. 1982. "To Smile or Not to Smile? That Is the Question." *Boston Globe,* Aug. 11, pp. 25, 27.

Vetter, B., and Babco, E. 1987. *Professional Women and Minorities.* 7th ed. Washington, D.C.: Commission on Professions in Science and Technology.

White, M. 1970. "Psychological and Social Barriers to Women in Science." *Science* 170(3956):413–16.

Zikmund, W. G., Hitt, M. A., and Pickens, B. A. 1978. "Influence of Sex and Scholastic Performance on Reactions to Job Applicant Resumes." *Journal of Applied Psychology* 63(2):252–54.

Zincone, L. H., Jr., and Close, F. A. 1978. "Sex Discrimination in a Paramedical Profession." *Industrial and Labor Relations Review* 32(1):74–85.

Beauty Is the Beast: Psychological Effects of the Pursuit of the Perfect Female Body

Elayne A. Saltzberg and Joan C. Chrisler

AMBROSE BIERCE (1958) once wrote, "To men a man is but a mind. Who cares what face he carries or what he wears? But woman's body is the woman." Despite the societal changes achieved since Bierce's time, his statement remains true. Since the height of the feminist movement in the early 1970s, women have spent more money than ever before on products and treatments designed to make them beautiful. Cosmetic sales have increased annually to reach $18 billion in 1987 ("Ignoring the economy . . . ," 1989), sales of women's clothing averaged $103 billion per month in 1990 (personal communication, U.S. Bureau of Economic Analysis, 1992), dieting has become a $30-billion-per-year industry (Stoffel, 1989), and women spent $1.2 billion on cosmetic surgery in 1990 (personal communication, American Society of Plastic and Reconstructive Surgeons, 1992). The importance of beauty has apparently increased even as women are reaching for personal freedoms and economic rights undreamed of by our grandmothers. The emphasis on beauty may be a way to hold onto a feminine image while shedding feminine roles.

Attractiveness is prerequisite for femininity but not for masculinity (Freedman, 1986). The word *beauty* always refers to the female body. Attractive male bodies are described as "handsome," a word derived from "hand" that refers as much to action as appearance (Freedman, 1986). Qualities of achievement and strength accompany the term *handsome;* such attributes are rarely employed in the description of attractive women and certainly do not accompany the term *beauty,* which refers only to a decorative quality. Men are instrumental; women are ornamental.

Beauty is a most elusive commodity. Ideas of what is beautiful vary across cultures and change over time (Fallon, 1990). Beauty cannot be quantified or objectively measured; it is the result of the judgments of others. The concept is difficult to define, as it is equated with different, sometimes contradictory, ideas. When people are asked to define beauty, they tend to mention abstract, personal qualities rather than external, quantifiable ones (Freedman, 1986; Hatfield & Sprecher, 1986). The beholder's perceptions and cognitions influence the degree of attractiveness at least as much as do the qualities of the beheld.

Because beauty is an ideal, an absolute, such as truth and goodness, the pursuit of it does not require justification (Herman & Polivy, 1983). An ideal,

The authors thank Jo Freeman, Sue Wilkinson, and Paulette Leonard for their helpful comments on an earlier version of this paper and Barbara Weber for locating the business and industry statistics.

by definition, can be met by only a minority of those who strive for it. If too many women are able to meet the beauty standards of a particular time and place, then those standards must change in order to maintain their extraordinary nature. The value of beauty standards depends on their being special and unusual and is one of the reasons why the ideal changes over time. When images of beauty change, female bodies are expected to change, too. Different aspects of the female body and varying images of each body part are modified to meet the constantly fluctuating ideal (Freedman, 1986). The ideal is always that which is most difficult to achieve and most unnatural in a given time period. Because these ideals are nearly impossible to achieve, failure and disappointment are inevitable (Freedman, 1988).

Although people have been decorating their bodies since prehistoric times, the Chinese may have been the first to develop the concept that the female body can and should be altered from its natural state. The practice of foot binding clearly illustrates the objectification of parts of the female body as well as the demands placed on women to conform to beauty ideals. The custom called for the binding of the feet of five-year-old girls so that as they grew, their toes became permanently twisted under their arches and would actually shrink in size. The big toe remained untouched. The more tightly bound the feet, the more petite they became and the more attractive they were considered to be (Freedman, 1986; Hatfield & Sprecher, 1986; Lakoff & Scherr, 1984). The painful custom of foot binding finally ended in the twentieth century after women had endured over one thousand years of torture for beauty's sake (Brain, 1979).

In the sixteenth century, European women bound themselves into corsets of whalebone and hardened canvas. A piece of metal or wood ran down the front to flatten the breasts and abdomen. This garment made it impossible to bend at the waist and difficult to breathe. A farthingale, which was typically worn over the corset, held women's skirts out from their bodies. It consisted of bent wood held together with tapes and made such simple activities as sitting nearly impossible. Queen Catherine of France introduced waist binding with a tortuous invention consisting of iron bands that minimized the size of the waist to the ideal measurement of thirteen inches (Baker, 1984). In the seventeenth century, the waist was still laced, but breasts were once again stylish, and fashions were designed to enhance them. Ample breasts, hips, and buttocks became the beauty ideal, perhaps paralleling a generally warmer attitude toward family life (Rosenblatt & Stencel, 1982). A white pallor was also popular at that time, probably as an indication that the woman was so affluent that she did not need to work outdoors, where the sun might darken her skin. Ceruse, a white lead-based paint now known to be toxic, was used to accentuate the pallor.

Tight corsets came back into vogue in Europe and North America in the mid-nineteenth century, and many women were willing to run the risk of developing serious health problems in order to wear them. The tight lacing often led to pulmonary disease and internal organ damage. American women disregarded the advice of their physicians, who spoke against the use of corsets because of their potential to displace internal organs. Fainting, or "the vapors," was the result of wearing such tightly laced clothing that normal breathing became impossible. Even the clergy sermonized against corsets; miscarriages were known to result in pregnant women who insisted on lacing themselves up too tightly. In the late nineteenth century, the beauty ideal required a tiny waist and full hips and bustline. Paradoxically, women would go on diets to gain weight while, at the same time, trying to achieve a smaller waistline. Some women were reported to have had their lower ribs removed so that their waists could be more tightly laced (Brain, 1979).

In the twentieth century, the ideal female body has changed several times, and American women have struggled to change along with it. In the 1920s, the ideal had slender legs and hips, small breasts, and bobbed hair and was physically and socially active. Women removed the stuffing from their bodices and bound their breasts[1] to appear young and boyish. In the 1940s and 1950s, the ideal returned to the hourglass shape. Marilyn Monroe was considered the epitome of the voluptuous and fleshy yet naive and childlike ideal. In the 1960s, the ideal had a youthful, thin, lean body and long, straight hair. American women dieted relentlessly in an attempt to emulate the tall, thin, teenage model Twiggy, who personified the 1960s' beauty ideal. Even pregnant women were on diets in response to their doctors' orders not to gain more than twenty pounds, advice physicians later rejected as unsafe (Fallon, 1990). Menopausal women begged their physicians to prescribe hormone replacement therapy, which was rumored to prevent wrinkles and keep the body youthful, and were willing to run any health risk to preserve their appearance (Chrisler, Torrey, & Matthes, 1989). In the 1970s, a thin, tan, sensuous look was "in." The 1980s' beauty ideal remained slim but required a more muscular, toned, and physically fit body. In recent decades the beauty ideal has combined such opposite traits as erotic sophistication with naive innocence, delicate grace with muscular athleticism (Freedman, 1988), and thin bodies with large breasts. The pressure to cope with such conflicting demands and to keep up with the continual changes in the ideal female body is highly stressful (Freedman, 1988) and has resulted in a large majority of American women with negative body images (Dworkin & Kerr, 1987; Rosen, Saltzberg, & Srebnik, 1989). Women's insecurity about their looks has made it easy to convince them that small breasts are a "disease" that require surgical intervention. The sophisticated woman of the 1990s who is willing to accept the significant health risks of breast implants in order to mold her body to fit the beauty ideal has not progressed far beyond her sisters who bound their feet and waists.

The value of beauty depends in part on the high costs of achieving it. Such costs may be physical, temporal, economic, or psychological. Physical costs include the pain of ancient beauty rituals such as foot binding, tatooing, and nose and ear piercing as well as more modern rituals such as wearing pointy-toed, high-heeled shoes, tight jeans, and sleeping with one's hair in curlers. Side effects of beauty rituals have often been disastrous for women's health. Tatooing and ear piercing with unsanitary instruments have led to serious, sometimes fatal, infections. Many women have been poisoned by toxic chemicals in cosmetics (e.g., ceruse, arsenic, benzene, and petroleum) and have died from the use of unsafe diet products such as rainbow pills and liquid protein (Schwartz, 1986). The beauty-related disorders anorexia nervosa and bulimia have multiple negative health effects, and side effects of plastic surgery include hemorrhages, scars, and nerve damage. Silicone implants have resulted in breast cancer, autoimmune disease, and the formation of thick scar tissue.

Physical costs of dieting include a constant feeling of hunger that leads to emotional changes, such as irritability; in cases of very low caloric intake, dieters can experience difficulty concentrating, confusion, and even reduced cognitive capacity. The only growing group of smokers in the United States are young women, many of whom report that they smoke to curb their appetites (Sorensen & Pechacek, 1987). High heels cause lower back pain and lead to a variety of podiatric disorders. Furthermore, fashion trends have increased women's vulnerability in a variety of ways; long hair and dangling earrings have gotten caught in machinery and entangled in clothing and led to injury. High heels and tight skirts prevent women from running from danger. The *New York Times* fashion reporter Bernadine Morris was alarmed to see in Pierre Cardin's 1988 summer fashion show tight wraps that prevented the models from moving their arms (Morris, 1988).

Attaining the beauty ideal requires a lot of money. Expensive cosmetics (e.g., makeup, moisturizers, and hair dyes and straighteners) are among the most popular and are thought to be the most effective, even though their ingredients cost the same (and sometimes are the same) as those in less expensive products (Lakoff & Scherr, 1984). Health spas have become fashionable again as vacation spots for the rich and famous, and everyone wants to wear expensive clothing with designer labels. Plastic surgery has become so accepted and so common that, although it's quite expensive, surgeons advertise their services on television. Surgery is currently performed that can reduce the size of lips, ear lobes, noses, buttocks, thighs, abdomens, and breasts; rebuild a face; remove wrinkles; and add "padding" to almost any body part. Not surprisingly, most plastic surgery patients are women (Hamburger, 1988).

Beauty rituals are time-consuming activities. Jokes about how long women take to get ready for a date are based on the additional tasks women do when getting dressed. It takes time to pluck eyebrows, shave legs, manicure nails, apply makeup, and arrange hair. Women's clothing is more complicated than men's, and many more accessories are used. Although all women know that the "transformation from female to feminine is artificial" (Chapkis, 1986, p. 5), we conspire to hide the amount of time and effort it takes, perhaps out of fear that other women don't need as much time as we do to appear beautiful. A lot of work goes into looking like a "natural" beauty, but that work is not acknowledged by popular culture, and the tools of the trade are kept out of view. Men's grooming rituals are fewer, take less time, and need not be hidden away. Scenes of men shaving have often been seen on television and in movies and have even been painted by Norman Rockwell. Wendy Chapkis (1986) challenges her readers to "imagine a similar cultural celebration of a woman plucking her eyebrows, shaving her armpits, or waxing her upper lip" (p. 6). Such a scene would be shocking and would remove the aura of mystery that surrounds beautiful women.

Psychological effects of the pursuit of the perfect female body include unhappiness, confusion, misery, and insecurity. Women often believe that if only they had perfect looks, their lives would be perfectly happy; they blame their unhappiness on their bodies. American women have the most negative body image of any culture studied by the Kinsey Institute (Faludi, 1991). Dissatisfaction with their bodies is very common among adolescent girls (Adams & Crossman, 1978; Clifford, 1971; Freedman, 1984), and older women believe that the only way to remain attractive is to prevent the development of any signs of aging. Obsessive concern about body shape and weight have become so common among American women of all ages that they now constitute the norm (Rodin, Silberstein, & Streigel-Moore, 1985). The majority of women in the United States are dieting at any given time. For them, being female means feeling fat and inadequate and living with chronic low self-esteem (Rodin, et al, 1985). Ask any woman what she would like to change about her body and she'll answer immediately. Ask her what she likes about her body and she'll have difficulty responding.

Those women who do succeed in matching the ideal thinness expected by modern beauty standards usually do so by exercising frenetically and compulsively, implementing severely restrictive and nutritionally deficient diets, developing bizarre eating habits, and using continuous self-degradation and self-denial. Dieting has become a "cultural requirement" for women (Herman & Polivy, 1983) because the ideal female body has become progressively thinner at the same time that the average female body has become progressively heavier. This cultural requirement remains in place despite the fact that physiology works against weight loss to such an extent that 98 percent of diets fail (Chrisler, 1989; Fitzgerald, 1981). In fact, it is more likely for someone to fully recover from cancer than for an obese person to lose a significant amount of weight and maintain that loss for five years (Brownell, 1982). Yet a recent study (Davies & Furnham, 1986) found that young women rate borderline anorexic bodies as very attractive. Thus, even the thinnest women find it nearly impossible to meet and maintain the beauty ideal.

The social pressure for thinness can be directly linked to the increasing incidence of anorexia nervosa and bulimia among women (Brumberg, 1988; Caskey, 1986). There are presently at least one million Americans with anorexia nervosa, and 95 percent of them are women. Between sixty thousand and 150,000 of them will die as a result of their obsession (Schwartz, 1986). Although cases of anorexia nervosa have been reported in the medical literature for hundreds of years (Bell, 1985), it was considered to be a rare disorder until the 1970s. Today's anorexics are also thinner than they were in the past (Brumberg, 1988). It is estimated that at least seven million American women will experience symptoms of bulimia at some point in their lives (Hatfield & Sprecher, 1986). A recent study (Hall & Cohn, 1988) found that 25 to 33 percent of female first-year college students were using vomiting after meals as a method of weight control. An accurate estimate of the number of women who are caught in the binge-purge cycle is difficult because women with bulimia are generally secretive about their behavior and the physical signs of bulimia are not nearly as obvious as those of anorexia nervosa.

Exercise has become for many women another manifestation of their body dissatisfaction. Studies have found that most men who exercise regularly do so to build body mass and to increase cardiovascular fitness; most women who exercise do so to lose weight and to change the shape of their bodies in order to increase their attractiveness (Garner, Rockert, Olmstead, Johnson, &

Coscina, 1985; Saltzberg, 1990). Exercise has lost its status as a pleasurable activity and become yet another way for women to manipulate their bodies, another vehicle for narcissistic self-torture. Reports of the number of women exercising compulsively are increasing and may become as widespread as compulsive calorie counting and the compulsive eating habits of anorexics and bulimics.

Beauty ideals are created and maintained by society's elite. Racism, class prejudice, and rejection of the disabled are clearly reflected (Chapkis, 1986) in current American beauty standards. For example, women from lower socioeconomic groups typically weigh more than women in higher socio-economic groups (Moore, Stunkard, & Srole, 1962); they are thus excluded by popular agreement from being considered beautiful. The high costs of chic clothing, cosmetics, tanning salons, skin and hair treatments, weight loss programs, and plastic surgery prevent most American women from access to the tools necessary to approach the ideal. Furthermore, the beauty standard idealizes Caucasian features and devalues those of other races (Lewis, 1977; Miller, 1969). In recent years, Asian American and African-American women have sought facial surgery in order to come closer to the beauty ideal (Faludi, 1991), and psychotherapists have noted increased reports from their black women clients of guilt, shame, anger, and resentment about skin color, hair texture, facial features, and body size and shape (Greene, 1992; Neal & Wilson, 1989; Okazawa-Rey, Robinson, & Ward, 1987). Obviously, women with visible disabilities will never be judged to have achieved "perfection." Whoopi Goldberg's routine about the black teenager who wrapped a towel around her head to pretend it was long, blonde hair and Alice Walker's (1990) essay about her psychological adjustment after the eye injury that resulted in the development of "hideous" scar tissue provide poignant examples of the pain women experience when they cannot meet beauty standards.

The inordinate emphasis on women's external selves makes it difficult for us to appreciate our own internal selves (Kano, 1985). The constant struggle to meet the beauty ideal leads to high stress and chronic anxiety. Failure to meet the beauty ideal leads to feelings of frustration, low self-worth, and inadequacy in women whose sense of self is based on their physical appearance. The intensity of the drive to increase attractiveness may also contribute to the high rate of depression among women.[2]

Insecurity is common even among beautiful women, and studies show that they are as likely as their plain sisters to be unhappy about their looks (Freedman, 1988). Beautiful women are all too aware of the fleeting nature of their beauty; the effects of aging must be constantly monitored, and these women worry that the beauty ideal they've tried so hard to match may change without warning. When such women lose their beauty due to illness or accidents, they often become depressed and are likely to have difficulty functioning in society and to believe that their entire identity has been threatened.

Given the high costs of striving to be beautiful, why do women attempt it? Attractiveness greatly affects first impressions and later interpersonal relationships. In a classic study titled "What Is Beautiful Is Good," psychologists Kenneth Dion, Ellen Berscheid, and Elaine Hatfield (Dion, Berscheid, &

Walster, 1972) asked college students to rate photographs of strangers on a variety of personal characteristics. Those who were judged to be attractive were also more likely to be rated intelligent, kind, happy, flexible, interesting, confident, sexy, assertive, strong, outgoing, friendly, poised, modest, candid, and successful than those judged unattractive. Teachers rate attractive children more highly on a variety of positive characteristics including IQ and sociability, and attractive babies are cuddled and kissed more often than unattractive babies (Berscheid & Walster, 1974). Attractive people receive more lenient punishment for social transgressions (Dion, 1972; Landy & Aronson, 1969), and attractive women are more often sought out in social situations (Walster, Aronson, Abrahams, & Rottman, 1966; Reis, Nezlek, & Wheeler, 1980).

Furthermore, because unattractive people are more harshly punished for social transgressions and are less often sought after social partners, failure to work toward the beauty ideal can result in real consequences. Television newswoman Christine Craft made the news herself when she was fired for being too old and too unattractive. Street harassers put women "in their place" by commenting loudly on their beauty or lack of it. Beauty norms limit the opportunities of women who can't or won't meet them. Obese women, for example, have experienced discrimination in a number of instances including hiring and promotion (Larkin & Pines, 1979; Rothblum, Miller, & Gorbutt, 1988) and college admissions (Canning & Mayer, 1966). Obese people even have a harder time finding a place to live; Lambros Karris (1977) found that landlords are less likely to rent to obese people. Even physicians view their obese patients negatively (Maddox & Liederman, 1969).

There is considerable evidence that women's attractiveness is judged more harshly than men's. Christine Craft was fired, yet David Brinkley and Willard Scott continue to work on major television news shows; their abilities are not thought to be affected by age or attractiveness. Several studies (Adams & Huston, 1975; Berman, O'Nan, & Floyd, 1981; Deutsch, Zalenski, & Clark, 1986; Wernick & Manaster, 1984) that asked participants to rate the attractiveness of photographs of people of varying ages found that although attractiveness ratings of both men and women decline with age, the rate of decline for women was greater. In one study (Deutsch, Zalenski, & Clark, 1986), participants were asked to rate the photographs for femininity and masculinity as well as attractiveness. The researchers found that both the attractiveness and femininity ratings of the female photographs diminished with age; the masculinity ratings were unaffected by the age or attractiveness of the photographs. Women are acutely aware of the double standard of attractiveness. At all ages women are more concerned than men about weight and physical appearance and have lower appearance self-esteem; women who define themselves as feminine are the most concerned about their appearance and have the lowest self-esteem (Pliner, Chaiken, & Flett, 1990). In fact, women are so concerned about their body size that they typically overestimate it. Women who overestimate their size feel worse about themselves, whereas men's self-esteem is unrelated to their body size estimates (Thompson, 1986). In a review of research on the stigma of obesity, Esther Rothblum (1992) concluded that the dieting industry, combined with Western attitudes toward weight and attractiveness, causes more pain and problems for women than for men.

Thus, the emphasis on beauty has political as well as psychological consequences for women, as it results in oppression and disempowerment. It is important for women to examine the effects that the pursuit of the perfect female body has had on their lives, challenge their beliefs, and take a stand against continued enslavement to the elusive beauty ideal. Women would then be able to live life more freely and experience the world more genuinely. Each woman must decide for herself what beauty really is and the extent to which she is willing to go to look attractive. Only a more diverse view of beauty and a widespread rebellion against fashion extremes will save us from further physical and psychological tolls.

Imagine an American society where the quality and meaning of life for women are not dependent on the silence of bodily shame. Imagine a society where bodies are decorated for fun and to express creativity rather than for self-control and self-worth. Imagine what would happen if the world's women released and liberated all of the energy that had been absorbed in the beautification process. The result might be the positive, affirming, healthy version of a nuclear explosion!

REFERENCES

Adams, Gerald R., & Crossman, Sharyn M. (1978). *Physical attractiveness: A cultural imperative.* New York: Libra.

Adams, Gerald R., & Huston, Ted L. (1975). Social perception of middle-aged persons varying in physical attractiveness. *Developmental Psychology, 11,* 657–58.

Baker, Nancy C. (1984). *The beauty trap: Exploring woman's greatest obsession.* New York: Franklin Watts.

Bell, Rudolph M. (1985). *Holy anorexia.* Chicago: University of Chicago Press.

Berman, Phyllis W., O'Nan, Barbara A., & Floyd, Wayne. (1981). The double standard of aging and the social situation: Judgments of attractiveness of the middle-aged woman. *Sex Roles, 7,* 87–96.

Berscheid, Ellen, & Walster, Elaine. (1974). Physical attractiveness. *Advances in Experimental Social Psychology, 7,* 158–215.

Bierce, Ambrose. (1958). *The devil's dictionary.* New York: Dover.

Brain, R. (1979). *The decorated body.* New York: Harper & Row.

Brownell, Kelly. (1982). Obesity: Understanding and treating a serious, prevalent, and refractory disorder. *Journal of Consulting and Clinical Psychology, 55,* 889–97.

Brumberg, Joan J. (1988). *Fasting girls.* Cambridge, MA: Harvard University Press.

Canning, H., & Mayer, J. (1966). Obesity: An influence on high school performance. *Journal of Clinical Nutrition, 20,* 352–54.

Caskey, Noelle. (1986). Interpreting anorexia nervosa. In Susan R. Suleiman (Ed.), *The female body in western culture* (pp. 175–89). Cambridge, MA: Harvard University Press.

Chapkis, Wendy. (1986). *Beauty secrets: Women and the politics of appearance.* Boston: South End Press.

Chrisler, Joan C. (1989). Should feminist therapists do weight loss counseling? *Women & Therapy, 8*(3), 31–37.

Chrisler, Joan C., Torrey, Jane W., & Matthes, Michelle. (1989, June). *Brittle bones and sagging breasts, loss of femininity and loss of sanity: The media describe the menopause.* Paper presented at the meeting of the Society for Menstrual Cycle Research, Salt Lake City, UT.

Clifford, Edward. (1971). Body satisfaction in adolescence. *Perceptual and Motor Skills, 33,* 119–25.

Davies, Elizabeth, & Furnham, Adrian. (1986). The dieting and body shape concerns of adolescent females. *Child Psychology and Psychiatry, 27,* 417–28.

Deutsch, Francine M., Zalenski, Carla M., & Clark, Mary E. (1986). Is there a double standard of aging? *Journal of Applied Social Psychology, 16,* 771–85.

Dion, Kenneth K. (1972). Physical attractiveness and evaluation of children's transgressions. *Journal of Personality and Social Psychology, 24,* 285–90.

Dion, Kenneth, Berscheid, Ellen, & Walster [Hatfield], Elaine. (1972). What is beautiful is good. *Journal of Personality and Social Psychology, 24,* 285–90.

Dworkin, Sari H., & Kerr, Barbara A. (1987). Comparison of interventions for women experiencing body image problems. *Journal of Consulting and Clinical Psychology, 34,* 136–40.

Fallon, April. (1990). Culture in the mirror: Sociocultural determinants of body image. In Thomas Cash & Thomas Pruzinsky (Eds.), *Body images: Development, deviance, and change* (pp. 80–109). New York: Guilford Press.

Faludi, Susan. (1991). *Backlash: The undeclared war against American women.* New York: Crown Publishers.

Fitzgerald, Faith T. (1981). The problem of obesity. *Annual Review of Medicine, 32,* 221–31.

Freedman, Rita. (1984). Reflections on beauty as it relates to health in adolescent females. In Sharon Golub (Ed.), *Health care of the female adolescent* (pp. 29–45). New York: Haworth Press.

Freedman, Rita. (1986). *Beauty bound.* Lexington, MA: D. C. Heath.

Freedman, Rita. (1988). *Bodylove: Learning to like our looks—and ourselves.* New York: Harper & Row.

Garner, David M., Rockert, Wendy, Olmstead, Marion P., Johnson, C., & Coscina, D. V. (1985). Psychoeducational principles in the treatment of bulimia and anorexia nervosa. In David M. Garner & Paul E. Garfinkel (Eds.), *Handbook of psychotherapy for anorexia nervosa and bulimia* (pp. 513–62). New York: Guilford.

Greene, Beverly. (1992). Still here: A perspective on psychotherapy with African American women. In Joan C. Chrisler & Doris Howard (Eds.), *New directions in feminist psychology: Practice, theory, and research* (pp. 13–25). New York: Springer.

Hall, L., & Cohn, L. (1988). *Bulimia: A guide to recovery.* Carlsbad, CA: Gurze Books.

Hamburger, A. C. (1988, May). Beauty quest. *Psychology Today, 22,* 28–32.

Hatfield, Elaine, & Sprecher, Susan. (1986). *Mirror, mirror: The importance of looks in everyday life.* Albany: State University of New York Press.

Herman, Peter, & Polivy, Janet. (1983). *Breaking the diet habit.* New York: Basic Books.

Ignoring the economy, cosmetic firms look to growth. (1989, July 13). *Standard and Poor's Industry Surveys, 1,* 37–38.

Kano, Susan. (1985). *Making peace with food: A step-by-step guide to freedom from diet/weight conflict.* Danbury, CT: Amity.

Karris, Lambros. (1977). Prejudice against obese renters. *Journal of Social Psychology, 101,* 159–60.

Lakoff, Robin T., & Scherr, Raquel L. (1984). *Face value: The politics of beauty.* Boston: Routledge & Kegan Paul.

Landy, David, & Aronson, Elliot. (1969). The influence of the character of the criminal and his victim on the decisions of simulated jurors. *Journal of Experimental Social Psychology, 5,* 141–52.

Larkin, Judith, & Pines, Harvey. (1979). No fat person need apply. *Sociology of Work and Occupations, 6,* 312–27.

Lewis, Diane K. (1977). A response to inequality: Black women, racism, and sexism. *Signs, 3*(2), 339–61.

Maddox, G., & Liederman, V. (1969). Overweight as a social disability with medical implications. *Journal of Medical Education, 44,* 214–20.

Miller, E. (1969). Body image, physical beauty, and color among Jamaican adolescents. *Social and Economic Studies, 18*(1), 72–89.

Moore, M. E., Stunkard, Albert, & Srole, L. (1962). Obesity, social class, and mental illness. *Journal of the American Medical Association, 181,* 138–42.

Morris, Bernardine. (1988, July 26). Paris couture: Opulence lights a serious mood. *New York Times,* p. B8.

Neal, Angela, & Wilson, Midge. (1989). The role of skin color and features in the black community: Implications for black women and therapy. *Clinical Psychology Review, 9,* 323–33.

Okazawa-Rey, Margo, Robinson, Tracy, & Ward, Janie V. (1987). Black women and the politics of skin color and hair. *Women & Therapy, 6*(1/2), 89–102.

Pliner, Patricia, Chaiken, Shelly, & Flett, Gordon L. (1990). Gender differences in concern with body weight and physical appearance over the life span. *Personality and Social Psychology Bulletin, 16,* 263–73.

Reis, Harry T., Nezlek, John, & Wheeler, Ladd. (1980). Physical attractiveness in social interaction. *Journal of Personality and Social Psychology, 38,* 604–17.

Rodin, Judith, Silberstein, Lisa, & Streigel-Moore, Ruth. (1985). Women and weight: A normative discontent. In Theo B. Sonderegger (Ed.), *Nebraska symposium on motivation: Psychology and gender* (pp. 267–307). Lincoln: University of Nebraska Press.

Rosen, James C., Saltzberg, Elayne A., & Srebnik, Debra. (1989). Cognitive behavior therapy for negative body image. *Behavior Therapy, 20,* 393–404.

Rosenblatt, J., & Stencel, S. (1982). *Weight control: A national obsession.* Washington, DC: Congressional Quarterly.

Rothblum, Esther D. (1992). The stigma of women's weight: Social and economic realities. *Feminism & Psychology, 2*(1), 61–73.

Rothblum, Esther D., Miller, Carol, & Gorbutt, Barbara. (1988). Stereotypes of obese female job applicants. *International Journal of Eating Disorders, 7,* 277–83.

Saltzberg, Elayne A. (1990). *Exercise participation and its correlates to body awareness and self-esteem.* Unpublished master's thesis, Connecticut College, New London, CT.

Schwartz, Hillel. (1986). *Never satisfied: A cultural history of diets, fantasies, and fat.* New York: Free Press.

Sorensen, Gloria, & Pechacek, Terry F. (1987). Attitudes toward smoking cessation among men and women. *Journal of Behavioral Medicine, 10,* 129–38.

Stoffel, Jennifer. (1989, November 26). What's new in weight control: A market mushrooms as motivations change. *New York Times,* p. C17.

Thompson, J. Kevin. (1986, April). Larger than life. *Psychology Today,* pp. 41–44.

Walker, Alice. (1990). Beauty: When the other dancer is the self. In Evelyn C. White (Ed.), *The black women's health book: Speaking for ourselves* (pp. 280–87). Seattle: Seal Press.

Walster, Elaine, Aronson, Vera, Abrahams, Darcy, & Rottman, Leon. (1966). Importance of physical attractiveness in dating behavior. *Journal of Personality and Social Psychology, 4,* 508–16.

Wernick, Mark, & Manaster, Guy J. (1984). Age and the perception of age and attractiveness. *Gerontologist, 24,* 408–14.

Williams, Juanita H. (1985). *Psychology of women: Behavior in a biosocial context.* New York: Norton.

NOTES

1. Bras were originally designed to hide breasts.

2. Statistics indicate that women are far more likely than men to be diagnosed as depressed. The ratio is at least 3:1 (Williams, 1985).

Sex, Lies, and Advertising

Gloria Steinem

Suppose archaeologists of the future dug up women's magazines and used them to judge American women. What would they think of us—and what can we do about it?

TOWARD THE END OF THE 1980s, as *glasnost* was beginning and *Ms.* seemed to be ending, I was invited to a press lunch for a Soviet official. He entertained us with anecdotes about new problems of democracy in his country. Local Communist leaders were being criticized in their media for the first time, he explained, and they were angry.

"So I'll have to ask my American friends," he finished pointedly, "how more *subtly* to control the press." In the silence that followed, I said, "Advertising."

The reporters laughed, but later, one of them took me aside: How *dare* I suggest that freedom of the press was limited? How dare I imply that his newsweekly could be influenced by ads?

I explained that I was thinking of advertising's mediawide influence on most of what we read. Even newsmagazines use "soft" cover stories to sell ads, confuse readers with "advertorials," and occasionally self-censor on subjects known to be a problem with big advertisers.

But, I also explained, I was thinking especially of women's magazines. There, it isn't just a little content that's devoted to attracting ads, it's almost all of it. That's why advertisers—not readers—have always been the problem for *Ms.* As the only women's magazine that didn't supply what the ad world euphemistically describes as "supportive editorial atmosphere" or "complementary copy" (for instance, articles that praise food/fashion/beauty subjects to "support" and "complement" food/fashion/beauty ads), *Ms.* could never attract enough advertising to break even.

"Oh, *women's* magazines," the journalist said with contempt. "Everybody knows they're catalogs—but who cares? They have nothing to do with journalism."

I can't tell you how many times I've had this argument in twenty-five years of working for many kinds of publications. Except as moneymaking machines—"cash cows" as they are so elegantly called in the trade—women's magazines are rarely taken seriously. Though changes being made by women have been called more far-reaching than the industrial revolution—and though many editors try hard to reflect some of them in the few pages left to them

 Reprinted from Ms. Magazine, vol. 1, no. 1.

after all the ad-related subjects have been covered--the magazines serving the female half of this country are still far below the journalistic and ethical standards of news and general interest publications. Most depressing of all, this doesn't even rate an exposé.

If *Time* and *Newsweek* had to lavish praise on cars in general and credit General Motors in particular to get GM ads, there would be a scandal—maybe a criminal investigation. When women's magazines from *Seventeen* to *Lear's* praise beauty products in general and credit Revlon in particular to get ads, it's just business as usual.

I.

When *Ms.* began, we didn't consider *not* taking ads. The most important reason was keeping the price of a feminist magazine low enough for most women to afford. But the second and almost equal reason was providing a forum where women and advertisers could talk to each other and improve advertising itself. After all, it was (and still is) as potent a source of information in this country as news or television and movie dramas.

We decided to proceed in two stages. First, we would convince makers of "people products" used by both men and women but advertised mostly to men—cars, credit cards, insurance, sound equipment, financial services, and the like—that their ads should be placed in a women's magazine. Since they were accustomed to the division between editorial and advertising in news and general interest magazines, this would allow our editorial content to be free and diverse. Second, we would add the best ads for whatever traditional "women's products" (clothes, shampoo, fragrance, food, and so on) that surveys showed *Ms.* readers used. But we would ask them to come in *without* the usual quid pro quo of "complementary copy."

We knew the second step might be harder. Food advertisers have always demanded that women's magazines publish recipes and articles on entertaining (preferably ones that name their products) in return for their ads; clothing advertisers expect to be surrounded by fashion spreads (especially ones that credit their designers); and shampoo, fragrance, and beauty products in general usually insist on positive editorial coverage of beauty subjects, plus photo credits besides. That's why women's magazines look the way they do. But if we could break this link between ads and editorial content, then we wanted good ads for "women's products," too.

By playing their part in this unprecedented mix of *all* the things our readers need and use, advertisers also would be rewarded: ads for products like cars and mutual funds would find a new growth market, the best ads for women's products would no longer be lost in oceans of ads for the same category, and both would have access to a laboratory of smart and caring readers whose response would help create effective ads for other media as well.

I thought then that our main problem would be the imagery in ads themselves. Carmakers were still draping blondes in evening gowns over the hoods like ornaments. Authority figures were almost always male, even in ads for products that only women used. Sadistic, he-man campaigns even won industry praise. (For instance, *Advertising Age* had hailed the infamous Silva Thin cigarette theme, "How to Get a Woman's Attention: Ignore Her," as "brilliant.") Even in medical journals, tranquilizer ads showed depressed housewives standing beside piles of dirty dishes and promised to get them back to work.

Obviously, *Ms.* would have to avoid such ads and seek out the best ones—but this didn't seem impossible. *The New Yorker* had been selecting ads for aesthetic reasons for years, a practice that only seemed to make advertisers more eager to be in its pages. *Ebony* and *Essence* were asking for ads with positive black images, and though their struggle was hard, they weren't being called unreasonable.

Clearly, what *Ms.* needed was a very special publisher and ad sales staff. I could think of only one woman with experience on the business side of magazines—Patricia Carbine, who recently had become a vice president of *McCall's* as well as its editor in chief—and the reason I knew her name was a good omen. She had been managing editor at *Look* (really *the* editor, but its owner refused to put a female name at the top of his masthead) when I was writing a column there. After I did an early interview with Cesar Chavez, then just emerging as a leader of migrant labor, and the publisher turned it down because he was worried about ads from Sunkist, Pat was the one who intervened. As I learned later, she had told the publisher she would resign if the interview wasn't published. Mainly because *Look* couldn't afford to lose Pat, it *was* published (and the ads from Sunkist never arrived).

Though I barely knew this woman, she had done two things I always remembered: put her job on the line in a way that editors often talk about but rarely do, and been so loyal to her colleagues that she never told me or anyone outside *Look* that she had done so.

Fortunately, Pat did agree to leave *McCall's* and take a huge cut in salary to become publisher of *Ms.* She became responsible for training and inspiring generations of young women who joined the *Ms.* ad sales force, many of whom went on to become "firsts" at the top of publishing. When *Ms.* first started, however, there were so few women with experience selling space that Pat and I made the rounds of ad agencies ourselves. Later, the fact that *Ms.* was asking companies to do business in a different way meant our saleswomen had to make many times the usual number of calls—first to convince agencies and then client companies besides—and to present endless amounts of research. I was often asked to do a final ad presentation, or see some higher decision-maker, or speak to women employees so executives could see the interest of women they worked with. That's why I spent more time persuading advertisers than editing or writing for *Ms.* and why I ended up with an unsentimental education in the seamy underside of publishing that few writers see (and even fewer magazines can publish).

Let me take you with us through some experiences, just as they happened:

- Cheered on by early support from Volkswagen and one or two other car companies, we scrape together time and money to put on a major reception in Detroit. We know U.S. carmakers firmly believe that women choose the upholstery, not the car, but we are armed with statistics and reader mail to prove the contrary: a car is an important purchase for women, one that symbolizes mobility and freedom.

But almost nobody comes. We are left with many pounds of shrimp on the table and quite a lot of egg on our face. We blame ourselves for not guessing that there would be a baseball pennant playoff on the same day, but executives go out of their way to explain they wouldn't have come anyway. Thus begins ten years of knocking on hostile doors, presenting endless documentation, and hiring a full-time saleswoman in Detroit: all necessary before *Ms.* gets any real results.

This long saga has a semihappy ending: foreign and, later, domestic carmakers eventually provided *Ms.* with enough advertising to make cars one of our top sources of ad revenue. Slowly, Detroit began to take the women's market seriously enough to put car ads in other women's magazines, too, thus freeing a few pages from the hothouse of fashion-beauty-food ads.

But long after figures showed a third, even a half, of many car models being bought by women, U.S. makers continued to be uncomfortable addressing women. Unlike foreign carmakers, Detroit never quite learned the secret of creating intelligent ads that exclude no one and then placing them in women's magazines to overcome past exclusion. (*Ms.* readers were so grateful for a routine Honda ad featuring rack and pinion steering, for instance, that they sent fan mail.) Even now, Detroit continues to ask, "Should we make special ads for women?" Perhaps that's why some foreign cars still have a disproportionate share of the U.S. women's market.

• In the *Ms.* Gazette, we do a brief report on a congressional hearing into chemicals used in hair dyes that are absorbed through the skin and may be carcinogenic. Newspapers report this too, but Clairol, a Bristol-Myers subsidiary that makes dozens of products —a few of which have just begun to advertise in *Ms.*—is outraged. Not at newspapers or newsmagazines, just at us. It's bad enough that *Ms.* is the only women's magazine refusing to provide the usual "complementary" articles and beauty photos, but to criticize one of their categories—*that* is going too far.

We offer to publish a letter from Clairol telling its side of the story. In an excess of solicitousness, we even put this letter in the Gazette, not in Letters to the Editors where it belongs. Nonetheless—and in spite of surveys that show *Ms.* readers are active women who use more of almost everything Clairol makes than do the readers of any other women's magazine— *Ms.* gets almost none of these ads for the rest of its natural life.

Meanwhile, Clairol changes its hair coloring formula, apparently in response to the hearings we reported.

• Our saleswomen set out early to attract ads for consumer electronics: sound equipment, calculators, computers, VCRs, and the like. We know that our readers are determined to be included in the technological revolution. We know from reader surveys that *Ms.* readers are buying this stuff in numbers as high as those of magazines like *Playboy;* or "men eighteen to thirty-four," the prime targets of the consumer electronics industry. Moreover, unlike traditional women's products that our readers buy but don't need to read articles about, these are subjects they want covered in our pages. There actually *is* a supportive editorial atmosphere.

"But women don't understand technology," say executives at the end of ad presentations. "Maybe not," we respond, "but neither do men—and we all buy it."

"If women *do* buy it," say the decision-makers, "they're asking their husbands and boyfriends what to buy first." We produce letters from *Ms.* readers saying how turned off they are when salesmen say things like "Let me know when your husband can come in."

After several years of this, we get a few ads for compact sound systems. Some of them come from JVC, whose vice president, Harry Elias, is trying to convince his Japanese bosses that there is something called a women's market. At his invitation, I find myself speaking at huge trade shows in Chicago and Las Vegas, trying to persuade JVC dealers that showrooms don't have to be locker rooms where women are made to feel unwelcome. But as it turns out, the shows themselves are part of the problem. In Las Vegas, the only women around the technology displays are seminude models serving champagne. In Chicago, the big attraction is Marilyn Chambers, who followed Linda Lovelace of *Deep Throat* fame as Chuck Traynor's captive and/or employee. VCRs are being demonstrated with her porn videos.

In the end, we get ads for a car stereo now and then, but no VCRs; some IBM personal computers, but no Apple or Japanese ones. We notice that office magazines like *Working Woman* and *Savvy* don't benefit as much as they should from office equipment ads either. In the electronics world, women and technology seem mutually exclusive. It remains a decade behind even Detroit.

• Because we get letters from little girls who love toy trains and who ask our help in changing ads and box-top photos that feature little boys only, we try to get toy-train ads from Lionel. It turns out that Lionel executives *have* been concerned about little girls. They made a pink train and were surprised when it didn't sell.

Lionel bows to consumer pressure with a photograph of a boy *and* a girl—but only on some of their boxes. They fear that, if trains are associated with girls, they will be devalued in the minds of boys. Needless to say, *Ms.* gets no train ads, and little girls remain a mostly unexplored market. By 1986, Lionel is put up for sale.

But for different reasons, we haven't had much luck with other kinds of toys either. In spite of many articles on child rearing; an annual listing of nonsexist, multiracial toys by Letty Cottin Pogrebin; Stories for Free Children, a regular feature also edited by Letty; and other prize-winning features for or about children, we get virtually no toy ads. Generations of *Ms.* saleswomen explain to toy manufacturers that a larger proportion of *Ms.* readers have preschool children than do the readers of other women's magazines, but this industry can't believe feminists have or care about children.

• When *Ms.* begins, the staff decides not to accept ads for feminine hygiene sprays or cigarettes: they are damaging and carry no appropriate health warnings. Though we don't think we should tell our readers what to do, we do think we should provide facts so they can decide for themselves. Since the antismoking lobby has been pressing for health warnings on cigarette ads, we decide to take them only as they comply.

Philip Morris is among the first to do so. One of its brands, Virginia Slims, is also sponsoring women's tennis and the first national polls of women's opinions. However, the Virginia Slims theme, "You've come a long way, baby," has more than a "baby" problem. It makes smoking a symbol of progress for women.

We explain to Philip Morris that this slogan won't do well in our pages, but they are convinced its success with some women means it will work with *all* women. Finally, we agree to publish an ad for a Virginia Slims calendar as a test. The letters from readers are critical—and smart. For instance: Would you show a black man picking cotton, the same man in a Cardin suit, and symbolize the antislavery and Civil Rights movements by smoking? Of course not. But instead of honoring the test results, the Philip Morris people seem angry to be proven wrong. They take away ads for *all* their many brands.

This costs *Ms.* about $250,000 the first year. After five years, we can no longer keep track. Occasionally, a new set of executives listens to *Ms.* saleswomen, but because we won't take Virginia Slims, not one Philip Morris product returns to our pages for the next sixteen years.

Gradually, we also realize our naiveté in thinking we *could* decide against taking cigarette ads. They became a disproportionate support of magazines the moment they were banned on television, and few magazines could compete and survive without them; certainly not *Ms.*, which lacks so many other categories. By the time statistics in the 1980s showed that women's rate of lung cancer was approaching men's, the necessity of taking cigarette ads has become a kind of prison.

• General Mills, Pillsbury, Carnation, DelMonte, Dole, Kraft, Stouffer, Hormel, Nabisco: you name the food giant, we try it. But no matter how desirable the *Ms.* readership, our lack of recipes is lethal.

We explain to them that placing food ads *only* next to recipes associates food with work. For many women, it is a negative that works *against* the ads. Why not place food ads in diverse media without recipes (thus reaching more men, who are now a third of the shoppers in supermarkets anyway) and leave the recipes to specialty magazines like *Gourmet* (a third of whose readers are also men)?

These arguments elicit interest, but except for an occasional ad for a convenience food, instant coffee, diet drinks, yogurt, or such extras as avocados and almonds, this mainstay of the publishing industry stays closed to us. Period.

• Traditionally, wines and liquors didn't advertise to women: men were thought to make the brand decisions, even if women did the buying. But after endless presentations, we begin to make a dent in this category. Thanks to the unconventional Michel Roux of Carillon Importers (distributors of Grand Marnier, Absolut Vodka, and others), who assumes that food and drink have no gender, some ads are leaving their men's club.

Beermakers are still selling masculinity. It takes *Ms.* fully eight years to get its first beer ad (Michelob). In general, however, liquor ads are less stereotyped in their imagery—and far less controlling of the editorial content around them—than are women's products. But given the under-representation of other categories, these very facts tend to create a dispro-portionate number of alcohol ads in the pages of *Ms.* This in turn dismays readers worried about women and alcoholism.

• We hear in 1980 that women in the Soviet Union have been producing feminist *samizdat* (underground, self-published books) and circulating them throughout the country. As punishment, four of the leaders have been exiled. Though we are operating on our usual shoestring, we solicit individual contributions to send Robin Morgan to interview these women in Vienna.

The result is an exclusive cover story that includes the first news of a populist peace movement against the Afghanistan occupation, a prediction of *glasnost* to come, and a grass-roots, intimate view of Soviet women's lives. From the popular press to women's studies courses, the response is great. The story wins a Front Page award.

Nonetheless, this journalistic coup undoes years of efforts to get an ad schedule from Revlon. Why? Because the Soviet women on our cover *are not wearing makeup.*

• Four years of research and presentations go into convincing airlines that women now make travel choices and business trips. United, the first airline to advertise in *Ms.*, is so impressed with the response from our readers that one of its executives appears in a film for our ad presentations. As usual, good ads get great results.

But we have problems unrelated to such results. For instance: because American Airlines flight attendants include among their labor demands the stipulation that they could choose to have their last names preceded by "Ms." on their name tags—in a long-delayed revolt against the standard "I am your pilot, Captain Rothgart, and this is your flight attendant, Cindy Sue"—American officials seem to hold the magazine responsible. We get no ads.

There is still a different problem at Eastern. A vice-president cancels subscriptions for thousands of copies on Eastern flights. Why? Because he is offended by ads for lesbian poetry journals in the *Ms.* Classified. A "family airline," as he explains to me coldly on the phone, has to "draw the line somewhere."

It's obvious that *Ms.* can't exclude lesbians and serve women. We've been trying to make that point ever since our first issue included an article by and about lesbians, and both Suzanne Levine, our managing editor, and I were lectured by such heavy hitters as Ed Kosner, then editor of *Newsweek* (and now of *New York Magazine*), who insisted that *Ms.* should "position" itself *against* lesbians. But our advertisers have paid to reach a guaranteed number of readers, and soliciting new subscriptions to compensate for Eastern would cost $150,000, plus rebating money in the meantime.

Like almost everything ad-related, this presents an elaborate organizing problem. After days of searching for sympathetic members of the Eastern board, Frank Thomas, president of the Ford Foundation, kindly offers to call Roswell Gilpatrick, a director of Eastern. I talk with Mr. Gilpatrick, who calls Frank Borman, then the president of Eastern. Frank Borman calls me to say that his airline is not in the business of censoring magazines: *Ms.* will be returned to Eastern flights.

- Women's access to insurance and credit is vital, but with the exception of Equitable and a few other ad pioneers, such financial services address men. For almost a decade after the Equal Credit Opportunity Act passes in 1974, we try to convince American Express that women are a growth market—but nothing works.

  Finally, a former professor of Russian named Jerry Welsh becomes head of marketing. He assumes that women should be cardholders and persuades his colleagues to feature women in a campaign. Thanks to this 1980s series, the growth rate for female cardholders surpasses that for men.

  For this article, I asked Jerry Welsh if he would explain why American Express waited so long. "Sure," he said, "they were afraid of having a 'pink' card."

- Women of color read *Ms.* in disproportionate numbers. This is a source of pride to *Ms.* staffers, who are also more racially representative than the editors of other women's magazines. But this reality is obscured by ads filled with enough white women to make a reader snowblind.

  Pat Carbine remembers mostly "astonishment" when she requested African-American, Hispanic, Asian, and other diverse images. Marcia Ann Gillespie, a *Ms.* editor who was previously the editor in chief of *Essence,* witnesses ad bias a second time: having tried for *Essence* to get white advertisers to use black images (Revlon did so eventually, but L'Oréal, Lauder, Chanel, and other companies never did), she sees similar problems getting integrated ads for an integrated magazine. Indeed, the ad world often creates black and Hispanic ads only for black and Hispanic media. In an exact parallel of the fear that marketing a product to women will endanger its appeal to men, the response is usually, "But your [white] readers won't identify."

  In fact, those we are able to get—for instance, a Max Factor ad made for *Essence* that Linda Wachner gives us after she becomes president—are praised by white readers, too. But there are pathetically few such images.

- By the end of 1986, production and mailing costs have risen astronomically, ad income is flat, and competition for ads is stiffer than ever. The 60/40 preponderance of edit over ads that we promised to readers becomes 50/50; children's stories, most poetry, and some fiction are casualties of less space; in order to get variety into limited pages, the length (and sometimes the depth) of articles suffers; and, though we do refuse most of the ads that would look like a parody in our pages, we get so worn down that some slip through. Still, readers perform miracles. Though we haven't been able to afford a subscription mailing in two years, they maintain our guaranteed circulation of 450,000.

  Nonetheless, media reports on *Ms.* often insist that our unprofitability must be due to reader disinterest. The myth that advertisers simply follow readers is very strong. Not one reporter notes that other comparable magazines our size (say, *Vanity Fair* or *The Atlantic*) have been losing more money in one year than *Ms.* has lost in sixteen years. No matter how much never-to-be-recovered cash is poured into starting a magazine or keeping one going, appearances seem to be all that matter. (Which is why we haven't been able to explain our fragile state in public. Nothing causes ad flight like the smell of nonsuccess.)

My healthy response is anger. My not-so-healthy response is constant worry. Also an obsession with finding one more rescue. There is hardly a night when I don't wake up with sweaty palms and pounding heart, scared that we won't be able to pay the printer or the post office, scared most of all that closing our doors will hurt the women's movement.

Out of chutzpah and desperation, I arrange a lunch with Leonard Lauder, president of Estée Lauder. With the exception of Clinique (the brainchild of Carol Phillips), none of Lauder's hundreds of products has been advertised in *Ms.* A year's schedule of ads for just three or four of them could save us. Indeed, as the scion of a family-owned company whose ad practices are followed by the beauty industry, he is one of the few men who could liberate many pages in all women's magazines just by changing his mind about "complementary copy."

Over a lunch that costs more than we can pay for some articles, I explain the need for his leadership. I also lay out the record of *Ms.*: more literary and journalistic prizes won; more new issues introduced into the mainstream, new writers discovered, and impact on society than any other magazine; more articles that became books, stories that became movies, ideas that became television series, and newly advertised products that became profitable; and, most important for him, a place for his ads to reach women who aren't reachable through any other women's magazine. Indeed, if there is one constant characteristic of the ever-changing *Ms.* readership, it is their impact as leaders. Whether it's waiting until later to have first babies or pioneering PABA as sun protection in cosmetics, *whatever* they are doing today, a third to a half of American women will be doing three to five years from now. It's never failed.

But, he says, *Ms.* readers are not *our* women. They're not interested in things like fragrance and blush-on. If they were, *Ms.* would write articles about them.

On the contrary, I explain, surveys show they are more likely to buy such things than the readers of, say, *Cosmopolitan* or *Vogue*. They're good customers because they're out in the world enough to need several sets of everything: home, work, purse, travel, gym, and so on. They just don't need to read articles about these things. Would he ask a men's magazine to publish monthly columns on how to shave before he advertised Aramis products (his line for men)?

He concedes that beauty features are often concocted more for advertisers than readers. But *Ms.* isn't appropriate for his ads anyway, he explains. Why? Because Estée Lauder is selling "a kept-woman mentality."

I can't quite believe this. Sixty percent of the users of his products are salaried and generally resemble *Ms.* readers. Besides, his company has the appeal of having been started by a creative and hardworking woman, his mother, Estée Lauder.

That doesn't matter, he says. He knows his customers, and they would *like* to be kept women. That's why he will never advertise in *Ms.*

In November 1987, by vote of the Ms. Foundation for Education and Communication (*Ms.*'s owner and publisher, the media subsidiary of the Ms. Foundation for Women), *Ms.* was sold to a company whose officers, Australian feminists Sandra Yates and Anne Summers, raised the investment money in their country that *Ms.* couldn't find in its own. They also started *Sassy* for teenage women.

In their two-year tenure, circulation was raised to 550,000 by investment in circulation mailings, and, to the dismay of some readers, editorial features on clothes and new products made a more traditional bid for ads. Nonetheless, ad pages fell below previous levels. In addition, *Sassy,* whose fresh voice and sexual frankness were an unprecedented success with young readers, was targeted by two mothers from Indiana, who began, as one of them put it, "calling every Christian organization I could think of." In response to this controversy, several crucial advertisers pulled out.

Such links between ads and editorial content were a problem in Australia, too, but to a lesser degree. "Our readers pay two times more for their magazines," Anne explained, "so advertisers have less power to threaten a magazine's viability."

"I was shocked," said Sandra Yates with characteristic directness. "In Australia, we think you have freedom of the press—but you don't."

Since Anne and Sandra had not met their budget's projections for ad revenue, their investors forced a sale. In October 1989, *Ms.* and *Sassy* were bought by Dale Lang, owner of *Working Mother, Working Woman,* and one of the few independent publishing companies left among the conglomerates. In response to a request from the original *Ms.* staff—as well as to reader letters urging that *Ms.* continue, plus his own belief that *Ms.* would benefit his other magazines by blazing a trail—he agreed to try the ad-free, reader-supported *Ms.* you hold now and to give us complete editorial control.

II.

Do you think, as I once did, that advertisers make decisions based on solid research? Well, think again. "Broadly speaking," says Joseph Smith of Oxtoby-Smith, Inc., a consumer research firm, "there is no persuasive evidence that the editorial context of an ad matters."

Advertisers who demand such "complementary copy," even in the absence of respectable studies, clearly are operating under a double standard. The same food companies place ads in *People* with no recipes. Cosmetics companies support *The New Yorker* with no regular beauty columns. So where does this habit of controlling the content of women's magazines come from?

Tradition. Ever since *Ladies Magazine* debuted in Boston in 1828, editorial copy directed to women has been informed by something other than its readers' wishes. There were no ads then, but in an age when married women were legal minors with no right to their own money, there was another revenue source to be kept in mind: husbands. "Husbands may rest assured," wrote editor Sarah Josepha Hale, "that nothing found in these pages shall cause her [his wife] to be less assiduous in preparing for his reception or encourage her to 'usurp station' or encroach upon prerogatives of men."

Hale went on to become the editor of *Godey's Lady's Book,* a magazine featuring "fashion plates": engravings of dresses for readers to take to their seamstresses or copy themselves. Hale added "how to" articles, which set the tone for women's service magazines for years to come: how to write politely, avoid sunburn, and—in no fewer than twelve hundred words—how to maintain a goose quill pen. She advocated education for women but avoided controversy. Just as most women's magazines now avoid politics, poll their readers on issues like abortion but rarely take a stand, and praise socially approved life-styles, Hale saw to it that *Godey's* avoided the hot topics of its day: slavery, abolition, and women's suffrage.

What definitively turned women's magazines into catalogs, however, were two events: Ellen Butterick's invention of the clothing pattern in 1863 and the mass manufacture of patent medicines containing everything from colored water to cocaine. For the first time, readers could purchase what magazines encouraged them to want. As such magazines became more profitable, they also began to attract men as editors. (Most women's magazines continued to have men as top editors until the feminist 1970s.) Edward Bok, who became editor of *The Ladies' Home Journal* in 1889, discovered the power of advertisers when he rejected ads for patent medicines and found that other advertisers canceled in retribution. In the early twentieth century, *Good Housekeeping* started its Institute to "test and approve" products. Its Seal of Approval became the grandfather of current "value added" programs that offer advertisers such bonuses as product sampling and department store promotions.

By the time suffragists finally won the vote in 1920, women's magazines had become too entrenched as catalogs to help women learn how to use it. The main function was to create a desire for products, teach how to use products, and make products a crucial part of gaining social approval, pleasing a husband, and performing as a homemaker. Some unrelated articles and short stories were included to persuade women to pay for these catalogs. But articles were neither consumerist nor rebellious. Even fiction was usually subject to formula: if a woman had any sexual life outside marriage, she was supposed to come to a bad end.

In 1965, Helen Gurley Brown began to change part of that formula by bringing "the sexual revolution" to women's magazines—but in an ad-oriented way. Attracting multiple men required even more consumerism, as the Cosmo Girl made clear, than finding one husband.

In response to the workplace revolution of the 1970s, traditional women's magazines—that is, "trade books" for women working at home—were joined by *Savvy, Working Woman,* and other trade books for women working in offices. But by keeping the fashion/beauty/entertaining articles necessary to get traditional ads and then adding career articles besides, they inadvertently produced the antifeminist stereotype of Super Woman. The male-imitative, dress-for-success woman carrying a briefcase became the media image of a woman worker, even though a blue-collar woman's salary was often higher than her glorified secretarial sister's, and though women at a real briefcase level are statistically rare. Needless to say, these dress-for-success women were also thin, white, and beautiful.

In recent years, advertisers' control over the editorial content of women's magazines has become so institutionalized that it is written into "insertion orders" or dictated to ad salespeople as official policy. The following are recent typical orders to women's magazines:

- Dow's Cleaning Products stipulates that ads for its Vivid and Spray 'n Wash products should be adjacent to "children or fashion editorial," ads for Bathroom Cleaner should be next to "home furnishing/family" features, and so on for other brands. "If a magazine fails for 1/2 the brands or more," the Dow order warns, "it will be omitted from further consideration."
- Bristol-Myers, the parent of Clairol, Windex, Drano, Bufferin, and much more, stipulates that ads be placed next to "a full page of compatible editorial."
- S.C. Johnson & Son, makers of Johnson Wax, lawn and laundry products, insect sprays, hair sprays, and so on, orders that its ads *"should not be opposite extremely controversial features or material antithetical to the nature/ copy of the advertised product."* (Italics theirs.)
- Maidenform, manufacturer of bras and other apparel, leaves a blank for the particular product and states: "The creative concept of the _____ campaign, and the very nature of the product itself appeal to the positive emotions of the reader/consumer. Therefore, it is imperative that all editorial adjacencies reflect that same positive tone. The editorial must not be negative in content or lend itself contrary to the _____ product imagery/message (e.g. *editorial relating to illness, disillusionment, large size fashion, etc.*)." (Italics mine.)
- The De Beers diamond company, a big seller of engagement rings, prohibits magazines from placing its ads with "adjacencies to hard news or anti/love-romance themed editorial."
- Procter & Gamble, one of this country's most powerful and diversified advertisers, stands out in the memory of Anne Summers and Sandra Yates (no mean feat in this context): its products were not to be placed in *any* issue that included *any* material on gun control, abortion, the occult, cults, or the disparagement of religion. Caution was also demanded in any issue covering sex or drugs, even for educational purposes.

Those are the most obvious chains around women's magazines. There are also rules so clear they needn't be written down: for instance, an overall "look" compatible with beauty and fashion ads. Even "real" nonmodel women photographed for a women's magazine are usually made up, dressed in credited clothes, and retouched out of all reality. When editors do include articles on less-than-cheerful subjects (for instance, domestic violence), they tend to keep them short and unillustrated. The point is to be "upbeat." Just as women in the street are asked, "Why don't you smile, honey?" women's magazines acquire an institutional smile.

Within the text itself, praise for advertisers' products has become so ritualized that fields like "beauty writing" have been invented. One of its frequent practitioners explained seriously that "it's a difficult art. How many new adjectives can you find? How much greater can you make a lipstick sound? The FDA restricts what companies can say on labels, but we create illusion. And ad agencies are on the phone all the time pushing you to get their product in. A lot of them keep the business based on how many editorial clippings they produce every month. The worst are products," like Lauder's as the writer confirmed, "with their own name involved. It's all ego."

Often, editorial becomes one giant ad. Last November, for instance, *Lear's* featured an elegant woman executive on the cover. On the contents page, we learned she was wearing Guerlain makeup and Samsara, a new fragrance by Guerlain. Inside were full-page ads for Samsara and Guerlain antiwrinkle cream. In the cover profile, we learned that this executive was responsible for launching Samsara and is Guerlain's director of public relations. When the *Columbia Journalism Review* did one of the few articles to include women's magazines in coverage of the influence of ads, editor Frances Lear was quoted as defending her magazine because "this kind of thing is done all the time."

Often, advertisers also plunge odd-shaped ads into the text, no matter what the cost to the readers. At *Woman's Day,* a magazine originally founded by a supermarket chain, editor in chief Ellen Levine said, "The day the copy had to rag around a chicken leg was not a happy one."

Advertisers are also adamant about where in a magazine their ads appear. When Revlon was not placed as the first beauty ad in one Hearst magazine, for instance, Revlon pulled its ads from *all* Hearst magazines. Ruth Whitney, editor in chief of *Glamour,* attributes some of these demands to "ad agencies wanting to prove to a client that they've squeezed the last drop of blood out of a magazine." She also is, she says, "sick and tired of hearing that women's magazines are controlled by cigarette ads." Relatively speaking, she's right. To be as censoring as many advertisers for women's products, tobacco companies would have to demand articles in praise of smoking and expect glamorous photos of beautiful women smoking their brands.

I don't mean to imply that the editors I quote here share my objections to ads: most assume that women's magazines have to be the way they are. But it's also true that only former editors can be completely honest. "Most of the pressure came in the form of direct product mentions," explains Sey Chassler, who was editor in chief of *Redbook* from the 1960s to the 1980s. "We got threats from the big guys, the Revlons, blackmail threats. They wouldn't run ads unless we credited them.

"But it's not fair to single out the beauty advertisers because these pressures came from everybody. Advertisers want to know two things: What are you going to charge me? What *else* are you going to do for me? It's a holdup. For instance, management felt that fiction took up too much space. They couldn't put any advertising in that. For the last ten years, the number of fiction entries into the National Magazine Awards has declined.

"And pressures are getting worse. More magazines are more bottom-line oriented because they have been taken over by companies with no interest in publishing.

"I also think advertisers do this to women's magazines especially," he concluded, "because of the general disrespect they have for women."

Even media experts who don't give a damn about women's magazines are alarmed by the spread of this ad-edit linkage. In a climate *The Wall Street Journal* describes as an unacknowledged Depression for media, women's products are increasingly able to take their low standards wherever they go. For instance: newsweeklies publish uncritical stories on fashion and fitness. *The New York Times Magazine* recently ran an article on "firming creams," complete with mentions of advertisers. *Vanity Fair* published a profile of one major advertiser, Ralph Lauren, illustrated by the same photographer who does his ads, and turned the life-style of another, Calvin Klein, into a cover story. Even the outrageous *Spy* has toned down since it began to go after fashion ads.

And just to make us really worry, films and books, the last media that go directly to the public without having to attract ads first, are in danger, too. Producers are beginning to depend on payments for displaying products in movies, and books are now being commissioned by companies like Federal Express.

But the truth is that women's products—like women's magazines—have never been the subjects of much serious reporting anyway. News and general interest publications, including the "style" or "living" sections of newspapers, write about food and clothing as cooking and fashion and almost never evaluate such products by brand name. Though chemical additives, pesticides, and animal fats are major health risks in the United States, and clothes, shoddy or not, absorb more consumer dollars than cars, this lack of information is serious. So is ignoring the contents of beauty products that are absorbed into our bodies through our skins and that have profit margins so big they would make a loan shark blush.

The truth is that individuals are fair game for the media and corporations are not—individuals don't advertise.

Should *Ms.* have started out with no advertising in the first place? The odd thing is that, in retrospect, I think the struggle was worth it. For all those years, dozens of feminist organizers disguised as *Ms.* ad saleswomen took their courage, research, slide shows, humor, ingenuity, and fresh point of view into every advertising agency, client office, and lion's den in cities where advertising is sold. Not only were sixteen years of *Ms.* sustained in this way, with all the changeful words on those thousands of pages, but some of the advertising industry was affected in its imagery, its practices, and its understanding of the female half of the country. Those dozens of women themselves were affected, for they learned the art of changing a structure from both within and without, and are now rising in crucial publishing positions where women have never been. *Ms.* also helped to open nontraditional categories of ads for women's magazines, thus giving them a little more freedom—not to mention making their changes look reasonable by comparison.

But the world of advertising has a way of reminding us how far there is to go.

Several years ago, as I was finishing this exposé in its first version, I got a call from a writer for *Elle*. She was doing an article on where women parted their hair: Why, she wanted to know, did I part mine in the middle?

It's all so familiar. I could imagine this writer trying to make something out of a nothing assignment. A long-suffering editor laboring to think of new ways to attract ads for shampoo, conditioner, hairdryers, and the like. Readers assuming that other women must want this stuff.

I could imagine a whole chain of women—all of us missing sources of information, insight, creativity, humor, anger, investigation, poetry, confession, outrage, learning, and perhaps more important, a sense of connection to each other; and a gloriously diverse world being flattened by a velvet steamroller.

I ask you: Can't we do better than this?

Sexism and the English Language: The Linguistic Implications of Being a Woman

Karen L. Adams and Norma C. Ware

To ANALYZE SEXISM IN the English language—what it looks like, and how it affects the way women think, feel, and act in our society[1]—we must look at two aspects of the relationship of language to society: reference and usage. First, how are female human beings referred to in English, what are the cultural attitudes these kinds of references suggest, and what are their implications for the ways women see themselves and their role in society? Second, what are characteristic speech habits of both women and men, and how do these speech habits affect the way women lead their lives? Then we can take up the question of change: What is being done to combat linguistic sexism, and what more could be done?

Referring to Women

One of the most intriguing characteristics of language is that it acts as a kind of social mirror, reflecting the organization and dynamics of the society of which it is a part. Because of this, we can learn a great deal about our society by looking at some of the words used in English to refer to women.

THE SEXUALIZATION OF WOMEN

English words used to refer to women are often "sexually weighted." This is evident in some sex-specific pairs of nouns that are similar in meaning but in which the female form has taken on sexual overtones. A prime example is the set of terms *master* and *mistress*. Both of these words refer to someone who possesses or has power over someone or something else, as in "He is the master of his fate," or "She is the mistress of a great fortune." However, as Lakoff has pointed out, the word *mistress* has acquired a sexual connotation that its masculine counterpart has not.[2] Thus, we can use a sentence like "Jane is Tom's mistress" to report the fact that Jane and Tom are sleeping together and be understood perfectly, while to attempt to describe the same situation with the expression "Tom is Jane's master" is to invite communicational disaster. The latter sentence fails to express its intended meaning because the word *master* is devoid of sexual connotations.

This kind of asymmetrical relationship between what are ostensibly male–female equivalents is not restricted to a single example. In the pair *sir* and *madam,* the latter refers to the proprietor of a brothel as well as serving as a term of address. Even the words *man* and *woman* may be seen to conform to this pattern. The sexual overtones inherent in the word *woman* show through clearly in a sentence such as: "After six months at sea, the first thing Bill wanted to do on leave was to find a woman." Then there is the case of the male academician who objected to the title of a new course because it was "too suggestive"—the title was "Women in the Social Order."[3]

Another indication of the sexualization of women in English is that the language seems to have so many more ways of describing women in terms of their sexuality than it has for men. Schulz reports the findings of two investigators who, as part of a larger study of slang, managed to collect over five hundred synonyms for *prostitute,* but only sixty-five for the masculine sexual term *whoremonger,* and she herself "located roughly a thousand words and phrases describing women in sexually derogatory ways. There is nothing approaching this multitude for describing men."[4] A 1989 dictionary of college slang shows the same pattern persisting since Schulz's article appeared over fifteen years ago. The dictionary contains over five times as many terms (fifteen versus five) for sexually active women as for men and twice as many terms (six versus three) with sexual overtones for unpleasant women.[5]

Many once quite neutral terms relating to women have degenerated into terms that have sexual or negative connotations or both. Schulz explains how the word *hussy,* for example, is derived from the Old English *huswif* (housewife), whose meaning was simply "female head of the household." A *spinster* was originally someone who operated a spinning wheel. A *broad* was simply a young woman, and *tart* and *biddy* were terms of endearment![6]

Linguists generally agree that an elaborate vocabulary on a given topic in a language means that this topic is of particular concern or importance to a particular group or to the society as a whole. What, then, can we conclude from the fact that English has so many terms describing women in specifically sexual ways, including its slang terminology, which is largely considered a male creation?[7] Is it that a woman's sexuality is considered the most salient aspect of her being, rivaling or even outweighing her humanity in importance? Furthermore, why are so many of these terms pejorative? Is it due to the well-know "sex is dirty" attitude that is characteristic of our culture? If this is true it leaves women in the position of having the essence of their existence defined in terms of something that is considered unclean and distasteful. The implications of this are sobering at best.

THE TRIVIALIZATION OF WOMEN

A look at the kinds of people and things with which women tend to be grouped in the English language can also tell us a great deal about how our culture regards the female sex. Consider, for example, stock phrases such as *women and children first,* or *wine, women, and song.* Less proverbial but no less significant classifications have been offered by various prominent individuals. For instance, during the Vietnam War former Harvard President Nathan Pusey is reputed to have lamented the draining effect of the draft on male brainpower at the university with the words, "We shall be left with *the blind, the lame and the women.*"[8]

Examples like these are not difficult to find. The question is, what do these groupings imply about the kind of people women are considered to be? For us, at least, the implication is that women are immature (like children), frivolous (to be indulged in for entertainment purposes, like wine and song), and handicapped (like the blind and the lame). Singly or in combination, these presumed female attributes provide a convenient excuse for not taking women seriously; they serve to trivialize the female sex.

This trivialization effect appears elsewhere in the language as well. The college dictionary of slang mentioned above has ten times as many words for stupid and/or superficial women, e.g., *dimbo* and *fifi,* than for men. More formal, nonslang situations also provide examples of trivialization. Lakoff has pointed out, for example, "that if, in a particular sentence, both *woman* and *lady* might be used, the use of the latter tends to trivialize the subject matter under discussion, often subtly ridiculing the woman involved." The expressions *lady atheist* (which appeared in the *San Francisco Chronicle,* January 31, 1972) and *lady sculptor,* with their connotation of eccentricity and frivolousness, are cited as cases in point.[9]

Similar in effect to the substitution of *lady* for *woman* is the common practice of referring to adult females as *girls.* Although the suggestion of youth may be a desirable one in our youth-oriented culture, it is also true that the association carries certain decidedly negative connotations- –irresponsibility, immaturity, "smallness" of body or mind, etc. What is associated with youth tends to lack stature, and therefore importance, almost by definition.

The parallel terms for men, *gentlemen* and *boys,* can have the same sort of trivializing effect, as in *gentleman scholar,* for example. However, the issue here is one of frequency. Males are referred to as *boys* or *gentlemen* much less often than females are called *girls* or *ladies.*[10]

WOMAN IN TERMS OF MAN

The English language also has a tendency to define women as a sort of male appendage. A woman's linguistic existence is in many cases expressed in essentially male terms, from a male point of view, or with male interests in mind. One example of this tendency is the fact that many of the nouns that refer to women performing various activities or roles are linguistically marked as derivatives of the basic (male) form. Thus, we have poet*ess* and actr*ess,* songstr*ess,* steward*ess,* usher*ette,* major*ette,* and stud*ette* (slang), not to mention proper names such as *Jeannette.* Only in matters of marriage and the few female-dominated professions is the female form the primary one. Thus, we have widow*er, male* nurse, and *male* prostitute.

Another way in which English tends to classify women in essentially male terms is in social titles that make the declaration of a woman's marital status— – i.e., her relationship to a man—obligatory. Until very recently, women had no choice but to reveal whether they were single or (ever) married every time they wanted to refer to themselves in the conventional title-plus-last-name manner. A woman was either *Miss* Somebody-or-other, or *Mrs.* Somebody-or-other.[11] Now, of course, one can be *Ms.* Somebody-or-other and supposedly avoid the whole issue. However, the use of *Ms.* is on occasion interpreted to mean "unmarried, and slightly ashamed of the fact." As one writer reports, "After four attempts to convince a travel agent that I was not 'Miss' or 'Mrs.' but 'Ms.,' she finally responded with 'Oh, I'm not married either, but it doesn't bother me.'"[12]

One of the more subtle ways in which the English language represents the female as a derivative, or subset, of the male is by means of the linguistic convention known as "generic man." In English, the same word that is used to refer to male human beings is also used in the generic sense to refer to all human beings: that word is, of course, *man.* English grammar books assure us that persons of both sexes are meant to be included in expressions such as *man the hunter, the man in the street, goodwill to men,* and *all men are created equal.* But is this really the case? If *man* is really generic, why is there something decidedly funny about the sentence, "My brother married a spaceman who works for NASA"?[13]

That generic man is not always quite what he appears to be is particularly well illustrated by the following incident: at the end of one of the hour-long segments of Jacob Bronowski's highly acclaimed series "The Ascent of Man," "the host of the series chatted for a few minutes with a guest anthropologist about what women were doing during this early period in the ascent of man."[14]

The same generic principle that makes *man* both male and female is supposed to apply to pronouns as well. We have all been taught that the third person singular pronoun *he* is both masculine and sex-indefinite. But again, if this is true, shouldn't the following statement sound perfectly natural: "No person may require another person to perform, participate in, or undergo an abortion against his will"?[15]

Research provides experimental evidence of the male bias in generic *man.* Two sociologists at Drake University asked college students to submit appropriate photographs for the various chapters of an introductory sociology textbook. One group of students was given a list of chapter titles, in which the generic term was not used (e.g., "Culture," "Family," "Urban Life," "Political Life," "Social Life"). Another group was given a list in which some of the titles had been changed to read "Urban Man," "Political Man," "Social Man," etc. Sixty-four percent of the students given the *man* titles submitted male-only pictures, whereas only 50 percent of the students given neutral labels submitted male-only pictures.[16]

Studies on generic *he* also offer clear evidence that, despite what the grammar books tell us, in actual use this generic term does not apply equally to men and women. Khosroshahi compared the images drawn by female and male students after they read paragraphs with sex unspecified for the person involved. The paragraphs were composed using generic *he, he or she,* or *they.* The students had been divided according to use in their own compositions of generic *he* and sex-inclusive pronouns such as *he or she.* According to the study generic "*He* was found to be least likely to evoke female referents, *he or she* most likely, and *they* in between." Only the women who used sex-inclusive pronouns in their own writing drew more images of women than men.[17] As reported twenty years ago by Bem and Bem, the use of generic *he* and the masculine images it evokes can have practical consequences. High school women in their study responded to job advertisements with generic *he* less often than to those with *she* even though they were qualified for jobs in both types of advertisements.[18]

All this is not to say, however, that generic terms are never interpreted generically. Grammar-book definitions and years of English composition classes have presumably had some impact, and sentences such as the following may well be taken as referring to both sexes:

1. Man the life boats!
2. Each student should pick up his paper upon entering the room.

But the impact appears to be minor. In Khosroshahi's study, the interpretation of *he* as generic accounted for less than an eighth of the images drawn by the students.[19]

The continued use of the so-called generic sense exacerbates, rather than solves, the problem. Because *man* and *he* are both generic and nongeneric, women find themselves caught in a linguistic contradiction of rather formidable proportions: they discover that they are being defined as both *man* and *not man* at the same time.[20] The generic *man* convention sets up a linguistic structure whereby women can be portrayed in English *either* as women *or* as people, but not both.

Finally, we note that other words can be used in such a way as to exclude females from human groups. A television commentator was heard to say: "People won't give up power. They'll give up anything else first—money, home, wife, children—but not power."[21]

IMPLICATIONS AND CONSEQUENCES (OR, SO WHAT?)

How does all this affect the way women live in the world? There are two views of the relationship of language to society and its effect on society. Some people maintain that the relationship between language and society is one of representation only, whereby language serves as a social mirror, reflecting the implicit values, attitudes, and prejudices of the society in which it is embedded but having no power to influence the perceptions or interactions of the people in that society. From this argument it follows that, while the picture the English language paints of women may be distasteful to us, that picture has no real effect on the way women think, the way they feel about themselves, or the way they lead their lives.

A considerable number of people disagree with this position, however. These people maintain that language not only reflects social values, attitudes, etc., but also reinforces them. In any language, it is easier to talk about some things than about others. Since many of the words that English offers for referring to women also have sexual connotations, it is easy to talk about women in a sexual way.

With the habit of talking about things in certain ways comes the habit of thinking about them in those ways. Thus, the language-based predisposition to talk about women in sexual terms makes it more likely that a speaker will think about them in those terms. It is in this sense, then, that language may be said to reinforce, as well as to reflect, prevailing social opinion.

One implication of this argument is that the ability of language to reinforce the status quo helps to perpetuate sexist attitudes and practices and to inhibit social change. Another implication is that, according to this theory, women are likely to come to "see themselves as the language sees them"—in the case of English, as sex objects, as trivial, as ambivalent about their status as complete human beings, etc.

Consider again the use of generic *he*. In Khosroshahi's study all men and the women who did not normally use sex-neutral pronouns drew more male than female images in all contexts. They drew the most with generic *he* and the fewest with *he or she*. The results fit studies on memory that show that the presentation of a word brings to mind all its associated meanings; thus, generic *he* will bring to mind the nongeneric sex-specific interpretation; *he or she* will introduce female-specific images. The women who used sex-neutral pronouns in their own writing and drew more female than male images in all cases show that a speaker can consciously override an image in a controlled context. The use of generic male terminology is so ubiquitous that this override process requires vigilance.[22]

The consequences of this relationship of language to society can be even more serious for minority women. Not only are sexist attitudes perpetuated through language, but so also are racist attitudes. Moreover, in bilingual communities, women may have to deal with additional stereotyping in another language. The result of this ability of language to reinforce negative attitudes and practices can be overwhelming in such cases.[23]

Female and Male Differences in Usage

Just as there are differences in the words that refer to women and men, so are there differences in the ways that women and men talk. In English, the same words, the same grammatical forms, and the same conversational strategies can be and are used by both women and men. However, the frequency of the usage of these words and strategies and the situations in which they are used differ depending on the speaker's and listener's sex as well as other characteristics of the speaker and the situation.[24]

SEX ROLES AND SPEAKING "PROPER" ENGLISH

In society at large, the manner in which some people talk is more "prestigious" than the way others do. In the United States, as in other countries, it is generally the language of the urban, well-educated, and wealthier speakers that is held in higher esteem. These people's upper-middle-class speech is the most acceptable and carries the label *standard English*. This standard language is taught in schools and is used by broadcasters and newspaper reporters.

Given the acknowledged existence of a standard language, one might expect all speakers of English to strive to use the standard in an effort to sound more prestigious. However, one consistent finding of studies on sex-based variations in English usage has been that women typically use more grammatically correct forms than do men and pronounce words in more acceptable ways. This means that they succeed in sounding more like standard-English speakers than men do. In the case of bilingual communities, the effort to sound prestigious can mean that women use English more than they do the non-English language—Spanish, for example.[25]

Trudgill, in a study of Norwich English (a form of British English), found that there, too, women used prestigious speech forms more often than did men.[26] He also found that, when speakers were asked about their use of standard and nonstandard forms, differences between actual and perceived behavior appeared. It seems that speakers "perceive their own speech in terms of the norms at which they were aiming rather than the sound actually produced,"[27] so that there were always cases of overreporting and underreporting of actual usages. These instances were strongly correlated with sex differences, no matter what the class of the speaker. Women claimed that they used standard forms more frequently than they actually did, and men reported that they used them less frequently than they actually did. As Trudgill convincingly argues, the actual differences between female and male speech, combined with the differences in reporting, indicate that women and men identify with different role models of behavior and seek to talk like those models.

Thorne and Henley point to research by Goffman[28] demonstrating that inferior status leads to careful and circumscribed behavior. They claim that women's usage of standard English is an example of this circumscribed behavior. Eckert, however, claims that it is a strategy for empowerment. She says that traditionally a woman's value is determined by her control over her domestic environment, which she gains through the indirect use of a man's power or through the development of personal influence. To secure personal influence without power, women must create an image of themselves as worthy of moral authority. Such worthiness includes their knowledge and use of language forms.[29]

What of the male usage of less standard forms? Why does behaving like a man mean using less correct and even lower-class speech? According to Eckert's analysis, men are not status bound and need not attend to these language forms for power. Other linguists have also argued that the prevalent socialization of males includes a male sex role of competitiveness, independence, and toughness, characteristics that working-class males are thought to embody. Speaking the less acceptable or nonstandard language associated with working-class males then becomes a way for all males to be tough and independent.

Differences between women and men in the use of contentious language also relate to women's more correct language behavior. Several studies have found that African-American girls know and even use forms of verbal dueling common in the African-American community, but that they use these forms with greater restraint or often not in the context of dueling.[30] Moreover, swearing, a way of shocking and antagonizing others as well as of releasing anger, is more frequent in the speech of males. Many of the terms used for swearing, such as *son of a bitch*, vilify women and thus show swearing to be a male domain. When women do swear, many tend to limit themselves to milder terms, such as *shit, hell,* and *damn,* and most men and women consider swearing improper in female speech.[31]

WEAKNESS AND WOMEN'S SPEECH

It is often claimed that women more frequently use certain language patterns that make their speech sound weak, tentative, and emotional. Examples are the use of fillers and hesitation markers, such as *ah, well,* and *um-m-m;* the use of hedges such as *sort of, I think, you know,* and *I guess;* the use of intensifiers, such as *really* and *very;* the use of tag questions at the ends of statements, such as "It's a nice day, *isn't it*"; and the use of certain models like *would* and *could* in nonpast contexts, as in *Would you answer the phone?* However, studies attempting to verify these claims have resulted in inconsistent findings.

A study by Erickson, Lind, Johnson, and O'Barr on the use of such forms in the testimony of courtroom witnesses verified that these patterns of speech are judged to be a sign of weakness and of a lack of competence and believability whether used by a male or by a female.[32] But the study found that all these forms were used by men as well as by women, and some were used even more by men than by women.

Why did this study fail to demonstrate the predicted language pattern? In this case, the expert witnesses, both female and male, used fewer of these forms than did the less experienced witnesses. Women and men who have high-status roles and who are familiar with the event in question are less likely to use such forms than are inexperienced witnesses of either sex.

In other studies where the results do not fit earlier claims, the differences arise from a previously oversimplified treatment of the language form in question. In language, the same expression can be used to convey different kinds of social and structural effects. Dubois and Crouch found in their study of academic discussions that men used tag questions more than women.[33] The men used them to make a question sound more like an assertion and to make the speaker sound less uninformed. This effect was the opposite of Lakoff's suggestion that tag questions weakened women's assertions.[34] Moreover, tag questions can also be a way to encourage someone else to talk. Preisler, in another study of women and men of different ages employed in different positions in the same British firm, found forms such as *I think,* which might be construed as tentative and weak in one context, to be part of a style for women managers of "careful deliberation and reflective weighing" in a task-oriented context.[35]

Women's voice quality or intonation is another attribute of women's speech that has been associated with weakness. Intonation can be viewed as a musical scale, with a high point (a note), a low point (a note), and steps (notes) in between. Women's intonation range is wider than men's, sometimes giving what is interpreted as an emotional, and therefore weak, quality to the voice. This characterization comes about because large fluctuations in voice level can be used to convey emotion. Being emotional is a devalued behavior in our society. An additional difference in women's and men's intonation patterns is that women use more patterns that end at higher levels, as intonation patterns for questions do, thus giving rise to the claim that women have a hesitant quality to their speech.[36]

As with tag questions and other phrases, women's use of these intonation patterns do not necessarily derive from women's lack of power but are as likely to be strategies designed to engage the listener in conversation. For example, wider variations in pitch also can indicate to listeners a speaker's high involvement in the topic, thus encouraging the listener's attention. The questionlike intonation at the end of sentences may also be "simply indicating desire for a continuation of the discourse," not uncertainty in the statement itself.[37]

The picture of weak forms and women's language is complicated further by the fact that even when women and men use the equivalent expressions, they are not always evaluated in the same way. A woman's utterance may be responded to as weak just because a woman is doing the talking. When women adjust their speaking habits to those of their male colleagues, as they often do,[38] that does not always make the interpretation more positive. Sometimes it results in criticism of them as women. While we can and should monitor our speech for these "weak" forms and assert them to be the positive strategies that they often are, the responses we get to the changes will not always be what we expect.

DIFFERENCES IN CONVERSATIONAL STRATEGIES AND THEIR EFFECT ON WOMEN

Another category of linguistic behavior that is relevant for understanding women's position in our society is conversational interaction. Sacks, Schegloff, and Jefferson[39] refer to conversation as a system that is "party administered" and "interactionally managed." This means that conversations are under the control of the individuals participating in them, and the interaction that arises is a consequence of the relationship among the speakers. Therefore, we expect that the disparate statuses of females and males would show in these exchanges.

Interruptions. One characteristic of conversation is speaker change, or "turn taking." A speaker signals the finish of her or his turn in various ways: making eye contact, lowering the voice level, or calling on someone else to take over. One common strategy in conversations is for the listener to wait for one of these signals and then to start talking. However, people can also gain the floor by interrupting the speaker.[40]

Over the years, one of the most commonly reported findings in the literature on language and gender has been that men interrupt women more than vice versa because of males' more dominant status. A recent survey by James and Clark of the literature on interruptions in mixed-sex conversations reveals, however, "that it is not, in fact the case that most [studies] have found men to interrupt women more than the reverse."[41] Interruptions by speakers can be related to many factors. Not only is status a factor, but also how well people know each other, ethnicity and personality, the topic and the degree of conflict present, and even the number of people present. Interruptions can also have positive functions. For example, they can indicate a listener's involvement in a speaker's tale and a desire to show enthusiasm for the tale.

This active-listener interruption style is frequently employed by women and sometimes accounts for their doing more interrupting than men. From the studies that have been done, "it cannot be definitively concluded that no gender differences exist in this respect";[42] that is, it may in fact be that men interrupt women more in situations where status is at issue. What are needed are more carefully defined criteria for determining what is an interruption and when its function is to control and limit another speaker's participation.

Selective reinforcement.   As suggested by the reasons for women's interruptions, women and men also handle the role of listener differently. A listener is expected to signal attentiveness in any of several ways: nodding the head; interjecting expressions such as *right, um-hmm;* or making more extensive verbal comments. Inadequate response from a listener can bring the exchange to a halt or at least make the speaker ask a question such as "Are you listening?"

Evidence that men listen differently than women is reported by Fishman[43] and Hirschman.[44] Both found that males use significantly fewer interjections such as *um-hmm* than do females, in both same-sex and mixed-sex verbal exchanges.[45] This lack of reinforcement by males can be seen as part of the competitive style of the male sex role. In conversations, this competitive style is manifested by attempts to dominate the exchange. One way of accomplishing this domination is to interrupt. Another way is to give only limited reinforcement. As Aries reports in her data on all-male, small-group interactions,[46] rather than encouraging one another, males concern themselves with establishing a hierarchy. They accomplish this by "brain picking" to see who knows the most, by telling jokes at one another's expense, and by telling stories about such physically threatening topics as castration and riots. It is easy to see how this difference in the use of reinforcers could make a woman, used to a supportive interaction style with other women, feel off-balance in mixed-sex interactions.

Another male strategy is to make a minimal or delayed response in an exchange. Speakers can infer from such a response that the listener thinks what they have to say is of little interest; they may then switch topics in an effort to engage the listener. In data collected by Zimmerman and West, this was the effect in three of the ten mixed-sex exchanges.[47] These results suggest that males use the strategy at least partially as a way to control the topic by changing it to one on which they can talk freely. This interpretation is supported by research by West and Garcia that found men making unilateral changes in topic and refraining "from other conversational activities, such as asking about women's potential 'tellables' or disagreeing with women's self-deprecations."[48]

Amount of talk.   Another difference between women and men in conversations is the length of the turn at talking. We all know the stereotypes of the talkative woman and the strong, silent man. However, data from a variety of sources invalidate these stereotypes. Men often talk longer during their turns than women do. This substantially larger volume of speech can afford them a dominant position in an interaction.[49] For example, Aries found that in mixed-sex groups the men initiated 66 percent of the conversations, compared to 34 percent for women, and those who initiated talk were also the ones who took up more of the available time for talk and were considered leaders by the others. Men were also the recipients of more of the talk; the women in the groups oriented their remarks toward the men, rather than toward the other women, and drew the men out.[50] Indeed, the "talkative" woman may be one who talks as much or nearly as much as a man.[51]

Conclusion

A few years ago, the principal question being asked by those who recognized and objected to sexism in the English language was can sexist language be changed? Is it in fact possible to legislate the changes necessary to wipe out language's sexist bias? The question is now well on its way to being answered affirmatively. In an attempt to eliminate sexist references to women, people have proposed many changes, and many of these are in use. Best known among them are the title *Ms.* to replace *Miss* and *Mrs.*; sex-indefinite substitutes such as sales*person,* mail *carrier,* spokes*person,* and *human*kind for the ambiguous generic *man* constructions; and substitutes for generic *he,* such as extension of the use of *they* to the singular, the alternation of *she* or *he* with *he* or *she,* and the newly coined *s/he.*

Some of these proposed changes have become institutionalized. For example, the U.S. Department of Labor's *Dictionary of Occupational Titles* has set the standard for nonsexist job designations. Since the publication of the *American Heritage School Dictionary* in 1972 (the first of its kind to employ definitions and sample sentences premeditatedly nonsexist in nature), efforts to eliminate sexism for the country's reading matter have also grown steadily. The *Random House Webster's College Dictionary* released in 1991 created some stir by including words like *herstory, waitron,* and *wimmin,* but its guidelines for avoiding sexist language did not. Newspaper policies developed in the mid to late 1970s for the most part have resulted in a uniform style of referring to women and men by name and title. Other major textbook publishers and professional organizations have also distributed guidelines for nonsexist writing to authors and editors. *Language, Gender, and Professional Writing,* published by the Modern Language Association, is a fine example of this. Library catalogers have worked to eradicate sexism in card catalogues, and various religious organizations have reworded hymnals and other materials used in their services.[52]

Along with these institutional efforts, the ongoing, day-to-day struggle of individual women to combat sexist language must be recognized. For example, more and more women are refusing to be called, or to call themselves, *girls* or to be referred to as *lady golfer* or addressed as *chairman.* Many professional women have also insisted upon the title *Ms.* A midwestern recruiting firm found that a majority of female executives under forty years of age preferred the title *Ms.,* and a recent study found that women using *Ms.* as a title as opposed to *Mrs.* or *Miss* are more likely to be perceived by other people as having the qualities of a manager.[53] These efforts have been all the more praiseworthy because they have often been undertaken knowing that one result may be ridicule by others.

The attack on the problems that women encounter in their use of language is also well under way at both institutional and personal levels. For example, assertiveness-training groups and workshops for working women on managerial skills and handling issues of power have as their goals (albeit often indirectly) changing the kinds of linguistic habits that we have described in this article. These groups are forming in all kinds of settings, from large corporations to informal workshops. In addition, an increasing number of articles in popular magazines and books describe sex differences in communication and assertive verbal behavior.[54] The popular success of Deborah Tannen's *You Just Don't Understand: Women and Men in Conversation* demonstrates that there is now widespread recognition that men and women have different conversational styles.[55] These publications often suggest how to break the patterns of male-dominated conversations, how to monitor the use of forms associated with "weak" and "hesitant" speech, and occasionally even teach men the verbal skills that women employ for more effective relationships.

The fact that many such changes are under way, however, only gives rise to another, equally important question: will the eradication of sexism in the English language help to eliminate this bias from other parts of society? The answer is yes. Language does, indeed, have the power to influence other parts of society; it can reinforce the status quo, or it can work to facilitate change. An awareness of sexist language is essential if we are to understand the traditional rules of interaction between women and men. Once we know these rules, we can work to modify them, to defy them, and to use them to our own advantage. Men and women can only benefit from the eradication of sexism in the English language.

NOTES

1. This article does not include information on the relationships between women and language in other societies, and what is true of English may not necessarily be true of other languages. Also, most of the data on usage that we describe are for white middle-class speakers, although when possible we have added data for women of color. Unfortunately, such research has often been neglected. A discussion of this neglect for Hispanic women can be found in D. Letticia Galindo, "Dispelling the Male-Only Myth: Chicanas and Caló," *The Bilingual Review/La Revista Bilingue* 17 (Jan.–April 1992), 3–35.

2. Robin Lakoff, *Language and Woman's Place* (New York: Harper and Row, 1975), 29. The extent to which the original meaning of *mistress* is still in use is open to question. Lakoff argues that it is "practically restricted to its sexual sense." However, one of us maintains that she quite comfortably refers to herself as mistress of her pet dog and cat. Also Betty Lou Dubois and Isabel Crouch, in "The Question of Tag Questions in Women's Speech: They Don't Really Use More of Them, Do They?" *Language in Society* 4 (1975), 289–94, criticize Lakoff and include the following quotes in which the word is used in a nonsexual sense: "It was not that she would make any demonstration; she just did not want to be looked at when she was not quite *mistress* of herself." (Italics added.) Oliver LaFarge, *Laughing Boy* (Boston: Houghton Mifflin, 1927, p. 26; reprinted 1957). "The walls are full of pictures of famous people, from President Nixon to President Sadat of Egypt, all of them autographed to the *mistress* of the house—former movie star Shirley Temple Black." (Italics added.) P. J. Oppenheimer, "Shirley Temple Black Talks About Her Times of Tears, Her Times of Triumph," *Family Weekly,* Nov. 1974, pp. 9–11.

3. Laurel Richardson Walum, *The Dynamics of Sex and Gender: A Sociological Perspective* (Chicago: Rand McNally College Publishing Co., 1977), 18. Walum also notes that the same word can have

both sexual and nonsexual meanings, depending on whether it is used to refer to a male or to a female. She points out that "a male *tramp* is simply a hobo but a female *tramp* is a slut." Ibid.

4. Muriel R. Schulz, "The Semantic Derogation of Women," in Barrie Thorne and Nancy Henley, eds., *Language and Sex: Difference and Dominance* (Rowley, Mass.: Newbury House Publishers, 1975), 72. The original study cited in Schulz, p. 75, is J. S. Farmer and W. E. Henley, *Slang and Its Analogues* (New York: Kraus Reprint Corporation, 1965 [reprint of seven volumes published 1890–1904]).

5. The dictionary in question, Pamela Munro et al., *Slang U* (New York: Harmony Books, 1989), contains words collected by and from UCLA students. Karen L. Adams, "Still a Dimbo After All These Years" (manuscript, Arizona State University, 1992), compared all nouns in the dictionary that referred specifically to either women or men and found that in addition to the sexually explicit vocabulary, words describing women as unattractive, e.g., *broomhilda* or *heifer,* were three times more common than words for unattractive men. Words for attractive men, e.g., *adonis* and *beauhunk,* were slightly more common than words for attractive women. The small numbers in this study in comparison to the one by Farmer and Henley mentioned above reflect the limited scope and specialized topic of the dictionary itself. A study of slang among Australian adolescents, Vivian de Klerk, "Slang: A Male Domain?" *Sex Roles* 22:9/10 (1990), 589–605, which also found an abundance of terms for girls rather than boys, supports the argument that the patterns of unevenness continue in contemporary society.

6. Schulz, "The Semantic Derogation of Women," 66–68.

7. De Klerk, "Slang: A Male Domain?" 592–93.

8. This example appears in Mary Ritchie Key, *Male/Female Language* (Metuchen, N.J.: Scarecrow Press, 1975), 82.

9. Lakoff, *Language and Woman's Place,* 23.

10. What is more likely to happen, we think, is that men will be referred to as *guys* rather than *boys*—a term that seems distinctly less trivializing somehow. This could be one reason why young women seem so often to refer to one another as *guys* as well.

11. Even more striking in this regard is the fact that a woman was and still is in many cases expected to take her husband's name upon marriage, so that she becomes not only *Mrs.* Somebody-or-other, but even *Mrs. John* Somebody-or-other. For example, Hillary Clinton initially kept her own name but was forced to assume her husband's when he ran for governor of Arkansas and her independence became a political liability. Related also is the familiar practice of referring to a married couple as "man and wife," now rapidly becoming obsolete.

12. Walum, *The Dynamics of Sex and Gender,* 19, note 2.

13. This example originally appeared in A. P. Nilsen, "Grammatical Gender and Its Relationship to the Equal Treatment of Males and Females in Children's Books" (Ph.D. dissertation, College of Education in the Graduate College, University of Iowa, Iowa City, 1973), 86–87. We discovered it in Casey Miller and Kate Swift, *Words and Women* (Garden City, N.Y.: Anchor Press/Doubleday, 1976), 29.

14. Miller and Swift, *Words and Women,* 20.

15. This example appears in Key, *Male/Female Language,* 89. It is interesting to note that *he* has not always been considered the correct third-person pronoun for referring to a single human being of indeterminate sex. Until about the eighteenth century, the correct choice of a pronoun for such a purpose was *they* or *he or she.* It was only when certain eighteenth-century grammarians decided that there was something inherently plural about *they,* and so prescribed a substitute for use in the singular, that our present generic *he* was born. Ann Bodine, "Androcentrism in Prescriptive Grammar: Singular 'They,' Sex-Indefinite 'He,' and 'He or She,'" *Language in Society* 4 (Aug. 1975), 129–46.

16. Joseph W. Schneider and Sally W. Hacker, "Sex Role Imagery and Use of Generic 'Man' in Introductory Texts: A Case in the Sociology of Sociology," *American Sociology* 8 (Feb. 1973), 12–18.

17. Fatemeh Khosroshahi, "Penguins Don't Care, but Women Do: A Social Identity Analysis of a Whorfian Problem," *Language in Society* 18 (Dec. 1989), 505. Khosroshahi's study is only one of many demonstrating the nongeneric interpretation of generic *he.* Donald G. MacKay, "Prescriptive Grammar and the Pronoun Problem," in Barrie Thorne, Cheris Kramarae, and Nancy Henley, eds., *Language, Gender and Society* (Rowley, Mass.: Newbury House Publishers, Inc., 1982), 38–53, is another such study, which also systematically addresses and counters linguistic arguments put forward as to why generic *he* should not or even cannot be changed. Mykol C. Hamilton, "Using Masculine Generics: Does Generic *He* Increase Male Bias in the User's Imagery," *Sex Roles* 19:11/12 (1988), 785–99, demonstrates that the bias in interpreting generic *he* as male occurs not only when students

are presented with sentences written by the experimenter but also, even more importantly, when students write their own generic *he* versus sex-inclusive sentences.

18. S. L. Bem and D. J. Bem, "Does Sex-Biased Job Advertising 'Aid and Abet' Sex Discrimination?" *Journal of Applied Social Psychology* 3 (1973), 6–18.

19. Khosroshahi, "Penguins Don't Care, But Women Do," 515.

20. Note that this same contradictory quality could also conceivably serve as a convenient way of covering up the exclusion of women. One can always claim to be using *man* in the generic sense, whether one actually is or not. Thus, the ambiguity inherent in the meaning and the usage of the word *man* effectively turns the term into yet another weapon in the arsenal of those who have an interest, for whatever reason, in keeping women in the social backwaters and out of the mainstream.

21. The late Frank McGee on *Today Show,* NBC-TV, June 19, 1972, quoted in Miller and Swift, *Words and Women,* 37.

22. Does the fact that the male students who used sex-neutral pronouns in their own writing but still drew consistently male images argue against the influence of language and thought? According to Khosroshahi, no. The relationship between change in action and change in thought is a complex one. Their use of sex-neutral pronouns is probably in response to external pressures that have not yet affected more unconscious processes. However, social theory accepts the notion that change in action can trigger change in ways of thinking (Khosroshahi, "Penguins Don't Care, But Women Do," 516–22).

23. For examples, see Patricia Bell Scott, "The English Language and Black Womanhood: A Low Blow at Self-Esteem," *Journal of Afro-American Issues* 2 (1974), 218–24.

24. This article focuses on speech differences that vary according to sex, yet the way people talk is affected by other considerations: for example, socioeconomic level—including education and occupation; the speaker's age; how well the speaker knows the listener; the topic discussed; the place of the conversation—such as a church or the speaker's own house; the method of communication—such as writing versus speaking; the speaker's personality; and the linguistic form used. As researchers acquire more understanding of language and gender issues, they have learned that the correct interpretation of findings depends on the context in which the data occurred.

25. The use of more standard speech by women is common in the African-American community as well as in the various bilingual communities in the United States. Examples of studies in which African-American women were found to use more standard forms than did African-American men include Roger D. Abrahams, "The Advantages of Black English," in Johanna DeStefano, ed., *Language, Society and Education: A Profile of Black English* (Worthington, Ohio: Charles A. Jones, 1973), 97–106; Frank Anshen, "Speech Variation Among Negroes in a Small Southern Community" (Ph.D. dissertation, New York University, 1969); Walter Wolfram, *A Sociolinguistic Description of Detroit Negro Speech* (Washington, D.C.: Center for Applied Linguistics, 1969). For studies about the preferred use of English over Spanish among some Hispanic women, see Victoria Patella and William Kuvlesky, "Situational Variation in Language Patterns of Mexican American Boys and Girls," *Social Science Quarterly* 37 (1979), 855–64; Yoland Sole, "Sociocultural and Sociopsychological Factors in Differential Language Retentiveness by Sex," in Betty Lou Dubois and Isabel M. Crouch, eds., "American Minority Women in Sociolinguistic Perspective," *International Journal of the Sociology of Language* 17 (1978), 29–44.

However, bilingual communities are very complex. Ana Celia Zentella, in "Language and Female Identity in the Puerto Rican Community," in Joyce Penfield, ed., *Women and Language in Transition* (Albany: State University of New York Press, 1987), 172–73, notes that in the Puerto Rican community in New York, girls receive "more exposure to and participation in Spanish [because of] greater restriction to the house and/or mother, play and friendships with females, caretaking responsibilities with infants, attendance at Spanish religious services, and inclusion in female discussions and activities." In school, girls may favor English, but marriage and motherhood make them responsible for Spanish language maintenance. Bea Medicine, "The Role of American Indian Women in Cultural Continuity and Transition," in Penfield, *Women and Language in Transition,* 159–66, describes a similarly complex role for Lakota women in the dual use of English and their native language.

26. Peter Trudgill, "Sex, Covert Prestige and Linguistic Change in the Urban British English of Norwich," *Language in Society* 1 (1972), 179–95, reprinted in Thorne and Henley, eds., *Language and Sex,* 88–104.

27. William Labov, *The Social Stratification of English in New York City* (Washington, D.C.: Center for Applied Linguistics, 1966), 455.

28. Erving Goffman, "The Nature of Deference and Demeanor," *American Anthropologist* 58 (1956), 473–502, reprinted in Erving Goffman, *Interaction Ritual* (New York: Anchor Books, 1967), 47–95, as discussed in Barrie Thorne and Nancy Henley, "Difference and Dominance: An Overview of Language, Gender and Society," in Thorne and Henley, eds., *Language and Sex,* 17–18.

29. Penelope Eckert, "The Whole Woman: Sex and Gender Differences in Variation," *Language Variation and Change* 1 (1989), 256. Eckert's explanation also covers those situations where women's speech is innovative as well as conservative.

30. Among such discussions are Edith Folb, *Runnin' Down Some Lines: The Language and Culture of Black Teenagers* (Cambridge, Mass.: Harvard University Press, 1980); Marjorie Harness Goodwin, "Directive–Response Speech Sequences in Girls' and Boys' Task Activities," in McConnell Ginet, Borker, and Furman, eds., *Women and Language in Literature and Society,* 157–73; Shirley Brice Heath, *Ways with Words: Language, Life, and Work in Communities and Classrooms* (Cambridge, Mass.: Cambridge University Press, 1983); and Claudia Mitchell-Kernan, "Signifying, Loud-Talking and Marking," in Thomas Kochman, ed., *Rappin' and Stylin' Out: Communication in Urban Black America* (Urbana: University of Illinois Press, 1972).

31. L. A. Bailey and L. A. Timm, "More on Women's—and Men's—Expletives," *Anthropological Linguistics* 18, no. 9 (1976), 438–49. The expectation that women should use more correct and nonshocking language also explains why women are discouraged from using varieties of slang. See, for example, Galindo's discussion on the use of Calo among Chicanas in the Southwest referred to earlier in note 1.

32. B. Erickson, E. A. Lind, B. C. Johnson, and W. M. O'Barr, *Speech Style and Impression Formation in a Court Setting: The Effects of "Power" and "Powerless" Speech,* Law and Language Project Research Report no. 13 (Durham, N.C.: Duke University, 1977).

33. Dubois and Crouch, "The Question of Tag Questions."

34. Lakoff, *Language and Woman's Place,* 14–17.

35. Brent Preisler, "Linguistic Sex Roles in Conversation: Social Variation in the Expression of Tentativeness in English," in Joshua Fishman, ed., *Contributions to the Sociology of Language* 45 (Berlin: Mouton de Gruyter, 1986), 289. For an excellent discussion of these issues with *you know,* see Janet Holmes, "Functions of *You Know* in Women's and Men's Speech," *Language in Society* 15:1 (1986), 1–22.

36. For further discussion of this notion, see Ruth Brend, "Male–Female Intonation Patterns in American English," in *Proceedings of the Seventh International Congress of Phonetic Sciences, 1971* (The Hague: Mouton, 1972), 866–69, reprinted in Thorne and Henley, eds., *Language and Sex,* 84–87.

37. Sally McConnell-Ginet, "Intonation in a Man's World," in Thorne, Kramarae, and Henley, eds., *Language, Gender and Society,* 79.

38. For an example of this adjustment, see Alice H. Deakins, "Talk at the Top: Topics at Lunch" (manuscript, William Paterson College, 1989) as reported in Tannen, *You Just Don't Understand,* 256.

39. Harvey Sacks, Emmanuel Schegloff, and Gail Jefferson, "A Simplest Systematics for the Organization of Turn-Taking in Conversation," *Language* 50.4 (1974), 696–735.

40. Interrupting is different from overlapping another's speech. Overlaps are instances in which the listener starts before the speaker has concluded, but the new speaker begins at or nearly at a signaled transition point. Interruptions do not occur at signaled transition points for speaker alternation and therefore are disruptions.

41. Deborah James and Sandra Clarke, "Women, Men, and Interruptions: A Critical Review," in Deborah Tannen, ed., *Gender in Conversational Interaction* (New York: Oxford University Press, 1993), 233.

42. Ibid., 231–32. Nicola Woods, in "Talking Shop: Sex and Status as Determinants of Floor Apportionment in a Work Setting," in J. Coates and D. Cameron, eds., *Women in Their Speech Communities: New Perspectives on Language and Sex* (London: Longman, 1988), 141–57, reports on a workplace where higher status women are interrupted less frequently, but in many other conversational strategies lower status males act in a more powerful way than higher status women. Therefore, isolating one factor may skew the real facts.

43. Pamela Fishman, "Interactional Shitwork," *Heresies* 2 (May 1977), 99–101.

44. Lynette Hirschman, "Analysis of Support and Assertive Behavior in Conversations" (paper presented at the summer meeting of the Linguistic Society of America, Amherst, Mass., July 1974).

45. It is interesting that, in mixed-sex exchanges, Hirschman found that both sexes use support forms less than they do when they are in same-sex situations. This is an indication that conversations do not flow as easily across sex boundaries.

46. Elizabeth Aries, "Interaction Patterns and Themes of Males, Females, and Mixed Groups," *Small Group Behavior* 7:1 (1976), 1–18.

47. Zimmerman and West, "Sex Roles, Interruptions and Silences in Conversation" in Thorne and Henley, eds., *Language and Sex,* 124. The article refers to only ten mixed-sex exchanges here, although earlier it referred to eleven.

48. Candace West and Angela Garcia, "Conversational Shift Work: A Study of Topical Transitions Between Women and Men," *Social Problems* 35:5 (1988), 568. Tellables are topics that the speaker could have clearly said much more about had there been the opportunity to pursue them.

49. For an example of how men can use silence to dominate, see Jack W. Sattel, "Men, Inexpressiveness, and Power," in Thorne, Kramarae, and Henley, eds., *Language, Gender, and Society,* 119–24.

50. Aries, "Interaction Patterns and Themes," 12–15.

51. For discussions on the effect of topic, participants, and setting on who dominates talk, see Philip Smith, "Sex Markers in Speech," in K. R. Scherer and H. Giles, eds., *Social Markers in Speech* (Cambridge, Mass.: Cambridge University Press, 1979), 109–46; Carole Edelsky, "Who's Got the Floor?" *Language in Society* 10 (Dec. 1981), 383–421.

52. Miller and Swift, *Words and Women,* 145–47, discuss some of the earlier efforts. Discussion of newspaper policies can be found in Ralph Fasold, Haru Yamada, David Robinson, and Steven Barish, "The Language Planning Effect of Newspaper Editorial Policy: Gender Differences in *The Washington Post,*" *Language in Society* 19 (1990), 521–39. Some variation in naming practice still occurs in nonnews type stories. See Lisa Mamula, "An Examination of Media Coverage of Gender-Related Differences Using Five 1990 Gubernatorial Races (undergraduate honors thesis, Arizona State University, 1990). However, Fasold et al., Mamula, and Michael Geis (*The Language of Politics* [New York: Springer-Verlag, 1987]) are among several studies demonstrating many other important differences in the description and amount of coverage given women and men in news stories. The full reference for the specific nonsexist guidelines mentioned here is Francine Wattman Frank and Paula A. Treichler, *Language, Gender, and Professional Writing: Theoretical Approaches and Guidelines for Nonsexist Usage* (New York: The Modern Language Association of America, 1989).

53. "Call Me Madam? No, Sir, Call Me Ms. and Smile When You Say It" *Canadian Business* 60:7 (1987), 12; and Kenneth L. Dion and Regina A. Schuller, "Ms. and the Manager: A Tale of Two Stereotypes," *Sex Roles* 22:9/10 (1990), 569–77. Karen L. Adams and Alleen P. Nilsen, "Multifaceted Self-Images: Terms of Address for Faculty in Academia" (manuscript, Arizona State University, 1992), found a similar pattern. Several women with Ph.D. degrees also preferred to use *Dr.* rather than *Ms.* or *Mrs.* to show their status and to avoid any controversy about marital status or political views. Other aspects of naming are related to these changes in title. Most women in Adams and Nilsen considered the use of *Mrs. John Smith* archaic and in a professional context maintained their own birthname or former last name upon marriage or remarriage.

54. Among such publications are Gloria Steinem, "The Politics of Talking in Groups," *Ms.* (May 1981), 43; Lynn Bloom, Karen Coburn, and Joan Pearlman, *The New Assertive Woman* (New York: Delacorte Press, 1975); and B. W. Eakins and R. G. Eakins, *Sex Differences in Human Communication* (Boston: Houghton Mifflin Co., 1975).

55. Deborah Tannen, *You Just Don't Understand: Women and Men in Conversation* (New York: William Morrow and Company, Inc, 1990).

Pornography: Conflict Among Feminists

Gloria Cowan

FEMINISTS DISAGREE about pornography. One issue concerns whether it contributes to violence against women. Susan Brownmiller (1975) argues that it provides the propaganda machine that teaches men to hate women. Deriving from this is a debate over whether the harm caused by pornography warrants government control.

A Historical Overview: The Politics of Pornography

In the late 1970s feminists rallied against pornography, first demonstrating against a movie, *Snuff,* in which a woman appeared to be tortured and mutilated and ultimately murdered for sexual stimulation. They also protested a billboard of a woman in chains with a caption reading "I'm black and blue from the Rolling Stones and I love it." Several antipornography organizations emerged, including Women Against Violence in Pornography and the Media (WAVPM), Women Against Violence Against Women (WAVAW), and Women Against Pornography (WAP). In 1978 WAVAW held a national conference in San Francisco on "Feminist Perspectives on Pornography," staging a "Take Back the Night March" through San Francisco's pornography district. The conference led to the publication of *Take Back the Night* (Lederer, 1980), a book of readings on pornography in which feminists were united in viewing pornography and pornographers as the enemy.

In the 1980s attorney Catherine MacKinnon and writer Andrea Dworkin proposed that laws be passed to provide victims of pornography the right to sue for damages. They framed their bill by defining pornography as the practice of sex discrimination and a violation of women's civil rights. Persons liable would be those who trafficked in pornography, coerced anyone into pornography, forced pornography on a person, or assaulted someone due to pornography (Dworkin, 1985; MacKinnon, 1985). Versions of this bill were passed in the cities of Minneapolis and Indianapolis. The former was vetoed by the mayor. The latter was found unconstitutional by a federal court because the definition of pornography as "graphic sexually explicit subordination of women, whether in pictures or words" was broader than the "obscenity" that the Supreme Court had held is not protected by the First Amendment (*American Booksellers Association v. Hudnut,* 1984, 1985, 1986).

About the same time, another group of feminists aligned themselves with civil libertarians and formed an organization called FACT (Feminist Anti-Censorship Task Force) to oppose censorship of pornography. While they acknowledge that pornography may be offensive and even harmful misogynist propaganda, they argue that the protection of individual rights and freedom of expression are more important. These anticensorship feminists also believe that banning pornography would not eradicate violence against women.

There is a third group—the "antiantiporn" or "prosex" feminists (Russo, 1987), such as writers Ellen Willis (1983), Kate Ellis (1984), Carole Vance (1984), and Gayle Rubin (1984)—who favor pornography. They argue that patriarchal culture represses women's sexual expression and that pornography liberates women by challenging traditional assumptions of female sexuality as monogamous, romantic, tied to procreation, and expressed only in committed relationships. They see the movement against pornography contributing to the belief that female sexuality is purer, naturally superior, and essentially different from violent male sexuality.

Critics of this point of view, such as Wendy Stock (1990), equate women's adoption of patriarchal sexual relations of dominance and submission as identification with the oppressor. She states: "We do not need to define our liberation as an acceptance of the erotic inequality that characterizes the turn-on of the patriarchy" (p. 151). The argument between pro- and antipornography feminists is about whether pornography itself enslaves or liberates women—whether pornography presents women as coerced, violated, and injured or whether it promises pleasure and freedom to women.

This increasingly heated debate led to two highly political conferences. At both the 1982 Barnard College conference on sexuality and the 1987 New York University's Law School conference, feminists vehemently attacked each other. At the Barnard conference, some feminist speakers criticized antipornography women as a sexually repressive force. At the New York University conference, antipornography feminists accused prosex feminists of colluding with pornographers (Leidholdt & Raymond, 1990).

The continuing controversy escalated in 1985 when U.S. Attorney General Edwin Meese created an eleven-member Commission on Pornography. The Commission was asked to examine information accumulated about pornography since a 1970 presidential panel reported that pornography was essentially harmless to society. The chairman of the commission, Henry E. Hudson, was a strong antipornography crusader, as were a number of other commissioners, including James C. Dobson, a radio evangelist. Only three of the commissioners had not previously publicly taken a position on pornography. Public hearings were held in six cities on general concerns about pornography, law enforcement, social scientific studies, production and distribution of pornography, child pornography, and the role of organized crime. The findings were released in 1986 (Attorney General's Commission on Pornography: Final Report, 1986). In ninety-two recommendations, the Commission proposed extensive remedies, including expansion and stronger enforcement of obscenity laws and actions such as community protests and boycotts.

The commissioners could not come to a unanimous decision as to whether pornography caused harm or even what constituted harm. For some conservative commissioners, harm included masturbation, homosexuality, and premarital sex. They saw all public portrayals of sexuality as harmful. Other commissioners, particularly Ellen Levine and Judith Becker, challenged the use of laboratory research as a basis for inferring that pornography causes sexual crimes against women. Despite their awareness of the limitations of this evidence, the commissioners concluded that both sexually explicit violent materials and sexually explicit degrading materials (though stated with less confidence) increase the likelihood of aggression toward women. The commissioners were most divided on whether harm was caused by pornography that was neither violent nor degrading. While researchers criticized the Commission for overgeneralizing and misrepresenting research findings, antipornography feminists found their position that pornography harms women endorsed by conservative members of the Commission.

Although antipornography feminists and religious conservatives find themselves on the same side of the pornography issue, their reasons are quite different. The conservatives believe that pornography erodes the moral climate of society and traditional values, whereas the antipornography feminists are concerned that pornography promotes misogynist attitudes and behaviors. Also, antipornography feminists and religious conservatives would not ban the same material. Religious conservatives would ban all explicit sexual expression, whereas antipornography feminists would ban only sexually explicit material that presents women as sexually degraded and/or subordinated. Civil libertarian feminists also find themselves in sometimes uncongenial company, defending pornographers and the voices of misogyny to preserve freedom of expression. At the present time, it is not possible to equate civil libertarian views with approval of pornography, nor should antipornography feminists be grouped with religious conservatives as antisex.

In summary, among feminist writers, there appear to be three distinct groups: an antipornography group, a propornography group, and a third group whose main issue is not pornography per se but rather freedom of expression. The current debate over pornography does not fit comfortably into a liberal versus conservative political context. As we have seen, proponents and opponents of pornography cannot be identified by political party or persuasion.

Definitions and Categories of Pornography

An underlying problem is that pornography does not mean the same thing to different people. Because religious conservatives view the portrayal of sexuality itself as immoral, they label an extremely broad range of material as pornographic, including the exposure of female breasts. In contrast, antipornography feminists tend to reserve the term *pornography* for sexually explicit material that degrades or dehumanizes women or presents women as physically abused in a sexual context.[1] Pornography can be contrasted with erotica. Gloria Steinem (1980) defined pornography as "any depiction of sex in which there is clear force, or an unequal power that spells coercion . . . its message is violence, dominance, and conquest" (p. 37). The Greek roots of the word, "porn" and "graphos," indicate graphic depictions of female sexual slaves or prostitutes. In contrast, erotica involves images, usually sensual, of sexual expression that are mutually pleasurable and freely chosen. The Williams Committee, established in Great Britain in 1977, defined pornography as public content that has two features: sexual explicitness and intent to arouse (in Einseidel, 1988). This commission distinguished also between erotica and pornography. In contrast to Steinem, erotica was defined as what *expresses* sexual excitement rather than *causes* it. In 1985, the Canadian Fraser Commission was unwilling to define pornography but was willing to consider identifying different types of representations. Similarly, the Meese Commission did not define pornography but chose to examine four types of sexually explicit material rather than pornography as a whole.

"Obscenity," in contrast to pornography, has a legal meaning as defined by the Supreme Court in *Miller v. California* (1973). Here, obscenity was defined as depictions or descriptions of sexual conduct presented in a manner found to be offensive by the average person in the community and appealing to prurient (lustful or lewd) interest. It is left to each community to define on its own what constitutes obscenity. The work must also lack "serious literary, artistic, political, or scientific value." Antipornography feminists insist that obscenity is not the appropriate term to use to refer to objectionable pornography because obscenity focuses on sex rather than on subordination.

Social science researchers (Donnerstein, Penrod, & Linz, 1987) and the Meese Commission (Attorney General's Commission on Pornography, 1986) have divided pornography into four primary categories: (1) nudity without force, coercion, sexual activity, or degradation; (2) sexually explicit material (sexual activity) without violence, degradation, submission, domination, or humiliation; (3) sexually explicit material or activity without violence but with degradation, submission, domination, or humiliation; and (4) sexually violent material, including rape and sadomasochistic themes. Both researchers and the Meese Commission include mild sexual activity paired with extreme or graphic violence (such as "slasher" films) either as special categories or as part of the sexually violent category.

Feminists define pornography as sexually explicit material that is violent and/or degrading. In a study of 119 National Organization for Women (NOW) Newsletter recipients (Cowan, 1992), considerable unanimity was found regarding what was considered to be pornographic: 13 percent considered nudity pornography, 33 percent explicit sexual activity, 96 percent degrading explicit sex, and 95 percent violent explicit sex.

Feminists are particularly concerned with degrading pornography because it is both insidious and common. It is also the category most lacking in definitional clarity. The Attorney General's Commission on Pornography (1986, p. 331) defined pornography as degrading when it was characterized by "degradation, domination, subordination, and humiliation." It is material that, although not violent, depicts "people, usually women, as existing solely for the sexual satisfaction of others, usually men, or that depicts people, usually women, in decidedly subordinate roles in their sexual relations with others, or that depicts people engaged in sexual practices that would to most people be considered humiliation."

One researcher (Zillmann, 1989) calls the material he has studied "common" nonviolent pornography rather than degrading pornography in order to avoid the assumption that the type of material that dehumanizes and degrades women is rare. Zillmann (1989) has defined common pornography as "messages that depict women as sexually insatiable, as socially nondiscriminating in the sense that they seem eager to accommodate the sexual desires of any man in the vicinity, and as hypereuphoric about any kind of sexual stimulation" (p. 135).

The problem with Zillmann's definition is the implication that rampant sexuality is itself degrading to women and that a woman is degraded by her sexual availability. The extent to which men's availability and insatiability is degrading to them is never discussed. When women, but not men, are said to be degraded or dehumanized by their display of sexuality, a double standard of sexuality is applied. To use availability and insatiability as the defining characteristics of what is degrading or dehumanizing also makes it difficult to distinguish sexual expression from sexual subordination. When different criteria are used by researchers to define degrading pornography, research results assessing the impact of this category of pornography are likely to be inconsistent, thereby adding to the controversy between antipornography and propornography feminists.

Another approach to defining degrading pornography is one I and Kerri Dunn (Cowan & Dunn, 1994) have used. College students were shown clips of nine common themes in pornography and then asked to rate them in terms of how degrading they are to women. Although women rated all nine themes more degrading than did men, both men and women rated dominance and objectification of women as the most degrading of the nine themes. Women also rated penis worship highly degrading. Status inequalities, availability, and submission (the classic rape myth, where the woman is portrayed as initially resisting but is transformed into a sex-crazed participant) were rated less degrading than dominance, objectification, and penis worship, and inequality was seen as much more degrading than sexually explicit material without inequality. Overall, the results of our research are consistent with feminist theory that suggests subordination is most degrading to women

The Content of Pornography

The Attorney General's Commission on Pornography (1986) concluded that pornography has become more violent since the 1970 commission found it to be harmless. However, others disagree. Linz, Donnerstein, and Penrod (1987) point out that analyses over a long period of time of violent imagery in different media (books, films, magazines) have not been conducted. Whether or not violence in pornography has increased, the fusion of sex and violence is common fare.

A significant number of sex scenes in X-rated videos contain acts of physical aggression and rape themes, as well as themes of dominance and inequality. Cowan, Lee, Levy, and Snyder (1988) assessed the prevalence of violence, dominance, and inequality in X-rated videos. From a catalog list of 121 X-rated videos available in video rental stores in Southern California, forty-five videos were randomly selected. The 443 sex scenes in these videos were analyzed for both blatant and subtle forms of violence, dominance, and inequality. Over half of the sexually explicit scenes were coded as predominantly concerned with domination or exploitation. Twenty-three percent of these scenes contained acts of physical aggression, such as the use of whips, pinching, slapping, hair-pulling, bondage, and kicking. Six percent contained rape themes, defined as the portrayal of an attack in which the victim did not stimulate the rapist, the attack was unexpected, and the victim was an unwilling participant. Fifty-one percent of the X-rated videos studied contained one such rape scene. Verbal aggression, defined as derogatory, abusive language, occurred in 29 percent of all sexually explicit scenes, and verbal dominance, defined as language reflecting inequality, occurred in 28 percent of the scenes. Thirty-eight percent of the sex scenes contained status inequalities (occupational, age, clothing, wealth). Ninety-seven percent of the heterosexual sex scenes showed a man ejaculating on a woman's face, stomach, or buttocks. This research indicated that a significant proportion of sex scenes in X-rated videos depict sexual subordination and inequality, those themes found most degrading to women. Given the prevalence and popularity of pornography, large numbers of women and men are being exposed to portrayals of sexual violence.[2] Even when the themes depicted are not violent, they frequently depict women in degrading and subordinate positions.

Brosnius, Weaver, and Staab (1993) analyzed fifty pornographic videotapes drawn from a German archive of all materials available in the international market from 1979 to 1988. Analysis of changes over time indicated an increase in males engaging in sex with female superordinates, female initiation of sexual activity, performance of fellatio as the initial sexual behavior, and portrayals of sex between casual acquaintances. Gender inequality was noted in the younger age of females, the common depiction of women performing fellatio while assuming a kneeling posture before her standing partner, the infrequent portrayal of female orgasm, and the common depiction of ejaculation on a woman's belly, breasts, buttocks, mouth, or face. Brosnius, Weaver, and Staab concluded that pornography portrays men and women in inequitable social and sexual roles.

Some may argue that pornography is degrading, if not violent, toward men as well as toward women. Direct comparisons of dominance and exploitation of women versus men in pornography are rare. Since most pornography is made for men and reflects male fantasies, greater attention has been paid to the dehumanization and degradation of women in pornography. In the content analysis performed by Cowan, Lee, Levy, and Snyder (1988), men did most of the domination and exploitation, where domination was defined broadly as one participant controlling the sex act, either physically or verbally. Exploitation included themes of one person exploiting another or others and typically portrayed inducements of various types (alcohol, hypnosis, aphrodisiacs, money, blackmail) and inequality (status, age, occupation, and clothing differences). In 78 percent of the domination scenes and in 68 percent of the exploitation scenes, men dominated women. Where women were the dominators and exploiters, over one-third of the instances were of women dominating and exploiting other women. In their content analysis of X-rated and R-rated videos, Yang and Linz (1990) found that females were more frequently the recipients than the perpetrators of violence and sexual violence in both types of videos.

A recent analysis of fifty-four X-rated interracial pornography videos (Cowan & Campbell, in press) demonstrated that both sexism and racism occur in the incidence of acts of verbal and physical domination. Verbal and physical acts of aggression per scene were over two times more frequently perpetrated by men than by women. African-American women were targets of nearly twice as many acts of verbal and physical aggression by white men than were white women. White women received more acts of aggression from African-American men than did African-American women. Overall, African-American women received more acts of physical and verbal aggression than did white women.

Does Violent Pornography Harm Women?

Social scientists do not agree about the effects of pornography on behavior or attitudes. Some researchers, such as Donnerstein, Linz, and Penrod (1987), believe that only violent pornography causes harm, while others (Zillmann, 1989) believe that nonviolent common pornography is harmful as well. Whether something is "harmful" depends, of course, on one's values. Harm may be physical—rape and other acts of sexual violence—or attitudinal, that which encourages rape-supportive beliefs, attitudes, and values in society at large. From a feminist framework, the primary issue is whether degrading and violent pornography *leads to* subordination of or violence toward women.

Different types of pornographic material have different effects. The evidence on violent pornography is less controversial than that on degrading/dehumanizing/common pornography. Research has shown that the viewing of violent sexually explicit material affects aggressive behavior, attitudes regarding the legitimacy of violence against women, and emotions and judgments regarding victims of violence.

In several studies using primarily male college student volunteers, exposure to violent pornography increased aggression toward females in a laboratory setting (in Linz, Donnerstein, & Penrod, 1987). The aggression, it should be noted, is typical of the type of aggression studied in experiments by social psychologists—administering electric shock to a (female) confederate under the guise of providing feedback in a learning experiment. Thus, this laboratory research has demonstrated a link between violent pornography and laboratory aggression, not between violent pornography and rape.[3]

Another effect of exposure to violent pornography is desensitization, which is the blunting or lessening of emotional responses after repeated exposure to some stimulus or event. When male college students are exposed to violent pornography and then given a mock rape trial to view or read about, those exposed to violent pornography are more likely to see the victim as less injured than those exposed to other types of films or to control groups (Linz, Donnerstein, & Penrod, 1984). Desensitization may be among the most important effects of repeated exposure to sexually violent pornography because if members of a community have been desensitized to sexual violence by viewing it in media, they might tend to see a real victim of sexual violence, e.g., a rape victim, as not injured.

Exposure to violent pornography also affects beliefs in rape myths. The scenarios in pornography that suggest women enjoy being dominated and respond orgasmically to violence support the rape myths that women may incite rape in various ways and even want or enjoy rape. Portrayals that show women enjoying rape and other forms of sexual violence lead to increased acceptance of rape myths in both men and women (Malamuth & Check, 1985). Men who initially expressed some proclivity to rape (who report they would rape if they would not be caught and punished) were most likely to increase in their level of rape myth acceptance after exposure to violent pornography (Malamuth & Check, 1985). The effects on rape myth acceptance have been shown to occur several days after exposure to sexually violent films (Malamuth & Check, 1981). The link between violent pornography and sexual violence is indirect, based as it is on controlled research in a laboratory setting. Although we cannot say that pornography causes rape, we can say that pornography causes the types of attitudes rapists hold. Violent pornography increases beliefs in rape myths, and belief in rape myths is a predictor of self-reported sexual aggression (Malamuth, 1986).

Nonlaboratory evidence is also available, though limited and often controversial. This includes testimonials by rapists of adult women, child molesters, and prostitutes of the role of pornography in their lives. For example, Silbert and Pines (1984), in a study of street prostitutes, discovered a significant relationship between violent pornography and sexual abuse in the reports of these prostitutes. Although they were not asked directly about pornography, of 193 prostitutes who had been raped, 24 percent mentioned that the rapist had insisted that the prostitutes perform and enjoy extreme acts of violence that the rapist had seen or had read. Diane Russell (1982), in a telephone study of rape incidence among a random sample of 930 women in the San Francisco area, found that 10 percent reported that they had been upset by being asked by their partners to imitate pornography seen or read. Twenty-four percent of the women who had been raped by their husbands or partners reported being asked to perform acts viewed or read in pornography.

Research on imprisoned sex offenders' use of pornography is inconclusive, although some suggest correlations between sex crimes and pornography consumption (Marshall, 1989). Sex offenders are exposed to explicit pornography at an earlier age (six to ten) than nonoffenders. Marshall (1988) found that over one-third of rapists and nonfamilial child molesters used pornography immediately prior to at least one of their offenses. Familial sex offenders (incest perpetrators) used pornography less than rapists and nonfamilial pedophiles. While a significant number of nonoffenders also use rape pornography and entertain thoughts of raping women, Marshall (1989) suggests that "pornography has a negative influence on these (rapists and child molesters) men" (p. 210).

A controversial area of research is on the relationship between availability of pornography and the incidence of sex crimes at the aggregate level. Court (1984) has shown a relationship between the availability of pornography and sex crimes, including rape, across selected societies. Kutchinsky (1991), however, found no relation between sexual violence and the availability of pornography in Denmark, Sweden, Germany, and the United States. Two U.S.

studies found a strong relationship between rape rates and the per capita sales of men's magazines such as *Playboy* even when important demographic differences were taken into account (Baron & Straus, in Marshall, 1989; Scott & Schwalm, 1988).[4] Using 1980 data, sociologists Jaffee and Straus (1987) examined reported rape rates in forty-one states as related to the circulation rates of eight leading sexually explicit magazines. Sex magazine circulation was found to have a significant relationship with the rate of reported rape even when important factors such as marital status, urban-rural location, socioeconomic status, and political liberalism were controlled.

The problem with studies of the relationship between sex crimes and the availability of, and likely exposure to, pornography is, of course, that we cannot draw the inference that the availability of pornography causes sex crimes because some third factor may cause both sex crimes and tolerance of pornography. The examination of the relationship between exposure to pornography and sex crimes is useful; however, much of this work has not yet precisely identified the category of pornography most related to sexual violence, nor has it examined the relationship between availability of pornography and desensitization and attitude effects.

Does Degrading Pornography Harm Women?

Various experimental studies have suggested that exposure to degrading/dehumanizing/common pornography has negative attitudinal and emotional effects, if not behavioral effects. Zillmann (1982, 1989) and Zillmann and Bryant (1984) have found that exposure to "common"[5] pornography for six sessions created a number of changes in both female and male viewers' attitudes and emotions. These effects include trivialization of rape and increased acceptance of sexual coercion, decreased support of the women's movement, promotion of sexual callousness toward women,[6] and changes in traditional values, such as promotion of pre- and extramarital sex, increased doubts about the value of marriage and of having female children, and the increased perception of popularity of less common sexual practices (sadomasochism and violent sex). Zillmann and Bryant (1988) also found that exposure to common pornography increased male and female viewers' dissatisfaction with their partner's sexual appearance, behavior, and affection.

Check and Guloien (1989) compared the effects of violent pornography, nonviolent but dehumanizing pornography,[7] and erotica on male college students and nonstudents in Toronto, Canada. They found that exposure to both sexually violent pornography and to dehumanizing pornography, but not erotica, increased the tendency of men to say they would rape if they could be assured that they would not be caught and punished compared to control participants who had not been exposed to pornography. These findings were strongest for men who scored high on a psychoticism scale[8] and men who habitually consumed pornography.

Recent unpublished work on the effects of degrading or dehumanizing pornography (Stock, 1993) shows negative emotional effects of this type of material. Wendy Stock (1993) found that for both male and female college students, the viewing of unequal sex, using the dominance, objectification, and penis worship materials from the Cowan and Dunn (1994) study cited previously, led to more negative mood states (depression, hostility, confusion) than exposure to either mere female availability without inequality (female hypersexuality, availability, and lack of discrimination), violent pornography, or sexually explicit erotica that depicts mutuality. Among the female students specifically, exposure to both nonviolent but degrading (unequal) pornography and violent pornography increased negative moods compared to erotica and availability. Negative ratings of unequal material were significantly higher than ratings of the violent material. Stock's research supports the conclusion that subordination, rather than sexual availability, degrades women. She found that women respond negatively to both violent and degrading material. Nonviolent material can have a stronger effect on mood and evaluation than violent material.

Wendy Stock (1993) has been exploring women's real world experiences with pornography. Among college women, 42.4 percent responded affirmatively to items related to partners either showing or describing pornography to them and either asking or forcing them to act out behaviors from pornography. Of 233 college women, 16.3 percent indicated they have been upset by someone trying to get them to do what they have seen in pornographic pictures, movies, or books. Many women reported experiencing negative feelings when exposed to pornography: uncomfortable, 74.7 percent; embarrassed, 73.4 percent; disgusted, 51.5 percent; repulsed, 41.2 percent; degraded, 38.6 percent; objectified, 29.6 percent; upset, 29.6 percent; nauseated, 26.6 percent; unattractive, 26.2 percent; inadequate, 26.2 percent; and angry, 25.3 percent.

The evidence on the effects of both violent and nonviolent but degrading pornography is as controversial among researchers as the issue of pornography is among feminists. Although it has not been demonstrated that exposure to pornography directly causes rape, the evidence that violent pornography and degrading pornography contribute to attitudes condoning and trivializing sexual violence is well documented. The source of disagreement among researchers is on what, specifically, in pornography is harmful. Is it the sex, the violence, the inequality, or the fusion of sex and violence? Researchers also disagree on the generality of the findings and the implications of the findings.

Who Consumes and Approves of Pornography?

Were pornography to be infrequently consumed and relegated to dirty little places, it would not be as significant a social problem. But it is no longer necessary to go to a designated pornography theater or sex shop to obtain pornography. The advent of the video rental industry and cable television have made sexually explicit material accessible to most adults. Many mainstream and family video rental outlets have special sections where adults can find X-rated[9] material.

Accurate statistics are difficult to obtain on who watches pornography or on how much of it is bought, rented, or otherwise available. One editor of a pornography trade publication, *Adult Video News,* claimed that there were almost 400 million X-rated tape rentals in 1988–89, which represents about 12 percent of all video rentals (in Johnson, 1991). A national survey conducted by the National Opinion Research Center, the General Social Survey (GSS), has asked questions about pornography for almost thirty years. In 1989, 22.8 percent of respondents said they had seen an X-rated movie in the previous year.[10] Since 1973 from 15 to 26 percent of all respondents have admitted viewing these films (Bryant & Brown, 1989). Variations may be due to changes in the ratings systems for X-rated films and the increased usage of X-rated motion pictures through video rental for VCRs. Male viewers have outnumbered women by as much as two to one and as little as 1.5 to 1 (Burton, 1989). In the 1989 GSS survey, 31 percent of men versus 16.6 percent of women had seen an X-rated movie in the last year. However, a survey performed in 1986 of one thousand stores stocking adult videos done by *Adult Video News* (Dullea, 1986) found that women (alone or with men) rent 63 percent of X-rated tapes. Another estimate (Johnson, 1991), citing industry figures, reported that 29 percent of X-rated videos are rented by women with men, 15 percent by women alone, and 3 percent by women with women.

Despite the exposure of adult women to pornography, surveys indicate that women view pornography as more dangerous than do men (Cowan and Stahly, 1992; Thompson, Chaffee, and Oshagan, 1990). Between 1973 and 1989 the percent of women who believed sexual materials cause rape went from 60 to 74 percent, while that of men went from 46 to 52 percent. Moreover, in 1989 half of the women favored making pornography illegal to all and another 47.2 percent would make it illegal to those under 18, compared to 29.5 percent and 63.6 percent of men, respectively. This remained constant from 1984 to 1989. Although a gender gap occurs in all groups, older, less educated, more religious respondents and nonfeminist housewives were more negative toward pornography and preferred to make pornography illegal (Burton, 1989). In the 1989 survey, among women and men, older, more conservative, and more religious individuals were more likely to want to make pornography illegal. Educational level was unrelated to the desire to ban pornography. The more recent differentiation of pornography into different categories, especially that involving sexual violence, may make a difference in the public attitudes toward pornography control. A *Newsweek* poll in 1985 (Burton, 1989) found that 73 percent of the respondents would ban magazines that depict sexual violence, 68 percent would ban sexually violent movies from theaters, and 63 percent would ban the sale or rental of sexually violent videocassettes.

In my work on attitudes toward pornography control (Cowan, Chase, & Stahly, 1989; Cowan & Stahly, 1992; Cowan, 1992), samples of female college students and feminist women (NOW Newsletter subscribers) were extremely negative toward both degrading and violent pornography, rating their feelings toward such material between one and two ("extremely negative") on a seven-point scale. Few, if any, women believed that pornography liberates women.

The age of viewers may affect attitudes toward pornography. In his testimony to the Meese Commission in 1985, Bryant (in Bryant & Brown, 1989) described his findings from a random-digit-dial telephone survey of six hundred people in the Midwest. Bryant asked two hundred junior high students, two hundred senior high students, and two hundred young adults (ages nineteen to thirty-nine) about their exposure to X-rated magazines with explicit sexual acts. The average reported age of first exposure to this material was 13.5 years. Ninety-two of the junior high students and 168 of the high school students had seen an X-rated film. Across the entire sample, females reported disgust and revulsion to their first exposure in a ratio of two to one, whereas males reported a positive effect by two to one. Gender differences were also found when the participants were asked whether these X-rated materials "made them want to try anything they saw," with two-thirds of the males and 40 percent of the females responding positively. The younger respondents were more likely to want to try something they had seen: 72 percent of junior high males and 44 percent of junior high females. One-quarter of the male students and 15 percent of female junior high students also reported that they had experimented with the behaviors depicted within a few days of having seen the materials (in Brown & Bryant, 1989).

Despite laws prohibiting rental of pornographic videos to adolescents in Canada, a recent survey of 276 ninth-grade students in Toronto found that nine of ten boys and six of ten girls had viewed them (Check & Maxwell, 1992). However, one-third of the boys said they did so at least once a month, compared to only 2 percent of the girls. Also, among these fourteen-year-olds, 30 percent of the boys versus 1 percent of the girls reported that pornography is the source of their most useful information about sex. The boys who were frequent consumers and who said that they learned about sex from pornography were also more accepting of rape myths and violence against women as well as more likely to believe that forcing girls to have intercourse is acceptable. In a sample of 453 high school students, mostly from southern California, (average age 14.5), Robin Campbell and I found that 83.3 percent of the boys and 48.3 percent of the girls have been exposed to explicit pornography videos. Of those students who have been exposed, 29 percent of the boys and 10 percent of the girls reported watching it at least once a month, and 60 percent of the boys and 37 percent of the girls reported learning "some" or "a lot" from it. Thus, in both the United States and in Canada, both boys and girls are exposed to pornography at a relatively young age, although boys acknowledge greater exposure. Adolescent boys appear to respond more positively to pornography than adolescent girls. These data are troubling, suggesting that at least in Canada, adolescent boys exposed to pornography are being socialized into attitudes supportive of violence toward women.

What Is to Be Done?

The question of what to do about pornography has become a debate over censorship. This has deflected attention from the issues of how to reduce violence against women. Concerns about freedom of speech have been especially acute in the United States, where an impossible dilemma is created for many feminists. Marilyn French (1991) notes:

> Even as women are told that restraining the pervasive violence against women in films means censorship, American culture censors other depictions of violence and *licenses* white male violence against all others; most particularly it licenses male violence against women. The subliminal message is clear; male violence is legitimate; the mark of a man; women are prey. Women face a dilemma: we can be nice and say nothing or we can join Jesse Helms and his fellow unpalatable puritans in demanding censorship. This is a false couching of the problem. We need to address the real one. (p. 32)

Pornography can be regarded as "hate" speech; it expresses hatred of women. Where to draw the line on hate speech has become an important issue in connection with political correctness and freedom of expression. In an article on racist speech, Mari J. Matsuda (1989) argues against an absolutist First Amendment position due to the harm experienced by victims of hate speech individually and the harm of perpetuating racism in general. Pornography is both sexist and racist.

Censorship of pornography in the United States exists now only in the area of child pornography. Although obscenity and pornography share sexual explicitness in common, pornography is a broad term and, as noted, can be broken into different categories. Obscenity, a legal term, is narrowly defined and is based on moral offensiveness to community standards, not potential harm to women. States have the right to enforce obscenity law, and some are doing so. Enforcement of obscenity law is not censorship because censorship involves the concept of *prior restraint*. Prior restraint means that the government cannot impose restraints on the publication of speech that has not been first proven illegal (Kaminer, 1980). Thus, each piece of pornography has to be individually judged obscene. While a harm-to-women interpretation that includes degrading and dehumanizing pornography as exceeding community standards could be added to obscenity law, as it has been in Canada, the enforcement procedure would still be tedious.

The civil legislation proposed by Catherine MacKinnon and Andrea Dworkin in the 1980s was ruled unconstitutional by a federal appeals court, although the court acknowledged that pornography leads to the subordination of women at work, at home, and on the streets. More limited versions of MacKinnon's and Dworkin's model bill have been proposed. One has been introduced in Massachusetts. Another has been introduced into the U.S. Senate. The Pornography Victims' Compensation Act would allow victims of sex crimes to sue the producers and distributors of obscenity or child pornography for damages if they could prove the crime was incited by the material and if the producers should have been able to foresee that pornography would be a substantial cause of a sex crime. Unlike pornography per se, the Supreme Court has held that restriction of obscenity and child pornography is not protected by the First Amendment. Called "the Bundy Bill" after serial killer Ted Bundy, who claimed that his addiction to hard-core pornography caused him to rape and murder, this bill has been narrowed several times in order to garner the support of more members of Congress. Its primary supporters are conservatives and fundamentalist Christian organizations, though some feminists also support it (Dezell, 1992).

Other regulations may be used to limit pornography, such as community zoning laws or antidisplay laws. In Fontana, California, concerned women were instrumental in getting their community to pass "rack cover" laws, which require that sexually explicit material be hidden from the view of children in convenience stores and on the streets. The Attorney General's Commission (1986) reminds us that the citizen's right to free speech entitles individuals to speak out against materials they find unacceptable. It recommended private actions, including pickets and boycotts against producers, distributors, and retailers of pornography, letter-writing campaigns, and educational media events. Feminists have engaged in various acts of civil disobedience, resistance, and other strategies, primarily during the 1970s, including defacing billboards, media campaigns, petitions, citizens' meetings, economic boycotts, antipornography advertising, demonstrations, public education, harassing theaters, training in self-defense, and seeking allies among opponents to media violence. Nikke Craft (Clark, 1981; Craft, 1981) destroyed a collection of ten photos in the special library collection at the University of California in Santa Cruz. These photos displayed eroticized nude dead women who apparently had been murdered. She tore them into pieces and poured chocolate syrup over them. Craft defended her act by stating that the mutilation of women's body and spirit is not art but part of the sexual violence that pervades women's lives. Another act of disobedience was the destruction of over 550 copies of *Hustler* in Santa Cruz in memory of Cindy Lee Hudspeth, victim of Kenneth Bianchi, the Hillside strangler (The Preying Mantis Women's Brigade, 1981). *Hustler* had joked about Bianchi and trivialized his murder of young women.

For many feminists, censorship and obscenity laws as they are currently defined are not the answers, but surely silence is not the answer either. As MacKinnon (1991, p. 11) said: "We are not supposed to talk about the way pornography hurts women. Pornography's actions are protected as speech, but our speech against it is silenced as action."[11] Women cannot afford to be silent about pornography in fear of being labeled as sexual prudes. Pornography is more about dehumanization and violence than it is about sex. As we have learned from the study of rape, incest, battering, and harassment, speaking out is the first step in resisting the victimization and devaluation of women.

NOTES

1. MacKinnon (1985) and Dworkin define pornography as the graphic sexually explicit subordination of women through pictures and/or words that also includes one of more of the following: (1) women are presented dehumanized as sexual objects, things, or commodities; or (2) women are presented as sexual objects who enjoy pain or humiliation; or (3) women are presented as sexual objects who experience sexual pleasure in being raped; or (4) women are presented as sexual objects tied up or cut up or mutilated or bruised or physically hurt; or (5) women are presented in postures of sexual submission, servility, or display; or (6) women's body parts—including but not limited to vaginas, breasts, and buttocks—are exhibited, such that women are reduced to those parts; or (7) women are presented as whores by nature; or (8) women

are presented being penetrated by objects or animals; or (9) women are presented in scenarios of degradation, injury, torture, shown as filthy or inferior, bleeding, bruised, or hurt in a context that makes these conditions sexual (pp. 1–2).

2. Palys (1986), in an examination of X-rated films (in which the sex is explicit) and adult films (where the sex is not explicit) in Canada, found that adult films contained more violence than X-rated films; however, he examined the non–sexually explicit scenes, as well as the sexually explicit scenes, and his definition of violence may have been more narrow than that of Cowan, Lee, Levy, and Snyder (1988).

3. In these studies, the aggressive behavior was measured almost immediately after subjects viewed the violent pornography (Donnerstein, Penrod, & Linz, 1987). Also, in the laboratory experimental studies of pornography effects, participants are randomly assigned to the film viewing conditions, sometimes a neutral nonsexual and nonviolent film, and, in other studies, a sexual but nonviolent film and a violent but nonsexual film, thus eliminating systematic differences between the different exposure groups. Outside the laboratory, people who choose to watch pornography are likely to be different in many respects than those who do not choose to watch pornography. In several studies (Malamuth, Check, & Briere, 1986; Demare, Briere, & Lips, 1988), the types of men most likely to be sexually aroused by depictions of sexual violence were more likely to say that they would rape and were more accepting of an ideology justifying male dominance over women and aggression against women.

4. Baron (1990) has reported that states having higher rates of pornography magazine circulation are also higher on indicators of gender equality. Baron suggests that both pornography and equality of women are more likely in states with greater political tolerance.

5. As noted previously, Zillmann (1989) attributes the effects in his studies to the portrayal of women as sexually insatiable and available.

6. Linz, Donnerstein, and Penrod (1988) report that they have been unable to replicate the Zillmann and Bryant findings regarding exposure to nonviolent pornography and sexual callousness toward women. Further, they found no effects of either the X-rated nonviolent or R-rated extremely violent films on such beliefs and attitudes about women.

7. Check and Guloien (1989) define dehumanizing pornography as that which portrays women as "hysterically responsive to male sexual demands, verbally abused, dominated, and degraded, and treated as a plaything with no human qualities other than her physical attributes" (p. 163).

8. Psychoticism measures include items that indicate feelings of isolation, thought control by others, obsessive thoughts, and other extreme ideations.

9. X-rated films refer to a rating system used by the Motion Picture Association of America (MPAA), with this designation indicating the presence of explicit sexual activity or extreme quantities and varieties of violence. Producers often attach X (or XXX) ratings to their sexually explicit films without subjecting them to MPAA review (Yang & Linz, 1990). No one under the age of eighteen is admitted to see these movies in theaters; however, video rental shops may not adequately monitor the age of those renting X- (or R-rated violent) material. This material is now labeled "NC-17."

10. Analysis of the 1989 GSS data was performed by the author of this chapter from data provided to the California State University system by the National Opinion Research Center.

11. The idea expressed by MacKinnon and her supporters is that pornography shows real violence happening to real people and is more than speech. This statement also implies that attempts to redress the harm done to women by pornography is taken more seriously than the harm of pornography itself.

REFERENCES

American Booksellers v. Hudnut, 598 F.Supp 1319 (S D. Ind. 1984), aff'd 771 F.2nd 323 (7th Cir. 1985), aff'd 475 U.S. 1001 (1986).

Attorney General's Commission on Pornography: Final Report. 1986, July. Washington, D.C.: U.S. Department of Justice.

Baron, Larry. 1990. Pornography and gender equality: An empirical analysis. *Journal of Sex Research* 27:363–80.

Brosnius, Hans-Bernd, James B. Weaver III, & Joachim F. Staab. 1993. Exploring the social and sexual "reality" of contemporary pornography. *Journal of Sex Research* 30:161–70.

Brownmiller, Susan. 1975. *Against our will: Men, women, and rape.* New York: Simon & Schuster.

Bryant, Jennings, & Dan Brown. 1989. Uses of pornography. In Dolf Zillmann & Jennings Bryant (Eds.), *Pornography: Research advances and policy considerations* (pp. 25–55). Hillsdale, NJ: Lawrence Erlbaum.

Burton, Doris-Jean. 1989. Public opinion and pornography policy. In Susan Gubar & Joan Hoff (Eds.), *The dilemma of violent pornography* (pp. 133–46). Bloomington: Indiana University Press.

Check, James V. P., and Ted H. Guloien. 1989. Reported proclivity for coercive sex following repeated exposure to sexually violent pornography, nonviolent dehumanizing pornography, and erotica. In Dolf Zillmann & Jennings Bryant (Eds.), *Pornography: Research advances and policy considerations* (pp. 159–84). Hillsdale, NJ: Lawrence Erlbaum.

Check, James V. P., & Dale K. Maxwell. July 1992. Pornography consumption and pro-rape attitudes in children. Paper presented at the 25th International Congress of Psychology, Brussels.

Clark, D. A. 1981. Stack O' Wheats: An exercise in issues. In Frederique Delacoste & Felice Newman (Eds.), *Fight back: A resource book on feminist resistance to male violence* (pp. 254–59). Minneapolis: Celis Press.

Court, John H. 1984. Sex and violence: a ripple effect. In Neil M. Malamuth & Edward Donnerstein (Eds.), *Pornography and sexual aggression* (pp. 143–72). New York: Academic Press.

Cowan, Gloria. 1992. Feminist attitudes toward pornography control. *Psychology of Women Quarterly* 16:165–78.

Cowan, Gloria, & Robin R. Campbell. In press. Racism and sexism in interracial pornography. *Psychology of Women Quarterly.*

Cowan, Gloria, Cheryl Chase, & Geraldine Stahly. 1989. Feminist and fundamentalist women's attitudes toward pornography control. *Psychology of Women Quarterly* 13:97–112.

Cowan, Gloria, & Kerri F. Dunn. 1994. What themes in pornography lead to perceptions of the degradation of women? *Journal of Sex Research, 31,* 11–21.

Cowan, Gloria, Carol Lee, Danielle Levy, & Debbie Snyder. 1988. Dominance and inequality in x-rated videocassettes. *Psychology of Women Quarterly* 12:299–312.

Cowan, Gloria, & Geraldine Stahly. 1992. Attitudes toward pornography control. In Joan Chrisler & Doris Howard (Eds.), *New directions in feminist psychology: Theory and research* (pp. 200–14). New York: Springer.

Craft, Nikki. 1981. The incredible use of the Stack O' Prints mutilations. In Frederique Delacoste & Felice Newman (Eds.), *Fight back: A resource book on feminist resistance to male violence* (pp. 247–49). Minneapolis: Celis Press.

Demare, Dano, John Briere, & Hilary M. Lips. 1988. Violent pornography and self-reported likelihood of sexual aggression. *Journal of Research in Personality* 22:140–53.

Dezell, Maureen. March 9, 1992. Bundy's revenge. *The New Republic,* 15–16.

Donnerstein, Edward, Daniel Linz, & Steven Penrod. 1987. *The question of pornography: Research findings and policy implications.* New York: The Free Press.

Dullea, Georgia. October 6, 1986. X-rated couples films finding a new market. *New York Times.*

Dworkin, Andrea. 1985. Against the male flood: Censorship, pornography and equality. *Harvard Women's Law Journal* 8:1–29.

Einseidel, Edna F. 1988. The British, Canadian, and U.S. pornography commissions and their use of social science research. *Journal of Communication* 38:108–21.

Ellis, Kate. 1984. I'm black and blue from the Rolling Stones and I'm not sure how I feel about it: Pornography and the feminist imagination. *Socialist Review* 14:103–25.

French, Marilyn. 1991. A choice we never chose. *The Women's Review of Books* 8(10–11):31–32.

Jaffee, David, & Murray A. Straus. 1987. Sexual climate and reported rape: A state-level analysis. *Archives of Sexual Behavior* 16:107–23.

Johnson, John. February 17, 1991. Into the valley of sleaze. *Los Angeles Times Magazine,* 9–18.

Kaminer, Wendy. 1980. Pornography and the First Amendment: Prior restraints and private actions. In Laura Lederer (Ed.), *Take back the night* (pp. 241–47). New York: William Morrow.

Kutchinsky, Berl. 1991. Pornography and rape: Theory and practice? *International Journal of Law and Psychiatry* 14:47–64.

Lederer, Laura. 1980. *Take back the night: Women on pornography.* New York: William Morrow.

Leidholdt, Dorchen, & Janice C. Raymond. 1990. Preface. In Dorchen Leidholdt & Janice C. Raymond (Eds.), *The sexual liberals and the attack on feminism* (pp. ix–xvii). New York: Pergamon Press.

Linz, Daniel, Edward Donnerstein, & Steven Penrod. 1984. The effects of multiple exposures to filmed violence against women. *Journal of Communication* 34:130–47.

Linz, Daniel, Edward Donnerstein, & Steven Penrod. 1987. The findings and recommendations of the Attorney General's Commission on Pornography: Do the psychological "facts" fit the political fury? *American Psychologist* 42:946–53.

Linz, Daniel, Edward Donnerstein, & Steven Penrod. 1988. Effects of long-term exposure to violent and sexually degrading depictions of women. *Journal of Personality and Social Psychology* 55:758–68.

MacKinnon, Catherine A. 1985. Pornography, civil rights, and speech. *Harvard Civil Rights–Civil Liberties Law Review* 20:1–70.

MacKinnon, Catherine A. Summer 1991. To quash a lie. *Smith Alumnae Quarterly,* 11–14.

Malamuth, Neil. 1986. Predictors of naturalistic sexual aggression. *Journal of Personality and Social Psychology* 50:953–62.

Malamuth, Neil, & James V. P. Check. 1981. The effects of mass media exposure on acceptance of violence against women: A field experiment. *Journal of Research in Personality* 15:436–46.

Malamuth, Neil, & James V. P. Check. 1985. The effects of aggressive pornography on belief of rape myths: Individual differences. *Journal of Research in Personality* 19:299–320.

Malamuth, Neil M., James V. P. Check, & John Briere. 1986. Sexual arousal in response to aggression: Ideological, aggressive, and sexual correlates. *Journal of Personality and Social Psychology* 50:330–40.

Marshall, W. L. 1988. The use of sexually explicit stimuli by rapists, child molesters, and non-offenders. *Journal of Sex Research* 25:267–88.

Marshall, W. L. 1989. Pornography and sex offenders. In Dolf Zillmann & Jennings Bryant (Eds.), *Pornography: Research advances and policy considerations* (pp. 215–34). Hillsdale, NJ: Lawrence Erlbaum.

Matsuda, Mari J. 1989. Public response to racist speech: Considering the victim's story. *Michigan Law Review* 87:2320–81.

Miller v. California, 413 U.S. 15 (1973).

Palys, T. S. 1986. Testing the common wisdom: The social content of video pornography. *Canadian Psychology* 27(1):22–35.

The Preying Mantis Women's Brigade. 1981. Actions against *Hustler.* In Frederique Delacoste & Felice Newman (Eds.), *Fight back: A resource book on feminist resistance to male violence* (pp. 264–65). Minneapolis: Celis Press.

Rubin, Gayle. 1984. Thinking sex. In Carole Vance (Ed.), *Pleasure and danger: Exploring female sexuality* (pp. 267–219). Boston: Routledge & Kegan Paul.

Russell, Diana H. 1982. *Rape in marriage.* New York: Macmillan.

Russo, Ann. 1987. Conflicts and contradictions among feminists over issues of pornography and sexual freedom. *Women's Studies International Forum* 10:103–12.

Scott, Joseph E., & Loretta A. Schwalm. 1988. Rape rates and the circulation rates of adult magazines. *Journal of Sex Research* 24:241–50.

Silbert, Mimi H., & Ayala M. Pines. 1984. Pornography and sexual abuse of women. *Sex Roles* 10:857–68.

Steinem, Gloria. 1980. Erotica and pornography: A clear and present difference. In Laura Lederer (Ed.), *Take back the night: Women and pornography* (pp. 35–39). New York: William Morrow.

Stock, Wendy. 1990. Toward a feminist praxis of sexuality. In Dorchen Leidholdt & Janice C. Raymond (Eds.), *The sexual liberals and the attack on feminism* (pp. 148–56). New York: Pergamon Press.

Stock, Wendy. 1993. The effects of pornography on women. Paper presented at Speech, Equality, and Harm Conference, Chicago, March 1993, and annual meeting of the Society for the Scientific Study of Sex, Chicago, November 5, 1993.

Thompson, Margaret E., Steven H. Chaffee, & Hayg H. Oshagan. 1990. Regulating pornography: A public dilemma. *Journal of Communication* 40(3):73–83.

Vance, Carole. 1984. *Pleasure and danger: Exploring female sexuality.* Boston: Routledge & Kegan Paul.

Willis, Ellen. 1983. Feminism, moralism, and pornography. In Ann Snitow, Christine Stansell, & Sharon Thompson (Eds.), *Powers of desire: The politics of sexuality* (pp. 160–67). New York: Monthly Review Press.

Yang, Ni, & Daniel Linz. 1990. Movie ratings and the content of adult videos: The sex-violence ratio. *Journal of Communication* 40(2):28–42.

Zillmann, Dolf. 1982. Pornography, sex callousness and the trivialization of rape. *Journal of Communication* 32:10–21.

Zillmann, Dolf. 1989. Effects of prolonged consumption of pornography. In Dolf Zillmann & Jennings Bryant (Eds.), *Pornography: Research advances and policy considerations* (pp. 127–57). Hillsdale, NJ: Lawrence Erlbaum.

Zillmann, Dolf, & Jennings Bryant. 1984. Effects of massive exposure to pornography. In Neil M. Malamuth & Edward Donnerstein (Eds.), *Pornography and sexual aggression* (pp. 115–38). New York: Academic Press.

Zillmann, Dolf, & Jennings Bryant. 1988. Pornography's impact on sexual satisfaction. *Journal of Applied Social Psychology* 18:438–53.

The Revolution for Women in Law and Public Policy

Jo Freeman

A REVOLUTION IN PUBLIC policy toward women happened in the 1960s and 1970s. Beginning with passage of the equal pay act in 1963 and the prohibition against sex discrimination in employment in 1964, Congress added numerous laws to the books that altered the thrust of public policy toward women from one of protection to one of equal opportunity. While implementation is incomplete, and equal opportunity by itself will not eradicate women's secondary position in society, the importance of this fundamental change should not be underestimated.

Parallel to this development the Supreme Court fundamentally altered its interpretation of women's position in society. Until 1971, the judicial approach to women was that their rights and responsibilities, opportunities and obligations, were essentially determined by their position in the family—the role of wife and mother. Women were viewed first and foremost as members of a dependent class whose individual rights were subservient to their class position. From this perspective virtually all laws that classified by sex were constitutional. Today most such laws have been found unconstitutional. The remaining laws and practices that treat the sexes differently are subject to more searching scrutiny than in the past, and the Court is particularly disapproving of rationalizations for them that encourage dependency.

The Tradition of Institutionalized Dependence

Until the 1930s the primary locus of governmental activity was in the states, not the federal government. Most of the laws that heavily affected people's lives were state laws. Article I, § 8 of the Constitution limits the areas in which the federal government may act, and the Tenth Amendment reserves all other powers to the states or to the people. Federal laws take precedence when there is a conflict, but it is only in the last fifty years that the Supreme Court has interpreted the Constitution to allow an expansion of federal authority. In the mid 1960s Congress elaborated on the means available to it to influence state policy, such as tying federal funds to the passage of specific laws. Despite this expansion, many policy arenas are still reserved to the states.[1]

The state legislature is not the only source of state law. This country inherited from Great Britain a large body of "common law," which was essentially the collective wisdom of individual judges deciding individual cases over hundreds of years, as collected and commented on by several great British jurists. This common law has remained operative in every state and any policy arena in which a state legislature has not passed a superceding statute. Although all new law is now supposed to be statutory in origin, the power of individual judges to interpret statutes as well as to reinterpret the original common law, and their willingness to adapt both to changing circumstances, has created an American common law in each state.

FAMILY LAW

Under the English common law a woman lost her legal identity upon marriage; it *merged* into that of her husband under the feudal doctrine of *coverture*. The result was succinctly stated by Justice Black in 1966 as resting "on the old common-law fiction that the husband and wife are one . . . [and] that . . . one is the husband."[2] The consequences were described by Edward Mansfield when he wrote the first major American analysis of *The Legal Rights, Liabilities and Duties of Women* in 1845.

> It appears that the husband's control over the person of his wife is so complete that he may claim her society altogether; that he may reclaim her if she goes away or is detained by others; that he may use constraint upon her liberty to prevent her going away, or to prevent improper conduct; that he may maintain suits for injuries to her person; that she cannot sue alone; and that she cannot execute a deed or valid conveyance without the concurrence of her husband. In most respects she loses the power of personal independence, and altogether that of separate action in legal matters.[3]

The merger of husband and wife into one person resulted in many common law principles that seem strange today. In the criminal law a husband and wife could not be guilty of conspiring together or of stealing one another's property. Husbands could not rape their wives. If a wife committed a criminal act in her husband's presence, it was assumed to be under his direction; he was the guilty party, not her. In the civil law, neither spouse could maintain a tort action (a civil wrong) against the other, nor could either testify against the other. A husband, but not a wife, could sue a third party for loss of consortium (services, society, companionship, and affection) resulting from injuries to the spouse.[4]

At common law these marital disabilities were offset by spousal obligations. The fundamental basis of the marital relationship was that husbands and wives had reciprocal—not equal—rights. The husband had to support the wife and children, and the wife had to render services as a companion, housewife, and mother in return. This doctrine did not mean wives could sue husbands for greater support, since by definition she did not have a separate legal existence. Nor did it give her a right to an allowance, wages, or income of any sort. But it did permit wives to obtain "necessaries" from merchants on their husbands' account. Even after all the states passed Married Women's Property Acts in the nineteenth century, permitting wives to retain control of their separate property, husbands were still obligated to pay their wives' debts when incurred for family necessities.[5] This spousal obligation continued after death or divorce. On marriage a wife obtained a *dower* right to the use, for her natural life, of one-third of the husband's property after his death, regardless of any will to the contrary. She retained that right even if he sold the property before he died, unless she specifically relinquished it to the purchaser. If the marriage ended in divorce, she was entitled to continued support, though not to the custody or guardianship of the children, unless she was at fault for the demise of the relationship.

Eight states that were originally controlled by France or Spain—California, Idaho, Texas, Washington, Arizona, Louisiana, Nevada, and New Mexico—did not inherit the English common law and thus followed rules developed in continental Europe. Under their *community property* systems each spouse is considered owner of half of the earnings of the other, and all property acquired during marriage (other than gifts and inheritances) is jointly owned by both spouses, regardless of who paid for it or whose name it is in. However, the result was often the same because the husband was considered to be the head of the household and as such could manage and dispose of the community property as he wished.

In 1979 Louisiana became the last state to give both spouses the legal right to manage the community property. The case that led to its revocation is a good example of how little protection joint ownership really gave to a wife. Louisiana's "head and master" law permitted a husband the unilateral right to dispose of jointly owned community property without his wife's knowledge or consent. In 1974 Joan Feenstra had her husband incarcerated for molesting their minor daughter. To pay the attorney who represented him in this action, he executed a mortgage on their home. Louisiana law did not require the husband to get his wife's permission to do this or even to inform her of his action, although the house had been paid for solely out of her earnings. After the charges were dropped, a legal separation was obtained, and the husband left the state, the attorney foreclosed on the mortgage, and Joan Feenstra challenged the constitutionality of the statute in federal court. During legal proceedings Louisiana changed the law to permit equal control, but only prospectively. However, the Supreme Court declared that the original statute had been unconstitutional and invalidated the mortgage.[6]

Several of the common law property states have occasionally adopted some of the community property rules. In the 1940s several passed laws to allow one-half of a husband's earnings to be considered as his wife's income in order to obtain more favorable income tax rates for married couples. When the federal government created joint filing in 1948 so couples could split their income, these states returned to common law rules.[7] In 1983 the Commission on Uniform State Laws proposed a Uniform Marital Property Act, which created a modern form of community property. Wisconsin adopted this with modifications in 1984, making it the ninth real community property state.[8]

Family law varies considerably from state to state because it is not an area in which the Constitution permits the federal government to act and thus impose uniformity. Between 1917 and 1947, thirty-three constitutional amendments were proposed to give Congress that authority, and twelve bills were introduced to provide for uniform marriage and divorce laws should such an amendment be ratified. None of these proposals were even voted on, let alone passed by Congress, and the idea faded. Nonetheless, states often follow each other's lead in changing their laws, and model laws are often proposed by nongovernmental entities and adopted by several states. After Mississippi passed the first Married Women's Property Act in 1839, the other states passed similar acts throughout the nineteenth century. These eventually removed the worst of women's legal disabilities. After Suffrage the National Woman's Party and the League for Women Voters proposed changes in the many state laws that affected men and women differently, though only a few were passed.

What was left prior to the beginning of the contemporary feminist movement in the mid 1960s was something of a patchwork quilt of common law dictates and statutory changes. In most states married women did not have the legal right to retain their own name or maintain a separate domicile. Husbands remained liable for support of their families, but a wife was responsible if the husband had no property and was unable to support them, or himself. Paternal preference in guardianship and custody of children had gradually shifted to the standard of what was in the best interests of the child, though several states provided that, all else being equal, the mother should be preferred if the child was of tender years and the father if the child was old enough to require education or preparation for adult life. Some states gave husbands a right equivalent to that of "dower," in effect requiring his permission before a wife could sell her separate property, just as hers was necessary for him to completely convey his. Half of the community property states provided that a wife could control her own earnings. In virtually all states wives could contract and sue independently of their husbands, though some states still required a husband's permission for a married woman to participate in an independent business, and a few denied wives the legal capacity to become a surety or a guarantor.[9] Indeed, in the 1920s Miriam Ferguson, elected governor of Texas after her husband had been impeached, had to secure a court order relieving her of her marital disabilities so there would be no doubt about the legality of her acts as governor.[10] And in the 1960s a married Texas woman successfully defended against the United States government's efforts to collect a judgment against her for an unpaid Small Business Administration loan on the grounds that her disability to bind her separate estate by contract had not been removed by court decree as required by Texas law.[11]

PROTECTIVE LABOR LEGISLATION

Protective labor legislation refers to numerous state laws that restricted the number of hours women could work, the amount of weight they could lift, occasionally provided for special privileges such as rest periods, and often excluded them entirely from night work or certain occupations. The first effective law, enacted in Massachusetts in 1874, limited the employment of women and children to ten hours a day. By 1900 fourteen states had such laws, and by the mid 1960s every state had some form of protective labor legislation.[12] There were two forces behind the drive for this legislation. One was organized labor, which saw women workers as competitors. Their policy was explicitly stated by President Strasser of the International Cigar Makers Union in 1879: "We cannot drive the females out of the trade, but we can restrict this daily quota of labor through factory laws."[13] The other was social reformers, who found the Supreme Court unreceptive to protective laws that applied to both sexes.

In 1905 the Supreme Court declared unconstitutional a New York law that prohibited bakers from working longer than ten hours a day or sixty hours a week. In *Lochner v. New York* the Court said that "the limitation necessarily interferes with the right of contract between the employer and employee . . . [which] is part of the liberty of the individual protected by the Fourteenth Amendment."[14] Three years later it upheld an Oregon law that restricted the employment of women in factories, laundries, or other "mechanical establishments" to ten hours a day on the ground that women's

> physical structure and a proper discharge of her maternal functions—having in view not merely her own health but the well-being of the race—justify legislation to protect her. . . . The limitations which this statute places upon her contractual powers . . . are not imposed solely for her benefit, but also largely for the benefit of all. . . . The reason . . . rests in the inherent difference between the two sexes, and in the different functions in life which they perform.[15]

With this precedent, the drive for protective legislation became distorted into a push for laws that applied to women only on the principle that half a loaf was better than none. Reformers eventually persuaded the Supreme Court that maximum hours and other forms of protective labor legislation were valid health measures for men as well as women,[16] but the opposition of organized labor to protective legislation for men focused their efforts on securing it for women. The 1938 Fair Labor Standards Act eventually provided federal protection for both sexes, but by then sex-specific laws governing the conditions under which women could work had gained a momentum of their own. The effect of these laws on women was controversial when they were passed and continued to be so long after they were in place. Those who supported them, particularly the Women's Bureau of the Department of Labor, claimed they effectively reduced the economic exploitation of women. Those who opposed them, including the National Woman's Party and the National Federation of Business and Professional Women, argued that they mostly protected men from female competition. These laws kept women out of jobs requiring night work and from promotions into positions requiring overtime or lifting more than the proscribed weights. During World War II protective labor laws were suspended to allow women to work in war industries and were reimposed after the war, when women were forced to leave.[17]

CIVIL AND POLITICAL RIGHTS

It is a common myth that when the Nineteenth Amendment extended suffrage to women on the same basis as men in 1920, all other civil and political rights automatically followed. In reality, few followed easily. Most required continual struggle. In the first few years after Suffrage there were even attempts to keep women from running for public office on the grounds that the right to vote didn't bring with it the right to be voted on.

One of the first uses to which women put their new right to vote was to change federal law to give women equal rights to citizenship with men.

Although the English common law allowed married women to retain their citizenship when they married foreign nationals, in the nineteenth century both Britain and the United States adopted the idea that a married woman's nationality should be that of her husband. In 1907 the United States made this principle automatic regardless of where the couple lived or the intentions of the husband to become a U.S. citizen. The first decade of the twentieth century was a period of heavy immigration, and the consequences of this law to native-born American women who married immigrants were quite onerous. Many states prohibited aliens from inheriting or buying real property or closed them out of some professions (e.g., law, medicine, teaching). During World War I, many American women married to foreign nationals found themselves classified as enemy aliens and their property confiscated.

Feminists achieved one of their first legislative successes in 1922, when Congress passed the Cable Act, separating a married woman's citizenship from that of her husband. However, it did not create equal citizenship rights or completely rectify major injustices. For example, in 1928 Ruth Bryan Owen's election to Congress was challenged by her opponent on the grounds that she had not met the constitutional requirement of seven years of citizenship. Owen, daughter of frequent Democratic Presidential candidate William Jennings Bryan, had lost her citizenship in 1910 when she married a British army officer. The 1922 act did not automatically restore her citizenship but only gave her the right to be renaturalized. The requirements were so burdensome that she was not renaturalized until 1925. This injustice, and continual lobbying by women's organizations, prompted several revisions in the law, until citizenship rights were finally equalized in the 1930s.[18]

The longest battle was over jury service, which feminists felt was an important indicia of citizenship, even though potential jurors are often less than enthusiastic over being called to serve. Traditionally, under the common law, juries were composed only of men, except in certain situations involving a pregnant woman. In this country the First Judiciary Act of 1789 mandated that federal jurors should have the same qualifications as those of the state in which the federal court was sitting, and no state permitted women to sit as jurors until Utah did so in 1898. In 1880 the Supreme Court found that the exclusion of blacks from jury service was unconstitutional but noted that this was not true of women.[19] Only twelve states conferred jury duty with enfranchisement. In the rest, many decades of trench warfare in the legislatures were necessary just to achieve the right to be in the jury pool; equal obligation to serve was the exception. By 1965 Alabama, Mississippi, and South Carolina still completely excluded women, and in only twenty-one states were women eligible on the same basis as men. In eighteen states and the District of Columbia, women were exempted based solely on their sex; in eight states, the exemption was limited to women with family responsibilities. It was not until the Civil Rights Act of 1957 that all citizens were deemed qualified to sit on federal juries, regardless of state law, and even this law was not implemented until the Federal Jury Selection and Service Act of 1968 specifically prohibited exclusion on the basis of race, color, religion, sex, national origin, or economic status.[20]

Women have often found employment opportunities in the state and federal civil service that they did not find in the private sector, but they have also found these opportunities limited by the law and by official rulings. In 1919, all federal civil service examinations were finally opened to women, but each department head could specify the sex of those he wished to hire for any position. This was not changed until 1962. Ironically, the right to specify sex was *not* opposed by most women in government. Civil service rules gave veterans preference over nonveterans, and since few women were veterans, many were concerned that they would not be hired for even the lowest level clerical jobs if sex could not be specified.

However, women were all opposed to laws and administrative rulings that prohibited both spouses from holding government jobs; even when the rulings did not explicitly state that the wife would be the spouse to lose her job, that was the practice. The first attempt to remove married women from the federal civil service was made in 1921. This effort failed, but a similar one was finally successful in 1932. Since federal employees included school teachers in the District of Columbia and military draftees, a teacher married to an army private could find herself dependent solely on his income. Many other states followed suit during the Depression, in the belief that hard times required that jobs be distributed as widely as possible. One job per family was the demand; removal of women was the outcome. Teachers were the hardest hit; by 1931 most school systems would not hire married women and would not retain women when they married. Although the federal law was repealed in 1937 and pressure on married women eased with World War II, when these women were needed in the labor force, state laws limiting their employment in government positions still existed as late as the 1950s.[21]

Sex and the Supreme Court

For many decades the courts made it clear that the traditional concern of public policy with women's family role went far beyond her legal rights and obligations within the marital relationship. Indeed, her family role formed the basis of her legal existence. The earliest case challenging a discriminatory law to reach the Supreme Court was instigated by Myra Bradwell, who objected to the refusal of Illinois to admit women to the practice of law. She and other women looked upon the newly ratified Fourteenth Amendment as an opportunity to remove some onerous legal barriers. In 1873 the Supreme Court rejected her argument that admission to the bar was a privilege and immunity of citizenship that could not be abridged by the states. Most telling was a concurring opinion by three justices which explained that

> [t]he natural and proper timidity and delicacy which belongs to the female sex evidently unfits it for many of the occupations of civil life. The constitution of the family organization, which is founded in the divine ordinance, as well as in the nature of things, indicates the domestic sphere as that which properly belongs to the domain and functions of womanhood. The harmony, not to say identity, of interests and views, which belong, or should belong, to the family institution is repugnant to the idea of a woman adopting a distinct and independent career from that of her husband. . . .
>
> It is true that many women are unmarried and not affected by any of the duties, complications, and incapacities arising out of the married state,

but these are exceptions to the general rule. The paramount destiny and mission of woman are to fulfill the noble and benign offices of wife and mother. This is the law of the Creator, and the rules of civil society must be adapted to the general constitution of things, and cannot be based upon exceptional cases.[22]

This rationale continued for almost a century. As late as 1961 Court decisions reflected a refusal to see women as individual people in preference to their identity as members of a class with a specific social role. That year a unanimous Court rejected a request by a Florida woman to overturn her conviction by an all-male jury for murdering her husband with a baseball bat during a "marital upheaval." Florida did not completely exclude women from jury service, but it was one of seventeen states that exempted women solely on the basis of their sex. This exemption took the form of assuming women did not wish to serve unless they registered a desire to do so with the court clerk, an assumption not made for men. Consequently, when Gwendolyn Hoyt's trial took place in 1957, only 220 women out of forty-six thousand eligible registered female voters had volunteered, and only ten of these were among the ten thousand people on the jury list constructed by the court clerk. The Court rejected her argument that "women jurors would have been more understanding or compassionate than men in assessing the quality of [her] act and her defense of 'temporary insanity.' " Instead it ruled that

> the right to an impartially selected jury . . . does not entitle one . . . to a jury tailored to the circumstances of the particular case, . . . It requires only that the jury be indiscriminately drawn from among those eligible in the community for jury service, untrammeled by any arbitrary and systematic exclusions. . . .
>
> . . . Despite the enlightened emancipation of women from the restrictions and protections of bygone years, and their entry into many parts of community life formerly considered to be reserved to men, woman is still regarded as the center of home and family life. We cannot say that it is constitutionally impermissible for a State, acting in pursuit of the general welfare, to conclude that a woman should be relieved from the civic duty of jury service unless she herself determines that such service is consistent with her own special responsibilities. . . .
>
> This case in no way resembles those involving race or color in which the circumstances shown were found by this Court to compel a conclusion of purposeful discriminatory exclusions from jury service. [cites omitted] There is present here neither the unfortunate atmosphere of ethnic or racial prejudices which underlay the situations depicted in those cases, nor the long course of discriminatory administrative practice which the statistical showing in each of them evinced.[23]

THE FOURTEENTH AMENDMENT

To understand the logic of the Court and to appreciate the significant change in orientation that the Supreme Court began in 1971, one has to understand the structure of legal analysis that has developed around the Fourteenth Amendment. The most far-reaching of the Civil War Amendments, the simple language of Section I imposed restrictions on State action that had previously only been imposed on the Federal government by the Fifth Amendment. These were that

> no state shall make or enforce any law which shall abridge the privileges or immunities of citizens of the United States; nor shall any State deprive any person of life, liberty, or property, without due process of law; nor deny to any person within its jurisdiction the equal protection of the laws.

The Supreme Court ruled very early that the "privileges and immunities" clause did not convey any rights that had not previously existed and thus shut that avenue of legal development. When Virginia Minor demanded suffrage as a right of citizenship, the Court said that since voting was not a privilege or immunity of national citizenship before the Fourteenth Amendment, it did not become one afterward.[24] The due process clause was for many decades used to undermine state economic regulations such as those found unconstitutional in *Lochner* as well as most of the New Deal legislation prior to 1937. This doctrine was called "substantive due process." Consequently, the quest for equality focused on the "equal protection" clause. Until 1971 this quest was a futile one for women. Initially the courts ruled that race and only race was in the minds of the legislators when the Fourteenth Amendment was passed. "We doubt very much whether any action of a state not directed by way of discrimination against negroes as a class or on account of their race will ever be held to come within the purview of this provision."[25] The prohibi-tion on racial discrimination was soon expanded to include national origin[26] and alienage.[27] Fundamental rights, such as voting, travel, procreation, criminal appeals, or those protected by the First Amendment, were eventually brought under the protective umbrella of the Fourteenth Amendment as well.[28]

This umbrella did not protect everyone or every right. Instead, in the post–New Deal era, two tiers of equal protection analysis emerged.[29] Not *all* legal discrimination was prohibited, only *invidious* discrimination. If a *compelling* state interest can be shown, distinct laws or state practices—such as those necessary to integrate school districts—based on race or nationality are permitted. The essence of this approach is that certain classifications are "suspect" and thus subject to "strict scrutiny" by the courts. Unless there is a "compelling state interest," they will be struck down. Classifications that are not suspect are not subject to the same searching inquiry. The state need only show that there is a *rational basis* for their existence, and the court will defer to the legislature.

In practice, classifications that are subject to strict scrutiny are almost always invalidated as unconstitutional. Classifications for which only a rational basis need be shown have almost always survived. The courts have shown great deference to the state legislatures and have gone out of their way to construct rationalizations for legal distinctions that to the untrained eye might seem to have only the flimsiest of reasons. For example, in 1948 the Court upheld a Michigan law that prohibited women from working in bars unless they were the wives or daughters of a male owner. Six justices felt this was an easy case to decide.

> The fact that women may now have achieved the virtues that men have long claimed as their prerogatives and now indulge in vices that men have long

practiced does not preclude the States from drawing a sharp line between the sexes, certainly in such matters as the regulation of the liquor traffic. . . .

While Michigan may deny to all women opportunities for bartending, Michigan cannot play favorites among women without rhyme or reason. . . . Since bartending by women may, in the allowable legislative judgment, give rise to moral and social problems against which it may devise preventive measures, the legislature need not go to the full length of prohibition if it believes that as to a defined group of females other factors are operating which either eliminate or reduce the moral and social problems otherwise calling for prohibition. Michigan evidently believes that the oversight assured through ownership of a bar by a barmaid's husband or father minimizes hazards that may confront a barmaid without such protecting oversight. . . . We cannot cross-examine either actually or argumentatively the mind of Michigan legislators nor question their motives. Since the line they have drawn is not without a basis in reason, we cannot give ear to the suggestion that the real impulse behind this legislation was an unchivalrous desire of male bartenders to try to monopolize the calling.[30]

The development of the two-tier system of jurisprudence meant that the outcome was determined by the level of analysis chosen rather than the reason for the classification. The "strict scrutiny" test was usually fatal, while the "rational basis" test was usually meaningless. Thus, in order to eliminate a legal classification, one has to convince the courts that it should be subject to strict scrutiny.

THE TURNING POINT: REED AND FRONTIERO

It was not until 1971 that the Court demonstrated displeasure at a State's "drawing a sharp line between the sexes,"[31] when it unanimously held unconstitutional an Idaho statute giving preference to males in the appointment of administrators of estates. In *Reed v. Reed* the Court found the "administrative convenience" explanation of the preference for males to have no rational basis.[32] Although unexpected, this development was not unforeseeable. During the previous few years the Court had been adding a bit of bite to the rational basis test by looking more closely at state rationalizations as they applied to *some* statuses or *some* interests that did not trigger strict scrutiny.[33] In the previous two years the emerging women's movement had become publicly prominent, and the Equal Rights Amendment had been battling its way through Congress.[34] Despite the Court's assertion that "the Constitution does not require legislatures to reflect sociological insight, or shifting social standards,"[35] the Court itself often does just that. A still stronger position was taken seventeen months later, when Air Force Lieutenant Sharon Frontiero challenged a statute that provided dependency allowances for males in the uniformed services without proof of actual economic dependency but permitted them for females only if they could show they paid one-half of their husband's living costs. Eight members of the Court found the statute unconstitutional, but they split as to the reason. Four applied strict scrutiny, using language very different from that of previous cases.

There can be no doubt that our Nation has had a long and unfortunate history of sex discrimination. Traditionally, such discrimination was rationalized by an attitude of "romantic paternalism" which, in practical effect, put women not on a pedestal, but in a cage. . . .

Moreover, since sex, like race and national origin, is an immutable characteristic determined solely by the accident of birth, the imposition of special disabilities upon the members of a particular sex because of their sex would seem to violate "the basic concept of our system that legal burdens should bear some relationship to individual responsibility. . . ." *Weber v. Aetna Casualty Surety Co.,* 406 U.S. 164, 175 (1972). And what differentiates sex from such nonsuspect statuses as intelligence or physical disability, and aligns it with the recognized suspect criteria, is that the sex characteristic frequently bears no relation to ability to perform or contribute to society. As a result, statutory distinctions between the sexes often have the effect of indiviously relegating the entire class of females to inferior legal status without regard to the actual capabilities of its individual members.[36]

Three justices found the statute unconstitutional on the authority of *Reed*—that administrative convenience was not a rational basis—while deliberately avoiding the characterization of sex as a suspect classification.[37] They gave as the compelling reason for such avoidance the fact that

the Equal Rights Amendment, which if adopted will resolve the substance of this precise question, has been approved by the Congress and submitted for ratification by the States. If this Amendment is duly adopted, it will represent the will of the people accomplished in the manner prescribed by the Constitution. By acting prematurely and unnecessarily, . . . the Court has assumed a decisional responsibility at the very time when state legislatures, functioning within the traditional democratic process, are debating the proposed Amendment. It seems . . . that this reaching out to pre-empt by judicial action a major political decision which is currently in process of resolution does not reflect appropriate respect for duly prescribed legislative processes.[38]

INTERMEDIATE SCRUTINY

In cases after *Reed* and *Frontiero* the Court applied a "strict rational basis" standard with greater and greater scrutiny, until in 1976 a new standard, subsequently referred to as one of "intermediate scrutiny," was articulated. On the surface, *Craig v. Boren* did not appear to be a potentially momentous case. It concerned an Oklahoma law that prohibited the selling of "3.2" beer to men under twenty-one but allowed its sale to women over eighteen. The state's rationale for this law was that more than ten times as many males as females between eighteen and twenty-one were arrested for drunk driving. The Court found the law unconstitutional, holding that "classifications by gender must serve important governmental objectives and must be substantially related to achievement of those objectives." It was not satisfied that "sex represents a legitimate, accurate proxy for the regulation of drinking and driving."[39]

After *Craig* the Court no longer wrote plurality opinions in which some justices supported use of strict scrutiny in gender cases and others concurred or dissented on a different basis. Instead, the "heightened scrutiny" of the new intermediate standard was applied consistently, though not unanimously, to strike down laws that made distinctions by sex in half the cases that came before the Court.[40] Yet even before *Craig* the language of the post-*Reed* decisions reflected a very different approach by the Court to women's status than that of previous cases. No longer was a woman's family status determinant of her legal status. Instead the very articulation by a State of the desirability of economic dependency or women's unique responsibility for family obligations to justify a sex-discriminatory law was viewed as irrational. Two cases decided in the spring of 1975 illustrate this profound transformation from the assumptions of *Hoyt* and earlier cases.

Weinberger v. Wiesenfeld challenged a provision of the Social Security Act that provided benefits for the surviving widow and minor children of a working man covered by the act but for only the minor children of a covered woman. Wiesenfeld's wife was the primary earner in the family. When she died in childbirth, he received fewer benefits than she would had he been the one to die. The unanimous opinion of the Court pointed out that

> since the Constitution forbids . . . gender-based differentiation premised upon assumptions as to dependency . . . [it] also forbids the gender-based differentiation that results in the efforts of female workers required to pay social security taxes producing less protection for their families than is produced by the efforts of men.

The Court further recognized the father's as well as the mother's responsibility for child care.

> It is no less important for a child to be cared for by its sole surviving parent when the parent is male rather than female. And a father, no less than a mother, has a constitutionally protected right to the "companionship, care, custody, and management" of "the children he has sired and raised."[41]

A month later the Court went further in *Stanton v. Stanton,* a Utah case in which a divorced father ceased paying child support to his daughter when she reached age eighteen but continued to pay child support for his son on the grounds that in Utah girls were no longer minors after eighteen, but boys were until age twenty-one. The Court found that

> no longer is the female destined solely for the home and the rearing of the family, and only the male for the marketplace and the world of ideas. . . . [I]f the female is not to be supported so long as the male, she hardly can be expected to attend school as long as he does, and bringing her education to an end earlier coincides with the role-typing society has long imposed.[42]

The Supreme Court continued to strike down state statutes that reinforced role-typing and economic dependency or rested on "archaic and overbroad generalizations." In doing so it invalidated statutes that provided for Social Security benefits payable to widows but not to widowers,[43] alimony for wives but not for husbands,[44] welfare benefits to families with unemployed fathers but not unemployed mothers,[45] and worker's compensation death benefits to widows, but to widowers only if they could prove economic dependency.[46]

JURY SERVICE

Even though intermediate scrutiny was not in place until 1976, by 1975 the Supreme Court was ready to take a new look at some state laws it had previously upheld. One of these concerned jury service. In the years since *Hoyt* more women had been added to the jury roles, and no state excluded them totally, but they did not serve equally everywhere.[47] Alabama's total exclusion was found unconstitutional under the Fourteenth Amendment by a three-judge federal district court in 1966.[48] That same year, the Supreme Court of Mississippi ruled that "the legislature has the right to exclude women so that they may continue their service as mothers, wives and homemakers, and also to protect them . . . from the filth, obscenity and noxious atmosphere that so often pervades a courtroom during a jury trial."[49] Mississippi's law was changed by the legislature in 1968, and South Carolina's by a voter referendum in 1967. The state of Louisiana had a statute limiting women's jury service that was virtually identical to the Florida statute upheld in *Hoyt* in 1961. Taylor had been sentenced to death for aggravated kidnapping by a jury chosen from an all-male pool of 175. Even before he was tried he claimed he was denied his Sixth Amendment right to a fair trial by "a representative segment of the community." This time the Court agreed. While it did not specifically overrule *Hoyt,* it did say it was out of date. Substantiating its position with a lengthy footnote on women's labor force participation, the Court concluded that "[i]f it was ever the case that women were unqualified to sit on juries or were so situated that none of them should be required to perform jury service, that time has long since passed."[50]

It was nineteen years before the Supreme Court decided another case on on gender discrimination in jury service. When it did so in 1994, it followed the path it had cut on race discrimination a few years earlier. In selecting a jury, both sides of every case have the right to challenge a certain number of individuals in the jury pool without giving a reason. These are called peremptory challenges. In four cases decided between 1986 and 1992 the Supreme Court ruled that race cannot be the basis of a peremptory challenge not only because defendants are entitled to a jury selected without the taint of race discrimination, but because potential jurors have a right to jury selection procedures that are free from stereotypes and "historical prejudices".[51]

The federal courts of appeal disagreed on whether peremptory challenges could be used to systematically eliminate all men or all women from a jury. In 1993 the Supreme Court granted certiorari to an Alabama man who was being sued for child support by a state agency. After the State used its peremptory challenges to remove 9 men, a jury of 12 women declared him to be the father. The State supported its action on the grounds that "men otherwise totally qualified to serve upon a jury might be more sympathetic and receptive to the arguments of a man alleged in a paternity action to be the father of an out-of-wedlock child, while women equally qualified to serve upon a jury might be more sympathetic and receptive to the arguments of the complaining witness who bore the child."[52]

Justice Blackmun, writing for the Court, expressed surprise that the State would so freely rely on "the very stereotype the law condemns." He went on to declare

Discrimination in jury selection, whether based on race or on gender, causes harm to the litigants, the community, and the individual jurors who are wrongfully excluded from participation in the judicial process. The litigants are harmed by the risk that the prejudice which motivated the discriminatory selection of the jury will infect the entire proceedings. (cites omitted) The community is harmed by the State's participation in the perpetuation of invidious group stereotypes and the inevitable loss of confidence in our judicial system that state-sanctioned discrimination in the courtroom engenders.[53]

The decision's sweeping language hid some fears that the traditional role of peremptory challenges—to limit jury bias by allowing both parties to remove jurors they did not feel good about even when a reason could not be articulated—was being eroded. Justice O'Connor voted with the majority reluctantly and urged that the decision be limited to the state as a party, not private litigants. Justices Rehnquist, Scalia, and Thomas dissented, on the grounds that the "heightened scrutiny" standard for sex cases was not the "strict scrutiny" required for race. Rehnquist went on to say that

Unlike the Court, I think the State has shown that jury strikes on the basis of gender "substantially further" the State's legitimate interest in achieving a fair and impartial trial through the venerable practice of peremptory challenges. (cites omitted) The two sexes differ, both biologically and, to a diminishing extent, in experience. It is not merely "stereotyping" to say that these differences may produce a difference in outlook which is brought to the jury room. Accordingly, use of peremptory challenges on the basis of sex is generally not the sort of derogatory and invidious act which peremptory challenges directed at black jurors may be.[54]

EDUCATION

Single-sex schools have presented particular challenges. Although most schools are now coeducational, neither the Court nor the Congress has decided that schools segregated by sex hold quite the stigma as those segregated by race. This is partially because sex-segregated schools have never been part of a state policy to denigrate a particular group in the way that racial segregation was. Even when single-sex schools were most common, there were still many coed ones available—though they didn't always offer the same educational advantages or weren't always the most prestigious. There is ambivalence also because of evidence that going to single-sex schools benefits at least some women.[55] Consequently, the judicial response to single-sex schools has been equivocal.

The Supreme Court faced the issue of the constitutionality of single-sex public schools in 1971, 1977, and 1982. In 1971 it merely affirmed without a written opinion the ruling of a District judge that men could not attend South Carolina's female-only state college.[56] The lower court had relied on the rational basis test—eight months before *Reed.* In 1982 the Court finally held that equal protection had been denied, but in a very limited context.

Mississippi University for Women, founded in 1884, had established a Nursing School in 1970. Like the rest of its programs, it was restricted to women only. Men could audit classes and participate as though they were students, but they could not matriculate. A male registered nurse who lived in the same town as MUW wanted a B.A. degree in nursing but didn't want to move to attend one of the other two schools in Mississippi that offered that degree coeducationally. In a five to four decision written by the newest member of the Court, Justice Sandra Day O'Connor, the Court held that "MUW's policy of excluding males from admission . . . tends to perpetuate the stereotyped view of nursing as an exclusively woman's job" and thus is not consistent with the State's claimed justification that the single-sex admissions policy "compensates for discrimination against women and, therefore, constitutes educational affirmative action." Instead the Court found that the "policy of permitting men to attend classes as auditors fatally undermines its claim that women, at least those in the School of Nursing, are adversely affected by the presence of men."[57]

Midway between these two cases a more ambivalent Court had split four to four (Rehnquist didn't participate) on whether or not Philadelphia could maintain sexually segregated public high schools. While the city had many coed schools, it had only two college preparatory high schools for academically superior students—one for boys and one for girls. Susan Vorchheimer did not want to be forced to choose between a coed environment and an academically enriched one. However, the schools were similar in their offerings except for a better science curriculum at the one for boys, and Vorchheimer did not maintain that she wanted to attend the boys high school to avail herself of science courses. The District Court found that the school board could not substantiate "separate but equal" schools, but the circuit court found otherwise. Placing great weight on Vorchheimer's failure to allege any educational deprivation and the fact that attendance at the superior schools was voluntary, it completely ignored the "intangible factors" upon which the Supreme Court had relied in dismantling racially segregated schools. "If there are benefits or detriments inherent in the system, they fall on both sexes in equal measure," it said. By dividing equally on appeal, the Supreme Court left the decision in force but without the precedential value of an affirmation.[58]

By 1992 very few single-sex public schools remained. Two of these were military colleges—the Citadel in South Carolina and Virginia Military Institute. The latter was one of fifteen public colleges in Virginia, most of which had been single-sex at one time. In 1970 the University of Virginia had integrated under threat of a federal District Court order;[59] in 1990 VMI was the only single-sex school left in the state. When VMI's male-only policy was challenged that year, the parties reflected a growing consensus that, whatever the benefits of single-sex education might be, it was not good government policy to support such schools. The plaintiff was the U.S. government, even though it was headed by a conservative Republican administration. Friend of the Court briefs were filed by over a dozen feminist and liberal organizations. The defendants were the State of Virginia, VMI itself, and its board. But the black Democratic Governor of Virginia and the female State Attorney General wanted no part of the case. Governor Wilder responded to the complaint by stating that "no person should be denied admittance to a state supported school because of his or her gender," VMI had to enlist the aid of an alumnus to act as its pro bono attorney.

Although the federal district court found VMI's male only policy "fully justified," the appeals court was ambivalent. Applying intermediate scrutiny it said that VMI offered a unique educational experience, based on mental and physical stress in a hostile, sexually homogeneous environment that "would be destroyed by coeducation." It also admitted that "[m]en and women are different" and that "it is not the goal of the Equal Protection Clause to attempt to make them the same. . . . [N]o one suggests that equal protection of the laws requires that all laws apply to all persons without regard to actual differences." However, it added, "While the data support a pedagogical justification for a single-sex education, they do not materially favor either sex." Therefore, the court asked, why does the Commonwealth of Virginia offer "the opportunity only to men"? The court could not find a policy statement that answered this question, apart from the Governor's opposition. Since the Constitutional standard required a substantial relation to an important governmental objective, and "evidence of a legitimate and substantial state purpose is lacking," the appeals court sent the case back to the District court to find a solution consistent with the guarantees of the Fourteenth Amendment. Although the appeals court didn't specify what this had to be, it suggested that the state admit women to VMI, set up a "separate but equal" educational opportunity, or "abandon state support of VMI, leaving [it] . . . to pursue its own policies as a private institution." An appeal to the Supreme Court was denied.[60]

VMI chose to fight. When the case was remanded to the District Court it presented a plan for women to take a "parallel program" called the "Virginia Women's Institute for Leadership" at nearby Mary Baldwin College for Women. Although the Justice Department opposed this plan as a poor substitute for VMI's rigorous and highly disciplined military environment, the disctrict court judge who had originally approved VMI's single-sex policy also approved the creation of a separate and admittedly unequal program for women. He said it was "justified pedagogically and . . . not based on stereotyping."

> [T]he controlling legal principals in this case do not require the Commonwealth to provide a mirror image of VMI for women. Rather, it is sufficient that the Commonwealth provide an all-female program that will achieve substantially similar outcomes in an all-female environment . . . which takes into account the differences and needs of each sex.[61]

NEW PROTECTIONS

The Constitution protects individuals only from action by the state, not from action by private parties. Thus private parties can discriminate on any basis they choose unless the state says otherwise. Many statutes have been passed prohibiting discrimination; sometimes those statutes are challenged as themselves violative of a Constitutional provision. The Supreme Court has heard three cases brought by private associations challenging restrictions on their membership policies as interfering with their First Amendment right of free association. California, Minnesota, and New York City all passed ordinances prohibiting sex (and some other) discriminations by some types of clubs often thought of as private. Their rationale was that many of these clubs were in fact arenas for the conduct of business or the exchange of information important to people's careers, and that therefore discrimination was "invidious." The Court has unanimously upheld all of these statutes, ruling that any "slight infringement on . . . members' rights of expressive association . . . is justified because it serves the State's compelling interest in eliminating discrimination against women."[62]

CURRENT RATIONALES FOR SEX-DISCRIMINATORY LAWS

The Court has relied on two different rationales for sex discriminatory statutes. The first is that women benefit. This was articulated in *Kahn v. Shevin,* which was decided in 1974, before *Craig* but after *Frontiero.* The Court upheld a Florida statute giving widows but not widowers a five-hundred-dollar property tax exemption. The majority ruled that the state law was "reasonably designed to further the state policy of cushioning the financial impact of spousal loss upon the sex for which that loss imposes a disproportionately heavy burden,"[63] without questioning whether there might be some more appropriate indicator than sex of financial incapacity. Even after *Craig* established a more stringent standard than reasonableness, the Court continued to look favorably upon statutes that it felt operate "to compensate women for past economic discrimination." *Califano v. Webster* upheld a Social Security provision that, prior to 1972, permitted women to eliminate more low-earning years from the calculation of their retirement benefits than men because it "works directly to remedy some part of the effect of past discrimination."[64]

Schlesinger v. Ballard introduced the second rationale, that men and women are not "similarly situated." Federal statutes that provided more time for female than for male naval officers to attain promotion before mandatory discharge were upheld as being consistent with the goal of providing women equitable career advancement opportunities. The Court found that because women were restricted from combat and most sea duty, it would take longer for them to compile favorable service records than for men. Therefore, "the different treatment of men and women naval officers . . . reflects, not archaic and overbroad generalizations, but, instead the demonstrable fact that [they] are *not* similarly situated with respect to opportunities for professional service."[65] This explanation was also relied upon to uphold a California statute that made statutory rape a crime that only males could commit against females. The state Supreme Court had already subjected the classification to "strict scrutiny" and found a "compelling state interest" in preventing teenage pregnancies. Applying the lesser standard of "important governmental objectives," the Supreme Court came to the same conclusion, but only by ignoring the dissent's objection that a sex-specific statute was not "substantially related" to the stated goal as long as a gender-neutral one could achieve the same result.[66]

THE DRAFT REGISTRATION CASES

This line of cases led inexorably to *Rostker v. Goldberg,* which contested the requirement that males but not females register for a potential draft. Draft registration had been discontinued in 1975, but was reactivated by President

Carter in 1980 as part of his response to the Soviet invasion of Afghanistan. In his request to Congress for funds for this purpose, Carter also asked that the statute be amended to permit registration and conscription of females. After extensive debate, Congress left the statute intact. This activated a lawsuit that had begun in 1971 but been dormant for many years. Three days before draft registration was to begin, a lower federal court found the Act unconstitutional and enjoined the government from further registration. Relying on the intermediate scrutiny test of *Craig*, the court concluded that "military opinion, backed by extensive study, is that the availability of women registrants would materially increase flexibility, not hamper it."[67] The injunction was lifted and registration continued while the Supreme Court pondered the effect of its new approach to gender cases on the oldest bastion of the male establishment. In this effort the Court was caught between the conflicting demands of two institutions to which it had traditionally deferred—the Congress and the military. The Court has always accorded great weight to the decisions of Congress, which had restricted registration to men. It has also deferred to judgments by the executive departments in the area of military affairs, and the military had testified before Congress that women should be registered (though not drafted). However, the Court noted that Congress's thorough consideration of the issue clearly established that its decision to exempt women was not the "accidental byproduct of a traditional way of thinking about females." It concluded that the "purpose of registration . . . was to prepare for a draft of *combat* troops" and that "[w]omen as a group, . . . unlike men as a group, are not eligible for combat." Because men and women were not "similarly situated" with regard to military service, it was not unconstitutional to distinguish between them. "The Constitution requires that Congress treat similarly situated persons similarly, not that it engage in gestures of superficial equality."[68]

On the surface it might seem desirable for the Court to require equality where men and women are similarly situated but make exceptions apparently in women's favor where they are not. However, since there are very few circumstances in which men and women are similarly situated, this line of thought could easily lead to a return of the inequitable protectionism of the *Muller* era. The different standards that that case legitimated for men and women provided only limited benefits. In the long run women were protected from better jobs, overtime, and the opportunity to compete with men rather than to be dependent on them.

An example of the consequences of protecting women from military service is to be found in *Personnel Administrator of Massachusetts v. Feeney*. While the Federal Government and almost all states give veterans preference for civil service jobs, Massachusetts is one of the few that gives them an absolute preference. After job candidates' scores have been computed on the basis of an examination and an assessment of their training and experience, those who pass are ranked. However, all passing veterans are ranked ahead of all nonveterans. Consequently, nonveteran Helen Feeney had never been able to secure one of the many civil service jobs she took exams for over a twelve-year period, even though she scored very high. During this period she held a lower level civil service job that was abolished in 1975, prompting her lawsuit. A lower federal court held the statute unconstitutional on the grounds that while it was not intended to discriminate against women, since only 1.8 percent of the veterans in Massachusetts were female the exclusionary impact was so severe that the State should be required to find a less extreme form of rewarding veterans. The Supreme Court found otherwise. Ignoring the fact that women were once restricted to only 2 percent of the armed forces, the Court nonetheless said that a neutral law with an adverse impact is unconstitutional only if discriminatory intent can be shown. It rejected the argument that the exclusion of women was such an inevitable and foreseeable consequence that the Massachusetts legislature must be held responsible for intending it even if that were not its primary objective. Instead the Court said that "the law remains what it purports to be: a preference for veterans of either sex over nonveterans of either sex, not for men over women."[69]

PREGNANCY AND PARENTHOOD

Pregnancy and parenthood have presented unique challenges to the Court, and the results have not been uniform. Gender-neutral statutes applying to pregnant persons may have a discriminatory impact on women even though all women do not get pregnant and even fewer are pregnant at any given time. Similarly, parenthood has a social and legal status in addition to its biological one, and the three do not always coincide. The rights of parents are further complicated by the assumption that in cases concerning children, the overriding principle should be the best interests of the child. The delicate balancing acts these conflicting concerns cause has led to inconsistent results and occasionally convoluted reasoning.

In 1974 the Court heard two cases against school boards in Virginia and Ohio that challenged policies that required pregnant teachers to take unpaid maternity leaves beginning several months before birth and continuing for several months afterward. The Court found these requirements to be discriminatory, but not on equal protection grounds. Instead the justices said that the women were denied due process because the rules created an irrebuttable presumption that pregnant teachers and recent mothers were incapable of performing their duties. Such a presumption put too heavy a burden on a woman's decision to have a child.[70] However, that same year it upheld the exclusion of pregnancy from coverage under the California disability insurance system. In *Geduldig v. Aiello* the Court said that the

> program does not exclude anyone from benefit eligibility because of gender but merely removes one physical condition—pregnancy—from the list of compensable disabilities. While it is true that only women can become pregnant, it does not follow that every legislative classification concerning pregnancy is a sex-based classification. . . . The program divides potential recipients into two groups—pregnant women and nonpregnant people.[71]

A year later the Court again looked to the due process clause to strike down a Utah statute that denied pregnant women unemployment benefits from twelve weeks before until six weeks after birth. In order to receive benefits from the Unemployment Insurance fund, claimants have to be able and willing to work at their usual occupation. As in the school board cases, it was the assumption that *no* woman could work during this period that the Court found unacceptable.[72] In 1976 Congress amended the Unemployment Compensation Act to prohibit denial of claims solely on the basis of pregnancy or termination of pregnancy.[73] This did not resolve the problems of women who quit their jobs because they were pregnant. Unemployment benefits are not given to anyone who quits a job unless it is for "good cause." When a Missouri woman who quit found no job openings after giving birth and was denied benefits, the Court upheld the State's judgment that childbirth was not a "good cause." In analyzing the statute, Justice O'Connor said that it should be construed "as prohibiting disadvantageous treatment, rather than mandating preferential treatment."[74]

By and large the Court has permitted the States to make distinctions between unwed mothers and fathers. A 1972 case appeared to be part of the emerging trend to look more closely at gender distinctions, but it was temporary. In *Stanley v. Illinois* a father who had intermittently lived with and supported his three children and their mother for eighteen years protested their automatic removal from his custody by the state after the mother's death. He demanded the same hearing on his fitness as a parent that the state accorded married fathers and all mothers. The state courts declined to give him this until the Supreme Court said the Constitution entitled him to equal protection with married fathers.[75] But in five subsequent cases only one more statute was invalidated. In 1977 the Court upheld an immigration statute giving preferred status to the children of unmarried mothers but not unmarried fathers.[76] It also upheld two Georgia statutes permitting unwed mothers but not unmarried fathers to veto the adoption[77] or sue for the wrongful death of a child.[78] Since fathers who subsequently legitimated their children had the same legal rights as other parents, the court found that the actual distinction in the law was not one of gender but one between fathers who did and did not legitimate their children.

In two New York cases raising the same issue—whether an unmarried father could block the adoption of his child—the Court split. The prospective adoptive parent in both cases, as in the Georgia one, had married the children's mother and wished to adopt her children over the objection of the biological father. The Court had to balance the traditional preference for "the best interests of the child" against claims of gender discrimination. In 1979 the Court ruled in favor of the biological father by five to four.[79] But in 1983 it returned to its earlier reasoning that the state had met its due process obligations by providing a means by which the father could legitimate his child and that a father who did not do so had no rights.[80] As legal doctrine, these decisions on the rights of unwed fathers are not consistent; the divided Court reflects the competing priorities it had to sort out and justify. However, if one reads the facts of the cases apart from the legal analysis, the crucial factor appears to be the kind of relationship the father had with his children and their mother. The more closely it approximated the social norm at some prior time—i.e., how long the father lived with the mother and supported the children—the more likely the Court was to rule in his favor.

ABORTION

The movement to change restrictive abortion laws began independently of and earlier than the women's liberation movement, but when that movement emerged it quickly captured the abortion issue as its own, energizing and publicizing it along the way. It was the impetus of the feminist movement that led to *Roe v. Wade,* the 1973 Supreme Court decision that eliminated most state abortion laws, after only a few years of public debate and state action on abortion. In some ways the Court was ahead of its time, because public debate had not yet created a consensus. The Court's sweeping removal of a century of legal restriction sparked massive efforts to reduce and reverse its effects. The legal and political controversy has become so polarized that it borders on civil war. It has also tainted many issues that are not obviously related to abortion, with the result that some legislation that might have passed or passed sooner has been stymied. The state battles over ratification of the ERA were infected by opponents' claims that restrictions on abortion would be precluded by it as a denial of equal rights on account of sex.[81] The Court decisions and legislative initiatives that followed *Roe v. Wade* can only be understood within a political context. Rather than reflect changes in legal doctrine that often follow social change, as exemplified by the reinterpretation of the Equal Protection Clause, new decisions and laws are best seen as the victories and defeats of an ongoing political struggle.

Laws prohibiting abortion were largely passed during the middle decades of the nineteenth century. Prior to that time the rules of the English common law prevailed, and those rules permitted abortion until the fetus moved. This was called quickening and occurred between the sixteenth and eighteenth weeks of pregnancy, or well into the second trimester. The movement for state laws prohibiting all abortions (except to save the life of the mother) was part of a larger movement by medical practitioners to institutionalize and professionalize their occupation.[82] Ironically, the medical profession also spearheaded the movement for legal reform in the middle of the twentieth century. By the 1950s several hundred thousand illegal abortions were being performed each year, with several thousand ending in death. Many physicians felt their ability to help their patients was limited by the strict laws; they sought ways of liberalizing them.

In 1967 Colorado became the first state to adopt a law permitting therapeutic abortions if the life or mental health of the mother was threatened, if pregnancy occurred from rape or incest, or if the fetus was deformed. That same year several referral services were set up by nonphysicians to direct women to safer illegal abortions. The public debate over abortion laws became more vociferous, and in the next couple years another ten states adopted therapeutic exceptions. Four states—Alaska, Hawaii, New York, and Washington—went further and repealed virtually all restrictions on abortion. Both of these developments were boosted by the women's movement and the injection into the medical debate of the idea that reproductive freedom was a woman's right. Cases began to reach the lower courts in the late 1960s.

Initially these just chipped away at the legal restrictions. Then, in 1969 and 1970, the California Supreme Court and several federal district courts declared their states' laws unconstitutional. In 1971 the Supreme Court granted certiorari to two cases from Texas and Georgia; seven justices heard oral argument in 1971, but the Court asked for a rehearing in 1972 with a full Court. Its decision was announced on January 22, 1973.[83]

Justice Blackmun, writing the majority opinion in *Roe v. Wade* and *Doe v. Bolton,* did not stick to legal analysis. Recognizing the "sensitive and emotional nature of the abortion controversy," he surveyed medical, religious, moral, and historical material before concluding that "this right of privacy, whether it be founded in the Fourteenth Amendment's concept of personal liberty . . . or, . . . in the Ninth Amendment's reservation of rights to the people, is broad enough to encompass a woman's decision whether or not to terminate her pregnancy." While asserting "that the word 'person,'" as used in the Fourteenth Amendment, "does not include the unborn," the Court did recognize that "a State may properly assert important interests in safeguarding health, in maintaining medical standards and in protecting potential life."[84] Therefore it adopted the medical division of pregnancy into three trimesters.

> (a) For the stage prior to approximately the end of the first trimester, the abortion decision and its effectuation must be left to the medical judgment of the pregnant woman's attending physician.
> (b) For the stage subsequent to approximately the end of the first trimester, the State, in promoting its interest in the health of the mother, may, if it chooses, regulate the abortion procedure in ways that are reasonably related to maternal health.
> (c) For the stage subsequent to viability, the State, in promoting its interest in the potentiality of human life may, if it chooses, regulate and even proscribe, abortion except where it is necessary, in appropriate medical judgment, for the preservation of the life or health of the mother.[85]

Antiabortion forces organized and tested *Roe's* limits by passing laws and bringing test cases. One group of laws restricted the use of public funds for abortions. Called the "Hyde Amendments" for their most outspoken sponsor, Cong. Henry Hyde (R. Ill.), these attachments to annual appropriations bills deny any federal money authorized by these bills to be used for abortions. Included are restrictions on abortions for military personnel, Peace Corps volunteers, Indians served by federal health programs, health benefits for federal employees, and foreign assistance programs for which abortion is a family planning method. These laws exempt abortions to save the life of the mother; some of them also exempt pregnancies from rape or incest. All of these laws have stimulated acrimonious conflict.

The most controversial have been the restrictions on federal funds for Medicaid recipients—poor people. Several states responded to *Roe* by refusing to pay for Medicaid abortions. In 1977 the Court held that the States did not have to fund abortions for Medicaid-eligible women and could choose to fund only "medically necessary" abortions without violating the Equal Protection clause.[86] The first Hyde Amendment passed Congress in 1976; it reached the Supreme Court in 1980. The Court held that the federal government had no constitutional or statutory obligation to fund abortions even when they were medically necessary.[87] As a result of the Hyde Amendments, the number of federally funded abortions went from 294,600 in 1977 to 165 in 1990. States still have the option of paying for the procedure with state money. In 1990 thirteen states spent sixty-five million dollars for 162,418 abortions. The District of Columbia used to be one of the biggest state funders of abortions, but because much of its budget comes from the federal government, it is subject to Congressional control. Since 1988 Congress has amended the annual appropriations bills to forbid the District to use locally raised funds for abortions.[88]

The other set of cases have tested the extent to which states can regulate the performance of abortion. The success of state restrictions has varied with the composition of the Court, which changed significantly during the Reagan and Bush administrations. Initially the Court affirmed *Roe* and applied strict scrutiny to state regulations. It upheld requirements that a doctor inform a woman about abortion and obtain written consent, but only if the requirements did not interfere with the physician-patient relationship. It found spousal consent statutes unconstitutional but parental notification requirements acceptable if a minor could present her request to a judge when a parent would not agree. Reporting requirements about abortions to the State were constitutional, but mandatory hospitalization and twenty-four-hour waiting periods were not. Advertising could not be restricted, and fetal protection statutes could apply only to viable fetuses.[89]

By 1989 enough conservatives had been added to the Court for the balance of opinions to shift. On July 3, 1989, the Court upheld Missouri's prohibition of abortions on public lands or by public employees and its requirement that viability tests be done on women more than twenty weeks pregnant by five to four. While it did not overrule *Roe,* the multiple opinions in *Webster* gave the states much more room for regulation than they had had before.[90] Several states quickly passed laws prohibiting or strictly regulating abortion in anticipation that this Court would overrule *Roe* when given the opportunity to do so. The Court agreed to hear only one of the three cases appealed to it and on June 29, 1992, declined to overrule *Roe,* again by five to four. Three of the Reagan appointees, O'Connor, Kennedy, and Souter, wrote the joint opinion in which they opted to follow the judicially conservative tradition of sticking to precedent. "The Constitution serves human values, and while the effect of reliance on *Roe* cannot be exactly measured, neither can the certain cost of overruling *Roe* for people who have ordered their thinking and living around that case be dismissed." However, this decision did away with the trimester framework and dropped strict scrutiny as the standard by which regulations must be judged. Instead it held that the state's interest in protecting human life extends throughout pregnancy; it may regulate at any stage provided that the regulation does not impose an "undue burden" on a woman's right to obtain an abortion.[91]

Lower Federal and State Cases

Not all cases challenging gender-based laws reach the Supreme Court. Sometimes the losing side decides not to appeal an adverse decision to the highest court because the costs of doing so are high and expectations of success may be low. Even if they do appeal, the Supreme Court, unlike the lower courts, can decide whether or not to grant certiorari, i.e., whether it wants to hear an appeal. Since *Reed* hundreds of cases have been resolved by lower or state courts. In most cases the Federal courts, following the lead of the Supreme Court, have held gender-based distinctions to be invalid. Sometimes they have not done so, and the case has not been appealed to the Supreme Court or it has denied review. When this happens, the geographical area over which that court has jurisdiction must abide by its decision, but courts elsewhere are free to formulate their own interpretation (though they are often influenced by other courts). Some courts have held laws to be constitutional that forbid a person of one sex to massage that of another, girls (but not boys) from soliciting patrons for drinks, topless female (but not male) dancers, and mothers from signing the driver's license applications of minors if the father was alive and had custody. A Maryland law that made it more difficult for husbands than wives to prove libel if accused of extramarital sexual activity was also upheld. Laws that have been held to be unconstitutional include those that denied a wife the right to sue a third party for loss of her injured husband's consortium, prohibited some bars from serving beverages to women, established different ages for males and females to be tried in juvenile court or different sentences for convicts, and required that the prefix "Miss" or "Mrs." appear before a woman's name on her voter registration affidavit.[92]

When State courts have had to rule on gender-based laws or other state actions, they have generally looked to the Supreme Court and its current equal protection analysis even when state ERAs might have provided a different standard. Fourteen states have added some form of equal rights provision to their State Constitutions or included it in a general Constitutional revision since 1968. Eight use language similar to that of the proposed Federal amendment. Most of the others have clauses patterned after the Equal Protection clause of the Fourteenth Amendment with sex included as a category. The ERA states are Alaska (1972), Colorado (1972), Connecticut (1974), Hawaii (1972), Illinois (1971), Maryland (1972), Massachusetts (1976), Montana (1973), New Hampshire (1974), New Mexico (1973), Pennsylvania (1971), Texas (1972), Virginia (1971), and Washington (1972). Utah and Wyoming included similar provisions in their original constitutions when they became states in 1896 and 1890, respectively. The judicial decisions are highly varied. Washington and Pennsylvania courts have taken an even stricter approach than the Supreme Court, striking down virtually all gender-based statutes, including ones that excluded women from contact sports dominated by men.[93] Several state supreme courts have avoided interpreting their ERA by deciding cases on other grounds or refusing to review them at all. Utah, Louisiana, and Virginia have followed a traditional "rational basis" standard and have found virtually all sex-based laws to be reasonable. Several states have applied the "strict scrutiny" standard,[94] and others have relied on lesser standards (usually derived from the latest Supreme Court language) or not articulated a specific standard. Thus laws that have been held violative of the ERA in some states have been upheld in others. Even in states where the highest court has held sex to be a suspect class, such as Illinois, lower state courts have applied the rule inconsistently, with the result that statutes invalidated in one jurisdiction are upheld in another.[95]

Of those states that do not have ERAs, only California and Oregon have declared sex to be a suspect class, and California did so a few months before *Reed*.[96] Oregon did not even rely on the Federal Constitution; in 1982 the state supreme court interpreted a long-standing state constitutional prohibition against granting any citizen or class of citizens special privileges to invalidate legal classifications by sex.[97] Several others have followed the Supreme Court in finding many sex-based statutes to be unreasonable. Yet even these states have found statutes to be rationally related to reasonable goals such as those permitting wives to share in their husband's property after divorce but not vice versa[98] and prohibiting girls from having paper routes before age eighteen.[99]

Some issues, such as maternal preference in custody cases, have provoked extremely varied responses. The Utah Supreme Court found it "wise" that children should be in the care of their mother. Maryland permits the use of maternal preference as a tiebreaker. But in New York, where voters rejected a state ERA, a court held the maternal preference rule violated the Fourteenth Amendment.[100]

While courts acting under a state ERA are not limited to standard equal protection analysis, few have chosen to break new paths. Those with ERAs are likely to apply a stricter standard than those without, but most tend to follow the lead of the Supreme Court. Judges also respond to legislative history, the political culture of their own geographic area, current public debate, and their perception of the customs and mores about proper sex roles. The decisions interpreting state ERAs demonstrate that the courts are not institutions removed from society responding only to legislative dictate and abstract legal analysis. The law is neither static nor apolitical. Instead it is a tool, viable only when it is actively used and often reflecting the views of those who use it. The changes in judicial attitude of the last two decades have not occurred in a vacuum. They have been as much a response to the women's liberation movement as the many legislative changes have been.

Legislative Gains

The legislative changes in public policy have been as vast as the judicial changes, but they began earlier.

EQUAL PAY

As early as 1923 equal pay was required in the federal civil service, but the federal government did not mandate it for the private sector until passage of the 1963 Equal Pay Act. First proposed in 1868 at the National Labor Union Convention, equal pay for equal work did not become a national issue until World War I. During the war women held jobs previously held by men, creating concern that they would depress the wage rates and men would be forced to work at the lower rates after the war. Montana and Michigan enacted the first state equal pay laws in 1919, but it was not until after World War II that a major bill covering 61 percent of the labor force was placed before Congress, and another fifteen years before it was passed.[101]

Passage was preceded by a great deal of debate on exactly what "equal pay" and "equal work" meant, but it took the federal courts to flesh out the meaning of the law. Federal courts ruled that work did not need to be identical, only "substantially equal." For example, male orderlies could not be paid more than female nurses' aides because they occasionally had to perform additional tasks such as tending to the intimate needs of male patients. However, the Equal Pay Act does permit differences in pay when based on seniority, merit, productivity, or "any other factor other than sex." Thus men selling men's clothes could be paid more than women selling women's clothes because the former were more profitable.[102] The Court has ruled that wage differentials created by prior compliance with protective labor laws or collective bargaining agreements were a violation of the Equal Pay Act. It was not enough to abolish separate seniority lists and pay scales; the base pay of the disadvantaged women workers must also be increased.[103] However, wage differentials based on the going market rate for the job, even when that market rate is affected by the sex of the workers, do not have to be equalized.

TITLE VII AND THE EEOC

When Congress debated the 1964 Civil Rights Act, one of the most controversial sections in it was Title VII, which prohibited discrimination in employment. At the urging of the National Woman's Party, Rep. Howard W. Smith of Virginia, an ERA supporter but a civil rights opponent, proposed a floor amendment to add "sex" to "race, religion, color, and national origin." While this provision was strongly supported by the women of the House, most of the House liberals opposed it, as did the Women's Bureau of the Labor Department. They were concerned that this additional responsibility would dilute enforcement efforts for minorities. Nonetheless, neither side felt strongly enough about it to spend more than a few hours in debate, and little of this was serious. Sex was added to Title VII through the combined votes of Republican supporters and southern Democratic opponents of the civil rights bill.[104] The Equal Employment Opportunity Commission, created to enforce Title VII, responded to this ambiguous mandate by ignoring the sex provision. This led several people within the EEOC, and many without, to feel that it was necessary to create an organized group supporting women's rights to put pressure on the government. As government employees they could not organize such a group, but they spoke privately with those whom they thought could do so, including Betty Friedan and many members of the state commissions on the status of women. Partially as a result of their efforts, the National Organization for Women was formed in 1966 and directed a good portion of its initial energies at changing the guidelines of the EEOC and supporting legal cases to obtain favorable court rulings.[105]

Initially the EEOC supported protective labor laws, largely because organized labor had fought for them for decades and argued that they were a necessary protection for women. Despite this lack of support, many blue-collar women, who felt their denial of job opportunities was justified by employers on the basis of state protective laws, saw Title VII as an opportunity to take their cases to court. The court decisions were repeatedly in their favor. Within a few years virtually all such laws were rendered void or were subsequently applied to men as well.[106]

Even with protective laws out of the way, there were many long-standing practices that treated women differently than men. The initial court decisions were not as consistently in women's favor. For example, Martin-Marietta Corporation would not employ the mothers of preschool children on its assembly lines, even though it would hire the fathers of those children. Since the company did in fact hire lots of women, the lower federal courts ruled that it did not discriminate. Although the Supreme Court rejected this "sex-plus" theory, it did not do so unequivocally. Instead it remanded the case to a lower court to ascertain whether having preschool children actually interfered with a woman's job performance.[107] Despite this ambiguity, the Court's rejection of "sex-plus" was used by lower courts to relieve women of burdens not imposed on male employees even when the job was restricted to women. Flight attendants, for example, had to be not only female but also unmarried and under thirty-two, and they could not wear glasses or be even slightly overweight. Several federal courts ended these restrictions as well as the prohibition on men.[108]

Other traditional practices that channeled women into sex-typed jobs were overturned after several years of struggle. For example, newspapers once listed Help Wanted ads separately by sex. Early EEOC guidelines were silent on this practice, though the EEOC forbade newspapers to advertise by race, religion, and national origin. When the agency finally ruled, it permitted sex-segregated ads provided a nondiscriminatory disclaimer was placed at the beginning of each heading. In *Pittsburgh Press v. Pittsburgh Commission on Human Relations,* the Supreme Court rejected the newspaper's argument that placement of the ads was a form of speech protected by the First Amendment. Instead the Court said it was at best commercial speech, which could be regulated, and furthermore speech that furthered the illegal activity of sex discrimination.[109]

One of the biggest hurdles for feminist litigators was an exception put in Title VII for jobs for which sex was a *bona fide occupational qualification* (bfoq). If defined broadly, the bfoq would become a very large loophole. Early decisions were mixed. The courts ruled that men could be flight attendants[110] but women could not be guards in male prisons.[111] However, under pressure from feminists, the EEOC defined the bfoq narrowly, and the federal courts largely followed suit. Although assessing if sex was a bfoq for a particular job had to be done on a case-by-case basis, by 1991 the Supreme Court had repudiated the last vestiges of protection. Johnson Controls, Inc., would not employ women in its battery-manufacturing operations unless they were beyond childbearing age or could prove they were sterile. The company was concerned that exposure to lead would harm any fetus carried by a female employee before she knew she was pregnant. In *UAW v. Johnson Controls* the

Court ruled that the Pregnancy Disability Act, which had amended Title VII in 1978 to require that pregnant women be treated like other women, precluded potentially pregnant women from being singled out for discrimination. Since only women were required to prove infertility, the company's policy was therefore in violation of Title VII.

> Fertile women, as far as appears in the record, participate in the manufacture of batteries as efficiently as anyone else. Johnson Controls professed moral and ethical concerns about the welfare of the next generation do not suffice to establish a BFOQ of female sterility. Decisions about the welfare of future children must be left to the parents who conceive, bear, support, and raise them rather than to the employers who hire those parents or the courts.[112]

For several years women tried to use the Equal Pay Act and Title VII to combat wage disparities between male- and female-dominated jobs before the courts finally refused to extend these laws that far. It is practically a truism that male-dominated jobs pay more than female-dominated jobs, regardless of the job's content, location, or working conditions. This leaves open the questions of *why* this is so and how it can be remedied. During the 1980s, women and labor unions demanded "equal pay for work of equal value," otherwise known as comparable worth or pay equity. Assessing the relative value of different jobs to an employer in order to establish equitable pay rates was not a new idea. During World War II, under pressure from the War Labor Board to stabilize wages and avoid strikes, many large companies turned to systems of job evaluation to determine wages. They hired consultants to evaluate jobs in their plants and assign them points based on the skill, effort, responsibility, and working conditions involved. Relative wages were determined by each job's relative point value.[113]

These job evaluation systems generally showed that male-dominated jobs paid 20 to 40 percent more than female-dominated jobs of equal point values. Since jobs were often segregated by sex, some plants even had separate pay scales that deliberately set the rate for women's jobs below men's jobs with equal points. During the 1970s labor unions began to argue that pay rates should be equalized. They did this because their usual demands for higher wages through collective bargaining were stymied by the poor economic climate. Demands for pay equity, with the possibility of a lawsuit lurking in the background, were one of the few ways available to improve at least some of their members' compensation without a strike. The leaders in making comparable worth claims and filing suits have been the unions of government employees, particularly the American Federation of State, County and Municipal Employees. This is partially because government jobs are heavily female and partially because political pressure could be put on governors and state legislatures to do the job evaluation studies necessary to illuminate wage disparities by sex. During the more affluent 1980s most states commissioned studies, and many raised wages as a result. There were some strikes and some litigation. When it looked like these cases might succeed in incorporating pay equity claims into Title VII law, the Reagan administration threw the weight of the Justice Department behind the opposition, with both the EEOC and the Civil Rights Commission joining the chorus. The ironic outcome was that pay equity was stopped at the national level even while it was succeeding at the state and local levels.[114]

THE EQUAL RIGHTS AMENDMENT

The Equal Rights Amendment was first introduced into Congress in 1923 at the instigation of the National Woman's Party. Many sex-specific laws were on the books, and the NWP felt that another constitutional amendment was the quickest and most thorough way to remove them. During World War II the NWP instigated a major campaign for congressional passage and rewrote the original language to read "equality of rights under the law shall not be denied or abridged by the United States or by any State on account of sex." It was voted on by the Senate three times—in 1946, 1950, and 1953. The first time the ERA passed the Senate by thirty-eight to thirty-five, without the two-thirds necessary to be sent to the states. In 1950 and 1953 the ERA received more than two-thirds of the votes, but only after a "rider" was added that "the provisions of this article shall not be construed to impair any rights, benefits or exemptions conferred by law upon persons of the female sex." This gutted the ERA, so supporters did not ask the House to vote on it.

The primary opposition to the ERA had always been from social reformers and labor unions, who feared it would eradicate protective labor laws. By 1970 federal court decisions on Title VII had mooted this issue. When the emerging feminist movement turned its attention to the ERA, the only major opposition was fading from the field. After a two-year battle led by Martha Griffiths (D. Mich.) in the House and Birch Bayh (D. Ind.) in the Senate, involving a potpourri of feminist, women's, establishment, and liberal organizations, the Equal Rights Amendment was sent to the states for ratification on March 22, 1972.

Initially the states rushed to ratify; twenty-two did so by the end of the year, and eight more in 1973. However, the ERA stimulated a backlash from the right, which had been looking on the growing feminist movement with apprehension. The ERA became a symbolic issue on which the right projected its worst fears about the goals of the new movement and mobilized public sentiment against it. Over time, support for the ERA faded; by 1978 only thirty-five of the needed thirty-eight states had ratified. On October 20, 1978, Congress passed a joint resolution extending the seven-year deadline for ratification. This bought more time, but not more states; the ERA expired on June 30, 1982.[115]

OTHER LEGISLATION

Although the ERA was not ratified, the two-year battle had some very beneficial side effects. It created a climate in Congress that there was a serious constituent interest in women's rights and established liaisons between feminist organizations and Congressional staff. With this impetus the 92nd Congress, which sent the ERA to the states, passed a bumper crop of women's rights legislation in 1971–72. In addition to the ERA there were laws that (1) expanded the coverage of Title VII and the enforcement powers of the EEOC; (2) prohibited sex discrimination in all federally aided education programs (Title IX); (3) added sex discrimination to the jurisdiction of the U.S. Commission on Civil Rights; (4) prohibited sex discrimination in state programs funded by federal revenue sharing; (5) provided free day care for children of poor families and a sliding fee scale for higher income families (which was vetoed by President Nixon); (6) provided for a child care tax deduction for some parents; (7) added prohibitions against sex discrimination to a plethora of federally funded programs, including health training, Appalachian redevelopment, and water pollution.

Subsequent Congresses have also been active. New laws included the Equal Credit Opportunity Act; the Women's Educational Equity Act, which provides grants to design programs and activities to eliminate stereotyping and achieve educational equity; creation of the National Center for the Control and Prevention of Rape; an amendment to the Foreign Assistance Act requiring particular attention be given to programs, projects, and activities that tend to integrate women into the national economies of foreign countries; prohibitions of discrimination in the sale, rental, or financing of housing; an amendment to Title VII to include pregnancy in employment disability insurance coverage; admission of women to the military academies; and the addition of still more antidiscrimination provisions to federally funded programs such as small business loans.

The States have also been active arenas. Laws have been passed in most states prohibiting sex discrimination in employment, housing, and credit and in some states prohibiting discrimination in insurance, education, and public accommodations. Most states now have no-fault divorce provisions; all but four have equal custody and support laws (two others have equal custody but provide support for only the wife). The changes have been partially a result of pressure from feminist and other public interest groups and partially in response to changes in federal legislation and Supreme Court decisions. Many states have followed the lead of the Federal government in conducting studies to identify gender-based distinctions in their laws and recommend changes. Most of these studies were in response to efforts to adopt a state ERA or ratify the federal amendment.

THE FAMILY—AGAIN

Toward the end of the 1980s both the federal and state governments turned their attention toward the family, which had undergone profound changes in the previous two decades. Although family law was traditionally a state prerogative, it had never been completely off limits to the federal government. Acts to abolish polygamy and punish those who engaged in it—largely aimed at Mormons—were passed between 1862 and 1887.[116] Immigration and citizenship laws have always taken family relationships into account, though not consistently. The Federal income tax law had to contend with the different ways the common law and community property states viewed marriage, with the result that income tax rates vary by marital status. But the primary stimulus behind the federalization of family law was welfare. As the federal government took more responsibility for the welfare of children, it paid more attention to the composition and regulation of the family.[117]

In 1935 the Social Security Act provided funds for Aid to Families with Dependent Children (AFDC), though it generally required that one parent be missing. As the welfare rolls rose, the states were required to establish programs to determine a child's paternity in order to locate and obtain funds from the missing father. By 1974 AFDC recipients were required to cooperate in identifying and locating the father in order to obtain benefits. Where there were court orders for support, the government could use the IRS to find the father and garnish the wages of federal and military employees. Further amendments expanded this to include families not receiving welfare and to increase the reach of the government into the income of the noncustodial parent.[118]

In 1990 Congress finally got serious about providing child care to working parents. For decades child care had a negative connotation as something resorted to by poor women who *had* to work. The federal government subsidized some child care during World War II when it wanted women in the factories so the men could go to war, but those funds were eliminated after the war. In 1971 President Nixon vetoed a two-billion-dollar child care bill because of its "family-weakening implications." Presidents Ford and Carter also expressed disapproval of bills in Congress during their Presidencies, though in 1976 some funds were made available to the States that could be used for day care. Finally, in 1988, after four decades of increasing labor force participation by mothers of young children, Congress proposed a major child care bill. It quickly became embroiled in turf battles between committees and conflicts over church and state (e.g., should federal money be used for church-sponsored day care). These were resolved by 1990, and Congress passed a five-year program of tax credits and state grants that President Bush signed into law on November 5, 1990.[119]

The President was not as enthusiastic about signing a bill to mandate unpaid leave for employees on the birth or adoption of a child or illness of a family member. His concern about increasing the costs to business outweighed his commitment to "family values," even though the United States was the only major industrialized country that did not provide such benefits. President Bush vetoed bills passed by Congress in 1990 and 1992 after eight years of wrangling; he said he would support only voluntary leave. However, once a new administration was elected, Congress rushed to pass H.R. 1, the Family and Medical Leave Act, which President Clinton signed on February 5, 1993.[120]

"Family values" also delayed government intervention into family violence. Traditionally, how a family conducted its internal affairs has been considered a private matter. Despite growing evidence of child and spousal abuse, it was many years before legislatures overcame opposition to mandate action where there was abuse of children, and even more before services were created for spouses—virtually always wives. By 1984, when Congress passed the Family

Violence Prevention and Services Act,[121] thirty-two states had domestic violence programs, usually funding for emergency shelters and other programs run by nonprofit organizations. Today virtually all states have such programs, though funding is inadequate.

Another development during the 1980s was the recognition of a pension as marital property rather than that of just the spouse who earned it. At one time the earning spouse kept a pension upon divorce and unilaterally decided if there should be a survivor's benefit upon death. Several federal laws passed during the 1980s made a survivor's annuity automatic for federal employees unless waived in writing by both partners. Some laws provided that a pro rata share of the pension goes to the nonearning spouse on divorce; others recognized court orders dividing pensions.[122]

Social Security benefits were also amended. When first enacted in 1935, the pension provisions of the Social Security law assumed everyone married and no one divorced; husbands worked but wives did not, at least not very much; and wives survived husbands. By the 1970s these assumptions were no longer true, and the Supreme Court was forcing the removal of blatant inequities. However, the new reality of working wives and frequent divorce still left wives earning much less in their lifetimes than husbands. Neither marriage nor earning patterns were stable enough for a truly equitable Social Security system to be created; some group was always penalized. Consequently, the eligibility rules were adjusted frequently to meet the latest political demands and fiscal mandates.[123]

During the 1980s courts and legislatures continued to alter the common law rules on the marital relationship. Economic obligations have become more equal. Some make both spouses equally liable for each other's debts. Some make the contracting spouse primarily liable and the other secondarily liable. Some have retained the common law rule with exceptions for specific circumstances.[124] Others found that "neither husband nor wife is liable for necessaries supplied to the other."[125] Most states now allow the criminal prosecution of a husband for raping his wife. Interspousal immunity for conspiracy and from lawsuits has been largely abolished. Immunity from testifying against a spouse is now at the option of the witness, except for "privately disclosed [information] in the confidence of the marital relationship."[126] Virtually all states permit both husband and wife to sue third parties for loss of consortium.

The federal courts have also moved into the realm of family law, but largely to prohibit rather than condone state invasions into family life. The primary vehicle for this was the Court's recognition of individual constitutional rights that superceded and abolished state laws. In 1965 the Supreme Court said married couples could not be sent to jail for using birth control.[127] In 1967 it found unconstitutional laws that prohibited interracial marriage.[128] In 1968 it overturned those that discriminated against the children of extramarital unions[129] or reduced the welfare benefits of needy children whose mothers were illicitly cohabiting.[130] In 1971 it said a State cannot provide grants to traditional families (i.e., married couple and related child) while denying such support to other family forms.[131] In 1976 it rejected an absolute parental veto over a minor's wish to obtain an abortion.[132] And in 1977 it decided that local zoning laws could not discriminate against extended families.[133] Most of these decisions relied on a modern form of "substantive due process"—the same doctrine that was used to overturn state labor laws earlier in the century. Just as prior Courts had read a "liberty to contract" into the Fourteenth Amendment's Due Process clause that preempted state regulation, this Court found a "right to privacy" in it which had the same effect.[134] As then, this is a right that inures to *individuals*, not groups. Thus the Court's more recent decisions do not further "family rights" so much as the rights of individuals to make family arrangements suitable to them.

There are exceptions to this trend. Federal Medicaid regulations "deemed" a portion of a spouse's income available to an applicant in determining eligibility. This regulation applied even when the spouses were separated and any support was purely hypothetical. In 1981 the Supreme Court did not apply a Constitutional standard but instead looked at the legislative history to determine what Congress had intended when it passed the Medicaid laws. It concluded that "deeming" was part of the legal scheme, even when no support was likely.[135]

The Challenges Ahead

The contemporary feminist movement finished the drive to remove discriminatory laws begun after Suffrage. It also altered public perceptions and public policy on the role of women to one that favors equality of opportunity and individual choice. This is reflected in the addition of "sex" to the pantheon of laws that prohibit discrimination in private conduct and in the Court decisions that recognize women's right to equal protection and due process. These changes, which largely occurred during the decade of the 1970s, are nothing less than a revolution in public policy. As late as 1963, the President's Commission on the Status of Women cautioned that "[e]xperience is needed in determining what constitutes *unjustified* discrimination in the treatment of women workers."[136]

As is true of any revolution, the changes that were made created new problems in their wake. Once equal opportunity became a possibility, the fact that it by itself would not lead to equality became clearer. Essentially this policy means that women who are like men should be treated equally with men. It accepts as standard the traditional male life-style, and that standard in turn assumes that one's primary responsibility should and can be one's job, because one has a spouse (or spouse surrogate) whose primary responsibility is the maintenance of house and family obligations. Women whose personal life-style and resources permit them to fit these assumptions could, in the absence of sex discrimination, succeed equally with men.

Most women cannot, however, because our traditional conception of the family, and women's role within the family, makes this impossible. Women still bear the primary responsibility for home and child care whether or not they are married and regardless of what their spouse does. The typical woman has more tasks to perform in a typical day than a typical man and thus has less time. Couples who equalize family responsibilities, or singles who take them all on, pay a price for deviancy. And women who spend the greater part of their lives as dependent spouses often find their "career" ended by death or divorce with little to show for it.

What is necessary is a total social reorganization that abolishes institutionalized sex role differences and the concept of adult dependency. It needs to recognize the individual as the principal economic unit, regardless of what combinations individuals do or do not choose to live in, and to provide the necessary services for individuals to support themselves and help support their children. In pursuit of these goals, programs and policies need to make participation by everyone in the labor force to the full extent of their abilities both a right and an obligation. They should also encourage and facilitate the equal assumption of family responsibilities without regard to gender, as well as develop ways to reduce conflict between the conduct of one's professional and private lives. While transition policies are necessary to mitigate the consequences of adult dependency, the goal should be abolition of the sexual division of labor. They should not be ones that permanently transfer dependency from "breadwinners" (male earners) to society in general, nor should they be ones that encourage dependency for a major portion of one's life by extolling its benefits and minimizing its costs. Instead, transitional policies should be ones that educate women to the reality that they are ultimately responsible for their own economic well-being but are entitled to the opportunities to achieve it.

This too is not enough. Even while the revolution was in process, the feminist movement was generating new public policies to address problems not solved by the mere removal of discriminatory laws and practices. The pervasiveness of violence, the degradation of pornography, and the lack of affordable, available child care are burdens particularly borne by women that equal opportunity programs do not address. As women moved into positions of power, feminist inquiry disclosed new or hidden discriminations, such as the "glass ceiling" and inadequate research into women's health needs. As the family became open to public inspection, a host of problems that more heavily affected women, such as incest, sexual abuse, and domestic violence, became apparent. As science created new ways of reproducing, it compelled reconsideration of the concept of motherhood. And as people diversified their ways of living together, the nature of the family was questioned.

Not all of the new problems can be mitigated by changes in law and public policy. But many can be. As the consequences of the legal revolution ripple throughout society, one task will be to identify where the law can be a useful tool for more social change and to devise appropriate policies to achieve it.

NOTES

1. For a discussion of the changing state of national/state relations, see the symposium on "Federalism: Aftermath of the 1980s and Prospects for the 1990s," in 26:2 *P.S.: Political Science and Politics,* June 1993, pp. 172–95.

2. *United States v. Yazell,* 382 U.S. 341, 361 (1966) (Black, J., dissenting).

3. Edward Mansfield, *The Legal Rights, Liabilities and Duties of Women* (Salem, MA: Jewett and Co., 1845), p. 273.

4. Leo Kanowitz, *Women and the Law: The Unfinished Revolution* (Albuquerque: University of New Mexico Press, 1969), Chapter 3.

5. 41 *American Jurisprudence Second,* 348. A husband was not chargeable for any debts other than necessities. There are many state court decisions on what constitutes a necessity and what proof must be offered that a husband failed to supply it.

6. *Kirchberg v. Feenstra,* 450 U.S. 455 (1981).

7. H.R. Rep. No. 1274, 80th Cong. 2nd Sess, pp. 241, 2258–59 (1948). Revenue Act of 1948, §§ 301–5, 62 Stat. 114–16 (1948), now Int. Rev. Code of 1954, § 6013. This is discussed in Kenneth M. Davidson, Ruth B. Ginsburg, and Herma Hill Kay, *Sex Based Discrimination: Text, Cases and Materials* (St. Paul, MN: West Publishing Co., 1974), pp. 528–33.

8. Harry D. Krause, *Family Law* (St. Paul, MN: West Publishing Co., 1988), p. 113. The Wisconsin statute is at Wis. Stat. Ann. § 766.001–766.97.

9. Since these laws have changed over time, there is no single source. The *Handbook on Women Workers,* published by the Women's Bureau of the Department of Labor every few years since its inception in 1920, usually has a section on state laws. In the early 1960s state commissions on the status of women compiled the laws of their states. Leo Kanowitz summarized their status in *Women and the Law* as it existed in the mid 1960s. Various legal reference works, such as *American Jurisprudence Second,* regularly compile and annotate state court decisions on different aspects of the law, including those affecting women. *Family Law Quarterly* publishes an annual compilation of "Family Law in the Fifty States."

10. *Equal Rights,* Nov. 8, 1924, p. 307; Jan. 31, 1925, p. 403.

11. *United States v. Yazell,* 382 U.S. 341 (1966).

12. Elizabeth Baker, *Technology and Women's Work* (New York: Columbia University Press, 1964), pp. 91–96.

13. Quoted in Alice Henry, *The Trade Union Woman* (New York: Appleton and Co., 1915), p. 24.

14. *Lochner v. New York,* 198 U.S. 45, 53 (1905).

15. *Muller v. Oregon,* 208 U.S. 412, 422 (1908).

16. *Bunting v. Oregon,* 243 U.S. 426 (1917). An exception was minimum wage legislation, which the Supreme Court would not uphold for either men or women until Justice Roberts's dramatic reversal of his opposition to Roosevelt's New Deal legislation in 1937 shifted the direction of the five to four decisions. Compare *Adkins v. Children's Hospital,* 261 U.S. 525 (1923), with *West Coast Hotel Co. v. Parrish,* 300 U.S. 379 (1937).

17. Baker, pp. 401–4.

18. J. Stanley Lemons, *The Woman Citizen: Social Feminists in the 1920s* (Urbana: University of Illinois Press, 1973), pp. 63–68, 235–36. The House Committee on Elections responded favorably to Owen's eloquent appeal and condemnation of the limitations of the 1922 Cable Act. It recommended she be seated, and the House concurred.

19. *Strauder v. West Virginia,* 100 U.S. 303, 310 (1880).

20. The common law doctrine was appropriately called "propter defectum sexus," or a "defect of sex." Lemons, pp. 69–73. William Blackstone, 2 *Commentaries* 362. The *Handbook of Women Workers* also lists the statutes on jury service. Federal law is at 28 U.S.C. § 1861.

21. Lemons, p. 79. Susan Ware, *Holding Their Own: American Women in the 1930s* (Boston: Twayne, 1982), p. 28; Lois Scharf, *To Work and to Wed: Female Employment, Feminism and the Great Depression* (Westport, CT: Greenwood Press, 1980), Chapter 4.

22. *Bradwell v. Illinois,* 83 U.S. (16 Wall.) 130, 141–42 (1873), (J. Bradley, concurring). See also *Ex parte Lockwood,* 154 U.S. 116 (1893).

23. *Hoyt v. Florida,* 368 U.S. 57, 59, 61, 62, 68 (1961).

24. *Minor v. Happersett,* 21 Wall. 162 (1875), relying on the *Slaughter House Cases,* 83 U.S. (16 Wall.) 36 (1873).

25. *Slaughter House Cases.*

26. *Yick Wo v. Hopkins,* 118 U.S. 356 (1886).

27. *Truax v. Raich,* 239 U.S. 33 (1915).

28. Laurence H. Tribe, *American Constitutional Law* (New York: The Foundation Press, 1978), pp. 1002–1110.

29. Judith A. Baer, *Women in American Law* (New York: Holmes and Meier, 1991), pp. 28–35.

30. *Goesaert et al. v. Cleary, et al., Members of the Liquor Control Commission of Michigan,* 335 U.S. 464 (1948).

31. Ibid.

32. *Reed v. Reed,* 368 U.S. 57 (1971).

33. Tribe, p. 1082. For example, in 1968 the Court overturned a Louisiana statute that denied children born out of wedlock the right to recover for the wrongful death of their mother. By six

to three, the Court held that the state's rationale that such a statute promoted morality and discouraged nonmarital births was not sufficient to deny the orphaned children the equal protection of the laws. *Levy v. Louisiana,* 391 U.S. 68 (1968).

34. Jo Freeman, *The Politics of Women's Liberation* (New York: McKay, 1975), pp. 147–48, 213–20.

35. *Goesaert* at 466.

36. *Frontiero v. Richardson,* 411 U.S. 677, 684, 686–87 (1973). This opinion was subscribed to by Justices Brennan, Douglas, White, and Marshall.

37. The three were Powell, Burger, and Blackmun. Justice Stewart concurred without joining either opinion, and Justice Rehnquist dissented for the reasons stated in the district court opinion, *Frontiero v. Laird,* 341 F.Supp. 201 (1972), that administrative convenience was a rational basis. If Stewart had joined the four justices who wrote the plurality opinion, sex would have become a "suspect" classification. This would have changed many subsequent judicial decisions, particularly by state and lower federal courts, and perhaps made the state and federal ERAs *legally* unnecessary.

38. *Frontiero v. Richardson,* 411 U.S. 677, 692 (1973).

39. *Craig v. Boren,* 429 U.S. 190, 197, 204 (1976).

40. Between 1971 and 1984 the Supreme Court applied equal protection analysis to twenty-five cases of sex-based classifications and found thirteen of them to be unconstitutional. Of the eight cases decided before *Craig,* five sex-specific statutes were struck. In the sixteen post-*Craig* cases the Court split evenly. Susan Gluck Mezey, *In Pursuit of Equality: Women, Public Policy and the Federal Courts* (New York: St. Martin's Press, 1992), has a summary chart of these cases on pp. 22–23.

41. *Weinberger v. Wiesenfeld,* 420 U.S. 636, 645, 652 (1975).

42. *Stanton v. Stanton,* 421 U.S. 7, 14–15 (1975).

43. *Califano v. Goldfarb,* 430 U.S. 199 (1977).

44. *Orr v. Orr,* 440 U.S. 268 (1979).

45. *Califano v. Westcott,* 443 U.S. 76 (1979).

46. *Wengler v. Druggists Mutual Insurance Company,* 446 U.S. 142 (1980).

47. According to the 1975 *Handbook of Women Workers,* at that time six states exempted women solely on the basis of sex, and ten allowed only women to be excused due to family responsibilities; p. 366.

48. *White v. Crook,* 251 F.Supp. 401 (M.D. Ala. 1966).

49. *State v. Hall,* 187 So.2d 861, 863 (Miss.), appeal dismissed 385 U.S. 98 (1966).

50. *Taylor v. Louisiana,* 419 U.S. 522, 537 (1975). Seven justices joined in the opinion. Burger concurred and Rehnquist dissented. Because the decision rested on the Sixth Amendment establishing the rights of criminal defendants, it applied only to women's participation in criminal juries. However, both criminal and civil juries are drawn from the same pool, so the practical effect of *Taylor* was to remove all sex-specific restrictions from all jurors.

51. *Batson v. Kentucky,* 475 U.S. 79 (1986); Powers v. Ohio, 499 U.S. 400, 111 S.Ct. 1364, 113 L.Ed.2d 411 (1991); *Edmonson v. Leesville Concrete Co.,* 500 U.S. 614, 111 S.Ct. 2077, 114 L.Ed.2d 660 (1991); Georgia v. McCollum, 505 U.S. ----, 112 S.Ct. 2348, 120 L.Ed.2d 33 (1992).

52. Brief for Respondent at 10 cited in *J.E.B. v. State of Alabama ex rel. T.B.,* 62 USLW 4219 (1994).

53. *J. E. B. v. State of Alabama ex rel. T. B.,* 62 USLW 4219 (1994).

54. *Ibid.*

55. This is argued by Janella Miller, "The Future of Private Women's Colleges," *Harvard Women's Law Journal* 7 (1984). See also Alexander W. Astin, *Four Critical Years: Effects of College on Beliefs, Attitudes and Knowledge* (San Francisco, CA: Jossey-Bass, 1977).

56. *Williams v. McNair,* 401 U.S. 951 (1971), affirming 316 F.Supp. 134 (D.S.C. 1970). Three lower federal courts upheld challenges to sex-segregated schools but under circumstances that did not lead to Supreme Court review. *Kirstein v. Rectors and Visitors of the University of Virginia,* 308 F.Supp. 184 (E.D. Va. 1970); *Bray v. Lee,* 337 F.Supp. 934 (D. Mass. 1972); *Berkelman v. San Francisco Unified School District,* 501 F.2d 1264 (9th Circ. 1974).

57. *Mississippi University for Women et al. v. Joe Hogan,* 458 U.S. 718 (1982). However, since Congress in Title IX of the 1972 Educational Amendments Act had specifically authorized the continuance of single-sex public undergraduate institutions that "traditionally and continually from

its establishment has had a policy of admitting only students of one sex," 20 U.S.C. § 1681(a), this ruling applied only to the School of Nursing and not to the entire University.

58. *Vorchheimer v. School District of Philadelphia*, 430 U.S. 703 (1977), 532 F.2d 880, 886 (3rd Cir. 1976), overturning 400 F.Supp. 326 (E.D. Pa. 1975).

59. *Kirstein v. Rectors and Visitors of the University of Virginia*, 308 F.Supp. 184 (E.D. Va. 1970).

60. *United States v. Virginia Military Institute*, 976 F.2d 980, 895, 897–900 (4th Cir. 1992), cert. denied, 113 S.Ct. 2431, 124 L.Ed.2d 651 (1993). On March 2, 1993, a lawsuit was filed against the Citadel by Shannon Richey Faulkner, who had been provisionally admitted by having references to her sex omitted from her high school transcript. The Citadel rejected her after discovering she was female. The Justice Department has joined the suit. *New York Times*, May 2, 1993, p. 24:5. The Fourth Circuit Court of Appeals ordered that she be allowed to attend day classes while the court considered her case [114 S.Ct. 87, 1994 WL 5621 (4th Cir. 1994), 210 F.3d 226 (4th Cir. 1993)].

61. *United States v. Commonwealth of Virginia*, 1994 WL 172275 at 10 (W D.Va., April 29, 1994) This time the Commonwealth of Virginia, now under a Republican administration, supported VMI. The previous fall the Democratic state attorney general had lost her campaign for governor. *Washington Post*, February 10, 1994, p. A-10.

62. *Roberts v. U.S. Jaycees*, 468 U.S. 609, 623 (1984). *Board of Directors of Rotary International v. Rotary Club of Duarte*, 481 U.S. 537 (1987). *New York State Club Association Inc., v. City of New York*, 487 U.S. 1 (1988). See *New York Times*, Dec. 8, 1991, p. 38:1, for a review of the impact of these decisions.

63. *Kahn v. Shevin*, 416 U.S. 351, 355 (1974).

64. *Califano v. Webster*, 430 U.S. 313, 318 (1977). Because Congress eliminated this exception in 1972, it applied only to men who reached age sixty-two before that time. The Court held similarly in *Heckler v. Matthews*, 465 U.S. 728 (1984), which concerned a technicality in the Social Security law that benefited women between 1977 and 1982.

65. *Schlesinger v. Ballard*, 419 U.S. 498, 508 (1975).

66. *Michael M. v. Superior Court of Sonoma County*, 450 U.S. 464, 472 (1981). Most states have gender-neutral statutory rape laws. Prior to this case three circuit courts had struck down gender-based statutory rape laws, and the Supreme Court had declined a request for review of one of them. See *Navedo v. Preisser*, 630 F.2d 636 (8th Cir. 1980), *U.S. v. Hicks*, 625 F.2d 216 (9th Cir. 1980), *Meloon v. Helgemoe*, 564 F.2d 602 (1st Cir. 1977), cert. denied 436 U.S. 950 (1978).

67. *Rostker v. Goldberg*, 509 F.Supp. 586, 603 (E.D. Pa. 1980).

68. *Rostker v. Goldberg*, 453 U.S. 57, 74, 76, 79 (1981). Until 1993 women were restricted from combat in the navy and air force by statute, 10 U.S.C. § 6015 and § 8549, and in the army and marine corps by internal policy. In April of that year Secretary of Defense Les Aspin lifted the ban on women in aerial combat and asked Congress to alter the law to permit women to serve on warships. *New York Times*, April 28, 1993, p. 1:6.

69. *Personnel Administrator of Massachusetts v. Feeney*, 442 U.S. 256, 280 (1979), overturning 451 F.Supp. 143 (Mass. 1978). In 1993 women were 11.5 percent of those in the active duty armed forces. *New York Times*, May 2, 1993, p. 4:4:5.

70. *Cohen v. Chesterfield County School Board* and *Cleveland Board of Education v. La Fleur*, 414 U.S. 632 (1974). Almost all of the lower courts that had heard similar cases found these rules to be discriminatory. See n. 8 for a list.

71. *Geduldig v. Aiello*, 417 U.S. 484, 496–97 n. 20 (1974).

72. *Turner v. Department of Employment Security*, 423 U.S. 44 (1975).

73. 90 Stat. 2667 (1976).

74. *Wimberly v. Labor and Industrial Relations Commission*, 479 U.S. 272, 281 (1987).

75. *Stanley v. Illinois*, 405 U.S. 645 (1972).

76. *Fiallo v Bell*, 430 U.S. 787 (1977).

77. *Quilloin v. Walcott*, 434 U.S. 246 (1978).

78. *Parham v. Hughes*, 441 U.S. 347 (1979).

79. *Caban v. Mohammed*, 441 U.S. 380 (1979).

80. *Lehr v. Robertson*, 463 U.S. 248 (1983).

81. Gilbert Y. Steiner, *Constitutional Inequality: The Political Fortunes of the Equal Rights Amendment* (Washington, DC: Brookings Institution, 1985).

82. James C. Mohr, *Abortion in America: The Origins and Evolution of National Policy, 1800–1900* (New York: Oxford University Press, 1978), is the definitive study of this movement.

83. Leslie Goldstein, *The Constitutional Rights of Women: Cases in Law and Social Change* (New York: Longman, 1979), pp. 272–74. Lawrence Lader, *Abortion II: Making the Revolution* (Boston: Beacon Press, 1973), Chapter 13.

84. 410 U.S. 113, 153 (1973).

85. Id. at 164–65.

86. *Beal v. Doe,* 432 U.S. 438 (1977), *Maher v. Roe,* 432 U.S. 464 (1977), *Poelker v. Doe,* 432 U.S. 519 (1977) (per curiam).

87. *Harris v. McRae,* 448 U.S. 297 (1980).

88. Rachel Benson Gold and Daniel Daley, "Public Funding of Contraceptive, Sterilization and Abortion Services, Fiscal Year 1990," *Family Planning Perspectives* 23:5 (Sept./Oct. 1991), pp. 198–99.

89. *Planned Parenthood v. Danforth,* 428 U.S. 52 (1976); *Bellotti v. Baird,* 443 U.S. 622 (1979); *Colautti v. Franklin,* 439 U.S. 379 (1979); *H.D. v. Matheson,* 450 U.S. 398 (1981); *City of Akron v. Akron Center for Reproductive Health, Inc.,* 462 U.S. 416 (1983); *Planned Parenthood Association of Kansas City, Missouri Inc. v. Ashcroft,* 462 U.S. 476 (1983); *Hodgson v. Minnesota,* 110 S.Ct. 2926 (1989); *Ohio v. Akron Center for Reproductive Health,* 110 S.Ct. 2972 (1989).

90. *Webster v. Reproductive Health Services,* 492 U.S. 490 (1989).

91. *Planned Parenthood of Southeastern Pennsylvania v. Casey.* 112 S.Ct. 2791, 120 L.Ed.2d 674 (1992). The Court declined to hear appeals from Louisiana and Guam, where laws banning most abortions had been found unconstitutional by lower federal courts. It also declined to hear a Mississippi case challenging restrictions similar to the Pennsylvania ones upheld in *Casey.*

92. These cases and others are reviewed by Daniel A. Per-Lee, "Validity, Under Equal Protection Clause of Fourteenth Amendment, of Gender-Based Classifications Arising by Operation of State Law—Federal Cases," 60 *Lawyer's Edition Second* (1979), p. 1188.

93. However, even Washington upheld the denial of a marriage license to two males on the grounds that both sexes were affected equally by the requirement that legal marriages be heterosexual. *Singer v. Hara,* 11 Wash. App. 247, 522 P.2d 1187 (1974). It also supported statutes requiring election of an equal number of men and women to Democratic party committees as a rational means to achieve desired equality. *Marchioro v. Chaney,* 90 Wash. 2d 298, 582 P.D. 487 (1978).

94. But this has not prevented them from upholding school regulations restricting the length of boys' but not girls' hair, *Mercer v. The Board of Trustees,* 538 S.W.2d 201 (Tex. Civ. App. 1976), or prison regulations that required women visitors to male prisons to wear brassieres, *Holdman v. Olim,* 581 P.2d 1164 (Hawaii 1978).

95. Comment, "Equal Rights Provisions: The Experience Under State Constitutions," *California Law Review* 65 (1977), pp. 1086–1112; Paul M. Kurtz, "The State Equal Rights Amendments and Their Impact on Domestic Relations Law," *Family Law Quarterly* 11 (1977), pp. 101–50; Dawn Marie Driscoll and Barbara J. Rouse, "Through a Glass Darkly: A Look at State Equal Rights Amendments," *Suffolk University Law Review* 12 (1978), pp. 1282–1311; Philip E. Hassman, "Construction and Application of State Equal Rights Amendments Forbidding Determination of Rights Based on Sex," *American Law Reports Third* 90 (1979), pp. 158–216.

96. *Sail'er Inn v. Kirby,* 5 Cal. 3rd 1, 485 P.2d 529, 95 Cal. Rptr. 329 (1971), invalidated a state statute prohibiting women from tending bar.

97. *Hewett v. State Accident Insurance Fund Corporation,* 294 Or. 33, 653 P.2d 970 (1982).

98. *M. v. M.,* 321 A.2d. 115 (Del. Sup. Ct. 1974).

99. *Warshafsky v. Journal Co.,* 63 Wis.2d 130, 216 N.W.2d 197 (Wis. 1974).

100. Compare *Cox v. Cox,* 532 P.2d 994 (Utah 1975); *Cooke v. Cooke,* 21 Md. App. 376, 319 A.2d 841 (Md. 1974); *State ex. rel. Watts v. Watts,* 77 Misc.2d 178, 350 N.Y.S.2d 285 (N.Y. Fam. Ct. 1973).

101. Cynthia Harrison, *On Account of Sex: The Politics of Women's Issues, 1945–1968* (Berkeley: University of California Press, 1988), Chapters 3 and 6.

102. *Schultz v. Wheaton Glass Company,* 421 F.2d 259 (3rd Cir. 1970); *Schultz v. American Can Co.,* 424 F.2d 356 (8th Cir. 1970); *Hodgson v. Brookhaven General Hospital,* 436 F.2d 719 (5th Cir. 1970); *Hodgson v. Robert Hall Clothes,* 473 F.2d 589 (3rd Cir. 1973).

103. *Corning Glass Works v. Brennan,* 417 U.S. 188 (1974).

104. Jo Freeman, "How Sex Got into Title VII: Persistent Opportunism as a Maker of Public Policy," *Law and Inequality: A Journal of Theory and Practice* 9:2 (March 1991), pp. 163–84. 110 *Congressional Record,* February 8, 1964, pp. 2577–84. The vote was 168 to 133 but was not a roll-call vote. Rep. Martha Griffiths (D. Mich.), who helped count the vote, identified its composition.

105. Freeman, 1975, p. 54.

106. The actual transition from protective labor laws to equal employment opportunity took several years; a few such laws still remain on the books. See U.S. Dept. of Labor, Women's Bureau, *State Labor Laws in Transition: From Protection to Equal Status for Women,* 1976, and compare it with *Time of Change: 1983 Handbook on Women Workers,* Bulletin 298 (Washington, DC: Government Printing Office), Chapter 7. The most important cases were *Weeks v. Southern Bell Telephone & Telegraph,* 408 F.2d 228 (5th Cir. 1969); *Rosenfeld v. Southern Pacific,* 293 F.Supp. 1219 (C.D. Cal. 1968), 444 F.2d 1219 (9th Cir. 1971); *Bowe v. Colgate,* 416 F.2d. 711 (7th Cir. 1969). See also Judith A. Baer, *The Chains of Protection: The Judicial Response to Women's Labor Legislation* (Westport, CT: Greenwood Press, 1978), pp. 166, 174, n. 137.

107. *Phillips v. Martin Marietta Corporation,* 400 U.S. 542 (1971).

108. This is discussed in Baer, 1991, pp. 83–84.

109. *Pittsburgh Press v. Pittsburgh Commission on Human Relations,* 413 U.S. 376 (1973).

110. *Diaz v. Pan American World Airways,* 442 F.2d 385 (5th Cir. 1971).

111. *Dothard v. Rawlinson,* 433 U.S. 321 (1977).

112. *UAW v. Johnson Controls Inc.,* 111 S.Ct. 1196, 1207 (1991).

113. Sara M. Evans and Barbara J. Nelson, *Wage Justice: Comparable Worth and the Paradox of Technocratic Reform* (Chicago: University of Chicago Press, 1989), pp. 24–26.

114. Evans and Nelson, pp. 32–41. The most successful pay equity case was *AFSCME v. State of Washington,* 578 F. Supp. 846 (W.D. Wash. 1983). It was reversed by the Ninth Circuit Court of Appeals in 770 F.2d 1401 (9th Cir. 1985). See Mezey, pp. 99–107, for more on the legal convolutions.

115. Janet K. Boles, *The Politics of the Equal Rights Amendment: Conflict and the Decision Process* (New York: Longman, 1979). Jane J. Mansbridge, *Why We Lost the ERA* (Chicago: University of Chicago Press, 1986). New resolutions have been introduced in each successive Congress. The House voted on one of these on November 15, 1983, but it did not receive the necessary two-thirds majority.

116. These were the Morrill Anti-Bigamy Act of 1862, 12 *Stat.* 501, the Edmunds Anti-Polygamy Act of 1882, 22 *Stat.* 30, and the Edmunds-Tucker Act of 1887, 24 *Stat.* 635. The latter annulled Utah laws allowing illegitimate children to inherit property and revoked woman suffrage in the Utah Territory on the premise that it increased the voting strength of Mormon husbands. Woman suffrage was restored by the Utah constitutional convention of 1895; Utah entered the Union in 1896 as the third full suffrage state. See Jean B. White, "Women's Place Is in the Constitution: The Struggle for Equal Rights in Utah in 1895," 42 *Utah Historical Quarterly* (Fall 1974), pp. 344–69.

117. Eva R. Rubin, *The Supreme Court and the American Family* (Westport, CT: Greenwood Press, 1986), pp. 12–13.

118. Social Security Act of 1935; 49 *Stat.* 620. Social Security Amendments of 1967; 81 *Stat.* 821. Social Service Amendments of 1974; 88 *Stat.* 2337. Child Welfare Act of 1980; 94 *Stat.* 500. Omnibus Reconciliation Act of 1981; 95 *Stat.* 357. Tax Equity and Fiscal Responsibility Act of 1982; 96 *Stat.* 324. Child Support Enforcement Amendments of 1984; 98 *Stat.* 1305.

119. 1990 *Congressional Quarterly Almanac* (Washington, DC: CQ Press, 1991), pp. 547–51.

120. *CQ Weekly Report,* Feb. 6, 1993, pp. 267–69.

121. P.L. 98-457.

122. Foreign Service Act (1980); 94 *Stat.* 2071. Central Intelligence Agency Appropriations Act (1982); 96 *Stat.* 1142. Department of Defense Appropriation Act (1982); 96 *Stat.* 718. Civil Service Spouse Retirement Equity Act (1984); 98 *Stat.* 3195. Retirement Equity Act (1983); 98 *Stat.* 494. Tax Reform Act (1986); 100 *Stat.* 2085. FY87 Department of Defense Military Functions and Personnel Levels Authorization Act (1985); 99 *Stat.* 583.

123. Social Security Amendments (1977); 91 *Stat.* 1509. Social Security Amendments (1983); 97 *Stat.* 65.

124. Jay M. Zitter, "Modern Status of Rule That Husband is Primarily or Solely Liable for Necessaries Furnished Wife," 20 *American Law Reports Fourth* 196.

125. *Condore v. Prince George's County,* 289 Md. 516, 425 A.2d 1011 (1981). Also, *Schilling v. Bedford County Memorial Hospital,* 225 Va. 539, 303 S.E.2d 905 (1983).

126. *Trammel v. United States,* 445 U.S. 40 (1980).

127. *Griswold v. Connecticut,* 381 U.S. 497 (1965).

128. *Loving v. Virginia,* 388 U.S. 1 (1967).

129. *Levy v. Louisiana,* 391 U.S. 68 (1968).

130. *King v. Smith,* 392 U.S. 309 (1967).

131. *New Jersey Welfare Rights Organization v. Cahill,* 411 U.S. 619 (1973).

132. *Planned Parenthood v. Danforth,* 428 U.S. 53 (1976).

133. *Moore v. City of East Cleveland,* 431 U.S. 494 (1977).

134. Tribe, 1978, Chapter 13.

135. *Schweiker v. Gray Panthers,* 453 U.S. 34 (1981).

136. Margaret Mead and Frances Balgley Kaplan, *American Women: The Report of the President's Commission on the Status of Women and Other Publications of the Commission* (New York: Charles Scribner's Sons, 1965), p. 49; my emphasis.

A Generation of Change
for Women in Politics

Ruth B. Mandel

WOMEN HAVE BEEN struggling for a voice in the public arena since our country was founded.[1] As early as 1776, Abigail Adams wrote a letter cautioning her husband, John Adams, to "remember the Ladies" as he and his collaborators held meetings to develop a new code of laws for a new nation. She urged him to avoid putting "unlimited power into the hands of the Husbands." He replied, "I cannot but laugh. . . . We know better than to repeal our Masculine systems . . . [and] completely subject Us to the Despotism of the Petticoat."[2] Over a half century later, the abolition activist Angelina Grimke wrote in a letter to a friend that the "investigation of the rights of the slave has led me to a better understanding of my own." She had come to believe that "it is woman's right to have a voice in all the laws and regulations by which she is to be *governed*" and that "woman has just as much right to sit in solemn counsel in Conventions, Conferences, Associations and General Assemblies, as man— just as much right to sit upon the throne of England, or in the Presidential chair of the United States."[3]

At the first U.S. woman's rights convention, held at a chapel in Seneca Falls, New York, for two days in July 1848, one hundred women and men signed the *Declaration of Sentiments*. Modeled on the *Declaration of Independence*, it called for the end of man's "absolute tyranny" over woman. Of the twelve resolutions attached to the declaration, only one was so controversial that it was adopted with less than a unanimous vote—the ninth resolution, which called on women to secure for themselves the right to vote. At the urging of Elizabeth Cady Stanton and Frederick Douglass, a small majority passed this radical resolution, which delegates feared would make them look ridiculous and, thereby, hurt the greater cause of women's rights.[4] The campaign for suffrage that this convention launched occupied women across the country for over seventy years. It did not conclude until August 26, 1920, when the Nineteenth Amendment to the U.S. Constitution, granting women the right to vote, was finally ratified.

During this period, women participated actively in a variety of social change and reform movements, including abolition, temperance, labor organizing, settlement house efforts, and birth control. The club movement in both

Special thanks are due to Lucy Baruch, director of information services at the Center for the American Woman and Politics, for collecting the data and for providing statistics and many of the tables that appear in this chapter.

the white and black communities led to the formation of many women's voluntary civic and service organizations. A few women even sought political office. Under the banner of a party that she created and called the Equal Rights Party, Victoria Claflin Woodhull ran for president in 1872. In 1884, Belva Lockwood, the attorney who won the right for women to practice before the U.S. Supreme Court, ran for president under the banner of the Woman's National Equal Rights Party.[5] Some years earlier, in 1866, suffragist Elizabeth Cady Stanton had tested women's constitutional right to run for office by seeking a seat in Congress as an independent candidate long before women could vote for her. Out of twelve thousand votes cast, twenty-four men marked their ballots for Stanton.[6] It took until 1917 for Jeannette Rankin, a Republican suffragist and pacifist from Montana, to become the first woman to serve in the Congress. She arrived in time to cast the sole vote against U.S. entry into World War I.

In the fifty years between 1920 and 1970, women steadily increased their voting rates and moved in small numbers into other political arenas. Women worked in election campaigns, in politicians' offices, and in the political parties, playing essential but largely supportive roles. A few rose to influential staff and political party positions, and some women were elected or appointed to offices. A substantial number of the women who served in the U.S. Congress before the 1970s were widows filling out the terms of husbands who died while in office.[7] Whether they arrived via the widow's way, won local or state office after raising their families and spending twenty years as community volunteers,[8] were sponsored by powerful men, or climbed a more typically male political ladder,[9] women in office were still the exception.

During the late 1960s and into the 1970s, when the women's movement raised the nation's feminist consciousness, feminists demanded that more women should hold positions of public leadership and exercise political power. Symbolically, the turning point came in July 1971, when the National Women's Political Caucus (NWPC) was founded. The Caucus, as it is called, was the first national membership organization established specifically to promote women into positions of political leadership. The phrase "in her own right" began to circulate as a way of distinguishing between a woman in public office by virtue of her marital affiliation and one who worked her way into political leadership. Thinking, speaking, and acting with self-conscious political goals and ambitions, women increasingly expressed the conviction that more women should be involved in politics—as voters, party activists, candidates, and officeholders.[10]

Voting

Women now outvote men, but they did not surge to the polls in overwhelming numbers after ratification of the national suffrage amendment. Women's voting rates at the national level increased slowly while they accustomed themselves to exercising their hard-won franchise. As women's educational levels rose and as more women entered the paid labor force, their numbers at the polls increased.[11] In presidential elections, women voted in lower numbers than men until 1964 and at lower rates until 1980. Since then, however, women's voting rates have exceeded men's in every presidential election (see Table 1). Women also have outnumbered men among registered voters by seven to eight million since 1984 (see Table 2).

Voting patterns differ somewhat among racial groups, but women consistently have outvoted men in each group. Among blacks, Hispanics, and whites, the *number* of female voters has exceeded the *number* of male voters for many years. The difference in voter turnout *rates* between women and men is greatest for African-Americans, but women voted at higher rates than men in all three groups in the presidential elections since 1984 (Table 1).

The Gender Gap

Antisuffragists feared that women would become a voting bloc with the power to change or control social policy. This was a special concern to the liquor interests, since women had been leading activists in the temperance movement. The dreaded block never materialized. Women voted in modest numbers; they voted in both parties. There was no sign that they voted alike. Conventional wisdom suggested that husbands, in particular, strongly influenced their wives' votes. Cartoons even depicted the presumably typical housewife wearing her apron as she answered the doorbell and responded to a pollster's (perhaps mythical) question about how she planned to vote: "I don't know. My husband hasn't told me yet." It was not until the 1980 presidential election that a persistent "gender gap" appeared. Between 1952 and 1976 preelection polls conducted by the Gallup organization indicated that women and men voted similarly in presidential races.[12] However, in 1980, 7 to 9 percent more women than men voted for Jimmy Carter. Since then, 4 to 9 percent more women have voted for the Democratic nominee (see Table 3). Although the gender gap decreased in the 1992 presidential vote, the pattern established in previous years remained. It was largest among the young. Single voters and women in the labor force voted more frequently for the Democrat than married voters and homemakers.[13]

The gender gap has appeared in a number of elections for the U.S. Senate and House as well as in several gubernatorial races and may well be in evidence in contests for lower offices for which election day polling data are not available. The data show that women are more likely than men to vote for Democrats.[14] The term *gender gap* has also been applied to differences in partisan identification, judgments about presidential performance, and opinions on public policy issues.[15] Women are more likely to identify as Democrats than as Republicans. Men identify as independents or Republican (see Table 4). During the Reagan and Bush administrations, women were less approving than men of the way the president performed in office (see Table 5). Finally, surveys show a difference in attitudes toward various issues. Compared with men, women express views that are less militaristic; less favorable to using force as a way of handling nonmilitary situations; more favorable to environmental protection policies and alternatives to the use of nuclear power; more supportive of programs to help the economically disadvantaged and to achieve racial equality; and more positive toward laws for regulating social problems such as drugs, gambling, and pornography.[16]

Table 1. Voter Turnout in Presidential Elections Since 1964

	Percentage of voting age population who reported voting		Number who reported voting (in millions)	
	Women	*Men*	*Women*	*Men*
1992				
All	62.3	60.2	60.6	53.3
Black	56.7	50.8	6.6	4.8
Hispanic	30.9	26.8	2.3	1.9
White	64.5	62.6	52.9	47.6
1988				
All	58.3	56.4	54.5	47.7
Black	54.2	48.2	5.9	4.2
Hispanic	30.1	27.4	2.0	1.8
White	59.8	58.3	47.7	42.7
1984				
All	60.8	59.0	54.5	47.4
Black	59.2	51.7	6.1	4.2
Hispanic	33.1	32.1	1.7	1.4
White	62.0	60.8	47.7	42.4
1980				
All	59.4	59.1	49.3	43.8
Black	52.8	47.5	4.8	3.5
Hispanic	30.4	29.2	1.3	1.1
White	60.9	60.9	44.0	39.9

1976				
All	58.8	59.6	45.6	41.1
Black	49.9	47.2	4.1	3.1
Hispanic	30.1	33.9	1.1	1.0
White	60.5	61.5	41.2	37.0
1972				
All	62.0	64.1	44.9	40.9
Black	57.1	52.1	3.9	3.1
White	63.4	65.6	40.7	37.5
1968				
All	66.0	69.8	41.0	38.0
Black	57.1	58.2	3.4	2.9
White	67.2	71.2	37.3	34.9
1964				
All	67.0	71.9	39.2	37.5
Black	58.0	59.1	3.3	2.8
White	68.2	73.4	35.7	34.5

Source: "Sex Differences in Voter Turnout," a fact sheet. Center for the American Woman and Politics (CAWP), Eagleton Institute of Politics, Rutgers University. This was taken from U.S. Bureau of the Census, Current Population Reports, *Population Characteristics*. Series P-20, Nos. 143, 192, 253, 322, 370, 405, 440, and 466. "Voting and Registration in the Election of November 1964, . . . 1992." These figures are from postelection responses to supplementary questions in the monthly Current Population Survey for a sample of households in November of each election year. Respondents to the survey report their own voting activity and that of other members of their household. This method overreports both voting and registration by several million people. Percents are calculated by dividing the number reporting that they have voted by the voting age population for that year. Prior to 1972 this included persons eighteen and over in Georgia and Kentucky, nineteen and over in Alaska, twenty and over in Hawaii, and twenty-one and over in all other states. The voting age population over-estimates those actually eligible to vote. Hispanic may be of any race.

Table 2. Voter Registration Since 1968

| Year | Number reporting they are registered voters (in millions) | |
	Women	Men
1992	67.3	59.3
1990	60.2	53.0
1988	63.4	55.1
1986	59.5	52.2
1984	62.1	54.0
1980	55.7	49.3
1976	51.5	46.3
1972	51.8	46.7
1968	45.2	41.4

Source: "Sex Differences in Voter Turnout," a fact sheet. Center for the American Woman and Politics (CAWP), Eagleton Institute of Politics, Rutgers University. This was taken from U.S. Bureau of the Census, Current Population Reports, *Population Characteristics,* Series P-20, Nos. 192, 253, 322, 370, 405, 440, and 466. "Voting and Registration in the Election of November 1968,…1992." These figures are from postelection responses to supplementary questions in the monthly Current Population Survey for a sample of households in November of each election year. Respondents to the survey report their own voting activity and that of other members of their household. This method overreports both voting and registration by several million people.

Table 3. The Gender Gap in Presidential Voting, 1980–1992

| Presidential candidates | ABC News/ Washington Post | | CBS News/NYT | | NBC News | |
	Women	Men	Women	Men	Women	Men
1980						
Ronald Reagan	47%	53%	46%	54%	47%	56%
Jimmy Carter	42%	35%	45%	37%	45%	36%
John Anderson	9%	9%	7%	7%	8%	8%
1984						
Ronald Reagan	54%	62%	56%	62%	55%	64%
Walter Mondale	46%	38%	44%	37%	45%	36%
1988						
George Bush	50%	57%	50%	57%	51%	57%
Michael Dukakis	49%	42%	49%	41%	49%	43%

| 1992 | Voter research and surveys | |
	Women	Men
George Bush	37%	38%
Bill Clinton	45%	41%

Source: "The Gender Gap," a fact sheet. Center for the American Woman and Politics (CAWP), Eagleton Institute of Politics, Rutgers University. Data come from exit polls done by the major networks.

Table 4.   Party Identification of Women and Men

Poll	Date	Democrats		Republicans	
		Women	Men	Women	Men
CBS News/NYT	June 1983	43%	32%	21%	25%
CBS News/NYT	April 1984	40%	37%	28%	31%
CBS News/NYT	May 1985	38%	30%	31%	28%
CBS News/NYT	June 1986	40%	35%	29%	28%
CBS News/NYT	May 1987	44%	35%	30%	31%
CBS News/NYT	May 1988	41%	32%	29%	31%
CBS News/NYT	June 1989	36%	32%	31%	31%
CBS News/NYT	May 1990	38%	28%	30%	32%
CBS News/NYT	May 1991	38%	26%	28%	31%
CBS News/NYT	June 1992	36%	29%	32%	34%

Source: "The Gender Gap," a fact sheet. Center for the American Woman and Politics (CAWP), Eagleton Institute of Politics, Rutgers University. Data are from surveys conducted by CBS News and *The New York Times*.

Table 5.   Presidential Approval Ratings, 1981–1992

Date	Approve of the way Reagan is handling his job as president	
	Women	Men
July 1981	55%	63%
July 1982	38%	48%
July 1983	34%	51%
July 1984	49%	59%
July 1985	60%	65%
July 1986	58%	69%
July 1987	44%	54%
July 1988	43%	59%

Date	Approve of the way Bush is handling his job as president	
	Women	Men
July 1989	61%	72%
July 1990	61%	66%
July 1991	69%	72%
July 1992	30%	33%

Source: "The Gender Gap," a fact sheet. Center for the American Woman and Politics (CAWP), Eagleton Institute of Politics, Rutgers University. Data are from the Gallup report.

As the gender gap gained recognition for its potential power, political campaigns began to target their advertisements, direct mail, and literature to specific female constituencies. While the female vote has never determined the outcome of a presidential election, it has been responsible for some statewide contests. For example, in the 1990 gubernatorial race in Texas, women gave Ann Richards the state's top executive office. In the 1992 primary election in Illinois, crossover voting by Republican women into the Democratic primary and a sizable gender gap resulted in the unexpected defeat of Alan Dixon, an incumbent male U.S. senator, and the nomination of Carol Moseley-Braun. She won the general election in November, becoming the nation's first African-American female senator. The 1992 general elections also saw a gender gap in ten of the eleven U.S. Senate races with female candidates, with the women's vote making the margin of victory for one of them—Barbara Boxer of California.[17]

Historically, large segments of the female population have not seen themselves either as a voting bloc or as a separate coalition of diverse female constituencies joined in common purpose around a shared agenda. But as the politics of the 1990s take shape, women may be more likely to recognize their own political power, particularly in support of social issues that affect their lives and those of their families. The two patterns of the gender gap—more women than men vote for Democrats and more vote for women—reflect women's dual concerns with issues and with female candidates and their desire to support both.

Running for Office

Since the 1970s women candidates have become increasingly familiar contenders. However, the pace of growth has been more rapid for the lower offices than the higher ones, for lawmakers than for executives. As can be seen in Figure 1 and Table 6, women have steadily won greater numbers of major party nominations for state legislative and congressional races. Their success in gaining the nomination for Senate and governor has been more erratic. Between 1974 and 1984 women received zero to three gubernatorial nominations; in 1986 and again in 1990 an all-time high of eight women ran for governor of their states. Female candidates for Senate ranged from one to eleven between 1970 and 1992. Although the numbers are still small, the overall trend has been upward.

As the population of female candidates expands, so do the level and variety of political experience they bring to their campaigns. It is no longer unusual for a woman seeking election to have a political resume, including previous positions in elective, appointive, or political staff positions rather than the extensive backgrounds as volunteers in civic and community organizations typical of earlier cohorts.[18] In the last twenty years many have established public careers; far fewer are widows inheriting their husbands' seats.

Nonetheless, there are still hurdles to cross before women candidates will have the same opportunities as men. As are aspirants in other male-dominated fields, women candidates are greeted with greater skepticism. They are usually running against male incumbents. They have less money.[19] With greater

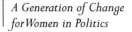

Figure 1. Major Party Female Nominees for State Legislatures, 1974– 1992.

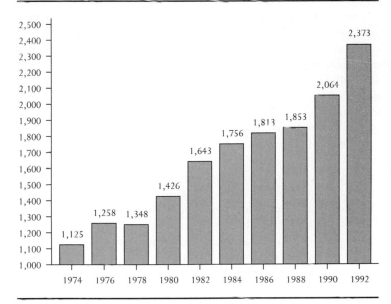

Source: "Women Moving into State Legislatures," a fact sheet. Center for the American Woman and Politics (CAWP), Eagleton Institute of Politics, Rutgers University.

Table 6. Major Party Female Nominees for the U.S. Congress, 1970– 1992

Year	Senate	House
1970	1 (0D, 1R)	25 (15D, 10R)
1972	2 (0D, 2R)	32 (24D, 8R)
1974	3 (2D, 1R)	44 (30D, 14R)
1976	1 (1D, 0R)	54 (34D, 20R)
1978	2 (1D, 1R)	46 (27D, 19R)
1980	5 (2D, 3R)	52 (27D, 25R)
1982	3 (1D, 2R)	55 (27D, 28R)
1984	10 (6D, 4R)	65 (30D, 35R)
1986	6 (3D, 3R)	64 (30D, 34R)
1988	2 (0D, 2R)	59 (33D, 26R)
1990	8 (2D, 6R)	70 (40D, 30R)*
1992	11 (10D, 1R)	108 (71D, 37R)*

* The 1990 figure includes one candidate for nonvoting delegate from Washington, DC; the 1992 figure includes two such candidates.
Source: "Summary of Women Candidates for Selected Offices," a fact sheet. Center for the American Woman and Politics (CAWP), Eagleton Institute of Politics, Rutgers University.

familiarity, female office seekers have lost some of their novelty and outsider status, at once a blessing and a curse. Any candidate prizes being taken seriously as a contender for public office, and the most readily credible are those who resemble incumbents—i.e., male lawyers. However, everyone also values appearing distinctive enough to remember on election day; women still stand out in a crowded field. Voters want change, but not too much change. Women candidates represent change because the overwhelming majority of elected officials are male; but they also must still prove that they have the know-how and ability to do a "man's job." Most women run against male incumbents who enjoy the benefits, privileges, and resources of incumbency status. Typically voters choose the familiar name on the ballot and return incumbents to office. At the congressional level, for example, the incumbency reelection rate is above 95 percent. Over the long run, female candidates cannot rely on a mood to "throw out the rascals" as a strategy for integrating what continues to be a man's political world.

Women considering a race for office still have a dollar disadvantage relative to male candidates, particularly since most are facing incumbent men. Women have found varying degrees of support in familiar places—namely, the political parties, business and labor associations, special interest groups, and civic and political networks traditionally associated with candidate endorsement and support. But political money and other campaign resources typically flow to political insiders, to familiar names and faces who have successfully withstood the tests of election and service in office. Because of this reality of political life, support from groups and organizations—particularly the women's political action committees (PACs)—that promote the expansion of women's political leadership has become key to female candidates' viability, especially to those candidates who agree with feminist policy objectives.

Since the early 1970s a number of feminist and partisan organizations at the national, state, and local levels have organized to support women candidates. Although this feminist political community is relatively small and underfunded in comparison with business, labor, and other traditional networks of political power, it has played a key role. Among its participants, the best known are the National Women's Political Caucus, the National Organization for Women, the National Women's Education Fund (defunct, but active in the 1970s and early 1980s), the Women's Campaign Fund, and EMILY'S List.[20] They promote women for public office who favor passage of the Equal Rights Amendment (ERA) and who take a prochoice position on abortion. These groups as well as several professional associations and issue-oriented groups (e.g., the American Nurses Association, the National Abortion Rights Action League, and other organizations fighting for abortion rights) have recruited and encouraged women candidates, sponsored training programs and workshops about running for office, and—critically important—raised and distributed money for campaigns.[21]

By 1992 there were forty-two PACs that gave money predominantly to women candidates or functioned with a predominantly female donor base. Thirty-five of these groups (twenty-two of which contributed exclusively to female candidates and thirteen of which contributed to both women and men) gave a total of $11.5 million to women running for office, making 1992 a year of extraordinary growth in dollar support for female candidates. The Women's Campaign Fund and the National Organization for Women distributed money to the most female candidates of all the PACs. EMILY'S List distributed the most money. It made national news and women's political history by raising and contributing $6.2 million to Democratic women candidates. Campaign money was also raised by state affiliates of national organizations. State PACs distributed much less than national ones, but the candidates they supported usually had smaller campaign budgets than those required for statewide or federal offices.[22]

By the first half of the 1990s women's political participation had expanded enormously. Voters were growing accustomed to more women on the ballot each election, and issues weighing on voters' minds—education, family and children's welfare, the environment, and health care—were closely associated with women's lives and experiences. In 1972, when feminist leader Gloria Steinem placed the name of Texas political activist Frances ("Sissy") Farenthold in nomination for the vice presidency at the Democratic national nominating convention, the act was viewed as a symbolic gesture. In 1984, only twelve years later, the Democrats nominated New York Congresswoman Geraldine Ferraro for vice president. In 1992, California—the nation's largest state—elected women to both of its United States Senate seats.

Women in Elective Office

The numbers of women in elective offices[23] increased steadily between the mid-1970s and the early 1990s (see Table 7). This was largely "incremental progress." Although women are 51 percent of the U.S. population, they do not hold even 25 percent of elected legislative or executive offices at any level.[24] Until 1974, no woman had been elected a state governor in her own right; since then, nine have been elected to governorships. In 1970, no state had an incumbent female lieutenant governor, and only one state had ever elected a woman to that office. By 1994, twenty-six women had been elected lieutenant governors; two of these went on to win their states' governorships.[25] The number of women in state legislatures has quintupled since 1969 (see Table 8 and Figure 2). In 1994, the 1,526 women represented 20.5 percent of the total 7,424 state legislators (see Table 8). State legislatures are important arenas for the politically ambitious. Although the size of constituencies, competition for seats, availability of staff support and offices, salary levels, length and frequency of legislative sessions, and distances to state capitals vary greatly across the country, in most states the legislature provides an opportunity to build a political career and sometimes serves as a springboard to higher office. In 1994, every state had at least six women in its state house and one woman in its senate. Representation by minority women remained low; the 154 African American women, eighteen Asian/Pacific Islander women, twenty-eight Hispanic women, and six Native American women accounted for 13.5 percent of all female state lawmakers.

At local levels women pushed their representation from 3 to 9 percent of elected county officials between 1975 and 1988 and from 4 to 14 percent of municipal officials between 1975 and 1985 (see Table 7). As of January 1994, 175 cities with populations over thirty thousand (or 18.1 percent of 966 such cities) had women mayors. In early 1994, women were mayors of eighteen of the one hundred largest U.S. cities.

Table 7. Percentages of Women in Elective Offices, 1975–1994

Level of office	1975	1977	1979	1981	1983	1985	1987	1989	1991	1993	1994
U.S. Congress	4%	4%	3%	4%	4%	5%	5%	5%	6%	10%	10%
Statewide elective[a]	10%	10%	11%	11%	13%	14%	15%	14%[b]	18%	22%	22%
State legislatures	8%	9%	10%	12%	13%	15%	16%	17%	18%	21%	21%
County governing boards[c]	3%	4%	5%	6%	8%	8%[d]	9%	9%[e]	NA	NA	NA
Mayors and municipal/township governing boards	4%	8%	10%	10%	NA	14%[f]	NA	NA	NA	NA[g]	NA

a. These numbers do not include officials in appointive state cabinet-level positions, officials elected to executive posts by the legislature, members of the judicial branch, or elected members of university boards of trustees or boards of education.

b. Although there was an increase in the number of women serving between 1987 and 1989, the percentage decrease reflects a change in the base used to calculate these figures.

c. The three states without county governing boards are Connecticut, Rhode Island, and Vermont.

d. Figure is for 1984.

e. Figure is for 1988.

f. Includes data from Washington, DC. States for which data were incomplete and therefore not included are Illinois, Indiana, Kentucky, Missouri, Pennsylvania, and Wisconsin.

g. While data for the more than one hundred thousand officials serving in towns and cities of all sizes have not been collected since 1985, figures are available for cities with populations over ten thousand. According to the National League of Cities, of the 23,729 mayors and municipal council members (and their equivalents) serving in cities with populations over ten thousand in April 1993, 4,657, or 19.6 percent, were women.

Source: "Women in Elective Office 1994," a fact sheet. Center for the American Woman and Politics (CAWP), Eagleton Institute of Politics, Rutgers University.

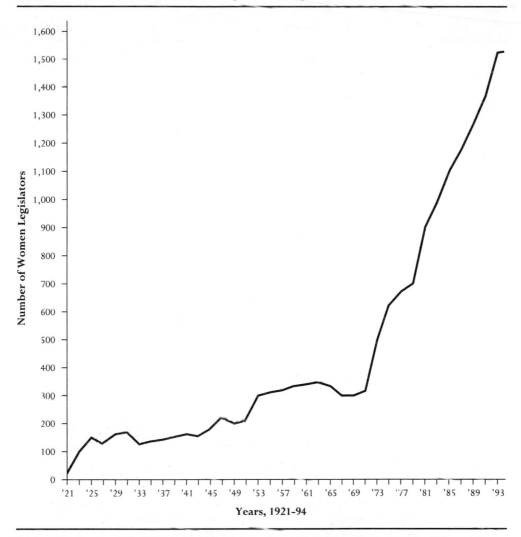

Figure 2. Number of Women Serving in State Legislatures, 1921–1994

Source: Data for years 1921–1967 cited in Naomi B. Lynn, "Women and Politics: The Real Majority," *Women: A Feminist Perspective,* ed. Jo Freeman. Mayfield, 1984. Data for years 1921–1967, Center for the American Woman and Politics (CAWP), Eagleton Institute of Politics, Rutgers University.

Progress has been slowest at the federal level, though the 1992 elections saw a major increase after an extraordinarily active election year. The 103rd Congress (1993–95) boasted an all-time high of seven women among the 100 U.S. senators and forty-seven women among the 435 members of the House of Representatives (Table 9 and Figure 3).

The most recent study of what kind of women are elected to public office was done in 1981. These were the pioneers. Women who won in the 1970s and early 1980s were predominately middle-aged, middle-class, Caucasian, married, mothers of children over twelve years old, relatively well educated, and employed at one time or another in traditional female fields.[26] The

Table 8. Women in State Legislatures, 1969–1994

Year	Women legislators	Percentage of total legislators
1969	301	4.0
1971	344	4.5
1973	424	5.6
1975	604	8.0
1977	688	9.1
1979	770	10.3
1981	908	12.1
1983	991	13.3
1985	1,103	14.8
1987	1,170	15.7
1989	1,270	17.0
1991	1,368	18.3
1992	1,375	18.4
1993	1,524	20.5
1994	1,526	20.5

The party breakdown for women serving in state legislatures in 1994 is

	Total legislators		State senators		State reps.	
	Number	Percentage	Number	Percentage	Number	Percentage
Democrats	931	61.0	211	61.7	720	60.8
Republicans	583	38.2	120	35.1	463	39.1
Nonpartisans	10	0.7	10	2.9	—	—
Independents	2	0.1	1	0.3	1	0.1
Total	1,526	100.0	342	100.0	1,184	100.0

Source: "Women in State Legislatures 1994," a fact sheet. Center for the American Woman and Politics (CAWP), Eagleton Institute of Politics, Rutgers University.

demographic profile of these early elected women was much like that of their male counterparts, but there were some differences. Women were more likely to have attended college but less likely to hold law or other graduate degrees. A smaller proportion held paid jobs prior to election, and these were concentrated in traditionally female occupations: the four most often cited by elected women in the early 1980s were secretarial/clerical, social work, elementary/secondary teaching, and nursing/health technical. While the great majority of all elected officials were married with children, more women were widowed, separated, or divorced, and fewer had young children. Among married office-holders, women were more likely to report strong spousal support for their political activities. Among parents, women reported that the age of their children was an important factor in their decision to run for office.[27] Their political profile was also similar but not identical. Among state legislators, women were less likely than men to have had previous experience in elective office but more likely to have held appointed office. Many of them had experience working for male politicians or in community projects and

Table 9.   Women in the U.S. Congress, 1917–1994

Congress	Dates	Women in Senate	Women in House	Total women
65th	1917–19	0 (0D, 0R)	1 (0D, 1R)	1 (0D, 1R)
66th	1919–21	0 (0D, 0R)	0 (0D, 0R)	0 (0D, 0R)
67th	1921–23	1 (1D, 0R)	3 (0D, 3R)	4 (1D, 3R)
68th	1923–25	0 (0D, 0R)	1 (0D, 1R)	1 (0D, 1R)
69th	1925–27	0 (0D, 0R)	3 (1D, 2R)	3 (1D, 2R)
70th	1927–29	0 (0D, 0R)	5 (2D, 3R)	5 (2D, 3R)
71st	1929–31	0 (0D, 0R)	9 (5D, 4R)	9 (5D, 4R)
72nd	1931–33	1 (1D, 0R)	7 (5D, 2R)	8 (6D, 2R)
73rd	1933–35	1 (1D, 0R)	7 (4D, 3R)	8 (5D, 3R)
74th	1935–37	2 (2D, 0R)	6 (4D, 2R)	8 (6D, 2R)
75th	1937–39	2 (1D, 1R)	6 (5D, 1R)	8 (6D, 2R)
76th	1939–41	1 (1D, 0R)	8 (4D, 4R)	9 (5D, 4R)
77th	1941–43	1 (1D, 0R)	9 (4D, 5R)	10 (5D, 5R)
78th	1943–45	1 (1D, 0R)	8 (2D, 6R)	9 (3D, 6R)
79th	1945–47	0 (0D, 0R)	11 (6D, 5R)	11 (6D, 5R)
80th	1947–49	1 (0D, 1R)	7 (3D, 4R)	8 (3D, 5R)
81st	1949–51	1 (0D, 1R)	9 (5D, 4R)	10 (5D, 5R)
82nd	1951–53	1 (0D, 1R)	10 (4D, 6R)	11 (4D, 7R)
83rd	1953–55	2 (0D, 2R)	12 (5D, 7R)*	14 (5D, 9R)*
84th	1955–57	1 (0D, 1R)	17 (10D, 7R)*	18 (10D, 8R)*
85th	1957–59	1 (0D, 1R)	15 (9D, 6R)	16 (9D, 7R)
86th	1959–61	2 (1D, 1R)	17 (9D, 8R)	19 (10D, 9R)
87th	1961–63	2 (1D, 1R)	18 (11D, 7R)	20 (12D, 8R)
88th	1963–65	2 (1D, 1R)	12 (6D, 6R)	14 (7D, 7R)
89th	1965–67	2 (1D, 1R)	11 (7D, 4R)	13 (8D, 5R)
90th	1967–69	1 (0D, 1R)	11 (6D, 5R)	12 (6D, 6R)
91st	1969–71	1 (0D, 1R)	10 (6D, 4R)	11 (6D, 5R)
92nd	1971–73	2 (1D, 1R)	13 (10D, 3R)	15 (11D, 4R)
93rd	1973–75	0 (0D, 0R)	16 (14D, 2R)	16 (14D, 2R)
94th	1975–77	0 (0D, 0R)	19 (14D, 5R)	19 (14D, 5R)
95th	1977–79	2 (2D, 0R)	18 (13D, 5R)	20 (15D, 5R)
96th	1979–81	1 (0D, 1R)	16 (11D, 5R)	17 (11D, 6R)
97th	1981–83	2 (0D, 2R)	21 (11D, 10R)	23 (11D, 12R)
98th	1983–85	2 (0D, 2R)	22 (13D, 9R)	24 (13D, 11R)
99th	1985–87	2 (0D, 2R)	23 (12D, 11R)	25 (12D, 13R)
100th	1987–89	2 (1D, 1R)	23 (12D, 11R)	25 (13D, 12R)
101st	1989–91	2 (1D, 1R)	29 (16D, 13R)	31 (17D, 14R)
102nd	1991–93	4 (3D, 1R)	29 (20D, 9R)**	33 (23D, 10R)**
103rd	1993–95	7 (5D, 2R)	48 (36D, 12R)**	55 (41D, 14R)**

* Includes a Republican delegate from prestatehood Hawaii.
** Includes a Democratic delegate from Washington, DC.
Please note: Table shows maximum number of women elected or appointed to serve in that Congress at one time. Some filled out unexpired terms, and some were never sworn in.
Source: "Women in the U.S. Congress 1994," a fact sheet. Center for the American Woman and Politics (CAWP), Eagleton Institute of Politics, Rutgers University.

Figure 3.   Women in the U.S. Congress, 1917–1994.

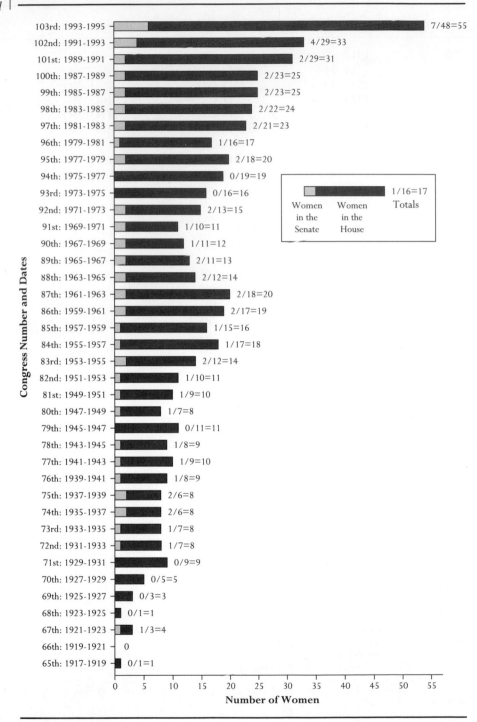

Source: "Women in the U.S. Congress 1994," a fact sheet. Center for the American Woman and Politics (CAWP), Eagleton Institute of Politics, Rutgers University.

Table 10. Previous Political Experience of Women and Men in State
Legislatures, 1981 (in percentages)

	State senators		State representatives	
Experience	Women	Men	Women	Men
Held one or more previous elective offices	47	49	25	34
Held one or more appointive government positions	55	43	42	26
Worked in a campaign	84	72	82	74
Worked on the staff of an elected official	25	12	24	16

Source: "Bringing More Women into Public Office," a project of the Center for the American Woman and Politics (CAWP), Eagleton Institute of Politics, Rutgers University.

charitable causes, or both. They had worked more often in someone else's political campaign before becoming candidates themselves (Table 10).

Substantial proportions of female officeholders were members of women's organizations; proportions ranged from one-third among local council members to over three-fourths of state legislators. These women belonged to at least one of five national organizations: the American Association of University Women (AAUW), the National Federation of Business and Professional Women's Clubs (BPW), the National League of Women Voters (LWV), the National Organization for Women (NOW), and the National Women's Political Caucus (NWPC). The higher her office, the more likely a woman official was to belong to such feminist groups as NOW and NWPC; for example, 58 percent of state senators and 46 percent of state representatives, but only 29 percent of county commissioners and 7 percent of local council members, were members of these feminist groups in 1981.[28]

Women were more likely than their male colleagues to credit an organization as an important factor in getting them to seek office and to attribute inspiration or assistance with their political careers to female role models, mentors, and the campaigns of other female candidates for whom they worked.[29] There were notable differences, at least as of 1981, in the organizations to which they belonged and gave this credit. By and large women were less likely to be affiliated with business groups and commercial associations. Few women elected officials belonged to veterans' organizations and, needless to say, none to fraternal organizations. Political women and men have much in common, but a gender-segregated and stratified society has meant that they have depended on different professional connections and bases of support.

African-American women have constituted a small yet distinctive group of elected women. In 1981 they were 6.5 percent of all women—sixty-three out of 967—in Congress, statewide elective executive positions, and state legislatures.[30] In 1994 they were 10 percent of all women—165 out of 1,653—in these offices. Even more than other women, they have acknowledged the important role in their careers played by various organizations, including civil rights groups, church groups, community groups, and women's groups (Table 11). Indeed, they have been more likely to be members of women's organizations, especially feminist organizations. African-American women more often than white women reported that women's organizations encouraged them to run and supported their candidacies.

At all levels of government, women officeholders have formed their own organizations. By 1992, women had established statewide associations for elected women in about a dozen states. The oldest of these is the California Elected Women's Association for Education and Research, formed in 1974.[31] The Congresswomen's Caucus, established in 1977 for women only, became the Congressional Caucus for Women's Issues in 1981 and admitted congressmen to its membership while retaining its primary goal of advocating a policy agenda of issues particularly important to women.[32] Women Executives in State Government was formed in 1985 for high-level officeholders in the states. Associations of women officials also formed within existing groups. For example, the National Conference of State Legislatures has a Women's Network, and women's caucuses exist in the National Association of Counties (Women Officials of NACo), the National Conference of Black Mayors (Black Women Mayors Caucus), and the National League of Cities (Women in Municipal Government). Organizations of women officials are not large, and not all eligible women choose to belong to them, but their very establishment is evidence of women officials' need for mutual support and to promote issues of special concern to them. The items on their policy agendas usually concern rights, justice, and equity for women. In addition, they seek clout and political advancement for women.

Table 11. The Role of Women's Organizations in the Political Careers of Black Women and All Women, 1981 (in percentages)

	State representatives		County commissioners		Local council members	
Role	Black women	All women	Black women	All women	Black women	All women
Member of a major women's organization	84	77	63	58	47	37
Member of a feminist organization	68	46	47	29	30	7
Encouraged by a women's organization to run for office	59	27	32	24	18	15
Received campaign support from a women's organization	54	54	32	18	13	7

Source: "Bringing More Women into Public Office," a project of the Center for the American Woman and Politics (CAWP), Eagleton Institute of Politics, Rutgers University.

The Impact of Women in Politics

Do women in politics make a difference in public policies, political processes, and public leadership? This cannot be definitively answered until women fill many more positions throughout the political system. However, initial surveys do reveal differences between political women and men in both attitudes and behavior.

In her 1976 study of women running for office, Susan Carroll found that "an overwhelming majority of women candidates, and of those elected, feel that they can do a better job of representing women's interests than their male counterparts."[33] In surveying elected women and men in 1977 and again in 1981, the Center for the American Woman and Politics (CAWP) found women's views to be more liberal and more feminist than men's on a number of public policy issues.[34] (A feminist attitude here, as in CAWP's surveys, refers to a position on an issue taken by the women's rights movement and endorsed by national feminist organizations such as NOW and NWPC.) In the 1981 survey officeholders were asked about their views on eight issues. A "gender gap" emerged on matters as diverse as whether the Equal Rights Amendment (ERA) should be ratified, whether the private sector could resolve our economic problems, and whether there should be a death penalty for murderers. Although the gap was smallest at the municipal level and largest at the state legislative level, women's attitudes differed from men's at all levels of office, both within political parties and across the ideological spectrum. Republican women, for example, expressed more liberal and feminist views than Republican men, and women who called themselves conservative appeared to be somewhat more liberal about policy issues and more feminist about "women's issues" than men labeling themselves conservative. Differences were most pronounced in attitudes toward women's issues, for example, whether there should be a constitutional ban on abortion and whether the ERA should be ratified. At all levels of office, black women were the most liberal.[35] In the fifteen states that did not ratify the ERA by the 1982 deadline, CAWP's 1981 survey of state legislators found an enormous forty-point gender gap. Seventy-six percent of the women legislators in these states, compared to 36 percent of their male counterparts, agreed that the ERA should be ratified.

A 1988 CAWP survey of state legislators demonstrated a continuing gender gap in attitudes toward some issues as well as a difference between women's and men's actions as lawmakers (see Figure 4).[36] In reporting their behavior in the legislature, women were more likely than their male colleagues to have established and worked for legislative priorities dealing with health care, children's and family issues, or women's rights regardless of party, ideology, feminist identification, constituency ideology, seniority, age, or political insider status. The study also provided evidence that women office-holders are having an impact on the way that government operates by bringing more citizens into the process, opting for government in public view rather than behind closed doors, and behaving more responsively to groups traditionally lacking access to the policy-making process (Figure 5).

Figure 4.   Women and Men Public Officials Have Different Policy Priorities.

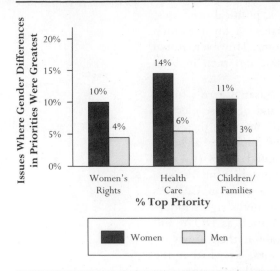

CAWP's National Survey of State Legislators asked officeholders about their top legislative priority in the most recent session.

• Women were more likely to give top priority to women's rights policies.
• Women were more likely to give priority to public policies related to their traditional roles as caregivers in the family and society—e.g., policies dealing with children and families and health care.

Source: *The Impact of Women in Public Office* (1991), a report of research conducted by the Center for the American Woman and Politics (CAWP), Eagleton Institute of Politics, Rutgers University.

In addition to survey data, there is anecdotal evidence that women bring something different to government and are having an impact on public policy. At the federal level, the bipartisan Congressional Caucus for Women's Issues has promoted such issues as the ERA, employment opportunities for women, women's health concerns, programs for displaced homemakers, assistance for women business owners, programs for victims of domestic violence, and dependent care and parental leave legislation. Members of women's groups in various state legislatures have worked together across party lines on agendas of particular interest to them as women. Such alliances range from formal women's legislative caucuses to informal networks meeting on issues and legislation affecting the lives of women and children, including the ERA, child care, equity in pensions and insurance, rights of divorced women, pay equity, counseling services for displaced homemakers, rape law, marital law, domestic violence, family leave, and sexual harassment.[37] Women legislators in West Virginia in 1987 persuaded the legislature to override the governor's veto of a bill providing medical care assistance for poor pregnant women and poor children. The women did this by "first, threatening to filibuster both houses of the legislature throughout the remaining week of the session; second, getting a resolution passed through the House on a unanimous voice vote calling on the Senate to reconsider the bill; and third, staging a quickly called candlelight vigil outside the Capitol by various advocacy groups."[38]

Similar signs of a feminist liberal consciousness among female elected officials were in evidence in late 1992, when the largest contingent of women ever to be elected to Congress arrived in Washington. Even before they were sworn in, the twenty-four new female House members of the 103rd Congress (twenty-one Democrats, three Republicans) issued a joint position statement calling

Figure 5. Women Officeholders Are Changing the Way Government Works.

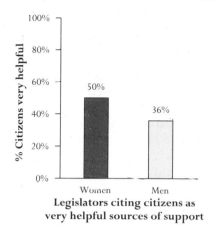

Women public officials are more likely than men to bring citizens into the process.

More women legislators reported that citizens were very helpful in working on their top priority bills.

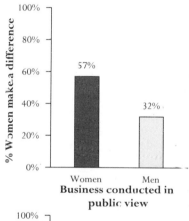

Women are more likely to opt for government in public view rather than government behind closed doors.

A majority of women legislators and a sizable minority of men legislators said women's increased presence had made a difference in the extent to which legislative business was conducted in public view rather than behind closed doors.

Women are more responsive to groups previously denied full access to the policymaking process.

Majorities of women and men legislators agreed that women have made a difference in the access of the economically disadvantaged to the legislature.

Source: *The Impact of Women in Public Office* (1991), a report of research conducted by the Center for the American Woman and Politics (CAWP), Eagleton Institute of Politics, Rutgers University.

for Congress to conform to sexual harassment laws, swift passage of a bill requiring employers to provide workers with family and medical leave, approval of full funding for Head Start, and passage of proposed abortion rights legislation.[39]

In local communities, women elected officials bring their own priorities to the towns and counties where they serve. Sometimes their impact manifests itself in a county shelter for battered women, sometimes a park for children or a local caregiving program for elderly people living alone. In 1985 the city of San Francisco, which had a woman mayor and several women supervisors, adopted an ordinance requiring developers building office space in central business areas to make provisions for on-site or nearby child care.[40]

Women in public office have also begun to make a difference through their powers to hire and appoint. Because they are likely to belong to women's organizations and to have worked and socialized with other women, female officials know where to find qualified women to recommend for positions on boards and commissions, to hire for their own staffs, and to suggest to others with positions to fill in politics or government. Like men, women turn automatically to familiar pools of talent for people with whom they share common experiences and can work comfortably. Moreover, political women in general make a point of hiring and promoting women. CAWP's 1981 national survey of officeholders found that large majorities of the women with staffs actively recruited women to fill openings.[41] During her three terms as governor in the 1980s, Vermont's Madeleine Kunin appointed large numbers of women to nontraditional governmental positions and left her mark on the state by creating a family court. In 1991, during her first ninety days in office, Texas Governor Ann Richards appointed more women and members of minority groups to boards and commissions than had any previous governors of Texas during their entire terms in office.

Women officials also take the time and trouble to encourage, educate, and advise other women about political life. CAWP's study concluded that political women "show evidence of a strong commitment when they take the time to educate women about political opportunities and to encourage women's political involvement. Contrary to the notion of the 'Queen Bee'—the woman who wants to keep all of the attention and power for herself to the exclusion of other women—the women in our studies and at our consultations welcome the chance to support other women."[42]

The evidence to date is that women do make a special contribution to the public world. If current trends continue, the long-term impact could be significant. First, women represent women's interests better than men have done. They do so collectively in caucuses and organizations, consciously as advocates of women's concerns, and unconsciously as people with a shared history and set of life experiences. Second, women inside the political system make it more open and responsive to larger sections of the citizenry and bring more women into public life. They do so directly by hiring, promoting, and appointing women and by serving as mentors; indirectly they are role models and educators who encourage women's participation by example and admonition.

At a grander and more abstract level, assessments of how much difference women will make must await a time when there are many more women establishing and implementing policy. In the closing years of the twentieth century, we are beginning a process of social evolution to incorporate more racial, ethnic, and gender diversity in political leadership than we have ever known. Perhaps a more caring and better-cared for society will be the result.

NOTES

1. Glenna Matthews, *The Rise of Public Woman: Woman's Power and Woman's Place in the United States 1630–1970* (New York: Oxford University Press, 1992), examines women's long struggle for a public voice and an acceptable public presence.

2. Quoted in Alice Rossi, ed., *The Feminist Papers* (Boston: Northeastern University Press, 1988), pp. 10–11.

3. Quoted in Rossi (pp. 320, 322) from Angelina Grimke, *Letters to Catherine Beecher* (Boston: Isaac Knapp, 1836).

4. Rossi, pp. 407–21.

5. Woodhull and Lockwood are described in Martin Gruberg, *Women in American Politics: An Assessment and Sourcebook* (Oshkosh, Wis.: Academia Press, 1968), p. 128; Edward T. James, ed., *Notable American Women 1607–1950* (Cambridge, Mass.: Harvard University Press, 1971), vol. 2, pp. 413–16, and vol. 3, pp. 652–55.

6. *Notable American Women* (1971), vol. 3, p. 345.

7. For a detailed discussion of what he calls "the matrimonial connection," see Irwin N. Gertzog, *Congressional Women: Their Recruitment, Treatment, and Behavior* (New York: Praeger, 1984), pp. 13–33.

8. Jeane J. Kirkpatrick discusses this pattern of entering office in middle age among female state legislators in *Political Woman* (New York: Basic Books, 1974), pp. 61–65 and passim.

9. Among Congresswomen during this period, New Jersey's Mary Norton is an example of the former, and the career of Michigan's Martha Griffiths illustrates the latter pattern. The highest appointive position held by a woman in this period went to Frances Perkins, Secretary of Labor in the administration of President Franklin Delano Roosevelt. Women in the Roosevelt administration, and the role of Democratic Party leader Molly Dewson and First Lady Eleanor Roosevelt in promoting women, are discussed in Susan Ware, *Beyond Suffrage: Women in the New Deal* (Cambridge, Mass.: Harvard University Press, 1981); Susan Ware, *Partner and I: Molly Dewson, Feminism and New Deal Politics* (New Haven, Conn.: Yale University Press, 1987).

10. This chapter does not examine women as party activists or in appointive public office. The general trend of slow and steady progress for women in politics between the early 1970s and the 1990s is as evident in the appointive arena as in the elective. More women than ever before were appointed by governors and by U.S. presidents to cabinet, subcabinet, and staff positions in their administrations. Research comparing the routes taken by women and men to appointive office in the late 1970s and early 1980s is reported in Susan J. Carroll and Barbara Geiger-Parker, *Women Appointed to the Carter Administration: A Comparison with Men* and *Women Appointed to State Government: A Comparison with All State Appointees* (New Brunswick, N.J.: Center for the American Woman and Politics, 1983). A fact sheet entitled *Women Appointed to Presidential Cabinets* is also issued by the Center for the American Woman and Politics.

11. For a detailed history and analysis of women as voters, see Sandra Baxter and Marjorie Lansing, *Women and Politics: The Visible Majority* (Ann Arbor, Mich.: University of Michigan Press, 1983).

12. "Exit polls" were first done in 1976. The preelection polls report how respondents *intended* to vote. See Gallup Opinion Index, December 1976, Report Number 137.

13. Data from exit poll conducted November 3, 1992, by Voter Research and Surveys, a consortium of ABC News, CBS News, CNN, and NBC News created in 1990 and reported in *The American Enterprise* Jan./Feb. 1993, p. 98. For more information, write VRS at 531 W 57 St., New York, NY 10019, or phone 212-975-5551.

14. For a compilation of information about "gender gap" races, see *The Gender Gap*, a fact sheet issued by the National Information Bank on Women in Public Office, Center for the American Woman and Politics, Eagleton Institute of Politics, Rutgers University, New Brunswick, N.J. 08901.

15. The "gender gap" is defined and examined by a number of scholars and political analysts in Carol M. Mueller, ed., *The Politics of the Gender Gap: The Social Construction of Political Influence*

(Newbury Park, Calif.: Sage Publications, 1988). See also Celinda C. Lake and Vincent J. Breglio, "Different Voices, Different Views: The Politics of Gender," in Paula Ries and Anne J. Stone, eds., *The American Woman 1992–93: A Status Report* (New York: W. W. Norton, 1992), pp. 178–201.

16. Sex differences in issue positions have been found by many polls. CAWP's *The Gender Gap* summarizes findings from Gallup, NY Times/CBS, Times Mirror Center, and NBC for 1990–92.

17. Data from these Voter Research and Surveys exit polls are reported in *The American Enterprise,* Jan./Feb. 1993, pp. 100–101, and *CAWP News and Notes,* vol. 9, no. 1, Winter 1993, pp. 8–9.

18. For a discussion of the backgrounds of women who ran for state legislative office before the mid-1970s, see Kirkpatrick's *Political Woman* (1974), pp. 29–58 and passim.

19. Women's experiences as political candidates in the 1970s and early 1980s are discussed in Ruth B. Mandel, *In the Running: The New Woman Candidate* (New York: Ticknor and Fields, 1981; Boston: Beacon Press, 1983), and Susan J. Carroll, *Women as Candidates in American Politics* (Bloomington: Indiana University Press, 1985). Personal accounts, analyses, and reflections on specific races include Bella Abzug, *Bella! Ms. Abzug Goes to Washington* (New York: Saturday Review Press, 1972); Shirley Chisholm, *Unbought and Unbossed* (New York: Avon, 1970) and *The Good Fight* (New York: Harper and Row, 1973); Barbara Jordan and Shelby Hearon, *Barbara Jordan: A Self-Portrait* (New York: Doubleday, 1979); Geraldine A. Ferraro with Linda Bird Francke, *Ferraro: My Story* (New York: Bantam, 1985); Congresswoman Pat Schroeder with Andrea Camp and Robyn Lipner, *Champion of the Great American Family* (New York: Random House, 1989); Ann Richards with Peter Knobler, *Straight from the Heart* (New York: Simon and Schuster, 1989); Celia Morris, *Storming the Statehouse: Running for Governor with Ann Richards and Dianne Feinstein* (New York: Charles Scribner's Sons, 1992).

20. The Women's Campaign Fund supports candidates on a bipartisan basis; established in 1974, it was the first women's PAC. EMILY'S List, a Washington-based donor network established in 1985, contributes money to selected female Democrats running for statewide and federal office. It is named after its philosophy of support—"Early Money Is Like Yeast, it makes the dough rise." With a donor base that grew from three thousand to twenty-four thousand members in 1992, EMILY is one of the most powerful political organizations in Washington.

21. For a review of the development of women's PACs, see Katherine E. Kleeman, *Women's PACs* (New Brunswick, N.J.: Center for the American Woman and Politics, 1983).

22. In 1992, NOW's PACs provided $460,000, including bundling and in-kind contributions, to 317 candidates. The Women's Campaign Fund contributed $1.5 million to 242 women. Information is from *CAWP News and Notes,* vol. 9, no. 1, Winter 1993, pp. 10–21. In the 1991–92 election cycle EMILY'S List and the Women's Campaign Fund were among the top fifty PAC money raisers reporting funds raised for federal candidates to the Federal Election Commission. FEC Press Release of April 29, 1993, p. 11.

23. Earlier versions of this and the next section appeared in *The American Woman 1988–89,* edited by Sara E. Rix (New York: W. W. Norton, 1988), and *The American Woman 1992–93,* edited by Paula Ries and Anne J. Stone (New York: W. W. Norton, 1992).

24. The United States is not a global leader in electing women, having one of the smaller proportions of women in its national legislative body. Global figures for female parliamentarians and legislators can be found in Ruth Leger Sivard, *Women . . . A World Survey* (Washington, D.C.: World Priorities, 1985), and in *The World's Women, 1970–1990* (New York: United Nations, 1991).

25. Nellie Tayloe Ross was elected governor of Wyoming in 1925 after the death of her husband, the governor. She served one two-year term. Miriam A. ("Ma") Ferguson replaced her husband, who had been impeached, in 1924. She served in 1925–26 and 1933–34. In 1966, Alabama Governor George Wallace, who was prohibited by the state constitution from running for reelection, had his wife Lurleen elected as his stand-in. Secretary of State Rose Mofford, an Arizona Democrat, succeeded Governor Evan Mecham in 1988 following his impeachment and conviction by the legislature. Only one woman, Consuelo N. Bailey of Vermont, was elected a lieutenant governor, serving from 1955–56, but two (in Michigan in 1940 and in Nevada in 1962) were appointed to fill unexpired terms. Gruberg, 1968, pp. 189–90.

26. For descriptions of the women elected to office in the 1970s and early 1980s, see Kirkpatrick (1974), Mandel (1983), Carroll (1985), and also Marilyn Johnson and Susan J. Carroll, "Profile of Women Holding Office, 1977," in *Women in Public Office: A Biographical Directory and Statistical Analysis,* 2nd ed. (Metuchen, N.J.: The Scarecrow Press, 1978); Susan J. Carroll and Wendy

S. Strimling, *Women's Routes to Elective Office: A Comparison with Men's* (New Brunswick, N.J.: Center for the American Woman and Politics, Eagleton Institute of Politics, Rutgers University, 1983).

27. Carroll and Strimling (1983), Chapter 1. Johnson and Carroll (1978), Part II, pp. 7A–20A.

28. Carroll and Strimling (1983), Chapter 4.

29. Ibid., pp. 44–50.

30. Chapters 7 through 12 of Carroll and Strimling (1983) look at the experiences of black women.

31. The oldest national organization of elected women is the National Order of Women Legislators. Established in 1938, NOWL's membership includes both current and former legislators.

32. The history, politics, and policy priorities of the Congressional Caucus for Women's Issues are described briefly in Mandel (1983), more fully in Gertzog (1984), and most recently in the four volumes entitled *The American Woman* (New York: W. W. Norton), pp. 19–23 (1987), pp. 310–29 (1988), pp. 325–46 (1990), pp. 441–60 (1992), a periodical series of reports on the status of women in the United States prepared by the Washington-based Women's Research and Education Institute (WREI).

33. Carroll (1985), p. 156.

34. See Johnson and Carroll (1978); also Kathy A. Stanwick and Katherine E. Kleeman, *Women Make a Difference* (New Brunswick, N.J.: Center for the American Woman and Politics, 1983).

35. See Stanwick and Kleeman (1983) for an overview of findings.

36. Results of this study, a survey of a national sample of state legislators in the summer of 1988, conducted under a grant from the Charles H. Revson Foundation, are presented in a series of reports summarized by Susan J. Carroll, Debra L. Dodson, and Ruth B. Mandel in *The Impact of Women in Public Office: An Overview* (New Brunswick, N.J.: Center for the American Woman and Politics, Eagleton Institute of Politics, Rutgers University, 1991).

37. Katherine E. Kleeman and Ruth B. Mandel, "Women Officials: A Singular Bond," *The Women's Economic Justice Agenda* (Washington, D.C.: The National Center for Policy Alternatives, 1987).

38. "Women Legislators Lead Stunning Revolt in WV," *National NOW Times,* May/June 1987, pp. 4, 7.

39. David S. Broder and Eric Pianin, "House Democrats Unseat Whitten, GOP Taps Armey," *The Washington Post,* December 8, 1992, p. A4.

40. For fuller discussion and examples of women officials making a difference in various jurisdictions across the United States, see Debra L. Dodson, ed., *Gender and Policymaking: Studies of Women in Office* (New Brunswick, N.J.: Center for the American Woman and Politics, Eagleton Institute of Politics, Rutgers University, 1991). This report is a collection of eleven essays written by scholars who investigated the impact of elected and appointed women in local, state, and national offices.

41. Stanwick and Kleeman (1983), p. 18.

42. Ibid., p. 19.

Out of Order: A Critical Perspective on Women in Religion

Martha J. Reineke

RELIGION EXPRESSES AND shapes the ideals, hopes, and needs of humankind. When humans wish to distinguish those ideas and experiences that are of utmost seriousness and value in their lives from those that are of secondary importance, they find in religious beliefs and practices answers to their questions of "ultimate concern."[1] Religion classifies and organizes such key aspects of experience as sexuality, birth, death, power, and violence. It grounds a people's deepest convictions and provides a basis for decisions based on a knowledge of good and evil, right and wrong. Religion, more than any other institution, "patrols the borders" that separate order from disorder in society, dispensing information, protection, and judgments. Interestingly, when religion attends to meaning and order, chaos and disorder, the human body is among its most common reference points. Why the body?

In her ground-breaking study of religion, *Purity and Danger: An Analysis of the Concepts of Pollution and Taboo,* anthropologist Mary Douglas notes that "the more personal and intimate the source of ritual symbolism, the more telling its message. The more the symbol is drawn from a common fund of human experience, the more wide and certain its reception."[2] Religion, engaged in mental "fence making," appeals to the human body, rather than to actual door posts, fence rows, and stone walls for images of order and meaning because the body is the most intimate and certain of boundaries.[3]

Significantly, religion does not symbolically account for order and proscribe disorder in the world by appeal to generic human bodies. Rather, religion most often demarcates order from disorder by appeal to the *female* body. The female body, site of processes men have perceived historically as mysterious and potentially dangerous, offers a most graphic symbolism of issues of ultimate concern. Women carry potential for order and meaning (life) and disorder or chaos (death) in their very bodies: menstruation (potential for life), reproduction (successful or miscarried creation), and aging (movement toward death) all testify to the triumphs and tragedies of existence. That religion, wanting to protect society from dangers that lurk on the margins of society, threatening disorder, acts most often against women is no wonder. Women, who symbolize with their bodies the powers and dangers to be contested, are also those humans least likely to have the power to protest the literal inscription of societal meaning on their bodies. Moreover, gender differences in women's and men's experience of religion can be traced to the role religion plays in advancing order and gaining control over the forces of disorder by controlling women and their bodies: power asserted over women is power asserted over the very powers of creation.

How does this happen? In this essay, I want to examine how those religious myths, rituals, and sacred symbols that are focused on the human body are among the primary vehicles for (1) socializing women to gender roles, (2) assigning women to subservient positions within a gendered caste system, and (3) controlling women's sexuality through use of power. I will also, in assessing a "verdict" on religion that will be sensitive to women's current concerns about sexism, point to instances in which women have experienced religion in nonoppressive ways. By way of contrast, such examples offer important insights for women scholars about the possible role for religion in the creation of nonsexist societies.

Religion and the Prescription of Gender Roles

Maleness and femaleness are culturally established, and religion is a primary vehicle for this socialization process. Classification systems that specify appropriate female behavior and distinguish it from that of males establish and enforce order in society. A good example is found in the religion of Hinduism.

Hinduism, the religion of India, is preoccupied with questions of order and disorder. Hindus believe that humans are locked into a cycle of suffering and disorder that persists across numerous lifetimes. This endless cycle of rebirth, which Americans sometimes call "reincarnation," is more properly called *samsara*. *Samsara* is countered by religious wisdom. Hindus, united in their desire to achieve an ordered unity of existence that they call *moksha*—liberation or salvation from *samsara*—differ from one another only in the variety of ways they seek *moksha*. The caste system, an elaborate hereditary division of labor among persons, places Hindus at different points along a common journey to *moksha*. Each person is born into one of four major castes: *brahmin* (priests), *kshatriya* (warriors), *vaiśya* (artisans and merchants), or *śūdra* (peasants). Upward mobility within one's own life is not possible: one's current life is the just product of one's previous lives. However, across a series of lifetimes, liberation is possible. Fit for the particular degree of freedom offered by one's present caste and gender, each Hindu makes his or her own way through *samsara,* toward *moksha.* For the priests, for example, wisdom that liberates is a product of meditation on the unity of all things in Brahman: Cosmic Principle or Ultimate Reality. For others—peasants, for example—*moksha* is a bliss attained in devotion to a god or a goddess. Sacrifices to the god or goddess, celebrations, and festivals free the devotee from enslavement in the prison of *samsara* and bring the devotee close to that god and to *moksha.*[4]

Women in Hinduism are traditionally socialized to find the fulfillment of their lives and their purpose in being good wives and the mothers of sons. A good wife treats her husband as a god.[5] She embodies the virtues of self-ﬄfﬓﬕ, submission, and patience. Her role in life is to facilitate her husband's spiritual journey to moksha. Because, according to Hinduism, a woman is defined solely in relation to her husband, an unmarried woman or a widow is a nonentity in Indian life. She falls outside the parameters of the classification system that describes appropriate female behavior. Consequently, the unmarried woman or widow poses a threat to societal order.

One consequence of this narrow definition of womanhood is the continuing practice of child marriages. Although the legal age of marriage is eighteen years, the most common age of females at the time of marriage, according to the most recent information, is nine.[6] To the extent that such early marriages are consummated and result in pregnancy, serious health problems may result. Another problem women face traditionally in India is widowhood. Because a husband's *karma* or spiritual status is intimately liked with his wife's, a widow enhances her husband's prospects for a higher rebirth or for *moksha* by either pursuing an ascetic life—begging for food, sleeping on the ground without shelter—or by joining her husband on his funeral pyre and dying with him. Although this latter custom has been outlawed, it continues in the form of "kitchen accidents." As a result of the often intolerable living conditions for widows, in the past three years some women have marched in New Delhi advocating the reinstatement of *sati,* or widow-burning.[7]

The experiences of women within Hinduism clearly illustrate the demarcation of order from disorder in Indian society through the inscription of order on female bodies. Hindu views of women mirror broad societal concerns about powers and dangers that lead Hindus who want to understand and control these powers and dangers to focus on the human body in general and on the female body in particular.

The human body provides the model for cultural order: the highest castes are associated with the human mind (meditation and knowledge); the lowest castes are associated with bodily waste (washers, barbers, sweepers). Crucial to the caste system is the control of order in the society by surveillance of body "borders." Disorder, in the form of pollution, lurks everywhere. For this reason, the society is particularly preoccupied with body orifices, which represent social exits and entrances.[8]

Bodily pollution threatens most at two points: material sustenance and reproduction. To share food is to share in the nature of another.[9] Yet, because food is produced through the combined efforts of persons of several castes—blacksmiths, carpenters, ropemakers, peasants—it is threatened by massive impurities. To counter impurity, elaborate precautions must be taken. Some food is, by definition, impure for the higher castes. Other food, potentially impure, is cleansed through rituals of preparation that constitute a symbolic break with the threat of disorder.[10]

More than those regarding food, concerns about women's roles in reproduction and about possible threats to hereditary purity constitute a central focus of Hinduism. Because cultural purity, which is the litmus test for cultural order, is transmitted biologically, Hinduism is to a great extent preoccupied with the protection and control of women's bodily orifices.[11] Children take their caste from their mother; hence, a woman who has sexual relations with a lower-caste man pollutes herself, endangers her future children, and subjects society as a whole to danger. For this reason, the chastity of unmarried female children is of great concern. Marriage prior to first menstruation is encouraged because the more likely virginity of the child-bride decreases the threat of pollution. The pressure is highest on Brahman (upper-caste) female children, for the threat of pollution from lower castes is greatest for them.

The caste system prescribes a hierarchy of order based on gender, which is no less significant than that based on the division of labor. Caste hierarchy, "writ large" in the world, is duplicated on a smaller scale within the family. There, when a woman treats her husband as a god, she duplicates the essence of the social hierarchy: those who are lower in life offer themselves to the higher.[12] The ethics of self-sacrifice structure order at every point. For this reason, each woman adopts a life of extreme asceticism (self-denial) and service to her husband. She is taught that a woman's strength lies in her submission to her husband and is marked by service, chastity, and devotion. So significant is this lesson that even the stories of the gods and goddesses confirm its truth: a woman's feminine behavior constitutes the pillar of stability that supports even the cosmos.[13]

For humans, death constitutes a fundamental threat to societal stability, one that religions attempt to counter with rituals enacted on behalf of order. In Hinduism, not all persons can be insulated from the experience of death, but a man acquires through marriage a kind of "insurance" against the brute reality of death: he who attends properly to the requirements of a "good marriage" (i.e., a marriage that produces a son and a grandson) advances toward *moksha*. Moreover, a man's spiritual status can also be advanced by his wife's actions: her devotion and sacrifices will enhance his prospects in his next life. A widow, assuming responsibility for her husband's death, feels guilt because she has failed as a result of lack of devotion or adequate sacrifice to ensure her husband's longevity.[14] The fundamental failure of human life—that we do not live forever—thus is made understandable (i.e., reasonable, orderly) when a woman takes responsibility for it, through ritual. Traditionally, that responsibility is exacted from a woman by widow-sacrifice: *sati*.[15] Less traditionally, and more commonly today, a widow lives on the margins of society. Greater asceticism is demanded from her than from a married woman. The widow shaves her head, lest her attractiveness create opportunities for sexual encounters that will bring impurities into the family. Eating as little as possible, demanding no shelter or material provisions, the widow will continue to live sacrificially, on the margins of life, on the verge of death.

Religious Legitimation of Caste

The hierarchy of male and female lives is one aspect of a caste system in India. Another kind of caste system, founded on a less systematic, but no less powerful, subordination of women to men, exists in cultures influenced by three religions that originated in the Near (Middle) East: Judaism, Christianity, and Islam.

These three religions share in common the tenets of "ethical monotheism." All worship only one God and share a historical tradition about this God, who communicates with humans through prophets. Judaism, the oldest of the three, and Christianity have a common scripture, which records the relationship between God and humans: the Hebrew Bible is the Christian Old Testament.[16] In the Moslem scriptures—the Qur'an—the prophet Muhammed proclaims the fundamental belief in one God and recounts revelations about religious forebears (e.g., Moses, Abraham, Isaac, Mary, Jesus) known also to Christians and Jews.

Judaism, Christianity, and Islam also share a common concern for ethical behavior. Indeed, all three religions link the words "response" and "responsibility": one who hears the word of God and *responds* is one who acts with *responsibility* to counter injustice and to create a more just world. Meaning and order are established in the world, and sin and disorder are challenged successfully to the extent that humans hear the word of God and are inspired to action.

Linked by a common focus on ethical behavior and the one God, Jews, Christians, and Moslems are distinguished from one another in their understandings of the word of God spoken to them. For Judaism, the definitive word of God is located in the Law (Torah). The Law constitutes a covenant (contract) between God and the people. Humans respond to God correctly when they keep the Law, for the basis of order and meaning in human existence is located there.

For Christianity, the word of God is decisively present in the life and teachings of Jesus. That Christianity is alone among the Western religions in divinizing its prophet accentuates the Christian claim that Jesus *is* God's presence and truth: he is the way, the truth, and the life. Meaning and order in human existence flow from Jesus, for in him "all things hold together" (Colossians 1:17).

Islam, the newest of the three religions that originated in the Near East, is distinguished from both Judaism and Christianity in its understanding of the word of God. According to Islam, because Judaism has increasingly misunderstood and distorted the authentic word of God spoken through Moses and recorded in the Torah, the word of God must be delivered to humans again. For Islam, the status of the word of God in Judaism is much like the status of a sentence at the end of the children's game of "telephone": at its origin, the Torah spoke truth, but in Muhammed's day, the message had been so altered by various interpreters of Torah that its original meaning had been lost. The game had to be called off and a new speaker (Muhammed) summoned to express God's word clearly in the Qur'an, so that humans could again serve God.

According to Islam, Christian beliefs are also in error. Christians wrongly dilute the rigor of monotheism when they treat the prophet Jesus as a divine being, the Son of God. Were Christians to attend rightly to the *message* of God, rather than to the *messenger,* they would be on the correct path of faith, a path that culminates, not with any incarnate messenger of the one God, but with the direct revelation in the Qur'an of God's word.

We can detect caste differences ascribed to gender in Judaism, Christianity, and Islam. A caste system is visible wherever we can locate "a social arrangement in which access to power and socioeconomic benefits are fixed, typically from birth, according to certain ascribed characteristics of the individual."[17] Symbols, myths, and rituals are primary vehicles for the teaching of caste differences that are ascribed to gender. The morning prayer of male Orthodox Jews makes this explicit. It includes the phrase "Praised are you, O Lord our God, King of the Universe, who has not created me a woman."[18] Creation stories often assign to women the responsibility for the presence of evil or

troubles in the present world. In these myths, women's presumed characteristics of sexual allure, curiosity, and gullibility are often blamed for humankind's
problems, primarily humankind's inattention to God's Law and word.

For example, folk Judaism attributes to Lilith, Adam's first wife, who
refused to obey him and fled from him, all kinds of evils and dangers to family
life. In this Jewish tradition, Lilith is contrasted with Eve, who, as the second,
and obedient, wife, was taken from Adam's side.[19] In Christianity, no Lilith
tradition functions to consign evil to a runaway wife. Instead, Christian
theology places the responsibility for evil squarely on Eve's shoulders. She
caused humankind's fall away from obedience to God's word into sin. The early
Christian theologian Tertullian, for example, writes about Eve:

> You are the Devil's gateway. You are the unsealer of that forbidden tree. You
> are the first deserter of the divine law. You are she who persuaded him whom
> the Devil was not valiant enough to attack. You destroyed so easily God's
> image man. On account of your desert, that is death, even the Son of God
> had to die.[20]

To the extent that the Christian theologian depicts all women as Eve's daughters, women are responsible, as a caste, for evil in the world and for all of
its consequences.

In other instances of Christian theology, the story of the fall of humans
into sin is interpreted not in a way that blames woman (Eve) for evil in the
world but rather in a way that justifies and legitimates a gendered hierarchy.
Women must be subordinate to man, but not so that she may be punished;
rather, because the social order of the world has been transformed by
human sin, woman's subordination to man is required for a return to order
and obedience.

The Christian theologian Luther, for example, believes that in original
creation Eve was the equal of Adam. Yet, through the fall into sin, Eve, and
all women after her, became inferior. For Luther, her subjugation is an
expression of divine justice that reorders the affairs of the world to counter
humans' earlier fall away from God into disobedience and disorder:

> This punishment too springs from original sin; and the woman bears it just
> as unwillingly as she bears those pains and inconveniences which have been
> placed upon her flesh. The rule remains with the husband, and the wife
> is compelled to obey him by God's command. He rules the home and the
> state, wages war, defends his possessions, tills the soil, builds, plants, etc.
> The woman, on the other hand, is like a nail driven into the wall. She sits
> at home . . . the wife should stay at home and look after the affairs of
> the household as one who has been deprived of the ability of administer-
> ing those affairs that are outside and concern the state. . . . In this way Eve
> is punished.[21]

The judgments that Luther wants to make about the origins of sin and about
the painful and disruptive consequences of evil in the world are made in view
of that most powerful of human symbols: the human body. Specifically, Eve's
body, source of willful disobedience, both symbolizes the plight of humanity
and points to the source of redemption. Redemption is possible for all
humanity only if women bear the pain placed on their flesh, a pain that, in

circumscribing their cultural position, effects the punishment necessary for humans to be returned to orderly relationship with one another and with God.

In statements of Jewish belief, located in important Jewish teachings called the Talmud, attitudes toward women also demonstrate the significance of caste hierarchy to societal order. Writings by the Pharisees and Flavius Josephus, for example, emphasize the inferiority of women to men. Women are "overcome by a spirit of fornication" and "plot in their hearts against men."[22] In both the *Book of Jubilees* and *The Testaments of the Twelve Patriarchs,* composed between 109 and 106 B.C.E., the danger of fornication with women (a danger to Judaism from within) is linked to the danger of foreign cultures (a danger to Judaism from without).[23] That all women are overcome with lust and harbor a predisposition for evil deeds becomes linked in the author's minds with impending seduction of the Jews by foreign cultures. Women's bodies symbolize the powers and dangers to be contested if the covenant with God is to be kept.

In the Diaspora exile after 70 C.E., which occurred as a result of conquest by the Roman Empire, misogynistic tendencies are extended, in part, as a result of the ever greater challenges to Jewish identity in the face of the dispersion of the Jewish people beyond the borders of Palestine. That the wild and unruly sexuality of women requires strict subordination of women, as a caste, to men, underscores the need for greater order in the Jewish Diaspora.[24] Talmudic prescriptions for order and identity, "writ large," repeat earlier inscriptions of a moral code on women's bodies: just as individual women must be discouraged from fornication, so also must Israel not play the harlot.

When compared with Judaism and Christianity, Islam most explicitly argues that social order depends on the careful attention to caste differences based on gender. Order in society is based on the separation of men's and women's lives into separate spheres. Men find their place in the public sphere and worship in the mosque; women find their place in the private sphere—the home—where they also pray. If a woman finds that she must leave the seclusion of the home to enter the public sphere, although such an act is discouraged in traditional Islam, she should be veiled from head to toe, so that no part of her body is displayed.[25]

The Islamic attribution of societal disorder to disobedient women is clearly visible in the Islamic imagery of Paradise: Paradise is "the Garden." It is a beautiful place with fountains, pastures, cool pavilions, fruits, and *hur:* lovely virgins. In the Garden, every male will have not only his wife but also seventy *hur.* The *hur* are never sick, never menstruate, and are never bad-tempered. Each time a man returns to a *hur,* he will find her virginity once again intact. Both daily human existence and imagery of the Judgment scene contrast dramatically with the Garden. In daily existence, women are sometimes sick and grumpy, they do menstruate, and their purity, after a single act of intercourse, is forever in doubt. In the Judgment scene, through which order is served and sinners are punished, the fantasy of Paradise is reversed: the sinful and disordered world condemned in the Judgment is a world in which women are in charge of men.[26]

Through use of such imagery, women are taught to conform to a caste role. They learn that good women are like the women of the Garden; bad women are like the women of the Judgment scene. Unfortunately, they also learn that women inevitably fall short of the required purity because they do menstruate and because, unlike the perpetually virginal *hur,* their virginity ends with the first act of intercourse. This sad truth, confirmed daily by women's bodies, serves in Islam both to justify men's wariness of women and to establish men's right to demand obedience of women, lest women's tendency toward immoral behavior throw the world into even greater disorder.

Of course, Judaism, Christianity, and Islam are not alone in ascribing order in society to women's obedience and decay to their disobedience. Hinduism's goddess tradition provides another mythic explanation of gender differentiation. Hindu religious myths tell us that an independent or autonomous goddess is dangerous and is prone to destructive use of her powers. Hence, Hindu goddesses are paired with male consorts—gods—by whom they are tamed and through whom their ambiguous powers are controlled.[27] To human women, goddesses represent the feminine ideal. They are chaste, virtuous, and obedient to their husbands. To depart from this ideal, by preserving one's autonomy through not marrying, is to flirt with danger. Just as demonic powers visit the independent goddess (e.g., Kali), so also will they visit independent human females. Dangers, large and small, are countered only as females—both divine and human—are obedient in their roles as wives. This symbolic message extends to a third area of primary linkage between religion and gender ideologies: power and sexuality.

Power and Sexuality

Religion—in ritual, word, and act—creates borders that separate societal order from disorder and protects these borders against threats from outside. To specify the boundaries of order, religion appeals to body symbolism, believing that a power asserted over the body is a power asserted in the social sphere and that a threat issued against the social body is a threat registered also by the human body. Religion acts to reinforce social order by controlling bodies and addresses fears about social disorder by appeal to fear of sexuality. Because the female body has been perceived historically as a source of dangerous power to be purified, controlled, and occasionally destroyed by men, women's bodies are the preferred focus in religious rituals and writings that aim to counter the forces of disorder.

One strong example of this thesis is visible in the Middle East between 800 and 500 B.C.E., when the Israelites moved into Canaan. The Canaanite society was agricultural and sedentary, and a large focus of Canaanite religious practice was symbols of fertility. Although the Canaanite society was not matriarchal in organization, power was diffused among both men and women.[28] Women took a primary role in the religious practices—assuming leadership in many temple rites devoted to gods and goddesses and celebrating fertility of land and people.[29] With the entrance of the Israelites into Canaan, military conflict was matched by cultural confrontation, for the Israelites were a strongly patriarchal, tribal society. Israelite leaders used religious rituals and beliefs—often focused on the female body—to distinguish ordered, approved beliefs and behaviors in Israel from those disruptive of order. Women, once major participants in temple rites and primary symbols of the celebrated sexuality of males and females, came to represent powers of fertility to be feared. Menstruating women were forbidden to enter the temple sites, now devoted to worship of the one God, Yahweh. After the birth of a child, women were forbidden to enter the temple for forty days in the case of a male child, for eighty in the case of a female child.[30] Rituals with water, enacted by the Canaanites to celebrate the life-giving powers of water, were transformed by the Israelites into rituals of purification. Much of the focus was purification from female pollution. Religion enabled the Israelites to transpose the Canaanite society's threat to Israelite identity and order to the female body. In turn, the Israelites could assert their power over the Canaanites by asserting control over women's bodies. If the female body—key site of mysterious, and potentially disorderly or polluting, processes—could be controlled and purified, then so could Israel. In each instance, a fundamental commitment to societal order was served.

Interestingly, one of the more significant dynamics between social order and sexuality is visible also in the religion of the people of Israel, as recorded in the writings of the prophets (e.g., Isaiah, Ezekiel), which both Jews and Christians include among their sacred writings. The prophets wrote during a time in which the ancient Israelites continue to define themselves as a monotheistic culture over against the polytheism of their neighbors. At times, the Israelites feel threatened by their neighbors, not only because the neighbors confront the Israelites with opposing, and potentially attractive, religious beliefs, but also because they pose a genuine military threat to the continued existence of Israel. Reacting to outside powers, the prophets, summoning the energies of the people against the outside threat, use language that correlates power and sexuality.[31] Isaiah, for example, inveighs against the moral decay of Israel, calling for a time when "the Lord shall have washed away the filth of the daughters of Zion" (Isaiah 3:16–26; 4:1–4), Ezekiel accuses Israel of playing the whore. God speaks through him to Israel in those terms:

> I will gather all your lovers, with whom you took pleasure . . . and I will judge you as women who break wedlock and shed blood are judged, and bring upon you the blood of wrath and jealousy . . . they shall strip you of your clothes and take your fair jewels, and leave you naked and bare. They shall bring up a host against you, and they shall stone you and cut you to pieces with their swords. (Ezekiel 16:37–40)

If we take anthropologist Mary Douglas's arguments seriously, the prophets' correlation of threats to power with sexuality is not merely coincidental. When societies perceive that their borders are threatened, they often try to redraw the boundaries of social order. Their "drawing exercises" often appeal to that most dominant of border images, the human body, and to that most mysterious and potentially threatening of bodies, the female body. To redefine appropriate sexuality and to distinguish it from "dirty" sexuality is to "clean house" in a larger sense: a society with sexual order is a society with political order as well.

Chinese religion offers an important variation on the negative theme of female sexuality. Religion in China, traditionally varied and diverse, includes Buddhism. The teachings of the Buddha direct a person in meditation toward enlightenment, which, not unlike Hinduism, frees one from the chains of an endless cycle of rebirth (*samsara*) and delivers one into the peace of *nirvana*. Mahayana Buddhism, a form of Buddhism found in China, teaches that the way to enlightenment may be difficult. Therefore, assistance is available from *bodhisattvas*—enlightened ones who labor on behalf of another's enlightenment. The *bodhisattvas* are often imaged as gods and goddesses who reside in various celestial Buddha-lands or Paradises. Their powers may be summoned on behalf of one's quest for enlightenment through devotion and ritual.

In China, a tradition of female, and not only male, *bodhisattvas* is melded with traditions of folk religion. "Folk religion" encompasses a variety of cultural expressions of religion in China. One does not "join" a folk religion; one becomes part of it by virtue of one's very existence in China. Central to these folk expressions of religion, the communist revolution notwithstanding, is ancestor veneration. For the Chinese, order in the present society is founded on the honoring of past order. Moreover, because those who lived in the past were more attuned to the fundamental order of existence, it is best, the Chinese believe, to give careful attention to the ancestors. Ritual evocation of the ancestors and their wisdom therefore constitutes a central aspect of Chinese culture. From daily activities such as farming, to medicine, to the opera, traditional Chinese life revolves around practices that display attentiveness to the ancestors. Ancestors who are significant, not only to an individual family, but also to a larger community, are referred to as gods and goddesses.

Thus, we can see that a strong goddess tradition stems from both Buddhism and folk religion in China. In this tradition, goddesses such as Kuan-Yin and Ma Tsu are portrayed in unambiguously positive language. Kuan-Yin, Goddess of Mercy, is often the principal deity in Buddhist temples. Ma Tsu, whose origins are located in folk religion, is a central figure for worship and the overseer of the fishing industry in Taiwan. Interestingly, while the goddesses exemplify wholly positive characteristics of care and compassion, they do so in sharp contrast to human females. Two messages dominate socialization of human females through religious ideologies. First, human females bear the marks of pollution through menstruation, sexual intercourse, and childbirth. Second, the greatest tragedy in a woman's life is to remain childless. Female identity is formed by childbearing, but that power is interpreted negatively as pollution, so as to circumscribe it. The goddesses, who become deities subsequent to earthly tragedies that prevent them from fulfilling their proper roles in earthly life as human wives and mothers, escape the marks of pollution and for that very reason attain their genuine and larger power as deities. In a sense then, while goddesses are identified as members of the human female gender, they also violate cultural definitions of the female gender and cultural restrictions on female power. That violation is conservatively interpreted within Chinese culture so as to exclude human females from identifying with the goddesses. Pollution ideologies and negative views of female sexuality and power are preserved, rather than challenged, by goddess mythology.[32]

The fear of sexuality is prevalent in Christianity as well. Mary, the mother of Jesus, has strong parallels with the compassionate goddesses of Chinese religion. She is distinguished, in her virginity, from all other women. In her purity she is the "new Eve," as contrasted with the sinful sexuality of the first Eve. Although the Bible documents that Mary and Joseph had other children after Jesus, church theology in later times conveniently ignores this, emphasizing Mary's complete break with sexuality and reproduction. Mary is always, and perpetually, a virgin.[33] As such, she can represent the virginity of the Christian church: i.e., its order and purity in relation to assaults from non-Christian influences.

Historically, whenever specific Christian groups have felt external pressures threatening their existence, Christian theologies, highlighting the dangers of sexuality, have reasserted the values of sexual asceticism and celibacy. For example, in the earliest years of Christianity, when it was a tiny and fragile religion, the Apostle Paul advocated celibacy. He recommended marriage only as a last resort (1 Corinthians 7:6–9). Later, Jerome articulated a quantitative measure of the value of perpetual virginity: marriage brings but a thirtyfold yield of virtue, widowhood sixtyfold, and virginity a hundredfold.[34] When the fragility of Christian communities is revisited later in the history of Christianity—for example, in the utopian experiment of the Shakers—asceticism and requisite celibacy become requirements of the Christian life.[35] The body comes to symbolize the necessity of impermeable, virgin walls of the new society.[36]

To be sure, celibacy and sexual asceticism often have been recommended for both men and women in the Christian religion. However, the dynamics are not the same for both genders; rather, the woman "plays the heavy." It is from the dangers of *her* sexuality that both man and woman are to be saved if they adopt the celibate life or practice sexual asceticism.

That religious sanctions can be used to enforce gender roles and specified forms of approved sexuality is nowhere more clearly visible than in that darkest chapter of the history of Christianity, when persecution of witches focused primarily on women. Women who deviated from religiously established norms for females—women of independent financial means, usually widows, women practitioners of folk medicine, poor women, and women who were single or who otherwise did not have the protection of propertied men—were the most likely victims. Although the issue was female power, the language of the witchcraft trials focused on the sexual behavior of the women accused of witchcraft. Trial records exhibit an exaggerated fear of female sexuality. Recent scholarly estimates suggest that several hundred thousand witches were killed between 1440 and 1770. There has not been a parallel persecution of men as men, although men have been persecuted in greater numbers as members of other minorities, primarily as Jews.[37]

Significantly, the witchcraft craze occurred during the Renaissance, a time of great cultural change and of challenges to traditional economic and political authority. As is so often the case, threats to power in a broad sense were responded to not only on a large social scale, but also on a smaller scale: women who had no decisive political power of their own were the most vulnerable to charges of witchcraft.

Christian theology's negative view of female sexuality illustrates that dominant religious images of women in Christianity are built on dualistic images of the human being. Women are universally devalued, based on the assumption of a hierarchy of culture over nature. As a realm of culture and reason is contrasted by Christian theologians with a realm of nature and emotion, women, because of their reproductive processes, are identified with nature and men are identified with culture and reason. Christian theology, identifying men with the cultural norm, measures women against that norm and finds them wanting. Men define culture and oppose themselves to women, whom they find inferior and beneath them. Associating women not only with nature but also with sexual passion, lack of reason, domestic activities, and reproduction, men propose to dominate and control women, just as they are mandated by scriptures (Genesis 1:28) to subdue and dominate the earth.

Female sexuality, interpreted according to this dualistic scenario, is highly problematic: the irrational, and potentially chaotic, sexuality of women is either controlled, in service to a Christian culture, or is dangerously out of control and is evil. Measured against the cultural and religious norm, female sexuality, in its evil mode, is that of the tempter, seducer, or polluter and, in its approved mode, is that of virgin, chaste bride, or mother. Although, according to Christian theology, both male and female are created in the image of God, Christian theologians, to the extent that they think dualistically, have placed women closer to the realm of nature, and hence to sexuality and death, than they have placed men.[38] Although human males obviously have bodies, in Christian theology they are "essentially" beings of reason and spirit; in contrast, women are "essentially" linked to nature and partake of the order of reason and spirit only secondarily. Moreover, even as men can bring their bodies under their conscious control in order to dominate both their bodies and their surroundings, women, according to the dualistic scenario, are subject to their bodies. If women are not ruled by men, they are ruled by their passions, and evil or chaos abounds. Hence, religiously approved roles for women, defined and legitimated by scripture and tradition, are narrowly limited to those clearly controlled by men (e.g., wife, daughter) or distinguished from nature and reproduction (e.g., the Virgin Mary or the celibate nun).

Exclusively masculine imagery for the deity in the Christian religion teaches the lessons of dualism: those who find themselves in the realm of culture are closer to God. In a Vatican declaration of 1976 against women's ordination, this dualistic vision was reconfirmed. The Roman Catholic Church hierarchy concluded that women cannot be priests because "there must be a physical resemblance between the priest and Christ."[39] The possession of male genitalia becomes the essential prerequisite for representing Christ, who in his maleness is the disclosure in earthly culture of the male God. The celibacy of the priest, confirming the celibacy of Jesus, links both to a realm distant from that of nature, embodiment, reproduction, and women.

Dualistic presuppositions even underlie the Christian Trinity: the three-part division of the deity speaks of a Father, Son, and Holy Spirit—but includes no Mother. The concept of the Trinity is a product of Christian reflection on God's relationship to the world and to humankind. Early Christian theologians wanted to preserve the unity of God (e.g., God's absolute power and knowledge) independent of the world and humankind. But they also wanted to acknowledge God's presence and power in the world and in individual human lives. The concept of the Trinity affirms both: even as the unity of the Godhead is maintained, God enters the world in the form of the Son and transforms the world because humans are empowered by the Spirit for new life.[40]

That female imagery is absent from the Trinity is a result of dualistic presuppositions shared by the theologians who shaped the concept of the Trinity over a period of years. The Spirit, the third member of the Trinity, was modeled on the Jewish concept of Wisdom, traditionally personified as female. In Jewish thought, Wisdom—a wise and beautiful woman—reveals God to humans and brings God's transforming possibilities to them. Remnants of the Jewish Wisdom tradition remain in early Christianity;[41] Luke, for example, mentions that the Wisdom (*Sophia*) of God sends prophets and apostles to humankind (Luke 12:49–50). Syriac Christianity (third century) maintained the feminine imagery of Wisdom when it translated Wisdom into the concept of the Holy Spirit. Including odes to a female Spirit among their hymns, Syriac Christians spoke of the spirit as the womb of rebirth and announced that they were nurtured on the milk of the Spirit.[42] Even so, Christian theologians, for the most part, excluded female imagery from their reflections about the Spirit, enforcing that dualistic presupposition that equates the male with God, the female with all that deviates or is separated from the divine. Thus, over a period of centuries, Christians lost all memories of the female Spirit–Wisdom celebrated by their Jewish forebears and the early Syriac Christians. According to later Christianity, female-associated images belonged to the realm of nature, not to that of God. Exclusively masculine imagery for the trinitarian relationship between God and the world prevailed.

Religion and the Subversion of Patriarchy

In this essay, I have shown that religion, that institution in society most likely to prescribe and defend the foundations of the social order, has regularly demarcated order from disorder by appeal to the female body. That women's bodies, more mysterious than men's, have been appropriated by religion, when it has wanted to circumscribe order and to find protection against the powers and dangers of chaos, has had onerous consequences for women. Granted that the female body has been religion's symbolism of choice, does that mean that religion has always oppressed women, or are there exceptions to patterns of oppression described in this essay?

Although the record is meager, a fact perhaps attributable to the predominance of men as recorders of history, we know that in some instances women, subverting both men's prescriptions for their orderly behavior and men's descriptions of their potential for disorderly behavior, have gained a measure of freedom. Instances of liberating behavior by women, associated with religious belief, fall into three categories.

First, some women have been able to interpret the religious demands on them in such a way as to countermand men's prescriptions for their behavior. Hindu women poet-saints, among whom we find Mahadeviyakka (1106–67 C.E.) and Lallesvari (fourteenth century C.E.), are a most dramatic example of this instance of patriarchal subversion. Both strove to live according to the *Bhagavad-gita,* a key devotional text in Hinduism. The *Bhagavad-gita,* according to the traditional interpretation, teaches that devotion (*bhakti*) to a god is not incompatible with the social obligations (*dharma*) one inherits by virtue of gender and caste, because performance of one's social role *is* an act of devotion to that god. But Mahadeviyakka's and Lallesvari's elaborations on this teaching offered a different interpretation. Both wrote that, if a woman's devotion to a god demands her complete attention, she may be exempted from her *dharma*—her inherited role as a wife and mother subservient to her husband, for *bhakti* has a higher value than *dharma*. Although in no way a conventional reading of the *Bhagavad-gita,* this "proto-feminist" interpretation provided these women with grounds for evading traditional women's roles. Their poetry describes their struggle to reconcile *dharma* and *bhakti,* highlights the resolution of the struggle in favor of renunciation of their marriages to human men in order to engage in an all-consuming devotion to a god, and conveys their intimate and erotic passion for their new, divine husband. Preserved to this day, the honored poetry of these women constitutes a remarkable record of emancipation.[43]

Appealing to a second strategy subversive of patriarchy, some women have exchanged the traditional female role, and its requirements, for that of an "honorary male." Both Buddhist and Christian nuns exemplify this possibility for liberation. In China, for example, biographies that date from 516 C.E. describe nuns who adopted an ascetic life-style that included the celibacy necessary for honorary-male status. In marked contrast to their lay counterparts, these Buddhist nuns are praised for their own worth, without regard to the quality of their relationships to husbands or sons, the traditional standard of valuation for Chinese women. Noted for their literary skill and erudition, these nuns are known to have lectured to other nuns and to large congregations of laypeople about the Buddha's teachings.[44]

A similar history of emancipated women can be traced in the early years of Christianity. Christian writings, dating from the same time period as the New Testament but not located in the Bible, record the leadership of celibate women—widows or virgins—in the Christian communities.[45] Among these early Christian groups, the titles "widow" and "virgin" referred to women's spiritual status rather than to their marital or physiological status: they signified women's complete devotion and commitment to Christ, in exclusion of marriage or remarriage to any man. For example, "the virgin Thecla," commissioned in ministry by the Apostle Paul, left home on the eve of her wedding to follow Paul. Her ministry became noted throughout Asia Minor.[46] Women in the first two centuries of the Christian era who committed themselves to service to Christ, like Thecla, could pursue vocations with considerable authority and autonomy. Even so, that they became equals in ministry with men only by becoming honorary males is graphically illustrated in stories about Thecla that note her rejection of marriage and her assumption of a male style of dress.

In later centuries, Christian women who accepted the celibate life-style lived together in monasteries. Granted considerable autonomy from domination by men, nuns rose to positions of authority not otherwise possible for women. Some abbesses were even accorded the right to authorize priests to serve in areas over which the abbesses had established ecclesiastical control.[47] Like their Buddhist counterparts, nuns experienced remarkable levels of freedom, both from the obligations traditionally imposed on women in their society and for the pursuit of vocational goals such as higher education; philosophical treatises, theological writings, plays, and poetry are attributed to them.[48]

In seeking a means of liberation from the constraints placed on women by patriarchy, some women have explored a third option: they have adorned the sphere to which they are allotted by patriarchy such that, although the parameters of that sphere have not been "recarved," in violation of patriarchal authority, the sphere has acquired, nevertheless, trappings of freedom. Women in Judaism and Islam, consigned to the home, have represented this possibility most often. For example, Moslem women, excluded from participation in religion at the mosque, sometimes have developed a ritual life that functions independently of men. In some rural areas of Iran, for example, women perform rituals that summon powers inherent in plants and minerals in order to overcome problems such as sickness or economic hardship. Within their own sphere, these women have authority in relation to other women, based on their abilities to summon powers on behalf of health and economic prosperity.[49] In certain sectors of Judaism, ambivalence toward the role of women has been balanced by an appreciation for women's leadership within the home. In their roles as leaders of religious life in the home, just as men are leaders of religious life in the outside world, some Jewish women may have approached the ideal of the "separate, but equal" sphere.[50]

Regrettably, despite their promise, all three categories that exemplify instances of liberating behavior for women in religion historically have had serious shortcomings. The subversion of religious teachings, exemplified by the Hindu women-saints, was successful, but only because these women's extreme devotion, so articulately expressed, was exceptional. As a distinct minority, these female poet-saints posed no substantive threat to the social order. Were Hindu women to have engaged in behavior such as theirs on a massive scale, it is likely that patriarchal authority would have been summoned against them.

Like the poet-saints, women who assumed the roles of honorary males were exceptions to the majority of women. Again, like the poet-saints, the price of freedom—celibacy—was high. That women were exempted from negative attributions of sexuality when they denied their sexuality and lived as celibate, honorary men could not constitute freedom from patriarchy, for these women gained freedom only because they accepted men's initial verdict about women: women harbor life-threatening powers of chaos and evil in their mysterious bodies, which can be countered only if they live celibate, cloistered lives. Moreover, to the extent that the role of honorary male did provide women with substantive power, the patriarchs moved swiftly to suppress it.

Denied continued economic support, Buddhist nuns gradually faded into social, economic, and intellectual obscurity.[51] As larger numbers of women in the early Christian communities modeled themselves on women such as Thecla, their quest for autonomy was thwarted and their movement repressed. Indeed, I Timothy in the New Testament was written apparently to counter the growing independence of Christian women. With its recommendation for women to keep silent (I Timothy 2:11) and its suggestion that churches support only "real" widows (I Timothy 5:3–16), I Timothy depicts a concerted effort to discourage young, never-married women and widows still in their childbearing years from pursuing vocations devoted to Christ.[52] So also did nuns in later centuries find their freedom constrained. In the late medieval era, centers of learning were transferred from the monasteries to the new universities, from which women were excluded. Convents were supervised by male bishops, and nuns' behavior was regulated by the requirement of regular confession before male priests. Nuns were strictly cloistered, and new religious orders, such as the Jesuits, did not include female branches.[53] A period of women's independence and autonomy was followed by a dramatic reassertion of patriarchal authority.

As for the third option elected by women in search of freedom, the autonomy of the home sphere, while making possible some freedom for women, has not been without its serious drawbacks: women who may have wished to participate in the public sphere, in order to pursue educations and careers, have been necessarily excluded from achievement of these aims. An absence of choice, rather than true freedom, has prevailed.

The three avenues to emancipation that we have examined share in common a fundamental conservatism: not disavowing the basic structure of patriarchy, they liberate women only because they promise subversion from within. Their failure to offer genuine possibilities for liberation suggests that women today must focus their critical attention on religion, not only when it is obviously acting as an institution of social control to oppress women—as described in the first part of this essay—but also when it is not obviously oppressive. Women must be wary, and not only because we have seen that women can opt for a liberating life-style only to the extent that their chosen role does not truly challenge patriarchal authority. Because the roles women elect, although apparently subversive, may be but contemporary versions of "the exceptional woman," "the honorary male," or "the guardian of the hearth," women must be prepared to be critical of roles that, on the surface, look emancipating. Each of those roles historically has extracted its price, offering liberation to only that minority of women willing to deny their sexuality, to forfeit motherhood, or to confine their expressions of freedom to the sphere of the home. To the extent that women today are not reconciled to making these sacrifices, they must summon their creative energies to envision life-styles and roles that will enable them to tell a happier tale about women in religion.

NOTES

1. Paul Tillich, *Systematic Theology,* vol. 1 (Chicago: University of Chicago Press, 1967), pp. 11–13.

2. Mary Douglas, *Purity and Danger: An Analysis of the Concepts of Pollution and Taboo* (Boston: Ark Paperbacks, Routledge & Kegan Paul, 1985), p. 114.

3. Ibid., p. 115.

4. Thomas J. Hopkins, *The Hindu Religious Tradition* (Belmont, CA: Wadsworth Publishing Co., 1971).

5. Katherine Young, "Hinduism," in *Women in World Religions,* ed. Arvind Sharma (Albany: State University of New York Press, 1987), pp. 59–105; pp. 73–74.

6. Joni Seager and Ann Olson, *Women in the World: An International Atlas* (New York: Simon & Schuster, 1986), p. 3.

7. Juthica Stangl, "India: A Widow's Devastating Choice," *Ms. Magazine,* September 1984, pp. 37–39.

8. Douglas, *Purity and Danger,* p. 123.

9. Ibid., p. 126.

10. Ibid., p. 127.

11. Ibid., pp. 125–26.

12. Young, "Hinduism," p. 75.

13. Ibid., pp. 78–79.

14. Ibid., pp. 84–85.

15. Ibid., p. 83. The word for good (i.e., obedient, self-denying) woman—*satī*—is identical, but for the diacritical mark, with the act of widow sacrifice: *sati* (p. 257, note 2).

16. The Hebrew Bible consists of the Torah (Genesis, Exodus, Leviticus, Numbers, and Deteuronomy), the Prophets (Joshua, Judges, 1 and 2 Samuel, 1 and 2 Kings, Isaiah, Jeremiah, Ezekiel, Josea, Joel, Amos, Obadiah, Jonah, Micah, Nahum, Habakkuk, Zephaniah, Haggai, Zechariah, and Malachi), and the Writings (Psalms, Proverbs, Job, Song of Solomon, Ruth, Lamentations, Ecclesiastes, Esther, David, Ezra, Nehemiah, and 1 and 2 Chronicles).

17. Meredith McGuire, *Religion: The Social Context,* 2nd ed. (Belmont, CA: Wadsworth Publishing Co., 1987), pp. 98–99. McGuire rightly notes that caste status confers necessary but not sufficient advantages to men's chances for recognition, power, and prestige: "Not all men obtain these privileges in the social system, but maleness is virtually a prerequisite. Some men suffer exploitation and discrimination, but not because of their gender. Religiously legitimated caste distinctions thus do not empower all men; they do, however, disempower all women by virtue of their gender identity" (ibid.).

18. Ibid.

19. Rosemary Ruether, *Sexism and God-Talk: Toward a Feminist Theology* (Boston: Beacon Press, 1983), p. 168.

20. Ibid., p. 167.

21. Martin Luther, *Lectures on Genesis,* Gen. 3:16, in *Luther's Works,* vol. 1, ed. Jaroslav Pelikan (St. Louis: Concordia Publishing House, 1958), pp. 202–3. As cited in Ruether, *Sexism,* p. 97.

22. Denise Carmody, "Judaism," in *Women in World Religions,* pp. 183–207; p. 193.

23. Ibid., p. 194.

24. Ibid.

25. Jane I. Smith, "Islam," in *Women in World Religions,* pp. 235–51; pp. 240–41.

26. Jane I. Smith and Yvonne Haddad, "Women in the Afterlife: The Islamic View as Seen from the Qur'an and Tradition," *Journal of the American Academy of Religion* 43:39–50, 1975; cited in Denise L. Carmody and John T. Carmody, *Ways to the Center: An Introduction to World Religions,* 2nd ed. (Belmont, CA: Wadsworth Publishing Co., 1984), pp. 333; 390, note 77.

27. Richard Brubaker, "The Untamed Goddesses of Village India," in *The Book of the Goddess: Past and Present,* ed. C. Olson (New York: Crossroad Press, 1983), pp. 145–61; pp. 158–59.

28. Judith Ochshorn, *The Female Experience and the Nature of the Divine* (Bloomington: Indiana University Press, 1981), pp. 24–34, 57–58, 89–90.

29. Ibid., p. 37.

30. Roslyn Lacks, *Women and Judaism* (Garden City, NY: Doubleday & Company, 1980), pp. 152–53.

31. Ochshorn, *The Female Experience,* pp. 161–63.

32. P. Steven Sangren, "Female Gender in Chinese Religious Symbols: Kuan Yin, Ma Tsu, and the 'Eternal Mother,'" *Signs: Journal of Women in Culture and Society* 9(11):4–25, 1983.

33. Ruether, *Sexism and God-Talk,* p. 150.

34. Ibid., p. 143.

35. Ibid., p. 196.

36. Douglas, *Purity and Danger,* p. 158.

37. McGuire, *Religion: The Social Context,* p. 107.

38. Ruether, *Sexism and God-Talk,* pp. 72–75. Ruether attributes her analysis to Sherry Ortner, "Is Female to Male as Nature is to Culture?" in *Woman, Culture and Society,* ed. M. Z. Rosaldo and L. Lamphere (Stanford, CA: Stanford University Press, 1974), pp. 67–87.

39. "Declaration on the Question of Admission of Women to the Ministerial Priesthood," Section 27, Vatican City, 15 October 1976, as cited in Ruether, *Sexism and God-Talk,* p. 275, note 10.

40. Rosemary Ruether, *Womanguides: Readings Toward a Feminist Theology* (Boston: Beacon Press, 1985), pp. 21–22.

41. Elizabeth Fiorenza, *In Memory of Her: A Feminist Theological Reconstruction of Christian Origins* (New York: Crossroad Press, 1983), pp. 132–36.

42. Ruether, *Womanguides,* pp. 24, 29–31.

43. David Kinsley, "Devotion as an Alternative to Marriage in the Lives of Some Hindu Women Devotees," in *Journal of Asian and African Studies* 15(1–2):83–93, 1980.

44. Nancy Schuster Barnes, "Buddhism," in *Women in World Religions,* pp. 105–35; pp. 123–25.

45. Dennis MacDonald, *The Legend and the Apostle* (Philadelphia: Westminster Press, 1983), is a book about one of these accounts, *The Acts of Paul and Thecla.*

46. Ibid., pp. 90–96.

47. Rosemary Ruether, "Christianity," in *Women in World Religions,* pp. 207–35; p. 219.

48. Ibid.

49. Erika Friedl, "Islam and Tribal Women in a Village in Iran," in *Unspoken Worlds: Women's Religious Lives in Non-Western Cultures,* eds. Nancy Falk and Rita Gross (San Francisco: Harper & Row, 1980), pp. 159–74; pp. 163–64.

50. Lacks, *Women and Judaism,* p. 124.

51. Barnes, "Buddhism," pp. 131–32.

52. MacDonald, *The Legend and the Apostle,* pp. 54–78.

53. Ruether, "Christianity," p. 219.

What Price Independence? Social Reactions to Lesbians, Spinsters, Widows, and Nuns

Rose Weitz

FOR SEVEN DAYS IN 1981, nineteen-year-old Stephanie Riethmiller was held captive by two men and a woman in a secluded Alabama cabin. During that time, according to Riethmiller, her captors constantly harangued her on the sinfulness of homosexuality, and one captor raped her nightly. Riethmiller's parents, who feared that their daughter was involved in a lesbian relationship with her roommate, had paid $8,000 for this "deprogramming"; her mother remained in the next room throughout her captivity. When the kidnappers were brought to trial, the jury, in the opinion of the judge, "permit[ted] their moral evaluations to enter into their legal conclusions" and failed to bring in a guilty verdict (Raskin 1982, 19).

As the Riethmiller case shows, the individual who identifies herself as a lesbian—or who is so labeled by others—may face severe social, economic, and legal sanctions. Along with communists, the diseased, and the insane, persons who openly acknowledge their homosexuality may be denied admission to the United States. In most U.S. jurisdictions, discrimination against homosexuals in housing, employment, child custody, and other areas of life is legal, while homosexual behavior is illegal. Gay persons are not covered under any of the national civil rights acts, and most court decisions have held that they are not covered under the equal protection clause of the United States Constitution. Moreover, in 1986 the U.S. Supreme Court ruled in *Bowers v. Hardwick* that state antisodomy laws are legal. (For an excellent, inclusive analysis of the legal status of homosexuality, see Achtenberg 1985.)

These legal restrictions reflect generally held social attitudes. National surveys in recent years have found that slightly more than half (51 percent) of American adults believe homosexuality should not be considered an acceptable life-style (*Gallup Report* 1982). A similar proportion (55 percent) believe homosexual relationships between consenting adults should not be legal—an increase of 12 percent since 1977 (*Gallup Report* 1987).

Cross-Cultural and Historical Views of Lesbianism

To most Americans, stigmatization and punishment of lesbianism seem perfectly natural. Yet such has not always been the case. In fact, a study of attitudes toward homosexuality in seventy-six cultures around the world found that in 64 percent of those cultures "homosexual activities of one sort or another are considered normal and socially acceptable for certain members of the community" (Ford and Beach 1951, 130).

In the Western world, male homosexuality, which had been an accepted part of Greek and Roman culture, was increasingly rejected by society as the power of the Christian church grew (Barrett 1979). Yet lesbianism generally remained unrecognized legally and socially until the beginning of the modern age. Instead, beginning with the Renaissance, intimate "romantic friendships" between women were a common part of life, at least among the middle and upper classes (Faderman 1981).[1]

> Women who were romantic friends were everything to each other. They lived to be together. They thought of each other constantly. They made each other deliriously happy or horribly miserable by the increase or abatement of their proffered love. They were jealous of other female friends (and certainly of male friends) who impinged on their beloved's time or threatened to carry away a portion of her affections. They vowed that if it were at all possible they would someday live together, or at least die together, and they declared that both eventualities would be their greatest happiness. They embraced and kissed and walked hand in hand, and some even held each other all night in sleep. But unless they were transvestites or considered "unwomanly" in some male's conception, there was little chance that their relationships would be considered lesbian. [Faderman 1981, 84]

We cannot know whether most romantic friends expressed their love for women genitally, and we do know that most were married to men (at least in part for economic survival). A reading of letters and journals from this period leaves no doubt, however, of the erotic and emotional intensity of these relationships between women and little doubt that in another era the relationships would have been expressed sexually (Smith-Rosenberg 1975; Faderman 1981). Yet belief in the purity of these relationships lingered even into the twentieth century. For example, when the British Parliament attempted in 1885 to add mention of lesbianism to its criminal code, Queen Victoria refused to sign the bill on the ground that such behavior did not exist (Ettorre 1980).

Given that lesbianism has not always elicited negative social reactions, the current intolerance of it cannot derive from some universal biological or ethical law. What, then, causes these negative social reactions? I suggest in this article that at least part of the answer lies in the threat that lesbianism presents to the power of males in society. Furthermore, I suggest that whenever men fear women's sexual or economic independence, all unmarried women face an increased risk of stigmatization and punishment. The experience of such diverse groups as lesbians, medieval nuns, and Hindu widows shows the interrelated social fates of all women not under the direct control of men.

Lesbians and the Threat to Male Power

Western culture teaches that women are the weaker sex, that they cannot flourish—or perhaps even survive—without the protection of men. Women are taught that they cannot live happy and fulfilled lives without a Prince Charming, who is superior to them in all ways. In the struggle to find and keep their men, women learn to view one another as untrustworthy competitors. They subordi-nate the development of their own psychological, physical, and professional strengths to the task of finding male protectors who will make up for their shortcomings. In this way, Western culture keeps women from developing bonds with one another, while it maintains their dependence on men.

Lesbians[2] throw a large wrench into the works of this cultural system. In a society that denigrates women, lesbians value women enough to spend their lives with women rather than with men. Lesbians therefore do not and cannot rely on the protection of men. Knowing that they will not have that protection, lesbians are forced to develop their own resources. The very survival of lesbians therefore suggests the potential strength of all women and their ability to transcend their traditional roles. At the same time, since lesbians do not have even the illusion of male protection that marriage provides, and since they are likely to see their fate as tied to other women rather than to individual men, lesbians may be more likely than heterosexual women to believe in the necessity of fighting for women's rights; the heavy involvement of lesbians in the feminist movement seems to support this thesis (Abbott and Love 1972).

Lesbians also threaten the dominant cultural system by presenting, or at least appearing to present, an alternative to the typical inequality of hetero-sexual relationships. Partners attempting to equalize power in a heterosexual relationship must first neutralize deeply ingrained traditional sex roles. Since lesbian relationships generally contain no built-in assumption of the superiority of one partner,[3] developing an egalitarian relationship may be easier. Lesbian relationships suggest both that a love between equals is possible and that an alternative way of obtaining such a love may exist. Regardless of the actual likelihood of achieving equality in a lesbian relationship, the threat to the system remains as long as lesbian relationships are believed to be more egalitarian. This threat increases significantly when, as in the past few years, lesbians express pride in and satisfaction with their life-style.

If lesbianism incurs social wrath because of the threat it presents to existing sexist social arrangements, then we should find that lesbianism is most negatively viewed by persons who hold sexist beliefs. Evidence from various studies (summarized in Weinberger and Millham 1979) supports this hypo-thesis. Homophobia (i.e., fear and hatred of homosexuals) appears strongly correlated with support for traditional sex roles. Survey data suggest that support for traditional sex roles explains homophobia better than do negative or conservative attitudes toward sex in general (MacDonald et al. 1973; MacDonald and Games 1974).

Historical data on when and under what circumstances lesbianism became stigmatized also support the contention of a link between that stigma and the threat lesbianism poses to male power. As described in the previous section, romantic friendships between women were common in both Europe and America from the Renaissance through the late nineteenth century. The women involved were generally accepted or at least tolerated by society even in the few cases where their relationships were openly sexual. That acceptance ceased, however, if either of the women attempted to usurp male privilege in some way—by wearing men's clothing, using a dildo, or passing as a man. Only in these circumstances were pre–modern-era lesbians likely to suffer social sanctions. In looking at both historical records and fiction from the thirteenth through the nineteenth centuries, Faderman (1981) found that women were, at most, lightly punished for lesbianism unless they wore male clothing.[4] She therefore concludes that "at the base it was not the sexual aspects of lesbianism as much as the attempted usurpation of male prerogative by women who behaved like men that many societies appeared to find most disturbing" (Faderman 1981, 17).

As long as the women involved did not attempt to obtain male privileges, romantic friends ran little risk of censure before the late nineteenth century. The factors behind the shift in attitude that occurred at that time again suggest the importance of the threat that lesbianism seemed to pose to male power.

Before the twentieth century, only a small number of independently wealthy women (such as the Ladies of Llangollen [Mavor 1973]) were able to establish their own households and live out their lives with their female companions (Faderman 1981). By the second half of the nineteenth century, however, the combined effects of the Civil War in this country and of male migration away from rural areas in both the United States and Europe had created a surplus of unmarried women in many communities. At the same time, the growth of the feminist movement had led to increased educational opportunities for women. These factors, coupled with the growth of industrialization, opened the possibility of employment and an independent existence to significant numbers of women.

Once female independence became a real economic possibility, it became a serious concern to those intent on maintaining the sexual status quo. Relationships between women, which previously had seemed harmless, now took on a new and threatening appearance. Only at this point do new theories emerge that reject the Victorian image of the passionless woman (Cott 1978), acknowledge females as sexual beings, and define lesbianism as pathological.

Stereotypes of lesbianism, first developed in the early twentieth century, reduce the threat to existing social arrangements by defusing the power of lesbianism as a viable alternative life-style. According to these stereotypes, all lesbians are either butches or femmes, and their relationships merely mimic heterosexual relationships. Lesbianism, therefore, seems to offer no advantages over heterosexuality.

Cultural stereotypes defuse lesbian sexuality by alternately denying and exaggerating it. These stereotypes hold that women become lesbians because of either their inability to find a man or their hatred of men. Such stereotypes deny that lesbianism may be a positive choice, while suggesting that lesbianism can be "cured" by the right man. The supposed futility of lesbian sexuality was summed up by best-selling author Dr. David Reuben in the phrase "one vagina plus another vagina still equals zero" (1969, 217). (Reuben further invalidated lesbianism by locating his entire discussion of the subject within his chapter on prostitution; male homosexuality was "honored" with its own chapter.) In other cultural arenas, lesbians and lesbianism are defined in purely sexual terms, stripped of all romantic, social, or political content. In this incarnation, lesbianism can be subverted into a vehicle for male sexual pleasure; in the world of pornographic films, men frequently construct lesbian scenes to play out their own sexual fantasies.

In sum, strong evidence suggests that the negative social reactions to lesbianism reflect male fears of female independence and that social sanctions and cultural stereotypes serve to lessen the threat that these independent women pose to male power.

If this hypothesis is true, then it should also hold for other groups of women not under direct male control. Next, I briefly discuss how, historically, negative social reactions to such women seem most likely to develop whenever men fear women's sexual or economic independence.

Spinsters, Widows, and Women Religious

The inquisition against witches that occurred from the fifteenth through the seventeenth centuries represents the most extreme response in the Western world to the threat posed by independent women. The vast majority of the persons executed for witchcraft were women; estimates of the number killed range from under one hundred thousand to several million (Daly 1978). Accusations of witchcraft typically involved charges that the women healed sickness, engaged in prohibited sexual practices, or controlled reproduction (Ehrenreich and English 1973). Such activities threatened the power of the church by giving individuals (especially women) greater control over their own lives, reducing their dependence on the church for divine intervention while inhibiting the natural increase of the Catholic population.

The witchcraft trials occurred in a society undergoing the first throes of industrialization and urbanization (Nelson 1979). The weakening of the rural extended family forced many women to look for employment outside the home. These unattached women proved especially vulnerable to accusations of witchcraft (Nelson 1979; Daly 1978). As Mary Daly points out, "The targets of attack in the witchcraze were not women defined by assimilation into the patriarchal family. Rather, the witchcraze focused predominantly upon women who had rejected marriage (Spinsters) and some who had survived it (widows)" (1978, 184).

Contemporary theological beliefs regarding female sexuality magnified the perceived economic and social threat posed by unmarried women. The medieval church viewed all aspects of female sexuality with distrust; unless a woman was virginal or proven chaste, she was believed to be ruled by her sexual desires (Ehrenreich and English 1973). Catholic doctrine blamed Eve's licentiousness for the fall from grace in the Garden of Eden. According to the most popular medieval "manual" for witchhunters, the *Malleus Maleficarum,* most witches were women because "all witchcraft comes from carnal lust, which is in women insatiable" (Kramer and Sprenger 1971, 120). Given this theology, any woman not under the direct sexual control of a man would appear suspect, if not outright dangerous.

For most women living before the nineteenth century who wished to or were forced to remain unmarried, entering the religious life was the only socially acceptable option.[5] During the Middle Ages, a woman could either become a nun or join one of the "secular convents" known as *Beguines* (Nelson 1979; Boulding 1976). Beguines arose to serve the population of surplus unmarried women that had developed in the early European cities. Residents of Beguines took a vow of chastity and obedience while living there, but they could marry thereafter. They spent their days in work and prayer.

Beguines threatened the monopolies of both the guilds and the church. The guilds feared the economic competition of these organized skilled women workers, while the church feared their social and religious independence (Nelson 1979); the Beguines' uncloistered life seemed likely to lead women into sin, while the lack of perpetual vows freed them from direct church supervision. For these reasons, the church in the fourteenth century ordered the Beguine houses dissolved, although some have continued nonetheless to the present day. Residents were urged either to marry or to become nuns (Boulding 1976).

The history of convents similarly illustrates the church's distrust of independent women (Eckenstein 1963). In the early medieval period, many nuns lived with their families. Some nuns showed their religious vocation through the wearing of a veil, while others wore no distinctive dress. Convents served as centers of learning for women, providing educational opportunities not available elsewhere. During this period, many "double monasteries" flourished, in which male and female residents lived together and shared decision-making authority.

Given medieval ideas regarding the spiritual weakness and inherent carnality of women, the independence of early medieval nuns could not be allowed to last long. The developing laws of feudalism increasingly restricted the right of women to own land, so that, by the Renaissance, women faced increasing difficulties in attempting to found or to endow convents, while friars began to take over the management of existing convents (Eckenstein 1963). The church gradually closed all double monasteries, pressuring nuns to enter cloisters and to wear religious habits. Education for nuns increasingly seemed unnecessary or even dangerous. For this reason, by the sixteenth century, church authorities had significantly decreased the educational opportunities available in most convents, although some convents did manage to preserve their intellectual traditions. Once Latin ceased to be taught to them, nuns were effectively excluded from all major church decisions.

As Protestant ideas began to infiltrate Europe, the status of unmarried women declined. One of the few areas in which Catholics and early Protestants agreed was the danger presented by independent women. Responding to flagrant sexual offenses in medieval monasteries, Protestants concluded that few men— let alone women, given their basically carnal nature—could maintain a celibate life. They therefore viewed "the religious profession [as] a thing of evil and temptation in which it was not possible to keep holy" (Charitas Perckheimer, quoted in Eckenstein 1963, 467). To Protestants, "marriage was the most acceptable state before God and . . . a woman has no claim to consideration except in her capacity as wife and mother" (Eckenstein 1963, 433). These beliefs, coupled with the political aims of Protestant rulers, culminated in the forced dissolution of convents and monasteries in many parts of Europe. In Protestant Europe, women were left without a socially acceptable alternative to marriage, while, in Catholic Europe, nuns had been stripped of their autonomy.

The belief in female carnality continued until the nineteenth century. At that point, while lower-class women were still considered sexually wanton by their social betters, prescriptive literature began to paint an image of upper-class women as passionless (Cott 1978). In this situation, unmarried lower-class women continued to suffer severe social sanctions as real or suspected prostitutes. Unmarried upper-class women continued to be stigmatized as unnatural, since they were not fulfilling their allotted role as wives and mothers. These upper-class women did not seem particularly threatening, however, since they were assumed, at least in public discourse, to be asexual beings. As a result, social sanctions against them diminished sharply, not to emerge again until women's newfound economic independence significantly changed the social context of romantic friendships among women.

In this historical overview, I have so far discussed only events in the Western world. In the West, widows probably evoke less of a sense of threat than do other unmarried women, since widows do not generally seem to have chosen their fate. It is instructive to compare the fate of Hindu widows, who are believed to have caused their husbands' deaths by sins they committed in this or a previous life (Daly 1978; Stein 1978).

Since a Hindu woman's status is determined by her relationship to a man, and since Hindu custom forbids remarriage, widows literally have no place in that society. A widow is a superfluous economic burden on her family. She is also viewed as a potential source of dishonor, since Hindus believe that "women are by nature sexually unreliable and incapable of leading chaste lives without a husband to control them" (Stein 1978, 255). For the benefit of her family and for her own happiness in future lives, a widow was in the past expected to commit suttee—to throw herself alive onto her husband's burning funeral pyre.[6] The horror of suttee was multiplied by the practice of polygamy and by the practice of marrying young girls to grown men, which resulted in the widowing of many young girls before they even reached puberty (Stein 1978; Daly 1978). Suttee, child marriage, and polygamy are illegal under the current government, but they still occur.

As her only alternative to suttee, a widow was allowed to adopt a life of such poverty and austerity that she rarely survived for long. Her life was made even more miserable by the fact that only faithful wives were permitted to commit suttee. The refusal to commit suttee might therefore be regarded as an admission of infidelity. If a woman declined to immolate herself, her relatives might force her to do so to protect both her honor and the honor of her family.

Stigmatization of Male Homosexuals

Reflecting the basic concerns of this book, this article has discussed male homosexuality only in passing. Nevertheless, we cannot ignore that the sanctions against male homosexuality appear even stronger than those against lesbianism. Why might this be so? First, I would argue that anything women do is considered relatively trivial—be it housework, mothering, or lesbianism. Second, whereas lesbians threaten the status quo by refusing to accept their inferior position as women, gay males may threaten it even more by appearing to reject their privileged status as men. Prevailing cultural mythology holds that lesbians want to be males. In a paradoxical way, therefore, lesbians may be perceived as upholding "male" values. Male homosexuality, in contrast, is regarded as a rejection of masculine values; gay males are regarded as feminized "sissies" and "queens." Thus, male homosexuality, with its implied rejection of male privilege, may seem even more incomprehensible and threatening than lesbianism. Finally, research indicates that people in general are more fearful and intolerant of homosexuals of their own sex than of homosexuals belonging to the opposite sex (Weinberger and Millham 1979). The greater stigmatization of male than female homosexuality may therefore simply reflect the greater ability of males to enforce their prejudices.

Conclusions

The stigmatization of independent women—whether spinster, widow, nun, or lesbian—is neither automatic nor natural. Rather, it seems to derive from a particular social constellation in which men fear women's sexual and economic independence. Sociological theory explains how stigmatizing individuals as deviant may serve certain purposes for the dominant community, regardless of the accuracy of the accusations leveled (Erikson 1962). First, particularly when social norms are changing rapidly, labeling and punishing certain behaviors as deviant emphasize the new or continued unacceptability of those behaviors. The stigmatization of "romantic friendships" in the early twentieth century, for example, forced all members of society to recognize that social norms had changed and that such relationships would no longer be tolerated. Second, stigmatizing certain groups as deviant may increase solidarity within the dominant group as it unites against its common enemy. Third, stigmatizing as deviant the individuals who challenge traditional ideas may reduce the threat of social change, if those individuals either lose credibility or are removed from the community altogether.

These principles apply to the stigmatization of independent women, from the labeling of nontraditional women as witches in medieval society to the condemnation of lesbians in contemporary society. Medieval inquisitors used the label *witch* to reinforce the normative boundaries of their community, to unite that community against the perceived source of its problems, and to eliminate completely women who seemed to threaten the social order. Currently, the word *lesbian* is used not only to describe women who love other women but also to censure women who overstep the bounds of the traditional female role and to teach all women that such behavior will not be tolerated. Feminists, women athletes, professional women, and others risk being labeled lesbian for their actions and beliefs. Awareness of the potential social consequences of that label exerts significant pressure on all women to remain in their traditional roles.

Antifeminist forces have used the lesbian label to denigrate all feminists, to incite community wrath against them, and to dismiss their political claims. In 1969 and 1970, some feminists responded to this social pressure by purging lesbians from their midst and proclaiming their moral purity (Abbott and Love 1972). This tactic proved extremely self-destructive, as movement organizations collapsed in bitterness and dissension. In addition, eliminating lesbian members had little effect, since lesbian-baiting by antifeminists was equally damaging to the movement, whether or not it was accurate.

By late 1970, many feminists had realized that trying to remove lesbians from their organizations was both self-destructive and ineffective. In response to this knowledge, various feminist organizations went on record acknowledging sexual preference as a feminist and a civil rights issue and supporting the rights of lesbians (Abbott and Love 1972). In a press conference held in December 1970, various women's liberation activists stated:

> Women's Liberation and Homosexual Liberation are both struggling toward a common goal: a society free from defining and categorizing people by virtue of gender and/or sexual preference. "Lesbian" is a label used as a psychic weapon to keep women locked into their male-defined "feminine role." The essence of that role is that a woman is defined in terms of her relationship to men. A woman is called a Lesbian when she functions autonomously. Women's autonomy is what Women's Liberation is all about. [quoted in Abbott and Love 1972, 124]

A leaflet distributed the same month by the New York branch of the National Organization for Women acknowledged that, when charges of lesbianism are made, "it is not one woman's sexual preference that is under attack—it is the freedom of all women to openly state values that fundamentally challenge the basic structure of patriarchy" (quoted in Abbott and Love 1972, 122).

It seems, then, that the fates of feminists and lesbians are inextricably intertwined. Unless and until women's independence is accepted, lesbians will be stigmatized, and unless and until the stigma attached to lesbianism diminishes, the lesbian label will be used as a weapon against those who work for women's independence.

NOTES

1. We have few firsthand data about the intimate lives of lower-class women. Few poorer women could write, and, even if they could and did record their lives, their letters and journals were rarely preserved.

2. I am using the terms *lesbian* and *heterosexual* as nouns simply to ease the flow of the writing. This article focuses on stigmatization, not on some intrinsic quality of individuals. Hence, in this article, *lesbian* and *heterosexual* refer to persons who adopt a particular life-style or who are labeled as doing so by significant others. These terms reflect shared social fates, not some essential, inflexible aspect of the individual.

3. Although there is no way to ascertain exactly what proportion of lesbian couples adopted butch–femme relationships in the past, recent studies suggest that such relationships have all but disappeared, especially among younger and more feminist lesbians (Tanner, 1978; Wolf, 1979; Peplau and Gordon, 1983; Harry, 1984; Lynch and Reilly, 1985/86).

4. The crime for which Joan of Arc was eventually condemned was not witchcraft but the heretical act of wearing male clothing.

5. However, it should be realized that convent life was not always a chosen refuge. Just as a father could marry his daughter to whatever man he chose, so too could he "marry" his daughter to the church.

6. Suttee was most common among the upper castes (where a widow meant an extra mouth, but not an extra pair of hands), but it occurred throughout Hindu society (Stein 1978).

REFERENCES

Abbot, Sidney, and Barbara Love. *Sappho Was a Right-on Woman: A Liberated View of Lesbianism.* New York: Stein and Day Publishers, 1972.

Achtenberg, Roberta (ed.). *Sexual Orientation and the Law.* New York: Clark Boardman Co., 1985.

Barrett, Ellen M. "Legal Homophobia and the Christian Church." *Hastings Law Journal* 30(4): 1019–27, 1979.

Boulding, Elise. *The Underside of History.* Boulder, Colo.: Westview Press, 1976.

Bowers v. Hardwick, 498 U.S. 186, 92, L.Ed. 2d 140, 106 S.Ct. 2841 (1986).

Cott, Nancy. "Passionlessness: An Interpretation of Victorian Sexual Ideology, 1790–1850." *Signs: Journal of Women in Culture and Society* 4(2):219–36, 1978.

Daly, Mary. *Gyn/ecology: The Metaethics of Radical Feminism.* Boston: Beacon Press, 1978.

Eckenstein, Lina. *Women Under Monasticism.* New York: Russell and Russell, 1963.

Ehrenreich, Barbara, and Deirdre English. *Witches, Midwives and Nurses: A History of Women Healers.* Old Westbury, N.Y.: Feminist Press, 1973.

Erikson, Kai T. "Notes on the Sociology of Deviance." *Social Problems* 9(Spring):307–14, 1962.

Ettorre, E. M. *Lesbians, Women and Society.* London: Routledge and Kegan Paul, 1980.

Faderman, Lillian. *Surpassing the Love of Men: Romantic Friendship and Love Between Women from the Renaissance to the Present.* New York: William Morrow and Co., 1981.

Ford, Clellan S., and Frank A. Beach. *Patterns of Sexual Behavior.* New York: Harper and Row, 1951.

Gallup Report. "Backlash Against Gays Appears to Be Leveling Off." 258:12–18, 1987.

Gallup Report. "Little Change in Americans' Attitudes Towards Gays." 205:3–19, 1982.

Glenn, Norval D., and Charles N. Weaver. "Attitudes Towards Premarital, Extramarital and Homosexual Relationships in the United States in the 1970s." *Journal of Sex Research* 15(2):108–17, 1979.

Harry, Joseph. *Gay Couples.* New York: Praeger, 1984.

Kramer, H., and J. Sprenger. *Malleus Maleficarum.* Translated by Montague Summers. New York: Dover Publications, 1971.

Lynch, Jean M., and Mary E. Reilly. "Role Relationships: Lesbian Perspectives." *Journal of Homosexuality* 12(2):53–69, 1985/86.

MacDonald, A. P., and R. G. Games. "Some Characteristics of Those Who Hold Positive and Negative Attitudes Towards Homosexuals." *Journal of Homosexuality* 1(1):9–28, 1974.

MacDonald, A. P., J. Huggins, S. Young, and R. A. Swanson. "Attitudes Towards Homosexuality: Preservation of Sex Morality or the Double Standard." *Journal of Consulting and Clinical Psychology* 40(1):161, 1973.

Mavor, Elizabeth. *The Ladies of Llangollen: A Study of Romantic Friendship.* New York: Penguin Books, 1973.

Nelson, Mary. "Why Witches Were Women." In Jo Freeman (ed.), *Women: A Feminist Perspective,* 2d ed. Palo Alto, Calif.: Mayfield Publishing Co., 1979, 451–68.

Peplau, Letitia A., and Stephen L. Gordon. "The Intimate Relationships of Lesbians and Gay Men." In Elizabeth R. Allgeier and Naomi B. McCormick (eds.), *Changing Boundaries: Gender Roles and Sexual Behavior.* Palo Alto, Calif.: Mayfield, 1983, 226–44.

Raskin, Richard. "The 'Deprogramming' of Stephanie Riethmiller." *Ms.,* Sept. 1982, 19.

Reuben, David. *Everything You Always Wanted to Know About Sex But Were Afraid to Ask.* New York: David McKay Co., 1969.

Rivera, Rhonda R. "Our Straight-Laced Judges: The Legal Position of Homosexual Persons in the United States." *Hastings Law Journal* 30(4):799–956, 1979.

Smith-Rosenberg, Carroll. "The Female World of Love and Ritual: Relations Between Women in Nineteenth Century America." *Signs: Journal of Women in Culture and Society* 1(1):1–29, 1975.

Stein, Dorothy K. "Women to Burn: Suttee as a Normative Institution." *Signs: Journal of Women in Culture and Society* 4(2):253–68, 1978.

Tanner, Donna M. *The Lesbian Couple.* Lexington, Mass.: D.C. Heath and Co., 1978.

Weinberger, Linda E., and Jim Millham. "Attitudinal Homophobia and Support of Traditional Sex Roles." *Journal of Homosexuality* 4(3):237–45, 1979.

Wolf, Deborah Goleman. *The Lesbian Community.* Berkeley: University of California Press, 1979.

Poverty and Welfare for Women

Alice Abel Kemp

On October 5, 1989, Fatima Ali, a thirty-two-year-old, black middle-class Muslim woman with five young children, was arrested for dropping her seven-year-old daughter and her three-year-old son out of a fifth-story window in Queens, New York. Ms. Ali was stopped before she could drop the other three children out the window and jump herself. Her husband had left her, and she had no doubt that she was heading for poverty, welfare, and homelessness. With no husband and no resources, taking herself and all her children back to Allah was the only alternative she saw. Although the city of New York has a multitude of programs for the poor, a homeless woman with children is likely to spend her days with her children in waiting rooms with scant food or facilities and her nights in "roach, lice, and rat infested welfare hotels" before returning the next day to more waiting in the public assistance office (Funiciello, 1993: p. 5).

Ms. Ali's feelings of hopelessness about the future are shared by many women, past and present. Among adults, women are twice as likely to be poor as are men, and often their poverty reflects the added economic responsibilities of providing for their children. Public assistance programs are available to only the very poor and provide low levels of support (Miller, 1990: p. 60; Udesky, 1990: p. 304). This chapter will examine why women are poor and why the official solutions to poverty fail to provide them with a minimally acceptable standard of living.

How Is Poverty Defined?

The official definition of poverty in the United States is an absolute measure based on a computation of the minimum level of income necessary for survival (Orshansky, 1969).[1] In 1955 the Department of Agriculture estimated the lowest cost for a nutritionally adequate diet using recommended dietary allowances and the calorie needs of adults and children. Relying on a 1955 consumer survey that showed the average family spends approximately one-third of its budget on food, the poverty line was established by multiplying the cost of the food plan by three.[2] In 1992, the annual threshold was $7,143 for one person and $14,228 for a family of four (two adults and two children under eighteen) (U.S. Bureau of the Census, 1993b: Table A).[3] The poverty rate is the share or percent of any given group with income below the poverty line.

Who Are the Poor?

Although the poverty population is very diverse, 57.4 percent are female. In 1992, 36.9 million persons, or 14.5 percent of our population, were officially defined as poor. Seventy-six percent of these people live in families, and 52.4 percent of these families are headed by women. More than one of every five children live in poverty, and over half of all children in female-headed families are poor (U.S. Bureau of the Census, 1993b: Tables 3, 4, and 5).[4] Poverty rates for black and Hispanic families are higher than the rates for comparable white families, but women are more likely to be poor than are men, regardless of race or Hispanic origin.[5]

POVERTY FOR INDIVIDUALS

Table 1 shows the poverty rate for adults age eighteen and older, by race. Among adults, the poverty rate for women is 14.3 percent versus 9.3 percent for men. The table also reports the sex/poverty ratio, which compares women's poverty to men's (McLanahan et al., 1989: p. 105). This ratio is 1.54 for all men and women, showing that women are 54 percent more likely to be poor than are men. Blacks and Hispanics experience more poverty overall than do whites in our society, but within each group women experience between 61 and 32 percent more poverty than men. Poverty for the other races (primarily Asian and Indian) is 13.1 percent for adult men and 15.2 percent for adult women, with a sex/poverty ratio of 1.16.

Figure 1 graphs the female share of the poverty population for several age groups. Girls are 49.8 percent of the children (under age eighteen) in poverty, but women are the majority in every other group. The risk of poverty is thus only relatively equal between the sexes for those under age eighteen. Women's share of poverty increases among young adults, declines slightly in the middle years, and increases substantially among those age sixty-five and older, where, after age seventy-five, women represent over 76 percent of the poor.

Figure 2 depicts the sex and age distribution of the entire poverty population by three age groups—children under eighteen, adults eighteen to sixty-four, and the elderly, sixty-five and older. Adult women constitute the single largest share of the poverty population.

POVERTY AND EMPLOYMENT

Our society assumes that employment is the path out of poverty. The poor are people who do not work. However, many people continue in poverty despite being employed. Over one-third of poor women and 51 percent of

Table 1. Poverty Rates in 1992 by Sex and Race

| Total Poverty Rate: | 14.5 percent | | | | |
| All Adults 18+: | 11.9 percent | | | | |

	All	*White*	*Black*	*Hispanic*[a]	*Other*[b]
Adult men	9.3	7.8	20.0	20.4	13.1
Adult women	14.3	11.7	32.1	27.0	15.2
Sex/poverty ratio[c]	1.54	1.50	1.61	1.32	1.16

a. Hispanic may be of any race.
b. Other includes Asian, American Indian, and any other nonwhite, nonblack races.
c. This is a ratio of the women's poverty rate to the men's poverty rate and shows women's greater risk when the ratio exceeds 1 (McLanahan et al., 1989: p. 105).
Source: U.S. Bureau of the Census, 1993b: Table 5.

Figure 1. Percent Female in Poverty by Age Cohort: 1992.

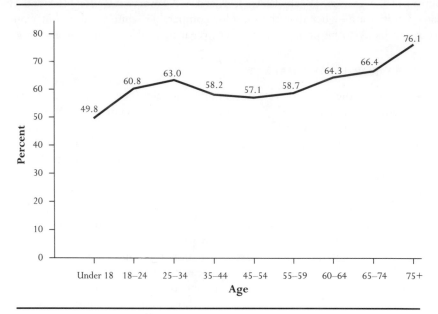

Source: Computed from U.S. Bureau of the Census, 1993b: Table 5.

poor men over sixteen had some employment during 1992. The proportion of the poverty population with some employment is highest for Hispanics (44.1 percent), lower for white persons (42.8 percent), and lowest for blacks (33.7 percent) (computed from U.S. Bureau of the Census, 1993b: Table 14).

POVERTY FOR FAMILIES

Poverty among families mirrors the relationship that exists among individuals.[6] Figure 3 shows poverty rates for different family types by race and the presence of children under eighteen. Poverty is higher among families headed by women, regardless of race. Furthermore, there is consistently more poverty for all families when the family includes children under eighteen, but female-headed families remain the poorest.

Trends in Poverty: Feminization of Poverty

Over time, poverty has become a *female* problem. Women are consistently more likely to experience poverty than men. In the last forty years, the overall poverty rate has gone down, but those escaping poverty have primarily been men and their families. Consequently, the share of poverty experienced by women and female-headed families has increased substantially. This trend is called the *feminization of poverty*. In reality, there are three different trends involved: (1) trends in poverty rates for persons, (2) trends in poverty rates

Figure 2. Persons in Poverty by Age and Sex: 1992.

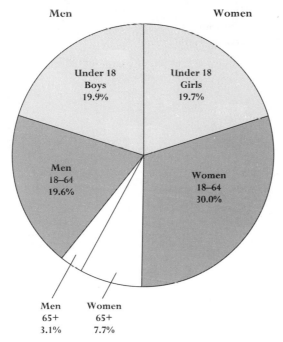

Total Poverty Population

Men   Women

Under 18
Boys
19.9%

Under 18
Girls
19.7%

Men
18–64
19.6%

Women
18–64
30.0%

Men
65+
3.1%

Women
65+
7.7%

Overall, women represent 57.4% of the poverty population.

Source: Computed from U.S. Bureau of the Census, 1993b: Table 5.

for families, and (3) trends in the *share* of the poverty population represented by different types of families.

TRENDS FOR PERSONS

Table 2 reports the sex/poverty ratio and male and female poverty rates for approximately the last forty years for white and black adults. In 1950, the ratio shows that women were only 10 percent more likely than men to be in poverty, even though the poverty rates for both men or women were considerably higher than in 1992. Thus, while the overall level of poverty has decreased substantially, adult poverty has become a *female* problem.

TRENDS FOR FAMILIES

Figure 1 graphs changes in the poverty rate for female-headed, married couple, and male-headed families from 1959 to 1992. All of these rates have declined, but the rate for female headed families continues to be the highest. Except

Figure 3.   Poverty Rates for Families by Family Type and Race and Hispanic Origin: 1992.

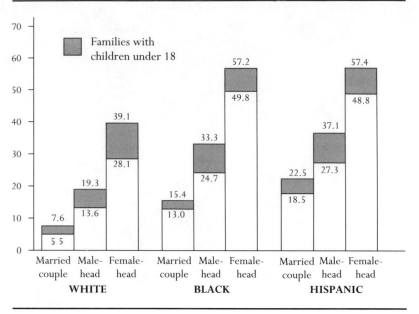

Hispanic may be of any race.
Source: U.S. Bureau of the Census, 1993b: Table 4.

Table 2.   Sex/Poverty Ratios and Poverty Rates for Whites and Blacks: 1950–1992

	1950	*1960*	*1970*	*1980*	*1992[a]*
Whites					
Adult men/adult women	1.10	1.23	1.46	1.48	1.50
Female poverty rate	35.9	18.2	12.4	9.8	11.7
Male poverty rate	32.7	14.8	8.5	6.6	7.8
Blacks					
Adult men/adult women	1.17	1.19	1.37	1.51	1.61
Female poverty rate	69.8	51.6	33.1	29.4	32.1
Male poverty rate	59.6	43.2	24.2	19.5	20.0

a. The 1992 data are not entirely comparable to the previous years since McLanahan et al. use data from the decennial census of the total U.S. population, and the 1992 data are from the Current Population Survey (March supplement) sample of sixty thousand households. See U.S. Bureau of the Census (1993b: Appendix A) for a discussion of comparability of the two sources of data.
Source: 1950 to 1980 from McLanahan et al. (1989: Table 2). 1992 data are computed from U.S. Bureau of the Census (1993b: Table 5).

Figure 4.   Trends in Poverty Rates for Family Types and Share of Poverty Families Headed by a Woman: 1959–1992.

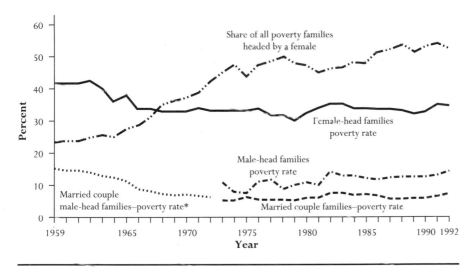

* Not reported separately
Source: Poverty rates from U.S. Bureau of the Census, 1993b: Table 4. Share of poverty families headed by a woman from same source.

for modest increases in the early 1980s, the three trends have remained at about the same levels for over twenty years.

SHARE OF POVERTY POPULATION

Figure 4 also graphs the *share* of poverty families headed by women. This calculation is the proportion of the total number of families in poverty that are headed by women. As Figure 4 shows, the share or percentage of all poor families that are headed by women has increased steadily since 1959. By 1992 over 52 percent of all families in poverty were headed by a woman.

The *feminization of poverty* refers both to the increases in the sex/poverty ratio since 1950, showing the relative increased risk to adult women, and to the increasing share of poor families headed by women. There are two other groups—the elderly and children—for whom trends in poverty show changes over the last forty years.

TRENDS FOR THE ELDERLY

In contrast to the poverty of female-headed families, poverty among those over age sixty-five has been substantially reduced since the 1960s, primarily because of increases in Social Security. Although 35.2 percent of the elderly population were in poverty in 1959, this had declined to 24.6 percent by 1970, and to only 12.9 percent in 1992. However, the Social Security benefits for elderly women are far below those for elderly men. The poverty rate for women went from 28.5 percent in 1970 to 15.7 in 1992, while the decline for men was from 19.0 percent to 8.9. The sex/poverty ratio for the elderly increased from 1.50 to 1.76 (U.S. Bureau of the Census, 1976: Table F; 1993b: Table 3, Table 5).[7]

TRENDS FOR CHILDREN

The poverty rates for children depend primarily on the type of family in which children live. For those children living in female-headed families, the poverty rate declined from 72.2 percent in 1959 to 53.0 percent in 1970 and fluctuated between 55 and 50 percent for the next twenty years. The rate in 1992 was 54.3 percent. Among children in married couple families, poverty has declined from 22.4 percent in 1959 to 9.2 percent in 1970; it was 10.9 percent for 1992 (Johnson et al., 1991: p. 34; U.S. Bureau of the Census, 1993b: Table 5).

However, the stability of the last twenty years is the result of opposing trends. On the one hand, there are today fewer children per family, and younger adults tend to have more education. These factors should have reduced the poverty of children. On the other hand, the number of families headed by women with children has increased, while the relative earnings of younger workers (despite their increased education) have declined (Duncan and Rodgers, 1991: pp. 548–49; Eggebeen and Lichter, 1991: p. 814).[8] The relative stability of children's poverty rates therefore obscures the fact that being dependent on the income of women increases the likelihood of poverty for children.

Duration of Poverty

For most of the poor population, being poor is a short-term condition. Approximately 60 percent of the people beginning a spell of poverty will be out of poverty in two years, and only 12 percent remain for over nine years (Bane and Ellwood, 1986: p. 10).[9] However, at any time, most of the poor have been so for many years.

These statements illustrate important differences in measuring the duration of poverty that are easily seen with a comparison to patients in a hospital. The majority of patients admitted in a year will be there only a short time, but a few are chronically ill and experience extended hospitalization. When the question is "How many entering will stay a long time?" the answer is very few. But if the question is "What share of the population at one point in time are chronically ill?" the answer is a much larger share (Bane and Ellwood, 1986: p. 11).[10]

The duration of a poverty spell is affected by its cause. Bane and Ellwood (1986: p. 18) report that 42 percent of those beginning poverty did so when the earnings of the head of the family or the wife declined, and the average duration was approximately three years.[11] Longer spells of poverty were found for both women and children when they began living in families headed by women (3.7 years for the women and four years for children). The longest spells of poverty were experienced by children born into poverty families (8.6 years).

Thus far, we have seen that women experience more poverty than men and that their poverty has more causes than men's. Women's likelihood of poverty is greater when they are heading their own families; they and their children experience longer durations of poverty than do persons in married couple and male-headed families.

Why Are Women Poor?

The predominant theories of poverty largely ignore the particular nature of women's poverty. Two explanations of poverty dominate the social science literature: individual and structural.

INDIVIDUAL EXPLANATIONS

The well-known report by Daniel Moynihan (1967: chap. 4, pp. 75–92) contends that the higher incidence of black families headed by women represents a "tangle of pathology" and contributes to higher poverty among blacks. Conditions in the black community such as a high divorce rate and unwed childbearing that result in more female-headed families are seen as part of a general breakdown of the family. While a larger proportion of black families than white families are headed by women, proponents of this perspective consider female-headed families deviant and maladaptive so that male children, particularly, are not raised to be full-fledged members of our society. For Moynihan, poor blacks have psychological flaws that produce the wrong kind of families. The Moynihan report represents an attempt to "blame the victim" (Baca Zinn, 1989: p. 868; Beeghley, 1983: chap. 6; Cerullo and Erlien, 1986: pp. 254–57). It failed to consider how a female-headed family could be an adaptation to poverty, one resulting from conditions beyond the woman's control, or even a preferable life-style.

Conservatives have argued that welfare programs, such as Aid to Families with Dependent Children (AFDC), encourage the establishment of female-headed households and out-of-wedlock childbearing so as to increase public assistance benefits (Murray, 1984: pp. 125–33; Gilder, 1981: chap. 11). Although research shows a modest decline in work effort in households where higher guaranteed incomes are available (Danziger et al., 1981: pp. 993–95), conservatives complain that the existence of welfare encourages people to avoid available employment. However, this argument appears to be based on the assumption that the amount of time people work is entirely under their own control. That is, conservatives want women with children to find employment, but they ignore how hard this may be due to a lack of jobs that do not accommodate women's child care responsibilities.[12] Furthermore, benefit levels for AFDC payments have been decreasing while the proportion of families headed by women has continued to increase (Ellwood and Summers, 1986: pp. 92–95; Darity and Myers, 1984: pp. 768, 774).[13] It is hard to believe that more and more women are establishing themselves as heads of a family in order to receive fewer and fewer benefits.

In general, individual explanations for poverty tend to treat the characteristics of the poor as causes of their poverty and implicitly to blame women for being poor.

STRUCTURAL THEORIES OF POVERTY

Structural views of poverty consider the socioeconomic structure of society as a part of the explanation. The very high unemployment experienced by young males (especially blacks) in urban areas is seen to contribute to more female-headed families (Ellwood and Summers, 1986: pp. 98–101; Wilson, 1987: p. 83). When fewer young men are economically viable, women establish households alone. These conditions affect Hispanic families as well as blacks (Sandefur and Tienda, 1988: p. 10). Critics (e.g., Baca Zinn, 1989: pp. 872–73), however, complain that to focus on men's unemployment results in a neglect of paths to socioeconomic independence for women, including pay equity and affordable child care.

Another structural explanation points to the increasing rates of divorce and unmarried childbearing as causes of poverty (e.g., Bane, 1986; Duncan and Hoffman, 1985).[14] Yet, despite a nearly 43 percent increase in the divorce rate from 1970 to 1982 (computed from U.S. Bureau of the Census, 1991b: Table 128), research for the same period shows that only 11 percent of all persons beginning a poverty spell were women and children moving into female-headed households.[15] Among just the poor female-headed families with children, 38 percent began poverty because of a divorce, and nearly another 21 percent because of the birth of a child (likely unmarried childbearing) (Bane and Ellwood, 1986: pp. 15–16).[16]

Research on race differences in family poverty rates represents a further structural explanation (e.g., Ricketts, 1989; Shulman, 1990; and Bane, 1986). Offering institutionalized racism as a primary explanation for the higher poverty of black families generally, Ricketts (1989: Table 2) shows that there is a strong link between family instability and economic instability for blacks, dating to the 1950s and the accompanying urbanization of blacks.[17] Shulman (1990: pp. 1000–1008) also argues that the economic differences between black and white married couple families are attributable to racism—racism in education that reduces the return on education for blacks, racism in employment that prevents qualified blacks from advancing, and racism "in the ability of blacks . . . to get jobs in the first place" (p. 1008). Bane (1986: pp. 214–20) finds that more black poverty is *not* produced by more female-headed families because the women are more likely to move from families that were already poor. Moving a poor woman from either the family of her parents or from a married couple family to a single-parent family does not change the amount of poverty when both groups are already poor. Bane (1986: p. 220) labels this "reshuffled poverty." For whites, however, Bane (1986: Table 9.6) finds that beginning poverty as a result of changing family structure accounts for 49 percent of beginning spells for female-headed families. Overall, racism appears to contribute to the higher poverty among black families relative to white families but does not account for the higher poverty of women within each race.

While a great deal of the changes producing poor female-headed families can be regarded as at least partly voluntary, Bane (1986: p. 231) concludes

> that the problem of poverty should be addressed by devoting attention to employment, wages, and the development of skills necessary for productive participation in the labor force rather than handwringing about the decline of the family.

Feminist Explanations for Women's Poverty

Feminists advance three major explanations for women's poverty: (1) women's labor market earnings are insufficient to support a family, (2) women heading their own families tend to be the sole support of their children, and (3) the lack of affordable child care limits and prevents the full labor market participation of many mothers (Garfinkel and McLanahan, 1986: p. 11; Robins, 1988: p. 122).

WOMEN'S LABOR MARKET EARNINGS

Women's labor market earnings are a function of both their hours of work and their wage rates. Among full-time, year-round workers, women earn 70.6 percent of what men earn. Improvements in this ratio in recent years are partly due to declines in men's earnings rather than improvements for women. In addition, of all women with labor market earnings in 1992, 53.5 percent were working full-time, year-round, as compared to 66.8 percent of the men with earnings (U.S. Bureau of the Census, 1993a: Table 24). The male-female gap in earnings is usually attributed to differences in worker characteristics (education, work experience, job skills) and to differences in characteristics of jobs (mainly occupational segregation by race and sex) (Kemp, 1994; Treiman and Hartmann, 1981: chap. 2). Most research on worker characteristics finds between 20 and 44 percent of the pay gap attributable to these differences, whereas the cost of being in a female-dominated occupation is estimated to reduce annual earnings by over $42 for each percentage point increase in females (Treiman and Hartmann, 1981: Table 4; Treiman et al., 1984: Figure 9.1). In short, women earn less than men, and their lower wages are due to a combination of not working full-time and being segregated into lower-paying, female-dominated jobs.

WOMEN HEADING FAMILIES ARE SOLE SUPPORT

Regardless of the reason why, in 1990 ten million women lived with their own children and the father was absent.[18] Only some of these absent fathers paid child support, and they didn't pay much. Government surveys show that 58 percent of these mothers had child support awards, but only 2.5 million received the full amount—an average of $2,995 per family. One-quarter received nothing.[19] The poverty rate for all women with children from absent fathers was 32 percent (U.S. Bureau of the Census, 1991a: p. 1).

Since 1975, the federal government has attempted to collect child support from absent fathers for women receiving welfare. The initial emphasis, however, was on recovering the funds spent on welfare. Beginning in 1984 welfare mothers kept only fifty dollars per month of child support received before their welfare grant would be reduced (Miller, 1990: pp. 79–85). In one research project, it was estimated that 7 percent of the dollar value of welfare payments were recovered from absent parents in 1985, while only about 10 percent of the women on welfare were receiving child support (Kahn and Kamerman, 1987: p. 13). Poor women, it appears, are trying to collect from poor men.

Child support programs are only minimally effective for any of the women with children from an absent father. In an analysis of a Wisconsin program from 1980 to 1986 that was not limited to poor families, researchers found child support payments for cases entering the court system increased between 11 and 30 percent. A gain of approximately 400 percent is estimated to be possible given the "difference between current child support payments and estimated ability to pay child support" (Garfinkel and Klawitter, 1990: p. 174). In addition, the amounts awarded

> tend not to cover expenses adequately, and are particularly deficient in taking into account expenses for child care, special medical care, or savings for college. (Miller, 1990: p. 81)

Courts generally base the amount of support awards on a percentage share of the man's income rather than on the amount needed to cover the costs of raising a child. Weitzman (1986: pp. 266–68) found California judges almost never awarded more than one-third of the man's income. Chasing absent fathers for child support will not solve women's poverty as long as child support awards and payments remain substantially below the ability of absent fathers to pay.

CHILD CARE

Without adequate and affordable child care, women with young children are effectively excluded from employment. Although we have no official data on how much a lack of child care reduces women's employment (Bloom and Steen, 1990: p. 25), research shows that making child care available to poor families increases employment rates and reduces welfare use (Robins, 1988: p. 122).

Nevertheless, 58 percent of working-age women with children under six in 1992 were in the labor force (U.S. Ways and Means Committee, 1993: p. 973). Data from 1988 showed nearly two-thirds of children under five whose mothers were employed were cared for in a home—their own home (28.2 percent) or the home of the provider (36.8 percent). Of the remaining proportion, 27.3 percent were in organized child care or kindergarten, 7.6 percent were cared for by their mother while at work, and approximately 0.1 percent were caring for themselves (U.S. Bureau of the Census, 1992: Table 1).

The history of child care in the United States demonstrates that a major shift in public acceptance occurred in the late 1980s (Norgren, 1989; Miller, 1990, pp. 101–7). Day care programs were first established in the nineteenth century as a charitable public service for poor working women. Run by upper-class women, these programs were one of the progressive reforms of that era, which included the temperance and birth control movements. Coinciding with the beginning of the social work profession, day care became associated with broken or troubled families. At the same time, kindergarten programs that emphasized learning and development for children, not merely custodial care, were begun for middle- and upper-class children so mothers could work (Norgren, 1989: p. 180).

Although the government was briefly involved in subsidizing day care during World War II, a subtle shift occurred through the employment of teachers in these programs. The distinction between day care and kindergarten became blurred. However, after the war, traditional beliefs about working mothers reemerged, and both public money and public support for day care disappeared. The federal government stayed out of day care until the 1960s, when the first Headstart programs were funded, targeting poor children. In 1967 amendments to Social Security legislation authorized unlimited matching funds to participants in the Work Incentive Program (WIN) and to potential and current recipients of welfare. A widespread expansion of high-quality, low-cost day care resulted, but this was short-lived.

Under the Nixon administration, federal support for day care was substantially reduced when, in 1971, Nixon vetoed the Comprehensive Child Development Act, signaling a return to the previous aversion to national assistance for working mothers. Funding ceilings were established for many social services in 1972, including child care programs. In general, only limited, means-tested programs for poor women on welfare remained until the 1980s (Norgren, 1989: p. 183). Under Reagan, tax credits for child care became available to middle- and upper-income families, but lower-income families were shut out because tax credits could not be turned into cash if a family did not owe taxes (Miller, 1990: p. 104). In the early 1980s, the United States was the only major industrialized country without a national child care policy (Joffe, 1983: p. 168).

In the late 1980s, however, child care was put on the national agenda. The debate shifted from whether child care was necessary to *how* to do it. Several bills provided for federal funding with different criteria for who would get it and who would administer it. Republicans generally favored less regulation and few standards for day care centers, particularly church-sponsored centers, which may discriminate in admissions and/or hiring. Democrats argued that states should establish regulations and set standards ("Child-Care Bill Dies Amid Partisan Sniping," 1988: pp. 365, 367).

Finally, in November 1990, the Child Care and Development Block Grant and Grants to States under Title IV-A of the Social Security Act for At-Risk Child Care (Public Law 101-508, HR 5835) passed and was signed in law. Under the Block Grant program states receive funds to supplement state programs based on the number of children under age five in their population. States must allocate 25 percent to before- and after-school care and 75 percent to "make child care more affordable or to improve quality and availability" (Blank, 1991: p. iii). Eligible families must have children under thirteen and a family income below 75 percent of the state median. Furthermore, parents need to be employed or participating in job training or educational programs.

One advantage of the Block Grant program is that families may use state vouchers to pay relatives, friends, or neighbors who provide home-based baby sitting. In addition, parents may use vouchers to pay for church-based child care, and religious groups can give preference to hiring workers and admitting children from their religious group (Blank, 1991: p. ii; "Families Gain Help on Child Care," 1990: p. 547). The Department of Health and Human Services has drafted regulations governing the implementation of this program that make parental choice a primary consideration. A concern among the states, however, is that this challenges the authority of the states to regulate child care providers and may result in taxpayers' money being used to support substandard and even unsafe day care (Frerking, 1992: pp. A-11, A-14).[20]

To summarize, feminists argue that women's poverty is different from men's because women are not treated the same as men in our culture.

Women's opportunities to solve their own poverty are limited by labor market discrimination and the lack of financial assistance from absent fathers. When women are economically responsible for children, the additional lack of affordable child care further inhibits their earnings. Contemporary policies that view women as the primary caretakers of children reinforce women's dependence on men and pressure women to marry or remarry (Hartmann, 1976: p. 139; Miller, 1990; Pearce, 1989: p. 504).

Solutions to Poverty

Until the advent of nationally funded public assistance programs during the Depression, the primary solution to women's poverty was marriage. Initially, public assistance programs in the United States were established with the Social Security Act in 1935 and were available only for children,[21] but it became increasingly difficult to assist children without also assisting their mothers. By the 1950s public assistance programs covered mothers as well as children. Mothers were subjected to regulations; states investigated their moral suitability to receive assistance and made sure that they were not cohabiting with any man who ought to be supporting the children. Many of these restrictions were removed with the reforms of the 1960s. The National Welfare Rights Organization worked to educate poor people about their rights and about the types of assistance programs available (Miller, 1990: p. 34).

CONTEMPORARY SOLUTIONS TO POVERTY

By the 1990s our society had a vast array of social insurance and assistance programs. They constitute a dual system, however. One consists of entitlement programs for the nonpoor, including workers, the elderly, and disabled persons; another system consists of means-tested programs that primarily serve poor women and their children. Table 3 describes the major ones, separating the entitlement programs from the means-tested ones. Entitlement programs have specific requirements for eligibility regarding age, employment, or disability. Those eligible are entitled to the benefits without any requirement that they be impoverished.[22] Means-tested programs, in contrast, require that persons prove they are poor in order to receive any benefits. A further distinction, also shown in Table 3, concerns whether a program provides cash payments or in-kind benefits. In-kind benefits are the use of services and facilities, such as medical care, where the payments are made directly to the providers—hospitals and physicians.

In 1992 the total federal outlay for social welfare programs was $705.3 billion, representing 51 percent of the total federal budget. Of the share to social welfare, 66.6 percent ($469.7 billion) went to entitlement programs for retired and disabled people—Social Security, Medicare, and other retirement programs, except for veterans. Only 19.6 percent ($138.1 billion) of the social welfare budget was for means-tested public aid programs, such as public assistance, Medicaid, supplemental security income, and food stamps. Entitlement programs for elderly and disabled persons cost three and one-third times more than public aid (U.S. Office of Management and Budget, 1991).[23]

Table 3. Types of Assistance Programs

Means-Tested Programs—*eligibility depends on demonstrating economic need:*
— Aid to Families with Dependent Children: AFDC or welfare, administered by the states with partial federal money
— Medicaid: health care for the poor, usually limited to AFDC participants, and state administered
— Food stamps: a federal/state program with different and less strict requirements for eligibility than AFDC
— Supplemental Security Income: SSI, a federal program of means-tested public assistance for the elderly or disabled when Social Security or pension income is insufficient
— Public housing: rent-free or rent-subsidized housing for poor persons

Entitlement Programs—*not based on economic need; rather participants need to meet age, employment, or disability requirements:*
— Social Security: federal retirement and disability payments for elderly or disabled persons and for widows and orphans
— Medicare: federal program of health care for the elderly and disabled persons
— Unemployment insurance: federal program for unemployed workers
— Worker's compensation: federal program for workers injured on the job

Cash Transfers—*recipients receive cash payments:*
— Aid to Families with Dependent Children
— Supplemental Security Income
— Social Security
— Unemployment insurance
— Worker's compensation

In-Kind Programs—*recipients use services and facilities, and payments are made directly to the providers*—*hospitals and physicians:*
— Medicaid
— Medicare
— Food stamps: eligible persons pay a portion of the value of the food stamps based on a sliding scale
— Public housing: eligible persons pay a portion of the value of the housing based on a sliding scale

---

Source: Kerbo, 1991: pp. 53–54.

PROGRAMS FOR THE NONPOOR

Workers are assisted by worker's compensation when injured on the job and by unemployment benefits when a job ends. Neither program requires that the recipient be impoverished. For the elderly and disabled, the predominant program is Social Security. In addition, when these persons are also poor, they are eligible for Supplemental Social Security (SSI). Social Security and SSI reduce poverty among the elderly primarily because Social Security payments increase as the inflation rate increases, but welfare grants are not adjusted for inflation (Beeghley, 1983: pp. 44–45).

Elderly women, however, are still at a disadvantage both from all income sources and from Social Security benefits. In 1992, of those over sixty-five who had income from *any* source, women's income was 56.3 percent of men's (U.S. Bureau of the Census, 1993a: Table 24). The average monthly income from Social Security for men age sixty-five and older was $740.20 in December 1992, while women age sixty-five and older received $551.19. In monthly benefits, then, women received 74.5 percent of what men received (U.S. Social Security Administration, 1993, Table 5.J3).

The amount of Social Security benefits are based on a person's previous earnings history or that of their spouse. Women's lifetime earnings tend to be lower than men's because women both have not worked as many years as men and have not earned comparable wages. Widows and wives, at age sixty-five, can collect one-half of their husbands' benefit or a benefit amount based on their own employment—whichever is greater. Either way, however, the woman's benefit is less than her husband's (Miller, 1990: pp. 117–20).

PROGRAMS FOR THE POOR

The major program for poor women is Aid to Families with Dependent Children (AFDC), better known as welfare. AFDC is administered by individual states, but the federal government pays between 50 and 80 percent of the benefit costs and 50 percent of the administrative costs (U.S. Ways and Means Committee, 1993: p. 615).

State-controlled AFDC benefit levels are substantially below federally controlled Social Security benefits. The average amount received by a female-headed family with children under eighteen in 1992 from Social Security was $6,676, but the same type of family received an average of $3,786 from AFDC (U.S. Bureau of the Census, 1993c, Table 7). The only difference for this 57 percent gap is that the woman receiving Social Security is a widow or maybe disabled, while the one receiving AFDC is not. Social Security is limited to elderly and disabled persons or widows and widowers with dependent children, while AFDC is available to only impoverished families with dependent children.

Welfare programs do not raise a family's income level above the poverty line. Benefits are so low in almost every state that a family receiving welfare remains in poverty. The median state benefit in 1993 for a one-parent family of three was $367 per month, and the median monthly amount for food stamps was $285. The lowest granting state is Mississippi, which supports recipients at 14 percent of the poverty line for a three-person family ($120 per month), and the highest is Alaska, where the benefits are 82 percent of the poverty line ($923 per month) (U.S. Ways and Means Committee, 1993: p. 657).

THE FAMILY SUPPORT ACT OF 1988

The Family Support Act of 1988 (Public Law 100-485) ties public assistance to required participation in job search, job training, and work experience programs. With this law, states have more authority for establishing the regulations than previously, and they are also required to provide more programs (Miller, 1990: pp. 62–70; Harlan and Steinberg, 1989: pp. 359–64; Gideonse and Meyers, 1989: pp. 38–39; U.S. Ways and Means Committee, 1993: pp. 617–20). There are several parts to this act.

First, the states are required to provide AFDC to intact two-parent families if the principal wage earner has a work history and the family is in need because of unemployment (U.S. Ways and Means Committee, 1993: p. 617). Many states excluded two-parent families in the past.

Second, states must deduct child support from the wages of absent parents. Women applying for AFDC are required

> to assign their child support rights to the State and to cooperate with welfare officials in establishing the paternity of a child and in obtaining support payments from the father. (U.S. Ways and Means Committee, 1993: p. 617)

Third, the act requires states to provide a mix of job search, job training, educational, and work experience programs for recipients, and participation is *required*. Beginning in 1990, states must offer a job opportunities and basic skills (JOBS) program, which replaces the previous work incentive (WIN) program (U.S. Ways and Means Committee, 1993: p. 617). When AFDC recipients obtain employment, their increased income makes them ineligible for assistance and for Medicaid. The act further includes provisions for a transition period within which both Medicaid and child care support are continued. Reports on several pilot JOBS programs show that employment rates among AFDC recipients increased through job search requirements (Goldman, 1989). But the educational programs, which are necessary for many uneducated poor women, are more expensive to establish. Evaluating pilot programs in Baltimore, Boston, and Philadelphia, Gittel and Moore (1989: p. 472) found most job training programs

> were fast-training sessions in traditional [women-dominated] job areas, such as clerical and secretarial skills, word processing, and typing. They are aimed at training AFDC women quickly and placing them in jobs.

The success of pilot programs was also clearly related to the demand for labor in the local economy; in areas of high unemployment, the programs produced no gains (Gueron, 1989: p. 376).

States are required to provide child care for custodial parents participating in the JOBS program. Women with children under three, with the option to make it children under one, are not required to participate. But if these women and other women with young children volunteer to participate, the programs are required to give volunteers first priority and to provide child care or at least vouchers for participants to purchase child care for themselves ("After Years of Debate, Welfare Reform Clears," 1988: p. 354; U.S. Ways and Means Committee, 1993: p. 617).

Evaluations of pilot programs, such as in Massachusetts, reveal problems for AFDC women in the use of child care. For example, women were required to have child care arrangements made before they could be enrolled in training classes, but vouchers for child care depended upon proof of enrollment (Gittel and Moore, 1989: pp. 457–58).

Lastly, states are to require one parent in two-parent welfare families to participate in unpaid, public-sector jobs a minimum of sixteen hours a week in order to receive AFDC ("After Years of Debate, Welfare Reform Clears," 1988: p. 356). This particular provision is referred to as *workfare*. While pilot programs showed these to be "feasible" (Garfinkel and McLanahan, 1986: p. 174), the evaluations were based on voluntary participants who did not need child care.

Despite the determination to make the poor earn their assistance, it remains to be seen whether job training and public-sector work experience will substantially reduce the poverty of women heading families. Even full-time work at a minimum wage job only brings a family of four to approximately 60 percent of the poverty line (Caputo, 1989: p. 91). Further, jobs obtained at this level of the labor market typically do not provide on-the-job training, advancement opportunities, or fringe benefits, such as health insurance (Gideonse and Meyers, 1989: p. 34). The combination of the low-wage employment of many women and the lack of health care and other benefits may leave women heading families in need of continued public assistance.

The Wisconsin Learnfare program represents another reform designed to make the poor more responsible (Corbett et al., 1989; Pawasarat et al., 1992). This program requires that all children age thirteen to nineteen covered by a public assistance AFDC grant be enrolled in school. When the child is not meeting the attendance requirements, the family's welfare grant is reduced. The idea is that children who stay in school will be less likely to become welfare dependent when they are adults. Evaluating the results after two years, Pawasarat et al. (1992) found not only that there was no improvement in attendance associated with Learnfare but also that attendance rates were worse in the second year than in the first. Other reforms being considered in California and Maryland include refusing additional benefits to unmarried women having babies while on welfare and paying new residents at the rate of the state from which they moved.

Generally, it appears welfare policies are still influenced by stereotypes of women as dependents and as the primary caretakers of children. Placing women in typical female-dominated jobs will not solve women's poverty, in spite of job-training and education programs designed to enhance their employment. More enforcement of child support will assist poor women, but when the state reduces the public assistance grant for amounts over fifty dollars, little movement out of poverty seems likely. Increases in child care assistance also serve poor women, but without access to better-paying jobs, child care is not going to solve poverty.

Conclusion

The issue of choice is at the center of the controversy about women's poverty. Even though Ms. Ali's attempt to take herself and her children back to Allah rather than face the horrors of poverty and homelessness represents a terrible choice, women with children are rational actors in an economic system that seems to give them few choices. Women are torn between voluntary, but devalued, domestic labor in the home and needed, but demeaning, low-wage labor market work, often without adequate child care. Women's employment is the preferred path to success, but marriage remains their primary route out of poverty when they have children. The pay for women's employment is insufficient to produce a family-level income except for a small proportion of women.

Women's poverty is a public issue, requiring solutions outside of the home. The community as a whole has a responsibility to ensure that all children receive adequate care. To accomplish this for their children, women should not have to be dependent either on men through marriage and/or child support or on the state through public assistance. Women have the right to earn their own independence. It has become a mockery that our society glorifies motherhood but regulates and even punishes poor mothers and their children.

NOTES

1. A major debate exists over the types of income that should be used in the computation of a poverty line. The Census Bureau defines income as money wages, salaries, net income from self-employment (farm or nonfarm), Social Security or railroad retirement, Supplemental Security income, public assistance or welfare payments, interest income, dividends, income from estates or trusts, net rental income or royalties, veterans' payments, survivor and disability benefits, unemployment and worker's compensation, private or government employee pensions, annuities, alimony or child support, other regular contributions from persons not in the household, and other periodic income (U.S. Bureau of the Census, 1993b: p. A-2). Excluded are capital gains, cash assets, gifts, the value of noncash benefits such as food stamps, public housing, Medicare and Medicaid, and all noncash job benefits, such as employee health benefits, pension contributions, and other job "perks." Further, income is measure before any taxes are paid, such as Social Security, federal and local income taxes, and sales taxes. Some analysts argue that since the official definition is based on pretax cash income, it overestimates the extent of poverty.

2. There are major disagreements about how to measure poverty. The official measure assumes poor households will spend their money the same way as average-income households and that relative expenses remain the same over time. Critics argue that the decision to multiply the cost of the food plan by three sets the poverty line at an unrealistically low level (e.g., Beeghley, 1983: chap. 2; Hagenaars and de Vos, 1988; Harrington, 1984: pp. 69–71). With food representing one-third of the poverty line budget, poor families are disadvantaged since they frequently spend as much as half of their income on food (Beeghley, 1983: p. 29).

3. Beginning in 1989 the Census Bureau began publishing a separate special report estimating the impact of taxes and noncash benefits on calculations of income and poverty (U.S. Bureau of the Census, 1989). Fourteen different poverty definitions are compared to the official measure. After extensive statistical calculations and estimations to produce these fourteen definitions (the methods for which are debated among social scientists, e.g., Harrington, 1984, especially chapter 4), these alterations do not eradicate poverty. For example, the 1992 rate for white female-headed families with children was reduced from 40.3 percent (with the official definition) to 29.3 percent. Overall, adding the value of noncash benefits (food stamps, housing, and Medicaid) to the official definition of income reduces the total poverty rate by only 2.2 percentage points. For everyone, the largest reduction in poverty results from the addition of non-means-tested cash benefits (mainly Social Security), which are counted in the official definition already (U.S. Bureau of the Census, 1993c: Table K). In spite of all the calculations, the resulting poverty rates for families headed by women with children remained between 2.6 and nearly five times the poverty of married couple families with children (U.S. Bureau of the Census, 1993c: Table K).

4. The population estimates are based on "the civilian noninstitutionalized population of the United States and members of the armed forces in the United States living off post or with their families on post, but excludes all other members of Armed Forces" (U.S. Bureau of the Census, 1993a: p. C-1). These estimates, however, exclude all the homeless in our population. See Wright (1989) for an extended discussion of homelessness.

5. The race breakdowns reported in the Census Bureau publications distinguish whites and blacks. Hispanic includes those who selected "Mexican, Puerto Rican, Cuban, Central or South American, or some other Hispanic origin" from a self-identification question in the census (U.S. Bureau of the Census, 1993a: p. C-6). Persons of Hispanic origin may be of any race, and Hispanic households represent 6.9 percent of all U.S. households in 1992. Total households in the U.S. are

85.2 percent white, 11.6 percent black, and 3.2 percent other races, which includes Asian or Pacific Islander, American Indian, Aleut or Eskimo, and others (computed from U.S. Bureau of the Census, 1993a: Table A). In both 1993 publications on income and poverty used in this chapter, Current Population Reports, Series P60-184 and Series P60-185, all races are included in the aggregate estimates, but detailed data are reported for whites and blacks only. Data for the nonwhite, nonblack races are only included in a few summary tables.

6. The Census Bureau defines a family as "groups of two or more persons (one of whom is the householder) related by birth, marriage, or adoption and residing together." Published data are also available for a household, which is defined as "all persons who occupy a housing unit" (U.S. Bureau of the Census, 1993b: pp. C-4, C-5). Thus, a household includes related family members and unrelated persons who are also in residence. A single person living alone is counted as a household but not as a family. In discussing poverty for families, we follow the Census Bureau definition. Since 1973, the Census Bureau has designated families and households as male- or female-headed when no spouse is present. Prior to that, married couple families were counted as male-headed.

7. The earliest computations of sex-specific poverty rates for the elderly are for 1959 (U.S. Bureau of the Census, 1967: Table 7). However, in that publication, the elderly are separated by family status. It reports the rate for families and the rate for unrelated individuals. A summary statistic for all men and women age sixty-five and older is not available. For two-person families with the head sixty-five and older, the poverty rate in 1959 was 32.5 percent. For unrelated individuals, the rate was 59.9 percent for men and 71.5 percent for women.

8. Duncan and Rodgers (1991) include food stamp benefits as income in their calculations of children's poverty. The Children's Defense Fund (Johnson et al., 1991) uses only cash income and reports a 21 percent increase in child poverty from 1979 to 1989. They attribute one-half of the increase in poverty among families with children to "the declining effectiveness of government cash payments . . . [to lift] such families out of poverty" (Johnson et al., 1991: p. 3).

9. It is very difficult to assess the movements of people in and out of poverty since a large part of the available research looks at cross-sections of the population. A cross-section is a sample of the population at one point in time; the next survey examines another different sample of people. Following people as they move in and out of poverty is not possible with this type of data. The Census Bureau data from the Current Population Surveys are based on cross-sectional samples.

Following the same group across time (longitudinal research) is necessary to evaluate movements in and out of poverty. One such study from the University of Michigan, the Panel Study of Income Dynamics (PSID), has followed a sample of five thousand families since 1968, and the majority of the information available about movements in and out of poverty is based on these data. The PSID may not be an accurate sample of the poverty population, however, because it began with a sample of only people living in families, and because those remaining in the panel are more likely to be in stable families. See Duncan et al. (1984: pp. 38–40) for a comparison of the PSID and the Current Population Survey. Bane and Ellwood (1986) and Duncan et al. (1984) use the PSID data and exclude persons over age sixty-four.

Another increasingly important longitudinal data source is the Survey of Income and Program Participation (SIPP), collected by the Census Bureau. However, the SIPP consists of several different panels, each one following the same people for only two and one-half years. A new report from these data (Short and Shea, 1991) reports transitions in poverty status for 1987 to 1988, but the report includes very little data for men and women separately or for family types.

10. Another distinction used in studies of the duration of poverty is between the persistently poor and the temporarily poor. Persistently poor are defined as those who were poor in at least eight of the ten years—1969 to 1978—covered in the research of Duncan and colleagues (1984). Temporarily poor are those who were poor one or two years. Duncan et al. (1984: pp. 41, 48) estimate that approximately 2.6 percent of the total U.S. population were persistently poor between 1969 and 1978, but 24.4 percent "experienced at least some poverty during that decade."

11. This is not comparable to the two years' duration referenced on p. 462. That duration is for the 60 percent beginning a spell. In this paragraph, the duration of three years is for the 42 percent who began poverty when the earnings of the family head fell.

12. Another difficulty for women with children is getting health care. While women receiving public assistance are usually covered by public health benefits (Medicaid), low-wage employment tends not to include health coverage, which may make public assistance preferable.

13. Research on duration and cycles of welfare use largely rely on the PSID data also used in studies of movements in and out of poverty (Duncan and Coe, 1984: pp. 71–94; Duncan et al.,

1988: pp. 467–68, Table 1). With the same distinctions between the population ever receiving welfare and those on welfare at a given time, the research shows that about 30 percent of the persons ever receiving welfare were recipients for one or two years, 40 percent for three to seven years, and 30 percent had eight or more years of participation. The median length of time was less than four years. Of the population receiving welfare at a given time, 7 percent have done so for one to two years, 28 percent for three to seven years, and 65 percent for eight years or more (Duncan et al., 1988: Table 1). Duncan and colleagues do not completely report sex differences in welfare use beyond Table 3.2 in Duncan and Coe (1984: p. 80). However, before the 1988 Family Security Act (implemented in 1990), 45 percent of all states limited eligibility to single parents with children— usually women (Shapiro and Greenstein, 1988: p. 1). Thus, sex differences in welfare use are largely a function of the eligibility restrictions and do not necessarily indicate a greater propensity among women to receive welfare.

14. This perspective is different from Moynihan's. He argued that psychological characteristics of blacks resulted in their greater propensity to set up female-headed families. Structural explanations, in contrast, focus on social forces that affect individual behaviors.

In addition to divorce and unmarried childbearing, another structural view is that women's increased labor force participation has also contributed to more female-headed families, but women's labor force participation increased substantially in the 1950s and 1960s, when the divorce rates were not increasing. Garfinkel and McLanahan (1986: Figure 5 and p. 66) show that the causal direction may be reversed; that is, marital instability may have increased married women's labor force participation.

15. The divorce rate for 1992 shows an increase of 34.3 percent from 1970 (computed from U.S. Bureau of the Census, 1991b: Table 128; and provisional data from U.S. Public Health Service, 1993: p. 1).

16. Using the PSID data for 1968 to 1982, Bane (1986: Tables 9.3 and 9.4) reports that 11.3 percent of all white persons beginning a spell of poverty and 10.9 percent of all black persons made transitions to female-headed households, but comparisons with Bane and Ellwood (1986: Table 3) regarding divorce and unmarried childbearing are not possible. Bane and Ellwood (1986) exclude the elderly and break down the data for types of families with children, whereas Bane's (1986) analysis includes the elderly and does not report separate estimates for families with children.

17. Structural or institutionalized racism refers to racially biased practices that are built into the structure of our society. Beeghley (1983: pp. 159–63) discusses structural mechanisms that reduce the employment opportunities of blacks and women—recruitment into jobs and screening for employment (such as testing, use of educational credentials, and the discretion of employers to avoid "unsuitable" candidates).

18. Data are based on women age fifteen and older with children under age twenty-one (U.S. Bureau of the Census, 1991a: p. 1). Not all of these women are unmarried, however. The Census Bureau population for this report is women with children who are not living with the child's father. Of the ten million in 1990, 25.4 percent are currently married, 30.7 divorced, 13.6 separated, 0.6 widowed, and 29.6 never married (U.S. Bureau of the Census, 1991a: Table A).

19. Approximately 1.25 million mothers received some of what they were owed. Another eight hundred thousand women had child support awards in 1989 but did not expect to receive anything because the payments were not yet due, the father had died, or the children were too old (U.S. Bureau of the Census, 1991a: p. 1).

20. There are now four different programs providing funding for child care: the new Block Grant program for low-income families, the program from the 1988 Family Support Act for AFDC recipients participating in the JOBS programs, the transitional child care for families leaving AFDC (one year of assistance with different guidelines and eligibilities), and the new child care for families "at risk" of needing AFDC (which also passed in 1990). The regulations for administering these various programs are in process and will likely require some time to be finalized. See Greenberg (1991) for a detailed discussion of each program.

21. See Garfinkel and McLanahan (1986: pp. 92–119), Katz (1986, 1989), and Nelson (1990) for history of public assistance and poor relief programs.

22. All of these entitlement programs are partly funded by contributions and payments from workers and employers. However, the total costs exceed the amounts contributed or collected.

23. The remaining 11.8 percent ($97.5 billion) of the federal social welfare budget consists of unemployment, health, and medical programs for nonelderly, nonpoor persons, assisted housing, and other social services (U.S. Office of Management and Budget, 1991).

REFERENCES

"After Years of Debate, Welfare Reform Clears." *Congressional Quarterly Almanac:* 94. Washington, D.C.: Congressional Quarterly, Inc., 1988, pp. 349–57.

Baca Zinn, Maxine. "Family, Race, and Poverty in the Eighties." *Signs: Journal of Women in Culture and Society* 14 (Summer 1989): pp. 856–74.

Bane, Mary Jo. "Household Composition and Poverty." In Shelton H. Danziger and Daniel H. Weinberg, eds., *Fighting Poverty: What Works and What Doesn't.* Cambridge, Mass.: Harvard University Press, 1986, pp. 209–31.

Bane, Mary Jo, and David T. Ellwood. "Slipping Into and Out of Poverty: The Dynamics of Spells." *Journal of Human Resources* 21 (Winter 1986): pp. 1–23.

Beeghley, Leonard. *Living Poorly in America.* New York: Praeger Publishers, 1983.

Blank, Helen. *The Child Care and Development Block Grant and Child Care Grants to States Under Title IV-A of the Social Security Act.* Washington, D.C.: Children's Defense Fund, January 14, 1991.

Bloom, David E., and Todd P. Steen. "The Labor Force Implications of Expanding the Child Care Industry." *Population Research and Policy Review* 9 (January 1990): 25–44.

Caputo, Richard K. "Limits of Welfare Reform." *Social Casework: The Journal of Contemporary Social Work* 70 (February 1989): pp. 85–95.

Cerullo, Margaret, and Marla Erlien. "Beyond the 'Normal Family': A Cultural Critique of Women's Poverty." In Rochelle Lefkowitz and Ann Withorn, eds., *For Crying Out Loud: Women and Poverty in the United States.* New York: Pilgrim Press, 1986, pp. 248–61.

"Child-Care Bill Dies Amid Partisan Sniping." *Congressional Quarterly Almanac:* 94. Washington, D.C.: Congressional Quarterly, Inc., 1988, pp. 365–68.

Corbett, Thomas, Jeannette Deloya, Wendy Manning, and Liz Uhr. "Learnfare: The Wisconsin Experience." University of Wisconsin–Madison, Institute for Research on Poverty, *Focus* 12 (Fall and Winter 1989): pp. 1–10.

Danziger, Sheldon, Robert Haveman, and Robert Plotnick. "How Income Transfer Programs Affect Work, Savings, and the Income Distribution: A Critical Review." *Journal of Economic Literature* 19 (September 1981): pp. 975–1028.

Darity, William, Jr., and Samuel L. Myers, Jr. "Does Welfare Dependency Cause Female Headship? The Case of the Black Family." *Journal of Marriage and the Family* 46 (November 1984): pp. 765–79.

Duncan, Greg J., with Richard D. Coe. "The Dynamics of Welfare Use." In Greg J. Duncan, ed., *Years of Poverty, Years of Plenty: The Changing Economic Fortunes of American Workers and Families.* Ann Arbor: Survey Research Center, University of Michigan, 1984, pp. 71–94.

Duncan, Greg J., with Richard D. Coe and Martha S. Hill. "The Dynamics of Poverty." In Greg J. Duncan, ed., *Years of Poverty, Years of Plenty: The Changing Economic Fortunes of American Workers and Families.* Ann Arbor: Survey Research Center, University of Michigan, 1984, pp. 33–70.

Duncan, Greg J., Martha S. Hill, and Saul D. Hoffman. "Welfare Dependence Within and Across Generations." *Science* 239 (January 1988): pp. 467–71.

Duncan, Greg J., and Saul D. Hoffman. "A Reconsideration of the Economic Consequences of Marital Dissolution." *Demography* 22 (November 1985): pp. 495–98.

Duncan, Greg J., and Willard Rodgers. "Has Children's Poverty Become More Persistent?" *American Sociological Review* 56 (August 1991): pp. 538–50.

Eggebeen, David J., and Daniel T. Lichter. "Race, Family Structure, and Changing Poverty Among American Children." *American Sociological Review* 56 (December 1991): pp. 801–17.

Ellwood, David T., and Lawrence H. Summers. "Poverty in America: Is Welfare the Answer or the Problem?" In Shelton H. Danziger and Daniel H. Weinberg, eds., *Fighting Poverty: What Works and What Doesn't.* Cambridge, Mass.: Harvard University Press, 1986, pp. 78–105.

"Families Gain Help on Child Care." *Congressional Quarterly Almanac:* 96. Washington, D.C.: Congressional Quarterly, Inc., 1990, pp. 547–51.

Frerking, Beth. "Parents: Tie Subsidy to Standards." *Times Picayunne* (January 19, 1992): pp. A-11, A-14.

Funiciello, Theresa. *Tyranny of Kindness: Dismantling the Welfare System to End Poverty in America.* New York: Atlantic Monthly Press, 1993.

Garfinkel, Irwin, and Marieka M. Klawitter. "The Effect of Routine Income Withholding of Child Support Collections." *Journal of Policy Analysis and Management* 9 (Spring 1990): pp. 155–77.

Garfinkel, Irwin, and Sara S. McLanahan. *Single Mothers and Their Children: A New American Dilemma.* Washington, D.C.: The Urban Institute Press, 1986.

Gideonse, Sarah K., and William R. Meyers. "Why the Family Support Act Will Fail." *Challenge* 32 (September/October 1989): pp. 33–39.

Gilder, George. *Wealth and Poverty.* New York: Basic Books, Inc., 1981.

Gittel, Marilyn, and Janice Moore. "Denying Independence: Barriers to the Education of Women on AFDC." In Sharon L. Harlan and Ronnie J. Steinberg, eds., *Job Training for Women: The Promise and Limits of Public Policies.* Philadelphia: Temple University Press, 1989, pp. 445–79.

Goldman, Barbara S. "Job Search Strategies for Women on Welfare." In Sharon L. Harlan and Ronnie J. Steinberg, eds., *Job Training for Women: The Promise and Limits of Public Policies.* Philadelphia: Temple University Press, 1989, pp. 389–413.

Greenberg, Mark. "Toward Seamless Service: Some Key Issues in the Relationship Between the Child Care and Development Block Grant and AFDC-Related Child Care." Washington, D.C.: Center for Law and Social Policy, July 1991.

Gueron, Judith M. "Work Programs for Welfare Recipients." In Sharon L. Harlan and Ronnie J. Steinberg, eds., *Job Training for Women: The Promise and Limits of Public Policies.* Philadelphia: Temple University Press, 1989, pp. 365–88.

Hagenaars, Aldi, and Klaas de Vos. "The Definition and Measurement of Poverty." *Journal of Human Resources* 23 (Spring 1988): pp. 211–21.

Harlan, Sharon L., and Ronnie J. Steinberg, eds. *Job Training for Women: The Promise and Limits of Public Policies.* Philadelphia: Temple University Press, 1989.

Harrington, Michael. *The New American Poverty.* New York: Holt, Rinehart and Winston, 1984.

Hartmann, Heidi. "Capitalism, Patriarchy, and Job Segregation by Sex." *Signs: Journal of Women in Culture and Society* 1 (Spring 1976): 137–69.

Joffe, Carole. "Why the United States Has No Child-Care Policy." In Irene Diamond, ed., *Families, Politics, and Public Policy: A Feminist Dialogue on Women and the State.* New York: Longman, 1983, pp. 168–82.

Johnson, Clifford M., Leticia Miranda, Arloc Sherman, and James D. Weill. *Child Poverty in America.* Washington, D.C.: Children's Defense Fund, 1991.

Kahn, Alfred J., and Shelia B. Kamerman. "Child Support in the United States: The Problem." In Alfred J. Kahn and Shelia B. Kamerman, eds., *Child Support: From Debt Collection to Social Policy.* Newbury Park, Calif.: Sage Publications, 1987, pp. 10–19.

Katz, Michael B. *In the Shadow of the Poorhouse: A Social History of Welfare in America.* New York: Basic Books, 1986.

————. *The Undeserving Poor: From the War on Poverty to the War on Welfare.* New York: Pantheon Books, 1989.

Kemp, Alice Abel. *Women's Work: Degraded and Devalued.* Englewood Cliffs, N.J.: Prentice Hall, 1994.

Kerbo, Harold R. *Social Stratification and Inequality.* 2nd ed. New York: McGraw-Hill, 1991.

McLanahan, Sara S., Annemette Sorensen, and Dorothy Watson. "Sex Differences in Poverty, 1950–1980." *Signs: Journal of Women in Culture and Society* 15 (Autumn 1989): 102–22.

Miller, Dorothy C. *Women and Social Welfare: A Feminist Analysis.* New York: Praeger, 1990.

Moynihan, Daniel Patrick. "The Negro Family: The Case for National Action." In Lee Rainwater and William L. Yancey, eds., *The Moynihan Report and the Politics of Controversy.* Cambridge, Mass.: MIT Press, 1967.

Murray, Charles. *Losing Ground: American Social Policy 1950–1980.* New York: Basic Books, Inc., 1984.

Nelson, Barbara J. "The Gender, Race, and Class Origins of Early Welfare Policy and the Welfare State: A Comparison of Workmen's Compensation and Mothers' Aid." In Louise A. Tilly and Patricia Gurin, eds., *Women, Politics, and Change.* New York: Russell Sage Foundation, 1990, pp. 413–35.

Norgren, Jill. "Child Care." In Jo Freeman, ed., *Women: A Feminist Perspective,* 4th edition. Mountain View, Calif.: Mayfield Publishing, 1989, pp. 176–94.

Orshansky, Mollie. "How Poverty Is Measured." *Monthly Labor Review* 92 (February 1969): pp. 12–19.

Pawasarat, John, Lois M. Quinn, and Frank Stetzer. *Evaluation of the Impact of Wisconsin's Learnfare Experiment on the School Attendance of Teenagers Receiving Aid to Families with Dependent Children.* Employment and Training Institute, University of Wisconsin–Milwaukee, February 5, 1992.

Pearce, Diana. "Farewell to Alms: Women's Fare Under Welfare." In Jo Freeman, ed., *Women: A Feminist Perspective,* 4th edition. Mountain View, Calif.: Mayfield Publishing, 1989, p. 493–506.

Ricketts, Erol. "The Origin of Black Female-Headed Families." University of Wisconsin–Madison, Institute for Research on Poverty, *Focus* 12 (Spring and Summer 1989): pp. 32–36.

Robins, Philip K. "Child Care and Convenience: The Effects of Labor Market Entry Costs on Economic Self-Sufficiency Among Public Housing Residents." *Social Science Quarterly* 69 (March 1988): pp. 122–36.

Sandefur, Gary D., and Marta Tienda, eds. *Divided Opportunities: Minorities, Poverty, and Social Policy.* New York: Plenum Press, 1988.

Shapiro, Isaac, and Robert Greenstein. *Holes in the Safety Nets: Poverty Programs and Policies in the States.* National Overview. Washington, D.C.: Center on Budget and Policy Priorities, April 1988.

Short, Kathleen, and Martina Shea. *Transitions in Income and Poverty Status: 1987–88.* Current Population Reports, Household Economic Studies, Series P-70, No. 24. U.S. Department of Commerce, Bureau of the Census. Washington, D.C.: U.S. Government Printing Office, 1991.

Shulman, Steven. "The Causes of Black Poverty: Evidence and Interpretation." *Journal of Economic Issues* 24 (December 1990): pp. 995–1016.

Treiman, Donald J., and Heidi I. Hartmann, eds. *Women, Work, and Wages: Equal Pay for Jobs of Equal Value.* Washington, D.C.: National Academy Press, 1981.

Treiman, Donald J., Heidi I. Hartmann, and Patricia A. Roos. "Assessing Pay Discrimination Using National Data." In Helen Remick, ed., *Comparable Worth and Wage Discrimination.* Philadelphia: Temple University Press, 1984, pp. 137–54.

Udesky, Laurie. "Welfare Reform and Its Victims: How Workfare Hurts Kids." *The Nation* 251 (September 24, 1990): pp. 302–6.

U.S. Bureau of the Census. Department of Commerce. *Income in 1966 of Families and Persons in the United States.* Current Population Reports, Consumer Income, Series P-60, No. 53. Washington, D.C.: U.S. Government Printing Office, 1967.

———. *Characteristics of the Population Below the Poverty Level: 1974.* Current Population Reports, Consumer Income, Series P-60, No. 102. Washington, D.C.: U.S. Government Printing Office, 1976.

———. *Measuring the Effect of Benefits and Taxes on Income and Poverty: 1986.* Current Population Reports, Consumer Income, Series P-60, No. 164-RD-1. Washington, D.C.: U.S. Government Printing Office, 1989.

———. *Child Support and Alimony: 1989.* Current Population Reports, Special Studies, Series P-60, No. 173, by Gordon H. Lester. Washington, D.C.: U.S. Government Printing Office, 1991a.

———. *Statistical Abstract of the United States: 1991.* 111th edition. Washington, D.C.: U.S. Government Printing Office, 1991b.

———. *Who's Minding the Kids? Child Care Arrangements: Fall 1988.* Current Population Reports, Household Economic Studies, Series P70-30. Washington, D.C.: U.S. Government Printing Office, 1992.

———. *Money Income of Households, Families, and Persons in the United States: 1992.* Current Population Reports, Consumer Income, Series P-60-184. Washington, D.C.: U.S. Government Printing Office, 1993a.

———. *Poverty in the United States: 1992.* Current Population Reports, Consumer Income, Series P60-185. Washington, D.C.: U.S. Government Printing Office, 1993b.

———. *Measuring the Effect of Benefits and Taxes on Income and Poverty: 1992.* Current Population Reports, Consumer Income, Series P-60-186RD. Washington, D.C.: U.S. Government Printing Office, 1993c.

U.S. Office of Management and Budget, Executive Office of the President. *Budget of the United States Government: Fiscal Year 1992.* Washington, D.C.: U.S. Government Printing Office, 1991.

U.S. Public Health Service. Centers for Disease Control, Department of Health and Human Services. Centers for Disease Control, Department of Health and Human Services. *Monthly Vital Statistics Report:* 41, January 15, 1993.

U.S. Social Security Administration. *Social Security Bulletin.* Annual Statistical Supplement, 1993. SSA Publication No. 13-11700, U.S. Department of Health and Human Services. Washington, D.C.: U.S. Government Printing Office, 1993.

U.S. Ways and Means Committee. House of Representatives. *Overview of Entitlement Programs: 1993 Green Book.* Washington, D.C.: U.S. Government Printing Office, July 7, 1993.

Weitzman, Lenore. *The Divorce Revolution: The Unexpected Social and Economic Consequences for Women and Children in America.* New York: The Free Press, 1986.

Wilson, William Julius. *The Truly Disadvantaged: The Inner City, the Underclass, and Public Policy.* Chicago: University of Chicago Press, 1987.

Wright, James D. *Address Unknown: The Homeless in America.* New York: Aldine de Gruyter, 1989.

Lady Versus Low Creature: Old Roots of Current Attitudes Toward Homeless Women

Stephanie Golden

IN JANUARY 1989 THE Homeless Women's Rights Network, an advocacy group organized to respond to the fearsome conditions in the New York City shelters for single homeless women, issued a report documenting the "unique forms of discrimination and abuse" faced by the residents of two notorious shelters in Brooklyn.[1] Two of the report's charges in particular exemplify issues that are unique to women's homelessness—historically as well as today—and thus make it different from that of men.

The first involves sexual abuse. The homeless women reported that shelter staff paid residents for sex and had sex with them in dormitories. Residents were also extremely vulnerable to rape and assault by men in the surrounding neighborhoods, not least because shelter staff refused to let women in after curfew and frequently threw them out onto the streets at night. Second, the shelter system created obstacles that helped prevent women from becoming employed. One such obstacle was that women who were trying to find jobs were not provided with the means to obtain appropriate, presentable clothing. As a result they often wound up postponing job interviews because they felt they could not dress properly.

While the report's authors, and commentators on homelessness generally, focus on the immediate need to remedy these and other abuses, it is also valuable to look at them from a historical perspective. The women described by the investigators could have been speaking a hundred years ago, raising much the same issues. For centuries, the experience of homeless women has been shaped not only by the factors that also made men homeless but also by issues that are central to the lives of all women, especially those clustering around sexuality.

Although much research has been done and many books have been written about homeless men, hardly any works treat homeless women as a group in themselves; they have generally been assimilated into the study of men and subsumed into generalizations based on that study. But two themes distinguish female homelessness: like other women, those who were homeless have always had more difficulty than men in earning a living, and they have been particularly victimized by ideologies about women.

While men have been outcasts, and more often than women, not only have they had more options, but—as is still true today—the male outsider has been defined in terms of work, and the female in terms of sexuality. That is, if a woman did not belong to a family or live within some other restrictive social context (such as a convent), her sexuality was seen as anarchic and threatening. At the same time sexuality was often the instrument of her economic survival—sometimes as a wise woman or midwife, but most often as a prostitute.

Although the history of homeless women is intertwined with that of two other venerable social phenomena not related to sex—begging and vagabondage—it is also closely related to one activity men generally do not share: prostitution, an option almost always open to a destitute woman. Although beggars, vagabonds, and prostitutes all evoke in the members of settled society similar mixtures of fear, envy, loathing, attraction, and moral disapproval, the element of sexuality and the mystery associated with it have entered into the public perception of homeless women and made them seem special in a way that has not been true for men.

The basic problem is one of category. Whereas a homeless man fits comfortably into a variety of categories (hobo, tramp, bum, vagrant), a homeless woman evokes intense discomfort. Women have always been defined so entirely in terms of whom they belong to that no category exists for a woman without family or home. If one thinks of society as a pattern of social forms that create categories into which its members fit, such a woman must be marginal, in the sense that because she fits into the pattern nowhere she has to exist at its edge. According to Mary Douglas, "Danger lies in transitional [that is, marginal] states, simply because transition is neither one state nor the next, it is undefinable." A person who exists at the margin is therefore automatically regarded as dangerous and unreliable.[2]

What is more, when someone moves outside society, she appears to those inside as "fundamentally different . . . perhaps even a different species"—and therefore capable of anything.[3] As a result *all* kinds of antisocial attitudes, qualities, and behavior are easily ascribed to her. At the same time, the images of very different outsiders tend to blur together, just because they are outside, so that little distinction is made among them. This is one reason why all types of outcasts have generally been shut up together in the same institutions, and why today various groups of homeless people with different needs and problems are still thrust indiscriminately into the same shelters.[4]

These problems of marginality are compounded for homeless women. First, they violate a specifically sex-based norm: women should not be alone. For a woman, being alone equals being outside because she is not in a relationship to a man. Second, the danger posed by such women appears especially potent because their living at the margin means that their sexuality is not under society's control—which also means that any woman whose sexuality appears unregulated must perforce become marginal in order for society to feel safe. In fact, all the forms of female marginality collapse into this one issue, which comes to define any female deviant. Thus any single homeless woman is immediately suspected of promiscuity, since thanks to the blurring effect she becomes virtually indistinguishable from a prostitute. The only way she can avoid this label is to exhibit an appearance and demeanor that put her unquestionably into an acceptable category.

To show how such issues have affected the treatment of actual women, this essay describes incidents in which the inability of homeless women in nineteenth- and early twentieth-century England and America to maintain a style of dress signaling that they occupied their proper "place"—that is, category—as women wound up perpetuating their homelessness. The deep fear of women who seem to live outside social control is further revealed by the reactions to a few homeless women who were discovered to be dressed like men.

Nineteenth-century responses to single homeless women were shaped by an ideology current in both Britain and America that established the home as a separate feminine sphere, where women both functioned as moral guardians of society and were themselves protected from the dangers of the world outside. According to this "cult of domesticity," women's nature was such that their proper place was exclusively in the home; by implication, women who were not in homes were not even real ("true") women.[5]

Women who did not remain sheltered in a home but ventured alone into city streets could be ensnared by scheming men into sexual immorality. Society itself was supposedly endangered by the loss of their virtue, for the existence of a population of promiscuous women would lead, as one British reformer put it, straight to the "decay of manhood and the family."[6] Like earlier ages, the nineteenth century found it essential to create an absolute distinction between the "true woman" and the prostitute, who was "her antithesis"—not only not a woman, but not even human.[7]

Prostitutes have always been set explicitly apart from other women, with their status signaled by clothing regulations. In ancient Rome and later in Europe, for example, prostitutes were required to wear specific clothing or badges, or to dye their hair a certain color.[8] In the nineteenth century the prostitute's style of dress was self-chosen but no less easily recognizable; she favored gaudy, flamboyant clothes that covered less of her body than was deemed proper for "respectable" women. Yet because of the blurring effect, even women who did not dress this way, but merely failed to appear "respectable," came under suspicion. Thus mid nineteenth-century New Yorkers, for example, "closely associated female homelessness and poverty with depravity."[9]

Even a woman who simply went out alone, without being shabbily dressed, could be taken for a prostitute or at least assumed to be "issuing a sexual invitation."[10] And once the suspicion of promiscuity took hold, it was easy to suspect her of other forms of immorality: "Once a woman has descended from the pedestal of innocence, she is prepared to perpetuate [sic] every crime," asserted a British reformer.[11]

The homeless woman looking for work, then, faced suspicion and hostility arising from powerful fears. To make things worse, few occupations were open to women, and generally they required an appearance clearly signaling that a woman remained within the boundaries of conventional respectability—something a woman without access to soap and water, as well as other amenities of shelter, could not maintain. For example, a thirty-three-year-old dressmaker interviewed by Henry Mayhew, the chronicler of the poor of Victorian London, told him that after her husband deserted her she could not earn enough money at her trade and "was obliged to sell my things to pay off my rent and get myself something to eat." Now she was staying at a shelter.

When I leave here (and they'll only keep me for three nights) I don't know what I shall do, for I have so parted with my things that I ain't respectable enough to go after needlework, and they do look at you so. My clothes are

all gone to live upon. If I could make myself look a little decent, I might perhaps get some work. I wish I could get into service again. . . . but I want things.[12]

Two Englishwomen who investigated female homelessness in the early
twentieth century concluded that the inability to dress respectably was a
significant cause of homelessness. Mary Higgs, a Christian missionary who ran
a small shelter for destitute women in London, based her conclusions largely
on her own experiences tramping through various towns and cities to find
out what options a woman on the road had. Her account and that of Ada
Chesterton, who did the same thing twenty years later in London, are intensely personal reactions to conditions on the street as no mere observer can
understand them—in Chesterton's case constituting a real identification with
the homeless prostitutes, match vendors, unwed mothers, and occasional
charwomen who lived a floating, outcast street life. While Higgs, around 1905,
made a series of three- to five-day excursions in different parts of the country,
Chesterton launched herself penniless from Euston Station into London one
night around 1925 "to see what would happen if I started from zero with
nothing but my personality to stand on. . . . I proved beyond the shadow of a
doubt that for a woman to get employment, in any recognised calling, without
reference or status of some sort, is tragically impossible."[13]

The women Higgs and Chesterton met had become homeless through the
death of a provider, illness, bad luck, or a rent increase that forced them out of
their lodgings. A severe housing shortage prevented them from getting a new place
even if they had work, and they had to live in cheap lodging houses or charity
shelters. The final alternative was the casual ward, a separate part of the workhouse
reserved for transients ("casuals"—purportedly laborers looking for work), who
spent at most a few nights there.[14] Accounts of conditions in the casual wards agree
that these institutions were deliberately designed to be as unpleasant as possible
in order to discourage people from using them, and that as a consequence most
of those on the road went there only as a last resort.

Beyond aesthetics or comfort, however, the main objection both writers
had to all of these alternatives was that they were degenerative. Higgs and
Chesterton raised much the same objections as do the women in the Brooklyn
shelters. Both laid great stress on the impossibility of staying clean in lodging
houses, a factor they found central to the inability to find work. Higgs, after
describing the terribly crowded and dirty conditions at one house, where there
was only one public sink for both men and women—so that one could not
undress to wash—commented, "Single women frequently get shaken out of a
home by bereavements or other causes, and drift, unable to recover a stable
position if once their clothing becomes dirty or shabby." The discovery of how
differently the world regarded them once they no longer looked middle-class
impressed these two women deeply. "It is not likely that a woman will get
employment unless she has character [a written reference] and clothes," by
Higgs's account:

> An unemployed man may obtain work at various occupations to which dirt
> is no hindrance, . . . but a woman must "look tidy," or no one will employ
> her. Therefore conditions destructive to cleanliness are for her equivalent to
> forcing her down lower and lower into beggary and vice. Once at a certain

stage she cannot rise, "no one would have me in their house," say, rightly enough, poor miserable creatures with scarcely a rag to their back.

In the minds of most people, Chesterton said, summarizing the wide range of suspicions that homeless women evoked, "Bedraggled garments not only spell destitution, but incapacity, dishonesty, and a total lack of sex morals."[15]

Chesterton, who had great self-confidence and considerable talent as a cook, assumed she could land a job, even without references, by sheer force of personality. She was outraged to discover that she was as much disregarded and brushed aside as the most pathetically incompetent or self-doubting derelict: "Neither the officials nor the individuals to whom I applied could persuade themselves that I was not a thief." As she and Higgs both discovered, the homeless woman was reduced to the image her clothes presented, in a much more radical way than was true for male vagrants. Chesterton commented that while the sight of a homeless man arouses compassion and the idea that something is wrong with society, a female vagrant arouses "distrust, if not hostility." Higgs concurred: "I do not believe that even women from the higher ranks can well help drifting to destitution if from any cause friends and foothold are lost. Most people distrust a friendless woman. Yet in many cases it is a matter of clothes!"[16]

On one occasion, Chesterton could not find a bed and had to spend the entire night in the streets. Sometime after midnight she found a food stall still open, but the proprietor refused to serve her. "The most abject specimen of man is quite welcome if he has the pence to pay. . . . But in the case of women there is the rooted belief that they must be bad lots or they would have a home; if they are not thieves they are prostitutes, and either way, even a commercial connection with them might cause trouble with the police." The public is indignant if a shabby man is refused beer in a bar. "But no one seems to think it unjust or even strange that a coffee stall keeper should 'shoo' off a woman who wants to buy food or drink in the watches of the night." The same man who said when she was destitute that he didn't serve women was very friendly when she came back well dressed. "Dirt, in a man," she commented elsewhere, "not infrequently suggests romance—in a woman it implies degradation, neglect and an obstinate refusal to undertake the obligations of her sex."[17]

The Brooklyn women who in 1989 complained that they could not dress properly for a job interview were, therefore, not being finicky or unreasonable; they just knew the rules—rules that also explain the ease with which middle-class women, once they had lost the essentially flimsy supports that maintained their social position, could (and still can) fall through the holes in the social fabric. Mayhew gave a telling example in which the clothes principle operated in reverse to save a woman from homelessness. Known as the "Lady Lurker" (a "lurk" was the ruse or trick a beggar used to induce people to give money), this woman was the daughter of a minister. She had been married to a schoolteacher, then a physician; after her second husband's death she "passed through various grades, till she is now a cadger."

She dresses becomingly in black, and sends in her card . . . to the houses whose occupants are known, or supposed, to be charitable. She talks with them for a certain time, and then draws forth a few boxes of lucifers, which, she says, she is compelled to sell for her living.[18]

Clearly this mode of survival depended entirely on her ladylike appearance.

Not only were homeless women objects of greater distrust than homeless men; the most negative responses came from "respectable" women. Both Chesterton and Caroline Kirkland, writing in 1853 on behalf of the Home for Discharged Female Convicts operated by the women of the New York Prison Association, lament the fact that although women themselves might seem to be, as Kirkland put it, "the natural and God-appointed aid" of other women in need, in practice they turn out to have less sympathy than do men. "Sad it is," Kirkland continued, "that fallen woman hopes less from her sisters than from her brothers; that it is more difficult to convince her of woman's forgiveness than of man's or God's." Chesterton, who took up match selling (essentially a discreet form of begging) to get some money, said she never found a woman who would buy from her: "It was not only their refusal to spend a penny that was hurtful, but their very obvious belief in my utter worthlessness." She thought that women would have been willing to help her only if they had seen her in a clean room, "in obvious but decent destitution."[19]

The respectable woman's hostility derived from an awareness that the norm that supposedly kept her safe at home actually rendered her quite vulnerable. Chesterton explained why homeless women did not go from door to door, as men did, offering plants in exchange for clothes: "The enthusiastic young wife who joyfully surrenders her husband's favourite jacket" to a man would suspect a woman of "sinister designs. . . . While the bare notion that any of her pretty garments should go to the clothing of the vagrant would be so distasteful as to induce the abrupt closing of the door."[20] That is, the idea of one's own coat on the other woman's back brings her too close for comfort. Women, lacking social and economic power as they do, have a particularly acute sense of the fragility of the social apparatus that keeps those who are economically dependent inside.[21]

American women made newly homeless by the Depression were also aware of the importance of appearance to their survival. In 1933 a reporter, Marlise Johnston, described the difficulties faced by a relatively new group: unattached, self-supporting white-collar working women. "The problem of the self-respecting, independent young girl out of work is one of the gravest in the whole tragic picture of unemployment," she said, and went on to describe the young middle-class women in New York who, "when their landlady wearies of having them stay on without benefit of rent, ride the subways all night. . . . Some girls live in this precarious way for weeks. Some hire out as domestic help for free room and board. Some go on the streets."

The pride of these young women, Johnston wrote, made them

> hate the idea of charity. . . . When they lose their jobs they make every sacrifice, they exhaust every resource, before they turn to society for help. . . . They half-starve themselves. But they do not go to bread lines, nor do they eat at soup kitchens. Any one who has marveled because there are no women in bread lines should realize that it is not because there are no hungry

women. It is because they believe that any public parade of poverty is degrading.

And, by instinct, they observed the familiar principle: "Food is the first thing that goes when a woman gets up against it, and appearance and clothes are the last. This is not vanity as much as self-preservation. They know that 60 per cent. of their chances of getting a job depends on their appearance."

What is remarkable is that the very fact of being poor and jobless rendered even these young women suspect. Affirming that these "whitecollar girls" were not the same as "the drifting type of woman" who used the Municipal Lodging House and the Salvation Army shelter, Johnston felt compelled to reassure her readers that, though poor through no fault of their own, these young women were still worthy of sympathy:

> The woman out of work in the big city is not merely the ghetto child. She is more likely of good breeding and education. . . . They are not potential Communists and Reds, nor soap-box orators against the civilization which made their new poverty possible. They are not even filled with self-pity. They have the same courage as men, but are more sensitive.[22]

The remarkable logic of this rescue operation demonstrates how easy it was for a woman to step over the line into the outsider's oblivion the moment her poverty became a "public parade."[23]

The United States also had another kind of homeless woman, whose existence posed a somewhat different threat. In this country, industrialization created the hobo and briefly made him a hero. Although quite a number of women were hoboes, homeless women do not possess the tramp/hobo tradition as part of a history, either in their own minds or in those of others. Thus they have always appeared to Americans as a shocking anomaly.

Women tramps seem to have been uncommon before the Depression; in 1880 the discovery of one was sufficiently noteworthy to rate equal treatment in the *Railway Age Gazette* (under the heading "Tramps") with a report of an attempted holdup by male tramps. The entire item reads: "A tramp, captured at Rahway, N.J., turned out to be a woman in man's clothes, and was handed over to the police."[24] It is possible that the number of female tramps was somewhat larger than such reports would indicate, since those who were not caught would have been counted as men.

Commentators seem to have been particularly disturbed by the phenomenon of women dressing as men. A *New York Times* report from August 1902 pays more attention to this than to the spectacular exploits of the woman in question: " 'Jimmie' McDougall, the handsome leader of the large and dreaded band of marauders and tramps who have long been the terror of Monroe County farmers, is now safe behind the bars of a jail, and has turned out to be a woman." When discovered by police, " 'Jimmie' was attired in white cloth shoes several sizes too large, blue overalls, and a red flannel shirt." It was after being put in a cell that she "broke down, and . . . disclosed her sex." Her true name was Theresa McDougall, and she had been an actress in Cleveland. "Later she was married to . . . a stage carpenter, with whom she led a tempestuous life, finally running away. She adopted man's attire in order to beat her way from Cleveland to Rochester."[25] The point of this article is not to reveal that a woman had led a gang of (presumably male) thieves, but to explain why she dressed as she did. It focuses on the catalogue of her garments; her criminal career is only a subsidiary to the real offense.

A similar catalogue figures in the report of another incident. In January 1901 the *Railway Conductor* denounced "the escapade of Susan Shelly of York Springs, Pa., who made her way from her home to Chicago, Illinois, disguised as a tramp, and riding in true hobo style in box and stock cars, clad in male attire." According to a Philadelphia newspaper account,

> Miss Shelly . . . has posed variously as a homeless tramp, girl of education and refinement in search of work, a young author on the hunt of material for a book and a detective. Whenever possible she appeared in men's clothing.
> . . . Dressed in a ragged pair of trousers, blue flannel shirt and thread-bare coat, she would slouch into a town in the typical hobo gait, and there levy on the citizens for food, clothing and money in the true tramp style. She delighted in having the police on her trail and seemed to get great enjoyment out of their peremptory orders to move on to another town.

The mayor of Harrisburg, having investigated her "queer case," stated that she "has no intention of violating any law, but that she is consumed by a desire to become famous."

The outrage of the *Railway Conductor* arose from a "full knowledge of the possibilities of a fate worse than death, which encompassed her on all sides"— a knowledge (the editor chooses to assume) Shelly lacked; otherwise "she would have shrunk in horror from attempting" such an exploit. "We assume she is a lady," he wrote, "from the fact that she has long occupied a prominent place as a teacher and from her candid acknowledgment that the trip was made with the purpose of gathering matter for a book"; but, he pointed out, by doing what she did she abrogated the rights and privileges of that status:

> for men in train service cannot, or do not conceive virtue traveling in a garb that would indicate only the lowest of creatures. Pity alone was perhaps the incentive which induced trainmen to permit her to remain upon their trains, but it is safe to say that they felt under no necessity of offering her any protection because of her sex. Thus it will be seen that she was wholly without protection, and, if possible, more obnoxious than the male hobo whom she impersonated.[26]

Note that her extra obnoxiousness lay in her having been "without protection"—that is, alone. Translating "protection" as control, one can see that what male clothing did was release her from the behavioral controls imposed by "ladyhood" and thereby break down the all-important distinction between "real" women and the other kind; this transgression prompted the familiar accusation that Shelly's act made her no better than a prostitute ("lowest of creatures"). The editor's anger derived from the concealment not so much of her female-ness (especially since it appears that the trainmen knew she was a woman) as of her *true status* as a female. There is real horror behind the self-righteous justification of the possibility that the trainmen could have unknowingly imposed their sexual urges on a "lady." When a man can no longer distinguish between ladies and low creatures, society itself is in danger.

The image of the male tramp or hobo commonly involved forceful action and power (the hobo is a heroic worker; the tramp may be a criminal plotting against society) and (as a considerable body of hobo literature attests) a sexual component sublimed into a form of noble conquest, with his personal erratic mobility blended into the nation's manifest destiny.[27] The female tramp, in contrast, was immediately and completely defined by her sexuality. Since the definition of "lady" included passivity, any woman exhibiting power and forceful action (which naturally included any woman traveling alone and wearing men's clothing) automatically belonged to the sphere of the "lowest creatures." Thus while a male tramp had a certain place in relation to society, a woman *had no place* as a tramp unless she could be defined as a prostitute—that is, degraded and marginalized.

The sense of total upheaval of the social order that Shelly's escapade provoked in the editor of the *Railway Conductor* becomes clearer if we look at some aspects of the meaning of transvestism. Transvestism has been used ceremonially to deal symbolically with the dangers of the indeterminate world of the margins. Medieval society, for example, institutionalized cross-dressing by both women and men during the great seasonal carnivals, as part of a temporary suspension of social norms and structures, including sex roles.[28]

In most contexts, however, transvestism is tolerable only in someone who is already marginal. In fact, in ancient Rome the distinctive clothing that prostitutes had to wear was specifically not the standard women's garment but the toga—men's dress; it signaled their status as not-really-women.[29] Joan of Arc wore male dress to preserve her virginity and thereby her divine inspiration; significantly, the act that ultimately triggered her execution was her insistence on once again putting on men's clothes after having been ordered to wear a woman's dress. The question for Joan's contemporaries was whether she was a saint or a witch; but in either case, she would remain marginal.[30]

"Real" women who violate the boundaries of their category but cannot easily be defined as marginal are even more threatening. The attempt to introduce the "bloomer dress" in the United States in 1851, for example, evoked outraged associations with prostitution, criminality, and madness, as the image of the trousered woman blurred into those of other creatures at the margins of humanity. For the rest of the century, long pantaloons were worn only by young girls (who, being sexually immature, were no threat), dancers, and—of course—prostitutes.[31]

Because homelessness forces a woman outside the narrow limits of her acceptable category, with her deviation necessarily signaled by her appearance, it shakes the very foundations of the social order. She must therefore be defined as marginal and treated as less than fully human. Most homeless women hate this experience, want to reenter society, and will put considerable effort into trying to become "real" women again. But there is always the possibility that, once shaken from their "place," some women might find an alternative so appealing that they are disinclined to return to it. One such lasting transformation occurred in the case of a thirty-seven-year-old woman hobo interviewed around 1934 by Walter C. Reckless, a sociologist. Mrs. Metzger, as he called her, had an eighth-grade education, was separated from her husband, and had worked in a semiskilled job for five years. She had been unemployed for two years before taking to the road, which she decided to do because "her savings were gone, . . . she could live cheaper on the road, . . . she wanted to travel, . . . to be free of her lover, . . . and . . . to be rid of the people who bothered her about her religion (she was a Seventh Day Adventist)."

"Yes, I am real happy on the road," Mrs. Metzger herself said. "I don't want any assaults, but outside of that I have been real happy. . . . It is pleasant to go from town to town. All my thirty-seven years I have never traveled." She felt that her "mind [was] more developed" as a result of her experiences. The most difficult part of being on the road, she told Reckless, was "when I can't find any water and want to get clean. . . . being dirty means more to me than being hungry." Mrs. Metzger liked to wear a dress, although all the other women on the road wore pants so as to pass for men and avoid molestation. A certain female pragmatism enabled her to reconcile her sexual encounters with her faith: "You have to put up on the road with certain things and you got to give in when forced. But that doesn't mean I don't keep up my religion."

So powerful is the value of appearance for women that even this female hobo internalized it. But she did more. By maintaining the appearance of respectability yet accepting the casual promiscuity required by the road, Mrs. Metzger created a kind of middle ground between the categories of "real" woman and prostitute—a territory that disconcerted her interlocutor, as did his perception that she inhabited it quite successfully. At the time of the interview she was headed back east, to her sister's family, and thought she might stay with them: "I can entertain people with travel talk now." But "if I don't like it at home with my sister, I can still go on the road again." In fact, as Reckless commented, "She seems to have the notion that the road is now her career—something on which she can fall back, something at which she had made a success." He looked on this as an indication of a new "social pathology"—the possible "growth of a chronic female hobo class." Indeed, his original purpose in the interview was to gauge "the extent of demoralization among unemployed and homeless women," and the only consolation for his discovery that "women are making pretty good hoboes as hoboes go" was the prerogative of labeling Mrs. Metzger deviant. But by his own account, the changes that the road had wrought in her character hardly seem pathological: "She likes the independence of the road and the sense of power she gets from making a go of life on the road. I believe she is proud of herself and thinks that she is a much superior person to the one she was previously."[32]

Mrs. Metzger, however, is an exception. Most homeless women have not been able to "make a go" of life outside. For them, no middle ground has been possible. The discomfort evoked by a woman whose appearance proclaimed that she lived outside the boundaries of true womanhood has prevented perception of the reality of a person trying to find work. Although female homelessness is largely a function of the same factors as male homelessness— the need for jobs and housing—it is also partly determined by a society's *image* of Woman. And our society still maintains the basic distinction between "real" and other women, though nowadays it takes less obvious forms.

Because of their lack of category, homeless women in the past either disappeared into invisibility or evoked suspicion, hostility, and blame. Even today, when the ideology of "woman's place" has a much weaker hold, the Brooklyn shelter residents suffer both of these effects, for they live under dehumanizing and degrading conditions that go largely unrecognized at a time of public outcry over the conditions in shelters for homeless families and for single homeless men.

In 1988, the director of a twenty-four-hour drop-in center for women in Manhattan told a visitor that both male guards in the city shelters and men on the streets around the center commonly assumed that "homeless women are fair game." "Men who harass homeless women feel the women belong to them because they're on the streets," she said. At the same time, these men left shoppers and businesswomen alone.[33] To this writer's imagination they seem like the very same men who rudely ogled the shabbily dressed Mary Higgs on a tramping expedition in the summer of 1903: "I had never realized before that a lady's dress, or even that of a respectable workingwoman, was a *protection*. The bold, free look of a man at a destitute woman must be felt to be realised."[34] Or they could be the trainmen who felt no obligation to "protect" Susan Shelly or the New York workingmen who felt free to assault nineteenth-century factory girls asking for directions on the street.[35] All knew the difference between the "real" women whom one must respect and those who, being outside, had no conventions protecting them.

While men may see homeless women as open sexual targets, women, as we have seen, may react with even greater hostility out of fear of becoming like them. Since the presence of homeless women raises issues that go right to the heart of our society, both these types of reaction are powerful and deeply ingrained. They can shape policy decisions about services for homeless women as well as the actual manner in which assistance is provided. It is therefore essential to develop a conscious awareness of such reactions so that services can be better designed to meet homeless women's real needs. If, for example, we know with what profound suspicion they will be viewed and we want them to find jobs, we will provide them not just with any clothing but with clothing suitable for an interview. And if we realize that almost any man will make certain assumptions about their sexuality, we will build in ongoing education for security guards (as the drop-in center did) or hire female guards—as well as prosecute the men who abuse them.

Beyond this, however, the treatment of homeless women—as of all homeless people—depends on how society at large sees them. And in fact, it is difficult to look at homeless women clearly. I think this is because their condition, not veiled like other women's by the gratuities of life inside society, reveals so nakedly our long-standing ambivalence toward female sexuality and the associated precariousness of most women's position that we turn away—like Chesterton's young wife, who would slam the door on a female plant seller—in order to preserve a reassuring distinction between them and us.

The sense of separation created by such a distinction is what enables institutions that warehouse and abuse women to exist in the first place. Recognizing the culturally determined component in our reaction to homeless women is one step toward creating, instead, a sense of community between "us" and "them." On such a feeling effective advocacy and true service both depend.

NOTES

1. Homeless Women's Rights Network, "Victims Again: A Report on the Conditions of Homeless Women in the New York City Shelter System" (photocopy, January 1989), unpaged.

2. This analysis is based on Mary Douglas, *Purity and Danger: An Analysis of Concepts of Pollution and Taboo* (London: Routledge & Kegan Paul, 1966), 94–98; quotation from p. 96.

3. Thomas J. Scheff, *Being Mentally Ill: A Sociological Theory* (New York: Aldine Publishing Co., 1966), 77.

4. For the European precedent of mixing different types of deviants in a single institution, see Michel Foucault, *Madness and Civilization: A History of Insanity in the Age of Reason* (New York: Random House, Vintage Books, 1973), chap. 2, "The Great Confinement"; for the United States in the nineteenth century, see Lucy Komisar, *Down and Out in the USA: A History of Public Welfare,* rev. ed. (New York and London: Franklin Watts, 1977), 17; and Michael Katz, *In the Shadow of the Poorhouse: A Social History of Welfare in America* (New York: Basic Books, 1986), 28–30.

The situation in shelters for the homeless in New York City was documented by a 1987 report prepared by the New York State Psychiatric Institute, whose investigation disclosed people ranging in age from eighteen to eighty, with a wide range of physical and/or mental health problems, among residents of single-adult shelters. Elmer L. Streuning, "A Study of Residents of the New York City Shelter System" (New York State Psychiatric Institute, 1987), photocopy. The New York Coalition for the Homeless has reported on large congregate shelters (now closed) where unrelated women, men, and children lived all together in open dormitories (*Safety Network/NY: The Newsletter of the Coalition for the Homeless,* November 1987, n.p.), and on HIV-positive homeless people put at greater risk by having to stay in armory shelters among the general population (*Safety Network/NY,* January and April 1990).

5. Kathy Peiss, *Cheap Amusements: Working Women and Leisure in Turn-of-the-Century New York* (Philadelphia: Temple University Press, 1986), 7, 165–66; Barbara J. Berg, *The Remembered Gate: Origins of American Feminism* (New York: Oxford University Press, 1978), 65–71; Christine Stansell, *City of Women: Sex and Class in New York, 1789–1860* (1986; Urbana and Chicago: University of Illinois Press, 1987), xii, 41, 155–56, 191. For a full description of the construct of domesticity, see Nancy F. Cott, *The Bonds of Womanhood: "Woman's Sphere" in New England, 1780–1835* (New Haven and London: Yale University Press, 1977), chap. 2, "Domesticity."

The centrality of "home" to the concept of "woman" is further illustrated by Susan B. Anthony's 1877 speech "Homes of Single Women," which assails those who might doubt that single women as much as the married possess "the true womanly home instinct." *Elizabeth Cady Stanton/Susan B. Anthony: Correspondence, Writings, Speeches,* ed. Ellen Carol DuBois (New York: Schocken Books, 1981), 151.

6. Peiss, *Cheap Amusements,* 166; Stansell, *City of Women,* 125; Joanne J. Meyerowitz, *Women Adrift: Independent Wage Earners in Chicago, 1880–1930* (Chicago and London: University of Chicago Press, 1988), 49; quotation from Mary Higgs, *Glimpses into the Abyss* (London: P. S. King & Son, 1906), 248. See also Higgs, 312: "In the case of women the moral danger is a grave additional reason for prevention of vagrancy."

7. Stansell, *City of Women,* 93, 97. See also Berg, *The Remembered Gate,* 179–80: the prostitute was "a creature so degraded that she did not and could never deserve the glorious name of 'woman'"; she was "a negative image of the quintessential female."

8. Gideon Sjoberg, *The Preindustrial City: Past and Present* (Glencoe, Ill.: Free Press, 1960), 135; Fernando Henriques, *Stews and Strumpets: A Survey of Prostitution,* vol. 1, *Primitive, Classical and Oriental* (London: MacGibbon & Kee, 1961), 131; Vern L. Bullough and Bonnie L. Bullough, *The History of Prostitution* (New Hyde Park, N.Y.: University Books, 1964), 114.

9. Judith R. Walkowitz, *Prostitution and Victorian Society: Women, Class, and the State* (Cambridge: Cambridge University Press, 1980), 26; Stansell, *City of Women,* 93, 173.

10. Stansell, *City of Women,* 97. See also Peiss, *Cheap Amusements,* 114.

11. J. B. Talbot, *The Miseries of Prostitution* (London, 1844), quoted in Walkowitz, *Prostitution and Victorian Society,* 39.

12. Henry Mayhew, *London Labour and the London Poor: A Cyclopaedia of the Condition and Earnings of Those That Will Work, Those That Cannot Work, and Those That Will Not Work,* 4 vols. (1861–62; reprint, New York: Dover, 1968), 3:416–17.

13. Mrs. Cecil Chesterton, *In Darkest London* (New York: The Macmillan Co., 1926), 11.

14. Mary Higgs, *Down and Out: Studies in the Problem of Vagrancy*, rev. ed. of *My Brother the Tramp* (London: Student Christian Movement, 1924), 48.

15. Higgs, *Glimpses*, 106, 250; Chesterton, *In Darkest London*, 220.

16. Chesterton, *In Darkest London*, 92, 120; Higgs, *Glimpses*, 190.

17. Chesterton, *In Darkest London*, 170–71, 120–21.

18. Mayhew, *London Labour and the London Poor*, 1:246.

19. Mrs. C. M. Kirkland, *The Helping Hand: Comprising an Account of the Home, for Discharged Female Convicts, and an Appeal in Behalf of That Institution* (New York: Charles Scribner, 1853), 51; Chesterton, *In Darkest London*, 57.

20. Chesterton, *In Darkest London*, 125.

21. "For though we always pretended to be exceptional, the truth was, now that we were a family we were increasingly like any other couple: with one toddler and one newborn I was only a divorce away from welfare." Alix Kates Shulman, *Burning Questions: A Novel* (New York: Bantam Books, 1979), 146.

22. Marlise Johnston, "The Woman Out of Work," *Review of Reviews* 87 (February 1933): 30–32.

23. The importance of appearance for these young city women is echoed by another Depression account, which describes "as many as half a dozen girls crowded into one room apartments, sleeping in relays, and pooling their clothes to assemble one outfit presentable enough to pass muster with a prospective employer." Agnes V. O'Shea of the New York City Central Registration Bureau for Women, quoted in Joan M. Crouse, *The Homeless Transient in the Great Depression: New York State, 1929–1941* (Albany: State University of New York Press, 1986), 111.

24. "Tramps," *Railway Age Gazette* 12 (23 April 1880): 217.

25. "Tramps' Leader Found to Be a Woman," *New York Times*, 7 August 1902, 1.

26. "An Unsophisticated Hobo," *Railway Conductor* 18 (January 1901): 26–27.

27. A good example of the hobo mystique appears in Hart Crane's epic poem *The Bridge*, where the sexual and heroic components come together in the image of the "rail squatters ranged" behind his father's cannery: they are "the ancient men" who in their travels "know a body under the wide rain; . . . They lurk across her, knowing her yonder breast. . ." (from the section called "The River" in part 2, "Powhatan's Daughter").

Glen H. Mullin, a university graduate who hoboed for a few months in the mid-1920s to see what "the Road" was like, commented: "To the genuine hobo a train is a thing compounded of magic and beauty. . . . The rattle and swank of a long freight pulling out of the yards, the locomotive black and eager, shoving hard a snorting muzzle along the rails." Quoted in Kenneth Allsop, *Hard Travellin': The Hobo and His History* (London: Hodder and Stoughton, 1967), 249.

28. Rudolf M. Dekker and Lotte C. van de Pol, *The Tradition of Female Transvestism in Early Modern Europe*, trans. Judy Marcure and Lotte van de Pol (Basingstoke and London: Macmillan Press, 1989), 6–7. The fundamental tension between the transvestite (and other marginal figures) and the basic principles that hold society together is described by William Willeford, *The Fool and His Scepter: A Study in Clowns and Jesters and Their Audience* (Evanston: Northwestern University Press, 1969). See, for example, 86: "The transvestism so common in ceremonial clowning and in saturnalian festivals has deep roots in fertility magic. . . . The reversal of sex roles activated the demonic . . . since these roles are fundamental to the cultural life that holds the demonic at a distance."

29. Henriques, *Stews and Strumpets*, 1:131.

30. Bonnie S. Anderson and Judith P. Zinsser, *A History of Their Own: Women in Europe from Prehistory to the Present*, vol. 1 (New York: Harper & Row, 1988), 156–59; Dekker and van de Pol, *Female Transvestism*, 43. Joan followed in the tradition of a long line of female saints who adopted male dress to preserve their virginity and thereby their saintly state (45).

31. Lois W. Banner, *American Beauty* (New York: Knopf, 1983), 94–96.

32. Walter C. Reckless, "Why Women Become Hoboes," *American Mercury* 31 (February 1934): 175–80.

33. Stephanie Golden, "Single Women: The Forgotten Homeless," *City Limits*, January 1988, 15.

34. Higgs, *Glimpses*, 94.

35. Stansell, *City of Women*, 97.

Feminists Before Feminism: Origins and Varieties of Women's Protest in Europe and North America Before the Twentieth Century

Marlene LeGates

THE WORDS *FEMINIST* AND *feminism* are of surprisingly recent origin, appearing for the first time a scant one hundred years ago, but advocates for women's interests have been active for centuries. As Karen Offen has noted, ". . . the ideas and the growth of organized movements for women's emancipation preceded the birth of the words, and consciousness of women's oppression through their subordination to men, . . . preceded both."[1]

Can we find this consciousness as far back as Jesus? He has been described as a feminist, who promoted "the dignity and equality of women in the midst of a very male-dominated society."[2] In the early Christian churches of the second and third centuries, women were probably in the majority[3] and by their presence and their prominence may have persuaded the Church Fathers to adopt their values on celibacy and virginity.[4] Was this an early women's movement? A few centuries later, the medieval church honored such women as Hildegard of Bingen, outstanding artist and theologian, who successfully challenged male authority to assert her leadership over her monastic community; and St. Catherine of Siena, a fourteenth-century prophet and mystic, who denounced church authorities as "fools, worthy of a thousand deaths!"[5] Were these women feminists?

Although these figures may have been conscious of women's oppression, none of them can be called feminists in the sense of conforming to the dictionary definition of *feminism* as "the theory of the political, social, and economic equality of the sexes."[6] Such a definition was foreign to traditional European society, where equality was commonly thought of in only moral or spiritual terms. Not until the late seventeenth and eighteenth centuries did new revolutionary ideas circulate about the possibility of actual equality *between men*. These ideas were to justify the French Revolution of 1789. Before then, however, it was rare to find the idea of full equality between the sexes.

Rather than reject the term *feminism* altogether as inapplicable to traditional Europe, I propose instead to use it to describe "the advocacy of women's interests." This working definition will allow flexibility in describing a feminist consciousness in European society before the nineteenth century. In spite of oppression women found a voice to protest their secondary status. Later, in the nineteenth century, women were able to use ideas inspired by the French

|

Revolution and the Industrial Revolution to lay the foundations of modern feminist theory and the feminist movement. The arguments they raised echo within contemporary feminism.

Traditional Europe

European society before the nineteenth century was self-consciously patriarchal. Authority was invested in men; women were assumed to be inferior. The justification for this assumption came from the two roots of European civilization, the Greco-Roman heritage and the Judeo-Christian tradition.

To the ancient Greeks, women were biologically inferior. Men enjoyed a natural advantage in their ability to reason, which was the foundation of intellectual and political life, because, among other disabilities, women's colder and wetter humors kept blood from rising to their brains. The second-century Greek physician Galen wrote, "The female is less perfect than the male for one, principal reason, because she is colder."[7] Unlike slaves, who lacked judgment because of their unfree status, or children, who lacked it because of their age, women's deficiency was inherent. Aristotle asserted that "the male is by nature fitter for command than the female. . . ."[8]

The Judeo-Christian tradition added to this idea the Genesis account of woman's creation after Adam and from his rib and of Eve's punishment for succumbing to the temptation of the serpent's speech. Accordingly, St. Paul was able to draw on Hebrew law and custom to enjoin women to silence in church. Divine law thus reinforced natural law in excluding women from the public realm and in placing them under male authority. In seventeenth-century England, for example, a woman who left her husband was reprimanded by the Court of the Exchequer Chamber, which referred to "the judgment of Almighty God inflicted upon women, for being first in the transgression."[9]

Women's intellectual and moral inferiority meant that authority was vested in men, but it was vested in some men more than in others since traditional Europe was hierarchical as well as patriarchal. The monarch was the apex of society, mirroring the authority of God, which was further reflected in the authority of every husband and father as head of his family, no matter how low his status in the social hierarchy was. Georges Duby has described medieval marriage as "a miniature monarchy in which the man ruled as king." Indeed, the whole social order was based on the subordination of female to male, as symbolized by the wife's prostration at her husband's feet in the medieval marriage ceremony. Marriage was thus

> the cornerstone of the social edifice. The whole universe was hierarchical, with order maintained throughout all levels by the presumption that every superior could expect reverence and obedience from his subordinate. . . . [10]

Philosophers, theologians, and legal theorists all drew heavily on this tradition. Based on specific commands in both Genesis and St. Paul, the sixteenth-century English "Homily on Matrimony" for the official use of preachers performing marriage ceremonies admonished women, ". . . ye wives be in subjection to obey your husbands . . . for the husband is the head of the woman, as Christ is the head of the Church."[11] In the eighteenth century, the Age of Enlightenment, a subscriber to the English journal *The Spectator* continued the theme: "You must have observed . . . that nothing is more gratifying to the Mind of Man than Power or Dominion, and this I think my self amply possessed of, as I am the Father of a Family."[12] Even after the beginning of the Industrial Revolution, which was to erode traditional society socially and economically, just as the French Revolution was to do ideologically, a British parliamentary committee of 1800 reported, "In his own house [the lowest cottager] finds those who respect him, who obey him; those, to whom he says go, and they go, and come, and they come."[13]

RESTRICTIONS ON WOMEN

In this society, "masterless" women, that is, single women not living under direct male authority, were considered to be a major social problem. Merry Wiesner has described how sixteenth- and seventeenth-century German and French towns enacted legislation intended to prevent unmarried women from taking up residence.[14] There is good evidence to suggest that these masterless women were the main victims of the witch hunt that gripped Europe in the same time period. While older, often widowed women were condemned as witches, young, unmarried women were convicted of infanticide, resulting in "misogynistic campaigns of unique savagery."[15]

If marriage meant some security against these charges, consider that the actions and rights of married women were often restricted. In Duby's study of marriage practices among the medieval nobility, women are reduced to pawns in strategic alliances; they are abducted, raped, and discarded at the whim of men. The only recourse women had was to exploit men's fear of their revenge.[16] Law codes traditionally described a married woman as a minor under her husband's guardianship. In 1768, the English jurist William Blackstone summarized her legal status:

> By marriage the very being or legal existence of a woman is suspended, or at least it is incorporated and consolidated into that of her husband, under whose wing, protection, and cover she performs everything.[17]

Under English common law, married women could not control their own property or earnings or enter into contracts, nor could they claim custody of their children. Under the Napoleonic Code of 1804, married women were ranked with children, felons, and the insane.[18]

LEARNED WOMEN

Any challenge to assumptions about the differences between women and men was seen as inherently threatening to the social order. When the women of the Renaissance dared to acquire an education, they could be described by contemporaries only as contradictions in terms or, as historian Patricia Labalme puts it, as "intellectual transvestite[s]."[19] The late fifteenth-century Italian prodigy Cassandra Fedele was called " 'the miracle of the age'; for a male soul had been born in one of female sex."[20] Earlier in the century, in France, Christine de Pisan was described by contemporaries as a *virilis femina*, or "manly woman," because of her "masculine" literary pursuits. She even said of herself, ". . . now I am truly a man."[21]

These were admirers speaking. Detractors attacked such women as sexually immoral. The fifteenth century scholar Isotta Nogarola was praised by one contemporary as having "overcome your own nature," but another went on to warn, "An eloquent woman is never chaste. . . ."[22] A seventeenth-century Italian doctor wrote, "It is a miracle if a woman in wishing to overcome her sex and in giving herself to learning and the languages, does not stain her soul with vice and filthy abominations."[23]

This association between female learning and lasciviousness was not coincidental. Norman Cohn has described how the early Christians and, later, medieval heretics were inevitably viewed by their enemies as sexually immoral, since anyone challenging any aspect of the status quo was held to be morally deviant as well.[24] In addition, women had to contend with the biological teachings of the ancient Greeks on the insatiable sexual appetite of women. This conviction of female lust sustained the assumption in the witch hunt that women commonly engaged in sexual intercourse with the devil.[25]

Attempts at Protest

In vain did learned women protest. Anna Maria van Schurman, who wrote a book advocating female education in 1639, announced on the title page that the author was a virgin. Later in the seventeenth century, Margaret Cavendish, Duchess of Newcastle, tried to assure her readers, "I am chaste, both by nature and education. . . ." Nonetheless her boldness in writing a book (albeit with her husband's permission) was interpreted by contemporaries as madness. Known as Mad Madge, she retired to the countryside, shunning society.[26]

A sad story is told of Elena Cornaro, who mastered six languages and received a degree in philosophy from the University at Padua in the late seventeenth century, no small feat, considering that women had been barred from universities since their inception. The degree-granting ceremony was attended by huge crowds, since "so learned a woman was a miracle, one might also say a freak." Her comment on all the fuss was that "the highest ornament of woman is silence," and she retired from public view, to work in silence until she died six years later.[27]

The biographer of Aphra Behn, a seventeenth-century English writer who defended the right of women to an education and urged the abolition of the double standard in sexuality, summarizes that a woman if "lucky, if willing to surrender respectability, comfort, approval, perhaps even love; if prepared to risk ridicule, loss of reputation, vilification or attack—might declare her autonomy. . . ."[28]

It is not surprising that, in the face of such social pressure and dependent upon male relatives for their education, many women gave up. Of the approximately thirty women humanists of the Italian Renaissance who can be named or identified, few continued to write or study as older women. The only ones who did were either widowed or nuns.[29]

Some women did take pride in their achievement. The sixteenth-century French writer Louise Labé offered these words of support:

And if anyone reaches the stage at which she is able to put her ideas into writing, she should do it with much thought and should not scorn the glory, but adorn herself with this rather than with chains, rings, and sumptuous clothes, . . ."[30]

Her contemporary Madeleine Nevue told her daughter to "seek out fame and immortality through her writings, . . ."[31] Another French writer, Hélisenne de Crenne, confessed, "Oh, what an inestimable felicity it is to me when I think that my books are circulating in that noble city of Paris: . . ."[32] Such women, however, were the exception rather than the norm.

Opportunities for Empowerment

It is thus difficult to find any practical argument for women's rights or any organized movement to promote them in traditional society. But, in addition to the individuals described above, we do find less self-conscious advocates of women's interests, often in unlikely places. For as well as the dominant traditions subordinating women, there were also traditions empowering them. Periods of social and political change created a more fluid society that offered opportunities that women could exploit.[33]

The history of early Christianity in the second and third centuries reveals a striking influence of women. In contrast to many other religions, where heroic asceticism was confined to men, Christian women could gain renown as virgins and celibates: "As Christians, women and the uneducated could achieve reputations for sexual abstinence as stunning as those achieved by any cultivated male." By dedicating themselves to the church, they rejected traditional social roles as wives and mothers, a revolutionary step in a demographically fragile society where each woman needed to produce five children just to maintain the population.[34] Jo Ann McNamara argues, "Their rejection of husbands, homes, and children was a genuine revolution, which they accomplished despite the preference of the Christian fathers of this period for a more traditional social morality."[35]

Women were also influential as patronesses and teachers, especially within the heretical sects, where they participated equally with men in intellectually intense study groups. Even within the orthodox church, "as distributors of wealth and patrons of individual writers, aristocratic Latin women acted as arbiters of intellectual life to a degree unparalleled in the Greek East."[36]

The centuries following the collapse of the Roman Empire in the West brought political and economic changes that opened up opportunities for propertied women. The disappearance of a centralized state transferred power to aristocratic families, based on land ownership. Changes in inheritance and dowry laws, the usual uncertainty over which son would succeed the monarch, and the tendency of women to outlive their husbands in an age of violence benefited in particular the queens of the early Middle Ages. Pauline Stafford has called the tenth century "a century of women," where for a brief period "Western Europe was ruled by queen-regents." She warns against singling out these women as exceptions: "Societies that favor and permit female rights at all levels offer the greatest opportunities to queens."[37]

Some medieval women were attracted to a group life that challenged patriarchal norms. In the early Middle Ages, nunneries offered women an opportunity to exercise skills as rulers over independent territory as well as to become administrators, scholars, and artists. Although as a result of the eleventh-century papal reform movement, most nunneries were brought under male control, some women created alternatives. Joan Kelly has suggested that the Beguines, celibate laywomen who began forming their own communities in the twelfth century, were "certainly feminist in their opposition to male subjection of women."[38]

As well, women were once again disproportionately attracted to heretical groups. The Guglielmites, thirteenth-century heretics, believed they could be saved only through a woman, their leader, Guglielma of Milan, whose life supposedly paralleled the life of Jesus.[39] We know little about Bloemardine in the Low Countries, whose followers tried to set up a female church.[40] Even more traditional heresies, which counted many women among their followers, must be considered subversive in their denunciation of accepted marital and sexual practices. Duby describes heresy in general as "seen by its contemporaries, and represented to them by its enemies, as a kind of feminist movement." The heretical tendency to treat men and women as equals went "completely counter to the fundamental structure of society."[41]

A more subtle appreciation of women's resistance to male norms emerges from Caroline Bynum's study, *Holy Feast and Holy Fast: The Religious Significance of Food to Medieval Women*. On the basis of her analysis of the food practices of female saints and mystics from the thirteenth to the fifteenth centuries, Bynum concludes that

> by means of food women controlled themselves and their world. Bodily functions, sensations, fertility, and sexuality; husbands, mothers, fathers, and children; religious superiors and confessors; God in his majesty and the boundaries of one's own "self"—all could be manipulated by abstaining from and bestowing food.

In manipulating their circumstances, women either appropriated the dominant patriarchal values for their own use or ignored them in favor of values taken from their own experience. They were not "constrained and impelled by society's notions of the female as inferior." Bynum is in fact describing a woman's culture, in many ways autonomous and liberating.[42]

Even women who confirmed in their own words "society's notions of the female as inferior" were not necessarily constrained by those notions in their behavior. The extraordinary twelfth-century abbess and mystic Hildegard of Bingen, mentioned at the beginning of this article, summarized the dominant ideology:

> For when God looked upon man he was well pleased, for man was made in his image and likeness. . . . But at her creation woman partook of a mixture of the two [man and God]; she is a different creature, created through another than God. . . . The man therefore presides over the tribunal of the world, ruling all creatures, while the woman is under his mastery and subject to him.[43]

Hildegard's life as an administrator, writer, consultant, and traveling preacher defies any notion of subordination. In fact, her biographer conjectures that Hildegard used the notion of female inferiority to justify her role as a prophet, since it was particularly appropriate for God to speak through the weak and despised.[44] When her decision to move her nuns to Rupertsberg was opposed by the local populace and by the authorities, she claimed authority for her, or rather God's, decision from a divine vision to overcome her opposition.

THE *QUERELLE DES FEMMES*

From the fifteenth century on, however, there was a philosophical and literary challenge to patriarchal traditions in the form of the prowoman side of the *querelle des femmes,* or the debate about woman. This discussion about the virtues and vices of women goes back to the ancient Greeks and Romans and was conducted entirely by men as an often abstract literary exercise. However, "the result of [the misogynists'] repeated attacks was a truly hostile opinion of women that was not exclusively 'literary' but affected the mentality of readers and consequently attitudes between the sexes." The result was to spur women to enter the debate and to lead the "prowoman" participants, both male and female, to examine patriarchal traditions.[45]

The first known woman to participate was Christine de Pisan, who wrote in 1404 that she was plunged into depression after reading misogynistic accounts of woman's infamy. Eventually her own experience and that of other women led her to discredit the misogynistic descriptions and to see them as products of a male culture rather than as eternal and applicable truths. Her feminism was a refusal "to accept insults and contempt in silence. . . ."[46] Historians Katherine Henderson and Barbara McManus have described similarly the contributions of prowoman writers in the debate in sixteenth- and seventeenth-century England who followed Pisan's example: "Women had to find a sense of self esteem within established value systems and to play the game by men's rules before they could challenge the old values and create their own rules."[47]

The prowoman arguments in the debate were surprisingly wide ranging. Most commentators argued for a theoretical equality between the sexes, based on the religious assumption of spiritual equality or equal capacity for virtue. The specific justification came from the alternate account of woman's creation in Genesis, that woman and man were created simultaneously and equally in God's image.[48]

Further, inequalities were thought to be the result of social conditioning. Woman's lack of access to education, rather than her lesser capacity for reason, was commonly denounced as responsible for her perceived inferiority. Some writers went further and attributed her inferior status to men's control of economic resources. A few writers even argued for the superiority of innate female virtues such as piety, compassion, and pacifism, but most argued for the determining importance of environment as opposed to biology.[49]

The debate ranged across Europe from the fifteenth to the eighteenth centuries. But its arguments remained theoretical and without practical importance. The context was literary and philosophical, and writers who advanced a seemingly radical justification for woman's intellectual equality often followed it with a conservative justification for the continuance of male govern-ance.[50] For example, whereas Pisan criticized misogyny as unjust and inaccurate, she nonetheless endorsed the divine order that sanctioned women's subordination: "God has . . . ordained man and woman to serve Him in different offices . . . each in their ordained task," and she urged women to "be humble and patient."[51]

Similarly, Mary Astell, a late seventeenth-century advocate of the right of women to education, urged that they have access to education as good in quality as that offered to men. She nonetheless noted that "she then who Marrys, ought to lay it down for an indisputable Maxim, that her Husband must govern absolutely and intirely, and that she has nothing else to do but to Please and Obey."[52] Her goal for women was quite modest: "to choose a husband wisely, to live with him on a basis of mutual respect and to educate her children properly."[53]

Since patriarchy was so closely tied to hierarchy and authoritarianism, any more thorough attempt at attacking the former would have to wait until the other components of traditional society were under attack as well. The political ideology of liberalism launched this challenge in the course of the seventeenth and eighteenth centuries in the context of the English, American, and French Revolutions. Against the justification of absolute monarchy as divine in origin and of social privilege as based on birth, liberalism argued that society is based on consent and that all men are created equal. As Karen Offen noted, "The vocabulary of feminism—liberty, equality, emancipation, liberation, justice, sisterhood—is directly appropriated from the vocabulary of the European Enlightenment and the French Revolution."[54]

However, while challenging authoritarianism and hierarchy, liberals stopped short of criticizing patriarchy, since *man* was never taken to mean *human being*. The seventeenth-century English political philosopher John Locke followed Aristotelian notions of women's inherent inferiority and denied that women had rational faculties equal to those of men. Both Locke and the framers of the 1789 French "Declaration of the Rights of Man and the Citizen" understood *man* to mean a small percentage of propertied males.[55] Herself an opponent of liberalism, Mary Astell summed up its hypocrisy: ". . . if absolute Sovereignty be not necessary in a State, how comes it to be so in a Family? . . . *if all men are born free,* how is it that all Women are born Slaves?"[56]

Mary Wollstonecraft, in her *Vindication of the Rights of Woman* in 1792, called "the first major work of feminist theory in history,"[57] challenged the gender bias of liberalism, which insisted on "considering females rather as women than human creatures." In contrast Wollstonecraft proposed to consider them "part of the human species" by applying to them the same standards of reason and virtue required for men. "I shall first consider women in the grand light of human creatures, who, in common with men, are placed on this earth to unfold their faculties; . . ." She appealed, "Let them be taught to respect themselves as rational creatures."[58] At the same time, Wollstonecraft went further than her predecessors by calling on the state to recognize women's claim to equality by implementing free universal primary education and demanding the right for women to achieve financial independence if they chose. However, Wollstonecraft was not interested in political rights or in challenging traditional gender roles. John Charvet summarizes her goal:

> Wollstonecraft's new woman with an educated mind, independent character and capacity for self-support will marry for affection and with respect for

her husband and, instead of being idolized as a pure angel while being despised as an inferior mind, will be a better companion to her husband and mother to her children.[59]

In both her demand for equal treatment with men and in her demand for respect for women's role within the family, Wollstonecraft foreshadowed the two currents of the nineteenth-century women's movement, or, as it was called in North America at the time, the woman movement.

The Woman Movement

American women who participated in the movement to abolish slavery were among those who carried Wollstonecraft's ideas on women's rights further. The abolitionist Lucretia Mott kept a copy of Wollstonecraft's book on display in her home for forty years.[60] She and her coworkers, kept from participating fully in the movement because of their sex, extended the language of liberalism to apply to women. In 1848 at Seneca Falls, New York, over two hundred women and men organized a Woman's Rights Convention, which drafted a Declaration of Sentiments modeled on the Declaration of Independence. In Britain John Stuart Mill, who successfully ran for public office on a platform of female suffrage, used the same language of equality to argue in 1869 that

> the legal subordination of one sex to the other—is wrong in itself, . . . and ought to be replaced by the principle of perfect equality admitting no power or privilege on the one side nor disability on the other . . . we ought . . . not to ordain that to be born a girl instead of a boy, any more than to be born black instead of white, or a commoner instead of a nobleman, shall decide the person's position through all life—. . .[61]

These reformers organized campaigns for the right of married women to control their property, the right of women to an education and suitable employment opportunities, and the right of women to vote. But many feminists went further. Elizabeth Cady Stanton criticized the Bible as "the central force in perpetuating an ideology of women's subjection" and addressed her prayers to a Heavenly Mother as well as to a Heavenly Father.[62] Both she and Amelia Bloomer called for and adopted dress reform, enjoying two years of "incredible freedom" before abandoning it because of "the persistent persecution and petty annoyances suffered at every turn."[63] British feminists attacked the double standard by seeking to repeal laws that permitted the detention and compulsory medical examination of prostitutes. Unlike their contemporaries who condemned prostitutes as morally flawed, feminist repealers regarded prostitutes as victims of male oppression and denounced the laws that unjustly "punish the sex who are the victims of a vice, and leave unpunished the sex who are the main causes, . . ."[64] Even after these laws were repealed in 1884, feminists continued to challenge the popular assumption of an uncontrollable male sex drive. They protested marital rape and the sexual abuse of children and lobbied to make incest a crime under English law.[65]

Unlike earlier protesters, nineteenth-century women had both the idea and the opportunity. The political and economic revolutions of the late eighteenth and early nineteenth centuries made it possible to challenge the idea of hierarchical human relationships as God-given and unalterable. Reformers could envision a world in the making, a future of human design, based on human needs and desires. In this environment women were not slow to demand changes for themselves. The German reformer Louise Otto-Peters declared in 1849, "In the midst of the great revolution in which we find ourselves, women will find themselves forgotten, if they forget to think of themselves!"[66]

The opportunity was provided by the Industrial Revolution and the changes it effected in society. Leisure, affluence, and education were possible now for a growing segment of middle- and upper-class women. While preindustrial upper-class women may have enjoyed wealth and perhaps learning, their lives as managers of complex households provided scant leisure. Although working-class women became involved in the suffrage campaign near its end, the women's movement was composed for the most part of a relatively privileged and homogeneous group. It was their shared culture, rooted in domesticity, that informed the other strand of nineteenth-century feminism.

Throughout the nineteenth century in Europe, Canada, and the United States, feminists exhibited a tendency to shift from an equal rights argument based on the similarity of the sexes to a position that stressed the differences between women and men. While it is impossible to know to what extent this shift came from tactical considerations or from ideological conviction, by the end of the century most feminists emphasized the importance of real or potential motherhood in endowing woman with special qualities, namely, a spirit of service and selflessness. These proponents of maternal, social, or relational feminism, as it has been variously called, stressed the importance of winning the vote in order to give women the opportunity to use their talents for the benefit of society as a whole.

One origin of maternal feminism was the separate spheres of ideology that accompanied the Industrial Revolution and the separation of home and work. The home was seen as a sanctuary from the competitive struggles of the business and political worlds; women in their capacity as wives and mothers came to symbolize the virtues of selflessness and compassion that men had had to renounce. For women the idealization of the female was perhaps also a way to compensate themselves for their economic marginalization as the Industrial Revolution moved production from the home to the factory. The idea of separate male and female spheres endowed women with a sense of moral superiority, reinforced a female network and culture, and created a sense of gender solidarity.

It did more. It encouraged reformers to see the problems caused by industrialism and urbanization and, in North America, large-scale immigration as male-created, as the results of allowing the masculine traits of individualism and competitiveness to flourish unchecked. The American reformer Mary E. Lease spoke what many thought: "Thank God we women are blameless for this political muddle you men have dragged us into. . . ."[67]

There were other influences as well. In the United States evangelical Christianity popularized the idea of a female morality. In the religious revivals of the 1820s and 1830s, the image of the suffering Christ epitomized feminine virtue based on suffering, loving, and forgiving.[68] In Europe a more conservative political culture made arguments based on women's familial and communal role more sympathetic than arguments based on an individualist ethic.[69]

All of these ideas were rooted in conservative traditions. But whereas antifeminists argued that women were special because they were unsullied by the dirt of politics and business and should remain so, feminists turned the argument around to justify political activity. Because women had the ability to make a difference, they also had the moral obligation to use their virtues to clean up the mess men had made. In the words of Nellie McClung, a Canadian suffragist:

> Women have cleaned up things since time began; and if women ever get into politics there will be a cleaning-out of pigeon-holes and of forgotten corners, on which the dust of years has fallen, and the sound of the political carpet-beater will be heard in the land.[70]

Reformers arguing in this tradition channeled most of their efforts into the temperance or municipal housekeeping movements, working to reduce drinking and to provide social welfare for their communities. Many became more rigorous proponents of sexual purity, arguing for the end of legalized prostitution or for censorship in the arts. The *Woman's Journal,* edited by American suffragist Lucy Stone, attacked Sarah Bernhardt as an unmarried mother and upheld legislation in the 1870s that restricted discussion of sexual subjects.[71] Historian Olive Banks has suggested that in Britain men were reluctant to give women the vote precisely because they feared the effects of such stringent morality.[72]

The tension within the woman movement between arguments based on similarity and arguments based on difference is echoed in contemporary feminism. Equal rights language is still used in the fight to end economic, legal, and sexual discrimination. The logical extension of equal treatment is a gender-free society. In contrast, those who are today called cultural feminists recognize and advocate an identifiable and specifically female ethic and experience. Although they are more concerned than their predecessors with rooting these differences in culture rather than biology, their sentiments may not be that different from those of Margaret Fuller, a nineteenth-century American transcendentalist, who claimed, "Were [women] free, were they wise fully to develop the strength and beauty of Woman; they would never wish to be men, or manlike."[73]

Many contemporary cultural feminists have been inspired by Carol Gilligan's description of women's pattern of moral reasoning in terms of connection and relationships, distinct from the male model of separation and rights.[74] Three-quarters of a century earlier Charlotte Perkins Gilman described "the basic feminine impulse" as "to gather, to put together, to construct; the basic masculine impulse is to scatter, to disseminate, to destroy."[75] Contemporary feminists who apply Gilligan's insights to subjects ranging from politics to science would fit right into the earlier movement. Josephine Donovan, for example, has recently explored the possibility "that a feminist political ethic may be derived from women's traditional culture, practice and experience";[76] and Margaret Benston, among others, argued that a feminist critique of science would correct the reductionist and mechanistic bias that has helped to dehumanize our social world.[77] Are these ideas so different from those expressed by Elizabeth Cady Stanton, who declared that if women were "once again permitted to rule, we would have a civilization at last in which ignorance, poverty and crime will exist no more . . . ."?[78] Even the claim in 1915 of Dr. Augusta Stowe, the first woman to graduate from medical school in Canada, that "when women have a vote in national and international affairs, war will cease forever"[79] is not so far removed from those who link women and pacifism today.

What is different, however is that nineteenth-century feminists seem not to have been unduly concerned about the tension between the two positions. Many of them in fact argued from both. For example, Stanton made a more consistent argument from equal rights than most feminists and lambasted the "law-makers and savants of the republic," who "can not take in the idea that men and women are alike; . . ."[80] Nancy Cott has quoted Harriet Laidlaw, who argued in 1912 that "insofar as women were like men, they deserved the same rights, and insofar as they differed, women ought to represent themselves."[81] It has been pointed out by many historians that feminists could not afford to set the terms of the debate and that their equivocacy was in fact a "functional ambiguity" that allowed them to adapt their arguments to the situation.[82]

One should note, however, that the term *feminism* first gained currency in the United States among women who reacted against the emphasis in the women's movement on morality and duties rather than on individualism and rights.[83] Today feminists are split as to whether the term properly applies to those who have espoused an individualist ethic and who embrace "gender justice" rather than "woman justice" or whether it can incorporate those who argue for equality while celebrating difference.[84] The homogeneous background of earlier feminists made it easier for them to refer to "woman" as a unity and to ignore the differences of class, ethnicity, and status that inform feminist debates today.[85]

Conclusion

Feminism took so long to develop because it challenged the most fundamental assumptions about social order. Throughout traditional society there are many examples of individual protest, but until the order itself was challenged by liberal ideas of legal equality between men, there was little possibility of conceiving of an alternative to patriarchal institutions. In its earliest form, the *querelle des femmes,* feminism could only counter misogyny.

The eighteenth-century political revolutions and the nineteenth-century Industrial Revolution created new foundations for feminism and gave it its two-sided aspect, arguments from equality and arguments from difference. The ability of feminists to utilize different grounds indicates their strength and determination as well as their flexibility. Whatever the context, women managed to articulate a reasoned argument for increased respect and better treatment.

Patriarchal assumptions die hard. The still pervasive association of feminists as "unfeminine" echoes the "unsexed women" of the nineteenth century and the "virile" women of the Renaissance. In its demand for gender equity, feminism continues to pose a challenge to the social order. In understanding its revolutionary challenge, we can the more appreciate the efforts of earlier feminists.

NOTES

1. Karen Offen, "Liberty, Equality, and Justice for Women: The Theory and Practice of Feminism in Nineteenth-Century Europe," in R. Bridenthal, C. Koonz, and S. Stuard, eds., *Becoming Visible: Women in European History* (Boston: Houghton Mifflin, 1987, Second Edition), 356, quote on p. 336.

2. Leonard Swidler, "jesus was a feminist," *Catholic World* (January 1971), 183.

3. Robin Lane Fox, *Pagans and Christians in the Mediterranean World from the Second Century AD to the Conversion of Constantine* (London: Penguin Books, 1986), 310.

4. See below, 496.

5. For Hildegard, see below, 297–298; Joseph Berrigan, "The Tuscan Visionary: Saint Catherine of Siena," in Katharina Wilson, ed., *Medieval Women Writers* (Athens, Ga.: University of Georgia Press, 1984), 261, 262.

6. *Webster's Third New International Dictionary of the English Language Unabridged,* vol. 1 (Chicago: Encyclopedia Britannica, Inc., 1986), 837.

7. Quoted in Bonnie Anderson and Judith Zinsser, *A History of Their Own: Women in Europe from Prehistory to the Present,* vol. 1 (New York: Harper & Row, 1988), 30.

8. Aristotle, "Politics," Book 1, Chapter 12, in *The Works of Aristotle,* vol. 2 (Chicago: Encyclopedia Britannica, Inc., 1952), 453.

9. Julia O'Faolain and Lauro Martines, eds., *Not in God's Image: Women in History from the Greeks to the Victorians* (New York: Harper & Row, 1973), 230.

10. Georges Duby, *The Knight, the Lady and the Priest: The Making of Modern Marriage in Medieval France* (New York: Random House, 1983), 152, first quote p. 99, second quote p. 215.

11. Quoted in Lawrence Stone, *The Family, Sex and Marriage in England 1500–1800* (New York: Harper & Row, 1977), 198.

12. Donald F. Bond, ed., *The Spectator* (Oxford: Clarendon Press, 1965), 273.

13. Quoted in Harold Perkin, *The Origins of Modern English Society 1780–1880* (Toronto: University of Toronto Press, 1972), 39.

14. Merry Wiesner, "Spinning out Capital: Women's Work in the Early Modern Economy," in Bridenthal, Koonz, and Stuard, 228–29.

15. William Monter, "Protestant Wives, Catholic Saints, and the Devil's Handmaid: Women in the Age of Reformations," in ibid., 213.

16. Duby, 106.

17. Quoted in Marilyn J. Boxer and Jean H. Quataert, "Overview, 1750–1890," in Marilyn J. Boxer and Jean H. Quataert, eds., *Connecting Spheres. Women in the Western World, 1500 to the Present* (Oxford: Oxford University Press, 1987), 126.

18. Bonnie Anderson and Judith Zinsser, *A History of Their Own: Women in Europe from Prehistory to the Present,* vol. 2 (New York: Harper & Row, 1988), 149.

19. Patricia Labalme, "Introduction," in Patricia Labalme, ed., *Beyond Their Sex: Learned Women of the European Past* (New York: New York University Press, 1980), 5. Much earlier a "masculine" education was thought to make women more holy in thus making them more like men (Anderson and Zinsser, vol. 1, 184).

20. Margaret King, "Book-Lined Cells: Women and Humanism in the Early Italian Renaissance," in Labalme, 76.

21. Quoted in Labalme, "Introduction," 5.

22. Both quoted in King, 76–77.

23. Quoted in Patricia Labalme, "Women's Roles in Early Modern Venice: An Exceptional Case," in Labalme, 139.

24. Norman Cohn, *Europe's Inner Demons: An Enquiry Inspired by the Great Witch-Hunt* (New York: Basic Books, 1975), 12, 15.

25. See J. Sprenger and H. Kramer, *Malleus Maleficarum,* trans. M. Summers (London: Pushkin Press, 1928), 41–47; and Ilza Veith, *Hysteria: The History of a Disease* (Chicago: University of Chicago Press, 1965).

26. Angeline Goreau, "Aphra Behn: A Scandal to Modesty (c. 1640–1689)," in Dale Spender, ed., *Feminist Theorists: Three Centuries of Key Women Thinkers* (London: The Women's Press, 1983), 20, 17 (quote), 18.

27. Quoted in Labalme, 142–43; see also Anderson and Zinsser, vol. 2, 86–87.

28. Goreau, 8–9.

29. King, 67–69.

30. Jeanne Prine, "Poet of Lyon: Louise Labe," in Katharina M. Wilson, ed., *Women Writers of the Renaissance and Reformation* (Athens, Ga.: University of Georgia Press, 1987), 149.

31. Anne R. Larsen, "The French Humanist Scholars: Les Dames de Roches," in ibid., 234.

32. Kittye Kelle Robbins-Herring, "Champion of Women's Rights: Hélisenne de Crenne," in ibid., 211.

33. For a discussion of the former, see Anderson and Zinsser, vol. 1, 52–77. Examples of more fluid conditions of which women took advantage occurred in the early Middle Ages (Bridenthal, Koonz, and Stuard, 131) and in the sixteenth and seventeenth centuries (Anderson and Zinsser, vol. 1, 182).

34. Peter Brown, *The Body and Society: Men, Women and Sexual Renunciation in Early Christianity* (New York: Columbia University Press, 1988), 61, 6.

35. Jo Ann McNamara, *A New Song: Celibate Women in the First Three Christian Centuries* (New York: Harrington Park Press, 1985), 65.

36. Brown, 345.

37. Pauline Stafford, *Queens, Concubines, and Dowagers: The King's Wife in the Early Middle Ages* (Athens, Ga.: University of Georgia Press, 1983), 141.

38. Joan Kelly, "Early Feminist Theory and the Querelle des Femmes, 1400–1789," *Signs* 8, no. 1 (Autumn 1982), 6fn.

39. Stephen Wessley, "The Thirteenth-Century Guglielmites: Salvation Through Women," in Derek Baker, ed., *Medieval Women* (Oxford: Basil Blackwell, 1978), 299.

40. Caroline Bynum, *Holy Feast and Holy Fast: The Religious Significance of Food to Medieval Women* (Athens, Ga.: University of Georgia Press, 1987), 229.

41. Duby, 109.

42. Bynum, 193–94, 295.

43. Quoted in Carolly Erickson, *The Medieval Vision: Essays in History and Perception* (New York: Oxford University Press, 1976), 211.

44. Sabina Flanagan, *Hildegard of Bingen, 1098–1179: A Visionary Life* (London: Routledge, 1989), 13–15.

45. The following account relies mainly on Constance Jordan, *Renaissance Feminism: Literary Texts and Political Models* (Ithaca, N.Y.: Cornell University Press, 1990). The quote is from E. V. Telle, *Marguerite d'Angouleme* (Toulouse: Lion, 1937), 23, quoted in Jordan, 87.

46. Beatrice Gottlieb, "The Problem of Feminism in the Fifteenth Century," in Julius Kirshner and Suzanne Wemple, eds., *Women of the Medieval World: Essays in Honor of John H. Mundy* (Oxford: Basil Blackwell, 1985), 346.

47. Katherine Henderson and B. McManus, *Half Human Kind: Contexts and Texts of the Controversy About Women in England 1540–1640* (Urbana: University of Illinois Press, 1985), 45.

48. Jordan; see, for example, 89, 122, 132, 200, 243, 283–84, 293.

49. Ibid., passim.

50. Jordan, 287, 295.

51. Quoted in Gottlieb, 354.

52. Mary Astell, "Some Reflections upon Marriage," in Bridget Hill, ed., *The First English Feminist: Reflections upon Marriage and Other Writings* (Aldershott, England: Gower/Maurice Temple Smith, 1986), 116.

53. Florence Smith, *Mary Astell* (New York: Columbia University Press, 1916), 102. Astell's educational goals weren't achieved until Girton College for Women was established at Cambridge in 1874.

54. Offen, "Liberty, Equality, and Justice," 340.

55. C. B. Macpherson, *The Political Theory of Possessive Individualism* (Oxford: Oxford University Press, 1962), 262; Teresa Brennan and Carol Pateman, "'Mere Auxiliaries to the Commonwealth': Women and the Origins of Liberalism," *Political Studies* 27, no. 2 (June 1979), 195; Zillah Eisenstein, *The Radical Future of Liberal Feminism* (New York: Longman, 1981), 33–54.

56. Astell in Hill, 76.

57. Josephine Donovan, *Feminist Theory: The Intellectual Traditions of American Feminism* (New York: Frederick Ungar, 1985), 1.

58. Mary Wollstonecraft, *A Vindication of the Rights of Woman* (New York: W. W. Norton & Company, 1967), first quote p. 31, second quote p. 84, third quote p. 33, fourth quote p. 150.

59. Ibid., 20.

60. Olive Banks, *Faces of Feminism: A Study of Feminism as a Social Movement* (Oxford: Basil Blackwell, 1986), 29.

61. John Stuart Mill, "The Subjection of Women," in Alice Rossi, ed., *Essays on Sex Equality: John Stuart Mill and Harriet Taylor Mill* (Chicago: University of Chicago Press, 1970), 125, 145.

62. Quoted in Donovan, 38.

63. Elizabeth Cady Stanton, *Eighty Years and More: Reminiscences 1815–1897* (New York: Schocken Books, 1971), 201–2.

64. Patricia Hollis, *Women in Public: The Women's Movement 1850–1900: Documents of the Victorian Women's Movement* (London: George Allen & Unwin, 1979), 208.

65. At this time under English law, father-daughter incest was often punished less severely than stealing a loaf of bread. Sheila Jeffreys, *The Spinster and Her Enemies: Feminism and Sexuality 1880–1930* (London: Pandora, 1985), 57. This feminist campaign had success, and an anti-incest law was achieved in 1908 (Jeffreys, 79).

66. Susan Groag Bell and Karen M. Offen, eds., *Women, the Family, and Freedom: The Debate in Documents,* vol. 1, 1750–1880 (Stanford, Calif.: Stanford University Press, 1983), 263.

67. Quoted in Mari Jo Buhle, *Women and American Socialism, 1870–1920* (Urbana: University of Illinois Press, 1981), 89.

68. Sara Evans, *Born for Liberty: A History of Women in America* (New York: The Free Press, 1989), 72–73.

69. Offen, "Liberty, Equality, and Justice," 336–38, 343.

70. Nellie McClung, *In Times Like These* (Toronto: Toronto University Press, 1972), 48.

71. Banks, 70.

72. Banks, 70, 131.

73. Quoted in Donovan, 34.

74. Carol Gilligan, *In a Different Voice: Psychological Theory and Women's Development* (Cambridge, Mass.: Harvard University Press, 1982).

75. Quoted in Donovan, 46.

76. Ibid., 171.

77. Margaret Benston, "Feminism and the Critique of Scientific Method," in A. Miles and G. Finn, eds., *Feminism in Canada: From Pressure to Politics* (Montreal: Black Rose Books, 1982), 55–58.

78. Quoted in Donovan, 39.

79. Quoted in R. C. Brown and R. Cook, *Canada, 1896–1921: A Nation Transformed* (Toronto: McClelland and Steward, 1974), 298.

80. Ellen Carol DuBois, ed., *Elizabeth Cady Stanton, Susan B. Anthony: Correspondence, Writings, Speeches* (New York: Schocken, 1981), 50.

81. Nancy Cott, *The Grounding of Modern Feminism* (New Haven, Conn.: Yale University Press, 1987), 21.

82. Cott, 20. See also Offen, "Equality, Liberty, and Justice," 339, 357, 361; and Deborah Gorham, " 'Singing up the Hill,' " in R. Francis and D. Smith, eds., *Readings in Canadian History: Post-Confederation* (Toronto: Holt, Rinehart and Winston, 1990), 168.

83. Cott, 39ff.

84. See Judith Stacey, "Are Feminists Afraid to Leave Home? The Challenge of Conservative Pro-Family Feminism," in Juliet Mitchell and Ann Oakley, eds., *What Is Feminism?* (New York: Pantheon, 1986), 208–37; and also the exchange between Ellen Dubois, Karen Offen, and Nancy Cott in "Comment and Reply," in *Signs* 14, no. 1 (Autumn 1988), 195–209.

85. Cott, 9.

From Suffrage to Women's Liberation: Feminism in Twentieth-Century America

Jo Freeman

THE SUFFRAGE movement was not a united movement. It was a coalition of different people and organizations that worked together for a few intense years around the common goal of votes for women. Approximately 95 percent of the participants in the movement were organized under the umbrella of the National American Woman Suffrage Association. Throughout most of its history this organization pursued the vote on a state-by-state basis. In 1916 NAWSA President Carrie Chapman Catt presented her "winning plan" to focus on a federal amendment while continuing with state work. She mobilized the coalition into high gear until success was achieved in 1920.

Her plan was stimulated by the challenge of Alice Paul, who had returned to the United States in 1913 after an apprenticeship in the British suffrage movement. There she had learned the value of publicity to be obtained by marches, civil disobedience, and hunger strikes. Paul persuaded NAWSA to let her organize a congressional committee to pursue a federal amendment, and when she felt support for her activities was insufficient, broke off to create a separate Congressional Union. One of Paul's strategies was to mobilize women in the states where women could vote. From her British experience she adopted the idea of holding the party in power responsible for failing to pass the federal amendment. Since President Wilson was a Democrat, she organized enfranchised women to vote against *all* Democrats in 1914, including those members of Congress who supported suffrage. In 1916 a separate National Woman's Party was created for this purpose, but Wilson was reelected, carrying ten of the twelve states in which women could vote for president by significant margins.

During World War I NAWSA leaders worked both for Suffrage and in support of the war effort. The congressional union worked only for Suffrage. They flouted Wilson's slogan that the purpose of the war was "to make the world safe for democracy" by standing outside the White House with banners reading "How long must women wait for democracy?" The rate of state enfranchisement of women accelerated, and pressure on the president and Congress intensified. In January 1918 President Wilson declared his support for a federal amendment, and later that month the House passed the amendment without a single vote to spare. It was not until May of 1919 that the Senate did likewise. A ferocious state-by-state battle ensued to get the three-fourths necessary to ratify the Suffrage Amendment. It almost didn't make it, but by two votes Tennessee became the thirty-sixth state. On August 26, 1920, the Nineteenth Amendment joined the Constitution, and twenty-six million American women became eligible to vote. Carrie Chapman Catt calculated that it took

57 years of campaigning

56 referenda to male voters

480 efforts to get state legislatures to submit suffrage amendments

277 campaigns to get state party conventions to include women's suffrage planks

47 campaigns to get state constitutional conventions to write women's suffrage into state constitutions

30 campaigns to get presidential party conventions to adopt women's suffrage planks into party platforms

19 successive campaigns with nineteen successive Congresses

NAWSA disbanded. Some of its members reorganized into a nonpartisan, nonsectarian League of Women Voters to provide women with political education and work for a broad range of social reforms. Other members, including Catt, turned their energies to working for peace. Many more returned to the organizations from whence they had come, such as the Women's Trade Union League, the General Federation of Women's Clubs, and the National Consumer's League. Still others founded new organizations, such as the National Federation of Business and Professional Women, and separate women's organizations within different occupations. These and several other women's organizations joined together to form the Woman's Joint Congressional Committee, which was described by the *Ladies Home Journal* as the "most highly organized and powerful lobby ever seen in Washington." Among their major achievements on the federal level were the Sheppard-Towner Maternity and Infancy Protection Act (1921), equal nationality rights for married women (1922), and the Child Labor Amendment (1925). The WJCC along with other progressive organizations were repeatedly attacked as socialist and subversive. These attacks took their toll; as the progressive impulse faded, many women returned to private life. The Congressional Union–National Woman's Party reorganized itself into a new National Woman's Party and continued its work for women's equality with men.

Survival During the Doldrums

Between the suffrage movement and the women's liberation movement, the paramount feminist issue was the Equal Rights Amendment. It was first proposed in 1921 by Alice Paul, who had decided that the next step was removal of all *legal* discrimination against women and that the most efficient way to do this was with another federal amendment. The ERA was aimed at the plethora of state laws and common law rules that restricted women's jury service; limited their rights to control their own property, contract, sue, and keep their own name and domicile if married; gave them inferior guardianship rights over their children; and generally stigmatized them as lesser citizens. It was vigorously opposed by progressive reformer Florence Kelley and her allies in the National Consumers' League, the Women's Trade Union League, and the League of Women Voters, because she feared it would also destroy the protective labor laws for which she had fought all her life.

The preponderance of these laws limited the hours women could work each day and each week, prohibited night work for women, and removed women from certain occupations altogether. Some states also required minimum wages for women only, though the Supreme Court declared this unconstitutional in 1923. Although many of these laws had passed before suffrage, Kelley and other progressives had joined the suffrage movement only after they became convinced that women must have the vote in order to pass more laws to improve the condition of working women. They were not about to see their decades of effort undermined by the utopian ideals of the militants.

The NWP was not initially hostile to protective labor laws; many members had fought for such laws in their home states. Early versions of the ERA exempted these laws from coverage. However, Kelley could not be convinced that *any* version would not be misinterpreted by the courts, and after much thought Paul and her colleagues decided that *any* exemption would become a universal exemption. Besides, she concluded, protective labor laws really hurt women more than they helped, because they encouraged employers to hire men. By the time the ERA was first introduced into Congress in December 1923, it had divided women's organizations into two warring camps, who fought each other to a stalemate for almost five decades.

The battle was more than a disagreement over what women wanted. Behind it was a fundamental disagreement over the meaning of equality. The NWP favored absolute equality of opportunity. Women would never achieve economic independence as long as laws treated them like children in need of protection. The reformers accepted fundamental differences in physiology and family role as incontrovertible. They noted that the female labor force was largely young, unmarried, and transitional. Labor unions did not want to organize women because they were not permanent workers and did not earn enough to pay dues. Thus collective bargaining did not offer the same protection for women workers that it potentially could for men. Only legislation could save women workers from gross exploitation by industrial capitalism.

Though both women, their followers, and allies had roots in the progressive movement, they came from different generations and had different world views. Kelley called herself a socialist, though her allies in the women's organizations would not have used that term after it became tainted by the red scare of the 1920s. Yet her view of women was solidly grounded in the conservative conception of the sexes that saw each as fundamentally different from the other and properly occupying separate spheres. Whereas Kelley accepted the status quo, Paul was a feminist visionary; she saw what women could be, undistracted by their current reality. She pursued this vision monolithically. With rare and minor exceptions she ignored any political issue other than removal of all legal barriers to women's equality and economic independence. During the 1920s she stifled any discussion within the NWP on the disenfranchisement of black women or the suppression of birth control information. Despite her commitment to anticommunism, during the 1950s she thwarted an attempt to broaden the base of the now minuscule NWP by including patriotic issues.

Hindered by declining numbers and influence, the NWP kept the feminist faith burning through some very hard times. The Depression led to an upsurge of extant public opinion against the employment of married women, or any woman who had a male relative to support her. Such women were thought to be taking jobs away from men, who had families to support. The advent of the Roosevelt administration brought to power Kelley's disciples Frances

Perkins and Molly Dewson, not to mention Eleanor Roosevelt, who, while a role model for activist women, thought the NWP "a perfectly useless organization." Their strong opposition to the ERA was based in part on their perception that it was primarily a class issue and not one of sex equality. As social reformers, they argued that requiring equal rights under law would favor upper-class professional and executive women at the expense of working-class women who needed legal protection. While they acknowledged that there were many state laws that unfairly distinguished between men and women, they felt that these should be eliminated state by state and law by law.

World War II saw the suspension of protective labor laws and a renewed interest in both the ERA and working women. Several organizations shifted their opinion from con to neutral to pro, following the lead of the National Federation of Business and Professional Women (BPW) in 1937. Many of the opposing organizations ceased to be active. The Republican party first endorsed the ERA at its 1940 national nominating convention; the Democrats followed in 1944. The Senate voted on the ERA for the first time in 1946. It failed, and when it came up again in 1950, opponents were ready with a crippling "rider" to exempt all laws for the protection and benefit of women. This was added on the Senate floor in both 1950 and 1953; after that the ERA never left committee. In the meantime, the NWP went through two crippling internal disputes involving purges and lawsuits. Leadership of the opposition was taken over by the AFL-CIO and traditional liberal organizations such as the ACLU. The Women's Bureau of the Department of Labor, a leading opponent since the ERA's inception, briefly withdrew during the Eisenhower administration (the only sitting president to endorse the ERA before 1972) but resumed its leadership role with vigor when Kennedy appointed Esther Peterson as its director after he became president in 1961.

Peterson had two items on her agenda for women: passage of an Equal Pay Act and derailment of the ERA. The first was achieved in 1963 after two years of concerted lobbying and compromises. Her strategy for attaining the second was the creation of a President's Commission on the Status of Women, which would propose a program of constructive action that would make the ERA unnecessary. The PCSW's final report urged "judicial clarification" of women's legal rights rather than a blanket declaration of legal equality via a constitutional amendment, along with a lengthy list of other objectives. In the process of reaching these conclusions, the commission thoroughly documented women's second-class status; its 1963 report, *American Women,* became something of a Government Printing Office best seller. It was followed by the formation of a citizen's advisory council and fifty state commissions. Many of the people involved in these commissions, dissatisfied with the lack of progress made on their recommendations, became founders and early activists in new feminist organizations.

Origins of the Women's Liberation Movement

By the 1960s the ERA was a nonissue. It had even been dropped from the platforms of the Democratic (1960) and Republican (1964) parties, despite continual lobbying by the NWP. Founders of the new feminist movement had no idea how much they owed to the lengthy battle over the ERA. Few had even heard of the NWP. Their focus was on the elimination of discriminatory practices and sexist attitudes, not legal rights. Their role model was the civil rights movement, not the old feminist movement.

The women's liberation movement was the bastard child of the civil rights movement. Unplanned, unwanted, and unloved by its parent, it nonetheless bore its stamp. During the 1950s and early 1960s, the civil rights movement captured the public imagination and educated it on the immorality of discrimination and the legitimacy of mass protest. As such, it became the mother of *all* the movements of the 1960s and 1970s. For women, however, it provided not only a model for action but also a very different world view from that of the "separate spheres" that had been the reigning ideology since the previous century. The idea that different people had a different place in society was in part a product of the Victorian era. It was accepted by the dominant force for social change of that period—the progressive movement—which sought to make government the protector of the unfortunate and the downtrodden, not their equalizer. The Supreme Court's 1896 decision in *Plessy v. Ferguson* (163 U.S. 537) that separate facilities by race could be equal reflected this view. It was rejected by the Supreme Court in 1954, when *Brown v. Board of Education* (347 U.S. 483) declared that separate was inherently unequal. The civil rights movement popularized this view and in so doing undermined the rationalization behind the sexual division of labor. The analogy that was often made by 1960s feminists between the status of women and the status of blacks was one that had been made frequently in the nineteenth century and, like then, was part of the process of educating American women to the inequities inherent in separate statuses.

The movement actually had two origins, from two different strata of society, with two different styles, orientations, values, and forms of organization. In many ways there were two separate movements, which only began to merge in the mid 1970s. Although the composition of both branches was predominantly white, middle-class, and college-educated, initially the median age of the activists in what I call the older branch of the movement was about twenty years greater. The difference in age between the participants in the two branches reflected an often-noted characteristic of society in the 1960s known as the generation gap. Over time the gap declined. Younger women joined older branch organizations, and the women in the younger branch became older. Today age is no longer a defining characteristic of different feminist groups (except for those organized into OWL—originally Older Women's Liberation, now the Older Women's League).

The first new feminist organization was the National Organization for Women (NOW), which was founded in 1966. Its key progenitor and first president was Betty Friedan, who came to national prominence by publishing her best seller *The Feminine Mystique* in 1963. Many of NOW's founders and early participants were members or staff of the president's and state Commissions on the Status of Women. The Women's Bureau held annual conferences for commission members; it was at the third such conference that NOW was proposed. The immediate stimulus was the refusal of the Bureau to permit a resolution urging the Equal Employment Opportunity Commission to enforce the provision of the 1964 Civil Rights Act prohibiting sex discrimination in employment.

The addition of "sex" to a section of a major bill aimed at eradicating race discrimination had at the time seemed more of a diversionary tactic than one geared to improving the status of women. With little notice and no hearings, it was added during the last week of floor debate by Rep. Howard W. Smith of Virginia, whose antagonism to civil rights was well known. What was not well known was that Smith had been a supporter of the ERA and the NWP for over twenty years and proposed the sex amendment at its request. This was not the first time for this tactic. The NWP had a longstanding policy of demanding rights for women that were given to any other group. It had been lobbying for two decades to add sex to executive orders that prohibited discrimination on the basis of race by federal contractors. And it had successfully added sex amendments to two previous civil rights bills—in 1950 and 1956. These bills did not pass, but the 1964 bill did, creating a tool to attack sex discrimination that piggybacked on the civil rights struggle. Although the Women's Bureau had initially opposed the sex provision, it quickly changed its attitude. Its objection to the resolution by the conference it sponsored emanated less from concern about the EEOC than that the NWP would demand a resolution on the ERA.

The NWP's initial attitude toward NOW was not sisterly. It did not want its role as the preeminent feminist organization to be usurped, particularly by women who had a broader agenda than the ERA. However, it knew an opportunity when it saw one. It infiltrated NOW as it had BPW and many other organizations, and in 1967 NOW endorsed the ERA. The debate was spirited but not acrimonious. Although labor union women felt compelled to withdraw from NOW because their unions opposed the ERA, most participants at the NOW conference were strong supporters. They were unaware of the decades of debate over protective labor legislation and were very attuned to the importance of equality as a result of the civil rights movement. The latter had created a different frame of reference than that of the struggle to protect workers against industrial exploitation at the turn of the century.

Just as important, by 1967 the world was a very different place than it had been in the 1920s. Women were one-third of the labor force; the fastest growing segment were mothers of young children. The idea that they were merely transitory was rapidly receding into the past. Despite the "back to the home" propaganda of the "feminine mystique" era of the 1940s and 1950s, women's participation in the labor force had risen steadily, while their position within it had declined. Opportunities to work, the trend toward smaller families, plus a change in preferred status symbols from a leisured wife at home to a second car and a color television set helped transform the female labor force from one of primarily single women under twenty-five, as it was in 1940, to one of married women and mothers over forty by 1950. Simultaneously, the job market became even more rigidly sex-segregated, except for traditionally female professional jobs such as teaching and social work, which were flooded by men. Women's share of professional and technical jobs declined by a third, with a commensurate decline in women's relative income. The result of this was the creation of a class of well-educated, underemployed, and underpaid women. These women became the social base of the new movement.

Many of them joined NOW, but as with any social movement, there was a mushroom effect that resulted in numerous new organizations within a few years. In 1968 women who were unhappy with NOW's support of women's right to choose abortion left to form the Women's Equity Action League (WEAL) in order to focus on economic and educational issues. The same year Federally Employed Women (FEW) organized for equal opportunity within the government. In 1969 men and women who wanted to devote their energies to legalizing abortion founded the National Association to Repeal Abortion Laws (NARAL). Between 1969 and 1971 women's caucuses formed in professional associations that did not already have separate women's organizations from the suffrage and postsuffrage era. In 1971 women who wanted to work within the political parties founded the National Women's Political Caucus (NWPC). And in 1974 unionized women formed the Coalition of Labor Union Women.

In the late 1960s, unaware of and unknown to NOW or to the state commissions, the younger branch of the movement was taking shape. While it did not begin on the campuses, its activators were on the younger side of the generation gap. Although few were students, all were under thirty and had received their political education as participants in or concerned observers of the social action projects of the preceding decade. Many came directly from new left and civil rights organizations, where they had been shunted into traditional roles and faced with the contradiction of working in a freedom movement but not being very free. Others had attended various courses on women in the multitude of free universities springing up around the country during those years.

During 1967 and 1968 at least five groups formed spontaneously and independently in five different cities—Chicago, Toronto, Detroit, Seattle, and Gainesville, Florida. They arose at a very auspicious moment. The blacks had just kicked the whites out of the civil rights movement, student power had been discredited by Students for a Democratic Society (SDS), and the organized new left was on the wane. Only draft-resistance activities were on the rise, and this movement more than any other of its time exemplified the social inequities of the sexes. Men could resist the draft; women could only counsel resistance.

There had been individual temporary caucuses and conferences of women as early as 1964, but it was not until 1967 that the groups developed a determined, if cautious, continuity and began to expand. In 1968 they held a national conference attended by over two hundred women from around this country and Canada on less than one month's notice. For the next few years, they expanded exponentially.

This expansion was more amoebic than organized, because the younger branch of the movement prided itself on its lack of organization. Eschewing structure and damning leadership, it carried the concept of "everyone doing her own thing" almost to its logical extreme. The thousands of sister chapters around the country were virtually independent of one another, linked only by journals, newsletters, and cross-country travelers. Some cities had a coordinating committee that tried to maintain communication among local groups and to channel newcomers into appropriate ones, but none of these committees had any power over the activities, let alone the ideas, of the groups it served.

One result of this style was a very broadly based, creative movement, to which individuals could relate as they desired, with no concern for orthodoxy or doctrine. Another result was political impotence. It was impossible for this branch of the movement to organize a nationwide action, even if there could have been agreement on issues. Fortunately, the older branch of the movement had the structure necessary to coordinate such actions and was usually the one to initiate them.

The Small Groups

The younger branch of the women's movement was able to expand rapidly in the beginning because it could capitalize on the new left's infrastructure of organizations and media and because its initiators were skilled in local community organizing. Since the primary unit was the small group and no need for national cooperation was perceived, multitudinous splits increased its strength rather than drained its resources. Such fission was often "friendly" in nature and, even when not, served to bring ever-increasing numbers of women under the movement's umbrella.

Unfortunately, these newly recruited masses lacked the organizing skills of the initiators, and, because the very ideas of "leadership" and "organization" were in disrepute, they made no attempt to acquire them. They did not want to deal with traditional political institutions and abjured all traditional political skills. Consequently, the growth of movement institutions did not go beyond the local level, and they were often inadequate to handle the accelerating influx of new people into the movement. Although these small groups were diverse in kind and responsible to no one for their focus, their nature determined both the structure and the strategy of the movement.

The major, although hardly exclusive, activities of the younger branch were organizing rap groups, putting on conferences, putting out educational literature, running service projects such as bookstores and health centers, and organizing occasional marches to "Take Back the Night." This branch contributed more in the impact of its ideas than in its activities. It developed several ideological perspectives, much of the terminology of the movement, an amazing number of publications and counterinstitutions, numerous new issues, and even new techniques for social change.

Nonetheless, its loose structure was flexible only within certain limits, and the movement never transcended them. The rap groups were excellent for changing individual attitudes, but they were not very successful in dealing with social institutions. Their loose, informal structure encouraged participation in discussion, and their supportive atmosphere elicited personal insight, but neither was very efficient for handling specific tasks. Thus, although the rap groups were of fundamental value to the development of the movement, the more structured groups were more politically effective. Individual rap groups tended to flounder when their members exhausted the virtues of consciousness raising and decided they wanted to do something more concrete. The problem was that most groups were unwilling to change their structure when they changed their tasks. They accepted the ideology of structurelessness without recognizing the limits on its uses.

Because structurelessness provided no means of resolving political disputes or carrying on ideological debates, the younger branch was wracked by internal disputes and personal attacks. "Trashing" sometimes reached epidemic proportions. The two most significant crises were an attempt by the Young Socialist Alliance (YSA), youth group of the Socialist Workers' Party (SWP), to take over the movement, and the gay/straight split. The Trotskyist YSA saw the younger branch of the movement as a potential recruiting ground for socialist converts and directed its members to join with that purpose in mind. Although YSA members were never numerous, their enormous dedication and their contributions of time and energy enabled them to achieve positions of power quickly in many small groups whose lack of structure left no means of resisting. However, many new left women had remained within the younger branch, and their past experience with YSA predisposed them to distrust it. Not only did they disagree with YSA politics, but also they recognized that, because YSA members owed their primary allegiance to a centralized national party, those members had the potential to control the entire movement. The battle that ensued can euphemistically be described as vicious, and it resulted in YSA being largely driven from the younger branch of the movement. (Several years later, in their SWP guise, YSA members began to join NOW, but NOW's structure made it more difficult to control.) However, the alienation and fragmentation this struggle left in its wake made the movement ill prepared to meet its next major crisis.

The gay/straight split occurred not because of the mere presence of lesbians in feminist groups but because a vocal group of those present articulated lesbianism as the essential feminist idea. They argued first that women should identify with, live with, and associate only with women and eventually that a woman who actually slept with a man was clearly consorting with the enemy and could not be trusted. When this view met the fear and hostility many straight women felt toward homosexuality, the results were explosive. The gay/straight struggle raged for several years and consumed most of the time and energy of the younger branch. By the time the tensions eased, most straight women had either become gay or left the younger branch. Some joined NOW, some rejoined the new left, and many simply dropped out of women's groups altogether. After gay women predominated (by about four to one) in the small groups, their anger toward straight women began to moderate. However, the focus of both the gay and straight women who remained was no longer directed at educating or recruiting nonfeminists into the movement but rather was aimed at building a "women's culture" for themselves. While a few groups engaged in outreach through public action on issues of concern to all women (e.g., rape) or even on issues concerning straight women primarily (e.g., domestic violence), most of the small groups concerned themselves with maintaining a comfortable niche for "women identified women" and with insulating themselves from the damnation of the outside world.

By the mid 1970s the small groups had disappeared or melded into women's culture. Most of the publications they had created folded, though a few remain to this day. Some of the service projects "institutionalized" by getting government funding (e.g., battered women's shelters and rape crisis centers), and others survived as small businesses (e.g., bookstores and abortion clinics). Many women remained active in "submovements" focused on specific issues such as battered women, rape, health, etc. Some women did burn out and retreat to their private lives. Others took their feminist consciousness with them into other arenas of activity. In particular, the prochoice, environmental, and antinuclear movements were energized and informed by feminists, creating such hybrids as ecofeminism. Many other feminists moved into academia, where they built campus women's centers and women's studies departments. And a lot of newly politicized women who would have joined a small group in the 1960s joined NOW and other older branch groups, bringing with them some of the free-wheeling style and desire for new ideas that had characterized the younger branch.

The Older Branch

Older branch organizations have stayed with traditional forms of organization, including paid memberships, elected officers, and national boards. Some experimented with new forms such as joint holding of offices. Some have paid staff. All started as top-down organizations lacking a mass base. Only NOW subsequently developed a mass base, though not all members wanted one. The NWPC tried to build a mass membership, but its success has been limited. Some of the service projects that originated as small groups but then obtained government funding joined together into national coalitions such as the Displaced Homemakers Network and the National Coalition Against Domestic Violence (NCADV). WEAL became a Washington-based lobbying group until it folded in 1989. Women who wanted to work full time on feminist issues without the burdens of servicing members created staff-based organizations that sought support through contributions, foundations, and government contracts for research or services. These include the Center for Women's Policy Studies, National Committee on Pay Equity, and Women's Legal Defense Fund. In addition, some longstanding women's organizations such as the American Association of University Women and the National Federation of Business and Professional Women became explicitly feminist, and still others such as the American Nurses Association and the National Education Association are implicitly so. They often join with feminist groups to pursue different items on the feminist agenda.

All have functioned largely as pressure groups, sometimes on the government, and sometimes within their professions. Those based in Washington created a feminist policy network, often working with labor, civil rights, and liberal organizations to obtain their goals. Collectively these organizations have used the legal, political, and media institutions of the country with great skill, bringing about major changes in law, public policy, and many institutional practices. There has been some specialization of function. Lawsuits have been largely handled by the Women's Rights Project of the ACLU, with other legal defense groups joining with amicus curiae briefs. NOW has organized most of the large marches. The NWPC has focused on campaign training of women to run for elected office.

As a result of their activities, the Equal Employment Opportunity Commission changed many of its originally prejudicial attitudes toward women. Numerous lawsuits were filed under the sex provision of Title VII of the 1964 Civil Rights Act. The Equal Rights Amendment passed Congress in 1972; the passage of many other laws continued throughout the 1970s and even into the less hospitable 1980s. The Supreme Court legalized most abortions in 1973 and radically rewrote constitutional law on women by 1976. Complaints were filed against several hundred colleges and universities, as well as many businesses, charging sex discrimination. Articles on feminism appeared in virtually every news medium, and a host of new laws were passed prohibiting sex discrimination in a variety of areas.

The organizations of the older branch have been able to sustain themselves longer than those of the younger branch, but they have had their ups and downs, and some (e.g., WEAL, NCADV) no longer exist. Funding is a continual problem. Assaults by the right wing have forced many to choose between staying on the cutting edge of social change or paying their staff. Controversy aids fundraising by direct mail but reduces support from government and foundations. Direct mail is very expensive to initiate and siphons off a lot of time. Memberships rise during controversies but fall when they are over; members also require expensive servicing and sometimes want to participate in decision making. Staff-based organizations are the most flexible and efficient but also the most dependent on the goodwill and policy preferences of foundations and government contracts. Few contemporary feminist organizations can rely on rich donors, as the National Woman's Party did for so long. The Feminist Majority Foundation is virtually the only one primarily supported in this way.

Although NOW began as a Washington pressure group, it is the only new feminist organization to develop a mass membership. Its early history was a convoluted one. NOW suffered three splits between 1967 and 1968. As the only action organization concerned with women's rights, it had attracted many different kinds of people with many different views on what to do and how to do it. With only a national structure and, at that point, no local base, individuals found it difficult to pursue their particular concerns on a local level; they had to persuade the whole organization to support them. This top-down structure, combined with limited resources, placed severe restrictions on diversity and, in turn, severe strains on the organization. Local chapters were also hampered by a lack of organizers to develop new chapters and the lack of a program into which they could fit.

These initial difficulties were overcome as NOW grew to become the largest single feminist organization. Although it never hired organizers to develop chapters, the enormous geographical mobility of its members and their desire to create chapters wherever they moved had the same results. NOW also benefited greatly from the publicity the movement received in the early 1970s. Although much of that publicity was a response to the eye-catching tactics of the younger branch or was aimed at "media stars" (none of whom were NOW leaders), NOW was often the only organization with a telephone and a stable address that incipient movement participants could find. Consequently, its membership grew at the same exponential rate that the younger branch had experienced in the late 1960s.

With its first contested presidential election in 1974, NOW developed two major factions that fought for control of the organization and very nearly split it into two. Although these factions articulated their concerns ideologically, the fight in fact was not over issues but rather was a very ordinary attempt by "outs" to become "ins." By 1975 the insurgent faction had established solid control of the national organization, and, in spite of an occasional contested election, it has remained in power ever since. Over the next few years control of NOW was centralized. A national office was established in Washington, the bylaws were rewritten, and state organizations were created. Dues were collected directly from members, not all of whom were members of local chapters, and used to fund a national staff and national projects. While this centralization did drain resources and energy from the chapters, it allowed NOW to focus its efforts and thus to increase its power on the national level. Major national projects, such as ratification of the ERA and opposition to restrictions on abortion, helped recruit money and people.

Although NOW remains the preeminent national feminist organization, it has only been a tangential part of the feminist policy establishment in Washington. This is partially from its own choice; NOW has usually stayed out of coalitions that it did not run. But it is also because NOW has often chosen controversy over caution. It adopted from the younger branch not only most of its ideas but also a lot of its flamboyant style: organizing demonstrations, sit-ins, and other activities designed to catch the public eye. Its size and its actions made it a lightning rod for attacks from the right. Its prominence makes "NOW-bashing" a favorite sport in the left. Even among feminists NOW is often in the unenviable position of always being an outsider. The establishment dismisses NOW as too radical, while those who call themselves radical disdain it as part of the establishment.

The Feminist Agenda

The contemporary feminist agenda has always been a lengthy one, but has not always stayed the same. In this it differed from its predecessor. Suffrage was the consuming passion of the woman movement. After it was achieved, the National Woman's Party deliberately stuck to one issue—congressional passage of the ERA; Alice Paul viewed occasional diversions into other concerns as "sideshows." The founders of the women's liberation movement thought concentration on a single issue had been a mistake; most conscientiously sought to be as broad ranging and inclusive as possible.

From the beginning it has been popular to differentiate the older and younger branches ideologically. The terms *reformist* and *radical* were often used, particularly by members of the younger branch, for whom the distinction was of critical importance to their identity as radicals. Labels such as *liberal* and *socialist* were also used to distinguish among different types of feminism. All of these labels were derived from traditional male ideological frameworks. They hide more than they reveal because they imply fundamental differences in analysis that simply are not there. Structure and style rather than ideas more adequately distinguished the two branches. Indeed, had there been fundamental ideological differences, it would not have been so easy for ideas, and eventually people, to move among groups in both branches. In reality, feminism in all its manifestations is radical in that it seeks to redefine the basic human relationships between the sexes and to redistribute power and other social goods. It is also conservative in that its driving forces are the concepts of liberty and equality that have been part of our civic culture for over two hundred years. There are ideological differences within the overall feminist movement, but they don't correspond to the organizational forms.

Ideology aside, there were some differences in how participants in the two branches approached feminism, which reflected their past experiences more than their understanding of what feminism meant or what a feminist world would look like. Older branch members were willing to work with existing institutions and were issue oriented. They identified problems and demanded specific changes in laws, policies, and private practices to improve women's status and opportunities. Younger branch members adopted from the new left a suspicion of existing institutions. "Working within the system" was to them inherently suspect. While they rarely disagreed with the issues identified by the older branch organizations and made similar demands within the institutions of which they were a part (other social movement organizations, academia, etc.), they were more concerned with articulating broad conceptual frameworks that would explain women's oppression and point to far-reaching solutions.

Younger branch feminists were also more concerned with process, espousing principles of inclusion and participation. From the very beginning a "feminist way" of doing things was often more important than feminist goals. That is why the structure and style of the two branches continued to differ even though issues and ideas readily diffused throughout the entire movement. Long after the two branches had merged to the point that such a distinction was no longer relevant, organizational form and process continued to be a priority and often a source of conflict. Such concerns were neither new nor radical. An "antipower ethic" has a long and honorable tradition in American history. Even though it is not a specifically feminist one, many feminists have incorporated it into their concept of feminism to the point where it became part of their ideology.

Within the younger branch a basic difference of opinion developed quite early. It was disguised as a philosophical difference, was articulated and acted on as a strategic one, but actually was more of a political disagreement than anything else. The original issue was whether the fledgling women's liberation movement should remain a branch of the radical new left movement or become an independent women's movement. Proponents of the two positions became known as "politicos" and "feminists," respectively, and traded arguments about whether the enemy was capitalism or male-dominated institutions and values. In some ways this argument recapitulated that between Florence Kelley and Alice Paul. As did Kelley and her allies, politicos saw women's problems lodged in an inequitable economic system that had to be changed before women could be free. Feminists in both eras acknowledged the role of economics but saw improving *women's* opportunities as their priority. However, unlike Kelley, politicos had no faith in the power of law to rectify these problems or the willingness of the state to improve the position of women. They and their feminist counterparts were alienated from traditional political institutions and put their faith only in an undefined revolution. The debate faded after 1970, when the influx of large numbers of previously apolitical women made an independent, autonomous women's liberation movement a reality instead of an argument. The spectrum shifted toward the feminist direction, but the basic difference in orientation remained until wiped out by the debate over lesbian feminism. Those women who maintained their allegiance to the left then created their own socialist feminist groups or united in feminist caucuses within left organizations.

At NOW's 1966 founding convention it passed a broad statement of purpose that articulated a general philosophy of equality and justice under law. It emphasized that "women's problems are linked to many broader questions of social justice; their solution will require concerted action by many groups." The following year it passed a Bill of Rights for women to be presented to candidates and parties in the 1968 elections. The first six planks were quickly passed. They were enforcement of sex discrimination laws; paid maternity leave; tax deductions for child care; establishment of readily available public child care facilities; equal and unsegregated education; and equal job training opportunities, housing, and family allowances for women in poverty. Proposals to support the Equal Rights Amendment and reproductive control were controversial; they passed, but several members quit as a result. By the time NOW organized the first national feminist march down New York City's Fifth Avenue on August 26, 1970, one of these—abortion—had become accepted as a major concern. The central demands were equal opportunity in employment and education, free abortion on demand, and twenty-four-hour child care centers. It was not until 1975 that ratification of the Equal Rights Amendment became the dominant motif. Even this was true only for the national office and in the unratified states. Most NOW chapters were in ratified states, and they worked on a plethora of local issues, often ones that were first brought to public consciousness by the younger branch. When the ERA was not ratified by the 1982 deadline, NOW vowed not to let it die. However, it was soon clear that the ERA no longer commanded the passion it once did; instead it was abortion that became the primary public demand. Here, NOW found itself in competition with NARAL and Planned Parenthood; it could not take the lead as it had on the ERA struggle.

As it did in the younger branch, lesbianism as an issue generated enormous hostility in older branch organizations. Even NOW initially rejected sexual preference as a legitimate feminist concern. However, by 1977 all feminist and most women's organizations acknowledged it as an important part of the feminist agenda. That year a government-sponsored women's conference was held in Houston to commemorate International Women's Year (which was actually in 1975). It passed a National Plan of Action that included elimination of discrimination on the basis of sexual preference and laws on private sexual behavior. Although the overall plan identified over two dozen concerns, the ERA, abortion, and sexual preference were the lead issues; all were passed over the vehement opposition of right wing women, who were about 20 percent of the delegates. Since then lesbianism has not been an issue within the movement; many estimate that most activists are lesbians. However, to the outside world homosexuality by either sex is stigmatized, and feminist support for lesbian and gay issues is used to discredit the movement. Many nonfeminists agree with the earlier radicalesbians, who said that "feminism is the theory; lesbianism is the practice."

By the mid 1970s real ideological differences were emerging in the women's (no longer called liberation) movement—not the false ones implied by the radical and reform labels. These differences replicated the debate over equality versus difference that had split women during the 1920s. The initial emphasis on equality that had bonded feminists of all stripes in the early movement was challenged by the values of what came to be called cultural feminism. Cultural feminism grew out of the web of relationships and alternative institutions that made up women's culture, but many of its most vocal adherents were women who had nurtured their politics in the new left until they reacted against its chauvinism. Cultural feminism was an attempt to identify and extol what women had in common, to put substance on the concept of sisterhood. It became a celebration of all things female without concern for whether these things came from hormones, socialization, or social status. As had happened earlier in the prior woman movement, difference between the sexes was elevated to a primary principle, with female characteristics claiming the moral edge.

Cultural feminism emerged in the mid 1970s as a dissenting voice; by the mid 1980s its concerns were structuring the major debates. New issues, such as male violence, pornography, sexual desire, divorce, and surrogacy, were often argued as conflicts over the importance of equality versus difference. It was also generating its own reaction by women for whom the idea of a universal sisterhood undermined their own identity. Race in particular became a heated issue, as minority women challenged the assumption that women had common characteristics and shared a common oppression. These women, particularly African-Americans, derived their identity from their race; their racial group, including the men, was their primary community. Initially most minority women had rejected feminism has having nothing relevant to say to their lives; they called it "white women's liberation" or the "white women's movement." However, as the sexism in their own communities as well as the dominant culture sensitized them to the feminist critique, they tried to fuse both feminist and racial concerns, often creating new labels, such as "womanist," to distinguish themselves. In the process they emphasized the differences among women, not those between women and men, and denounced white women for daring to speak for all women.

Although the ideas of cultural feminism appeared to take the movement almost 180 degrees from the original egalitarian impulse, such a transformation is not uncommon to radical social movements. Most movements based on group identity, including but not limited to those of minorities, have two competing impulses: that for assimilation and that for affirmation. The former demands inclusion on an equal basis with the dominant group; the latter relies on exclusivity to maintain group identity and the sense of community that goes with it. The assimilationist impulse is usually the driving force behind the emergence of a new movement. Insofar as it succeeds in gaining concessions and bringing its members into the dominant culture and its institutions, it does so at a cost to group identity and cohesion. Insofar as it fails to make such inroads, it reacts against rejection by claiming superiority for what makes it different from the dominant culture. Most movements both succeed and fail; either way affirmation of and identification with group characteristics become the dominant motifs at a later stage. This idea in turn leads to a form of encapsulation, in which activity is directed inward rather than outward and boundaries between insiders and outsiders are guarded jealously. To the outside world the movement seems becalmed, even dead. It usually takes a new generation of activists, at some later time, to bring it back into the public eye by once again demanding entry.

THE EQUAL RIGHTS AMENDMENT

The Equal Rights Amendment was the dominant issue of the women's movement during the 1970s and part of the 1980s. This was not by choice. Had it not been waiting in the wings for the right historical moment, none of the founders would have proposed it. Nonetheless, the ERA became the dominant issue because it captured the public's imagination—pro and con—as no other issue had. It was the quintessential symbolic issue. It meant what people thought it meant, and all involved projected onto it their greatest fears and their greatest hopes for the future of women.

In 1970 feminist moles in the federal government urged Congresswoman Martha Griffiths (D. Mich), the ERA's chief sponsor in the House of Representatives, to file a petition to discharge it from the House committee in which it had been buried for almost two decades in order to commemorate the fiftieth anniversary of Suffrage. Massive publicity on the rise of the new feminist movement encouraged a groundswell of support for the ERA within the government. The Senate Judiciary Committee held hearings after some pressure from NOW. A Women's Bureau conference endorsed it, as did the Secretary of Labor. The president of the National Federation of Republican Women and the (women's) vice chair of the Democratic National Committee wrote their state affiliates urging resolutions of support. After delegates attending the national conference of the Business and Professional Women deluged their Representatives with telegrams, a discharge petition was signed by enough Members of Congress to bring the issue to the floor. Nonetheless, it took two years and several votes before it was sent to the states for ratification on March 22, 1972.

Passage of the ERA came at a unique point in its history. It had been debated for years by mutual antagonists who would not compromise an inch. In the meantime, social and legal changes intervened to undermine the basis of the opponents' position. Between 1970 and 1972 opposition was greatly attenuated. With a few notable exceptions, the ERA became a symbolic issue on which everyone could agree. Yet even as this agreement was reached, a new opposition was developing. Ironically, it was from the right, which had mostly supported the ERA during its lengthy stay in Congress. This opposition grew and eventually consumed more moderate forces, even while the ERA gained support from ancient foes to the left.

While not a new issue, the ERA became newly public at the end of a major period of social reform and at the beginning of the women's movement. The timing couldn't have been worse. The 1960s saw a major transformation in American society, and like previous social reform movements, it stimulated a backlash. The initial focus of that backlash was on busing, but it quickly spread to encompass the new issues of feminism, abortion, and gay rights, all of which were interpreted as an attack on the family and the American way of life. At the time the Right arose, feminism was still riding on the crest of enthusiasm that accompanies all new social movements. This enthusiasm was sufficient for the two-year Congressional campaign, but it was not uniform throughout the states. The new feminist organizations were not yet sufficiently organized to transfer resources to where they were most needed or to deal with practical political problems. By the time they were, it was too late.

Twenty-two states that already had strong feminist movements quickly ratified the amendment. In January 1973, a national "stop ERA" campaign surfaced, headed by noted right-winger Phyllis Schlafly. Drawing on a network of readers of her newsletter, *Eagle Forum,* Republican women's clubs, and fundamentalist churches, she was able to bring to the anti-ERA campaign a political expertise the feminist organizations did not yet have. The kind of constituent pressure that Congresspeople had felt at the national level, local legislators felt at the state level—but for the opposite position. By 1975 only another twelve states had ratified, and the major women's groups realized that the ERA would require a long, hard political fight in southern and rural states. It took another three years to create viable, knowledgeable ERA coalitions in those states, largely, but not always, led by NOW. In 1978 only one more state was added to the ratification list, but Congress agreed to extend the seven-year deadline until June of 1982. It was too late. The "antis" were well organized and able to scare several state legislators into believing that the ERA would bring women into combat, unisex toilets, and abortion on demand. When the final deadline passed, the ERA had failed by the loss of seven votes in three states.

Nonetheless, the war fared better than the battle. Feminism made the personal political and, in the process, raised everyone's consciousness about the importance of family issues, sexuality, and the role of women. It also stimulated major strides toward the legal equality that the ERA was originally written to achieve. Many state equal rights amendments were passed, discriminatory laws were changed, and the Supreme Court reinterpreted the basic premise against which laws affecting women were to be judged from one of protection to one of equal opportunity. But this time the debate was different than it was sixty years ago. The argument concerned not the meaning of equality but the role of women. This time the opponents rejected equality of any kind as desirable for women, favoring instead protection of women to pursue the goals of wife and motherhood in a traditional way. To them the ERA symbolized not equal legal rights but the entire women's liberation movement, which, along with the other social movements of the 1960s, was, they felt, a severe threat to their basic values and way of life.

ABORTION

The movement to change restrictive abortion laws began independently of and earlier than the women's liberation movement, but when that movement emerged, it quickly captured the abortion issue as its own, energizing and publicizing it along the way. Since then, the two movements have proceeded along parallel tracks. The abortion, or prochoice, movement, as it prefers to be called, has distinct organizations devoted solely to that issue. The most prominent of these is NARAL (National Abortion Rights Action League). Planned Parenthood (which has a broader agenda) is the most powerful. Before *Roe v. Wade* legalized abortions, the younger branch nourished many referral groups. Since then, local prochoice organizations still exist in many cities, though their activities vary enormously. These organizations are sustained by a separate set of activists whose primary energies are focused on reproductive freedom, even though virtually all are sympathetic to other feminist concerns. The parallel tracks are tied together by these sympathetic activists and their equivalents in feminist organizations. Some activists "cross over" as staff of feminist and prochoice organizations, but most concentrate on one. All feminists support national mobilizations, whether by feminist or prochoice groups. Although there are feminists who are antiabortion, they are a small minority within the women's movement and are ignored. All of the feminist organizations see reproductive freedom as an intrinsic part of the feminist agenda. Everyday organizing and lobbying are handled by the prochoice organizations; demonstrations may be organized by any group; during crises everyone pitches in.

Prochoice activity can be divided into three periods. Before *Roe* the emphasis was on reforming or repealing state laws (NARAL's acronym at its 1969 founding stood for National Association for Repeal of Abortion Laws). The initiators in the early 1960s were largely professionals—doctors, lawyers, clergy—and mostly men. Aided by several public crises (a german measles epidemic, the Thalidomide scare), they stimulated vociferous debate. Four states repealed their abortion restrictions, and several others loosened them. Referral services mushroomed. Although feminists were attuned to this debate as early as 1967, they didn't begin to impact on it until 1970. By the time *Roe* was decided in 1973, feminists and feminist consciousness permeated the entire prochoice movement. The argument had shifted from the right of physicians to counsel their patients to the right of women to control their bodies. This approach changed the abortion debate from one of freedom of professional decision making to a fundamental constitutional right. *Roe* itself was the project of a small feminist group in Austin, Texas, and the lawyer who argued *Roe* before the Supreme Court was one of its participants.

After *Roe* the movement grew complacent. It was the antis—calling themselves the right-to-life movement—who were the activists. Even while states debated liberalizing their abortion laws, the United States Catholic Conference and local dioceses had organized right-to-life leagues and urged parishioners to lobby their local legislators. In 1973 the Church created the National Right to Life Committee, which was a separate organization but received a lot of Church support. In 1975 the National Conference of Catholic Bishops presented its Pastoral Plan for Pro-Life Activities. It urged every Catholic to get involved in prolife activities and outlined a political strategy of lobbying elected officials to support a prolife constitutional amendment and oppose their reelection if they didn't. The NRLC eventually became independent of the Church, but while its leadership was often Protestant, its base was largely among Catholics. As in the feminist movement, the right-to-life movement fought, factioned, and fractured, leading to the formation of new organizations such as the American Committee for Life, the American Life Lobby, March for Life, and several different political action committees. It was also courted and eventually coopted by the new right, who saw opposition to abortion as an issue that could mobilize voters to conservative candidates. New right leaders were also recruiting fundamentalist Protestant ministers to get involved in politics and encourage their followers to actively oppose abortion as one of several conservative causes. They succeeded to the point that fundamentalist Protestants now outnumber Catholics among the activists. Education, elections, and lobbying were the predominant tactics in the 1970s, though sidewalk counseling of clinic patients, mass marches, and demonstrations were also used. While there had been sporadic civil disobedience and harassment of abortion clinics during the 1970s, in the 1980s more militant tactics became prevalent. In 1984 these escalated in response to the Supreme Court's reaffirmation of *Roe* the year before. Two dozen clinics were bombed or set on fire, clinic employees received death threats, and several letter bombs were sent to clinics.

The climate changed in 1989, when the Supreme Court handed down its *Webster* decision. Although the Court had permitted greater state regulation of abortion throughout the 1980s, it had not questioned the basic premise of *Roe*. By the time of *Webster* enough new, antichoice justices had been added to the court that that decision rang the firebell of alarm. Even though the decision was not unexpected and could have been worse, within a few hours after it was announced on July 3, 1989, prochoice supporters were committing civil disobedience all over the country. For the first time young women and men who had not known the fear of unwanted pregnancy that was so common before *Roe* realized how tenuous reproductive freedom was. Funds poured in and phones rang at the offices of NOW, NARAL, and Planned Parenthood. That fall abortion became an issue in local elections, with prochoice candidates winning against openly prolife opponents. In 1993 the court once again had an opportunity to overturn *Roe,* this time with enough conservative justices to do so. However, in *Casey* it backed away from this option, instead increasing the permissible scope of state regulation.

When prochoice activists were roused from their complacency, it escalated the conflict between them and the prolifers. Even before *Webster,* a new, more militant group calling itself Operation Rescue had brought thousands of people to Atlanta during the 1988 Democratic convention to block abortion clinics. Although hundreds were arrested, they continued their strategy of targeting a specific city for massive blockades continuing for weeks at a time. When local police proved inadequate to protect the clinics, they asked the federal courts for injunctions to keep Operation Rescue away from their doors. Many federal judges complied by invoking an 1871 statute passed to protect blacks from the Ku Klux Klan. This had a temporary effect. Arrests of clinic blockaders dropped from over twelve thousand in 1989 to one thousand to three thousand for the next three years. However, in 1993 the court overturned these injunctions, saying the statute was not intended to be used for this purpose. Shortly thereafter, Operation Rescue held "rescues" in ten cities.

Less than a year later it upheld another attempt to use laws created for one purpose to protect abortion clinics from harassment. NOW and several clinics filed suit under the Racketeer Influenced and Corrupt Organizations Act (RICO), which was passed in 1970 to provide a way of curbing large-scale criminal "enterprises" whose individual participants might themselves commit only small crimes. They claimed that blockading and other illegal activities outside the clinics were a form of extortion; those engaged in them were part of a nationwide conspiracy who could be challenged by private RICO suits as racketeers. Both the federal district and appeals courts dismissed the case on the grounds that there was no economic motive behind the prolife protestors. However, the Supreme Court unanimously reversed in January of 1994, holding that interstate commerce was affected whether the motive was economic or not.

The Next Revolution

The ERA was ahead of its time in the 1920s. The NWP saw it as a legal revolution but did not realize that an economic revolution had to come first. Women had only just won the right to work outside the home; they had not achieved the right for their work to be taken seriously. The real revolution of the contemporary women's movement is that the vast majority of the public no longer questions the right of any women, married or unmarried, with or without children, to work for wages or to achieve her fullest individual potential.

The next revolution is a social one—a revolution in personal and family relationships. Although women have finally won the right to work, there is still a fundamental assumption that the principal social unit is the two-parent family, only *one* of whom is a primary wage earner. There is still a basic division of labor in which men are expected to be the "breadwinners" and women are expected to focus their energies on the family, though each may "help" with the other's task.

The women's liberation movement began the social revolution with its critique of established sex roles. But it raised more questions than answers, and the backlash clearly indicates that, like the NWP in the 1920s, the movement is ahead of its time. Our society is not yet ready for the vast changes in the organization of work and in social policies that will be required to bring about this next step. These changes, like those that constituted the economic revolution, will probably accrue over time. They will come about as more women, and more men, adjust their lives to the conflicting pressures of family and work until a threshold of incompatibility is reached. At that time a new feminist movement will be needed to propose a new vision that can confront the problems of the social revolution.

Toward an Afra-American Feminism

Carol Wayne White

Introduction

The black woman, wrote Zora Neal Hurston, is the mule of the world.[1] This sentiment candidly depicts the plight of African-American women in the United States, a nation besieged by diverse forms of sexual and racial oppression. Yet, as entrenched are American social institutions in unjust practices based on gender and racial identity, so even more tenacious have been the efforts of African-American women to dignify their existence through acts of resistance and empowerment. The historical accounts and theoretical critiques given by black women themselves constitute an Afra-American feminism.[2]

Generally speaking, Afra-American feminism designates the perspectives of black women struggling to overcome sexist and racist assumptions and practices. Many articulate black women have addressed the harmful socio-political, economic, and psychological effects of these practices on black women as a whole and have worked toward their eradication through a wide range of means, i.e., community work, scholarship, political organizations, etc. They have advanced certain principles at one time or another in the progress toward racial and sexual equality in this country. Here I will identify four.

First is the basic assumption that although the experiences of individual black women may differ, they share a heritage of race and gender oppression. This insight has often led to the formation of organizations and networks geared toward the needs and concerns of black women. A second conviction states that progress of neither race nor sex can be secured without incorporating the black woman's voice. Because they have often been an unacknowledged factor in race and gender issues, black women have had to position themselves at a pivotal point in the discussion of equality in North America. In these settings they have presented a voice that refuses to be ignored by white feminists, black men, or the larger society. A third critical principle contends that the feminist energies of black women must always be understood and appreciated alongside the racial struggle of blacks in North America. At its center is the belief that the status of black women is one true measure of racial progress. In this sense, black women's personal and professional advances are consistently interpreted within a larger communal framework that establishes an inextricable link between individual and collective struggles. Finally, there is an awareness that to be black and female is to be more than just burdened with oppression. There is much to celebrate. In this respect, Afra-American feminism attempts to show the strengths and joys of being black and female in North America.

Part One: The Emergence of Afra-American Feminism

HISTORICAL CONTEXT

Afra-American feminism arises from the larger and more complex historical matrix of black and white race relations in North America created by the institution of slavery. By the early eighteenth century, slavery had become the dominant vehicle through which social, legal, and racial structures were established. Women were second-class citizens; blacks were chattel. Interracial marriages and sexual liaisons were prohibited; white men who impregnated black women were punished; black men who impregnated white women were lynched.[3]

Spurred by the spirit of capitalism, slavery became an economic and political structure that manipulated and exploited African-American women and men as a permanent labor force. Within this structure, the status of the black female slave was quite precarious; as an African, she was deemed intellectually and morally inferior; as a woman, she was viewed as a valuable commodity used to increase the slave population. She not only worked in plantation fields and the masters' houses but also was forced to produce children.[4] In this context, the right to choose when, and with whom, to be sexually active was denied the black woman. As some female slave narratives indicate, however, she often resisted the violations of her body, her reproductive rights, and her sexual and social relations.[5] These historical accounts provide insight into an inherent feminist consciousness among black women who had to survive harrowing conditions.

NINETEENTH-CENTURY AFRA-AMERICAN FEMINISM

During and after slavery, as opportunity presented itself, black women attempted to overcome the restrictions placed upon them. Through issues ranging from social reform to the formation of Black Women's Clubs to the call for educational reform and economic prosperity, black women called attention to the interlocking systems of race and gender oppression. In the racial struggle in slavery and freedom, black women fought alongside black men. Black women also echoed the demands of white feminists to redefine the role of women within the family and in the public sphere. Although the black woman's needs were partly espoused by these movements for blacks and women, they were not fully represented by either. These nineteenth-century social reform movements brought forth the first major opportunities for blacks and women to work toward emancipation. But freedom for whom? And at what costs?

The plight of black women within these social reform movements is illustrated in the controversy surrounding the Fifteenth Amendment. The American Equal Rights Association (AERA), an organization founded by Elizabeth Cady Stanton, Susan B. Anthony, and Frederick Douglass in 1866, brought together abolitionists and feminists to advocate black and woman suffrage. When, however, it became clear that only one goal could be achieved, they collided. Black women activists had to choose whether or not to support the Fifteenth Amendment, which gave only black men, not black women, the right to vote. Sojourner Truth recognized the problem this posed for black women. In a now famous speech given in 1867 at an AERA convention, she said:

> There is a great stir about colored men getting their rights, but not a word about the colored women; and if colored men get their rights, and not colored women theirs, you see the colored men will be masters over the women, and it will be just as bad as it was before.[6]

As a staunch advocate of black women's rights, Truth articulated the essence of Afra-American feminism, i.e., a consciousness of the need to address diverse forms of oppression. Unfortunately, in the nineteenth century, this approach was systematically thwarted by the overall structure of American society, which bred separatist politics and ideologies. All black female activists were burdened with the problem of how to address the uneasy tension between racial and sexual politics.

Frances Harper, another black female member of the AERA, also advocated a prorace and prowoman perspective. She, however, supported the amendment because she saw white racism—including that of her white sisters—as the greatest obstacle to the progress of black women. She wrote in 1869, "The white woman all go for sex, letting race occupy a minor position. Being a black means that every white, including every white working-class woman, can discriminate against you."[7] In this context, Harper's decision was based upon what she deemed to be the most salient issue: her race's survival. If the race had no rights, the women's struggle was meaningless. Despite this controversy, Harper had a deep commitment to women's issues. She was active in both the American Woman Suffrage Association and the Women's Christian Temperance Union (WCTU).

KEY IDEAS WITHIN NINETEENTH-CENTURY AFRA-AMERICAN FEMINISM

The separatist politics of the social reform movements of the nineteenth century challenged black women to speak for themselves. In their speeches and writings, those in leadership positions continually confronted "a woman question and a race problem."[8] In 1904 Mary Church Terrell, president of the National Association of Colored Women, wrote, "Not only are colored women . . . handicapped on account of their sex, but they are almost everywhere baffled and mocked because of their race. Not only because they are women, but because they are colored women."[9] Yet this somber image did not lead to hopelessness or passive resignation. Black women recognized the need for transformation and change.

Maria Stewart, an abolitionist speaking on behalf of the Afric-American Female Intelligence Society of Boston in the 1830s, believed that black women were the "fundamental agency" by which racial progress was secured.[10] She emphasized the role of black women within the family as well as their visibility and effectiveness within the public sphere. Stewart critiqued the social caste system that pitted black and white women against each other for material stability and economic favors. Understanding that silence was seen as tacit approval of this system, she urged black women to work for their own emancipation, for "it is of no use for us to wait any longer for a generation of well-educated men to rise. . . . Now all we have to do is, by a spirit of virtuous ambition to strive to raise ourselves."[11] Stewart's feminism was an admixture of racial pride and black female solidarity. In her speeches she argued that the black woman's perspective is crucial to the understanding of racial discrimination. Her ideas reflected a distinct analysis of black womanhood as the center of social and political change in North America.

In the nineteenth century several women expressed this view. In the words of Anna Julia Cooper, "To be a woman in such an age carries with it a privilege and an opportunity never implied before. But to be a woman of the Negro race in America, and to be able to grasp the deep significance of the possibilities of the crisis, is to have a heritage, it seems to me, unique, in the age."[12] In 1892 Cooper composed a classic text of black feminist ideology, *A Voice from the South*. Countering the assumption that the black problem was epitomized in the experience of black men, she wrote, "The 'other side' has not been represented by one who 'lives there.' And not many can more sensibly recognize and more accurately tell the weight and the fret of the long 'dull pain' than the open-eyed but hitherto voiceless Black Woman of America."[13] She maintained that women must play an important role in the elimination of racial oppression.

> Every attempt to elevate the Negro, whether undertaken by himself or through the philanthropy of others, cannot help but prove abortive unless so directed as to utilize the indispensable agency of an elevated and trained womanhood. . . . Only the Black woman can say "when and where I enter, in the quiet, undisputed dignity of my womanhood, without violence and with-out suing or special patronage, then and there the whole race enters with me."[14]

Cooper conceived a societal framework based upon equality, coexistence, and respect between the races and the sexes. However, she felt that this vision would not occur until the subordination of women was eliminated in all its forms. She believed strongly in the power of the woman's movement to challenge patriarchal power. She notes, "It is not the intelligent woman vs. the ignorant woman, nor the white woman vs. the black, the brown, and the red—it is not even the cause of women vs. man. Nay, 'tis woman's strongest vindication for speaking that the world needs to hear her voice. It would be subversive of every human interest that the cry of one-half the human family be stifled."[15] Cooper's inclusive feminism advocated legislative action that would secure the rights and interests of all its marginalized groups. Her belief that women of all races and backgrounds should come together to transform and generate a more humane and free society is reflected in her address to the World Congress of Representative Women:

Let woman's claim be as broad in the concrete as in the abstract. We take our stand on the solidarity of humanity, the oneness of life, and the unnaturalness and injustice of all special favoritism, whether of sex, race, country, or condition. If one link be broken, the chain is broken. . . . We want, then, as toilers for the universal triumph of justice and human rights, to go to our homes from this Congress, demanding an entrance not through a gateway for ourselves, our race, our sex, or our sect, but a grand highway for humanity.[16]

Black women's convictions concerning the rights of women were deeply rooted in experience as well as theory. Their status as the least important (and least privileged) group in North American society enabled them to advance ideas that helped all women. Once, during an antislavery meeting where someone was praising the Constitution, Sojourner Truth offered the following response:

Children, I talks to God and God talks to me. I goes out and talks to God in de fields and de woods. Dis morning I was walking out and I got over de fence. I saw de wheat a holding up its head, looking very big. I goes up and takes holt of it. You b'lieve it, dere was no wheat dare. I says, "God, what is de matter wid dis wheat?" and he says to me, "Sojourner, dere is a little weasel in it." Now I hears talkin' about de Constitution and de rights of man. I come up and I takes holt of dis Constitution. It looks mighty big, and I feels for my rights, but dere ain't any dare. Den I say, "God, what ails dis Constitution?" He says to me, "Sojourner, dere is a little weasel in it."[17]

This sentiment is echoed in the words of Nannie Helen Burroughs, a prominent churchwoman, who noted that "when a woman went to court in defense of her virtue, she is looked upon with contempt. She needs the ballot, to reckon with men who place no value upon her virtue, and to mould healthy sentiment in favor of her own protection."[18]

POLITICAL AND SOCIAL ACTIVISM OF EARLY AFRA-AMERICAN FEMINISM

Black women responded to these ideas in many ways. Some participated in the woman suffrage movement. Astute black women recognized that women's enfranchisement would enable black women and men to work more effectively for racial progress: for educational opportunities, fuller representation and protection in the labor force, and civil liberties. It was also necessary to eradicate the black woman's peripheral and exploited status. In 1870 in South Carolina, Lottie Rollins, a member of the South Carolina's Women's Rights Association in Columbia, said, "We ask suffrage not as a favor, not as a privilege, but as a right based on the ground that we are human beings and as such, entitled to all human rights."[19] In 1880, Mary Ann Shadd Carey organized the Colored Women's Progressive Association. Created to "take an aggressive stand against the assumption that men only begin and conduct industrial and other things," the association advocated equal rights for women. With the franchise, Carey believed women would gain "independence of thought and action."[20]

Other women worked in small charitable organizations like the Independent Order of Saint Luke, one of thousands of mutual benefit societies serving the black communities since the eighteenth century.[21] These mutual self-help organizations attempted to expand the economic base of black communities and promote social and political activities. Its founders were usually individuals who had accumulated enough wealth to make investments, make "personal loans," or help establish other financial institutions. The Order of Saint Luke was a mass-based organization whose members were represented by all occupational segments: professional/managerial, entrepreneurial, and working-class.

The women of Saint Luke sponsored boycotts, rallied against segregation and lynching, and promoted educational opportunities for black children. One of Saint Luke's most prominent members was Maggie Lena Walker, who founded the St. Luke Penny Savings Bank in Richmond, Virginia, in 1903.[22] The intersection between economic and political gain for black women was keenly emphasized by Walker. She argued that the only way in which black women would be able to "'avoid the traps and snares of life,' would be to 'band themselves together, organize, . . . put their mites together, put their hands and their brains together and make work and business for themselves.'"[23] Walker's concern for the economic status of black women was further evidenced in her affiliation with the National Association of Wage Earners (NAWE) in the 1920s. Believing that it was important for all black women to support themselves, this women's organization sought to pool the energies and resources of housewives, professionals, managerial, domestic, and factory workers to protect and expand the economic base of black women.[24] The activities initiated by Walker and other black women emphasized their inherent feminist tendencies. In the context of community work they combined efforts to confront the forces of racism and sexism.

This was also indicative of the women involved in the Universal Negro Improvement Association, one of the more radical groups of the mid 1920s that attempted to represent the interests of impoverished and working-class blacks. Led by Marcus Garvey, this grass-roots organization instilled its members with a sense of pride, racial dignity, and the dream of a better life. From its inception, women were an integral part of the organization. Women's rights were guaranteed through the Constitution. Amy Jacques Garvey, second wife of the leader, was also active in the organization. One of her responsibilities was editing the Woman's Page in the UNIA newspaper, *Negro World*. According to Amy Jacques Garvey, the new negro woman would "work on a par with men in the office and the platform; practice thrift and economy; teach constructive race doctrine to children, and demand absolute respect of the race from all men."[25] By 1925, when the organization began to lose its radicality, tensions arose between its male and female members as some of the men began to complain of women's ascendancy and advocated women being kept in their place. At one UNIA convention, Amy Jacques Garvey offered the following criticism:

> If the United States Senate and Congress can open their doors to White women, we serve notice on our men that Negro women will demand equal

opportunity to fill any position in the Universal Negro Improvement Association or anywhere else without discrimination because of sex. We are sorry if it hurts your old-fashioned tyrannical feelings, and we not only make the demand but we intend to enforce it.[26]

SOCIAL REFORM AND BLACK FEMALE SOLIDARITY

The organization of social clubs by and for black women in the late nineteenth and early twentieth centuries was the third major response. Generally speaking, these black clubs were composed of well-educated middle-class females steeped in the Protestant ethic. They shared some goals in common with their white counterparts: moral reform, aid to the poor and aged, and self-improvement. Yet neither were these clubs imitations of white women's groups, nor were they formed solely as reaction to racial discrimination. According to one prominent club member, Fannie Barrier Williams, they arose from "the organized anxiety of women who have become intelligent enough to recognize their own low social condition and strong enough to initiate the forces of reform."[27]

Many were local service organizations. In 1890 the Harper Women's Club (named after Frances Ellen Watkins Harper, an antislavery lecturer) in Jefferson City, Missouri, instructed women in the latest child care techniques, advocated temperance, and offered classes in sewing and millinery. In 1892 the Colored Woman's League of Washington, D.C., was created in order to improve education and promote the interests of black women. In 1893 the Woman's Era Club of Boston, organized by Josephine St. Pierre Ruffin, collected data, published tracts and leaflets, and initiated the first monthly magazine published by black women: *The Woman's Era*. Legislation, family life, health, and fashion were among its concerns.[28]

Black women contributed goods and services to local communities through such organizations as the Dorcas Home Missionary Society of Concord Baptist Church in Brooklyn and the One Thousand Women of Bethel Church in New York City in the mid 1890s.[29] Some projects were geared toward the elderly. In Louisville, Kentucky, the Society of St. James was established in 1893 to care for the aged. The Alpha Home in Indianapolis, Indiana, provided health care for aged ex-slave women. Originally created in 1883, it was expanded to an eight-room house accommodating both women and men in 1893. In 1896 the Cleveland Home for Aged Colored People was incorporated. Its motto, "Let us not be weary in well-doing," inspired the women to channel their energies toward positive goals. To build financial stability, they charged membership fees, held socials, and provided entertainment. Similar activities were abundant in black communities across the nation, i.e., the creation of the Sarah Ann White Home in 1896 in Wilmington, Delaware; the Colored Aged Home in Newark, New Jersey, in 1895; and the Phillis Wheatley Home for Aged Colored Women under the leadership of Mary E. McCoy.[30]

The clubs proliferated throughout the Northeast and parts of the South and Midwest. In 1896 they joined together in the National Association of Colored Women (NACW) to (1) address the social problems of poverty, joblessness, and increasing racial hostility; (2) establish a black female reform network, necessitated by the rejection of black women as equal participants in the reform movements led by white women; and (3) counter attacks on black women promulgated in the popular literature and scientific writings.[31] According to one such article, black women had "the brain of a child and the passions of a woman, steeped in centuries of ignorance and savagery and wrapped about with immemorial vices."[32] Black women were made the scapegoat of the lowly conditions of the entire race. According to another source, they were "the chief instruments of the degradation of the men of their own race. When a man's mother, wife, and daughter are all immoral women, there is no room in his fallen nature for the aspiration of honor and virtue."[33]

As black women began to clearly define their goals, racial advancement came to the fore. The NACW's mission was "to furnish evidence of the moral, mental, and material progress made by people of color through the efforts of our women."[34] From 1896 to 1910, the NACW's main interest was in moral and educational reform. It sponsored activities ranging from kindergartens and mothers' meetings to domestic science and rescue work. After 1910 it became more politically active, often concerning itself with the elimination of Jim Crow laws and lynching, advocating voting rights and better education for blacks, and seeking improvements within the justice and prison systems.[35]

The black women's club movement refused to divorce women's interests from the struggle for racial equality. Its underlying belief was that the black woman's talents, skills, and educational and social achievements were integral to furthering racial progress. Although her moral and intellectual capacities were questioned by the wider culture, they were visibly recognized within these club activities. Here black women exerted power and acted as creative and responsible agents. In 1933 Mary McCloud Bethune, a civil rights leader and pioneer in the cause for black women's education, offered the following observation on the leadership role of black women:

> By the very force of circumstance, the part she played in the progress of the race has been of necessity, to a certain extent, subtle and indirect. She has not always been permitted a place in front ranks where she could show her face and make her voice heard with effect. . . . But she has been quick to seize every opportunity which presented itself to come more and more into the open and strive directly for the uplift of the race and nation.[36]

Part Two: Contemporary Issues and Voices

ENCOUNTERING BLACK MALE SEXISM IN THE 1960S AND 1970S

Early Afra-American feminism ranged from the radical woman-centered feminism of Sojourner Truth and Maria Stewart to the universal humanism of Anna Julia Cooper to the "racial advancement" reformism of the black women's club movement. During the first half of the twentieth century, black women participated in such major organizations as the National Association for the Advancement of Colored People (NAACP) and the National Urban League. In the 1950s and 1960s black women were not only supporters of the civil rights movement but also leaders, organizers, and strategists who helped shape the movement's direction. In the 1970s many were actively involved in such Afrocentric grass-roots movements as the Black Panthers and the Black

Muslims. In all of these movements black women and men shared a common goal and sense of unity in addressing the racial problem. However, black male leaders often did not fully appreciate or welcome the strengths and insights of black women. Awareness of this sexism created a dilemma for black women and caused tensions in black male-female relationships.

Black female activists, working with men who refused to acknowledge their own sexist assumptions toward black women and who chose rather to focus exclusively upon racial discrimination imposed by the wider culture, faced a dilemma: either curb natural energies or talents to appease the male leaders or demand respect and possibly jeopardize the overall project toward racial advancement. Ella Baker faced this problem in the civil rights movement. She was one of the founders of the Southern Christian Leadership Conference (SCLC) and the initiator of the Student Nonviolent Coordinating Committee (SNCC). SNCC was an independent student-led organization within the civil rights movement that set much of the agenda for the civil rights movement. While Martin Luther King, Jr., was the designated leader of the SCLC, Baker's organizational skills kept the organization going. Baker understood the patriarchal structure of the SCLC:

> There would never be any role for me in a leadership capacity with SCLC. Why? First, I'm a woman. Also, I'm not a minister. And second . . . I knew that my penchant for speaking honestly . . . would not be well tolerated. The combination of the basic attitude of men, and especially ministers, as to what the role of women in their church setups is—that of taking orders, not providing leadership—and the . . . ego problems involved in having to feel that here is someone who . . . [has] . . . more information about a lot of things than they possessed at that time. . . . This would never have lent itself to my being a leader in the movement there.[37]

In the black militant grass-roots organizations the problem was even more acute. Author and activist Angela Davis wrote of her experiences participating in the Los Angeles chapter of SNCC:

> Some of the brothers came around only for staff meetings (sometimes), and whenever we women were involved in something important, they began to talk about women taking over the organization—calling it a matriarchal coup d'etat. All the myths about black women surfaced. We were too domineering; we were trying to control everything, including the men—which meant by extension that we wanted to rob them of their manhood.[38]

Similar problems were reported by Kathleen Cleaver, an officer in the Black Panther Party, and wife of Panther leader and author Eldridge Cleaver, who also advocated women's liberation. She writes, "If I suggested [ideas], the suggestion might be rejected; if they were suggested by a man the suggestion would be implemented. It seemed throughout the history of my working with the Party, I always had to struggle with this. . . . The fact that the suggestion came from a woman gave it some lesser value."[39]

The personal and often subtle forms of sexism recounted by Baker, Davis, and Cleaver became institutionalized in the Black Muslim movement, which sprang up in urban centers during the 1970s. Led by Elijah Muhammad and thrust into the national spotlight by Malcolm X, the Black Muslims were a distinctive Afrocentric grass-roots organization with an established independent economic base through restaurants, food stores, schools, and newspapers. The movement had great appeal for those interested in racial advancement and racial pride. However, it was highly patriarchal. In *Message to the Black Man,* Muhammad unabashedly spoke of women as property and as "man's field to produce his nation."[40] Promoting a masculinist ideology, he wrote, "To become good Muslims, black women must become chattel once again, with good and loving masters, to be sure, but chattel nevertheless."[41] Because the question of race was paramount in the concerns of black women in the late 1960s and 1970s, most attempted to ignore these forms of sexism. Whether in the mainstream or militant Afrocentric movements, a politicized prowoman perspective was often lost or marginalized in the march toward racial advancement.[42]

STRATEGIC ORGANIZING IN THE 1970S

In the aftermath of the civil rights movement a notable change in perspective occurred among some black women. Black anthropologist Diane Lewis observed that "as the bulk of the higher-status, authoritative positions meted to blacks went to black men, a number of black women, particularly in the middle class, became more sensitive to the obstacle of sexism and to the relevance of the women's movement."[43] In 1970 *The Black Woman* was one of several emerging publications where the faint glimmer of a black feminist consciousness could be detected. While the contributors cited awareness of the dangers in patterning sex roles after dominant models found in white society[44] and the detrimental effects of the dominant society on black male-female relations,[45] they still saw as their aim "to demand rights as blacks first, women second."[46] A 1972 poll indicated that 62 percent of black women favored "efforts to strengthen or change women's status in society," compared with only 45 percent of white women. Moreover, 67 percent of black women expressed "sympathy with efforts of women's liberation groups," compared with only 35 percent of white women.[47] A growing number of black women noted a lack of commitment from black male leaders toward addressing sexism within the black community and the rights of black women overall. As Eudora Pettigrew wrote in 1974, "The black man grapples to achieve social justice and parity with the white male—essentially to attain white male power, privilege and status—while black women are shoved to the back of the bus."[48]

The need to recognize black women as a separate entity with their own concerns and interests became the driving force behind the formation of groups designed to build solidarity and cohesion among black women themselves. Many of these groups, such as the San Francisco–based Black Women Organized for Action (BWOA), were organized to help black women find employment, enter the political process, and provide general support against discrimination. Other groups included the League of Black Women (in Chicago), Black Women Concerned (in Baltimore), National Black Women's Political Leadership Caucus (in Detroit), and Sisters Getting Ourselves Together (in Davis, California).[49] When the first conference of the National Black Feminist Organization (NBFO) convened in New York in December

1973, it was the first black women's organization that used the term *feminist*. Its agenda was succinctly stated in one participant's words: "While we share with our men a history of toil and dignity, it is categorically different to be Black and a woman in this society than it has been to be Black and male."[50] Among its concerns were many goals central to the women's liberation movement: day care, abortions, maternity leaves.[51]

Other groups, like the Combahee River Collective, represented a class-conscious politicized activism.[52] A self-described group of black lesbian feminists who have been meeting since 1974 in Boston, Massachusetts, the collective views its primary goal as building coalition with other progressive organizations and movements. With an active commitment to "struggling against racial, sexual, heterosexual, and class oppression," this group of black women works to combat the manifold and simultaneous oppression that all women of color face.[53] Its members promote nonhierarchical distribution of power within the group and believe that "the liberation of all oppressed peoples necessitates the destruction of the political-economic systems of capitalism and imperialism, as well as patriarchy."[54] They have worked on many issues of particular relevance to black women, such as sterilization abuse, battered women, rape, health care, and abortion rights. The collective has also published writings and conducted workshops on black feminism as a means of reaching black women nationwide.

KEY IDEAS AND EXPRESSIONS OF THE 1980S

More recently Afra-American feminism has come to the fore with a proliferation of sociopolitical analyses, theoretical critiques, and literary and artistic expressions.[55] Central to all of these is the argument that a poor black woman is triply disadvantaged in a society that values "whiteness," "maleness," and "money." Race, gender, and class intersect to cause tridimensional oppression. To separate them is to treat any one system of oppression as the most important key. For instance, those who consider class oppression to be the main cause of black women's subordinate status focus exclusively upon economics.[56]

Afra-American feminism also seeks to celebrate black womanhood within the North American cultural setting. Negative and oversimplified views of black women are debunked in favor of more positive ones that show black women as more than the sum of victimizations.[57] For example, one dominant image of the black woman has been as a beast of burden, in contrast to the American ideal of womanhood: fragile, white, and not too bright.[58] Afra-American feminism acknowledges that this black female image is derived from the historical role of black women as laborers in a society where ideals of femininity were equated with protected domesticity. Yet it contends that this representation of the black female laborer not only manifests the oppressive experiences of work and the economic forces that have exploited the energies of black women but also underscores the liberating attitudes of personal autonomy and sexual equality assumed by black women.[59] Moreover, Afra-American feminism challenges the myth of the "emasculating matriarch" found in traditional marriage and family literature, where it is argued (either explicitly or implicitly) that the social problems arising in black communities have come as a result of black women's dominance over black men.[60] Instead it presents models of black womanhood that are strong and independent.

In 1983 novelist Alice Walker coined the term *womanist*.[61] Its origin is from the black folk expression "you acting womanish," meaning "wanting to know more and in greater depth than is good for one . . . outrageous, audacious, courageous and willful behavior."[62] Its usage conveys the cultural codes (beliefs, meanings, and values) that have crystalized in the African-American community around women's activity. It celebrates the passage of wisdom between women (mothers, daughters, sisters, friends, lovers) for the sake of survival—in the white world, in the black community, and with men. While this concept allows women to claim their roots in black history, religion, and culture, it also suggests their connection with feminism.[63] As a popular term among many black feminists, *womanist* honors the culture-specific feminism of black women that has existed from the eighteenth century to the present time. As one writer states, it is a philosophy that concerns itself with both sexual equality in the black community and "with the world power structure that subjugates both blacks and women."[64] Womanist ideology contains a pluralistic liberationist perspective that has always been part of the black female activist tradition. It provides a lens that portrays how all oppressions are interlocked and may be approached through the collective efforts of all marginalized groups. In 1971 Fannie Lou Hamer, the daughter of sharecroppers and a civil rights activist in Mississippi, epitomized this insight in her address to the National Association for the Advancement of Colored People (NAACP) Legal Defense Fund.

> You know I work for the liberation of all people because when I liberate myself, I'm liberating other people . . . her [the white woman's] freedom is shackled in chains to mine; and she realizes for the first time that she is not free until I am free.[65]

Conclusions: Goals for Afra-American Feminism

Black women must continue to critique the dominant institutional forms of oppression within the United States. However, it is just as imperative that we address the inadequacies of social institutions operative in African-American culture and life, in particular our families and churches.[66] Some black feminists have already identified the misogynist values in the image of the emasculating matriarch. Some have pointed to the rates of sexual and physical abuse of black women and to the tradition of black men assuming the visible leadership positions in many black social institutions while women do the work.[67]

While these insights are critical, they have not reached popular black culture. Current studies indicate that within black families, mothers continue to assume the primary role for child care, household maintenance, and socialization, despite earlier assumptions of role flexibility.[68] In this context, black women are still expected to perform the domestic roles as well as provide economic support. Coping with multiple competing demands has created serious health problems for black women.[69]

The black church has been a powerful institution providing a network of supportive relations against a hostile white society. Advocating collective consciousness and collective responsibility, it has produced civic and political leaders as well as a distinct ethical and social value system for African-Americans. Historians and scholars of religion have documented its important leadership role in the quest for social justice in North America. Generally missing from these writings, generated predominantly by men, are critiques of its hierarchical and sexist structure.[70] Inundated with a hierarchy of male clergy, theologians, and professionals leading female congregations, the "black church" presents a model where "the women are consistently given responsibilities in the kitchen, while the men are elected to the important boards and leadership positions."[71] Furthermore black theology remains largely hostile to developments inclusive of women's rights, perspectives, and critiques. Mutually enriching male and female relations are jeopardized by distorted views of masculinity that objectify women as utilitarian props within the man's domain. Theologian Pauli Murray has underscored the limitations of black theology.

> In reveals little understanding of the problems of black women as women and almost totally ignores feminist theology. Black women are torn between their loyalty to their racial community and growing conscious-ness of the need to struggle against sexism. . . . There is a dearth of black women theologians—due in part to the strong patriarchal tradition of the black Church—who can bring to bear their influence upon the development of black theology. The interlocking factors of racism and sexism within the black experience awaits analysis.[72]

The invisibility of black women within the black church and black theology reflects and reinforces their invisibility in black history. Traditional studies of African-American history, family, and life have focused upon only outstanding, often legendary, male subjects who are portrayed as the key players in decisive events and who alone are esteemed as having lasting historical significance.[73] In these scenarios black women are seldom recognized as subjects whose actions and thoughts helped to shape an epoch. There has been a lack of interest in finding the authentic voices of women through primary sources (narrative writings, impressionistic accounts such as novels, autobiography) or secondary sources (historical essays, travel journals).

In the struggle for wholeness, black feminists must demand an ethic of accountability and caring, not only from the dominant culture but also from their black brothers, fathers, and sons; they also must encourage all black females to incorporate womanist politics in their daily lives. The underlying rationale of Afra-American feminist ideology must become the dominant ethic of contemporary black society. This is the notion that both white culture and African-American communities share the responsibility for "righting the wrongs" of racism/sexism.[74] We must demand that black men acknowledge the reality of sexual oppression; we must challenge our educators and clergy who would reeducate "our" people on every issue to advocate the dignity and equality of women.

Whether in religious training, familial structures, or educational pedagogy, there is a need to secure the rights of black women. I suggest that this agenda include, but not be limited to, the following strategic measures:

1. transforming misogynist and homophobic conceptions of sexuality
2. challenging the patriarchical elements within traditional African-American religion
3. overcoming the inherent sexist assumptions of all Afrocentric ideologies
4. providing feminist strategies and pedagogical insights within classroom settings
5. eradicating social forms or patterns of dating/sexual encounters among young black males that condone sexism or violence against females

Accordingly, the role of black feminists continues to be the same: engaging in brave acts of resistance, defiance, and empowerment. We must continue to break the silence.

> And when we speak we are afraid
> our words will not be heard
> nor welcomed
> but when we are silent
> we are still afraid.
>
> So it is better to speak
> remembering
> we were never meant to survive.

—Audre Lorde, "A Litany for Survival"

NOTES

1. See Zora Neal Hurston, *Their Eyes Were Watching God* (New York: Negro Universities Press, 1969), 29. Hurston's view of black women's status in America is found in the folk wisdom given to Janie Sparks by her grandmother, who says, "De white man throw down the load and tell de nigger man to pick it up. He pick it up because he have to, but he don't tote it. He hand it to his womenfolks. De nigger woman is de mule of the world so far as Ah can see."

2. This term suggests a distinct cultural continuum dating from the eighteenth century to the present day of brave and articulate black women. For usage of this term, I am indebted to Joanne Braxton and Andree N. McLaughlin, eds., *Wild Women in the Whirlwind* (New Brunswick, N.J.: Rutgers University Press, 1990), xxii. For accounts of black women's myriad acts of resistance against the dominant culture, see Paula Giddings, *When and Where I Enter* (New York: William and Co., 1984); Sharon Harley and Rosalyn Terborg-Penn, eds., *The Afro-American Woman: Struggles and Images* (New York & London: Kennikat Press, 1978); Bert James Lowenberg and Ruth Borgin, eds., *Black Women in Nineteenth-Century American Life: Their Words, Their Thoughts, Their Feelings* (University Park: Pennsylvania State University Press, 1976); Gloria T. Hull, Patricia Bell Scott, and Barbara Smith, eds., *All the Women Are White, All the Blacks Are Men, But Some of Us Are Brave: Black Women's Studies* (Old Westbury, N.Y.: Feminist Press, 1982); Rosalyn Terborg-Penn, "Discontented Black Feminists: Prelude and Postscript to the Passage of the Nineteenth Amendment," in *Decades of Discontent: The Women's Movement, 1920–1940,* ed. Lois Scharf and Joan M. Jensen (Westport, Conn.: Greenwood, 1983); Hazel V. Carby, *Reconstructuring Womanhood: The Emergence of the Afro-American Woman Novelists* (New York: Oxford University Press, 1987); Gerda Lerner, ed., *Black Women in White America: A Documentary History* (New York: Vintage, 1973).

3. See Winthrop D. Jordan, *White Over Black: American Attitudes Toward the Negro, 1550–1812* (New York: W. W. Norton & Company, 1968), 35, 77; A. Leon Higginbotham, Jr., *In the Matter of Color: Race and the American Legal Process, The Colonial Period* (New York: Oxford University

Press, 1978), 23, 43ff. For further discussions, see James C. Ballagh, *A History of Slavery in Virginia* (Baltimore: John Hopkins Press, 1902); Ronald T. Takaki, *Iron Cages: Race and Culture in Nineteenth-Century America* (Seattle: University of Washington Press, 1979); John Hope Franklin, *From Slavery to Freedom: A History of Negro Americans* (New York: Vintage Books/Random House, 1969).

4. Mamie E. Locke, "From Three-Fifths to Zero: Implications of the Constitution for African-American Women, 1787–1870," in *Women and Politics* 10, no. 2 (1990): 36.

5. Paula Giddings, *When and Where I Enter* (New York: William Morrow and Co., 1984), 39–46. For further discussions also see Erlene Stetson, "Studying Slavery: Some Literary and Pedagogical Considerations on the Black Female Slave," in *All the Women Are White, All the Blacks are Men, But Some of Us Are Brave,* ed. Gloria T. Hull, Patricia Bell Scott, and Barbara Smith (Old Westbury, N.Y.: The Feminist Press), 61–84; Angela Davis, "The Black Woman's Role in the Community of Slaves," *The Black Scholar* 3 (December 1971): 2–16; Darlene Hine and Kate Wittenstein, "Female Slave Resistance: The Economics of Sex," in *The Black Woman Cross-Culturally,* ed. Filomina Chioma Steady (Boston: Schenkman, 1981); Deborah Gray White, *Ar'n't I a Woman? Female Slaves in the Plantation South* (New York: Norton, 1985).

6. Sojourner Truth, "I Suppose I Am About the Only Colored Woman That Goes About to Speak for the Rights of Colored Women," in *Black Women in White America: A Documentary History,* ed. Gerda Lerner (New York: Vintage Books, 1973), 569.

7. Giddings, 68.

8. Anna Julia Cooper, *A Voice from the South* (Ohio: Aldine Printing House, 1892), 134.

9. Mary Church Terrell, "The Progress of Colored Women," *Voice of the Negro* 1, no. 7 (July 1904): 292.

10. Maria Stewart, *Productions of Mrs. Maria W. Stewart* (Boston, 1835), 28.

11. Ibid., 69.

12. Cooper, 144.

13. Ibid., ii.

14. Ibid., 29, 31.

15. Ibid., 121.

16. May Wright Sewall, ed., *World's Congress of Representative Women* (Chicago, 1893), 715, cited in Lowenberg and Borgin, 330–31.

17. Lerone Bennet, *Before the Mayflower: A History of the Negro in America, 1619–1964* (Baltimore: Penguin Books, 1964), 146.

18. Nannie H. Burroughs, "Black Women and Reform," *The Crisis* 10 (August 1915): 187.

19. Rosalyn Terborg-Penn, "Afro-Americans in the Struggle for Woman Suffrage" (Ph.D. dissertation, Howard University, 1977), 55.

20. Mary Ann Shadd Carey, "The Colored Women's Progressive Association," *Mary Ann Shadd Cary Papers* (Moorland-Spingarn Research Center, Howard University, Washington, D.C.), cited in Giddings, 75.

21. Elsa Barkley Brown, "Womanist Consciousness: Maggie Lena Walker and the Independent Order of Saint Luke," *Signs: A Journal of Women and Culture and Society* 14, no. 3 (Spring 1989), reprinted in *Black Women in America: Social Science Perspectives* (Chicago: The University of Chicago Press, 1990), 179.

22. Ibid.

23. Maggie Lena Walker, "Addresses," 1909, *MLW Papers,* cited in Celia Jackson Suggs, "Maggie Lena Walker," *Truth: Newsletter of the Association of Black Women Historians* 7 (Fall 1985): 6.

24. Brown, 1990, 186.

25. Mark D. Matthews, " 'Our Women and What They Think': Amy Jacques Garvey and the Negro World," *Black Scholar* (May–June 1979): 11.

26. Ibid.

27. Fannie Barrier Williams, "The Club Movement Among Colored Women in America," in J. E. MacBrady, ed., *A New Negro for a New Century* (Chicago: American Publishing, 1900), 383.

28. Dorothy Salem, *To Better Our World: Black Women in Organized Reform, 1890–1920,* vol. 14 in sixteen-volume series *Black Women in United States History* (Brooklyn, N.Y.: Carlson Publishing Co., 1990), 16ff. See Lerner, *Black Women in White America,* 450–58.

29. Ibid., 14.

30. Ibid., 71ff. For further discussion of the women's club movement, see Cynthia Neverdon-Morton, "The Black Woman's Struggle for Equality in the South, 1895–1925," in Sharon Harley

and Rosalyn Terborg-Penn, eds., *The Afro-American Woman: Struggles and Images* (Port Washington, N.Y.: Kennikat Press, 1978); Ruby M. Kendrick, "They Also Serve: The National Association of Colored Women, Inc., 1896–1964," *Negro History Bulletin* 17 (March 1954): 171–75; Gerda Lerner, "Early Community Work of Black Club Women," *Journal of Negro History* 59 (April 1974): 158–67.

31. On the national front, black clubwomen presented a type of social reform that was reflective of major feminist developments within this period. Many prominent members of the NACW believed in the woman's sphere, which emphasized women's moral superiority, nurturance of children, and imposition of middle-class standards on the economically disadvantaged. For further discussion, see Salem, 17, 29ff.

32. Eleanor Taylor, "The Negro Woman: Social and Moral Decadence," *Outlook* 76 (January 1904): 270.

33. "The Negro Problem by a Colored Woman and Two White Women," *The Independent* 64 (March 17, 1904): 589.

34. Elizabeth Davis, *Lifting as They Climb* (Washington, D.C.: The National Association of Colored Women, 1933), 41.

35. Salem, 50ff.

36. Mary Bethune, "A Century of Progress of Negro Women," address before the Chicago Women's Federation, June 30, 1933, cited in Lerner, *Black Women in White America,* 580.

37. Ella Baker, interview, June 19, 1968, *The Civil Rights Documentation Project* (Moorland-Spingarn Collection, Howard University, Washington, D.C.), 34–35.

38. Angela Davis, *Angela Davis: An Autobiography* (New York: Random House, 1974), 161.

39. Julia Herve, "Black Scholar Interviews Kathleen Cleaver," *Black Scholar* (December 1971): 56.

40. Barbara A. Sizemore, "Sexism and the Black Male," *Black Scholar* (March–April 1973): 6. See Bibi Amina Baraka, "Coordinator's Statement," in Imamu Amiri Baraka, ed., *African Congress: A Documentary of the First Pan-African Congress* (New York: William Morrow, 1972), 177.

41. Sizemore, 6.

42. With a few notable exceptions, most black women were not interested in publicly tackling sexism. Among those who attempted to discuss the full effects of racism and sexism on black women are Linda LaRue, "The Black Movement and Women's Liberation," in *The Black Scholar* 1 (May 1970): 36–42; Francis Beal, "Double Jeopardy: To Be Black and Female," in Robin Morgan, ed., *Sisterhood Is Powerful: An Anthology of Writings from the Women's Liberation Movement* (New York: Vintage Books, 1970); Pauli Murray, "The Negro Woman in the Quest for Equality," address delivered to the leadership Conference of the National Council of Negro Women, Nov. 14, 1963, Washington, D.C., printed as "The Liberation of Black Women," in Jo Freeman, ed., *Women: A Feminist Perspective* (Palo Alto, Calif.: Mayfield Publishing Co., 1975), 354; Aileen Hernandez, "Small Change for Black Women," *Ms.* 3 (August 1974): 16–18.

43. Diane K. Lewis, "A Response to Inequality: Black Women, Racism, and Sexism," *Signs: A Journal of Women and Culture and Society* 3, no. 2 (Winter 1977), reprinted in *Black Women in America: Social Science Perspectives* (Chicago: The University of Chicago Press, 1990), 42.

44. Toni Cade, "On the Issue of Roles," in *The Black Woman* (New York: New American Library, Signet Books, 1970), 102–3.

45. Francis Beale, "Double Jeopardy," in *The Black Woman,* 90–92.

46. "Preface," in *The Black Woman,* 10.

47. See Louis Harris and Associates, *The 1972 Virginia Slims American Women's Opinion Poll: A Survey of the Attitudes of Women on Their Roles in Politics and the Economy,* pp. 2, 4, cited in Lewis, 1990, 41.

48. See Geraldine Rickman, "A Natural Alliance: The New Role for Black Women," *Civil Rights Digest* 6 (Spring 1974): 62.

49. Lewis, 1990, 42, 49.

50. Eleanor H. Norton, quoted on p. 86 in Bernette Golden, "Black Women's Liberation," *Essence* 4 (February 1974): 35–36, 75–76, 86.

51. See Beverly Davis, "To Seize the Moment: A Retrospective on the National Black Feminist Organization," *Sage* 5, no. 2 (Fall 1988): 44.

52. The Combahee River Collective, "A Black Feminist Statement," in *But Some of Us Are Brave,* 13.

53. Ibid.

54. See Combahee River Collective, *Combahee River Collective Statement: Black Feminist Organizing in the Seventies and Eighties* (New York: Kitchen Table Press, 1986), 12–13.

55. For a sampling of contemporary black feminism, see Audre Lorde, "The Master's Tools Will Never Dismantle the Master's House," in *This Bridge Called My Back: Writings by Radical Women of Color*, ed. Cherie Moraga and Gloria Anzaldua (Watertown, Mass.: Persephone Press, 1981); Bell Hooks, *Ain't I a Woman? Black Women and Feminism* (Boston: South End Press, 1981); Bell Hooks, *Feminist Theory: From Margin to Center* (Boston: South End Press, 1984); Bell Hooks, *Talking Back: Thinking Feminist, Thinking Black* (Boston: South End Press, 1989); Delores Williams, "Black Women's Literature and the Task of Feminist Theology," in Clarissa W. Atkinson, Constance H. Buchanan, and Margaret R. Miles, eds., *Immaculate and Powerful: The Female in Sacred Image and Social Reality* (Boston: Beacon Press, 1985); "The Combahee River Collective: A Black Feminist Statement," in Zillah Eisenstein, ed., *Capitalist Patriarchy and the Case for Socialist Feminism* (New York: Monthly Review Press, 1979); Barbara Christian, *Black Feminist Criticism: Perspectives on Black Women Writers* (New York: Pergamon, 1985); Jacquelyn Grant, "A Black Response to Feminist Theology," in Janet Kalvern and Mary I. Buckley, eds., *Women's Spirit Bonding* (New York: Pilgrim Press, 1984), 117–24, and "Black Feminist Theology: Celebrating in the Midst of Struggle," unpublished keynote address, Women's Inter-Seminary Conference, Denver, Colorado, 1986.

56. Deborah K. King, "Multiple Jeopardy, Multiple Consciousness: The Context of a Black Feminist Ideology," *Signs: A Journal of Women and Culture and Society* 14, no. 1 (Autumn 1988), reprinted in *Black Women in America*, 270.

57. Joyce Ladner, *Tomorrow's Tomorrow: The Black Woman* (Garden City, N.Y.: Doubleday, 1971), 280. For further discussions upon this paradigm of black womanhood, see Patricia Hill Collins, "The Social Construction of Black Feminist Thought," *Signs: A Journal of Women and Culture and Society* 14 (1989): 746.

58. Bonnie Thornton Dill, "The Dialectics of Black Womanhood," *Signs: A Journal of Women and Culture and Society* 4, no. 3 (Spring 1979), reprinted in *Black Women in America*, 75.

59. Ibid., 76.

60. See E. Franklin Frazier, *The Negro Family in the United States* (Chicago: University of Chicago Press, 1966); Daniel P. Moynihan, *The Negro Family: The Case For National Action* (Washington, D.C.: Department of Labor, 1965); Lee Rainwater, *Behind Ghetto Walls* (Chicago: Aldine Publishing Co., 1970).

61. Alice Walker, "In Search of Our Mother's Gardens," *Womanist Prose* (New York: Harcourt, Brace, Jovanich, 1983).

62. Ibid., xi–xii. Walker also offers the following nuances for the term: (2) A woman who loves other women, sexually and/or nonsexually. . . . Committed to survival and wholeness of entire people, male and female....Traditionally capable, as in: "Mama, I'm walking to Canada and I'm taking you and a bunch of other slaves with me." Reply: "It wouldn't be the first time." (3) Loves music. Loves dance. Loves the moon. *Loves* the Spirit. Loves love and food and roundness. Loves struggle. Loves herself. *Regardless.* (4). Womanist is to feminist as purple to lavender.

63. For theological formulations of womanist thought, see Katie Geneva Cannon, *Black Womanist Ethics* (Atlanta: Scholars Press, 1988); Jacquelyn Grant, *White Women's Christ and Black Women's Jesus: White Feminist Christology and Womanist Response* (Atlanta: Scholars Press, 1989); Delores Williams, "Womanist Theology," in *Weaving the Visions* (San Francisco: Harper & Row, Publishers, 1989).

64. See Chikwenye Okonjo Ogunyemi, "Womanism: The Dynamics of the Contemporary Black Female Novel in English," *Signs: A Journal of Women and Culture and Society* 11, no. 1 (Autumn 1985): 63–80.

65. Lerner, *Black Women in White America*, 609–11.

66. Pamela T. Reid and Lillian Comas-Diaz, "Gender and Ethnicity: Perspectives on Dual Status," in *Sex Roles* 22, nos. 7/8 (1990): 402. Reid and her associates note that although recent profiles of the contemporary black family emphasize its diversity, they also note central themes that underlie such diversity and provide coherence for blacks. Among these are strong kinship bonds among a variety of households; strong work, education, and achievement orientation; and strong commitment to religious values and church participation. See R. Hill, *The Strength of Black Families* (New York: Emerson-Hall, 1972); M. K. Ho, *Family Therapy with Ethnic Minorities* (Newbury Park, Calif.: Sage, 1987).

67. For discussions on sexual violence, see Barbara Smith, "Notes for Yet Another Paper on Black Feminism, or Will the Real Enemy Please Stand Up," *Conditions* 5 (1979): 123–27. Concerning

politics, see Linda LaRue, "The Black Movement and Women's Liberation," in Sue Cox., ed., *Female Psychology: The Emerging Self* (Chicago: Science Research Association, 1976). See also Jacquelyn Grant, "Black Women and the Church," in *But Some of Us Are Brave*, 141–52.

68. See Melvin N. Wilson et al., "Flexibility and Sharing of Childcare Duties in Black Families," *Sex Roles* 22, nos. 7/8 (1990): 409–23; E. E. Macoby, *Social Development: Psychological Growth and the Parent-Child Relationship* (San Diego, Calif.: Harcourt, Brace, & Jovanovich, 1988).

69. For further discussions of the complex of factors (social, economic, and cultural) factors affecting black women's health, see "Health Factsheet on Black Women: National Black Women's Health Project," in *Sage* 2, no. 2 (Fall 1985): 76–77; Mirian Wright Edelman, "The Black Family in America," in Evelyn C. White, ed., *The Black Woman's Health Book* (Seattle, Wash.: Seal Press, 1990), 128–48; Darielle Watts Jones, "Towards a Stress Scale for African-American Women," *Psychology of Women Quarterly* 14 (1990): 271–75. Jones points to the role and relationship stressors confronting many black women who must parent as single mothers, are dissatisfied in primary relationships with men who do not provide monetary or emotional support, and must grapple with race and ethnicity problems.

70. E. Franklin Frazier, *The Negro Church in America*; C. Eric Lincoln, *The Black Church Since Frazier* (New York: Schocken Books, 1974).

71. Jacquelyn Grant, "Black Women and the Church," in *But Some of Us Are Brave*, 142.

72. Ibid.

73. For discussions of black women's invisibility in historiography, see Gerda Lerner, *The Majority Finds Its Past* (New York and Oxford: Oxford University Press, 1979), 60; For nontraditional approaches to historiography, see Illene Alexander, Suzanne Bunkers, and Cherry Nuhanju, "A Conversation on Studying and Writing About Women's Lives Using Nontraditional Methodologies," *Women's Studies Quarterly* 3/4 (1989): 99–114.

74. This is one of many strategies specified by the Leadership for Black Women program. For further discussion, see Nora Hall and Karen Gray, "Leadership for Black Women: Strategies for the Future," *Sage* 5, no. 2 (Fall 1988): 54.

Keep Us on the Pedestal: Women Against Feminism in Twentieth-Century America

Susan E. Marshall

IN RECENT DECADES, A growing body of feminist research has delineated the structure, strategy, and political ideology of women's rights movements in the United States (Flexner 1973; Kraditor 1968, 1971; Freeman 1975; Cott 1987). We know surprisingly little, however, about the organization of opposition to proposed changes in female status. The astounding defeat of the Equal Rights Amendment (ERA) in 1982 (see Boles 1979; Berry 1986; Mansbridge 1986) underscores the continuing significance of antifeminist movements.

This article compares the American antisuffrage movement that flourished between 1910 and 1918 and the recent anti-ERA movement spearheaded by Phyllis Schlafly to suggest a conceptual framework for understanding antifeminist movements in the United States. Much of the popular and scholarly work on American antifeminism has emphasized the powerful resistance of business interests to progress in women's rights for the purpose of maintaining an abundance of cheap female labor (Firestone 1970; Scott and Scott 1975; Carabillo 1978). While the profit motive may explain corporate financial contributions to the antifeminist cause, a large part of the organizing and lobbying activities has been performed by antifeminist females, many of whom are not in the labor force and thus not in a position to exploit directly members of their own sex (Brady and Tedin 1976; Tedin et al. 1977).

This analysis attempts to explain the emergence and growth of female countermovements to feminism through an examination of the rhetorical strategies used to define the movement, to establish goals, and to attract adherents. A comparison of female antisuffrage and anti-ERA literature suggests that strikingly similar arguments have been utilized to justify the maintenance of traditional gender roles. In particular, the passage of legislation mandating gender equality was perceived as a threat to the privileged status of homemaker, which excuses women from the responsibilities of financial support, political participation, and military service. In both historical periods, the sacred symbols of family, God, and country were evoked frequently to emphasize the importance of female domestic roles for the perpetuation of American society. Conversely, this potent rhetoric discredited feminists as selfish, unpatriotic, irreligious, antifamily, and both antimale and antifemale.

547

This article explores these common rhetorical themes and analyzes the two female antifeminist movements in terms of status politics (see Gusfield 1963; Lipset 1965).

Historical Background

Although the first formal antisuffrage organization was established in the United States as early as 1872, organized antisuffrage activity remained sporadic and limited in scope until 1910, when suffragist victories began to mount in the form of state constitutional amendments giving women the vote. By 1913, there were sixteen state antisuffrage organizations and a National Association Opposed to Woman Suffrage. Many of these groups existed with acknowledged male financial support, but their leadership and membership were overwhelmingly female. Their activities included public speaking to advertise the cause, legislative lobbying at state and federal hearings on the suffrage issue, and the publication and distribution of antisuffrage literature. Their journals delineated the arguments against woman suffrage, reported the progress of antisuffrage campaigns, rejoiced at suffragists' defeats, and trivialized suffragists' victories. By 1918, however, the heyday of the antisuffrage movement had passed, weakened by the success of a suffrage amendment in the key eastern state of New York and the imminent ratification of the Susan B. Anthony amendment to the U.S. Constitution, which enfranchised twenty-six million women in 1920.

Similarly, the organization of contemporary antifeminists was in large part a response to the success of the women's movement in gaining state ratification of the ERA. Twenty-eight states ratified the ERA in 1972, the first year of eligibility. During that year, a countermovement began to coalesce, dedicated to halting ratification in additional states and rescinding the amendment where it had already been ratified. Reportedly backed by corporate interests, the countermovement nonetheless had a rank and file predominantly composed of women. Local and regional groups appeared, with such attention-getting names as Eve Reborn, HOT DOG (Humanitarians Opposed to Degrading Our Girls), AWARE (American Women Are Richly Endowed), and POW (Protect Our Women), but the most prominent national antifeminist organization was clearly Phyllis Schlafly's STOP-ERA, an offshoot of Eagle Forum, a conservative organization that Schlafly also founded. The contemporary antifeminist movement proved more successful than its predecessor. After 1977 no additional states ratified the ERA, several states voted to rescind ratification, and the lapse of the June 30, 1982, deadline found the ERA three states short of the thirty-eight needed to add it to the U.S. Constitution.

The Ideology of Antifeminism

Why would women organize to oppose actively a women's rights movement? A comparative historical analysis of American antisuffrage and anti-ERA literature suggests that the ideology of antifeminism embodies three related arguments: reaffirmation of divinely ordained sex differences, support for the traditional family as a necessary basis for the continuation of society, and alignment of antifeminism with unselfish patriotism. Issues of women's rights have been recast as a moral battle over the basic institutions and values of American society.

NATURE'S PLAN: SPECIALIZATION BY SEX

Antifeminist arguments for the maintenance of differential laws by sex rest ultimately on a belief in inherent and hence immutable sex differences. By this argument, the superior intellectual and physical endowments of men intend them for the public sphere, the world of economics and politics, as the providers and protectors of women and children. Women, by contrast, are guided by sentiment rather than reason and are thus designed for the domestic sphere of childbearing and child rearing, keeping the home, and instilling morality. This specialization of function, it is argued, is ordained by God and nature, as supported by both scientific theories of evolution and religious tenets. Impertinent feminists who wish to tamper with the laws of nature thus threaten the continuation of civilization.

The antisuffragist view of woman's role was a reflection of middle-class values—"to be tender, loving, pure, and inspiring in her home, . . . to raise the moral tone of every household, to refine every man, . . . to mitigate the harshness and cruelty and vulgarity of life everywhere" (*Anti-Suffragist* 1908d, 8). The delicate female nervous system renders woman without "staying qualities, continuity of purpose, or affinity for the rough and tumble warfare in political life" (*Anti-Suffragist* 1910b, 2). Moreover, "woman does not think, she feels, she does not reason, she emotionalizes," and hence a female electorate is likely to "do injury to itself without promoting the public good" (*Woman's Protest* 1915c, 15; 1915e, 19). Because they believed in these inherent limitations, antisuffragists believed that feminists were asking not for equality but for special favors. "Women cannot consistently ask for a place in men's political race and then insist that they be helped over all the hurdles because they are naturally handicapped in the contest by their sex and their mission as mothers" (Heron 1915, 6). Paradoxically, however, antisuffragists repeatedly insisted, "We acknowledge no inferiority to men. We claim to have no less ability to perform the duties which God has imposed upon us than they have to perform those imposed upon them" (Illinois Association 1909, 3).

Contemporary antifeminists assert similar "fundamental inherent differences between men and women" (Schlafly 1977, 21). Male intellectual and physical superiority and female maternal instinct "must be recognized as part of the plan of the Divine Architect for the survival of the human race through the centuries" (p. 11). By opposing such sex-based roles, the women's movement and the ERA are "opposing Mother Nature herself" (p. 87). Specifically, legal mandates for equal employment opportunity rapidly degenerate into "reverse discrimination," given their blatant disregard for "the inadequacy of female qualifications" (p. 131). Gender-free laws will also remove traditional female protections from physically demanding jobs, thus increasing female injury and unemployment, and women's athletic opportunities will be virtually eliminated if they have to compete with men because of legal challenges to sex-segregated sports programs. While insisting that attempts to eradicate inherent sex differences cannot succeed, antifeminists also predict that experiments that undermine the traditional sex-based division of labor will "further confuse a generation already unsure about its identity," ominously conjuring up the specter of rampant homosexuality (p. 22).

In both countermovements, antifeminists portrayed themselves as women who accepted these sex differences and embraced their femaleness. Anti-suffragists were "women who are proud of their womanhood and their relationship to men" (*Woman's Protest* 1915a, 3). They were the true ladies, the "patient, self-sacrificing women" who carry on their work "quietly and unostentatiously," with "grace of manner, dignity of bearing, purity of spirit, and nobility of conduct" (*Anti-Suffragist* 1908b, 5; Sebring 1915, 11; George 1915, 5). These qualities are also cited in more recent antifeminist literature, such as Andelin's *Fascinating Womanhood* (1966), Morgan's *Total Woman* (1973), and Schlafly's "Positive Woman," who "understands that men and women are different, and that these differences provide the key to her success as a person, and fulfillment as a woman" (Schlafly 1977, 9).

In sharp contrast, feminists have been characterized as malcontents, women who have failed at being women and are trying, somewhat childishly, to spoil the happiness of others of their sex. In the early decades of this century, suffragists were variously called "Amazons," "mannish," "unwomanly," "vulgar," and "viragoes"; in short, they were a disgrace to "Fair Womanhood" (*Anti-Suffragist* 1909a, 3; 1912a, 2; 1912b, 7; White 1915b, 9; *Woman's Protest* 1915e, 19). According to Schlafly, feminists are "disgruntled," "whining," "straggly-haired" women who downgrade their sex and ultimately reject it, as evidenced by their campaign to adopt male prerogatives and jobs (Schlafly 1977, 34, 35, 37). Paradoxically, the sexual stereotypes of dependence and emotionality embraced by antifeminists are the very ones used to further discredit their adversaries. Feminists are "hysterical"; they are "howling dervishes" who "cry copiously" about supposed injustices and seek "silly" corrective measures such as the elimination of sexist words from laws and textbooks (*Anti-Suffragist* 1909c, 5; *Woman's Protest* 1915b, 7; Schlafly 1977, 28, 45). The use of the diminutive term *suffragette* is a notable example of the derogatory application of feminine stereotypes.

THE CULT OF DOMESTICITY

To antifeminists, immutable sex differences dictate a traditional family structure, in which male breadwinners support female homemakers. Patriarchal marriage is the ultimate goal for the normal woman. "Marriage and motherhood give a woman new identity and the opportunity for all-round fulfillment as a woman" (Schlafly 1977, 56), and "if she does not think and plan to this end herself someone does it for her" (Bannister 1910, 6). Comparing domestic and career roles, they argued that motherhood offers the satisfaction of achievement at an early age, while marriage provides a boss (the husband) who is more tolerable than a supervisor or an office manager (Schlafly 1977, 57, 60). Feminist demands are perceived as a threat to this fundamental social order. Increased female participation in the economic and political spheres causes women to neglect their domestic responsibilities and erodes patriarchal power, which "will tend to the disintegration of the home and the hurt of the nation and the race" (*Anti-Suffragist* 1909b, 2).

Antisuffragists claimed that the female vote was unnecessary and redundant, for male family heads adequately represented the wishes of their wives. Moreover, women had considerable political influence through their charity work and especially through motherhood. "Raise good and able men and in one generation the world will be governed by good and able men," counsels one antisuffragist (Arnold 1915, 14). If women adequately perform their domestic duties, there is no time for active political participation. It is thereby implied that good wives and mothers are disinterested in the vote. Conversely, voting females neglect their family responsibilities, producing ill-mannered or delinquent children and exacerbating antagonism between the sexes to the point of marital dissolution. Political activity also strains the delicate female reproductive organs, "making [women] childless or mothers of a weak-kneed race" (*Anti-Suffragist* 1911, 7). This, of course, is the greatest threat to the continuance of society.

Contemporary antifeminists contend that the equal employment opportunity platform of the women's liberation movement "deliberately degrades the homemaker" (Schlafly 1977, 86). Equality of treatment under the ERA "would wipe out the most basic and precious legal right that homemakers now enjoy: the right to be a full-time homemaker" (p. 98). The ERA was labeled "an elitist upper-middle class cause" (p. 149), perpetrated by selfish professionals who "betray" other women for a "brief high" or "fix" of political power (Schlafly 1973, 12). Feminists' destructive antifamily activities harm both sexes. The eradication of sex-discriminatory employment practices eliminates protection for females from overtime work, making it more difficult for women to perform their domestic duties. In addition, feminist pressure for "reverse discrimination . . . means that employers are being forced to hire and train inexperienced single women with no dependents in order to achieve some arbitrary quota . . . rather than a more qualified man with dependents" (Schlafly 1977, 118). This unjust displacement of married males presumably forces more wives out of the home and into the labor force. Women's liberation thus represents a concerted attack on the family, on female homemakers, and on male providers.

In both historical periods, feminists have been cast as the antithesis of the generous, self-sacrificing maternal figure. They are possessed of "intense egotism" and driven by "personal indulgence," promoting a "do your own thing" attitude that "is eroding the fabric of our families" and inculcating dangerous, individualistic values in our children (Armstrong 1915, 3; Brazzil 1915, 18; Schlafly 1977, 77). Feminists are "marital misfits" whose refusal to have babies is responsible "for the apparent disintegration of the institution of marriage" (Schlafly 1977, 65, 212). At the extreme, suffragists were portrayed as advocates of un-Christian and un-American life-styles, supporting activities such as free love and communal child rearing (*Anti-Suffragist* 1909d, 8; Illinois Association 1911, 1). Schlafly similarly charged that feminist support of abortion on demand represents an ominous revitalization of Hitler's genocidal policies (1977, 11) and that "lesbianism is logically the highest form in the ritual of women's liberation" (p. 208). "NOW [the National Organization for

Women] is for prolesbian legislation giving perverts the same legal rights as husbands and wives—such as the rights to get marriage licenses, to file joint income tax returns, and to adopt children" (p. 228).

PRO PATRIA

The explicit intentions of suffragists and ERA advocates to alter U.S. laws for the attainment of gender equality enabled antifeminists to monopolize the sacred symbols of God, family, and country in defense of the status quo. The two countermovements adopted the role of patriot and portrayed feminists as radical socialists who would overthrow the government in their single-minded desire to press their minority views on an unwilling electorate. Paradoxically, while condemning feminists for their "enshrinement of individuality," antifeminists explained their own rejection of constitutional amendments as the patriotic defense of individual and state rights from the imposition of federal mandate (Schlafly 1977, 77). During both eras, feminists were charged with duplicity for demanding equal rights when they were unable or unwilling to shoulder equal responsibilities of citizenship.

Antisuffragists were quite insistent that the female vote would cause the downfall of democracy. The cult of domesticity does not prepare women for the job of running the country. With little knowledge of finance, protected by their husbands from taxpaying responsibilities, enfranchised women would presumably support expensive referenda and ultimately bankrupt the government (Tucker 1911, 6; White 1915a, 9). The greater emotionality of females would prompt them to cast impulsive votes for candidates and issues. "National obligations would be piled up under some outburst of pity. . . . International alliances and menaces would be 'happy thoughts' of some moment of great excitement. And without intending it or providing against it, the nation would be plunged into war" (*Anti-Suffragist* 1908c, 8). Not only would this be unjust to males, who are singularly burdened with the duties of military service, but it would also threaten democratic rule. "To extend suffrage to women would be to introduce into the electorate a vast noncombatant party incapable of enforcing its own rule. . . . To make possible a majority which a minority could safely defy would be to overthrow the idea of Republican Government" (*Anti-Suffragist* 1908a, 3). During this wave of feminism, however, neither suffragists nor their adversaries debated the issue of female participation in warfare. Both sides expected women to support the war effort from the sidelines via voluntary relief work and temporary employment in defense industries.

The contemporary feminist movement has recast the issue of female military duty. The exclusion of women from combat positions is viewed as an example of sex discrimination in employment. The ERA would make women subject to a draft and to equal participation in warfare. The countermovement claims that this issue demonstrates the hypocrisy of feminists. "They will exercise *their* freedom of choice to avoid military service"—through legal loopholes such as age restrictions, conscientious objector status, etc.—"but they are willing to inflict involuntary military duty on all other eighteen-year-old girls" (Schlafly 1977, 124). In contrast, antifeminists are true patriots. "It is the task of the Positive Woman to keep America Good"—that is, in accordance with the principles of "Judeo-Christian civilization" (pp. 213, 219). This includes support for capitalist free enterprise and freedom from excessive government intervention. Schlafly supports local control of educational facilities that honor the traditional family; the right of employers to prefer, among equal job candidates, wage earners with dependents; the right to life of all innocent persons from conception to natural death; and the right of society to protect itself by designating different roles for males and females in the military, police, and fire protection services. The ERA is thus viewed as a "federal grab for power," an undemocratic erosion of the rights of individual citizens and states (p. 166).

The antithesis of God-fearing, democratic society is socialism, and feminists are frequently portrayed as seditious radicals who "agitate and demonstrate and hurl demands at society" (Schlafly 1977, 10). Antisuffragists made much of the political alliance between women's suffrage organizations and the Progressive and Socialist parties, as well as the feminist establishment of a Woman's Peace party during World War I (Illinois Association 1913; Conroy 1915; *Woman's Protest* 1915f; Repplier 1915). The continuation of militant suffragist activity during the war years was further evidence of the tendency of feminists to place self above country, in contrast to the patriotic contributions of antisuffrage organizations to the war effort (*Woman's Protest* 1915d). During both eras, feminist attacks on the traditional patriarchal institutions of marriage, work, and politics were perceived as evidence of "the rabid determination of militant radicals" to "evade" their domestic responsibilities at the expense of increased government "spending and control" (Schlafly 1977, 27, 204, 206). For antifeminists, socialism represents the greatest danger to women. Its emphasis on equality ignores inherent sex differences and makes the individual rather than the family the fundamental unit of society, thus reducing not only male power but also male responsibility for female dependents.

Antifeminism as Status Politics

The antisuffragist and anti-ERA literature illustrates how countermovements to feminism frequently embrace masculine and feminine stereotypes to legitimate the preservation of sex-discriminatory legislation. Females should not vote because they do not have the emotional, cognitive, or physical abilities necessary for active political participation, and they cannot compel obedience to their mandate via military force. The ERA should not be passed because it legalizes "reverse discrimination," the displacement of male workers by less qualified females. In both periods, female advocates of gender equality were derided for their lack of competence in the male sphere as well as for their loss of femininity.

However, the antifeminist belief in a rigid sexual division of labor admits no inequality with males. Females are uniquely suited for their domestic duties of home maintenance and child care, and conversely the domination of the public sphere by males is justified by males' inherently superior aggressive, analytical, and logical abilities. This ideology of "separate but equal" means that feminists who complain of gender inequality in American society are guilty of derogating their own sex. Antifeminist rhetoric thus adeptly reversed the images of women's liberation and antifeminism. The former now presents negative images of woman as victims, while the latter promises hope and fulfillment.

Both countermovements carried this argument one step further. Females not only have attained equality with males but also enjoy special privileges, which are threatened by feminist pressures to integrate traditional male and female roles. These asymmetrical rights and responsibilities are derived directly from the gender-based division of labor. As breadwinners, males are required to support their families and must pay their wives alimony in the event of divorce. As the stronger and more aggressive sex, males must also go to war. The physical inferiority of females thus works to their advantage, for women are spared the drudgeries and responsibilities of the male role. The insulation of females within the home preserves their special feminine qualities of gentleness, purity, and morality. It keeps them on the pedestal, above the harshness and vulgarity of the masculine public domain.

American antifeminist movements can thus be explained with reference to Gusfield's (1963) concept of status politics. Countermovements to feminism represent a defense of the dominant status of homemaker, which is perceived as threatened by demands to tear down the rigid separation of male and female spheres. Thus, antisuffragists warn that "if women claim equality, they must lose their privileges" (*Anti-Suffragist* 1910a, 8). Schlafly's STOP-ERA organization was reportedly an acronym for "Stop Taking Our Privileges" (Solomon 1978, 49), and Schlafly labeled the ERA the "Extra Responsibilities Amendment" (Schlafly 1977, 104). The Nineteenth Amendment and the ERA thus became symbolic battlegrounds for the issue of which female life-styles will dominate American society (Scott 1985; Marshall 1986). It is not surprising, therefore, that the rhetoric of antifeminism is so saturated with the sacred myths of God, family, and country. As Gusfield observed, the language of status politics is the language of moral issues. At stake is the "symbolic conferral of respect upon the norms of the victor and disrespect upon the norms of the vanquished" (1963, 174). Antifeminist movements represent the attempt of one group to legitimate publicly its concept of woman's proper place in the social order.

Despite the rhetorical similarities of the two antifeminist movements, significant social changes during this century have given each movement a distinct historical context, manifested by the differences in membership of the groups. In 1910, the status defense of the homemaker was led by wealthy, elite women, the wives of eminent eastern politicians and industrialists, such as Mrs. Elihu Root, Mrs. Schuyler Van Renssalaer, and Mrs. Lowell Putnam. The founder and first president of the National Association Opposed to Woman Suffrage, Mrs. Arthur M. Dodge, traced her American ancestry to the first colonists, and her husband was reported at the time to be New York's wealthiest merchant. Newspaper accounts of mass antisuffrage fund-raisers described the assemblage as "prosperous-looking" and reported large donations in response to requests from the dais to "forgo theatre or opera tickets" for the defeat of suffrage ("Suffragists" 1914, 20; "Mormons" 1915, 5). Antisuffrage publications made frequent reference to the social imperative for the "redemptive influence of a lady" to "displace vulgarity with refinement, bad taste with propriety," and "bad manners with fine breeding" during these trying times of social upheaval (Sebring 1915, 11). Not surprisingly, corporate contributors to the antisuffrage cause reportedly included liquor, railroad, and oil interests, and northern legislators who led the fight against suffrage in the U.S. Senate were also well-known spokespersons for the interests of big business (Flexner 1973, 297–305).

The status conflict that spawned the antisuffrage movement may be better understood within a broader class context as an attempt to preserve the cultural hegemony of the eastern industrial elite from the onslaughts of uneducated foreign immigrants and western pioneers. A common argument used against suffrage by these organizations, for example, was the deleterious consequence of expanding the political power of the foreign-born by granting the vote to immigrant women (Scott 1909, 1; *Woman's Protest* 1915g, 7). It is interesting to note that antisuffrage leader Dodge founded the National Federation of Day Nurseries for the dual purpose of alleviating the burdens of the working woman while achieving the broader social goal of inculcating American middle-class values in immigrant children. Moreover, the parallel growth of support for woman suffrage and political reform in the western states was denounced as irrelevant to the East, which contained, after all, the bulk of American population and its moral center. While racist and classist rhetoric was not exclusive to one side of the suffrage issue (See Kraditor 1971, Chapters 6–7), the antisuffragists went further in their efforts to define motherhood and female domesticity as the solution to the political and cultural threat facing native-born Americans. Furthermore, although the predominantly middle-class suffrage movement also received its share of support from wealthy eastern socialites, the suffragists made greater efforts to reach working-class women. They courted prominent union leaders, spoke in immigrant neighborhoods, passed resolutions in support of women workers, and held public rallies to support female strikers and to protest poor working conditions in the wake of disasters, such as the Triangle Fire of 1911, which killed 146 women garment workers in New York City (see Gompers 1920; Schaffer 1962). While one might argue that the suffragists' motives were primarily instrumental, the suffragists were noticeably more likely than were the antisuffragists to target appeals to employed women of the lower classes.

In the contemporary era, antifeminism appears to receive its greatest support from a different segment of society. Surveys have generally found that female anti-ERA activists are more likely to come from lower-class backgrounds and to have lower levels of educational attainment than members of the pro-ERA movement; they are also less likely to have spouses with professional occupations (Tedin et al. 1977; Arrington and Kyle 1978). Female antifeminist activists are also less likely to be employed and, when employed, are less likely to be found in professional occupations than are pro-ERA activists (Mueller and Dimieri 1982). Other surveys assessing the correlates of women's attitudes about the ERA have similarly found that ERA opponents tend to be less educated (Huber, Rexroat, and Spitze 1978) and are less likely to be employed (Scott 1985) than those favoring the proposed amendment.

While the evidence is inconclusive, due to the small number of empirical studies, it does suggest that contemporary antifeminism is more likely to receive support among working-class, nonemployed women. Perhaps the attraction of this ideology lies in its defense of the traditional middle-class family with male as provider and female as homemaker, long a symbol of upward mobility in the United States. Seen in this light, the movement's charges that affirmative action programs threaten the male breadwinner role and force wives into the labor force to support families contain a powerful class appeal. Anti-ERA rhetoric portrayed feminists as "smooth-talking college women who have never seen a factory production line" and are thus far removed from and little concerned with the economic problems of working-class women (Schlafly 1977, 148, 145). Significantly, Phyllis Schlafly herself came from a modest family background, grew up during the Depression, worked her way through college, and achieved upward mobility through marriage to a successful attorney (Felsenthal 1981).

These divergent historical circumstances of the status politics of anti-feminism point to tentative explanations for the failure of the antisuffragists to halt ratification of the Nineteenth Amendment in one era and the success of the anti-ERA movement fifty years later. During the second decade of this century, the status conflict favored the rising middle classes, as other popular reform movements—such as temperance, labor rights, and progressivism—joined with suffrage in chipping away at the hegemony of the eastern industrial elite. In addition, political support for the suffrage amendment increased after 1918, in recognition of women's contribution to the war effort and the embarrassing absence of female political rights in the aftermath of President Wilson's pledge to make the world safe for democracy. Suffragist leaders highlighted these incongruities in the media. They also demonstrated considerable political expertise when, after two decades of campaigns for the passage of state woman suffrage referenda, during which time an effective network of state organizations was developed, they followed up with a coordinated national effort singlemindedly focusing on the issue of the vote. (It has been suggested, however, that this single-issue strategy ultimately impeded expansion of the movement to other feminist concerns after suffrage was secured.)

By contrast, the success of the contemporary stop-ERA movement may be traced partly to the economic problems of the 1970s, which engendered a backlash against affirmative action programs designed to promote employment opportunities for women and minorities. Given the membership composition of the anti-ERA movement, it is likely that what is perceived as threatening to the male breadwinner role may concomitantly be seen as endangering the position of the female as homemaker as well as the family's middle-class status. One survey, for example, found that both sexes were more likely to oppose the ERA if they believed that its passage would make it harder for males to find good jobs, and the authors predicted that a stagnating economy would have deleterious effects on ratification (Huber, Rexroat, and Spitze 1978). This is indeed what happened. According to national opinion surveys, public support for the ERA generally declined throughout the 1970s, although a majority of Americans continued to support it (Daniels, Darcy, and Westphal 1982). Interestingly, 1980 marked the nadir of ERA support, the same year that the Republican party withdrew its longstanding support of the amendment at its national convention and nonetheless swept the presidential elections later that year. In the rising conservative political tide, antifeminist leaders such as Schlafly wasted no time in integrating the anti-ERA movement with other powerful new right political organizations. Feminists, in contrast, may inadvertently have weakened support for the ERA by addressing a broad spectrum of issues, including the right to abortion, during the ratification struggle. The stop-ERA movement adeptly seized the opportunity to recruit new members through local churches and antiabortion groups (Brady and Tedin 1976; Mueller and Dimieri 1982). Postmortems conducted in the wake of the June 1982 ratification deadline identified other strategic errors by the pro-ERA movement—most notably, the failure to develop cohesive state organizations until the opposition had already mobilized, redefined the amendment, and scored some impressive state legislature defeats of the ERA (see Marshall and Orum 1986). The proponents had lost momentum as early as 1974, and they "were essentially fighting a rearguard action" (Boles 1982, 576). By the time the National Organization for Women (NOW) finally took charge of a focused national ratification campaign in the latter 1970s, it may have already been too late for the ERA.

Since defeating the federal Equal Rights Amendment in 1982, Schlafly's Eagle Forum continues to monitor the progress of state ERAs, remobilizing Stop-ERA whenever necessary to combat referenda in Maine (1984), Vermont (1986), and Iowa (1992). Schlafly has actively opposed most recent feminist policy demands, including comparable worth, subsidized child care, family leave, and abortion, frequently testifying at congressional hearings and appearing on network news programs (Marshall 1991, 56–61). Eagle Forum opposed the activation of women soldiers during the Gulf War, citing the harm done to mothers and their young children by a military policy acceding to elitist feminist demands for equal treatment (Schlafly 1991, 1).

The 1980s witnessed the rise of another women's antifeminist organization. Concerned Women for America (CWA) was founded in 1979 by Beverly LaHaye, the wife of prominent new right minister Tim LaHaye. Headquartered in the nation's capital for maximum political impact and claiming a membership far larger than Eagle Forum, CWA addresses similar issues but with a stronger religious focus (Marshall 1991, 57–60). For example, both organizations seek to restore "profamily" values to public education, but CWA also wants to reinstate prayer in school and makes greater use of sexual morality themes to discredit the opposition. While both groups rely heavily on grass-roots lobbying, CWA's tactics include members' prayer chains and legal challenges to the separation of church and state. Although Eagle Forum and CWA are competing for the same constituency and disagree on tactics and goals, they never engage in public bloodletting, wisely presenting a united front to their feminist adversaries.

The new right coalition scored some impressive victories during the Reagan and Bush administrations. The 1989 Supreme Court decision *Webster v. Reproductive Services* upheld Missouri's restrictive abortion law, inspiring several other state legislatures to pass similar laws limiting women's reproductive freedom. A series of conservative appointments to the Supreme Court increased the likelihood of overturning *Roe v. Wade,* and feminist attempts to circumvent the courts with the proposed Freedom of Choice Act will probably not withstand the strong counterattack by antifeminist and prolife groups. The 1992 election of President Clinton altered feminist political opportunities, as illustrated by the 1993 passage of the Family Leave and Medical Act, previously vetoed by President Bush, which mandates unpaid leaves for many employees due to childbirth, adoption, or family illness. Antifeminist organizations responded to the loss of White House support with battle cries and emergency appeals to their constituencies, mobilizing sufficient protests to successfully block a number of key Clinton appointments.

With each victory, antifeminist leaders proclaimed the death of feminism. In truth, the evidence is less conclusive than either group will admit. Feminist organizations reported surges in membership and financial support after the *Webster* decision and the Clarence Thomas confirmation hearings, but repeated crises tend to weaken organizations in the long run. Americans did become more socially conservative in the 1980s, but this reversal generally excluded women's roles (Mason and Lu 1988, 45). For example, over two-thirds of Americans favor efforts to change women's status, and a majority of both sexes agree that a strong women's movement is still needed (Sapiro 1991, 21; Simon and Landis 1989, 276). While Faludi (1991) convincingly charged the mass media with orchestrating a backlash against women's rights, her feminist call to arms was a national best-seller. Although Eagle Forum continues to bestow its annual Fulltime Homemaker Award, it has moderated its stance against women's employment, supporting the "mommy track" and other policies that create "family-friendly workplaces" (Schlafly 1990, 2). These mutual adjustments illustrate the complexity of the struggle for women's rights and the continuing interaction between social movements and their countermovements.

REFERENCES

Andelin, Helen B. 1966. *Fascinating Womanhood: A Guide to a Happy Marriage.* San Luis Obispo, Calif.: Pacific Press.

Anti-Suffragist. 1908a. 1 (July): 3.

———. 1908b. "Salutatory." 1 (July): 4–5.

———. 1908c. 1 (Dec.): 3.

———. 1908d. 1 (Dec.): 8.

———. 1909a. "The Suffragettes' Midnight Raid." 1 (Mar.): 3.

———. 1909b. "Extracts from Papers Read at Albany, N.Y., February 24, 1909." 1 (June): 1–8.

———. 1909c. 2 (Sept.): 5.

———. 1909d. 2 (Sept.): 8.

———. 1910a. "Madame Bell-Ranske." 2 (Mar.): 8.

———. 1910b. "Statement of Miss Phoebe W. Couzins, L.L.B., in Opposition to Woman Suffrage." 2 (June): 2.

———. 1911. "Australia." 3 (Sept.): 7.

———. 1912a. "The Taste of Woman Suffrage." 4 (Jan.): 2.

———. 1912b. "Subjects for the Alienist." 4 (Apr.): 7.

Armstrong, Eliza D. 1915. "Woman Suffrage and the Saloon." *Woman's Protest* 7 (May): 3.

Arnold, Mrs. George F. 1915. "Ignorance of the Real Issues at Stake." *Woman's Protest* 6 (Apr.): 14.

Arrington, Theodore S., and Patricia A. Kyle. 1978. "Equal Rights Amendment Activists in North Carolina." *Signs* 3 (Spring): 666–80.

Bannister, Lucy E. 1910. "Extracts from Paper Read Before Judiciary Committee." *Anti-Suffragist* 2 (June): 6.

Berry, Mary Frances. 1986. *Why ERA Failed.* Bloomington: Indiana University Press.

Boles, Janet K. 1979. *The Politics of the Equal Rights Amendment: Conflict and Decision Process*. New York: Longman.

————. 1982. "Building Support for the ERA: A Case of 'Too Much, Too Late.'" *PS* 15 (Fall): 572–77.

————. 1991. "Form Follows Function: The Evolution of Feminist Strategy." *Annals of the American Academy of Political and Social Science* 515 (May): 38–49.

Brady, David, and Kent L. Tedin. 1976. "Ladies in Pink: Religion and Political Ideology in the Anti-ERA Movement." *Social Science Quarterly* 56 (Mar.): 564–75.

Brazzil, Ruth. 1915. "The False Foundation of the Suffrage Argument." *Woman's Protest* 7 (June): 17–18.

Carabillo, Toni. 1978. "The New Right." *National NOW Times* (Mar.): 6.

Conroy, George R. 1915. "An Indissociable Alliance: Socialism, Suffragism, Feminism." *Woman's Protest* 7 (July): 8–9.

Cott, Nancy F. 1987. *The Grounding of Modern Feminism*. New Haven, Conn.: Yale University Press.

Daniels, Mark R., Robert Darcy, and Joseph W. Westphal. 1982. "The ERA Won—at Least in the Opinion Polls." *PS* 15 (Fall): 578–84.

Faludi, Susan. 1991. *Backlash: The Undeclared War Against American Women*. New York: Crown.

Felsenthal, Carol. 1981. *The Sweetheart of the Silent Majority: The Biography of Phyllis Schlafly*. Garden City, N.Y.: Doubleday.

Firestone, Shulamith. 1970. "The Women's Rights Movement in the U.S.: A New View." In *Voices from Women's Liberation*, ed. Leslie B. Tanner, pp. 433–43. New York: Signet (New American Library).

Flexner, Eleanor. 1973. *Century of Struggle: The Women's Rights Movement in the United States*. New York: Atheneum.

Freeman, Jo. 1975. *The Politics of Women's Liberation*. New York: Longman.

George, Mrs. A. J. 1915. "Why We Are Anti-Suffragists." *Woman's Protest* 7 (Oct.): 5–6.

Gompers, Samuel. 1920. "Labor and Woman Suffrage." *American Federationist* 27 (Oct.): 936–39.

Gusfield, Joseph R. 1963. *Symbolic Crusade: Status Politics and the American Temperance Movement*. Urbana: University of Illinois Press.

Heron, Mrs. John B. 1915. "Feminism a Return to Barbarism." *Woman's Protest* 6 (Apr.): 5–6.

Huber, Joan, Cynthia Rexroat, and Glenna Spitze. 1978. "A Crucible of Opinion on Women's Status: ERA in Illinois." *Social Forces* 57 (Dec.): 549–65.

Illinois Association Opposed to Woman Suffrage. 1909. *To the Voters of the Middle West*. 1 (Sept.).

————. 1911. *Man for the State; Woman for the Home*. 8 (June).

————. 1913. *Woman Suffrage a Socialist Movement*. 17 (May).

Kraditor, Aileen S., ed. 1968. *Up from the Pedestal: Selected Writings in the History of American Feminism*. New York: Quadrangle/New York Times.

————. 1971. *The Ideas of the Woman Suffrage Movement, 1890–1920*. New York: Anchor/Doubleday.

Lispet, Seymour Martin. 1965. "The Sources of the Radical Right." In *The New American Right*, ed. Daniel Bell, pp. 166–234. New York: Criterion.

Mansbridge, Jane J. 1986. *Why We Lost the ERA*. Chicago: University of Chicago Press.

Marshall, Susan E. 1986. "In Defense of Separate Spheres: Class and Status Politics in the Antisuffrage Movement." *Social Forces* 65 (Dec.): 327–51.

————. 1991. "Who Speaks for American Woman? The Future of Antifeminism." *Annals of the American Academy of Political and Social Science* 515 (May): 50–62.

Marshall, Susan E., and Anthony M. Orum. 1986. "Opposition Then and Now: Countering Feminism in the Twentieth Century." In *Research in Politics and Society*, vol. 2, eds. Gwen Moore and Glenna D. Spitze, pp. 13–34. Greenwich, Conn.: JAI Press.

Mason, Karen Oppenheim, and Yu-Hsia Lu. 1988. "Attitudes Toward Women's Familial Roles: Changes in the United States, 1977–85." *Gender and Society* 2: 39–57.

Morgan, Mirabelle. 1973. *The Total Woman*. Old Tappan, N.J.: F. H. Revell.

"Mormons Control Eight Suffrage States." 1915. *New York Times*, Jan. 15, 5.

Mueller, Carol, and Thomas Dimieri. 1982. "The Structure of Belief Systems Among Contending ERA Activists." *Social Forces* 60 (Mar.): 657–75.

Repplier, Agnes. 1915. "Women and Peace." *Woman's Protest* 7 (Oct.): 5–6.

Sapiro, Virginia. 1991. "Feminism: A Generation Later." *Annals of the American Academy of Political and Social Science* 515 (May): 10–22.

Schaffer, Ronald. 1962. "The New York City Woman Suffrage Party, 1909–19." *New York History* 43 (July): 268–87.

Schlafly, Phyllis. 1973. *Phyllis Schlafly Report* 6 (July): 2, 12.

———. 1977. *The Power of the Positive Woman.* New York: Jove, HBJ Books.

———. 1990. *Phyllis Schlafly Report* 24 (Dec.): 2.

———. 1991. *Phyllis Schlafly Report* 24 (Mar.): 1.

Scott, Anne F., and Andrew M. Scott. 1975. *One-Half of the People: The Fight for Woman Suffrage.* Philadelphia: Lippincott.

Scott, Wilbur J. 1985. "The Equal Rights Amendment as Status Politics." *Social Forces* 64 (Dec.): 499–506.

Scott, Mrs. William Forse. 1909. "Extracts from Papers Read at Albany, N.Y., Feb. 24, 1909." *Anti-Suffragist* 1 (June): 1–2.

Sebring, Emma G. 1915. "The Call of the New Lady." *Woman's Protest* 6 (Apr.): 10–11.

Simon, Rita J., and Jean M. Landis. 1989. "Women's and Men's Attitudes About a Woman's Place and Role." *Public Opinion Quarterly* 53 (Summer): 265–76.

Solomon, Martha. 1978. "The Rhetoric of STOP ERA: Fatalistic Reaffirmation." *Southern Speech Communication Journal* 44 (Fall): 42–59.

"Suffragists Spice Anti Mass Meeting." 1914. *New York Times,* Jan. 9, 20.

Tedin, Kent L., David W. Brady, Mary E. Buxton, Barbara M. Gorman, and Judy L. Thompson. 1977. "Social Background and Political Differences Between Pro- and Anti-ERA Activists." *American Politics Quarterly* 5 (July): 6.

Tucker, Gilbert M. 1911. "Female Taxpayers Should Object." *Anti-Suffragist* 3 (Mar.): 6.

White, Mrs. George P. 1915a. "Taxation Without Representation—Misapplied." *Woman's Protest* 6 (Feb.): 8–9.

———. 1915b. "The Recent Rejection of Radicalism." *Woman's Protest* 7 (May): 8–9.

Woman's Protest. 1915a. "Must All Women Bear the Burden of the Ballot to Give Some Women Political Prominence?" 6 (Jan.): 3.

———. 1915b. "The Futility of a Woman's Peace Party." 7 (May): 5–7.

———. 1915c. "New Suffragist Plea—Give Us Jury Duty." 7 (June): 14–15.

———. 1915d. "The Rise of Militancy in America." 7 (June): 16–17.

———. 1915e. "A Noisy and Selfish Propaganda." 7 (June): 19.

———. 1915f. "The Suffragist Peace Party Fiasco." 7 (July): 6–7.

———. 1915g. "Cold Logic Applied to 'Inalienable Rights.' " 6 (Apr.): 6–7.

Misogynists, Masculinist Mentors, and Male Supporters: Men's Responses to Feminism

Michael S. Kimmel

THERE'S A NEW "MEN'S" movement" in America. Triggered in part by Robert Bly's best-selling book, *Iron John,* men across America have been gathering together to experience male bonding, to grieve for absent fathers, to heal the wounds that come from being a man in modern society (Bly, 1991). That men are participating in these weekend retreats to retrieve their "deep" manhood has been the subject of significant media attention and, occasionally, ridicule. What has it got to do with women?

To hear Bly and his followers tell it, the new men's movement has nothing to do with women. Feminist women, they say, have spent the past twenty years finding their voices, their female energy, the source of their power. Now, these men say, it's our turn. Men have to find their deep masculine energy, their "inner warrior," to restore and revitalize American manhood. This mythic quest through male initiation rituals and male bonding retreats has nothing to do with women. It's about men.

Not so, says Susan Faludi, in her recent best-seller (Faludi, 1991). Faludi sees Bly's work and the new men's movement as part of the "backlash" against feminism, an effort to undermine the modest gains women have made in the past two decades. Actually, the new men's movement is only one of several reactions by American men to feminism, both historically and in the contemporary era. By tracing several of these responses historically, since the beginning of the women's movement in the middle of the nineteenth century, we can better understand these current movements among American men.

Three types of men's responses can be identified from their speeches, sermons, pamphlets, and magazine articles, as well as from political organizations and voluntary associations in both the nineteenth and twentieth centuries.[1] The *antifeminist* response relied on traditional religious ideas to demand women's return to the private sphere of home and hearth. Antifeminist men yearned nostalgically for the traditional separation of spheres that had kept women from explicitly challenging men's dominance in the public sphere. "Get back to the home, where you belong!" might have served as the antifeminist battle cry. A *masculinist* response, by contrast, was less concerned with women's participation in the public sphere than with her dominance in the private realm. Masculinists claimed that women's control over childhood socialization had "feminized" American manhood, and they tried to develop islands of untainted virility so that boys could once again grow up to be "real men." Finally, a *profeminist* response provided support for women's increased participation in the public realm, joining with women in agitating for educational, labor, and political reforms. Many men also supported women's demands for changes in the private realm, such as in marriage and sexual relations; these men tried to live in their personal lives the alternative the women were demanding. Profeminists believed that feminism would benefit men as well as women, because relating to equals was healthier, and, as one profeminist man put it simply, "more fun" (O'Neill, 1978: 50).

These three responses did not simply emerge the moment feminist women began to agitate for changes. Rather, they reflected several longer-term changes in the organization of work, social mobility, and political rights that had fundamentally altered the traditional psychological and social foundations of masculinity. One pillar of nineteenth-century masculinity was economic autonomy, as a shopkeeper, farmer, or independent craftsperson. Owning the shop, being one's own boss, and controlling the labor process were central, but rapid industrialization and the closing of the frontier led to these men's replacement in the late nineteenth century with factory workers and dispossessed farm laborers. Before the Civil War, almost nine-tenths of American men were farmers or self-employed businesspersons; by 1870, that figure had dropped to two-thirds, and by 1910, less than one-third were independent (Trachtenberg, 1982). In Kansas alone, there were over eleven thousand foreclosures on independent family farms from 1889 to 1893 (Shannon, 1945: 313). At the same time, women's entry into the work force and the professions and the rise of women's colleges all had a dramatic impact on the traditional definition of femininity. In 1880 2.6 million women were employed. That figure more than doubled by 1900 (5.3 million), and by 1920 it had climbed to 8.5 million (*Abstract of the Fourteenth Census,* 1920: 481). No longer were women supposed to manifest "learned helplessness." They could be as competent and capable as any man.

These trends have continued in our own era, as plant closings and the decline of the small shopkeeper and the American family farm have continued to erode the possibility of economic autonomy. Simultaneously, women have been flooding the labor force, the professions, and higher education. And just as the closing of the frontier eliminated the physical space in which men could test and prove their manhood, contemporary movements to impel military withdrawal from Vietnam, Iran, and other countries suggest a closing of the global imperial frontier. When President John F. Kennedy labeled his program "the New Frontier," could he have known what was at stake for American manhood?

The Antifeminist Response

Although the crisis in American masculinity had its roots in the structural transformation of the American economy and political arena, some men have confused women's simultaneous claims for a larger presence in the public sphere with the cause of their problems. Feminism, they believe, has caused the collapse of the "natural" order, which guaranteed them the superior position over women, and they seek to reverse this trend. In the nineteenth century, men often opposed women's suffrage on biological grounds. One writer claimed that women would be physiologically damaged if they got the vote, growing larger, developing heavier brains, and losing their unique feminine mannerisms and features (Bushnell, 1870). It was not so much that women should be deprived of the vote as that they should be *exempted* from it, because of their lofty position:

> The privilege of voting for and holding public elective oYces is not denied to the women of this country for being inferior in intellect to the men, or for ranking lower as human beings than the men, or because the principle of equal rights to all in matters of public concern was not as applicable to them as to the men, but solely for natural reasons, nature having assigned the home and not the State to woman as her sphere. America's women would gain nothing by the suVrage; on the contrary they would lose their peace and happiness by it. Womanhood teaches them this. (Hertwig, 1883: 11–12)

Another writer fused military service and the franchise, arguing that "no one should take part in government who was not ready to defend, by force, if necessary, the institutions of the country" (Frothingham, 1894: note on 1). This position was best summed up by one anonymous antifeminist, who argued in a debate about the question in Sacramento, California, in 1880:

> I am opposed to woman's suVerage [sic] on account of the burden it will place upon her. Her delicate nature has already enough to drag it down. Her slender frame, naturally weakened by the constant strain attendant upon her nature is too often racked by diseases that are caused by a too severe tax upon her mind. The presence of passion, love, ambition, is all too potent for her enfeebled constitution and wrecked health and early death are all too common. (California Historical Society Library, San Francisco, ms. #2334)

(The debate was decided in favor of the opponents to suffrage.)

Men also used the "natural" division between the sexes as the justification for opposition to women's education. "I think the great danger of our day is forcing the intellect of woman beyond what her physical organization will possibly bear," wrote John Todd in 1867; he counseled giving women "all the advantages and all the education which her organization, so tender and delicate, will bear; but don't try to make the anemone into an oak, nor to turn the dove out to wrestle with storms and winds, under the idea that she may just as well be an eagle as a dove" (Todd, 1867: 23, 25). And female labor force participation was attacked on similar grounds. "The growing demand for female labor is an insidious assault upon the home; it is the knife of the assassin aimed at the family circle and the divine injunction. It excludes women from nature's dearest impulse," wrote Edward O'Donnell in 1897 (O'Donnell, 1897: 186).

Medical texts abounded with details of the horrors of women's equal participation in the public world. "Certain women seek to rival men in manly sports, and the strongminded ape them in all things, even in dress," observed Dr. Alfred Stille in his presidential address to the American Medical Association in 1871. "In doing so, they may command a sort of admiration such as all monstrous productions inspire, especially when they tend towards a higher type than their own" (cited in Ehrenreich and English, 1979: 65).

Today's antifeminist argument differs little. Biology is still destiny, and women's presumed "natural" function is to produce children. Feminism has duped women into abandoning marriage and children, argue contemporary antifeminists, who elevate women onto the proverbial pedestal. Women ought to be exempted from public participation because they are the bearers of morality, and only they can constrain men's antisocial amoral impulses. "No man with gumption wants a woman to fight his nation's battles," noted General William C. Westmoreland, one of the architects of America's Vietnam War (cited in Freedman, 1985: 110). And conservative theorist George Gilder writes that "a woman may even do more good without a job than with one" (1986: 41). "I'd just as soon keep her at home dependent on me rather than be dependent on her bringing in so much a week," one working man told a journalist, while another expressed fears at the consequences of women's entry into the work world, when he commented that "if women work and they're married, they get too independent. Before long there's trouble at home" (Astrachan, 1986: 96).

Contemporary antifeminists also rely on a strange reading of anthropological literature to inveigh against women for their challenges to "the inevitability of patriarchy" (Goldberg, 1975; Amneus, 1979). If men have historically oppressed women in most cultures, they argue, there must be something natural and inevitable about patriarchy, which is therefore sacrosanct and unchallengeable.

Feminist arguments for equality are countered by antifeminists who point to areas in which equality would socially challenge the biological imperative. In employment, for example, C. H. Freedman attempts to frighten readers, asserting that "the forcing of the fire departments of this country to lower their standards to accommodate women amounts to nothing less than the offering of human sacrifices" (Freedman, 1985: 109). Many leaders of the religious right wing, including Jerry Falwell's Moral Majority, campaigned vigorously against the Equal Rights Amendment, because, they argued, woman would be forced to relinquish the rights and privileges she now possesses. One antifeminist man called Phyllis Schlafly "the most outstanding American in our history" for leading the fight against that "irresponsible and dangerous" amendment (Freedman, 1985: 250).

Organizationally, the National Organization for Men (NOM), led by divorce lawyer and *Playboy* columnist Sidney Siller, opposes feminism, which it claims is "designed to denigrate men, exempt women from the draft and to encourage the disintegration of the family" (Siller, 1984). NOM opposes affirmative action, imprisonment of men for nonpayment of alimony, and preference to women on child-custody issues. In the antifeminist scheme, it's time for men to stand up to the "libbers' stridency and the brain damaged man-hating" that characterizes modern feminism (cited in Freedman, 1985: 284).

The Masculinist Response

Another group of men have been less distressed about women's increased power than with men's reduced significance. They mourned the disappearance of "real men" from the political scene and sought frantically to reassert a vigorous virility in a world that "feminized" manhood. A century ago, as well as today, American men were concerned about "wimps."

The masculinist response differed from the antifeminist response in several important ways. Antifeminists saw women as the cause of men's problems and sought to press women back into the private sphere where, they argued, women belonged. Masculinists were often indifferent to women in the public sphere and sought instead to dislodge women's dominance in the home, and especially in the raising of young boys. It was here that boys were distracted from becoming men.

It was the presence of girls that distracted them. Masculinists believed there was "something enervating in feminine companionship," so the separation of boys and girls was essential to retrieve masculinity from women's clutches (Dubbert, 1979: 97). Several child-rearing manuals cautioned against mixed dancing, coed classrooms, and even feather beds for boys, since these beds' softness and warmth led to impure thoughts (Barker-Benfield, 1976: 232). At the same time, a new "muscular Christianity" hailed a remasculinized Jesus: he was "no lick-spittle proposition," proclaimed preacher Billy Sunday in the 1890s, but "the greatest scrapper who ever lived" (cited in Douglas, 1977: 327). Thomas Hughes's *The Manliness of Christ* (1880) and Carl Case's *The Masculine in Religion* (1906) echo this theme.

Masculinists were terrified that men were turning into women; that is, that men were becoming "inverts." Throughout their writings, both then and now, one senses a terror of male homosexuality, which supposedly saps the virility of the nation. This fear is a response to the increased visibility, since the late nineteenth century, of a viable gay subculture in American cities. Today's gay and lesbian urban subculture provokes irrational hatred and fear among many, even as their contribution to American culture grows. One antidote was homosociality, a rigorously enforced single-sex social life. If the sexes mingled, it was reasoned, the boys would become feminized, and hence homosexual.[2] As G. Stanley Hall argued in his 1904 textbook, *Adolescence,* familiarity and camaraderie produced a disenchantment and diluted the "mystic attraction of the other sex" (Hall, 1904: 641). Such notions also fueled masculinist arguments against coeducation and against women's education in general. An article in *Educational Review* ("The Woman Peril," 1914: 109) blamed women teachers for creating a "feminized manhood, emotional, illogical, noncombative against public evils."

But perhaps the most significant answer to the perceived feminization of American boyhood was the number of organizations devoted to a boy's proper upbringing that sprang up around the country. The YMCA, the Boy's Club, and the Boy Scouts of America were devoted to reclaiming American boyhood from the feminizing influences of women, who were turning "robust, manly, self-reliant boyhood into a lot of flat chested cigarette smokers with shaky nerves and doubtful vitality," according to Ernest Thompson Seton, the founder of the Boy Scouts of America in 1910 (cited in Macleod, 1983: 49). The Boy Scouts celebrated a masculinity tested and proven against nature and other boys. Here was a "boy's liberation movement to free young males from women, especially from mothers" (Dubbert, 1979: 152). If boys could be provided with a haven away from all feminizing influences, a place to redirect male anxieties and to sublimate adolescent sexual yearnings, then these boys could become the "real men" required by early-twentieth-century industrial capitalism.

The symbolic hero to the masculinist cause was President Theodore Roosevelt, whose triumph over youthful frailty and transformation into a robust vigorous warrior served as a template for a revitalized American social character. Roosevelt elevated compulsive masculinity and military adventurism to the level of national myth and "symbolized a restoration of masculine identity at a time . . . when it appeared to be jeopardized" (Dubbert, 1980: 313).

These themes resonate through the contemporary masculinist response. Some masculinists seek to dislodge women's primacy in the private sphere, claiming "equal" rights for men in such areas as child custody, spousal consent to abortion, and elimination of alimony and child support. Men's challenges to women's perceived parental monopoly come from "men's rights" and "fathers' rights" groups such as the Coalition of Free Men, Men's Rights International, and Men Achieving Liberation and Equality (MALE). As one critic summed up this position:

> Men, they say, are emotionally and sexually manipulated by women, forced into provider roles where they work themselves to death for their gold-digger wives, kept from equal participation and power in family life, and finally dumped by wives only to have the courts and lawyers give all the property, money and child custody to the women. (Messner, 1986: 32)

One writer advises men who feel powerless in the face of divorce-court proceedings to "fight dirty and win" by exploiting their wives' vulnerabilities (Robinson, 1986: 175).

Not all masculinists are so vicious, nor do they all slide so casually close to the antifeminist position. Most masculinists today, like their forbears, are less concerned with what women are doing, in either the public or private sphere, and more concerned with rescuing men from the feminizing clutches of an emasculating culture. Some echo Muscular Christians, recasting Jesus as a religious Rambo. Televangelist Jerry Falwell, for example, insists that "Christ wasn't effeminate. . . . The man who lived on this earth was a man with muscles. . . . Christ was a he-man!" (cited in Fitzgerald, 1986: 166).

By far the most common theme among contemporary masculinists is the recovery of "deep manhood" by the "mythopoetic" men's movement. This diverse group consists of men who follow the teachings of Robert Bly, Jungian therapists like Robert Moore and Douglas Gillette (1991, 1992), participants in "wildman" retreats, men who are active in twelve-step and recovery movements, and many new age therapies. These men believe that by exploring ancient legends, myths, poems, and fairy tales, they can extract new archetypes for men, new models for manhood. Their workshops and retreats draw on anthropological evidence of male bonding rituals in non-Western traditional societies and reinvention of rituals of initiation to manhood.

Many masculinists today rely on the psychoanalytic claim that American men have not fully separated from their mothers and have not achieved a healthy gender identity by bonding with their fathers. Thus they carry with them the "father wound," a gaping hole in the depth of men's psyches that yearns for closure. Mythopoetic rituals are designed to facilitate men's separation from the world of women and to present contemporary men with "mentors" who can facilitate the secure grounding of a healthy masculine identity. (For a fuller discussion and critique of the mythopoetic men's movement, see Kimmel and Kaufman, 1993.)

The Profeminist Response

Although less visible and less influential than their antifeminist or masculinist counterparts, both in the late nineteenth century and today, some American men have openly embraced feminist principles, believing that women's increased public participation—symbolized by suffrage or the ERA, women's increased personal autonomy, and women's right to birth control and sexual freedom—would be a significant gain for both women and men. In every feminist struggle, from Seneca Falls through the campaign for the ERA, profeminist men have supported women's demands. Some have even examined their own lives and have struggled to develop more egalitarian and mutually supportive relationships (see Kimmel and Mosmiller, 1992).

In the mid-nineteenth century, profeminist men supported women's suffrage. Several men were signers of the original Declaration of Sentiments in 1848, among them Frederick Douglass, the celebrated black abolitionist. Other abolitionists, such as William Lloyd Garrison, Samuel Gridley Howe, and Thomas Wentworth Higginson, also campaigned actively for women's rights. Many mid-century communal-living experiments were organized by men, such as Robert Dale Owen, John Humphrey Noyes, and Moses Harmon, who saw the communes as retreats from female sexual slavery and as locations to develop new relations between women and men and new forms of family organization based on mutuality and equality. And many of the men who founded and led the new women's colleges, such as Matthew Vassar, William Allan Neilson and Joseph Taylor (both of Smith College), and Henry Durant (of Wellesley), as well as the men who supported coeducation at Cornell, Oberlin, Wesleyan, and other schools, believed that men would also benefit from the ability to relate to strong, whole people, capable of complementary relations. Durant wrote that the "real meaning" of higher education for women was "revolt against the slavery in which women are held by the customs of society—the broken health, the aimless lives, the subordinate position, the helpless dependence, the dishonesties and shams of so-called education. The Higher Education of Women . . . is the cry of the oppressed slave. It is the assertion of absolute equality" (cited in Horowitz, 1984: 44).

By the end of the nineteenth and the beginning of the twentieth centuries, many men actively participated in the state campaigns for woman suffrage, believing that political equality might relieve the world of oppressively masculine politics. (What the masculinists wanted to restore, the profeminists wanted to eliminate.) The Men's League for Woman Suffrage had both American and English branches. In the United States, it was headed by Oswald Garrison Villard, publisher of the *New York Evening Post,* and Rabbi Stephen Wise, and was administered by the young Greenwich Village radical Max Eastman. His pamphlet "Is Woman Suffrage Important?" linked a socialist economic critique of the leisured class with a feminist-inspired analysis of male–female relationships; capitalism and sexism had turned women's "enforced feebleness into a holy thing" (Eastman, 1916: 8).

Profeminist men also marched in suffrage demonstrations. An editorial from *La Follette's* in May 1911 praised the eighty-five "courageous and convinced men" who marched in a suffrage demonstration in New York City. One marcher counted being "booed and hissed down the Avenue a very thrilling and inspiring experience" and indicated his determination that "if I can help to that end, there shall be a thousand men in line next year." And he was not far off target. An article in the *New York Times* the next year estimated that about eight hundred men marched in a suffrage demonstration in New York (*New York Times,* 11 May 1912, p. 15), although Eastman's estimate was much higher, considering the Men's League took up five blocks of marchers, four abreast (Eastman, 1936: 351).

Within the growing labor movement, women's rights also found support, especially from Eugene V. Debs. In his pamphlet "Woman—Comrade and Equal," published by the Socialist party (undated), Debs proclaimed himself "glad to align myself with a party that declares for absolute equality between the sexes. Anything less than this is too narrow for twentieth century civilization, and too small for a man who has a right conception of manhood" (Debs, 1948: 454). Debs concluded by linking the social emancipation of women to the end of male violence against women and the transformation of masculinity:

> Under our brutal forms of existence, beating womanhood to dust, we have raged in passion for the individual woman, for use only. Some day we shall develop the social passion for womanhood, and then . . . we shall lift woman from the mire where our fists have struck her, and set her by our side as our comrade and equal, and that will be love indeed.

Within the personal sphere, turn-of-the-century profeminist men supported women's claims for autonomy in marriage and demands for sexual freedom, including divorce and birth control. William Sanger, husband of birth-control advocate Margaret Sanger, was arrested in 1915 for distributing his wife's pamphlet, *Family Limitation.* At home, he was equally supportive. "You go ahead and finish your writing," she quotes him as saying that year, "and I'll get the dinner and wash the dishes" (cited in Forster, 1985: 252). (Apparently, she used to draw the curtains in their apartment when he did so, lest anyone take notice of this gender reversal [Reed, 1977: 136].)

Many of the young radicals who gathered in Greenwich Village in the first two decades of this century supported women's equality and wrestled with these issues in their own lives. Max Eastman and Ida Rauh caused a scandal when they married in 1911 and she retained her own name on their apartment mailbox. Eastman, editor of *The Masses* and founder of the Men's League for Woman Suffrage, saw in feminism a blueprint for changing *men's* as well as women's lives. In the March 1914 issue of the magazine, Eastman reported a conversation with the new stenographer:

> "Are you a feminist?" we asked the stenographer.
> She said she was.
> "What do you mean by Feminism?"
> "Being like men," she answered.
> "Now you are joking!"
> "No, I'm not. I mean mental independence. And emotional independence too—living in relation to the universe rather than in relation to some other person."
> "All men are not like that," we said sadly.
> "Then they ought to join the Feminist movement!"

Perhaps the most articulate of these radicals was Floyd Dell, who argued that the liberation of women from the oppressive bonds of traditional femininity implied the liberation of men from the restrictive trappings of traditional masculinity. Feminism was more than "a revolt of women against conditions which hamper their activities; it is also a revolt of women and men against the type of woman created by those conditions" he wrote in 1921 (Dell, 1921: 349). In "Feminism for Men," Dell made this clear:

> The home is a little dull. When you have got a woman in a box, and you pay rent on the box, her relationship to you insensibly changes character. It loses the fine excitement of democracy. It ceases to be companionship, for companionship is only possible in a democracy. It is no longer the sharing of life together—it is a breaking of life apart. Half a life—cooking, clothes, and children; half a life—business, politics and baseball. . . . It is in the great world that a man finds his sweetheart, and in that narrow little box outside of the world that he loses her. When she has left that box and gone back into the great world, a citizen and a worker, then with surprise and delight he will discover her again and never let her go. (1914: 32)

To Dell, the woman's movement signaled the hope of all humankind, because it included both women and men; he wrote in 1913:

> If the woman's movement means anything, it means that women are demanding everything. They will not exchange one place for another, nor give up one right to pay for another, but they will achieve all rights to which their bodies and brains give them an implicit title. They will have a larger political life, a larger motherhood, a larger social service, a larger love, and they will reconstruct or destroy institutions to that end as it becomes necessary. They will not be content with any concession or any triumph until they have conquered all experience. (Dell, 1913: 51)

Today's feminist woman also has male allies, some of whom recall their century-old forebears. For example, organizations such as Men Allied Nationally for the Equal Rights Amendment (MAN for ERA) sponsored rallies and marched in ERA demonstrations behind a banner, just as the Men's League for Woman Suffrage had done in suffrage parades. And many prominent American men campaigned for the amendment. Predictably, men long identified with feminist causes, such as Phil Donahue and Alan Alda, were visibly supportive. Alda argued that men would benefit from the passage of the ERA, as wider role options available to women can relieve men of a lot of pressure:

> As women fill traditionally male roles as police chiefs, gas station attendants, baseball players, and bankers, we may also begin to realize that wisdom, aggressiveness, and physical courage are not solely male attributes. The pressure to provide these qualities all by ourselves will be taken from men's shoulders. We can still be strong and brave, but we won't have to feel we're the only ones who are. (Alda, 1976: 93)

Men will benefit from feminism, Alda contends, because current standards of masculinity are often pathological, locking men into behavior that is destructive to women, to children, and to other men. As a prisoner of masculinity, as a sufferer of "testosterone poisoning," a man is "not someone you'd want to have around in a crisis—such as raising children or growing old together" (Alda, 1975: 16).

If appeals to men's self-interest do not convince, however, Alda resorts to moral arguments as well. "How long can we stand by and watch qualified people excluded from jobs or denied fair payment for their labor? How long can we do nothing while people are shut out from their fair share of economic and political power merely because they're women?" (Alda, 1976: 93). Moral claims also convinced journalist Howard Cosell, the sportscaster American fans most love to hate, who stated that he supported the ERA

> because, simply, it's right and necessary. It relates to the betterment of society, it relates to the principles upon which the nation was supposed to be founded, principles which have not been lived up to. You do what is right and you stand for what is right. And the way you do that is with your mind, your heart, your vocalizations, and your general influence. It's very simple. (Cosell, 1975: 78)

Several organizations work with men around some area identified as important to the feminist movement. Several, such as R.A.V.E.N. in St. Louis (which stands for Rape and Violence End Now), EMERGE in Boston, and MOVE in San Francisco, are devoted to ending men's violence against women, both by supporting the battered-women's movement and by counseling violent men. Many cities have established men's centers or have ongoing men's support groups to help men understand and support women's demands. And the National Organization for Men Against Sexism (NOMAS) is a network of profeminist men across the country who are involved in everything from profeminist men's music and art to political organizing about rape and violence.[3] The organization applauds "the insights and positive changes that feminism has stimulated for both women and men" and opposes continued economic and legal discrimination, rape, domestic violence, and sexual harassment (NOMAS, 1990). Profeminist magazines such as *Changing Men* provide personal and analytic articles about these issues to both male and female readers.[4]

A number of profeminist men are also academic men, and their research on the history of masculinity (Dubbert, 1979; Filene, 1976; Kimmel, 1987a, 1987b, 1987c; Pleck and Pleck, 1980), on the formulation of the male sex role (Pleck, 1981, 1986; Brannon and David, 1976), on masculinity and sports (Fine, 1987; Messner, 1987), on sexuality (Kimmel, 1990), and on themes of masculinity in literature (Morgan, 1987; Murphy, 1987) have all challenged the notion of masculinity, taking a feminist perspective. Often, male students pick up the feminist message as well. One national fraternity, for example, recently produced a poster against date rape (Pi Kappa Phi, 1985). Others are running workshops on date rape and sexual harassment (see Scher, Stevens, Goode, and Eichenfield, 1987).

In many different arenas, contemporary profeminist men are confronting prevailing notions about the ways women and men should relate, are opening up and are learning how to listen to their women friends and lovers, and are trying to integrate feminist ideas into their own lives. Sometimes they are even trying to talk with other men about these ideas. In breaking ranks with men's silence about the position of women in American society, profeminist men also face hostility and isolation from other men. But profeminist men believe that the social changes already accomplished by feminism, and the changes that feminism will bring, contain significant and desirable changes for men as well and that the feminist vision of sexual equality and gender justice is both practically and morally a vision of a world in which we would want to live.

NOTES

1. This essay is based on an ongoing research project on men's responses to feminism in the United States. Earlier essays have been published in *The Making of Masculinities: The New Men's Studies,* Harry Brod, ed. 1987. Boston: Allen and Unwin; Barbara Risman and Pepper Schwartz, eds. 1987. *Gender in Intimate Relationships: A Microstructural View.* Belmont, CA: Wadsworth; and *Gender & Society* 1(3), 1987. I am grateful to Harry Brod, Martin Duberman, Cynthia Fuchs Epstein, Jo Freeman, John Gagnon, Judith Gerson, Frances Goldin, Cathy Greenblat, Michael Kaufman, Barbara Laslett, Judith Lorber, Gina Morantz-Sanchez, Joseph Pleck, and Catharine Stimpson for comments and criticisms on earlier drafts.

2. Such insistence on homosociality as insurance against possible homosexual behavior is ironic, especially when one recalls that, as Kinsey revealed in his classic studies (Kinsey, 1948), most men who have had homosexual experiences first did so precisely in these homosocial realms, such as summer camp, Boy Scouts, the military, or religious institutions.

3. Contact the National Organization for Men Against Sexism at 54 Mint St., #300, San Francisco, CA 94103.

4. Contact *Changing Men* at 306 N. Brooks St., Madison, WI 53715.

REFERENCES

Alda, Alan. 1975. "What Every Woman Should Know About Men." *Ms.,* October.
Alda, Alan. 1976. "Alan Alda on the ERA." *Ms.,* July.
Amneus, Daniel. 1979. *Back to Patriarchy.* New Rochelle, NY: Arlington.
Anonymous editorial. 1914. "The Woman Peril." *Educational Review* 47, February.
Anonymous participant in debate held at Elk Grove, Sacramento, California. 22 January 1880. California Historical Society Library, San Francisco, Ms. 2334.
Astrachan, Anthony. 1986. *How Men Feel.* Garden City, NY: Anchor Books.
Barker-Benfield, G. J. 1976. *The Horrors of the Half Known Life: Male Attitudes Toward Women and Sexuality in Nineteenth Century America.* New York: Harper and Row.
Bly, Robert. 1991. *Iron John: A Book About Men.* Reading, MA: Addison-Wesley.
Brannon, Robert, and Deborah David, eds. 1976. *The Forty-Nine Percent Majority.* Reading, MA: Addison-Wesley.
Bushnell, Horace. 1870. *Woman Suffrage—The Reform Against Nature.* New York: Scribner's.
Case, Carl. 1906. *The Masculine in Religion.* N.p.
Cosell, Howard. 1975. "Why I Support the ERA." *Ms.,* October.
Debs, Eugene. 1948. *Writings and Speeches of Eugene V. Debs,* edited by Arthur Schlesinger, Jr. New York: Hermitage Press.
Dell, Floyd. 1913. *Woman as World Builders—Contemporary Studies.* Chicago: Forbes.
Dell, Floyd. 1914. "Feminism for Men." *The Masses,* July.
Dell, Floyd. 1921. "Feminism and Socialism." *New Masses.*
Douglas, Ann. 1977. *The Feminization of American Culture.* New York: Alfred Knopf.
Dubbert, Joe. 1979. *A Man's Place: Masculinity in Transition.* Englewood Cliffs, NJ: Prentice-Hall.
Dubbert, Joe. 1980. "Progressivism and the Masculinity Crisis." Pp. 303–20 in *The American Man,* edited by E. Pleck and J. Pleck. Englewood Cliffs, NJ: Prentice-Hall.
Eastman, Max. 1916. "Is Woman Suffrage Important?" New York: Men's League for Woman Suffrage.
Eastman, Max. 1936. *The Enjoyment of Living.* New York: Harper and Row.
Ehrenreich, Barbara, and Deirdre English. 1979. *For Her Own Good: 150 Years of Medical Advice to Women.* New York: Anchor Books.
Faludi, Susan. 1991. *Backlash: The Undeclared War Against American Women.* New York: Crown.
Filene, Peter. 1976. *Him/Her Self: Sex Roles in Modern America.* New York: Harcourt, Brace (revised edition, Baltimore: Johns Hopkins University Press, 1986).
Fine, Gary Alan. 1987. *With the Boys.* Chicago: University of Chicago Press.
Fitzgerald, Frances. 1986. *Cities on a Hill.* New York: Simon and Schuster.
Forster, Margaret. 1985. *Significant Sisters: The Grassroots of Active Feminism.* New York: Alfred Knopf.
Freedman, C. H. 1985. *Manhood Redux: Standing Up to Feminism.* Brooklyn, NY: Samson Publishers.
Frothingham, O. B. 1894. *Woman Suffrage: Unnatural and Inexpedient.* Boston: privately printed.
Gilder, George. 1986. *Men and Marriage.* Gretna, LA: Pelican.
Goldberg, Steven. 1975. *The Inevitability of Patriarchy.* New York: Morrow.

Hall, G. Stanley. 1904. *Adolescence,* vol. 2. New York: Appleton.

Hantover, Jeffrey P. 1980. "The Boy Scouts and the Validation of Masculinity." Pp. 285–302 in *The American Man,* edited by E. Pleck and J. Pleck. Englewood Cliffs, NJ: Prentice-Hall.

Hertwig, John George. 1883. "Woman Suffrage." Washington, DC: Eckler Printers.

Horowitz, Helen L. 1984. *Alma Mater: Design and Experience in the Women's Colleges from Their Nineteenth Century Beginnings to the 1930's.* New York: Alfred Knopf.

Hughes, Thomas. 1880. *The Manliness of Christ.* Boston: Houghton Mifflin.

Kimmel, Michael S. 1987a. "The 'Crisis' of Masculinity in Historical Perspective." Pp. 121–54 in *The Making of Masculinities: The New Men's Studies,* edited by Harry Brod. Boston: Allen and Unwin.

Kimmel, Michael S. 1987b. "The Cult of Masculinity: American Social Character and the Myth of the Cowboy." Pp. 235–49 in *Beyond Patriarchy: Essays by Men on Pleasure, Power, and Change,* edited by Michael Kaufman. New York: Oxford University Press.

Kimmel, Michael S., ed. 1987c. *Changing Men: New Directions in Research on Men and Masculinity.* Beverly Hills, CA: Sage Publications.

Kimmel, Michael, ed. 1990. *Men Confront Pornography.* New York: Crown.

Kimmel, Michael, and Michael Kaufman. 1993. "Weekend Warriors: Robert Bly and the Politics of Male Retreat." *Feminist Issues* 13(2), Fall.

Kimmel, Michael, and Tom Mosmiller, eds. 1992. *Against the Tide: Pro-Feminist Men in the United States, 1776–1990.* Boston: Beacon Press.

Macleod, David. 1983. *Building Character in the American Boy: The Boy Scouts, YMCA, and Their Forerunners, 1870–1920.* Madison: University of Wisconsin Press.

Messner, Michael. 1986. Book review of *Men Freeing Men,* in *Changing Men,* 16.

Messner, Michael. 1987. "The Life of a Man's Seasons: Sports and Masculinity in the Lifecourse of the Jock." In *Changing Men: New Directions in Research on Men and Masculinity,* edited by Michael S. Kimmel. Beverly Hills, CA: Sage Publications.

Moore, Robert, and Douglas Gillette. 1991. *King, Warrior, Magician, Lover.* New York: HarperCollins.

Moore, Robert, and Douglas Gillette. 1992. *The King Within.* New York: William Morrow.

Morgan, David. 1987. "Masculinity and Violence in American Fiction." Paper presented at Third International Interdisciplinary Congress on Women, Dublin, Ireland, July.

Murphy, Peter. 1987. *John Hawkes: Toward a Radical Theory of Male Heterosexuality.* Ph.D. dissertation, Dept. of English, S.U.N.Y. at Buffalo, NY.

National Organization for Men Against Sexism. 1992. "Statement of Principles." P. 477 in *Against the Tide: Pro-Feminist Men in the United States, 1776–1990,* edited by M. S. Kimmel and T. Mosmiller. Boston: Beacon Press.

New York Times. 1912. "The Heroic Men." Editorial, May 11.

O'Donnell, Edward. 1897. "Women as Bread Winners—The Error of the Age." *The American Federationist,* October.

O'Neill, William L. 1978. *The Last Romantic: A Life of Max Eastman.* New York: Oxford University Press.

Pi Kappa Phi (fraternity). 1985. "Statement of Position on Sexual Abuse" and poster "Today's Greeks Call It Date Rape."

Pleck, Joseph. 1981. *The Myth of Masculinity.* Cambridge, MA: MIT Press.

Pleck, Joseph. 1986. *Working Wives/Working Husbands.* Beverly Hills, CA: Sage Publications.

Pleck, Joseph, and Elizabeth Pleck, eds. 1980. *The American Man.* Englewood Cliffs, NJ: Prentice-Hall.

Reed, James. 1977. *From Private Vice to Public Virtue: The Birth Control Movement and American Society Since 1830.* New York: Basic Books.

Robinson, G. P. 1986. "When All Else Fails and the War Is On: How to Fight Dirty and Win." Pp. 174–76 in *Men Freeing Men,* edited by Francis Baumli. Jersey City, NJ: New Atlantis Press.

Scher, Murray, Mark Stevens, Glenn Goode, and Greg Eichenfield, eds. 1987. *Handbook on Counseling and Therapy with Men.* Newbury Park, CA: Sage Publications.

Shannon, Fred A. 1945. *The Farmer's Last Frontier: Agriculture, 1860–1897.* New York: Holt, Rinehart.

Siller, Sidney. 1984. "National Organization for Men." Privately printed pamphlet.

Todd, John. 1867. *Woman's Rights.* Boston: Lee and Shepard.

Trachtenberg, Alan. 1982. *The Incorporation of America: Culture and Society in the Guilded Age.* New York: Hill and Wang.

The Experiences of Minority Women in the United States: Intersections of Race, Gender, and Class

Elizabeth M. Almquist

MINORITY WOMEN confront all the issues and problems that white women face. They know the joys and sorrows of children, housework, jobs, and relationships with men and other women. They experience the pain and trauma associated with rape, sexual harassment, exclusion, discrimination, and every other kind of mistreatment of women. Minority women share many of the same feminist goals that majority women seek and are increasingly aware that their smaller paychecks and constricted job opportunities reflect gender discrimination as much as race discrimination. Despite all these commonalities, minority women are likely to interpret their experiences within a different framework than white women do, to assign different priorities to feminist goals, and to view white women with some suspicion and feelings of apartness.

Race (or ethnicity) and race discrimination erect enormous barriers between minority and white women and among various groups of minority women. There are a number of different minority groups in the United States. Within each group, women's identity and experiences are further subdivided by differences in age, marital status, social class, and the like. To expose some of the barriers that have divided different groups of women, I first describe the unique historical experiences of Native American, African-American, Hispanic, and Asian women.

The Forces That Divide: Racial Divisions in the United States

Historically, the major racial groups were geographically distant from one another, with African-Americans concentrated in the Southeast, Mexican Americans—as the largest Hispanic group—in the Southwest, and Asians on the West Coast. Only Native Americans were dispersed throughout the North American continent. Historically as well, the white majority used the different groups to fill different economic functions. Social definitions of race, ethnicity, and color were imposed on top of geographic distances and economic divisions. Therefore, women from the different groups lived apart from one another.

While the particular circumstances of the groups were enormously varied, we find similarities. Women played crucial productive, family, and community

573

roles, working very hard and seeing themselves as partners with their husbands and brothers. Contact with whites disrupted family life in every instance, and women were too often defined as sexual property. The history of minority women involved continuous struggles to survive and to protect entire groups against the onslaughts of the white majority. Today, we find further similarities among different groups of women: increasing similarities in family situations and work lives, increasing activism in both minority group and feminist movements, increasing efforts to understand and transcend barriers of race, gender, and class.

The following sections provide brief glimpses of the larger groups, locating them in social time and space, highlighting key points in women's history, and identifying some of the commonalities and divergences in women's lives.[1] The material presented here is not as complete as I would like, because the 1990 census data (see Table 1) are available for only broad groupings by race and Hispanic origin, and because traditionally social scientists and historians have not paid much attention to women within these groups. Still, the recent flowering of research and feminist literature by and about racial-ethnic women provides a wealth of detail, only some of which can be presented here.

NATIVE AMERICAN WOMEN: THE INVISIBLE MINORITY

Before the coming of Europeans, Native American[2] women played crucial productive and social roles in hundreds of diverse and separate groups. The European invaders neither noticed nor appreciated differences among tribal cultures. They swept across the North American continent, killing native people either deliberately or accidentally by spreading smallpox, diphtheria, whooping cough, and other diseases to which native people had no immunities. Native Americans who survived were herded onto reservations that were perceived as having few natural resources, and the much-hated Bureau of Indian Affairs was established to protect and control these groups. In the process, most groups lost their traditional means of earning a living; significant social and family distinctions among the tribes were obliterated,[3] Native Americans were denied the right to vote, and only a few were allowed to obtain a formal education. These policies and practices combined to ensure that Native Americans would be largely confined to rural areas where jobs are few and far between, that they would have few opportunities to influence political affairs, and that they would become the most invisible of minority groups.

Government policies and practices significantly reduced Native American women's status by destroying their traditional patterns of contributing greatly to the group's basic subsistence. The examples are numerous. In the horticultural groups, farming provided the main source of food, and hunting was supplementary. Women did much of the farming, and in some of these societies, such as the Choctaw and Iroquois,[4] women controlled their own labor, controlled the food and other products of their labor, and played major roles in tribal decision making. Traditionally, land was "owned" by the entire group or by large extended families. Christian missionaries were appalled when they saw women doing agricultural work and thought that men did not care about providing for their families. In cooperation with the federal government,

Table 1. Population Characteristics by Race and Hispanic Origin, 1990[a]

	White	African-American	American Indian	Asian or Pacific Islander	Other race[b]	Hispanic origin[c]
Total population (in thousands)	199,686	29,986	1,959	7,274	9,805	22,354
Sex ratio (aged 18+)[d]	92.4	84.1	94.2	92.6	NA	103.2
Marital status (women aged 15+)						
% Never married	20.8	38.3	29.7	27.6	NA	29.9
% Now married	55.6	30.9	44.7	58.7	NA	49.4
% Other status[e]	23.6	30.8	25.6	13.7	NA	20.7
% Family households female headed[f]	18.4	48.0	26.1	17.9	NA	27.6
Median household annual income[g]	$31,435	$19,758	$20,025	$36,784	$22,813	$24,156
% All persons below poverty level	9.8	29.5	30.9	14.1	25.3	28.2
% High school graduates	77.9	63.1	65.5	77.5	43.4	49.8
% College graduates	21.5	11.4	9.3	36.8	6.0	9.2

a. **Sources:** Income, poverty, and education data from U.S. Bureau of the Census, Minority Economic Profiles, Tables CPH-L-92 through CPH-L-95. All other data from U.S. Bureau of the Census, C-P-1, 1990 Census of Population, General Population Characteristics, United States, 1993, Tables 42 through 46.

b,c. One question from the census asks respondents to identify their race. "Other race" includes all persons who did not classify themselves as "white," "Native American," "African-American," or "Asian or Pacific Islander." A separate question asks about the ethnic identity of respondents, who select from a wide variety of ethnic backgrounds such as English, French, Canadian, Spanish, etc. The Hispanic origin population is derived from this ethnic identity question, and these persons may be of any race.

d. Sex ratio=number of males per one hundred females.

e. Other status includes separated, widowed, and divorced.

f. Households may be composed of families, one individual, two or more unrelated individuals, or a combination of these. The percentage given is of family households that are headed by a woman rather than a man.

g. Minority Economic Profiles provides income data for all households only; income data are not provided for different types of households.

policies were introduced that made individual men the property holders and reduced women's participation in food production.

Women also played very important roles in food production in foraging societies, including the buffalo-hunting tribes of the Great Plains. Women were responsible for preserving and cooking the meat, for making clothes and shelters from the hides, and for supplementing the meat by gathering many kinds of wild plant foods. In other hunting and gathering societies, meat was less important and women's foraging for plant foods was even more important. All the groups that relied on hunting and gathering lost their traditional sources of food and were expected to learn to farm according to "white" methods, which always included only secondary roles for women.

In some herding societies, such as the Navajo, women traditionally tended the sheep and wove blankets from the wool. Beginning in the 1930s, government policy parceled out land to men only and limited the number of sheep that a family could own. Women lost their major source of wealth, and their sense of security and bargaining power within the family was taken away.[5] Seeking work in town was frowned on for women, and they could choose only restaurant work, seasonal agricultural employment, or domestic service. Men left the reservation to find jobs, and divorce and desertion rates skyrocketed. Women's difficulties were compounded because women lost their traditional culture but did not perceive Anglo (white)[6] culture as worthy of being emulated.[7] Shirley Hill Witt[8] suggests that the loss of meaningful roles for women is a factor promoting the high birthrate among the Navajo.

Today, Native American women juggle numerous responsibilities with limited resources. Poverty and unemployment pervade the reservation areas, where white-owned corporations eagerly gobble up land but offer few jobs for native people. Only a very few tribal groups have been able to negotiate lucrative contracts for their mineral resources that provide a high income; much more common are reservations where the unemployment rate exceeds 50 percent, especially in the winter months.[9] The economic situation produces devastating social consequences, with large numbers of families unable to adequately feed, clothe, and house their members.

The picture has improved very little in the past decade: more women are working for pay, but fewer men are employed, and the poverty rate has increased.[10] Women have been able to leave jobs as maids and domestic workers, but, as with African-American women and Hispanics, nearly one-fourth are employed in service occupations (see Table 2), performing work outside the home that had formerly been done inside the home. These food preparation, cleaning, and personal service jobs are characterized by low pay, few fringe benefits, little opportunity for advancement, and employment that fluctuates with the state of the economy. Like all groups of women, regardless of race or ethnicity, another one-fourth of Native American women are employed as administrative support (clerical) workers. Native American clerical workers are frequently employed by the federal government, which has become, almost by default, the largest employer of Native American women.[11] Public-sector employment strongly influences the type of jobs women are able to obtain; most professional Native American women are teachers or nurses, and most managers are in lower level positions. Women are underrepresented

Table 2. Occupational Distribution by Gender, Race, and Hispanic Origin

	White	American Indian	African American	Asian or Pacific Islander	Hispanic origin
Employed women, 1990[a]					
Executives, administrators	11.7%	7.6%	8.7%	11.1%	7.2%
Professionals	16.9	12.4	11.6	16.6	8.9
Technologists and technicians	3.6	3.5	3.1	5.2	2.5
Sales	13.2	10.0	11.7	12.6	11.6
Administrative support (clerical)	27.9	25.3	24.2	22.2	24.4
Service	15.7	25.6	24.5	16.4	23.5
Farming	0.9	0.4	1.2	0.6	2.1
Precision production, craft, and repair	2.2	2.4	3.2	4.2	3.5
Operators, fabricators, and laborers	7.9	12.8	11.8	11.3	16.3
TOTAL	100.0%	100.0%	100.0%	100.0%	100.0%
Employed men, 1990[a]					
Executives, administrators	13.8%	6.7%	7.2%	13.4%	6.3%
Professionals	12.3	6.7	6.7	18.6	5.2
Technologists and technicians	3.6	2.6	2.7	6.7	2.2
Sales	11.8	6.0	6.1	11.2	7.2
Administrative support (clerical)	6.3	10.0	5.8	9.4	6.9
Service	9.0	19.3	14.5	13.7	16.1
Farming	3.8	2.9	5.9	1.9	7.6
Precision production, craft, and repair	19.8	14.6	23.2	11.5	19.8
Operators, fabricators, and laborers	19.6	31.2	27.9	13.6	28.7
TOTAL	100.0%	100.0%	100.0%	100.0%	100.0%

a. Includes persons who had a job at the time of the census; excludes unemployed persons.
Source: U.S. Bureau of the Census, CP-S-1-1, 1990 Census of Population, Supplementary Reports, Detailed Occupation and Other Characteristics from the EEO File for the United States. Hispanic origin from Table 1; all others from Table 2.

among top-level executives, and they are severely underrepresented in the high-status professions (see Table 3). Native American men are more heavily concentrated in precision production, craft, repair, factory operative, transportation, and manual labor jobs than any other group of men. They do not fare much better in white-collar occupations than Native American women.

In the face of these conditions, Native American women work very hard to add to family resources through raising gardens and livestock, making clothing, making and selling souvenirs, or other informal employment. Traditional roles encompass caring for the old and the infirm and helping friends and relatives in times of distress. Many women spend a great deal of

Table 3.   Labor Force Status, by Race and Hispanic Origin, 1990[a,b]

	White	Native American	African-American	Asian or Pacific Islander	Other race	Hispanic origin
Women's employment						
Percent in labor force	56.3	55.1	59.5	60.1	55.5	55.9
Percent unemployed	5.0	13.1	12.1	5.5	12.8	11.2
Share of total U.S. jobs	37.1	0.3	5.6	1.4	1.4	3.4
Share executives	33.4	0.2	3.0	1.0	0.6	1.7
Ratio	**90.0**	**66.7**	**53.6**	**71.4**	**42.5**	**50.0**
Share high-status professions	18.0	0.1	1.4	1.4	0.2	0.8
Ratio	**48.4**	**33.3**	**25.0**	**100.0**	**14.3**	**23.5**
Men's employment						
Percent in labor force	75.2	69.4	66.5	75.5	80.1	78.7
Percent unemployed	5.3	15.4	13.7	5.1	10.5	9.8
Share of total U.S. jobs	45.1	0.4	5.1	1.6	2.2	4.8
Share executives	56.1	0.3	2.9	1.8	0.8	2.6
Ratio	**124.4**	**67.6**	**56.3**	**115.5**	**40.5**	**55.4**
Share high-status professions	64.3	0.2	2.4	1.8	0.6	2.3
Ratio	**142.5**	**51.4**	**47.2**	**118.1**	**27.9**	**47.4**

a. The occupations used here are a subset of the larger occupational categories shown in Table 2. A subset was chosen in order to examine more closely the highest paying, most prestigious occupations, which carry high levels of authority. Still, because of data limitations, the categories defined here are not necessarily homogeneous. As defined for this table, executives include managers and administrators but exclude management-related occupations such as accountants; personnel, training, and labor relations specialists; purchasing agents, etc. High-status professions include engineers, architects, and surveyors; mathematical and computer scientists; natural scientists; health-diagnosing professions (physicians, dentists, etc.); postsecondary (college) teachers; and lawyers and judges. This category excludes all other professional and technical occupations.
b. Definition of other terms:
Share of total U.S. jobs: The percent of the total jobs in the United States held by a particular group; e.g., white women hold 37.1 percent of all jobs in the United States. Note: Hispanics can be of any race; therefore, the shares of the total U.S. jobs for all groups of men and women—except Hispanics—add to 100 percent.
Share executives: A group's share of the total executive jobs in the United States; e.g., African-American women hold 3.0 percent of all executive and administrative positions in the U.S.
Share high-status professions: A group's share of the total high-status professional jobs.
Ratio: A group's share of the total jobs in an occupational category divided by that group's share of the total U.S. jobs. For instance, African-American women hold 3.0 percent of all executive and administrative positions but hold 5.6 percent of the total U.S. jobs. Therefore, their ratio status for this occupational category=3.0 divided by 5.6=53.6. Ratios above 100 indicate the group holds a larger share of the occupational category than they do of the total jobs and are overrepresented in that category. Scores below 100 indicate the group is underrepresented in the occupational category.
Source: U.S. Bureau of the Census, Census of Population 1990, CP-S-1-1, Supplementary Reports, Detailed Occupation and Other Characteristics from the EEO File for the United States, Tables 1 and 2.

time working on behalf of the Pan-Indian movement, which is concerned with maintaining or regaining traditional tribal culture, including language, customs, dress, religion, and ceremonies. In choosing to be the keepers of the culture,[12] women make a lifelong commitment.

The Native American movement is designed to maximize Native American self-determination. Federal control over Native American affairs is exercised through the Bureau of Indian Affairs (BIA). Technically, the tribes own their reservation lands and the natural resources these lands contain. But contracts with the oil, uranium, and coal mining companies must be negotiated through the BIA, and Native Americans rightfully believe they are being cheated in the process. The large companies, the federal government, and tourists encroach on native lands, destroying the beautiful mother earth, turning farmland and sacred shrines into mines or tourist facilities, and relocating thousands of Native Americans away from their ancestral homes. To confront these massive changes requires running a gauntlet of twisted legal and bureaucratic procedures. The Native American movement is concerned not with achieving material gains but with educating doctors, lawyers, and other professionals to regain some control. Women are active participants, readily taking leadership roles and often forming the majority of protest marchers.[13] On a day-to-day basis, they work to maintain movement organizations, to educate the people in both traditional and "white" lifeways, to provide health care, and to reduce alcoholism, suicide, and violence. These activities have been labeled *retraditionalization,* as women extend their family and community caretaking roles in professional and political activities.[14] They might equally well be termed *politicization,* taking an activist, public role in their own tribal affairs and in dealing with external groups. Women have formed feminist organizations, such as Women of All Red Nations, and their feminist activity is shaped by an ever-present concern for the multiple oppressions people of color face.

Over half of the nearly two million Native Americans now reside in cities and towns. The city is a cold and lonely place. Native Americans socialize mainly with other Native Americans, avoiding contact with whites who are antagonistic toward them. A large number return to their rural homes periodically to renew contacts with family and friends. Caught between native and white lifeways, Native American women specifically choose to remain bicultural in orientation.[15] This means accepting enough Anglo culture to get a job, to communicate with employers and with the children's teachers, to establish residence and to vote, and to negotiate the intricacies of federal bureaucracies. It also means rejecting the materialistic values of Anglo culture and retaining an emphasis on native values, such as sharing material goods, being noncompetitive, avoiding manipulation of other people, and not criticizing them.[16] This communal orientation works well in establishing shared bonds with other Native Americans, and it helps to ease the burdens and tensions of life in the often-hostile white city. Women get along by being politely formal toward whites and reserving warmth and emotional responsiveness for family and friends. Most Native American women are first- or second-generation urban residents. They are making life choices now that will affect all future generations.

AFRICAN-AMERICAN WOMEN: THE LARGEST MINORITY

My mother used to say that the black woman is the white man's mule and the white woman is his dog. Now, she said that to say this: we do the heavy work and get beat whether we do it well or not. But the white woman is closer to the master and he pats them on the head and lets them sleep in the house, but he ain't gon' treat neither one like he was dealing with a person. Nancy White[17]

African women were brought to the United States to work, to produce, and to reproduce. At first male slaves had been preferred for work in the fields and in the skilled jobs demanded by the expanding agricultural economy. When the United States committed itself to ending the slave trade, large numbers of black women were imported to increase the slave population. Thus, there was an early definition of black women as sexual property, a definition that was enlarged because slave women had no power to prevent sexual assaults by white men. In their ignorance, many white men came to believe that black women actually enjoyed their sexual assaults. Slave women performed multiple roles. They worked as both field hands and domestic servants; they were required to have children, sometimes through forced breeding with selected male slaves; and they cared for their families and children in the slave quarters after all their other work was finished.[18] Women were sometimes given a few days off after childbirth to nurse their children, but this was not done in recognition of their needs for rest and recovery. Instead, the slave owner was protecting his or her investment in human chattel.

After slavery, black women continued to work as domestic servants or as hired labor in the fields owned by their former masters. Two world wars lured thousands of blacks to the North with promises of work in defense-related industries. For women, the change of venue meant little in the way of real employment gains. They continued to work as maids and babysitters in white homes, and as cooks, dishwashers, and janitors in hotels, restaurants, and office buildings. The few women who were able to obtain a college education concentrated heavily in teaching because they could find jobs in segregated schools. It was long after World War II before enough school doors were open to allow black women to move out of domestic and service work and into professional and clerical occupations. In the last two decades, black women have scored impressive increases in educational attainment and strong gains in professional fields previously dominated by white women. Despite this, no group has shattered white male control over the elite professions that offer the highest pay and the most prestige (see Table 3).[19] Further, black women, like all other groups of women, are still notably absent from managerial occupations, from the skilled crafts, and from factory supervisory work. Employers are especially unwilling to place women of color in positions where these women would supervise or work alongside white men.

African-American women have always had exceptionally high rates of paid employment. Sheer necessity compels many to work, because high unemployment rates create economic insecurity for both sexes and because the sex ratio (number of men per one hundred women) has been and still is very low. Historically, male scarcity was created when black men moved out of the South more rapidly than did black women, suffered heavy casualty rates as front-line troops in various wars, and experienced high death rates from poor health and poor health care.[20] Contemporary conditions recreate male scarcity. Poverty and discrimination take a heavy toll in apathy, alcoholism, drug abuse, crime, poor health, early deaths, unemployment, and low wages. Coupled with longer prison sentences and more frequent enactment of the death penalty for blacks compared to whites,[21] these factors result in proportionately fewer men to marry and to fill breadwinner roles.

After slavery, whites imposed a different system of social control, including segregated housing, workplaces, and schools. They tried to impose a stronger set of stereotypes, portraying black women as docile, obedient creatures who existed to serve the interests of whites and alternately as emasculating matriarchs who dominated black men. African-American women never accepted these stereotypes; indeed, the very act of defining and valuing self in the face of such caustic stereotyping is explicit testimony to the strength that these women possessed.[22]

Black women coped with oppression in myriad ways,[23] and their coping strategies continue in the present day. They frequently form extended households, with three generations living together and pooling resources. Black relatives and friends seem more willing than white ones to adopt informally children whose mothers are experiencing financial or emotional distress. The mothers see informal adoption as a much better alternative than formal adoption, because they do not have to relinquish custody and the children are placed with people whom the mothers know and trust.[24] These customs may have originated as a response to the uncertainties of family life during the time immediately following slavery, or they may be seen as adaptive patterns that are continuously made necessary by current conditions. In either case, black women have had to be very resourceful to survive. Yet they are stereotyped and ridiculed by outsiders because their assertiveness is a threat to the status quo.[25]

During slavery, free black women fought for its abolition. After slavery, many black women fought for suffrage, organized clubs to extend their own education, sought better schooling for their children, and formed groups to help the sick and impoverished.[26] The last few decades have brought new varieties of activism. Just as Native American women formed a critical mass to carry out the Native American movement, so black women organized through the churches and provided a solid foundation for the civil rights movement.[27] During the 1960s and 1970s, they organized and led the National Welfare Rights Organization.[28]

During those decades as well, the Black Power movement brought a variety of cross-currents and conflicting pressures. Above all else, that movement sought to reassert the masculinity of black men. Thus, women who practiced birth control and sought abortion rights were denounced as contributing to racial genocide. Advocates of increased education and better jobs for black women were put down as threats to black men's self-esteem, which was already undermined by racism.[29] Black women were becoming increasingly feminist in attitude, but they saw organized feminism as unreceptive to their interests.[30] Consequently, they formed their own feminist organizations, including the Combahee River Collective.[31]

Today, African-American women scholars are producing a variety of insightful analyses of their own position and of the entire society. These writings assert the need for black women to define themselves and their priorities; to refuse any simplistic explanations of the conditions in which they live;[32] to combine with other groups to achieve specific changes that are mutually beneficial; and to recognize that race, class, and gender oppression are inseparable.[33]

> Anglo women sensitive to Chicanas as members of a minority must guard against a very basic conceptual mistake. All minorities are not alike. To understand the black woman in not to understand the Chicana. To espouse the cause of minority women, Anglos must recognize our distinctiveness as separate ethnic groups. Consuelo Nieto[34]

Mexican American women comprise the largest and oldest Hispanic origin group. Contrary to stereotype, a large but unknown number are the descendants of Spanish and Spanish–Native American ancestors who lived in the Southwest long before Mexico ceded that territory to the United States. Only some are illegal aliens or recent migrants. Throughout this century, turbulent economic and political conditions in Mexico have constantly encouraged Mexicans to cross the Rio Grande River—a border that they regard as artificial. Therefore, many Mexican Americans have dwelt in the United States for several generations.

The Spanish conquistadores arrived in the New World largely without women. The first Mexicans were created by the union of Spanish men and Native American women. The Spaniards bartered trade goods for women or captured the women by force. In at least one incident, native women were baptized as Catholics before they were systematically raped by the Spanish soldiers.[35]

The Spaniards looked down on the indigenous women, both because these women were natives and because they were women. They treated them as sexual, domestic, and laboring servants. Indigenous men began to emulate the Spaniards. Women were to be taken by conquest, treated as property, and used to bolster the men's status as property holders. The Catholic church helped to institutionalize a very unequal relationship between women and men. The Spaniards had discovered that they could control Native American women servants and keep them laboring in the *encomienda*[36] system by teaching them to venerate the Virgin Mary. The *Marianisma* ideal taught women to be silent, to endure pain and sorrow, and to think in fatalist terms. Good women were identified as virgins, saintly mothers, and martyrs. To follow Mary, women had to be submissive, altruistic, and self-denying. The only alternative was to follow in the footsteps of the self-serving temptress Eve. These ideals were incorporated into the culture of the new nation of Mexico, part of which was taken over by the United States.

The dichotomy between woman as Mary and woman as Eve continues today in somewhat modified form. Real people do not fit either category, but they are pressured to do so. There is some security in accepting a role as a good mother who unconditionally loves her children and places their needs before her own, "but this acceptance lends itself to a subtle pernicious undermining of women's self-esteem."[37]

The Marianisma concept for women complements the machismo concept for men. In the popular image, a macho male is a virile person who conquers and exploits women sexually. But "machismo also consists of manliness in a broader sense than just sexual prowess. It includes the elements of courage, honor, and respect for others, as well as the notion of providing fully for one's family."[38] Machismo supports the pattern of male dominance and promotes large families because children are evidence of the husband's machismo. Meanwhile, the Marianisma ideal stresses that "bearing and rearing children are the woman's most important function, symbolizing her maturity."[39]

Current debate effectively challenges the Marianisma and machismo stereotypes, and women lead the opposition through their feminist research and organizing.[40] First, women oppose sexist behavior within the Chicano community and urge everyone to redefine "manliness" to incorporate positive, useful attributes. Second, they review history to show that many native groups originally had highly equalitarian relationships between women and men. Patriarchal images were imposed on native people by the Spanish conquerors, who used the suppression and silencing of women as a tool to achieve control over the peasant class, both women and men.[41] Third, feminist scholars assert that macho attitudes are not a necessary part of Mexican American culture. Instead, male oppression of women stems from misguided, exaggerated imitations of Anglos as well as from structural conditions imposed on Mexican Americans.[42]

Betty Garcia-Bahne[43] shows how Anglo exploitation and domination created conditions favoring male dominance. When Mexico ceded the Southwest Territory in 1848, Anglos poured into the territory, displacing Spanish-Mexican landowners and turning peasants into a semicolonized labor force to build the infrastructure for the developing capitalist industry. Mexican Americans struggled to survive. They could not rely on Anglo courts for justice or on Anglo capitalists for steady work and adequate pay. They had to rely on themselves and their extended families for support and assistance. Garcia-Bahne suggests that the Mexican American worker faced a tough, competitive, and authoritarian situation on the job and tended to reproduce this relationship in his family. He had little reason to be certain that he could continue to fill the breadwinner role; the low wages that he did earn undermined his manliness. For these reasons, he demanded extra obedience and respect from his wife.

Throughout this century, Mexican American women and men workers were regarded as a supply of cheap, exploitable, and dispensable labor. In the huge agribusinesses, in the fields and the canneries, entire families worked together, because the work was seasonal and the wages of all members were required to support the family. Women and girls worked under the watchful eye of husbands and fathers, who made certain that they did not violate traditional norms of behavior and were protected from unwelcome sexual advances.[44] As industrialization developed, Mexican Americans were increasingly employed as factory operatives. Women especially were preferred for sewing jobs in garment factories. By the 1930s, about one-half of employed Chicanas were in domestic- and personal-service work, one-fifth were agricultural laborers, and another one-fifth were employed in manufacturing.[45]

In recent years, Mexican Americans have dispersed somewhat around the country, becoming more urbanized and better educated. Mexican American women's rates of labor force participation have increased. Unfortunately, these women have not been able to exchange their educational qualifications for jobs and salaries at the same level that Anglos have. In 1980 Mary Romero[46] found that Mexican American women and men still confronted stereotypes and barriers that prevented full occupational assimilation. They were still more heavily concentrated in blue-collar and lower white-collar occupations than were Anglos, and they were particularly excluded from higher status professional and managerial work. Affirmative-action legislation has only minimal impact on these patterns. Contemporary data for all Hispanic women suggest little had changed by 1990 (see Tables 2 and 3).

For the last several decades, Mexican Americans have been active in a variety of social movements to enhance their political, educational, and economic opportunities. These activities spawned an awareness of sexism and often served as the springboard for feminist organizing. With roots in the working-class union movement as well, the Chicana feminist movement includes a growing number of local and regional associations that publish newsletters, encourage labor activities and strikes, work to secure better health care, and support women candidates for public office.[47]

Chicana feminist consciousness also emerged as a struggle for equality with Chicano men, and it was shaped by different political ideologies and different social class backgrounds. While all recognize that women will be liberated only when Mexican Americans are liberated as a group, some enclose their feminist activity almost entirely within the struggle against racist oppression. These women perceive Anglo feminists as too narrow and individualistic and too much in opposition to men.[48] Other Chicanas appear much more outspoken about the ways in which Chicano men oppress women individually.

A middle position recognizes that the Mexican American population is quite diverse, with large segments highly acculturated to Anglo middle-class patterns and other segments relatively aloof from them. In the face of this diversity, there is a strong need to stress Chicano unity to mobilize the population in pursuit of human-rights goals. Many Mexican Americans see themselves as a colonized population. Maxine Baca Zinn[49] argues that the main strategy for achieving decolonization and for forming the New La Raza is to use the family as the basic organizational unit of the movement. In this "political familism," machismo is being redefined to mean active striving for the good of the Mexican American people. All members, young and old, men and women, are urged to contribute to the movement. Women are valued for their contributions to the family as well as for their activities outside the home. Chicana feminism places little stress on liberation for women alone; it emphasizes instead the benefits that can be obtained for Chicanos as a group.

PUERTO RICAN WOMEN ON THE CONTINENT

> [My mother] once told me her idea of hell was to be a single mother of two children under five in the South Bronx. I'm afraid of ever knowing what she meant. Aurora Levins Morales[50]

Puerto Ricans have been citizens of the United States since 1917; this facilitates frequent movement back and forth between the island and the continent. Puerto Rico is an island colony belonging to the United States, with a weakly developed economy.[51] Migrants to the United States tend to be from rural areas and to lack advanced education or job skills specifically applicable in an urban setting. Still, Puerto Ricans perceive the mainland as offering a wealth of opportunities, and they choose to concentrate in the New York City area. Puerto Ricans who move to other cities receive better jobs and pay than do those in New York,[52] but that city remains the major point of arrival and of departure for the journey home.

Many factors contribute to the decision to return to the island: a Puerto Rican's lack of English language skills, hostility expressed toward dark-skinned people, and the Anglo emphasis on competition and material gain. Puerto Rican values stress generosity, personalism, and spiritual rather than material matters. These conflict with the emphasis on efficiency and rationality of the Anglo-Protestant culture Puerto Ricans encounter.[53] In addition, friends and family, sometimes even young children, are back home on the island. Migrants know that they can return to people who care about them.

Women experience migration, transience, and discrimination in ways that are personally disruptive and that make family life difficult. More women than men return to Puerto Rico. Some are women who have lost their jobs, older women whose children are grown, or women whose marriages have dissolved. As Lourdes Miranda King points out,

> it is not unusual to find women working in the United States whose children are cared for by grandmothers or other relatives in Puerto Rico, or to find wives and children living in Puerto Rico while their husbands find work in the mainland, or to find working wives in Puerto Rico "pioneering the resettlement" of husband and children—different patterns yet with the same divisive effect on families. The woman is thrust into the role of sole supporter, creating the new immigrant woman and incidentally destroying the myth of the passive female.[54]

It is impossible to understand the lives of Puerto Rican women on the mainland without examining their lives on the island. "Despite the dramatic changes experienced by Puerto Rico since industrialization and the changing role of women, sexism and male chauvinism remain deeply rooted in Puerto Rican culture and society."[55] Island culture is a mixture of Spanish, African, and Native American antecedents, resulting in a blend that is uniquely Puerto Rican. The culture emphasizes macho values for men, virginity and honor for women. Girls experience many more restrictions in dress, conduct, movement, and language use than do boys. A girl is not permitted to be openly aggressive and must channel her ambitions into narrowly defined areas—marriage, some schooling, and a limited range of jobs. These include the helping professions—nursing and teaching—if she is well educated, and service work and manufacturing jobs if she is not.[56] Marriages are not particularly equalitarian. Marya Munoz Vasquez points out that men will do housework only if the windows are closed and the curtains drawn. "If someone learned that the husband was helping his wife or catering to her wishes, he would be described as *sentado en el baul* (the implication is that his wife dominates him)."[57] Wives defer to husbands by consulting them about everyday decisions. Men strive to maintain a public image of being dominant and macho even if their personal values are at variance with the social norm. The emotional distance between husband and wife and the unbalanced power structure contribute to women's deep psychological investment in their children.

In a unique study, Rosemary Cooney and her colleagues[58] documented how male dominance persists among married couples in the United States. They studied an older parental generation who were born in Puerto Rico and who had moved to New York City many years ago, as well as their adult children who were born and reared in the United States. The extent of patriarchal attitudes varied from couple to couple; however, the two distinct generations exhibited virtually identical levels of male dominance in family decision making. Male dominance had a different foundation in the two generations. Among the parents' generation, men's influence was embedded in patriarchal beliefs, and the less well educated the husband, the more control he exerted over family affairs. A different pattern emerged among the adult children; in this generation the men were moving ahead of women in education and the job market, and the higher a man's standing in these arenas, the more dominance he exhibited.

Puerto Rican women confront a variety of issues: racism from both inside[59] and outside the Puerto Rican community; discrimination in housing, education, and jobs; and urban poverty created by racism and exaggerated by the declining textile industry and the disappearance of factory jobs in the urban Northeast.[60] Women are especially vulnerable to unemployment, yet a myth persists that they have an easier time finding jobs than men do, echoing the false rhetoric that African-American women encounter. A further concern shared with African-Americans is high-pressure sterilization programs, as studies in New York and Hartford show that nearly half of Puerto Rican women have been sterilized.[61] Women are often pressured to consent to sterilization during the labor and trauma of childbirth, a time when they are most vulnerable to persuasion. Such imposed sterilization violates religious beliefs for many, raises the fear of racial genocide, and denies women the right to control their own bodies. Women fight all these issues on several fronts, using their mothers as models and extending their mothering roles into a concern for the well-being of the entire Puerto Rican community.[62]

CUBAN WOMEN IN THE UNITED STATES

> Work gives color to life. In Cuba, it was not common that women worked, although I was a teacher myself. But things have changed here. Most Cuban women work and are very active. I am not saying all these nice things about work because I have a nice job. I worked in a factory many years ago when I came to the United States and I still would say that work, no matter what kind, is good for human beings.[63]

Cuban immigrants began arriving in the United States soon after the fall of the Batista government and Castro's rise to power. The Wrst groups were people who had been prominent in the Batista regime, from well-educated aZuent families. Castro's policy was to allow almost everyone who wanted to leave Cuba to do so. More recent migrants have been less well educated. The special programs that were instituted to settle Cuban refugees outside the Miami area have been all but abandoned now, so that a large proportion remain where they Wrst entered the country.[64]

The early Cuban women immigrants had been well educated but were not oriented toward working for pay. The tradition of *vergenza* (female dignity and honor) prevailed in Cuba. Women from the middle and upper classes were expected to be bright and energetic but not to traffic too frequently in men's affairs of business and politics. These women were accustomed to having domestic servants to do housework and to care for their children.[65]

The transition to the United States was abrupt and disorienting. Many wives came with their children to face an uncertain future in this country. The early immigrants believed that their stay here would be temporary and that they would soon return to Cuba. Later immigrants did not share this illusion, as the Castro government showed no signs of failing. Regardless of marital status, the era in which they immigrated, or their level of preparation, many Cuban women were thrust into the labor force. Lacking English language skills, they were unlikely to find secretarial and clerical jobs; and lacking the specific credentials, even highly educated women were unable to enter teaching, medicine, and law. Most found jobs only as factory operatives and in domestic service, as did their husbands and brothers, but many men were eventually able to acquire credentials and to resume professional careers.[66]

The ranks of Cuban women are constantly replenished by recent immigrants. Working may be a relatively permanent adaptation for Cuban women in the United States, and the occupational patterns of these women increasingly resemble those of Anglo women. Myra Marx Ferree[67] emphasizes that many of the first immigrant groups worked only to regain the socioeconomic status their families lost in moving to this country. She found few differences between working and nonworking Cuban women in Florida. Working women were more interested in issues of pay and working hours, but they expected to continue to do most of the household work. Women's attitudes toward family and gender roles were determined more by the age at which they entered this country than by their labor force status. Women who came as children or who were born here were less likely to accept restrictions on women's roles than were women who migrated as adults. The younger women looked forward to more equalitarian family roles than those their mothers and grandmothers had experienced.

Recent evidence confirms Ferree's predictions concerning intergenerational differences. Prieto[68] finds older Cuban American women especially concerned about their daughters remaining virginal and uncorrupted, while younger women are eager to blend in with U.S. society, adopting a less restricted lifestyle. Both Ferree and Prieto studied women who live in New York and New Jersey. Apparently no research has explored gender issues in Miami, where the presence of large numbers of Cubans may facilitate enforcing traditional norms and values. Further, Cubans are more economically advantaged than Mexican Americans and Puerto Ricans, and my research[69] shows that occupational inequality is greatest within those racial and ethnic groups who have higher education and incomes.

ASIAN AMERICAN WOMEN

Fueled by thousands of recent immigrants, the Asian population in the United States is growing very rapidly. Among the six largest specific groups of Asian and Pacific Islanders, five—all but the Japanese—doubled in population between 1980 and 1990.[70] With figures given in thousands, these groups and their decade changes in population are

Chinese from 812 to 1,645
Filipino from 782 to 1,407
Japanese from 716 to 848
Asian Indian from 387 to 815
Korean from 357 to 799
Vietnamese from 245 to 615

The U.S. Census Bureau has not yet released detailed data on specific groups of Asian Americans, but the composite portrait of all Asians in 1990 (see Tables 1 to 3) shows them to be the most advantaged of all race groups, having more education and higher family incomes even than white Americans. The Asian "advantage" over Anglos stems from several sources—immigration of very highly educated Asians in the past two decades, concentration in the high-income states of California and New York, employment of several members in each family, and continuous hard work and struggle against racism.[71] Though not always present in large numbers, women have participated in every stage of Asian American history.

In the nineteenth century, most Chinese and Japanese immigrants were male sojourners intent on making money and returning to their native lands. Few prospered in the mines, railroads, and canneries of the West Coast because they had to compete with white migrants for jobs and resources. Consequently, prejudices and stereotypes were formed, and sometimes open hostilities erupted. The Chinese Exclusion Acts and other restrictive legislation affected the numbers of Asian women entering the country and the subsequent forma-tion of families.[72] The Japanese were more likely to bring wives with them than were the Chinese; nonetheless, some sent back to their homeland for "picture brides."[73]

There was an unbalanced sex ratio among Asian groups. The figures are startling. In California in 1920, there were 529 Chinese men and 171 Japanese men for every 100 women of their respective nationalities.[74] The presence of so many single men created a need for services typically performed in families. A sizable segment of the population, especially among the Chinese, ran boardinghouses, laundries, and restaurants. Chinese women were imported to serve as prostitutes. The demand for their services was high among the single men who had no other form of sexual outlet. The wages of prostitutes, camp cooks, and laundry workers were low, however, because the wages of the men they served were low.[75]

Japanese women were able to come to the United States and to establish families before the restrictive Immigration Act of 1924. Some were able to buy land and to establish truck farms on the West Coast. Japanese women worked side by side with their husbands in the fields throughout the long day and returned to the household at night to do all the housework. Men did not participate in housework and child care. Japanese women were expected to sacrifice their own well-being so that the family could gain a foothold in the new land. They were to defer to their husbands, even to go hungry so that men could eat when food was scarce.[76] The more prosperous the Japanese became, the more resentment other groups directed toward them. Anti-Japanese sentiment climaxed during World War II, when people of Japanese ancestry were forced to move to relocation camps in the interior. After the war, there were very few new Japanese immigrants of either sex.

In contrast, Chinese women did not arrive in great numbers until after World War II, when they came as the wives of returning servicemen, both Anglos and Chinese Americans.[77] The 1952 McCarran-Walter Act established quotas for immigrants from specific nations and allowed persons who were close relatives of immigrants already in the United States to enter as well. "More than 30,000 Chinese women, many of whom had been separated from their husbands for decades, entered as nonquota immigrants by 1960."[78] Contemporary immigrants of Chinese ancestry come from many different countries; they are often students of both sexes who elect to stay in the United States. Consequently, the Chinese American population has increased dramatically, and the sex ratio has evened out.

Evelyn Glenn[79] traced the adaptation of the Chinese to their varying historical conditions in the United States. In the early years, when Chinese women were all but barred from entering this country, a "split household" developed with women remaining in China. Chinese men returned to their homeland to marry and sire children and then returned alone to the United States. Later, as new brides and older married women were admitted to the United States, a "small producer" strategy emerged. The Chinese established family businesses, saving up money to start, and managing to stay in business by having all family members work long, hard hours. Today, Chinese Americans, together with many other Asian groups, exhibit a dual wage earner strategy. Wives and husbands—and often children as well—are employed for pay, because it is deemed necessary for survival.

Filipino men were initially attracted to Hawaii to work as farm laborers; after World War II, large numbers began migrating to the continental United States. For a long time, the men were laborers and typically single, either because they could not afford to return home to secure a wife or because various state laws forbade Orientals from marrying Caucasians.[80] Many Filipino women came to the United States under the family reunification provisions of the 1952 and 1965 immigration legislation. Between 1965 and 1980, a large number of Filipino women migrated on their own, under provisions that specified that immigrants who were qualified to work in occupations badly needed in the United States were to be given first preference in admission quotas. These Filipino immigrants were highly trained professionals, especially in medicine; a large proportion of women are nurses. In 1980 Filipino women were more likely than any other group except Asian Indians to be professional workers.[81] However, recent analyses show that the proportion entering under occupational quotas is declining while those entering under family reunification provisions is increasing, suggesting that the number of weakly educated immigrants with poorer job prospects will continue to increase.[82]

A very high proportion of other groups of Asians—Indians, Koreans, and Vietnamese—immigrated to the United States within the past twenty years. As voluntary immigrants, people from India and Korea often arrive with strong educational credentials to enter the professions or with capital to begin businesses.[83] Unsure of succeeding financially, these immigrants stress achievement for men and hard work for women and children. Wives are encouraged to work for pay outside the home but to maintain traditional patterns within the home, doing the bulk of the housework and being deferential to husbands. As recent arrivals, Asians cling to customs from their home countries; for instance, Indian parents continue to prefer arranged marriages for their daughters and sons because they believe they will choose more satisfactory spouses than the young people will.[84]

As political refugees, Vietnamese women had little choice in coming to the United States. In 1980, the most recent year for which nationality-specific data are available, Vietnamese women were less well educated than Vietnamese men and less likely to be working for pay than other Asian women. In addition, Vietnamese income was lower than any other minority group, and unemployment and poverty rates were higher.[85] It is unclear whether they have been able to overcome these rather desperate circumstances in the intervening years. It is clear that the Vietnamese brought strong patriarchal values from their homeland and cling rather fiercely to them. Nazli Kibri[86] studied lower income Philadelphia women who suffered when their husbands made major financial decisions unilaterally, ordered the women around, or physically abused them. The women's only recourse was to tell friends about the problems and to try to have their friends' husbands influence the errant husbands to mend their ways. Kibri describes this response as one of "negotiating patriarchy," where the worst suffering was alleviated but the patriarchal authority system remained intact.

For all Asians, continuing immigration provides a constant infusion of traditional values. Among those who migrated earlier, there are marked differences between the older generation born abroad and the younger generation reared in the United States. For instance, Japanese parents worry about their children remaining faithful to traditional religious beliefs and are especially concerned about their daughters marrying Anglos.[87] Children of both sexes, but girls particularly, are supposed to be modest, unassuming, and strongly oriented toward family. This means that younger women who espouse feminist values, who place individual desires over family needs, or who merely pursue a chosen career actively are in danger of coming into conflict with their parents. There is little social support for the independent, assertive woman.

The traditional Chinese family had roles rigidly prescribed on the basis of sex and age. The father—"the terrible old one"—was a patriarch with supreme authority. Wives and daughters were expected to serve the male head of the family and to produce male heirs. Education was not necessary for women; in fact, it might endanger feminine virtues of modesty, inconspicuousness, patience, gentleness, and sensitivity to others. This stark picture of family roles was the ideal model in traditional China.[88] Many Vietnamese immigrants are of Chinese ancestry and hold equivalent views, believing that a girl should obey her father when she is a child, her husband when she is married, and her son when she is widowed.[89] Similar sentiments echo in other groups; Dasgupta[90] points out that Indian women in the United States experience less authoritarian marriages than in their native country, but the family remains hierarchical, with husbands firmly in charge. Women are expected to be good mothers, understanding, supportive, good-natured, and self-sacrificing. Throughout Asian communities, individuals are expected to sacrifice their own interests to the well-being of the family, yet sons are given more freedom to deviate from these expectations. Today, Asian American daughters are encouraged to obtain an education so they can help support the family, but not to venture very far outside its confines. Asian American women are likely to have foreign-born parents and grandparents and to experience conflict with them over proper demeanor, dress, regard for elders, dating, mate selection, and career choice. Women face a primary conflict between the assertiveness and activism needed to succeed in a chosen career and the reserve and modesty demanded by Chinese culture.

In the popular and scholarly literature, Asian Americans are depicted as a "model" minority: polite, deferential, hard-working, achievement-oriented, and economically well placed.[91] Indeed, Asians have had to be many of these things to survive against hostile stereotypes and repeated harassment. Their struggles have enabled each successive generation to attain more education and higher status occupations than the previous one. Despite their upward movement, Asian Americans have had difficulty entering management careers in white-owned businesses, and they do not receive the same rates of pay within occupations as whites do.[92]

In the last two decades, Asian American groups organized to protest negative stereotyping, to counteract employment discrimination, and to reclaim Asian identity. Whites are puzzled by these efforts because they do not know the history of Asians in this country and they fail to recognize the depths of hostility and humiliation that Asians have experienced.[93]

Esther Ngan-Ling Chow[94] describes women's participation in Asian American movements designed to eliminate racism, to improve the well-being of deprived Asians, and to foster pride in Asian cultural heritage. Because Asians have been segregated from whites, women's strongest ties are to their specific Asian group. They have felt somewhat aloof or estranged from the feminist movement. Recent events encourage women to become more radical in pursuit of women's interests. These include the hostility of Asian men toward independent women; the vicious stereotyping applied specifically to Asian women by whites; and the mistreatment, desertion, and physical abuse of Asian women by Anglo and Asian husbands. Asian feminism is tempered by concern over the well-being of impoverished Asians and the need to identify as Asians in a race-conscious society. Hence, similar to African and Mexican Americans, Asian feminists place more emphasis on jobs and health and give lower priority to abortion rights or political office-holding for women.[95]

Gender and Jobs

Jobs are important for everyone because they are the primary source of income for most individuals in the United States, they give individuals a sense of place and of identity, and they set the stage for forming friendships. Jobs are an avenue for obtaining financial security and alleviating poverty for minority groups; they are the major point of contact with the dominant group as well. For women, paid employment helps reduce dependence on men and leads to more assertive behavior. For all these reasons, employment and job level are of crucial significance for minority women.

Table 2 describes the distribution of all groups of women and men across the major occupational categories. Some disparities are readily apparent. Whites and Asians are much better represented in the upper white-collar jobs than are Native, African, or Hispanic Americans. Compared to men, women are very weakly represented in the elite blue-collar jobs identified as "precision production, repair and crafts." These jobs generally pay more than any of the service occupations and many of the clerical occupations in which women are so heavily concentrated. At the top of the prestige hierarchy, it may appear as if women are better represented in managerial and especially professional jobs than are men. But the extreme heterogeneity of these occupations must be kept in mind. The professional category includes seventy-five different occupations that vary enormously in the power, pay, and prestige attached to them. Women and minorities are more heavily concentrated in the lower paying, less prestigious occupations than are Anglo and Asian men. The executive or managerial jobs also differ greatly and follow the rule that the higher the prestige, pay, and authority of an occupation, the fewer the women—especially minority women—found in it.[96] For this reason, Table 3 presents more refined occupational categories: the professions include only the very high-status positions, and management-related occupations are omitted from the executive category. The division better separates out the high-paying jobs in the professions than in executive positions, as the latter category still includes a number of jobs in which workers manage very few people and have little authority. As a result, women appear to be *less* underrepresented among executives than they appear among high-status professionals.

Table 3 provides a closer look at the labor force status of women and men. Rates of labor force participation vary significantly across the different race and ethnic groups and between women and men. One way to understand these differences is to recognize that job opportunities strongly influence labor force participation rates; the better the jobs available, the more men and women enter the labor market. Further, the unemployment figures record only individuals who are actively seeking work; large numbers of individuals may become so discouraged that they give up the job search and are not counted at all.

Because of varying population size and different rates of labor force participation, the various race and ethnic groups differ greatly in the numbers who are employed. Table 3 shows the share of the total labor force each group of women and men comprise. Native American women and men are least numerous, holding less than 1 percent of the total jobs in the United States. White men are the most numerous group, holding 45.1 percent of the total jobs, yet they hold 56.1 percent of the executive positions and 64.3 percent of the high-status professional positions. The disparity between each group's share of each occupational category and its share of the total labor force is shown in the ratios calculated by dividing the former by the latter and multiplying by 100. Ratio scores below 100 indicate a group is under-represented in the occupation, scores above 100 indicate a group is over-represented in the occupation, and ratio scores that are precisely 100 indicate that a group's representation in the occupation equals their representation in the total labor force. White men have the highest ratio scores; for executives they achieved a ratio of 124.4 and for high-status professions a whopping 142.5. Asian men are also more heavily involved in these elite positions than they are in the total labor force. Asian women have a ratio score of 100 in the high-status professions. *All other race-sex groups are underrepresented in the highest paying, most prestigious jobs this country has to offer.* African, Native American, and Hispanic women are especially underrepresented in the high-status professions.

One can assess degrees of gender inequality by comparing women's and men's scores within each group. In all but one comparison (Native American executives), men's ratio scores are higher than women's. More importantly, the greatest disparities appear among the two groups—Anglos and Asians—who are generally the most advantaged groups in the labor force. There are smaller gaps between women and men, especially in executive positions, among Native Americans, African-Americans, and Hispanic origin groups. This is strong evidence that gaining good educations and high-paying jobs does *not* reduce gender inequality within groups; relative affluence in fact increases disparities between women and men.

I was able to explore occupational gender inequality in more detail using 1980 data for the eleven largest racial and ethnic minority groups, examining occupations separately for Native Americans, African-Americans, Mexican Americans, Cubans, Puerto Ricans, Chinese, Japanese, Filipinos, Koreans, Asian Indians, and Vietnamese.[97]

The groups with the *least* gender inequality in professional and managerial jobs were those with the lowest sex ratios (few men), low educational levels so that men had only a slight advantage over women in school years completed, large numbers of women who have never married or were divorced, somewhat larger families, and lower female labor force participation rates. These groups that possess the least educational and financial resources and also have the least gender inequality include Native Americans, African-Americans, Mexican Americans, and Puerto Ricans. These are the large, indigenous minority groups who continue to experience significant economic discrimination in this society.

In contrast, smaller groups with high proportions of recent well-educated immigrants and with high levels of self-employment exhibit the *highest* levels of inequality. These include the Chinese, Asian Indians, Koreans, and, to a lesser extent, Japanese and Cubans. These are groups in which men have an enormous educational advantage over women, which shows up in much higher proportions of men attaining high-status positions. In these groups as well, men become the self-employed doctors, lawyers, counselors, and accountants in private practice and the managers of the family business. Women, in contrast, become secretaries or receptionists in their husband's offices or unpaid service workers in the family grocery store, motel, or repair shop.

The findings suggest several conclusions:

1. *Gender, race, and class intertwine in numerous ways.* For instance, large racial and ethnic groups are typically indigenous groups who experience greater discrimination and acquire limited economic resources. Smaller immigrant groups have higher class standing; they shun government employment and provide men with greater educational advantages over women. The higher

the overall level of educational attainment of a group, the greater the disparity between women and men in school years completed.

2. *Employers, both public and private, play a part in producing varying levels of gender inequality in jobs.* They choose which groups to employ, and they assign men and women to different job levels, with commensurate differences in prestige, pay, and opportunities for advancement.

3. *The actual level of gender inequality in jobs reflects the opportunities and achievements of men as much as it does those of women.* Across minority groups, there are greater differences among men in the absolute level of occupational achievement than there are among women. Men are exceptionally advantaged in some groups (e.g., Asian Indians) and exceptionally disadvantaged in others (e.g., Mexican Americans, blacks), but the percent of women who are in professional and managerial jobs varies within a much more limited range. This finding implies that people in general and employers in particular make distinctions among different groups of men, but tend to lump women together in an undifferentiated mass.

4. *Groups with the greatest economic resources (higher social class) exhibit the greatest disparities between women and men, whereas groups with the fewest economic resources exhibit the smallest disparities between women and men in occupational achievement.*

I interpret the connection between higher social class and greater gender inequality in the following way.[98] In all groups, men and women share equally the goods and resources necessary for basic survival (food, clothing, shelter), but men tend to control surplus goods and resources and to use these surpluses to enhance their advantaged position. Men's control over surplus goods and resources is reflected in the higher and more specialized education obtained for sons rather than for daughters and in the priority assigned to husbands' over wives' careers.

Men have more privileges than do women in all groups, but men's privileges are greatest in the groups with highest social class standing. Minority groups with the lowest levels of education, jobs, and income in American society have the fewest surplus resources. Women contribute a large share of the family income and are respected accordingly. The limited resources must be used for survival needs and are shared equally. Neither sons nor daughters are able to attain much advanced schooling, and the level of gender inequality in occupations remains relatively low.

By contrast, minority groups with higher levels of education, jobs, and income display more male dominance, especially over the surplus. Sons and daughters are equally highly likely to be sent to college, but sons are encouraged to complete graduate-level professional, technical, or business training. The specialized credentials of the sons translate into more high-status professional and managerial jobs than daughters are able to attain. Because of their greater income, husbands in the more advantaged groups can command more support, personal care taking, and services from their wives than can men in the less advantaged groups. These men may be more consciously egalitarian in attitudes than are men in lower level jobs; nonetheless, they have the power to exert more authority in household affairs."[99]

Voices from Within

There are many ways of viewing reality. In this section, I try to echo the themes and concerns expressed primarily by the minority women whose views are recorded in the book *This Bridge Called My Back: Writings by Radical Women of Color.*[100] These authors and scholars and leaders do not represent all the different communities of minority women. Yet their voices ring loud and true as they speak frankly of how they interpret the constraints imposed on their lives by the forces of race, class, gender, and sometimes homophobia and describe their visions of the better world they hope to build.

GROWING UP: DUAL IDENTITIES

Many themes are interwoven throughout the book and throughout other writings by women of color.[101] We can usefully begin with the earliest memories of these women, which are frequently of racist experiences involving denial or denigration of their identity as a minority-group member. Aurora Morales[102] remembers going from place to place in New York with her mother pretending to be an Italian, hiding their Puerto Rican identity, in order to rent an apartment. Barbara Cameron's[103] childhood was marred by many incidents of white terrorism; she watched as Anglos senselessly gunned down Native Americans who were her friends and relatives. The experience of even a little violence, whether based on ethnicity or not, engenders feelings of helplessness. As Naomi Littlebear writes, "I need to feel control of my own life—violence has on some level rendered me helpless and given me a deep fear of being powerless."[104] It was many years later before Littlebear could state with equanimity, "I've been through so much pain that I've popped out the other side."[105]

Growing up and establishing a satisfactory sense of self is often traumatic for any youngster. But whites in American society do not have to contend with the issue of racial identity. Their whiteness is a given, an established fact that is comfortable and never questioned. This is not the case for people of color, whose identities are dual in nature. On one side are the pressures to identify as an American, to try to achieve a taken-for-granted identity as an ordinary citizen. People of color must identify with general American or Anglo culture just to survive. From an ethnic perspective, however, Anglos and Anglo culture are not very desirable. For a Puerto Rican woman, Anglos may be perceived as too harsh, constrained, limited, and uptight. A Japanese woman might see the same people as too loose, unrestrained, and noisy. The only point on which the two might agree is that Anglos are uncommonly selfish.

At the same time that people of color must outwardly identify with and accept Anglo culture, they must carefully portray themselves within the minority community as a true member of their own group. Aurora Morales describes the intricate juggling of identity: "Where I grew up, I fought battles to prove I was Puerto Rican with the kids who called me 'Americanita' but I stayed on the safe side of that line: Caribbean island, not Portah Rican; exotic tropical blossom, not spic—living halfway in the skin and separating myself from the dark, bad city kids in Nueva York."[106]

LANGUAGE AND CULTURE

Growing up in a distinctive ethnic community means learning two different cultures and two very different modes of speaking. Language is more than a series of words and sounds put together to establish sentences. Language includes subtle inflections, symbols, and nuances. Language conveys a whole world of meaning. One's native language—whether it is standard American English or black English, Tex-Mex or Puerto Rican Spanish—reminds one of home, family, and community. Even the women of color who are most acculturated to Anglo culture yearn to return to their own origins via language, to hear the words spoken by their loved ones in the rhythms they have known since childhood.

As professionals or executives, acculturated women are successful in the Anglo-dominated career world; they appear to move easily in what is, for them, a foreign existence. These women are often asked to be spokespersons for their group, to describe their own culture for Anglo outsiders. They believe that such token roles are traps. If they speak from their hearts and describe the crushing experiences of racism, the Anglo audience will feel guilt; if they describe what they really want—a sense of autonomy within a community built around their own values—the Anglos will feel threatened.[107] A hostile audience is not an inviting prospect. Equally daunting is the probability of being dismissed as not typical of the group or of finding the work a complete waste of time:

> When Third World women are asked to speak representing our racial or ethnic group, we are expected to move, charm, or entertain, but not to educate in ways that are threatening to our audiences. We speak to audiences that sift out those parts of our speech (if what we say does not fit the image they have of us), come up to shake our hands with "That was lovely my dear, just lovely," and go home with the same mind set they come in with.[108]

Minority women perceive that portraying their own lives to outsiders is an impossible task. Even when they try, they have to do so in their *second* language.[109]

GROWING UP FEMALE

People of color endure growing-up experiences that are confounded by the issue of gender. All cultures prescribe different roles for women and men. Gender roles often contain internal contradictions.

Women's prescribed gender roles are particularly fraught with dualisms in regard to sexuality. To be successful as a woman means being able to attract and keep a man. Thus, just like many Anglo women, minority women have to negotiate the tricky labyrinth of displaying a "come hither" attitude to men but stopping those men before they get too close, of exuding an alluring sensuality for all men but reserving actual intercourse for the one and only special man, and sometimes of using sexuality to entice men while having been taught that they will not enjoy actual intercourse at all.[110]

These hide-and-seek games concerning sexuality are as familiar to white women as they are to women of color. Yet women of color experience some additional twists on the dating–rating–mating contests. For instance, it may be even more difficult for a minority woman than for her white counterpart to accept her sexuality as a lesbian and to identify herself publicly as gay. This is so because of the special concern of minority groups to at least appear to conform to Anglo culture and the very great efforts expended by minority group members to stamp out any signs of nonconformity.[111]

Heterosexual minority women face the quandary of becoming attached to white men much more frequently than Anglo women consider linking up with minority men. In some respects, white men are very attractive to minority women. They carry the comfort of full-fledged acceptance in white-dominated society, and frequently they have the glamour of more money and resources than minority men. Yet the man's very whiteness erects a barrier. His own growing-up experiences may render him incapable of understanding the minority woman. Furthermore, men of all groups come to view women as sexual property, i.e., as nonpersons whom the man may possess, treat, and dispose of as he sees fit. Given that the dominant group has been accustomed to seeing minority groups as instruments for reaching their own ends, as slaves, or as inferior persons, how tempting it must be for the white man to regard minority women especially as sexual property, as unfit for marriage, or as having no need or right to be treated decently.

Suppose that, in spite of all this, a minority woman chooses to align herself with a white man. Then minority men feel betrayed because they believe the white man has not only emasculated the black man, the Hispanic man, the Asian man, the Native American man, or whomever, but also the white man has stolen his sexual property.

And what of minority women's relationships with minority men? Anglo culture virtually equates masculinity with money, whiteness, and sexual prowess. Many minority persons of both sexes believe that Anglos have conspired to rob minority men of each of these. Therefore, minority women feel especially concerned to support men's egos and to help men build a strong sense of masculinity.[112]

Gender roles reach far beyond issues of love and sex. Gender-type proscriptions and prescriptions pervade every nook and cranny of human life. In all cultures, women are viewed as less valuable and less powerful than men. Growing up for all girls means coming to terms with these negative views and stereotypes.

Typically, the mother is charged with teaching these lessons to her daughter. Gloria Anzaldua describes the multiple contradictions she learned from her widowed mother:

> Though she loved me she would only show it covertly—in the tone of her voice, in a look. Not so with my brothers—there it was visible for all the world to see. They were male and surrogate husbands, legitimate receivers of her power. Her allegiance was and is to her male children, not to the female.
>
> Seeing my mother turn to my brothers for protection, for guidance— a mock act. She and I both knew she wouldn't be getting any from them. Like most men they didn't have it to give, instead needed to get it from women. . . .

Yet she could not discount me. "Machona—india ladina" (masculine—wild Indian), she would call me because I did not act like a nice little Chicanita is supposed to act: later, in the same breath she would praise and blame me, often for the same thing—being a tomboy and wearing boots, being unafraid of snakes or knives, showing my contempt for women's roles, leaving home to go to college, not settling down and getting married, being a politica, siding with the Farmworkers. Yet, while she would try to correct my more aggressive moods, my mother was secretly proud of my "waywardness." (Something she will never admit.) Proud that I'd worked myself through school. Secretly proud of my paintings, of my writing, though all the while complaining because I made no money out of it.[113]

DIVISIONS WITHIN THE MINORITY COMMUNITY

Generational differences erect barriers among women. The speed of social change in this country guarantees that contemporary women will inhabit a world that is different from that of their mothers. And mothers and daughters can inhabit different worlds *at the same time* within this country. The possibilities are endless: mother came to this country as a foreign immigrant to the West Coast while daughter grew up as an American citizen in the interior; or mother battles the legacy of slavery in the rural South while daughter copes with sexism and racism in the urban North; or mother lives on the Lakota Sioux Indian Reservation while daughter lives and works in the dry heat of Los Angeles; "or" (but probably "and") mother scrubs floors, waits on white people, and struggles with poverty so that daughter might go to college and have a professional career.

But it is not just the separate worlds that divide mother and daughter; it is the separate thinking as well. The mothers taught daughters to survive in a racist, classist, sexist, and homophobic society, for which the daughters are grateful. The mothers also counseled patience, tolerance, occasional deceit, and suppression of anger—for to recognize all the injustices would make a difficult situation intolerably worse. Yet the daughters are coming to a full realization of their own anger at the injustice that they suffer, that their mothers and fathers endured, and that their brothers speak against, although often for men only. The daughters can no longer accept stereotyped and negative definitions of themselves based on either race or gender. They perceive that their mothers did accept those hatreds in order to survive, that their mothers do not understand their own thinking about injustice, and that their mothers are afraid that the daughters will be disillusioned or harmed by the views they have chosen.[114] The mothers perceive their daughters' lives as rejections of their own. To reach across these barriers, to heal and soften the divisions between mother and daughter, is a top priority for minority women.

A minor theme in the personal writings of minority women concerns the barriers between sisters, i.e., between them and other women within their own group. Minority women are painfully aware that whites and men control the bulk of the resources and most of the power in all situations in American society. As minority women, they control little of either. They understand that it is frequently advantageous and often critical to ally themselves with the powerful others (whites or men). Minority women struggle against this system of power and, privately at least, provide plenty of support for one another. How painful it is, then, to find that the same women who supported them in private sometimes go over to the other side in public where the support would really count.

Another minor theme concerns relationships with brothers (men in the same group). Minority feminism frequently originated from participation in minority-group movements, where women gained in courage to strike out against racial oppression and developed a strong sense of the injustice of sexism. Yet to pursue feminism is to invite rejection from minority men. Merle Woo describes the complex web of gender and race:

> Some of the male writers in the Asian American community seem never to support us. They always expect us to support them. . . . We almost always do. Anti–Yellow men? Are they kidding? We go to their readings, buy and read and comment on their books, and try to keep up a dialogue. And they accuse us of betrayal, are resentful because we do readings together as Women, and so often do not come to our performances. And all the while we hurt because we are rejected by our brothers. . . . These men of color . . . fight the racism in white society, but they have bought the white male definition of "masculinity." . . .
>
> Some Asian men don't seem to understand that by supporting Third World women and fighting sexism, they are helping themselves as well. I understand all too clearly how dehumanized Dad was in this country. To be a Chinese man in America is to be a victim of both racism and sexism. He was made to feel he was without strength, identity, and purpose. He was made to feel soft and weak, whose only job was to serve whites. Yes, Ma, at one time I was ashamed of him because I thought he was "womanly." . . . I didn't know that he spent a year and a half on Angel Island; that we could never have our right names; that he lived in constant fear of being deported; that, like you, he worked two full-time jobs most of his life; that he was mocked and ridiculed because he speaks "broken English." And Ma, I was so ashamed (of his being humiliated by whites) when I was only six years old that I never held his hand again.[115]

ATTITUDES TOWARD WHITE WOMEN

To grow up as a minority group member is to learn self-hatred through the vicious racism in American society. Minority women struggle to replace self-hatred with love, respect, and esteem for themselves, for their parents, and for other members of their own group. They also acknowledge their feelings toward other minority groups: several authors in *This Bridge Called My Back* point out that they could not help but learn to be racist in a society that uses racism "both to create false differences among us and to mask very, very significant ones—cultural, economic, political."[116] In discussing the racist images she derived from television, books, movies, and magazines, Barbara Cameron says, "We are all continually pumped with gross and inaccurate images of everyone else and we all pump it out."[117] To transcend such false images requires performing painful self-analysis,[118] recognizing the differences in historical experience among different groups of women, allowing each group time and space to separate and come to terms with their own lives and experiences, and finally uniting across the barriers of race, class, and sexual preference.[119]

At this stage of feminist consciousness among minority women, identifying with other women of color is difficult; identifying with white women is doubly so. Some of the worst instances of racism are suffered through the hands of white women. Even without those instances, perceptions of whites and feelings toward whites are greatly mixed. Each view is grounded in reality and is thought out with awareness of its implications.

Some women of color believe that white women can never know the full horror of brute racism or the grinding desperation of intense poverty.[120] In this view, racial divisions are so strong that white women can never relinquish the advantages they have by being white; in a crisis, they will inevitably support white men or the capitalist economic system that white men control. This perception coincides with having experienced the white feminist movement as "elitist, crudely insensitive, and condescending" and white women as "limited, bigoted, and myopic."[121]

Other minority women believe that it is wrong to judge white women on the basis of their race; in fact, that kind of racism is precisely what all women must work to eradicate. In this view, white women are racist because they have been linked with the white power structure and oppressed by white men.[122] This perception accompanies the hope that, through intense efforts, women of all groups can come to understand one another and the forces that divide them and ultimately can work together to build a better society.

Conclusion: Minority Women and Feminism

This essay has ranged widely over the historical experiences of diverse groups, through an examination of gender inequality in jobs, toward some of the ideas expressed by minority women themselves. Each approach offers a different perspective of the lives of minority women. Yet I believe each approach leads to the same findings and implications, and these have distinct consequences for the kind of feminism minority women choose.

The first finding is that, while there are many forces that divide, individual women do not and cannot compartmentalize their lives. They cannot neatly separate their experiences into distinct categories and label some "racial," some "gender," and some "social class." They are not members of minorities first and women second. Nor are they women first and members of minorities second. They are individuals who have incorporated a whole constellation of roles, characteristics, and experiences into their self-concepts. Yet gender and race are master statuses, channeling these women into certain roles and impinging on their lives at every turn.

Second, what is true for the individual is true for the society. The forces of race, gender, and class are inseparable. Where minority women have been feminist activists, their activities and viewpoints are affected by a deep concern for the well-being of their own ethnic group. Women have been exceptionally active in all types of minority-group movements as well. For many, their treatment as second-class citizens in minority movements crystalized their awareness of sexism, galvanizing them into action on that front. Yet the experience of racism makes them reluctant to form enduring links with white feminist groups, and the experience of sexism often puts them at loggerheads with minority males. The experience of class oppression may turn their immediate attention to crushing financial issues. Thus gender, race, and class intertwine, weaving patterns that both unite minority women with and separate them from other groups.

Third, minority women must be free to define themselves, their priorities, and their goals based on their own analysis of their condition in American society. In the near future, producing such an analysis requires some separatism, so that various individuals and groups may sort out their unique experiences, reclaim their own identities, and emerge with a fresh perspective on the many forces that shape American society.

Fourth, white women can know and understand the conditions of minority women, but it is their responsibility to find out. Minority women do not want the task of explaining themselves to anyone.

Finally, the white feminist movement can incorporate minority women, but for it to do so movement members must go far beyond merely expressing a desire to be inclusive. The movement must embrace all the issues that confront women, especially those of race and class. Barbara Smith put the matter very well:

> The reason racism is a feminist issue is easily explained by the inherent definition of feminism. Feminism is the political theory and practice to free all women: women of color, working-class women, poor women, physically challenged women, lesbians, old women, as well as white economically privileged heterosexual women. Anything less than this is not feminism, but merely female self-aggrandizement.[123]

NOTES

1. Teresa L. Amott and Julie A. Matthei, *Race, Gender and Work: A Multicultural Economic History of Women in the United States* (Boston: South End Press, 1991), contains a much more detailed economic and political history of European, American Indian, Mexican American, African-American, Asian American, and Puerto Rican women.

2. Native Americans prefer to be called by their own tribal names—Zuni, Hopi, Pueblo, etc.—but recognize that that is unlikely to happen. Therefore, they opt for "Native Americans" as a label. Few want to be called "Indians," because that is indeed a misnomer.

3. John Price, "North American Indian Families," in Charles H. Mindel and Robert W. Habenstein, eds., *Ethnic Families in America* (New York: Elsevier North-Holland, 1976), pp. 248–70.

4. Judith K. Brown, "Economic Organization and the Position of Women Among the Iroquois," *Ethnohistory* 17 (1970), pp. 151–63.

5. Laila Sheekry Hamamsy, "The Role of Women in a Changing Navajo Society," *American Anthropologist* 59 (1957), pp. 101–11.

6. The term *Anglo* is widely used in the Southwest to distinguish whites from Mexican Americans and from Native Americans. In this article, the terms *white, Anglo, majority,* and *dominant group* are used synonymously. They refer to the great bulk of U.S. citizens who, despite their specific ethnic backgrounds, participate in and are products of the mainstream culture.

7. Joan Ablon, "Relocated American Indians in the San Francisco Bay Area: Social Interaction and Indian Identity," in Howard M. Bahr, Bruce A. Chadwick, and Robert C. Day, eds., *Native Americans Today: Sociological Perspectives* (New York: Harper and Row, 1972), pp. 412–27.

8. Shirley Hill Witt, "Native Women Today: Sexism and the Indian Woman," in Sue Cox, ed., *Female Psychology: The Emerging Self* (Chicago: Science Research Associates, 1976), pp. 249–59.

9. Amott and Matthei, p. 57.

10. Comparison between 1980 and 1990 census data based on Elizabeth M. Almquist, "Labor Market Gender Inequality in Minority Groups," *Gender and Society* 1 (1987), pp. 400–414.

11. Amott and Matthei, p. 59.

12. Carol Cornelius Mohawk, "Native Women: Working for the Survival of Our People," *Akwesasne Notes* (Late Fall 1982), pp. 4–5.

13. Rosemary Ackley Christensen, "Indian Women: A Literature Search Through Historical and Personal Perspectives" (not dated, circa 1983), xeroxed publication of the Indian Education Department of the Minneapolis, Minnesota, public schools.

14. Pamela T. Reid and Lillian Comas-Diaz, "Gender and Ethnicity: Perspectives on Dual Status," *Sex Roles* 2 (1990), pp. 397–408; Rayna Green, "American Indian Women: Diverse Leadership for Social Change," in Lisa Albrecht and Rose M. Brewer, eds., *Bridges of Power: Women's Multicultural Alliances* (Philadelphia: New Society Publishers, 1990), pp. 61–73.

15. Rayna Green, *Women in American Indian Society* (New York: Chelsea House, 1992).

16. Reid and Comas-Diaz; Green, *Women in American Indian Society.*

17. A woman interviewed by John L. Gwaltney in *Drylongso: A Self-Portrait of Black America* (New York: Vintage, 1980). Quotation cited by Patricia Hill Collins in "Learning from the Outsider Within: The Sociological Significance of Black Feminist Thought," *Social Problems* 33 (1986), pp. 514–32.

18. Frances M. Beal, "Slave of a Slave No More: Black Women in Struggle," *The Black Scholar* 6 (1975), pp. 16–24; Elizabeth F. Hood, "Black Women, White Women: Separate Paths to Liberation," *The Black Scholar* 9 (1978), pp. 45–56.

19. Natalie J. Sokoloff, "Evaluating Gains and Losses by Black and White Women and Men in the Professions, 1960–1980," *Social Problems* 35 (1988), pp. 36–53. See also Patricia A. Gwartney-Gibbs and Patricia A. Taylor, "Black Women Workers' Earnings Progress in Three Industrial Sectors," *Sage* 3 (1986), pp. 20–25; and Mary Romero, "Twice Protected? Assessing the Impact of Affirmative Action on Mexican-American Women," *Ethnicity and Public Policy* 5 (1986), pp. 135–56.

20. Jacquelyne Jackson, "But Where Are the Men?" *The Black Scholar* 3 (1971), pp. 30–41.

21. A total of 1.6 percent of the total African-American population is in correctional institutions. Comparable figures for other groups are 0.2 percent of whites, 0.9 percent of Native Americans, 0.1 percent of Asians, and 0.9 percent of Hispanics. Source: U.S. Bureau of the Census, C-P-1, 1990 Census of Population, *General Population Characteristics.*

22. Patricia Hill Collins, "Learning from the Outsider Within: The Sociological Significance of Black Feminist Thought," *Social Problems* 33 (1986), pp. 514–32.

23. Elmer P. Martin and Joanne Mitchell Martin, "The Black Woman: Perspectives on Her Role in the Family," *Ethnicity and Public Policy* 5 (1986), pp. 184–205.

24. Norma Carson, "The Role of Informal Adoption in the Liberation of Black Women" (paper presented at the annual meeting of the Mid-South Sociological Association, Jackson, Miss., October, 1982).

25. Cheryl Townsend Gilkes, "From Slavery to Social Welfare: Racism and the Control of Black Women," in Amy Smerdlow and Helen Lessinger, eds., *Class, Race, and Sex: The Dynamics of Control* (Boston: G. K. Hall, 1981), pp. 288–300.

26. Martin and Martin, op. cit.; Hood, op. cit.

27. Aldon Morris, "The Black Southern Sit-In Movement: An Analysis of Internal Organization," *American Sociological Review* 46 (1981), pp. 744–67.

28. Guida West, *The National Welfare Rights Movement: The Social Protest of Poor Women* (New York: Praeger, 1981).

29. Linda J. M. LaRue, "The Black Movement and Women's Liberation," in Cox, ed., *Female Psychology,* pp. 216–25.

30. Diane K. Lewis, "A Response to Inequality: Black Women, Racism, and Sexism," *Signs: Journal of Women in Culture and Society* 3 (1977), pp. 339–61.

31. The Combahee River Collective, "A Black Feminist Statement," in Gloria T. Hull, Patricia Bell Scott, and Barbara Smith, eds., *All the Women are White, All the Blacks Are Men, But Some of Us Are Brave: Black Women's Studies* (Old Westbury, N.Y.: Feminist Press, 1982), pp. 13–22.

32. Barbara Cameron, "Entering the Lives of Others," in Cherrie Moraga and Gloria Anzaldua, eds., *This Bridge Called My Back: Writings by Radical Women of Color* (Watertown, Mass.: Persephone Press, 1981), p. 23.

33. Collins, op. cit.

34. Consuelo Nieto, "The Chicana and the Women's Rights Movement: A Perspective," *Civil Rights Digest* 6 (1974), pp. 36–42.

35. Anna Nieto-Gomez, "Heritage of *La Hembra*," in Cox, ed., *Female Psychology,* pp. 226–34.

36. The *encomienda* was a plantationlike enterprise, controlled by a Spanish landlord. The native people worked there in a relationship to the Spanish master that was semifeudal and semislave.

37. Betty Garcia-Bahne, "*La Chicana* and the Chicano Family," in Rosaura Sanchez and Rosa Martinez Cruz, eds., *Essays on la Mujer* (Los Angeles: University of California, Chicano Studies Center Publications, 1977), p. 39. See also Irene Blea, *La Chicana and the Intersection of Race, Class and Gender* (New York: Praeger, 1992).

38. David Alvirez and Frank D. Bean, "The Mexican-American Family," in Mindel and Habenstein, eds., *Ethnic Families in America* (New York: Elsevier North-Holland, 1976), pp. 270–89.

39. Leo Grebler, Joan W. Moore, and Ralph C. Guzman, *The Mexican-American People* (New York: Free Press, 1970), p. 366.

40. Alma M. Garcia, "The Development of Chicana Feminist Discourse, 1970–1980," *Gender and Society* 3 (1989), pp. 217–38.

41. Maria L. Apodaca, "The Chicana Woman: An Historical Materialist Perspective," *Latin American Perspectives* 12–13 (1977), pp. 75–89.

42. Maxine Baca Zinn, "Chicano Men and Masculinity," in Michael S. Kimmel and Michael A. Messner, eds., *Men's Lives* (New York: Macmillan, 1989), pp. 87–97; Maxine Baca Zinn, "Family, Feminism, and Race in America," *Gender and Society* 4 (1990), pp. 68–82.

43. Garcia-Bahne, op. cit.

44. Nieto-Gomez, op. cit.

45. Romero, op. cit. See also Vicki L. Ruiz, "'And Miles to Go . . .': Mexican Women and Work, 1930–1950," in Lillian Schlissel, Vicki L. Ruiz, and Janice Monk, eds., *Western Women: Their Land, Their Lives* (Albuquerque: University of New Mexico Press, 1988), pp. 117–36.

46. Romero, op. cit.

47. Garcia, op. cit.

48. Terry Mason, "Symbolic Strategies for Change: A Discussion of the Chicana Women's Movement," in Melville, ed., *Twice a Minority* (St. Louis: C. V. Mosby, 1980), pp. 95–108.

49. Maxine Baca Zinn, "Political Familism: Toward Sex Role Equality in Chicano Families," *Atzlan* 6 (1975), pp. 13–26.

50. Aurora Levins Morales, "And Even Fidel Can't Change That," in Moraga and Anzaldua, eds., *This Bridge Called My Back,* p. 53.

51. Michael Myerson, "Puerto Rico, Our Backyard Colony," in Francesco Cordasco and Eugene Bucchioni, eds., *The Puerto Rican Experience* (Totowa, N.J.: Rowman and Littlefield, 1973), pp. 114–24. See also Eva E. Sandis, "Characteristics of Puerto Rican Migrants to and from the United States," in Cordasco and Bucchioni, eds., *The Puerto Rican Experience,* pp. 127–49.

52. Lois Gray, "The Jobs Puerto Ricans Hold in New York City," *Monthly Labor Review* 28 (1978), pp. 12–16.

53. Joseph P. Fitzpatrick, "The Puerto Rican Family," in Mindel and Habenstein, eds., *Ethnic Families in America,* pp. 192–217.

54. Lourdes Miranda King, "*Puertorriquenas* in the United States: The Impact of Double Discrimination," *Civil Rights Digest* (1974), p. 24.

55. Edna Acosta-Belen, "Puerto Rican Women in Culture, History and Society," in Edna Acosta-Belen, ed., *The Puerto Rican Woman,* 2nd ed. (New York: Praeger, 1986), pp. 14–15.

56. Edward W. Christensen, "The Puerto Rican Woman: A Profile," in Acosta-Belen, ed., *The Puerto Rican Woman,* 1st ed. (New York: Praeger, 1977), pp. 51–63.

57. Marya Munoz Vasquez, "The Effects of Role Expectations on the Marital Status of Urban Puerto Rican Women," in Acosta-Belen, ed., *The Puerto Rican Woman,* 2nd ed., pp. 110–19.

58. Rosemary S. Cooney, Lloyd H. Rogler, Rosemarie Hurrell, and Vilma Ortiz, "Decision Making in Intergenerational Puerto Rican Families," *Journal of Marriage and the Family* 44 (1982), pp. 621–31.

59. Social standing in Puerto Rico is based on a number of factors, including skin color. Girls are taught that it is preferable to marry lighter skinned men in order to "whiten" the race. This not-so-subtle message is reemphasized in the United States, especially because of the racism whites direct toward any person with African ancestry. See Angela Jorge, "The Black Puerto Rican Woman in Contemporary American Society," in Acosta-Belen, ed., *The Puerto Rican Woman,* 2nd ed., pp. 180–88.

60. Christine E. Bose, "Puerto Rican Women in the United States: An Overview," in Acosta-Belen, *The Puerto Rican Woman,* 2nd ed., pp. 147–69.

61. Cited in Amott and Matthei, op. cit., p. 287.

62. Nancy A. Naples, "Activist Mother: Cross-Generational Continuity in the Community Work of Women from Low Income Urban Neighborhoods," *Gender and Society* 6 (1992), pp. 441–63.

63. Interview excerpt from Yolanda Prieto, "Cuban Women in New Jersey: Gender Relations and Change," in Donna Gabaccia, *Seeking Common Ground: Multidisciplinary Studies of Immigrant Women in the United States* (Westport, Conn.: Praeger, 1992), pp. 185–202.

64. Thomas D. Boswell and James R. Curtis, *The Cuban-American Experience* (Totowa, N.J.: Rowman and Allanheld, 1983).

65. Myra Marx Ferree, "Employment Without Liberation: Cuban Women in the United States," *Social Science Quarterly* 60 (1978), pp. 35–50.

66. Alexjandro Portes and Alex Stepick, "Unwelcome Immigrants: The Labor Market Experiences of 1980 (Mariel) Cuban and Haitian Refugees in South Florida," *American Sociological Review* 50 (1985), pp. 493–514.

67. Myra Marx Ferree, op. cit.

68. Prieto, op. cit.

69. Almquist, op. cit. Also, see below, "Gender and Jobs."

70. U.S. Bureau of the Census, 1990 Census of Population and Housing, C-P-1, *General Population Characteristics,* 1993.

71. Deborah Woo, "The Socioeconomic Status of Asian American Women in the Labor Force: An Alternative View," *Sociological Perspectives* 28 (1985), pp. 307–38.

72. Norris Hundley, Jr., *The Asian American: The Historical Experience* (Santa Barbara, Calif.: ABC-Clio, 1976).

73. Rose Hum Lee, "Chinese Americans," in Francis Brown and Joseph S. Roucedk, eds., *One America* (New York: Prentice-Hall, 1951), pp. 309–18; Harry L. Kitano, *Japanese Americans: Evolution of a Subculture* (Englewood Cliffs, N.J.: Prentice-Hall, 1976).

74. Monica Boyd, "Oriental Immigration: The Experience of the Chinese, Japanese, and Filipino Populations in the United States," *International Migration Review* 5 (1971), pp. 48–80.

75. Lucie Cheng Hirata, "Free, Indentured, Enslaved: Chinese Prostitutes in Nineteenth Century America," *Signs: Journal of Women in Culture and Society* 5 (1979), pp. 3–79.

76. Irene Fujitomi and Diane Wong, "The New Asian-American Woman," in Stanley Sue and Nathan Wagner, eds., *Asian Americans: Psychological Perspectives* (Palo Alto, Calif.: Science and Behavior Books, 1973).

77. Boyd, op. cit.

78. Harry H. L. Kitano and Roger Daniels, *Asian Americans: Emerging Minorities* (Englewood Cliffs, N.J.: Prentice-Hall, 1988), p. 15.

79. Evelyn Nakano Glenn, "Split Household, Small Producer and Dual Wage Earner: An Analysis of Chinese-American Family Strategies," *Journal of Marriage and the Family* 45 (1983), pp. 35–46.

80. Kitano and Daniels, op. cit.

81. Almquist, op. cit.

82. Kitano and Daniels, op. cit.

83. Won Moo Hurh and Kwang Chung Kim, *Korean Immigrants in America* (London: Associated University Presses, 1984); Arthur W. Helweg and Usha M. Helweg, *An Immigrant Success Story: East Indians in America* (Philadelphia: University of Pennsylvania Press, 1990); Parmatma Saran, *The Asian Indian Experience in the United States* (Cambridge, Mass.: Schenkman, 1985).

84. Sethi Dasgupta, *On the Trail of an Uncertain Dream: Indian Immigrant Experience in America* (New York: AMS Press, 1989).

85. Almquist, op. cit. See also Paul J. Rutledge, *The Vietnamese Experience in America* (Bloomington: Indiana University Press, 1992).

86. Nazli Kibria, "Power, Patriarchy, and Gender Conflict in the Vietnamese Immigrant Community," *Gender and Society* 4 (1990), pp. 9–24.

87. R. Brooke Jacobsen, "Changes in the Chinese Family," *Social Science* 51 (1976), pp. 26–31; Fujitomi and Wong, op. cit. For a fascinating fictional account of the relationships within families with one or more parents born abroad, see Maxine Hong Kingston, *China Men* (New York: Ballantine, 1980).

88. Lucy Jen Huang, "The Chinese American Family," in Mindel and Habenstein, eds., *Ethnic Families in America,* pp. 124–47.

89. Kibria, op. cit.

90. Dasgupta, op. cit.

91. Charles Hirschman and Morrison G. Wong, "The Extraordinary Educational Attainment of Asian-Americans: A Search for Historical Evidence and Explanations," *Social Forces* 65 (1986), pp. 1–27; Victor Nee and Jimy Sanders, "The Road to Parity: Determinants of the Socioeconomic Attainments of Asian Americans," *Ethnic and Racial Studies* 8 (1985), pp. 75–93.

92. Robert M. Jiobu, "Earnings Differentials Between Whites and Ethnic Minorities: The Cases of Asian Americans, Blacks, and Chicanos," *Sociology and Social Research* 61 (1976), pp. 24–38.

93. Mitsuye Yamada, "Invisibility Is an Unnatural Disaster: Reflections of an Asian American Woman," in Moraga and Anzaldua, eds., *This Bridge Called My Back*, pp. 35–40.

94. Esther Ngan-Ling Chow, "The Development of Feminist Consciousness Among Asian American Women," *Gender and Society* 1 (1987), pp. 284–99. See also Bok-Lim Kim, "Asian Wives of U.S. Servicemen: Women in Shadows," *Amerasia Journal* 4 (1977), pp. 91–115; and Chalsa Loo and Paul Ong, "Slaying Demons with a Sewing Needle: Feminist Issues for Chinatown Women," *Berkeley Journal of Sociology* 27 (1982), pp. 77–88.

95. Similar patterns distinguish blacks and whites. See Elaine J. Hall and Myra Marx Ferree, "Race Differences in Abortion Attitudes," *Public Opinion Quarterly* 50 (1986), pp. 193–207; and H. Edward Ransford and Jon Miller, "Race, Sex and Feminist Outlooks," *American Sociological Review* 48 (1983), pp. 46–59.

96. These conclusions are drawn from considering the 1990 data in some detail. See also Barbara F. Reskin and Catherine E. Ross, "Jobs, Authority and Earnings Among Managers: The Continuing Significance of Sex," *Work and Occupations* 19 (1992), pp. 342–65; Denise A. Segura, "Chicana and Mexican Immigrant Women at Work: The Impact of Class, Race, and Gender on Occupational Mobility," *Gender and Society* 3 (1989), pp. 37–52; Wu Xu and Ann Leffler, "Gender and Race Effects on Occupational Prestige, Segregation, and Earnings," *Gender and Society* 6 (1992), pp. 376–92.

97. Almquist, op. cit. In hindsight, I wish I had included whites in the analysis. At the time, I thought that whites were too heterogeneous to comprise a distinct ethnic group.

98. Gerhard Lenski has proposed similar views about class stratification in whole societies. See *Power and Privilege: A Theory of Social Stratification* (New York: McGraw-Hill, 1966).

99. Janice M. Steil, "Marital Relationships and Mental Health: The Psychic Costs of Inequality," in Jo Freeman, ed., *Women: A Feminist Perspective,* 4th ed. (Palo Alto, Calif.: Mayfield, 1984), pp. 138–48.

100. As already indicated, *This Bridge Called My Back: Writings by Radical Women of Color* was edited by Cherrie Moraga and Gloria Anzaldua and was published in Watertown, Massachusetts, by Persephone Press in 1981. Subsequent references to articles in this book refer to it simply as "*This Bridge.*"

101. See Angela Davis, *Women, Race and Class* (New York: Random House, 1981); Paula Giddings, *When and Where I Enter: The Impact of Black Women on Race and Sex in America* (New York: Bantam, 1984); Margaret C. Simms and Julianne M. Malveaux, eds., *Slipping Through the Cracks: The Status of Black Women* (New Brunswick, N.J.: Transaction, 1986).

102. Morales, op. cit., pp. 53–57.

103. Barbara Cameron, "Gee, You Don't Seem Like an Indian from the Reservation," *This Bridge,* pp. 46–52.

104. Naomi Littlebear, "Earth-Lover, Survivor, Musician," *This Bridge,* p. 158.

105. Ibid.

106. Morales, op. cit., p. 53.

107. Doris Davenport, "The Pathology of Racism: A Conversation with Third World Wimmin," *This Bridge,* pp. 85–91.

108. Mitsuye Yamada, "Asian Pacific American Women and Feminism," *This Bridge,* p. 71.

109. Barbara Smith and Beverly Smith, "Across the Kitchen Table: A Sister to Sister Dialogue," *This Bridge,* pp. 113–27.

110. Morales, op. cit., p. 56.

111. Morraga, "La Guera," *This Bridge,* pp. 27–34.

112. The authors in *This Bridge* actually say very little about the need to build or restore the threatened masculinity of minority men. I suspect radical and lesbian women have moved beyond this issue in the 1980s and 1990s.

113. Gloria Anzaldua, "*La Prieta,*" *This Bridge,* p. 201.

114. Yamada, op. cit., describes the painful process of coming to grips with her identity as an Asian woman.

115. Merle Woo, "An Open Letter to Ma," *This Bridge,* p. 145.

116. Mirtha Quintanales, "I Paid Very Hard for My Immigrant Ignorance," *This Bridge,* p. 153.

117. Cameron, op. cit., p. 49.

118. Quintanales, op. cit., p. 154.

119. Smith and Smith, op. cit., p. 126.

120. Ibid., p. 113.

121. Davenport, op. cit., p. 86.

122. Smith and Smith, op. cit.

123. Quoted at the beginning of the section "Entering the Lives of Others: Theory in the Flesh," in *This Bridge,* p. 23.

Feminist Consciousness and Black Women

Pauline Terrelonge

LIKE THE POPULIST movement at the turn of the century, and the prohibition and antiwar movements of subsequent decades, the contemporary feminist movement is having an enormous impact on black America. It is not so much that black people have embraced the feminist movement or that they have even begun to identify with it. Rather its effect is seen in the controversy it has engendered within the race concerning the exact status of black males and females and what the ideal role of each should be. A common (and, some would argue, the dominant) view within the black community at the present time is that blacks have withstood the long line of abuses perpetrated against them ever since their arrival in this country mainly because of the black woman's fortitude, inner wisdom, and sheer ability to survive. As a corollary to this emphasis on the moral, spiritual, and emotional strength of the black woman in offsetting the potential annihilation of the race, proponents of this view stress the critical role that she plays in keeping the black family together and in supporting black males. Indeed, many blacks regard the role of uniting all blacks to be the primary duty of the black woman, one that should supersede all other roles that she might want to perform, and certainly one that is essentially incompatible with her own individual liberation.[1] Pursuit of the latter is generally judged to be a selfish goal detrimental to the overall welfare of the race. In short, sexism is viewed by many blacks, both male and female, to be a factor of minimal importance in the overall oppression of the black woman. The brunt of culpability for her unequal condition is accorded to racism.[2]

The object of this essay is to challenge this point of view. It is my belief that the foregoing view of black female subordination expresses a narrow perspective on the nature of social oppression in American society, and, because of this, the solutions that are commonly proposed—e.g., correcting the imbalance in the black sex ratio or building stronger black families—are doomed to serve as only partial palliatives to the problems facing black women.

The first fact that must be grasped is that the black female condition in America has developed in a society where the dominant economic form is the market economy and the sole purpose of economic activity is the making of a profit on the part of large corporations. Because profit maximization is the superordinate goal to which all other social goals are merely subsidiary, labor is a premium. Labor must not only be made as highly productive as possible but also be obtained at the cheapest possible cost. The manipulation of the labor market is essential to attain these dual goals and provide for the effective functioning of the American economic order.

A major strategy for manipulating labor has been the maintenance of a sexual division of labor, i.e., a situation where certain roles are designated as male, others as female. The allocation of societal functions according to gender has been based on certain biological factors that objectively differentiate the sexes and the way those factors are interpreted through the ideology of sexism. The fact that women bear children has been used to justify their relegation to the domestic sphere. Their ability to reproduce has been made a duty, to which have been added the responsibilities of nurturing the offspring, serving the spouse, and performing or supervising all domestic-related chores. It is easy to see how the pattern of female responsibility for the domestic sphere is useful to the economic system; it has allowed certain critical societal functions to be performed without the need of providing monetary remuneration.[3]

It is generally recognized that the ideology of racism has functioned to maintain blacks in a subordinate economic state.[4] Less readily recognized, however, are the similarities of the process of racial subordination to that of female subordination. In both cases the rationale for subordination resides in characteristics ascribed by the large capitalist interests, which are almost totally white male. Moreover, both forces—sexism and racism—create an occupationally segregated labor market, thereby giving rise to a situation where there are male jobs and female jobs, white jobs and black jobs.

From a cursory view, the white female has appeared historically to enjoy a privileged status; after all, as a result of sharing the bedrooms of white males, to her fall many of the material privileges and benefits of the society. But it is essential to recognize that rarely has she achieved these amenities on her own merit; nearly always it has been through the efforts and good graces of her spouse. The apparent freedoms and material well-being enjoyed by many white women depend not on women earning them but on women fulfilling a nurturant and supportive role and, of course, maintaining a distinctive sexual identity through a socially defined image of female attractiveness. Thus, beauty and sexual attractiveness are essential to woman's economic survival, and maintaining these assets has become a major concern, second only to fulfillment of her domestic functions.

The cult of the home, like so many other aspects of white America, has unfortunately permeated the culture of Afro-America. While the cult in black society has been subjected to indigenous permutations,[5] in essence it bears close similarities to the white pattern, as would be expected in view of the fact that the economic forces affecting the larger society also impinge on the black subculture. Thus, within Afro-American culture (and I emphasize within), maleness creates privileges—that is, certain freedoms and rights are attached to being male. Certain sexually specific behaviors are part of the black socialization process. The result is that marriage among blacks is just as much a union of unequals as it is in the larger society; child rearing, domestic chores, and custody of children are largely female concerns. Hence, it is erroneous to argue that the domestic patterns of white society are not replicated in the black community. The "housewife" model may not fit completely, but it is closely approximated in the sense that black women must bear the brunt of the domestic-related chores, even when they also work outside the home.

What has historically differentiated black women from most white women is the peculiar way in which the racial and sexual caste systems have interfaced. Throughout their history in America, black women have had to face a condition of double dependency- -(1) on their spouses or mates and (2) on their employers. Although these dependencies have also been the lot of many employed white women, proportionately fewer of the latter faced both of them. Double dependency has practically always been the onus of black women. Moreover, because of the racial caste system, a significant proportion of black married women, both historically and contemporaneously, have not had the economic support of their husbands—because their husbands are either absent or underemployed or unable to find employment. What is significant about the fact that so many black women have had to contribute to their families' financial support is that society's reaction to their plight has been sexist. Because they are more economically independent of a male breadwinner than is the societal norm, many black women have been made to feel that they usurped the male role, as though they—and not society—were ultimately responsible for the black man's inability to be the main breadwinner.

It is sometimes argued that the black woman's lack of choice over whether she should or should not work renders her condition totally dissimilar to that of a white woman. While it is true that black men have had a more difficult time providing for their families than white men and that this has forced more black women to be in the labor force than white women, it must be recognized that the roles of both groups of women were ultimately conditioned by larger economic forces: white women were conditioned not to work in the productive sector; black women were conditioned to work. Those white women who were forced by economic circumstances to work outside the home were made to feel that their behavior was somehow deviant, and in most cases they abandoned their occupational participation when it was no longer absolutely necessary to their families' financial well-being. Thus, neither group of women, white or black, had an option. Consequently, the behavior of both groups of women was a direct consequence of economic forces over which they exercised little or no control.

The foregoing picture of the different though mutually consistent roles played by black and white women has not remained static over the years. In the last twenty-five years, dramatic changes have taken place in the composition of the female labor force. Increasing numbers of married white women have sought paid employment, and black women have made major gains in earnings. In short, the labor force profiles of both groups of women have become more and more similar, especially for young women.[6]

The movement of white females into the labor sphere has been partially caused by inflation, which has made it increasingly difficult for white males to maintain a middle-class standard of living solely from their earnings. This situation bears stark similarity to the one that has traditionally prevailed in black society, where familial economic survival- -in both the working and the middle classes—generally depends on both spouses' income.

For white women, like black women, labor force participation has not relieved them of performing traditional female domestic chores. For both groups of women, this has had a significant impact on the nature of their occupational participation, as it is generally interpreted by employers as a sign of the inherent unreliability of female labor—i.e., as a source of potential absenteeism and turnover—and is used as an added rationale for relegating women to the least prestigious, least financially remunerative, and most menial tasks. Even working women who are not wives or mothers find their occupational destinies affected by employer expectations that they do or will perform dual roles.

The entrance of more women into the productive sphere of the society has not brought about the demise of occupational segregation based on sex; indeed, economists reveal that occupational segregation based on sex is highly resistant to change.[7] Thus, women continue to predominate in those jobs that are least secure; least subject to unionization; least lucrative in terms of compensation, working conditions, and fringe benefits; and least conducive to career advancement.[8] So the influx of women into the labor market has not appreciably reduced the chances of males to find employment in a labor market that continues to be occupationally segregated. Women can be absorbed by the economy as a result of the fact that in the past thirty years there has been a phenomenal increase in some traditional female jobs, primarily in the clerical and service sectors of the economy.

Women are judged by employers to be particularly suited for clerical and service jobs for three basic reasons: (1) because of their socialization, they are assumed to prefer these jobs despite the low wages;[9] (2) female socialization trains them to display the attitudes of docility and compliance essential to the functioning of bureaucracies; and (3) because women are assumed to be ultimately supported by men, employers think they will not resist being shunted into or out of the economy according to its boom and bust cycle. The latter is particularly detrimental to black women, since a considerable proportion of them are the sole or major suppliers of family income.

What is interesting about most female-dominated jobs is that they increasingly demand two credentials that are more difficult for black women than white to attain. One is a relatively high level of education, at least a high-school diploma. The other is the facility to read, write, and communicate verbally in mainstream English. Although it is not readily acknowledged, jobs such as telephone operator, typist, and secretary commonly require an ability to use the language of white middle-class society. Because of their subcultural status and the low quality of education they receive, black women historically have been at a distinct disadvantage in manipulating the cultural symbols of the larger society. Thus, the deprecatory societal evaluation of black linguistic patterns and the institutional racism of the nation's educational system have worked to black women's disadvantage in the competition between black and white female workers for clerical jobs. In 1992 the proportions of black and white working women in administrative-support and clerical jobs were 25.7 and 27.9 percent, respectively.[10] Nonetheless, the rapid infiltration of black women into the clerical sphere in recent years seems to indicate that the discrimination against black women holding clerical jobs is declining. Whether they are actually achieving total equality with white women in this sphere or whether white women hold relatively more prestigious jobs is a question that needs further investigation. What is clear is that the wage levels of black and white women workers have now almost completely converged.

Although black men are also victims of white ethnocentrism and poor education, their chances of earning higher pay than do black women are enhanced as racial barriers fall, because many high-paying male occupations— e.g., in craft unions, municipal services, and the military—do not place such demand on the communication skills that are the sine qua non for advancement in clerical jobs. Indeed, the military offers many black men the chance of making up the deficiencies they incurred in the nation's educational system, as well as the opportunity to gain significant social benefits that are, for many, the route to upward occupational mobility. The continued sexual stereotyping of positions in those areas that have belatedly opened up to blacks reduces the chances for black women to move out of the traditionally female, clerical jobs. Thus, the erosion of racial barriers in employment is working more to the advantage of black men than black women.[11]

It is important to recognize this point, because it contradicts the commonly held view that the black woman fares infinitely better in American society than does the black man. Those who advance this claim generally rest their arguments on two facts. First, a greater proportion of black women than men hold jobs that are designated *professional* in the Bureau of the Census classification schema, and, second, historically, black women are more likely to have graduated from high school and college than are black men.

Yet it must be recognized that black women have never held high-status professional jobs in any great numbers. This is because, even in the professional occupational category, rigid sex segregation persists. Black women are able to find relatively easy access to such female occupations as nursing and teaching, but have a hard time, particularly in comparison to black men, gaining access to higher-status occupations such as law, medicine, and dentistry.[12] The latter are just as much male fields among blacks as among whites.

Black women's greater educational attainment is similarly misleading. First, in the society at large, women are more likely to have graduated from high school than are men, so that this is not an aberration among blacks. Moreover, although the number of black female college graduates has historically exceeded that of black male graduates,[13] this was not the case in all parts of the nation.[14] Since the advent of a whole gamut of minority programs designed to boost black college enrollment in the 1970s, black males have made strides in attaining a college education and are now 43.7 percent of all black students attending college.[15] Nor does attending college necessarily have the same impact on women as on men. A study of historically black colleges in the 1960s, containing half of all black college students, showed that the women significantly lowered their aspirations for professional achievement by the time they were seniors, whereas the men maintained or increased theirs.

These black college-educated women appeared to be significantly limited by sexual constraints in their career aspirations. They consistently chose traditionally feminine occupations and very few planned to venture into occupations dominated by men. Even more significantly, perhaps, the women saw the "feminine" jobs they selected as having lower status and demanding less ability than the "masculine" occupations—a telling com-ment on how they viewed what they had to offer in the job world.[16]

The association of femaleness with a distinctive economic function transcends racial lines. This fact is often obscured by certain racial differences in female labor force participation, such as the higher unemployment rate of black women than of white women, as well as the tendency of black women to begin their careers in jobs lower in status, their greater expectations of working, and their tendency to value higher wages above job satisfaction.[17] Although these differences should not be underestimated, it is myopic to focus on them exclusively in assessing the black female condition. The observation by Gump and Rivers, based on an extensive review of the literature on black/white differences in labor force participation, is particularly poignant here:

> Much data has been presented portraying the black woman as more likely to enter the labor force, more interested in doing so, more likely to work full time and continuously, and more necessary to the financial welfare of her family. . . . While such facts suggest a woman much less constricted by the traditional role than her white counterpart, it is equally true that black women choose occupations traditional for women, are motivated perhaps more by a sense of responsibility than by achievement need, are much more traditional in their sex-role attitudes than are young white women, and to some extent seem burdened by the responsibility they carry.
>
> Thus it appears that black women have *not* escaped many of the constraints imposed upon white women, though they are free of some of them. . . . There are those who would assert too quickly the freedom of black women, and they must be reminded of her bondage.[18]

If there is much in the objective condition of black women that warrants the development of a black feminist consciousness, why have so many black women failed to recognize the patterns of sexism that directly impinge on their everyday lives? Why have they failed to address a social force that unremittingly thwarts their ability to compete on an equal basis in the society?

Five factors have contributed to this situation. The most formidable is that many black intellectuals and spokespeople have ignored the issue of sexism, largely because it has been viewed as a racially divisive issue. That is, a feminist consciousness has been regarded as a force that could generate internal conflict between black males and black females. It is this writer's firm conviction that, far from being a source of internecine conflict, a feminist consciousness would contribute to the welfare of the race in a variety of ways:

1. It would enable black men and women to attain a more accurate and deeper level of understanding of many of the social problems that are currently undermining the viability of the race. Such problems as the black male unemployment rate, the absence of the black male in the family, the large representation of black women among those on welfare, and the high black "illegitimacy" rate are just a few of the many social problems afflicting blacks that are, in part at least, attributable to the operation of sexism in our society.

2. Elimination of sexism on the interpersonal level within black culture would result in each sex developing its individual talents and capacities unhindered by societal definitions of appropriate sexual behavior, thus increasing the general pool of black abilities.

3. A feminist consciousness, in ridding black males and females of their socially conditioned anxieties concerning masculinity and femininity, would foster greater psychological well-being and thereby strengthen the interpersonal bonds that are constantly being eroded and loosened by the impact of interpersonal sexism.

A second factor that helps to explain the absence of feminist consciousness among black women is the ideology of racism. Racism is so ingrained in American culture and so entrenched among many white women that black females have been reluctant to admit that anything affecting the white female could also affect them. Indeed, many black women have tended to see all whites, regardless of sex, as sharing the same objective interest, and clearly the behavior of many white women vis-à-vis blacks has helped to validate this reaction.

A third factor is the message that emerged in the black social movement of the sixties. In one sense, this movement worked to the detriment of black women, because they were told in many different ways that the liberation of the black man was more important than was their own liberation. In fact, they were often given to believe that any attempt on their part to take an equal place with the black man in the movement would contribute to his emasculation.[19]

The idea of black matriarchy, another ideological ploy commonly introduced to academicians and policymakers, is a fourth factor that has suppressed the development of a feminist consciousness among black women. In a nutshell, this view holds that in their conjugal and parental relationships black women are more dominant than black men, and so black and white women relate to their mates in altogether different ways.[20] It is easy to see how this view of black women could be used by some to negate the fact of black female oppression: if the black woman were indeed found to be more dominant than is the black man, this could be construed as meaning that she is not dependent on him and thus not in need of liberation. In fact, scholarly exploration of the issue has revealed the idea of black matriarchy to be mythical and has shown that the relationship of black and white women to their mates is fundamentally similar. And even if a black matriarchy did exist, it would be fallacious to infer from this that the black woman is not sexually oppressed, for her subordination is a derivative of both her family-related role and her position in the productive sphere of the economy. Thus, single and married black women are both placed in positions of subservience whenever they seek employment. Both are subjected to the manipulative tactics that are used to keep all female laborers—white and black, married and unmarried—in a low economic state compared to male laborers.

What the participants in the debate on black matriarchy fail to recognize is the white bias of their viewpoints. Implicit in their arguments is the idea that any matriarchy is unnatural and deviant. To attach such a pejorative label to matriarchy, and to view the patriarchal form as a positive good or an index of normality, is to accept the normative standard of the larger white society. Given the role that the family plays in supporting and perpetuating existing unequal economic arrangements, it may be fitting for us to question whether it would not be in the best interests of blacks to work out familial relationships that deviate from the conventional patriarchal norm and approximate a more egalitarian pattern, thereby challenging the racial and sexual status quo.

A final factor that has inhibited the development of a feminist consciousness among women in American society in general, and black females in particular, has been the church. Biblical support for sexual inequality is as strong today as it ever was, and the Christian church has played a preeminent role in validating the patriarchal nature of Western culture.[21] This is as true in black churches as it is in white ones, although the role of black religion in enchaining black women has been little subject to discussion.[22] The persistence of patriarchal views in black churches is undoubtedly due in some measure to the fact that most of our noted black theologians are men. But a more important point is that it persists because of the deep religiosity of black people today and the fact that most black religions are basically Christian despite some deviations and modifications. For whatever reason, it is significant that the church is the most important social institution in the black community and the one in which black women (in contrast to black men) spend most of their time and energy. This dedication undoubtedly has contributed in no small part to the black female's passive acceptance of her subservient societal role. Even so-called black nationalist religions, which proffer a different view of the world and a substitute for the teachings of Christianity, have failed to come to terms with the subordination of black women in our society. Indeed, some have even adopted theological preachments designed to stultify the development of female talents and to push women yet further into the traditional servile roles of mother and wife.[23]

In sum, black women in America have been placed in a dependent position vis-à-vis men. The source of their dependence is dual: it originates in the role they have been socialized to play in the family and the discrimination they face when they seek remunerative employment outside the home. Because sexual dependence works to the detriment of the entire race—both male and female—all blacks, regardless of sex, need to recognize the way in which their behavior, be it familial, marital, occupational, or otherwise, is subject to social control. From this realization they need to develop alternative behavioral norms for themselves and socialization patterns for their offspring that will challenge the distribution of power in America.

The view that racism is the sole cause of black female subordination in America today exhibits a very simplistic view of the black female condition. The economic processes of the society subordinate different groups of workers in different ways, but always for the same end. Because white supremacy and male chauvinism are merely symptoms of the same economic imperatives, it is facile to argue that white pigmentation is the sine qua non for the attainment of power in America, that white women share the same objective interests as white men, and that white women thus have nothing in common with black women. Although whiteness may be a contributory condition for the attainment of social privilege, sex and socioeconomic status are contingent conditions. Because color, gender, and wealth are at the present time collective determinants of power and privilege in America, it is almost impossible to disentangle their individual effects. Thus, those who would assert that the elimination of one type of social discrimination should have priority over all others display a naive conceptualization of the nature of power in American society and the multifaceted character of social oppression.

NOTES

1. Examples of literature supporting this perspective are Mae King. "Oppression and Power: The Unique Status of the Black Woman in the American Political System," *Social Science Quarterly,* 56 (1975), 116–28; Linda La Rue, "The Black Movement and Women's Liberation," *Black Scholar,* 1 (May 1970), 36–42; and Julia Mayo, "The New Black Feminism: A Minority Report," in *Contemporary Sexual Behavior: Critical Issues in the 1970's,* Joseph Zubin and John Money, eds. (Baltimore: John Hopkins University Press, 1973), 175–86.

2. Notable exceptions are Barbara Sizemore, "Sexism and the Black Male," *Black Scholar,* 4 (Mar.–Apr. 1973), 2–11; Aileen Hernandez, "Small Change for Black Women," *Ms.,* 3 (Aug. 1974), 16–18; Elizabeth Almquist, "Untangling the Effects of Race and Sex: The Disadvantaged Status of Black Women," *Social Science Quarterly,* 56 (1975), 129–42; Charmeyne D. Nelson, "Myths About Black Women Workers in Modern America," *Black Scholar,* 6 (Mar. 1975), 11–15; and William A. Blakely, "Everybody Makes the Revolution: Some Thoughts on Racism and Sexism," *Civil Rights Digest,* 6 (Spring 1974), 11–19.

3. Margaret Bentsen, "The Political Economy of Women's Liberation," *Monthly Review,* 21 (Sept. 1970); Juliet Mitchell, *Women's Estate* (New York: Random House, 1971), 99–158; Paul Baran and Paul Sweezy, *Monopoly Capital* (New York: Monthly Review Press, 1966); Gayle Rubin, "The Traffic in Women: Notes on the 'Political Economy' of Sex," in *Toward an Anthropology of Women,* Rayna Reiter, ed. (New York: Monthly Review Press, 1975), 3; Jean Gardiner, "Women's Domestic Labor," *New Left Review,* 89 (Jan.–Feb. 1975), 47–59; Sheila Rowbotham, *Woman's Consciousness, Man's World* (Baltimore: Penguin Books, 1974).

4. See, among others, Harold Baron, "The Demand for Black Labor: Historical Notes on the Political Economy of Racism," *Radical America,* 5 (Mar.–Apr. 1971), 1–46.

5. For further discussion of black sex-role socialization see, among others, Diane K. Lewis, "The Black Family: Socialization and Sex Roles," *Phylon,* 34 (Fall 1975), 221–37; Carlfred Broderick, "Social Heterosexual Development Among Urban Negroes and Whites," *Journal of Marriage and the Family,* 27 (May 1965), 200–203; Alice R. Gold and M. Carol St. Ange, "Development of Sex-Role Stereotypes in Black and White Elementary Girls," *Developmental Psychology,* 10 (May 1974), 461; and Boone E. Hammond and Joyce Ladner, "Socialization into Sexual Behavior in a Negro Slum Ghetto," in *The Individual, Sex, and Society,* Carlfred B. Broderick and Jesse Bernard, eds. (Baltimore: Johns Hopkins University Press, 1969), 41–52.

6. See Elizabeth Almquist's article in this book for more data on this point.

7. See Thornborrow and Sheldon, this volume.

8. See Thornborrow and Sheldon, this volume.

9. Edward A. Nicholson and Roger D. Roderick, *Correlates of Job Attitudes Among Young Women* (Columbus: Ohio State University Research Foundation, 1973), 10.

10. *Employment and Earnings,* January 1992, Table 21, p. 194.

11. Stuart H. Garfinkle, "Occupation of Women and Black Workers, 1962–74," *Monthly Labor Review,* 98 (Nov. 1975), 25–35.

12. Elizabeth Almquist, "Untangling the Effects of Race and Sex"; Marion Kilson, "Black Women in the Professions, 1890–1970," *Monthly Labor Review,* 100 (May 1977), 38–41; Diane Nilsen Westcott, "Blacks in the 1970's: Did They Scale the Job Ladder?" *Monthly Labor Review,* 105 (June 1982), 29–38.

13. Women are 55.2 percent of all black college graduates. Bureau of Labor Statistics, unpublished data, annual averages of the 1992 Current Population Surveys. Part of the reason for this is that until recently blacks were basically a rural people, and it is generally the case for farmer families to withdraw males from school to work the farm but not females, since farming is

considered to be a male occupation. For further discussion of how this has contributed to present-day disparities in black male and female occupational status, see E. Wilbur Bock, "Farmer's Daughter Effect: The Case of the Negro Female Professionals," *Phylon* (Spring 1969), 17–26.

14. Andrew Billingsley, *Black Families in White America* (Englewood Cliffs, N.J.: Prentice-Hall, 1968), 79–82.

15. Bureau of Labor Statistics, unpublished data, annual averages of the 1992 Current Population Surveys.

16. Patricia Gurin and Carolyn Gaylord, "Educational and Occupational Goals of Men and Women at Black Colleges," *Monthly Labor Review,* 99 (June 1976), 13–14.

17. Patricia Cayo Sexton, *Women and Work,* Employment and Training Administration, R. & D. Monograph no. 46 (Washington, D.C.: Department of Labor, 1977), 15; Joyce O. Beckett, "Working Wives: A Racial Comparison," *Social Work,* 21 (Nov. 1976), 463–71.

18. Janice Porter Gump and L. Wendell Rivers, *The Consideration of Race in Efforts to End Sex Bias* (Washington, D.C.: Department of Health, Education and Welfare, National Institute of Education, 1973), 24–25.

19. Joyce A. Ladner, *Tomorrow's Tomorrow: The Black Woman* (Garden City, N.Y.: Doubleday and Co., 1971), 284; Robert Staples, *The Black Woman in America* (Chicago: Nelson-Hall Publishers, 1975), 174–76; Janice Gump, "Comparative Analysis of Black Women's and White Women's Sex Role Attitudes," *Journal of Consulting and Clinical Psychology,* 43 (1975), 862–63; Cellestine Ware, *Woman Power: The Movement for Women's Liberation* (New York: Tower Publications, 1970), 75–99.

20. S. Parker and R. J. Kleiner, "Social and Psychological Dimensions of Family Role Performance of the Negro Male," *Journal of Marriage and the Family,* 31 (1969), 500–506; John H. Scanzoni, *The Black Family in Modern Society* (Boston: Allyn and Bacon, 1971); Katheryn Thomas Dietrich, "A Re-examination of the Myth of Black Matriarchy," *Journal of Marriage and the Family,* 37 (May 1975), 367–74; H. H. Hyman and J. S. Reed, "Black Matriarchy Reconsidered: Evidence from Secondary Analysis of Sample Surveys," *Public Opinion Quarterly,* 33 (1969), 346–54; Robert Staples, "The Myth of Black Matriarchy," in *The Black Family,* Robert Staples, ed. (Belmont, Calif.: Wadsworth Publishing Co., 1971), 149–59; Alan Berger and William Simon, "Black Families and the Moynihan Report: A Research Evaluation," *Social Problems,* 33 (Dec. 1974), 145–61.

21. Simone de Beauvoir, *The Second Sex* (New York: Vintage Books, 1974); Susan Bell, *Women, from the Greeks to the French Revolution* (Belmont, Calif.: Wadsworth Publishing Co., 1973); Alan Cuming, "Women in Greek and Pauline Thought," *Journal of the History of Ideas,* 34 (Dec. 1973), 517–28.

22. Notable exceptions are Rosemary Reuther, "Crisis in Sex and Race: Black vs. Feminist Theology," *Christianity and Crisis,* 34 (Apr. 15, 1974), 67–73; "Continuing the Discussion: A Further Look at Feminist Theology," *Christianity and Crisis,* 34 (June 24, 1974), 139–43.

23. Barbara Sizemore, "Sexism and the Black Male," *Black Scholar,* 4 (Mar.–Apr. 1973), 2–11; Harry Edwards, "Black Muslim and Negro Christian Family Relationships," *Journal of Marriage and the Family,* 30 (Nov. 1968), 604–11.

Chicana Feminisms: Their Political Context and Contemporary Expressions

Denise A Segura[1] and Beatriz M. Pesquera

Because I, a *mestiza*,
continually walk out of one culture
and into another,
because I am in all cultures at the same time,
alma entre dos mundos, tres, cuatro,
me zumba la cabeza con lo contradictorio.
Estoy norteada por todas las voces que me hablan
simultaneamente.[2]

—Gloria Anzaldua (1987, 77)

CHICANAS,[3] WOMEN OF Mexican heritage in the United States, are bilingual, bicultural women of color who weave diverse paths through multiple social terrains. Chicana feminists strive to maintain racial-ethnic unity while contesting patriarchal domination. This struggle poses many contradictions: "Estoy norteada por todas las voces que me hablan simultaneamente [I am guideless for the many voices that speak to me simultaneously]."

This essay explores historical and contemporary expressions of Chicana feminisms.[4] We begin with a brief profile of Chicanas. We follow this with an exploration of the political context of Chicana feminisms. Then, we profile three Chicana feminist organizations that embody various aspects of the Chicana movement. We conclude with a discussion of contemporary Chicana feminist perspectives.

Who Are Chicanas?

Chicanas' membership in a historically subordinated racial-ethnic group, their concentration among the poor and working class, and their gender have resulted in a situation of "triple oppression" (Segura 1986; Apodaca 1986; Mirande and Enriquez 1979). As Mexicans, Chicanas have been treated as "second-class citizens" since their incorporation into the United States in 1848 (Acuna 1981; U.S. Commission on Civil Rights 1972). Historically, they have encountered racial-ethnic and gender discrimination, limiting their access to education, jobs, and political participation. They are overrepresented among the poor and lower working classes. Concurrently, Chicanas have maintained a distinct Chicano/Mexican culture (Garcia 1982; Keefe and Padilla 1987).

A profile of Chicana education, employment, earnings, and income reveals key differences by gender and race-ethnicity that place them in disadvantageous situations vis-à-vis the majority white population. In 1992, approximately 14 million people of Mexican heritage lived in the United States. They were 63.6 percent of the U.S. Hispanic population (U.S. Bureau of the Census 1992, Table 1).[5] Chicano families have a substantially lower median income ($23,019 in 1990) than non-Hispanic white families ($39,240 in 1991). Moreover, in 1992 over one-quarter (27.4 percent) of Chicano families lived below the poverty line, compared to 7.1 percent of non-Hispanic white families (U.S. Bureau of the Census 1992, Table 4).

Chicanas' employment experiences inform their political consciousness or sense of themselves as racial-ethnic women. In 1992 the Chicana labor force participation rate was at 51.6 percent for persons sixteen and over, which is slightly lower than the 58 percent rate of non-Hispanic white women but substantially lower than that of either non-Hispanic white men (74.6 percent) or Chicano men (80 percent) (U.S. Bureau of the Census 1992, Table 2). Their 1992 unemployment rate was higher (10.5 percent) than that of non-Hispanic white women (5.4 percent), but lower than that of Chicano men (12.4 percent). These differences reflect several phenomena: high fertility among young Chicanas, lower levels of education, inadequate affordable child care, and employment in relatively unstable or seasonal jobs. Like all women, Chicanas tend to work in administrative support (clerical) jobs. But only 14 percent of Chicanas, compared to 29.7 percent of non-Hispanic white women, work in managerial or professional occupations (U.S. Bureau of the Census 1992, Table 2). In this regard Chicanas appear more similar to Chicano men, of whom 9.3 percent worked as managers or professionals. Far more Chicanas (16.2 percent) than non-Hispanic white women (6.5 percent) worked in low-paying, often unstable jobs as operators, fabricators, and laborers (14.9 percent and 7.5 percent, respectively). At the same time 29.2 percent of Chicano men worked in these jobs. The median 1991 earnings of all full-time Chicana workers was $15,637. This was substantially lower than that of Chicano men ($18,156), non-Hispanic white women ($21,098), and non-Hispanic white men ($31,161) (U.S. Bureau of the Census 1992, Table 2). This brief comparison demonstrates how the intersection of gender and race-ethnicity negatively affects Chicana employment and earnings. This unique set of circumstances informs a distinct Chicana perspective, a world view that guides their assessment of the relevancy of social reforms or movements, including American feminism.

The Political Context for Chicana Feminisms

Contemporary Chicana feminism emerged during the turbulent social movements of the 1960s and early 1970s that challenged existing power relations on the basis of race-ethnicity and gender/sexuality. The "second wave" of the American women's movement called into question patriarchal relations—systemic male domination and female subordination. Social movements by people of color, including the Chicano movement, opposed the structuring of power and privilege on the basis of race-ethnicity. Central to these movements was a critique of power relations in social institutions and the prevailing cultural ideologies that justified them. However, each differed in their focus (women, the Chicano community), their understanding of oppression, overall ideological orientations, and political programs to eliminate social inequality.

Many Chicanas perceived that their realities did not readily "fit" into the perspectives and programs of either social movement. Chicanas' needs and aspirations for liberation were typically ignored, subsumed, or trivialized within both the American women's movement and the Chicano movement. Chicana feminists took exception to the framing of oppression based primarily on gender. In addition, they criticized the reformist character espoused by many prominent mainstream feminist groups such as NOW and *Ms.* magazine. By *reformist* they meant a focus on incorporating women into existing, highly stratified socioeconomic structures (e.g., women accessing male domains) as opposed to changing race-ethnic, class, and gender relations in these structures. Chicanas perceived this reformism as inadequate in that it would not change all forms of social inequality (Del Castillo 1974; Nieto-Gomez 1973, 1974; Martinez 1972; Flores 1973).

In October 1970, at the "Women's Workshop" of the Mexican American Issues Conference, Chicana participants identified the absence of organizations that met their needs as a serious obstacle to their empowerment. To address this issue, a resolution was passed to establish a Chicana-centered organization, Comision Femenil Mexicana Nacional, Inc. Part of the resolution stated:

> The efforts and work of Chicana/Mexicana women in the Chicano Movement is generally obscured because women are not accepted as community leaders either by the Chicano Movement or by the Anglo establishment. (Comision Femenil Mexicana Nacional, Inc., 1986)

The Chicana movement developed during the late 1960s and early 1970s. Chicanas formed numerous groups at the grass-roots level and on college campuses. They also developed state and national organizations. Some of these groups published newspapers, pamphlets, and magazines. Hijas de Cuauhtemoc arose at California State University, Long Beach, and published a newspaper with the same title. With women from other campuses and community groups, they published *Encuentro Femenil.* Comision Femenil Mexicana Nacional, Inc., formed in Los Angeles, California, in 1970 and published the magazine *Regeneracion.* At the national level, MANA (Mexican American Women's National Association) formed in 1974 in Washington, D.C. Many pamphlets and other magazines were also published during this time by various groups and Chicana activists (e.g., Martha Cotera's *Diosa y Hembra* and *The Chicana Feminist*). Others published articles on Chicanas in student newspapers and leftist publications of the period (e.g., Marta Vidal in *International Socialist Review;* Magdalena Mora in *Sin Fronteras*). Few articles appeared in mainstream feminist outlets (e.g., *Ms.* magazine).

For their organizations and publications, Chicanas often adopted names rooted in a revolutionary heritage from Mexico. Hijas de Cuauhtemoc, for example, was a women's organization founded in 1910 in Mexico City that opposed the Diaz dictatorship (Macias 1982). *Regeneracion* was the official journal of the Partido Liberal Mexicano, a progressive Mexican political party (Macias 1982). These quintessential images of revolutionary struggle provided Chicanas with one way to frame their local agendas within a larger critique of race, class, and gender domination.

Chicanas sought various ways to reconcile their critique of male domination within the Chicano community to the Chicano movement agenda. Unwilling to be dismissed as political actors, Chicanas formed caucuses within Chicano movement organizations, formed Chicana women's groups, and organized conferences on *la mujer* (women). They argued that these groups were necessary in order for women to develop their political consciousness free from male-centered ideas and influences.

Although Chicana women's groups were exclusively female, they were viewed as essential parts of the "larger" Chicano movement. Adelaida del Castillo, editor of *Encuentro Femenil,* a Chicana feminist journal, articulated this perspective in 1974:

> We're not a separatist movement, that would be suicidal. We as Chicanas and Chicanos are oppressed. We're not going to ally ourselves to white feminists who are part of the oppressor. I mean, that would be a contradiction. It also hurts when Chicano men don't recognize the need for this specialization which is called "Chicana Feminism."

Chicanas focused on expanding the boundaries of the Chicano movement and argued that their activities were for *la Raza* (the people), with a special emphasis on *la mujer.* Fashioning the discourse in this manner, Chicanas, as many women have done throughout history, gave formal recognition to patriarchal contours while eroding its base through underground subversive separatism. These activities did not, however, go unchallenged, given the powerful ideological hegemony of Chicano cultural nationalism.

The term *Chicano* arose as the symbolic representation of the struggle for self-determination and betterment of the Chicano community (Chicano Coordinating Committee on Higher Education 1969; Alvarez 1971; Acuña 1981). Chicano cultural nationalist ideology locates Chicano oppression in the colonial domination of Mexican Americans following the annexation of northern Mexico by the United States after the U.S.-Mexico War of 1846–48, which limited Chicano access to education, employment, and political participation (Almaguer 1971; Barrera, Muñoz, and Ornelas 1972; Blauner 1972; Estrada, Garcia, Macias, and Maldonado 1981). Ideologically, cultural differences between Anglos and Mexicans were used to legitimate racial inequality (e.g., Mexicans were viewed as intellectually and culturally inferior) (Blauner 1972; Takaki 1979; Montejano 1987). One example is the popularity of using a "cultural deficiency" framework to explain an array of characteristics (e.g., lower levels of education, higher unemployment rates) as part of an ethnic or cultural tradition. Such a framework depicts Mexican American culture as lagging behind American culture in developing behaviors and attitudes conducive to achievement (Baca Zinn 1979, 1980, 1982).

Within a cultural nationalist ideology that celebrated Chicanos' cultural heritage from Mexico and their indigenous roots, *la familia, la Virgen de Guadalupe* (the patron saint of Mexico), and *la Adelita* (women who fought during the 1910 Mexican Revolution and nurtured the troops) symbolized ethnic pride and resistance. Concurrently, these cultural symbols recognized both women's importance within the confines of their traditional roles and insurgent activities in social change. Chicanas were exalted as self-sacrificing mothers (*la madre*) and as caretaker-fighters in revolutionary struggle (*la Adelita*).

Chicano movement groups often organized around the ideal of *la familia.*[6] A high value was placed on family solidarity, with individual desires subsumed to the collective good. Critiques of gender relations in the family, the Chicano community, and movement groups met with hostility. Cynthia Orozco asserts, "When Chicanas raised the issue of male domination, both the community and its intellectual arm, Chicano Studies, put down the ideology of feminism and put feminists in their place" (1986, 12). Feminists, in contrast, argued that the struggle against male domination was central to the overall Chicano movement for liberation. Anna Nieto-Gomez, one of the most prolific Chicana feminist writers of the late 1960s and early 1970s, proclaimed:

> What is a Chicana feminist? I am a Chicana feminist. I make that state-ment very proudly, although there is a lot of intimidation in our com-munity and in the society in general against people who define themselves as Chicana feminists. It sounds like a contradictory statement, a *Malinche*[7] statement—if you are a Chicana you're on one side, if you're a feminist, you must be on the other side. They say you can't stand on both sides—which is a bunch of bull. (Nieto-Gomez 1974)

Chicanas who departed from the nationalist political stance were labelled *vendidas* (sell-outs), *agabachadas* (white identified), or *Malinche* (betrayer/collaborator) (Lopez 1977; Nieto-Gomez 1973, 1974). Labelling was a tool of repression against Chicanas who advocated a feminist position. Martha Cotera points out that the label *feminist* was also a social control mechanism:

> We didn't say we were feminist. It was the men who said that. They said, "Aha! Feminista!" and that was a good enough reason for not listening to some of the most active women in the community. (1977, 31)

Such social and political sanctions were meant to discourage women from articulating a feminist standpoint.

In the Chicano community, the labels *vendida, agabachada, Malinche,* and *feminista* denoted cultural betrayal and assimilation into non-Chicano values and life-style. These labels accused Chicanas of acting "like white women"—a disloyal act to *la cultura* and community politics anchored in a cultural nationalist sense of racial-ethnic unity. Moreover, these charges implied that Chicanas' critiques of gender relations were antifamily, antimen, and pro-Anglo. Within this formulation, feminism is irrelevant at best; at worst it is divisive of the "greater" Chicano struggle.

The antagonism toward American feminism of this period can be understood in light of the antithetical characterizations of "the family" in both movements. The American women's movement argued that the subordination of women within the patriarchal family is a primary form of oppression. Furthermore, feminist critiques of patriarchal relations often identified men as the enemy. Both formulations (the family as a locus of female oppression and the specter of men as the enemy) stood in direct opposition to the cultural nationalist ideology that eulogized the traditional role of women in the family, the Chicano family as an agent of resistance, and *carnalismo* (brotherhood of *La Raza*).

In light of the political milieu of the 1960s and 1970s, it is not surprising that many Chicanas felt ambivalence toward American feminism. They tended to perceive the women's movement predominantly white, middle-class leadership as largely unable or unwilling to articulate a vision of women's empowerment sensitive to race-ethnic and class differences (Cotera 1980). During this period, few Anglo or Chicana feminists moved to build coalitions between both communities of women (Del Castillo 1974; Martinez 1972; Nieto 1974; Cotera 1973; Flores 1973; Gonzalez 1977). Chicanas questioned the feminist call to "sisterhood," arguing that unity based on only the subordination of women overlooked the historical race-ethnic, class, and cultural antagonisms between women. They opposed American feminist writings that equated sexism with racism as ahistorical, inasmuch as gender and race are not analogous systems of oppression (Nieto-Gomez 1973; Apodaca 1986). Chicanas expressed skepticism that eliminating sexual oppression would end class and race-ethnic inequality. Instead, they argued that feminism was irrelevant to Chicanas until it addressed race-ethnic and class concerns. Chicanas doubted, however, that such an integrative approach would emerge in light of racism and "maternal chauvinism" among women's movement activists, as Anna Nieto-Gomez states:

> Chicanas, having to deal with racism in the feminist movement and sensing that Anglo women believe they can solve the problems of minority women, have tried to circumvent this maternal chauvinism. (1973, 46)

Concern with what Nieto-Gomez termed *maternal chauvinism*,[8] or the idea that white feminists can comprehend, analyze, and devise the best solutions to Chicanas' concerns, reverberates throughout the writings of early Chicana feminists.

Chicanas also decried the articulation of feminist concerns and proposals for solutions to gender inequality that omitted them and other women of color. Reviews of key feminist writings of the late 1960s and early 1970s by Chicana feminists such as Martha Cotera (1977, 1980) and Alma Garcia (1989) confirm the accuracy of this perception. In the rare instances Chicanas were included within feminist writings, their experiences tended to be cast in ways that reinforced cultural stereotypes of them as women who "did not want to be liberated" (Longeaux y Vasquez 1970). Most often, however, Chicanas have been silent objects within feminist writings—neither included nor excluded by name. Thus, Chicanas in this period concluded they were not "equal" sisters in the struggle against gender oppression.

Chicana Feminist Organizations

A theme that spans the past decade is the framing of Chicana feminisms in the collective struggles of the Chicano community. Chicanas at various levels of society, class locations, sexual preferences, and political perspectives share a collective identity as Mexican women but diverge on how best to address the historical inequality of Chicanas. At the state and national levels, Comision

Femenil Mexicana Nacional, Inc., and MANA have continued their organizational efforts to empower Chicanas. However, as in the past, most work is done by numerous small and localized groups on college campuses, in community-based organizations, and workplaces.

COMISION FEMENIL MEXICANA NACIONAL, INC.

Founded in 1970, Comision is the largest Chicana organization and includes twenty-three chapters nationwide, with the majority in California. Francisca Flores, a founder of Comision, stated in 1971:

> The time has come to quit quibbling and start mingling with other women. A movement of Mexican women such as has never been seen before. That is what we are going after. No more will anyone say to us . . . you are not organized . . . [her spacing; there is no missing text] there is no national organization to represent women from the migrant farms to the tall urban centers in the cities. There will not be an agency which will not know of our existence. (Flores 1971, 7)

Comision promotes Chicana leadership in education, employment, economic development, community, and electoral politics. In the Los Angeles area (the area with the highest concentration of Mexicans in the United states), Comision currently runs numerous social service delivery programs, including the Chicana Service Action Center, which provides job training; Casa Victoria, a community-based alternative to Chicana juvenile incarceration; and Centro de Niños, a bilingual/bicultural child development center geared to the needs of the working poor. They publish a newsletter, hold annual conferences, and participate in national and international women's conferences. Comision works with such organizations as Planned Parenthood Foundation and local and state agencies to promote health and reproductive rights for Chicana/Latina women. The following quote from the *1985–86 Annual Report* embodies Comision's spirit:

> Student, mother, wife, professional, farmworker, homemaker, single parent, it doesn't matter. *Comision Femenil Mexicana Nacional, Inc.* is there for all Latinas to take, to hold, to embrace, to learn, to share, to advocate, but most of all, it is a vehicle for change for Latinas in the United States. (1986, 6)

MEXICAN AMERICAN WOMEN'S NATIONAL ASSOCIATION

The Mexican American Women's National Association (MANA) was founded in Washington, D.C., in October 1974, "when Mexican American women of different political, educational, professional and geographic backgrounds met to discuss the need for a self-identifying organization which would focus on the concerns of the more than five million Chicanas in the United States" (Mexican American Women's National Association 1982). Since its inception, MANA has been "striving for parity between Chicanas and Chicanos as they continue their joint struggle for equality . . . creating a national awareness of the presence and concerns of Chicanas and the active sharing of its Mexican American heritage" (Mexican American Women's National Association 1982).

In practice, MANA supports efforts to strengthen families while advocating for equal rights for women. MANA supported the passage of the Equal Rights Amendment (ERA). Moreover, MANA has collaborated with the Women's Legal Defense Fund, the National Organization for Women, the National Council of La Raza, Mexican American Legal Defense and Educational Fund, and other national Chicano/Latino and women's organizations to advocate for programs that benefit women of color. MANA prepares position papers on areas of concern to the organization (e.g., reproductive rights, the ERA) to attempt to publicize Chicanas' perspectives on these issues.

MANA's collaborative efforts with other feminist groups are not undertaken without tension. For example, at a major five-hour prochoice "Mobilization for Women," organized by NOW on November 12, 1989, at the Lincoln Memorial, Irma Maldonado, president of MANA, was the only Latina invited to speak. As time passed, the rally's organizers tried to scratch her from the scroll of invited speakers to "speed up" the event (*Hispanic Link Weekly Report* 1989).

Several MANA chapters run Hermanitas Programs (Little Sisters), which link MANA members to teenage Chicanas/Latinas to nurture leadership and self-esteem among these young women (Mexican American Women's National Association 1990). In 1984 MANA founded a national scholarship program to help support high-achieving Latinas in higher education. Currently, MANA's Washington, D.C., chapter operates the Economic Equity Project, which is funded by the Ford Foundation, to research and develop issue papers on the economic plight of Hispanic women for dissemination to policymakers and Hispanic organizations at the state, local, and federal levels (Mexican American Women's National Association 1991). MANA organizes and conducts annual training conferences to develop leadership among the members and promote a greater awareness of Chicana/Latina heritages. MANA publishes a newsletter that helps provide information on national issues and programs to members.

MUJERES ACTIVAS EN LETRAS Y CAMBIO SOCIAL

In California, Chicanos/Latinos comprise approximately one-quarter of the state's population, yet Chicanas constitute less than 2 percent of the faculty of the prestigious, nine-campus University of California system. In 1983 Chicana faculty and graduate students from northern California founded Mujeres Activas en Letras y Cambio Social (Women Active in Higher Education and Social Change) (MALCS) in Berkeley. MALCS is dedicated to the recruitment and retention of Chicanas/Latinas in higher education. The organization is particularly interested in supporting collaborative ventures that can challenge institutional racism, sexism, and homophobism.

Adaljiza Sosa Riddel, the first chair of MALCS, describes its purpose as

> empowerment of *mujeres* as *mujeres* is what MALCS is all about. Our empowerment efforts are in the realm of ideas, values, analysis, and the translation of those ideas from our minds and hearts onto acts of lasting benefit, writings, creative acts, and, we fervently hope, structural change. Our efforts are aimed directly at bridging the gap between the academic environment

within which we work and the communities from whence we came and in which we live. We want to improve the quality of life for us all, but especially for the overwhelming majority of Chicanas who have little economic, academic, cultural, or political power over their own lives. (Mujeres Activas en Letras y Cambio Social 1989)

Most MALCS organizers had been active in the insurgent feminist politics situated within the Chicano movement. Although critical of the American women's movement and feminist theories for their inattention to the intersection of race, class, *and* gender/sexuality, many critiqued patriarchal relations. MALCS works toward the support, education, and dissemination of Chicana issues. As one MALCS member states:

> Chicana scholarship is going to impact the intellectual world and also the work at the practical level to help the 95 percent of our sisters who are not at the university and aren't going to be unless we make it happen. So, Chicana scholarship has to reach out and push the intellectual boundaries and reach back to its roots—the community.

Chicanas' efforts to promote research on their community have sometimes met with considerable resistance and, at other times, been subjected to indifference. As one response to this problem, MALCS published a Working Paper Series cosponsored by the Chicano Studies Program and Women's Resource and Research Center at the University of California, Davis. In 1992 the Working Paper Series gave way to a yearly anthology of Chicana scholarly writings.

To combat the marginalization of Chicana studies within traditional disciplines and Chicano studies as well as women's studies, MALCS institutionalizes alternative avenues and "safe spaces" to develop intellectually and continue the tradition of political dissent. One mechanism to accomplish this is through the annual Chicana/Latina Summer Research Institute, where Chicanas/Latinas from various institutions (academic and nonacademic) come together to network, share information, offer support, and reenergize. The 1991 "Statement" from the MALCS Conference organizers in Laredo, Texas, states:

> The MALCS Institute is one of the few places Chicanas can come together without the influences of male and/or Anglo consciousness or opinion. For most Chicanas, this is the only place to come together. While some charge that this is separatist, the MALCS reply is not one of apology. This is our space. The dynamics of this Chicana space are worth guarding, even in the face of criticism from those we respect and work with in our home institutions. It is our sincere hope that the critics outside MALCS will understand the above position and respect the reasons this space has been created. (*MALCS Annual Research Institute Program* 1991)

MALCS is committed to the development of Chicana feminist discourse that validates, nurtures, and empowers Chicanas. Chicana feminists in MALCS insist on posing Chicana questions grounded in the objective conditions of the Chicano community (e.g., poverty, rising rates of households headed by women, immigration, lack of educational equity, cultural suppression, etc.). This kind of intensive inquiry is best accomplished in an autonomous space that is Chicana-centered. MALCS allies itself with groups within the academy and the larger community that share similar interests and concerns (e.g., employment rights, reproductive and health care rights, immigrant rights). Alliances with women's studies and women's centers vary across campuses. The intellectual work that MALCS members are responsible for, however, is facilitated by their relative autonomy and the creation of a Chicana intellectual community within the academy.

Contemporary Chicana Feminisms

Chicanas, like other women in our society, vary in their level of knowledge and attitudes regarding feminism. Chicanas' feminisms are mediated by their social locations (e.g., region, education, immigrant status, employment, and social class) and life experiences. Chicanas are concerned with female empowerment and social change to better their lives.

Rosario Torres Raines conducted a study in 1985 of 185 middle-class Chicana mothers and daughters and 130 Anglo mothers and daughters in south Texas. She found considerable support for (what she terms) "materially relevant related issues encompassed within the agenda of the American women's movement," particularly equal employment rights, day care, and the ERA. Her study also found less support for abortion among Chicanas than Anglo women because it was conceptualized as a family issue. Torres Raines argues that the high level of support for "materially-based issues" provides one potential base for feminist unity. However, different beliefs concerning the role of women in the family and the "sacred" nature of *la familia* can be a source of tension among women.

Similar to Chicanas in the Torres Raines study, a 1990 study of feminism among Chicana white-collar workers (Pesquera and Segura forthcoming) showed they supported such issues as training opportunities, equal pay, and affirmative action. Their support for these issues was not just gender-based but stemmed from their awareness of the unique social vulnerability of Mexicans in the United States. They believed that "Mexicans do not share equally in the good life" and cited institutional discrimination in education and employment as key barriers to social equality. They spoke poignantly of their own struggles and those of their families to make it through high schools where their abilities were often questioned and undermined by insensitive curriculums and inadequate counseling. By and large Chicanas reject individualistic explanations for the persistent low social status of Mexicans in this society and advocate group solutions such as bilingual education and family health care to be able to bring healthy children into the world.

Chicana white-collar workers demonstrated strong support for reproductive rights. They felt warmly toward feminism, and over half felt comfortable calling themselves "feminists." Although many of the women had advocated for Chicana and Chicano rights, few felt comfortable with the idea of joining a feminist organization.

Women in this study familiar with the women's movement tended to feel that it has tried to empower *all* women. One clerical worker stated:

> At the beginning, I felt it was more for white women, trying to get equal pay for equal work, at the material level. But now, I feel that it's more inclusive of all cultures, of all women.

While many women believed they benefited from the women's movement's agendas, they also argued that the movement has not advocated specifically for Chicana/Latina women:

> I think they categorize [the movement] as all women. What they don't realize is that there are real barriers that Latinas have additionally to being a woman. I've never heard the minority thrust at all.

The sentiments by Chicana white-collar workers regarding the women's movement and Chicana concerns resemble those articulated in the previous decades by Chicana activists. That is, Chicanas want feminists to listen to their concerns and incorporate them into women's movement agendas.

A 1988 study of 101 Chicanas/Latinas in MALCS (Segura and Pesquera, 1992) explored their attitudes toward the women's movement, the Chicano movement, and Chicana feminism. Similar to the Chicana white-collar workers, the majority of MALCS Chicanas supported features of American feminism, especially the struggle for gender equality. By and large, MALCS Chicanas refer to themselves as "Chicana feminists" and see themselves as distinct from other feminist traditions. Since they also feel that American feminism has not been sensitive to important race-ethnic or class concerns of Chicana/Latina women, they tend not to join mainstream feminist groups such as NOW.

MALCS Chicana feminist expressions revolve around the principles of collectivity and insurgent analysis but differ in their strategies for social change. Of the women who called themselves Chicana feminists, sixty-two discussed what this meant. From their descriptions of Chicana feminism, the following typology was developed: *Chicana Liberal Feminism, Chicana Cultural Nationalist Feminism,* and *Chicana Insurgent Feminism.* Each category is grounded in the material condition of the Chicano people and highlights different aspects of Chicana feminism. Each encompasses diverse ways of interpreting oppression and advocating strategies for social change.

The Chicanas within the liberal feminist tradition espoused an "equal rights" approach. They advocate strategies that empower Chicanas ranging from personal support to policy initiatives and affirmative action. They feel that Chicana subordination can be redressed through institutional reforms that bring Chicanas into the political and social mainstream.

Chicana cultural nationalist feminism describes the attitudes of women who identify as feminists but are committed to a cultural nationalist ideology. They believe that change in gender relations should be accomplished without destroying traditional cultural values. For example, one forty-one-year-old Chicana graduate student wrote:

> I want for myself and for other women the opportunities to grow, and develop in any area I choose. I want to do this while upholding the values (cultural, moral) that come from my being a part of the great family of Chicanos.

Reminiscent of the slogan popularized during the Chicano movement (that all Chicanos are members of the same family—*la gran familia de la raza*), Chicana cultural nationalism articulates a feminist vision anchored in the ideology of *la familia*. While advocating feminism, this perspective retains allegiance to cultural nationalism that glorifies Chicano culture. Chicana cultural nationalism, however, downplays how cultural traditions often uphold patriarchy. It ignores the difficulty of reconciling a critique of gender relations within the Chicano community with the preservation of Chicano culture.

Other women, in the tradition of insurgent feminism, argue that "real liberation" for Chicanas is not possible without a radical restructuring of society. They seek to expose unequal and exploitative relations of power and privilege in our society and champion revolutionary change to end all forms of oppression. They want more than "special emphasis" on *la mujer*, arguing that the liberation of the community can be accomplished only with the elimination of gender/sexuality oppression. For example, one MALCS member stated:

> I believe that the impact of sexism, racism and elitisms, when combined result in more intensely exploitative, oppressive and controlling situations than when these conditions exist independently of one another. The status and quality of life of the Chicano community as a whole can only improve/change when that of women within that community changes/improves. Any revolutionary change must include a change in relationships between men and women.

This woman, like the majority of MALCS Chicanas, views political activism as a critical component of Chicana feminisms. Political activism in this context ranges from fighting for the educational rights of Chicanos to marching in the streets for family health care as well as reproductive rights to creating safe spaces (such as MALCS) that foster the development of intellectual frameworks grounded in Chicanas' lived experiences.

Conclusion

Chicana feminist expressions are rooted in their diverse social locations. Across the span of history, political ideologies, and organizational strategies, Chicana feminists struggle to eradicate all forms of social inequality. This struggle is anchored within the social and political struggles of the Chicano/Latino community at large. Chicana feminist organizations, whether at the grass-roots, state, national, or academic level, advocate Chicana empowerment. Although Chicanas credit the American women's movement for their efforts to eradicate gender inequality, they are critical of its exclusionary practices and reluctance to address the contradictions posed by race-ethnicity and class. Rather, Chicana feminists seek ways to better their community and maintain their ethnic identity. Their actions and words echo what Chicana feminist Martha Cotera stated in 1977:

> There has always been feminism in our ranks and there will continue to be so as long as Chicanas live and breathe in the movement, but we must see to it that we specify philosophical directions and that our feminist directions will be our own and coherent with our Raza's goals in cultural areas which are ours. Chicanas will direct their own destiny. (Cotera 1977, 13)

NOTES

1. Author's names are listed randomly. Our research has been supported by grants from the academic senates of the University of California at Davis and at Santa Barbara. Dr. Pesquera acknowledges the support of a Humanist-in-Residence Rockefeller Fellowship at the University of Arizona, Tucson, and Dr. Segura acknowledges the support of a Ford Foundation Postdoctoral Fellowship at the University of California, Los Angeles.

2. The English language translation for the second half of the quote is "my soul between two, three, four worlds, my head spins with contradiction. I am guideless for the many voices that speak to me simultaneously." The term *mestiza* refers to a woman of mixed blood—typically the mixture of the Indian and the Spanish. We thank Dr. Francisco Lomeli, professor of Spanish and Portuguese at the University of California, Santa Barbara, for his help in translating this passage. We also note his concern that English does not convey the full meaning of the metaphoric *norteada* (lost, seeking guidance [as if] by the North Star to find the way).

3. The terms *Chicana* and *Chicano*, respectively, refer to a woman and to a man of Mexican descent residing in the United States without distinguishing immigrant status. *Chicano* also refers generically to the category of persons (male and female) who claim Mexican heritage (e.g., the Chicano community). These labels offer an alternative to the more common ethnic identifiers *Mexican* and *Mexican American*. Other terms associated with people of Mexican descent include *Hispanic* and *Latino*. Both of these terms typically include Spaniards and a variety of ethnic groups who were colonized at one time by Spain. Readers interested in the history and significance of different labels used by the Mexican origin popula-tion are referred to Portes and Truelove (1987, 359–85), Garcia (1981, 88–98), and Peñalosa (1970, 1–12).

4. We use the plural *feminisms* to underscore how there is no one universally accepted understanding of Chicana oppression and empowerment.

5. Most of the data in this publication were collected by the Bureau of the Census in the March 1992 supplement to the Current Population Survey (see Thornborrow and Sheldon in this volume for more on the CPS). Hispanic origin was determined by a question asking for self-identification of a person's origin or descent. Race is determined by a separate question. "Hispanics" normally include persons of any race. This is the first CPS report to separate persons who are white but not of Hispanic origin. Persons of Mexican, Puerto Rican, Cuban, Central and South American, and other Hispanic are also shown. However, the social and economic characteristics provided are not given separately by sex for all groups.

6. The intertwined notions of *familia* and *community* as integral to different types of Chicano political activism are discussed in Muñoz and Barrera (1982, 101–19), Gonzalez (1982, 146–49), Segura and Pesquera (1992, 69–92), and Pardo, (1990, 1–7).

7. In Mexican culture, the word *Malinche* has become synonymous with *betrayal*. The word is rooted in the conquest of Mexico by the Spaniards. *Malinche* was applied to Malintzin, an Indian woman who was given to the Conquistador Hernan Cortes by a tribe antagonistic to the powerful Aztecs. Cortes called her Doña Marina. In later years, Doña Marina/Malintzin became villified as a collaborator with the Spaniards who facilitated the downfall of the Indian way of life (as opposed to the incompetence of the male leadership of the Aztecs) and was called "Malinche." This image was resurrected in the days of the early Chicano movement and used to discourage Chicana feminists from critiquing sexism in the Chicano community. Chicana feminists have been actively reexamining the pejorative image of Malinche and reclaiming her as "Malintzin," a strong, creative woman who challenged the boundaries of her life and that of other Indian women. For additional information on this topic, we advise readers to consult Del Castillo (1977, 124–49) and Alarcon (1983, 182–90).

8. Nieto-Gomez' use of the term *maternal* can be regarded as a metaphor for *paternal*. Specifically, she critiques the notion that one group (e.g., "woman") is most capable of solving social problems. Essentially, she is charging white women with paternal behaviors but gendering her critique, hence the word *maternal*.

REFERENCES

Acuña, Rodolfo. 1981. *Occupied America: A History of Chicanos*, Second Edition. New York: Harper and Row.

Alarcon, Norma. 1983. "Chicana's Feminist Literature: A Re-Vision Through Malintzin/or Malintzin: Putting Flesh Back on the Object." Pp. 182–90 in *This Bridge Called My Back: Writing by Radical*

Women of Color, Second Edition, edited by Cherrie Moraga and Gloria Anzaldua. New York: Kitchen Table, Women of Color Press.

Almaguer, Tomas. 1971. "Toward the Study of Chicano Colonialism." *Aztlan, Chicano Journal of the Social Sciences and Arts* 2:7–22.

Alvarez, Rodolfo. 1971. "The Unique Psycho-Historical Experience of the Mexican American." *Social Science Quarterly* 52:15–29.

Apodaca, Maria Linda. 1986. "A Double Edge Sword: Hispanas and Liberal Feminism." *Critica, a Journal of Critical Essays* 1(Fall):96–114.

Baca Zinn, Maxine. 1979. "Chicano Family Research: Conceptual Distortions and Alternative Directions." *Journal of Ethnic Studies* 7:59–71.

———. 1980. "Employment and Education of Mexican-American Women: The Interplay of Modernity and Ethnicity in Eight Families." *Harvard Educational Review* 50:1 (February):47–62.

———. 1982. "Mexican-American Women in the Social Sciences." *Signs: Journal of Women in Culture and Society* 8:259–72.

Barrera, Mario, Carlos Muñoz, and Charles Ornelas. 1972. "The Barrio as an Internal Colony." Pp. 465–99 in *People and Politics in Urban Society, Urban Affairs Annual Review,* Vol. 6, edited by Harlan H. Hahn. Beverly Hills, CA: Sage Publications.

Blauner, Robert. 1972. *Racial Oppression in America.* New York: Harper and Row.

Chicano Coordinating Committee on Higher Education. 1969. *El Plan de Santa Barbara: A Chicano Plan for Higher Education.* Santa Barbara, CA: La Causa Publications.

Comision Femenil Mexicana Nacional, Inc. 1986. *1985–86 Annual Report.* Los Angeles, CA: Comision Femenil Mexicana Nacional, Inc.

Cotera, Martha P. 1973. "Mexicano Feminism." *Magazin* 1:30–32.

———. 1977. *The Chicana Feminist.* Austin, TX: Information Systems Development.

———. 1980. "Feminism: The Chicana and Anglo Versions, A Historical Analysis." Pp. 217–34 in *Twice a Minority: Mexican American Women,* edited by Margarita Melville. St. Louis: C. V. Mosby Co.

Del Castillo, Adelaida R. 1974. "La Vision Chicana." *La Gente* 8, 3–4.

———. 1977. "Malintzin Tenepal: A Preliminary Look into a New Perspective." Pp. 124–49 in *Essays on la Mujer,* edited by Rosaura Sanchez and Rosa Martinez Cruz. Los Angeles: University of California, Los Angeles, Chicano Studies Center Publications.

Estrada, Leobardo F., F. Chris Garcia, Reynaldo Flores Macias, and Lionel Maldonado. 1981. "Chicanos in the United States: A History of Exploitation and Resistance." *Daedalus* 110:103–31.

Flores, Francisca. 1971. "Comision Femenil Mexicana." *Regeneracion* 2:6–7.

———. 1973. "Equality." *Regeneracion* 2:4–5.

Garcia, Alma M. 1989. "The Development of Chicana Feminist Discourse, 1970–1980." *Gender and Society* 3(June):217–38.

Garcia, John A. 1981. "'Yo Soy Mexicano . . .': Self-Identity and Socio-Demographic Correlates." *Social Science Quarterly* 62(March):88–98.

———. 1982. "Ethnicity and Chicanos: Measurement of Ethnic Identification, Identity, and Consciousness." *Hispanic Journal of Behavioral Sciences* 4:295–314.

Gonzalez, Cesar A. 1982. "La Familia de Joaquin Chinas." *De Colores, Journal of Chicano Expression and Thought* 2:146–49.

Gonzalez, Sylvia. 1977. "The White Feminist Movement: The Chicana Perspective." *Social Science Journal* 14:67–76.

Hispanic Link Weekly Report, November 27, 1989.

Keefe, Susan E., and Amado M. Padilla. 1987. *Chicano Ethnicity.* Albuquerque: University of New Mexico Press.

Longeaux y Vasquez, Enriqueta. 1970. "The Mexican-American Woman." Pp. 379–84 in *Sisterhood Is Powerful,* edited by Robin Morgan. New York: Vintage.

Lopez, Sonia A. 1977. "The Role of the Chicana Within the Student Movement." In *Essays on La Mujer,* edited by Rosaura Sanchez and Rosa Martinez Cruz. Los Angeles: Chicano Studies Center Publications.

Macias, Anna. 1982. *Against All Odds.* Westport, CT: Greenwood Press.

Martinez, Elizabeth. 1972. "La Chicana." Pp. 130–32 in *Third World Women.* San Francisco, CA: Third World Communications.

Mexican American Women's National Association (MANA) [Newsletter]. Fall 1991, Spring 1990, 1982. Washington, DC: MANA.

Mirande, Alfredo, and Evangelina Enriquez. 1979. *La Chicana.* Chicago: University of Chicago Press.

Montejano, David. 1987. *Anglos and Mexicans in the Making of Texas, 1836–1986.* Austin: University of Texas Press.

Mujeres Activas en Letras y Cambio Social. *Noticiera de MALCS* [Newsletter]. Winter 1989. Davis: Chicano Studies Program, University of California, Davis.

Muñoz, Carlos, Jr., and Mario Barrera. 1982. "La Raza Unida Party and the Chicano Student Movement in California." *The Social Science Journal* Vol. 19, No. 2 (April):101–19.

Nieto, Consuelo. 1974. "Chicanas and the Women's Rights Movements." *Civil Rights Digest* 4 (Spring):38–42.

Nieto-Gomez, Anna. 1973. "La Femenista." *Encuentro Femenil* 1:34–47.

———. 1974. "Chicana Feminism." *Encuentro Femenil* 1:3–5.

Orozco, Cynthia. 1986. "Sexism in Chicano Studies and the Community." Pp. 11–18 in *Chicana Voices: Intersections of Class, Race, and Gender,* edited by Teresa Cordova, Norma Cantu, Gilberto Cardenas, Juan Garcia, and Christine M. Sierra. National Association for Chicano Studies, Conference Proceedings. Austin: Center for Mexican American Studies, University of Texas, Austin.

Pardo, Mary. 1990. "Mexican American Women Grassroots Community Activists: (Mothers of East Los Angeles)." *Frontiers, A Journal of Women's Studies* 11: 1–7.

Peñalosa, Fernando. 1970. "Toward an Operational Definition of the Mexican American." *Aztlan, Chicano Journal of the Social Sciences and Arts* 1:1–12.

Pesquera, Beatriz M., and Denise A. Segura. Forthcoming. "There Is No Going Back: Chicanas and Feminism." In *Critical Issues in Chicana Studies: Temas Criticos en Estudios Chicanas,* edited by Norma Alarcon, R. Castro, M. Melville, E. Perez, Tey D. Rebolledo, C. Sierra, and A. Sosa Riddell. Berkeley, CA: Third Woman Press, 1993.

Portes, Alejandro, and Cynthia Truelove. 1987. "Making Sense of Diversity: Recent Research on Hispanic Minorities in the United States." *Annual Review of Sociology* 13:359–85.

Segura, Denise A. 1986. "Chicanas and Triple Oppression." Pp. 47–65 in *Chicana Voices: Intersections of Class, Race, and Gender,* edited by Teresa Cordova, Norma Cantu, Gilberto Cardenas, Juan Garcia, and Christine M. Sierra. National Association for Chicano Studies, Conference Proceedings. Austin: Center for Mexican American Studies, University of Texas, Austin.

Segura, Denise A., and Beatriz M. Pesquera. 1992. "Beyond Indifference and Antipathy: The Chicana Movement and Chicana Feminist Discourse." *Aztlan, International Journal of Chicano Studies Research* 19:69–92.

Takaki, Ronald, T. 1979. *Iron Cages: Race and Culture in Nineteenth Century America.* New York: Albert A. Knopf.

U.S. Bureau of the Census. 1992. "The Hispanic Population in the United States: March 1992." *Current Population Reports,* Series P-20, No. 465. Washington, DC: U.S. Government Printing Office.

U.S. Commission on Civil Rights. 1972. *Education for Mexican Americans: The Excluded Student.* Report III: Mexican American Education Study. Washington, DC: U.S. Government Printing Office.

A Cloak of Many Colors: Jewish Feminism and Feminist Jews in America

Ilsa M. Glazer

THE FEMINISM OF American Jewish women is a nubby-textured cloak of many colors. It is a fabric woven of an unbroken thread of thousands of years of history that asks the Jewish people, individually and collectively, to follow the Hebrew moral imperative *tikkun olam,* meaning "repairing the world," by a commitment to sociopolitical activism in the *global* village. This involves struggle against injustice for Jews, women, and all others scarred by oppression.

In order to understand the multiple voices of American Jewish feminism, the "cloak of many colors,"[1] it is necessary to understand something of Jewish history and practice. The term *Jewish* encompasses both a religion, Judaism, and an ethnic group, Jews. Judaism developed in Israel, the Promised Land, four thousand years ago. Some elements of the religion have remained unchanged since that time. Yet survival depended on Judaism's capacity to evolve and change over the millennia from the religion of nomadic pastoralists under the Patriarch Abraham, to a state religion under the biblical kings, to the religion of a people living both under conquest in Israel and in exile from their land. Jews today live in Israel, a modern state reborn as a Jewish homeland in 1948, and in what is called the Diaspora, Jewish communities outside Israel.

Jews have settled in all the continents in their long history. Over time, they took on many of the cultural and racial characteristics of the dominant population. Jews who migrated to America came mostly from Europe, North Africa, and the Middle East and therefore tend to be Caucasian. Those who migrated to the modern state of Israel from subsaharan Africa, India, and elsewhere have made that country a multiracial and multicultural mosaic united by religion.

In the United States as of 1990, 4,395,000 people identified themselves as Jews by religion, 1.8 percent of the total population. Of these 60 percent are members of congregations. Another 1,120,000 people describe themselves as "secular" Jews. For them, being Jewish is a matter of ethnic identity alone and has no religious content.[2] Jewishly identified people consider themselves united as *Beit Yisrael,* the House of Israel. They feel they belong to and take responsibility for *klal Yisrael,* all Jews, which includes both genders, all ages, the ancestors, and the souls not yet born. Belonging to *Beit Yisrael* is like being in a family.

There is no "Jewish community" anywhere. Rather, there are many Jewish communities based on diverse religious ideologies and practices. In America there are three major denominations: Orthodox, Conservative, and Reform, and numerous smaller ones, such as Reconstruction.[3] The Orthodox denomination believes that God revealed the religion in its totality to Moses on Mount Sinai and that it cannot be changed, yet the Orthodox are divided into subgroups based on differences of interpretation of how to practice God's law. Conservative, Reform, and Reconstructionist Jews consider only some of God's law revealed. To them, many of the rituals, customs, and practices associated with religious law were constructed by humans over the course of history and are therefore amenable to change. Conservatives emphasize close study of holy texts to find within them justification for changing details of observance. Reform and Reconstruction reject many traditions and holy texts, substituting new forms of prayer, ritual, and practice in adapting to modern social life and assimilating in American society. Reform believes that as long as Jews adhere to the religious and ethical postulates of the ancient prophets, they can disregard most of the laws and even some of the biblical commandments. Reconstruction seeks to develop Jewish practice to coincide with American ideals.[4] Most American Jews find a comfortable home within these latter three denominations.

While practice of the Jewish religion is based in the home and community and is intensely interactional, it is also a highly personal negotiation between the individual and God. Religious leaders, called rabbis, are teachers who can advise but have no authority to compel. In addition to the Ten Commandments, there are religious laws called *mitzvot,* "good deeds," governing virtually every aspect of daily life. The individual freely chooses which of the *mitzvot* to practice.

The remainder of this chapter describes how American Jewish feminists variously interpret *tikkun olam,* repairing the world. The first part, "Jewish Feminism," describes the work of American feminists who happen to be Jews. The next part, "Feminist Jews," describes the work of Jewishly identified feminists within American Jewish religious and communal life.

Jewish Feminism

Jewish feminists are those who work toward a feminist agenda as Americans and whose identity as Jews is a private matter, imbued with a range of shades of meaning. While Jewish feminists include religiously committed Jews, the category also incorporates women born to Jewish mothers (and therefore Jewish according to traditional law)[5] but who have no religious identity or affiliation. It also includes women who were born Jewish but have converted to other religions.

Converts to other religions are included because many still tend to identify themselves as *ethnically* Jewish. Their identification largely results from the experience of European Jewry in World War II, when a person with any traceable Jewish ancestry was hunted by the Nazis and murdered in the Holocaust.[6] America is one of the few societies in the Diaspora in which Jews feel welcome and reasonably secure despite sporadic manifestations of anti-Semitism.[7] Yet the psychological scar of being of a people whose history has long been that of a despised minority, vulnerable to false accusation, extortion, rape, massacre, expulsion, and second-class status in Christian Europe and

Muslim North Africa and the Near East, makes Jews nervously watchful, even as converts. Because of their historical experience, despite their successful acculturation and assimilation in American society, many Jews continue to feel themselves to be an ethnic minority.

Jews traditionally have valued literacy. Hebrew literacy was expected of men, for this was the language of prayer in which women were nonpartici- pants. Respect for literacy carried over, when conditions permitted, to valuing literacy in one of the two languages of Jewish communal life, Ladino and Yiddish, as well as the languages of the host society. Women, though illiterate in Hebrew, were tutored in these languages when families could afford private teachers.[8] A rich body of literature for women developed in Jewish languages. Literacy in host languages depended largely on whether Jews were permitted access to secular study and were in a socioeconomic position to take advantage of the opportunity. The majority were impoverished. Unable to afford school- ing, they were illiterate and ashamed of it. For them, literacy in a host language was valued in part because it could lead to marketable professions when migration was necessary, thus providing some measure of security. No matter how quickly Jews had to leave, they took their knowledge with them.[9] Since most societies excluded women from professional life, Jews generally followed the dominant preference of providing professional education to sons.

The historical experience of the Jewish Diaspora promoted feelings of insecurity. Jews had always to be ready to leave at any moment, abandoning their material goods, when anti-Semitism threatened their lives. In this century, flight from massacre occurred in countries in which Jews had lived con- tinuously for two thousand years.[10] They migrated mainly to the United States and Israel.

In contemporary America, as a result of the feminist movement, Jewish women began clamoring for higher education and professional training equal to that of their men. Today, although there certainly exist pockets of impoverished inner-city Jewish female-headed households of poorly educated women with many children,[11] Jewish women are among the nation's most highly educated women. Jews educate daughters in higher percentages than do Catholics and Protestants, partly an artifact of Jewish preference for urban living and partly because of aspirations for upward social mobility. The result it that a high proportion of Jewish feminists have entered the professions. As scholars, artists, journalists, lawyers, politicians, psychotherapists, and development specialists, Jewish feminists have made major contributions to feminist theory and practice nationally and internationally.[12]

Jewish feminists have often achieved professional status despite hindrances put in their way by Jewish men, who are often critical of feminism. In fact, the price many Jewish feminists pay for their professional success is the alienation, and sometimes hostility, of Jewish men. Hostility between the genders is not new and is certainly not unique to Jews. What bears analysis is the changing cultural style of Jewish male hostility. In the past, it was fashionable for American Jewish male writers and comedians to mock their Jewish wives and mothers for an "overbearing" interactional style that, in fact, was characteristically Eastern European and shared by both genders.[13] The latest target of mockery is the "Jewish American Princess," stereotyped as highly materialistic, demanding, sexually cold, and intellectually vacuous. "JAP" jokes, initially created by Jewish men, have passed into the general population and are now considered a new form of anti-Semitism, particularly on college campuses.

Jewish men show their alienation from Jewish women by their ever-increasing preference for marrying non-Jews. Rarely in the course of thousands of years of Jewish history has there been so strong a rejection by Jewish men of tribeswomen.[14] Men from groups deemed "inferior" to those who set the social norms often feel they gain by rejecting women of their own group. By marrying women of the dominant group, they "get back" at men of the dominant group. Interestingly, Jews follow this pattern at a period of American history in which they are least excluded from mainstream society. Self-hate is frequently discussed in Jewish society.[15] It may explain some intermarriage, but since many Jewish men expect their wives to convert to Judaism, intermarriage seems at least as much of a rejection of Jewish women as it is an expression of self-hate. This is a serious issue for feminist Jews, to whom we now turn.

Feminist Jews

Feminist Jews are women who identify as members of *Beit Yisrael,* the House of Israel, and define their mission within Jewish religious and communal contexts to give voice to women's interests. They unite across denominations in mixed-gender American Jewish voluntary organizations to ensure incorporation of a feminist agenda.[16] Feminist Jews work within each of the major denominations in diverse ways that reflect religious differences. All express an overarching commitment to the continuity and survival of *Beit Yisrael* and diverse interpretations of *mitzvot, good deeds.*

Traditional Judaism is deeply patriarchal, and feminists share the common anguish of disempowerment, of "otherness." To Miriyam Glazer,[17] the feminist spiritual quest "heals the scars of religious sexism." The scars come from Jewish women's status as "exiles in a culture and a tradition that marginalizes and trivializes (their) needs and desires."

Feminist Jews unite to explode the myth of emotionally strong, economically successful, and religiously sacred Jewish family life by increasing awareness in Jewish social service agencies, synagogues, and community organizations of problems of wife battering, substance abuse, child abuse and incest, the feminization of poverty, difficulties of finding suitable mates, and neglect of the special needs of single-parent households and of the aged. These social problems, long denied, afflict Jewish communities just as they do those of other Americans.[18]

In spiritual matters, feminist Judaism is expressed in various ways. Among Conservative, Reform, and Reconstructionist congregations and *havurot* (fellowships), the first major struggle was to gain equality with men in religious ritual and in positions of religious leadership.[19] Gaining equality in a patriarchal religion requires a radical reconceptualization of theology. This is more easily accomplished by Reform and Reconstructionist Judaism, which are ideologically predisposed to change in that they value acculturation and assimilation to American society. The ordination of women as rabbis began with these two denominations; Conservatives followed.[20] Another change is the ordination of those gifted with beautiful voices as cantors, who lead the chanting of prayer in the synagogue.

The status of women in communal prayer services is in the process of becoming egalitarian.[21] Women now "count in the *minyan*" and are called for *aliyot*. A *minyan* traditionally consists of a quorum of ten post–*bar mitzvah* males necessary for the recitation of communal prayer. *Aliyot* (singular, *aliyah*) refers to the honor of being called to read from the holy texts during the prayer service. Seventy percent of Conservative congregations are now egalitarian.[22] Women counting in the *minyan* is fiercely resisted by the remaining 30 percent of Conservative congregations, even though they may have difficulty gathering a *minyan*. Resistance to *aliyot* sometimes comes from women, who may be embarrassed by their ignorance of chanting.[23]

An important change, unthinkable in the past, is a commitment to egalitarian prayer service. This entails revision of what is called "the God-language of prayer." Hebrew is the holy language. Easiest to change are prayers honoring the male God and the founding patriarchs repeated throughout each service. Today honor is given to the matriarchs and to the *Shechinah,* the female aspect of God. Because Hebrew classifies all words by gender, desexing God-language is a complex undertaking that has only just begun, and it is unlikely that it can ever be fully achieved. Prayers conducted in English, found prominently in Reform and Reconstructionist services, have been desexed.

The spiritual quest that rejects "otherness" in patriarchal traditional Judaism leads feminists to what Miriyam Glazer (op. cit.) calls the healing, nourishing, and strengthening function of creating new rituals. New rites celebrating the female life cycle are now developing for use within the synagogue and in women-only gatherings. Some parallel male rituals. The naming ceremony for a newborn girl parallels the *brit mila,* the circumcision ceremony marking infant male identity as a Jew. The *bat mitzvah* for adolescent girls and women parallels the *bar mitzvah* that marks entree into the adult male community. Other new rites are uniquely for women, such as the *Rosh Chodesh* ceremony celebrating the new moon (and new month) of the lunar Hebrew calendar. Women's groups are now in the process of creating new rites that speak to women's needs: for example, for menopause or acknowledging the pain of loss of a husband. A feminist *Hagaddah,* the text used at the Passover holiday celebrating the Jews' freedom from slavery in ancient Egypt, has been written to strengthen resolve to work for the freedom of all oppressed people. Creating new *Midrash,* feminist commentaries on holy text, is an important transformative scholarly activity shared by Conservative and Orthodox feminists.[24]

The feminist challenge is accepted among what are known as the "Modern" Orthodox and rejected by the "Ultra" (extreme) Orthodox.[25] In Orthodox thought, females and males complement each other; no one is considered a complete person without a mate.[26] The Orthodox woman's role, embraced by feminists, is to sanctify the home by various activities.[27] Some Orthodox women join the work force in order to enable their husbands to dedicate themselves to the study of holy text. The result is that in many Orthodox communities in America and abroad, more women than men mediate between the outside world and their own closed world. They and not their men are the innovators and modernizers.

Orthodox feminists seek change in the framework of Jewish code of personal status law (included in *halacha,* the legal exegesis of Judaism governing every aspect of life). Orthodox women are disadvantaged by the strongly patriarchal bias of *halacha.*[28]

The challenge for Orthodox feminists is to create a climate sympathetic to women within a community that abides by the decisions of exclusively male-run religious courts. Orthodox feminists create this climate by intensive study of the holy texts to gain expertise equal to that of male legal experts. For the first time in Jewish history, they have established formal training institutes that can produce feminist *Midrash;* they also form informal study groups. They examine texts for case studies that can be used as precedents for releasing women from marriages to husbands who refuse to divorce their wives and for releasing "anchored wives" (see note 28). They form self-help organizations to advise women and to assemble rosters of sympathetic rabbis to provide legal counsel for women in the religious courts.

Increasing numbers of American Jewish women are now spending a good part of their lives single, often childless, sometimes by deliberate choice and sometimes because they cannot find suitable Jewish mates.[29] The challenge for childless feminist Jews is to further Jewish continuity and survival in ways other than childbearing. They believe their contribution is to enhance the *quality* of Jewish life. By making Jews more responsive to *tikkun olam,* repairing the world, they lessen the rate of assimilation and thus increase the size of the Jewishly identified population. Their feminist commitment is therefore in service roles in Jewish political, community, and social welfare organizations. Jews are only a tiny minority in America and in the global village and have been so throughout history. These feminist Jews, together with their family-oriented feminist Jewish sisters, strive for justice for Jews and for all humankind. The essential messages of Judaism and feminism, a yearning for universal peace and justice, are the same.

NOTES

1. The "cloak of many colors" is a biblical reference to Joseph, who was, paradoxically, tricked by his brothers into exile and by his eventual success there was able to save the Jewish people. It is used here as a symbol of multivocality, ambiguity, paradox: in continually questioning the meaning of Jewish identity, one authenticates the process of continuity through change.

2. This figure includes 4,210,000 Jews by birth and 185,000 converts. There are 210,000 Jewish Americans who have converted to other religions and 415,000 who are of Jewish parentage or descent but were raised in a religion other than Judaism. The source for figures is *Highlights of the CJF 1990 National Jewish Population Survey,* published in 1991 by the Council of Jewish Federations in association with the Mandell Berman Institute North American Jewish Data Bank, the Graduate School and University Center, CUNY.

3. According to the 1990 *Yearbook of American and Canadian Churches,* no census has ever been taken of the number of Orthodox houses of worship. There are approximately 600,000 Orthodox Jews in America. Estimates of the number of Conservative Jews vary considerably. The *Yearbook* provides figures of 850 congregations and 1.5 million members. The denomination's umbrella

organization, United Synagogue of America, estimates eight hundred congregations and 890,000 members. Bernice Balter, executive director of the Women's League for Conservative Judaism (personal communication), theorizes that the discrepancy comes from different criteria for membership. Some congregants pay dues only until their children undergo adolescent rites of passage but identify as members because they use the synagogue for rituals. The Reform denomination has 839 congregations of 1.3 million members. There are seventy Reconstructionist congregations and an uncounted number of *havurot* (fellowships). Estimates of membership range from ten thousand (*Yearbook*) to fifty thousand (Lani Moss, program coordinator, Federation of Reconstructionist Congregations, and Havurot, personal communication).

Robert M. Seltzer, *Jewish People, Jewish Thought: The Jewish Experience in History* (New York: Macmillan, 1980), is an excellent source for discussions of the theological differences among the denominations.

4. For a discussion of denominational differences, see Leo W. Schwartz, ed., *Great Ages and Ideas of the Jewish People* (New York: Modern Library, Random House). See also "Who Is a Reconstructionist Jew?" pamphlet of the Reconstructionist Rabbinical College, Wyncote, PA.

5. In defining a Jew as a person born to either a Jewish mother or a Jewish father, the Reform movement has broken with this tradition.

6. The two core events that Jews believe mark Jewish history of the twentieth century are the Holocaust, in which the Nazis murdered six million European Jews, one-third of the world's Jewish population, and the creation of the modern state of Israel.

7. An important American Jewish organization dedicated to the struggle against anti-Semitism is the Anti-Defamation League.

8. See Schwartz, *Great Ages and Ideas,* who writes (p. 364) that in the Enlightenment period of the eighteenth century, the upper bourgeois Jewish women of France and Germany were educated in foreign languages and general science, whereas men's education was limited to religious studies.

9. The greatest number of refugee Jews came to America from Eastern Europe between 1880 and 1920. To understand the dynamics of their adaptation to American life, see Neil Cowan and Ruth Cowan, *Our Parents' Lives: The Americanization of Eastern European Jews* (New York: Basic Books, 1989).

10. Jews lived in such cities as Alexandria in Egypt, Cologne in Germany, Avignon in France, Rome in Italy, and Baghdad in Iraq from early Roman times. Jews lived elsewhere—Ethiopia and Poland are examples—for at least one thousand years before having to flee. See Seltzer, *Jewish People, Jewish Thought.*

11. Jews as well as non-Jews tend to view Jewish Americans as a highly successful immigrant group (see, for example, Charles E. Silberman, *A Certain People: American Jews and Their Lives Today* [New York: Summit Books, 1985]). While the majority have entered the mainstream, there are significant numbers of poor Jews, mainly women, whose plight feminist Jews have brought to light (see *Jewish Women and Children at Risk,* a report of the Task Force on the Jewish Woman, Subcommittee on Jewish Women in Poverty, United Jewish Appeal-Federation of New York, Spring 1991).

12. Many of the founders of the feminist movement are Jews, including Betty Friedan, whose *Feminine Mystique* sparked the movement. Many scholars who brought the feminist message to academe happen to be Jewish. A bibliography on Jewish women in the Diaspora is Aviva Cantor's *The Jewish Woman 1900–1985* (New York: Biblio Press, 1987).

13. For a discussion of this, see "From Veneration to Vituperation," in Charlotte Baum, Paula Hyman, and Sonya Michel, *The Jewish Woman in America* (New York: New American Library, 1976). Excellent examples of oppressive stereotypes masquerading as humor are Dan Greenberg's *How to Be a Jewish Mother* (Los Angeles: Price, Stern, Sloan, 1966), Leslie Tonner's *Nothing But the Best: The Luck of the Jewish Princess* (New York: Coward, McCann and Geoghegan, 1975), Bruce Jay Friedman's *A Mother's Kisses* (New York: Simon and Schuster, 1966), and Philip Roth's *Portnoy's Complaint* (New York: Random House, 1967).

14. The Council of Jewish Federations (CJF) survey statistics show that more than half the Jewish male population intermarries today. Twenty years ago intermarriage was relatively rare. Men who marry non-Jewish women reject Jewish women but not Judaism. Two-thirds of all converts to Judaism are women. Most convert on their marriage to Jewish men, and nearly all—99 percent—raise their children as Jews. CJF statistics show the majority of Jewish women prefer not to marry at all rather than intermarry.

15. Jewish male self-hate is discussed in Raphael Patai, *The Jewish Mind* (New York: Charles Scribner's Sons, 1977), and Alan M. Dershowitz, *Chutzpah* (Boston: Little, Brown and Company,

1991). A sterling example of rejection of Jewish women is David Greenwald, "Jewish, Single and Male," in *Jewish Marital Status,* ed. Carol Diament (Northvale, NJ: Jason Aronson, 1989).

16. For example, the Federation-United Jewish Appeal established a Task Force on Women, and the American Jewish Congress established a Commission on the Status of Women. The former is a comprehensive body promoting both religious and social change; the latter includes issues of political concern, such as free choice on abortion, and works to build an international network of feminist Jews. The organization U.S./Israel Women to Women promotes a feminist agenda in Israel.

17. Miriyam Glazer, "Orphans of Culture and History: Gender and Spirituality in Contemporary Jewish-American Women's Novels," *Tulsa Studies in Women's Literature* (Spring 1994). See also Thena Kendall, "Memories of an Orthodox Youth," and Sara Reguer, "Kaddish from the 'Wrong' Side of the *Mehitzah*," in Susannah Heschel, ed., *On Being a Jewish Feminist: A Reader* (New York: Schocken Books, 1983).

18. See, for example, Susan Weidman Schneider, *Jewish and Female: A Guide and Sourcebook for Today's Jewish Woman* (New York: Simon and Schuster, 1985).

19. Feminist Jewish scholarship now flourishes and takes a multiplicity of forms. Sally Priesand, the first ordained woman rabbi, wrote a comprehensive account of Jewish women's place in history and society, *Judaism and the New Woman* (New York: Behrman House, 1975). For excellent discussions of feminist Judaism socially and theologically, see Heschel, *On Being a Jewish Feminist;* for an agenda for radically transforming Judaism, see Judith Plaskow, *Standing Again at Sinai: Judaism from a Feminist Perspective* (San Francisco: Harper and Row, 1990). For Jewish women in history, see Sondra Henry and Emily Taitz, *Written Out of History: Our Jewish Foremothers,* 2nd ed. (New York: Biblio Press, 1983). For poems, stories, and essays, see Melanie Kaye/Kantrowitz and Irena Klepfisz, *The Tribe of Dina: A Jewish Women's Anthology* (Montpelier, VT: Sinister Wisdom, 1986).

20. The Reform movement ordained its first woman rabbi in 1972. The Conservative movement followed in 1985. It seems unlikely that the Orthodox movement will ever ordain women rabbis, because their religious service requires separation of the genders and women have no roles in public religious rites. Informal observation suggests that far more women are ordained than find employment leading congregations. For an accounting, see Laura Geller, "Reactions to a Woman Rabbi," in Heschel, *On Being a Jewish Feminist.*

21. For an analysis of the difficulties of transforming a service, see Riv-Ellen Prell, "Sacred Categories and Social Relations: The Visibility and Invisibility of Gender in an American Jewish Community," in Harvey E. Goldberg, ed., *Judaism Viewed from Within and from Without: Anthropological Studies* (Albany: State University of New York Press, 1987).

22. Source: Bernice Balter, executive director, Women's League for Conservative Judaism (personal communication). See also National Survey of Women in Ritual, Women's League for Conservative Judaism.

23. In a survey conducted by the Women's League for Conservative Judaism at their November 1988 convention, although 70.5 percent read Hebrew, only 15 percent could chant a portion of holy text, 9.8 percent could lead in prayer, and 9.4 percent could read the Bible in Hebrew. Source: Rabbinical Assembly Newsletter, May 1989.

Such statistics suggest that women's struggle for equality has only just begun. Now they must struggle for that rigorous training that will enable them to perform the ritual. See Arleen Stern, "Leaning to Chant the Torah: A First Step," in Heschel, *On Being a Jewish Feminist.*

24. *Midrash* is the body of interpretation that has been developed over the centuries to relate Old Testament rules of personal and social conduct to changing conditions of everyday life since biblical times.

25. Modern Orthodoxy arose in America as the three denominations became differentiated in adapting to American life. Ultra Orthodoxy retains the communal structure and ideology brought to this country from Eastern Europe. The Ultra Orthodox reject as much as they can of modern life, including birth control.

26. The belief that no one is complete without a mate is deeply embedded in Jewish thought and is shared by Conservative Jews. Many contemporary Jewish women prefer to remain single rather than marry a non-Jewish mate because they adhere to the traditional Jewish custom of endogamy. Non-Jewish men are thus not seen as potential spouses.

27. These include maintaining the complicated system of dietary laws known as *kashrut* and ushering in the Sabbath, the cherished holy day of rest, by lighting and blessing the Sabbath candles. In the name of modesty, some Modern Orthodox wives and all Ultra Orthodox cover their hair and wear clothing that covers arms and legs and observe various taboos associated with menstruation.

28. For example, according to *halacha,* only men can sue for divorce: women cannot initiate divorce proceedings. Widows cannot remarry unless the husband is proven to have died. This law creates a problem for widows whose soldier husbands are missing in action or who desert them and cannot be located. These women are *agunot* (singular, *agunah*), "anchored" wives. Another legal problem is that widows cannot remarry unless ceremonially "released" by the late husband's brother. This creates a problem if he is under age, for the widow must wait until the brother reaches the age of thirteen and undergoes the ritual *bar mitzvah,* which welcomes him into the community of men. If he is already adult, he may set conditions for her release that she cannot fulfill.

29. Carol Diament's edited volume *Jewish Marital Status* documents the various types of situations of women alone.

For a comprehensive account of lesbian Jews, see Evelyn Tornton Beck, ed., *Nice Jewish Girls: A Lesbian Anthology* (Waterloo, MA: Persephone Press, 1982).

Lesbian Feminism and the Feminist Movement

Lisa Ransdell

LESBIANS ARE AMONG the distinctive groups of women who have contributed to and gained from the contemporary women's movement. Yet unease over lesbian involvement provoked conflict from the movement's beginnings in the late 1960s, when *lesbian, dyke,* and *man-hater* were used as epithets by anti-feminists to assail the character of activists as well as to dissuade more women from becoming involved. This rampant stigmatizing of participants had repressive internal effects as well, as movement leaders initially emphasized their heterosexuality and discouraged open lesbian involvement. Despite the ambivalence of many over their visible presence, lesbians persevered in their activism, creating dissonance while contributing energy, ideas, and a woman-centered culture that continues to sustain the movement. In this article I profile lesbian participation in the women's movement, explore the substance of lesbian feminist ideology, and consider the impact lesbians have had on the movement as a whole.

Lesbian Feminist Activism

The early involvement of lesbians in the women's movement was motivated foremost by the relevance of feminist issues to lesbians as women. Limited jobs, low pay, restricted reproductive rights, and inadequate child care, as well as sexual harassment and rape are problems common to women as a group; lesbians are no exception. There was also a hope that problems unique to lesbians—debilitating stereotypes, discrimination in housing and employment, and the predisposition of most courts against awarding custody to lesbian mothers—could be logically linked with the feminist critique of oppressive, gender-based ideologies and societal hostility to strong, independent women. Many lesbians found that neither women's issues nor lesbian issues were effectively addressed in the 1950s homophile movement, a movement dedicated to improving the public image of homosexuals, or the more militant gay rights movement of the 1960s. The sexism of male-dominated gay organizations like Mattachine Society and the Gay Liberation Front, and the conservatism of female homophile groups, which began as secretive social clubs in the repressive atmosphere of the 1950s, led some lesbians in the late 1960s to look to the emerging women's movement for a broader platform for change (Faderman, 1991:197; Phelan, 1989:37; D'Emilio, 1983:228).

While many of the first feminists who were lesbian kept their lesbianism secret and worked for generic feminist goals, others participated as open lesbians, demanding that feminist organizations publicly espouse lesbian rights. Del Martin and Phyllis Lyon, founders of the female homophile organization Daughters of Bilitis, came to believe that societal hostility to lesbians was ultimately rooted in sexism, joining the San Francisco chapter of the National Organization for Women as open lesbians in the late 1960s.[1] While some local chapters of NOW were tolerant of lesbian members, this was not the case with the national organization, where there were fears that any acknowledgment by NOW of lesbian issues would damage the credibility of the movement. NOW founder Betty Friedan fanned the flames of controversy by referring to lesbians as a "lavender menace,"[2] and many of the most militant lesbian members either were purged from the group[3] or resigned out of frustration. One of those who resigned during this early period was author/activist Rita Mae Brown, editor of the New York NOW newsletter at the time she left in 1970.[4]

Brown and other lesbian feminists found that the ideology, structurelessness, and grass-roots orientation of the women's liberation sector of the movement resulted in a greater openness to lesbian participation than was the case with large organizations like NOW. The radical feminist focus on sexual politics[5] and revolutionary social change appealed to younger activist lesbians, whose identities were influenced more by the sexual liberalism and militant politics of the 1960s than the severely repressive atmosphere of earlier decades (Faderman, 1991:204). However, stereotypes of lesbians held by radical feminists and the preoccupation of many of these women with interpersonal struggles with men meant that lesbian concerns did not automatically fit their agendas (Marotta, 1981:236).

Ultimately, lesbian feminism found its greatest flowering in independently established lesbian organizations like the Furies, a group Brown helped to form. In these lesbian-only groups the fundamentals of radical feminist philosophy and practice were applied to lesbian reality, and a distinctive viewpoint began to emerge that identified institutionalized heterosexuality as a key feature of women's oppression. Concepts like "woman-identified"—the orientation of women to other women in the name of solidarity—seemed obviously to encompass lesbians, whose solidarity with women extended one step further into the sexual realm (Buechler, 1990:117). Increasingly, lesbian feminism redefined the essence of lesbianism in political rather than sexual terms. Lesbians were idealized as the embodiment of woman identification: women whose political, emotional, and sexual needs were exclusively met by other women (Freeman, 1975:137).

The first salvo of a militantly political lesbian feminist ideology came in the 1970 Second Congress to Unite Women, when a group of women wearing "Lavender Menace" T-shirts disrupted the meeting to demand that lesbian issues be addressed (Hole and Levine, 1971:239–42; Freeman, 1975:137–39).

During this event, the protesters, members of a group calling itself Radicalesbians, distributed the tract "The Woman-Identified Woman":

> What is a lesbian? A lesbian is the rage of all women condensed to the point of explosion. . . . Our energies must flow toward our sisters, not backward toward our oppressors. As long as women's liberation tries to free women without facing the basic heterosexual structure that binds us in one-to-one relationship with our oppressors, tremendous energies will continue to flow into trying to straighten up each particular relationship with a man. . . . It is the primacy of women relating to women, of women creating a new consciousness of and with each other, which is at the heart of women's liberation and the basis for the cultural revolution.[6]

The ascendance of lesbian vanguardism—the view that lesbians stood at the forefront of the movement because of the inherently liberatory nature of their life-styles—stemmed from several sources. First, lesbian feminists initially sought to depict lesbian sexuality in stereotypically feminine ways as diffuse, romantic, and nurturing, leading to the portrayal of lesbianism as a positive, affirming choice a woman could make in a deeply sexist society. This effectively reduced much of the stigma associated with lesbianism and the fears of many heterosexual feminists (Echols, 1989:218). Second, radical feminists' critical examination of women's private experiences—practiced in consciousness-raising groups and embodied in the slogan "the personal is political"—led to consideration of the ways in which women's nurturing roles in heterosexual relationships helped to perpetuate male dominance. Thus, lesbian feminism was depicted as a logical solution to a dilemma faced by many straight radical feminists: the tension caused by battling sexist oppression publicly while still encountering it in interpersonal relationships with men. In this context a number of straight feminists experimented with lesbianism or adopted a lesbian identity initially for political rather than erotic reasons. Third, lesbian feminism coalesced at a point when the radical feminist segment of the movement was highly fragmented and bitterly divided over ideology and strategies. Increasingly, then, the energy and idealism of lesbian feminists filled a void in the radical feminist sector of the movement for cohesiveness and vision in political theory and practice. These developments, along with the success lesbian feminists had in creating and sustaining an alternative lesbian counterculture of music, art, literature, and social services, led to lesbian feminist dominance of radical feminist politics and discourse by the mid 1970s.

The lesbian feminist counterculture—usually referred to as "women's culture"—reflected the essence of lesbian feminism in the 1970s and was instrumental in its proliferation. As a counterculture, it fit the spirit of the radical feminist call for the creation of a new, egalitarian social order to replace the sexist social order of patriarchal society. Unlike radical feminism, it suggested that liberation and fulfillment could be achieved through immersion in the lesbian feminist community rather than requiring that women struggle to overturn the present system. Besides its idealization of lesbian life-styles, women's culture promoted separatism, or a commitment to live, work, and do politics with only other lesbians, and reinforced the desirability of politically correct behavior: the notion that only certain ways of thinking, speaking, dressing, and behaving were acceptable.

The politicization of lesbianism generated enormous conflict. Many heterosexual feminists resented the suggestion that they were guilty of participating in oppressive, counterproductive relationships. Also, many premovement lesbians were uncomfortable with lesbian feminist rhetoric, viewing their politicized sisters as usurpers who had not paid their dues (Snitow, Stansell, and Thompson, 1983:31). The crisis over lesbian vanguardism culminated in the gay-straight split, a serious schism that rocked the movement between 1970 and 1972 as straight feminists reacted defensively to the elevation of sexual preference as the ultimate gauge of feminist commitment (Freeman, 1975:134–42).

Besides helping to splinter the movement, lesbian vanguardism may have contributed to other problems. In the view of some it led radical feminism further away from a focus on social change and toward cultural feminism, or the creation and maintenance of a depoliticized, separatist women's culture, and "personal solutionism." "With the rise of lesbian feminism, the conflation of the personal with the political, long in the making, was unassailable. More than ever, how one lived one's life, not one's commitment to political struggle, became the salient factor" (Echols, 1989:240). It also led to antagonism in lesbian communities as apolitical lesbians and those who engaged in "politically incorrect" activities like butch/femme role-playing were dismissed by lesbian feminists as being "male-identified" (Adam, 1987:94).[7]

During this same period the National Organization for Women began to yield to pressure from lesbian activists and their supporters, formally recognizing lesbian oppression in 1971, establishing a task force on sexuality and lesbianism in 1973, and passing a resolution in 1975 that made lesbian rights one of the priorities of the organization (Freeman, 1975:99; Buechler, 1990:66).[8] Ironically, these measures were enacted without the universal support of moderate lesbians left in the organization, many of whom were still enmeshed in the legacy of passing as heterosexual left over from the repressiveness of the 1950s lesbian subculture (Snitow, Stansell, and Thompson, 1983:30).

The gay-straight split continued to fade in importance later in the decade as differences among feminists and among lesbians challenged the practicality of woman identification as the sole foundation for feminist consciousness, and as an increasingly repressive social and political climate led to a powerful antifeminist backlash. Lesbianism became less an issue as the energies of the movement were redirected outward to the struggle to pass the ERA and preserve reproductive rights, and as conflicts within lesbian communities over issues of difference absorbed the energies of lesbian feminists. During the 1970s lesbians integrated all strata of the feminist movement, successfully demanding that their issues be taken seriously. In 1970, when women marched down Fifth Avenue in the first mass march of the contemporary movement, their demands were equal opportunity in employment and education, free abortion on demand, and twenty-four-hour child care centers. At the 1977 National Women's Conference in Houston to commemorate International Women's Year, the three main issues were the ERA, abortion, and gay and lesbian rights. In only a few years lesbians had gone from being pariahs to being a priority.

By the beginning of the 1980s it was clear that the idealism and inflexibility of early radical lesbian feminist theory and practice sowed the seeds for its decline as a viable political force. The chauvinism of lesbian vanguardism alienated many lesbians who were uncomfortable with its narrow vision of feminism. Lesbians of color reacted strongly against the emphasis on separatism as a political strategy because of ties with men from their racial and ethnic groups in the struggle against racism. Working-class lesbians were put off by the focus on political correctness, since features of their own culture like role playing and remaining in the closet were condemned through its enforcement. The 1980s also saw the emergence of what became known as the "lesbian sex wars," as lesbian sexual libertarians challenged romanticized conceptions of lesbian sexuality. They argued for the appropriation of male-defined forms of sexuality as a means of empowering women, favoring experimentation with pornography, sadomasochism, butch/femme role-playing, and even public sex to counter what they viewed as the repressiveness of lesbian feminist prescriptions for sexual behavior (Faderman, 1991; Raymond, 1989).

As lesbian feminists struggled to incorporate the perspectives of diverse constituencies of lesbians, they became more moderate and less rigidly insistent on politically correct behavior. The diminishment of separatism as a strategy led lesbians increasingly to contribute their idealism and organizing skills to other progressive social movements of the 1970s and 1980s such as the nonviolent direct action movement, where their knowledge and commitment resulted in the assumption of important leadership positions (Epstein, 1991). Many lesbians returned to the *gay/lesbian* movement in response to the rightwing backlash against gay rights initiatives and the AIDS crisis of the 1980s, adding feminist concerns to the agenda of the movement and taking on roles of greater leadership and public visibility than before (Cavin, 1990:325–30).

In the 1990s it appears that lesbian feminists will continue their broad-based activism: a diverse constituency of lesbians, united in their loose conjoining of feminist precepts with a commitment to gay/lesbian civil rights and with ties to other movements for progressive social change. As lesbian feminist political participation has broadened, so has the essence of lesbian feminist ideology, although fundamental features are identifiable. These are important to point out, for the philosophy of lesbian feminism is one of the most significant legacies of lesbian participation in the women's movement.

The Essence of Lesbian Feminist Ideology

Lesbian feminist ideology was most clearly and consistently expressed at the point when lesbian vanguardism was at its peak in the mid 1970s. During this period, lesbian feminism was characterized by woman identification, romanticized beliefs about gender and female sexuality, and identification of institutionalized heterosexuality as a central mechanism of sexual inequality (and an assumption that lesbianism is an act of political resistance). While the idealism and parochialism of these early radical lesbian feminist beliefs became muted over time, the most common understanding of the ideas of "lesbian feminism" flow from these philosophical underpinnings.

Woman identification—used to describe personal and political solidarity with other women and sometimes as a nonthreatening euphemism for lesbianism (e.g., the "woman-identified woman")—was a critical component of early lesbian feminism and a good illustration of its idealism, for although lesbians were thought to exemplify woman identification, the benefits of such an orientation were clearly intended to encompass all women: "If we are lesbian feminists, we feel and act on behalf of women as women" (Raymond, 1989:155). The woman identification of lesbians was thought to be enhanced by their independence from intimate relationships with men and greater freedom from institutionalized gender roles and ideologies. Because woman identification was part of the philosophical justification for separatism, its place as a defining feature of lesbian feminism diminished as separatism fell into disfavor. A small number of lesbians still practice separatism, living and working as independently of mainstream society as possible, often deeply involved in sustaining the alternative institutions of women's culture. Most lesbians who are currently active in the women's or gay/lesbian movements have expanded their definition of woman identification, believing that the goals of lesbian feminism can best be served through joining together in coalition with other groups, including gay men and heterosexual feminists, to promote change.

The lesbian feminist inclination toward promotion of *romanticized conceptions of gender and sexuality*—sometimes expressed in a belief in the superiority of female traits and values over those of men—was a means of creating a positive image of the lesbian in a society that formerly characterized her solely in terms of sexual deviance. Essentialism, or the view that females and males have radically different temperaments because of biological sex, was one feature of lesbian feminism that most sharply delineated it from the radical feminist call for an end to the sex role system (Freeman, 1975:142), aligning it with the cultural feminist critique of masculine culture and values (Buechler, 1990:118). While lesbian essentialism promoted a new, positive identity for lesbians and encouraged the development of the lesbian counterculture as a haven where gentleness, empathy, and egalitarian relationships would prevail, it also had the effect of almost completely desexualizing lesbian identity. Because of the popularity of essentialist beliefs, lesbian identity was increasingly defined in terms of anger, politics, and resistance to institutionalized heterosexuality rather than desire. Adrienne Rich exemplified lesbian essentialism in her famous essay "Compulsory Heterosexuality and Lesbian Existence," where she asserted that lesbianism exists on a continuum that includes nonsexual forms of woman-identified experience. In her view, lesbian existence involves the breaking of a taboo and rejection of a compulsory way of life (1980:649).

Idealized conceptions of lesbianism such as these were later assailed by the strident objections of lesbian sexual libertarians, who argued that female (and lesbian) sexuality is not essentially different from male sexuality. As a result, the romanticized, desexualized conceptualizations of lesbianism that characterized early lesbian feminist theorizing slowly began to give way to consideration of the complexities of sexual desire and pleasure between women (Vance, 1984). While on the one hand these developments led to bitter conflicts and debates, on the other hand it also moved the movement closer to an analytical framework truly inclusive of women's differing experiences (Smith, 1989:414).

The final premise of lesbian feminism, and the one that has changed least over time, is the *belief that lesbianism challenges the norm of compulsory heterosexuality,* which is thought by lesbian feminists to undergird the oppression of women. As both an ideology and an institution, compulsory heterosexuality perpetuates male dominance by tying women intimately to their oppressors, a condition of dependency maintained through a variety of mechanisms, including force, finances, and the promotion of false consciousness (Rich, 1980). The concept of compulsory, or institutionalized, heterosexuality expanded radical feminist analysis of sexual politics and established the "inherent feminism of lesbianism and the anti-feminism of lesbian persecution" (Faderman, 1991:212).

The view that lesbianism is an act of resistance is predicated on the placement of compulsory heterosexuality within a male-dominated social system in which women are dependent on men for economic survival and social approval. From this perspective, lesbians undermine the institution of heterosexuality and patriarchal control of women by rejecting male definitions of female gender roles and women's sexuality (Kitzinger, 1987:114). Despite wide acceptance among lesbian feminists of the premise that lesbianism has a political dimension, lesbian theorists differ as to whether lesbianism is inherently political or whether a further commitment to activism is necessary before the potential for radical change is realized. Cheryl Clarke's views illustrate the former position:

> For a woman to be a lesbian in a male-supremacist, capitalist, racist, homophobic culture, such as that of North America, is an act of resistance. . . . No matter how a woman lives out her lesbianism—in the closet, in the state legislature, in the bedroom—she has rebelled against becoming the master's concubine, viz. the male-dependent female, the female heterosexual. (1983:128)

Adrienne Rich took a mid-range position, arguing that lesbianism in and of itself does not directly threaten male power:

> We can say that there is a nascent feminist political content in the act of choosing a woman lover or life partner in the face of institutionalized heterosexuality. But for lesbian existence to realize this political content in an ultimately liberating form, the erotic choice must deepen and expand into conscious woman-identification—into lesbian/feminism. (1980:659)

Finally, Anne Koedt assumed a hard-line position early on, arguing that lesbian feminism must align itself with radical feminism before it can have a truly political function:

> The act of rebellion inherent in lesbianism is only radical if it is placed in the context of destroying the sex role system instead of rejecting men. (1973:251)

While ideological consistency and idealism sustained lesbian feminism in the early 1970s, a number of tensions and points of disagreement have fueled its elaboration in succeeding years. Reaction against the idealization of lesbian relationships, lesbian vanguardism, the politicization of lesbian identity, and overapplication of the concept "the personal is political" resulted in considerable broadening of the meaning of lesbian feminism and greater heterogeneity among the women who identify with this part of the movement. Because of the changes more than two decades of struggle have brought to the philosophy of lesbian feminism, the legacy of lesbian involvement in feminism is perhaps best assessed through consideration of their contributions to the movement over the long term, a question to which I now turn.

The Impact of Lesbian Feminism on the Women's Movement

Through feminist activism and the articulation of lesbian feminist ideology, lesbians have contributed to the women's movement in five distinctive ways: by reinforcing and extending radical feminist interpretations of gender and female sexuality, by providing leadership and carrying out a significant amount of the work of the movement, by creating and sustaining an alternative women's culture, by contributing to the articulation of a more complex feminist agenda sensitive to the experiences and needs of diverse groups of women, and by helping to legitimize nontraditional life-styles and the importance of choice at every level in women's lives.

REINFORCEMENT AND EXTENSION OF RADICAL FEMINIST INTERPRETATIONS OF GENDER AND FEMALE SEXUALITY

Philosophical points of connection between radical and lesbian feminism include a conceptualization of gender as a fundamental category of oppression, the premise that the oppression of women is accomplished in part through the social construction of norms regulating gender and sexuality that place women in a position of dependence and inferiority with respect to men, and the notion that the oppression of lesbians is at root a form of sexist oppression. By actively challenging conventional notions of gender behavior and sexual expression, lesbians exemplify radical feminist views. Thus lesbians embody the goals of women's liberation with their independence from men, sexual self-determination, and defiance of gender roles (Abbott and Love, 1972:136).

Additionally, lesbian feminism significantly expanded the radical feminist critique of sexual politics by demonstrating the centrality of the institution of compulsory heterosexuality to women's oppression. By codifying the idea that male and female gender roles are opposites that find their natural expression in heterosexual relationships, and with the placement of these roles and relationships in a social system characterized by male dominance, compulsory heterosexuality reinforces the dependence of women on men at the same time that it stigmatizes sex and gender behaviors that are nonnormative. Viewed from this perspective, the negative social reaction to lesbianism and the frequency with which feminists are accused of being lesbian result from the threat posed by lesbianism and feminism to the foundations of male power (Weitz, 1989:450).

Lesbian feminism also suggests that straight women are further oppressed by compulsory heterosexuality in that alternative versions of heterosexual relationships are suppressed and discouraged, and through cultural denigration of woman-identified experiences such as female friendship and bonding between women.

PROVISION OF LEADERSHIP AND ACCOMPLISHMENT OF SIGNIFICANT FEMINIST WORK

Despite the ambivalence of many over the visible presence of lesbians in the women's movement, lesbians have consistently supported the goals of feminism. Some feminist organizations like NOW and the National Women's Studies Association have lesbian constituencies large enough to sustain special interest caucuses and other structures to serve the needs of lesbian members. NOW itself has moved a long way from the days of the "lavender menace"; its current president, Patricia Ireland, is publicly known to be lesbian. In many ways lesbians may be seen as a natural feminist constituency, since their intimate partners and comrades share similar interests in female liberation and are unlikely to be threatened by the loss of social privileges if the movement succeeds. Lesbians also may be less conflicted by the tension between their private, social selves and their public, political selves, and they are unlikely to avoid protest because of the illusion of male protection (Epstein, 1991:182; Valverde, 1987:104; Weitz, 1989:448).

CREATION AND SUSTENANCE OF "WOMEN'S CULTURE"

One vestige of radical feminism that persists to the present day is the network of feminist countercultural institutions and projects that were begun for the purpose of spreading feminist values, providing services to women in a nonoppressive environment and linking localized feminist communities across the country. Rape crisis centers, battered women's shelters, feminist bookstores, women's health clinics, women's studies programs, feminist recording and printing companies, women's music festivals, coffeehouses, and other venues provide services and products to women that reflect feminist sensibilities. While these are by no means the sole province of lesbians, they have over time increasingly been sustained by lesbian feminist commitment. While a diverse cross-section of women may make use of these services, they also perpetuate a semblance of structure for lesbian communities and radical feminist ideals (Taylor and Whittier, 1992).

In the more formal domain of academic scholarship, feminist theories and research increasingly make reference to sexual identity as a determining component of female experience. Studies of lesbian subcultures speak of these "women's worlds" as social spaces where women are empowered to define their own experiences (Stimpson, 1986:37–38). The popular culture of the women's movement is also rich with lesbian voices. Critically acclaimed and publicly revered writers like the white lesbian poet and essayist Adrienne Rich and the late black lesbian poet, essayist, and novelist Audre Lorde have been open about their lesbianism, citing the parallel and synergistic effects of sexism, racism, and homophobia. Lesbian musicians and artists celebrate lesbian lives and feminist values, sustaining the culture of the women's movement along with the legitimacy of lesbian presence within it.

CONTRIBUTIONS TO A FEMINIST AGENDA SENSITIVE TO THE EXPERIENCES AND NEEDS OF DIVERSE GROUPS OF WOMEN

The rhetoric of universal sisterhood characteristic of the early years of the women's movement began to give way to challenges by lesbians and working-class women in the 1970s and women of color in the 1980s (Echols, 1989:203; Ferree and Hess, 1985:90, 104; Snitow, Stansell, and Thompson, 1983:36). By articulating their unique experiences as outsiders in multiple contexts, lesbians of color have furthered understanding of the effects of homophobia across cultures, expanding theoretical analyses of the linkages between sexuality and power (Collins, 1990:192).[9] Increasingly, feminist theory incorporates themes of difference between groups of women, prompting a more complex understanding of the interlocking nature of systems of oppression. As Lorde said:

> Our future survival is predicated upon our ability to relate within equality. As women, we must root our internalized patterns of oppression within ourselves if we are to move beyond the most superficial aspects of social change. Now we must recognize differences among women who are our equals, neither inferior nor superior, and devise ways to use each others' difference to enrich our visions and our joint struggles. (1992:407)

LEGITIMATION OF NONTRADITIONAL SEXUALITY AND THE IMPORTANCE OF CHOICE AT EVERY LEVEL OF WOMEN'S LIVES

Despite the controversy their open participation sometimes provoked for the women's movement, both internally and externally, the political work of lesbian feminists and the philosophy of lesbian feminism significantly preserved the focus on sexual politics of radical feminist analysis. Both lesbian feminism and radical feminism are critical of traditional sex roles and affirm nonreproductive sexuality (D'Emilio, 1983:237). Lesbian feminist contributions to the feminist discourse on sexuality led to legitimation of lesbian life-styles in the movement and to increased affirmation of the importance of sexual choices for all women:

> All women who long for a woman-centered sexuality will find it in their best interests to take an active interest in the development of lesbian culture. . . . To fight for lesbian rights and against heterosexism is to fight against male-defined female roles, and for autonomy. (Valverde, 1987:105)

To conclude, the integration of lesbian issues and lesbian participation in the women's movement has resulted in conflicts and tensions that persist to the present; however, lesbian feminism has also added important energy and concepts to the feminist agenda. The manner in which lesbian feminism influenced the agenda of the movement demonstrates that lesbians have something to offer rather than merely something to gain from feminism (Weitz, 1984). In the long run, feminist involvement has had more of a positive than a negative effect on lesbians as well. One positive by-product of participation is that it helped establish lesbianism as a legitimate, honorable identity, at least in the context of the women's movement. Another positive result of participation is that it provided a broad and nonstigmatizing context for coming out to lesbians, who lack the economic and social resources available to gay men (D'Emilio, 1983:236; Adam, 1987:89).

Not everyone accepts the notion that lesbian vanguardism led to the decline of radical feminism and the fragmentation of the movement. Some argue that radical feminism gave way to new forms of feminist activism sustained by lesbian feminist communities (Taylor and Whittier, 1992). Because these communities often socialize new members into a feminist consciousness, they are actually a route *to* personal transformation and political activism. It is unlikely that radical feminism could have been sustained as a mass movement during the political, social, and economic hostilities of the 1980s even without the controversies surrounding lesbian feminism. It may prove to be the case that lesbian feminism represents a survival mode for radical feminism during periods of social hostility (Taylor and Rupp, 1993).

NOTES

1. See Del Martin and Phyllis Lyon, *Lesbian Woman* (San Francisco: Glide Publications, 1972), for more on the Daughters of Bilitis and the relationship between the female homophile movement and the early women's movement, pp. 262–76.

2. Friedan's early views on lesbian involvement, which ranged from acknowledgment of the significance of lesbian contributions to fears that lesbians were "agents provocateurs" out to destroy the movement from within, are recounted in her book *It Changed My Life: Writings on the Women's Movement* (New York: Random House, 1976), pp. 139–41.

3. Marotta (1981:259) recounts a 1970 "purge" led by Friedan and other conservative NOW leaders that involved efforts to keep lesbians from being elected or reelected to offices in the national organization and the New York chapter.

4. See Rita Mae Brown, *A Plain Brown Rapper* (Baltimore: Diana Press, 1976), pp. 79–95.

5. In her book *Sexual Politics,* Kate Millett (1970:24–25) used the concept of sexual politics to characterize the relationship between the sexes as one of male dominance and female subordinance. The concept is also used by radical feminists to identify patterns of gender inequality in relationships between men and women.

6. Radicalesbians, "The Woman Identified Woman," in Anne Koedt, Ellen Levine, and Anita Rapone, eds., *Radical Feminism* (New York: Quadrangle Books, 1973), pp. 240–45.

7. This was particularly a problem for lesbians of color, who were less inclined than white women to embrace separatism as a viable political strategy, and for working-class lesbians, whose culture was less politicized and more oriented toward closeted eroticism and role-playing (Snitow, Stansell, and Thompson, 1983:30–34).

8. A current NOW pamphlet, "Why Should You Support Lesbian and Gay Civil Rights?" connects feminism and lesbianism in the following way: "Discrimination against lesbians and gays undermines the fight for women's equality. Women who dare to step out of traditionally 'acceptable' roles are often labeled as lesbians, regardless of their sexual orientation. Used as a threat, this label is meant to invalidate women and their fight for equality. As long as being labeled a lesbian can be used as a threat, women will not be able to achieve full equality."

9. See the following for more on the perspectives of lesbian feminists of color: Gloria T. Hull, Patricia Bell Scott, and Barbara Smith, eds., *All the Women are White, All the Blacks Are Men, But Some of Us Are Brave: Black Women's Studies* (New York: The Feminist Press, 1982); Barbara Smith, ed., *Home Girls: A Black Feminist Anthology* (New York: Kitchen Table: Women of Color Press, 1983); and Cherríe Moraga and Gloria Anzaldua, eds., *This Bridge Called My Back: Writings by Radical Women of Color* (New York: Kitchen Table: Women of Color Press, 1983).

REFERENCES

Abbott, Sidney, and Barbara Love. 1972. *Sappho Was a Right on Woman: A Liberated View of Lesbianism.* New York: Stein and Day.

Adam, Barry D. 1987. *The Rise of a Gay and Lesbian Movement.* Boston: Twayne.

Brown, Rita Mae. 1976. *A Plain Brown Rapper.* Baltimore: Diana Press.

Buechler, Steven M. 1990. *Women's Movements in the United States: Woman Suffrage, Equal Rights and Beyond.* New Brunswick, NJ: Rutgers.

Cavin, Susan. 1990. "The Invisible Army of Women: Lesbian Social Protests, 1969–1988." In Guida West and Rhoda Lois Blumberg, eds., *Women and Social Protest.* Oxford: Oxford University Press.

Clarke, Cheryl. 1983. "Lesbianism: An Act of Resistance." In Cherrie Moraga and Gloria Anzaldua, eds., *This Bridge Called My Back: Writings by Radical Women of Color.* New York: Kitchen Table: Women of Color Press.

Collins, Patricia Hill. 1990. *Black Feminist Thought: Knowledge, Consciousness and the Politics of Empowerment.* New York: Routledge.

D'Emilio, John. 1983. *Sexual Politics, Sexual Communities: The Making of a Homosexual Minority in the United States 1940–1970.* Chicago: University of Chicago Press.

Echols, Alice. 1989. *Daring to Be Bad: Radical Feminism in America 1967–1975.* Minneapolis: University of Minnesota Press.

Epstein, Barbara. 1991. *Political Protest and Cultural Revolution: Nonviolent Direct Action in the 1970's and 1980's.* Berkeley: University of California Press.

Faderman, Lillian. 1991. *Odd Girls and Twilight Lovers: A History of Lesbian Life in Twentieth Century America.* New York: Columbia University Press.

Ferree, Myra Marx, and Beth B. Hess. 1985. *Controversy and Coalition: The New Feminist Movement.* Boston: Twayne.

Freeman, Jo. 1975. *The Politics of Women's Liberation.* New York: David McKay.

Friedan, Betty. 1976. *It Changed My Life: Writings on the Women's Movement.* New York: Random House.

Hole, Judith, and Ellen Levine. 1971. *Rebirth of Feminism.* New York: Quadrangle Books.

Hull, Gloria T., Patricia Bell Scott, and Barbara Smith, eds. 1982. *All the Women Are White, All the Blacks Are Men, But Some of Us Are Brave: Black Women's Studies.* New York: Feminist Press.

Kitzinger, Celia. 1987. *The Social Construction of Lesbianism.* London: SAGE Publications.

Koedt, Anne. 1973. "Lesbianism and Feminism." In Anne Koedt, Ellen Levine, and Anita Rapone, eds., *Radical Feminism.* New York: Quadrangle Books.

Lorde, Audre. 1992. "Age, Race, Class, and Sex: Women Redefining Difference." In Paula S. Rothenberg, ed., *Race, Class and Gender in the United States: An Integrated Study.* Second Edition. New York: St. Martin's Press.

Marotta, Toby. 1981. *The Politics of Homosexuality.* Boston: Houghton Mifflin.

Martin, Del, and Phyllis Lyon. 1972. *Lesbian Woman.* San Francisco: Glide Publications.

Millett, Kate. 1970. *Sexual Politics.* Garden City, NY: Doubleday and Company.

Moraga, Cherrie, and Gloria Anzaldua, eds. 1983. *This Bridge Called My Back: Writings by Radical Women of Color.* New York: Kitchen Table: Women of Color Press.

Phelan, Shane. 1989. *Identity Politics: Lesbian Feminism and the Limits of Community.* Philadelphia: Temple University Press.

Radicalesbians. 1973. "The Woman Identified Woman." In Anne Koedt, Ellen Levine, and Anita Rapone, eds., *Radical Feminism.* New York: Quadrangle Books.

Raymond, Janice G. 1989. "Putting the Politics Back into Lesbianism." *Women's Studies International Forum* 12(2):149–56.

Rich, Adrienne. 1980. "Compulsory Heterosexuality and Lesbian Existence." *Signs: A Journal of Women in Culture and Society* (Summer):631–57.

Smith, Barbara, ed. 1983. *Home Girls: A Black Feminist Anthology.* New York: Kitchen Table: Women of Color Press.

Smith, Elizabeth A. 1989. "Butches, Femmes, and Feminists: The Politics of Lesbian Sexuality." *NWSA Journal* 1(3):398–421.

Snitow, Ann, Christine Stansell, and Sharon Thompson. 1983. *Powers of Desire: The Politics of Sexuality.* New York: Monthly Review Press.

Stimpson, Catharine R. 1986. *Women's Studies in the United States.* New York: Ford Foundation.

Taylor, Verta A., and Leila Rupp. 1993. "Women's Culture and Lesbian Feminist Activism: A Reconsideration of Cultural Feminism." *Signs: A Journal of Women in Culture and Society* 19(1):32–61.

Taylor, Verta A., and Nancy E. Whittier. 1992. "Collective Identity in Social Movement Communities: Lesbian Feminist Mobilization." In Aldon Morris and Carol Mueller, eds., *Frontiers of Social Movement Theory*. New Haven, CT: Yale University Press.

Valverde, Mariana. 1987. *Sex, Power and Pleasure*. Philadelphia: New Society Publishers.

Vance, Carole S. 1984. "Pleasure and Danger: Toward a Politics of Sexuality." In Carol S. Vance, ed., *Pleasure and Danger: Exploring Female Sexuality*. Boston: Routledge & Kegan Paul.

Weitz, Rose. 1989. "What Price Independence? Social Reactions to Lesbians, Spinsters, Widows, and Nuns." In Jo Freeman, ed., *Women: A Feminist Perspective*. Mountain View, California: Mayfield.

Weitz, Rose. 1984. "From Accommodation to Rebellion: The Politicization of Lesbianism." In Trudy Darty and Sandee Potter, eds., *Women-Identified Women*. Palo Alto, California: Mayfield.

Subject Index